A DICTIONARY OF
MILITARY
AND TECHNOLOGICAL ABBREVIATIONS AND ACRONYMS

Bernhard Pretz

A DICTIONARY OF
MILITARY
AND TECHNOLOGICAL
ABBREVIATIONS AND
ACRONYMS

Routledge & Kegan Paul

London, Boston, Melbourne and Henley

First published in 1983
by Routledge & Kegan Paul Plc
39 Store Street, London WC1E 7DD,
9 Park Street, Boston, Mass. 02108, USA,
296 Beaconsfield Parade, Middle Park,
Melbourne, 3206, Australia, and
Broadway House, Newtown Road,
Henley-on-Thames, Oxon RG9 1EN
Printed in Great Britain by
Thetford Press, Thetford, Norfolk

Library of Congress Cataloging in Publication Data

Pretz, Bernhard, 1943-
    Dictionary of military technological acronyms.

    Bibliography:p.
    1. Military art and science - Acronyms.
2. German language - Acronyms. 3. Russian language -
Acronyms. I. Title.
U26. P73 1983   355'.00148   82-18634
ISBN 0-7100-9274-1

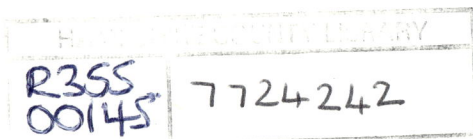

A

A acting rank; admiral; airman; apprentice; artificer; assistant; Australian; ampere; answer; annual (report); antenna; area; assault/attack (aircraft (US)
A-bomb atomic bomb
A-day announcement day (US); assault day (US)
A-echelon vehicles and stores to replenish F-echelon (UK)
A-gear arresting gear (aircraft)
A-level advanced level GCE (UK)
A-scope linear radar display
A-staff Adjutant General staff (UK), discipline, promotion, welfare
A1C Airman First Class
A-1D Skyraider, strike bomber by Douglas
A-2D Skyshark, attacker aircraft by Douglas
A-3 Falcon, ground attack aircraft by Curtiss
A-3 Skywarrior, atomic bomber by Douglas
A-4 V-2, Vergeltungswaffe, rocket (GE) 1944
A-4M Skyhawk, naval fighter/bomber by McDD
A-5 Vigilante, atomic bomber Mach 2 by Rockwell
A-6E Intruder, naval fighter/bomber by Grumman
A-7A Corsair II, tactical attack jet by Vought
A-7E " " by Rockwell
A-7P " " for Portugal
A-9A close support aircraft, jet by Northrop
A-10A Thunderbolt II, twin turbofan close support aircraft by Fairchild
A-11 SR-71 by Lockheed
A-17 attack aircraft 1939 by Northrop
A-18 Hornet/Cobra, attack version of F-18 by Northrop/McDD
A-19 gun, 122mm (SU)
A-20G Havoc, attack bomber by Douglas

A-24 dive bomber by Douglas
A-26 Invader, attack bomber by Douglas
A-37B Dragonfly, counter-insurgency aircraft by Cessna
A-39 Tortoise, heavy assault tank (UK) WW2
A-69 class, corvettes, SAR and pollution control (FR)
A-109 Hirundo, light helicopter by Agusta Bell
A-129 Mangusta/Mongoose, armed helicopter by Agusta Bell
A-244/S acoustic homing torpedo by Whitehead-Motofides
A-300 Airbus, transport aircraft (UK-FR-GE)
AA acting appointment; administrative assistant (US); air attache; aircraft apprentice (UK); aircraft artificer (UK); armament artificer (UK); artificer apprentice (UK); authorized allowance; absolute altitude; air armament; air-to-air (missile); analysis of account; anti-aircraft (artillery); armature accelerator; arrival angle
A/A angle of attack; any acceptable (codification)
AA-1 Alkali, air-to-air missile (SU)
AA-2 Atoll, " (SU)
AA-2-2 Advanced Atoll, " (SU)
AA-3 Anab, " (SU)
AA-3-2 Advanced Anab, " (SU)
AA-4 Awl, " (SU)
AA-5 Ash, " (SU)
AA-6 Acrid, " (SU)
AA-7 Apex, " (SU)
AA-8 Aphid, " (SU)
AA-52 arme automatique transformable, light machine gun 7.5mm (FR)
AAA Anti-aircraft Artillery (US); Army Appropriation Account; Army Athletics Association (UK); Awaiting Aircraft Availability (US)

1

AA&A   Armor, Armament and Ammunition (US)
AAAC   Australian Army Aviation Corps
AAAIS   Anti-aircraft Artillery Intelligence
        Service (US) WW2
AAArty Anti-aircraft Artillery (UK)
AAAS   American Association for the Advance-
        ment of Science (US)
AAAT   Anti-aircraft armoured truck, twin
        gun, 6x6 by Krauss-Maffei
AAB   Aircraft Accident Board (US); Anti-
        aircraft Battery; Army Air Base
        (US); Australian Army Book
AA/B   Anti-aircraft balloon
AABNCP E-4B, Advanced National Command Post
        by Boeing
aaby   as amended by (US)
AAC   Acting Armourer Corporal; Acting
        Assistant Commissioner; Aerial
        Ambulance Company (US); Aeronauti-
        cal Advisory Council; Alaskan Air
        Command (US); ALLA Annual Confer-
        ence Nato; anti-aircraft cannon
        (projectile); Army Air Corps (UK);
        Army Apprentices' College, (Harro-
        gate UK); Air (traffic) Area Con-
        trol (US); automatic amplitude
        control; automatic approach control
AACB   Aeronautics and Astronautics Coordi-
        nating Board (US)
AACC   Administrative Area Control Centre
        (UK); area approach control centre
AACD   antenna adjustable current distribu-
        tion
AACE   Airborne Alternate Command Echelon
        Nato
AACE   Air-to-air Combat Environment
AAcft   Army aircraft (US)
AAComs Army Area Communications System (US)
AACP   E-4, Advanced Airborne Command Post
        by Boeing
AACS   Airways and Air Communications Ser-
        vice (US); Army Air Communications
        System; Army Air Corps Squadron;
        Asynchronous Address Communications
        System; Automatic Address Communi-
        cations System
AACU   Anti-aircraft Cooperation Unit
AAD   admission and disposition (US);
        Advanced Ammunition Depot; Anti-
        aircraft Division; Armoured Auto-
        mobile Detachment; Army Air Defense
        (US)
A&AD   Applications and Analysis Division
AAD-5   AN- airborne infra-red line-scanner
        by Honeywell
AAD   Type L, (naval) anti-aircraft defence
        system, parachute and cable appara-
        tus (UK) WW2
AADA   anti-aircraft defended area Nato
AADC   Air Aide-de-Camp; All Applications
        Digital Computer; Anti-aircraft
        Defence Commander; Area Air
        Defense Commander (US); Army Air
        Defense Command (US)
AADCCS Army Air Defense Control and Coor-
        dination System
AADCom Army Air Defense Command (US)
AADCP   Army Air Defense Command Post (US)
AADS   Army Air Defense Site (US)
AADS-70 Army Air Defense System for the
        1970s US programme SAM-D
        XMIM-104
AADT   Anti-aircraft Dome Trainer by RFD
AAE   Army Aviation Element (US); All
        American Engineering Co. (Wilming-
        ton, Del.); Automatische
        Antworteinrichtung (automatic
        answering equipment)
AAEC   Australian Atomic Energy Commission
AAEE   Aircraft and Armament Experimental
        Establishment (Boscombe Down, UK)
AAES   Aldershot Army Equipment Show (UK)
AAEW   Atlantic Airborne Early Warning
        Nato
AAF   American Air Force; Army Air Force
        (US) WW2; Army airfield (US);
        Atlantic Amphibious Force (USN);
        Auxiliary Air Force (UK)
AAFC   anti-aircraft fire control
AAFCE   Allied Air Forces Central Europe,
        Ramstein, Nato
AAFCWF Army and Air Force Civilian Welfare
        Fund (US)
AAFEMPS Army and Air Force Exchange and
        Motion Picture Service (US)
AAFES   Army and Air Force Exchange Service
        (US)
AAFIS   Army and Air Force Intelligence
        Staff (US)
AAFM   anti-aircraft field mount (for MG)
AAFMPS Army and Air Force Motion Picture
        Service (US)
AAFNDA Army, Air Force and Naval Disci-
        pline Acts (UK)
AAFNE   Allied Air Forces Northern Europe
        Nato
AAFSE   Allied Air Forces Southern Europe
        Nato
AAFSS   AH-56, Advanced Aerial Fire
        Support/Suppression System (gun-
        ship helicopter)
AAFU   augmented assault fire units
AAFWB   Army and Air Force Wage Board (US)
AAG   Air Adjutant General; Assistant
        Adjutant General; anti-aircraft
        gun
AAGF   Advanced Aerial Gun for Future
        Fighters (US) programme
AAGFS   anti-aircraft gunfire simulator
AA&GM   anti-aircraft and guided missiles
        (branch)

AAGR	air-to-air gunnery range
AAGRA	Anti-aircraft Group, Royal Artillery
AAGS	Army Air Ground System (US)
AAGW	air-to-air guided weapon
AAH	Advanced Attack Helicopter (US) programme; Advanced Armed Helicopter
AAHQ	Allied Air Headquarters
AAI	Allied Armies in Italy; angle of approach indicator; American Aerospace Industries (US); Aircraft Armament Industries (Baltimore, US); Ausbildungs-ausstattung für Instandsetzung (maintenance training simulator)
AAIC	Allied Air Intelligence Centre
AAIE	American Association of Industrial Editors
AAI-ELO	Ausbildungs-ausstattung für Instandsetzung - Elektronik (maintenance training simulator - electronics)
AAI-EVA	Ausbildungs-ausstattung für Instandsetzung - Energie-Versorgungs-Anlage (maintenance training simulator - power plant)
AAIS	Anti-aircraft Intelligence Service (US)
AAL	Aircraft Assignment Letter
AAL	Aircraft Approach Limitations
AALC	Air-cushioned Assault Landing Craft (US), Amphibious Assault Landing Craft
AALD	Australian Army Legal Department
AALMG	anti-aircraft light machine gun
AALO	Army Air Liaison Officer
AALR	anti-aircraft laser range-finder
AALS	Active Army Locator System (US); advanced approach and landing system
AAM	air-to-air missile (US); anti-aircraft missile (battery); Army Aircraft Maintenance (US); Australian Air Mission
AAMB	anti-aircraft missile battery
AAMC	Australian Army Medical Corps
AAMG	anti-aircraft machine gun
AAMREP	air-to-air missile weapons system flight report (US)
AAMS	Army aircraft maintenance shop (US)
AAMsBN	Anti-aircraft Missile Battalion (USMC)
AAMWS	Australian Army Medical Women's Service
AANC	Automatic ATRAN Nose Checker (automatic terrain recognition and navigation)
AANS	Australian Army Nursing Service
AAO	Authorized Acquisition Objective (US)
AAOA	Ambulance Association of America
AAOC	Anti-aircraft Operations Centre (SHAPE); Australian Army Ordnance Corps
AAOD	Army Aviation Operating Detachment (US)
AAOR	anti-aircraft artillery operations room
AAP	analyst assistance programme; Apollo Applications Program (US)
AAP	Army Ammunition Plant (US); Allied Administrative Publication Nato
AAPC	All African People's Conference; Assault Amphibian Personnel Carrier
AAPIU	Allied Aerial Photographic Interpretation Unit
AAPM	Army Aviation Planning Manual (US)
AAPO	All African People's Organization
AAPP	auxiliary airborne power plant
AAPSO	All African People's Solidarity Organization
AAPU	auxiliary airborne power unit
AAQ-6	airborne forward-looking infra-red FLIR by Hughes
AAQ-9	airborne infra-red detector by TI
AAQMG	Acting/Assistant Quartermaster General
AA&QMG	Assistant Adjutant and Quartermaster General
AAR	after action report; aircraft accident report; aircraft accident record (US); air-to-air refuelling; Army Area Representative (US)
AAR-42	airborne infra-red warning receiver
AAR-44	" " by Cincinnati Electronics
AARB	advanced aerial refuelling boom by McDD
AARC	Army Attrition Rates Committee Nato
AARDAC	Army Air Reconnaissance for Damage Assessment in the Continental US
AARDC	Army Aviation Research and Development Command (US)
AARS	Airborne Armoured Reconnaissance Squadron; automatic acquisition radar seeker
AAS	Administrative Airlift Service; Aeromedical Airlift Squadron (US); amphibious assault ship; Annual Average Score (US); Army Apprentices' School (UK); Army Air Services (US) 1928; atomic absorption spectroscopy; Auxiliary Ambulance Service
AAS-35	Pave Penny, airborne laser target acquisition equipment
AAS-36	airborne maritime surveillance equipment
AAS-37	" " + laser target marker
AASA	Administrative Assistant to the Secretary of the Army (US)
AASC	Allied Air Support Command; Army Area Signal Center (US); Australian Army Signal Corps

AASE   Army Aviation Support Element (US)
AASF   advanced air striking force (RAF day
        bombers WW2)
AASGP   amphibious assault ship, general
        purpose
AASH   Army Advanced Scout (US programme)
        (helicopter)
AAslt   air assault (US)
AASO   Afro-Asian Solidarity Organization
AASS   "   "   "   Secretariat
AASR   airport and airways surveillance
        radar
AASTA   Army Aviation Systems Test Activity
        (US)
AAT   analytic approximation theory; arme
        automatique transformable (machine
        gun FR)
AATB   Advanced Amphibious Training Base
        (US)
AATC   Advanced Air Training Command (US);
        anti-aircraft Training Center
        (US); Army Aviation Test Command
        (US); automatic air traffic control
AATCO   Army Air Traffic Coordinating Office
        (US)
AATDC   Army Airborne Transport Development
        Centre (UK)
AATH   automatic approach-to-hover (heli-
        copter flight control system)
AATMS   Advanced Air Traffic Management
        System
AATO   Army Air Transport Organization
AATOC   Airhead Air Traffic Coordination
        Center (US)
AATraCen anti-aircraft Training Center (US)
AATRI   Army Air Traffic Regulation and
        Identification (system) (US)
AATS   automatic altitude trim (system)
        (for helicopters)
AATTV   Australian Army Training Team,
        Vietnam
AAV   airborne assault vehicle; amphibious
        assault vehicle; armoured anti-
        aircraft vehicle; Arab-American
        Vehicles (company) Cairo (AMC +
        AOI)
AAVC   Australian Army Veterinary Corps
AAvn   Army Aviation
AAVS   Aerospace Audiovisual Service MAC
        (US)
AAW   Advanced Attack Weapon (USAF pro-
        gramme); Aeromedical Airlift Wing
        (USAF); airborne assault weapon
        (SP gun); anti-aircraft warfare;
        anti-aircraft weapon
AAWC   Anti-air Warfare Center (US); Austra-
        lian Advisory War Council
AAWEx   Anti-air warfare exercise
AAWSSC Army Atomic Weapons Safety/Systems
        Committee (US)

AA-X-9 air-to-air missile (nuclear)
        (SU)
AAYSO   Afro-Asian Youth Solidarity
        Organization (Djakarta)
AB   air base; Air Branch RN; able
        bodied (seaman); aerial burst
        (bomb); air break; air blast;
        antenna beam; after-burner;
        airborne A/B; crane ship (USN);
        Agusta Bell, Gallarate IT
a/b   airborne
AB-47   light helicopter by AB, Sioux
AB-204 anti-submarine helicopter by AB
AB-205 heavy helicopter by AB (license
        CH-47)
AB-206 Jet Ranger, light helicopter by AB
AB-212 heavy helicopter, ASW by Agusta Bell
ABA   American-British-Australian
ABAR   advanced battery acquisition radar
        (US)
Abbey Hill naval ECM equipment by Decca RN
Abbot   FV-433, 105mm SP gun by Vickers
ABBV   Allgemeine Bedingungen für
        Beschaffungsverträge (des BMVg)
        (general conditions for procure-
        ment contracts) (GE)
ABC   America-Britain-Canada; Argentina-
        Brazil-Chile; Atomic-Biological-
        Chemical (warfare); advanced bio-
        medical capsule; automatic back-
        ground control; Advanced Blade
        Concept (helicopters); automatic
        brake control; assessment, bio-
        logical and chemical
ABCA   America-Britain-Canada-Australia
        (Armies standardization pro-
        gramme); Army Bureau of Current
        Affairs (UK) (now: BCA)
ABCAirStd American-British-Canadian Air
        Standardization Agreement
ABCC   Atomic Bomb Casualty Commission
ABCCC   airborne battlefield command and
        Control Centre Nato
ABCCo   American Buckle & Cartridge Company
ABCCTC Advanced Base Combat Communications
        Training Center (US)
ABCD   America-Britain-China-Dutch East
        Indies; American-British-Chinese-
        Dutch (powers in the Pacific WW2);
        Advanced Base Construction Depot
        (US); atomic, biological and
        chemical defence (UK); atomic,
        biological and chemical protection
        and damage control; awaiting bad
        conduct discharge (US)
ABCR   atomic, biological, chemical and
        radiological (warfare) Nato
ABD   Advanced Based Depot (US); average
        body dose (radiation)
abd   aboard

ABDA   American-British-Dutch-Australian
          Supreme Command WW2
ABDACom   Advanced Base Depot Area Command
          (US); American-British-Dutch-
          Australian Supreme Command WW2
ABDAFloat American-British-Dutch-Australian
          Naval Operations Command WW2
ABDAir   American-British-Dutch-Australian
          Air Operations Command WW2
ABDArm   American-British-Dutch-Australian
          Army Operations Command WW2
ABDS   Army Bomb Disposal Squad
ABECo   Arab British Engine Company (Rolls-
          Royce daughter)
ABEWS   Army Battlefield Electronic Warfare
          Simulator
ABF   Annullar blast fragmentation (war-
          head); Aircraft Battle Force (US);
          Army Benevolent Fund (UK); avail-
          ability balance file (US)
ABFC   Advanced Base Functional Components
ABF/Lw   Ausbildungsflugzeut der Luftwaffe
          (GE), Air Force trainer aircraft
ABG   Air Base Group (US)
ABI   American-British Intelligence Nato
ABIOL   Advanced Base Initial Outfitting
          List (US)
ABL   Alleghenny Ballistics Laboratory
          (Cumberland Md); Atlas Basic Lang-
          uage
ABLE   Activity Balance Line Evaluation
          PERT (programme evaluation review
          technique)
ABM   anti-ballistic missile; automatic
          batch mix
ABM-1   Galosh, anti-ballistic missile (SU)
ABMA   Army Ballistic Missile Agency
ABMC   American Battle Monuments Commission
          (US)
ABMEWS   anti-ballistic missile early warning
          system Nato
ABMM   anti-ballistic missile missile Nato
ABMTM   Associated British Machine Tool
          Makers Ltd
ABN   anti-bolshevik bloc of nations;
          aerodrome beacon
abn   airborne
AbnCP   Airborne Command Post Nato
AbnOC   Airborne Operations Centre (SHAPE)
          Nato
ABOD   Advanced Base Ordnance Depot
ABPA   Advanced Base Personnel Administra-
          tion (US)
ABPG   Advanced Base Proving Ground (US)
ABPO   Advanced Base Personnel Office(r)
          (US)
ABPT   air brake position transmitter
ABPU   Advanced Base Personnel Unit (US)
ABR   Additional Billet Requirements (US);
          amphibian boat reconnaissance
          (aircraft) (USN)

ABRACADABRA Abbreviations and Related
          Acronyms associated with
          Astronautics, Defence, Busi-
          ness and Radio Electronics by
          Raytheon
Abrams   XM-1, experimental battle tank by
          Chrysler
ABRB   Advanced Base Receiving Barracks (US)
ABRD   Advanced Base Receiving Depot (US),
          "   "   Reshipment Depot (US)
ABRES   Advanced Ballistic Re-entry System
          (US)
ABRO   Army in Burma Reserve of Officers
ABS   Acrylonitrile Butadiene Styrene
          (plastic); American Bureau of
          Shipping
abs   absent; absorbent
ABSAP   airborne search and attack plotter
ABSD   Advanced Base Sectional Dock (USN);
          "   "   Supply Depot; Army Base
          Supply Depot
ABSIE   American Broadcasting Station in
          Europe WW2
abstee   absentee (US)
ABT   all body type (US)
ABTU   Arms Basic Training Unit; Advanced
          Base Training Unit (US); Advanced
          Base Torpedo Unit (USN); Air
          Bombers Training Unit (US)
ABV   Assault Bridging Vehicle
ABZ   Autophon-BBC-Zellweger (consortium),
          Postfach CH-5401 Baden
AC   Atlantic Council Nato; Advisory Com-
          mittee; Army Corps; Army Council;
          Air Control; Air Command; Air Corps
          (US); Ambulance Corps; Army Co-op-
          eration (squadron); armed cargo
          (aircraft) (US); attack cargo
          (vessel) (USN); collier (USN);
          armoured car; aircraft; aircraft
          carrier; alternating current; anti-
          clutter; analog computer; airframe
          change; air control; Advisory Cir-
          cular
AC   anti-char (anti-tank) FR
AC-47   Magic Dragon, gunship aircraft,
          armed cargo by Douglas
AC-119   armed cargo aircraft by Fairchild
AC-123   Provider, armed cargo aircraft by
          Fairchild
AC-130   Spectre, gunship Hercules,
          by Lockheed
AC-224   Atlantic Council Document No. 224
          Nato
ACA   Adjacent Channel Attenuation;
          Advanced Combat Aircraft; Advisory
          Committee on Aeroballistics (US);
          Agence Centrale des Approvisione-
          ments (Central Acquisitions Agency)
          Nato; Airlift Clearance Authority

(US); Allied Commission for Austria; Allied Control Authority; Alternate Command Authority Nato; American Communications Association; Armaments Control Agency; Australian Council on Aeronautics; Awaiting Combat Assignment (US)

ACAB   Army Contract Adjusting Board (US)

ACAC   Allied Container Advisory Committee

ACACA   Army Command and Administration Communication Agency Nato

ACAG   Allied Control Authority for Germany

ACAN   Army Command and Administrative Network Nato

ACAP   Advisory Committee on Airports Policy BAA (UK)

ACAS   Assistant Chief of the Air Staff

ACAU   automatic calling and answering unit

ACAV   armoured cavalry assault vehicle

ACB   Amphibious Construction Battalion (US); Army Classification Battery (US)

ACBD   Active Commission Base Date (US)

ACBWS   Automatic Chemical-Biological Warning System

ACC   Administrative Co-ordination Committee; air control centre; Air Co-ordinating Committee (US); aircraft climb corridor; Allied Control Centre; Allied Control Commission; Allied Control Council; Amphibious Command Car Nato; Amphibious Control Center LCC (USMC); Area Control Centre ATC; Area Co-ordination Centre; armoured car company; Army Cadet College (UK); Army Catering Corps (UK); Army Chemical Corps (US); artillery control console; artillery control computer; automatic combustion control

acc   acceleration, acceptance, accumulation

ACCA   Ad-hoc Crypto Co-ordinative Agency Nato; Asynchronous Communications Control Attachment

ACCB   Airframe Change Control Board

ACCC   American Communications Components Corp. (Costa Mesa, Cal.); Army Catering Corps Colonel Commandant (UK)

ACCD   Accelerated Construction Completion Date Nato

ACCHAN   Allied Command, Channel Nato

ACCIS   Automated Command Control and Information System

ACCLAIMS   Army ComSec Commodity, Logistical and Accounting Information Management System (US) (communications security)

ACCNET   Army Command and Control Network (US)

ACCO   Tcc-39, Automatic Communications Central Office

ACCOR   Army ComSec Central Office of Records (US) (communications security)

ACCS   acoustic communication with submarines; Air Command and Control System Nato by Siemens

ACCSIP   Air Command and Control System Improvement Plan Nato

AccStr   accountable strength (US)

ACCV   Armored Cavalry Cannon Vehicle (US) by Emerson

ACD   adapter control detector; Administrative Commitment Document (US); Atlantic Community for Defence (proposal) Nato; automatic chart display

ACDA   Arms Control and Disarmament Agency (UN); Aviation Combat Development Agency (US)

AC/DC   alternating current/direct current

ACDiv   assault craft division (USN)

ACDO   Air Carrier District Office (US)

ACdre   Air Commodore

ACDS   Assistant Chief of the Defence Staff Nato

acdt   accident

AcDu   active duty (US)

ACDuObli   active duty obligation (US)

ACDuTra   active duty training (US)

ACE   Airspace Control Element (US); Airspace Co-ordination Element; Allied Command Europe Nato; altimeter control equipment; Army Certificate of Education (UK); assessment of combat effectiveness (US); automatic clutter elimination; automatic computing engine

ACEA   Action Committee for European Aerospace

ACE/ACCIS   Allied Command Europe/Automated Command Control and Information System Nato

ACEB   Army Combat Engineer Battalion (US)

ACEC   Ateliers de Constructions de Charleroi, B-6000 Charleroi

ACED   Advanced Communicating Equipment Depot Nato

AceHigh   Allied Command Europe Troposcatter Communications System Nato

CEL   Aerospace Crew Equipment Laboratory (Philadelphia, Pa)

ACEMF   Allied Command Europe Mobile Force Nato

ACEMIS   Automated Communications-Electronics Management Information System (US)

ACEN   Assembly of Captive European Nations

ACENet   Allied Command Europe
          Communications Network
          (Nato)
ACEORP   Automotive and Construction Equip-
          ment Overhaul and Repair Plant
          (US)
ACEPD   Automotive and Construction Equip-
          ment Parts Depot (US)
ACERep   Allied Command Europe Reporting
          System Nato
ACES   Annual Cycle Energy System (US),
          heat pump for heating and cooling)
ACES-2   aircraft ejection seat by McDD
ACET   Advisory Committee on Electronics
          and Telecommunications; automatic
          cancellation of extended targets
          (US)
ACEur   Allied Command Europe Nato ACE
ACEval   Air Combat Evaluation (US)
ACF   Active Citizen Force (South Afr.);
          Air Combat Fighter; Area Confine-
          ment Facility (US); Army Cadet
          Force (UK); Army Club Fund (US);
          Army Council Form; auto-correla-
          tion function; Avions de Combat
          Future (future combat aircraft)
          (FR)
ACFA   Army Cadet Force Association (UK)
ACFR   Air Combat Fighter Radar
acft   aircraft
AcftC   aircraft carrier
ACG   Amphibious Control Group (US); Area
          Control Group (US); Airborne Co-
          ordinating Group; Assistant Chap-
          lain General (UK); automatic con-
          trol gear
ACGB   Aircraft Corporation of Great Britain
ACGM   Aircraft Carrier General Memorandum
          (US)
ACGp   Army Carrier Group (US)
ACGS   Acceleration Control Guidance
          System
ACHE   acethyl cholinesterase (enzyme con-
          trolling muscular movement)
ACHS   American Camp and Hospital Service
          (US)
ACI   Air Combat Intelligence (US); Army
          Council Instruction (UK); American
          Craftsmen Incorporated (US);
          Alliance Co-operative Internation-
          ale (International Cooperative
          Alliance)
ACIC   Aeronautical Chart and Information
          Center (St Louis, Mo.); Allied
          Auxiliary Intelligence Centre
          (US-UK)
ACID   automatic classification and inter-
          pretation of data
ACIGS   Assistant Chief of the Imperial
          General Staff

ACIIB   American Civilian Internee Informa-
          tion Bureau (US)
ACIM   axis crossing interval meter
ACIMS   Aircraft Component Intensive
          Management System (US)
ACIntel   Assistant Chief of Staff, Intelli-
          gence Nato
ACIO   Aeronautical Chart and Information
          Office (US)
ACIP-300 light unguided anti-tank missile
          by Thomson-Brandt
ACIPR   Allied Committee on Intellectual
          Property Rights Nato
ACIR   Aviation Crash Injury Research
ACIS   Amphibious Command Information
          System (USN)
ACISq   Aeronautical Chart and Information
          Squadron (US)
ACL   action centred leadership; Aero-
          nautical Computer Laboratory
          NADC (Johnsville Pa.); allowable
          cargo load (US); allowable cabin
          load; application control lang-
          uage; Atlas Computer Laboratory;
          authorized consumption list
ACLant   Allied Command Atlantic Nato
ACLC   Air Cadet League of Canada
ACLog   Assistant Chief of Staff, Logistics
          Nato
ACLOS   automatic command to line of sight
          (guided missiles)
ACLS   air cushion landing system; all-
          weather carrier landing system
          (USN); automatic carrier landing
          system; automated control landing
          system
ACLU   American Civil Liberties Union
ACM   additional crew-members (US); Air
          Chief Marshal (UK); air combat
          manoeuvering; American Campaign
          Medal (US); Army Commendation
          Medal (US); Association for Com-
          puting Machinery (US); associative
          communication multiplexer; anti-
          armour cluster munition (US);
          authorized controlled material;
          auxiliary mine-layer (USN)
AC/M   aircraft, meteorological Nato
ACMA   Army Class Manager Activity
ACMC   Area Combined Movements Center (US)
ACMF   Air Corps Medical Forces (US);
          Allied Central Mediterranean
          Forces; Australian Commonwealth
          Military Forces
ACMI   Air Combat Manoeuvering Instrumenta-
          tion by Kelvin
ACMO   Allied (Command Europe) Communica-
          tion Management Organization Nato
ACMP   Assistant Commissioner of the Metro-
          politan Police (UK)

ACMR	Advanced Computer for Medical Research
ACMR/I	Air Combat Manoeuvring Range Instrumentation (Philippines)
ACMRR	Advisory Committee on Marine Resources Research FAO
ACMS	Army Command Management System (US
ACN	Air Commander Norway Nato; assigned control number (US); asbestos cloth, neck
acn	all concerned notified (UK)
ACNA	Advisory Council on Naval Affairs (US)
ACNB	Australian Commonwealth Naval Board
ACNIP	Auxiliary Communications Navigation and Identification Panel for AV-8 by Conarc
ACNN	Air Commander North Norway Nato
ACNO	Assistant Chief of Naval Operations (US)
ACNO(Comm)/DNC	Assistant Chief of Naval Operations (Communications) Director of Naval Communications
ACNO(GenPlanProg)	Assistant Chief of Naval Operations (General Planning and Programming)
ACNP	Assistant Chief of Naval Personnel (USN)
E&T	Education and Training
F-C	Finance Comptroller
MS	Morale Services
NR&NDA	Naval Reserve and Naval District Affairs
P	Plans
PC	Personnel Control
Perf	Performance
PM	Property Management
PPM	Personal Program Management
R	Records
ACNS	Assistant Chief of Naval Staff
OPS	Operations
Pol	Policy
OR	Operational Requirements
Ops&Air	Operations and Air
ACO	Administrative Contracting Officer (US); Admiralty Compass Observatory (Slough, UK); Airborne Control Officer; Air Contact Officer; Air Controller Officer AEW; Army Careers Office (UK); attack cut out
ACOC	Air Command Operations Centre Nato
ACOCC	Atlantic (Fleet) Commander Operational Control Center (USN)
ACofS	Assistant Chief of Staff (US)
ACOG	aircraft on ground (US); Agence Civile OTAN du temps de guerre (Nato Civil Wartime Agency)
ACONA	Advisory Council on Naval Affairs (US)

ACOP	Airborne Corps Operation Plan (US)
ACORD	Advisory Council on Research and Development
ACORN	Associative Content Retrieval Network; Automatic Check-out and Recording Network
ACOS	Assistant Chief of Staff Nato
ACOT	Assistant (Chief of Staff), Organization and Training Nato
AcoustInt	acoustical intelligence (US)
ACP	Advanced Command Post (US); airborne Advanced Command Post (US); air control point (US); airlift Advanced Command Post; Allied Communications Procedure Nato; Allied Communications Publication Nato; Alternate Command Post (US); Assistant Credit Planning (Dept DSAA); Automatic Colt Pistol; azimuth change pulse
A-CP	Anti-Concorde Project
ACPD	Army Control Program Directive (US)
ACP&P	Assistant Chief (of Staff), Plans and Policy Nato
ACProg	Assistant Chief (of Staff), Programmes Nato
acpt	acceptance
ACPU	Aerial Coast Patrol Unit (USN)
ACQ	Admiral Commanding, Battle Cruisers (RN)
acq	acquisition
ACR	Admiral Commanding Reserves (RN); advanced capabilities radar; aircraft control room; Air Control and Reporting Nato; anti-circular run; air-field control radar; Armored Cavalry Regiment (US); Armored Cruiser (USN); approach control radar; Allied Commission on Reparations; ammunition condition report
ACRA	anti-char rapide autorepulse (anti-tank missile, laser) (FR)
ACRE	Acting Commander, Royal Engineers; advanced cyrogenic rocket engineering; automatic check-out and reading equipment
ACRO	Area Chief Recruiting Officer
Acrow	Heavy Bridge (UK) bridging equipment, Panel Bridge (UK) bridging equipment, Uniflote (UK) light floating bridge equipment by Mabey & Johnson
ACRP	Army Cost Reduction Program (US)
acrs	across
ACRS	Advisory Council for Reactor Safeguards (US)
ACRt	Analysis Control Routine
ACRV	Armored Command and Reconnaissance Vehicle (US)

ACS   acoustic communication with sub-marines; active communications satellite; Admiral Commanding, Sub-marines; Admiralty Computing Service; aerodrome control service; airlift coordination staff; airways communication station; Alaskan Communications System; altitude control system; amphibious command ship; Army Community Service (US); Artillery Computer System (USMC) Fadac; assembly control system; Assistant Chief of Staff; automatic control system

acs   anodal closing sound

A/CS   aircraft security (vessel)

ACSA   Adaptive Channel-Selective Address (communications system) by ABZ; Allied Communications Security Agency Nato Brussels

ACSC   Army Command and Staff College (US)

ACSEA   Allied Command, South East Asia

ACSFor   Assistant Chief of Staff, Force Development (US)

ACSI   Assistant Chief of Staff, Intelligence (US)

ACSIL   Admiralty Centre for Scientific Information and Liaison NSTIC

ACSM   Advanced Conventional Stand-off Missile (US) programme; Allied Cadre Group on Material Standardization Nato; American Congress of Surveying and Mapping

ACSM/CM/UW   Advanced Conventional Stand-off Missile/Cratering Munition/Unitary Weapon (USAF) programme

AC/SOF   Air Commando/Strategic Offensive Forces (US)

ACSP   Advisory Council on Scientific Policy; Aircraft Cross-servicing Program Nato

ACSS   automated colour separation system

ACST   Army Clerical Speed Test (US)

ACT   Advisory Council on Technology; air contact team; air control team (US); aircraft commander time (US); Allied Control Team; armored cavalry trainer (US); analogical circuit technique; associated container transportation; automatic code translation; Aviation Classification Test (US)

Act   action Nato, activity (US)

ACTA   Advanced Combat Training Academy (US); air combat training area

ACTC   Air Corps Training Centre

Act/Conv   Activation/Conversion (US)

ActDu   Active Duty (US)

ActDuTra   Active Duty for Training (US)

ACTF   altitude control test facility

ACTG   Advanced Carrier Training Group (US)

actg   acting (rank)

ACTH   arbitrary correction to hit

Act/IC   Active (vessel) in Commission (USN)

Act/OC   Active (vessel) out of Commission

Act/IS   Active (vessel) in Service

Act/OS   Active (vessel) out of Service

ACTICE   Authority Coordinating the Transport of Inland Continental Europe

ACTISUD   Authority Coordinating the Transport of Inland Southern Europe

ActgLt   Acting Lieutenant

ActgSubLt   Acting Sub-lieutenant

ActO   Action Officer (US)

ACTP   Advanced Computer Techniques Project

ActPO   Accountable Property Officer (US)

ActRep   activities report (shipping) (USN)

ACTS   Acoustic Control and Telemetry System (US)

ACU   arithmetic control unit; Army Canoe Union (UK); Assault Craft Unit (US); automatic calling unit

ACV   Air Cushion Vehicle, Armored Command Vehicle (US); Auxiliary Aircraft Carrier (USN)

ACVC   Army Commercial Vehicle Code (US)

ACVFA   Advisory Committee on Voluntary Foreign Aid (US)

ACVT   Armored Combat Vehicle Technology (US) programme

ACW   Aircraftwoman

acw   alternating continuous waves; automatic car wash

AC&W   Aircraft Control and Warning Nato; air communications and weather

ACWF   Army Central Welfare Fund (US)

ACWRon   Aircraft Control and Warning Squadron (USN)

ACWS   Aircraft Control and Warning System Nato

AD   Administrative Department; airborne doppler (radar) (UK); advisory direction CEAC Nato; assured destruction; Air Defence; average deviation; Airworthiness Directive; air despatch; Armoured Division (UK); ammunition dump; Alliance Defence Nato; Armament Depot; Army Depot; Air Depot; Active Duty; Assistant Director; Destroyer Tender (USN)

A/D   analog-to-digital (computer)

AD-1   Ames/Dryden, pivot-wing aircraft project by NASA 1979

AD-70   Study of the Alliance Defence Problems in the 1970s Nato

AD-650   airborne doppler navigation radar for helicopters by Marconi-Elliott

ADA   Air Defence Area; Army Discipline
         Act (UK); Active Duty Agreement
         (US); air defensive artillery; Air
         Defense Agency (US); Atomic Devel-
         opment Authority; Action Data
         Automation; acoustic data analysis;
         automatic data acquisition
Ada   US DoD programming language (Ada
         Byron 1816-62 Lady Lovelace)
ADAA   Air defence action area (Nato)
ADAC   Acoustic Data Analysis Center (US);
         Air Defence Artillery Commander;
         automated direct analog computer;
         avion à décollage et atterissage
         courts (short take-off and landing
         aircraft) (FR)
ADAD   air defence artillery director
ADAH   Assistant Director of Army Health
AdAllCon advise all concerned (US)
ADAM   Area Denial Artillery Munition (US)
ADAMS   Airborne Data Acquisition and Manage-
         ment System by Collins
Adamsite DM, sneezing gas
ADAOD   air defense artillery operation
         detachment (US)
ADAPCP   Alcohol and Drug Abuse Prevention
         and Control Program (US)
ADAPT   Active Duty Assistance Program Team
         (US); analog-digital automatic
         programme tester
ADAPTS   Air-deliverable Anti-pollution
         Transfer System (USCG)
ADAR   Advanced Design Army Radar; advanced
         data acquisition routine; air
         defense area (US)
ADARCO   advise date of reporting in compli-
         ance with orders
ADAS   auxiliary data annotation set; air
         deployable array system (USN)
ADASP   Air Defense Annual Service Practice
         (US)
ADAT   Army Dependants' Assurance Trust (UK)
ADATE-1500 Automatic Dynamic Assembly Test
         Equipment by Watkins
ADatP   Allied Data Processing Publication
         (Nato)
ADAV   avion à décollage et à atterissage à
         la vertical (vertical take-off and
         landing aircraft) FR
AdAval   advise availability (US)
ADAWS   Assistant Director of Army Welfare
         Services (UK)
ADAWS-1 Action Data Automation Weapon
         System (naval) by Ferranti
ADB   Air Defence Battery; RA (UK), Adrian
         de Backer (visual landing systems)
         (Leuwensteenweg 275 B-1930
         Zaventen)
ADBD   Active Duty Base Date (US)
ADBMS   Available Data Base Management
         System

ADBZ   Air Defence Battle Zone (Nato)
ADC   Aide-de-Camp (UK); Army Dental Corps
         (RADC); Assistant Division Comman-
         der; Aerospace Defense Command
         (US); Active Duty Commitment (US);
         Aerodrome Defence Corps; aerodrome
         control; air data computer; auto-
         matic digital computer; analog-to-
         digital computer; analog-to-digi-
         tal converter; ammunition dumping
         craft
AD&C   Ammunition Distribution and Control
         (US); advice duration and charge
         (UK)
AdCap   Mk-48, advanced capabilities
         (torpedo)
AdCashAl advance cash allowance (US)
ADCC   Air Defence Control Centre (Nato)
ADCCCS   Air Defense Command, Control and
         Coordination System (US)
ADCO   Air Defense Communications Office
         (US); alcohol and drug control
         office(r) (US)
ADCoC   Area Damage Control Center (US)
ADCom   Aerospace Defense Command (US)
AdComd   Administrative Command (US)
AdCon   advise (all) concerned (US)
AdConSen Advice and Consent of the Senate
         (US)
ADCoP   Area Damage Control Party (US);
         Associate Degree Completion Pro-
         gram (US)
ADCor   Applied Devices Corporation (US) -
         Hawk
ADCP   Air Defense Command Post (US)
ADCS   Advanced Defence Communications
         System; Aerospace Defense Command
         Squadron (USAF)
ADCSP   Advanced Defense Communications
         Satellite Program (US)
ADD   Air Defence District (Nato); ancil-
         lary data display; artificer deep
         diver (RN)
ADDAS   automatic digital data assembly
         system
ADDC   Air Defense Direction Center (US)
AdDelRep additional delay in reporting (US)
AdDev   advanced development
ADDF   Abu Dhabi Defence Forces
ADDIC   Alcohol and Dependency Intervention
         Council (US)
ADDL   aircraft dummy deck landing
ADDP   air defense defended point (US)
AddPla   additional places
AdDu   additional duty
ADDR   Annual Defense Department Report
         (US)
ADDS   Assistant Director of Dental Ser-
         vices (UK); Automatic Data Dis-
         tribution System (US)

ADE   air defence emergency; Assistant
          Division Engineer (US)
ADELA   Atlantic (Community Office) for the
          Development of Latin America
Adelco   Elektronik GmbH, D-2085 Quickborn
ADEN   30mm cannon by ROF Enfield
ADEP   Air Defence Electronic Partnership
          (ICL+HSA+SINTRA+Westinghouse)
          (39 South Ealing Road, London
          W5 4QU)
ADepRep   Army Deployment Reporting System
          (US)
ADEPT   Automated Direct-entry Packaging
          Technique
ADEU   Automatic Data Entry Unit
ADEW   air defense early warning (US)
ADEX   air defence exercise (airspace)
          (Nato); ASEAN Defence Exposition
          (Singapore)
ADF   automatic direction finder; airborne
          direction finder; auxiliary deto-
          nating fuse
ADFS-320/922 airborne direction finder
          system by OTC
ADFS-347 automatic (vehicular) direction
          finder system VHF by OAS
ADFS-348 automatic (vehicular) direction
          finder system UHF by OAS
ADFSC   Automatic Data Field Systems Command
          (US)
ADFW   Assistant Director of Fortifications
          and Works
ADG   Advanced Development Group (US);
          Air Defence Group (Canada); Assis-
          tant Director General; Degaussing
          Ship (USN)
ADGB   Air Defence of Great Britain
ADGBC   Air Defence of Great Britain Command
ADGE   Air Defence Ground Environment
          (Nato); Air Defence Group Environ-
          ment (Nato)
ADGES   Air Defence Ground Environment
          System (India)
ADGMS   Assistant Director General of Medical
          Services
AdGru   Advisory Group,
ADH   Assistant Director of Hygiene; auto-
          mated data handling
ADHC   Air Defence Hardware Committee
          (Nato)
          SC1 Subcommittee 1
          SC2 Subcommittee 2
ADHWP   Automated Data Handling Working Party
          (Nato)
ADI   airborne direction indicator; atti-
          tude director indicator; automatic
          direction indicator; alien declared
          intention (US); approved driving
          instructor; American Documentation
          Institute ASIS

ADIE   acquisition data input equipment
AdIntelCen advanced intelligence center
          (US)
ADIS   automatic data interchange system
ADISP   Aeronautical Data Interchange
          Systems Panel
ADIZ   Air Defence Identification Zone
          (Nato)
Adj   Adjutant
ADJAG   Assistant Deputy Judge Advocate
          General
AdjGen   Adjutant General
Adjt   Adjutant
ADK   anti-dipole compensation; Autodreh-
          kran (vehicular crane) (EG)
ADL   activities of daily living; Assis-
          tant Director of Labour; Army
          Dental Laboratory; automatic data
          link; Authorized Data List (US)
Adler   Artillerie-Daten, Lage und Einsatz
          Rechner (artillery data location
          and combat computer) (GE)
ADLIPS   Advanced Data Link Processing System
          (Canadian Navy); Automatic Data
          Link Plotting System by Leigh
AdLog   Advanced Logistic Command
ADLS   air despatch letter service
ADM   advanced development model; air
          decoy missile; Air Defence Medal;
          American Defense Medal; atomic
          demolition munition
Adm   administration, admiral
ADM-20   Quail, air decoy missile
ADMAR/ADKAR Abgesetzte Darstellung der
          Maastricht/Karlsruhe
          Radardaten (EUROCONTROL
          remote display of ATC radar
          data)
ADMC   Air Defense Missile Command (US)
AdmCen   Administration Center (US)
AdminI   administrative instructions
AdminO   administrative officer; administra-
          tive orders
AdmM   administrative memorandum (Nato)
ADMMO   Atomic Demolition Munition Mission
          Officer (Nato)
AdmO   administrative order
ADMO   Assistant Director of the Meteoro-
          logical Office; (CA) Assistant
          Director of the Meteorological
          Office, Civil Aviation
ADMRL   application data material readiness
          list
ADMS   advanced depot medical stores;
          Assistant Director of Medical Ser-
          vices (UK); automatic digital mes-
          sage switch
ADMSC   automatic digital message switching
          centre
AdMsg   advise by message

ADMs1Bn Air Defense Missile Battalion (US)
Admty   Admiralty
ADNA   Assistant Director of Naval Accounts
ADNAC   Air Defence of the North American
          Continent
ADNC   Air Defence Notification Centre
          (Nato); Air Defence National
          Centre (Nato); Assistant Director
          of Naval Construction
ADNI   Assistant Director of Naval Intelli-
          gence
ADO   administration duty officer;
          Advanced Development Objective
          (US); air defence operations
          (Nato); air defence officer;
          Assistant District Officer
ADOA   Air Defence Operation Area (Nato)
ADOC   Air Defence Operations Centre
ADOF   Assistant Director of Ordnance Fac-
          tories
Adolf   50.6cm railway gun (GE) WW2
ADOS   Assistant Director of Ordnance Ser-
          vices
ADOT   air defence operation team; automatic
          digital optical tracker
ADP   Advanced Development Plan; air
          defence position; Allied Defence
          Publication (Nato); automatic data
          processing
ADPA   American Defense Preparedness Assoc-
          iation (US)
ADPC   automatic data processing centre
ADPE   automatic data processing equipment
ADPESO   Automatic Data Processing Equipment
          Selection Office
ADPFB   Automatic Data Processing Field
          Branch
ADPG   Air Defence Planning Group (Nato)
AdPlan   advanced planning
ADPM   automatic data processing machine
ADPPB   Automatic Data Processing Production
          Branch (US BUPERS)
ADPP&PB   Automatic Data Processing, Program-
          ming and Production Branch (BUPERS)
ADPR   Assistant Director of Public Rela-
          tions
ADPS   automatic data processing system
ADPSC   automatic data processing service
          centre
ADPSO   Association of Data Processing Ser-
          vice Organizations (US)
ADR   accident data recorder; Air Defence
          Region; Air Defence Regiment RA;
          aircraft direction room; aircraft
          discrepancy report
AdR   advisory route
Adrm   aerodrome
AdroBn   aerodrome battalion (US)
adrp   airdrop
ADRS   automatic data reporting system

ADS   accessory drive system; accurately
          defined systems (computers); air
          data sub-system; air defence
          system; air defence sector; air
          defence ship; aircraft development
          service; aeronautical systems
          division; Air Despatch Squadron
          RCT; Advanced Dressing Station;
          audio distributing system; auto-
          matic depressurization system;
          automatic door seal; Ammunition
          Delivery System for M-109; Aerial
          Delivery Section
ADSAF   Automatic Data Systems within the
          Army in the Field (US)
ADSARM   Advanced Defense-Suppression Anti-
          radiation Missile (USAF programme)
ADSC   Aeronautical Division of the Signal
          Corps (US) WW1, Air Defence Soft-
          ware Committee (Nato), -SO, Air
          Defence Software Committee Support
          Office, Army Distinguished Service
          Cross (US)
AdSec   advanced section
AdSel   Address selective (radio system)
          DABS (UK)
ADSID   Air Defense Systems Integration
          Division (USAF)
ADSL   authorized depot storage list
ADSM   Air Defence Suppression Missile by
          GD; American Defense Service Medal
          (US); Army Distinguished Service
          Medal (US)
ADSO   Assistant Division Signal Officer
AdSOC   Administrative Support Operations
          Center (US)
ADSS   Australian Defence Scientific Ser-
          vice
ADS&T   Assistant Director of Supplies and
          Transport
ADSTAR   automatic document storage and re-
          trieval
ADSU   advanced direct support unit (Nato)
ADSW   advanced direct support workshop (Nato);
          augmented direct support workshop
ADT   active duty for training; admission
          discharge and transfer (computer);
          air-data terminal; amphibious
          training demonstrator; Assistant
          Director of Transport; atomic
          damage template (US); average
          daily traffic
ADTA   Airborne Division, Territorial Army
          (UK)
ADTC   Air Defence Technical Centre (Nato);
          Armament Development and Test
          Center AFSC Eglin AFB (US)
ADTech   advanced decoy technology
ADTn   Assistant Director of Transportation
ADTP   Accelerated Development Test Pro-
          gramme (Nato)

ADU	aircraft delivery unit (US); army dog unit (UK); automatic data unit; auxiliary display unit	AECL	Atomic Energy of Canada Ltd
ADUM	automated data unit movement (US)	AECMA	Association Européenne des Constructeurs de Materiel Aerospatial (Association of European Aerospace Manufacturers) (88 Boulevard Malesherbes, F-75008 Paris)
ADUNI	Army Dog Unit in Northern Ireland		
ADvCP	advanced command post		
ADvHed	advanced headquarters		
AdvIntelCen	advanced intelligence centre	AECO	Aeromedical Evacuation Control Officer (US)
AdvMOS	advanced military occupational speciality (US)	AECP	Army Extension Course Program (US)
Advon	advanced echelon (US)	AED	aeronautical engineering duty; astro electronics division; automated engineering design
ADVS	Assistant Director of Veterinary Services		
AdvScol	advanced School (US)	AEDC	Arnold Engineering Development Center (US AFSC)
ADW	Air Defence Warning; Assistant Director of Works	AEDS	Atomic Energy Detection System
ADWC	Air Defence Warning Condition yellow: probable red: imminent/in progress white: improbable	AEDU	Admiralty Experimental Diving Unit
		AEE	airborne evaluation equipment; Aircraft Energy Efficiency (NASA programme); Army Entrance Examination; Atomic Energy Establishment
ADWE&M	Assistant Director of Works Electrical and Mechanical	AeE	Aeronautical Engineer
ADWEPS	Air Defense Weapons Cost Effectiveness Study (US)	AEEC	Airlines Electronic Engineering Committee
ADWOC	Air Defence Weapons Operations Centre	AEEE	Army Equipment Engineering Establishment (CA)
ADX	Advanced Development Experimental; air defence exercise; automatic data exchange; automatic digital exchange;	AEEL	Aeronautical and Electronic Engineering Laboratory NADL (Johnsville Pa)
		AEEMS	automatic electric energy management system
ADZ	air defence zone (Nato)	AEEP	Aircraft Energy Efficiency Program (US)
AE	adult education; Army Education; Air Electrical STANAG; ammunition ship (Nato); atomic energy; atmospheric explorer; aeronautical engineering; ammunition examiner	AEEW	Atomic Energy Establishment Winfrith
		AEF	Advanced Electronics Field (training programme) (US); aircraft engine fitter; Allied Expeditionary Forces; American Expeditionary Forces; Australian Expeditionary Forces
A&E	armament and electronics (Nato); analysis and evaluation (US)		
AEA	Air Efficiency Award (UK); air entraining agent (concrete); assignment, eligibility and availability (US); Atomic Energy Authority (UK)	AEG	active element group; Allgemeine Elektrizitätsgesellschaft (General Electricity Society) (AEG-Telefunken, Lyoner Str. 26, D-6000 Frankfurt 71)
AEAC	Atomic Energy Authority Constabulary (UK)		
AEAF	Allied Expeditionary Air Force	AEGIS	An Existing General Information System; Airborne Early Warning Ground Integration Segment by Hughes
AEARC	Army Equipment Authorizations Review Center (US)		
AEC	automatic exposure control; Atomic Energy Commission; American Engineering Council (US); Army Educational Certificate (UK); Army Education Centre; Army Educational Corps (US); Arab Electronics Company Al Khar (AOI+Thomson CSF); Aviation Electric of Canada; Associated Equipment Ltd (Southall)	Aegis	naval anti-aircraft system by RCA (SPY-1+Standard)
		AEI	acrylic eye illustrator; aerial exposure index; annual efficiency index; Associated Electrical Industries; automatic error interrogation
AECA	Arms Export Control Act (US) 1976		
AECB	Atomic Energy Control Board (CA)	AEL	Admiralty Engineering Laboratory (West Drayton UK); Aero Electronics Ltd (UK); Aeronautical Engineering Laboratory (US NAPTC),
AECC	Aeromedical Evaluation Control Center (US)		

AEL   Aeronautical Engine Laboratory
          (US); Aircraft Engineering Labora-
          tory; American Electronic Labora-
          tories (US); Associated Engineer-
          ing Ltd (UK); Authorized Equipment
          Listings (US); automation engineer-
          ing laboratory
AEL-4012 Falcon, small RPV by AEL (UK)
AEL-4019 airborne camera for RPVs by AEL
AEL-4020 Merlin, small RPV by AEL
AEL-4041 Mosette, small RPV
AELE   Association Européenne de Libre
          Échange (European Free Trade Assoc-
          iation)
AElP   Allied Electrical Publication (Nato)
AEM   air escort mission; missile support
          ship (Nato)
AEM-422   atomic energy munition (nuclear
          shell)
AEngrServ Army Engineer Service (US)
AEO   Air Engineer Officer (US); Assistant
          Experimental Officer (UK)
AEOB   advanced engine overhaul base; alter-
          nate escort operating base
AEOO   aeromedical evacuation operations
          officer
AEOP   Allied Explosive Ordnance (dispatch)
          Publication (Nato)
AEP   Allied Engineering Publication
          (Nato); Apollo Extension Program
          (US); Agence Européenne de Produc-
          tivité (European Productivity
          Agency)
AEPB   Active Enlisted Plans Branch BUPERS
          (US)
AEqP   Allied Equipment (Army) Publication
          (Nato)
Aequare   surveillance and target designation
          by RPVs for bombers (USAF program)
AER   Army Emergency Relief (US); Army
          Emergency Reserve (UK); Assault
          Engineer Regiment (US)
aer   aeronautics; aeroplane
AERB   Army Educational Requirements
          Board (US)
AERDL   Army Electronics Research and Devel-
          opment Laboratory (US)
AerE   Aeronautical Engineer
AERE   Atomic Energy Research Establishment
          (Harwell UK)
AERNo   Aeronautical Equipment Reference
          Number (UK)
AERO   Air Education and Recreation Organi-
          zation (Upper Chobham Rd, Camber-
          ley, Surrey)
Aerobee   US experimental rocket
Aero-Caster heavy-lift fluid film system by
          Aero-Go Inc.
Aerodyne unmanned wingless experimental air-
          craft by Dornier

Aeros   research satellite 1972 by Dornier
AEROS   Artificial Earth Research and
          Orbiting Satellite
Aerosat   European communications satellite
          by GE Cosmos group
AERS   Aircraft Equipment Requirement
          Schedule (US)
AES   aeromedical evacuation system;
          Armoured Engineer Squadron (UK);
          Army Education Scheme;
          artificial earth satellite;
          Atmospheric Environment
          Service
AE&S   air equipment and support (US)
AESA   Astilleros Espanolas SA
AESAP   Army Entertainment Scholarship and
          Award Program (US)
AESC   automatic electronic switching
          centre
AESOP   artificial earth satellite observa-
          tion programme
AESOR   Association Européenne des Officiers
          de Reserve (European Reserve Offi-
          cers' Association)
AESRS   Army Equipment Status Reporting
          System (US)
AEtP   Allied Electronics Publication
          (Nato)
AETR   advanced engineering test reactor
AEv   air evaluation
AEV   Aero-thermodynamic Elastic Vehicle;
          armoured engineer vehicle
AEW   Admiralty Experimental Works, air-
          borne early warning, armoured
          electronic warfare (vehicle)
AEW-1   airborne early warning aircraft
          Nimrod by Hawker Siddeley
AEW-2   airborne early warning aircraft
          Shackleton (project)
AEW-3   airborne early warning aircraft
          Gannet (project)
AEW&C   airborne early warning and control
AEWP   Aerospace Education Workshop Project
          (US)
AEWRon   Airborne Early Warning Squadron
          (USN); Fleet Air Reconnaissance
          Squadron (USN)
AEWS   advanced earth satellite weapon
          system; airborne early warning
          system
AEWTF   aircrew electronic warfare tactics
          facility (multiple ground sites)
          (Nato); aircrew electronic warfare
          training facility
AEWTU   Airborne Early Warning Training Unit
          (US)
AEx   agreement to extend enlistment (US)
AF   Admiral of the Fleet; Asiatic Fleet
          (USN); accuracy figure; Air Force;
          Army Form; armoured force;

AF	auxiliary force; automatic following (radar); automatic (smoke) filter; air field; audio frequency; stores ship (USN)
A/F	anti-flooding
A&F	Abercrombie & Fitch
AFA	Armed Forces Act (UK); Air Force Act; Air Force Association (US); Army Flight Activity (US); Advanced Fleet Anchorage
AFAB	Army Families Advice Bureau (UK)
AFAC	airborne forward air controller; 120mm arrow-type anti-tank shot (FR)
AFADI	Air Force Air Defense Interceptors (US)
AFADL	Air Force Avionics Development Laboratory AFSC (US)
AFAFC	Air Force Accounting and Finance Center (US)
AFAITC	Air Force Intelligence Training Center (US); Armed Forces Intelligence Training Centre
AFAK	Armed Forces Assistance to Korea (US)
AFAL	Air Force Avionics Laboratory (Wright Patterson AFB, Ohio)
AFAO	approved forces acquisition objective (US)
AFAPL	Air Force Aero Propulsion Laboratory (US)
AFAR	advanced field array radar; Azores fixed acoustic range (Nato)
AFAS	Armed Forces Art Society (UK)
AFATL	Air Force Armament and Testing Laboratory (AFSC Eglin AFB, US)
AFB	Air Force Base (US); anti-friction bearing; Army Fire Brigade (UK)
AF&B	Accounting and Finance Branch (BUPERS USN)
AFBMD	Air Force Ballistic Missile Division (US)
AFC	Air Force Cross; Army Field Code; Australian Flying Corps RAAF; amplitude frequency characteristics; auto-correlation functions; automatic flight control; automatic frequency control
AFC	Alvis of Coventry (UK)
AFCA	Association Française pour la Communauté Atlantique (French Association for the Atlantic Community)
AFCC	Air Force Combat Command; assault fire command console
AFCCG	Atlantic Fleet Combat Camera Group (USN)
AFCE	Allied Forces Central Europe (Nato); Armed Forces Coin Exchange (US); automatic flight control equipment
AFCEA	Armed Forces Communications and Electronics Association US
AFCENT	Allied Forces Central Europe Brunssum (Nato)
AFCM	Air Force Commendation Medal (US)
AFCMD	Air Force Contract Management Division AFSC (US)
AFCO	Admiralty Fleet Confidential Order
AFCo	Andrew Fryberg & Co. (Hopkinton Mass.)
afco	automatic fuel cut-off
AFCRC	Air Force Cambridge Research Center (US)
AFCRL	Air Force Cambridge Research Laboratories (US)
AFCRS	Army Full Crew Research Simulator (for tanks) by GE
AFCS	active federal commissioned service (US); Air Force Communication Service (US); Army Facilities Components System (US); Armed Forces Courier Service (US); Air Force Communications System (US); artillery fire control simulator; adaptive flight control system; automatic flight control system; avionic flight control system
A/FCS	Armament and Fire Control Survey
AFCSC	Air Force Command and Staff College (US)
AFD	Air Force Depot; Armed Forces Day; accelerated freeze drying; auxiliary floating dock (USN); Admiralty floating dock
AFDA	Air Force Discipline Act (UK)
AFDB	Auxiliary, floating dock, big (USN)
AFDC	(Army) Airborne Forces Development Centre (Amesbury Abbey) 1943 (UK)
AFDCB	Armed Forces Disciplinary Control Board (US)
afdk	after dark
AFDL	auxiliary, floating dock, light (USN)
AFDL(C)	auxiliary, floating dock, light, concrete
AFDM	auxiliary, floating dock, medium (USN)
AFDO	assistant fighter director officer
AFDP	Armed Forces Development Plan (US)
AFDS	Air Fighting Development Squadron RAF; automatic flight direction system; auxiliary fighter director ship
AFDV	allwetterfähiges Flugführungssystem für Drehflügler und VSTOL by Dornier (all-weather flight direction system for rotary and VSTOL aircraft)
AFE	US Army program, electronic warfare helicopter
AFEB	Armed Forces Epidemiological Board (US)

AFEE	Airborne Forces Experimental Establishment (UK)	AFLC	Air Force Logistics Command (US)
AFEES	Armed Forces Examining and Entrance Stations (US)	AFLCM	Air Force Logistics Command Manual (US)
AFEM	Armed Forces Expeditionary Medal (US)	afld	airfield
AFES	Admiralty Fuel Experimental Station	AFLO	airborne force liaison officer
AFETR	Air Force Eastern Test Range AFSC (US)	aflt	afloat
		AFM	Air Force Manual (US); Air Force Medal (UK); Armed Forces Management
AFEX	Armed Forces in Europe Exchange (US)		
AFF	Army Field Force (UK)	AFMA	Armed Forces Management Association
AFFB	aluminium floating foot bridge (US)	AFMDC	Air Force Missile Development Center (US)
AFFDL	Air Force Flight Dynamics Laboratory AFSC Wright Patterson AFB	AFMed	Allied Forces Mediterranean (Nato)
AFFF	aqueous film forming foam	AFMFP	Aircraft, Fleet Marine Force, Pacific (US)
AFFRS	artillery free flight rocket system		
AFFSC	Air Force Flight Safety Committee (Nato)	AFML	Air Force Materials Laboratory (US)
		AFMPG	Atlantic Fleet Mobile Photographic Group (USN)
AFFTC	Air Force Flight Testing Center AFSC (US)	AFMSC	Armed Forces Menu Service Committee (US)
AFG	Allied Freighter Guard (Nato); analogue function generator; audio frequency gain	AFMTC	Air Force Missile Test Center (US)
		AFN	American Forces' Network
		AFNB	Armed Forces News Bureau (US)
AFGE	American Federation of Government Employees (US)	AFNE	Allied Forces Northern Europe (Nato); American Forces Network Europe; Astilleros y Fabricas Navales del Estado SA (Argentina)
AFGIS	Aerial Free Gunnery Instruction School (US)		
AFGR	approved for gross requirement		
AFGU	Aerial Free Gunnery Unit (US)	AFNorth	Allied Forces Northern Europe Oslo (Nato)
AFGWC	Air Force Global Weather Center (US)		
AFHA	Armed Forces Hostess Association (US)	AFO	Admiralty Fleet Order RN; Army Forwarding Officer (UK)
AFHC	Air Force Headquarters Command (US)		
AFHQ	African Force Headquarters; Allied Force Headquarters (US-UK)	AFOAR	Air Force Office of Aerospace Research (US)
AFHQCIC	Allied Force Headquarters Counterintelligence Corps	AFOAS	Air Force Office of Aerospace Science (US)
AFHQPS	Allied Force Headquarters Petroleum Section	AFOSR	Air Force Office of Scientific Research (US)
AFHRL	Air Force Human Resources Laboratory (US)	AFOEA	Air Force Organizational Excellence Award (US)
AFI	auxiliary functional item (data link); automatic fault isolation; Armed Forces Institute (US)	AFOMMIU	amphibious forces ordnance material mobile instruction unit (US)
		AFOUA	Air Force Outstanding Unit Award (US)
AfI	African-Indian (ocean area) (USN)	AFP	adiabatic fast passage; Air Force Police; Air Force Publication; annual firing practice; annual funding programme; armed forces police
AFI	automatisches Fahrplan-Informationssystem by Dornier (automatic timetable information system)		
AFInsPath	Armed Forces Institute for Pathology (US)	AFPA	American Fighter Pilots Association (US)
AFIO	approved for inventory objective	AFPAM	automatic flight planning and monitoring
AFIP	Armed Forces Institute for Pathology (US)		
AfI-RAN	Africa-Indian Ocean Region Air Navigation	AFPav	airfield pavement
		AFPCB	Armed Forces Pest Control Board (US)
AFIT	Air Force Institute of Technology (US)	AFPB	armed forces police detachment
		AFPEC	Armed Forces Product Evaluation Committee (US)
AFIW	Air Force Industrial Workshop		
AFJA	Armed Forces Judo Association	AFPEO	Armed Forces Professional Entertainment Office (US)
AFL	Air Force Letter (US); Air Force List (UK)	AFPR	Air Force Plant Representative (US); Armed Forces Procurement Regulations (US)
AFLant	Air Forces, Atlantic (US)		

AFPRB   Armed Forces Pay Review Body (UK)
AFPRO   Armed Forces Plant Representative
         Office(r); Air Force Plant Repre-
         sentative Office(r)
AFPS   American Forces Press Service;
         Armed Forces Press Service; Army
         Field Park Squadron (UK)
AFPT   artillery fire plan table
AFPU   Army Film and Photographic Unit
AFQT   Armed Forces Qualification Test
AFQTVA   Armed Forces Verbal Arithmetic Sub-
         test (US)
AFR   air fuel ratio; amplitude frequency
         response; artillery flash ranging;
         Air Force Regulation; Air Force
         Reserve
AFRA   Armed Forces Reserve Act 1952 (US);
         average freight rate assessment
AFRadBioRschInst Armed Forces Radio-biology
                  Research Institute (US)
                  AFRRI
AFRBA   Armed Forces Relief and Benefit
         Association
AFRC   Air Force Research Center (Cambridge
         Mass.); Armed Forces Reserve
         Center (US)
AFRCE   Air Force Regional Civil Engineer
         (US)
AFRes   Air Force Reserve (US)
AFRM   Armed Forces Reserve Medal (US)
afrm   airframe
AFROTC   Air Force Reserve Officer Training
         Corps (US)
AFRPL   Air Force Rocket Propulsion Labora-
         tory (US)
AFRRI   Armed Forces Radiobiology Research
         Institute (US)
AFRS   Armed Forces Radio Service (US)
AFRSC   Armed Forces Recipe Service Committee
AFRSF   Atlantic Fleet Range Support Facility
         (USN)
AFRTC   Air Force Reserve Training Center
         (US)
AFRTS   American Forces Radio and Television
         Service; Armed Forces Radio and
         Television Service (US)
AFRTS-LA American Forces Radio and Televi-
         sion Service, Los Angeles
AFRTS-W American Forces Radio and Television
         Service, Washington
AFS   advanced flying school; aeronautical
         fixed service; Air Force Station
         (US); Army Fire Service (UK);
         auxiliary fire service; Atlantic
         Ferry Service; Air Force Speciality
         (US); Air Force Supply; combat
         stores ship (USN)
AFSA   Africa South of the Sahara (USN);
         American Flagship Available;
         American Foreign Service Associa-

tion; Armed Forces Security
         Agency (US)
AFSARC   Air Force Systems Acquisition and
         Review Committee (US)
AFSatCom Air Force Satellite Communications
         System (US)
AFSC   Air Force Systems Command (US); Air
         Force Speciality Code (US); Armed
         Forces Staff College; American
         Friends Service Committee
AFSCIG   Air Force Systems Command Inspector
         General (US)
AFSCM   Air Force Systems Command Manual
         (US)
AFSCS   Army Field Stock Control System (US)
AFSD   Air Forces Service Division (Nato)
AFSE   Allied Forces Southern Europe
AFSJT   Air Force Strategic Jet Tankers
AFSOG   Air Force Special Operations Group
         (US)
AFSouth Allied Forces Southern Europe
         Naples (Nato)
AFSR   Argonne Fast Source Reactor
AFSS   Air Force Secret Satellite; auto-
         matic fire suppression system by
         Hughes
AFSSC   Armed Forces Supply Support Centre
         (Nato)
AFStaffCol Armed Forces Staff College (US)
AFSTC   Army Foriegn Science and Technology
         Center (US)
AFSU   Auxiliary Ferry Service Unit (US)
AFSWC   Air Force Special Weapons Center
         (US)
AFSWP   Armed Forces Special Weapons Project
         (US)
AFT   adaptive ferro-electric transformer;
         Atelier de Fabrication de Tou-
         louse (FR)
AFTA   Air Force Tactical Airlift; Air
         Force tactical aircraft
AFTAC   Air Force Technical Applications
         Center (US)
AFTDU   Airborne Forces Tactical Development
         Unit RAF 1943 Tarrant Rushton
AFTFA   Air Force Tactical Fighter Aircraft
AFTI   Advanced Fighter Technology Integra-
         tion (USAF programme); Allied
         Forces Technology Integration
         (Nato)
AFTIA   Armed Forces Technical Information
         Agency (Nato)
AFTN   aeronautical fixed telecommunica-
         tions network (for air traffic
         control)
AFTO   Air Force Technical Orders
AFTP   additional flight training period
AFTrnTraRonPac Auxiliary Service Force,
                Transportation Training
                Squadron, Pacific (USN)

AFTS	Advanced Flying Training School RAF; aeronautical fixed telecommunications service
AFU	advanced flying unit (UK); assault fire unit (US)
AFUS	Air Force of the United States
AFV	Armored Fighting Vehicle (USMC)
AFVG	Anglo-French variable geometry (aircraft programme)
AFVN	American Forces Vietnam Network
AFW	Army Field Workshop
AFWAB	Army Fixed Wing Aptitude Battery (US)
AFWAR	Air Force (personnel) with the Army (US)
AFWE	Air Forces Western Europe (Nato)
AFWL	Armed Forces Writers League (US); Air Force Weapons Laboratory (US)
AFWR	Atlantic Fleet Weapons Range (USN)
AFWST	Armed Forces Women's Selection Test (US)
AFWTR	Air Force Western Test Range (US); Atlantic Fleet Weapon Test Range (USN)
AG	Adjutant General (US); airman gunner (UK); Air Group (US); Army Group (Nato); advanced guard; armed guard; air-to-ground (communications); anti-gas; automatic gun; miscellaneous ship (USN)
A-G	arresting gear
A/g	air graph
AGA	Australian Garrison Artillery
a-g-a	air-to-ground-to-air
AGACS	automatic ground-to-air communications system; air-to ground-to-air communications system
AGAI	Army General and Administrative Instructions (UK)
AGARD	Advisory Group for Aerospace Research and Development (Nato)
Agave	airborne light-weight radar by Thomson-CSF; class, mine-sweepers IT
AGB	icebreaker (USN-USCG-Nato)
AGC	Adjutant General's Corps (US); aboard guidance computer; abort guidance computer; Armed Guard Center (US); automatic gain control; Amphibious Group Command (vessel) (USN); Aerojet General Corporation
AGCA	automatic ground-controlled approach
AGCF	air-ground correlation factor
AGCL	automatic ground-controlled landing
AGCM	Army Good Conduct Medal
AGCT	Army General Classification Test (US)
AGCTS	Armed Guard Center Training School (US)
agcy	agency

AGD	axial gear differential
AGD	sea-going dredge (USN)
AGDE	escort research ship (USN)
AGDok	Arbeitsgemeinschaft Dokumentation (working group on military technology documentation) (GE)
AGDS	American Gage Design Standard
AGE	aerospace ground environment; automatic ground equipment; associated ground equipment; automatic guidance electronics; Admiralty Gunnery Establishment
AGEH	hydrofoil research ship (USN)
Agena	space missile by Lockheed
AGEP	Advisory Group on Electronic Parts (Nato)
AGER	environmental research ship (USN)
AGF	Adjutant General to the Forces (US); Army Ground Forces (US); miscellaneous flagship (USN)
AGH	Australian General Hospital
AGI	Aeronautical & General Instruments Ltd (40 Purley Way, Croydon CR9 3BH), auxiliary (vessel) general intelligence (USN)
AGIC	Army General Institute Committee (UK)
Agiflite	airborne camera by AGI
Agile	short-range air-to-air missile (US) class, ocean mine-sweepers (USN)
AGIO	Armed Guard Inspection Officer
AGIS	Armed Guard Inspection Service
AGIS-143	Automatisches Gefechts und Informationssystem für Schnellboote der Klasse 143 (automatic combat information system for FPB of the 143 class) (GE)
AGL	above ground level; airborne gun laying (radar); lighthouse tender (USN)
AGLO	Air Ground Liaison Officer (USMC)
AGM	Admiralty General Message; missile range instrumentation ship (USN); air-to-ground missile; air-launched guided missile
AGM-12	Bullpup, air-launched guided missile by Martin Marietta
AGM-28	Hound-dog, air-launched guided missile, nuclear stand-off missile
AGM-45	Shrike, air-launched guided missile, anti-radar missile by TI
AGM-53	Condor, air-launched guided missile, TV-homing by Rockwell
AGM-62	Walleye, air-launched guided missile, TV-guided by Hughes/Martin
AGM-65	Maverick, air-launched guided missile, anti-tank role by Hughes A TV-guidance B TV-guidance with scene magnification C laser guidance D infra-red guidance

AGM-69   SRAM, air-launched guided missile, short-range missile nuclear warhead by Boeing

AGM-78   Standard, ARM, air-launched guided missile, anti-radar missile by GD

AGM-83   Bulldog, air-launched guided missile by Maxson

AGM-84   Harpoon, air-launched guided missile anti-ship missile by McDD

AGM-86   ALCM, air-launched guided missile, air-launched cruise missile, SCAD, subsonic cruise armed decoy, ECM-carrier by McDD

AGM-88   HARM, air-launched guided missile, high-speed anti-radiation missile by TI

AGMR   advanced gas-cooled maritime reactor; major communications relay ship (USN)

AGN   Articles for the Government of the Navy (USN)

AGO   air gunnery officer

AGOR   auxiliary general, oceanographic research (vessel) (USN)

AGOS   Air-to-Ground Operation System; Air-to-Ground School; Air Gunnery Officers School; auxiliary general, ocean surveillance (USN)

Agosta   class, conventionally powered attack submarines (FR)

AGP   automatic guidance programming patrol craft tenders (USN)

AGR   advanced gas-cooled reactor; radar picket ship (USN)

AGRA   Army Group, Royal Artillery

AGRE   Army Group, Royal Engineers

AGREE   Advisory Group on Reliability of Electronic Equipment

Agrion   surveillance and fire direction radar by Thomson CSF

Agrion-15   maritime surveillance radar by Thomson-CSF

AGRM   Adjutant General, Royal Marines

AGRS   American Graves Registration Service

AGS   abort guidance system (NASA); Advanced Guard Support; aircraft general standards; Aircraft Generation Squadron (USAF); Air Gunnery School (UK); Allied Geographic Section; Army General Staff (US); Army Gymnastics Staff (UK); Armed Guard School (US); automatic gain stabilization; auxiliary general, survey (vessel) (USN)

AGS-901   airborne anti-submarine warfare system (UK-AS)

AGSAN   astronomical guidance system for air navigation

AGSC   coastal surveying ship (USN)

AGSL   satellite launching ship (USN)

AGSM   Africa General Service Medal

AGSS   high-speed transport submarine (USN)

AGT   Avco-Lycoming Gas Turbine; Allison Gas Turbines (Detroit Diesel Allison, POB 894, Indianapolis In. 46206)

AGTR   technical research ship (USN)

AGUS   Ausbildungsgerät für U-Jagd und Sonar by KAE (training system for anti-submarine warfare and sonar)

AGUW   Ausbildungsgerät für Unterwasserwaffen (training system for underwater weapons)

AGVG   Anglo-German variable geometry (aircraft)

AGW   actual gross weight

AGWAC   Australian guided weapons and analogue computer

AGZ   actual ground zero

AH   ampere hour; analogue hybrid (computer); airfield heliport; hospital ship (USN); heavy attack aircraft (US); attack helicopter; armed helicopter; assault helicopter; anti-submarine helicopter

A/H   alter heading

AH-1   Huey Cobra, Sea Cobra, armed helicopter

AH-15   Cobra, anti-tank helicopter by Bell

AH-56   Cheyenne, armed helicopter

AH-64   AAH, advanced attack helicopter by Hughes

AHAM   advanced heavy anti-tank missile (US project)

AHAMS   advanced heavy anti-tank missile system by McDD

AHAWS   advanced heavy anti-tank weapon system

AHB   active hostile battery

AHC   Allied High Commissioner; Army Hospital Corps; assault helicopter company; assault helicopter carrier; Aerospatiale Helicopter Corporation (Dallas Tx.), Aerospatiale daughter

AHCT   ascending horizon crossing time

ahd   airhead, arrowhead (shot)

AHEC   Army's Higher Education Centre (UK)

AHF   anhydrous hydrofluric acid

AHFRAC   Army Human Factors Research Advisory Committee (US)

AHFRDC   Army Human Factors Research and Development Committee (US)

AHG   active homing guidance

AHGMR   ad hoc group on missile reliability

AH-IT   Sea Cobra, attack helicopter, naval anti-submarine warfare by Bell

AHIWG   ad hoc intelligence working group (Nato)

AHMEWG	ad hoc mixed exploratory working group	AIBS	American Institute for Biological Sciences
AHMWG	ad hoc mixed working group (Nato)	AIC	Adjutant, Intelligence Corps; Aeronautical Information Circular; advanced intelligence centre; air intercept control; Allied Intelligence Committee; action information centre; air information centre; automatic intersection control; Air Information Codification (Nato); Ammunition Identification Code
AHP	Allied Hydrographic Publication (Nato); air horse power; evacuation hospital ship (USN)		
AHp	Army heliport		
AHQ	Allied Headquarters; Army Headquarters; Air Headquarters; Area Headquarters; Alternate Headquarters		
AHQE	Air Headquarters Egypt (RAF) WW2	AICBM	anti-intercontinental ballistic missile
AHQWD	Air Headquarters Western Desert (RAF) WW2	AICC	air intercept control common (frequency) (Nato)
AHR	acceptable hazard rate	AICE	American Institute of Consulting Engineers
AHRS	altitude and heading reference system; attitude and heading reference system; automatic heading and reference system	AICO	action information control officer
		AICPOA	advanced intelligence center, Pacific Ocean area (US)
AHS	airborne hardware simulator; American Helicopter Society	AICS	air intake control system; Air Intercept Control School
AHT	Admiralty Health Trust; acoustic homing torpedo	AICT	Atlantic Information Centre for Teachers (37a High Street, Wimbledon, London SW19 5BY)
AHTAIWG	ad hoc technical air intelligence working group (Nato)		
AHTD	Army Headquarters Transport Division	AICV	Armoured Infantry Combat Vehicle
AHU	accumulated heat units; anti-halation undercoat (photogr.)	AID	Aeronautical Inspection Directorate (UK); Agency for International Development (US); Aircraft Intelligence Department (UK); Army Intelligence Department; automatic interrogation distorted
AHWG	ad hoc working group		
AI	Admiralty Instructions; airborne interception (radar); airborne interdiction (aircraft); aircraft instrument (aircrew stations); aircraft identification (radar); aircraft inspector; air intelligence; annoyance index (noise); anti-icing (agent, equipment); aptitude index; Army Intelligence; area of intersection; assistant instructor		
		AIDA	automatic intruder detection alarm
		AIDAS	advanced instrumentation and data analysis system
		AIDATS	Army In-flight Data Transmission System
		AIDC	Aircraft Industry Development Centre (Taiwan)
A&I	Alternation and Improvement (US programme)	AIDE	adapted identification decision equipment; automated image device evaluation
AI^2	Avionic Instruments Incorporated (943 East Hazlewood Ave., Rathway NJ)	AIDECS	automatic inspection device for explosive charge shell
AIA	anti-icing additive; Aerospace Industries Association of America; American Industry Association; Aviation Industry Association (NZ); Associazione Industrie Aerospaziale (IT); Atelier Industriel de l'Air (FR)	AIDJEX	Arctic Ice Dynamic Joint Experiment
		AIDRB	Army Investigational Drug Review Board (US)
		AIDS	Atlantic Institute for Defence Studies; airborne integrated data system; Air Force Intelligence Data System; Army Information and Data Systems (US)
AIAA	American Institute of Aeronautics and Astronautics; Aerospace Industries Association of America		
		AIDS-10	battlefield surveillance seismic equipment by Defence Electronics
AIAAM	Advanced Intercept air-to-air missile (USAF programme)	AIE	acceptance inspection, equipment; authorized 'in excess' (US)
AIB	Accident Investigation Branch (DoT); Admiralty Interview Board; Agency Investigation Board; Aircraft Instrument Bulletin		
		AIEA	Agence Internationale de l'Energie Atomique (International Atomic Energy Agency)

AIED	Aircraft Industries Engineering Division (Israel)
AIEE	American Institute of Electrical Engineers
AIER	American Institute of Economic Research
AIET	average instruction execution time
AIETA	airborne infra-red equipment for target analysis
AIF	Air Intelligence Force; Amphibian Imperial Forces; Australian Imperial Forces; Army Industrial Fund (US); Atomic Industrial Forum; automated intelligence file
AIFI	automatic in-flight insertion
AIFO	Army Instructions and Force Orders
AIFS	advanced instruction flying school; advanced indirect fire system by Norden
AIFV	armoured infantry fighting vehicle
AIG	Adjutant Inspector General; Assistant Inspector of Gunnery; address indication group
Aig	accident investigation
AIHS	Aspen Institute for Humanistic Studies (Princeton NJ)
AII	Army Intelligence Interpreter
AIIS	advanced infra-red imaging seeker by Rockwell
AIJD	Association Internationale des Juristes Democrates (International Association of Democratic Lawyers)
AIL	air intelligence liaison; airborne instruments laboratory; Aviation Instruments Ltd
AILAS	automatic instrument landing approach system
AILO	air intelligence liaison officer
AILS	advanced integrated landing system; automated instrument landing system
AIM	aerial independent models; air interception missile; airman's information manual; alarm indicator monitor; armored infantry mechanized (US)
AIM-4	Falcon, air interception missile, infra-red guidance by Hughes
AIM-7	Sparrow, air interception missile by Raytheon E standard version F extended range
AIM-9	Sidewinder, GAR-8, air interception missile, infra-red guidance missile by Philco/Raytheon
AIM-26	Falcon, air interception missile by Hughes
AIM-47	air interception missile by Hughes
AIM-54	Phoenix, air interception missile, long range by Hughes
AIMI	aviation intensive management items
AIMILO	Army-Industry Material Information Liaison Officer (Nato)
AIMIS	advanced integrated modular instrument system
AIMPA	Association Internationale de Meteorologie et de Physique de l'Atmosphere (International Association of Meteorology and Atmospheric Physics)
AIMS	Army Integrated Meteorological System (US); automatic industrial management system
AIMVAL	Air Intercept Missile Evaluation (Nato)
AIMVAL/ACEVAL	Air Intercept Missile Evaluation/Air Combat Evaluation (Nato)
AIMX	Air Intercept Missile Exercise
AIMXS	Aircraft IFF Mark XII Section (US)
AINO	Assistant Inspector of Naval Ordnance
AIO	Action Information Organization (RN system); Air Intelligence Organization (Nato); Allied Interrogation Organization (UK-US); Army Intelligence Organization; aviation information officer
AIP	Aeronautical Information Publication (US); Allied Intelligence Publication (Nato), Australian Industrial Participation
AIPC	Army Installations Planning Committee
AIPCN	Association Internationale Permanente des Congrès de Navigation (Permanent International Association of the Navigation Congress)
AIR	accelerated item reduction; aviation item reports; American Institute of Research; air-launched interception rocket; airborne intercept radar
AIR-2	Genie, airborne interception rocket nuclear
AiraCobra	P-39, fighter aircraft by Bell
AiraComet	P-59, jet aircraft by Bell 1942
AirAd	Air Administration (net) (US)
AirAF	Aircraft, Asiatic Fleet (USN)
AirAntiSubRon	aircraft Antisubmarine Squadron (USN)
AirASDevLant	Aircraft Anti-submarine Development Detachment, Atlantic
AIRBALTAP	Allied Air Forces Baltic Approaches (Nato)
AirBatForPac	Aircraft Battle Force Pacific Fleet (USN)
AIRBM	anti-intermediate range ballistic missile
Airbus	A-300, transport aircraft (UK-FR-GE)

AIRCA   air intake ramp control actuator
AirCdre   Air Commodore
AIRCENT   Allied Air Forces Central Europe
          (Nato)
AirCom   airways communications system
AirComd   Air Command (communications net)
          (US)
AirDef   Air Defence (division) (SHAPE)
AirDefCom   Air Defence Commander
AirDep   Air Deputy (SHAPE)
AirDevRon   air development squadron
AirDex   air defence exercise (Nato)
AIRE   American Institute of Radio Engineers
AIREASTLANT   Allied Naval Air Forces East
          Atlantic Area (Nato)
AirElo   air electrical officer
AirEngPropAccOvhl   Airplane, Engine, Propel-
          ler and Accessory Over-
          haul (US)
AirEO   Air Engineering Officer
AIREP   Air Reports (in plain language) (US)
AIRES   Advanced Imagery Requirements Exploi-
          tation System (USAF programme)
AirEvacWing   Air Evacuation Wing (US)
AIRF   assignment instructions remain firm
AirFam   aircraft familiarization
AirFerRon   Aircraft Ferry Squadron
AirFMFPac   Aircraft, Fleet Marine Force,
          Pacific (USN)
Air Horse   W-11, helicopter by Cierva
          (1 engine 3 rotors)
AirIS   aircraft store issuing ship (USN)
AIRLANT   Air Forces, Atlantic Fleet (USN)
AIRLO   Air Liaison Officer
AIRMEE   International Aircraft Maintenance
          Engineering Exhibition
AirMG   aircraft machine gunner
AirMiss   aircraft miss (reporting system for
          near misses)
AirNavO   air navigation officer
AIRNON   Allied Air Forces North Norway (Nato)
AirNorSols   Aircraft Northern Solomons (US)
AIRNORTH   Allied Air Forces Northern Europe
          (Nato)
AirOps   Air Operations; Air and Special
          Operations (division) (Nato)
AirPac   Air Forces, Pacific Fleet (USN)
AIRPASS   Airborne interception radar and
          pilot's attack sight system
AIRS   advanced inertial reference sphere by
          Northrop; aircraft inventory re-
          porting system
AirScoForPac   Aircraft Scouting Force,
          Pacific Fleet (USN)
AirShipGr   Airship Group
AIRSONOR   Allied Air Forces South Norway
          (Nato)
AirSoPac   Aircraft, South Pacific Force
AIRSOUTH   Allied Air Forces Southern Europe
          (Nato)

AirTac   air rendezvous system by LMT
AirtoS   short-range air-to-surface system
AirTrack   flight safety system by AEG-
          Telefunken
AirTransRon   Air Transport Squadron
AirTraRon   Air Training Squadron
AIS   advanced instructional system;
          Aeronautical Information Service;
          Air Intelligence Service; altitude
          indication system; Artillery
          Information Service WW2
AIS-pod   aircraft instrumentation sub-system
          pod
AI^2S Advanced Infra-red Imaging Seeker by
          Rockwell
AISA   Aeronautica Industrial SA (Spain)
AIST   hovercraft (SU)
AISV   Advanced Infantry Support Vehicle by
          Lockheed
AISV-L   Advanced Infantry Support Vehicle,
          light
AIT   advanced individual training; auto-
          ignition temperature; automotive
          information test; Airitalia
AITC   action information training centre
AITE   aircraft-integrated test equipment;
          automatic inter-city telephone
          exchange
AITS   automatic integrated telephone
          system
AIW   aural infrasonic wave
AIWC   Air Intelligence Watch Condition
          (Nato)
AIWM   American Institute of Weights and
          Measures
AIZ   air intercept zone (Nato)
AJ   anti-jamming; attack jet (aircraft);
          area junction
AJ-37   Viggen, strike aircraft by SAAB
AJ-168   Martel, air-to-ground missile, TV
          guided by BAC/Matra
AJAC   automatic jamming avoidance cir-
          cuitry
AJAG   Assistant Judge Advocate General (US)
          /Civ Civil Law
          /Mil Military Law
AJCC   alternate joint communications centre
          centre
AJD   anti-jamming display
AJEET   jet trainer aircraft (improved Gnat)
          by HAL
AJEX   Association of Jewish Ex-servicemen
          and Women
AJSS   Australian Joint Staff Service
AK   cargo ship (USN)
AK-47   Automat Kalashnikov, 7.62mm assault
          rifle (SU)
AKA   amphibious cargo attack (vessel)
          (Nato)
AKC   Army Kinema Corporation (UK)

AKD   cargo ship, dock; deephold cargo
          ship (USN)
AKF   cargo ship, refrigerated (USN)
AK-FBM   cargo ship, fleet ballistic missile;
          Polaris resupply ship (USN)
Akizuki   class, destroyers (JMSDF)
AKL   cargo ship, light (USN)
AKM   Automat Kalashnikov Modernizovannji
          assault rifle 7.62mm (SU)
AKMS   Automat Kalashnikov Modernizovannji
          with folding stock
AKN   cargo ship, net (USN); Automatisier-
          tes Korps-Stammnetz (automatic
          telephone net) (GE)
AKR   cargo ship, vehicles (USN)
AKS   cargo ship, general issue (USN)
AKS-74   assault rifle 5.46mm (SU)
Akshai   class, Indian patrol boats
AKSS   cargo submarine (USN)
AKV   cargo ship, aircraft ferry (USN)
AL   Admiralty Letter; American Legion;
          Army List; amplitude limiter;
          approach and landing; arrival
          locator; auxiliary, light (light-
          ship) (USN)
A/L   air liaison
al   airlift
AL-8-70   airborne rocket pod 8cal. 2.75" FFAR
AL-18-50 airborne rocket pod 18cal. 2" FFAR
ALA   American Land Army; Army Launch Area
ALAD   automatic liquid agent detector;
          Army Legal Aid Department
Aladin   Tiger, ground-based air surveillance
          system by Thomson-CSF
ALAF   Arme légère à fil (light wire-guided
          weapon) (FR)
AlAirC   Alaskan Air Command (US)
Alamak-Standard RPV launching and control
          system by Meteor
Alamac-Rid light-weight RPV launching and
          control system by Meteor
ALanF   Army Land Force (US)
ALAR   Avion légère d'attaque et de recon-
          naissance (light-weight strike
          reconnaissance aircraft)
AlArAct   All Army Activities (US)
ALARM   air-launched anti-radiation missile
          by BAe; air-launched advanced
          ramjet missile; alerting long-
          range airborne radar for MTI
          (moving target identification)
AlarmCom-80 alarm Communications system
ALARR   air-launched air-recoverable rocket
Alasca   all aspect capability (air-to-air
          missile) by BGT
ALAT   BQM-74, air-launchable aerial target
          by Northrop; Army Language Apti-
          tude Test (US); Aviation Légère
          d'Armée de Terre (French Army Air
          Corps)

ALATB   air-landing anti-tank battery
ALatd   assumed latitude
ALB   Army Language Bureau
Albacore torpedo bomber WW2 by Fairey
Albany   class, guided missile cruisers (USN)
Albatross helicopter; naval surface-to-air
          missile by Selenia; SA-16,
          amphibian SAR aircraft; L-39,
          jet trainer aircraft (Czech)
Albermarle transport aircraft WW2 by
          Armstrong
Albert Medal UK decoration for rescuers
ALBI   air-launched ballistic intercept
          missile; air-launched boost inter-
          cept missile
Albion   FV-13581, 3 ton 6x4 truck
ALBM   air-launched ballistic missile
AlBushra class, patrol boats (Oman)
ALC   adaptive logic circuit; Air Logis-
          tics Corporation (US); Army Legal
          Corps (UK); assault landing craft;
          automatic level control
alc   alcohol
ALCAN   Aluminium Company of Canada
AlCanUS   Alaska, Canada, United States
Alcatel   CIT Alcatel (FR)
ALCC   airborne launch control centre
ALCH   approach light contact height
ALCM   AGM-86, air-launched cruise missile
          by Boeing
ALCO   airlift liaison coordination
          office(r)
ALCom   Alaskan Command
ALCon   all concerned
ALCOR   ARPA/Lincoln C-band Observable Radar
          (Advanced Research Projects Agency)
ALCS   airborne launch control system
ALD   acquisition logistics division; at a
          later date
ALD-2   airborne ECM equipment by Rodale
ALD-5   airborne ECM equipment by Raytheon
Aldis lamp signal flashlight
ALDM-2   artillery laser range-finder by
          Iskra (Yugoslavia)
ALDPS   automatic logistic data processing
          system
ALE-19   airborne chaff dispenser
          (2. 6. 18. 23. 28. 29. 30. 32. 33.
          35. 38. 39. 40. 129.)
ALEMS   Apollo Lunar Excursion Module
          Sensors
ALESC   Amiral Commandant l'Escadre à la
          Mer (Admiral, French Fleet
          (afloat))
ALESCO   Amiral Commandant l'Escadre (Nato)
ALEX   alert exercise; anchor line exten-
          sion (kit)
ALF   advanced landing field; auxiliary
          landing field; automatic letter
          facer

ALFCE   Allied Land Forces, Central Europe
ALFCENT   Allied Land Forces, Central Europe
ALFSEA   Allied Land Forces South East Asia
ALFSH   Allied Land Forces Schleswig-
       Holstein (Nato)
ALG   advanced landing ground
ALGASM   Amiral Commandant le Groupe Anti-
       Sous-marine (Commander, Anti-
       submarine Force)
ALGOL   algebraic-oriented language
       (computers)
ALH   advanced light helicopter by HAL
ALHT   Apollo Lunar Hand Tool
ALICE   artillery line intercommunication
       equipment FACE+AWDATS
AlImpRemps   alert implementation reports
       (Nato)
ALLA   Allied Long Lines Agency (Nato
       Brussels)
ALLD   airborne laser locator designator
ALLEG   Amiral Commandant l'Escadre Légère
       à la Mer (Amiral, Light Squadron
       (afloat))
Allen lamp   portable fluorescent lamp (UK)
Allen Summer   class, destroyers (USN)
Alligator   M-2, Gillois-type floating bridge
       equipment by EWK; class, landing
       ships, tank (SU); LVT, landing
       vehicle, tracked wtih 1 ton
       demolition charge (UK) WW2
Alligator-5   radar jammer (FR)
ALM   American Legion of Merit; Atelier de
       Fabrications du Mons (FR)
ALM-175   portable countermeasures receiver
       teat set by GI
AlMajCom   all major commands
ALMC   Army Logistics Management Center (US)
ALMIDS   Army Logistics Management Integrated
       Data System (US)
AlMilAct   all military activities
ALMS   aircraft landing measurement system
ALMSA   automated logistics management
       systems Agency (US)
ALN   accounting line number (Nato);
       ammunition lot number
AlNav   all naval activities
AlNavSta   all naval stations
ALNOT   (search and rescue) alert notice
       (Nato)
ALNOTs   (search and rescue)
ALO   Air Liaison Office(r); Applied
       Liaison Office; authorized level of
       organization
ALON   Air Liaison Officer Net (Nato)
ALon   assumed longitude
ALOTS   airborne light-weight optical track-
       ing system
Alouette   II SA-3130 helicopter by AS
Alouette   III SA-319 utility helicopter by
       AS

ALP   air liaison party; allied logistics
       publication; ambulance loading
       point; automated learning process;
       automated library programme
ALPA   Alaskan long period array (radar);
       Amiral Commandant les Porte-Avions
       (Admiral, Aircraft Carriers
       (afloat))
ALPC   automatic language processing com-
       mittee
ALPC   Army Logistics Policy Council
ALPEC   ammunition loading production
       engineering center (US)
ALPHA   AMC Logistic Program Hardward,
       Automated (US) (Army Material
       Command)
Alpha Jet   jet aircraft, trainer, close air
       support (FR-GE)
ALPS   advanced linear programming system
ALPT   Army language proficiency test (US)
AlPurComs   all-purpose communications system
ALQ-80   airborne jammer by Hallicrafts
ALQ-92   airborne communications jammer
ALQ-99   airborne tactical jammer by Raytheon
ALQ-101   electronic warfare pod by
       Westinghouse
ALQ-103   airborne jammer by Sanders
ALQ-117   airborne ECM system by ITT
ALQ-119   airborne jammer pod by Westinghouse
ALQ-123   airborne infra-red countermeasures
       system
ALQ-125   TEREC, tactical electronic recce
       system
ALQ-126   airborne defensive jammer
ALQ-127   radar countermeasures system by
       Westinghouse
ALQ-131   airborne ECM pod by AIL Cutler-
       Hammer
ALQ-133   airborne electronic target locator
       system
ALQ-135   TEWS, tactical electronic warfare
       system by Northrop
ALQ-136   helicopter-borne radar jammer by
       ITT
ALQ-144   helicopter-borne IRCM set by
       Sanders
ALQ-147   airborne IRCM set
ALQ-152   airborne jammer by Xerox
ALQ-154   airborne tail-warning radar
ALQ-155   radar warning receiver by Westing-
       house
ALQ-157   airborne jammer by Xerox
ALQ-161   airborne ECM system by AIL
ALQ-199   airborne ECM pod
ALR   Amado Laguna des Rins SA (Av. de
       la Jota 34, Zaragoza 14 Spain)
ALR-41   airborne radar warning receiver
ALR-45   airborne radar warning receiver by
       Itek/Loral
ALR-47   wing-tip radar warning receiver

ALR-50   airborne missile launch warning
          receiver by Magnavox
ALR-56   radar warning system by Loral
ALR-59   naval radar passive surveillance
          system by Litton
ALR-67   radar warning receiver by Itek/
          Grummen
ALRAAM   advanced long-range air-to-air
          missile
ALRep   air-launch report
ALRI   airborne long-range input
ALRR   Ames Laboratory research reactor
ALRTF   Army long-range technological fore-
          cast
ALS   active laser seeker; advanced logis-
          tics system (USAF); air logistics
          service; air logistic support
          (Nato); Army Legal Service (UK)
          -ALC; approach lighting system;
          automatic landing system; azimuth
          laying set
ALSC   auxiliary library service collections
ALSE   aviation life support equipment
AlSeaFron Alaskan Sea Frontier
AlSec   Alaskan Sector
ALSEP   Apollo Lunar Surface Experiments
          Package
ALSETEX   Société Alsacienne d'Études et
          d'Exploitations (4 rue de
          Castellane Paris)
ALSO   Auxiliary Library Service Organiza-
          tion
ALSP   Army Logistics Study Programme
ALSS   airborne location and strike system
AlStaCon All Stations Continental (US)
AlStg   altimeter setting
ALT   airborne laser tracker; approach and
          landing test; administrative lead
          time
alt   altitude; alterations
ALTA   Army Lawn Tennis Association
ALTAIR   ARPA long-range tracking and instru-
          mentation radar (Advanced Research
          Projects Agency)
AltHQ   alternative headquarters
ALTEL   artillery-launched television camera
          by Fairchild
AltFFl   alternating fixed and flashing
AltFGpFl alternating fixed and group
          flashing
AltFl   alternating flashing
AlfGpOcc alternating group occulting
AltOcc   alternating occulting
AltRev   altitude reservation
ALU   arithmetic and logic unit (computer)
Aluminaut deep-ocean research submarine
ALUSLO   American Litigation US Liaison
          Officer
ALUSNA   American Litigation US Naval Attache
ALUSNOB   American Litigation US Naval
          Observer

ALVRJ   air-launched low-volume ramjet
          (US programme)
ALWT   advanced light-weight torpedo
AlZnMGl   high-strength aluminium alloy
AM   Active Militia; Air Ministry (UK);
          Air Marshal (UK); Air Medal (US);
          Albert Medal (UK) (lifesaving);
          Army Manual; Arms Material (US);
          Assignment Memorandum (US); air-
          lock module; amplifier; aluminium
          mat; analog monolithic (computer);
          air-launched missile; attack
          missile; auxiliary minesweeper
          (Nato); mine countermeasures
          tender (Nato); area multiplexer
          (module) SDMS; amplitude modula-
          tion (communications); associative
          memory (computer); Aer Macchi,
          Varese (IT)
AM-1   Mauler, carrier-borne attack air-
          craft by Martin
AM-2   aluminium mats, for rapid runway
          repair
AM-10   Lasso, SS/As-12, light-weight anti-
          surface semi-automatic optical
          missile by AS
AM-23   23mm airborne gun (SU)
AM-39   Exocet, anti-surface missile by AS
AM-50   120mm mortar by Brandt
AMA   Academy of Model Aeronautics; air-
          head maintenance area; Army
          maintenance area; air material
          area (US); American Management
          Association; American Medical
          Association; ASROC missile
          assembly
AMAA   Army Mutual Aid Association (US)
AMAB   Army Medical Advisory Board (UK)
AMAC   aircraft monitoring and control
          system (arms and fuses nuclear
          bombs) (USAF)
AMAD   aircraft mounted accessory drive
AMAMS   advanced medium-range anti-tank
          missile system (European pro-
          gramme) -AHAMS
AMARC   Army Material Acquisition Review
          Committee (US)
AMARS   automatic message address routing
          system
AMASCP   air material area stock control
          point
Amazon   class, frigates (RN)
AMB   Administrative Machine Branch; Air
          Ministry Bulletin (UK); Airways
          Modernization Board (US); Armament
          Material Bulletin (US); mini-
          sweeper, harbour (USN)
amb   ambulance
AMBD   automatic multiple blade damper
AMBF   asset master balance file

Ambidrome   amphibious bridging vehicle by
            CEFA
ambl   airmobile
AMBLADS   advise method, bill of lading and
            date shipped
AMC   air mail center (US); Air Material
            Command (US); Air Mounting Centre
            (UK) (South Cerney Oxf.); American
            Maritime Commission (cases); Ameri-
            can Motors Corporation (Detroit);
            Armament Material Change; armoured
            mortar carrier; Area de Material
            Cordoba (Argentina); Army Material
            (Missile, Mobility, Munitions)
            Command (US); Army Medical Centre;
            Army Medical Corps (RAMC); Avia-
            tion Maintenance Costs; Austin
            Motor Company (UK); automatic
            monitoring circuit; auxiliary
            minesweeper, coastal (USN); armed
            merchant cruiser (RN); Auto-
            mitraillause de Combat (tank by
            Renault)
AMCA   Advanced Material Concept Agency
AMCALMSA   Army Material Command Automatic
            Logistics Management Systems
            Agency (US)
AMCE   Aldershot Military Corrective
            Establishment
AMCEC   Allied Military Communications Elec-
            tronics Committee
AMCFASC   Army Material Command Facilities
            and Services Center (US)
AMCFSA   Army Material Command Field Safety
            Agency (US)
AMCI&SA   Army Material Command Installations
            and Services Agency (US)
AMCLDC   Army Material Command Logistics Data
            Center (US)
AMCLSSA   Army Material Command Logistics
            Systems Support Agency (US)
AMCM   airborne mine-countermeasures
AmCon   American Consul
AmConRepO   American Consular Reporting
            Officer
AMCOS   Aldermaston mechanised cataloguing
            and ordering system UKAEA
AMCP   Allied Military Communications Panel
AmCross   American (national) Red Cross
AMCS   airborne missile control system;
            Army Mobilization Capabilities
            Study (US)
AMCU   minesweeper, coastal, underwater
            locator (USN)
AMD   administrative machine division;
            Administrative Management Division
            (US); Admiralty Machinery Depot;
            Aerospace Medical Division USAFSC;
            aircraft maintenance department;
            air movement directive; air move-

ment designator; air movement
data; aviation maintenance depart-
ment; Army Medical Department;
Avions Marcel Dassault (46 ave.
Kleber, F-75116 Paris)
AMDC   Army Missile Defence Command (US)
AMDF   Army Master Data File (US)
AMDI   Admiralty Merchant Ships Defence
            Instructions
AMDO   Aeronautical Maintenance Duty
            Officer
AMDP   aircraft maintenance delayed for
            parts; ammunition distribution
            point
AME   aero-medical evacuation; Air
            Ministry Examination; angle meas-
            uring equipment; Atelier de
            Fabrication de Mulhouse (FR);
            average monthly earnings
AMedD   Army Medical Department (US)
AMedDPAS   Army Medical Department Property
            Accounting System (US)
AMedP   Allied Medical Publication
AMedS   Army Medical Science
AMedServ   Army Medical Service
AMEE   Admiralty Marine Engineering Estab-
            lishment
AmEmb   American Embassy
AMES   Air Ministry Experimental Station
AMETA   Army Management Engineering Train-
            ing Agency (US)
AMETS   Artillery Meteorological System by
            Plessey/MEL, Army Meteorological
            System (Nato)
AmEx   American Expeditionary Forces
AMF   airport mail facility; Allied
            (Command Europe) Mobile Force
            (Nato); Army Management Fund (US);
            Australian Marine Force;
            Amphibisches Mehrzweck-
            Fahrzeug by EWK, 4x4
            amphibious multipurpose vehicle
AMF(A)   Allied (Command Europe) Mobile
            Force Air Component
AMFAir   Allied (Command Europe) Mobile
            Force Air Component
AMF(L)   Allied (Command Europe) Mobile
            Force Land Component
AMFLand   Allied (Command Europe) Mobile
            Force Land Component
AMFUR   amplified failure or unsatisfactory
            report
AMG   Allied Military Government; American
            Military Government; automatic
            magnetic guidance
amgm   airmailgram
AMGO   Assistant Master General of Ordnance
AMGOT   Allied Military Government of the
            Occupied Territory
AMHS   automated materials handling system

AMI   advanced manned interceptor; air mileage indicator; annual military inspection; American Military Institute; auxiliary minesweeper, inshore (Nato)

AMIADB   Army Member, Inter-American Defense Board

AMIC   Air Movement Information Centre (Nato)

AMiCom   Army Missile Command

AmInCo   American Instrument Company

AMIO   Arab Military Industries Organization

AMIP   Army Management Information Programme

AMIR   air mission intelligence report (Nato)

AMIS   advanced management information system; air movements information section; aircraft movement information system; Army Management Information System (US)

AMK   anti-misting kerosene

AMkTU   Army Marksmanship Training Unit (US)

AML   Airfield Marking and Lighting STANAG; Aeronautical Materials Laboratory; Admiralty Materials Laboratory; applied mathematics laboratory; amplitude modulated link (cable TV by Hughes); amplitude modulation with noise limiter; armoured missile launcher; automated multi-channel link by Theta-Com; Allied Military Liaison

AML-60   Automitrailleuse Légère armoured car by Panhard

AML-90   Automitrailleuse Légère armoured car

AML-245   Automitrailleuse Légère armoured car

AML/M3   HOT anti-tank armoured car by Panhard

AML/M3   VDA anti-aircraft armoured car by Panhard

AML/M3   VPM mortar carrier by Panhard

AMM   American Military Mission; Ammunition and related equipment STANAG; anti-missile missile

AMMC   Aviation Material Management Center (US Army)

AMMI   American Merchant Marine Institute

AMMIP   Aviation Material Management Improvement Programme

AMMO   Air Ministry's Meteorological Office; Ammunition Interchangeability STANAG

ammo   ammunition (status)
     minus   less than half left
     plus   more than half left
     zero   no ammunition left

Ammonal   ammonium-nitrate + powdered aluminium

AMMRC   Army Materials and Mechanics Research Center (US)

AMMRL   aircraft maintenance material readiness list

AMNW   Air Ministry Navigational Warning

AMO   Administrative Medical Officer; Air Ministry Orders (UK); air movement officer; aircraft material officer; Allied Meteorological Office (Nato); Army Medal Office (UK); Army medical officer; assistant medical officer; aviation medical officer

AMOB   automatic meteorological and oceanographic buoy

AMOS   additionally awarded military occupational speciality (US); automatic meteorological observation station

AMOSC   Authorized Military Occupational Speciality Code (US)

AMP   advanced multipurpose (missile); advanced management programme; Air Member for Personnel (Air Council); Allied Mining and Mine-countermeasures Publication (Nato); Army Material Plan (US); American Military Police; automatic message processing

Amp   Ampere

amp   amplitude

AMPC   Auxiliary Military Pioneer Corps; automatic message processing centre

AMPD   Air Ministry Plans Department

AMPDR   advanced multi-mode pulse doppler radar by LMEricsson

AMPERE   Applied (Physics Laboratory) Management Planning and Engineering Resource Evaluation

AmpFUR   Amplified failure or unsatisfactory report

amph   amphibious

AmphibEx   amphibious Exercise

AmphibFor   amphibious force
     CenPac   Central Pacific
     Lant   Atlantic Fleet
     Med   Mediterranean (USN)

amphO   amphibious observation

Amp/hr   Ampere hours

AMPI   annual military personnel inspection

Ampligard   noise-protective earphones by RACAL

Ampliroll   special pick-up ramp for trucks by Foden

AMPPGD   Army Mobilization Planning and Programming Guidance Document (US)

AMPR   aeronautical manufacturer's planning report

AMPS   automatic message processing system by MEL

AMPSS   advanced manned precision strike system

AMQ	American medical qualification; Army married quarters
AMR	advanced material requirement; Atlantic missile range; automatic map reader (airborne, computerised) by Marconi Elliott; automatic message routing
AMR-33	Automitrailleuse de Reconnaissance by Renault
AMR-701	ground-to-air communications system by AGA
AMRAAM	advanced medium-range air-to-air missile by Northrop
AMRAC	Anti-missile Research Advisory Council
AMRAD	ARPA measurements radar (Advanced Research Projects Agency)
AMRD-NASC	Army Missile and Rockets Directorate, Nato Supply Centre
AMRL	Aerospace Medical Research Laboratory
AMRS	Army Medical Reserve Store (Woolwich); Air Ministry Radio Station
AMRSS	advanced medium-range sonar system
AMS	Assistant Military Secretary; advanced monopulse seeker by Raytheon; Aeronautical Material Specification; Apollo mission simulator; Army Management Structure (US); Army Map Service (US); Army Medical Service (UK); Army Medical Staff (UK); American Meteorological Society; Avionics Maintenance Squadron (USAFE); Accommodation and Messenger Service (Admiralty); high-speed minesweeper (USN); auxiliary, minesweeper (Nato; ABC-Messtelle, NBC reporting post
AM&S	Administration, Mess and Supply (US)
AMSA	advanced manned strategic aircraft (US programme); area maintenance support activity
AMSAA	Army Material Systems Analysis Agency (US)
AMSAM	anti-missile surface-to-air missile
AMSAT	amateur radio satellite, GE, 70 Kgs
AMSC	Allied Military Staff Conference; Army Medical Speciality Corps; Army Medical Speciality Code
AMSD	anti-missile, ship-defence by Raytheon
AMSE	aeronautical material support equipment
AMSEF	anti-minesweeping explosive float; area maintenance supply facility; Army Morale Support Fund
AMSI	Admiralty Merchant Shipping Instructions; Atlantic Merchant Shipping Instructions
AMSL	above mean sea level
AMSO	Air Member for Supply and Organization (Air Council)
AmSO	ammunition shipment order
AMSP	Allied Military Security Publications (cryptography) (Nato); Army Maintenance and Supply Publication (Nato); Army Master Study Program (US)
AMSR	automatic missile site radar
AMST	advanced medium STOL transport (US programme) -YC-15
AMSU	amphibious maintenance support unit (US) Lant Atlantic Pac Pacific
AMT	advanced materials technology (armour plates); aerial mail terminal; aerial mail transfer; Air Member for Training (Air Council)
AmTank	amphibious tank
AMTC	Army Mountain Training Centre
AMTCL	Association for Machine Translation and Computational Linguistics
AMTF	airmobile task force
AMTI	airborne moving target indicator; adaptive moving target indicator; area moving target indicator
AmTk	amphibious tank
AmTracBn	amphibious tractor battalion
AmTrack	amphibious tracked vehicle (US); landing vehicle, tracked (US); amphibious tractor (Nato)
AMTS	air movement traffic section; Army Mechanical Transport School
AMTSD	Air Ministry Technical and Stores Department
AMTT	active moving target tracking
AMU	advanced marksmanship unit; astronaut manoeuvering unit; atomic mass unit
AMVER	Atlantic merchant vessel report
AMVERS	automatic merchant vessel report system
AmVets	American Veterans of WW2 and Korea
AMVM	administrative motor vehicle management
AMVOP	Army Motor Vehicle Operator's Permit
AMWDD	Admiralty Miscellaneous Weapons Development Department
AMX	automatic message exchange; close support aircraft by Aerit+AM, Atelier de Construction d'Issy-le-Moulineaux (FR) (tanks)
AMX-10AMB	ambulance tank
AMX-10	Crecce tank 105mm gun
AMX-10 ECH	mobile workshop, armoured
AMX-10 H	armoured bridgelayer

AMX-10 M missile-armed killer tank
AMX-10 P infantry combat vehicle
AMX-10 PC command post vehicle
AMX-10 Ratac radar vehicle
AMX-10 RC wheeled recce tank 105mm gun
AMX-10SOA artillery observation vehicle
AMX-10 TM personnel carrier/mortar tractor
AMX-10 VOA artillery observation vehicle
AMX-13 light tank
AMX-13 Bitube, twin 30mm anti-aircraft tank
AMX-13 DCA anti-aircraft tank
AMX-13 PC command post vehicle
AMX-13 VCA support vehicle for 155mm guns
AMX-13 Ratac surveillance radar vehicle
AMX-13 Sanitaire, armoured ambulance
AMX-13 VTP/VTI infantry combat vehicle
AMX-30 main battle tank
AMX-30 D recovery tank by EFAB
AMX-30 GCT self-propelled 155mm gun
AMX-30 H armoured bridgelayer by EFAB
AMX-30 R Roland launcher anti-aircraft tank
    by EFAB
AMX-30 SA twin 30mm anti-aircraft tank by
    EFAB
AMX-32 improved AMX-30 105mm gun by EFAB
AMX-50 main battle tank prototype 1950
    120mm gun
AMX-56 VCI infantry combat vehicle
AMX-105 self-propelled howitzer 105mm
AMX-155 self-propelled howitzer 155mm
AMX-155 GCT self-propelled howitzer
AMX M-55 engineer tank
AMX VCG recovery-tank
AMX VTP infantry combat vehicle
AMZ ABC-Meldezentrale, NBC reporting
    center
AN Air Force/Navy, Army Navy (code)
    (Nato); Astro Navigation STANAG;
    Army Number; net laying ship (USN)
An Antonov, aircraft (SU)
An-2 Colt, single-engined biplane
An-8 Camp, transport plane
An-10 transport plane
An-12 Cub, 4-turbo-prop tactical transport/
    EW
An-14 Clod, transport plane
An-22 Cock, Antei, long-range heavy
    transport
An-24 transport plane
An-26 Curl, transport plane
An-30 survey aircraft
An-32 Cline, transport plane
AN-52 ammunition, nuclear 10-15 kilotons
An-72 Coaler, twin turbofan STOL aircraft
ANA Air Navigation Act; appropriate
    national authorities; Assistant
    Naval Attache
ANARE Australian National Antarctic
    Research Expedition
ANB air navigation bureau

ANBS Air Navigation and Bombing School;
    air navigation and bombing
    system
ANC Air Navigation Commission; Air
    Navigation Committee (Nato); Air
    Navigation Conference; Air Naviga-
    tor's Certificate; African
    National Council; Army Nurse Corps
    (US); area Naval Commander; all
    numbers calling
ANCA Allied Naval Communications Agency
    (Nato London)
ANCE Assemblée des Nations Captives
    d'Europe (Assembly of Captive
    European Nations)
Anchorage class, assault transports LSD
    (USN)
ANCR aircraft non-combat ready (Nato)
ANCU airborne navigation computer unit
ANCUN Australian National Committee for
    the United Nations
AND air navigation directions; Army/Navy
    design; Air Force/Navy design;
    Army/Navy (Aeronautical) Design
    Standard (US)
ANDB Air Navigation Development Board
    (US)
Andover HS-748 transport aircraft by HS
Andromeda RPV by Aerosystem Electronic
AnDUS Anglo-Dutch-United States
ANDVT advanced narrow-band digital voice
    terminal TRI-TAC by ITT
ANEEG Army/Navy Electronics Evaluation
    Group
A-New airborne electronics - new integra-
    ted ASW programme (USN)
ANF anti-nuclear factor; Allied Nuclear
    Force; Atlantic Nuclear Force;
    Army News Features
ANFE aircraft not fully equipped
ANG Air National Guard (US); Atlantique
    Nouvelle Génération by Breguet,
    improved Atlantic maritime
    Patrol/ASW aircraft
ANGAU Australian New Guinea Administration
    Unit
ANGB Air National Guard Base (US)
ANG-CE Air National Guard Civil Engineering
ANGFS Air National Guard Flying Squadron
ANGLICO Air and Naval Gunfire Liaison
    Company
ANGUS Air National Guard of the United
    States
ANHT American Naval Historical Team
ANIK telecommunications satellite by
    Hughes Can.
ANIM Association of Nuclear Instrument
    Manufacturers
ANIP Army/Navy Instrumentation Program
    (US)

ANJSB	Army/Navy Joint Specifications Board
ANL	Argonne National Laboratory (US); automatic noise landing; auxiliary, net laying (USN)
ANM	Admiralty Notices to Mariners
ANMB	Army/Navy Munitions Board
ANMC	American National Metric Council
ANMCC	Alternative National Military Command Center (Washington)
ANMI	Allied Naval Manoeuvering Instructions (Nato)
ANNA	Army/Navy/NASA/Air Force (geodetic satellite programme) (US)
Annapolis	class, helicopter-carrying destroyers (RCN)
AnnFlyQuire	annual flying requirements
AnnNo	announcement number
AnnRept	annual report
ANO	air navigation order 1949; air navigation office(r)
ANORS	anticipated not operationally ready supply
ANP	aircraft nuclear propulsion; Allied Navigation Publication (Nato)
ANPB	Army/Navy Petroleum Board
ANPP	Army Nuclear Power Programme
ANPPPC	Army/Navy Petroleum Pool Pacific Coast
ANPT	air navigation procedures trainer by Litton
ANR	active noise reduction; air navigation regulations
ANRAC	aids, navigation radio control
ANRC	American National Red Cross; Australian National Research Council
ANS	Air Navigation School; Air/Naval surveillance; Army Nursing Service; Army/Navy Stores; American Nuclear Society; area navigation system
ANS-351	aircraft area navigation system by Collins
ANSI	American National Standards Institute; Army/Navy safety instruction
ANSIA	Army/Navy Shipping Information Agency
ANSL	American National Standard Labels; Australian National Standards Laboratory
ANSO	Assistant Naval Stores Officer
Anson	bomber/maritime recce aircraft WW2 by Avro
ANT	Arme Nucleaire Tactique (Pluton) (tactical nuclear weapon) (FR)
AnTac	Air Navigation, Tactical (control system)
Antar	FV-12000, tractor for semi-trailers by Thornycroft
AntDefCom	Antilles Defence Command
Antilope	airborne radar mapping and targeting system by EMD
Antipilarkos Laskos	class, Greek guided missile patrol boats by CMN
Antiradar	anti-radar drone (GE)
AntiSubWarWysProjOfc	Anti-submarine Warfare Systems Project Office (USN)
Antoinette	first flight simulator by Levasseur 1909
ANTS	Advanced Naval Training School
ANTU	Air Navigation Training Unit
ANU	airplane nose up
ANU	automatische Netzüberwachung (automatic network monitoring)
ANUDS	Army Nuclear Data System (study) (US)
ANV	advanced naval vehicles (USN programme); armoured NBC defence vehicle
ANVIS	aviator's night vision imaging system by Bell & Howell
ANZAC	Australian New Zealand Army Corps WW1
ANZAM	Australia-New Zealand and Malaya 1963
ANZUK	Australia, New Zealand, United Kingdom
ANZUS	Australia, New Zealand, United States
AO	Admiralty Orders; Army Orders; Air Ordnance; accounts office; area of operation; administrative office(r); appointing order; auxiliary, oiler (Nato)
AOA	Air Office in charge of Administration; American Ordnance Association; amphibious objective area
AOAD	Army organic air defence
AOATC	Atlantic Ocean air traffic control (Nato)
AOB	advanced operational base; air order of battle; approved operating budget
AOC	Air Officer Commanding USMC (Nato); Army Ordnance Corps - RAOC; air operator's certificate; airhead ordnance company (RAOC); automatic overload control; agreed operational characteristics (Nato)
AOC-document	agreed operational characteristics
AOCan	aviation officer candidate (US)
AOCI	airport operators council international
AOCinC	Air Officer Commanding in Chief (Nato); BAFO British Air Force of Occupation

AOCM	aircraft out of commission awaiting maintenance (Nato)	AOS	azimuth orientation system; acquisition of signal; advanced operations systems (computers); algebraic operations system (computer)
AOCO	Atomic Ordnance Cataloging Office (US)		
AOCP	aircraft out of commission awaiting parts (Nato)	AOSL	authorized organizational st ckage list
AOCR	aircraft operating cost report	AOSO	advanced orbiting solar observatory
AOD	advanced ordnance depot; Army Ordnance Depot; Army Ordnance District (Nato); Aerodrome Officer of the Day	AOSP	advanced on-board signal processor
		AOSS	submarine oiler (USN)
		AOT	alignment optical telescope
AOE	aerodrome of entry; auxiliary, oiler, explosives (USN); fast combat support ship (USN)	AOTC	Aviation Officers Training Corps
		AOTD	active optical target detector (missile)
AOER	Army Officers' Emergency Reserve	AOTE	amphibious operational training element
AOEW	air operating empty weight		
AofF	Admiral of the Fleet; adjustment of fire	AOTEA	Army Operational Test and Evaluations Agency (US)
AOFU	Army Operational Film Unit	AOTU	amphibious operational training unit
AOG	aircraft on ground; American Operational Group; auxiliary, oil, gasoline (USN-Nato)	AOU	automated offset unit; azimuth orientation unit
		AOV	artillery observation vehicle
AOGM	Army of Occupation of Germany Medal (US)	AOWF	Army Officers' Widows' Fund (UK)
AOH	accepted on hire; awaiting overhaul; aircraft requiring overhaul	AOWS	aircraft overhaul work stoppage
		AP	airman pilot; ammunition point; aircraft park; auxiliary patrol; assumed position; air position; air publication; approaches; Advisory Panel on Administration (Nato); ammonium perchlorate (propellant); air pollution; armour-piercing (shot); anti-personnel (mine); attack, propeller (aircraft); application programme; array processor; autopilot; transport ship (USN)
AOI	Arab Organization for Industrialisation (Egypt, UAEs, Saudi Arabia, Qatar); area of interest	
AOil	aviation oil	
AOIV	automatically operated inlet valve	
AoL	absent over leave; absent over liberty	
AOL	Admiralty Oil Laboratory; Atlantic Oceanographic Laboratories	
AOM	Army of Occupation Medal (US)	
AOMC	Army Ordnance Missile Command (Nato)	AP	bouncing mine by GIAT
AOMSC	Army Ordnance Missile Support Centre	AP-32Z	rifle grenade by FN
AOND	Administrative Officer, Navy Department	AP-1640	rifle grenade
		APA	advance of pay and allowance; Aircraft Procurement, Army (US); appropriation purchases account (US); Army Parachute Association (UK); additional personal allowance; attack transport LPA (USN-Nato); Albanian People's Army
AONS	Air Observers Navigation School	
AOO	aviation ordnance officer	
AOP	Allied Ordnance Publication (Nato); air observation post; artillery observation plane; atomic ordnance platoon	
		APAAF	Albanian People's Army Air Force
AOP-10	Skeeter, light helicopter by Saunders-Roe	APACS	airplane position and altitude camera system
AOPB	Active Officer Promotion Branch BUPERS	APAG	Atlantic Policy Advisory Group
AOQ	average out-going quality; aviation officers' quarters	APAM	anti-personnel and anti-material (bomb) by Honeywell; array processor access method
AOQL	average out-going quality limit	A-part	alpha particle
AOR	air operations room; auxiliary, oiler, replenishment (USN)	APATS	automatic programmer and test system; antenna pattern test system
AORE	Army Operational Research Establishment DOAE	
AORG	Army Operational Research Group	APB	air portable bridge (UK); all points bulletin (US); antiphase boundary
AOS	Air Observers' School; Army Ordnance Service; amphibious objective study	

APB	Army Packaging Board (US); barracks ship (self-propelled) (USN)
APBC	armour-piercing, ballistic cap (shot), anti-tank round
APBS	Automated PEMA Budget System (US) (Procurement of Equipment and Missiles, Army)
APC	abbreviated performance characteristics; activity processing code; assistant principal chaplain (UK); armour-piercing, capped (shot); armoured personnel carrier; all-purpose capsule (Aspirin, Phenedrine, Caffeine); automatic power compensator; approach power compensator; area of position control; automatic phase control; antenna positioning and control (system); amplitude phase conversion; automatic pressure control; Air Priority Committee; small coastal transport (USN)
APC-30-10	antenna positioning and control system by Koor
APCABC	armour-piercing, carbide, ballistic cap (shot) (Nato)
APCC	ACLANT Preliminary Coordinating Conference (Nato)
APCCLA	Aviation Petroleum Coordinating Committee (Latin America)
APCEC	Army Precommission Extension Course (US)
apch	approach
APCHE	armour-piercing, capped, high-explosive
APCM	Asiatic Pacific Campaign Medal (US)
ApCon	approach control
APC&PCCB	Active Plans Costing and Program Change Control Branch BUPERS
APCS	associative processor computer system; Army Postal and Courier Service (UK); Air Photographic and Charting Service (US)
APC-T	armour-piercing, capped with tracer (shot)
APD	advanced planning document; administrative planning division; air procurement district; air pollution division; area postal directory; Army Pay Department; Admiralty Press Division; avalanche photo-diode; high-speed transport LPR (USN); Ausschuss für Patentdokumentation (Patents Documentation Committee)
APD-7	SLAR, side-looking airborne radar
APDMS	Sparrow, aerodrome point defence missile system
APDS	armour-piercing, discarding sabot (UK), anti-tank shot

APDSFS	armour-piercing, discarding sabot fin stabilised
APDSMS	advanced point defence surface missile system (3rd generation Sea Sparrow)
APDS-T	armour-piercing, discarding sabot with tracer (anti-tank shot)
APE	Army Preliminary Evaluation; advanced production engineering; ammunition peculiar equipment; automatic photographic equipment; amphibisches Pionier-Erkundungsfahrzeug by EWK (amphibious engineer recce vehicle 4x4)
APEER	aircrew performance enhancement and error reduction program (FAA)
APEL	Aeronautical Photographic Experimental Laboratory (Johnsville Pa)
Aper	anti-personnel
apers	anti-personnel
APEX	Association of Professional Executive Clerical and Computer Staff
apexer	approach indexer
APF	acid-proof floor; administrative flagship (USN)
APFD	auto-pilot flight director
APFSDS	armour-piercing fin-stabilised discarding sabot (anti-tank shot)
APG	ACLANT Planning Guidance (Nato); Army Planning Group; Aberdeen Proving Ground; anti-personnel grenade; automatic programme generation; azimuth pulse generator; support gunnery ship (USN); automatisches Prüfgerät (automatic test set)
APG-30	airborne radar gunsight
APG-63	airborne radar gunsight by Hughes
APG-65	airborne radar gunsight, digitalized by Hughes
APG-66	airborne radar gunsight for F-16
APGC	air proving ground command; air proving ground centre
APH	hospital transport (USN)
APHE	armour-piercing, high-explosive (shell)
APHEI	armour-piercing, high explosive incendiary
APHG	anti-personnel hand grenade
APHHW	all-purpose hand-held weapon
API	American Petroleum Institute; armour-piercing, incendiary projectile; air position indicator; automatic priority interruption
APIC	Allied Press Information Centre (Nato)
APICS	American Production and Inventory Control System
APID	air photograph interpretation detachemnt

APIS   Army Photographic Interpretation
        Section; Army Photographic Intelli-
        gence Service
API-T   armour-piercing, incendiary with
        tracer, anti-aircraft projectile
APIU   Army Photographic Interpretation Unit
APJI   Army parachute jumping instructor
APL   Army Promotion List; allowance parts
        list; applied physics laboratory;
        Aero Propulsion Laboratory (USAF);
        barracks ship (USN)
APLA   aviation pilot, lighter than air
        (airship licence) (US); airplane
        lighter than air (airship)
APM   assistant provost marshal (UK);
        assistant paymaster (USMC); ALLA
        Plenary Meeting (Nato) (Allied
        Long Lines Agency); applicable
        material assets; Army Program
        Memorandum (US); mechanized
        artillery transport (USMC)
APMC   Allied Political and Military Commis-
        sion
APMG   Assistant Postmaster General
APMO   Avion Patrouilleur Maritime de
        l'OTAN (Nato maritime patrol air-
        craft)
APMS   advanced power management system
        (airborne electronic warfare)
APMT   antenna pattern measurement test
APN   non-mechanized artillery transport
        (USMC)
APN-59 airborne navigation radar by Sperry
APN-91 airborne weather radar
APN-182 airborne ASW radar
APN-195 helicopter-borne ASW radar
APN-209 radar altimeter by Honeywell
APO   aerospace projection operation;
        acting pilot officer (RAF); annual
        programme objectives; Army Pensions
        Office (Stanmore, Middlesex); Army
        Pay Office (Ashton); Army Post
        Office; Anton Piller KG, Osterode
        (Postfach 1860, D-3360 Osterode)
APOC   Army point of contact
APOD   aerial port of debarkation
APOE   aerial port of embarkation
apogee furthest distance to the earth
        (satellites) -perigee
APOR   Advisory Panel on Operations Research
        (Nato)
APOTA   automatic positioning telemetry
        antenna
APP   air parcel post; Allied Procedures
        Publication (Nato); advanced pro-
        curement plan; armour-piercing,
        proof (projectile); approach (con-
        trol service) (Nato); auxiliary
        power plant; Army Procurement Pro-
        cedure; troop barge class A (USN)

app   apparatus; approach; apparent;
        approved; approximate
APPAC   Aviation Petroleum Products Alloca-
        tion Committee (London)
APPCFI All Party Parliamentary Committee
        for Freedom of Information (UK)
AppCon approach control
appd   approved
APPG   adjacent phase pulse generator
APPLAUSE appeal, plain facts, personali-
        ties, local angle, action,
        uniqueness (universality), sig-
        nificance, energy DINFUS NEC
        (US)
APPLE   Apollo payload exploration; Ariane
        passenger payload experiment;
        associative processor programming
        language evaluation
appn   appropriation
APPR   Army Package Power Reactor
AppRes applied research
appro   approbation, approval
approx approximate, approximation
approp appropriation
appt   appointment, appointed
APP-T   armour-piercing, proof with tracer
        (projectile)
APQ-120 airborne fire-control radar
APQ-144 FLR, airborne forward-looking radar
        by GE
APQ-146 airborne terrain-following radar by
        TI
APQ-706 helicopter-borne ASW radar by SMA
APR   airborne profile recorder; alterna-
        tive path re-try; automatic power
        reserve (aircraft engines); annual
        progress report; Army Public Rela-
        tions; rescue transport (vessel)
        (USN)
APR-25 airborne radar warning receiver by
        Applied Technologies
APR-27 airborne radar warning receiver by
        Magnavox
APR-35 36 37 airborne radar warning
        receiver by Itek
APR-38 airborne radar homing and warning
        system by McDD
APR-39 airborne radar warning receiver by
        Melpar
APR-46 airborne radar warning receiver by
        Itek
APRE   Army Personnel Research Establish-
        ment (UK)
APRFR   Army pulse radiation facility
        reactor
APRIL   aqua planing risk indicator for
        landing
A/Prin assistant principal
APRO   Army Pay Record Office (Worthy Down)
APRS   acoustic position reference system

aprt   airport
aprx   approximate
APs   Allied Publications (Nato)
APS   Army Postal Service; assistant pri-
          vate secretary; automatic programme
          system; auxiliary power supply;
          auxiliary power system; minelaying
          submarine (USN); 9mm automatic
          pistol, Stechkin (SU)
APS-20   airborne surveillance radar AEW-1
          AEW-2
APS-85   SLAR, side-looking airborne radar
APS-94   SLAR, side-looking airborne radar
APS-111   airborne surveillance radar E-2B
APS-116   airborne surveillance radar
APS-120   ARPS advanced radar processing
          system by GE
APS-125   ARPS for Hawkeye by-GE
APS-128   airborne search radar by AIL
APS-171   airborne rotodome-mounted antenna
APS-500   GPWS, ground proximity warning
          system by TRT
APS-503   504 airborne search radar by Litton
APS-705   airborne search and navigation radar
          SMA
APS-707   helicopter-borne anti-surface radar
          for SAR missions by SMA
APSL   acting paymaster sub-lieutenant
APSA   automatic particle size analyser
APSI   aircraft propulsion subsystem inte-
          gration
APSP   array processor sub-routine package
APSPS   all-purpose submarine periscope
          System by Kollmorgen
APSS   Army Printing and Stationery Service
          (UK); transport submarine LPSS
          (USN)
APSVDS   armour-piercing super-velocity dis-
          carding sabot (shot)
APT   airman proficiency test; airport con-
          trol tower; advanced passenger
          train; after peak tank; automatic
          picture transmission; automatic
          position telemetry; automatic pro-
          grammed tool; automatic powerplant
          test (and monitoring equipment,
          airborne) by Marconi; allowed pro-
          ject time; troop barge class B
          (USN)
AP-T   armour-piercing, tracer (projectile)
APTC   Army Physical Training Corps
APT-DI   armour-piercing, tracer - dark igni-
          tion (anti-aircraft projectile)
APTS   Army physical training staff;
          Australian Parachute Training
          School; automatic picture trans-
          mission, sub-system (NASA)
APU   Army Postal Unit; additional propul-
          sion unit; auxiliary power unit
APUS   Area Production Urgency Committee

APV   transport and aircraft ferry (USN)
APVO   air defence (SU)
APW   American Prisoner of War; action
          programme for women; Air Proving
          Wing (USAF)
APWD   Army Psychological Warfare Division
APWO   assistant public works officer
APX   Atelier de Construction de Puteaux
          (FR)
APX-100   airborne IFF transponder by Bendix
APX-103   airborne IFF transponder
APX-409   optical sight, tanks by APX
APX/M-371 tank episcope against ground
          targets
APX/M-508 Cotac, laser sight by APX
APX/M-520 optical periscope sight by APX
APY   giant Y-boat (USN)
APY-1   airborne search radar AWACS by
          Westinghouse
AQ   assistant quartermaster; accomplish-
          ment quotient; achievement quo-
          tient
AQAP-1   Allied Quality Assurance Publication
          (Nato)
AQAPs   Allied Quality Assurance Publica-
          tions
AQB   Army Qualification Battery
AQE   Airman Qualification Examination
AQH   Air Headquarters ... Nato
AQH-4   airborne sonar recorder by Precision
          Data
Aquilon   FR designation Sea Venom
AQL   acceptable quality level
AQM   air quartermaster
AQM-34   *Firebee*, target drone RPV
AQM-34L   RPV, recce, TV-camera + IR line-
          scanner
AQM-34M   RPV low-altitude recce by *Teledyne*-
          Ryan
AQM-34Q   Combat Dawn, RPV, ELINT by
          Teledyne-Ryan
AQM-34R   Compass Dwell, RPV, ELINT by
          Teledyne-Ryan
AQM-37A   Sea Skimmer, target drone by Beech
AQM-91A   RPV long-distance surveillance
AQMG   assistant quartermaster general
AQMS   armourer/artificer/artisan quarter-
          master sergeant
AQS-13   helicopter-borne low-frequency
          dipping sonar by Bendix
AQS-14   airborne mine-hunting sonar
AQS-18   heliccpter-borne dipping sonar by
          Bendix
AQS-901   airborne sonobuoy data processor
          BARRA system
AQT   aviation qualification test; appli-
          cant qualification test
Aquacom   underwater radio telephone system
          by Zodiac
Aquatone U-2, high-altitude reconnaissance
          aircraft by Lockheed

Aquila XMQM-105, RPV TV camera by Lockheed

AR   air radio (officer) (UK); air
         reserve; annual review (Nato);
         allocated reserve; Army Regula-
         tions; aerial reconnaissance;
         ammunition reserve; Army Reserve;
         allowance regulations; aspect
         ratio; advice of receipt; auto-
         matic rifle; automatic rim
         (cartridge); anti-reflection;
         acrylic rubber; acid resisting;
         artillery radar; arithmetic regis-
         ter; associative register; assault
         rifle; air rescue; air refuelling;
         amphibious reconnaissance; repair
         and maintenance ship (USN-Nato);
         Alfa Romeo (IT); Abeking &
         Rasmussen D-2874 Lemwerder

A&R   Assembly and Repair

AR-3D   artillery radar, air defence by
         Plessey

AR-10   assault rifle

AR-15   M-16, automatic rifle 5.56mm

AR-18   assault rifle 5.556mm by Armalite

AR-51   55 59 Alfa Romeo, jeep (IT)

AR-70.223 assault rifle 5.56mm by Beretta

Ar-81   Arado, dive-bomber WW2 by Arado

AR-90   coastal defence vessel by DTCN

Ar-95   recce aircraft WW2 by Arado

Ar-23i   light-weight submarine-borne float-
         plane WW2 by Arado

Ar-234   jet long-range recce 900km/h WW2 by
         Arado

Ar-234   Blitz, jet bomber WW2 by Arado

ARA   accelerated readiness analysis;
         aerial rocket artillery; air re-
         fuelling area; aircraft research
         association; aircraft replaceable
         assembly; airborne radar approach;
         American Reloaders Association;
         Army Rifle Association; assigned
         responsible agency

ARAA   aerodrome radar approach aid;
         Atelier Régional de l'Armée de
         l'Air (Air Force Regional Workshop)

ARAAV   M-551, armoured reconnaissance air-
         borne assault vehicle (Sheridan
         tank)

ArabSat Arabian regional communications
         satellite

ARAC   Army radar approach control

ArADCom Army Air Defense Command (US)

ARAF   Angolan Republic Air Force FAPA

ARAR-13 radar detection, analysis and iden-
         tification system for airborne
         maritime recce by Thomson-CSF

ARAR/ARAX ARAR-13 forerunner by Thomson-CSF

ARATU   class, fast mine-sweepers for Brazil
         by AR

ArAv   Army aviation; Army aviator

Arava   IAI-201, light tactical transport
         STOL by IAI

ARB   Air Research Bureau (Brussels); Air-
         worthiness Requirements Board
         (Cranwell); Air Registration Board
         (UK); Aeronautical Research Board;
         Air Reserve Base (US); Armored
         Rifle Battalion (US); Army release
         bock; auxiliary, repair, battle
         damage (Nato)

ARBS   angle rate bombing system by Hughes

ARC   advanced re-entry concept; Aero-
         nautical Research Committee;
         Aeronautical Research Council
         (UK); Airworthiness Requirements
         Committee; Ames Research Center
         (NASA); air radio communication;
         anti-riot cartridge (rubber
         bullet) (UK); automatic remote
         control; automatic reception con-
         trol; automatic relay calculator;
         augmentation research centre;
         American Red Cross; Army Regula-
         tions with Changes (US); Annual
         Review Committee (Nato); area of
         responsibility center (US); Air-
         craft Radio Corporation (US);
         Atlantic Research Corporation
         (US); auxiliary, repair, cables
         (USN)

ARC-114 LOHAP, light observation helicopter
         avionics pack by GTE Sylvania

ARC-115 SLAE, standard light-weight
         avionics equipment

ARC-191 JTIDS, joint tactical information
         distribution system by Hughes

ARC-340 VHF/FM airborne communications and
         homing system by GEC/Marconi

ARCADS   advanced rocket control and
         delivery system by Bendix

ARCAM   Army Reserve Components Achievement
         Medal (US)

ARCAS   automatic radar chain acquisition
         system

ARCB   Army Regular Commission Board (UK)

ARC-Coal heavy fuel substitute from coal/
         water by ARC

ARCE   amphibious river crossing equipment

ARCH   articulated computer hierarchy

Archer   self-propelled anti-tank gun WW2
         (UK)

ARCHS   Army Reactor Systems Health and
         Safety (Review Committee) (US)

ARCO   Army Requirements Control Office
         (US); Auxiliary Resources Control
         Office (US)

ARCom   Army Reserve Command (US)

ArCoM   Army Commendation Medal (US)

ArCoMet Area Commanders' Meeting (Nato)

ArCOV   Army Combat Operations, Viet Nam

ARCS	air raid casualties service; Army ration credit system (US); Australian Red Cross Society
ARCSA	aviation requirements for the combat structure of the Army (US)
ARCT	airborne radar coherent transmitter; Army radio code (aptitude) test (US)
Arcus	unmanned submarine by SPAR+ERNO
ARD	Armament Research Department; automatic release date; acute radiation dose; anti-recovery device (mine warfare); auxiliary, repair, dumb (dock) (USN)
ARDC	Air Research and Development Center AFSC; Air Research and Development Command (US); Air Research and Development Council (Nato); auxiliary, repair, dumb (dock) concrete (USN)
ARDE	Armament Research and Development Establishment
Ardhana	class, patrol boats by Vosper & Thornycroft
ARDIS	Army research and development information system
ARDM	auxiliary, repair dock, medium (USN)
ARDME	automatic radar distance measuring equipment
ARDP	Army requirements development plan
ARDS	advanced remote display station; aviation research and development service
ARE	Applicazioni Radio Elettroniche SpA (IT); Atelier de Construction de Rouanne (FR)
AreaCord	area coordination
AREE	Admiralty regional electrical engineer
ARELÇ	Army resettlement employment liaison cell (UK)
ArEnBd	armor and engineer board (US Army)
ARENTS	advanced research engineering nuclear test satellite ARPA
ARept	agent report
ARES	advanced radar environment simulator
Ares	3-dimensional surveillance radar by Thomson-CSF
ARF	all-round fire; automatic return fire
ARF/8M2	2" airborne rockets by SNIA
ARFA	Allied Radio Frequency Agency (Brussels, Nato)
ArFCoS	Armed Forces Courier Service (Nato)
ArFCoSta	Armed Forces Courier Station
ArFor	area forecast (weather)
ArForStat	armed forces status reporting system (US)
ARFPC	Army reserve forces policy committee (US)
ARG	amphibious ready group; anti-riot gun; armoured replacement group; auxiliary, repair, gasoline engines (USN); Anzeige und Rechen-Gerät (display and calculation equipment for FNA-4)
ARGADS	advanced radar-directed gun air defense system (US programme)
ARGMA	Army rocket and guided missile Agency, Redstone Arsenal (US)
Argo	naval search radar (IT)
Argocat	wheeled amphibious vehicle
Argos-10	long-range early warning radar by Selenia
Argos-12	3-dimensional early warning radar
ARGUS	analytical reports gathering and updating system; automatic routine generating and updating system M-700 computer by Ferranti; Autonomes Radar Gefechtsfeld-Uberwachungssystem (autonomous battlefield surveillance system, Kiebitz/Orphee)
Argus	tank commander's day/night sight by Rank; CL-28, CP-107, LRPA, long-range (maritime) patrol aircraft by Canadair
ARH	ammunition rail-head; auxiliary, repair, hull (heavy) (USN)
ArHoC	Army housing committee (US)
ARI	automatic return item; Aircraft Research Institute (UK); airborne radio instrument
ARI-5955	airborne ASW radar
ARI-23246	airborne ECM pod
ARIA	Administration, Ryukyu Islands, Army (US)
A/RIA	advanced range instrumentation aircraft
Ariadne	Klasse 393, mine-sweepers (FGN)
Ariane	orbital transport missile by AS
Arica	class Peruvian submarines by HDW 1977
Ariel	AS-30, Nord-5401, air-to-surface missile by Nord Aviation/AS; laser target seeker by Thomson-CSF
Ariel	I II III helicopter by SNCASO
Ariel-6	scientific satellite (UK)
ARInc	Aeronautical Radio Incorporated (US)
ARIP	automatic rocket impact predictor
ARIS	advanced range instrumentation ship (USN); airborne range instrumentation system ACMR (USAF)
Arisaka-38	Japanese 6.5mm rifle
ARISTOTLE	annual review and information symposium on the technology of training, learning and education (US)
Ark	tank-launched bridge system (UK)
ARL	Admiralty Research Laboratory (Teddington, Middx UK); Aerospace

research laboratory; Arctic Research Laboratory (Point Barrow, Alaska); Arlington Va Research Laboratory (USAF); (aeromedical, aeronautical), acceptable reliability level; auxiliary, repair landing crafts (USN)

ARL-66   airborne control receiver

ARLIS   arctic research laboratory Ice Station

ARLO   air reconnaissance liaison officer

ARM   Army ready material; accumulator read-in module; anhysteretic remnant magnetisation; AGM-45, Shrike, anti-radar missile; auxiliary, repair, machinery (USN)

arm   armament

A/RM   area/remote multiplexer (module) SDMS

ARMACS   aviation resources management and control system (US)

Armadillo   suit/bullet-proof suit

ArMatSC   Army material status committee (US)

Armbrust   hand-held anti-tank weapon by MBB

ArmCom   armored command (US Army); armament command (Rock Island Ill.)

armd   armoured

ArmDAS   Army damage assessment system (US)

armdC   armoured car

armdF   armoured force

ARMD-NASC   Army rockets and missile division Nato supply centre

Armed Porter   O-2TT, armed forward air controller aircraft by Cessna

ArmGrdCen   armed guard center (US)

ARMIP   accounting and reporting management improvement program (US)

ARMS   Army master data file reader microfilm system (US)

armt   armament

ARMSCOR   Armament Corporation (SA)

Army Mule   H-25, helicopter by Vertol

ARN   aids to radio navigation; air radio navigation; airborne radio navigation, air reporting net(work) (Nato)

ARN-101   Pave Tack, digital navigation and weapon delivery system pod by Lear Siegler

ARN-118   airborne radio navigation by Collins

ARN-124   airborne distance measuring equipment by Collins

ArNa   Army with Navy (US)

ARNG   Army National Guard (US); Army national grid (maps)

ARNGUS   Army National Guard of the United States

ARNO   Association of Retired Naval Officers

ArNot   area notices (navigation)

ARO   air radio officer; air refuelling operator; Army routine order; Army Research Office (US)

AROD   airborne range and orbit determination

ARODS   airborne radar orbital determination system

ARO-E   Army Research Organization (US) in Europe

ARO-FE   Army Research Organization (US) in the Far East

AROM   associative read-only memory

AROU   aviation repair and overhaul unit

ARP   advanced re-entry programme; air raid precaution; air raid protection; ammunition refilling point; anti-radiation projectile (Copperhead); anti-riot pistol; area radar plot; Army research plan; automatic reporting post (air defence) (Nato); azimuth reset pulse

ARPA   Advanced Research Projects Agency (US); area radar prediction analysis

Arpac   Arme Individuelle de Proximité Anti-Char (close-range anti-tank weapon)

ARPAT   advanced research projects agency terminal

ARPC   air reserve personnel center (US)

ARPICo   air raid protection institute company (UK)

ARPN   aircraft and related procurement, Navy (US)

ARP-RFL-40   rifle grenade by MECAR

ARP-RFL-40-BT   rifle grenade for 5.56mm rifle

ARPS   APS-116, advanced radar processing system by GE

arpt   airport

ARPV   advanced remotely piloted vehicle

ARQ   annual review questionnaire; automatic repeat request (Nato); automatic response query

ARR   armoured reconnaissance regiment; Army readiness regions; Army retail requirements

arr   arrival

ARR   airborne radio receiver; airborne radio relay; automatic request for repetition

ARR-78   ASCL, advanced sonobuoy communications link by Hazeltine

ArRADCom   Armament Research and Development Command (US Army, Picatinny Arsenal)

ARRC   Associate of the Royal Red Cross

ArRCom   Armament (material) Readiness Command (US Army)

ARRCS   air raid reporting control ship (Nato)

ARRDE   Army Radar Research and Development
        Establishment (UK)
ARRL   aeronautical radio and radar labora-
        tory
Arrowhead Shot/conical bore projectile,
        anti-tank
ARRS   aerospace rescue and recovery service
        MAC (US); aerospace rescue and
        recovery squadron (USN); airborne
        radar ranging system by Elta
ARS   airborne reconnaissance squadron;
        aerial reconnaissance and secur-
        ity; air regulatory squadron (USN);
        air rescue service; air refuelling
        squadron; Army radio school;
        azimuth reference system (gui-
        dance); auxiliary, repair, salvage
        (USN-Nato); American Rocket
        Society; Atelier de Construction
        de Rennes (FR)
ars   arsenal
ARSB   air reconnaissance support battalion
ARSD   aviation repair supply depot; auxil-
        iary, repair, salvage, dock (USN)
ARSEM   Army registry of special educational
        materials (US)
ArSO   armament supply officer
ARSpt   air reconnaissance support
ARSR   air route surveillance radar
ARST   aerial reconnaissance and security
        troop; auxiliary, repair, salvage,
        tender (USN)
ArStaf Army staff
ARSV   armored reconnaissance scout vehicle
        (US)
ART   aviation radio technician; arithmetic
        reasoning test; airborne radio,
        tactical; advanced research and
        technology; airborne radiation
        thermometer; average retrieval
        time; airborne radio transmitter;
        Artillery and related equipment
        STANAG; automated range tracking
ART-132 VHF airborne radio, tactical by
        Marconi
ART-151 VHF airborne radio, specially for
        helicopters
ArTaCom Army requirements for tactical com-
        munications
ArTaDS Army tactical data system
ARTC   air route traffic control; antenna
        rotation and target control
ARTC-100-1 antenna rotation and target con-
        trol system by Koor
ARTCC   air route traffic control centre
ArtFüInFelSys Artillerie Führungs- Informa-
        tions- und Feuerleitsystem
        (artillery command, infor-
        mation and fire-control
        system)

ARTG   azimuth range and timing group
ARTl   awaiting results of trial
artO   artificer officer
ARTOC   Army tactical operations Center (US);
        Area Route traffic operations
        (Nato)
ARTP   advanced resident training plan
ArtRak Artillerierakete (artillery rocket)
ArTrEP Army training and evaluation pro-
        gramme
artS   artificer sergeant
ARTS   Armed Forces Radio and Television
        Service (US); automated radar ter-
        minal system by Sperry Univac
ArtSF   Artillerie auf Selbstfahrlafette
        (self-propelled artillery)
ARTT   Annual Review travelling team (Nato)
arty   artillery
ARTY   Artillery Procedures STANAG
artyR   artillery reconnaissance
ARU   American Research Union; Army Rugby
        Union (UK); armoured reinforcement
        unit; audio response unit
arunk   arrival unknown
ARV   armoured recovery vehicle
ARV   auxiliary, repair, vessel, aircraft
        (USN)

ARVE   auxiliary, repair, aircraft engines
        (USN)
ARVH   auxiliary, repair, aircraft, heli-
        copters
ARVN   Army, Republic of Viet Nam
ARW   air raid warning; ammunition repair
        workshop
ARWAB   Army rotary wing aptitude battery
ARW/MTW Achtradwagen/Mannschaftstransport-
        wagen (8-wheeled personnel
        carrier by DB)
Aryabhatta satellite (India) 1975
AS   Admiral Superintendent; Africa Star;
        air staff; assistant secretary;
        Australia (Seato); arsenal sec-
        tion; ammunition store; Armed Ser-
        vice; Anglo-Saxon; Army surplus;
        anti-submarine; angle of sight;
        air-to-surface (missile); antenna
        site; alto-stratus (clouds);
        air-speed; anti-submarine;
        automatic switching; after sight;
        submarine tender (USN-Nato),
        Aerospatiale (FR firm)
A&S   ammunition and stores
AS-1   Kennel, air-to-surface missile (SU)
AS-2   Kipper, air-to-surface missile (SU)
AS-2L   Air-Sol Leger Laser by Euromissile,
        airborne anti-tank missile
AS-3   Kangaroo, air-to-surface missile (SU)
AS-4   Kitchen, air-to-surface missile (SU)

AS-5	Kelt, air-to-surface missile radar homing (SU)
AS-6	Kingfish, air-to-surface missile nuclear (SU)
AS-7	Kerry, air-to-surface missile radio-guided (SU)
AS-8	Kerry, helicopter-borne anti-tank missile (SU)
AS-9	helicopter-borne anti-tank missile 50 mile range
AS-11	SS-11, anti-tank guided weapon by AS
AS-12	SS-12, anti-tank guided weapon
AS-12	naval air-to-surface missile (GE); FAG, Feldarbeitsgerät, excavator (GE)
AS-15	naval air-to-surface missile 15km range by AS/Matra
AS-15TT	Air-Sol 15km Tous Temps, naval air-to-surface missile 15km range all-weather by AS/Matra
AS-20	Nord 5103, air-to-surface missile by Nord
AS-30	Nord-5401, Ariel, air-to-surface missile by Nord
AS-37	Martel, air-to-surface missile radar-homing by BAC/Matra
AS-61	heavy helicopter by Agusta
AS-202	Bravo, trainer aircraft by FFA
AS-332	Super Puma, helicopter by AS
AS-350	Ecureuil, utility helicopter by AS
ASA	air security agency; American Standards Association; anti-submarine aircraft; Army Sailing Association (UK); Army School of Ammunition; Army security agency (US); aviation supply annex
ASA	Assistant Secretary of the Army (US)
	FM financial management
	CW civil works
	I&L installations and logistics
	M&RA manpower and reserve affairs
	R&D research and development
ASAC	assistant special agent in charge (CIA); anti-submarine air controller; all-source analysis center (US Army); Army study advisory committee (US); alto-stratus and alto-cumulus (clouds)
ASACS	airborne surveillance and control system; anti-submarine air close-support
ASADS	anti-submarine air distant support
ASAECS	anti-submarine air escort and close-support
ASAES	Army small arms experimental station (UK)
ASAF	Australian Small Arms Factory
ASALM	advanced strategic air-launched missile by Martin-Marietta

asap	as soon as possible
ASAP	Army scientific advisory panel; anti-submarine attack plotter; applied systems and personnel
ASARC	Army systems acquisition review council (US)
ASARS	advanced (airborne) synthetic aperture radar system (high-altitude recce)
ASAS	all-source analysis system (US SigInt programme)
ASASAU	anti-submarine air search and attack unit
ASAT	anti-submarine attack teacher; air search and attack team (USN-Nato); advanced subsonic aerial target drone by FR
ASat	anti-satellite US killer satellite program
ASATTU	anti-submarine attack teacher training unit
ASAU	air search and attack unit
ASB	aircraft safety beacon; Air Safety Board; anti-submarine barrier; Aluminium Schnellbau-Behälter by EWK (rapid construction petroleum tank)
asb	asbestos
ASB-19	ARBS, angle-rate bombing system by Hughes
ASBCA	Armed services board of contract appeals (US)
ASBD	advanced sea-based deterrent
ASC	Army School of Cookery (UK); advanced surgical centre; Armed Services Committee; air service command (US); Army Service Corps -RASC --RCT; administrative service center (US); American Security Council; advanced scientific computer; air support control (US); air support carrier (RN); American Standard Code; analogue signal conditioning; Assistant Steering Committee (Nato); automatic switching centre
ASCA	automatic subject citation alert
ASCAC	anti-submarine classification and analysis center (USN)
ASCAT	anti-submarine classification and analysis test
ASCB	Army sports control board (UK)
ASCC	Air Standardization Coordinating Committee (Nato)
ASCE	Allied Supreme Commander Europe
ASCent	assembly system for central processor
ASCG	anti-submarine carrier group
ASCII	American standard code for information interchange

ASCL	ARR-78, advanced sonobuoy communications link by Hazeltine
ASCO	Arab Satellite Communications Organization
ASCom	Army service command
ASCON	automatic switched communications network by Rockwell
ASCP	Army strategic capabilities plan
ASCU	air support control unit
ASD	Admiralty Salvage Department; armament supply department; ammunition sub-depot; Army shipping document; artillery spotting division; aviation supply depot; Aeronautical systems division AFSC; aerospace systems division RCA, air surveillance drone
ASD	Assistant Secretary of Defense (US)
A	administration
C	Comptroller
EM&R	equipment maintenance and readiness
C^3I	command, control, communications installation
HA	health affairs
H&E	health and environment
I&L	installations and logistics
ISA	internal security affairs
ITCC	intelligence, telecommunications command and control
M&RA	manpower and reserve affairs
PA	public affairs
PA&E	program analysis and evaluation
ASDE	airport surface detection equipment
ASDeFor	anti-submarine defense forces (USN)
Lant	Atlantic
Pac	Pacific
ASDevDet	anti-submarine development detachment
ASDF	Air Self Defence Forces (Japan)
ASDIC	anti-submarine detection investigation committee WW2 (RN); sonar equipment; armed service documents intelligence centre
Asdic-193M	mine-hunting sonar
ASDIRS	Army study documentation and information retrieval system
ASDiv	advanced systems division
ASDPSim	advanced system data processing simulation
ASDS	air surveillance drone system
ASE	aviation support equipment; Army School of Education; Agence Spatiale Européenne ESA; Admiralty Signals Establishment; automatic stabilization equipment; air standard efficiency
AS&E	American Science and Engineering (Cambridge Mass.)

ASEAN	Association of South East Asian Nations (Philippines, Thailand, Indonesia, Singapore, Malaysia)
ASEB	aeronautics and space engineering board
ASecGS	administrative section, general staff
ASED	Army School of Education and Depot
ASEE	Anti-submarine Experimental Establishment
ASEG	all services evaluation group
ASEM	MM-100, anti-ship Euromissile consortium: AS, BAe, MBB
ASERL	Admiralty services electronic research laboratory (Baldock)
ASESA	Armed Services Electro Standards Agency (US)
ASESBd	Armed Services Explosives Safety Board (US)
ASET	aeronatuical services earth teminal
ASF	Army service forces; Army special forces; Army Stock Fund (US); additional selection factor; amphibious striking forces; air superiority fighter (aircraft)
ASFBM	auxiliary, submarines, fleet ballistic missile (USN)
ASFDO	anti-submarine fixed defences officer
ASFIR	active swept frequency interferometer radar
ASFTrnTraRon	Auxiliary service force, transportation training squadron (USN)
Lant	Atlantic
Pac	Pacific
ASG	aeronautical standards group; air safety group; Army service group; auxiliary service group; Assistant Secretary General; assessment sub-group (Nato)
ASG-21	air-to-surface gun, 6-barrels, 20mm
ASGRO	armed services graves registration office
ASGS	Assistant secretary of the general staff
ASH	Army School of Hygiene (Mytchett); assault support helicopter (USN); advanced scout helicopter, Black Hawk; anti-submarine helicopter
A&SH	Argyll and Sutherland Highlanders
ASH-8	airborne recorder by Litton
Asheville	class, fast patrol gunboats (USN)
ashp	airship
ASI	Advanced Study Institutes (Nato); additional skill identifier; armaments standardization and interoperability (Nato programme); advanced scientific instrument; air speed indicator; augmented spark igniter

ASIC   area security information centre;
         associated states of Indo-China
ASigCen area signal centre
ASIP   Army stationing and installation
         plan; aircraft structural integ-
         rity programme
ASIR   air speed indicator reading
ASIRC   aquatic sciences information re-
         trieval center (Rhode Island)
ASIS   abort sensing and implementation
         system; ammunition and stores
         issuing ship (USN)
ASJ   automatic search jammer
ASL   Acting Sub-lieutenant; authorized
         stockage list; aeronautical struc-
         tures laboratory; auxiliary, sub-
         marine, little (USN)
asl   above sea level
ASLADS   automatic shipboard launch aircraft
         data system
ASLEP   Apollo surface lunar experiment
         package
ASLL   Air-Sol Leger Laser by EM, air-
         launched laser-guided light anti-
         tank missile
ASLO   Australian scientific liaison office
aslt   assault
ASLT   advanced solid logic technology
ASM   Academy Sergeant Major (UK); arma-
         ment sergeant major; armourer
         sergeant major; artificer sergeant
         major; Antarctica Service Medal
         (US); aircraft survival measures
         (bomb-protected hangars) (Nato);
         anti-submarine missile ASRoc;
         air-to-surface missile
ASM-1   air-to-surface missile by Mitsubishi
ASM-607 maintenance and test equipment for
         airborne central computers by TI
ASMC   automatic systems management and
         control
ASMD   anti-ship missile defence (missile)
         by GD
ASME   American Society of Mechanical
         Engineers
ASMI   airfield surface movement indicator
ASMIO   Arabian States Military Industries
         Organization
ASMIS   (major) Army subordinate (command)
         management information system (US)
asmodee photographic reconnaissance drone
         by MBLE
ASMP   Army survival measures plan; Air-Sol
         Moyenne Portée by AS; air-to-
         ground tactical nuclear missile
ASMR   advanced short/medium range aircraft
ASMRO   armed services medical registration
         office (US)
ASMS   advanced surface missile system
ASMSA   Army signal material support agency
         (US)

ASMT   Army School of Mechanical Transport
         (UK)
ASMWS   Army Snow and Mountain Warfare
         School (UK)
ASN   Army Serial Number; Army Service
         Number; atomic strike net (US);
         average sample number;
         Arbeitsgemeinschaft für Spacelab
         Nutzung (Spacelab utilization co-
         operative); Assistant Secretary
         of the Navy (USN)
         FM   financial management
         I&L installations and logistics
         R&D research and development
ASN-92   Cains, carrier alignment inertial
         navigation system (airborne)
ASN-128 LDNS, light doppler navigation
         system for helicopters by
         Singer-Kearfott
ASNDT   American Society for non-destructive
         testing
ASNP   Army student nurse programme
ASO   American Society for Oceanography;
         area supply office; aviation
         supply office; assistant secre-
         tary's office; area specialist
         officer (CIA); area supply
         officer; area safety officer;
         aviation safety officer; air staff
         officer; air signal officer; air
         surveillance officer
ASOAP   Army spectrometric oil analysis pro-
         gramme
ASOC   air support operations centre (Nato)
ASO/ICP aviation supply office/inventory
         control point
ASOP   Army strategic objectives plan (US);
         Atomic standing operating proce-
         dures (Nato); automated structural
         optimization programme
ASOS   assistant supervisor of shipbuilding
         (US); automatic storm observation
         system)
ASOTS   Africa South of the Sahara
ASP   Annual Service Practice (Nato);
         anti-submarine patrol (Nato); air
         superiority programme; Army
         strategic plan; ammunition supply
         point; atomic strike plan; Allied
         Standing Procedure (Nato); aero-
         space plane (USAF); anti-submarine
         plane; accelerated surface post;
         attached support processor; air-
         craft standard parts, equipments
         and systems STANAG; acoustic
         signal processor
aspa   airspace
ASPAC   Asian and Pacific Council
ASPB   armed services petroleum board;
         assault support patrol boat (USN)

ASPCGA   atomic strike plan control group
          alternate (US)
ASPD   armed services police department
ASPECT   acoustic short-pulse echo classifica-
          tion technique (Nato)
ASPEP   association of scientists and profes-
          sional engineering personnel
ASPF   annual service practice firings
ASPIC   armed services interrogation centre
Aspide   anti-aircraft rocket by Selenia
ASPJ   airborne self-protection jammer
ASPO   avionics system planning office;
          aerospace projection operation
ASPPO   armed services procurement planning
          office(r)
ASPR   armed services procurement regula-
          tions
ASPRM   armed services procurement regula-
          tions manual
ASPRS   armed services procurement regula-
          tions supplement
ASPS   annular suspension and pointing
          system (Spacelab)
ASPT   Army School of Physical Training (UK)
ASptC   Army support centre
ASQ-81   airborne magnetic anomaly detector by
          TI
ASQ-151   airborne electro-optical viewing
          system
ASQ-166   IACS, integrated avionics control
          system by Grumman
ASR   Air Staff Requirement (RAF); air-sea
          rescue; armed strike reconnais-
          sance; Army status report; avail-
          able supply rate; Army Support
          Regiment (RE); airborne search
          radar; automatic send/receive;
          aviation safety regulation; air-
          port surveillance radar; auxiliary,
          submarine rescue (USN-Nato)
ASR-1300 Air Staff Requirement (for new
          command and control system) (RAF)
ASR-1585 (for 10cm-band UKADGE air surveil-
          lance radars)
ASR-1586 (for 23cm-band UKADGE air surveil-
          lance radars)
ASRA   automated (data processing) system
          requirement analysis
ASRAAM   advanced short-range air-to-air
          missile
ASRD   aircraft shipment readiness date
ASRE   Admiralty Signals Research Establish-
          ment; Admiralty Signal and Radar
          Establishment
ASRgn   altimeter setting region
ASROC   RUR-5A, anti-submarine rocket homing
          torpedo by Honeywell; ERA extended
          range ASROC
ASRPB   aviation selected reserve program
          branch BUPERS

ASRS   Anglo-Soviet recognition signals
          WW2; air surveillance radar
          system; automatic storage and re-
          trieval system; aviation safety
          reporting system
A/SRS   air-sea rescue service (UK)
ASRT   air surveillance radar team; air
          support radar team
ASS   assault supply ship; transport sub-
          marine (USN); Atelier de Charge-
          ment de Salbris (FR)
ASSA   area supply support activity, cargo
          submarine (USN)
Assault Breaker RGWS, radar-guided weapon
          system, air-to-air by
          Grumann; anti-tank
          missile system ground-
          launched aircraft-guided
ASSC   aviation section signal corps (USAF
          forerunner); airborne systems
          support centre
ASSESS   airborne science spacelab equipment
          system simulation (NASA/ESA);
          analytical studies of surface
          effects of submerged submarines
ASSET   aerothermodynamic structural sys-
          tems environmental tests
AS&SL   all ships and stations letters
ASSM   anti-ship supersonic missile;
          anti-surface ship missile
ASSO   anti-submarine support operations
ASSOTW   airfields and seaplane stations of
          the world
ASSP   transport submarine (USN)
ASSR   Autonomous Socialist Soviet Republic
ASST   anti-ship surveillance and targeting
          (mission); advanced supersonic
          transport (aircraft)
asst   assistant
ASSU   air support signal unit
assy   assembly
AST   air supported threat; Army School of
          Transport (Langmoor UK); air ser-
          vice training; advanced simulator
          technology; automatic shop tester;
          auxiliary segment table; advanced
          supersonic transport (aircraft)
ast   assistant
AST-403   Air Staff Target RAF requirement
          for ECA, European combat aircraft
AST-404   Air Staff Target for light trans-
          port helicopter
AST-409   Air Staff Target for Harrier
AST-1227 Air Staff Target for air-launched
          anti-tank weapon
AST-1228 Air Staff Target for ALARM, air-
          launched anti-radiation missile
          by BAe
ASTA   association of short circuit testing
          authorities (standard)

A-Star   US designation for AS-350 utility helicopter
ASTC   airport surface traffic control
ASTD   air supported threat defence
ASTEC   advanced solar thermo-electric conversion
ASTer   anti-submarine Terrier (missile)
ASTF   astro-propulsion system test facility
ASTI   advanced systems technology integration (USAF programme)
ASTIA   armed services technical information agency
ASTM   American Society for Testing Materials (standard); American Society for Tropical Medicine
ASTMC   American (rocket society) structures and materials committee
ASTO   Arab satellites telecommunications organization
ASTOR   anti-submarine torpedo ordnance rocket
ASTP   Apollo-Suyuz test project; Army specialist training programme
ASTR   application technological satellite range
ASTRA   application of space techniques relating to aviation
Astrant   class, South African designation for France-built Agosta class submarines
ASTraP   Army specialized training programme
Astre   airfield surface detection equipment by Thomson-CSF
ASTRO   air-space travel research organization
Astrolite light-weight noise-defending earphones by Racal
AstSecNav Assistant Secretary of the Navy
          FinMgmt   financial management
          InsLog   installations and logistics
          ResDev   research and development
ASTT   action-speed tactics trainer by Singer
AstT   astronomical time
ASTU   air support training unit
ASU   aircraft scheduling unit; aircraft starting unit; Arab Socialist Union; automatic switching units
ASU-85   air-transportable self-propelled anti-tank gun 85mm (SU)
ASU-57   air-transportable self-propelled anti-tank gun 57mm (SU)
ASubjScd Army subject schedule
ASup   air supply
ASuW   anti-surface warfare
ASV   armoured support vehicle; aerothermodynamic structural vehicle; automatic self-verification; anti-surface vessel, radar WW2 (RAF); air-to-surface vessel (radar) WW2 (RAF)
ASVAB   armed services vocational aptitude battery
ASVCN   automatic secure voice communications network
ASVU   Army security vetting unit
ASW   anti-submarine warfare; weapon Anti-Shelter-Waffe (rocket-assisted follow-on charge bomb) (GE); air-sea warfare
ASWACS   anti-submarine warfare air close support
ASWADS   anti-submarine warfare air distant support
ASWAECS   anti-submarine warfare air escort and close support
ASWBPL   armed services whole blood processing laboratory
ASWC   airport surface weather conditions; anti-submarine warfare centre SACLANT
ASWCR   airborne surveillance warning and control radar
ASWD   Army special weapons depot
ASWDU   air-sea warfare development unit
ASWE   Admiralty surface-weapons Establishment (Portsdown, Portsmouth)
ASWEPS   anti-submarine warfare environmental prediction system; anti-submarine warfare environmental prediction studies (Nato)
ASWEx   anti-submarine warfare exercise (Nato)
ASWFitRon anti-submarine warfare fighter squadron (USN)
ASWG   American steel wire gauge
ASWGru   anti-submarine warfare group (USN)
ASWI   anti-submarine warfare installations (Nato)
ASW-LR   anti-submarine warning, long range (Nato)
ASWORG   anti-submarine warfare operations research group
ASWO   air stations weekly orders
ASWRC   anti-submarine warfare research centre
ASWS   anti-submarine warfare system; airport surface weather system; automated surface weather system
ASWSAG   anti-submarine warfare systems analysis group
ASWSC&CS anti-submarine warfare ship command and control system
ASW-SOW   anti-submarine warfare stand-off weapon
ASWSPO   anti-submarine warfare systems project office

ASW-SR   anti-submarine warning, short-range
ASWTacScol   anti-submarine warfare tactics
      school
ASWTC   anti-submarine warfare training
      centre
ASWTraCen   anti-submarine warfare training
      centre
ASWTNS   anti-submarine warfare tactical
      navigation school
AS-X-9   air-to-surface radar homing missile
      (SU)
AS-X-10   air-to-surface TV homing missile
      (SU)
AsyG   assistant secretary general (Nato)
ASZ   air surface zone
AT   achievement test; air transfer; Army
      transport; annual training;
      artillery training; anti-tank;
      anti-torpedo; antenna; atomic time;
      air temperature; apparent time;
      automatic test; auxiliary, tug
      (ocean), USN; artillery tractor
      (SU)
at   atomic, attitude
A/T   anti-tank
A&T   acceptance and transfer
AT-1   Shmel. Snapper, anti-tank missile
      (SU)
AT-I   DM-701, Pandora, rocket-launched 8-
      fold anti-tank mine (GE)
AT-2   Swatter, radio guided anti-tank
      missile (SU)
AT-II   DM-711, Medusa, Larat II, rocket-
      launched 5-fold hollow-charge mines
      (GE)
AT-3   Maliotka, Sagger, wire-guided a/t
      missile (SU)
AT-4   Spigot, anti-tank missile (SU)
AT-5   Spandrel, anti-tank missile (SU)
AT-6   Spiral, anti-tank missile air-
      launched (SU)
AT-26   Xavante, close-support aircraft
      (Brazil)
At-100   armoured riot control car by GKN-
      Snakey 4x2
AT-104   armoured riot control car 4x4
AT-105   armoured riot control car 4x4
ATA   air training area; air training
      advisor; Air Transport Auxiliary;
      air transport association; actual
      time of arrival; Atlantic Treaty
      Association (Nato, Paris); addi-
      tional training assemblies; ad-
      vanced test accelerator (laser);
      airport traffic area; auxiliary
      ocean tug (USN); Aviation Training
      Aids Ltd (High Street, Hartley
      Wintney RG27 8PE)
ATAAD   anti-tank/assault/air defence
      (weapon)

ATAB   air transport allocation board;
      aviation training aids branch
ATAC   Army tank automotive centre; air
      transport advisory council
ATACC   alternate tactical air command
      central
ATACS   Army tactical area communications
      system by ITT
ATAD   air technical analysis division
2ATAF   2nd Allied Tactical Air Force (Nato)
      (Mönchen Gladbach)
4ATAF   4th Allied Tactical Air Force (Nato)
      (Ramstein)
5ATAF   5th Allied Tactical Air Force (Nato)
      (Vicenza IT)
ATAFCS   Army tactical airborne fire-control
      system (helicopter) by Ford
ATAFS   Army tactical airborne fire-control
      system
ATAG   air training advisory group
atak   attack
ATAM   air-to-air missile
ATAR   anti-tank air(-launched) rocket
ATAS   air transport auxiliary service
ATASM   advanced tactical air-to-surface
      missile
ATAU   aviation training aids unit
ATB   Army tank battalion; amphibious
      training base; aircraft technical
      bulletin; access type bits; air
      transport board
ATBM   anti-tactical ballistic missile;
      advanced tactical ballistic
      missile
ATC   air transport command; approved type
      certificate; aquatic training
      centre; Army training corps; air
      training corps; advanced training
      command; air training command;
      Army training centre; armament
      training camp; air traffic control
      STANAG; anti-torpedo craft; auto-
      matic track control; automatic
      train control; analogue training
      computer; armoured troop carrier;
      automatic temperature control;
      aircraft technical committee;
      Analog Training Computers Ltd,
      185 Manmouth Parkway, West Long
      Branch, NJ 07764 USA)
ATC-610   training computer for aircraft by
      ATC
ATCA   Allied Tactical Communications
      Agency (Brussels, Nato); advanced
      tanker/cargo aircraft (USAF pro-
      gramme); automatic trunk circuit
      adjustment
ATCAC   air traffic control advisory commit-
      tee
ATCAP   air traffic control automation
      panels

ATCC	air traffic control centre; Atlantic (division) transport control center (HQ) (US)
ATCCC	advanced tactical command and control capability
ATCC	Allied tanker coordinating Committee WW2
	L London
	W Washington
ATCE	ablative thrust chamber engine
ATCEU	air traffic control experimental unit
ATCH	armored troop carrier, helicopter (USN)
ATCL	air traffic control line
ATCLO	amphibious training command liaison officer
ATCO	air traffic control office(r)
ATCo	air traffic coordinator
ATComS	airport tower communications system
ATCorEu	air traffic coordinator, Europe
ATCorUS	air traffic coordinator, US
ATCRBS	air traffic control radar beacon system
ATCS	air traffic communications system; air traffic control service
ATCSS	air traffic control signal system
ATCT	air traffic control tower
ATCU	air-transportable communications unit
ATD	actual time of departure; academic training division; annual training duty; air turbine drive
ATDA	Army training device agency; augmented target docking adapter NASA
ATDMA	advanced time division multiple access (communications system)
ATDR	aeronautical technical directive requirement
ATDS	airborne tactical data system
A/Tdsm	apprentice/tradesman (UK)
ATDU	air transport development unit (RAF); armoured trials and development unit (UK)
ATDV	advanced technology demonstrator vehicle (missile) --SRAM
ATE	automatic test equipment; altitude transmitting equipment; advanced technology engine; Alfred Teves GmbH, Rebstöcker Str. 41, D-6000 Frankfurt 19 (ITT daughter), Atelier de Fabrication de Toulouse
ATEC	Atlantic Treaty Education Committee (Nato); air transport electronics council; automatic test equipment complex; aircraft/avionics test equipment complex by AS
ATECMA	Agrupacion Tecnica Espanola de Constructores de Material Aerospacial (Spanish aerospace manufacturers technical association)

ATEGG	advanced turbine engine gas generator
ATEL	Aviation Traders Engineering Ltd (Stansted Airport, Essex)
ATEM	anti-tank Euromissile consortium: BAe+AS+MBB
ATEP	Army training equipment pool
ATerm	air terminal
ATEx	Atlantic Tradewind experiment
ATF	amphibious task force; airborne task force; Australian task force in Viet Nam; Allied task force (Nato); automatic transmission fluid; fleet ocean tug (USN-Nato)
ATFCNN	allied task force commander North Norway (Nato)
ATFOS	alignment and test facility for optical systems
ATG	air transport group (CA); antenna test group; air-to-ground
ATGM	anti-tank guided missile
ATGW	anti-tank guided weapon
ATH	autonomous terminal homing
ATHOC	automatic target hand-off computer by Goodyear
athodyd	aero thermo-dynamic duct (ramjet)
ATI	Army training instruction; average total inspection; air technical intelligence
ATI-2	Fantrainer, Anfangstrainer mit Turbine und integrierter Luftschraube by RFB (initial trainer aircraft with turbine and integrated propeller)
ATII	advanced techniques for imagery interpretation
Atila	Automatisation de Tir de l'Artillerie (artillery computer system) by CIMSA
Atilay	class, submarines for Turkey by HDW 1977
ATIS	Allied translation and intelligence section; airport terminal information system; automatic terminal information system
ATIU	air technical intelligence unit SWP South West Pacific
ATJ	automatic through junction
ATk	anti-tank
AtkCarAirWing	attack carrier air wing (USN)
AtkEch	attacking echelon
AtkRon	attack squadron
AtkSC	attack surveillance coverage
ATL	air transport liaison; ocean-going tank landing craft (USN)
Atl	Atlantic
AT-L	artillery tractor 8.3 tons (SU)
Atlantic	BR-1150, maritime patrol aircraft anti-submarine warfare by Breguet

ATLAS   a tactical logistical and air simu-
         lation STC; abbreviated test lang-
         uage for avionic systems; anti-tank
         laser-assisted system (Anglo-
         Belgian project)
ATLAS-group Air France, Alitalia, Iberia,
         Lufthansa and Sabena
Atlas   SM-62, intercontinental ballistic
         missile
Atlas/Centaur orbital transport missile by
         GD
ATLB   air transport licensing board
ATLIS   airborne/automatic tracking laser
         illuminating system by Martin
ATLO   air transport liaison officer
ATLP   Army-wide training literature pro-
         gramme
ATLS   air transport liaison section (Army)
ATM   anti-tank mine; anti-tank missile;
         Apollo telescope mount NASA; air
         turbine motor; air training memo-
         randum
atm   atmosphere
A&TM   ammunition and toxic material
ATMAC   air traffic management automated
         centre
ATMC   air transport movement control
ATMCC   air transport movement control centre
ATMOS   ammunition and toxic material open
         space (store)
ATMP   air target materials programme
ATMS   air traffic management system
ATMU   aircraft torpedo maintenance unit
ATN   augmented transition network
AtNo   atomic number
ATO   ammunition technical officer RAOC;
         Allied travel office; aircraft
         transfer order; assisted take-off;
         automatic trunk office; ocean tug,
         old (USN)
AtoA   air-to-air
ATOC   air transport operation centre;
         allied tactical operations centre
         (Nato)
ATOM   Apollo telescope orientation mount
ATOMAL   Atomic information (Nato classifica-
         tion)
AtomStasRep atomic status report (Nato)
Atorp   anti-torpedo
ATOS   assisted take-off system
ATP   allied technical publication; air
         technical publication; accepted
         test procedure; allied tactical
         publication; Army training pro-
         gramme; authority to proceed
ATP-33   Allied Tactical Publication, tactical
         doctrines for allied air forces
ATP-35   Allied Tactical Publications (Nato),
         tactical doctrines for allied
         ground forces

ATP-ASCP Army transportation plan in the
         support of the Army strategic
         capabilities plan
ATPL   airline transport pilot license
ATR   air traffic regulations; aircraft
         trouble report; aviation training
         record; anti-transmitting receiv-
         ing (radar); automatic test and
         repair (module); advanced
         thermic reactor; air transport
         radio; automatic target recogni-
         tion; air-transportable racking
         (system) (UK); auxiliary, tug,
         rescue (USN)
ATRAN   automatic terrain recognition and
         navigation (system) by Goodyear
ATRem   average time remaining
ATReps   air traffic control representatives
AtRon   Atlantic squadron USN before 1941
ATrP   Allied Training Publication (Nato)
ATS   (Women's) Auxiliary Territorial
         Service (UK) now: WRAC; armament
         training station; Army transport
         service; Air transport service;
         air traffic services; advanced
         training school; Army topographic
         station; application technology
         satellite; automatic tactical
         switchboard; automatic test
         system; anti-tetanus serum; air-
         transportable sonar; air-to-
         surface (tactical fighter/bomber);
         air turbine starter; automatic
         traffic signal; astronomical time
         switch; advanced technology satel-
         lite; salvage and rescue ship
         (USN); Atelier de Construction de
         Tarbes; Advanced Technology
         Systems Ltd (Austin daughter) (UK)
AT-S   artillery tractor, tracked 15 tons
         (SU)
ATSD   air traffic situation display;
         assistant to the secretary of
         defence
ATSDT   assistant to the secretary of
         defence telecommunications
ATSM   air transport squadron, medium
ATSR   Army transport service regulations
ATSS   advanced time sharing system;
         auxiliary training submarine (USN)
ATSU   air traffic service unit; air trans-
         port security unit
Atsumi   class, amphibious attack vessels
         (JMSDF)
ATT   Army training test; advanced techni-
         cians test; air training team;
         advanced technology transport
         (aircraft); American Telephone &
         Telegraph Company
AT-T   artillery tractor, tracked 25 tons
         (SU)

Attack class, fast patrol boats (RAN)
Attacker jet fighter 1949 by Supermarine
ATTC aviation technical training centre
ATTD aviation technical training division
ATTDU air transport tactical development
    unit (RAF)
Attila artillery rocket 80.5mm (IT)
ATTITB Air Transport and Travel Industry
    Training Board (158 High Street,
    Staines Middx TW18 4AS)
attn attention
    dir directed
    inv invited
ATTP advanced transport technology pro-
    gramme
ATTW aircrew training and test wing (USAF)
ATU advanced training unit; antenna
    tuning unit
ATURM amphibious training unit (Royal
    Marines)
ATV armoured transport vehicle; all-
    terrain vehicle; Alliierter
    Truppenversuch (Allied troop test)
AtVol atomic volume
ATVR armoured transport vehicle, recon-
    naissance
ATVS advanced television seeker
ATW advanced training wing; adventure
    training wing (UK); air transport
    wing; anti-tank weapon
AtWt atomic weight
AU air university; astronomical unit
    (93 million miles); all-up
    (weight); amplifier unit; arith-
    metic unit
AU-23 Peacemaker, counter-insurgency plane
    by Cessna
Audace class, missile cruisers (IT)
Audax light plane WW2 by Hawker
AUDIT automated un-attended detection
    inspection transmitter
AUG Armee Universal Gewehr, 5.56mm by
    Steyr (army universal rifle)
AugU augmenting unit
AUM air-to-underwater missile
Aurora CP-140, maritime surveillance + ASW
    aircraft (CA)
AUS Army of the United States; aircraft
    utilization section (UK) (staffed
    by RAF, RN, USAF, CAA); assistant
    under-secretary
Aus Australian
AUS-50/5 anti-personnel mine (IT)
AUSA Association of the United States Army
    (annual meeting of the)
Auster light plane (UK)
Austin class, assault transport ship LPD
    (USN)
AUT advanced unit training
AUTEC Atlantic undersea test and evaluation

    center (USN); American undersea
    test and evaluation center
AuthAb authorized abbreviation
AUTOCAT automatic control of air trans-
    missions
AUTODIN automatic digital network; auto-
    matic distribution network
AutoFüNLw Automatisches Führungsfernmelde-
    netz der Luftwaffe (automatic
    telecommunications and command
    network of the German Air
    Force)
AutoKo Automatisches Korpsstammnetz
    (automatic corps telephone net-
    work)
AutoMaP automatic machining programme
AutoMet automatic meteorological compensa-
    tion
AutoNet automatic network
AutoPIC automatic personal identification
    code
AutoPlan-2081 automatic flight planning
    system by Ferranti
AutoProMT automatic programming of machine
    tools
AutoSeVoCom automatic secure voice communi-
    cations
AutoSTraD automatic system for transporta-
    tion data
AutoVoN automatic voice network
AutoWeap automatic weapon
AUV administrative use vehicle, armoured
    utility vehicle
AUW all-up weight; advanced underwater
    weapon
AUWC advanced undersea weapon circuitry
AUWE Osborne, advanced underwater equip-
    ment (acoustic mine-sweeping
    system); Admiralty underwater
    weapons establishment (Portland)
aux auxiliary
AV anti-vapour (filter); anti-varmin
    (cartridge); armoured vehicle;
    austere version (tank); audio-
    visual; atomic volume; seaplane
    tender (USN)
AV-8 Harrier, license-built by McDD
AV-115 aviation gasoline for Navy aircraft
AV-145 aviation gasoline for Air Force
    aircraft
AVA Aerodynamische Versuchsanstalt
    (aerodynamic experimental estab-
    lishment)
AVADS automatic Vulcan air defence system
AVAS automatic VFR advisory service
    (visual flight rules)
AVASI abbreviated visual approach slope
    indicator
AVB advanced aviation base (ship) USN
avblt availability

AVC   American Veterans Committee; Army
        Veterinary Corps --RAVC; auto-
        matic volume control; automatic
        voltage compression; automatic
        voltage control; large catapult
        lighter (USN)
AvCad   aviation cadet
AvCAL   aviation consolidated allowance list
AVCAT   aviation fuel, high flash point
AvCert aviator's certificate
AVCS   assistant vice chief of staff;
        advanced vidicon camera system
AVCSA   assistant vice chief of staff (US
        Army)
AVD   Army veterinary department; seaplane
        tender, destroyer (USN)
Avenger TBF-1, carrier-borne aircraft by
        Grumman; GAU-8, gatling gun 30mm
        by GE
AVFR   available for reassignment
avg   average
AVG   aircraft escort vessel (USN)
AvGas   aviation gasoline
AVGP   armoured vehicle, general purpose
        (CA)
AVH   aircraft rescue boat (USN)
AVHRR   advanced very high resolution
        radiometer
Aviaskop endoscopic inspection system (GE)
Avibras X-40, Sonda III, tactical missile
        (Brazil)
AVId   airborne vehicle identification
Aviocar C-212, light transport plane by
        CASA
Aviojet C-101, jet trainer by CASA
avionics aviation electronics
AVIS   audio-visual information system
Avisa   infra-red warning receiver by
        Siemens
AVIT   audio-visual instructional technol-
        ogy
AVK   Artillerieversuchskommando, Kiel
        (naval artillery experimental com-
        mand)
AVKP   armoured vehicle kill potentials
AVLA   amphibious vehicle launching area
AVLB   armoured vehicle launched bridge
AVLF   airborne very low frequency
AvLub   aviation lubricant
AVM   Allied Victory Medal; automatic
        vehicle monitoring system by
        Hazeltine (for police cars); air-
        borne vibration monitor; guided
        missile ship (USN)
AVN   automatic voice network
AvnCdt aviation cadet
AvnEngBn aviation engineer battalion (USMC)
AVNL   automatic video noise limiting;
        automatic video noise landing
AvnMed aviation medicine

AvnU   aviation unit (USMC)
AVO   administrative veterinary officer
AvOil   aviation oil
AvOpTech aviation operations technician
AvOrdTech aviation ordnance technician
AVOX   analog voice-operated switch
AVP   Army validation programme; small
        seaplane tender (USN)
AVQ-22 airborne low light level television
        equipment by Westinghouse
AVQ-23 Pave Spike, airborne pod, day-only
        TV/laser designator system by
        Westinghouse
AVR   Army Volunteer Reserve, aircraft
        rescue vessel (USN)
AVRE   armoured vehicle, Royal Engineers;
        assault vehicle, Royal Engineers;
        (Petard, Carpetlayer, Bullshorn
        Plough, Goat, Onion, Skid Bailey
        Bridge) WW2
Avro-504 trainer aircraft WW2 (UK)
AVROC   aviation reserve officer candidate
        program (US)
AVRP   audio-visual recording and presenta-
        tion
AVRS   Army Veterinary and Remount Service
AVS   Advanced vertical STOL aircraft
        (US programme); aviation supply
        ship (USN)
AVSCom aviation system command (US Army)
        (St Louis Mo.)
AvStar hand-held flight computer by
        Jeppesen
AVT   auxiliary, aircraft transport (USN)
AVTAG   aviation fuel, turbine kerosene
AVTC   Army vocational training centre
avtr   aviator
AVTR   airborne video-cassette tape
        recorder by TEAC
AVTUR   aviation turbine fuel
AW   atomic warfare; acoustic warfare;
        articles of war; air warning;
        Army-wide; atomic weight; auto-
        matic weapon; all water (trans-
        port); actual weight; above water
        (height); all-weather; distilling
        ship (USN)
A/W   air worthy
AW-391 airborne ASW radar
AWA   air warfare analysis; Army Wives'
        Association; airspace warning
        area; Armstrong Whitworth Aircraft
        Ltd; Amalgamated Wireless Austra-
        lasia Ltd (North Ryde, NSW
        Australia)
AWAC   American Women's Army Corps
        Amalgamated Wireless of Austra-
        lasia Company
AWACS   E-3, airborne warning and control
        system by Boeing

AWADS   adverse-weather aerial delivery system
AWAS   air warfare analysis section, Australian Women's Army Service
AWASP   advanced weapons ammunition supply point
AWB   amphibious warfare board
AWC   Army War College
AWCLS   all-weather carrier landing system
AWCCM   acoustic warfare counter-counter-measures
AWCO   area wage and classification office
AWCS   airborne weapons control system
AWCSSI   Army War College Strategic Studies Institute
AWCTA   atomic weapon carrying tactical aircraft
AWCW   airborne warning and control wing (USAF)
AWD   advanced workshop detachment, air worthiness division ICAO
AWDATS   artillery weapon data transmission system by Marconi
AWF   all-weather fighter (aircraft)
AWG   American wire gauge; airborne weapon group
AWG-9   airborne radar fire-control system by Hughes
AWG-10   airborne pulse-doppler radar
AWG-25   command launch computer and control panel for HARM by TI
AWHA   Australian Women's Home Army
AWI   Air Works India (Bombay)
AWI-2   Fantrainer, Anfangstrainer mit Wankelmotor und integrierter Luftschraube by RFG (initial trainer aircraft)
A&WI   Atlantic and West Indies, America and WW
AWIC   Army warfare inquiry committee (UK)
AWK   water tender (USN)
AWL   administrative weight limitation; all-weather landing (system)
AWLog   Army wholesale logistic system
AWN   automated weather network
AWOC   all-weather operations committee
AWOL   absent without leave
AWOP   all-weather operations panel
AWP   Allied weather publications
AWRE   atomic weapons research establishment (Aldermaston UK); Australian weapons research establishment
AWrnCo   aircraft warning company (USMC)
AWS   air warning service; Army welfare service; air wing staff; aircraft warning squadron; amphibious warfare school (Poole UK); air weather service; atomic warning system; air weapon system
AWS-2   naval long-range surveillance radar by Plessey
AWS-4   naval surveillance radar for small craft by Plessey
AWS-5   naval surveillance radar for corvettes and frigates by Plessey
AWSM   acoustic warfare support measures
AWSCom   advanced weapons support command
AWSP   The Army's Wilkinson Sword of Peace (UK)
AWST   atomic weapons special transport
AWSta   all-weather station
AWT   alternate water terminal
AWTI   air weapons training installation
AWTS   Army-wide training support
AWTSS   all-weather tactical strike system (radar) (USAF)
AWU   atomic weight unit; Ausbildungsgerät Waffensystem U-Boot by KAE (submarine weapon system simulator)
AWVS   American Women's Volunteer Service
AWX   all-weather aircraft
awy   airway
AX   experimental auxiliary (vessel) (USN); armed spotter aircraft FAC
AXP   Allied exercise publication (Nato)
AXQ-14   data link weapon control system by Hughes
AxSigCom   axis of signal communications
Ayanami   class, destroyers (JMSDF)
AYK-10   airborne digital computer by Univac
AYK-14   general purpose computer by Univac
AYK-15   miniaturized AYK-14
AyrYeo   The Ayrshire Yeomanry
AYS-901   airborne acoustic data processing system ASW
AYT   Army youth team (UK)
AZ   airship tender (USN); Aufschlagzünder (impact fuse)
az   azimuth
AZ5C   high-strength aluminium alloy
AZBw   Alarmzentrum der Bundeswehr
AZ/EZ   Ausbildungszentrum Erprobungszentrum (training and evaluation centre)
AzI   azimuth instrument (theodolite)
AZnV   Aufschlagzünder mit Verzögerung (delayed impact fuse)
Azon   azimuth-only bomb (guided)
Azor   transport aircraft by CASA; class, combat hydrofoils (SU)
AZP-23   anti-aircraft gun, 23mm (SU)
AZS   automatic Zero set
Azteca   class, patrol vessel (Mexico)

B

B	Brigadier (UK); bombardier; biennal (report); British; bomber; battery; base
B-echelon	vehicles and men not required at short notice
B-Munition	Brandmunition, incendiary ammunition
B-Patrone	Beobachtungspatrone (ranging-sounding projectile), V verbessert (product-improved)
1830-B	naval computer
B-1	bomber, variable-sweep Mach 2 by Rockwell
B-1	heavy infantry tank (FR)
B-3	Lancaster, bomber (UK)
B-3LA	light attack aircraft by SAAB
B-IV	SdKfz 301, remote-controlled demolition tracked vehicle WW2 (GE)
	a 3500 kgs
	b 4000 kgs
	c 5000 kgs
B-5	bomber, Chinese-built Il-28
B-6	bomber, Chinese-built Tu-16
B-9	XB-901, twin-engined bomber 1930 by Boeing
B-10	XB-10, XB-907, twin-engined bomber 1934 by Martin
B-11	recoilless gun 107mm (SU)
B-15	Black Widow, night fighter/bomber WW2 by Northrop
B-17	YB-17, Flying Fortress, bomber WW2 by Boeing
B-18	bomber 1938 by Douglas
B-24	Liberator, bomber WW2 by Consolidated
B-25	Mitchell, twin-engined bomber WW2 by North American
B-26	Invader, A-26, attack bomber by Douglas, took this designation after Marauder had been phased out
B-26	Marauder, bomber WW2 by Martin
B-29	XB-29, Superfortress, bomber WW2 by Boeing
B-36	Vultee, 6-engined bomber 1946, piston-engined jet-boosted, D RPV director aircraft
B-45	Tornado, jet bomber 1949 by North American
B-47	Stratojet, medium bomber by Boeing
B-50	strategic bomber 1951
B-52	Stratofortress, strategic bomber 1955 by Boeing
B-57	Intruder, Night Intruder, bomber by Martin, UK-designation Canberra
B-58	Hustler, Mach 2 bomber 1960 by Corvair
B-66	Destroyer, tactical bomber 1970 by McDD
B-70	Valkyrie, Mach 3 bomber by North American
B-250	Beschleunigungsmesser by Litef (acceleration meter)
B-707/307C	4-jet long-range transport aircraft by Boeing
BA	British Admiralty; British Army; budget activity; bomb aimer; able-bodied (seaman) (RN); breathing apparatus; battery (dry); battery adjust; buffer amplifier; British Aerospace
B/A	braking action
ba	blind approach
BAA	brigade administrative area; British Airports Authority; budget activity account; broadband antenna amplifier
BAAM	basic administration and management (programme)
BAAN	budget authorization account number
BABS	blind approach beacon system; beam approach beacon system
BAC	base area commandant; British Air Commission (Washington); battleship, aircraft carrier; barometric altitude control; British Aircraft Corporation Ltd, later: British Aerospace Corporation, ---BAe; Boeing Aerospace Company
BAC-167	Strikemaster, light trainer/attack aircraft by BAC

bac   bacteriological
BACC   British-American Coordination
           Committee
BACCHUS   British Aircraft Corporation Commer-
           cial Habitat under the sea
BACE   basic automatic check equipment
Bachstelze FA-330, rotor-kite towed behind
           submarines WW2 by Focke-
           Achgelis
BACo   British Aluminium Company Ltd
BACO-liner barge-container liner
BACSA   British Association for Cemeteries
           in South Asia
bact   bacteriological
BAD   base ammunition depot; base air
           depot; British Admiralty Delegation
           (Washington)
BADG   British Aerospace Development Group;
           British Aerospace Dynamics Group
           (POB 5, Bristol BS12 7QW)
BADGE   base air defence ground environment
Badger   tank drivers' passive night vision
           system by Pilkington
BAE   Bendix Aviation Electric (CA)
BAe   British Aerospace (Richmond Road,
           Kingston upon Thames KT2 5QS)
BAEA   British Atomic Energy Authority
BAeD   British Aerospace Dynamics (Group)
BAeDG   British Aerospace Dynamics (Group),
           (POB 5, Filton, Bristol BS12 7QW)
BAEE   British Army Equipment Exhibition
           (Aldershot)
BAERE   British Atomic Energy Research
           Establishment
BAF   Belgian/British/Bulgarian/Burma
           Air Force
BAFO   British Air Force of Occupation;
           British Army Forces Overseas
Bafs   British Armed Forces Service
           (vouchers) NAAFI-money
BAFSV   British Armed Forces Service
           vouchers (NAAFI-money)
BAG   ballistic attack game
BagAir   baggage for air travel
BAGR   Bureau of Aeronautics, General Rep-
           resentative (US)
           CD Central District
           ED Eastern District
           WD Western District
BAGS   Bullpup all-weather guidance system
Bagshot   bomber (RAF) by Bristol

BAIB   British Accidents Investigation
           Branch
Bailey   Universal bridge (UK) by Mabey
BAIO   Brigade Artillery Intelligence
           Officer
BAIS   British Air Intelligence Service
BAK   British auxiliary, cargo (USN)
baks   barracks

BAkWVT   Bundesakademie für Wehrverwaltung
           und Wehrtechnik, Mannheim (Federal
           GE   Academy for Defence, Admin-
           istration and Technology)
BAL   Ballistics STANAG; British Anti-
           Lewisite; basic assembler lang-
           uage; Bristol Aerospace Ltd (CA)
bal   ballistic, balance
Balao   class, submarines (USN)
BalDny   ballistic density
ball   ballistics, ballast
Ballistite propellant
Ballute   balloon and parachute (retarding
           system for TGSM)
BallWin   ballistic winds
BalMi   ballistic missile
BaLog   Base Logistic Command
BALS   blind approach landing system
BalSpaCon balance of space-to-space control
           agencies (US)
Balt   Baltic
BaltAp   Allied Command Baltic Approaches
           Karup Denmark; Allied Forces
           Command Baltic Approaches
Baltyk   class, intelligence collecting craft
           (Poland)
BalWnd   ballistic winds
BAM   British Air Ministry; Baikal Amur
           Mainline (railway) (US); bitumin-
           ous aggregate mixture; British
           auxiliary, minesweeper (USN);
           Bundesanstalt für Materialprüfungen
           (Federal GE   Establishment for
           Materials Testing)
BAMA   British Army Motorists' Association
BAMBI   ballistic (anti-) missile boost
           intercept
BAMO   Bureau of Aeronautics Material
           Officer (US)
BAMRO   Bureau of Aeronautics Maintenance
           Repair Officer
BAMS   Broadcast to Allied Merchant Ships
BAMSR   British Admiralty Maintenance and
           Supply Representative
BaNavAvnOffScol Basic Naval Aviation Offi-
           cers School (USN)
Bandeirante EMB-110, light transport air-
           craft by EMB
Banderulha EMB-111, maritime surveillance
           aircraft by EMB
Bangor   class, minesweepers WW2 (RN)
BANS   Basic Air Navigation School; bright
           alpha-numeric sub-system
Banshee   F-24, naval jet fighter 1949 (USN)
Bantam   anti-tank guided weapon by Bofors
BANU   British Army News Unit
BANZARE   British-Australian-New Zealand
           Arctic Research Expedition
BAOR   British Army of the Rhine
BAP   battery aiming point; basic assembler

BAP   programme; Bildschirmarbeitsplatz
          (data display)
BAP-100   airfield demolition rocket (FR)
BAPD   base ammunition and petroleum depot
BAPO   British Army Post Office
BAPRept   beds and patients report
BAQ   basic allowance for quarters (US)
          AC   adopted child(ren)
          DisRet   disability retirement
          F   father
          H   husband
          LC   legitimate children
          M   mother
          SC   stepchild(ren)
          W   wife
BAR   Bureau of Aeronautics Representative;
          British Army Review; Browning
          Automatic Rifle; battery acquisi-
          tion radar; base address register
          (computer)
bar   barometer
Barbarossa-2 bus missile study by Orlando
Barbel   class, auxiliary submarines AGSS
          (USN)
BARBICAN battlefield automated radar bearing
          intercept classification and
          analysis (system) EW by MEL-
          Ferranti
BARC   barge, amphibious, resupply, cargo
          (USN)
BarCAP   barrier combat air patrol
Barcelo   class, guided missile patrol boats
          for Spain by Lüerssen
BARDAY   Bureau of Aeronautics Representative
          (Dayton Ohio)
BarDoc   barrier doctrine (Nato)
BarFor   barrier force
Barker   rifle British 1800
BarLant   Barrier Force, Atlantic (USN)
BARM   British Admiralty Repair Mission
BarMine   anti-tank mine bar-shaped (UK)
baro   barometer
Baron   mine-sweeping (flail) tank WW2
BarPac   Barrier Force Pacific (USN)
Barra   SSQ-801, CAMBS, helicopter-borne
          sonobuoy by AWAC command-active
          multi-beam sonobuoy system
BarraBridge instant Infantry bridge by
          Barracuda
Barracuda universal bomber WW2 by Fairey;
          TSR torpedo spotter reconnais-
          sance
Barrier-S barbed wire coil by Graepel
Barrier-Z barbed wire coil by Graepel
BARRO   Bureau of Aeronautics Resident Repre-
          sentative Officer
Bart   Baronet
BART   Bay area rapid transit(system) (San
          Francisco) (USN)
BARV   beach armoured recovery vehicle (RM)

BAS   British Army Staff; basic allowance
          for subsistence; basic air speed;
          bomb assembly spares; blind
          approach system
BasBr   basic branch (training course) (US)
BASC   Berlin Air Safety Centre (Nato)
BASCA   Bay Area Supply Corps Association
          (San Francisco)
BASD   basic active service date
BASE   basic Army strategic estimates
BaSec   base section
BASEC   British Approval Service for Elec-
          tric Cables
BASEEFA   British Approval Service for Elec-
          trical Equipment in Flammable
          Atmospheres
BaseOps   base Operations
BASIC   battle area surveillance and inte-
          grated communications; beginners
          all-purpose symbolic instruction
          code (computer language)
BASO   Brigade Air Support Officer
BASOC   Brigade Air Support Operations
          Centre
BasOpS   base operating information system
BasPM   basic planning memorandum
Bastard   armoured truck
BAT   branch assistance team; battalion
          anti-tank (gun); basic air temp-
          erature; British ocean-going tug
          (USN); Bureau d'Assistance Tech-
          nique (Technical Assistance
          Bureau) (FR); Buldozerniy Artil-
          leriskiy Tyagatch (artillery
          tractor dozer) (SU)
bat   battle; battalion
Bat   radar-guided air-to-surface missile
          (USAF) WW2
BatCruLant Battleships and cruisers,
          Atlantic Fleet (USN)
BatCruPac Battleships and cruisers, Pacific
          Fleet (USN)
BatDiv   Battleship Division (USN)
BaTelCo   Bahamas Telecommunications Corpora-
          tion
BATES   battlefield artillery target engage-
          ment system by Marconi
BatFor   battle force (USN)
Bathy   SSQ-36, helicopter-borne sonar buoy
BatLant   battleships, Atlantic Fleet (USN)
BatPac   battleships, Pacific Fleet
BATLSK   British Army Training Liaison Staff,
          Kenya
BATO   balloon-assisted take-off
Batral   class, light landing and transport
          vessel (FR)
BatRecon battlefield reconnaissance
BatRon   battleship squadron
BATS   basic additional teleprocessing sup-
          port

BatShipBatForLant   battleships, battle force,
                    Atlantic Fleet (USN)
BatShipBatForPac   battleships, battle force,
                    Pacific Fleet
BatShipsLant   battleships, Atlantic Fleet
BatShipPac   battleships, Pacific Fleet
BATT   British Army Training Team
batt   battery, battalion
BattEffPrize   Battle Efficiency Prize
Battle   bomber WW2 by Fairey
BATTS   British Army Training Tean, Sudan
BATUS   British Army Training Unit, Suffield
         Canada
Baung   class, fast patrol boats (Malaysia),
         by Hong Kong Lürssen
BAV   basic air vehicle RPV ALCM
BAV-485   wheeled amphibious vehicle (SU)
BAVG   British aircraft carrier escort (USN)
Bazooka   M-20, anti-tank rocket launcher
BB   Bescherming Bevolking (Civil Defence)
      (Dutch); below bridge; bedding
      book; bevel base (bullet); Bailey
      bridge; battery (accumulator);
      bullet breech (rimfire cartridge);
      back bearing; balloon barrage;
      battleship (USN)
B/B   baby (incendiary) bomb
B&B   Brüggemann & Brand (D-3552 Wetter/
       Lahn)
BBB   basic boxed base
BBC   Bromolbenzyl Cyanide; broad-band chaff;
       British Broadcasting Corporation;
       Bitterroot Bullet Company; Brown
       Boverie & Cie (D-6800 Mannheim)
BBC-York   Brown Boverie York, Kälte & Klima-
            technik (Lerchenstr. 16, D-2
            Hamburg 50)
BBG   battleship, guided missiles (USN)
BBH   battalion beachhead; Blend-Brand-
       Handgranate by Buck (dazzling and
       incendiary hand-grenade)
BBIS   Brass Band Insurance Services
bbl   barrel; barrels; barrel lengths
BBoD   Bullpup Board of Directors
BBP   bulk breaking point
BBV   Besondere Bedingungen für Beschaf-
       fungsverträge BWB (special condi-
       tions for procurement contracts)
BC   Battery Commander; Bomber Command
      (RAF); Budget Committee (civilian)
      (Nato); biological and chemical
      (warfare); bathy-conductograph;
      bottom - contour; back course
      (localizer); battle cruiser (RN);
      Bren gun carrier (UK)
B/C   broadcast
BCA   Bureau of Current Affairs; battery
       control area
BCAI   broadcast-controlled air intercep-
        tion

BCAL   British Civil Air Lines
BCAN   bureau control activity number
BCAP   barrier combat air patrol
BCAR   British Civil Airworthiness Require-
        ments
BCATP   British Commonwealth Air Training
         Programme WW2
BCATS   British Commonwealth Air Training
         Scheme WW2
BCC   basic crypto-analysis course;
       battery control centre; British
       Crown Colony; battery/battalion
       command centre; ballistic control
       computer; BETA correlation centre
       (battlefield exploitation and
       target acquisition)
BCD   bad conduct discharge; binary coded
       decimal (computer); Broadcast and
       Communications (products) Divi-
       sion (RCA)
BCDC   binary coded decimal computer;
        binary coded decimal counter
BCDD   British Chemical Defence Department;
        Base construction depot detachment
BCE   basic civil engineering; baseline
       cost estimate
BCEL   British Commonwealth Ex-service
        League
BCF   Battle Cruiser Force; British
       Commonwealth Forces
BCF-gas   Bromo-Chloro-di-Fluoromethane (for
           fire extinguishers)
BCFK   British Commonwealth Forces in Korea
bch   beach
BCI   International Broadcasting System;
       Broadcast Interference
BCIRA   British Cast Iron Research Associa-
         tion
BCL   Burroughs Common Language
BCLO   Bomber Command Liaison Officer
BCM   ballistic correction of the moment;
       basic control manoeuvres (flying);
       beyond capability of maintenance;
       British Composite Materials Engi-
       neering Ltd (Avonmouth Bristol
       BS11 9DU)
BCN   British Commonwealth of Nations;
       bureau control number
bcn   beacon
BCO   battery control officer
BCOF   British Commonwealth Occupation
        Force (Association)
BCP   battery command post
BCRA   Bureau Central de Renseignements
        Allie (French Central Intelligence
        in Exile) WW2
BCS   Battle Cruiser Squadron; battery
       commander's station; British Civil
       Service; British Calibration Ser-
       vice; British Computing Society;

BCS	battlefield computer system by Norden; (artillery) battery (level) computer system by Norden
bcst	broadcast
BCT	basic combat training; battalion combat train; battery control trailer
BCU	battery coolant unit (IR seeker); big close-up (camera mode)
BCV	battery control van
BCW	biological and chemical warfare
BD	base depot; battle dress (UK); boom defence; base detonating (fuse); bomb disposal (Nato); blocking device; blowing dust (weather); blocker deflector; bottom down
bd	board; boundary; bundle
BD-1	bomb dispenser by Bölkow (GE)
BDA	battle/bomb damage assessment
BDB	base development board
BDC	Bomb Disposal Company (RE); bottom dead centre; binary decimal counter
BDCC	British Defence Coordinating Committee
	ME Middle East
BDD	boom defence depot
BDD&M	Board of Decorations and Medals
BDE	British destroyer escort (USN)
bde	brigade
bdeHQ	brigade headquarters
bdeLT	brigade landing team
BdeMaj	Brigade Major
BDF	British Defence Forces; Belize Defence Forces; Bangla-Desh Forces; base detonating fuse
BDHI	Bearing-Distance-Heading-Indicator
BDI	bearing deviation indicator (sonar)
BDL	battery data link
bdl	bundle
BDLI	Bundesverband der Deutschen Luft- und Raumfahrtindustrie (Federal Association of the German Aerospace Industry)
BDM	bomber defence missile
Bdmr	bandmaster
BDMS	base depot medical stores
BDNMSSS	Board of Directors Nato Maintenance Supply Service System
BDO	boom defence officer
BDP	base development plan; break-down pressure
BDr	Bodendruck (ground pressure)
bdr	Brigadier; Bombardier; border
BDR-610	transceiver HF SSB 20 W, by MBLE
BDRA	basic daily food (ration) allowance
BDRK	bomb damage repair kit (for runways)
bdry	boundary
BDS	British Defence Staff; Bomb Disposal Squad; bomb damage survey
BDSA	Business and Defence Services Administration

BDSH-5	15 smoke pot (SU)
bdsm	bandsman
BDSO	British Defence Sales Organization (St Chrisopher House, Southwark Street, London SE1 0TD)
BDST	British Double Summer Time
BDSW	British Defence Staff (Washington DC)
BDSWashDC	British Defence Staff (Washington DC)
BDU	battery display unit; bomb disposal unit
BDV	boom-defence vessel (RN); tracked tractor (Sweden); breakdown vehicle
BDVeh	breakdown vehicle
BDX	wheeled armoured personnel carrier by Beherman Demoen
bdy	boundary
BdZ	Bodenzünder (base detonating fuse)
BE	British Electric; Belgium (Nato); British Embassy; Board of Education; basic encyclopedia; British Empire; British Element; base ejection (smoke shell); base exploding (projectile)
B&E	breaking and entering
Be-6	Madge, seaplane by Beriev (SU)
Be-12	Mail, Tchaika, seaplane, ASW, recce (SU)
BEA	British East Africa
BEAB	British Electrical Approvals Board
Beacotron	beam coupling tube
BEAIRA	British Electrical and Allied Industries Research Association
BEAMA	British Electrical and Allied Manufacturers' Association
Bearcat	F-8F, naval fighter by Grumman
Bear Trap	tethered deck-landing system for naval helicopters
Beaufighter	naval night-fighter aircraft by Bristol
Beaufort	torpedo bomber by Bristol
Beaver	light helicopter; artillery observation plane (CA); Canadian designation for Biber; armoured vehicle launched bridge
BEBC	big European bubble chamber
BEC	basic education centre
BECAMP	ballistic environmental characteristics and measurement programme
BECO	booster engine cut-off
Bedford	FV-13100, truck (UK)
BedOc	beds occupied
BedsHerts	The Bedfordshire and Hertfordsshire Regiment
BE&E	basic electricity and electronics (course)
BEEF	business and engineering enriched FORTRAN (computer)

Beemoth   HDH-11, chemical spraying RPV by
          HDH
Beeswing   Infantry Swingfire anti-tank
           missile
BEF   British Expeditionary Forces; band
          elimination filter; blunt end for-
          ward
Begbie lamp   signal flash lamp (UK)
BEGR   bore erasion gauge reading
BeGr   Beton-Granate concrete-piercing
          grenade
BEL   bureau equipment list
BelAir   Belgian Air Staff
BelAirbus   Belgian Airbus Industry (SABCA +
            SOCATA)
Belfast   transport aircraft (UK)
Belknap   class, guided missile cruisers (CG-
          USN)
Bell-204   universal helicopter by Bell
Bell-205   transport helicopter by Bell
Bell-206   Jetranger, light helicopter by Bell
Bell-209   SeaCobra, AH-1 attack helicopter by
           Bell
Bell-214   BigLifter, SAR helicopter by Bell
BelNav   Belgian Naval Staff
Belouga   keel sonar 48 hydrophones by
          Thomson-CSF
BelTer   Belgian Army Staff
Beluga   scatter bomb by Matra
Beluga-Dispenser   parachute retarded dispen-
                   ser for 151 Belugas
Belvedere   naval patrol helicopter, tandem
            rotors by Westland
BEM   British Empire Medal
BEMA   Business Equipment Manufacturers'
          Association
BEMAR   backlog of essential maintenance and
          repair
BEME   Brigade Electrical and Mechanical
          Engineer
BEMO   bare equipment mechanization officers
BeNeChan   Benelux Channel Subarea (Nato)
BeNeLux   Belgium-Netherlands-Luxembourg
BEng   basic engineering
BenGurion   tank 50 tons (Israel)
BennySuggs   beneficial suggestions (pro-
             gramme)
BenSug   beneficial suggestions (programme)
BENT   beginning evening nautical twilight
Beob   Beobachtung (surveillance)
BeobPzArt   Beobachtungspanzer der Artillerie
            by Thyssen (artillery surveil-
            lance tank)
BEP   budget evaluation plan
BEPN   Betriebs- und Erhaltungs-Perioden
          Norm (operation and maintenance
          cycle standard)
BEQ   bachelor enlisted quarters
BER   British experimental rocket; beyond
          economic repair; budget execution
          review

BerCon   Berlin Contingency (Nato)
BERH   Board of Engineers for Rivers and
          Harbours
Berka   Berlin-Karlsruher Industriewerke
          GmbH (IWKA subsidiary)
Berka-Weste   bullet-proof jacket by Berka
BerSeaPat   Bering Sea Patrol
BERt   bit error rate
BESA   British Engineering Standards
          Association, --BSI
Besa   machine gun 7.92mm (Czech)
BesAnVH   Besondere Anweisung für die Ver-
          sorgung des Heeres (special Army
          procurement directive)
BESD   basic enlisted service date
BESI   bus electronic scanning indicator
BESL   British Empire Service League
BESO   British Executive Service Overseas
BESRL   Behaviour and Systems Research
          Laboratory
BEST   basic electronics training (pro-
          gramme); ballastable earth-moving
          sectionized tractor
Bestmann   Bü-181   training aircraft by
           Bücker
BETA   battlefield exploitation and target
          acquisition (programme) (US)
          (SOTAS, Quick Look, ELS, REMBASS);
          Business Equipment Trade Associa-
          tion
Betalight   phosphorescent tritium light by
            SRDL
BETRO   British Export Trade Research Organ-
          ization
BEU   basic encoding unit
BEV   billion electron volts
Beverley   bomber by Blackburn
BEW   Board of Economic Warfare
BEx   broadband exchange
BExec   budget execution
BEZU   optical fire control system for
          missiles
BF   battle fleet; battery fire; bayonet
          fighting; brought forward; blue
          flag; blue force; beat frequency;
          base frequency; basse fréquence;
          audio frequency
Bf-...   see Me-... Bayerische Flugzeugwerke
          later: Messerschmitt AG design,
          Me-...
BFA   Ballonfabrik Augsburg (Postfach 280,
          D-8900 Augsburg 31)
BF-ABS   howitzer 155mm (FR)
BFAP   British Forces Arabian Peninsular
BFBS   British Forces Broadcasting Service
BFD   blind fire director; budget formula-
          tion directive
BFDC   battalion fire distribution centre
bf dk   before dark
BFE   battle field estimate

BFES	British Forces Education Service
BFF	Berlin Field Force
BFG	British Forces in Germany
bfg	briefing
BFK	Borfaserkunststoff (boron fibre reinforced plastic)
BFM	basic fighter manoeuvres (USAF); basic field manual (US Army)
BFMA	British Force Maintenance Area
BFMB	British Field Message Book
BFN	British Forces Network
BFNE	British Forces Near East
BFO	beat frequency oscillator
BFP	British Forces Programme
BFPO	British Forces Post Office
bfr	before; briefer
BFS	British Frontier Service (in Germany); Base Facilities for SACLANT; Bundesanstalt für Flugsicherung (Federal Authority for Air Safety) (GE)
BFT	basic fitness test
BFWTT	boilerwater/feedwater test and treatment
BFYSG	British Forces Youth Service, Germany
BG	Brigadier General; beach group; broad gauge; Bloc de Guidage (guidance unit)
bg	bearing
Bgbv-82	recovery tank by Hägglund & Söner
BGDA	Blue Grass Depot Activity (US)
BGE	Bloc de Guidage d'Engine (missile guidance unit)
BGEA	Bloc de Guidage d'Engine type A
BGen	Brigadier General
BGGS	Brigadier General General Staff
BGL	below ground level
bglr	bugler
bgm	buglemaster
BGM-34A	RPV HOBOS-carrier by Teldyne-Ryan
BGM-34B	RPV strike support system (Pathfinder + LLLTV) by Teldyne-Ryan
BGM-34C	advanced RPV carrying TV + terminally guided missile by Northrop
BGM-71	TOW, tube-launched optically-tracked wire-guided anti-tank missile by Hughes
BGM-109	Tomahawk, cruise missile by GD
BGOH	Bureau de Gestion OTAN Hawk (Nato Hawk Management Office)
BGPP	beneficiary government production programme
BGRV	boost-glide re-entry vehicle
BGS	Brigadier, General Staff; Bombing and Gunnery School
BGSS	battalion ground surveillance section
BGT	Bodenseewerk Gerätetechnik (Postfach 1120 D-7770 Uberlingen)
BGWS	Brigade of Grukhas Welfare Scheme
BH	Base hospital; Brinell hardness; British Hovercraft (Corporation)
B/H	bill of health
bh	barrels per hour
BH-7	combat hovercraft (Iran) by BHC
BH-gun	naval gun 40mm by RR
Bhaskara	earth surveillance satellite 1979 (India)
BHC	Battle Honours Committee; British High Commissioner; British Hovercraft Corporation; ballistic height correction; benzene-hexachloride (insecticide)
bhd	beachhead; bulkhead
BHDM	British Home Defence Measures
BHN	Brinell hardness number
bhnd	behind
BHO	Branch Hydrographic Office; black hole ocarina (helicopter-borne IR radiation suppressor)
BHP	brake horse power
BHQ	brigade/battalion headquarters
BHRA	British Hydromechanics Research Association
BHS	Bayerische Berg-, Hütten- & Salzwerke (München, D-8972 Sonthofen); Bordhubschrauber (naval helicopter)
BHT	blow-down heat transfer
BHVG	British Honduras Volunteer Guard
BI	background investigation; branch immaterial; Bermuda Islands; Biological Inventory; battlefield interdiction; battlefield illumination; base ignition; block-in; black iron
BIA	barrack inventory accounter; Bureau des Informations Aeronautiques (Aeronautics Information Bureau)
BIAC	Business and Industry Advisory Committee (Nato)
BIB	British Intelligence Bureau; baby incendiary bomb
Biber	midget submarine WW2; armoured vehicle launched bridge by MaK
BIC	battlefield information centre; battery interconnection cables
BICC	battlefield information control centre
Bickford	safety fuse (US)
BICT	Bundesinstitut für Chemisch-Technische Untersuchung Federal (GE) (Chemical and Technical Tests Institute)
BID	British Intelligence Department
BIDS	battlefield information distribution system (US Army) JTIDS
BIEE	British Institute of Electrical Engineers

BIET   British Institute of Engineering
          Technology
BIF   British Invasion Forces
BIFF   battlefield IFF system
Big Ben FV-11400, 6x4 truck by Thornycroft
Big Bird military recce satellite by Lock-
          heed
Big Lifter Bell-214, helicopter by Bell
Big Willie Mother, first British tank WW1
BII   basic issue items
BIIL   basic issue items list
bil   billet
BILI   basic issue list items
BIM   blade inspection method; basic indus-
          trial materials (programme); BETA
          interface module (battlefield
          exploitation and target acquisi-
          tion)
BIMRAB Bureau (of Naval Weapons) Industry
          Material Reliability Advisory
          Board
Binary gas two component nerve gas
BinOvc breaks in overcast
BInSum brief intelligence Summary
BIO   Brigade/Branch Intelligence Officer
BIOc   British Indian Ocean (Territories)
biol   biological
BiolDef biological defence
BiolOps biological operations
BiolRept biological report
BiolRsch biological research
BiolWpn biological weapons
BiolWpnSys biological weapon systems
BioPack biological pack(s)
BIOS   British Intelligence Objectives Sub-
          committee
BIOS   biological investigation of space
          satellite (NASA)
BIOT   British Indian Ocean Territories
BIP   binary image processor, bomb impact
          plot
BIPOLT bulk inland POL transport (Nato)
Bird   class, fishery protection vessels
          (RN)
BirdCAP rescue combat air patrol
Bird Dog L-19, forward air controller air-
          craft by Cessna
BIRDIE battery integration and radar display
          equipment
BIRO   Base Industrial Relations Office(r)
BIS   British Intelligence Service; British
          Information Service; Board of
          Investigation and Survey; business
          information systems; battlefield
          identification system
BiscLant Bay of Biscay Atlantic Subarea
Bishop self-propelled gun (UK)
BISS   battlefield identification system
          study; base installation security
          system by ComDev

BJT   built-in test (equipment)
bit   binary digit
BITE   built-in test equipment
bit/s   bits per second
Bittern helmet night vision goggles by
          Pilkington
biv   bivouac
BiV   Bildverstärkung, (image intensifica-
          tion)
BiV-TV-Kamera Bildverstärkung (low light-
          level TV camera)
BIW   battle injury or wound
Bizerte class, guided missile patrol boats
          by SFCN
BJCEB   British Joint Communications Elec-
          tronics Board
BJCO   British Joint Communications Office
BJSM   British Joint Services Mission
          WASHDC Washington DC
BJU   beach jumper unit
bk   blinker
BK   Bordkanone,(airborne/vehicular gun)
BK-1H   Blendkörper, Hand (hand grenade,
          smoke)
BK-117 utility helicopter by Bölkow/
          Kawasaki
bkdg   background
bkry   bakery
BKPA   British Kidney Patients Association
BKS   bruchsichers Kraftstoffsystem (leak-
          proof petrol system)
bks   barracks
bkt   blinker tube
BL   British Legion, -- RBL; bomb line;
          breech loader; bomb load; basic
          load; base line; breaking load;
          building line
B/L   bill of lading
bl   bale, barrel
Bl   blinde Munition (inert ammunition)
BL-755 scatter bomb 273 kgs, 147 bomblets
          (UK)
BLA   British Liberation Army, --BAOR
BLAC   British Light Aviation Centre
Blackbird SR-71, special strategic recce
          aircraft by Lockheed
Black Courtain Super Mirage jet interceptor/
          fighter (Israel)
Blacker Bombard anti-tank weapon, spigot
          principle WW2 Home Guard
Black Fly maritime surveillance RPV by
          Fairchild
Black Hawk S-67, UH-60 attack helicopter by
          Sikorsky
Black Hole IR emission suppressor for heli-
          copters by Hughes
Black-Hot IR viewing system by Marconi
Black Knight HH-53, SAR helicopter by
          Sikorsky
Black Knights RHA free-fall team

Black Prince   Infantry tank (UK)
Black Swan   class, escort ships WW2 (RN)
Black Widow   P-61, B-15, night fighter/
          bomber WW2 by Northrop
BLading   bill of lading
BLATS   built-up low-cost advanced titanium
          structure by Rockwell
BLB   Boothby, Lovelace & Bulbulian (nasal
          oxygen mask)
BLC   Bengal Light Cavalry; boundary layer
          control (flap blowing); breech-
          loader carriage; battery level
          computer TACFIRE by Norden
BLD   Bande Laterale Double (double side
          band)
bld   building
bldg   building
BldgFor   building foreman
Blenheim   twin-engined medium bomber by
          Bristol
BlERt   block error rate
BLESMA   British Limbless Ex-servicemen's
          Association
BLEU   Belgian-Luxembourg Economic Union;
          blind landing experimental unit
BLF   band limiting filter
B-L-FK   Blowpipe, portable anti-aircraft
          missile by Short
BLG   breech loading gun
BLG-60   Brückenlegegerät (EG) AVLB
bl gef   blind gefüllt (inert charge)
BLH   British Legion Headquarters
Blimp   non-rigid airship
Blindfire   DN-181, tracking radar by Marconi
Blindicide   shoulder-fired anti-tank rocket
          by Mecar
Blitz   Ar-234, jet bomber WW2 by Arado
blk   blank, block, bulk, black
blkd   blocked
BLM   Bureau of Land Management (NASA);
          blind landing machine; basic lang-
          uage machine
BLMC   British Leyland Motor Corporation
bln   baloon
blo   below (US)
BLO   British Liaison Officer; Bombardment
          Liaison Officer
bloc   blockade
Bloodhound   ground-to-air missile by BAC
Blowpipe   B-L-FK, portable anti-aircraft
          missile by Short
BLP   back loading point; bomber, land
          plane
BL&P   blind loaded and plugged (projectile)
BLR   beyond local repair; breech-loading
          rifled (mortar)
BLS   Bureau of Labor Statistics
BLSJICP   beam lead sealed junction integrated
          circuit package
BLSS   base level self sufficiency spares

BLT   battalion landing team
BL&T   blind-loaded and traced (projectile)
BLTC   bottom loading transfer cast
BLU   bomb, light universal; Bande
          Laterale Unique (single side band)
BLU-3   bomb load, universal
BLU-27   880 lbs bomb napalm
BLU-63   bomblet, cluster bomb
BLU-81   Grasshopper, air-launched land mines
BLU-82   Daisy Cutter, 7.5 tons fire bomb
BLU-86   bomblets
BLU-91   Gator air-dropped mine system, anti-
          tank
BLU-92   Gator, air-dropped mine system,
          anti-personnel
BLU-181   Grasshopper, air-dropped multi-
          sensor land mines, runway bomb
Blue Baron   airborne IR recce pod by FFV
Blue Box   flight trainer by Link
Blue Crew   nuclear-powered submarine
Blue Eagles   helicopter display team (AAC)
Blue Fox   air-to-air/air-to-ground radar
          by Ferranti
Blue Kestrel   helicopter-borne ASW search
          radar by Ferranti
Blue Ridge   class, command ships (CC-USN)
Blue Steel   airborne stand-off missile (UK)
Blue Streak   ballistic missile (UK)
Blue Water   tactical missile (UK)
BLV   British Legion Village
BM   Boatswain's Mate; Beachmaster;
          Brigade Major; Bronze Medal;
          branch material; ballistic
          missile; breech mechanism; bench
          mark; back marker; boundary
          marker; bending moment; bending
          margin; Monitor (USN); pistol
          0.45 in. by Hispano
B/M   bill of material
BM-Boot   Binnen-Minensuchboot (inshore river
          mine-sweeper)
BM-13   rocket launcher 132mm 16 tubes (SU)
BM-14   rocket launcher 140mm 17 tubes (SU)
BM-21   rocket launcher 122mm 40 tubes (SU)
BM-24   rocket launcher 240mm 12 tubes (SU)
BM-59   FAL, self-loading rifle 7.62mm by
          Beretta
BM-8005   driver's viewer, light intensifying
          by Eltro
BM-8021   helicopter night landing system by
          Elektro Spezial
BM-8025   night aiming equipment for ICV
          Marder by Elektro Spezial
BM-8028   night vision goggles by Elektro
          Spezial
BMA   British Military Attache; beach
          maintenance area; basic mainten-
          ance allowance (clothing)
BMAA   barracks master-at-arms
BMAC   Boeing Military Aircraft Company;

computerized automatic maintenance and test bench for anti-
aircraft missiles

BMARCo   British Manufacture & Research Com-
         pany (Oerlikon subsidiary)
BMASR   Bureau of Military Application of
         Scientific Research (Nato)
BMAT   British Military Advisory Team
BMat   bill of material
BMATB   British Military Advisory Team,
         Bangla-Desh
BMatKatZ Bundes-Material-Katalogisierungs-
         Zentrale (Federal (German)
         Material Cataloguing Centre)
BMB   Breda Meccanica Brescna (IT)
BMC   basic missile checker; British Motor
         Corporation
BMCS   Bureau of Motor Carrier Safety
BMCT   beginning morning civil twilight
BMD   base maintenance division; ballistic
         missile defence; ballistic missile
         division EDP; light air-transport-
         able tank (SU)
BMD-20   rocket launcher 200mm 4 tubes (SU)
BMD-25   rocket launcher 250mm (SU)
BMD-34   mine detector by BETA
BMDAT   ballistic missile defence advanced
         technology (US programme)
BMDATC   Ballistic Missile Defence Advanced
         Technology Center
BMDC   ballistic missile defence centre
BMDCP   ballistic missile defence command
         post; battalion mortar and Davy
         Crocket platoon
BMDEAR   ballistic missile defence emergency
         action report
BMDITP   ballistic missile defence integrated
         training plan
BMDMB   ballistic missile defence missile
         battalion
BMDMP   ballistic missile defence master
         plan
BMD-NEAT ballistic missile defence nuclear
         effects and threat committee
BMDO   ballistic missile defence operations
BMDOA   ballistic missile defence operations
         activity
BMDPM   ballistic missile defence programme
         manager
BMDPO   ballistic missile defence programme
         office
bmdr   bombardier
BMDS   ballistic missile defence system
BMDSB   ballistic missile defence surveil-
         lance battalion
BMDSCom ballistic missile defence systems
         command
BME   ballistic measurement equipment by
         AVL; bulk memory element (airborne
         tape recorder for ALCM)

BMEC   British Marine Equipment Council
BMEP   brake mean effective pressure
BMEWS   ballistic missile early warning
         system
BMF   basic main force; Belgian Mechanical
         Fabrication (ASCO+Cockerill+
         Lambert) (Brussels)
BMFBuT   Bundesministerium für Bauten und
         Technik, Federal (Austrian) (Minis-
         try for Civil Engineering and
         Technology)
BMfLV   Bundesministerium für Landesvertei-
         digung Federal, (Austrian) (Ministry
         for Defence
BMFT   Bundesministerium für Forschung und
         Technologie, Federal (German)
         (Ministry for Research and Tech-
         nology)
BMG   budget and manpower guidance;
         Browning machine gun
BMH   British Military Hospital
BMI   British Military Intelligence;
         ballistic missile intercept(or)
BMJ   basic military journalist (course)
BMK-20   Bordmaschinenkanone 20mm (tank-borne
         machine cannon 20mm)
BML   ballistic missile launcher
BMM   British Military Mission
BMNT   beginning morning nautical twilight
BMO   business machines operator;
         Ballistic Missile Office (Nato)
BMOW   boatswain's mate of the watch
BMP   brake mean power
BMP-1   tracked armoured personnel carrier
         (SU)
BMP-73   tracked armoured personnel carrier
         amphibious (SU)
Bmr   beachmaster
BMR   basic military requirements;
         amphibious wheeled infantry
         combat vehicle by British
         Alcan
bmr   bomber
BMR-600 6x6 armoured personnel carrier by
         ENASA
         PP   Portapersonal
         PM   Portamortero
         VEC Vehiculo de Exploration de
              Caballeria
BMRA   Brigade Major, Royal Artillery
BMRB   British Market Research Bureau
BMRSyst ballistic missile re-entry system
BMS   Bureau Militaire de Standardisation
         (Military Agency for Standardiza-
         tion) (Nato)
BMSM   British Merchant Ship Mission
Bmstr   bandmaster
BMT   British Mean Time; Basic Motion Time
         (study); Bureau Mouvements et
         Transport (Movement and Transport
         Office) Nato)

BMTD	base medical transport depot
BMTT	buffered magnetic tape transport
BMU	beachmaster unit
BMV	Bundesministerium für Verkehr Federal (German) (Ministry for Transport)
BMVg	Bundesministerium für Verteidigung Federal (German) (Ministry for Defence)
BMWS	ballistic missile weapon system
BMY	base marshalling yard; Bowen McLaughlin (York US)
BN	bottle necked (cartridge); Brazilian Navy; Constructions Ferroviaires et Metalliques Brugeoise-Nivelles (Belgium)
B/N	bombardier/navigator
bn	battalion, beacon
Bn	Baron
BN-2	Islander, light aircraft by Britten-Norman
BN-21	light-intensifying binocular by AEG
BNA	British Naval Attache
BNAF	British North African Force
BNAO	basic naval aviation officers' (school)
BNAS	British Naval Air Service
BNCSR	British National Committee on Space Research
BnCTn	battalion combat train
BndrSL	Bandmaster Sub-lieutenant
bndry	boundary
bndy	boundary
BNEA	British Naval Equipment Association (BMEC daughter)
BNEC	British Nuclear Energy Conference
BNEP	basic naval establishment plan
BNES	British Nuclear Energy Society
BNFL	British Nuclear Fuels Ltd (Sellafield)
BNFMRA	British Non-ferrous Metals Research Association
BNGM	British Naval Gunnery Mission
BNHQ	battalion headquarters
BNI	Bengal Native Infantry
BNLO	British Naval Liaison Officer
BNS	British Naval Staff; British Naval Security; Bangla-Desh Naval Ship
BNP	Bureau of Naval Personnel, Bureau of Naval Publications
BNPCL	Bureau of Naval Personnel Circular Letters
BNRL	British Nuclear Reactor Ltd
BNS	bathymetric navigation system
BnSFCP	battalion shore fire control party
BNX	British Nuclear Export Executive
BO	bombing officer; black out; block out; base order; brigade ordnance
bo	bomber

Bo-105	light utility helicopter by MBB
Bo-105C	PAH-1, anti-tank helicopter by MBB
Bo-107	BK-117, 6-12 seat utility helicopter by MBB
Bo-125	medium transport helicopter by MBB
Bo-810	Cobra-2000, anti-tank guided weapon by MBB
BOA	break-off altitude
BOADICEA	British Overseas Airways Digital Information Computer for Electronic Automation
BOA-MILS	broad ocean area missile impact location system
BoatSuppU	boat support unit
BOB	beginning of business; Branch Office Boston ONR; Bureau of the Budget
Bobbin	carpet-like instant road built by AVRE
BOBC	British Outward Bound Centre (Kristiansand Norway)
BOC	battalion orderly corporal; battalion operations centre; Branch Office Chicago ONR; British Oxygen Company
BOCCA	Board for Coordination of Civil Aviation
BOD	base ordnance depot; beneficial occupation date NADGE; basic occupational date; bureau of ordnance design; biochemical oxygen demand
BoD	bottom of duct; board of directors
Bodan	type, river ferries (GE)
BODU	Bureau of Ordnance Design Unit
BOF	basic oxygen furnace
Bofi	anti-aircraft system by Bofors gun+radar+proximity fuse
Bofors	-40/70 anti-aircraft gun 40mm by Bofors
Bofors-77	gun 155mm by Bofors
Bofors-4140	gun 105mm by Bofors
BofR	board of review
BOH	break-off height
BOI	basis of issue; Bulletins of Ordnance Information NOB NWB
BOIMARS	basis of issue monitoring and recording system
BOIP	basis of issue plan
BOL	Branch Office London ONR; bearing-only launch
BoM	bills of materials
bom	bomb(ing)
bomb	bombardment
Bomarc	strategic intercept missile by Boeing
Bomb	bombardier, Bombay
BombCS	Bombay Civil Service
BombSC	Bombay Staff Corps
Bombay	transport aircraft WW2 (UK)
BombRep	bomb report (hostile)
BomCom	bombing command (US Army)
BOMEX	Barbados Oceanographic and Meteorological Experiment

BOMID	Branch Office Military Intelligence Division
BomRept	bombing report (by aircraft) (Nato)
BomRon	bombing squadron
bomst	bombsight
bon	battalion
BOO	brigade ordnance officer
Boomerang	fighter aircraft by Commonwealth AF
Boozer	listening device into German frequencies (RAF) WW2
BOP	Branch Office Pasadena ONR; basic operation plan; balance of payments
BOPA	balance of payments act
BOPP	balance of payments programme
BOQ	bachelor officers' quarters; base officers' quarters
BoR	board of review
Bora	artillery rocket 198mm by SAI
BORAD	British Oxygen Research and Development Organization
BORAM	block-oriented random access memory
BORU	boat operating and repair unit
BOS	battalion orderly sergeant
BoS	bombing section
BOS	basic operating system; basic oxygen steel(making)
BOSEY	Board of Supply Executive Yuan
BosGrp	Boston Group
Bos'n	boatswain
BoSS	Bureau of State Security (RSA)
BOSS	Bio-astronautic Orbiting Space Station
Boston	DB-7, twin-engined attack bomber by Douglas
BoT	Board of Trade; beginning of tape
BoT-unit	Board of Trade unit (electricity)
BOU	boat operating unit
Boughton	RB-44, 4x4 cross-country vehicle (UK)
Bouncing Bomb	dam busting spinning bomb WW2 (RAF)
BOV	brown oil of vitriol (sulphuric acid 75 per cent)
BOW	base ordnance workshop; Bureau of (Naval) Weapons
BOWACA	Bureau of (Naval) Weapons Advisory Committee on Aeroballistics
BoWag	Bombenwagen (bomb transport vehicle)
BOWO	Brigade Ordnance Warrant Officer
Boxcar	C-119, cargo aircraft by Fairchild
boxtrol	fuel (methanol+acetone)
BP	basic pay; beach party; beginning period; Budget Programme; back projection; band pass; base point; boiling point; bronze point; black powder; between perpendiculars
B/P	bills payable

b/p	blue print
BPA	budget programme account; British Parachute Association; basic pressure altitude
BPAM	basic proportional access method
BPB	Base Planning Board
BPCD	barrels per calendar day
BPCO	British Passport Control Office
BPD	basic planning document; barrels per day
BPDMS	basic point defence missile system Sparrow
BPDRC	multiple rocket launcher (IT)
BPDSMS	basic point defence surface missile system
BPE	Board of professional engineers
BPED	base pay entry date
BPF	British Pacific Fleet; band pass filter
BPFA	Bureau des Programmes Franco-Allemand (Paris) (Franco-German Projects Agency)
BPFILO	British Pacific Fleet Intelligence Liaison Officer
BPFLO	British Pacific Fleet Liaison Officer
BPG	Bordprüfgerät (built-in test equipment)
BPhI	boost phase intercept
BPI	binary bits per inch
BPM	barrels per minute
BPMS	blood pressure measuring system
BPN	bureau project number
BPO	British Post Office; base post office
BPOS	basic psychological operations study
BPPG	bureau planned procurement guide
BPR	Bureau of Public Records; bridge plotting room
BPrf	bullet-proof
BPRO	blind persons resettlement officer
BPS	border patrol sector; border patrol station; basic programming system; basic programming support; batch processing system
BPS-15	submarine navigation radar
BPSD	barrels per steam day
BPSP	bi-polar signal processing
BPT	battle practice target; blade passing tone (noise)
BPt	boiling point
BPU	base production unit
B&Q	barracks and quarters
BQL	basic query language
BQH-4	passive sonar, for submarines
BQM	base quartermaster
BQM-34	Firebee RPV launching Maverick, HOBOS or Shrike by Teledyne-Ryan
BQM-74	ALAT, air-launched aerial target by Northrop

BQMS   battery quartermaster sergeant
BQQ-2   sonar system for submarines
BQQ-5   active/passive multi-beam hull-
          mounted ASW sonar+towed array by
          Hughes
BQR-15 towed sonar for submarines
BQR-20 sonar for attack submarines
BQS-13 Active/passive sonar for submarines
BQS-15 short-range sonar for submarines
br   bugler; bridge; bridging; bombar-
          dier; brevet; branch; bomber
BR   barrage rocket; barrack regulations;
          Board of Review; book for refer-
          ence; bomber reconnaissance; block
          release; breeder reactor; box
          respirator
Br   Brandgeschoss (incendiary projectile)
BR-Gerät Bord-Raketen-Gerät (air-to-ground
          rocket launcher)
BR-51   multi-rocket launcher 158mm by Breda
BR-250 bomb, general purpose 250 kgs
BR-500 Mk-83, bomb, general purpose, 500 kgs
Br-1150 Atlantic, maritime patrol aircraft
          by Breguet
BRA   Brigadier, Royal Artillery
BRAMIS base resource airfield management
          information system
BranchHydro Branch Hydrographic Office
BraNik Brazilian Navy Ikara air-to-sea
          missile
BRAS   ballistic rocket air suppression
Bras   class, fast patrol boats for Nigeria
          by Lürssen
BRASCO Brigade Royal Army Service Corps
          Officer
Brasilia EMB-120, turboprop transport air-
          craft by EMB
Brasilsat regional communications satellite
          (Brazil)
BrASO   Branch Aviation Supply Office
Brassboard air-defence giant display panel
          (US)
Bravo   AS-202, trainer aircraft by FFA
Brayton-telescope distance measuring tele-
          scope
Brazo   radar homing anti-aircraft missile
          by Hughes
BRC   Budget Review Committee; base resi-
          dence course; British Research
          Council
BRCA   British Red Cross Association
Br&Cl   branch and class
BRcn   battle reconnaissance
BRCS   British Red Cross Society
brcst   broadcast
BRD   base remount depot; binary rate
          divider; bomb release distance;
          Bundesrepublik Deutschland
          (abbreviated only in East German
          usage) (Federal Republic of Ger-
          many) FRG better: GER or D

BRDC   British Research and Development
          Corporation
BRDM-1 reconnaissance vehicle 5.6 tons (SU)
BRDM-2 BTR-40, reconnaissance vehicle
          7 tons 4x4 (SU)
BRDMA   wheeled tank destroyer, 3 missiles
          (SU)
BRE   Building Research Establishment
Brecon class, minesweepers FRP (RN)
Breguet-1150 Atlantic, maritime patrol air-
          craft by Breguet
BREL   Boeing Radiation Effect Laboratory
BREMA   British Radio Equipment Manufactu-
          rers Association
Bren   Brno-Enfield machine gun (UK)
Bren-carrier Brno-Enfield machine gun
          tracked carrier vehicle
BrestChan Brest Channel Subarea (Nato)
brev   brevet(ted)
brf   brief(ing)
BRFA   runway demolition bomb (parachute+
          rocket) (Spain)
BRG   beacon reply group
brg   bearing; bridge; barrage
BrgBln barrage balloon
BRGW   brake release gross weight
brh   bridgehead
BrHon   British Honduras
BrI   British India; British Isles
BRI   bearing range indicator
BridgeCo bridge company (USMC)
Brig   brigade, Brigadier
BrigGen Brigadier General
BrInsMat Branch Officer, Inspector of Naval
          Material
Bristol-171 Sycamore, helicopter by Bristol
Brit   Britain, British
Britannia transport aircraft by Bristol
BritCon British Contingent (UN)
brkwtr breakwater
BRL   battalion reserve line; bomb release
          line; breech-loader; Ballistics
          Research Laboratory (Aberdeen
          Proving Ground)
brl   barrel
br-l   breech-loader
brm   barometer
BRMC   Band of the Royal Military College
BrN   broadcast net(work)
BRNC   British Royal Naval College (Dart-
          mouth)
brng   bearing
BRO   brigade routine order
Broadsword class, patrol vessels (RN)
Brobv-941 Brobandvagn (armoured vehicle
          launched bridge) by Hägglund &
          Söner
BROILER Biopedagogical Research Organiza-
          tion on Intensive Learning
          Environment Reactions

Bromide airborne ECM equipment WW2 (RAF)
Bronco OV-10, LARA/COIN, twin turboprop
      light armed recce/counter-insur-
      gency aircraft by North American
Brooklyn class, cruisers WW2 (USN)
Brown Bess musket 1770 (UK)
Browning machine gun 12.7mm (US)
BRP   bomb release point
BRP-250 bomb, retarded, parachute 250 kgs
BRP-500 bomb, retarded, parachute 500 kgs
BRQM   Brigade Quartermaster (USMC)
BRR   Batelle Research Reactor; brigade
      receiving room
BR/RL   bomb rack/rocket launcher
BRS   British receiving station
BrSprGr BrandSprenggranate, high-explosive
      incendiary grenade
BrT   British Time
BRTF   battery repair and test facility
BrTn   bridge train (US) (vehicles)
BRU   boat repair unit; bomb rack unit;
      British recovery unit
BrÜbsM-80 Brücken und Übersetzmittel der
      80er Jahre (bridging and river-
      crossing equipment of the 1980s)
Bruin   tactical trunk communications system
      (UK)
Bruin-MIS tactical trunk mobile informations
      system (UK)
Brummbär SP assault gun 150mm WW2
Bruno   railway cannon 280mm WW2
BruPz-68 Brückenpanzer (armoured vehicle)
      launched bridge by Arsenal Thun
      SW
BrUSA   British-US-agreement
BRUTE   British Universal Trolley Equipment
BRW   British relay wireless
Brybo-harness assault abseil harness (UK)
BS   British Standard; bomb store; Burma
      Star; back space; battleship (RN);
      below specification; blowing sand
      (weather); broadcast station
B/S   balance sheet; bill of sale
bs   bags; bales
B&S   Brown & Sharpe (wire gauge)
BS-1015Y weather map teleprinter by Hell
BSA   Birmingham Small Arms Company Ltd;
      bi-metal steel aluminium;
      Basic Standardization Agreement;
      base sub-area;
      British South Africa;
      Boy Scouts of America
BSACM   British South African Campaign Medal
BSAM   basic sequential access method
BSAP   British South Africa Police
BSAS   British Special Air Service

BSB   British standard beam
BSC   Balkan Supply Centre; billet
      sequence code; broadcast
      specialist course DINFUS; British
      Safety Council; Bengal Staff
      Corps; British Supply Council;
      binary synchronous communication;
      British Steel Corporation
BSCA   Bureau of Security and Consular
      Affairs
BSCB   British Signal Communications Board
BSD   base supply depot; Biological Sci-
      ences Division ONR; Ballistics
      Systems Division; British Space
      Development; barrels per steam day
BSDL   Boresight datum line
BSE   base support equipment; regional
      communications satellite (Japan)
BSerBn base service battalion
BSF   blade slap factor; blade slip
      factor
BSFC   brake specific fuel consumption
BSG   British Standard Gauge
bsh   bushel
BSI   British Solomon Islands; British
      Standards Institution; battery
      status indicator
BSIB   Boy Scouts International Bureau
BSIP   British Solomon Islands Protec-
      torate
BSL   Boatswain Sub-lieutenant; British
      Service League
BSM   battery sergeant major; Bronze Star
      Medal
BsnADSect Boston Air Defense Sector
BSO   bomb store officer; bomb safety
      officer; base supply officer;
      battalion standing order;
      British Supply Office
BSOT   basic sonar operator trainer by
      Gould
BSP   Bering Sea Patrol; border security
      police; bi-polar signal proces-
      sing; British Standard Pipe
      (thread)
BSR   Bristol simplified re-heat
BSRA   British Ship Research Association
BSRC   British Science Research Council
BSS   British Standard Sizes; British
      Standard Specifications
BSSO   Bureau of Ships Shipping Order
B/St   bill of sight
BST   British Standard Time; British
      Summer Time (1 hr ahead of GMT)
BSTAS   battlefield surveillance and target
      acquisition system
bstr   booster

bstr rkt booster rocket
BSU   base service unit; boat support unit;
         blood supply unit
BSW   British Standard Whitworth (thread);
         barrels of salt water
BS&W   basic sediment and water
BSWB   Boy Scouts World Bureau
BSWE   British Scouts in Western Europe
BT   boat tail (projectile); bathy-
         thermograph; bomber/transport
         (aircraft); basic trainer (air-
         craft); tank (SU)
bt   baronet; boat; beat; brevet
BT-001   Tornado, British Trainer (aircraft)
         by BAC
BT-5   Yak-18 aircraft Chinese designation
BT-33   artillery fire control simulator by
         Saab
BT-39   anti-aircraft gunfire simulator by
         Saab
BTA   British Troops in Austria; best
         technical approach
BTAM   basic telecommunications access
         method
BTB   British Troops in Berlin; basic test
         battery; ballistic training bomb;
         bus tie breakers
BTC   buried trench concept missile -X;
         bola tipo culher (spoon-type
         bullet);
         Bahamas Telecommunications Corpora-
         tion
BTCA   basic tables of commissioning allow-
         ances
BTD   bomb testing device
BTDC   before top dead centre
BTDCPF   bathy-thermograph data collecting
         and processing facility
BTDPAF   bathy-thermograph data processing
         and analysis facility
BTE   British Troops in Europe; British
         Troops in Egypt; British Transport
         Executive; battery terminal equip-
         ment; built-in test equipment
BTF   barrels of total fuel; bomb tail fuse
BThU   British Thermal Unit
BTI   British Technical Index
BTL   Bell Telephone Laboratories
BTM   blast test missile; missile test
         bench; batch time-sharing monitor;
         bromo-trifluoro-methane (fire ex-
         tinguisher); tracked trench digger
         (SU)
btm   bottom
BTMF   block type manipulation facility
btn   between
BTO   branch transportation office(r);
         basic tactical organization;
         brigade transport officer; bombing
         through overcast

BTPC   Brussels Treaty Permanent Commission
BTR   -40 BRDM-2, 4x4 recce vehicle 7 tons
         (SU)
BTR-50   tracked amphibious armoured person-
         nel carrier (SU)
BTR-60   8x8 amphibious APC (SU)
BTR-152 wheeled APC (SU)
btry   battery
BTRE   British Telecommunications Research
         Establishment
BtryEx   Battery Executive (US) (gun position
         officer)
BTS   blood transfusion service
BTSS   basic time sharing system
btswn   boatswain
BTT   battle group tactical trainer
         (Bovington)
BTU   tank-mounted dozer blade (SU); base
         transfusion unit; British Thermal
         Unit; Board of Trade Unit (UK)
BtW   boat wave
BTX   benzene toluene xylene
bty   battery
BU   bread unit; base unit; bottom up
Bü-181   Bestmann, trainer aircraft by
         Bücker WW2
BuAer   Bureau of Aeronautics
BUAF   British United Air Ferries
Buccaneer transsonic fighter/bomber by
         Hawker-Siddeley; target air-
         craft by Flight Refuelling Ltd
Buckeye T-2, trainer aircraft by Rockwell
Buck Private XA-6, ultra-light helicopter
         by American Helicopters
BucLaSP buckling of laminated stiffened
         plates
BUCo   built-up control WW2 D-day prepara-
         tions
BuCon   Bureau of Construction
BuC&R   Bureau of Construction and Repair
BUCS   back-up control system (helicopters)
BudFin   Budget and Finance Division (Nato)
BUDWSR   Brown university display for working
         set references
Buddy Pack airborne stream-lined fuel tank
BUEC   back-up emergency communications
BuEng   Bureau of Engineering
BuDocks Bureau of Yards and Docks
BUFF   B-52, bomber, big ugly fat fellow
Buffalo F-2, naval fighter WW2 by Brewster;
         amphibious personnel carrier,
         LVT-family DHC-5; STOL transport
         aircraft by DHC
Büffel   armoured recovery vehicle by MaK
BUFORA   British Unidentified Flying Objects
         Research Association
BUGS   Brown university graphic system
BUIC   back-up interceptor control (air
         defence radar --SAGE)
Bulldog AGM-83, air-to-ground missile by

Maxson, M-41, light tank by Walker; trainer aircraft by Scottish Aviation, Gatling gun 1877

Bullfinch   light aircraft by Scottish Aviation

BullJAG   Bulletin of the Judge Advocate of the US Army

Bullpup   AGM-12, air-to-ground missile; EM-1, EM-2, assault rifle by RSAF

Bullshorn Plough   mine-clearing equipment tank-mounted (UK) WW2

BUM   back-up mode

BuLoGa   business logistics game

BuMed   Bureau of Medicine and Surgery

BuM&S   Bureau of Medicine and Surgery

BUMS   Befehls- und Meldesystem (U-Bootführung) (submarine command and reporting system) (FGN)

BuNa   butadiene+natrium (artificial rubber)

BuNav   Bureau of Navigation

BuNo   Bureau of Shipping Number (identification)

BuOrd   Bureau of (Naval) Ordnance

BuPers   Bureau of (Naval) Personnel

BuPubAff Bureau of Public Affairs

BUPS   beacon, ultra-portable, S-band

Bur   Burma; Bureau

BÜR   Boden Überwachungs Radar (ground surveillance radar) by SEL

Burney-gear   minesweeping equipment (RN) (--Paravane)

Burney-gun   recoilless gun (UK)

Burney-Paravane   explosive minesweeping equipment (RN); explosive ASW equipment (RN)

BuSandA   Bureau of Supplies and Accounts

BUSCI   British-US convoy instructions WW2

BuShips   Bureau of Ships

BuShipsMgtOWesPac   Bureau of Ships Management Office Western Pacific

Bushmaster   specification, automatic gun for Infantry support (US), 25mm GLAAD, gun low-level anti-air defense (US)

Bushmaster   powered single-axle trailer for Land Rover by Scottorn (UK)

BUSRA   British-US routing agreement

BUSRAT   battle unit short-range anti-tank weapon system

Bussard   A-32, transport aircraft WW2 by Fw; terminally guided cannon-launched shell by Martin/BGT/AEG/Diehl

BUT   basic unit training; broadband unbalanced transformer

BUTEC   British Underwater Test and Evaluation Centre

Butt   class, Klasse-520, landing ships universal FGN

BUV   back-scatter ultra-violet

BUWC   basic underseas weapon circuit

BuWeps   Bureau of (Naval) Weapons.

FltReadRep   Bureau of (Naval) Weapons Fleet Readiness Representative

Rep   Bureau of (Naval) Weapons Representative

SuppRepNATraCom Bureau of (Naval) Weapons Support Representative Naval Air Training Command

ResRep   Bureau of (Naval) Weapons Resident Representative

TechLO   Bureau of (Naval) Weapons Technical Liaison Officer

Buzz-bomb   V-1, flying bomb WW2 (GE)

BV   bureau voucher; Blohm & Voss (POB 100720 D-2000 Hamburg)

bv   balanced voltage

BV-076   Bauvorschrift für Schiffe der Bundesmarine (construction directives for ships of the FGN)

BV-137   dive-bomber by BV WW2

BV-138   long-range recce aircraft by BV

BV-139   float-plane by BV

BV-140   long-range recce aircraft by BV

BV-141   short-range recce aircraft by BV

BV-222   long-range recce aircraft by BV

BV-238   transport aircraft by BV

BV-246   Radieschen, anti-radiation missile WW2 by BV

BV-202   Bandvagn (articulated tracked transport vehicle) by Bolinder-Munktell

BV-206   Bandvagn (articulated tracked transport vehicle) by Hägglund & Söner

BVC   ballistic velocity computer

BVE   binocular visual efficiency

BVG   Belize Volunteer Guard

BV-P-170 Blohm & Voss Projekt 170 high-speed bomber WW2

BV-P-203 Blohm & Voss Projekt 203 jet fighter aircraft

BV-P-213 Blohm & Voss Projekt 213 jet miniature interceptor

BV-P-215 Blohm & Voss Projekt 215 jet night interceptor

BVR   beyond visual range (missile)

bvt   brevetted

BW   The Black Watch; biological warfare; bacteriological warfare; band width; body weight; below water

B&W   bread and water, black and white

BWA   British West Africa, backward wave amplifier

BWAR   budget workload analysis report

BWB   Bundesamt für Wehrtechnik und Beschaffung Federal (German) (Agency for Defence Technology and Procurement (Koblenz)

BWC   British War Cabinet

B/WCC   bomb-to-warhead conversion components

BW/CW	biological warfare/chemical warfare	BWSO	Bureau of (Naval) Weapons Shipping Order
BWD	barrels of water per day	BWTF	bank wire transfer of funds
BWE	Bureau of (Naval) Weapons Evaluation; Besondere und Witterungs Einflüsse (special and meteorological influences, artillery)	BW-TV	black and white television
		BWV	back water valve
		BWVA	British War Veterans of America
BWFRR	Bureau of Naval Weapons Fleet Readiness Representative	BX	base exchange (store) (USAF)
		bx	unfit man (UK)
BWG	Birmingham wire gauge	BY	budget year
BWI	British West Indies	ByF	battery fire
BWIR	British West India Regiment	BYMA	Baltimore Yard minesweeper
BWksp	base workshop	byp	bypass
BWM	British War Medal WW1	BZ	British Zone; incapacitating war gas
BWO	backward wave oscillator		
BWP	basic war plan, brown wrapping paper	Bz	Bronze (US); Brazil(ian)
BWPA	backward wave power amplifier	BZ	Brennzünder (igniting fuse, time fuse)
BWPD	barrels of water per day		
BWPH	barrels of water per hour	BZÜ	Bauzustandsüberwachung (monitoring of the progress of construction)
BWR	boiling water reactor		
BWRS	British War Relief Society		

C

C   Canadian; change; control; corps;
         combat; confidential (classifica-
         tion); Command Paper (1870-99)
         (UK); Captain; chief; commander;
         controller; comptroller; constable;
         consul; curate; cargo (aircraft);
         copper (plated); controls (elec-
         tronics); Centigrade; Cordite
         (powder); cubic; climb; Cruiser
         (RN)

C-Abwehr chemical defence

C-day   commence day; deployment operation
          commences

C-Schutz chemical protection

2C   command and communications (system);
          command and control (system)

C^2 command and control (system)

3C   command, control and communications
          (system)

C^3 command, control and communications
          (system)

4C   command, control, communication and
          computation (system)

C^4 command, control, communication and
          computation (system)

C-1   medium-range cargo aircraft by
          Kawasaki

C-1   Trader, naval cargo aircraft (USN)

C-2   Greyhound, carrier on-board delivery
          plane by Grumman

C-2   Wasserfall, anti-aircraft rocket WW2

C-2   submachine gun 9mm by Echeveria

C-5   An-4, cargo aircraft Chinese designa-
          tion

C-5   Galaxy, cargo aircraft by Lockheed

C-6   autogyro aircraft 1924 by Cierva

C-8   autogyro aircraft 1928 by Cierva

C-9   Nightingale, cargo aircraft by McDD
          DC-9

C-12   SuperKingAir, light transport air-
          craft by Beech

C-22   target drone by AS

C-30   Rota, autogyro aircraft by Cierva

C-44   jeep by Citroen

C-46   Commando, transport aircraft by
          Curtiss

C-47   Dakota, Skytrain, DC-3, Gooney Bird
          tactical transport aircraft by
          Douglas

C-54   Skymaster, 4-engined cargo by
          Douglas

C-70   class, corvettes, guided missile
          (FR)

C-71   project, corvettes, 700 tons by
          Lürssen

C-74   Globemaster, cargo aircraft by
          Douglas

C-82   Packet, cargo aircraft by Fairchild

C-97   Stratofreighter strategic transport
          aircraft by Boeing

C-83   project, corvette 1160 tons by
          Lürssen

C-101   jet trainer/light attack aircraft by
          CASA

C-118   DC-6, 4-engined cargo aircraft by
          Douglas

C-119   Boxcar, cargo aircraft by Fairchild

C-121   Super Constellation, cargo aircraft

C-123   Provider, cargo aircraft by Fair-
          child

C-124   Globemaster, strategic transport
          aircraft by Douglas

C-130   Hercules, cargo aircraft by Lockheed

C-133   Cargomaster, heavy strategic trans-
          port aircraft by Douglas

C-135   Stratolifter, cargo aircraft by
          Boeing

C-137   transport aircraft by Boeing

C-140   JetStar, VIP transport aircraft by
          Lockheed

C-141   Starlifter, transport aircraft by
          Lockheed

C-160   Transall, European transport air-
          craft by Nord/HFB/VFW

C-212   Aviocar, light transport aircraft by
          CASA

CA   Crown Agent; chartered accountant;
          command accountant; chief accoun-
          tant; Assistant Commandant (USMC);
          conflict alert; corps area; com-
          manding artillery; coast

CA	artillery; civil aviation; colonial allowance; civil affairs; concealed aircraft; Canada (Nato); (offensive) counter-air; heavy cruiser (USN); combat assault; combined arms; civil authorities; cost account; civic action; Canite (tear gas); control air, (computer programme); conflict alarm; collision alarm (system); controlled airspace; command action (net); Conseil Atlantique (Atlantic Council); Courant Alternatif (alternating current)
C/A	coarse/acquisition (code NAVSTAR)
C-A	conventional alloy; (North Atlantic) Council Agenda (for meetings) (Nato)
CA-1	Caesar, anti-aircraft tank by Oerlikon/Philips/Krauss-Maffei
CAA	chief air artificer; Civil Aeronautics Administration (US); Civil Aviation Authority (UK); concepts analysis agency; crypto access authorization; combat available aircraft
CAAB	Commandement Allie des Approches de la Baltique (Allied Command, Baltic Approaches)
CAADRP	civil aircraft airworthiness data recording procedures
CAAES-450	WFA-420, modular command and fire-control system by Ferranti
CAAF	Combined Allied Air Forces WW2
CAAFOI	Civil Aviation Authority's Flight Operations Inspectorate
CAAG	cotton aerodynamic anti-gravity (flying suit)
CAAIS	computer-assisted action information system by Ferranti
CAAM	conventional airfield attack missile (US programme)
CAAR	compressed air accumulator rocket
CAARC	Commonwealth Advisory Aeronautical Research Council
CAAS	Canadian Army Administration Service; combined arms and support; computer-aided approach sequencing
CAATC	coastal anti-aircraft training centre
CAAvn	Commander, Army Aviation
CAB	Civil Aeronautics Board; Career Activities Branch; captured air bubble
CABATM	Civil Aeronautics Board Air Transport Mobilization
CABM	Commonwealth of Australia Bureau of Meteorology
C-ABM	Chinese-oriented anti-ballistic missile system
CAC	Commander, Air Centre; contact area commander; Chief Artillery Controller; Coast Artillery Corps; Canadian Armoured Corps; Combined Arms Centre; control and coordination; combat air crew; combined action company; Central Advisory Council; control analysis centre by RCA; Commonwealth Aircraft Corporation (Australia); Computer Avionics Corporation; Curtiss Aircraft Corporation (Buffalo); Centre d'Achat de Coblence (Koblenz Procurement Centre)
CACAC	Civil Aircraft Control Advisory Committee (UK)
CAC/ASAS	control analysis centre/all-source analysis system by RCA
CACC	Civil Aviation Communications Centre
CACD	computer-aided circuit design
CACDA	Combined Arms Combat Development Activity
CACFE	Central Advisory Council for Forces' Education
CACHE	computer-controlled automated cargo handling envelope
CACM	Central American Common Market
CACO	casualty assistance calls officer
CACo	Chicago Arms Company
CACP	casualty assistance calls programme
CACS	CinCent Airlift Coordination Staff; computer-assisted command system (RN) by Ferranti
Cactus	South African designation for Crotale surface-to-air guided weapon
CACW	Chinese-American Composite Wing
CAC&W	continental aircraft control and warning
CAD	Central Accounts Division; Central Aircraft Dispatch; Civil Affairs Division; Civil Air Defence; Central Ammunition Depot; computer-assisted design; cushion augmentation devices; cartridge actuated device (fuse); centre aiming disc
Cad	cadet
CADA	computer-assisted designer analysis
CADAM	computer-augmented design and manufacturing (graphics)
CADC	Canadian Army Dental Corps; Continental Air Defence Command; central air data computer; colour analysis display computer
CADD	computer-assisted design drafting
CADE	computer-assisted data evaluation
CADF	commutated antenna direction finder
CADI	Centre Annexe de Direction d'Interceptions (Control and reporting post) (air defence)

Cadillac-Gage -system, Add-On, gun stabiliz-
             ing gear by CG
CADIN   Continental Air Defense Integration
             North (US-Canada)
CADIZ   Canadian air defence identification
             zone
Cadloy   high-hardness armour plating alloy
             by CG
CADM   SUU-54, clustered airfield demolition
             munition, scatter bomb
CAdminI computer administration instruction
CADOP   Continental Air Defence Operation
             Plan
CAD/PAD cartridge actuated device/propellant
             actuated device (fuse)
CADPO   communications and data processing
             operation
CADRE   completed active duty requirements,
             enlisted
CADS   containerized ammunition distribution
             system; cushion augmentation devi-
             ces
CAdSame callsigns and Address group remain
             the same
CADW   civil air defence warning
CAE   Canadian Army, Europe; Canadian Avia-
             tion Electronics Ltd (Montreal);
             Commandement Alliee en Europe
             (Allied Command, Europe) (Nato)
CAEM   Conseil d'Assistance Economique
             Mutuelle (Mutual Economic Aid
             Council)
Caernarvon main battle tank WW2 (UK)
Caesar   CA-1, anti-aircraft tank by
             Oerlikon/Philips/Krauss-Maffei
CAEWW   Carrier Airborne Early Warning Wing
CADO   Central Air Documents Office (USAF)
CAF   Canadian Armed Forces; clerical,
             administrative and fiscal; Central
             African Federation; completely
             assembled for ferry
CAFAC   Commander all Forces Aruba-Curacao
CAFAF   Commander, Amphibious Forces,
             Atlantic Fleet (USN)
CAFDA   Commandement Aerien des Forces de
             Defense Aerienne (Air Command Air
             Defence Forces)
CAFE   corporated average fuel economy (US
             programme for car manufacturers)
CAFIC   Combined All Forces Information
             Centre
CAFM   commercial air freight movement
CAFO   Confidential Admiralty Fleet Order
             (RN)
CAFPF   Commander, Amphibious Forces, Pacific
             Fleet (USN)
CAFT   consolidated advance field teams
CAFTA   Central American Free Trade Associa-
             tion
CAFU   Civil Aviation Flying Unit (ILS
             calibration aircraft)

CAG   Commander, Army Group; Comptroller
             and Auditor General; civil air
             guard; carrier air group; combat
             arms group; heavy guided missile
             cruiser (CA-USN); Canadian Aero-
             space Group
CAGO   cargo apparent good order
CAGRA   Commander, Army Group, Royal Artil-
             lery
CAGRE   Commander, Army Group, Royal
             Engineers
CAGSigs Commander, Army Group, Signals
CAH   helicopter cruiser
CAI   Canadian Aeronautic Institute;
             configuration audit inspection;
             computer-assisted instruction;
             close-controlled air interception;
             close approach indicator
CAIB   Canadian Army Identification Bureau
CAIC   computer-assisted instruction centre
CAINS   ASN-92, carrier aircraft/alignment
             inertial navigation system
CAIO   Corps Artillery Intelligence Officer
CAirC   Caribbean Air Command
CAIS   Computer-assisted action information
             system
CAK   command access keys
CAL   Canadian Arsenals Ltd; Cornell Aero-
             nautical Laboratory; conversation-
             al algebraic language; computer-
             assisted learning; confined area
             landing; Carabine Automatique
             Légère 5.56mm light automatic
             carbine by FN
cal   calorie; calibre; calibration
CALA   Civil Aviation Licensing Act
CALC   cargo acceptance and load control
calc   calculator; calculation
CALE   Canadian Army Liaison Executive
California class, nuclear-powered cruisers
             guided missiles CGN (USN)
CallAlert mast-mounted millimetre-wave
             warning receiver by AIL
Calliope multiple artillery rocket launcher
             WW2
Calypso surveillance radar for submarines
             by Thomson-CSF
CAM   Civil Actions Medal (Viet Nam);
             Civil Affairs Mission; commercial
             air movement (number); Catapult
             Aircraft (armed) Merchantman;
             cockpit area microphone; Camou-
             flage STANAG; cement aggregate
             mixture; Civil Aeronautics Manual;
             computer-assisted manufacturing;
             content addressable memory
cam   camouflage
CAMA   centralized automatic message
             accounting
CAMAC   computer application for measurement
             and control (standard)

CAMAE   Central Air Material Area, Europe
         (Nato)
CAMAL   continuous airborne missile launched
         and low level system
Cam-Al-gun Cambridge Aluminium anti-tank
         gun
CAMANF   6x6 armoured amphibious truck by
         Biselli
CAMAR   common aperture multi-function array
         radar
CamBn   camouflage battalion
CAMBS   command active multi-beam sonobuoy
         (helicopter-borne) (RN)
CAMC   Canadian Army Medical Corps
CamCo   camouflage company
CAMEL   critical aeronautical material
         equipment list
CamnHighrs The Cameron Highlanders
CAMI   continuing action maintenance in-
         structions; contingency action
         maintenance instructions; Civil
         Aero-Medical Institute; Civil
         Aviation Medical Institute
Camillino armoured personnel carrier (IT)
CAML   cargo aircraft mine-laying (system)
CAMLS   cargo aircraft mine-laying system
         by Lockheed
CAMOPac Central Ammunition Management
         Office Pacific
CAMP   Coast Artillery Mine Planters
Campagnole jeep by FIAT
CAMPS   centralized automated military pay
         system; computer-assisted message
         processing system
CAMS   communication area master station
CAMSI   Canadian American Merchant Shipping
         Instructions; Confidential Admir-
         alty Merchant Shipping Instruc-
         tions
CAN   custons assigned numbers
Can   Canada; Canadian
can   cancel; cancellation
CANA   Canadian Army (Nato)
CanAirDiv Canadian Air Division
CanAirFax Canadian Maritime Air Command
         Halifax
CanAirHed Canadian Air Force Headquarters
         (Ottawa)
CanAirLant Canadian Maritime Air Command
         Atlantic (Halifax)
Canasta low light level television system
         for tank fire control by Thomson-
         CSF
CaNavHed Canadian Naval Headquarters
         (Ottawa)
CaNavUS Canadian Naval Representative of
         the Canadian Joint Staff in the
         US (Washington)
Canberra EB-57, RB-57, twin-jet multi-role
         recce aircraft by BE

CaCASS   Canadian Command active sonobuoy
         system
CanCoMarLant Canadian Commander Maritime
         Atlantic
CanComFlt Canadian Commander Afloat; Senior
         Canadian Officer Afloat
CanCon   Canadian Control (system)
cand   candidate
CandE   communications and electronics
CandR   convoy and routing (USN); control
         and reporting (Nato)
CanDU   Canadian Deuterium Uranium (reactor)
         BLW boiling light water
CANE   computer-assisted navigation equip-
         ment (RN)
CANEL   Connecticut Advanced Nuclear
         Engineering Laboratory
CanEWS   Canadian (Naval) electronic warfare
         system by Westinghouse
CANF   Combined Allied Naval Forces WW2
CanFlag Lant Canadian Flag Officer Atlantic
         Coast (Nato)
CanForceHed Canadian Forces Headquarters
CANFSWPA Combined Allied Naval Forces
         South West Pacific Area WW2
         OPlan operating plan
CANGO   Committee for Air Navigation and
         Ground Organization
Canite   CA, tear gas
CanLant Canadian Atlantic Subarea
Canopus optical fire control system by
         Thomson
CANP   civil aircraft notification proce-
         dure
CANSG   Civil Aviation Navigational Services
         Group
CanTASS Canadian towed array surveillance
         system by ComDev
CanTran cancel (in) transmission
Canuck   CF-1000, Canadian fighter aircraft
         by AVro (Canada)
Can-UK-US Canada-United Kingdom-United
         States
CAO   commanding air officer; commissioned
         armament officer; chief adminis-
         trative officer; chief aeronauti-
         cal officer; collateral action
         officer; civil affairs officer;
         change of administrative office
CAOC   counter-air operations centre
CAOF   Canadian Army Occupation Force
CAORB   Civil Aviation Operational Research
         Branch
CAORG   Canadian Army Operational Research
         Group
CAP   combat air patrol; civil air patrol;
         combined action platoon; combined
         action programme; communications
         afloat programme; contingency
         amphibious plan; current assess-

ment plan; Cariolis acceleration platform; Civil Aviation Publication; Code Adresse Primaire, (primary address code)

Cap   Captain

cap   captured; capacity

CAPC   Canadian Army Provost Corps; Civil Aviation Planning Committee

CapCom   capsule communicator (NASA)

CAPCP   civil air patrol coastal patrol

CAPDAC   computer-assisted piping design and construction

CAPE   communications automatic processing equipment

CAPER   cost of attaining personnel requirement

CAPI   computer-administered programmed instruction

CAPM   combat air patrol mission

CAPO   Canadian Army Post Office

CAPPS   centralized Army passenger port call system

CaPr   catalogue of programme

CAPRI   coded address private radio intercommunications (system); computerized advanced personnel requirements information (system)

CAPRIS   combat active/passive radar identification system by SEL

Capt   Captain

CaptLB   Captain, landing barges

CapTor   MK-60, capsuled torpedo sleeping ASW torpedo mine

CAPUC   coordinating area production urgency committee

CAPWSK   collision avoidance, proximity warning, station keeping (equipment)

CAR   Chief Army Reserve; Committee for Aeronautical Research; Civil Air Regulations; condition and recommendation; channel address register; Colt Automatic Rifle; cloudtop altitude radiometer; collision avoidance radar

Car   Caribbean; carrier

CARA   Combat Air(crew) Rescue Aircraft; Cargo and Rescue Aircraft

CARAC   Civil Aviation Radio Advisory Committee

CarAEWRon   Carrier Airborne Early Warning Squadron VAW (USN)

CarAntSubAirGru   Carrier Anti-submarine Warfare Air Group CVSG (USN)

CarAntiSubGru   Carrier Antisubmarine Warfare Group

CarASWAirGru   Carrier ASW Air Group CVSG

carb   carbine; carburettor; carbon

CarBagAir   baggage for air cargo

CarBasOrd   carry out basic orders

CarbSeaFron   Caribbean Sea Frontier

Carcara   X-1, main battle tank 90mm gun by Bernardinin/Biselli

CarCslr   career counsellor

CARD   Campaign against Racial Discrimination; compact automatic retrieval device; compact automatic retrieval display; computer-augmented road design

CARDA ConUS   airborne reconnaissance for damage assessment

CARDE   Canadian Armament Research and Development Establishment

CarDiv   carrier division

CARDS   computer-assisted radar display system

CARE   Cooperative for American Relief to Europe; Cooperative for American Relief Everywhere; continuous aircraft reliability evaluation

CARF   central altitude reservation facility

Cargo   transport tracked vehicle by Hotchkiss

Cargocat   light Infantry support vehicle by Crayford

Cargomaster   C-133, heavy strategic transport aircraft by Douglas

CaribDiv   Caribbean Division (USN)

Caribou   DHC-4, STOL transport aircraft by DHC

CaribSeaFron   Caribbean Sea Frontier

CarInfo   Career information

CarInfoCen   Career Information Centre

Carl Gustav   recoilless anti-tank gun 84mm; machine pistol 9mm

CARN   conditional analysis for random networks

CARP   computed air release point

CarPac   carriers, Pacific WW2

Carpetlayer   instant road (carpet) launched by AVRE WW2

CarQuals   carrier qualifications

carr   carrier (vehicle)

CARS   combat arms regimental system

CarStrikFor   carrier strike force

CarStrikGruOne   carrier strike group one

CART   collision avoidance radar trainer (aircraft)

CarTaskFor   carrier task force

cartog   cartographer

CarTransRon   carrier transport squadron

CARTU   combat aircrew refresher training unit

CAS   Chief of Air Staff; Coordinator of Army Studies; coincidence adjusting scale; Children's Army School; Coast Artillery School; Coastguard Air Service; Civil Affairs Section; completely assembled for strike; controlled American source;

CAS   (visual) close air support; calibrated air speed; (stability) command augmentation system (helicopters); collision avoidance system; controlled air space; central amplifier station
cas   casualty
CASA   Commander Antarctic Support Activities; close air support aircraft Thunderbolt II; Construcciones Aeronauticos SA (Spain)
CASB   Cost Accounting Standard Board
CASC   captive air-space craft (minesweeper)
Cascavel EE-9, wheeled recce vehicle by Engesa
CASCP Caribbean area small craft project
CASCU Commander aircraft support control unit
CASD   carrier aircraft service detachment
CASDAC computer-assisted ship design and construction
CASD   carrier aircraft service division
CASDiv carrier aircraft service division
CASE   Commission on Accreditation of Service Experience (American Council of Education); Counter-agency for Sabotage and Espionage
CasEvac casualty evacuation
CASEx combined aircraft submarine exercise
CASF   Canadian Active Service Force, composite air strike force
CshDep cash deposit
CASI   Canadian Aeronautics and Space Institute
CASigs Commander Army Signals
CaSL   Catering Sub-lieutenant
CASPAR Cambridge analog simulator for predicting atomic reactions
CasPmt casual payment
CasRep casualty (summary) report
CASS   SSQ-50, command active sonobuoy system (helicopterborne)
CAST   Canadian Air/Sea Transportation (reinforcement) (Nato); computerized automatic system tester; Council for Agricultural Science and Technology
CASTCG Canadian Air/Sea Transportation Combat Group (Nato)
CASTE Civil Aviation Signals Training Establishment
CASThe Hague Chief, Army Staff, Netherlands (Nato)
CASTE computer-assisted system for theatre engineering
Castor rapid Infantry bridging system by GIAT
Castor-IIB tracking/fire control radar by Thomson-CSF
Castor-1000 sonar by ELAC

CASU   carrier aircraft service unit
CASUF carrier aircraft service unit fighters; combat aircraft service unit
CASum civil affairs summary
CASWO confidential and secret weekly orders
CASWS close air support weapon system (USAF programme)
CAT   combined acceptance trials; Canon auto-tuning; civil air transport; Central Analysis Team; compressed air tunnel; clear air turbulence; clear air temperature; carburettor air temperature; cartridge assembly test; computer-assisted typesetting; coast artillery training; city air terminal; container anchorage terminal; Cible Aerienne Telecommandée (remote-controlled aerial target)
cat   category
Cat   aerial navigation ground station WW2
CATA   Compania Argentina de Trabajos Aeros
CATAC Commandement Aerien Tactique (tactical air command)
CATAF Commandement Aerien Tactique Français (French tactical air command)
Catafighter naval Hurricane
Catalina PBY, flying boat by Consolidated
CATC   crashed aircraft transit centre; computerised air traffic control; Commonwealth Air Transport Council; Commonwealth Air Transport Committee
CATCC carrier air traffic control centre
CATCO carrier air traffic control officer
CATCUSAF Commander Amphibious Training Command (US) Atlantic Fleet
CATF   Commander Amphibious Task Fleet; Combined Amphibious Task Fleet
CATI   Canon Anti-char d'Infanterie (sans recul) (Infantry anti-tank recoilless cannon
catk   counter-attack
CATO   civil air traffic officer
CATOR combined air transport operations room
CATS   Civil Affairs Training School; communications and tracking system
CATU   combat aircrew training unit
Catulle naval Javelot
CATV   community antenna television; cable television
CATVS cable television system
CAU   crypto ancillary unit
CAV   construction assistance vehicle (subaqua); composite analog video
Cav   Cavalry

Cavalier tank WW2 (UK) ex-Cromwell I
CAVU   ceiling and visibility unlimited
CAW   carrier air wing; channel address
         word
CAWC   Central Advisory Water Committee
CAWCS   Centre for the Automation of Weapon
         and Command Systems (Netherlands)
CAWS   common aviation weather system;
         cannon artillery weapon system
CAWSE   casualty analysis (for the determi-
         nation of) weapons system effec-
         tiveness
CAX   community automatic exchange
Cayuse   OH-6, observation helicopter by
         Hughes
CB   Companion of the Most Noble and
         Ancient Order of the Bath; confi-
         dential book; carrier-borne;
         counter-bombardment; counter-
         battery; confinement to barracks;
         cryptographic bureau; construction
         battalion; coastal battery;
         casualty branch; citizens' band
         (frequencies); chemical biological
         (warfare); centre of buoyancy;
         chloro-bromo (methane) fire ex-
         tinguisher; common battery; central
         battery; conical ball (projectile);
         crash boat; cruiser, big (USN);
         compass bearing; sneezing gas
CBAIC   chemical biological accident and
         incident control
CBAICP   chemical biological accident and
         incident control plan
CBALS   carrier-borne air liaison section
CBC   Construction Battalion Centre; Civil
         Budget Committee; cruiser, big,
         command (USN); Companhia Brasileira
         ce Cartuchos
CbC   Contraband control
CBCO   Central Board of Conscientious
         Objectors
CBD   construction battalion detachment;
         cash before delivery
CBE   Commander of the Most Excellent
         Order of the British Empire;
         command budget estimates; chemical,
         biological and environmental
CBFBS   Cyprus British Forces Broadcasting
         Service
CBFC   Commander British Forces Cyprus
CBFCA   Commander British Forces Caribbean
         Area
CBFHK   Commander British Forces Hong Kong
CBGLO   carrier-borne ground liaison officer
CBGLSect carrier-borne ground liaison
         section
CBI   China-Burma-India (theatre) WW2;
         Central Bureau of Identification;
         complete background investigation

CBIO   counter-battery intelligence officer
CBIS   Communist Bloc Intelligence Service;
         computer-based information system
CBL   commercial bill of lading; central
         bidders' list
cbl   cable
CBLO   chief bombardment liaison officer;
         carrier-borne (air) liaison
         officer
CBLS   carrier bombs light store
CMB   Comité du Budget Militaire (Military
         Budget Committee)
CBMIS   computer-based management informa-
         tion system
CBMU   construction battalion maintenance
         unit
Cbn   construction battalion
cbn   carbine; cabin
CBnDet   construction battalion detachment
CBNS   Commander, British Naval Staff
         (Washington DC)
CBO   counter-battery officer; coding
         board officer; computer burst
         order
CBo   coastal bombardment
CBOI   complete basis of issue
CBOIP   complete basis of issue plan
CBOR   current break-off and memory
CBOSS   count back order and sample select
CBP   contact burst preclusion (fuse)
CB&PGNCS circuit breaker and primary gui-
         dance navigation control system
CBR   Coast Guard Budget and Requirements;
         chemical bacteriological and
         radiological; chemical biological
         and radiological (warfare); cloud
         base recorder
CBR-1...12 California Bearing Ratio
            (runway conditions)
         12 metal plates
         10 grass runway
          4 loose sand
CBRD   Canadian base reinforcement depot;
         construction battalion replacement
         depot
CBRE   chemical biological and radiological
         element
CBRCC   chemical biological radiological
         centre
CBrF   chloro-bromo-fluoro (fire exting-
         uisher)
CBRN   chemical biological radiological
         and nuclear
CBRW   chemical biological and radiological
         warfare
CBS   central battery signalling; Columbia
         Broadcasting System (US)
CBT   core block table
cbt   combat
CbtI   combat intelligence

C-Btry	counter-battery
CBU	container bomb unit; cluster bomb unit
CBU-2	bomb dispenser for BLU-30
CBU-52	cluster bomb
CBU-55	bomb FAE (fuel air explosives)
CBU-58	cluster bomb
CBU-71	cluster bomb
CBU-72	bomb FAE
CBudFin	Chief of Budget and Finance Division
CBW	Canadian Black Watch; chemical and biological warfare
CC	Corps Commander; combat commander; company commander; county clerk; commodore commanding; chief constable; county commissioner; chief controller; camp commandant; cumulative changes; Companion of the Order of Canada; Construction Corps; Cadet Corps; civil control; civil commotion; confinement camp; combat clothing; control council; control centre; command centre; correspondence course; (tactical) command ship (USN); Sea Sea (submarine) (USN); cruiser (Nato); battle cruiser; correlation centre (intelligence); Cruiser Command; cushion craft (RN); card column; Combat Clothing and Equipment STANAG; continuous current; cirro-cumulus (cloud); counter chronograph; carbon copy; common carrier; change course; cyanogen chloride; compass course; chronometer correction; control computer; colour compensation; comparison circuit; configuration control
cc	chapters
CC-7	cushioncraft (RN)
CCA	Chief Clerk of the Admiralty; Commander, Coast Artillery; Combat Command A (US) WW2; court of criminal appeal; Commission for Conventional Armament; cash clothing allowance; Continental Control Area FAA (US); collision course attack (missile); carrier-controlled approach; carrier-controlled airspace
CCAC	Combined Civil Affairs Committee L London S Supply
CCAI	close-controlled air interception
CCAL	Centre de Controlle d'Artillerie Anti-aerienne Légère (light anti-aircraft artillery control centre)
CCAM	Canadian Civilian Association of Marksmen
CCANAFI	Citizens' Committee for the Army Navy and Air Force Inc.
CCAO	Chief Civil Affairs Officer (US-UK)
CCAR	carrier-controlled approach radar
CCAS	close-combat anti-armour system (US) now IMAAWS
CCATF	Commander, Combined Amphibious Task Force
CCATNA	Combined Committee on Air Training in North America
CCB	company conduct book; Central Control Board; Combat Command B (US) WW2; Configuration Control Board NADGE; Combined Communications Board; contraband control base; control and command boat (USN); command communications boat (USN); command control block (computer); cubic capacity of bunkers
CCBO	Corps counter-bombardment officer
CCBP	Combined Communications Board Publications
CCBW	Committee on Chemical and Biological Warfare
CCC	Central Criminal Court; Control Commission Court; Combat Cargo Command; Civilian control commission; Commodity Credit Corporation; classified control clerk; Chief Cable Censor; Cognizant Controlling Custodian; Combat Command C WW2 (reserve); Civilian Conservation Corps; Combined Co-ordinating Committee; command control and communications (system); central computer complex; computer control complex; Connecticut Cartridge Company; Communications Components Corporation; Canadian Commercial Corporation
CCCA	commander corps coastal artillery
CCCC	Communications Components Corporation California; command control communications and computation (system)
CCCCI	command control communication computation and identification (system)
CCCCS	command control communication and computation system
CCCI	command control communication and identification
CCCME	Comité de Coordination des Communications Militaires en Europe (European Military Communications Coordinating Committee)
CCCMMM	closed chest cardiac massage and mouth-to-mouth (resuscitation)
CCCO	Central Cartridge Company; Creedmore Cartridge Company
CCCS	command control and communications system; Compatibility of Command and Control Systems (Nato)

CCD	Commander Coastal Defence; civil censorship division; central commissioning detail; conference of the committee of disarmament (UN); Command and Control Division STC (Nato); charge-coupled devices; controlled current distribution; construction completion date; Centre de Contrôle et de Detection (Control and reporting centre)
CCDD	command and control development division
CCDG	Civil Coordination Detachment General ATC (Nato)
CCDL	Commander Cruiser-Destroyer (Force) Atlantic Fleet (USN)
CCE	chief construction engineer, commercial construction equipment
CCEC	Chairman Communications Electronics Committee
CCEAF	Commander Central European Air Forces
CCECA	Consultative Committee on Electronics for Civil Aviation
CCEEP	Canada Committee for Coordination of Emergency Economic Planning
CCEGF	Commander Central European Ground Forces
CCEI	composite cost effectiveness index
CCESF	Commander Central European Sea Forces
CCEW	Communauté Centre Europe des Wagons (Central Europe Wagon Pool)
CCEWG	Civil Communications-Electronics Working Group
CCF	Captain Coastal Forces; The Camerons of Canada Fusiliers; Combined Cadet Force (UK); Corps Contingency Force; correctional custody facility; Centre de Coordination des Feux (fire support coordination centre); central control facility; central communications facility; cross-correlation function
CCFA	Combined Cadet Force Association
CCFET	Captain Coastal Forces, Eastern Theatre
CCFR	Commonwealth Committee on Fuel Research
CCG	Combat Camera Group; Control Commission for Germany BE British Element; Comité de Coordination des Experts Budgetaires Gouvernementaux (Co-ordinating Committee for Government Budget Experts)
CCGD	Commander Coast Guard District
CCGE	cold cathode gauge experiment
CCh	Chief of Chaplains
CCH	computerized criminal history (files) FBI; channel check handler; cubic capacity of holds

CCHMS	Central Committee for Hospital Medical Services
cchr	cubic centimetres per hour
CCI	command control interface MSR; collision course interception; command control and identification (system); Cascade Cartridge Incorporated
CCIF	Comité Consultatif International Téléphonique des Fréquences (International Telephone Consultative Committee)
CCIL	commander's critical items list
CCIP	continuously computed impact point
CCIR	Comité Consultatif International Radiophonique International (Radio Consultative Committee)
CCIS	command control and information system
CCIT	Comité Consultatif International Téléphonique/Télégraphique (International Telephone/Telegraph Consultative Committee)
CCITT	Comité Consultatif International Télégraphique et Téléphonique (International Telephone and Telegraph Consultative Committee)
CCK	channel control check
CCL	communications circular letter; contamination control line; core current layer
CCLSAF	Central Command for Land Sea and Air Forces
CCM	confidential code message; Crimean Campaign Medal 1854 (UK); counter-counter measures; combined cipher machine; combined coding machine; constant current modulation; controlled carrier modulation; chain crossing model (semi-conductor); Centre de Contrôle Mixte (joint control centre)
CCMA	Commander Corps Medium Artillery, civilian clothing maintenance allowance
CCMD	continuous current monitoring device
CCME	Contre-Contre Mesures Electroniques ou Anti-brouillage Electronique (electronic counter-counter measures
CCmptC	central computer centre
C&CMRB	Clemency and Court Martial Review Branch BUPERS
CCMS	Committee on the Challenges of Modern Society (Nato)
CCMT	Citizens' Committee for Military Training YM of Young Men
CCN	command control number; contract change notification; contract change notice

CCNDT   Canadian Council for Non-destructive
        Testing

CCNR   Consultative Committee for Nuclear
        Research, European Council
CCO   chief of combined operations;
        casualty clearing officer; classi-
        fied control officer; combat cargo
        officer; commercial contracting
        officer; convoy control officer;
        central coding office; current-
        controlled oscillator
CCOC   command control operations centre
CCOK   Central Chancery for the Orders of
        Knighthood
CCP   casualty collecting post; cross-
        check procedure; code of civil
        procedure; consolidated cryptologic
        programme; contamination control
        point; critical compression pres-
        sure; communication control
        package; console control package
CCPC   Comité de Coordination des Plans
        Civil d'Urgence (Civil Emergency
        Coordinating Committee) (Nato);
        Civil Communications Planning
        Committee (Nato)
CCPT   Comité de Coordination des Plans de
        Transport (Coordinating Committee
        for Transport Planning)
CCR   Centre de Contrôle Régional de la
        Circulation Aerienne (Regional Air
        Traffic Control Centre); Code de
        Categorie de Référence (Reference
        number category code)
CCR   Commission of Civil Rights; Combat
        Command, Reserves; closed circuit
        radio; Common Centre of Research;
        critical compression ratio; coher-
        ent change request
CCr   combat crew
CCRA   Commander Corps Royal Artillery
CCRCT   Commander Corps Royal Corps of Trans-
        port
CCRE   Commander Corps Royal Engineers
CCRKBA Citizens' Committee for the Right to
        Keep and Bear Arms (US)
CCRP   continuously computed release point
CCrP   Code of Criminal Procedure
CCRS   Commander Corps Royal Signals
CCRTD   Committee for the Coordination of
        Cathode Ray Tube Development
CCRU   common cold research unit
CCS   casualty clearing station; combat
        cargo service; Combined Chiefs of
        Staff; collective call sign; Ceylon
        Civil Service; central computer,
        ship; central computer station;
        command and control system; con-
        trolled combustion system; commu-
        nication control system

C/CS   commodities, coal and steel
CCS-750 electro-magnetic compatibility
        testing system by Electro Metrix
cc/sec cubic centimetres per second
CCSF   Commander Caribbean Sea Frontier
CCSSA   Control and Command Systems Support
        Agency
CCST   Centre for Computer Sciences and
        Technology
CCT   command cadet team; correct corps
        time; communications control
        team; comprehensive college test;
        combat control team; coastal
        cargo, tanker (USN); continuous
        coding transformation; coated
        cargo tanks (tanker); Comité de
        Coordination des Télécommunica-
        tions (Coordinating Committee for
        Telecommunications)
cct   circuit
CCTA   Coordinating Committee for Technical
        Assistance; Centre de Contrôle
        Tactique Aerien (tactical air
        control centre); Comission de
        Coopération technique pour
        l'Afrique au Sud (Commission for
        Technical Cooperation with Africa
        South of the Sahara)
CC&TC   Chamberlain Cartridge and Target
        Company
CCTks   cubic capacity of tanks
CCTP   Coordinating Committee for Transport
        Planning
CCTS   combat crew training squadron
CCTV   closed circuit television
CCTW   closed circuit television wing
        RAEC
CCU   common control unit; chart compari-
        son unit; contaminant collection
        unit
CCUI   combined common user items
CCV   control configured vehicle (air-
        craft)
CCVS   COBOL computer validation system
CCW   channel command word;
        counter-clockwise
        BAD bottom angular down
        BAU bottom angular up
        BH   bottom horizontal

CCWDB   counter-clockwise down blast
CCWTAD counter-clockwise top angular down
CCWTAU counter-clockwise top angular up
CCWTH   counter-clockwise top horizontal
CCWUB   counter-clockwise up blast
CCZA   Canadian Coastal Zone Atlantic
CCZP   Canadian Coastal Zone Pacific
CD   Captain of the Dockyard; clearance
        diver; Canadian Forces Decoration;
        clothing depot; corps duty;

central department; combat development; contract definition (phase); card distribution; comptroller division; confidential document; corrections division; Council Deputies (Nato); convalescent depot; coastal defences; civilian duty; Civil Defence; certificate of discharge; Code de Denomination (Item Name Code) Control Data GmbH (Stresemannallee 30 D-6000 Frankfurt 70)

Cd	Command Paper 1900-18; command
C/D	consular declaration; customs declaration
.c&d	collection and delivery
cd	carried down; candella; current density
CD	coast defence; chemcial defence; count down; cage dipole; check digit; coherent detector; common digitizer; displaced central (trajectory); classification of defects
C^2D^2	Command and Control Development Division
CDA	Civil Defence Act, Canada; civil damage assessment; command and data acquisition (station); Centre de Direction (Tactique) (Air forward director post (Nato)
CDAAA	Committee to Defend America by Aiding the Allies
CdAEng	commissioned air engineer
CDAP	Civil Damage Assessment Programme
CSAPU	central data acquisition and processing unit
CdArmn	commissioned airman
CDAS	Civil Defence Ambulance Service
CDB	concrete dibber bomb (runway demolition)
CdB	commissioned boatswain
cdbd	cardboard
CdBndr	commissioned bandmaster
CdBPR	commissioned boatswain, plotting and radar
CDBS	command data buffer system (for ICBM in-flight re-targeting)
CDC	Civil Defence Committee; Canadian Dental Corps; Colonial Development Corporation; Commonwealth Development Corporation; Canada Development Corporation; Centre for Disease Control; combat data coordinator; Caribbean Defence Command; Combat Development Command; career development course; command and data (handling) console; central digital computer; Cost Determining Committee; contract data coordina-

tor; Computing Devices Company Canada (Ottawa); Control Data Corporation (Ottawa); Control Data Canada (Ottawa)

CDCE	commander disaster control element
CDCF	commander disaster controlforce
CDCG	commander disaster control group
CdCmyO	commissioned commissary officer
CdCO	commissioned communications officer
CdCon	commissioned constructor
CDD	certificate of disability for discharge; Code de Disponibilité de Document (document availability code)
CdD	Comité des Directeurs (Board of Directors)
CDE	Chemical Defence Establishment (Porton UK); Coal Development Establishment
CDEC	Combat Development and Experimentation Command (US Army) Hunter Liggett Military Reservation (Cal.); Combat Development Experimental Center
CDEE	Chemical Defence Experimental Establishment
CdeG	Croix de Guerre
CdElO	commissioned electrical officer
CdEng	commissioned engineer
CDF	coastal defence force; class determinations and findings; combination distribution frame
CDFC	Commonwealth Development Finance Company
CDFS	The Chief of the Defence Force Staff (AS)
CDG	coder-decoder group
CdGr	commissioned gunner
CDH	constant delta heigh
CDI	command driver increment; cargo disposition instructions; Civil Defence Intelligence; course deviation indicator; course director indicator; Centre de Direction des Interceptions (Control and reporting centre) (Nato)
CdInO	commissioned instructor officer
CDK	channel data check
CDL	Central Dental Laboratories; canal defence light (illuminating tank D-day WW2); Central Dockyard Laboratory (RN); computer design language; Centre de Detection Lointaine (reporting post) (Nato)
CDM	Common Defence Market (proposal) (Nato); command detonated mine
CDMA	code division multiple access
CdMAA	commissioned master-at-arms
CDMS	command and data management system;

CDMS	COMRADE data management system (computer-aided design environment)
CDN	Comité de Direction du NADGE (NADGE Policy Board); Chambre des Destinations de Navires (Ship destination room)
Cdn	Canadian
CDNA	Conférence des Directeurs Nationaux des Armaments (Conference of National Armaments Directors (Nato)
CD/NC	computer-assisted design/numerical control
CDNRS	chaff dispensing naval rocket system
CDO	command duty officer (US)
CdO	commissioned officer
cdo	commando (UK)
CdObs	commissioned observer
CdOE	commissioned ordnance engineer
CDOG	combat developments objective guide
CdOO	commissioned ordnance officer
CDP	company distributing point; contract definition phase; camouflage detection photography; compressor discharge pressure
CDPE	continental daily parcel express
CDR	cargo delivery receipts; complete design release; contract definition report; critical design review; coast defence radar; composite damage risk
Cdr	commander
cdr	conductor
CDR-430	coast defence radar by Plessey
CDRA	Committee of Directors of Research Associations
CdRadO	commissioned radio officer
CDRB	Canadian Defence Research Board
CDRC	Civil Defence Regional Commissioner; civil disturbance readiness conditions
CDRD	Chemical Defence Research Department; Committee of Defence Research Directors (Nato)
CDRE	Chemical Defence Research Establishment (Porton UK)
Cdre	commodore (RN)
CdreIC	commodore in charge (RN)
CdreLCBP	Commodore commanding landing craft bases Portsmouth (RN)
CdreSupt	commodore superintendent (RN)
CdrF	Commander, Flying (RN)
CDRF	Canadian Dental Research Foundation
CDRL	Chemical Defence Research Laboratory; contractor data requirement list
CDRS	Civil Defence Rescue Service
CdrSBU	Commander, Special Boat Units (RN)
CDS	Chief of the Defence Staff, Canada; Commander, Destroyer Squadron (USN); Civil Defence Services; Civil Direction of Shipping; Chamber of Destination of Ships; central distribution system; control distribution system; container delivery system (USAF); capability design specifications; command destruct signal
CdSB	commissioned signals boatswain
CDSD	Civil Defence Support Detachments
CDSE	computer-driven simulation environment
CDSF	COMRADE data storage facility (computer-aided design environment)
CdSh	commissioned shipwright
CDSM	Comité sur le Défis de la Société Moderne (Committee on the Challenges of Modern Society) (Nato)
CDSO	Companion of the Distinguished Service Order
CdSO	commissioned supply officer; commissioned stores officer
CDSR	controlled deployment specular reflector
CDSU	coastal defence signal unit
CDT	central daylight time (US)
Cdt	Commandant; cadet
CDTA	Chrysler's Detroit Tank Arsenal
CdtMid	cadet midshipman
CDU	command destruct unit; control and display unit; computer display unit
CDV	cash debit voucher; Civil Defence Volunteers
CDW	Civil Defence Warning; cold drinking water
CdWdr	commissioned wardmaster
CdWo	commissioned writer officer
CDWS	Civil Defence Warning Service
CDX	control differential transmitter
CE	chief engineer; civil engineer; chemical engineer; construction electrician; counter-espionage; combat exhaustion; Corps of Engineers (US); civil employment; commercial enterprise; Council of Europe; Central Europe; compression engine; chemical energy (shell); composition exploding; carbon equivalent; centre of effort; circular error; compass error; channel end; critical examination; Cincinnati Electronics Corp. (Cincinnati Ohio); Carco Electronics; Centre d'Evaluation (evaluation centre)
C&E	clothing and equipment; customs and excise (UK); communications and electronics
C-E	communications electronics
CE-2F	Wet Chariot, swimmer delivery vehicle by Cosmos (IT)

CEA	control electrical artificer; control electronics assembly (autopilot); Canadian Electrical Association; Commissariat à l'Energie Atomique (Atomic Energy Commission)
CEAA	Council of European-American Associations
CEAC	Committee for European Airspace Coordination (Nato)
CEADI	coloured electronics altitude director indicator
CEAM	Centre d'Experimentations Aeriennes Militaires à Mont-de-Marsen (Landes) (Military Aerospace Experimental Centre)
CEASC	Committee for European Airspace Coordination (Nato)
CEAT	Centre Européen Aerospatial (Toulouse) (European Aerospace Centre)
CEB	combined effects bomblet (USAF); Communications Electronics Board (Nato)
CEBAR	chemical biological and radiological
CEBMCO	Corps of Engineers ballistic missile construction office
CEC	Central Economic Committee; Civil Engineers Corps; Commonwealth Economic Committee; Commonwealth Education Conference; Commonwealth Engineering Committee; Commander in Chief (FR); centralized electronic control; Communications Electronics Committee (Nato); Canadian Electrical Code (standard)
CECA	Communauté Européenne du Charbon et de l'Acier (European Coal and Steel Community)
CECAI	Committee on Education Cultural Affairs and Information (Nato)
CECDC	cost estimate control data centre
CEch	combat echelon
CECLANT	Commandant en Chef des Forces Françaises Atlantique (Brest) (French Commander in Chief, Atlantic)
CECMED	Commandant en Chef des Forces Françaises Méditerranée (Toulon) (French Commander in Chief, Mediterranean)
CECORE	Centre de Commandement du Reseau (automatic communications system)
CECS	communications-electronics coordinating section, Nato Standing group --CEC; civil engineering computing system
CECSA	Compania de Electronica y Comunicaciones SA (Spain)
CED	captured enemy document; Committee for Economic Development; current enlistment date; communications

	engineering department; carbon equivalent difference; computer entry device; Communauté Européenne de Défense (European Defence Community)
CEDA	Committee for Economic Development of Australia
CEDC	Committee for the European Defence Community
CEDM	Common European Defence Market (proposal) (Nato)
CEDO	Captured Enemy Documents Organization (Nato)
CEE	communications electronics element; common entrance examination; captured enemy equipment; Central Engineering Establishment; combat emplacement excavator; Communauté Economique Européenne (European Economic Community); Comité Economique pour l'Europe (Economic Commission for Europe)
CEEB	college entrance examination board
CEEC	Council for European Economic Cooperation
CEF	Captain, Escort Forces; Canadian Expeditionary Forces; Chinese Expeditionary Forces; critical experiments facility
CEFA	Chaudronnerie et Forges d'Alsace (F-67250 Soultz-sous-Forêts) (EWK daughter)
CEFAC	Civil Engineering Field Activities Centre
CEFDA	Central European Forces Distribution Agency
CEFI	contractor engineer-furnish and install
CEG	Centre Experimentelle de Gramat (explosives) (experimental centre) DTAT
CEGB	Central Electricity Generating Board (UK)
CEI	cost effectiveness index; communications electronics instruction; Council of Engineering Institutions; Commission Electrotechnique Internationale (International Electrotechnical Commission)
CEIF	Council of the European Industrial Federation
ceil	ceiling
CEinC	Civil Engineer in Chief
CEIP	communication electronics implementation plan
CEIS	cost and economic information system
CE/IWT	Central Europe/Inland Waterways Transport (working group) (Nato)
CEJEDP	Central Europe Joint Emergency Defence Plan (Nato)

CEL   carbon equivalent liquids; Cossor
         Electronics Ltd (Elizabeth Way,
         Harlow Essex); Centre d'Essais des
         Landes (missile proving ground
         near Bordeaux)
cel   celestial
celscope celestial telescope
CEL-850 IFF equipment by Cossor
CELC   Commonwealth Education Liaison
         Committee
CelIntRep accelerated intelligence report
Celloband A2785CV, isophtalic polyester
         resin for glass-reinforced
         plastic by BP
Celtic   tactical message terminal (portable)
         by Cossor
CEM   cost effective method; computer edu-
         cation for management
cem   cemetery; cement
CEMA   Council for Mutual Economic Assis-
         tance
CEMF   counter-electromotive force
CEMIRT   civil engineering maintenance
         inspection repair and training
CEMN   control electrical mechanician
CEN   Comité Européen de Normalisation
         (European Standards Committee)
         Captive European Nations
cen   centre; centigrade
CenCATS Central (Pacific) Combat Air Trans-
         port Service (US TAG)
CenDraftO central drafting officer
CenPac   Central Pacific (area)
CenPacFor Central Pacific Forces
CENTAG   Central European Army Group (Secken-
         heim) (Nato)
Centaur space missile by GD; assault tank
         57mm gun (RM) WW2; half-track
         Land Rover by Laird
Centaure towed anti-aircraft gun by GIAT/
         CETME
CentCom Central (Pacific) Communications
         (Instructions) (US)
Centerline aircraft landing system by Narco
CentLant Central Atlantic Subarea
CENTO   Central Treaty Organization (Turkey-
         Iran-Pakistan-UK-US)
CentPacBaCom Central Pacific Base Command
Centurion main battle tank (UK)
         Ark Centurion AVLB
CENW   controlled effects nuclear weapon
CEO   chief education officer; casualty
         evacuation officer; control of
         engagement order; chief engineer's
         office
CEOA   Central European Oil Agency (Nato)
         (managing agency for CEPS); Central
         Europe Operating Agency (Nato)
         formerly: CEPA
CEOAS   Corps of Engineers Office of
         Appalachian Studies

CEOI   communication-electronics operation
         instructions
CEOinC   Civil Engineer Officer in Charge
CEP   Custodian of Enemy Property;
         Civil Emergency Planning (Nato);
         Central Engineer Park (Long
         Marston UK); circular error proba-
         bility; command executive proce-
         dures
CEPA   Central European Pipelines Agency
         (Nato), --CEOA
CE/PB   Central Europe Ports and Beaches
         (Nato working group)
CEPB   Civil Emergency Planning Board
         (Nato)
CEPC   Civil Emergency Planning Committee
         (Nato); Central European Pipelines
         Committee (Nato)
CEPD   Central European Pipelines Direc-
         torate; Communications electronics
         policy directive
CEPE   Central Experimental and Proving
         Establishment (RCAF)
CEPES   Comité Européen pour le Progrès
         Economique et Social (European
         Committee for Economic and Social
         Progress)
CEPO   Central European Pipeline Office
         (Nato); Central European Projects
         Office (engineering)
CE/POL   Central Europe POL Transport (Nato
         working group)
CEPPC   Central Europe Pipeline Policy
         Committee (Nato)
CEPS   Central Europe Pipeline System
         (Nato)
CEPT   Conférence Européenne des Adminis-
         trations des Postes et Télécommu-
         nications (European Conference of
         Postal and Telecommunications
         Administrations)
CER   combat effectiveness report; com-
         plete engineering release; cost
         estimation relationship; complete
         engine repair; control of electro-
         magnetic radiation
CERA   Civil Engineering Research Associa-
         tion
CERB   Coastal Engineering Research Board
         (US)
Cerbere towed anti-aircraft gun 20mm by
         GITA
CERC   Coastal Engineering Research Center
         (US Army)
CERCA   Commonwealth and Empire Radio for
         Civil Aviation
CERE   Centre d'Essais Regional Européenne
         (European Regional Test Centre)
Ceres   ELINT monitoring and surveillance
         system

CERF   Commander Emergency Recovery Force
CERG   Commander Emergency Recovery Group
CERL   Central Electricity Research Laboratories; Coastal Engineering Research Laboratory
CerMet ceramic-to-metal
CERN   Centre Européen de Recherches Nuceaires (European Nuclear Research Centre); Conseil Européen de Recherches Nucleaires (European Nuclear Research Council)
CERNA   Centre d'Essais Régional Nord-Americain (North American Regional Test Centre)
CE/RRT Central Europe Rail Road Transport (Nato working group)
CERS   commander emergency recovery section
CERS   Centre Européen de Recherches Spatiales (European Space Reseacch Centre ESTEC
CE/RT   Central Europe Road Transport (Nato working group)
CERU   commander emergency recovery unit
Cervantes mortar locating radar (UK)
CES   Conference on European Security; Centre for Environmental Studies; coordinated evaluation system; Cooper Engineering Service
CESA   Canadian Engineering Standards Association
CESDEN Centre for Advanced Studies of the Spanish National Defence
CESE   communications equipment support element TRI-TAC; Comité Economique de Secours Européen (European Economic Relief Committee)
CESEMI computer evaluation of scanning electron microscope images
CESF   Commander Eastern Sea Frontier
CESI   communications-electronics standing instructions; Centro Elettrotecnico Sperimentale Italiano
CESO   Canadian Executive Service Overseas
CESSAC Church of England Soldiers' Sailors' and Airmen's Clubs
CESSAIA Church of England Soldiers' Sailors' and Airmen's Institutes' Association
CEST   Central European Summer Time
CET   common external tariff; Central European Time; FV-180, combat engineer tractor
CETEX   Committee on Extra-terrestrial Exploration
CETI   communications with extra-terrestrial intelligence
CETME   Centro de Estudios Tecnicos de Materiales Especiales (Spain)
CETS   contractor engineering and technical services

CETZ   Central European Tactical Zone
CEU   communications expansion unit
CEV   combat engineer vehicle; convoy escort vessel (USN); Centre d'Essais en Vol (Bretigny sur Orge)
CEWA   Combined Economic Warfare Agencies
CEWCSL Corps of Engineers Waterborne Commerce Statistic Centre
CEWI   combat electronic warfare and intelligence
CEWP   Central European Wagon Pool (railways)
CEWRC   Civilian Employee Welfare and Recreation Committee)
CEx   central excitation
CF   Chaplain to the Forces; Colonial Forces; Commonwealth Fund; copies furnished; carry forward; centre-fire (cartridge); cable firing; cable fusing; correlation factor; consistency figure; concept feasibility; centre of floatation; cathode follower; combined function; correlation function; carrier frequency; communication factor; cruiser, flying deck (USN)
cf   counter-fire
CF-5   F-5, Canadian fighter aircraft, --F-5
CF-98   compact frigate by DTCN
CF-100 Canuck, all-weather fighter/interceptor by Avro (Canada) 1950
CF-101 F-101, Voodoo, Canadian fighter, --F-101
CF-104 F-104, Canadian fighter
CFA   cognizant field activity; current files area; Canadian Field Artillery; covering force area; cross field amplifier
C/FA   commodities, food and agriculture
CF&A   Chief of Finance and Accounting
CFAE   Contractor furnished aircraft equipment
CFAD   Commander Fleet Air Detachment, Commander Fleet Air Defence
CFADC   Canadian Forces Air Defence Command
CFANS   Canadian Forces Air Navigation School
CFAP   Copenhagen Frequency Allocation Plan
CFAR   constant false alarm rate (processor) radar computer
CFAW   Commander Fleet Air Wing
CFAWL   Commander Fleet Air Wing Atlantic
CFAWP   Commander Fleet Air Wing Pacific
CFB   Canadian Forces Base, Combined Forces Base
CFC   Combined Federal Campaign; central fire control; consolidation freight classification; controlled force circulation (boilers)

CFCC	Canadian Forces Communications Command
CF/CD	concept formulation/contract definition (procurement procedure)
CFCEB	Canadian Forces Communications and Electronics Branch
CFCF	Central Flow Control Facility FAA (Washington)
CFCU	central fire control unit
CFD	constant fraction discriminator; cubic feet per day
CFE	Canadian Forces Europe; college of further education; contractor furnished equipment; Central Fighter Establishment
CFER	collector field effect register
CFF	critical fusion frequency, critical flicker frequency
CFG	cubic feet of gas
CFGD	cubic feet of gas per day
CFGH	cubic feet of gas per hour
CFGM	cubic feet of gas per minute
CFH	cubic feet per hour
CF/HP	constant flow/high pressure (oxygen system)
CFI	chief flying instructor; cost freight and insurance
CFK	Carbonfaserverstärkter Kunststoff (carbon-reinforced plastic)
CFL	cease-fire line; clear flight level
CFM	Cadet Force Medal (UK); contingency for movement; cubic feet per minute; centrefire magnum (projectile)
CFMA	central financial management activities
CFMEB	Canadian Forces Military Engineers Branch
CFMS	Canadian Forces Medical Services
CFMS	chained file management system
Cfn	craftsman
CFN-90	semi-smooth bore 90mm gun (FR)
CFNA	Commander Naval Forces Atlantic
CFO	Central Forecasting Office; critical flash-over; chief fire officer; commissioning and fitting out; connection fitting out; central forecasting office; calling for orders
CFOC	contractor fin opener crank
CFOR	ComSec field office of record (communications security)
CFOU	commander forward observation unit (RA)
CFP	centre of filtering and plotting; control filter post; combined filter and plotting (room); concept formulation package
C-F/PCM	course-fine/pulse code modulator
CFPF	central food preparation facility

CFPHT	constant fraction of pulse height trigger
CFPS	Captain, fishery protection squadron; central food preparation system
CFR	Code of Federal Regulations (aeronautics); Council on Foreign Relations; Committee for Fuel Research; commercial fast reactor; contact flight rules
CFRP	carbon fibre reinforced plastic
CFS	Central Flying School WW1 (Upavon UK); central forecasting station; contract field services; cubic feet per second
CFSG	Cometary Feasibility Study Group ESRO
CFSR	contract food status report
CFSTI	Clearinghouse for Federal Scientific and Technical Information
CFT	constant fraction trigger; contract field technician
cft	cubic feet; craft
CFTD	constant fraction timing discriminator
cftmn	craftsman
CFTS	Canadian Forces Training System (Trenton, Ontario)
CFTH	Canadian Forces Training Thomson-CSF
CFU	control functional unit (data link); current file user
CFV	cavalry fighting vehicle
CFWIS	Central Fighter Weapons Instructor School
CFWS	Coordinated Federal Wage System
CG	Chaplain General; Consul General; Commissary General; Coast Guard; Commanding General; Captain of the Guard; Consultative Group (Nato) (east-west trade); centre of gravity; computer graphics; cargo glider (aircraft); cruiser, guided missiles (Nato); Phosgene (war gas)
C-G	Captain General
CG-4	cargo glider by Waco
CG-15	Hadrian, cargo glider by Waco
CGA	Coast Guard Academy; Coast Guard auxiliary (vessel); Compagnie Generale d'Automatisme
CGAB	Coast Guard air base
CGAC	Coast Guard Air Corps
CGADC	Commanding General Air Defence Command
CGAirFMFLant	Commanding General Air Fleet Marine Force Atlantic
CGAirFMFPac	Commanding General Air Fleet Marine Force Pacific
CGAS	Coast Guard air station

CGC   Coast Guard Cutter; cruiser, guided
        missile and command (Nato);
        Cadillac Gage Company (Warren
        Michigan)
CGCArC Commanding General, Continental Army
        Command
CGConARC Commanding General, Continental
        Army Command
CGD   Coast Guard District
CGds   The Coldstream Guards
CGE   certificate of general education;
        Canadian General Electric (Corp.);
        Compagnia Generale die Elettricita
        SPA (Milan IT)
CGen   Chaplain General
CGF   coast garrison force
CGFF   Commander Gurkha Field Force
CGFMFLant Commanding General, Fleet Marine
        Force Atlantic
CGFMFPac Commanding General, Fleet Marine
        Force Pacific
CGForTrpsFMFLant Commanding General, Force
        Troops, Fleet Marine
        Force Atlantic
CGForTrpsFMFPac Commanding General, Force
        Troops, Fleet Marine
        Force Pacific
CGG   Canadian Grenadier Guards
CGGCM   Coast Guard Good Conduct Medal
CGH   Cape of Good Hope; centre of gravity
        hook
CGI   chief gunnery instructor; chief
        ground instructor; corrugated
        galvanized iron; computer-genera-
        ted image (simulators)
CGIVS   computer-generated image visual
        system
CGL   Colt grenade launcher; centre of
        gravity limits
CGLanForTraComLant Commanding General,
        Landing Force Training
        Command Atlantic
CGLanForTraComPac Commanding General,
        Landing Force Training
        Command Pacific
CGLO   Commonwealth Geological Liaison
        Office
CGM   Conspicuous Gallantry Medal (RN)
CGM-13 Mace, ground-launched cruise missile
        by Martin
CGMAG   Commanding General Marine Aircraft
        Group
CGMarBrig Commanding General Marine Brigade
CGMAW   Commanding General Marine Aircraft
        Wing
CGMB   Commanding General Marine Base
CGN   cruiser, guided missile, nuclear-
        powered
cgo   cargo
CGOP   Coast Guard operating base

CGOS   Combat Gunnery Officers School
CGOU   Coast Guard Oceanographic Unit
CGP-200 tape cassette recorder by Uher
CGPS   Canadian Government Purchasing
        System
CGR   Coast Guard Reserve, Committee's
        General Report (Nato)
CGR-1020 Cossor ground-to-air radio,
        emergency radio VHF/UHF (RAF)
        by Cossor
CGRAM   clock generator random access
        memory
CGRM   Commandant General, Royal Marines;
        Commando Group, Royal Marines
CGRS   central gyro reference system
CGS   Chief of the General Staff; Court of
        General Sessions; Central Gunnery
        School; Coast and Geodetic Survey;
        centimetre, gramme, second
        (system); control guidance sub-
        system
C&GS   command and general staff; coast
        and geodetic survey
CGSAC   Commanding General Strategic Air
        Command
CGSB   Canadian Government Specifications
        Board
CGSC   Command and General Service/Staff
        College (Fort Leavenworth)
CGSThe Hague Chief of the General Staff,
        Netherlands
CGSE   centimetre gramme second electro-
        magnetic
CGT   capital gains tax
CGT-1148 Cossor ground teleprinter
        electronic teleprinter by Cossor
CGT-1054 Celtic, Cossor ground terminal,
        tactical message terminal by
        Cossor
CGTAC   Commanding General, Tactical Air
        Command
CGTS   Coast Guard Training Station
CGU   ceramic glazed units
CGUSAComZEur Commanding General US Army
        Communications Zone Europe
CGUSACDC Commanding General US Army Combat
        Development Command
CGUSAMC Commanding General US Army Material
        Command
CGUSArAl Commanding General US Army Alaska
CGUSArADCom Commanding General US Army Air
        Defense Command
CGUSArMC Commanding General US Army
        Material Command
CGUSConArC Commanding General US Continen-
        tal Army Command
CGYd   Coast Guard Yard
CH   Member of the Order of the Compan-
        ions of Honour; Captain of the
        Horse; cross hairs (sights);

CH   critical height (landing minimum);
            compass heading; ceiling height;
            Chain Home (WW2 UK radar early
            warning); combat helicopter;
            candle hour; central heating
Ch   Chaplain to the Forces (UK); Chief
ch   charge; chain; chart; check; chemi-
            cal; choke; channel
C&H   Curtis & Harvey
CH-3   combat helicopter by Sikorsky
CH-19   S-55, cargo helicopter by Sikorsky
            (USMC)
CH-26   anti-tank gun 57mm (SU)
CH-46   Sea Knight, naval helicopter by
            Boeing/Vertol
CH-37   Mojave, heavy transport helicopter
            by Sikorsky
CH-47   Chinook, transport helicopter by
            Boeing/Vertol
CH-53   S-65, Sea Stallion, heavy helicopter
            by Sikorsky
CH-54   Tarhe, Skycrane, heavy transport
            helicopter by Sikorsky
CHA   Committee of Heads of Administration
ChaCom   chain of command
Chaff   radar reflective foil for ECM
Chaffee   M-24, recce tank by Cadillac
ChaffRoc   naval chaff and other decoy
            launching rocket
CHAG   compact high-performance aerial gun
            30mm by Ford, ---GAU-8;
            chain arrester gear
Chain-Gun   XM-230, XM-242, 30mm electric-
            motor driven gun by Hughes
Chain Home radar early warning system WW2
            (UK) Chain Home Low,
            Chain Home Extra Low
Challenger FV-4030/3 main battle tank by
            Vickers; twin jet by Canadair
Chamois Flir tank night vision system by
            SAT
CHAMPION   compatible hardware and milestone
            programme for integrating organi-
            zational needs (US)
CHAMPUS   civilian health and medical pro-
            gramme of the United States
Chan   Channel and Southern North Sea
            (Nato)
ChanCom   Channel Committee (Nato); Channel
            Command (Nato)
CHANCOMTEE Channel Committee (Nato)
Channel Hunter minesweepers (Nato project)
ChanSec   Channel Committee Secretary
            ISC informal staff communication
            ISL informal staff letter
            ISM informal staff memo
Chap   Chaplain; Chapparral (missile) (US)
Chapaev   class, 15000 ton cruisers (SU)
ChapGen   Chaplain General
CHAPI   (three) colour helicopter approach
            path indicator (UK)

Chapparral MIM-72, SHORADS, short-range
            air defence system (missile)
            by Ford
char   character
CharGuid   character guidance
Chariot   CCE-2, swimmer delivery vehicle WW2
            (RN); tank (Israel)
Charioteer tank destroyer (UK)
Charles F Adams class, destroyers guided
            missiles (DDG-USN)
Charleston class, amphibious cargo ships
            AKA (USN)
CHARM   Civil Aeronautics Agency high-alti-
            tude remote monitoring
CHART   Clearing House for Augmenting Resour-
            ces for Training
ChAvMainTech chief aviation maintenance
            technician
CHB   cargo handling battalion
ChB   Chief of the Bureau (USN)
ChBAer   Chief of the Bureau of Aeronautics
ChBDocks   Chief of the Bureau of Yards and
            Docks
ChBMed   Chief of the Bureau of Medicine and
            Surgery
ChBOrd   Chief of the Bureau of Ordnance
ChBPers   Chief of the Bureau of Naval
            Personnel
ChBSandA   Chief of the Bureau of Supplies
            and Accounts
ChBShips   Chief of the Bureau of Ships
ChBWeps   Chief of the Bureau of Weapons
ChBosn   Chief Boatswain
ChC   Chaplain Corps
CHC   cartridge head clearance; choke coil
ChCarp   chief carpenter
ChCk   chief cook
ChClk   chief clerk
ChCom   chain of command (reporting system)
CHD   correctional holding detachment;
            coronary heart disease
ChDLG   Chief, Defence Liaison Group
            Indo Indonesia
ChE   chief engineer; chemical engineer
CHE   cargo handling equipment
Cheetah   tracked armoured personnel carrier
            by Krauss-Maffei; helicopter by
            HAL; combat support vehicle by
            Teledyne Continental
Checkov   target tracking radar for anti-
            ballistic missiles (SU)
ChElec   chief electrician
ChElecTech chief electronics technician
chem   chemical
ChemE   chemical engineer
ChemBomb   chemical bomb
Chemitek   explosive residue collecting and
            analysis system by SAS
ChemWar   chemical warfare
Chenilette tracked machine gun carrier WW2
            by Renault

Cherokee   jeep (US)
Cheyenne   AH-56, combat helicopter by Lock-
           heed
ChF   Chaplain to the Fleet
chf   chief
CHF   critical heat flux
ChfTech   chief technician
ch/fwd   charges forward
chg   charge, change
CHG   cruiser, helicopter, guided missiles
           (Nato)
ChGun   chief gunner
Chicksaw   H-19, S-55, transport helicopter
           by Sikorsky
ChiCom   Chinese Communist
Chieftain main battle tank (UK) 1965;
           commuter aircraft by Piper
Chikugo   class, frigates (JMSDF)
CHIL   consolidated hazardous items list
ChiNat   Chinese Nationalist
ChInfo   chief of information
Chinook   CH-47, medium transport helicopter
           by Boeing/Vertol
CHIP   (Allied Command) Channel Intelli-
           gence Plan
Chip   miniature computer part (EPROM)
Chipmunk   light trainer aircraft (UK)
ChkPt   check point
CHL   Chain Home Low early warning radar
           WW2 (UK), confinement at hard
           labour
chlo   chloride, chloroform
Chm   chairman
ChMach   chief machinist
ChMEDT   Chief, military equipment delivery
           team
           Bur Burma
Chmn   chairman
ChNavAirshipTra Chief of Naval Airship
           Training
ChNavCom   Chief of Naval Communications
ChNavMat   Chief of Naval Material
ChNavMis   Chief of US Naval Mission
ChNavSecMAAG Chief, Naval Section, Military
           Assistance Advisory Group
CHNI   combat helmet Northern Ireland (UK)
Chobham-armour composite armour by ROF
           (Chobham)
ChoD   Chief of Defence
ChofF   Chaplain of the Fleet
CHOL   common high-order language
           (computers)
ChOp   change of operational control (Nato)
ChOPln   change of my operation plan
ChOrd   change of my operation order
CHORI   Chief of Office of Research and
           Inventions
CHPL   civil helicopter pilot licence
ChPClk   chief pay clerk
ChPhar   chief pharmacist

ChPhot   chief photographer
CHQ   Commonwealth Headquarters; corps
           headquarters; company headquarters
chq   cheque
ChREle   chief radio electrician
Chrm   chairman
chron   chronicle; chronology
CHS   Canadian Hydrographic Service
ChSClk   chief ship's clerk
ChSked   change of my operation schedule
ChSkr   chief skipper
ChSupClk   chief supply clerk
Cht   chemist
CHT   cylinder head temperature; cyclo-
           hepta-triene (laser)
ChTemp   charge temperature
ChTorp   chief torpedoman
CHU   centigrade heat unit
Chukar   MQM-74, propeller-driven target
           drone by Northrop
ChUM   chart updating manual
Chunnel   Channel Tunnel (project) (UK)
Churchill flame-thrower WW2; main battle
           tank WW2; Twaby Ark AVLB WW2
chute   parachute
ChV   check valve
CHW   constant hot water
CI   Imperial Order of the Crown of India;
           corps instructions; Commerce Inter-
           national SA (Brussels); concealed
           installation; counter-intelligence;
           counter-insurgency; configuration
           item; chief inspector; chief
           instructor; cost inspector;
           Channel Islands; Chemical Inspec-
           torate; consular invoice; compres-
           sion ignition; cast iron; corruga-
           ted iron; colour index; call indi-
           cator; configuration inspection
C^2I command, control and identification
C^3I communications, command, control and
           identification
C^4I command, control, communication,
           computation and identification
C&I   commercial and industrial
CIA   chief inspector of accidents; chief
           inspecting armourer; chief inspect-
           ing artificer; Chief Inspector of
           Armaments; Central Intelligence
           Agency; certified internal auditor
CIAA   Coordinator of Inter-American Affairs
Ciacio-S   active/passive acoustic homing
           torpedo head by Selenia
CIAP   climatic impact assessment plan;
           Comité International de l'Alliance
           pour le Progrès (International
           Committee for the Alliance for
           Progress)
CIAS   Conference of Independent African
           States

CIB   combat information bureau; command information bureau; criminal investigation branch; central intelligence board; combat infantryman's badge; controllable interface box

C&IB   curriculum and instruction branch

CIBS   CERN/IHEP Boston spectrometer

CIC   Counter-Intelligence Corps; combat information centre; combat intelligence centre; civil internment camp; criminal investigation court; customer identification code; combat intercept control; Combined Intelligence Committee; content indication code; Commonwealth Information Centre; Commander in Chief; command information centre; Critical Issues Council; communication intelligence channel

CICR   Conférence Internationale de la Croix Rouge (International Red Cross Conference)

CICRIS   Cooperative Industrial and Commercial Reference and Information Service

CICS   Committee for Index Cards for Standards; customer information control system

CID   Criminal Investigation Department; Committee for Imperial Defence; command information division; combat information and detection; charge injection device; Council for Industrial Design; change in design

CIDA   current input differential amplifier

CIDB   communications intelligence data base

CiDCon   civil disturbance (readiness) condition

CiDeRe   civil defence report

CIDG   civilian irregular defence group (RVN)

CIDIN   common ICAO data interchange network

CIDNO   contractor's identification number

CIDNP   chemically induced dynamic nuclear polarization

CIDST   Committee for Information and Documentation of Science and Technology (UK)

CIDP   Confédération Internationale pour la Désarmament et la Paix (International Confederation for Disarmament and Peace)

CiDStat   civil disturbance status report

CIE   Companion of the Most Eminent Order of the Indian Empire; compression ignition engine

CIEM   Conseil International pour l'Exploitation de la Mer (International Council for the Exploration of the Sea)

Cierva   autogyro aircraft (Spain) 1924

CIF   central issue facility; cost, insurance, freight

CIFE   central index file - Europe

CIF&C   cost, insurance, freight and commission

CIF&I   cost, insurance, freight and interest

CIFLT   cost, insurance, freight London terms

CIFRR   common instrument flight rules room

CIFV   Chief of Fighting Vehicles

CIG   central intelligence group (US); current intelligence group (Nato); computer image generation; cyrogenic in-ground

cig   ceiling

CIGMA   Centre International de Gestion du Materiel du Breguet Atlantique (International Centre for Handling Atlantic (aircraft) equipment)

CIGS   Chief of the Imperial General Staff

CII   commonality, interchangeability and interoperability (concept) (Nato); Compagnie Internationale pour l'Informatique (FR)

CIIA   Canadian Institute of International Affairs

CIJ   Cour Internationale de Justice (International Court of Justice)

CIL   Canadian Industries Ltd

CILAS   Compagnie Industrielle du Lasers (F-91400 Marcoussis)

CILSA   Chief Inspector of Land Service Ammunition

CIM   Channel Islands Militia; combination influence mine; computer interface module

CIMAS   continuous iron making and steel making

Cimbeline   mortar locating radar by EMI

CIME   Comité Inter-gouvernemental pour la Migration Européenne (Intergovernmental Committee for European Migration)

CiMiC   civilian-military cooperation

CIMS   civilian information management system; communications instructions for merchant ships

CIMSA   Compagnie Informatique Militaire Spatiale et Aeronautique (Thomson daughter) (1) Avenue de l'europe F-78141 Velizy)

CIMT   Chief Inspector of Mechanical Transport

CINA   Commission Internationale de la
        Navigation Aerienne (International
        Air Navigation Commission)
CinC   commander in chief
CinCAF commander in chief Allied Forces WW2;
        commander in chief Asiatic Fleet
        WW2
CinCAFE commander in chief Air Forces
        Europe (Nato)
CinCAFLant commander in chief US Air Forces
        Atlantic
CinCAFMed commander in chief Allied Forces
        Mediterranean (Nato)
CinCAFPac commander in chief US Army Forces
        Pacific WW2
CinCAFStrike commander in chief US Army
        Forces Strike
CinCAirCent commander in chief Allied Air
        Forces Central Europe
CinCAirEastLant commander in chief Allied
        Air Forces Eastern
        Atlantic Area (Nato)
CinCAl commander in chief Alaska
CinCarib commander in chief Caribbean
CinCArLant commander in chief US Army
        Forces Atlantic
CinCArStrike commander in chief US Army
        Forces Strike
CinCA&WI commander in chief Atlantic and
        West Indies
CinCAWI commander in chief American West
        Indies Stations
CinCBomber Command commander in chief (RAF)
CinCBPF commander in chief British Pacific
        Fleet WW2
CinCCoastalCommand commander in chief (RAF)
CinCEastLant commander in chief East
        Atlantic Area (Northwood UK)
CinCent commander in chief Allied Forces
        Central Europe (Brunssum)
CinCEur commander in chief US Forces in
        Europe, ---USCinCEur
CinCFE commander in chief US Forces Far East
        Command
CinCFighter Command commander in chief (RAF)
CinCFlt commander in chief Fleet (RN)
CINCH compact inertial navigator combined
        with head-up display by Marconi
CinChan Commander in Chief Channel and
        Southern North Sea (Nato)
CinCHF commander in chief Home Fleet (RN)
CinCHomeFlt commander in chief Home Fleet
        (RN)
CinCIberLant commander in chief Iberian
        Atlantic Area (Nato)
CinCLant commander in chief Atlantic Fleet
        (RN)
CinCLantFlt commander in chief Atlantic
        Fleet (USN-Nato)
CinCMAirChan commander in chief Allied Mari-
        time Air Channel (Nato)

CinCMEAF commander in chief Middle East
        Air Forces
CinCMEAFSA commander in chief Middle East,
        South Asia and Africa South of
        the Sahara (US)
CinCMed commander in chief Mediterranean
        (USN-Nato); commander in chief
        British Naval Forces in the
        Mediterranean
CinCMELF commander in chief Middle East
        Land Forces
CinCNE commander in chief North East
        Command
CinCNeFE commander in chief Netherlands
        Forces in the East WW2
CinCNELM commander in chief Naval Forces
        Eastern Atlantic and Mediter-
        ranean (USN-Nato)
CinCNethHome commander in chief Netherlands
        Home Station
CinCNORAD commander in chief North American
        Air Defense Command
CinCNorth commander in chief Allied Forces
        Northern Europe (Kolsaas
        Norway)
CinConAD commander in chief Continental Air
        Defence Command
CinCPac commander in chief Pacific Fleet
        (RN)
CinCPacAF commander in chief Pacific Air
        Forces (US)
CinCPac-CinCPOA commander in chief US
        Pacific Fleet and Pacific
        Ocean Area
CinCPacFlt commander in chief Pacific Fleet
        (USN)
CinCPacHedPearl commander in chief US
        Pacific Fleet Headquar-
        ters Pearl Harbour
CinCPacRep commander in chief Pacific Rep-
        resentative (US)
        M-BI Marianas-Bonin Islands
        Phil Philippines
CinCPOA commander in chief Pacific Ocean
        Area
CinCRDAF commander in chief Royal Danish
        Air Force (Nato)
CinCRDN commander in chief Royal Danish
        Navy (Nato)
CinCRNAF commander in chief Royal Norwegian
        Air Force (Nato)
CinCRNorN commander in chief Royal Norwegian
        Norwegian Navy (Nato)
CinCSA commander in chief South Atlantic
        (RN)
CinCSAC commander in chief Strategic Air
        Command
CinCSouth commander in chief Allied Forces
        Southern Europe (Naples IT)
        (Nato)

CinCSpeComME   commander in chief Specified
              Command Middle East
CinCStrike   commander in chief US Strike
             Command
CinCUNC   commander in chief United Nations
          Command
CinCUS   commander in chief USN Fleet WW2,
         US Command (Nato)
CinCUSAFE   commander in chief US Air Forces
            Europe
CinCUSArEur   commander in chief US Army
              Europe
CinCUSArPac   commander in chief US Army
              Pacific
CinCUSNavEur   commander in chief US Naval
               Forces Europe
CinCWestLand   commander in chief Western
               Atlantic Area (Norfolk)
               (Nato)
CINECA   Cooperative Investigation of the Nato
         of the Eastern Central Atlantic
CInfo   Chief of Information (USN)
CINO   Chief Inspector of Naval Ordnance
c-insgcy   counter-insurgency
CINTAC-4   naval intercommunications system
           by Redifon
CIntC   Canadian Intelligence Corps
CIO   combat information officer; combat
      intelligence officer; command
      issuing office
CIOCS   communications input/output control
        system
CIOM   communications input/output multi-
       plexer
CIOMR   Confédération des Officiers Medicaux
        de Réserve International (Federa-
        tion of Medical Reserve Officers)
CIOR   Confédération Interallies des
       Officiers de Réserve (Inter-allied
       Confederation of Reserve Officers)
CIOS   Combined Intelligence Objectives
       Subcommittee; Combined Intelligence
       Operations Section
CIOT   international telegraph operation
       centre
CIOU   custom input/output unit
CIP   central information post; component
      improvement programme; common
      infrastructure programme (Nato);
      command information programme;
      consolidated intelligence pro-
      gramme; class improvement plan;
      combined instrument panel; combat
      intelligence plan (naval); civil
      institution programme
CIP-67   communication improvement programme
         (Nato) (secure directional radio
         system)
CIPA   Corrupt and Illegal Practices Act;
       Canadian Industrial Preparedness
       Association

CIPASH   Committee for International Pro-
         gramme in Atmospheric Sciences
         and Hydrology
CIPC   Combined Intelligence Priorities
       Committee (US-UK)
CiPhony   ciphered telephony
CIPR   corporate industrial preparedness
       representative
CIR   Compagnie Industrielle Radioelec-
      trique (Bundesgasse 17 CH-3000
      Bern); Canada India Reactor; cost
      information report; characteristic
      instants of restitution; Commis-
      sion on Industrial Relations;
      Council on Industrial Relations;
      Committee on Industrial Relations
cir   circle; circuit; circular; circum-
      ference
CIRA   Committee on International Reference
       Atmospheric; Centro Italiano de
       Ricera Aerospaziale
Circe   mine-hunting sonar by Thomson-CSF;
        class, mine-hunters
CircLtr   circular letter
CirEP   circular error probable
CIRES   communications instructions for
        reporting enemy sightings
CIRIA   Construction Industry Research and
        Information Agency
CIRIS   complete integrated reference
        instrumentation system
C/IRM   Commodities - Industrial raw mate-
        rials
CIRO   Consolidated Industrial Relations
       Office; Centre Inter-armées de
       Recherche Operationelle (Joint
       Operational Research Centre)
CIRSEA   Company Italian for Research and
         Development of Aerospace Equip-
         ment (Microtecnica, Oleodinamica,
         Secondo Mona, Magnaghi, Nardi,
         OMI)
CIRVIS   communications instructions for
         reporting vital intelligence
         sightings;- visual -
CIS   Centre for International Studies;
      Central Information Service;
      counter-information service;
      cost inspection service;
      cataloguing in source; Chartered
      Industries of Singapore
CISA   Canadian Industrial Safety Associa-
       tion
CISCO   construction information system,
        cost and operation
CI/SERE   counter-insurgency/survival,
          evasion, resistance, escape
CISET   Compagnia Italiana Servici Tecnici
        Spa
CISIR   Ceylon Institute of Scientific and
        Industrial Research

CISM   Conseil International du Sports Militaire (International Council for Military Sports)

CISSB   Civil Service Selection Board

CIST   Chief Inspector of Subsidized Transport

CIT   configuration identification table; compressor inlet temperature; compression in transit; California Institute of Technology (US); Cranfield Institute of Technology (UK); Convention Internationale des Télécommunication

cit   citizen; citation

cita   citation

Citation   jet aircraft VIP transport by Cessna

CITE   compression ignition and turbine engine (fuel); contractor independent technical effort

CITel   Committee for the Inter-American Telecommunications

CIU   central interpretation unit; control indicator unit

CIV   certificate issue voucher; City Imperial Volunteers

civ   civil; civilian

CivClo   civilian clothing

CivConf   civilian confinement

CivDef   civil defendent

CivE   civil engineering

CivEmp   civil employee

CivEngLab   civil engineering laboratory

Civ-M-MARP   Civilian-Mobilization-Manpower Allocation Requirements Plan (US)

CivPersInS   civilian personnel management information system

Civ-Sub   civilian substitution (programme) (US)

CIWS   Close-in weapon system (naval anti-aircraft turret Vulcan/Phalanx)

CJ   Chief Justice

CJ-800   tracked tractor (Yugoslavia)

CJA   Criminal Justice Act

CJCAE   Congress Joint Committee on Atomic Energy

CJCC   Commonwealth Joint Communications Committee

CJCS   Chairman, Joint Chiefs of Staff

CJS   Canadian Joint Staff

CJSATC   Cyprus Joint Service Adventure Training Centre (Dhekelia)

CJSW   Canadian Joint Staff Washington

CJTF   commander joint task force

CJTG   commander joint task group

CKD   completely knocked down

CKMTA   Cape Kennedy Missile Test Annex (NASA)

ckpt   cockpit

ckw   clockwise

CL   communication lieutenant; centre line; Canadian Legion; cable layer; cruiser, light (USN); core lokt (projectile); calendar line; craft loss; critical list; compiler language; cutter location; cut lengths; cable links; car load; chemi-luminescence; connecting lines; control leader; current layer; Cammel Laird & Co. Ltd (Birkenhead); Creusot-Loire (FR); Canadair Ltd (Montreal)

C&L   control and line

C/L   craft loss; circular letter

cl   class; classification; clearance; climb

CL-28   Argus, LRPA, long-range patrol aircraft by Canadair

CL-44   Skymaster, transport aircraft by Canadair

CL-51   truck by Lancia

CL-89   USD-501, surveillance drone by Canadair/Dornier

CL-100   class corvettes by DTCN

CL-215   amphibian aircraft by Canadair

CL-289   USD-502, surveillance drone by Canadair/Dornier

CLAA   cruiser, light anti-aircraft (Nato)

CLAC   Combined Liberated Areas Committee (US)

CLAFB   Classified List of Army Forms and Books

CLAG   computerized land/air game (simulation)

CLAM   chemical low-altitude missile (ramjet)

CLAMS   counter-measures launch and monitoring system (sub-launched anti-torpedo decoys)

Clansman   series of ground radio equipment (UK)

Claribel   GS-20, hostile fire indication radar by MESL

CLARITY   conciseness, lively details, action relationship, intelligence, talk, youthfulness (news features goal)

CLAS   China Lake Astronomical Society

clas   classified; classification

C-LAS   C-band light-weight acquisition system

CLASS   computer-based laboratory for automated school systems

Classic Fox   naval ELINT data processing system by GTE Sylvania

Claymore   mine (UK)

CLB   central land-board; crash locator beacon

CLBRP   cannon-launched beam-rider projectile by Ford/Northrop

CLC	Commonwealth Liaison Committee; central logic control; constant light compensation; course line computer; tactical command ship (USN)
CLD	constant level discriminator
cld	cloud; cancelled; coloured; cooled; cleared
CLCr	Communications Lieutenant Commander
CLCU	civil labour control unit
CLD	heavy recovery vehicle by Berliet
CLDC	ComSec logistic data centre (communications security)
CLE	Central Landing Establishment Ringway (UK); composite leading edge (Starlifter wings)
Clearscan	naval surveillance radar by Decca
CLES	Canadian Legion Educational Service; Comité de Liaison des Exposants de Satory (Liaison Committee for Satory Expositors)
CLF	Commander, landing force; combined landing force
CLFC	Commander Land Forces Cyprus (UK)
CLG	change to lower grade; light cruiser, guided missiles (Nato-USN)
CLGC	civilian labour group centre
CLGM	cruiser, light guided missiles (SSM+ SAM) (Nato)
CLGN	cruiser, light, guided missiles nuclear-powered (USN)
CLGP	cannon-launched guided projectile
CLGSO	civilian labour group special order
CLH	Croix de la Légion d'Honeur
CLI	command language interpreter
CLIFS	costs, life interchangeability function and safety
CLIN	contract line item number
ClipperBow	ocean monitoring satellite (US)
CLIRA	closed loop in-reactor assemblies
CLK	hunter-killer ship (USN)
clk	clerk; clock
clkw	clockwise
clkwz	clockwise
CLL	Chief of Legislative Liaison
cllr	councillor
clm	column
ClMA	clothing monetary allowance
CLMAS	China Lake Mutual Aid Society
CLN	Comité Logistique du NADGE (NADGE Logistics Committee)
clnc	clearance
CLO	central legal office; civil liaison office(r); command liaison officer; chief liaison officer
clo	clothing
CLOCE	contingency lines of communications Europe
CLOGE	Comité Liaison OTAN sur la Guerre

	Electronique (NATO Electronic Warfare Liaison Committee)
CLOS	command to line of sight (missiles)
CLR	Commando Light Regiment RA (Marines); converted leave rate; centre of lateral resistance; constant load rupture; computer language recorder; Code de Longue Référence (long reference number code)
clr	clear; colour; cooler
CLS	Central Landing School Ringway (UK) WW2; closed loop support; control and launch sub-systems
C/Ls	carrier landings
CLSA	cooperative logistics support arrangements
CLSC	ComSec logistics support centre (communications security)
clsd	closed
CLSS	combat logistic support system agreement (US-Germany)
CLSU	ComSec Logistic Support Unit (communications security)
CLSX	close loop support, extended
CLT	computer language translator
CLTE	commissioned loss to enlisted status (revocation of appointment) (US)
cltgl	climatological
CludActDat	include accounting data
CLUSA	Continental Limits of the USA
CM	Coronation Medal (UK); certified master; Court Martial; counter-measures; counter-mortar; Canadian Milita; Certificate of Merit; controlled minefield; command module; camera module; common mode; cross modulation; communications multiplexer; cruise missile; minelayer (Nato); Comité Militaire (Military Committee)
C-M	Council Memorandum (Nato)
C&M	construction and machining
cm	centimetre; central meridian; centre of mass
CM-60	gun/mortar 60mm by Brandt
CM-170	trainer aircraft Super Magister
CMA	controller of military accounts; corps maintenance area; court of military appeals; clothing maintenance allowance; civil-military affairs
CMA-734	airborne navigational aid VLF system by Canadian Marconi
CMAA	Chief Master-at-Arms
CMAB	clothing monetary allowance, basic
CMAC	Capital Military Assistance Command
CMAIIss	clothing monetary allowance, initial issue
CMAIWAC	clothing monetary allowance, initial, Women's Army Corps

CMAO	court martial appointing order
CMAS	clothing monetary allowance, standard
CMAT	Commonwealth Military Advisory Team (Ghana)
CMB	Central Medical Board; coastal motor boat; concrete median barrier
cmbd	combined
CMBG	Canadian Mechanized Brigade Group
CMBL	commercial bill of lading
cmbt	combat
CMC	Commandant, Marine Corps; Command Meteorological Centre; Chinese Maritime Customs; Combined Meteorological Committee (Canadian); Cheyenne Mountain Complex; command module computer; contact-making clock; coordinated manual controls; Canadian Marconi Company; Computer Machinery Company
CMCA	cruise missile carrier aircraft
CMCM	Chairman Military Committee Memorandum (Nato)
CMD	Capital Military District; contract management district; coupled mobility devices
Cmd	Command Paper 1919-56, command; commendation
CM&D	counter-measures and deception (EW)
cmdg	commanding
CMDN	catalog management data notification
Cmdr	Commander; Commodore
Cmdre	Commodore
Cmdt	Commandant
CMEA	Council for Mutual Economic Assistance
CMET	Council on Middle East Trade
CMF	Canadian Military Forces; Central Mediterranean Forces; career management field; court martial forfeiture; Commonwealth Military Forces; Ceylon Military Forces; Citizen Military Forces (Australian Army Reserve); coherent memory filter
CMG	composite maintenance group; Corps maintenance group; computer management group; Companion of the Most Distinguished Order of St Michael and St George (UK); Congress Medal for Gallantry (US); Chief Marine Gunner; control moment gyroscopes (Skylab)
CMG-2	Colt Machine gun 5.56mm
CMH	combined military hospital; Centre of Military History; Congressional Medal of Honor
CMHQ	Canadian Military Headquarters
CMI	cruise missile interception (aircraft); computer manager instruction

CMIA	command management inventory accounting
CMIC	Communications and Mission Integration Centre (ASW Edinburgh South Australia)
CMIF	career management individual file
CML	Coffret à Message Local (local message box); current mode logic; coastal mine layer
cml	chemical; commercial
CmlOps	chemical operations
CMM	Commander of the Order of Military Merit (Canada); Chuong My Medal (US-Viet Nam); computerized modular monitoring; control maintenance management; Commission for Maritime Meteorology WMO; coordinated measuring machines
CMMA	clothing monetary maintenance allowance
CMME	command maintenance management evaluations
CMMG	civil manpower management guides (US)
CMMI	civil manpower management instructions
CMML	civil manpower management letters
CMMR	confirmed and made matter of record
CMN	Canadian Merchant Navy; Constructions Mécaniques de Normandie
cmn	commission
Cmnd	Command Paper 1956-
CNES	Centre National d'Etudes Spatiales (National Space Centre) (Toulouse)
Cmnr	commissioner
CMO	Chief Medical Officer; Controlled Materials Officer; Court Martial Officer; confidential monthly order; civil-military operations; minelayer, ocean (Nato)
CMOS	complementary metal-oxide semiconductor
CMOS/SOS	complementary metal-oxide semiconductor silicon-on-sapphire
CMP	civilian medical personnel; Corps of Military Police (UK) --CRMP; controlled materials plan; Commissioner of the Metropolitan Police; command module pilot; cost of maintaining project; Common Module Programme (UK-IR) (components); Conseil Mondial de la Paix (World Peace Council)
CmpCtr	computer centre
cmpd	compounded
CMPF	central meat processing facility
CMPI	civilian marine personnel instructions
cmps	centimetres per second
cmpt	computer; computation

CMR configuration management review; common mode rejection; court martial reports; Cape Mounted Rifles Rgt; communications moon relay

CMRI command maintenance readiness inspection

CMRR common mode rejection rate

CMRST Committee on Manpower Resources for Science and Technology

CMS central material service; coastal mine-sweeper; Centre for Measurement of Science; Cambridge monitor system; Ca-Mg-Silicate

CMS-27 military computer language

CMSC Corps of Military Staff Clerks

CMSER Commission of Marine Science Engineering and Resources

CMSgt Chief Master Sergeant

CM/SM command module/service module (NASA)

CMT corrected mean temperature; cadmium mercury telluride

cmt cement; comment

CMTC Citizens' Military Training Corps (US); Combined Military Transportation Committee; coupled monostable trigger circuit

CMU computer memory unit

CMV common mode voltage; contact-making voltmeter

CMY civil man-years

CN chloro-aceto-phenone (Chemical Mace tear gas); cellulose-nitrate (celluloid); cascade nozzle

C/N consignment note; contract note; circular note; credit note; cover note

CN-120 armour-piercing arrow-type shot 120mm (FR)

CNA Centre for Naval Analysis; code not allocated; commander's narrative analysis; Canadian Northwest Atlantic (Force); Chief of Naval Air (Forces); Canadian Nuclear Association; cosmic noise absorption

CNAAdTra Chief of Naval Air Advanced Training

CNAB Commander Naval Air Bases

CNABaTra Chief of Naval Air Basic Training

CNAD Conference of National Armaments Directors (Nato)

CNAF Chinese Nationalist Air Force

CNAIntermTra Chief of Naval Air Intermediate Training

CNAIT Chief of Naval Air Intermediate Training

CNAL Commander Naval Air Force Atlantic

CNAO combined naval air operation

CNAOpTra Chief of Naval Air Operational Training

CNAOT Chief of Naval Air Operational Training

CNAP Commander Naval Air Force Pacific

CNAPrimTra Chief of Naval Air Primary Training

CNAPT Chief of Naval Air Primary Training

CNAResTra Chief of Naval Air Reserve Training

CNAS Chief of Naval Air Services

CNAT Chief of Naval Air Training

CNATE Chief of Naval Airship Training and Experimentation

CNATecLTA Commander, Naval Air Technical Training, lighter-than-air

CNATechTra Chief of Naval Air Technical Training

CNATra Chief of Naval Air Training

CNATT Chief of Naval Air Technical Training

CNB Canadian Naval Board, Commander Naval Base

CNC Chief Naval Censor; Chief of Naval Communications; change notice card; computer numerically controlled

CN-CA cellulose nitrate/cellulose acetate

CNCE TSQ-111, communications nodal control element TRI-TAC by Martin-Marietta

cncl council

cnclr councillor

CNCS Central Navigation Control School

CND Chief of Naval Development; campaign for nuclear disarmament

CNDC Canadian National Defence College

CNDI commercial non-development items

CNDO Chief Navy Disbursing Officer

CNDRD Canadian National Defence Research Department

CNE compare numeric equal; Chantiers Navals de l'Estrel

CNEAF Commander of Northern European Air Forces

CNEGF Commander of Northern European Ground Forces

CNEngO Chief Naval Engineering Officer

CNEO Chief Naval Engineer Officer

CNES Centre National d'Etudes Spatiales (National Space Research Centre (Toulouse); Comité National d'Etudes Spatiales (National Space Research Committee)

CNESF Commander of the Northern European Sea Forces

CNEXO Centre National pour l'Exploration des Oceans (Paris) (National Ocean Exploration Centre)

CNF central NOTAMS facility (notice to airmen)

CNG Commander Northern Group; compressed natural gas

CNGB	Chief National Guard Bureau
CNI	Chief of Naval Intelligence; Chief of Naval Information; communication, navigation, identification (system avionics); communication, navigation, information
CNIM	Constructions Navales et Industrielles de la Méditerrané
CNIS	Channel navigation information system
CNJA	Chief Naval Judge Advocate
cnl	cancel; cancellation
CNL	Cantieri Navali Liguri (IT)
CNM	Chief of Naval Material
CNMO	Canadian Naval Missions Overseas
CNO	Chief of Naval Operations
CNOB	Commander Naval Operating Base
CNP	Chief of Naval Personnel; celestial north pole
CNR	Chief of Naval Research; civil nursing reserve; changes to Navy regulations; carrier-to-noise ratio; composite noise rating; combat net radio; Cantieri Navali Riuniti (Genoa IT)
CNRS	Centre National de la Recherche Scientifique (National Centre for Scientific Research)
CNS	Canadian Naval Service; Chief of the Naval Staff; central navigation school
CNSA	Chief of the National Security Agency
CNSG	consolidated nuclear steam generator
CNSSO	Chief Naval Supply and Secretariat Officer
CNSTheHague	Chief, Navy Staff, Netherlands
CNSTurkey	Chief, Navy Staff, Turkey
cntclkwz	counter-clockwise
cntr	container
cntrf	centrifugal
CNTS	Chief of Naval Transportation Service
CNU	compare numeric unequal
CNWDI	critical nuclear weapons design information
CO	commanding officer; control officer; communications officer; clerical officer; chief officer; conscientious objector; change order; combined operations; commando operations; Colonial Office, since 1966: Commonwealth Office; Crown Office; Criminal Office; crystal oscillator
co	corps; county; company
COA	commanding officer area; controller of ordnance accounting; current operating allowances; change of assignment; Centre OTAN d'Approvisionement (Nato Procurement Centre)
COAA	Centre d'Operations Anti-aeriennes (Anti-air Operations Centre)
COAC	Commanding Officer Atlantic Coast
COAD	command and administrative data system
COAirEvacRon	Commanding Officer Air Evacuation Squadron
COAM	customer-owned and maintained
COAMP	cost analysis and maintenance programme
COAR	Centre d'Operations Aeriennes Régional (Regional Air Operations Centre)
Coastguarder	HS-748, maritime patrol aircraft by HS
COAT	correct outside air temperature
COB	close of business; command operating budget; Committee of Combined Boards; Collocated Operating Bases (Nato Air Forces)
COBB	combined operations bombardment battery
COBE	Commander of the Most Excellent Order of the British Empire
COBELDA	integrated fire control system by SABCA
COBOL	common business-oriented language (computer)
Cobra	diesel-electric APC by ACEC; fire suppression system (UK); AH-15, Huey Cobra, helicopter by Bell
Cobra-2000	Bo-810, anti-tank guided weapon by MBB
CobraBall	airborne laser/radar tracking system
CobraDane	FPS-108, satellite and ICBM tracking radar by Raytheon
CobraJudy	naval phased array radar (USN-USAF)
COBTU	combined over-the-beach terminal unit
COC	combined operations command; combat operations centre; Chief of Chaplains; certificate of competency; Corps of Commissionaires
COCEEE	Committee on captured enemy electronic equipment
$COCl_2$	Phosgene (war gas)
COCO	contractor-owned contractor-operated
CoCom	Coordinating Committee (on East-West Trade) (Nato Paris)
COCOS	Chief of combined operations
COD	Central Ordnance Depot (UK); composite ordnance depot; cash on delivery; collect on delivery; carrier on-board delivery (aircraft) naval; clean out door; chemical oxygen demand

CODA	Centre d'Opérations de Défense Aerienne (air defence operations centre)
CODAG	combined diesels and gas turbines
CodAn	coded analysis (weather)
CODAP	Comprehensive occupational data analysis programme
CODAR	correlation display analysing and recording
CoDaSyL	Conference on Data Systems Languages
CoData	Standing Committee for Data on Science and Technology
CODCAVE	Committee on Decentralization of Controls after V-E-Day (US)
Coddress	coded address
CoDef	Chairman of the Defence Committee (Nato)
CodeJ	Code de Justification
CoDES	computer design and evaluation system
CoDiPhase	coherent digital phased array system
CODIS	coded discharge; controlled digital simulator
CODOG	combined diesel or gas turbines
CODOT	classification of occupations and directory of occupational titles
Codress	coded address
CODSNorway	Chief of the Defence Staff, Norway
COE	Corps of Engineers; Chief of Engineers; certificate of eligibility
COEA	cost and operational effectiveness analysis
COEC	CONAD operational employment concept (Continental Air Defence Command); Council Operations and Exercises Committee (Nato)
COECWG	Council Operations and Exercises Committee Working Group (Nato)
COED	computer operated electronic display
coeff	coefficient
CoEnCo	Committee for Environmental Conservation
COESA	Committee on Extension to the Standard Atmosphere
COEV	Canadian Ocean Escort Vessel
CoF	Captain of the Fleet
COF	correct operation factor
CofA	certificate of airworthiness
CofC	coefficient of correlation
CofE	Church of England; coefficient of elasticity
CofF	Chaplain of the Fleet; Chief of Finance; coefficient of friction
Coff	cut off
CofG	convenience of government; centre of gravity

CofI	court of inquiry
CofM	correction of the moment
CofO	Chief of Ordnance
CofR	commencement of rifling
COFRAS	Compagnie Française d'Assistance Specialisée (arms trade) (Paris)
CoFron	coastal frontier
CofS	Church of Scotland, Chief of Staff; condition of service
CofSA	Chief of Staff US Army
CofSAF	Chief of Staff US Air Force
CofT	Chief of Transportation
CoFT	Commander Fleet Train
COG	centre of gravity; course over the ground; Centre d'Opérations de Groupe (battalion operations centre); convenience of government
COGAG	combined gasturbine and gasturbine
COGB	certified official government business
COGD	circular outlet gas duct
COGOG	combined gasturbine or gasturbine
COGS	continuous orbital guidance system
COGSA	carriage of goods by sea act
COH	combined operations headquarters
COHQ	combined operations headquarters
COHO	coherent (pulse) oscillator
COI	Central Office of Information; communication operation instructions; cooperative for information OSS-CIA; course of instruction
COIC	combined operational intelligence centre; Canadian Oceanographic Identification Centre
COID	Council on Industrial Design
CoIn	counter-insurgency (operations); counter-intelligence (service)
COINS	Committee on Improvement of National Statistics
CoInt	commands interested (mailing)
COJO	Conference of Jewish Organizations
Col	Colonel; colonial; collective (ranging); column
COL	computer oriented language
COLA	cost of living allowance
COLAC	Central Organization of Liaison of Allocation of Circuits
CoLanForASCU	Commanding Officer, Landing Force Air Support Control Unit
COLB	cost of living bonus
ColComd	Colonel Commandant
Cold	(cold crew) nuclear powerd submarine (USN)
cold	coloured
ColdmGds	Coldstream Guards (UK)
Colibri	ESM equipment for anti-tank helicopters (warning receiver) by Elettronica

COLIDAR   coherent light detection and
          ranging
ColinCh   Colonel in Chief
CollSta   (casualties) collecting station
colm   column (US)
ColmGP   column gap
coln   column (UK)
COLOS   command off the line of sight
          (missiles)
COLS   communications for on-line systems
ColSgt   Colour Sergeant
COLT   conventional on-line translator
Columbus vehicle mat by Columbus
COLY   City of London's Yeomanry
COM   computer output microfilm;
          commissioned officers' mess
Com   commander; Commonwealth; common;
          committee; commodore; commissioner;
          Communications (division) STC
COMA   Court of Military Appeals
ComAAFCE Commander, Allied, Air Forces
          Central Europe
ComADC   Commander, Air Defence Command
ComAEWW   Commander airborne early warning
          wing
ComAFFor Commander Air Force forces
CoMaint   command maintenance
ComAir   commander, aircraft; Commander, Air
          Forces
ComAirBaltAp Commander, Allied Air Forces
          Baltic Approaches (Karup
          Denmark)
ComAirCanLant Air Commander, Canadian
          Atlantic Subarea (Nato)
ComAirCent Commander Allied Air Forces
          Central Europe (Nato)
ComAirCentLant Air Commander Central
          Atlantic Subarea (Nato)
ComAirChan Maritime Air Commander Channel
ComAirEastLant Air Commander Eastern Atlan-
          tic Area
ComAirLant Commander Allied Air Forces
          Atlantic (Nato); Commander Air
          Forces Atlantic Fleet (US)
ComAirNoN Commander, Allied Air Forces North
          Norway
ComAirNoreChan Air Commander North Channel
ComAirNorLant Air Commander North Atlantic
          Subarea (Nato)
ComAirNorth Commander, Allied Air Forces
          Northern Europe (Nato)
ComAirPlymChan Air Commander Plymouth
          Channel Subarea (Nato)
ComAirSoNor Commander, Allied Air Forces
          South Norway (Nato)
ComAirSouth Commander Allied Air Forces
          Southern Europe (Naples Nato)
ComAlAirC Commander, Alaskan Air Command
ComALFSouth Commander Allied Land Forces
          Southern Europe (Verona Nato)

ComALFSouth East Commander Allied Land
          Forces South East Europe
          (Izmir Nato)
ComAlSeaFron Commander Alaskan Sea Frontier
ComAMF(L) Commander ACE Mobile Force Land
          Component (Nato) (Allied
          Command Europe)
ComAntDefCom Commander Antilles Defence
          Command
ComAntarcticSuppAct Commander Antarctic
          Support Activities
          CASA
CoMarCasa Commander French Maritime Forces
          Morocco
ComArFor Commander Army Forces
CoMarRhin Commander Maritime Rhine
CoMART   Commander Marine Air Reserve Train-
          ing
ComASWFor Commander Anti-submarine Warfare
          Force
          Lant Atlantic
          Pac   Pacific
ComASWGru Commander Anti-submarine Warfare
          Group
ComAT   Commander Air Training
ComATF   Commander Amphibious Task Force
ComAtkCarAirWing Commander Attack Carrier
          Air Wing
ComAtkCarStrikeFor Commander Attack Carrier
          Striking Force
CoMATS   Commander Military Air Transport
          Service
comb   combined; combustible
combn   combustion
ComBaltAp Commander Allied Forces Baltic
          Approaches (Karup Denmark)
ComBarForLant Commander Barrier Forces
          Atlantic
ComBaseFrance Commander US Bases in France
ComBat   Commander of the US Battlefleet
Combat Angel AQM-34, chaff dispenser EW
          ECM
ComBatCruLant Commander Battleships/
          Cruisers Atlantic Fleet
Combat Dawn AQM-34Q, Firebee family RPV
          for electronic intelligence
Combat Grande Spanish national air defence
          system
Combattante class, I-III fast patrol boats,
          guided missiles (FR) by CMN
ComBeNeChan Commander, Belgian and Nether-
          lands Channel Subarea
ComBisLant Commander Bay of Biscay Atlantic
          Subarea
ComBlackBase Commander Black Sea Defence
          Sector
ComBosFort Commander Bosphorus Fortifica-
          tions
CombQuarForce Combined Quarantine Force
ComBrestChan Commander Brest Channel Sub-
          area

ComBritElbe   Commander British Naval Elbe
              Squadron
ComBritRhin   Commander British Naval Rhine
              Squadron
CombSecGS   Combat Section General Staff
ComCanLant   Commander Canadian Atlantic Sub-
             area
ComCaribSeaFron   Commander Caribbean Sea
                  Frontier
ComCarStrikFor   Commander Carrier Striking
                 Force
ComCarStrikGru   Commander Carrier Striking
                 Group
ComCBLant   Commander Construction Battalions
            Atlantic
ComCBPac   Commander Construction Battalions
           Pacific
ComCen   Communications Centre
ComCenSect   Commander Central Section
ComCentAG   Commander Central Army Group
            Europe (Nato)
ComCentLant   Commander Central Atlantic Sub-
              area
ComCherChan   Commander Cherbourg Channel
              Subarea
ComCM   communications counter-measures
ComCortDiv   Commander Escort Division
ComCortRon   Commander Escort Squadron
ComCosDiv   Commander Coastal Division
ComCosRon   Commander Coastal Squadron
ComCoSurFor   Commander Coastal Surveillance
              Force
ComCruDesLant   Commander Cruiser/Destroyer
                Force Atlantic
ComCruDesPac   Commander Cruiser/Destroyer
               Force Pacific
        ElecRep   Electronic Represen-
                  tative
        G&HRep   Gunnery and Hull
                 Representative
        MaintRep Maintenance Repre-
                 sentative
        MatRep   Material Representa-
                 tive
        PersRep   Personnel Represen-
                  tative
        SupRep   Supply Representa-
                 tive
        M&ERep   Machinery and Elec-
                 trical Representa-
                 tive
ComCruFor   Commander of the Cruiser Force
ComCruLant   Commander Cruisers Atlantic
comd   Commander (UK); commanding
ComD   Commander Destroyers
ComDWA   Commander Destroyers Western
         Approaches
ComDarFort   Commander Dardanelles Fortifica-
             tions
ComDesDevGru   Commander Destroyer Development
               Group

ComDesDiv   Commander Destroyer Division
ComDesFlot   Commander Destroyer Flotilla
ComDesGru   Commander Destroyer Group
ComDesRon   Commander Destroyer Squadron
ComDestr   Commander of the Destroyer Force
ComDev   Commonwealth Development Finance
         Company; Computing Devices Company
         (Ottawa) (Control Data Canada
         daughter)
comdg   commanding
Comdr   Commander
ComdSgtMaj   Command Sergeant Major
Comdt   Commandant
ComdtCoGard   Commandant Coast Guard
ComdtMCS   Commandant Marine Corps Schools
ComDWA   Commodore Destroyers Western
         Approaches
COME   Chief Ordnance Mechanical Engineer;
       Cultural Organization for the
       Middle East
ComEastConADReg   Commander Eastern Continen-
                  tal Air Defence Region
ComEastLant   Commander Eastern Atlantic
              Force
ComEastSeaFron   Commander Eastern Sea
                 Frontier
CoMECon   Council of Mutual Economic Coopera-
          tion with the USSR
COMED   Combined (moving) map and electronic
        display for aircraft by Ferranti
CoMedBase   Commander Mediterranean Defence
            Sector
CoMedCent   Commander Mediterranean Central
            Area
CoMedEast   Commander Mediterranean Eastern
            Area
CoMedNorEast   Commander Mediterranean North
               Eastern Area
CoMedOc   Commander Mediterranean Occidental
          (Western) Area
CoMedSouEast   Commander Mediterranean South
               Eastern Area
ComEight   Commandant Eighth Naval District
ComEleventh   Commandant Eleventh Naval
              District
COMESA   Committee on the Meteorological
         Effects of Stratospheric Aircraft
         (UK)
COMET   Council on Middle East Trade;
        Committee for Middle East Trade;
        computer-operated management eval-
        uation technique; CONUS Meteoro-
        logical Teletype (system); trans-
        port aircraft by deHavilland,
        tank (UK)
ComExDiv   Commander Experimental Division
ComExO   Committee for the Exploration of
         the Oceans
ComFAir   Commander Fleet Air
ComFAirELM   Commander Fleet Air Eastern
             Atlantic and Mediterranean

ComFAirWing   Commander Fleet Air Wing
ComFAirWingLant   Commander Fleet Air Wing
          Atlantic
ComFAirWingNorLant   Commander Fleet Air Wing
          North Atlantic
ComFAirWingsLant   Commander Fleet Air Wings
          Atlantic
ComFAirWingsPac   Commander Fleet Air Wings
          Pacific
ComFive   Commandant Fifth Naval District
ComFiveATAF   Commander Fifth Allied Tactical
          Air Force (Southern Europe
          Nato)
ComFldCom-DASA   Commander Field Command -
          Defence Atomic Support
          Agency
ComFleTraGru   Commander Fleet Training Group
ComFour   Commander Fourth Naval District
ComFourATAF   Commander Fourth Allied Tactical
          Air Force (Central Europe
          Nato)
ComFourteen   Commander Fourteenth Naval
          District
ComGen   Commanding General; Commissary
          General
ComGenEuCom   Commanding General European
          Command
ComGenMed   Commanding General US Army Medit-
          erranean Theatre WW2
ComGenPOA   Commanding General US Army Pacific
          Ocean Area WW2
ComGenTen   Commanding General Tenth US Army
ComGenThirdAir   Commanding General Third US
          Air Division
ComGenUSAFE   Commanding General US Air
          Forces Europe
ComGenUSArEur   Commanding General US Army
          Europe
ComGerNorSea   Commander German North Sea
          Subarea
ComGib   Naval Commander Gibraltar
ComGibLant   Commander Atlantic Approaches
          Gibraltar
ComGibMed   Commander Gibraltar Mediterranean
          Command
ComGrePat   Commander Greenland Patrol
ComGtmoSect   Commander Guantanamo Section
ComHawSeaFron   Commander Hawaiian Sea
          Frontier
ComIberLant   Commander Iberian Atlantic Area
          (Lisbon)
ComIceASWGru   Commander Iceland ASW Group
ComIceDeFor   Commander Iceland Defence Force
ComMidEastFor   Commander Middle East Force
ComIFSDiv   Commander Inshore Fire Support
          Division
CoMil   Chairman of the Military Committee
          (Nato)
COMilDept   Commanding Officer, Military
          Departments

CoMin   Commander Minecraft
CominCh   Commander in Chief
CoMinDiv   Commander Minecraft Division
CoMinFlot   Commander Minecraft Flotilla
ComInform   Communist Information Bureau 1947
CoMinGrp   Commander Mine Group
CoMinLant   Commander Minecraft Atlantic
CoMinPac   Commander Minecraft Pacific
ComInst   Communications Instructions
ComInt   Communications Intelligence
ComIntern   Communist International
CoMish   Congo (Military) Mission
COMIST   modernization of communications in
          the short term (Nato)
ComJam   communications jamming
ComJTF   Commander Joint Task Force
ComJUWaTF   Commander Joint Unconventional
          Warfare Task Force
ComKWest   Commander Key West
          EvDet   Test and Evaluation
          Detachment
          For   Force
coml   commercial
ComlAirAuth   commercial air travel is
          authorized
ComlAirDir   commercial air travel is
          directed
ComLandCent   Commander Allied Land Forces
          Central Europe
ComLanDenmark   Commander Allied Land Forces
          Denmark
ComLandFor   Commander Land Forces
ComLandJut   Commander Allied Land Forces
          Schleswig-Holstein and Jutland
          (Nato)
ComLandNoN   Commander Allied Land Forces
          North Norway
ComLandNorway   Commander Allied Land Forces
          Norway
ComLandSchleswig   Commander Allied Land
          Forces Schleswig-
          Holstein
ComLandSoNor   Commander Allied Land Forces
          South Norway
ComLandSouth   Commander Allied Land Forces
          South Europe
ComLandSouthEast   Commander Allied Land
          Forces South Eastern
          Europe
ComLandZealand   Commander Allied Land
          Forces Zealand
ComLanShipFlot   Commander Landing Ship
          Flotilla
ComLanShipRon   Commander Landing Ship
          Squadron
ComLantFltWpnRan   Commander Atlantic Fleet
          Weapons Range
ComLink   communications link
COMLO   Combined Operations Material Liaison
          Officer

ComLo   compass locator
ComLogNet   command logistics network;
          combat logistics network
ComLSTDiv   Commander landing ship tank
          division
comm   communications; commission
Comm   Department of Commerce (US)
CoMAirCentLant   Commander Maritime Air
          Forces Central Atlantic
          Subarea
ComMAirChan   Commander Allied Maritime Air
          Forces Channel (Nato)
ComMAirCentLant   Maritime Air Commander
          Central Atlantic Subarea
ComMAirEastLant   Commander Maritime Air
          Forces Eastern Atlantic
          Area
ComMAirGibLant   Commander Maritime Air
          Forces Gibraltar Subarea
ComMAirNoreChan   Commander Maritime Air
          Forces North Channel
          Subarea
ComMAirNorLant   Commander Maritime Air
          Forces Northern Atlantic
          Subarea
ComMAirPlymChan   Commander Maritime Air
          Forces Plymouth Channel
          Subarea
Commander   tractor for semi-trailers by
          Scammell (UK); jet aircraft by
          IAI
Commando   C-46 cargo aircraft WW2 by Curtiss;
          mortar 60mm by Thomson-Brandt;
          helicopter by Westland;
          amphibious armoured car by
          Cadillac-Gage; rapid interven-
          tion vehicle by Leyland;
          submachine gun 5.56mm by Colt
Commando   VI attack rubber boat with 60mm
          gun/mortar by Angeviniere
Commando   Ranger, 4x4 armoured personnel
          carrier by Cadillac-Gage
Commando   Scout, XM-966, 4x4 recce vehicle
          by CG
ComMarFor   Commander Marine Forces
CommBn   communications battalion
CommCen   communications centre
commd   commissioned
CommDet   commissioning detail
Commer   heavy truck (UK)
Commer/Unipower   10 tons 6x4 truck
commie   communist
Commiss   Commissary
comn   commission
Commo   Commodore
Commr   Commissioner
CommSta   communications station
ComTech   communications technician
commun   communications
commZ   communications zone

ComNASEA   Commodore Naval Air Stations
          East Africa
ComNATODefCol   Commandant NATO Defence
          College
ComNavAirLant   Commander US Naval Air Forces
          Atlantic
ComNavAirPac   Commander US Naval Air Forces
          Pacific
ComNavAirTransWing   Commander Naval Air
          Transport Wing
          Pac Pacific
ComNavBaltAp   Commander Allied Naval Forces
          Baltic Approaches (Karup
          Denmark)
ComNavBase   Commander Naval Base
ComNavBrem   Commander Bremen Naval Group
ComNavCAG   Commander Naval Forces Central
          Army Group Area and Bremerhaven
ComNavCent   Commander Allied Naval Forces
          Central Europe
ComNavEastLantMed   Commander US Naval Forces
          WW2 Eastern Atlantic
          and Mediterranean
ComNavFE   Commander US Naval Forces Far East
ComNavFor   Commander US Naval Forces
          Azores
          Ice   Iceland
          Japan
          Korea
          Marianas
          Phil   Philippines
          V   Viet Nam
ComNavGer   Commander US Naval Forces Germany
ComNavGerBalt   Commander German Naval Forces
          Baltic (Nato)
ComNavIdent   communication, navigation,
          identification (equipment)
ComNavNAW   Commander US Naval Forces North-
          west African Waters WW2
ComNavNoN   Commander Allied Naval Forces
          North Norway (Nato)
ComNavNorCent   Commander Naval Forces North-
          ern Area Central Europe
ComNavNorth   Commander Allied Naval Forces
          Northern Europe (Nato)
ComNavScAp   Commander Allied Naval Forces
          Scandinavian Approaches (Nato)
ComNavOpSuppGru   Commander Naval Operations
          Support Group (USN)
          Lant Atlantic
          Pac   Pacific
ComNavSoNor   Commander Allied Naval Forces
          South Norway (Nato)
ComNavSouth   Commander Allied Naval Forces
          Southern Europe (Naples Nato)
ComNavSuppFor   Commander Naval Support Force
          (USN)
ComNEastLant   Commander North East Atlantic
ComNine   Commander Ninth Naval District
ComNLonTEVDet   Commander New London Test and
          Evaluation Detachment

COMNO   Combined Office of Merchant Navy
            Operators
ComNoN   Commander Allied Forces North Norway
ComNoNor   Commander Allied Forces North
            Norway (Bodo Norway)
ComNorASDefLant   Commander North American
                Anti-submarine Defense
                Force Atlantic
ComNoreChan   Commander Nore Channel Subarea
ComNorLant   Commander Northern Atlantic
            Subarea
ComNorPac   Commander US Naval Forces Northern
            Pacific
ComNorSeaCent   Commander North Sea Subarea
                Central Europe
ComNorSect   Commander Northern Section
ComNorthAG   Commander Northern Army Group
            Europe
ComNorVATEVDet   Commander Norfolk VA Test
                and Evaluation Detachment
                (USN)
comnZ   communications Zone
COMO   commissioned officers' mess open
Como   Commodore
ComO   communications officer
ComOceanLant   Commander Oceanic Atlantic
                Subarea
ComOceanSys   Commander Oceanographic Systems
            Lant   Atlantic
            Pac   Pacific
ComOff   communications officer, commissioned
            officer
ComOne   Commandant First Naval District
ComOpConCen   Commander Operational Control
                Centre
ComOpTEVFor   Commander Operational Test and
            Evaluation Force
            Lant   Atlantic
            Pac   Pacific
ComOrTexGrp   Commander Orange Texas Group
                (Inactive Reserve Fleet
                Atlantic)
Comp   Comptroller of the Treasury;
            companion; composite; complement;
            comprehensive; computer; compass;
            compiler; compression; compound;
            composition; component
ComPac   Commonwealth Trans-Pacific Telephone
            Cable
ComPAC   computer Programme for Automatic
            control
Compack   light-weight satellite communica-
            tions terminal by Marconi
COMPACT   consolidation of military personnel
            activities; compatible algebraic
            compiler and translator
ComPaSect   Commander Panama Section
                CaribSeaFron
                WestSeaFron
COMPASS   computerized moving planning and

status system; computer-orientierte
            Methode für Planung und Ablauf-
            steuerung in Seehäfen (computer-
            oriented method for planning and
            control in ocean terminals)
CompassCope   YQM-94, long-range recce RPV
                by Boeing
CompassCope   R YQM-98A, long-range recce
                RPV by Teledyne Ryan
CompassDawn   electronic intelligence drone
                by Teledyne Ryan
CompassDwell   AQM-34, Firebee, electronic
                intelligence RPV by Teledyne
                Ryan
Compass Island   class, fast cargo ships
                (USN)
Compass Tie   ESM equipment for close support
                aircraft
ComPatFor   Commander Patrol Forces (USN)
Compatto   naval automatic gun by OM
ComPay   computer payroll
compet   competitive
CompEX   competitive evaluation exercise
CompGen   Comptroller General
ComPhibFor   Commander Amphibious Force
                Lant   Atlantic
                Pac   Pacific
ComPhibLant   Commander Amphibious Force US
                Atlantic Fleet
ComPlymChan   Commander Plymouth Channel
                Subarea
CompoRon   composite squadron
CompRon   composite squadron
Compt   Comptroller
Comptr   Comptroller
CompuScene   computer (generated) scene
                simulator by GE
COMRADE   computer-assisted design environment
ComRat(s)   commuted ration(s)
ComRedAtkCarAirWing   Commander Readiness
                    Attack Carrier Air
                    Wing
ComRel   community relations
ComRedDesRon   Commander Reserve Destroyer
                Squadron
ComRivDiv   Commander River Division
ComRivFlot   Commander River Flotilla
ComRivPatFor   Commander River Patrol Force
ComRivSuppRon   Commander River Support
                Squadron
ComRoute   Commander in Chief US Fleet Convoy
            and Routing Section WW2
ComSAMar   Commander Straits and Marmara
                Defence Sector
ComSaT   communications satellite; global
            commercial satellite
ComSat General   Communications Satellite
                Corporation (US),
                --Intelsat
ComSec   communications security

ComSec I   communications security course
        phase I
ComSecondFlt   Commander US second Fleet
COMSER   Commission on Marine Science and
        Engineering Research (UNO)
ComServFor   Commander USN Service Force
            Lant   Atlantic
            Pac   Pacific
            SoPacSubCom   South Pacific
            Subordinate Command
ComServLant   Commander Service Force Atlantic
        (USN)
ComServPac   Commander Service Force Pacific
        (USN)
            PetScol   Petroleum School
ComSeven   Commander Seventh Naval District
ComSix   Commander Sixth Naval District
ComSixATAF   Commander Sixth Allied Tactical
        Air Force, Southern Europe
        (Nato)
ComSixFlt   Commander Sixth US Fleet
comn   commission
ComSoLant   Commander South Atlantic Force
        (USN)
ComSoNor   Commander Allied Forces Southern
        Norway (Oslo Nato)
ComSoSect   Commander Southern Section
ComSOTFE   Commander Support Operations Task
        Force Europe
ComSqn   communications squadron (USMC)
COMSTAR   Commendation for Signals Transmit-
        ted Accurately and Rapidly (Nato)
ComStar   communication satellite by Hughes
ComStratResCent   Command Strategic Reserve
            Allied Land Forces
            Central Europe
ComStrikeFltLant   Commander Striking Fleet
            Atlantic
ComStrikFltLant   Commander Nato Striking
            Fleet Atlantic
ComStrickFLant   Commander Striking Fleet
            Atlantic
ComStrikFLantRepEur   Commander Striking
                Fleet Atlantic Repre-
                sentative in Europe
ComStrikForSouth   Commander Naval Striking
            and Support Forces
            Southern Europe
ComSTS   Commander Military Sea Transporta-
        tion Service
            FE   Far East
            Lant   Atlantic
            Pac   Pacific
ComSubACLant   Commander Submarines Allied
            Command Atlantic
ComSubDevGru   Commander Submarine Develop-
            ment Group
ComSubDiv   Commander Submarine Division
ComSubEastLant   Commander Submarine Forces
            Eastern Atlantic

ComSubFlot   Commander Submarine Flotilla
ComSubFronDef   Commander Sub-Frontier
            Defence
ComSubLant   Commander Submarine Forces
        Atlantic
ComSubPac   Commander Submarine Forces
        Pacific
ComSubMed   Commander Submarine Forces
        Mediterranean
ComSubMedNorEast   Commander Submarine Forces
            Mediterranean North East
ComSubRon   Commander Submarine Squadron
ComSubWestLant   Commander Submarine Force
            Western Atlantic Area
ComSuComLantFlt   Commander Subordinate
            Command US Atlantic Fleet
COMSUFRHIN   Commander French Rhine River
        Squadron
comsystr   commissary store
comt   commitment
ComTACGru   Commander Tactical Air Control
        Group
ComTACRon   Commander Tactical Air Control
        Squadron
ComTAFDen   Commander Tactical Air Force
        Denmark
ComTAFNorNor   Commander Tactical Air Force
            North Norway
ComTAFSoNor   Commander Tactical Air Force
            South Norway
ComTaiwanPatFor   Commander Taiwan Patrol
            Force
ComTaskForNoN   Commander Allied Task Force
            North Norway
CoMTBFlot   Commander Motor Torpedo Boat
        Flotilla
CoMTBRon   Commander Motor Torpedo Boat
        Squadron
CoMTBTraCen   Commander Motor Torpedo Boat
        Training Centre
ComTechRep   complementary technical report
ComThree   Commandant Third Naval District
ComThirteen   Commandant Thirteenth Naval
        District
ComTonGru   Commander Tongue Point Group
        (inactive Fleet Pacific Fleet)
ComTrainCarRonPac   Commander Carrier Train-
            ing Squadron Pacific
            Fleet
ComTraLant   Commander Training Force Atlantic
ComTraPac   Commander Training Force Pacific
ComTwelve   Commandant Twelfth Naval District
ComTwo   Commandant Second Naval District
ComTwoATAF   Commander Second Allied Tactical
            Air Force, Central Europe
ComUKADR   Commander United Kingdom Air
        Defence Region (Nato)
ComUSAFFor   Commander US Air Force Forces
ComUSAFSo   Commander US Air Force Southern
        Command

ComUSAFSS Commander US Air Force Security
    Service
ComUSAFTF Commander US Air Force Task
    Force
ComUSArFor Commander US Army Forces
ComUSArSo Commander US Army Forces Southern
    Command
ComUSArTF Commander US Army Forces Task
    Force
ComUSBasFrance Commander US Ports and Bases
    in France WW2
ComUSFAirWingMed Commander US Fleet Air
    Wing Mediterranean
ComUSForAZ Commander US Forces Azores
ComUSForIce Commander US Forces Iceland
ComUSForJapan Commander US Forces Japan
ComUSForKorea Commander US Forces Korea
ComUSJapan Commander US Forces Japan
ComUSJTF Commander US Joint Task Force
ComUSJUWTF Commander US Joint Unconvention-
    al Warfare Task Force
ComUSKorea Commander US Forces Korea
ComUSLandFor Commander US Land Forces
ComUSMACThai Commander US Military Assis-
    tance Command Thailand
ComUSMACV Commander US Military Assistance
    Command Viet Nam
ComUSMarFor Commander US Marine Forces
ComUSMarianas Commander US Forces Marianas
ComUSMarTF Commander US Marine Task Force
ComUSMilGP Commander US Military Group
ComUSMilGru Commander US Military Group
ComUSNavFor Commander US Naval Forces
ComUSNavSo Commander US Naval Forces
    Southern Command
ComUSNavTF Commander US Naval Task Force
ComUSRhin Commander US Rhine River Patrol
ComUSTDC Commander US Taiwan Defense
    Command
ComWashADSect Commander Washington Air
    Defense Section
ComWestSeaFron Commander Western Sea
    Frontier
ComyGen Commissary General
ComZ Communications Zone
ComZone Communications Zone
Con Constabulary; control; Congress;
    Consul; confidential
CONAB Commanding Officer Naval Air Base;
    Commanding Officer Naval Advanced
    Base
ConAC Continental Air Command (US)
ConActD continuous active duty
ConAD Continental Air Defense Command (US)
ConAF conceptual design for the Army in
    the field
CONAir Commanding Officer Naval Air Wing
conalog contact-analog (computer)
ConAlt construction and repair alteration
ConArC Continental Army Command (US)

Conar Fieldguard, Contraves artillery
    radar (fire control rocket
    artillery)
CONAS Commanding Officer Naval Air Station
Conbat Infantry anti-tank weapon 122mm
ConC Constructor Captain
conc concentration
Concertina barbed wire coils
Concorde European supersonic transport air-
    craft
ConCr Constructor Commander
concr concrete
cond condenser; conductor; conductivity
ConDEC Consolidated Diesel Electric Corp.
    (US)
ConDeCa Council for the Defence of Central
    America
Condor passive night viewer by Pilkington;
    AGM-53A, TV-guided air-to-surface
    stand-off missile Naval (US) by
    Rockwell; NBS-4, night bomber,
    short range by Curtiss; UR-425,
    4x4 amphibious armoured vehicle
    by Henschel; Fw-200, long-range
    recce aircraft by Focke-Wulf
CONDOR Connaissance et Detection des
    Orages (storm monitoring and
    detection)
conec connection
ConElRad control of electro-magnetic
    radiations
ConEstab connection establishment
ConEx container express; container export
conf conference; confinement, confiden-
    tial
ConFAD concept of a Family of Army Divi-
    sions
ConfBul confidential bulletin
confd confidential
Confessor Sea Cat, GWSk-22, naval anti-
    aircraft missile or sea-skim-
    ming anti-ship missile study by
    Short/RAE/ASWE
config configuration
Conf-MH confidential modified handling
Cong Congress
ConGen Consul General
Conger mine-clearing hose, rocket-propelled
    nitro-glycerine filled WW2 (UK)
CongInt interest by Member of Congress
CongR Congressional Record
ConHan contextual harmonic analysis
ConHydroLant confidential Hydrographic
    Office Reports Atlantic
ConL Constructor Lieutenant
ConLCr Constructor Lieutenant Commander
conn connection
ConnRang The Connaught Rangers
ConObjtr conscientious objector
ConOps Continental Operations (by US Army
    Intelligence Command)

ConPresDu continue present duty
ConPy contact party
Conqueror heavy tank (UK) WW2
conR contact reconnaissance
ConRoute convoy and routing system (USN) WW2
Cons Consul; Constable; conservative; construction
ConSA consular shipping adviser
ConShelf continental shelf
ConShip control (of fighters) from ship
ConShore control (of fighters) from shore
ConSL Constructor Sub-lieutenant
consol consolidate(d)
Consol long-range radio aid to navigation
Const Constable; construction
Constab Constabulary
ConSStocks contingency support stocks
ConstElec construction electrician
Constructor FV-12000, 6x6 truck by Scammell
cont continue; continuation; contract(or)
contam contamination
contbd contraband
Contractor tank transporter truck by Scammell
ConTrail condensation trail
ConTran control translator
ConTreat continue treatment (hospital)
CoNuBS compact nuclear Brayton system
ConUS Continental United States
ConUSA Continental United States Armies
MDW in the Military District of Washington
conv convertible; convict
convate connection reservation
ConvDD converted destroyer (USN)
convers connection conversion
ConvEx convoy exercise (Nato)
convl conventional
COO Chief Ordnance Officer; Chief of Ordnance; Controller of Ordnance
Coontz class, guided missile destroyers (DDG-USN)
COOP continuity of operations plan; contingency operations plan
coop cooperative
COOPCOM Communications Facilities in Support of the Department of the Army Continuity of Operations Plan
Cooper bomb WW1 (UK)
COOPlan contingency of operations plan
CoorAuth coordinating authority
coord coordinating; coordination
CoORS communications outage restoral section
COP combat outpost; command operating programme; commanding officer's punishment; change over panel
CoP Co-pilot

cop copper
COPAG Collision Prevention Advisory Group
COPE Custodian of Postal Effects; covert observation and photography equipment by Handland low light level surveillance camera
COPEP Committee of Public Engineering Policy
COPERS Commission on the Preparation of European Space Research, --ESRO
COPL combat outpost line
COPO Chief of Personnel Operations
COPP combined operations pilotage party
Copperhead XM-712, CLGP, cannon-launched guided projectile 155mm by Martin
COQC commanding officers qualification course
Coquelet teleprinter system (FR)
COR contracting officer's representative; cargo outturn report; circular of requirements (Nato); carrier wave operated reception
cor corrector; correction; corridor
Cor Corps
CoRA coherent radar array
Cora digital computer by Contraves (--Conar, --Fieldguard)
CORADCom Communications Research and development Command (US Army)
Corail automatic radar landing system by SEL
Coral 66 computer real-time application language
CorC Cornell computing language
CorCen Correlation Centre (Nato)
Cord coordinator; coordination
CORD Coordination of Research and Development; computer with on-line remote devices
CORDS Civil operations revolutionary development support (Viet Nam); coherent-on-receive doppler system
CORE Congress of Racial Equality (US)
CoRE Company of Royal Engineers (UK)
CoRep control repair (organization)
CORep combined overload and repair control
CORF Committee on Radio Frequencies
CORG Combat Operations Research Group
Cornwell Decoration for Boy Scouts (UK)
Coronado PB-2Y, flying boat by Consolidated
Corp Corporal; corporation
Corporal surface-to-surface tactical missile (US)
corr correct(ion); correspondence
CORRA combined overseas rehabilitation relief appeal
CORS Chief of the Regulations Staff; Conversion/Overhaul reporting System, --Hawk

Corsair   USN naval fighter aircraft WW2;
          F-4U by Chance Vought,
          FG-1 by Goodyear
Corsair II   A-7, jet attack bomber by Vought
CORschOpsDet   Commanding Officer Research
          Operations Detachment
CorSec   Corresponding Secretary
Cort   Escort
CortDiv   Escort Division (USN)
CortRon   Escort Squadron (USN)
CORTEX   communications-oriented real-time
          executive
Corvette   VIP transport jet by Aerospatiale
Corvus   broad band chaff dispensing rocket
          (RN)
COS   Chief of Staff; Controller of
          Ordnance Services; civilian occu-
          pational specialty; change over
          switch; Centre d'Opérations de
          Secteur (sector operations centre)
COSA   Chief of Staff, Army; Corps service
          area; combat operational support
          aircraft
COSAG   combined steam and gas turbines
COSAL   coordinated ship allowance list
COSAMREG   consolidation of supply and main-
          tenance regulations
COSAR   compression scanning array radar
COSATI   Committee on Scientific and Techni-
          cal Information -- COSI (US)
COSBA   Computer Service and Bureau Associa-
          tion
COSD   combined operations supply depot
COSEC   Coordination Secretariat of National
          Associations of Students; Culham
          on-line single experimental
          console
COSI   Committee on Scientific Information
          COSATI (US)
Cosinor   Companhia Siderurgica do Nordeste
          (Brazil) (OTO-Melara daughter)
COSIS   care of supplies in storage
COSMD   combined operations signal mainten-
          ance depot; combined operations
          signal maintenance division
COSMIC   Chief of Staff Military Intelligence
          Committee (Nato) (top secret clas-
          sification); Computer Software and
          Management Information Centre
COSMO   combined operations signal mainten-
          ance office(r)
COSMOS   centralization of supply management
          operations; coast survey marine
          observation system; computer
          optimization and simulation
          modelling for operating super-
          markets
Cosmos   European space probe --ISPM by
          MBB; satellites, Soviet
COSO   combined operations signal officer

COSPAR   Committee on Space Research (of the
          International Council of Scienti-
          fic Unions)
COSOUMAT   Commandant des Forces Sous-
          Marines (Françaises) de
          l'Atlantique) (Commander French
          Submarines Atlantic)
COSSAC   Chief of the Staff of the Supreme
          Allied Commander WW2
CoSSAct   Command Systems Support Activity
COST   Committee for Overseas Science and
          Technology; Continental Offshore
          Stratographic Test (Alaska)
COSTAC   Conduite de Tir Stabilisée Anti-
          Char (simplified and miniaturized
          COTAC)
CoSTAr   combat service to the Army
COSU   combined operations scout unit
COSVN   central office for South Viet Nam
CoSy   compiler system; correction system
COT   consecutive overseas tour; coordi-
          nated operability test
CoT   company transport
COT   cockpit orientation trainer; card
          or tape (reader)
COTA   confirming telephone (message)
          authority
COTAC   Conduite de Tir Automatique pour
          Char (automatic fire control
          system for tanks + laser range-
          finder (FR)
COTAR   correlation tracking and ranging
          (system)
COTC   Canadian Officers' Training Corps;
          Commander (Fleet) Operational
          Training Command (USN)
          Lant   Atlantic
          Pac   Pacific
          SubCom Subordinate Command
          Canadian Overseas Telecommunica-
          tions Corp.
CoTn   company train
COTP   Captain of the Port (USCG)
COTR   contracting officer's technical
          representatives; core and two
          rings
CoTug   control tugs (organization)
Cougar   Canadian Infantry fire support
          vehicle; F-9F, swept-wing naval
          fighter aircraft by Grumman 1951;
          anti-aircraft missile tank pro-
          ject, Rapier + Leopard by HSA and
          Krauss-Maffei
County   class, flotilla leader vessels (RN)
Courier   delayed repeater communications
          satellite (US)
COUSNAB   Commander of US Naval Advanced
          Bases
COUSS   Commanding Officer US Ship
COV   concealed vessel; concentrated oil
          of vitriol (acid)

COVE   Committee on Value and Evaluation
COW   Coventry Ordnance Works
Cox   Coxswain
Coy   company
COZ   Centre d'Opérations de Zone (zone operations centre)
COZI   communications zone indicator
CP   Chief of Police; co-pilot; command paymaster; cost and performance; command post; connecting post; communications personnel (USMC); control post; constant pressure; centre of pressure; cross and point (sights); chemically pure, calorific power; central pivot; candle power; continental polar (air mass); central processor; clock pulse; coherent potential; colour print; collision probability; command processor; control panel; continuous phase; communication processor; Canadian Patrol (aircraft); concrete piercing (bomb)
C&P   care and preservation; cost and performance
CP-1   low-cost night vision goggles by EA
CP-107   Argus, Canadian maritime patrol aircraft by Canadair
CP-121   Tracker, ASW/surveillance aircraft by Grumman
CP-140   Aurora, ASW/surveillance patrol aircraft
CPA   certificated public accountant; Chief of Public Affairs; Civilian Production Administration; Cost Planning and Appraisal; closest point of approach; contract price adjustment; critical path analysis; coherent potential approximation; concurrent photon amplification
CPAD   central pay accounts division
CPB   civilian personnel branch; centre of pressure back; channel programme block
cpbl   capable
CPC   Canadian Postal Corps; criminal procedures code; civilian personnel circular; Combined Policy Committee (Nato); Chief Pay Clerk; Clerk of the Privy Council; Chief of Planning and Control (USMC); City Policy Commissioner; craft, protective and custodial; constant pressure cycle; channel programme command; controlled potential coulometry
CPCS   coast phase control system; cheque processing control system
CPCU   custody pending completion of use

CPD   central postal directory; Central Procurement Division (USMC); Counter-Propaganda Directorate (UK) WW2; communication processor and display (system); Comité de Défense (Defence Planning Committee)
CPE   cloud processing equipment; collective protective equipment; cardinal point effect (radar); contractor performed evaluation; circular probable error
CPEB   Central Postal Enquiry Bureau
CPED   continuous particle electrophoresis device
CPEP   contractor performance evaluation plan
CPES   contractor performance evaluation system
CPF   Canadian Permanent Force; Central Post Fund; Contributory Pensions Fund; centre of pressure forward
CPFF   cost plus a fixed fee (contract)
CPFLP   contingency planning facilities list program (US)
CPFMS   COMRADE permanent file management system
CPG   Commander Amphibious Group; clock pulse generator
CPH   cycles per hour
CPI   Chief Pilot Instructor; consumer price index; crash position indicator; characters per inch
CPIC   combined photographic interpretation centre
CPID   computer programme integral document
CPIF   cost plus incentive fee (contract)
CPI/FDR   crash position indicator/flight data recorder
CPILS   correlation protected instrument landing system
CPK   central pastry kitchen
CPL   Computer Projects Ltd; Commander Amphibious Force Atlantic (USN); common programme language; contractor performance list; contractor procurement list
Cpl   Corporal
CPL&D   civilian personnel letters and dispatches
CPLEE   changed particle lunar environment experiment
CPM   Colonial Police Medal (for Gallantry); critical path method (computers); central processor module; cycles per minute; cards per minute

CPMI	command personnel management inspections
CPO	Chief Petty Officer; command pay office(r); civilian personnel officer; compulsory purchase order; component pilot overhaul; concurrent peripheral operations
CPOIC	Chief Petty Officer in Charge
CPOUKLF	Chief Petty Officer in Charge United Kingdom Land Forces
CPOS	civilian personnel occupational standards
CPOW	Chief Petty Officer of the Watch
CPP	Commander Amphibious Force Pacific (USN); civilian personnel pamphlet; controllable pitch propeller
CPPC	cost plus percentage of cost (contract)
CPPM	civilian personnel procedures manual
CPPS	critical path planning and scheduling
CPR	Commander Amphibious Squadron (USN); civilian personnel regulations; carrier performance rating; continuing property records; component pilot rework
cpr	copper
CPRB	Combined Production and Resources Board (UK-US)
CPRC	Central Price Regulating Committee
CPRI	Canadian Peace Research Institute
CPRO	Chief Public Relations Officer
CPS	carrier pigeon service; command personnel summary; Contract Plant Services; cycles per second; characters per second; CERN proton synchrotron; conversational programme system
CPSC	Consumer Product Safety Commission (US)
cpse	counter-poise
CPSIM-E	central programme simulator-extended
CPSM	critical path scheduling method
CPSNA	Consel Permanent pour la Securité de la Navigation Aerienne (Permanent Commission for the Safety of Air Navigation)
CPSU	Communist Party of the Soviet Union
CPT	central planning team; co-pilot time; critical path technique
Cpt	Captain
cpt	cockpit; counter-point
CPTP	civil pilot training programme
CPU	computer processor unit; central processing unit; central packaging unit; central protection unit
CPubInfo	Chief of Public Information
CPU/IOU	central processor unit/input-output unit
CPUSA	Communist Party of the USA
CPV	command post vehicle
CPVA	Chemisch- Physikalische Versuchs-Anstalt Dänisch Nienhof (Chemical and Physical Experimental Establishment, Navy)
CPVC	critical pigment volume concentration
CPW	complanar wave guide
CPX	command post exercise (Nato)
CQ	(NCO) in charge of quarters; change of quarters; call to quarters
C/Q	certificate of assignment to quarters (US)
CQ&AB	correspondence qualifications and appointments branch BUPERS
CQB	close quarter battle
CQDN	Comité des Questions de Défense Nucleaire (Nuclear Defence Affairs Committee)
CQM	Chief Quartermaster; Company Quartermaster
CQMS	Company Quartermaster Sergeant
CR	Commendation Ribbon; clothing regulations; composite regiment; combat ready; confidential report; commencement of rifling; consultant report; credit record; control relay; compression ratio; continuous rod; card reader; carriage return; ceiling register; communication register; constant rate; control routine
cr	cruiser; crossroads; circular; creek
Cr	Commander; crystals
C/R	change of rating; change request
C&R	(Bureau of) Construction and Repair (USN); convoy and routing; control and reporting
CR-62	Cossor radar, precision approach radar
CRA	Commander Royal Artillery; command relationships agreement; continuing-resolution authority; composite research aircraft; combat ready aircraft
CrAA	Commander-at-Arms
CRAAM	Centre of Radio Astronomy and Astrophysics Mackenzie University (Sao Paulo)
Crab	mine-sweeping Sherman tank (flail tank)
CRAC	careers research and advisory centre
CRACC	Communications and Radar Assignment Coordinating Committee
CRAD	Committee for Research into Apparatus for the Disabled
CRAF	civilian reserve air fleet
CRAG	carrier replacement air group; combat readiness air group

Craig   standard container for radar stations (US)

CRALOG   Council of Relief Agencies Licensed to Operate in Germany

CRAM   contractual requirements recording analysis and management; card random access memory

CRAOC   Commander Royal Army Ordnance Corps

CRASC   Commander Royal Army Service Corps

CRAW   combat ready air wing

CRB   Central Radio Bureau; chemical radiological biological (warfare)

CRBFD   close range blind fire director

CRBW   chemical radiological biological warfare

CRC   Canadian Retraining Centre; control and reporting centre; command reporting centre; condition reservation code; Central Requirements Committee; Combined Rubber Committee; cyclic redundancy check-sum; coordinating research council; Communications Research Centre

CrC   Crew Chief

CRCC   Canadian Red Cross Committee; consolidated record communications centre; cyclic redundancy check character

CRCom   Change Review Committee

CRCP   continuously reinforced concrete pavement

CRCS   Canadian Red Cross Society; clinical record cover sheet

CRCT   Commander Royal Corps of Transport

CRD   Central Recruiting Depot (Whitehall); central repair depot; computer read-out device; chronic radiation dose; Centre de Recherches pour la Défense National (Research Centre for National Defence)

CRd   card read

CRDA   Cantieri Riuniti dell'Adriatico (IT)

CRDF   cathode ray direction finder

CRDS   component repair data sheet

CRDT   Centre de Renseignement et de Direction de Tir (A/A Operations Centre)

CRE   Commander Royal Engineers; combat readiness evaluation; Commission for Racial Equality; Chemical Research Establishment (Porton UK)

CREC   ComSec Research and Engineering Coordinating Group

CRecon   Counter-reconnaissance

CREES   Centre for Russian and East European Studies (University of Birmingham)

CREME   Commander Royal Electrical and Mechanical Engineers

CRESS   centre for research in social systems

CREST   combat readiness by electronic service testing

CRETC   combined radiating effects test chamber

CRF   cryptological repair facilities; capital recovery factor

CRH   calibre radius head (of projectile)

CRI   code relationship index

CRIL   consolidated repairable items list

crim   criminal

CRIME   censorship records and information Middle East

CRIMP   consolidated RVNAF improvement and modernization plan

CRIO   ComSec regional issuing officer

CRIS   command retrieval information system; current research information system

CritCom   critical communications system

CritHous   critical housing shortage

Critic   critical (intelligence)

CritiCom   critical intelligence communications

CRJE   conversational remote job entry

CRL   chemical research laboratory

CRM   counter-radar missile; count rate meter

CrM   cruise missile

CRMB   Combined Raw Materials Board (UK-US)

CRMC   certified round missile concept (US standards)

crmn   crewman

CRMP   Corps of Royal Military Police

CRN   continuous random network

CRNL   Chalk River Nuclear Laboratories (CA)

CRNSS   Chief of the Royal Naval Scientific Service

CRO   corps routine order; carded for record only; civilian repair organization; criminal records office; Chief Recruiting Officer; Commonwealth Relations Office; cathode ray oscilloscope; cathode ray oscillograph

Crocodile   flame thrower tank (UK) WW2

CROCS   contingency re-routing of communications

Cromwell   tank WW2 (UK)

Cross Cocktail   improvised hand grenade (UK)

Crossfire   A-6A aircraft spare parts expediting programme

Crotale   R-440, R-460, low-level air defence system by Thomson-CSF/Matra

CRP   control and reporting post; community relations program (US); cost reduction programme; constant rate of penetration; ComSec resources programme

CrP   criminal procedure
CRPL   central radio propagation laboratory
CRPM   combined registered publication
             memoranda; Communication register-
             ed publication memoranda
CRR   constant ratio rule
CRRC   Constructions Requirement Review
             Committee
CRS   combat ready status; corps rest
             station; camp reception station;
             container recovery service; com-
             ponent repair squadron; cold-
             rolled steel; control and report-
             ing system; Compagnies Republi-
             caines de Securité (French anti-
             terrorist squads)
crs   course
CRSD   contractor required shipping date
CRSigs   Commander Royal Signals
CRT   combat readiness training; cathode
             ray tube
crtn   correction
CRTS   Commonwealth Reconstruction Training
             Scheme
CRU   Canadian Reinforcement Unit; control
             register user; compass reference
             unit; civil resettlement unit;
             composite reserve unit
Cru   cruiser
CruBatFor   cruiser battle force
CruDesFlot   cruiser-destroyer flotilla
CruDesLant   cruiser-destroyer force Atlantic
CruDesPac   cruiser-destroyer force Pacific
CruDiv   cruiser division
CruLant   cruisers Atlantic
CruLantFlt   cruisers Atlantic Fleet
CruPac   cruisers Pacific
CruPacFlt   cruisers Pacific Fleet
CruScoFor   cruisers scouting force
Cruise Missile AGM-86A
Crusader 6x4 articulated tractor by
             Scammell tank WW2 (UK);
             F-8, Mach 1.7 jet aircraft by
             Vought 1955
CRV   combat reconnaissance vehicle
CRV-7   unguided airfield attack rockets
             275mm Canadian
CRVO   Commander of the Royal Victorian
             Order
CRWMP   Commendation Ribbon with Metal Pen-
             dant (US)
CRWO   coding room watch officer
CRWPC   Canadian Radio Wave Propagation
             Committee
crypto   classification cryptomaterial;
             cryptoanalysis; cryptography
CryptoCom   cryptographic communications
             equipment by Crypto
Cryptomatic (equipment) by Crypto
             HC-520, hand-held set;

             HC-580, computer crypto set;
             HC-590, teleprinter crypto set
Cryptoplex   bus cryptographic device by
             Crypto
Cryptovox HC-330, language scrambler by
             Crypto
Cryptrol T-450, teleprinter scrambler by
             Crypto
Cryptronic digital scrambler by Crypto
cryst   crystal(lized)
CRZ   close reconnaissance zone
CS   Chief of Staff; cruiser squadron;
             civil service; close support;
             continuous service; composite
             service; counter-sabotage; cost
             sharing (contract); current
             series; commissary store; communi-
             cations station; communications
             satellite by NASDA; cruiser,
             scout (USN); command system;
             common shell; cast steel; carbon
             steel; coal and steel; cirro
             stratus (clouds); (rotating)
             cassegrain system antenna; con-
             crete slab; cycles per second;
             cyclo-stationery; tear gas
C/S   Chief of Staff; call sign; certifi-
             cate of service; cycles per
             second
C&S   charges and specifications; clean
             and sober
60-CS   breech-loading mortar by DTAT
CS-90   gun by GIAT
CSA   Chief of Staff US Army; Consular
             Shipping Adviser; close support
             aircraft; Central Supplies Agency;
             Canadian Standards Association;
             chloro-sulphoric acid
CSA-1   Chinese surface-to-air missile
             (like Soviet SA-2)
CSAB   Combined Shipping Adjustment Board
             (US-UK)
CSAC   combat support aviation company (US);
             central ship's alignment console
CSAF   Chief of Staff US Air Force
CSAFM   Chief of Staff US Air Force Memor-
             andum
CSAR   communications satellite advanced
             research
CSARC   component search and rescue con-
             troller
CSArmy   Chief Scientist, Army (UK)
CSAS   Canadian Small Arms School; command
             and stability augmentation system
             -- Tornado; control support and
             augmentations system (for heli-
             copters); Command support and
             augmentations system
CSAT   Civil Service Arbitration Tribunal
CSB   Central Statistical Board;

CSB   chemical stimulation of the brain; calcium silicate brick

C&SB   Correspondence and Services Branch BUPERS

CSBL   consolidated site base loading

CSC   Civil Service Commission(er); combat support company; Combined Ship-building Committee; Command and Staff College (USMC); continuous service certificate; certificate of security clearance; Conspicuous Service Cross; Chief Sector Controller; Commonwealth Scientific Committee; common signalling channel; course and speed computer; Computer Systems Corporation (Moorestown NJ); Communications Satellite Corporation; Computer Sciences Corp. (Calif.)

C-SCAN   carrier system for controlled approach of naval aircraft

CSCBS   Commodore Superintendent, Contract-built Ships

CSCE   Conference on Security and Cooperation in Europe; communications system control element Tri-Tac by Martin-Marietta

CSCMC   The Chief Scout's Certificate of Meritorious Conduct (UK)

CSCS   Civil Service Cooperative Stores

CSD   Communications Systems Division (RCA); computer sciences division; constant speed drive

CSDE   Central Servicing Development Establishment (RAF)

CSDF   command supply discipline programme

CSDIC   combined services detailed interrogation centre 'NOI non-operational intelligence

csdrbl   considerable

CSE   combined services entertainment; certificate of secondary education; combat support element (US); communications security equipment; Central Signals Establishment; containment systems experiment

CSEAF   Commander Southern European Air Forces

CSect   control section

CSED   consolidated ships electronic design; coordinated ships electronic design

CSEDS   combat systems engineering development site (USN)

CSEE   Compagnie de Signeaux et d'Enterprises Electriques (rue Caroline Paris)

CSEF   current switch emitter follower

CSEGF   Commander Southern European Ground Forces

CSESF   Commander Southern European Sea Forces

CSF   community service file; Caribbean Sea Frontier; close supporting fire

CSFPSC   Commander, Service Force, Pacific Fleet, Subordinate Command (USN)

CSFS   Commander Naval Striking and Support Forces, Southern Europe (Nato)

CSG   combat service group; combined studies group (CIA); combat support group; commando submachine gun; course and speed over the ground

CSGM   Chairman Standing Group Memorandum (Nato)

CSGN   cruiser, strike, guided missiles nuclear-powered (USN)

CSgt   Colour Sergeant (UK)

CSH   combat support hospital

CSHFTC   The Chief Scout's Highland Field-craft Training Centre (Glenfeshie UK)

CSHS   Chief Superintendent of Hydrographic Services; Chief Superintendent of Hydrographic Supplies

CSI   Companion of the Most Exalted Order of the Star of India; ConUs sustaining increment; coelliptic sequence initiation; Constructions Specifications Institute; Computer Systems International

CSID   Computer Sciences International Deutschland GmbH (Munich)

CSigO   Chief Signals Officer

CSIR   Council for Scientific and Industrial Research (POB 395 Pretoria 0001, RSA)

CSIRO   Commonwealth Scientific and Industrial Research Organization (Sydney)

CSL   complete service life; Communications Sub-lieutenant; Commander, Service Force Atlantic (USN); common specification language; control and simulation language; computer simulation language; constant scattering length; Chemical Systems Laboratory (US Army Aberdden Proving Ground)

CSLO   combined services liaison officer; Canadian Scientific Liaison Office

CSM   China Service Medal 1937-9; Company Sergeant Major (UK); Command Sergeant Major (US); Commodore Superintendent (Malta RN); calendar maintenance supervisor; Chief of Staff Memorandum (US); command and service module (NASA); communications security material; communications security monitoring; critical supplies and materials

CSMP	current ships' maintenance project (USN)
CSML	continuous self mode locking
CSMP	continuous system modelling programme
CSn	Contract Surgeon
CSO	Chief Signals Officer; Command Signals Officer; Chief Staff Officer; Club Safety Officer; Central Statistical Office; Commonwealth Scientific Office
CSOC	Consolidated Space Operations Center (Peterson AFB)
CSOF	Chief Superintendent of the Ordnance Factories (UK)
CSofA	Canadian School of Artillery
CSP	Commander, Service Force, Pacific (USN); Combat Supplies Platoon (RAOC); Council on Scientific Policy; concurrent (initial) spare parts; control switching point
CSPC	Coal and Steel Planning Committee (Nato)
CSPE	communications system planning element Tri-Tac
CSPM	Communications Security Publication Memorandum
CSPS	coherent signal processing system
CSQ	cryptofacility security questionnaire
CSR	Chief of Staff Regulations; civil service retirement; The Canadian Scottish Regiment; council situation room; combat surveillance radar
CSRDF	civil service retirement and disability fund (US)
CSRO	consolidated standing route order
CSS	Civil Secret Service; Confederated States Ship (US); Central Security Service (US); combat service support (US); computer systems simulator; Computer Sales and Services; computer sub-system
C&SS	clothing and small stores
CSS-1	Chinese surface-to-surface MRBM 1, 800 km
CSS-2	Chinese surface-to-surface IRBM, 4,000 km
CSS-3	Chinese surface-to-surface ICBM 6,500 km
CSSA	Civil Service Supply Association
CSSB	Civil Service Selection Board
CSSD	Central Sterile Supply Department DMed (UK)
CSSE	Central Security Service, Europe (US); combat service support element
CSSM	compatible single side-band modulation

CSS-N-1	Chinese surface-to-surface naval missile
CSSpt	common supply support
CSSS	combat services support system
CSSX-4	Chinese surface-to-surface nuclear missile ICMB 11,000 km, 3MT warhead like Soviet SS-9
CST	combat support training; central standard time; College of Science and Technology
cst	coast
CSta	consolidating station
CSTA	combat surveillance and target acquisition
CSTC	Canadian Signals Training Centre
CSTI	Council of Science and Technology Institutes
CStJ	Commander of the Order of St John of Jerusalem
CSTR	Committee on Solar Terrestrial Research
CSTV	control system test vehicle (USN) by Lockheed (remote controlled miniature submarine)
CSU-3	sonar equipment by KAE
CSU	civilian search unit; central statistical unit; constant speed unit
CSups	combat supplies
CSV	Community Service Volunteer; combat support vehicle
CSW	course and speed through water; channel status word
CSWC	crew served weapons captured
CSWS	corps support weapon system (US missile)
CT	communications technician; certificated teacher; correct time; combat team; communications trench; corps troops; combined trials; confirmatory test; current transactions; cruiser tank; controlled target (aircraft); dual trainer aircraft; conning tower; centre tap; charge transfer; control transformer; cooling tower; current transformer; cable transfer
ct	current; carat; circuit
CT-movement	communist terrorist movement
C&T	contingency and training
CT-2	controlled target aircraft by AS
CT-4B	trainer aircraft by NZAI
CT-10	controlled target aircraft by AS
CT-20	controlled target aircraft propeller-driven by AS
CT-40GM	fire control radar by Contraves
CT-41	target drone by AS
CTA	common table of allowances; Chaplain, Territorial Army; Brazilian Aerospace Centre

CtA	controlled airspace
CTAB	Commonwealth Technical Advisory Bureau; Commerce Technical Advisory Board (US)
CTB	coastal torpedo boat; Commonwealth Telecommunications Board; computer time bookers; combined travel board; commercial traffic bulletin
C/TB	Cargo/Tanker Branch MSTS
CTBT	comprehensive (nuclear) test ban treaty
CTC	combat training centre; cadet training centre (UK); Civil Technical Corps; Canadian Transport Commission; Communications Transistor Corporation (US); carbon tetrachloride (fire extinguisher); centralized traffic control; compact transpiration cooling
CTCI	Classification Type pour le Commerce International (Standard International Trade Classification)
CTD	Central Training Depot; classified telephone directory; convalescent training depot; cross track distance
ctd	coated
CTDAS	Centre Technique de la Défense Aerienne du SHAPE (SHAPE Air Defence Technical Centre)
CTDC	Civil Transport Development Corporation, Japanese Boeing 767 production firm; control track direction computer
CTDO	Central Technical Doctrine Officer
CTE	Commander, Task Element
CTEB	Council of Technical Examining Bodies
CTF	Commander, Task Force; combined task force; carrier (borne) task force; Chaplain to the Territorial Forces; coal tar fuel; controlled thermonuclear fusion
ctf	certificate
CTFM	continuous transmission frequency modulated
CTG	Commander, Task Group; combined task group
CTGds	company's trench guards
ctg	cartridge
CTH	The Cape Town Hussars (Regiment); Corporation of Trinity House
CTI	command technical inspection; complaint type investigation; contract technical instructor; Canadian Technical Industries (ammunition); Chemisch Technisches Institut BICT
CTL	CTL constructive total lost
ctl	central

CtlZ	control zone
C&TM	clothing and textile material
ctms	counter-measures
ctn	centre
CTO	Chief Tower Operator; Chief Treasury Officer; central telegraph office; Central Treaty Organization CENTO; Chief Technical Officer; Conventional take-off (aircraft); Controle Technique Officiel (Government Quality Assurance)
CTOC	corps technical operations centre
CTOL	conventional take-off and landing (aircraft)
CTP	coordinated test programme; consolidated telecommunications programme; combat training programme
CTps	corps troops
CTR	Cambridge Territorial Regiment; Controlled thermonuclear reaction; certified test records; certified test requirements; collective television reception
Ctr	contribution; contributor; controlled (airspace) Zone CEAC; control (zone message traffic)
CTRU	Colonial Thermite Research Unit
CTS	Cosmic top secret (Nato); contractor technical services; common test subroutines; computerized training system; contralateral threshhold shift; controlled thermal severity; communications technology satellite (Canadian regional system); Centre Technique du SHAPE (SHAPE Technical Centre)
CTS/RTS	clear-to-send/request-to-send
CTSS	compatible time-sharing system
CTT	Cadet Training Team (UK); combined tactical trainer (RN) by Ferranti
CTTB	Central Trade Test Board (RAF)
ctte	committee
CTTL	complementary transistor-transistor logic
CTU	Commander, Task Unit; channel testing unit; centigrade thermal unit
CTV	control(led) test vehicle
CTVA	Chemisch-Technische Versuchsanstalt (Chemical Technological Experimental Establishment)
CTW	course through water
CTX	fleet support transport aircraft (USN)
CTZ	corps tactical zone
CtZ	control zone
CU	control unit; close-up
cu	couplers (electronics); cubic; cumulus (clouds)
CU-10	infra-red night vision binoculars
CUAS	Cambridge University Air Squadron; common user airlift service

CUCB	cumulus and cumulonimbus (clouds)	CVC	consecutive voyage charter; Vice Chief of Staff (US); combat vehicle crewman; Consolidated Vacuum Corporation (US); current voltage characteristics
Cuckoo	torpedo bomber WW2 by Sopwith		
cucm	cubic centimetre		
CUDAT	common user data terminal		
CUDWR	Columbia University Division of War Research		
		CVCR	control van connecting room
CUE	control unit end; computer update equipment	CVD	Central Vehicles Depot (Ludgershall UK); common valve development; creative visual dynamics; chemical vapour deposition
CUEA	coastal upwelling ecosystems analysis		
CUED	Cambridge University Engineering Development	CVE	aircraft carrier, escort (USN)
		CVeh	combat vehicle
cuft	cubic feet	CVF	controlled visual flight
CUH-1	Canadian Utility Helicopter Bell-212	CVFR	controlled visual flight rules
CUICat	common user item catalogue	CVG	carrier air group (USN)
cum	cumulative	cvge	coverage
CUMLT	common user military land transportation	CVH	aircraft carrier, helicopters (USN)
		CVHA	aircraft carrier, helicopters assault
CUNet	common user network		
CUO	credit union office	CVHC	aircraft carrier, helicopters coastal
CUOT	common user ocean terminal		
cur	current	CVHE	aircraft carrier, helicopters escort
CURA	Cambridge University Rifle Association		
		CVHQ	Central Volunteer Headquarters (UK); Civilian Volunteer Headquarters TAVR (UK)
CURAC	Coal Utilization Research Advisory Committee (Australia)		
curr	current; currency	CVIS	computerized vocational information system
CURTS	communications user radio transmission sounding		
		CVK	centre vertical keel
CURV	cable-controlled under-water recovery vehicle	CVL	aircraft carrier, little (USN)
		CVL/CVE	aircraft carrier, little/ aircraft carrier, escort
cus	course		
cusec	cubic (feet) per second	CVLGN	night fighter air group (USN)
CUSR	Central US Registry; Canada-US Region	CVN	aircraft carrier, nuclear powered (USN)
CUSRPG	Canada US Regional Planning Group (Nato Washington)	CVO	Commander of the Royal Victorian Order
cust	custody; custodian	CVR	controlled visual (flight) rules; cockpit voice recorder
custr	customer		
cut	cutter	C-VR	verbatim record of North Atlantic Council Meeting (shorthand)
CUTC	Cambridge University Training Corps		
Cutlass	F-7U, twin jet naval fighter aircraft by Vought 1948; naval ECM system by Decca	CVRT	combat vehicle, reconnaissance, tracked
		CVRW	combat vehicle, reconnaissance, wheeled
CV	collection voucher; corvette (RN); corner velocity; command vehicle; continuous vision; conversation voice; calorific value; common valve; aircraft carrier (USN); Code Variante (reference number); variation code	CVS	aircraft carrier, seaplanes (USN); aircraft carrier, antisubmarine warfare support; constant volume sampling
		CVSD	continuously variable slope delta (modulation)
C-V	capacitance - voltage	CVSG	carrier anti-submarine warfare group
CV-440	Metropolitan, twin-engined liaison aircraft by Convair	CVSGR	reserve carrier anti-submarine warfare group
CVA	attack aircraft carrier (USN)	CVSM	Canadian Volunteer Service Medal
CVAN	attack aircraft carrier nuclear-powered (USN)	CVTR	Carioland-Virginia tube reactor
		CVT	aircraft carrier, training (USN)
CVANX	attack aircraft carrier nuclear-powered experimental (USN)	CVU	aircraft carrier, utility
		CVV	aircraft carrier for vertical take-off aircraft
CVB	aircraft carrier, big (USN)		

CVW	attack carrier air wing (USN)	CWRR	Committee on Water Resources Research
CVWS	combat vehicle weapons system		
CVX-396	cryptographic equipment by Crypto	CWS	Canadian War Services; Chemical Warfare School; central wireless station; continental wage schedule (US); control wheel steering
CW	chemical warfare; carrier wave; continuous wave; commercial weight; chain wheel; call waiting; clipping weight		
CW-detector	chemical warfare detector	CWSF	Commander Western Sea Frontier (USN)
C&W	Cable & Wireless Ltd (London)	CWSO	command weapons system orientation
CW-1	(2, 3, 4) Chief Warrant Officer W-1 (US)	CWSP	communications with and service to the public
CWA	Civil Works Administration; Canadian Western Approaches	CXT	common extended tariff (EC)
		CWT	chief water tender; critical water temperature; central war time
CWAC	Canadian Women's Army Corps		
CWAcq	continuous wave acquisition (radar)	cwt	hundredweight
CWAEC	Country War Agricultural Executive Committee	CWTAD	clockwise top angular down
		CWTAU	clockwise top angular up
CWAR	continuous wave acquisition radar	CWTD	continuous wave target detection (radar)
CWAS	contractor's weighted average share (in cost risk)		
		CWTDC	continuous wave target detection console
CWB	Central Wages Board		
CWBAD	clockwise bottom angular down	CWTG	Computer World Trade Group (UK)
CWBAU	clockwise bottom angular up	CWTH	clockwise top horizontal
CWBW	chemical warfare/biological warfare; chemical warfare bacteriological warfare	CWUB	clockwise up blast
		CWW	cruciform wing weapon --GBU-15
		CX	cable assemblies; non-radio frequencies control transmitter
CWC	Chemical Warfare Committee		
C&WCk	caution and warning (system) check	C-X	cargo aircraft next generation (USAF)
CWD	civilian war dead		
CWDB	clockwise down blast	cx	convex
CWE	current working estimate	CXT	common extended tariff (EC)
CWED	cold weld evaluation device	CY	Chief Yeoman; communications yeoman; calendar year; cubic yards; cases and cabinets (electronic components)
CWF	civilian wllfare fund		
CWFO	Chief Woman Fire Officer in the NFS		
CWGC	Commonwealth War Graves Commission (UK)		
		cy	capacity; copy; cyanide
CWI	continuous wave illuminator (radar)	cyber	cybernetics
CWIll	continuous wave illuminator	CyberLog	cybernetic logistics planning control and management information system
CWINC	Central Waterways Irrigation and Navigation Commission (India)		
		CYC	Company of Young Canadians
CWInj	cold water injury	Cyclonite	explosive, cyclo-trimethylane-trinitramine
CWIR	continuous wave illuminator radar		
CWM	commercial water movement (number)	Cyclop	single-tube double-eyepiece night vision goggle by Oldelft
CWMN	commercial water movement (number)		
CWMTU	cold weather material test unit	Cyclops	millimetre-wave seeker for terminal guidance (USAF); air-launched anti-armour missile (USAF programme abandoned)
CWO	Chief Warrant Officer; chemical warfare officer; chief watch officer; commissioned warrant officer; communications watch officer; cash with order		
		CYEE	Central Youth Employment Executive
		cyl	cylinders
		Cymbeline	RFA no. 15, mortar locating radar by EMI
CWO-1	(2, 3) Chief Warrant Officer W-1 (US)		
CWOp	cold weather operations	CYn	communications yeoman
CWPI	configuration work package item; coast watching and communications in the South Pacific Islands (RN)	Cyrano	multi-function digital monitoring radar
		CYS	Chief Yeoman of Signals
CWR	continuous welded rail	CYW	Chief Yeoman Warder (UK)
CWRD	Chemical Warfare Research Department	CZ	combat zone; canal zone
CWRE	Chemical Warfare Research Establishment		
CWREME	Command Workshop, Royal Electrical and Mechanical Engineers	CZC	chromated zinc chloride

CZD	calculated zone distance	CZF	Canal Zone Forces
CZE	compare zone equal	CZU	compare zone unequal

D

D   Director; Deputy; District; Distinguished; deserter; destroyer; died; desert; drill (cartridge); diode; disintegrating; depth charge; dust

d   density; degree; diameter; distance; diopter; diagram; dose; drizzle; differential

(d)   attached to depot

D-day   debarkation day 6 June 1944; decimal day (UK) 15 February 1971; day on which operations commence (Nato)

D-notices   defence notices

D-ration   (combat) day ration

D-regulations   dress regulations (uniform)

D-site   decoy site

3-D   three-dimensional

D-1   howitzer 152mm (SU)

D-1   infantry tank by Renault (FR)

D-2   Skyservant, Do-28, twin-engined transport aircraft by Dornier

D-3   rocket launcher, 10 tubes 300mm (Spain)

D-5X   Turbo Sky, Do-28, turbo version Skyservant by Dornier

D-VII-B   Fledermaus, anti-aircraft fire control system by Contraves

D-20   field howitzer 152mm (SU)

D-30   field howitzer 122mm (SU)

D-44   anti-tank gun 85mm (SU)

D-74   field gun 122mm (SU)

D-566   truck 9.5 tons (Hungary)

D-921   anti-tank low-pressure smooth-bore gun 90mm (FR)

DA   dental apprentice; district attorney; dope addict; Defence Aid (lend-lease) WW2; discrete address; Denmark (Nato); Department of the Army (US); dispensing allowance; divisional artillery; Defence Act; double action (revolver); delayed action (fuse); direct action; dissolved acethylene; data adapter; di-phenyl chlor-arsine; drift

angle; director angle; define area; delay amplifier; direct access; Défense Aerienne (air defence); long-range aviation (SU)

D/A   digital-to-analog (data converter), discharge afloat

DA-08   naval air surveillance radar by HSA

DAA   divisional administrative area; Dependents' Assistance Act; di-acetone alcohol; di-acetone acrylamide; data access arrangement

DAAA   Defense Appropriation Authorization Act (US) 1977

DAA&AM   Defence Aid (lend-lease) Aircraft and Aeronautical Materials WW2

DAACA   Department of the Army, Allocation Committee, Ammunition (US)

DAACE   Department of the Army, Alternate Command and Control Element (US)

DAAE   Defence Aid (lend-lease) Administration Expenses WW2

DAAG   Deputy Assistant Adjutant General

DA-AHEW   Department of the Army Plan for Assistance to the Department of Health Education and Welfare (US)

DAAI&OC   Defence Aid (lend-lease) Agricultural, Industrial and Other Commodities

DAAMP   Department of the Army Avionics Master Plan

DAAP   dependents' allowance and assigned pay

DAAPMP   Defence Analysis and Aircraft Penetrations Mission Planning

DAA&QMG   Deputy Assistant Adjutant and Quartermaster General

DAAS   defence automatic addressing system

DAB   Dependents' Allowance Board; Destroyer Advisory Board; Design Appraisal Board; Disbursing and Accounting Branch

DABLC   Director, Advanced Bases Logistic Control

DABOA	Director, Advanced Base Office, Atlantic (US)
DABOP	Director, Advanced Base Office, Pacific (US)
dabrk	daybreak
DABS	discrete address beacon system ADSEL
Dabur	class, patrol boat by IAI
DAC	divisional artillery commander; divisional ammunition column; Director of Army Contracts; Deputy Assistant Controller; Department of the Army, Civilian; Development and Aid Committee; document availability code (Nato); digital-to-analog converter; data analysis and control; distance amplitude correction
DAc	data acquisition
DAcAN	Distribution and Accounting Agency (Nato), Military Committee Standing Group ... (Nato)
DACC	Department of the Army Communications Centre; Dangerous Air Cargoes Committee
DACCEUR	Defence Area Communications Control Centre Europe
DACCS	Department of the Army Command and Control System
DACG	Deputy Assistant Chaplain General
DaCom	data communication
DACOS	Deputy Assistant Chief of Staff
DACOWITS	Defense Advisory Committee on Women in the Services (US)
dacr	dacron
DACRP	Department of the Army Communications Resources Programme
DACS	Disarmament and Arms Control Section (Nato)
DACT	Dissimilar Air Combat Training (USAF)
DACTA	national air defence and air traffic control system (Brazil)
DACTT	defensive air combat tactics test (USAF)
DACU	digitizing and control unit
DAD	dockyard armament depot; Deputy Assistant Director
DADAC	Department of the Army Distribution and Allocation Committee; digital-to-analogue deck angle converter
DADAH	Deputy Assistant Director of Army Health
DADB	data analysis data base
DADC	digital air data computer
DADCAP	dawn and dusk combat air patrol
DADCMI	Department of the Army (policy) for Disclosure of Classified Military Information (to foreign government)
DADG	Deputy Assistant Director General
DADGMS	Deputy Assistant Director General of Medical Services
DADH	Deputy Assistant Director of Hygiene
DAdm	Director of Administration
DADME	Deputy Assistant Director of Military Engineering
DADMS	Deputy Assistant Director of Medical Services
DADOS	Deputy Assistant Director of Ordnance Services; Deputy Assistant Director of Ordnance Stores
DADPTC	Defence Automatic Data Processing Training Centre (Blanford, Dorset UK)
DADQ	Deputy Assistant Director of Quartering
DADS	Deputy Assistant Director of Supplies; Director of Army Dental Service; digital air data system; data acquisition and display system
DADST	Deputy Assistant Director of Supplies and Transport
DADT	Deputy Assistant Director of Transportation
DAE	Director of Army Education
DAEDARC	Department of the Army Equipment Data Review Committee
DAER	Department of Aeronautical and Engineering Research (Admiralty)
DAF	Department of the Air Force; departure airfield; delayed action fuse; direct action fuse; double apron fence; Dominion Aluminium Fabrication (Canada); van Doorne Automobil Fabriek (Eindhoven NL)
DAFC	departure airfield control
DAFCG	departure airfield control group
DAFD	Department of the Army Forward Depot
DAF&E	Defence Aid (lend-lease) Facilities and Equipment WW2
DAFFD	Department of the Army Forward Floating Depot
DAFIE	Directorate of Armed Forces Information and Education OIAF (US)
DAF-Indal Ltd	Dominion Aluminium Fabricating Indal (Canada)
DAFS	direct aerial fire support
DAFT	digital analogue function table
DAF YP	reconnaissance vehicle by DAF
DAG	Deputy Adjutant General; development assistance group
Dagaie	Dispositif d'Autodefense pour la Guerre Antimissile Infrarouge et Electromagnetique (naval anti-missile missile IR and radar-homing) by CSEE
DAGO	district aviation gas office
DAH	Director of Army Hygiene
DAI	Director of the Atlantic Institute (Nato Paris); death from acciden-

DAI   tal injuries; Direction Affaires Internationales (French arms trade)

DailySitRep   daily situation report SHAPE

Daimler   Ferret, scout car by Daimler (UK)

DAIO   divisional artillery intelligence officer

DAIP   Department of the Army Intelligence Plan

DAIR   driver aid information and routing; dynamic allocation interface routine

DAIS   digital avionics information system; defence automatic integrated switching

Daisy Cutter   BLU-82B, fire bomb

DAJAG   Deputy Assistant Judge Advocate General

DAK   Director of Army Kinematography

DAk   decision acknowledge

Dakin Medal   decoration for animals (UK)

Dakota   DC-3, C47, RC-47, transport aircraft by Douglas

DAL   Dominion Arsenals Ltd

DALC   deployment area location code

dalgt   daylight

Dalia-500   radar pulse analyser by Thomson-CSF

DALRLV   Department of the Army Logistics Readiness Liaison Visits

DALS   Director of Army Legal Service; data acquisition logging system

DALT   Department of the Army Liaison Team

DAlt   drop altitude

DAM   defended area model

dam   damage

DAM   distortion adaptive model Tri-Tac; dual absorption model

DAMA   Department of the Army Material Annex, demand assign multiple access

DamBuster   spinning bomb (RAF) WW2

DamCon   damage control

DAM II-EE   defended area model II engagement evaluation

DAM II-EP   defended area model II engagement planning

DAMIS   Department of the Army Management Information System

Da-Mon-Yr   day month year

DAMP   downrange anti-missile measuring project

DAMPL   Department of the Army Master Priority List

DAMPMT   Department of the Army Military Personnel Management Team

DAMP/TVPP   Department of the Army Motion Picture/Television Production Programme

DAMRIP   Department of the Army Management Review and Improvement Programme

DAMR(N)   Director of Aircraft Maintenance and Repair (Navy)

DAMR(W)   Director of Aircraft Maintenance and Repair (Washington)

DAMS   Deputy Assistant Military Secretary; defence against missile systems

DAMSA   Dépôt Avancé des Materiels du Service de Santé de l'Air (advanced air medical equipment depot)

DAMTI   digital airborne moving target indicator

DAMWO   Department of the Army Modification Work Order

Dan   Denmark (Nato)

DAN   Dépenses Administratives Nationales (national administration expenses)

DANC   decontamination agent, non-corrosive

Dannert Concertina   barbed wire drum

DANS   AD-660, doppler airborne navigation system by GEC-Marconi

DAO   division ammunition officer; district aviation officer; district accounting officer; district advisory officer

DAO&OS   Defence aid (lend-lease) ordnance and ordnance stores WW2

DA-OPRR   Department of the Army Plan for Possession, Control and Operation of Railroads

DAOPS   daylight aiming and observation periscope system (for tanks)

DAOT   Director of Air Organization and Training (RN)

DAP   Director of Army Psychiatry; Director of Army Programs (US); Director of Administrative Planning; documents against payment; do anything possible; distant aiming point; data automation proposal

DAPD   Directorate of Aircraft Production Development

DAPF   data analysis and processing facility

Daphne   class, submarines (FR-Portuguese)

DAPHNE   Dido and Pluto handmaiden for nuclear experiments

DAPM   Deputy Assistant Provost Marshal; directional anti-personnel mine

DAPP   data acquisition and processing programme

DAPS   Director of Army Postal Services

DAQ   Director of Army Quartering

DAQMG   Deputy Assistant Quartermaster General

DAQS-13   helicopter-borne dunking sonar by Bendix

DAR   Director of Army Recruiting; Director of Atomic Research; defence acquisition radar; digital avionics recorder; data automation requirements; deficiency action report (Nato); Directorate of Atomic Research (Canada); damage assessment routine

DAr   Detroit Arsenal

DARC   data acquisition and reports control; direct access radar channel

DARCom   (US Army Material) Development and Readiness Command (Alexeandria Va)

DARD   Directorate of Aircraft Research and Development

Dardo   naval point defence anti-aircraft system (Bofors twin 40mm + Orion radar by Selenia)

Daring   class, destroyers (RAN)

DARK   discrimination analysis technique adapted and refined at Kwajalein

DArmE   Directorate of Armament Engineering

DARMS   digital alternate representation of music symbols

DARPA   Defense Advanced Research Projects Agency (US)

DARR   Department of the Army Regional Representative

DARRIS   Department of the Army Requisition Receipt and Issue System

DARS   Department of the Army Relocation Sites

DART   development advanced rate techniques; daily automatic rescheduling technique; disappearing automatic retaliating targets (simulator) by ATA; dual axis rate tranducer (gyro) by BAC

Dart   towed aerial target by ATA; anti-tank missile (US) abandoned 1958

DArty   Director of Artillery

DAS   Deputy Assistant Secretary; Director of Armament Supply; direct air support; direct automotive support; divisional armourer's shop; development advisory service; Directorate of Armament Supply; DME-based azimuth systen (landing system); data acquisition (sub) system; data analysis system

DASA   Defence Atomic Support Agency

DASC   direct air support centre

DASD   Director of Army Staff Duties; direct access storage device

DAS&E   defence aid (lend-lease) services and expenses WW2

DASER   Department of the Army Suitability Evaluation Report

DASF   defence aid (lend-lease) special fund WW2

DASH   QH-50, drone anti-submarine helicopter (carrying two homing torpedoes by Gyrodyne); destroyer, anti-submarine, helicopter;DHC-7, Ranger, aircraft by DHC

DASL   Department of the Army Strategic Logistics

DASM   delayed action space missile

DASO   Department of the Army Special Order; demonstration and shakedown operations

DASPO   Department of the Army Special Photographic Office

DASS   demand assigned signalling and switching

DASSO   Department of the Army Systems Staff Officer; data systems support office

DASSO/FMSO   Department of the Army Systems Staff Officer/Fleet material support office (USN)

DAST   division for advanced systems technology; design, architecture, software and testing (of electronic components)

DASTARD   destroyer, anti-submarine, transportable array detector

DASWE   Director Admiralty Surface Weapons Establishment

DAT   Director of Army Telegraphy; Director of Army Training; development acceptance test; design approval test; dynamic address translator; Défense Aerienne du Territoire (territorial air defence); helicopter-borne scatter mine system (IT)

DATA   Defense Air Transportation Association (US)

DATAC   Development Areas Treasury Advisory Committee

DATAP   data transmission and processing

DATEL   data telecommunications

DATI   Director of Army Technical Information

DATICO   digital automatic tape intelligence check-out

DATM   Department of the Army Technical Manual

DATO   disbursing and transportation office

DATOR   Data Operational Requirements (board) (Nato Military Committee)

DAT&OV   defence aid (lend-lease) tanks and other vehicles WW2

DATRDA   defence aid (lend-lease) testing reconditioning of defence articles WW2

DATS   data transmission system; Dornier aerial target system

DATSC   Department of the Army Training and Support Committee

DAtt   Defence Attache

Dauntless SBD, naval dive bomber by Douglas
Dauphin SA-360, utility helicopter by AS
Dauphin II SA-365, utility helicopter by SA
DAUWE Director, Admiralty Underwater Weapons Establishment
DAV Disabled American Veterans
DAVIE Department of the Army Vocabulary of Information Elements
DAVID digital action video intrusion detection by ComDev
David field artillery computer (Israel)
DAVIE digital alpha-numeric video insertion equipment
Davis apparatus submarine escape apparatus
Davis gun recoilless aircraft gun WW2
DAV&OW defence aid (lend-lease) vessels and other watercraft WW2
DAV&RS Director of Army Veterinary and Remounts Service
DAW-1 infra-red homing system for Chapparral
DAWS design of aircraft wing structures; Director of Army Welfare Services
DAXREP Department of the Army Command and Control Reporting System
DB daily bulletin; disciplinary barracks; distribution branch; double barrelled; double base; double buttons; double bottom; double butted; dive bomber; Division Blindee (armoured division); Daimler Benz AG (D-6090 Rüsselsheim)
dB decibel
DB-7 Boston, dive bomber by Douglas
DB-3163 self defence jammer
DBA data base administrator; design basic accident; doing business as
DBB Director of the Bureau of the Budget; deals, battens, boards (ships' cargo)
DBC District Base Commandant; Deputy Brigade Commander
DBE Dame Commander of the Most Excellent Order of the British Empire; Daughters of the British Empire
DBF data base file
DBGM Deutsches Bundesgebrauchsmuster (GE trade mark)
DBH division beachhead; diameter at breast height
DBHP draw bar horse-power
DBk data bank
dbl double (reduction gear)
DBM de-activation of beach mines
dBm decibel meter
DBMS data base management software
DBMSPSM data base management system problem specification model
DBO district barracks officer

DBOI development basis of issue
DBP diastolic blood pressure; draw bar pull
DBRN decibel based reference noise
DBS doppler beam sharpening (radar); direct broadcast satellite
DBSO district base services office
DBST Double British Summer Time
DBTG data base task group
DBU digital buffer unit
DBV doppler broadening velocity
DC divisional commander; detachment commander; district commissioner; defence counsel; Dental Corps (US); damage control; discarded clothing; deck court; depot company; Defence Committee (Nato); document confidential; district constabulary; death certificate; deputy chief; disarmament conference; development characteristics; depth charge; dual core (bullet); disappearing carriage; dead centre; direct current; directional control; double crochet; double crown; dual capable; decimal classification; director cargo (aircraft); despatcher console; device control; direct connections; drift correction; deviation clause; Dominion Cartridge Company
DC-central damage control central (US)
DC-3 Dacota, C-47, AC-47, transport aircraft by Douglas
DC-4 Skymaster, Sphinx, C-54, four-engined cargo aircraft by Douglas
DC-6 C-118, four-engined cargo aircraft by Douglas
DC-10 transport aircraft by Douglas
DC-130 Hercules, director aircraft for RPVs by Lockheed
DCA Defence Communications Act; Defence Communications Agency; Director of Civil Affairs; damage control assistant; direction control aid; drift correction angle; Department of Civil Aviation (Australia); Digital Computer Association; driver control area; di-cholroacetic; Défense Contre Avions (anti-aircraft defence)
DCAA Defense Contracts Audit Agency (US)
DC/AC direct current/alternating current
DCadets Director of Army Cadets
DCAEur Defence Communications Agency Europe
DCAI Defence Communications Agency Instructions
DCAN Direction des Constructions et Armes Navales
DCAOC Defence Communications Agency Operations Centre

DCAS	Deputy Chief of Air Staff (Air Council); data collection and analysis system NASA, Defence Contract Administration Services
DCASD	Defence Contract Administration Services District
DCASO	Defence Contract Administration Services Office
DCASPR	Defence Contract Administration Services Plant Representative
DCASAPRO	Defence Contract Administration Services Plant Representative Officer
DCASQ	Defence Contract Administration Services Quarters
DCASR	Defence Contract Administration Services Region
DC-Automet	directional control automatic meteorological compensation --Lance
DCB	Defence Communications Board; data control block; define control block; draw-out circuit breakers; Défense Contre-blindée (anti-tank defence); Système Decimal Code Binaire (binary coded decimal)
D&CB	debt and correspondence board
DCBD	define control block dummy
DCBDM	Defence Commander, Base Defence Mediterranean
DCBE	Dame Commander of the Order of the British Empire
DCBO	divisional counter-bombardment officer
DCC	damage control centre; defence control centre; district communications centre; division computer centre; digital cross correct; direct computer control; display channel complex; double cotton covered
DCCAN	Direction Centrale des Constructions et Armes Navales (Central Directorate of Naval Construction and Weapons)
DCCAO	Deputy Chief Civil Affairs Officer (US-UK)
DCCB	Defence Control Centre Building
DCCD	Deputy Commissioner for Civil Defence
DCC-MSF	direct contact condensation multi-stage flash
DCCo	Delaware Cartridge Company
DCCP	Directorate of Communications Components Production
DCCU	data communication control units
DCD	Director of Civil Defence; Director of Combat Development; Directorate of Communications Development; digital coherent detector
DCDP	defence centre data processing
DCdr	Deputy Commander
DCDS	Deputy Chief of Defence Staff I Intelligence OR Operational Requirements
DCDU	data collection and distribution unit
DCE	data communications equipment; defensive capacity (equipment); defence combat evaluation
DC-E	Director of Communications - Electronics
DCE&ME	Director of Clothing, Equipment and Manufacturing Establishments
DCF	dependency certificate filed; disaster control force
DCFEM	dynamic crossed field electron multiplication
DCG	disaster control group; Deputy Chaplain General (UK); Deputy Commanding General (US)
DCGO	District Coast Guard Officer
DCGS	Deputy Chief of the General Staff
DCh	District Chaplain; depth charge
DCHQ	damage control headquarters
DCI	damage control instructor; Director, Central Intelligence; Defence Council Instructions; Directorate of Chemical Inspections; data communication interrogate
DCIC	Defence Ceramic Information Centre
DCIGS	Deputy Chief of the Imperial General Staff
DCII	Defence Central Index of Investigation
DCJ	District Court Judge
dcl	declaration
DCL	design capability line; data check list; dual current layer
DCLA	Deputy Chief of Staff, Logistics and Administration SHAPE
DCLI	The Duke of Cornwall's Light Infantry
DCLogA	Deputy Chief of Staff Logistics and Administration
DCLTC	Dry Cargo Loading Technical Committee
DCM	Distinguished Conduct Medal; Director of Civilian Marksmanship; district court martial; Directorate for Classification Management DoD (US); defence combat manoeuvring
DCMA	digital communications with multiple access
DCMD	District of Columbia Military District
DCMG	Dame Commander of the Order of St Michael and St George

DCMS	Deputy Commissioner, Medical Services; depot command management system	DCRO	district civilian readjustment office(r)
DCN	document control number; design change notice; drawing change notice	DCRP	disaster control recovery plan
		DCS	Deputy Chief of Staff; Director, Comptroller Systems; Defence Construction Service; defence communications system; data communications system; direct coupled system; distributed computer system
DCNATO	Deputy Council of NATO		
DCNG	District of Columbia National Guard		
DCNI	Department of the Chief of Naval Information		
DCNM	Deputy Chief of Naval Management, Deputy Chief of Naval Material	DCS-Autodin	Defence Communications System Automatic Digital Network

DCNM   Deputy Chief of Naval Management,
       Deputy Chief of Naval Material
    D   Development
    M&F   Material and Facilities
    M&O   Management and Organization
    P&FM Programme and Financial
          Management

DCNO   Deputy Chief of Naval Operations
    Air   Air
    D   Development
    L   Logistics
    P&P   Plans and Policy
    R   Readiness
    FO&R Fleet Operations and Readiness
    P&R   Personnel and Naval Reserves

DCNS   Deputy Chief of Naval Staff

DCO   director control officer; deputy commanding officer; district camouflage officer; district clothing officer; district communications officer; duty cipher officer; Deputy Chief of Staff, Operations SHAPE; depth cut-out; Director of Combined Operations
    I   India
    ME   Middle East

DCofS Deputy Chief of Staff

DCOS   Deputy Chief of Staff

DCP   Director of Civilian Personnel; Deputy Controller, Polaris (UK); defensive capacity (personnel); development concept paper; dental continuation pay; design change proposal; data collecting platform

DCPA   Defence Civil Preparedness Agency

DCPG   Defence Communications Planning Group

DCPO   district civilian personnel office(r); Deputy Chief of Staff, Personnel and Organization SHAPE

DCPR   defence contractor's planning report

DCPSK differentially coherent phase shift keying

DCPU   display control and processing unit

DCR   dual cycle rifle (US) future rifle system; data communications read

dcr   decoration; decrease

DCRA   Dominion of Canada Rifle Association

DCRE   Deputy Commander, Royal Engineers

DCSC   defence construction supply centre

DCSCD Deputy Chief of Staff for Combat Developments

DCSC-E Deputy Chief of Staff for Communications-Electronics

DCSI   Deputy Chief of Staff for Intelligence

DCSO   Deputy Chief of Staff for Operations; deputy chief signals officer; deputy chief scientific officer

DCSOI Deputy Chief of Staff, Operations and Intelligence

DCSCompt Deputy Chief of Staff, Comptroller

DCSFor Deputy Chief of Staff, Force Development

DCSLog Deputy Chief of Staff, Logistics

DCSMIS Deputy Chief of Staff, Management Information System

DCSOps Deputy Chief of Staff, Operations and Plans

DCSOT Deputy Chief of Staff, Operations and Training

DCSPA Deputy Chief of Staff, Personnel and Administration

DCSPer Deputy Chief of Staff, Personnel

DCSARDA Deputy Chief of Staff of the Army for Research Development and Acquisition

DCSRM Deputy Chief of Staff for Resource Management

DCSROTC Deputy Chief of Staff, Reserve Officers' Training Corps

DCSS   Damage Control Suit System

DCST   Deputy Chief of Supplies and Transport

DCSTS Deputy Chief of Staff, Training and Schools

DCT   director, control tower; depth charge thrower

dct   document; direct

DCTL   direct coupled transistor logic

DCU   drum control unit; device control unit

DCVO   Dame Commander of the Royal Victorian Order

DCW   data communications write

DCW&S Director of Chemical Warfare and Smoke

DC-X-200 project aircraft 200 passengers by McDD

DD deputy director; duty driver; displaced diplomat; Defence Department; dishonourable discharge; discharged dead; departure date; development directive; determination of dependency; destroyer; double drift; data definition; dry dock; duplex drive (amphibious); di-chloro-propylene and di-chloro-propane; definite decoding; detergent dispersant; day's date; delayed delivery

D/D days after date; demand draft

dd dated; delivered; drilled

D&D drunk and disorderly; drunk and dirty

DD-2 second development decade 1971-80

DDA designated deployment area; dangerous drugs act; Detroit Diesel Allison (Indianapolis Ind.) (GM daughter); digital drive amplifier (missile site radar); digital differential analyser; data differential analyser; District de Défense Aerienne (air defence district)

DDALv days delay enroute chargeable as leave

D'DAS digital data acquisition system

DDAS(ET) Deputy Director of Armament Supply (Eastern Theatre) WW2

DDC Defence Documentation Centre (for Scientific and Technical Information); deck decompression chamber; direct digital control; Corvette (USN)

DDCA Deputy Director of Civil Aviation

DDCO(I) Deputy Director of Combined Operations, India WW2

DDD deadline delivery date, diesel direct drive; distance direct dialling

DDDS Deputy Director of Dental Services

DDE Destroyer Escort (USN); Class I anti-submarine escort (Nato)

DDEM Directorate of Design of Equipment and Mechanization

DDEP Defence Development Exchange Programme

DDFO Deputy Director of Fighter Operations

DDG Deputy Director General; destroyer, guided missiles

DDGSE Deputy Director of Signals Equipment

DDGSR Division of the Director General of Scientific Research

DDH destroyer, carrying helicopters (Canada); destroyer, anti-submarine helicopters (Nato); anti-submarine destroyer

DDI divisional detective inspector; direct dial in

DDK destroyer, hunter-killer (USN)

DDL Deputy Director of Labour; digital data link; data description language

DDM difference in depth modulation

DDME Deputy Director of (Electrical and Mechanical Engineering)

DDMI Deputy Director of Military Intelligence

DDMOI Deputy Director of Military Operations and Intelligence

DDMS Deputy Director of Medical Services

DDMT Deputy Director of Military Transport

DDMT-1A RASIT, Rapiere, medium-range battlefield surveillance radar by LCT

DDN defence data network (Canada); Département de la Défense National (Department of National Defence)

DDNI Deputy Director of Naval Intelligence

DDO District Dental Officer; dummy delivery order; destroyers disbursing office

DDocks Director of Docks

DDODI Deputy Director Operation Division, Irregular, Admiralty

DDOS Deputy Director of Ordnance Services

DDP design data package; declaration of design performance; Department of Defence Production (Canada); data distribution point

DDPL demand deposit programme library

DDPR Deputy Director of Public Relations

DDPS Deputy Director of Personal Services; Deputy Director of Postal Services; discrimination data processing system

DDPU digital display processing unit

DDR The Devonshire and Dorset Regiment; Deutsche Demokratische Republik (GDR); dynamic device reconfiguration; destroyer, radar picket (USN)

DDRA Deputy Director, Royal Artillery

DDRB Danish Defence Research Board

DDRD Deputy Director of Research and Development; Director of Defence Research and Engineering; Danish Defence Research Establishment

DDRM Deputy Director of Repair and Maintenance

DDRR directional discontinuity ring radiator

DDS Deputy Defence Secretary; Deputy Director of Science; Director of Dental Services; display and de-briefing system; deep diving system; digital data service

dd/s   delivered sound
DDSD   Deputy Director of Staff Duties
DD&Shpg   dock dues and shipping
DDSR   Deputy Director of Scientific
          Research
DDST   Deputy Director of Supply and Trans-
          port
DDT   dichloro-diphenyl-trichloro-ethane
          (insecticide)
DDTO   District Domestic Transportation
          Office(r)
DDTV   dry diver transport vehicle
DDUS   date departed United States
DDV   deep diving vehicle
DDVS   Deputy Director of Veterinary
          Services
DDWE&M   Deputy Director of Works Electrical
          and Mechanical
DDWO   Deputy Director of War Organization
DDX   destroyer, experimental (USN)
DE   District Establishment; direct
          entry; defence emergency; double
          entry; Denmark (Nato); destroyer
          escort (USN); ocean escort (Nato);
          device end; deflection error;
          diesel-electric; digestible energy;
          differential equation; damage
          expectancy
D&E   development and engineering
DE-1160B modular light-weight active/passive
          ASW sonar by Raytheon (export
          version SQS-56)
DE-1164   modular light-weight active/passive
          + variable depth sonar
DEA   Department of Economic Affairs;
          Department of External Affairs;
          data exchange annex; Davis escape
          apparatus
DEAC   Defence Economics Analysis Council
DeADS   Detroit air defense sector
DEASC   Defence and External Affairs Sub-
          committee (UK)
DEB   digital European backbone; data
          extension block
DEC   disaster emergency committee;
          Development and Education Command
          (USMC); Digital Equipment Corpora-
          tion; Escort Control vessel (USN)
dec   decoration; deceased; deciphering;
          decision; decoding; decoppering;
          declination; decimal
DECB   data event control block
Decca   UK firm, radio phase comparison
          system for ground positioning
DECCC   Defence commercial communications
          centre
DECCO   Defence commercial communications
          office; Defence Communications Con-
          tracting Office
DECEA   Defence Communications Engineering
          Agency

DECEO   Defence Communications Engineering
          Office DCA
DECM   Defence electronics counter-
          measures
decn   decision; decontamination (UK)
DECO   Development Engineering Corporation
DeCoM   delay cost model
decom   decommissioned
decomd   decommissioned
decon   decontamination
DECOR   digital electronic continuous
          ranging
DECTRA   Decca tracking and ranging
DECUS   Digital Equipment Computers Users
          Society
DED   Director of Engineering Development;
          diesel engine driven
ded   deduct
DEdn   Director of Education
DEDS   digital error detection subsystem;
          data entry and display subsystem
Deep Quest rescue submersible by Lockheed
DeepSubSys deep submergence system
DeepSubSysProjTechO Deep Submergence
                     Systems Project Tech-
                     nical Office (USN)
Deeptow   deep sea towing system by Dornier
DEER   directional explosive echo ranging
DEF   disarmed enemy forces, Defence
          (specification)
def   defend; defence; defensive; define;
          definition; defective; deflagrate;
          deflection; defrost; defoliate
DEFA   Direction des Etudes et Fabrications
          d'Armaments (Directorate of Arma-
          ments Research and Development)
          (FR) (cannon 30mm)
DEFA/ADEN airborne gun 30mm
DefCloth&TexSupCen Defence Clothing and
                    Textile Support Center
                    (US)
DefCom Defence Command
DefComSys Defence Communications System
DefCon Defence (readiness) condition
DefConstrSupCen Defense Construction Supply
                 Center (US)
DefElecSupCen Defence Electric Supply
               Centre
Defender OH-6, Hughes-500, Cayuse, light
          helicopter TOW-armed by Hughes;
          cheap light-plane by Britten-
          Norman
DefEx Defence Exports (Madrid)
DefGenSupCen Defence General Supply Centre
Defiant fighter aircraft WW2 by Boulton
         Paul
DefIndPlantEquipCen Defense Industrial
                     Plant Equipment
                     Center (US)
DefIndSupCen Defence Industrial Supply
              Centre

DefIndSupDep Defence Industrial Supply Depot
DefIntelAgcy Defence Intelligence Agency
defl   deflect(ion), deflate, deflation
DefLOWH Defense Liaison Officer to the
         White House
defn   deficiency
DefPerSuppCen Defence Personnel Support
         Centre
DefRepNAMA Defence Representative, North
         Atlantic Mediterranean Area
DEFREP Defence Readiness Posture; Defence
         Representative (Nato)
DefSec Defense Section (US)
DEF STAN (quality assurance) Standard of
         the British MoD
DefSubSupCen Defense Subsistence and Supply
         Center (US)
DEFT   dynamic error free transmission
DefWeapSysMgtCen Defence Weapons Systems
         Management Centre
DEG   Destroyer, escort, guided missiles
         (Nato); Deutsche Entwicklungs
         Gesellschaft GMBH (German Develop-
         ment Company)
deg   delegation; degree
D&EG   Development and Engineering Group
Deg&Dep degaussing and deperming
DeGeSch Deutsche Gesellschaft zur
         Schädlingsbekämpfung WW2 (war gas)
Deg/range degaussing range
Degtyarev RPD, self-loading rifle 7,62mm
         (SU); PTRD machine gun;
         DShK-38 heavy machine gun
DEH   hydrofoil 2500 tons by Boeing
DEI   Dutch East Indies
Deirdre class, Irish corvettes
DEL   directly employed labour
del   delivery; delegate; delegation
Delfin L-29, Czech trainer aircraft by Aero
DelGru Delaware Group
Delphin floatplane by Dornier
DELRAC Decca long-range area coverage
DelRivePOE delay in arriving at port of
         embarkation
DELTA   detailed labour and time analysis
Delta   orbital transport missile by McDD
Delta   Dagger F-102, super-sonic fighter;
         interceptor by Convair
Delta   Dart F-106, supersonic fighter;
         interceptor by Convair (mach 2)
DELTIC delay-line time compression
DelWU   Delegate to the Western Union
dem   demodulator
DemBomb demolition bomb
demil   demilitarized
DEME   Director of Electrical and Mechanical
         Engineering
DEMIZ   DEW east military identification
         zone (distant early warning) (US)
DEML   detached enlisted men's list

demo   demolition (bomb); demonstration
demon   demonstration
demob   demobilization
DeMod   deployment model
demon   demonstration
Demon   F-38, naval fighter by McDD
DEMS   defensively equipped merchant ship
         (US)
DEMSS   defensively equipped merchant ship
         school
den   dental
DenCo   Dental Company (USMC)
dens   density
DentCAP Dental Civic Action Programme
denyg   denying
DEO   district engineer officer; The Duke
         of Edinburgh's Own (Gurkha Rifles)
DEOS   Director of Equipment and Ordnance
         Service
DEP   Director of Equipment and Policy;
         deflection error probable; defence
         electronics products RCA
dep   deputy; deployment; departure;
         depot; dependent; department
DEPA   Defence Electric Power Administra-
         tion
DepActv depot activity
DepAir Air Deputy to SHAPE
DEPC   Defence Equipment Policy Committee
DepChfofNavMat Deputy Chief of Naval
         Material
DepChfofNavMat&Fac Deputy Chief of Naval
         Material and Facili-
         ties
DepCom DeputyCCommander
DepComOpTEvFor Deputy Commander, Operation-
         al Test and Evaluation
         Force
         Lant Atlantic
         Pac Pacific
DepComStrikForSouth Deputy Commander, Naval
         Striking and Support
         Forces Southern
         Europe (ashore)
DepComSTS Deputy Commander Military Sea
         Transport Service (USN)
DepDir Deputy Director
DEPE   double escape peak efficiency
DepEvacPay Dependents evacuation pay
DepEX   Deployment Studies on Nike X
DepMilSec Deputy Military Secretary
depn   dependent
DepNav Department of the Navy (US);
         Naval Deputy to SHAPE
DepnoAuth dependents not authorized (at
         overseas duty station)
DepRep Deployment reporting system
DepSACLant Deputy Supreme Allied Commander
         Atlantic
DepSecDef Deputy Secretary of Defence

DepSecLantFAP Deputy Secretary ACLANT
            Frequency Allocation Plan
DepStAr deployment status of Army units
DEPSum daily estimated position summary
dept department, departmental
DeptAr Department of the Army
DER radar picket escort ship (USN)
DerbyYeo The Derbyshire Yeomanry
DERD diesel electric reduction drive
DERE Dounreay Experimental Reactor Estab-
            lishment
DERI deep electric research investigation
DEROS date eligible for return from over-
            seas
DERP deficient equipment reporting proce-
            dures
DERR The Duke of Edinburgh's Royal Regi-
            ment
DERV diesel engined road vehicle
DES Department of Education and Science;
            Director of Educational Services;
            Director of Engineering Stores;
            diesel electric ship; data encryp-
            tion standard; dynamic environment
            simulator; dispersed emergency
            station
des destroyer; desert; deserter; deser-
            tion; design; designation; desig-
            nated; desired; desirable
DesAccts Destroyer's Accounts (USN)
DesAF Destroyers, Asiatic Fleet (USN)
DesBatFor destroyer battle force
desc descend; describe
DESC Defence Electronic Supply Centre
DeScoFor destroyer scouting force
DesCruPac Destroyers/Cruisers, Pacific
DesDevDiv Destroyer Development Division
DesDevGru Destroyer Development Group
DesDevRon Destroyer Development Squadron
DesDiv Destroyer Division
DesEff Deserters' Effects
DesFlot Destroyer Flotilla
DesFltSurg designated student Naval flight
            surgeon
desig designate; designation
DesigDisbAgent designated special disbursing
            agent
DesLant Destroyers, Atlantic
DesPac Destroyers, Pacific
DesNavAv designated student naval Aviator
DESO District Educational Services
            Office(r)
desp despatch
DESPort daily equipment status report
DesRep Destroyer Representative; Destroyer
            repair
DesRon Destroyer Squadron
DesSoWesPac Destroyers, South East Pacific
            Fleet
DEST Directorate of Engineering and
            Standardization

dest destroyer; destination; destruction
destn destination
Destroyer RB-66, radar jammer aircraft by
            Douglas
DET Division des Engines Tactiques
det detachment; detective; detach;
            detect; detain
DETA di-ethylene-tri-amine
DetCon Detective Constable
DetD detached duty
Dete naval radar WW2 (Germany)
DeTeWe Deutsche Telephonwerke und Kabelin-
            dustrie
DetInsp Detective Inspector
detn determination, detention
DetPay detained pay
DetRIns detailed routing instructions
DetSgt Detective Sergeant
DetSup Detective Superintendent
DetSupt Detective Superintendent
DEU data exchange unit; data entry unit
DEUCE digital electronic universal com-
            puting engine
DeuGra Deutsche Graviner Brandschutzsysteme
            GmbH (Elisabethstr. 21, D-4030
            Ratingen 2)
dev deviation; development
DevA development acceptance
Devastator TBD-1, naval torpedo bomber by
            Douglas
DEVIL development of integrated logistics
Devon The Devonshire Regiment; artillery
            observation plane by De Havilland
devpt development
DEW distant early warning (system) (US-
            Can)
DeWaT deactivated war trophy
DEWIZ distant early warning identification
            zone
DEX deferred execution
DEXAN digital experimental airborne navi-
            gator
DF direct fire; defensive fire; direc-
            tion finder; direction finding;
            disposition form; delay fuse; drop
            forging; director fighter aircraft
            (USAF); disk file; distribution
            feeders; Doppelfernrohr (binocu-
            lars); Dauerfeuer (sustained fire)
df draft; dead freight; decontamination
            factor
D&F determination and finding
DF-laser deuterium fluoride laser
DF-1 DF-2, direction finding course (USN)
            phase 1 (phase 2)
DF-3 tank fire control system by Barr &
            Stroud
DF-4 Corsair, fighter aircraft by Vought
DF-8 Crusader, jet aircraft by Vought
DF-100 Super Sabre, jet aircraft RPV

director by North American
Rockwell

DFA designated field activity;
Department of Foreign Affairs

DFaE Director of Facilities Engineering

DFC Distinguished Flying Cross; disk
file check

DFCO duty flying control officer

DFCU disk file control unit

DFDR digital flight data recorder

DFE division force equivalents

DFEC Defence Finance Economic Committee

DF/ESM direction finder for electronic
support measures

DFH defence family housing

DFI Directorate of Food Investigation;
disk file interrogator

DFL Deutsche Forschungsanstalt für Luft-
und Raumfahrt (German Research
Establishment for Aeronautics and
Spaceflight)

DFLS day fighter leaders school

DFM Distinguished Flying Medal;
Director for Food Management;
direct force mode (control)

DFMA Director for Military Assistance

DFMO doppler filter mixer oscillator

dfndt defendant

DFO district finance officer; Defence
Field Office (Thailand)

DFP divisional foot police; di-isopropyl-
fluoro-phosphate (war gas)

DFR Dounreay fast reactor; dropped from
rolls; decreasing failure rate;
distribution feeders rack; disk
file read

DFRA Drop Forging Research Association
(UK)

DFRIF Defence Freight Railway Interchange
Fleet

DFS dual flight simulator; direction
finder system

DFS-15 direction finder system; portable
by ESL

DFS-230 DFS-231, combat and cargo glider
WW2 by Deutsche Forschungsanstalt
für Segelflug

DFSB defence force section base

DFSC defence fuel supply centre

DFSR detailed functional system requirement

DFStn direction finding station

DFSU disk file storage unit

DFT Director, Fleet Training (USN);
diagnostic function test

dftmn draftsman

DFUA Datenfernübermittlungsanschluss
(data transmission connection
module)

dfus diffuse

DFVLR Deutsche Forschungs- und Versuchs-
anstalt für Luft- und Raumfahrt
(German Research and Experimental
Establishment for Aeronautics and
Spaceflight)

DFW Director(ate) of Fortifications and
Works; diesel fuel waiver; disk
file write

DFWES direct fire weapons effects simulation (for helicopters) by Solarton

DG Dragoon Guards; Dutch Guilder
(florin),
Director General
A(N)   aircraft (Naval)
NMT   Naval manpower and training
PS(N)   personal services (Naval)
Ship   ship department
ST   supply and transport
W(N)   weapons (Naval)
directional gyro; de-gaussing;
destroyer, guided missiles a/a
(Nato)

dg diagnosis

3-DG The Third Carabiniers, The Prince of
Wales's Dragoon Guards

4/7 DG The 4th/7th Royal Dragoon Guards

5 DG The 5th Royal Inniskilling Dragoon
Guards

7 DG The 7th Dragoon Guards

DG-91 hand grenade with percussion fuse
by Italmeccanica

DGA Director General Aircraft; Delegation Générale pour l'Armament
(Armaments General (trade) Delegation of the French MoD)

DGAA Distressed Gentlefolks' Aid Association

DGAMS Director General of Army Medical
Services

DGAR Director General of Army Requirements

DGAVS Director General of Army Veterinary
Service

DGBC digital geo-ballistic computer

DGCA Director General of Civil Aviation

DGCE Director General of Communications
Equipment (UK)

DGCStJ Dame Grand Cross of the Order of
St John of Jerusalem

DGCVO Dame Grand Cross of the Royal
Victorian Order

DGD Director Gunnery Division; diesel
geared drive; Deutsche Gesellschaft fur (Patent) Dokumentation
(German Association for Documentation) (patents)

DGD&M Director General, Dockyards and
Maintenance

DGDC Deputy Grand Director of Ceremonies

DGE Directorate General of Equipment

DGFVE	... aluminium-zinc-magnesium alloy	DGTO	de-gaussing technical officer
DGH	Director General of Hygiene	DGW	Director General of Weapons; Director General of Works
DGI	Director General of Information; Director General of Inspection	DGWO	de-gaussing wiping officer
DGISD	Director General of Intelligence Service Department	DGZ	desired ground zero
DG/L	computer language	DGzRS	Deutsche Gesellschaft zur Rettung Schiffbrüchiger (German Associa- tion for the Rescue of the Ship- wrecked)
DGLR	Deutsche Gesellschaft für Luft und Raumfahrt (e. V. Goethestr. 10, D-500 Köln) (German Association for Aeronautics and Spaceflight)	DH	Director of Hygiene; de Havilland (aircraft company) (UK); decision height; desired height; desired heading; dead heat
DGM	Director General for Manpower; Defence Guidance Memorandum; destroyer, guided missiles SAM + SSM (Nato); digital group multi- plexer Tri-Tac by Raytheon	DH-4	reconnaissance bomber by de Havilland
		DH-110	Sea Venom, naval all-weather fighter by de Havilland
DGME	Director General of Military Educa- tion	DH-112	Venom, all-weather fighter by DH
DGMEA	Director General of Management Engineering and Automation (CA)	DH-132	tank crew helmet by Gentex
		DH-152	noise-protective tank crew helmet by Gentex
DG-MG	diesel-geared motor-geared	DH-178	combined ear-defender + ballistic helmet by Gentex
DGMP	Director General of Munitions Pro- duction	DHA	dependent housing area
DGMS	Director General of Medical Services	DHC	De Havilland Aircraft of Canada Ltd (Downview, Ontario M3K 1Y5)
DGMT	Director General of Military Train- ing	DHC-4	Caribou, STOL transport by DHC
DGMW	Director General of Military Works	DHC-5	Buffalo, tactical transport by DHC
Dgn	Dragoon	DHC-7	Ranger, maritime patrol plane by DHC
DGO	daily general order; de-gaussing officer	DHE	data handling equipment; dump heat exchangers
DGOC	divisional general officer command- ing	DHEW	Department of Health Education and Welfare (US)
DGON	Deutsche Gesellschaft für Ortung und Navigation (German Association for Location and Navigation)	DHIRS	District Headquarters Induction and Recruiting Station (USMC)
DGP	Director General of Personnel; Director General of Production	DHJ	Diensthalbjahr NVA DDR (servie half year)
DGP	Deutsche Grenzpolizei (DDR) (German Border Police) (GDR)	DHMPGTS	Department of Her (His) Majesty's Procurator General and Treasury Solicitor
DGPS	Director General of Personal Services (and Officer Appointments)	DHO	District Historical Office(r)
DGR	Director of Graves Registration	DHP	developed horse power
DGRO	de-gaussing range officer	DHQ	Division Headquarters, District Headquarters
DGrtP	death gratuity payment	DHS	data handling system; dual hardness steel
DGS	divisional general survey; Director General, Ships; Director General, Signals; destroyer, guided missiles SSM (Nato)	DHSS	Department of Health and Social Security; data handling sub-system
DGSC	Defence General Supply Centre	DHU	detector head unit
DGSRD	Director General of Science Research and Development (UK)	DHX	dump heat exchangers
DGStJ	Dame of Grace of the Order of St John of Jerusalem	DI	drill instruction; drill instructor; district inspector; defence intel- ligence; Director of Infantry; detective inspector; divisional inspector; diplomatic immunity; document identifier; distinctive insignia; due in; daily inspec- tion; de-icing; dark ignition (tracer); Division d'Infanterie, infantry division
DGT	Director General of Transportation; Director General of Training		
DGTA	Director General of the Territorial Army		
dgtl	digital	D&I	disassembly and inspection

di   diameter
DIA   date of initial appointment;
            Defence Intelligence Agency;
            Detachement d'Intervention Air
            (air control team)
dia   diameter; diagram
DIAC   data interpretation and analysis
            centre by Litton; Defense Indus-
            trial Advisory Council (US)
Diad   US defence policy (strategic bombers
            + ballistic missile submarines) →
            Triad
DIADC   Defence Intelligence Agency Dissem-
            ination Centre
Diademe   mobile electronics repair station
            by SFENA
diag   diagonal; diagnosis; diagram
Dial   diallyl-barbituric acid (hypnosis)
DIALEX   differential absorption laser exper-
            iment LIDAR --- Spacelab
DIAM   data independent architecture module
diam   diameter
Diamond-T   tank transporter vehicle (UK)
DIAN   Decca integrated airborne naviga-
            tion
DIANE   digital integrated attack and navi-
            gation equipment (avionics) (UK);
            distance indicating automatic
            navigation equipment
diaph   diaphragm
DIAS   digital avionics information system
DIBA   digital integrated ballistic analy-
            ser
Dibber   bomb retarded bomb (retro rockets)
DIC   detailed interrogation centre;
            defence identification code;
            digital interior communications by
            Ford
dic   dictionary
DICASS   SSQ-62, directional command-active
            sonobuoy system (helicopter-borne)
DICAT   digital computer assisted targeting
            unit ---XM-1
DICBM   defence intercontinental ballistic
            missile; depressed trajectory
            intercontinental ballistic missile
Dicke Berta mortar 42cm (GE) WW1
DICON   digital communications network

DICORAP   directional controlled rocket-
            assisted projectile
DICU   data interface control unit; driver
            indicator control unit
DID   detailed issue depot; data item
            descriptions
DIDAS   dynamic instrumentation data auto-
            mobile system
Di/Des   vessel disposed of by destruction
            (USN)

DIDS   defence integrated data systems;
            digital information display
            system; DLSC integrated data
            system (defence logistics service
            centre); defence information dis-
            tribution system
DIDS-CD   defence information distribution
            system - civil defence
DIDU   defense item data utilization (pro-
            gramme) (US)
DIE   Defence Industries Exhibition (UK)
DIECO   defence item entry control office
DIECP   defence item entry control pro-
            gramme
DIEME   Directorate of Inspection of Elec-
            trical and Mechanical Equipment
DIER   department instrument equipment
            reserve
Dieso   diesel oil; diesel fuel
DIF   duty involving flying
DiF   direction finding
dif   differential; difference
DIFAR   SSQ-53, directional low-frequency
            analyser and ranging system;
            direction finding and ranging
            (sonobuoy)
DiffPay   difference in pay
Di/FLC   disposition of vessel by foreign
            liquidation corporation (USN)
DifKin   diffusion kinetics
DIFOT   duty in flying status involving
            operational or training flights
            (USN)
            Crew   as crewmember
            Dorse   effective at endorsed
                        date
            Tech   as technical observer
            Exist   existing detail
                        continues
            Ins   under instruction
            InsCrew   under instruction as
                        crew member
            NonCrew   as non crewmember
            InsNonCrew under instruction as
                        non crewmember
            Relas   as his relief
            Rept   upon reporting
            Rvk   revoked
DIG   Deputy Inspector General; disable-
            ment income group; delivery indi-
            cator group; digital image genera-
            tion; digital input gate
dig   digit; digital
DigiCom   digital communications terminal by
            E-Systems
DigiTac   digital tactical aircraft control
            (USAF programme)
digl   di-glycol-di-nitrate
DigOps   Digest of Operations
DIGS   Dornier inter-active graphics system
            (computer-drawn maps) by Dornier

Di/Int   disposition of vessel by Department
         of the Interior (USN)
DIIO   District Industrial Incentive
         Office(r)
DIL   Defense Industries Ltd
DiLaG   differential laser gyro(scope) by
         Sperry
Dilbert Dunker air-sea emergency trainer
DILS   doppler inertial IORAN system
DIM   district industrial manager; defence
         information memorandum; device
         interface module; vehicular mine
         detector (SU)
DIMES   defence integrated management
         engineering systems; development
         and improved management engineer-
         ing systems
DIMS   Director of the International Mili-
         tary Staff (Nato)
DIMUS   digital multi-beam steering
DIMPLE   deuterium moderated pile; low energy
         (atomic reactor)
DIN   Deutsches Institut für Normung
         (German Institute for Standardiza-
         tion)
DINA   direct noise amplifier; di-oxy-
         ethyl-nitramine-di-nitrate
         (Cordite N)
DInfoS   Defense Information School (US)
DINO   Deputy Inspector of Naval Ordnance
         (US)
Dingo   reconnaissance vehicle
Dinkum Digger trench digging machine
DIO   Divisional Intelligence Officer;
         District Intelligence Officer;
         District Information Office(r);
         Director of Industrial Operations;
         data input/output; direct input/
         output
Diodon   keel sonar (24 hydrophones) by
         Thomson-CSF
dion   division
DIOP   di-ido-octyl-phtalate (plasticizer)
DIOS   distribution information and optimi-
         zing system
DIP   detailed issue park; defamation,
         identification and publication
         (elements of libel); Defence Indus-
         try Productivity (Ca); dual incline
         package; display information pro-
         cessor
DIPD   double inverse pinch device
DIPEC   Defence Industrial Plant Equipment
         Centre
dipl   diplomat
DIPR   Departmental Industrial Plant
         Reserve
DIPS   dissent propulsion system NASA;
         Director of the International
         Planning Staff (Nato)

DIPSM   Director of the International Plan-
         ning Staff Memorandum (Nato)
DIR   depot inspection and repair; dis-
         assembly inspection report; dis-
         charge instrument recorder;
         development inhibitor releasing
         (phot)
dir   direction; directed; director
Dira   artillery rocket 81mm twin 15 cell
         launcher by Oerlikon
DIRAFIED Director, Armed Forces Information
         and Education Division (US)
DIRACDA Director US Arms Control and Dis-
         armament Agency
DirBy   when directed by
DirCaribDocks Director, Bureau of Yards and
               Docks, Caribbean Division
               (USN)
DirChesDocks Director, Bureau of Yards and
              Docks, Chessapeake Division
DirCruit Director of Recruiting (USN)
DirDet   when directed detach
DirEastCenDocks Director, Bureau of Yards
                 and Docks, East Central
                 Division
DirEast Docks Director, Bureau of Yards and
               Docks, Eastern Division
               (USN)
direc   direction
DirEurDocks Director, Bureau of Yards and
             Docks, European Division (USN)
DirFldSuppAct Director, Field Support
               Activity
DirFM   Director, Field Maintenance
DirGen   Director General
DirGulfDocks Director, Bureau of Yards and
              Docks, Gulf Division (USN)
DirLantDocks Director, Bureau of Yards and
              Docks, Atlantic Division
DirLAuth direct liaison authorized (Nato);
         direct line of authority (US)
DirMidWestDocks Director, Bureau of Yards
                 and Docks, Midwest Divi-
                 sion (USN)
DirNavCom Director of Naval Communications
DirNavHis Director of Naval History
DirNavPubPrintServ Director, Navy Pulica-
                    tions and Printing
                    Service (US)
DirNIMS Director of the Nato International
         Military Staff
DirNorEastDocks Director, Bureau of Yards
                 and Docks, Northeast
                 Division (USN)
DirNorWestDocks Director, Bureau of Yards
                 and Docks, Northwest
                 Division (USN)
DirNSA   Director, National Security Agency
         (US)
DIRO   Director, Industrial Relations Office
         (US) DLRO

DirOCD   Director, Office of Civil Defense (US)
DirPA   Director of Personnel and Administration (US)
DirPacDocks   Director, Bureau of Yards and Docks, Pacific Division (USN)
DirPro   when directed proceed
DirSoEastDocks   Director, Bureau of Yards and Docks, Southeast Division (USN)
DirSoWestDocks   Director, Bureau of Yards and Docks, Southwest Division (USN)
DirWestDocks   Director, Bureau of Yards and Docks, Western Division (USN)
DirSP/ProjMangrFBM   Director, Special Projects Project Manager, Fleet Ballistic Missile (USN)
DIS   Defence Intelligence Staff; Defence Intelligence School; Defense Investigation Service (US)
dis   disconnect; dismount; distribute; discipline; distance; distant
DiSal   disposition of vessel by sale
disb   disbanded; disburse
DISC   Director of Information Service Control; Defence Industrial Supply Centre; delay in separation code; district information service control; differential isochronous self-collimating
disc   discontinue
DISCC   district information service control command
disch   discharge
DISCO   Defence Industrial Security Clearance Office; digital scan converters airfield, surveillance radar by HSA
DisCom   division support command
discon   discontinue
DISCON   Defence Integrated Secure Communications Network (Australia)
DISCOS   Disturbance Compensation System for NOVA satellite
DiScp   disposition of vessel by scrapping
DiscRep   discrepancy report
discr   discriminate
discrp   discrepancy
DISD   Defence Industrial Supply Depot
disem   disseminate
disemb   disembark
DisGrat   discharge gratuity
dishon   dishonourable
DisLine   dispersal line
dismd   dismissed
DisOp   discharge by operator
DISP   Defence Industry Studies Programme; DoD Industrial Security Programme

disP   dispersal point
disp   dispensary; disposal; dispatch
disqual   disqualify
disre   disregard
DisRep   discrepancy in shipment report
DisRet   disability retirement
DisSevr   disability severance
DISS   digital interface switching system
diss   dissolved
dist   distance; distilled; district
DistDentalO   District Dental Officer
Distel   Digitales Informationsverarbeitungssystem für taktische Einsatzzentralen der Luftwaffe (digital information processing system for tactical operations centres of the German Air Force)
DistEngr   District Engineer
DistMedO   District Medical Officer
DISTO   Defence Industrial Security Education and Training Office
distr   distribution
DistrA   distribution authority
DISTRAM   digital space trajectory measurement system
DisTreat   upon discharge treatment
distrib   distribute
DistRo   distribution rotation
DISUB   duty involving submarine operations
DIT   Detroit Institute of Technology
DITC   Department for Industry Trade and Commerce (Canada)
DiTes   disposition of vessel by using as target and for tests
DiTrn   disposition of vessel for transfer to other government agency
div   division(al); diversion; diving; divergence
DIVAD   division air defence (radar guided twin anti-aircraft gun by Ford)
DivCom   Division Commander
DivEngr   Division Engineer
DivHQ   divisional headquarters
DivInfo   division of information
DivPay   diving pay
DivSigs   divisional signals
DiWSA   disposition of vessel by War Shipping Administration
Dixie   class, destroyer tenders (USN)
DJA   Deputy Judge Advocate of the Fleet
DJAG   Deputy Judge Advocate General
Djinn   single seater helicopter by SNCASO
DJS   Director, Joint Staff
DJSM   Director, Joint Staff Memorandum
DJStJ   Dame of Justice of the Order of St John of Jerusalem
DJUOL   daily JUMPS update output listing (joint uniform military pay system)
DK   Danish Krone

dk	dock; deck; dark
DKF/KM	Dokumentation Kraftfahrwesen/Krauss Maffei (automotive documentation by Krauss Maffei)
DKI	data key idle
DKQN-11	river crossing sonar equipment for engineer reconnaissance by Elac
DL	Deputy Lieutenant; driving licence; Department of Labor (US); deadline; direct layer; de luxe; deck log; data link; departure locator
D/L	data link
DL	destroyer leader (USN) frigate; delay line; dynamic loader
DLA	dislocation allowance; depot level activity; Defence Liaison Agency; distributed lumped active
DLat	difference of latitude
DLBD	digital light beam deflecting (display)
DLC	divisional land commissioner; deep look capability (radar); direct lift control (system/aircraft)
DLCC	division logistics control centre
DLCS	data line concentrator system
DLD	dead line date
dld	delivered
DLE	date link escape
DLF	development loan fund
DLG	defence liaison group; destroyer leader; guided missiles (Nato) (frigate)
DLGN	destroyer leader, guided missiles nuclear-powered (Nato)
DLI	The Durham Light Infantry; Defence Language Institute
DLIEC	Defence Language Institute East Coast Branch
DLIEL	Defence Language Institute English Language Branch
DLIS	desert locust information service
DLISDA	Defence Language Institute Systems Development Agency
DLISW	Defence Language Institute Southwest Branch
DLIWC	Defence Language Institute West Coast Branch
DLL	design limit load
DLM-3	Datenleitungsmessgerät (data link) testing system by Goltermann)
DLNC	Deputy Local Naval Commander
DLO	District Legal Office(r); Divisional Legal Officer; dead letter office
DLOC	division logistical operation centre
DLogS	division logistics system
DLong	difference of longitude
DLOY	The Duke of Lancaster's Own Yeomanry
DLP	deck-landing practice; defence language programme; double large post
DLPT	defence language proficiency test
DLR	driving licence regulations
dlr	dealer
DLRO	Director, Labor Relations Office
DLRV	dual module lunar roving vehicle NASA
DLS	debt liquidation schedule, DME-based landing system
DLS-A	DLS station azimuth
DLSC	defence logistics services centre
DLSD	Director, Logistics and Security Directorate
DLS-E	DLS station elevation
DLST	division logistics system test
DLT	deck-landing training; decision logic table; data loop transceiver
DLTS	deck-landing training school
DLU	data line unit
dlvd	delivered
dlvr	deliver
dly	daily
DM	District Manager; Defence Medal; Director of Mechanization; destroyer minelayer (USN); fast minelayer (Nato); delta modulation; design manual; demonstration mission (Spacelab); demand meter; differential mode; digital monolithic (computer); Adamsite (sneezing gas)
D&M	driving and maintenance
DM	Deutsches Modell (German model)
DM-11	fuse for 175mm HEI shell by Diehl; 9mm x 19 cartridge; anti-tank mine, dispersal mine; 175mm HEI shell by Diehl
DM-12	anti-tank dispersal mine; electronic time fuse by Honeywell; HE charge; 84mm HEAT cartridge for Carl Gustav by Energa
DM-14	110mm solid-propellant rocket motor by DNAG
DM-15	smoke warhead by Buck for LARS
DM-15 HC	high-capacity 76mm smoke pot by Buck
DM-18	7.62mm practice cartridge; 110mm practice warhead by Buck
DM-19	HEI grenade by Buck
DM-21	fuse for 155mm HEI shell by Diehl; 7.62mm cartridge with tracer
DM-21	anti-tank mine; 155mm HEI shell by Diehl
DM-22	hollow-charge rifle grenade by Hispano
DM-25	smoke warhead for LARS by Buck
DM-28	practice warhead for LARS by Diehl
DM-29	HE charge
DM-31	hand grenade by Diehl; fuse for LARS by Junghans; anti-personnel mine
DM-33	mechanical fuse for smoke warhead DM-15 by Junghans/Diehl

DM-38	110mm practice warhead by Buck	DME	Director of Mechanical Engineering; distance measuring equipment; distance monitoring equipment; design margin evaluation; di-methyl-ethanol-amine
DM-41	hand grenade fragmentation		
DM-43	fuse for LARS by Junghans		
DM-45	155mm smoke shell (hexa-cholro-ethane)		
DM-48	practice hand grenade	DMED	Defence Medical Equipment Depot (Ludgershall UK); digital message entry device by Cincinnati
DM-48A1	20mm TP-T projectile by Diehl		
DM-51	hand grenade by Diehl (Sprengrohr) (Bangalore Torpedo)	DMedA	Director of Medical Activities
DM-53	electrical fuse for DM-25; electronic double fuse by Honeywell; incendiary shell by Buck	DMET	distance measuring equipment touch-down; distance measuring equipment TACAN
DM-54	cannon shot simulation charge by IWKA; 110mm canister warhead with proximity fuse by AEG; RAZ Raketenannäherungszünder	DMF	digital matched filter
		DMG	distinguished military graduate; Defense Marketing Group (US)
		dmg	damage
DM-58	practice hand grenade	DMGO	divisional machine gun officer
DM-81	20mm HEI projectile; mechanical nose fuse by Diehl	DMHS	Director of Medical and Health Services
DM-91	20mm multi-purpose projectile	DMI	Director(ate) of Military Intelligence BWO
DM-101	20mm HEI projectile with mechanical base fuse by Diehl	DMIC	Defence Metals Information Centre
DM-105	155mm smoke shell 4 charges by Buck	DMIS	Director, Management Information Systems
DM-143	time fuse 150 seconds by Diehl		
DM-153	time fuse by Diehl	DMISA	depot maintenance interservice support agreement
DM-301	20mm impact fuse by Diehl		
DM-701	Pandora, AT-1, artillery bar mine by DNAG	DML	Defence Medal for Leningrad; data manipulation language
DM-711	Medusa, AT-2, artillery hollow charge mine	dml	demolition
		DmlO	demolition officer (US Army)
DMA	Director of Military Assistance; division of military application AEC; divisional maintenance area; Defense Mapping Agency (US); Division of Military Aeronautics (US Army) 1918; direct memory access; di-methyl-acetamine; Defence Manufacturers' Association (UK); Delegation Ministerielle pour l'Armament (Armaments Ministerial Delegation)	DMLS	doppler microwave landing system by Plessey
		DMM	Defence Medal for Moscow; data manipulation mode
		DMMB	Defence Medical Material Board
		dmn	dimension
		DMO	Director of Military Operations (UK); debarkation medical officer; district medical officer; Directory of Mortuary Operations; Defence Medal for Odessa; Dependent Meteorological Office; Defense Mobilization Order (US); district marine officer; district material officer; Director, Meteorological Office MoD London
DMAAC	Defence Mapping Agency Aerospace Centre		
DMAHC	Defence Mapping Agency Hydrographic Centre		
DMAO	District Management Assistant Office		
DMAP	di-methyl-amino-pyridine	DMOI	Director of Military Operations and Intelligence
DMAT	Dictionary of Military and Associated Terms DoD (US)		
		DMO&I	Director of Military Operations and Intelligence
DMATC	Defence Mapping Agency Topographic Centre	DMOS	duty military occupational specialty
D&MB	Decorations and Medals Branch BUPERS		
DMC	digital micro-circuit; direct manufacturing costs; direct multiplexed control	DMO&P	Director of Military Operations and Planning
		DMOS	Director of Meteorological and Oceanographical Services (N) Naval
D-MC	Deputy Chairman, Military Committee (Nato)		
		DMov	Director of Movements
DMCC	depot maintenance control centre	DMP	Director of Manpower Planning; disarmed military personnel
DMD	Director of the Mobilization Department; digital message device; PSG-2 by Magnavox		
		DMPD	Director of Dockyard Manpower and Productivity

DMPI	desired mean point of impact	DMV	Department of Motor Vehicles (US)
dmpr	damper	DMX	data multiplex units TDDL (time division data link)
DM/PRT	dual mode personal rapid transit		
DMQ	Director of Movements and Quartering	DMZ	de-militarized zone
DMR	Director of Military Research; Director of Materials Research; date material required	DN	Department of the Navy (US); Dynamit Nobel AG
		dn	dragoon
dmr	drummer	DN-181	Blindfire, tracking radar for Rapier by Marconi
DMRA	dual mode rolling airframe, naval anti-aircraft missile	DNA	Director of Naval Accounts; Deputy for Nuclear Affairs; Defense Nuclear Agency (US)
DMRD	Directorate of Materials Research and Development		
DMRI	date material required increasing (urgent)	DNAD	Director of Naval Air Division
		DNAG	Dynamit Nobel AG D-5210 Troisdorf
DMRL	Defence Metallurgical Research Laboratory (India)	DNAP	Director of Naval Administrative Planning
DMRN	Director of Materials Research, Naval	DNAR	Director of Naval Air Radio
DMS	Directorate of Military Survey; Director of Medical Services; distinguished military student; Department of the Military Secretary; Defence Mapping School; Defence Materials System; difference of messing subscription (allowance) (UK); documentation of molecular spectroscopy; data management system; defence meteorological satellite; direct moduled sole (boot); defence management simulation; differential manoeuvring simulator; display management system; defence management system; daily movement summary; destroyer minesweeper (high speed) (USN); Defense Marketing Services (100 Northfield Str. Greenwich CT USA 06830)	DNAW	Director of Naval Air Warfare
		DNB	died, non-battle
		DNC	Director of Naval Constructions; Director of Naval Communications; direct numerical control
		DNCCC	Defence National Communications Control Centre
		DND	Department of National Defence (Canada); Director of Navigation and Direction
		DNDS	Director of Naval Dental Service
		DNE	Director of Naval Equipment; di-nitro-ethane
		DNEC	distribution Navy enlisted classification (USN code)
		DNEdS	Director of Naval Education Service
		DNES	Director of Naval Education Service
		DNET	Director of Naval Engineering Training
		DNFCT	Director of Naval Foreign and Commonwealth Training
DMSC	Defence Material Standardization Committee (UK)	DNFPS	Director of Naval Future Policy Staff
DMSN	Director of Marine Services, Naval	DNI	Director of Naval Intelligence; division of naval intelligence; directorate of naval intelligence
DMSP	Defense Meteorological Satellite Program (US)		
DMSRAC	Driving and Maintenance School, Royal Armoured Corps (Bovington)	Dnjepr	class, intelligence collecting vessels (SU)
DMSS	Director of Medical and Sanitary Services; defence meteorological satellite system	DNL	differential non-linearity
		DNLS	day/night laser sight
dmst	demonstrate; demonstration	DNM	Director of Naval Manning
dmstn	demonstration	DNMP	Director of Manpower Planning
dmstr	demonstrator	DNMR	Director of Manpower Requirements; Director of Manpower Resources
DMSV	Defence Medal for Sevastopol		
DMT	Director of Military Training; digital message terminal PV-1641 Plessey; dimensional motion times	DNMS	Director of Medical Services
		DNMSP	Director of Manpower Structure Planning
DMTB	deployment mobilization troop basis	DNMT	Director of Manning and Training
DMWR	depot maintenance work requirements		E Engineering
DMTR	Dounreay materials testing reactor		S Supply and Secretariat
DM&TS	departure of mines and technical surveys		X Seaman
		DNO	Director of Naval Ordnance; District Naval Officer
DMU	dual purpose manoeuvring unit		

DNOA   Director of Naval Officer Appoint-
         ments
         E Engineering
         S Supply and Secretariat
         X Seaman
DNOP   Director of Naval Officer Procure-
         ment
DNOR   Director of Naval Operational
         Requirements
DNOrds   Director and Chief Inspector of
         Naval Ordnance
DNOS   Director of Naval Operational
         Studies
DNOT   Director of Naval Operations and
         Training
DNP   drill in non-pay status (reservists)
         (US); declared national programme
DNPlans Director of Naval Plans
DNPP   Director of Naval Program Planning
         (USN)
DNPTS   Director of Naval Physical Training
         and Sports
DNR   Director of Naval Recruiting,
         Director of Nuclear Research
DNRQ   did not receive questionnaire
DNS   Director of Naval Signals
dns   dense; density
DNSC   Director of Naval Service Conditions
DNST   Director of Naval Sea Transport
DNSy   Director of Naval Security
DNT   Director of Naval Training;
         di-nitro-toluene
DNTS   Director of Naval Transportation
         Service CNTS (USN)
DNV   minelayer destroyer (USN) MMD
DNVT   digital non-secure voice terminal
         Tri-Tac by E-Systems
DNW   Deutsch-Niederländischer Windkanal
         Nord-Ost Polder (NL) (wind tunnel)
         (Dutch-German aerodynamic research
         establishment); Director of Naval
         Warfare
DNWA   Director of Naval Analysis
DNWC   Director of Naval Weapons Contracts
DNWS   Director of Naval Weather Service
         MoD London
DNXT   Director of Naval Exercises and
         Training
DO   duty officer; dental officer;
         district officer; divisional
         officer; disbursing officer; demi-
         official; divisional order; due
         out; Defence Order (priority
         rating); delivery order; direct
         order; design office; drawing
         office
Do-17   fighter aircraft WW2 by Dornier
Do-18   mail aircraft WW2 by Dornier
Do-19   combat aircraft WW2 by Dornier
Do-22   multi-role aircraft WW2 by Dornier

Do-24   seaplane by Dornier,
         TT Technologieträger (experimental)
Do-26   cargo aircraft WW2 by Dornier
Do-27   STOL aircraft by Dornier
Do-28   Skyservant, light transport aircraft
         by Dornier
Do-31   experimental VTOL jet 1969 by Dornier
Do-34   Kiebitz, tethered reconnaissance
         helicopter platform by Dornier
Do-215   light bomber WW2 by Dornier
Do-217   combat aircraft WW2 by Dornier
Do-228   twin turboprop commuter aircraft
         1980 by Dornier
Do-317   combat aircraft WW2 by Dornier
Do-335   speed record plane (nose and rear
         propeller) by Dornier
DOA   Department of the Army (US); date of
         availability; direction of arri-
         val; day of ammunition; dead on
         arrival; dissolved oxygen analy-
         ser; differential operation ampli-
         fiers; dominant obstacle allow-
         ance;
         Director of Officer Appointments
         E Engineering
         S Supply and Secretariat
         X Seaman
DOAE   Defence Operational Analysis
         Establishment (UK)
DOB   dispersion operational base; date of
         birth; depth of burst
DOC   district officer commanding;
         Department of Commerce (US);
         Department of Communications
         (Canada); direct operating costs
doc   document
DOCA   date of change of accountability;
         date of current appointment;
         Defense Orientation Conference
         Association (US)
DOCE   date of current enlistment
docu   document
DOD   Director, Operations Division; date
         of death; died of disease
DoD   Department of Defense (US)
DoD-1   ADA, Department of Defense program-
         ming language project 1975
DODAAC   Department of Defense activity
         address code
DODAC   Department of Defense ammunition
         code
DODCI   Department of Defense computer
         institute
DODCLIPMI Department of Defense consolida-
         ted list of principal military
         items
DODDAC   Department of Defense Damage Assess-
         ment Center
DODEP   Department of Defense Emergency
         Plans

DODFDCO Department of Defense foreign dis-
         closure coordinating office
DODHGFO Department of Defense household
         goods field office
DODI   Department of Defense instruction
DODIC   Department of Defense identification
         code
DODIER   Department of Defense industrial
         equipment reserve
DODIIS   Department of Defense intelligence
         information system
DODIR   Department of Defense intelligence
         reports
DODMPAC Department of Defense military pay
         and allowance committee
DODMUL   Department of Defense master urgency
         list
DODNACC Department of Defense national
         agency check center
DODPM   Department of Defense military pay
         and allowances entitlement manual
DoDprt   date of departure
DODRE   Department of Defence Research and
         Engineering
DOE   Department of Energy (US); Depart-
         ment of the Environment (UK);
         Director of Education; date of
         enlistment
DOES   Defence Organizational Entry Stan-
         dards
DOF   degrees of freedom (artillery)
DOFA   details of agreement STANAG
DofA   Director of Artillery
DofC   Director of Contracts
DOFC   Defence orthopedic footwear clinic
DofCornLI The Duke of Cornwall's Light
         Infantry
DofDPlansN Director of Defence Plans, Naval
DOFL   Diamond Ordnance Fuse Laboratory
DofM   Director of Mechanization
DofP   Director of Plans
DofQN   Director of Quartering, Naval
DofS   Director of Stores
         W Washington
         date of supply; depot of supplies
         (USMC)
DofY   Director of Victualling
Dogan   class, fast patrol boats (Turkey)
         by Lürssen
DogEvent nuclear bomb experiment 1951
         Nevada
DOHC   dual overhead camshaft
DOI   Department of the Interior (US);
         Department of Industry (Canada);
         died of injuries; Director of
         Informations; dissent orbiter
         initiate NASA
Doka   dark-room goggles by Oldelft
DOL   Director of Laboratories AFSC (US);
         detached officers' list

Dolly   airborne data link equipment
DOME   District Ordnance Mechanical
         Engineer
Dominies VIP transport plane by BAe
Domino   airborne ECM equipment WW2 (UK);
         target acquisition system against
         low-flying aircraft by Thomson-
         CSF
DomRep   Dominican Republic
DOMS   Directorate of Military Support
DomSat   domestic communications satellite
DON   Department of the Navy (US); demand
         order number
Don   class, submarine depot ships (SU)
DONI   Director of Operations Northern
         Ireland
DOO   divisional ordnance office(r);
         divisional operations officer;
         district ordnance office;
         Director, Office of Oceanography
Doodlebug flying bomb WW2 German
DOOLAR   deep-ocean object location and
         recovery
DOP   designated overhaul point; develop-
         ing-out paper
DOPE   display, oral, printed, electronic
         (media)
Doppler-70 air navigation system by Decca
Doppler-80 air navigation system ACD +
         radar + PBDI by Decca
DoppZ   Doppelzünder, duplex fuse
DOR   Directorate of Operational Research;
         daily operational report;
         dropped own request; date of rank;
         digital output relay
DOR-4   Superwal, seaplane WW2 by Dornier
DORA   Defence of the Realm Act 1914,
         Directorate of Operational Analy-
         sis; dynamic operator response
         apparatus
Dora   80cm railway gun WW2 Germany
DORE   Defence officer record examination
DORF   Diamond Ordnance Radiation Factory
DOrg   Director of Organization
Dorina   class, small corvettes by VT
DORIS   direct order recording and invoicing
         system
DOS   Director of Ordnance Services;
         Director of Overseas Services;
         date of separation; day of supply;
         day of sale; dependents overseas
         (on station); disk operating
         system; decision outstanding
Dosco   HS-100-4, 4x4 2 ton truck (US)
DOSI   Directorate of Operational Services
         and Intelligence
DOSV   deep ocean survey vehicle
DOT   Department of Transport; Department
         of Treasury; Department of Tele-
         communications; Department of

Overseas Trade; Directory of Occupational Titles; Dependent Overseas Territory; designating optical tracker (IR sensors against ICBMs); deep ocean transponder; discrete ordinate transport

DOTCCS   Directorate of Telecommunications and Command and Control Systems (US)

DOTCOOP   Department of Transportation Continuity of Operations Plan

DOTI   Director of Operations, Training and Intelligence

DOV   disbursing officer's voucher

DOTIPOS   deep ocean test instrument placement and observation system

DOUCHE   description of underwater contacts hastily and exactly

DOV   double oil of vitriol (sulphuric acid)

DOVAP   doppler velocity and position (radar)

Dove   light transport plane

Dover Devil   XM-248, .5 cal squad automatic weapon by Dover Arsenal

DOW   died of wounds

DOWB   deep ocean work boat

DoX-1   seaplane, transport WW2 by Dornier

DP   displaced persons; distinguished pass; detained pay; duty paid; distributing point; delivery point; departure point; detention of pay; by direction of the President; Department of the Pacific (USMC); disabled person; deck-piercing (bomb); deep penetration (bomb, shell); drill purpose only (cartridge); dual purpose; double purpose; diametrical pitch; durable press; data processing; differential pressure; dispensed phase; display package; description pattern; damp proof(ing); dry powder; direct port; Direction des Poudres (gunpowder directorate)

dp   deep

D&P   development and printing (photo)

D.P   delivery against payment

DP-2E   Neptune, naval aircraft by Lockheed

DP-12000   Tallboy, deep penetration bomb 12000 lbs WW2 (UK)

DP-22000   Grand Slam, deep penetration bomb 22000 lbs WW2 (UK)

DPA   Defence Production Act; deferred payment account; Deutsches Patentamt (German Patents Office)

DPAO   District Public Affairs Officer (US)

DPB   Defence Production Board (Nato); deposit pass book

DPC   Defence Planning Committee (Nato); Defence Production Committee

(Nato); Defense Procurement Circular (US); Defense Plants Corporation (US); data processing centre; display processor code

DPCA   Director of Personnel and Community Activities; displaced phase centre antenna

DPCC   Director of Postal and Courier Communications

DPCM   differential pulse code modulation

DPC/MS   Defence Planning Committee, Ministerial Session (Nato)

DPC/PS   Defence Planning Committee, Permanent Session (Nato)

DPCT   differential protection current transformer

DPD   District Port Director (USN); Director Personnel Department (USMC); data project directive; data processing department

DPE   Director of Physical Education; data processing equipment

DPers   Director of Personal Services

DPEWS   dual-purpose electronic warfare system; naval dual-purpose electronic warfare system SLQ-32

DPFG   data processing functional group

DPG   data processing group; date of permanent grade; Dugway Proving Ground

DPGW   Defence Planning Working Group (of Defence Ministers)

DPH   Department of Public Health, Diamond Pyramid Hardness

DPI   Director of Public Instruction; Department of Public Information; data processing installation

DPIO   District Public Information Office(r)

DPL   Director of Pioneers and Labour

dpl   diplomat; deploy; duplex

DPLO   District Postal Liaison Office(r)

DPM   Deputy Provost Marshal, District Paymaster; Defence Programme Memorandum; Draft Presidential Memorandum; digital plotter map; digital panel meters

DPMA   Data Processing Management Association (US)

DPMC   Director of Personnel, Marine Corps

dpng   deepening

DPnr&Lab   Director of Pioneers and Labour

DPO   district pay office; distributing post office; depot property officer; duty petty officer; district personnel office(r); district plans office(r); district postal office(r)

DPOB   date and place of birth

DPolT   differential polarization telegraphy

DPost	Director of Postal Services
DPP	Director of Public Prosecutions
DPPG	Draft or Tentative Planning and Programming Guidance
DPPO	District publications and printing office
DPQ	Defence Planning (Review) Questionnaire
DPR	double pulse rating
DPRI	Disaster Prevention Research Institute
DPRN	Director of Public Relations, Navy
DPRO	District Public Relations Office(r)
DPRORM	Drafting, Pay and Records Office, Royal Marines
dprt	depart
DPS	Defence Priority System; Defence Planning Staff; Defence Printing Service; Department of Political Science; Directorate of Personal Services MoD (UK); Director of Postal Services; data processing system; descent propulsion system
DPSA	Data Processing Supply Association; Defence Production Sharing Arrangement (US-Canada); deep penetration strike aircraft
DPSB	Defence Production Supply Board
DPSC	Defence Personnel Support Centre
DPSD	Director of Dockyard Production and Support
DPSK	dual phase shift keying; differential phase shift keying
DPSS	Director of Printing and Stationery Service
dpst	deposit
DPT	Director of Plans and Training; distributed profit tax; development prototype
dpt	department
dptrk	dumptruck
dpty	deputy
DPU	data processing unit
DPW	Department of Public Works (Canada); Director of Prisoners of War
DPWG	Defence Planning Working Group
DPWM	double-sided pulse with modulation
DPWO	District Public Works Office(r)
dpx	duplex
DQ	detention quarters, depot quartermaster (USMC)
	N Norfolk
	P Philadelphia
	PH Pearl Harbour
	QQ Quantico
	R Richmond
	SF San Francisco
DQM	divisional quartermaster; depot quartermaster

DQMG	Deputy Quartermaster General
DQMS	Deputy Quartermaster Sergeant
DR	dispatch rider; drill regulations; dress regulations; daily relays; disposition report; discrepancy report; defence regulations; Destroyer (RN); dead reckoning; directional radio; doppler radar; deficiency report; data report; depression rangefinder; dynamic relaxation; design requirements; development report; deduced reckoning; defined readout; demolition rocket; Dessin de Référence (reference drawing)
dr	door; dram; drum; driver; drummer
DR-810	muzzle velocity radar by LSI
DR-2000-S3	naval radar warning receiver by Thomson-CSF
DRA	division rear area; de-rating appeal; dead reckoning analyser; Dansk Radio AS (DK-2630 Taastrup)
DRAAG	design review and acceptance group
DRAC	Director, Royal Armoured Corps
Dragon	twin 20mm anti-aircraft tank, Marder hull by Thyssen, GIAT, Thomson-CSF; FGM-77, XM-47, M-47, medium-range anti-tank guided weapon by McDD/Raytheon
Dragon-300	4x4 armoured vehicle by Southfield
Dragonfly	A-37B, counter-insurgency plane by Cessna; HR-1, helicopter by Westland
Dragon Wagon	high-mobility articulated work vehicle by Lockheed/Oshkosh
Dragoon-300	4x4 combat vehicle by Arrowpointe
Dragunov	rifle 7.62mm sniper's rifle (SU)
DRAI	dead reckoning analog indicator; dead reckoning analyser and indicator
Draken	SAAB-35, allweather Mach 2 Interceptor by SAAB
DRAPO	Definition et Réalisation d'Avions par Ordinateur by Dassault/Breguet
DRB	Disability Retirement Branch BUPERS; Defence Research Board (Canada)
DRBJ-11	naval phased array radar by Thomson-CSF
DRC	Defence Review Committee (Nato); deployment readiness condition; district recruiting command; deputy regional commander; damage risk contours
DRCA	Drill Regulations for Coast Artillery
DRCCC	Defence Regional Communications Control Centre
DRCL	dose rate contour line

drct   direct
DRCWR   Defence Review Committee Standing
        Sub-group on War Reserve Stocks
        (Nato)
DRD   Defence Research Directors
DRDO   Defence Research and Development
        Organization (India)
DRDTO   detection radar data take-off
DRE   district reserve equipment; Director
        of Radio Equipment; Directorate of
        Radio Equipment; data recording
        equipment;
        Defence Research Establishment
        (Canada)
        O Ottawa
        P Pacific
        S Suffield
        T Toronto
        V Valcartier
DRepat Director of Repatriation
DResearch Director of Operational Research
DREWS   direct read-out equatorial weather
        satellite
DRF   division ready force; depression
        rangefinder
drft   drift
DRG   Defence Research Group
drg   drawing
DRHC   drill regulations hospital corps
DRI   dead reckoning indicator; descent
        rate indicator
DRIC   Defence Research Information Centre
        (UK)
DRID   direct read-out image dissector
DRIDAC drum input to digital automatic com-
        puter
DRIFT   diversity receiving instrumentation
        for telemetry
DRILS   defence retail inter-service logis-
        tic support
DRIR   direct read-out infra-red
DRIVE   documentation review into video
        entry (computer terminals) by
        Ferranti
DRL   Defense Research Laboratories (US)
DRLA   Drill Regulations for Light Artillery
DRLMS   digital radar land-mass simulation
        system (Tornado flight simulator)
DRLS   dispatch rider letter service
DRM   direction of relative motion; direc-
        tion of relative movement
DrMaj   Drum Major (USMC)
DRME   Direction des Recherches et Moyens
        d'Essai
DRMO   District Records Management Officer
DRMT-1 battlefield surveillance radar (FR)
DRMU   Depot Régional de Munitions (region-
        al ammunition storage room)
DRN   dead reckoning navigation
DRO   disablement resettlement officer

        (UK); dining room orderly; daily
        routine order; daily report of
        obligations; divisional routine
        order
Drohne CL-89, reconnaissance drone
DRO-LA Defense Research Office, Latin
        America (US Army element)
drone   programmed pilotless aircraft not:
        RPV Nato: automatically or
        remotely controlled
Dror   machine gun (Israel)
DROS   date returned from overseas
DRP   dead reckoning plotter; Directorate
        of Radio Production; dense random-
        packed
DRPC   Defence Research Policy Committee
DRPC-1 RATAC, artillery fire control radar
        by LMT
DRpos   dead reckoning position
DRPP   Directorate of Research Programming
        and Planning
DrPr   drawing practice
DRPT-2 RASURA, battlefield surveillance
        radar by EMD
DRRF   division rapid reaction force
DRS   division restructuring study (US)
        detection ranging set
DRSC   direct radar scope camera
DRSHC   deletion reason/supply history codes
DRT   Director of Railway Transport; dead
        reckoning tracer
DRTD   disaster recovery training depart-
        ment (USN)
DRTE   Defence Research Telecommunications
        Establishment (Canada)
DRU   demolition research unit; design
        research unit; data recapture unit
DRUSIWAL Drucksimulationsanlage Wasser
        Land/Luft (detonation pressure
        simulation installation)
DRVN   Democratic Republic of Viet Nam
        (North)
DRVS   doppler radar velocity sensor
DRVT-3 RAPACE, battlefield radar by EMD
DRW   Dornier Reparaturwerft; defensive
        radio warfare
drwg   drawing
DRZ   deep reconnaissance zone
drzl   drizzle
DS   Drill Sergeant; Defence Secretary;
        dental surgeon; Deputy Secretary;
        directory staff; dressing station;
        distinguished service; driving
        school; defensive sector; direct
        support; date of service; document
        signed; decision sheet; detached
        service; daylight saving; digit
        select; digital signal; descent
        stage; data set; double slave
        (LORAN); Discarding sabot (shot)

DS-Veh   DS-Vehicle   driver seated vehicle
DSA   Defence Shipping Authority (Nato);
         Defence Supply Agency (Nato);
         division service area; designated
         security agency; digital signal
         analysis; dynamic structure
         analysis
DSAA   Defense Security Assistance Agency
         (US) (Arms Sales)
DSAA-4   active sonobuoy system by CIT-
         Alcatel
DsablSevP   disability severance pay
DSAC   Deputy Supreme Allied Commander
DSAEur   Deputy Supreme Allied Commander
         Europe
DSAD   Director, Systems Analysis Division
DSafSM   Deputy Safeguard Systems Manager
DSAO   diplomatic service administration
         office
DSAP   data systems automation programme;
         defence systems application pro-
         gramme
DSAR   Defence Supply Agency Regulation
DSARC   Defence Systems Acquisition Review
         Council
DSAS   direct support aviation section
DSASO   Deputy Senior Air Staff Officer
DSB   Defence Signal Board (UK); Defense
         Science Board (US); duty steam
         boat (RN); double side band;
         demand scheduled bus
DSC   divisional supply column; Defence
         Shipping Council; Defence Supply
         Centre; Defence Supply Corpora-
         tion; Distinguished Service Cross;
         down stage centre; digital signal
         conditioning; differential scan-
         ning calorimetry
DSCB   data set control block
DSCS   deep space communications satellite;
         defence satellite communications
         system
DSD   Director of Signals Division MoD
         London; Director of Staff Duties
DSDP   deep sea drilling project
DSDW   Director of Staff Duties, Weapons
DSE   distributed systems environment
         (computers by Honeywell); direct
         support equipment; data set exten-
         sion
DSEA   Davis submerged escape apparatus
DSEB   Defence Shipping Executive Boards
DSEB E/W Defence Shipping Executive Boards
         East or West
DSec   Director of Security
DSecDef Deputy Secretary of Defense (US)
DSelect Director of Personnel Selections
DSES   Defense Systems Evaluation Squadron
         (USAF)
DSFC   direct side force control

DSFT   detection scheme with fixed
         thresholds
DSG   Deputy Surgeon General; Deputy Sec-
         retary General; direct support
         group
dsg   designate
DSGM   Director Standing Group Memorandum
dsgn   designer; designation
DSGSCAR Deputy Secretary of the General
         Staff Coordination and Report
DShK   12.7mm machine gun (SU)
DSI   data systems inquiry; deep suppres-
         sion integer TIB
DSIATP   defence sensor imagery application
         training programme
DSIF   deep space instrumentation facility
DSIR   Department of Scientific and Indus-
         trial Research (UK)
DSK   Dauerschutzluftklimasystem (perma-
         nent protected air conditioning
         system)
DSL   deep scattering layer; data set
         label
dsl-elec diesel-electric
DSLT   detection scheme with learning of
         the thresholds
DSM   Distinguished Service Medal;
         Directorate of Servicing and
         Maintenance
DSM-61   anti-submarine under-water detona-
         tion charge
DSMA   Directorate of Supply Management,
         Army (UK)
DSMAC   digital scene-matching area correla-
         tor
DSMG   designated systems management group
DSMS   Defence systems management schools
dsmtd   dismounted
DSN   Director of Sales Negotiations DSAA
DSN   deep space network NASA
dsnt   distant
DSO   Companion of the Distinguished Ser-
         vice Order; divisional signals
         officer; district security officer;
         district service officer; district
         supply officer; district staff
         officer; Defence Sales Organiza-
         tion (of the Royal Ordnance
         Factories) (St Christopher House,
         Southwark Street London SE1 0TD)
DSOT   daily systems operability test
DSP   designated stock point; defence
         support programme; Director of
         Selection of Personnel
D&SPiers destroyer and submarine piers (USN)
DSQ   discharged service qualifications
DSQ-28   dual-axis seeker for Harpoon by TI
DSQC-11 underwater telecommunications
         equipment by Elac
DSQN-11 standard sonar by Elac

DSQQ-11   side-looking sonar by Elac
DSQS-21   sonar for destroyers by KAE;
          BZ with pitch and roll stabiliza-
          tion
DSR   document status report; Director of
          Scientific Research
DSRD   Directorate of Signals Research and
          Development
DSRV   deep submergence rescue vessel
          (Nato)
DSS   Drill Sergeant School; Department of
          Supplies and Services (Canada);
          Defence Signals Staff; direct
          support system; deep submergence
          systems; digital spectrum stabili-
          zer; digital sub-system
DSSA   direct supply support activity
DSSC   defence subsistence and supply centre
DSSCS   defence special security communica-
          tions system
DSSM   dynamic sequencing and segregation
          model
DSSN   disbursing station symbol number
DSSO   defence surplus sales officer;
          district ships' service officer
DSSP   direct supply support point; deep
          submergence systems project
DSSPTO   deep submergence systems project
          technical office
DSST   Director of Supply and Secretariat
          Training
DSSV   deep submergence search vehicle
DST   Director of Supply and Transport
          AS   Armament and Specialist Stores
          Fin Finance
          FM   Fuel, Movements and Transport
          GV   General and Victualling Stores
          MA   Management and Administration
          daylight saving time; double summer
          time; day spottable tracer (dark
          tracer); data summary tape; data
          system test; Direction de la Sur-
          veillance du Territoire (director-
          ate for the supervision of alien
          activity in France)
DSTA-3   active master sonobuoy by CIT-
          Alcatel
DStJ   Dame of Grace (of Justice) of the
          Order of St John of Jerusalem
DSTO   deputy sea transport officer
DS&TO   district supply and transport officer
DSTP   Director, Strategic Target Planning
dstr   deserter
DSTV-2   passive slave sonobuoy by CIT-Alcatel
DSTV-4   passive omnidirectional sonobuoy by
          Thomson-CSF
DSU   direct support unit; direct supply
          unit; data selector unit; data
          storage unit
DSV   deep submergence vehicle

DSVL   doppler sonar velocity log (for
          submarines) by Sperry
DSVT   digital subscriber voice terminal
DSvy   Director of Surveys
DSWP   Director of Surface Weapons Projects
DSWR   Director of Surface Weapons Research
DSyG   Deputy Secretary General
DT   Director of Training; divisional
          train; double time; day tracer
          (projectile); delayed time (fuse);
          detecting head (electronics); dis-
          persion time; development type;
          development testing; deep tank;
          daylight time; double throw; data
          transmission; drop top; deuterium
          and tritium; dummy target; dynamic
          tear; Doppeltrommel (double drum)
DT-1   development test phase 1
DT-11   HE hand grenade
DT-21   anti-tank mine by IWKA/Mauser
DT-551   REMBASS sensors
DT-573   REMBASS sensors
DTA   Detroit Tank Arsenal; differential
          thermal analysis
DTACCS   Director Telecommunications Command
          and Control Systems (US)
DTAO   during the temporary absence of
DTAS   data transmission and switching
          system by Litton
DTASW   Department of Torpedo and Anti-
          submarine Warfare
DTAT   Direction Technique des Armaments
          Terrestres (FR)
DTB   destroyer tactical bulletin; drogue
          target (towing aircraft) and
          bomber
DTC   desert test centre; Department of
          Technical Cooperation
DTCA   Direction Technique des Construc-
          tions Aeronautiques (FR)
DTCN   Direction Technique des Construc-
          tions Navales (2 rue Royale
          F-75200 Paris)
DTCP   diode transistor compound pair
DTCU   data transmission control unit
DTD   Director of Training Department;
          Director of Technical Development;
          data transfer done
dtd   dated
DTDMA   distributed time division multiple
          access
DTE   data terminal equipment
DT&E   development test and evaluation
DTEAS   detection, track, evaluation and
          assignment system
DTF   definite tape file
DTFP   deck-landing training and flying
          practice
DTG   date time group; dynamically tuned
          gyro by Sperry

DTI	Department of Trade and Industry (UK); Division of Technical Information AEC
DTIA	Direction Technique et Industrielle de l'Aeronautique (Ministry of Aviation) (FR)
DTL	diode transistor logic; down the line
dtlAvr	detailed as aviator (USMC)
DTM	Director of Torpedoes and Mining; 7.62mm tank-mounted machine gun (SU)
DTMB	Defence Traffic Management Board; David Taylor Model Basin (sub-marine simulator) NSRDC
DTMBPMMS	David Taylor Model Basin (sub-marine simulator) planar motion mechanism system
DTMF	dual-tone multi-frequency (proce-dures)
dtmn	draughtsman
DTMS	Defence Traffic Management Service
DTn	Director of Transportation
DTN	Defence Teleprinter Network; (world-wide) data transport network data transfer network
dtn	detain
DTNSRDC	David Taylor Naval Ship Research and Development Centre (sub-marine simulator)
DTO	district transportation office(r); district training office(r)
DTOA	differential time of arrival
DTOD	Director of Trade and Operations Division
DtoP	deployment day to production day; MRGR Material Gross Requirements (US)
DT/OT	development test/operational test
DTpt	Director of Transport
DTR	Director of Transport and Remounts; double taxation relief; demand totalizing relay; diffusion trans-fer; disposable tape reel; distri-bution tape reel; digital tape recorder
DTRA	Defence Technical Review Agency
DTRM	dual thrust rocket motor
DTRRCT	Driver Training Regiment Royal Corps of Transport
DTOC	division tactical operations centre
DTS	defence transportation system; digi-tal tandem switch; data transfer system; double thermostat and safety
DTSS	Dartmouth time sharing system
DTT	Director of Trades Training
DTTU	data transmission terminal unit
DTU	data terminal unit, data transfer unit
DTUPC	design to unit production cost
DTV	dynamic test vehicle; Deutscher Verband Technisch Wissenschaft-licher Vereine Düsseldorf
DTWJLRRCT	driver training wing, junior leaders regiment Royal Corps of Transport
DTWP	Director of Tactical and Weapons Policy Division
DTZ	division tactical zone
DU	dismounted unit; died unmarried; depleted uranium; display unit; delay unit
du	duplex (radio) duty
DUAP	depleted uranium armour-piercing (shot)
DUAV-4	light-weight dipping sonar by CIT-Alcatel
dub	dubious
DUBA-5	Tarpon, hull-mounted sonar by Thomson-CSF
DUBM-20	mine-hunting sonar by Thomson-CSF
DUBM-21	mine-hunting sonar by Thomson-CSF -41 mine-hunting sonar by Thomson-CSF
DUC	Distinguished Unit Citation (US)
Duck	DUKW, amphibious truck
DuCon	duty connection
DuDat	due date (deadline)
DUE	Distinguished Unit Emblem (US)
DuFly	duty involving flying
DuIns	duty under instruction
DUKW	Detroit United Kaiser Works amphibious truck WW2
Dumbo	flying boat SAR
DUNC	deep underwater nuclear counter
Dune Buggy	XR-311, cross-country vehicle by FMC
DUNSC	deep underground support centre
DUP	disk utility programme
dup	duplicate
Durance	class, supply ships (FR)
Durandal	runway busting bomb by Matra
DUSA	Deputy Under-Secretary of the Army; Defence Union of South Africa
DUSC	deep underground support center (USAF)
DuSign	duty assigned by
DuSta	duty station
Dust	M-42, twin 40mm anti-aircraft gun
DUSW	Director of Undersea Warfare MoD London
dut	duty
DUTE	digital universal test equipment
DUUA-2	search and attack sonar by CIT-Alcatel
DUUX-2	submarine passive accoustic range-finder by CIT-Alcatel
DUWPN	Director of Underwater Weapons Pro-jects, Navy

DV   distinguished visitor; disabled
          veteran (US); direct vision;
          double vision; Dienstvorschrift
          (service manual); Datenverarbei-
          tung (data processing)
dv   dive (bomber)
D&V   demonstration and validation
DV-56   plastic anti-personnel mine (FR)
DVA   Dunkirk Veterans' Association;
          Department of Veterans' Affairs
          (US); Dispositif de Visualisation
          Annexe (ancillary data display)
DVARS   doppler velocity altimeter radar set
DVDE   digitalized voice and data encoding
DvDy   diving duty
DVFR   defence visual flight rules
DVGC   Director of Veterans Guard of Canada
dvlp   development
DVM   digital voltmeter
DVO   district veterinary officer;
          divisional veterinary officer;
          direct view optics
DVOR   doppler VHF omnidirectional range
Dvora   class, patrol boats by IAI
DVP-810   voice security unit by Datotek
DVP-821   desktop voice security unit by
          Datotek
DVP-841   full duplex voice security system
          by Datotek
dvr   driver (UK); diver (USN)
DV&RS   Director of Veterinary and Remount
          Service
DvrMech   Driver and Mechanic (US)
          A   amphibious vehicles
          M   motorcycles
          Mech   mechanic
          Op   operator special equipment
          T   tracked vehicles
          W   wheeled vehicles
DVS   Director of Veterinary Services
DVSL   District Venture Scout Leader
DVST   direct view storage tube
DW   desert warfare; dock warrant;
          delivered weight
D/W   dust wrapper; dependent wife
DWA   died of wounds by (enemy) action
DWAC   Director Women's Army Corps (US)
DWB   development work book
DWBA   distorted wave-borne approximation
DWBO   district war bonds office(r)
DWC   dead weight capacity; Douglas World
          Cruiser, double-decker seaplane
          1924 by Douglas
DWCoordN Director of Weapons Coordination,
          Naval
DWD   Deutscher Wetterdienst, Offenbach
          (German Meteorological Service)
DWE   Deggendorfer Werft und Eisenbau GmbH
          (D-8360 Deggendorf/Donau)
DWESN   Director of Weapons Equipment,
          Surface, Navy

DWEUN   Director of Weapons Equipment,
          Underwater, Navy
dwg   drawing
DWI   descriptive word index
DWks   Director of Works
DWL   designer's water line; downwind
          localizer
DWNavN   Director of Weapons, Navigation,
          Naval
DWPN   Director of Weapons Production,
          Naval
DwPnt   dew point
DWPO   District War Plans Officer
DWProdN   Director of Weapons Production,
          Naval
DWQN   Director of Weapons Quality Assur-
          ance, Naval
DWR   The Duke of Wellington's Regiment
          (West Riding)
DWRAC   Director of Women's Royal Army Corps
DWRDSN   Director of Weapons Research and
          Development, Surface, Naval
DWRDUN   Director of Weapons Research and
          Development, Underwater, Naval
DWRNS   Director of Women's Royal Naval
          Service
DWRPN   Director of Weapons Resources and
          Programmes, Naval
DWSA   Director of Weapons Systems Analy-
          sis; Daedalian Weapon Systems
          Award (US)
DWSMC   Defence Weapons Systems Management
          Centre
DWT   deck-watch time; dead-weight tons;
          Deutsche Gesellschaft für Wehr-
          technnik (Deutschherrenstr. 157
          D-5300 Bonn 2) (German Association
          for Defence Technology)
dx   distance; duplex
DX-15/60 data multiplexer for tactical
          directional radios by SEL
DX-143   Milan simulator
DXDA-MC   ductile metals experimental diamond
          abrasive, metal clad
DX/DXG   experimental destroyer, guided
          missiles (USN programme)
DXI   direct exchange item
DXR   deep X-ray
dy   duty; delivery
DY   dockyard
DYA   Dependent Youth Association US
          Forces
dyn   dynamics, dynamite, dynamo
DYNAMO   dynamic action management operations
Dynasight second generation image intensi-
          fier by Dynavest Ltd (UK)
Dynatrac XM-571, snow vehicle by Flextrac
          (CA)
DYORBL   The Duke of York's Own Regiment of
          Bengal Lancers

DYRMS	The Duke of York's Royal Military School (Dover)	DZA	doppler Zeeman analyser
DYS	The Duke of York's Royal Military School (Dover)	DZSO	drop zone safety officer
DZ	drop(ping) zone; Doppelzünder (duplex fuse)	DZVR	Daimler Zugmaschine mit Vierradantrieb (4x4 Daimler tractor)

E

E	Enlisted Grades (US Army)
E-1	recruit
E-2	private 2
E-3	private 1
E-4	corporal specialist 4
E-5	sergeant specialist 5
E-6	staff sergeant specialist 6
E-7	sergeant 1st class specialist 7
E-8	master sergeant; first sergeant
E-9	staff sergeant major; command sergeant major
E	Efficiency Award (US); Engineering Officer (RN); Earl; East; Earth; experimental (UK); electronic aircraft (US); electronic (counter-measures)
e	elevation; electronics; extreme; engineering; elasticity; eccentricity; electromotive
E-boat	(fast) enemy boat WW2
E-day	embarkation day; exercise (begins day
E-Geschütz	Eisenbahngeschütz (railway gun)
E-Stelle	Erprobungsstelle (experimental establishment)
E_o	muzzle energy
3E	Economy; environment; energy
E-1	Tracer, naval radar platform, twin rotors (Nato)
E-2B	rocket launcher 108mm 20 tubes (Spain)
E-2C	Hawkeye, naval early warning aircraft by Grumman
E-3	rocket launcher, 216mm 21 tubes (Spain)
E-3A	Sentry, AWACS, airborne warning and control system by Boeing
E-3B	Sentry, AWACS, Nato version
E-4	Doomsday Jet, AABNCP, advanced airborne command post by Boeing
E-15	acoustic torpedo (FR)
E-45	miniature RPV by E-Systems
E-63	People Sniffer, by GE
EA	Engineer Admiral (RN); Equipment Assistant (RAF); electrical
	artificer; educational advisor (US); economic advisor; East African; Education Act; enemy aircraft; East Anglian; Espionage Act; electronic attack (aircraft) (US); effective address; exhaust air; experimental aircraft (UK); EuroAtlas (D-2800 Bremen 44)
EA-content	effective agent content
EA-6A	Intruder, ElInt aircraft by Grumman
EA-6B	Prowler, ECM aircraft ICAF by Grumman
EAA	East African Artillery
EAASC	East African Army Service Corps
EAB	Engineer Aviation Battalion
EAC	Eire Air Corps; Eastern Air Command WW2; Educational Advisory Committee (US); European Advisory Commission; expect approach clearance; Engineering Advisory Council; error alert control; European Atomic Commission; East African Command
EACH	East African Command Headquarters
EACP	European Area Communications Plan
EACS	electronic automatic chart system
EACSO	East African Common Service Organization
EAD	External Affairs Department (Canada); entry on active duty; extended active duty; effective air distance
EADF	Eastern Air Defense Force (US)
EADI	electronic attitude director indicator (for helicopters)
EADS	echelon above division study
EAE	Aeronautic Engineering Division USCG
EAEC	European Atomic Energy Commission
EAES	European Atomic Energy Society
EAEME	East African Electrical and Mechanical Engineers
EAF	East African Forces; Egypt Air Force; emergency action file
EAFB	Edwards Air Force Base (Mojave Desert Calif.); Eglin Air Force Base (Florida)

EAG ElInt Advisory Group; experimental firing ship (USN)

Eager Beaver field forklift truck (UK)

EAGLE elevation angle guidance landing equipment

Eagle 30mm anti-aircraft gun by ARes Inc.; F-15, supersonic, all-weather tactical fighter by McDD

EAHC East African High Commission

EAIR extended area instrumentation radar

EAIRO East African Industrial Research Organization

EAL Electronics Associates Ltd

EAM electronic accounting machine

EAMAS emergency action message authentication system

EAMEM European-African-Middle East (campaign) Medal (US)

EAMS Empire Air Mail Scheme

EAMTMTS Eastern Area, Military Traffic Management and Terminal Services

EAN expenditure account number

EANCO emergency actions non-commissioned officer

EANDC European American Nuclear Data Committee

EANS Empire Air Navigation School

EAO emergency actions officer

EAOC errors and omissions excepted

EAON except as otherwise noted

EAOS expiration of active obligated service

EAP Engineer Admiral, Personnel (RN); emergency actions procedures; East African Protectorate; effective air path

EAPD Europe Asia Pacific Division DSAA (US)

EAPG Eastern Atlantic Planning Guidance

EAPS engine air particle separators

EAR electronically agile radar by Westinghouse; employee appraisal record; energy absorbing resin

EARB European Airlines Research Bureau

EarlPraDate earliest practical date

EAROM electrically alterable read-only memory

EARPC East African Royal Pioneer Corps

EarthNet European Satellite ground stations

Earthquake 22000 lbs bomb (RAF) WW2

EAS estimated air speed; equivalent air speed, Electronique Aerospatiale (FR); Eingabe-Ausgabe-System (input-output-system)

EASA Electrical Apparatus Service Association (US)

EASAMS Ltd E-A Space and Advanced Military Systems (Marconi daughter) (UK)

EASC East African Service Corps

EASCON Electronics and Aerospace Systems Conference

EASEP Early Apollo Sceintific Experiments Package

EASI expanded additional skill identifier

EasTAF Eastern Transport Air Force (US)

EastCo East Coast (US)

EastCon Eastern Sea Frontier Control (US)

EastLant Eastern Atlantic Area

EastOMP East Ocean Meeting Point (USN)

EasTroPac Eastern Tropical Pacific

EastSeaFron Eastern Sea Frontier

EASy early acquisition system; efficient assembly system

EAT European Army Treaty; earliest arriving time; electronic angle tracking (radar); expected approach approach time

EATC East African Training Centre (Nakuru) (Nakuru)

EATP Empire Air Training Plan WW2

EATS European Air Transport Service; Empire Air Training Scheme WW2; expanded area test system (Point Mugu)

EAU electronics airborne unit

EAW equivalent average words

EAWP Eastern Atlantic War Plan

EAX electronic automatic exchange

EB equipment branch; enlistment bonus; evaluation branch BUPERS; epoxy-bonded; explosive boat; early burst (bomb); electron beam; equal brake; ElInt bomber, ECM bomber

EB-57 Canberra, ElInt aircraft by Martin

EB-66 Destroyer, ECM aircraft by Douglas

EBA electronic bay assembly

EBAILL European Bureau for the Allocation of International Long Lines (Nato)

EBAM electron beam address memory

EBCD extended binary coded decimal

EBCDIC extended binary coded decimal interchange code

Eber experimental tank composed of Leopard 1 + KPz 70

EBF externally blown flap

EBG Engin Blinde de Genie (engineer tank)

EBICON electron bombardment induced conductivity

EBIN Brazilian shipyard

Eblis laser target seeker (FR)

EBM electronic bearing marker

EBMat Entstehung und Beschaffung von Wehrmaterial (origination and procurement of defence material (procedures)

EBOR experimental beryllium oxide reactor

EBR experimental breeder reactor; electron beam recorder

EBR-75   Engin Blinde de Reconnaissance 8x8 recce car by Panhard
EBS   emergency broadcast system
Ebsicon   valve for low light level television
EBW   engineer base workshop
EBWR   experimental boiling water reactor
EC   embarkation commandant; Executive Committee (Nato); exercise commander, Engineer Captain; engagement controller; Economic Committee (Nato); European Community; emergency capability; engineering construction; Eastern Command; European Command; emergency commission; Engineer Corps; Executive Council; extension course; ElInt Cargo (aircraft); ECM Cargo (aircraft); electrical conductivity; error counter; evaluation centre; elevation correction; electronic calibration; electronic coding; enamel-covered; electromagnetic compatibility; electrolytic corrosion; electronic computer; error correction; extended coverage; Evansville Company (US) (ordnance)
EC-2   Hawkeye, ElInt aircraft by Grumman
EC-121   radar picket aircraft Super Constellation
EC-130   Hercules, TACAMO, take action and move out, electronic warfare aircraft by Lockheed
EC-137   earlier designation for E-3 AWACS airborne warning and control system by Boeing
EC-620   gun control and stabilization system for tanks by Marconi
EC-755   portable voice ciphering system by Philips
ECA   Economic Cooperation Administration; European Combat Aircraft (programme); target drone (FR)
ECAB   Executive Committee of the Army Board
ECAC   European Civil Aviation Conference; electromagnetic compatibility analysis centre; Engineering College Administrative Council
ECAD   European Civil Affairs Division (US)
ECAFE   Economic Commission for Asia and the Far East
ECAP   electronic circuit analysis programme
ECAR   European Civil Affairs Regulations (US), east central area reliability
ECB   excellence in competition badge
   P   Pistol
   R   Rifle (US)
ECB   Electronic Components Board; event control block

ECC   Equal Compensation Committee; equipment category code (US); enlisted classification code (US); enlisted correspondence course; European Coordination Committee; electronic check control; electronic components code; error checking and correction
ECCC   European Communications Coordinating Committee; European Command Coordinating Committee
ECCM   electronic counter-counter-measures
ECCS   emergency core cooling system
ECD   emergency category designator; estimated completion date; energy conversion devices; electronic components and devices
ECDI   electronic course deviation indicator
ECE   Economic Commission for Europe (UN)
ECEP   electronic converter electric power
ECF   emission contribution fraction
ECG   electrocardiogram; electrocardiograph; export credit guarantee
ECGB   East Coast of Great Britain
ech   echelon
ECI   East Coast of Ireland; extension course institute; error cause identification; Electronics Corporation of Israel (Tel Aviv)
ECIA   Esperanza y Cia SA (Vizcaya Spain)
ECIIB   enemy civilian internee information bureau
ECITO   European Central Inland Transport Organization
ECL   equipment component list; English comprehension level; emitter coupled logic; Elbit Computers Ltd (Haifa Israel); 105mm illumination shell (FR)
ECLA   Economic Commission for Latin America (UN)
Eclipse   military data system by Rolm
ECLO   emitter-coupled logic operator
ECLS   environmental control and life support system Spacelab by Dornier
ECM   European Common Market; electronic counter-measures; electronic coding machine; electronic cipher machine; electro-chemical machining; extended core memory; electronic control module; Elément de Commandement Mobile (mobile command element)
ECMA   European Computer Manufacturers' Association
ECME   Economic Commission for the Middle East (UN)
ECMO   electronic counter-measures operator
ECMP   electronic counter-measures plan

ECMT	European Conference of Ministers of Transport
ECN	engineering change notice
ECNG	East Central Nuclear Group
ECNOS	Eastern Atlantic, Channel and North Sea Orders for shipping (Nato)
ECNR	European Council for Nuclear Research
ECO	Emergency Commissioned Officer; engineering change order; electron coupled oscillator
ECom	US Army Electronics Command
econ	economy
EconAd	the Nato Committee of Economic Advisors
ECOR	Engineering Committee on Ocean Resources (US)
EcoSoC	Economic and Social Council (UN)
ECP	equipment collecting point; engineering change proposal
ECPD	Engineers' Council for Professional Development (US)
ECQAC	Electronic Components Quality Assurance Committee (Nato)
ECR	error cause removal (form); enemy contact report; engineering change request
Ecran	direct broadcast satellite Siberia (SU)
ECRS	economic and contingency reserve stock
Ecrylon	bullet-proof glass
ECS	European Communications Satellite; environment control system (heat exchanger outlet; aircraft); engineering change sheet
ECS^2	executive control and subordinate system by Dornier
ECSA	European Communications Security Agency (Nato)
ECS-b	experimental communications satellite (Japan)
ECSC	European Coal and Steel Community
ECSS	European communications satellite system; executive control and subordinate system by Dornier
ECT	electro-convulsant therapy; environment control table; Evans Clean Tunnel
ECU	environmental control unit; European currency unit; extreme close-up (photo)
ECUK	East Coast of United Kingdom
Ecureuil	AS-350, utility helicopter by AS
Ecureuil II	AS-355, Twin Star, utility helicopter by AS
ECV	Civil Engineering Division (USCG)
ECWA	Economic Commission for Western Asia (UN)
ECX	TACAMO replacement studies aircraft, ECM (take action and move out) (US)
ECX-130	TACAMO version C-130 aircraft
707-ECX	TACAMO version C-130 aircraft Boeing 707
ED	Efficiency Decoration; Education Department; employment department; existence doubtful; enemy dead; extra duty; Eastern District; engineering design; engineering duty; engineering development; engineering department; external deflector; electronic device; electronic director (aircraft) (USAF); edge distance; effective dose; error detecting
ed	edition; editorial
ED-135	Stratolifter, TDCA, tactical deployment and control aircraft by Boeing
EDA	estimated date of arrival; early departure authorized; (British) Electrical Development Association now BEDA; electronic design automation; electronic differential analyser
EDAC	equipment distribution and condition report; error detection and correction
EDATS	extra deep armed team sweep (RN)
EDAVR	enlisted distribution and verification report (US)
EDB	emergency dispersal bases; ethene-di-bromide
EDC	European Defence Community; Eastern Defense Command (US Army); estimated date of completion, equipment distribution and condition (report); Educational Development Centre; electronic digital computer; extra dark colour; error detection and correction; energy distribution curve
EdCen	Education Centre
EDCF	European Defence Community Forces
EDCL	electrical discharge connection lasers
EDCMR	effective date of change of morning report (US)
E/DCP	equipment/document change proposal
EDCPF	environmental data collection and processing facility
EDCSA	effective date of change of strength accountability
EDD	estimated date of delivery; expected date of delivery; electronic data display
EDDC	East Coast (Naval Publications) Distribution Center (USN)
Edenton	class, salvage and rescue ships ATS (USN)
EDF	European Defence Forces; Empire Defence Forces (Malaya)

EDFR	effective date of Federal recognition	EDVR	enlisted distribution and verification report (US)
EDGE	electronic data gathering equipment		
EDHE	experimental data handling equipment	Edward Medal	decoration for miners and workers (UK)
EDIC	European Defence Industries Council; European Defence Industries Committee	EE	electronic engineer(ing); electrical engineer(ing); electronic equipment; erros excepted; elements of expense; educational establishment; engagement effectiveness; expiration of enlistment; employment exchange; envoy extraordinary
EDIG	European Defence Industries Group (Nato)		
EDIP	European Defence Improvement Programme		
EDIS	engineering data information system		
EDITAR	electronic digital tracking and ranging	E&E	eyes and ears; evasion and escape
		EE-3	Jararaca, scout car by Engesa
EDM	equipment deadlined for maintenance; engineering development model; electro-discharge machining	EE-9	Cascavel, armoured car by Engesa
		EE-11	Urutu, armoured personnel carrier by Engesa
edn	education	EE-15	4x4 1.5 ton truck by Engesa
EDO	estate duty officer; employee development officer; engineering duty officer; engineering duty only	EE-17	Sucuri, wheeled anti-tank vehicle by Engesa
		EE-50	6x6 5 ton truck by Engesa
EDO-Corporation (College Point New York)		EEA	essential elements of analysis; estimated expenditure of ammunition (US); Electronic Engineering Association (UK)
EDO-610	medium-range keel sonar		
EDO-700	variable depth sonar		
EDOC	effective date of change		
EDOMP	educational development of military personnel	EEAIE	Electrical, Electronic and Allied Industries Europe
EDP	Emergency Defence Plan (US-Canada); equipment deadlined for parts; electronic data processing; European Defence Products (rue de Duc B-1150 Brussels) (MBB+PRB)	EEC	Emerson Electric Corp. (St Louis); European Economic Community; electronic engine control; Eurocontrol Experimental Centre
		EEC-1	electronic engine control by Ford 1978
EDp	experimental development	EECT	end evening civil twilight
EDPA	European Defence Procurement Agency (Nato)	EED	electro-explosive device
		EEE	economy, environment, energy
EDPLD	emergency defence plan Denmark		
EDPM	electronic data processing machine		
EDPS	equipment distribution planning studies; electronic data processing system	EEEC	electromagnetic energy environment criteria
		EEF	Egyptian Expeditionary Forces
EDR	electronic decoy rocket; employee data record; exploratory development requirement	EEFI	essential elements of friendly informations
		EEG	electro-encephalogram; electro-encephalograph
EDRL	effective damage risk level		
EDS	estimated date of separation; environmental data service	EE&H	electricity, electronics and hydraulics (school) (USN)
EDSAC	electronic delayed storage automatic computer	EEI	essential elements of information; Environmental Equipment Institute (US)
EdSat	educational televisional satellite		
EDSI	Engineering Department (Ships Installations) NAEC	EELS	electronic emitter location system
		EEM	earth entry module NASA
EDT	eastern daylight time; engineering design test; estimated delivery time; estimated departure time	EEMTIC	Electrical and Electronic Measurement and Test Instruments Conference
EDTI	explosives demolition technical installation	EEMTR	enhanced enlisted master tape record
	TaM traps and mines	EENT	eyes, ears, nose and throat
EDU	experimental diving unit (USN)	EEO	equal employment opportunity (US)
educ	education	EEOC	equal employment opportunity commission (US)
EDV	Elektronische Datenverarbeitung (electronic data processing)	EEOO	equal employment opportunity officer (US)

EEPNL	estimated effective perceived noise level
EER	enlisted efficiency report; equipment evaluation report; explosive echo ranging
EERC	explosive echo ranging charge
EERI	Earthquake Engineering Research Institute (US)
EERL	Earthquake Engineering Research Laboratory (US)
EE&RM	Elementary Electrical and Radio Material (school) (USN)
EES	European (Community) Exchange System; enlisted evaluation system; electronic emission security
EESA	Equipos Electronicos SA (Spain)
EESAFS	electric and electronic safety arming and fusing system
EEST/PD	emergency establishment supplement table of personnel distribution
EET	East European time; education equivalency test; engineering evaluation test
EETech	Electronics and Energy Technology (Sevenoaks, Kent UK)
EEV	English Electric Valve Co. Ltd (Chelmsford, Essex) (GEC group)
EEVC	English Electric Valve Co. Ltd
EEWT	elementary exercises without troops
EEZ	exclusive economic zone
EF	effective fire; enemy fire; expeditionary force; electrician fitter; emergency fleet; ElInt fighter aircraft; ECM fighter aircraft; EW fighter aircraft (US); elevation finder; extra fine; experimental flight; Einzelfeuer (single shot)
EF-4	Wild Weasel, Phantom electronic defence suppression aircraft by McDD
EF-111	two-seat electronic warfare aircraft by General Dynamics
EFA	Etudes et Fabrications Aeronautiques Clichy (FR)
EFAB	Etablissement d'Etudes et de Fabrications d'Armament de Bourges (FR)
EFAS	electronic flash approach system
E&FB	equipment and facilities branch BUPERS
EFC	Escort Force Commander; European Federal Constitution; Expeditionary Force Canteens; equivalent full charge; expect further clearance
EFCS	engineer functional components system (US); equivalent full charge shots
EFD	electronic frequency display
EFEA	European Free Exchange Area
eff	effective
effcy	efficiency

EFI	Expeditionary Force Institutes Naafi
EFIM	state-owned trust (IT)
EFL	emitter follower logic; equivalent focal length
EF&LTC	enemy fuels and lubricants technical emergency committee WW2 (US)
EFM	engineering field manual; expeditionary forces message
EFOB	emergency fleet operating base
EFPD	equivalent full power days
EFR	electronic failure report; emerging flux regions
EFRC	Edward Flight Research Center (US)
EFS	Engineer Field Squadron
EFT	electronic funds transfer
EFTA	European Free Trade Association
EFTO	encrypted for transmission overseas; encrypted for transmission only
EFTS	elementary flying training school
EFU	energetic feed unit
EG	escort group (USN); Exploratory Group (Nato); electron gun; ethylene glycol; Europäische Gemeinschaft (European Community); Eingabegerät (data input equipment)
EGD	electro-gas dynamics
EGDS	equipment group design specifications
EGIF	equipment group inter-face
EGM	Empire Gallantry Medal; extraordinary general meeting
EGO	eccentric geophysical observatory NASA
EGS	electronic glide slope
EGSP	Electronics Glossary and Symbols Panel
EGT	engine gas temperature; exhaust gas temperature
EH-101	anti-submarine helicopter by EHI
EH-608	SOTAS, stand-off target acquisition system for helicopters by Sikorsky
E-HA	enroute high altitude
EHC	escort helicopter carrier
EHD	electro-hydro-dynamic
EHES	Environmental Health Engineering Services
EHF	extremely high frequencies
EHI	European Helicopter Industries (Agusta + Westland)
EHI-101	Sea King replacement helicopter by EHI
EHIP	European Hawk Improvement Plan (Nato)
EHL	effective half-life
EHP	effective horse-power; electrical horse-power
EHSI	electronic horizontal situation indicator (avionics)

EHT	extra high tension
EHTR	emergency highway transport regulation
EHTRC	emergency highway traffic regulation centre
EHV	extra-high voltage
EHWS	extreme high water level spring tides; encapsulated Harpoon weapon system
EI	East Indies; East India; end item; electrical insulation; Earth (atmosphere) interface
EIA	Electronic Industries Association (US)
EIB	electronic information bulletin; export-import bank
EIC	employee identification code; equipment identification code; exercise intelligence centre; East India Company; Engineering Institute of Canada
EICAS	engine indication and crew alerting system (airborne) by Collins
EICM	employer's inventory of critical manpower
EICS	East India Company's Service
EID	Electrical Inspection Directorate
EIdLt	emergency identification light
EIDSO	engineer information and data systems office
Eifel	Elektronisches Informations- und Führungssystem für die Einsatzverbände der Luftwaffe (electronic information and command system for the operational German Air Force units)
EIG	exchange information group
Eihgr	Eihandgranate (egg-shaped hand grenade)
EIJC	Engineering Institutions Joint Council
EIL	Electronic Instruments Ltd; explosives investigative laboratory
EIMO	engineering interface management office
EinC	Engineer in Chief
EInd	East Indies
EinhG	Einheitsgeschoss (common/uniform projectile)
EIO	extended interaction oscillators
EIP	economic inventory procedures
EIPC	European Institute of Printed Circuits
EIPG	European Independent Planning Group; European Independent Programme Group (Nato)
EIR	earned income relief (tax); equipment improvement recommendation; electronic intelligence receiver; engineering investigation request

EIR/A	electronic intelligence receiver/analyser
EIRMA	European Industrial Research Management Association
EIRP	effective isotropic radiated power
EIS	Educational Institute of Scotland; environmental impact statement (US noise act); epidemic intelligence service; economic information system
EISA	Esperiencias Industriales SA (Madrid Spain)
EisbPzZug	Eisenbahnpanzerzug (armoured railway train)
EISO	Engineering and Integrated Support Office
EIT	engineer in training
EITB	Engineering Industry Training Board
EIU	economist intelligence unit
EIVT	European Institute for Vocational Training
EJC	Engineers Joint Council
EJT	extended joint test for Nato weapons
EKK	Erprobungskommando für Kriegsschiffneubauten (experimental command for Naval Constructions)
EL	Engineer Lieutenant; East longitude; education level; electric laboratory; electronic laboratory; electro-luminescent
el	elevation; element; electric
ELA	Eritrean Liberation Army
E-LA	enroute low altitude
Eland	South African designation AML armoured car
ELANE	Electronics Association for the North East
ELanR	The East Lancashire Regiment
ELAS	Elektronisches Luftbildauswertesystem (electronic aerial photography)processing system
elas	elasticity
Elbit	Computers Ltd (Haifa Israel)
ELCr	Engineer Lieutenant Commander
elect	electronics
ELD	electric-light driven; east longitude date; edge lit display
ElDatTraWP	electronic data transmission working party
Eldi-2	artillery rangefinder by Zeiss
ELDO	European Launcher Development Organization
Eldorado/Mira	search and tracking radar (FR)
Eldos	navigation system by SEL
ELE	engine life expectancy; equivalent logic element
elec	electric; electrical; electronic
ELECo	Engineering and Lighting Equipment Company

elect   electronics; election
ElecTech electronics technician
Electra   twin turboprop cargo aircraft by
          Lockheed
ElectrEngin electrical engineering
electro   electrotype
electron electronics
Eledone   passive submarine sonar by Thomson-
          CSF
Elefant   SLT, heavy-weight transport vehicle
          destroyer tank WW2
ElekLuft Elektronik und Luftfahrtgeräte
          (Justus v. Liebigstr. 18 D5300
          Bonn)
elem   element; elementary
elev   elevator, elevation
ELF   Eritrean Liberation Front; explosive
          (actuated) light filter; early
          lunar flare; extremely low fre-
          quencies; electro-luminescent
          ferro-electric
ELFC   electro-luminescent ferro-electric
          cell
ELG   European Liaison Group; emergency
          landing ground
ELIC   Electro Lamp Industry Council
ElInt   electronic intelligence; electro-
          magnetic intelligence
ElIntS   electronic intelligence ship
Elisa   ESM/ElInt receiver by Thomson-CSF
ELIT   electronics information test
EL/K-1001 miniaturized UHF radio by ELTA
ElL   Electrical Lieutenant
ELLA   European Long Lines Agency (Nato)
ElLCr   Electrical Lieutenant Commander
ELM   Eastern Atlantic and Mediterranean
          Element (USN)
elm   element
EL/M-2001 airborne range-only radar by ELTA
EL/M-2106 battlefield alerting radar against
          low-flying aircraft by ELTA
EL/M-2108 portable infantry radar by ELTA
EL/M-2200 surface radar system for sea-air
          surveillance by ELTA
ElMA   electro-mechanical aid
ElMer   electrical merchant
ElMInt   electro-magnetic intelligence
ElMn   Electrical Mechanician
          (A) Air
ELMS   electric loop mobility system
ELNA   Elektro Navigation und Industrie
          GmbH (Siemensstr. 35 D-2084
          Rellingen)
EloGM   elektronische Gegenmassnahmen
          (electronic counter-measures)
ELOI   emergency letter of instructions
ELOISE   European Large orbiting instrumenta-
          tion for Solar experiments
EloKa   elektronische Kampfführung (elec-
          tronic warfare)

ELOM   electro-optical light modulator
eLon   east longitude
eLong   east longitude
ELOp   Electro Optical Industry Ltd
elOp-5133 tank driver's night vision system
EloProg   electronic programming system for
          CL-89 by Dornier
ELOS   electronic line-of-sight
eloUM   elektronische Unterstützungsmassnahmen
          (electronic support measures)
ELOX   electrical oxidation; electrical
          spark erosion
ELP   emergency landing procedure;
          emergency loading procedure
ELR   export licensing regulations
ELS   emitter location system
EL/S-8600 military computing system by ELTA
ELSA   emergency life support apparatus
          breathing mask + alarm signal by
          Sabre Ltd (Aldershot)
ELSAG   Elettronica San Giorgio (Genova-
          Sestri IT)
Elsan   airborne dry toilet
ELSAP-2000 elektronische Schiessanlage für
          Panzer by Scherz SW (electronic
          fire control simulator for
          tanks)
ELSB   edge-lighted status board
ElSec   electronics security
ELSIE   electronic letter sorting and
          indicating equipment
ElSL   Electrical Sub-lieutenant
ELSS   extra-vehicular life support system
          NASA
elsw   elsewhere
ELT   engineering laboratory technician;
          emergency locator transmitter
ELTA   Electronics Industries Ltd (Ashod
          Israel) (IAI subsidiary)
ELTAD   emergency locator transmitter,
          automatic deployable
ELTAF   emergency locator transmitter
          automatic fixed
ELTAP   emergency locator transmitter
          automatic portable
ELTC   enlisted loss to commissioned
          (status) (US)
ELTR   emergency locator transmitter
          receiver
ELV   extra low voltage
ELWS   extreme low water level, spring
          tides
ELZZ   elektronischer Laufzeitzünder
          (electronic time fuse)
EM   electrician's mate (USN); Efficiency
          Medal; enlisted man; Edward Medal
          (UK) (lifesaving); Education Medal
          (US); Engineer of Mines (US);
          Equitum Magister (Master of Horse);
          education manual; European Move-

ment; External Memorandum; Etat Major (general staff) (FR); electrical and mechanical; electron microscope; engine maintenance; experimental model; Enfield Model; expanded metal; electro-magnetic; emergency maintenance; end of medium; Euromissile (MBB + Aerospatiale)

em   emission

E&M   electrical and mechanical

E/M   electro-mechanical

EM-1   EM-2, Enfield Model, 4.85mm buttless rifle

EM-4M   Entfernungsmessgerat 4m Basis (optical distance measuring equipment)

EM(A)   electrical mechanic Air

EMA   emergency movements, atomic; European Monetary Agreement

EMAS   Emergency message authentication system of USEuCOM

EMatKat   einheitliche Materialkatalogisierung (uniform material cataloguing)

EMATS   emergency message automatic transmitting system)

EMB   electronic material bulletin

emb   embarked; embarkation; embargo

EMB   Embraer (Brazil)

EMB-110   Bandeirante, light transport aircraft by EMB

EMB-111   Banderulha, maritime patrol aircraft by EMB

EMB-120   Brasilia, turboprop transport aircraft by EMB

EMB-312   turboprop trainer aircraft by EMB

EMBERS   emergency bed request system

EmbO   embarkation officer

EMBO   European Molecular Biology Organization

EMBRAER   Empresa Brasileira de Aeronautica

EMC   enlisted men's club; engineered military circuit; electronic material change; electro-magnetic compatibility; excess minority carriers

EMC-81   wheeled mortar carrier by Panhard

EMCCC   European Military Communications Coordination Committee AMCEC

EmCon   emission control; electro-magnetic radiation control

EMCP   electro-magnetic compatibility programme

EMCRO   Experimental Medical Care Review Organization

EMD   electronic map display; Electronique Marcel Dassault (St Cloud FR); Eidgenössisches Militärdepartement (Swiss MoD)

EMDG   Euromissile Dynamics Group (Paris) (BAe + MBB + Aerospatiale)

EMDP   electro-motive difference of potential

EME   Electrical and Mechanical Engineers (Engineering)

EMEC   Electronics Maintenance Engineering Centre

EMED   Embarkation Medical Equipment Depot (Netley)

emerg   emergency

EmergCon   emergency condition

Emerlec   Emerson Electric Company

Emerlec-30   twin automatic 30mm naval gun system by Emerson

EMES-12   Entfernungsme gerät (laser stereoscopic range-finder by Zeiss)

EMES-13   correlation range-finder by Leitz

EMES-15   binocular stabilized day/night laser/IR range-finder

EMETF   electro-magnetic environment test facility

EMF   experimental mechanized force; enlisted master file; electromotive force; evolving magnetic features

EMFC   electrical method of fire control

EMGDN   Etat-Major Général de la Défense Nationale (Defence General Staff)

EMI   extra-military instruction; Etat-Major Militaire International (International Military Staff); Electrical and Musical Instruments Ltd (UK); electro-magnetic interface

EMI-280   7mm assault rifle project (UK)

EMIC   emergency maternity and infant care

EMIE   Electrical and Musical Industry Electronics Ltd

EMIR   Elektronisches Management InformationsSystem der Rüstung, (Electronic Management Information System of Armament)

EML   equipment maintenance log; estimated month of loss; equipment modification list

EMM   Electronic Memories and Magnetics Corporation

Emma   40mm naval proximity fuse by Thomson

EMMA   electron manual metal arch (welding)

EMO   examining medical officer; electronics materials officer

EMOS   entry military occupational specialty; earth's mean orbital speed

Emp   Emperor; Empress

emp   employment; employee

EMP   electro-magnetic pulse (detection)

EMPco   Electronic Mechanical Products Company

empl   emplane(d); emplacement

EmPro   emergency proposal

EMR	equipment maintenance record; Eastern Mediterranean Region; electro-magnetic radiation; electro-magnetic resonance; engine mixture ratio
EMRIC	Educational Media Research Information Center (US)
EMRS	East Malling Research Station
EMS	Eire Marine Service; emergency medical service; equipment maintenance squadron (USAFE); European Monetary System; Ermüdungsmessstreifen (material fatigue measuring strip)
EMSA	Electron Microscope Society of America
EMSC	Electrical Manufacturers' Standards Council (US)
EmSec	emanations security
EmSked	employment schedule (US)
EMSO	European Mobility Service Office
EMSR	electronic material shipment request
EMT	emergency medical treatment; Efficiency Medal, Territorial; expanded mobility truck by Chrysler
EMU	electro-magnetic unit; European Monetary Union; expanded memory unit
EMux	electronic multiplexing
EMV	elektromagnetische Verträglichkeit (electro-magnetic compatibility)
EMZ	Eurometaal Zaandam (Holland)
ENA	European Nuclear Agency
enam	enamelled
ENASA	Empresa Nacional de Autocamiones SA (Spain)
EnC	enlistment cancelled
ENC	equivalent noise charge
ENCA	European Naval Communications Agency
encl	enclosure
ENCP	European Naval Communications Plan
end	endorse(ment)
endg	ending
ENDC	Eighteen Nations Disarmament Committee (UN Geneva) 1962
ENDOR	electron nuclear double resonance
ENDS	Euratom Nuclear Documentation System
ENE	estimated net energy
ENEA	European Nuclear Energy Agency
Energa	DM-22, rifle grenade by Energa
ENF	European Nuclear Force
Enfrac	engineer tank AMX-30 hull (FR)
eng	engineer; engine
EngCol	engineer column
Engesa	Engenheiros Espezializados SA (Sao Paulo Brazil)
ENGR	combat engineer STANAG
EngrE	engineer element

EngrCen	engineer centre
EngrFac	engineer facility
ENIAC	electronic numerical integrator and computer
Enigma	cryptographic machine (GE) WW2
ENJJPT	Euro/Nato Joint Jet Pilot Training Sheppard AFB
EnL	Engineer Lieutenant
enl	enlist(ment); enlarge(ment)
EnLCr	Engineer Lieutenant Commander
enlt	enlistment
ENMASA	Empresa Nacional de Motores de Aviacion SA (Spain)
Enmoth	HDH-10, target drone aiming and scoring system for Redeye by HDH
ENMR	Executive for National Military Representatives SHAPE
ENOSA	Empresa Nacional de Optica SA (Spain)
enq	enquiry
enr	en route
ENRC	European Nuclear Research Centre
ENRFOSComd	en route this station from Overseas Command
ENSA	Entertainment National Service Administration (UK) WW2
ENSB	Empresa Nacional Santa Barbara (Spain)
EnSL	Engineer Sub-lieutenant
ENSURE	expedited non-standard urgent requirements for equipment
EN&T	ear, nose and throat
Entac-58	Engin Téléguide Anti-Char (anti-tank guided missile) by SNIA
Enterprise	STS, Orbiter-101, Shuttle transportation system by NASA
EntNAC	entrance national agency check
EntPz	Entspannungspanzer, Entsatzpanzer (recovery tank) (SW)
EnvExt	Envoy Extraordinary
Envoy Target	7.62mm sniper's rifle by RSAF
Enzian	anti-aircraft missile 1944 by Messerschmitt
EO	executive officer; educational officer; engineer officer; embarkation officer; explosives officer; equipment operator; executive order; engineering order; electro-optical
EOA	examination, opinion and advice, end of address
EOAP	earth observations aircraft programme
EOARDC	European Office of the Air Research and Development Command (US)
EOB	electronic order of battle; estimated on berth; expense operating budget; end of block
EOC	Equal Opportunities Commission; emergency operations centre;

electronic operations centre; ElInt orientation course; end of construction; end of course (examination); Enemy Oil Committee

EOCM — electro-optic counter-measures

EOCM-reactor — electro-optic counter-measures automatic discharge towards the EO threat by Eichweber

EOD — entry on duty; entering office date; explosive ordnance disposal STANAG, every other day

EODB — explosive ordnance disposal bulletin

EODC — explosive ordnance disposal control

EODGru — explosive ordnance disposal group
Lant — Atlantic
Pac — Pacific

EODI — explosive ordnance disposal incident

EODP — explosive ordnance disposal procedures

EODS — explosive ordnance disposal school (US); explosive ordnance disposal squadron (RE UK); explosive ordnance disposal specialist (US)

EODSupv — explosive ordnance disposal supervisor (US)

EODT — explosive ordnance disposal team

EODU — explosive ordnance disposal unit

EODV — Wheelbarrow, explosive ordnance disposal vehicle

EOE — Enemy Occupied Europe

E&OE — errors and omissions excepted

EOF — emergency operating facility; end of file

EOGB — electro-optically guided bomb

EOGB-2 — electro-optically guided bomb by Rockwell

EOH — emergency operation headquarters; equipment on hand

EOHP — except otherwise herein provided

EOKA — Ethnike Organosis Kypriotikes Apeleutheroseos (Greek Cypriots)

EOJ — end of job

EOL — end of life

EOLM — electro-optical light modulation

EOM — end of month; end of message; electrical officer; minesweepers (RN); Egyptian Order of Merit; every other month

EONR — European Organization for Nuclear Research

EOP — Executive Office of the President (US)

EOPAP — earth and ocean physics application programme

EOQ — economic order quantity

EOQC — European Organization for Quality Control

EOR — equipment operationally ready; explosive ordnance reconnaissance; earth orbit rendezvous; end of reel

EORA — explosive ordnance reconnaissance agent

EORL — emergency officers' retired list

EOS — electro-optical system; earth observation satellite by ESA 1983

EOS-500 — electro-optic system tracker by SAAB

EOSD — equipment on station date

EOSM — electro-optic support measures

EOSO — escort oilers supervising officer

EOT — end of transmission; enemy occupied territory; engine order telegraph (ship); end of tape; end of task

EOTS-F — electro-optical tracking system for trajectory measuring by Contraves

EOU — enemy objective unit

EOV — economic order van; end of volume

EOW — electro-optical warfare; engine over the wing

EP — estimated position; enemy position; embussing point (UK); engineering practice; equipment publication; ending period; entrucking point (UK); engineering personnel; emergency planning; electroplated; expanding point (projectile); extreme pressure; expanded polystyrene; electronic patrol (aircraft); electrically polarized; extended play (record); environmental protection; epoxide resin

EP-3 — Orion, electronic patrol aircraft by Lockheed

EPA — emergency powers act (US president); European Procurement Agency; Environmental Protection Agency (US)

EPAC — Electronic Parts Advisory Committee

EPAG — elektronisches Programmier- und Abfeuergerät für MSM (electronic programming and launching device for mine dispenser)

EPAL — Explosivos Alaveses SA (Spain)

EPAM — externally powered armor/airborne machine gun 7.62mm (US)

EPAQ — electronic parts of assessed quality

EPC — European Political Community; European Prime Contractors; Economic and Planning Council; End Products Committee WPB; Engin Principal de Combat (French MBT for the 90ies; Erreur Probable Circulaire (circular probable error)

EPCE — (naval) electronic plant control equipment by Litton

EPCER — experimental patrol craft escort and rescue

EPCO   Engine Parts Coordinating Office
EPD   engineer plant depot; earliest prac-
          ticable date; Enlisted Personnel
          Directorate BUPERS; Extra Police
          Duty (US); Eastern Procurement
          Division (US); excess profits
          duty; Exercise Planning Directives
          (Nato); Ecart Probable en Direc-
          tion (probable error in direction)
EPD   electronic proximity detector
EPDA   Emergency Powers Defence Act
EPDL   Emergency Powers Defence Law
EPDM   ethylene propylene diene monomer
          (synthetic rubber)
EPDO   Enlisted Personnel Distribution
          Office (US)
EPDT   estimated project duration time
EPE   Electronic Parts and Equipment
          STANAG
EPers   enlisted personnel
Epervier drone semi-active homing missile
          or recce drone by MBLE
EPF   emergency plant facilities
EPG   European Planning Group (Nato);
          Enivetok proving ground (US);
          European Participating Government;
          electro-static particle guide;
          Elektronisches Prüfgerät (elec-
          tronic test set); Elektronisches
          Programmiergerät (electronic pro-
          gramming device --CL-89)
EPGA   Emergency Petroleum and Gas Adminis-
          tration Department of Transporta-
          tion
EPI   electronic position indicator;
          engine performance indicator;
          economic procurement item
EPIC   extended performance and increased
          capability; engineering and pro-
          duction information control; earth
          pointing instrument carrier
EPIDC   East Pakistan Industrial Development
          Corp.
EPIRB   emergency position indicating radio
          beacon
EpiRept   epidemiological report
EPLA   Electronic Precedence List Agency
          (US)
EPLF   Eritrean People's Liberation Front
EPLO   Swedish command control and informa-
          tion system
EPM   economic performance monitoring
EPMA   electron probe micro-analysis
EPMS   enlisted personnel management system
EPN   external priority number; equivalent
          perceived noise
EPNdB   equivalent perceived noise decibels
EPNG   El Paso natural gas (reactor)
EPNL   effective perceived noise level
EPNS   electro-plated nickel silver

EPO   Evershed Power Optics Ltd (Bridge
          Wharf, Chertsey Surrey)
EPOs   examination procedure outlines
EPOS   Electric Power on Sea (North Sea Gas
          German project)
EPP   effective programme projection;
          Ecart Probable en Portée (probable
          error in range)
EPPI   electronic programmed procurement
          information (US)
EPPP   emergency production planning pro-
          gram (US)
EPR   equipment performance report; engine
          pressure ratio; electron paramag-
          netic resonance; essential perfor-
          mance requirements
EPR-1.2   (3.6 6) electronic underwater mine
          by Tecnovar
EPROM   erasable programmable read only
          memory (computer chip)
EPS   exercise planning staff; emergency
          power supply; equipment policy
          statement; engineered performance
          standards; electromagnetic posi-
          tion sensor; Externes Prüfsystem
          (external testing system)
Epsilon   TB-30 primary trainer aircraft by
          AS
EPT   excess profits tax; ethylene propy-
          lene tar polymer (synthetic
          rubber)
EPTA   expanded programme of technical
          assistance
EPTS   existed prior to service
EPU   European Payments Union; European
          Political Union; emergency power
          unit; electrical power unit
EPW   enemy prisoner of war
EPWIB   enemy prisoner of war information
          bureau
EQ   educational quotient
Eq   equipment; equator; equalizer;
          equivalent
EqDD   equipment density data
eqpt   equipment
Equate   USM-407, electronic quality assur-
          ance test equipment by RCA
equil   equilibrium
equip   equipment
EQUIP   equipment usage information pro-
          gramme
equiv   equivalent
EQX   electronic warfare experimental
          aircraft
ER   Elizabeth Regina (UK); Edward Rex
          (UK); engineer regulations;
          equipment regulations; emergency
          regulations; engine room; enhanced
          radiation (warhead); extended
          range (missile); electronic recon-

naissance; en route (aircraft);
electronic ram; error recovery;
echo ranging; effectiveness
report; emergency rescue; estab-
lished reliability; external
resistance

E&R engineering and repair

ERA emergency relief administration;
external relations act; engine
room artificer; expenses on return
of absentee (US); Electrical Research Association BEAIRA; electronic reading automation; extended range ASROC

ERADCom Electronics Research and Development Command (US Army)

ERAM extended range anti-armor munition
(USAF programme)

ERAPS SSQ-75, expandable reliable acoustic
path sonobuoy

ERB emergency relief bureau; enlisted
record brief; ecclesiastical relations branch BUPERS

ERBF long-range projectile 155mm by SRL

ERBM extended range ballistic missile

ERBS earth radiation budget system
(satellite, ozone research NASA)

ERC enlisted reserve corps (US Army);
economic research council; electronics research center (US);
wheeled armoured recce vehicle by
Panhard

ERC-60-20 Serval wheeled armoured recce
vehicle with mortar

ERC-90 Serval wheeled armoured long-range
recce vehicle by Panhard 90mm gun

ERC-90S Sagaie, anti-tank recce vehicle,
90mm gun by Panhard

ERC TG-120 Guepard, recce vehicle by
Panhard

ERCO Electric Reduction Company of Canada

ERD Emergency Reserve Decoration (Army);
equipment readiness date; expenses
for return of deserter (US); emergency return device; equivalent
residual dose

ERDA Emergency Research and Development
Administration (US); Emergency Re-
search and Development Agency;
Electrical and Radio Development
Association of Australia

ERDC Electronic Research and Development
Command (US Army)

ERDE Engineering Research and Development
Establishment

ERDL extended range data link -- Walleye;
Engineering Research and Development Laboratory

ERDU Electronic Research and Development
Unit (US Army)

ERE extra-regimental employment

Edison responsive environment

erec erection

EREO extra-regimentally employed officer

EREP earth resources experimental
package; environmental recording
and editing and printing

ER&I Edward Rex et Imperator

ERF emergency reserve force

ERG emergency reserve group

ERFA European Radio Frequency Agency

ERFAA European Radio Frequency Allocation
Agency

ERFB extended range full bore 155mm
howitzer round by SRL

ERG emergency reserve group; emergency
recovery group; electrical resistance gauge; electro-retino-gram

ERGOM European Research Group on Management

ergon ergonomics

ERGS electronic route guidance system

ERIC energy rate input controller;
educational resources information
center (US)

Eridan class, Tripartite minehunter
(French, Dutch, Belgian)

ERISA Employees' Retirement Income
Security Act (US)

ERL European requirements list

ERMA Erfurter Maschinenwerke (GE) WW2

ERMISS explosion resistant multi-influence
sweep system (naval mines)

ERNIE electronic random number indicating
equipment (UK)

ERNO Entwicklungsring Nord der Deutschen
Raumfahrtinudstrie (Bremen)

ERO European Regional Organization;
European Research Organization;
European Research Office

EROP executive review of overseas programmes

EROPA Eastern Regional Organization for
Public Administration

EROS earth resources observation system;
earth resources observation satellite (ground station for Landsat,
Siowe Falls Dakota); giant X-ray
machine at AWRE

ERP European Recovery Plan; European
Recovery Programme; European requirements program (US); electronic requirement plan; equipment
requirements plan; effective
radiated power

ERPAL electronic repair parts allowance
list

ERPSL essential repair parts stockage
list

ErpSt Erprobungsstelle (experimental
establishment)

ErpSt	71	Eckernförde (naval equipment)
	91	Meppen (guns and ammunition)
	51	Koblenz-Metternich (engineer equipment)
	41	Trier (vehicles and tanks)
	81	Greding (electronics)
	61	Manching (air force equipment)
	52	Oberjettenberg (mountain warfare)

ERR electoral registration regulation; engineering release record; engine removal report

err error

ER-RB enhanced radiation - reduced blast (nuclear warhead) neutron bomb

ERS emergency relocation site; emergency recovery section; eastern range ships (USN); earth resources satellite; Ergonomics Research Society; Experimental Research Society (US); electrical resistance strain; engine repair shop; economic retention stock

ERSA Electronic Research Supply Agency (US)

ERSCRE Engine and Railway Staff Corps, Royal Engineers

ER&SD Employee Relations and Services Division (Industrial Relations Department US)

ERSOS earth resources survey operational satellite

ERT educational requirements test

ERTC European regional test centre

ERTS European rapid train system; earth resources technology satellite --Landsat (US)

ERU emergency recovery unit; ejector release unit

ERV electronic repair vehicle; extended range vehicle RPVs ALCMs

ERW electric resistance welding

ERY The East Riding Yeomanry

ery early

ERZ extended reconnaissance zone,

ES emergency service; engineer stores;, essential services; embarkation staff; eligible for separation; electro-static; engine-sized; electrical sounding; electronic switch

E-S en-route supplement

Es-32 smoke charge (GDR)

ESA European Space Agency; Eastern Atlantic Subarea (Nato); expiration of service agreement; European Supply Agency (Nato)

ESAR electronically steerable array radar

ESB educational service branch BUPERS; eligibility and screening branch BUPERS; electrical simulation of the brain; electrical storage battery

ESBA Eastern Sovereign Based Area (Dhekelia Cyprus)

ESBD engineer stores base depot

esc escort

ESC Electronic Systems Command (USAF Hanscom); equipment serviceability criteria; electronic structural calculator; extended core storage; European Space Conference, escape character

ESCA electron spectroscopy for chemical analysis

Esacpac ejection seat

EsCarFor escort carrier force (USN)

ESCES experimental satellite communication earth station

ESCO Educational Scientific and Cultural Organization (UN UNESCO)

EScoRon escort scouting squadron

EscortDiv escort division

EscortFightDiv escort fighter division

EscrG escort guard

ESD electronic systems division AFSC; engineer stores depot; estimated shipping date; earth sciences division ONR; employment services division; echo sounding device; ending sequence done

ESDAC European Space Data Centre

ESD(MSC) Employment Services Division of the Manpower Services Commission (UK)

ESE Engineer Stores Establishment

ESF Eastern Sea Frontier

ESFA Emergency Solid Fuels Administration

ESFC equivalent specific fuel consumption

ESFSWR extra special flexible steel wire rope

ESG English Standard Gauge; electrostatic gyro; electrically suspended gyro; Elektronik System Gesellschaft (München) (BDM/US, GEI/Aachen, IBM SG/Bonn, Logica/UK, SOBEMAP/Belgium)

ESGM electro-statically supported gyro monitors for Poseidon by Rockwell

ESH equivalent standard hours; electric strip heater

ESHP equivalent shaft horsepower

ESHU emergency ship handling unit

ESI   Electronic Systems International
          Inc. (Lancaster Pa USA); extremely
          sensitive information
ESIL   European Standard Inventory List
          (nomenclature) (Nato)
ESIST   European Security and its Inter-
          action with Science and Technology
          Committee (Nato)
ESL   Engineer Sub-lieutenant; expected
          significance level
ESLAB   European Space Laboratory
ESLO   European Satellite Launching Organi-
          zation
ESM   Emergency Service Medal; electronic
          support measures
ES&M   expandable supplies and material
ESME   excited state mass energy
ESN   English-speaking nations; European
          scientific notes; educationally
          sub-normal
esn   essential
ESNLw   Einsatzstammnetz der Luftwaffe
          (German Air Force tactical communi-
          cations network)
ESO   embarkation staff officer; educa-
          tional service office(r); elec-
          tronic supply office(r); emergency
          standby order
ESOC   European Space Operations Centre;
          European Satellite Operations
          Centre (Darmstadt)
ESONE   European Standards of Nuclear Elec-
          tronics
ESP   extra-sensory perception; electron
          spin polarization
ESPAR   electronically steerable phased
          array radar
ESPAWS   enhanced self-propelled artillery
          weapons system (US)
espg   espionage
ESPOL   executive systems problem oriented
          language
ESR   equivalent service rounds; estimated
          sedimentation rate; electron spin
          resonance; electro slag refined
          (steel)
ESRANGE   European Space Launching Range
          (Kiruna)
ESRD   equipment shipment ready date
ES&RD   enlisted services and records divi-
          sion BUPERS
ESRIN   European Space Research Institute
          (Frascati/Rome)
ESRO   European Space Research Organization
ESS   engineer and signals store; educa-
          tional services section; elec-
          tronic switching system; ESM signal
          sorter
ESSA   Environmental Sciences Services
          Administration (US); environmental

          service satellite; Environmental
          and Space Sciences Administration
          (US)
ESSCo   Electronic Space Structure Corpora-
          tion
Essex   class, aircraft carriers (USN)
ESSG   engineer strategic studies group
ESSM   emergency ship salvage material
ESSNSS   electronic supply segment of the
          Navy supply system (USN)
ESSPO   Electronics Supporting Systems Pro-
          ject Office (US)
ESSWACS   electronic solid-state wide angle
          camera system by AFAL
EST.   eastern standard time; electrical
          shock treatment; enlistment
          screening test; earliest start
          time
est   estimate(d); establish(ment)
EstAr   estimated arrival date
estb   establish(ment)
ESTEC   European Space Technology Centre
          (Nordwijk Netherlands); European
          Space Research and Technology
          Centre
estg   estimating
Esther   proximity fuse for 105mm-155mm (FR)
ESTI   European Space Technology Institute
E/STIEP   engineering/service test and inde-
          pendent evaluation programme
estn   estimation
ESTRACK   European Space Tracking System
ESTRIFF   encryptic secure tracking radar
          identification friend or foe
          (Nato)
ESU   electro-static unit
ESurr   The East Surrey Regiment
ESV   earth satellite vehicle
ET   European Theatre (of Operations);
          educational training; engineer
          training; engineering test;
          equivalent training; estimated
          time, elapsed time; electric tele-
          graphy
E&T   education and training
ET-001   radio surveillance system by R&S
ET-316   Rapier, clear weather anti-aircraft
          system (UK)
ETA   estimated time of arrival
ETACCS   European Theater Air Command and
          Control Study (US)
ETAR   European theatre air routes
ETAS   Etablissement Technique d'Angers
          (DTAT test centre); estimated true
          air-speed
ETB   enlisted training branch BUPERS;
          estimated time of blocks; end of
          transmission block; Entwicklung-
          stechnische Betreuung (technical
          assistance for development)

ETBS   Etablissement Technique des Bourges (DTAT test centre)

ETC   estimated time of completion; engineer training camp; European Translation Centre; European Traffic Committee; electro-thermal (integrated) circuits

ETCG   elapsed time code generator

ETCR   estimated time of crew's return

ETCRRM   electronic teleprinter cryptographic regenerative repeater mixer

ETD   estimated time of departure; electronic tactical display; extension trunk dialling; equivalent transmission density; Testing and Development Division (USCG)

ETDP   emergency traffic disposition plan

ETE   estimated time en-route; experimental tunnelling establishment

Etendard   carrier-based attack, tanker, recce aircraft by Dassault 1956

ETF   eastern task force; enhanced tactical fighter (USAF programme); estimated time of flight; engine test facility

eth   ether

Ethan Allen   class, nuclear ballistic missile submarine SSBN (USN)

ETI   elapsed time indicator; estimated time of interception

ETIC   estimated time in commission

ETim   elapsed time

ETJC   Engineering Trades Joint Council

ETKM   every test known to man

ETM   enlisted transfer manual (US); European Theatre Medal; electronic trajectory measuring; electronic test and measurement

ETMWG   Electronic Trajectory Measurement Working Group

ETN   equipment table nomenclature

Etna   inertial naval attack system by SAGEM

ETO   European Theatre of Operations; European Transport Organization; express transportation order; estimated time off

EtO   ethylene oxide

ETOUSA   European Theater of Operations (US Army)

ETP   equal time point; elevated training platform; estimated turnaround point; estimated turning point

ETPS   Empire Test Pilots School (London)

ETR   estimated time of return; export traffic release; export to repair; Eastern Test Range (Cape Canaveral); experimental test reactor

ETRA   estimated time to reach altitude

ETS   expiration of time of service; educational testing service; Employment Training School (RAOC); engineering and technical services; enlisted training section; European Telecommunications System; engineered time standards; estimated time of sailing; electronic test set; engineering test satellite (Japan); European Telephone System for US Forces by SEL+TN+DeTeWe

ETS-5   Engineering test satellite by Mitsubishi

ETSP   entitled to severance pay

ET/ST   engineering technical service test

ETST   electronics technician selection test

ETT   estimated travel time

ETTT   EA-6B Team Tactics Trainer by AAI

ETV   educational television

en   engine test vehicle (jet)

ETW   Europaischer Transschall Windkanal (European Transsonic Establishment); Ersttreffwahrscheinlichkeit (first hit probability)

ETX   end of test

EU   Europe; experimental unit; Etat-Unies (United States) (FR); electronic unit

EU-13   fragmentation bomb 120 kg by SAMP

EU-32   general-purpose bomb 125 kg by SAMP

EU-70   general purpose bomb 50 kg by SAMP

Euclid   loader, road construction machine

EuCom   European Command (Nato-US)

EUDAC   European Distribution and Accounting Agency of the Military Committee London Standing Group (Nato)

EUDDL   equivalent uniformly distributed dead load

Eule   night vision goggles by AEG

EUM   European Mediterranean Region

EUMS   engine usage monitoring system for jet engines

EUN   Long Tom, 155mm field gun (US)

Eupad   Edinburgh University pad, dry antiseptic dressing

Eur   Europe

EURATOM   European Atomic Energy Community

Eureca   beacon paratroopers' marker lights

EURO   European Regional Office of FAO

EUROC   European Rescue Operation Centre

EUROCAE   European Organization for Civil Aviation Electronics

EUROCEAN   European Oceanographic Organization

EUROCHEMIC   European Company for the Chemical Processing of Irradiated Fuels

EUROCOM   Eurogroup on cooperation of tactical communications systems (Nato); study on battlefield communications by EUROCOM

EUROCONTROL   air traffic control of European
(Nato countries)
EUROGROUP   Nato informal group of European
Defence Ministers (Be, DK, GE,
GR, IT, LUX, NL, NO, P, UK,
TUR)
EUROLAND   EUROGROUP study on aircraft landing
systems cooperation
EUROLOG   Eurogroup study on cooperation of
logistic support
EUROLONGTERM   Eurogroup for development and
harmonization of tactical
concepts
EUROMED   Eurogroup study on cooperation of
military medical services
Euromissile   (7 rue Beranger Chatillion),
MBB + Aerospatiale,
Roland missile
EURONAD   Eurogroup national armaments
directors
EUROP   European Railway Wagon Pool
Europackage   Eurogroup plans for introduc-
tion of major new equipment
Euro-SAM   Hawk replacement
Eurosatellite group   AS+Thomson-CSF+AEG+MBB+
ETCA+ACEC
EUROSCHED   Eurogroup study on cooperation
concerning major weapon systems
and national planning schedules
Eurospace   European Industrial Space Study
Group
EUROSTRUCTURE   Eurogroup exchange of informa-
tion on force structures of
member countries
EUROTOX   European Standing Committee for the
Protection of the Population
against Long-term Risks of
Intoxication
EUROTRAINING   Eurogroup study of cooperation
in training
EURPIR   SHAPE periodic intelligence review
EUSEC   European Communications Security
and Evaluation Agency of the
military committee (London)
Eutelsat   European telecommunications
satellite organization
--Marots --ECS
EUTTAS   European utility tactical transport
aircraft system programme
EUV   extreme ultra-violet
EV   escort vessel; emergency vessel;
electron volt
EV-1   Mohawk, ElInt plane by Grumman
EVA   Engineer Vice Admiral; electron
velocity analyser; extra-vehicular
activity (spaceflight); ethylene
vinyl acetate (plastic)
evac   evacuation

eval   evaluation
evap   evaporation
Evader   Mk-55, terminally guided warhead
ICBM (US)
EVCS   extra-vehicular communications
system (NASA)
eve   evening
evid   evidence
EVEC-20   Equipement de Visualisation et
d'Erengistrement de Chasse aux
Mines (mine-hunting sonar
computer)
EVR   electronic video recorder/reproduc-
tion
EVS   extra-vehicular suit (space);
electro-optical viewing system;
environmental science
EVT   effective visual transmission
EW   engineer works; enlisted women;
electronic warfare
E&W   England and Wales
EW   early warning (radar)
EWAD   early warning air defence
EWAS   economic warfare analysis section
EWD   economic warfare division
EWDT   early warning data transmission
EWE   electronic warfare element
EWG   Elektrischer Weggeber für FNA
(electric course and distance
sensor)
EW-GCI   early warning-ground controlled
intercept (radar)
EWI   education with industry
EWK   Eisenwerke Kaiserslautern Göppner
GmbH (Barbarossastr. 30, D-6750
Kaiserslautern)
EWO   essential works order; electronic
warfare officer
EWP   emergency war plan
EWQ   enlisted women's quarters
EWR   early warning radar;
Entwicklungsring (Süd) (MBB
daughter)
EWRC   European War Research Council
EWS   emergency water supply; electronic
warfare system; emergency welfare
service
E&WS   electrical and wireless school
EWS-900   electronic warfare system naval
chaff launcher by SAAB
EWSF   European Work Study Federation
EWSM   electronic warfare surveillance
measures
EWT   European war theatre; eastern war
time WW2; electronic (warfare)
weapon targeting (US Army)
EWTR   electronic warfare test range
ex   exercise; execution; excess;
exchange; except; examination
EX   experimental (radio station) (Nato)

ExAgt   executive agent
EXAPT   European Exchange automatic picture
            transmission
ExBedCap expected bed capacity
EXCC   exercise control centre
EXCG   exercise control group
exch   exchange
excl   excluded
excp   except
EXCOM   extended communications search (Nato)
EXCP   executive channel programme
ExDiv   experimental division
EX/DP   express/direct pack (US)
ExecAsst executive assistant
exer   exercise
exh   exhaust
ExLv   excess leave
ExMovRep expedited movement report
EXNMR   Executive National Military Represen-
            tative SHAPE
Exocet   surface-to-surface missile by AS
            MM-38 naval
            AM-39 helicopter-borne
            MM-40 vehicle-borne
EXOS   executive office of the secretary of
            the Navy
Exosat   x-ray satellite by ESA
EXP   exchange of persons office (UNESCO);
            expanding, experimental; express;
            expenses; specifications and
            methods of acceptance testing for
            explosives STANAG
ExPatr   Exerzierpatrone drill cartridge
ExpDivUnit experimental diving unit
exped   expeditionary
ExpEnl   expiration of enlistment
exper   experiment
EXPERT   extended PERT programme (programme
            evaluation review technique)

expl   explosives
explo   explosives
expr   expire; expiration
Explofoil expanded metal cells to fill
            tanks to prevent explosions
Explorer satellite NASA
Explosive Paravane Burney Paravane, explo-
            sweep, RN mine-sweeping equip-
            ment
Explosive Sweep RN mine-sweeping equipment
            or towed anti-submarine
            charge
expt   experimental
exptl   experimental
EXR   execute and repeat
ExRedCon exercise readiness condition
EcSpec   exercise specification
ExSta   experimental station
ext   external, extension, extend(ed)
ExTAl   extra time allowance
Extender KC-10, ATCA, advanced tanker/
            cargo aircraft by McDD
ExtEnl   eextension of enlistment
extn   extension
extrm   extreme
extsv   extensive
extv   extensive
EYorks   The Duke of York's Own East York-
            shire Regiment
EYR   The East Yorkshire Regiment
EZ   empfindlicher Zünder (sensitive
            fuse), Entlastungszünder (lift-up
            fuse)
EZSF   Entlastungszünder, Sofortzünder,
            metallfrei (lift-up fuse, instan-
            taneous, metal-free)
EZSM   Entlastungszünder, Sofortzünder aus
            Metall (metallic instantaneous
            lift-up fuse)

F

F	fitter; flag; field; fleet; Flying Officer (RAF); fighter (aircraft); frigate; full choke (bore); flat nose (projectile); Fahrenheit; Farad; fog; fuel; fire; frequency; filter; fluorine
f	fathoms; feet; focal length; filament
(f)	französisch French make WW2 (GE)
F-echelon	fighting part of a unit
F-1	anti-personnel hand grenade (SU); 20mm automatic gun by GIAT; mine detector by AFT; 9mm submachine gun by ASAF
F-2	20mm automatic gun by GIAT
F-2	Chinese-built MiG-15
F-2A	Buffalo, fighter aircraft WW2 by Brewster
F-2H	Banshee, jet fighter 1949 (USN)
F-3D	Skyknight, night fighter by Douglas
F-3H	Demon, transsonic fighter
F-4	Phantom II, twin-jet all-weather fighter/bomber by McDonnell
F-4	Chinese-built MiG-17; smoke rifle grenade by Ruggieri
F-4D	Skyray, fighter by Douglas
F-4E	Phantom, jet trainer aircraft by McDD
F-4F	Wildcat, naval fighter WW2 by Grumman; Phantom II, multi-role tactical fighter by McDD
F-4U	Corsair, naval fighter WW2 by Vought
F-5	Tiger II, Freedom Fighter, lightweight jet fighter by Northrup; Chinese-built MiG-17PF
F-6	Chinese-built MiG-19
F-6F	Hellcat, naval fighter WW2 by Grumman
F-7	Chinese-built MiG-21
F-7F	Tigercat, naval fighter WW2 by Grumman
F-7F-2N	Tigercat, night fighter WW2 by Grumman
F-7U	Cutlass, naval twin-jet fighter by Vought
F-8	Crusader, supersonic fighter 1955 by Vought
F-8	Chinese-built MiG-21
F-8F	Bearcat, naval fighter WW2 by Grumman
F-9F	Panther, jet fighter by Grumman
F-9F-6	Cougar, swept-wing Panther by Grumman
F-11	Tiger, YF-9F, jet fighter by Grumman
F-14A	Tomcat, variable sweep jet fighter by Grumman
F-15	Eagle, jet fighter by McDD
F-16	ACF, air combat fighter, lightweight fighter by General Dynamics
F-18	YF-17, Hornet, Cobra, low-cost air combat fighter by McDD+Northrop; Hornet carrier-based McDD; Cobra land-based Northrop
F-27	Maritime, turboprop aircraft by Fokker
F-28	VIP jet aircraft by Fokker
F-30	30mm automatic gun by Mauser
F-34	fuel for European military aircraft
F-40	fuel for US tactical aircraft
F-51D	Mustang, fighter aircraft by North-American
F-80C	Shooting Star, first US jet aircraft by Lockheed
F-82	Twin Mustang, fighter aircraft by North American
F-84F	Thunderstreak, jet fighter/bomber by Republic
F-84G	Thunderjet, jet fighter by Republic
F-86F	Sabre, jet fighter by North American
F-89	Scorpion, jet fighter by Northrop
F-94	Starfire, allweather fighter by Lockheed
F-100	Super Sabre, supersonic fighter by North American 1955
F-101	Voodoo, supersonic all-weather interceptor by McDonnell 1957
F-102	Delta Dagger, supersonic fighter/ interceptor 1953 by Convair
F-104	Starfighter, jet fighter/interceptor by Lockheed

F-104G Starfighter, jet fighter/interceptor by Lockheed German version

F-105 Thunderchief, tactical nuclear bomber by Republic

F-106 Delta Dart, fighter/interceptor 1959 by Convair

F-108 Rapier, Mach 2 interceptor

F-111 variable-sweep jet fighter/bomber by General Dynamics

F-122 frigate Federal German Navy

FA fitter/armourer; fireman apprentice; flight attendant; field allowance; field ambulance; field artillery; field activity; family allowance; fighter/attacker (aircraft); fire arms; free area; fresh air; frequency agility; fluorescent antibody; fighter alert; fire alarm; fuel air (ratio); Frankford Arsenal (Philadelphia); Fremdantrieb (externally powered)

F&A food and agriculture; fore and aft

FA-223 FA-225, rotocraft glider aircraft by Focke-Achgelis WW2

FA-330 Bachstelze (rotor kite towed behind submarines) WW2 by Focke-Achgelis

FAA Fleet Air Arm (RN); Federal Aviation Administration (US); family allowance class A; Foreign Assistance Act (US) 1961

FAAB family allowance class A and B

FAAC Food Additives and Contaminants Committee

FAACE Forces Aeriennes du Centre Europe (Allied Air Forces Central Europe)

FAAD forward area air defence

FAAM family of air-to-air missiles

FAANE Forces Aeriennes du Nord Europe (Allied Air Forces Northern Europe)

FAAO Fleet Aviation Accounting Office (USN)
    L Atlantic
    P Pacific

FAAP forward air ammunition park; Federal Aid to Airport Program (US)

FAAR TPQ-32, forward area alerting radar

FAAS forward area alerting system

FAASE Forces Aeriennes Allies du Sud Europe (Allied Air Forces Southern Europe)

FAATDC Federal Aviation Technical Development Center (US)

FAAWTC Fleet Anti-Air Warfare Training Center (USN)

FAB Fleet Air Base (USN); family allowance class B; Forces Aeronautical Broadcasting station; first aid box

fab fabric

FABMDS Field Army Ballistic Missile Defense System (US programme 1960)

FABU fleet air base unit

FABx fire alarm box

FAC forward air controller; Frequency Allotment Committee; Fleet Activities Command (USN); Fleet Augmentation Component (US); fast as can; final approach course; functional area code; Fairey Aviation Company Ltd

fac facility; factory; facsimile

FAC fast attack craft
    (M) missile boat
    (G) gun boat
    (T) torpedo boat

FACATS fleet area control and tracking system

FacConCen facilities control centre

FACE facilities and communication evaluation (US); field artillery computer equipment (UK); Fabrica Apparechiature per Communicazioni Elettriche (IT)

FACG fast attack craft, gunboat

FACI first article configuration inspection

FACM fast attack craft, missile boat

FACP forward air control post

FACR first article configuration review; force assessment in the central European Region (Nato)

FACS fast attack class submarine; field army communications system

facs facsimile

FACT fully automatic computing technique; fully automatic compiling technique; fully automatic computer translator; Flanagan aptitude classification test; fast attack craft, torpedo boat

FACTS FLIR-augmented Cobra TOW sight by Hughes (forward-looking infra-red)

FAD forward ammunition depot; field advanced dumps; fleet air detachment; flexible automatic depot; force activity designator

FADAC field artillery digital automatic computer (US)

FADAP fleet anti-submarine warfare data analysis program (US)

FADC fighter air direction centre

FADES fuselage analysis and design synthesis

FAdm Fleet Admiral

FAE fuel air explosives

FAESHED fuel air explosive system, helicopter delivered

FAETU fleet airborne electronics training unit

DET   detachment
Lant   Atlantic
Pac   Pacific

FAF   French Air Force, final approach
      fix; free at field (aircraft
      delivery)

FAFDC   force artillery fire direction
        centre ANF (Nato)

FAFT   first article factory tests STC

FAG   fleet assistance group;
      Feldarbeitsgerät (field excavator)

FAGAirTrans   first available government
              transportation

FAGLant   fleet assistance group Atlantic

FAGPac   fleet assistance group Pacific

FAGS   Federation of Astronomical and Geo-
       physical Services

FAGT   first available government surface
       transportation

FAGTrans   first available government surface
           transportation

Fah(r)   Fahrenheit

FAHD-960   computerized surveillance and
           location receiver by Schlumberger

FAI   fresh air inlet; fresh air intake;
      Fédération Aeronautique Inter-
      nationale

FAIO   field army issuing office

FAIR   fair and impartial random (selective
       service system) (US)

FAir   Fleet Air Command (USN)

FAirDEx   fleet air defence exercise

FAirReconRon   fleet air reconnaissance
               squadron

FAirELM   fleet air Eastern Atlantic and
          Mediterranean

FAirIntAugmU   fleet air intelligence augmen-
               tation unit

FAirIntSuppCen   fleet air intelligence sup-
                 port centre

FAIRS   Fairchild automatic intercept and
        response system (jammer)

FAirShips   fleet airships

FAirShipWing   fleet airship wing

FAirSuppU   fleet air support unit

FAirTrans   first available air transportation

FAirWestPac   fleet air wing western Pacific
              area

FAirWg   fleet air wing

FAirWing   fleet air wing

FAK   freight all kinds (ship)

FAKs   file access keys

FAL   Forces Armée Lao; Fuzil Automatique
      Légère 7.62mm,(light automatic
      rifle by FN)

Falcon   A-3, ground attack aircraft 1920 by
         Curtiss; AEL-4012, camera-carrying
         small RPV by Ael; AIM-26, AIM-4,
         air intercept missile by Hughes,
         heat-homing or radar-

guided, twin 30mm anti-aircraft
tank by Vickers

Falcon-10   maritime patrol aircraft by
            Breguet

Falcon-20   maritime patrol aircraft by
            Breguet

Falcon goggles   night vision goggles by
                 Pilkington

Falconet   Pocket Cannon, 24mm portable
           semi-automatic weapon by SARMAC

Falke   TR-84, artillery calculator by AEG;
        acoustic homing torpedo WW2

FallEx   fall exercises (Nato)

FALo   FAL with heavy barrel,light machine
       gun

FALT   field artillery logic tester

FALW   family of air-launched weapons
       (Nato)

FAM   field artillery missile; foreign air
      mail

fam   family allowance

FAMA   forward airhead maintenance area

FAMAS   Fuzil Automatique MAS 5.56mm rifle

FAmb   field ambulance

FAMC   Fitzsimons Army Medical Centre

FAMECE   family of military engineering con-
         struction equipment (US)

FAMF   floating aircraft maintenance
       facility

FAMIS   financial and management information
        system (US)

FAMOS   fleet air meteorological observation
        satellite (US); floating gate
        avalanche injection; metal oxide
        semi-conductor

FAMS   field army message system

FAMTO   first aid mechanical transport
        outfit (UK), vehicle repair kit

FAMU   fleet aircraft maintenance unit (US)

FandT   fuel and transportation (US)

FANK   Forces Armée National Kmer

FANS   food and nutritional system

Fantrainer   AWI-2, ATI-2
             ATI-2, Anfangstrainer mit
             Turbine und integrierter Luft-
             schraube by RFB (initial
             trainer with integrated turbo-
             fan)
             AWI-2, Anfangstrainer mit
             Wankelmotor und integrierter
             Luftschraube by RFB (initial
             trainer with Wankelmotor and
             integrated airscrew)

FANY   first aid nursing yeomanry,
       cover name WW2 British agents in
       France

FANYS   first aid nursing yeomanry service,

FAO   fleet aviation officer; fleet accoun-
      tant officer; fleet administrative
      officer; finance and accounting

FAO	officer; Food and Agricultural Organization (UN Rome); finish all over
FAP	forward ammunition post; first aid post; finance and accounting policy; family assistance programme; facilities assistance programme; financial analysis programme
FAPC	Food and Agriculture Planning Committee (Nato)
FAPG	fleet air photographic group
FAPRon	fleet air photographic squadron
FAPO	field army petroleum office
FAPUSJCEC	frequency allocation panel US joint communications electronics committee (Nato)
FAQ	fair average quality
FAQS	fair average quality of season
FAR	Federal Aviation Regulations (US); flight aptitude ratings test (US); foreign area research (coordination group) (Nato); forward acquisition radar; field array radar; frequency agile radar; false alarm rate; Federal Airworthiness Regulation (US)
FARA	Formula air racing association (Redhill Surrey)
FARELF	Far East Land Forces
FARP	forward arming and refuelling post
FARR	forward area refuelling and rearming
FARS	field army replacing system
FAS	forward area sector; field alert status; force accounting system; foreign agricultural service; free alongside; Ferranti autostabilizer system (helicopters); force augmentation system (helicopters); frequency agile system (radar); factor analysis system
FASA	field army service area; fleet airships, Atlantic (USN)
FASCAM	family of scatterable mines (US)
FASCO	forward area support coordination officer
FASCOM	field army support command
FASD	fleet anti-submarine duties
FASEB	Federation of American Societies of Experimental Biology
FASO	forward airfield supply organization; field aviation supply office
FASOC	forward air support operating centre (Nato)
FASOR	forward area sonar research
FASP	fleet airships, Pacific (USN)
FASR	frequency agile shipboard radar
FASRon	fleet aircraft service squadron
FASS	Federation of Associations of Specialists and Subcontractors

FAST	forward area support team (missile supply); fast automatic shuttle transfer; freight automatic system for traffic management; fence against satellite threats; first atomic ship transport; formulae for assessing the specifications of trains
FAST-pack	fuel and sensor tactical (airborne pods)
FAST Break	mobile unit SHAPE
Fast Mover	jet fighter/bomber for ground attack
fastnr	fastener
FASTP	foreign area specialist training programme
FASTULant	fleet ammunition ship training unit Atlantic
FASTUPac	fleet ammunition ship training unit Pacific
FAT	final acceptance trials; final assembly test; flight test station (telecommunications)
fat	fathoms
FA-T	flight attendant in training
FATA	Forces Aeriennes Tactiques Allies (Allied Tactical Air Force)
FATAB	field artillery target acquisition battery
FATAC	Forces Aeriennes Tactiques (tactical air force)
FATAG	field artillery target acquisition group)
FATCAT	film and television correlation assessment technique
FATIS	Food and Agriculture Technical Information Service (OEEC)
Fat Man	Nagasaki nuclear bomb
FATME	Fabbrica Apparechiature Telefoniche & Materiale Elettrico Brevetti Ericsson (SPA)
FATOC	field army tactical operations centre
FATrans	first available transportation (US)
FATSO	first aid technical stores outfit
FATU	fleet air tactical unit
FAU	Friends' Ambulance Unit (Quakers); flag administration unit (USN)
Faustpatrone	Panzerfaust-30, rocket-propelled anti-tank hollow-cahrge WW2
fav	favourable
FAV	fast acting valve
FAvO	fleet aviation officer
FAW	fleet air wing; forward area weapons
FAWOD	furnish assignment instructions without delay
FAWPRA	fleet air western Pacific repair activity (USN)
FAWPSC	frequency allocation and wave propagation sub-committee (Nato)

FAWS	flight advisory weather service	F&C	full and change (high water)
FAWTU	fleet all-weather training unit	F/C	facilities control
FAX	fuel air explosive; fuel and air explosion; fixed astronautical radio station	FCA	flight control assemblies; Faraday cup array; frequency control and analysis; freight consolidating activity
fax	facsimile; facts		
FAY	fleet activities, Yokosuka Japan (USN)	FCAD	field contract administration division ONM (US)
FAZ	automatic rifle (Yugoslavia)	FCAP	force combat air patrol
FB	film bulletin; fire brigade; feed back; fighter bomber; full bore; flying bomb; full back; flying boat (USN); flat bottom; flat bar; fog bell; fixed base (radio station)	FCB	facility clearance board WPB (US); foreign clearance base; frequency coordinating body ICAO; Marine Broadcast station (radio) (Nato)
		FCC	Federal Communications Commission (US); first class certificate; flight coordination centre; flight communications centre; fire control computer; fluid catalytic cracking; flat conductor cable; flight control centre
FB-111	variable sweep fighter/bomber by General Dynamics/Northrop		
FBA	fighter bomber aircraft (Nato); fluorescent brightening agent		
FB/A	fighter/bomber/attacker aircraft		
FBAA	flying boat alighting area		
FBC	foot-brake control	FCCB	field configuration control board
FBE	folding boat equipment		
FBH	force beachhead; fire brigade hydrant	FCDA	Federal Civil Defence Administration
FBhdL	force beachhead line	FCDC	fireccontrol digital computer
FBI	Federal Bureau of Investigation (fidelity, bravery, integrity)	FCE	Fleet Civil Engineer; fire control equipment
FBIS	foreign broadcast information service	FCe	fourth charge
FBL	fly-by-light; fly-by-laser	FCEAANo7	Yellow Fever, anti-aircraft fire control equipment
FBM	fleet ballistic missile		
FBMS	fleet ballistic missile system; fleet ballistic submarine	FCECA	Fishery Committee for the Eastern Central Atlantic
FBMTLL	fleet ballistic missile tender load list	FCG	foreign clearance guide; Federal Coordination Group
FBO	fixed base operation	FCGS	freight classification guide system
FBP	fleet boat pool; final boiling point	FCH	fine cross-hair (sights)
FBPO	forward base pay office	FCI	fire control instruments
FBR	fireball radius	FCIP	field cable installation platoon
fbr	fibre	FCJ	foreign criminal jurisdiction
FBRL	final bomb release line	FCL	fire coordination line, fuse cavity lining
FBS	forces' broadcasting service; Federal Bureau of Standards; forward based systems; full beam spread (illumination)	FCLP	field carrier landing practice
		FCLVT	fuse cavity lining variable time
		FCM	farrier corporal major
FB/S	fighter/bomber, strike	FCMV	fuel consuming motor vehicle
FBW	fighter bomber wing, fly-by-wire	FCNP	fire control navigation panel
FBWT	Forschungsberichte aus der Wehrtechnik (research reports of the defence technology)	FCO	fire control officer; flag communication officer; fleet communication officer; Foreign and Commonwealth Office; fighter control officer (RAF); flight clearance office; fire control operation; fire control operator (USN); flight communications operator; fire control order
FBY	future budget year		
FBZ	forward battle zone		
FC	fire controlman (US); flying cadet; fire commander; flag captain; field command; fighter command (RAF); flying commission; finance corps; fund code; flexible connection; fighter controller (RAF); file cabinet; fire clay; foot candle; fuel cell; fixed coast (radio station)		
		FCo	field company
		FCOAC	furnish copies of orders to appropriate commanders
		FCP	forward control post, fire control

FCP   personnel; file control procedure;
            fatigue crack propagation
fcp   foolscap (paper format) (UK)
FCPC   Federal Committee on Pest Control;
            flight crew plane captain;
            fleet computer programming centre
            Lant   Atlantic
            Pac   Pacific
FCPO   fleet chief petty officer
FCR   fire controlman, rangefinder opera-
            tor; fire control radar; facility
            change request
FCRA   fire control radar antenna
FCRC   federal contract research centre
FCRU   facilities control relay unit
FCS   fire controlman, submarine; field
            conduct sheet; forces courier
            service; fire control system;
            flight control system
FCS-1   (2, 3) tank fire control system by
            Ferranti
FCS-80   flight control system by Collins
FCS-870   light-weight flight control system
            by Bendix
FCSC   fire control systems coordinator;
            foreign claims settlement commis-
            sion; 30mm truncated cone hollow-
            charge anti-aircraft shell
FCSCWSL   fire control and small calibre
            weapons laboratory
FCSMA   flexible communications satellite
            for military applications
FC&SCWWL   Fire Control and Small Calibre
            Weapons Systems Laboratory (US
            Army)
FCSS   fire control sight system
FCST   Federal Council for Science and
            Technology (US)
fcst   forecast
FCT   fraction thereof; final contract
            trials; Federal Capital Territory
            (Australia); filament centre tap
FCTC   fuel centreline thermo couples
FCTG   fast carrier task group
fcty   factory
FCU   fuel control unit; fuel consumption
            unit, fighter control unit; field
            communications unit; fares calcu-
            lating units
FCZ   forward combat zone
FD   field dress; fleet duties; flight
            director; floating dock; fire
            direction; fighter direction (USN);
            Finance Department (US Army)
fd   field
FD   fire drop; flight deck; focal dis-
            tance; file directory; finite
            difference; fire damper; floppy
            disk; frequency demodulator; fre-
            quency doubler; frequency diversity

FD-2   Fairey Delta, fast aircraft by
            Fairey
FDA   Food and Drug Administration (US);
            freight distribution activity;
            Food Distribution Administration;
            fighter director aircraft;
            Fahrzeugdatenerfassungsanlage
            (vehicular data acquisition system
            by Dornier)
FDAA   Federal Disaster Assistance Adminis-
            tration
FDAI   flight direction and altitude indi-
            cator
FdArty   field artillery
FDAU   flight data acquisition unit
FdBchy   field butchery
FdBky   field bakery
FDC   field dental centre; fire direction
            centre; flight director computer
FD&C   food drug and color regulations (US)
FDCS   fighter direction control school
FDD   floating dry dock; fleet dry dock
FDDL   frequency division data link;
            Fiche Descriptive des Donnes
            Logistiques (item logistics data
            transmittal form)
FDDS   flight data distribution system
FDEP   flight data entry panel
FDHDB   flight deck hazardous duty billet
FDHDBP   flight deck hazardous duty billet
            pay
FDHO   Factory Department, Home Office
FdHygSect   field hygiene section
FDI   flight direction indicator
FDL   firearms development laboratories;
            forward defended locality;
            forward defence line; fast deploy-
            ment logistics; flight dynamics
            laboratory
FDLS   fault detection and location system,
            fast deployment logistics ship
FDM   frequency division multiplex
FDMA   frequency division multiple access
FDMC   Fiscal Director of the USMC
FDNet   fighter direction network
FDNR   frequency dependent negative resis-
            tor; frequency dependent negative
            register
FDO   fleet aircraft direction officer;
            fighter director officer; fire
            direction officer; fleet dental
            officer
FDP   foreign duty pay; funded delivery
            period; forward director post;
            forward defence post; fast digital
            processor; flight data processing;
            field deployment programme
FDR   facts, discussion, recommendations
            (letter construction); flight data
            recorder

FDRF   financial data record folder
FdRgt   field regiment (Royal Artillery)
FDS   forward dressing station; finance
         disbursing section; Fleet Dental
         Surgeon; fighter direction ship;
         frequency division separator;
         flight director system
FDS-1003 fibre-optic data system by Cossor
FDSC   fire direction survey calculator
         (hand-held for mortar crews) (US)
FDSU   flight data storage unit
FDT   fighter director tender (USN);
         formated data tapes
FDTE   force development testing and
         experimentation
FDV   fault detect verification
FDx   full duplex
FE   Far East; field expedient (US);
         fraudulent enlistment (US); Fleet
         Engineer; flight engineer; finite
         element (method); flash evapora-
         tion; format effector
F&E   Forschung und Entwicklung (research
         and development)
FEA   Foreign Enlistment Act; Federal
         Energy Administration (US);
         Foreign Economic Administration
         (US)
FeAA   ferric acetyl-acetonate
FEAF   Far East Air Forces
Fearless class, Royal Marines command ships
FEB   Financial and Economic Board;
         functional electronic block
FEBA   forward edge of the battle area
FEC   Far Eastern Command; Foreign Economic
         Coordination (US)
FEC-101 teleprinter error correction system
         by Siemens
FECA   future European combat aircraft
FECB   Far East Combined Bureau WW2
FECP   facility engineering change proposal
fed   federal (US)
Fed   Federal Cartridge Company
F&ED   Facilities and Equipment Department
         NSC (US)
F&EDCD   Facilities and Equipment Department
         Control Division NSC
F&EE   film and equipment exchange
FEFC   Far East Freight Control; Far East
         Freight Conference
FEGLI   Federal Employees' Group Life Insur-
         ance
FEHBP   Federal Employees' Health Benefits
         Program (US)
FEI   field engineer instructor;
         facilities engineering items;
         firing error indicator
FELF   Far East Land Forces
FEM   finite element method (computerized
         design)

FEMA   Federal Emergency Managing Agency
         (US)
Fenelon submarine-borne passive acoustic
         rangefinder by CIT-Alcatel
Fennec   jeep, by Lohr (FR)
FENSA   Film Entertainment National Service
         Administration
FEO   flag engineer officer (RN); fleet
         engineer officer
FEP   financial evaluation programme;
         front end packages; front end
         processor
FEPA   Fair Employment Practice Act
FEPC   Fair Employment Practices Code (US);
         Farm Employment Practices Commit-
         tee (US)
FEPE   full energy peak efficiency
FEPOW   Far East Prisoner of War
FEPP   foreign excess personal property
FER   field engineering representative
         (US)
fer   ferry
FERA   Federal Emergency Relief Administra-
         tion; Fieldguard, Feuerleitgerät
         für Raketenartillerie (fire con-
         trol equipment for rocket
         artillery)
Ferex-4021 portable magnetic mine detector
         by Dr Förster
FERI   optical warning device, sea skimmer
         detector by Eltro
FERO-51 hand-held infra-red equipment
Ferret   FV-712, scout car
ferret aircraft skyspy recce/ElInt
FerRon   ferry squadron (USN)
FES   Funktions-Einheits-System (function-
         al system code)
FET   fleet evaluation trial; Federal
         Excise Tax (US); Far East Time;
         field effect transistor
FETC   Far East training centre
FETS   further education and training
         scheme
FETs   field effect transistors
FETT   field effect tetrode transistor
FEVA   Federal Employees' Veterans'
         Association
FEX   fleet exercise
FF   field force; frontier force;
         foreign flag; frigate; force flag-
         ship; fire fighting; flip flop;
         form feed; failure factor; fuel
         flow; fixed focus
F&F   fittings and fixtures
FFA   for further assignment; free fire
         area; free foreign agency; free
         fatty acid; Forces Françaises en
         Allemagne (French Forces in Ger-
         many); Flug- und Fahrzeugwerke
         Altenrhein (Switzerland)

FFAR	folding fin air-launched rockets
FFB	fact finding bodies
FFC	field force conspectus; foreign funds control; for further clearance; fuse factor correction
FFCC	forward facing crew cockpit (airbus)
FFCoy	fire fighting company
FFD	friendly forward disposition
FFDO	force fighter direction officer
FFF	flight facilities flight; form fit function
FFFA	field force field ambulance
FFFG	treble fine grain (powder)
FFFK	Faser-feld-fernkabel by SEL (fibre-field long-distance cable)
FFG	double fine grain (powder); frigate guided missiles; Flensburger Fahrzeugbau Gesellschaft (Werftstr. 24 D-2390 Flensburg)
ffgt	fire fighting
FFGX	frigate, guided missiles, experimental
FFI	French Forces of the Interior WW2; free from infection
FFL	Federal Firearms Licence (US)
FFl	finished floor
F&Fl	fixed and flashing (light)
FFLOP	field fresnel lens optical platform
FFO	furnace fuel oil
FFMS	fuel flow metering system
FFP	fleet frequency plans; firm fixed price
FFPS	Forces' Family Pensions Scheme
FFR	forces fixed (exchange) rate (UK); foreign force reduction; free flight rocket; fleet fighter reconnaissance (aircraft); fitted for radio; fit for role
FFRR	full frequency range recording
FFSp	Feldfernsprecher (field telephone)
FFSS	full frequency stereophonic sound
FFT	for further transfer; fast Fourier transformation
F FTF	fast flux test facility
FFTFR	fast flux test facility reactor
FFU	field force unit (Gambia)
FFV	Förenade Febriksverken (Eskilstuna S-63187 Sweden)
FFV-013	area defence mine by FFV
FFV-028	hollow charge mine by FFV; towed automatic mine-laying plough
FFV-65	HEAT round for Carl Gustav
FFV-219	target practice bore 9mm for Carl Gustav by FFV
FFV-441	anti-personnel fragmentation shell for Carl Gustav by FFV
FFV-469	smoke shell for Carl Gustav by FFV
FFV-545	illumination shell for Carl Gustav by FFV
FFV-551	HEAT round for Carl Gustav
FFV-553	target practice bore 7.62mm for Carl Gustav by FFV
FFV-555	electro-optical sight for Carl Gustav by FFV
FFV-915	rifle grenade, smoke by FFV
FFWM	free floating wave meter
FFYeo	The Fife and Forfar Yeomanry
FFY	The Fife and Forfar Yeomanry
FFZ	free fire zone
FG	Federal Government; Foot Guards; fixed guidance; fire guard; fundamentals graduate; Firemaster to the Grenadiers (UK); fine grain (powder); field gun; fine granulation; friction glazed
fg	fog
FG-Zünder	Fliehgewicht Zünder (centrifugal fuse (a/a))
FG-1D	Corsair, naval fighter WW2 by Goodyear
FGA	fighter, ground attack
FGB	fast gun boat
FGCM	field general court martial
FGCS	flight guidance and control system
fgf	fully good fair (quality)
FGM	field guidance memorandum
FGM-77	Dragon, anti-tank guided weapon by McDD
FGN	Federal German Navy
fgn	foreign(er)
FGNS	Federal German Navy Ship
FGO	flag gunnery officer; fleet gunnery officer
FGpFl	fixed and group flashing (light)
fgt	freight
FH	field hospital; flag hoist; field howitzer; fire hydrant; fighter (aircraft); fog horn; fore hatch
F/H	freehold
FH-1	Phantom, jet fighter 1946 by McDD
FH-70	field howitzer 1970, 155mm towed UK-German-Italian design
FH-77	field gun/howitzer 15mm by Bofors
FH-155-1	FH-70, field howitzer 155mm British-Italian-German design
FHA	Federal Housing Administration
FHAI	Federal Housing Administration Insurance
FHD	family housing division
FHE	fast hydrofoil escort (USN)
FHG	Forces Headquarters Gibraltar
FHMA	family housing management account
FHP	friction horse power
FHR	Federal House of Representatives (Australia)
FHS	The Forces' Help Society and Lord Roberts Workshop (UK)
FHsg	family housing
FHTNC	Fleet Hometown News Center (USN)
FHWA	Federal Highway Administration

FI   Falkland Islands; Faroe Islands;
            fabrication instruction; fighter/
            interceptor (aircraft); Firearms
            International
Fi   fighter (aircraft)
Fi-5   trainer aircraft WW2 by Fieseler
Fi-98   Stuka, dive bomber WW2 by Fieseler
Fi-103   V-1, flying bomb WW2 by Fieseler
Fi-156   Storch, communications aircraft WW2
Fi-158   experimental aircraft WW2 by Fieseler
Fi-167   multi-purpose aircraft WW2 by Fieseler
FIA   financial inventory accounting; full
            interest admitted
FIAR   Fabbrica Italiana Apparacchiature
            Radioelettriche SpA (Milan)
FIAT   Fabbrica Italiana Automobili Torino;
            field information agency technical;
            first installed article test STC
            (Nato)
FIAT-6614   4x4 air-droppable amphibious
            vehicle by FIAT
FIAT-6616   4x4 amphibious air-droppable
            armoured car by FIAT
FIAT-6640   4x4 amphibious truck 7 tons by
            FIAT
FIB   flight information bulletin
FIBI   filed but impracticable (to transmit)
Fibrocon   fibre-optics connection by
            Hellerman Deutsch
FIC   flight information centre; fleet
            intelligence centre; fault isola-
            tion check-out (system); frequency
            interference control
FICA   Federal Insurance Contribution Act
FiCon   fighter reconnaissance
FIVPacFac   fleet intelligence centre Pacific
            facility
FID   field intelligence department;
            Falkland Islands Dependencies;
            fuse instantaneously detonating;
            four-round illumination diamond
FIDAC   film input to digital automatic
            computer
FIDACSys   film input to digital automatic
            computer System
FIDASE   Falkland Islands and Dependencies
            Aerial Survey Expedition
FIDO   Film Industry Defence Organization;
            fog, intensive, dispersal of;
            fog investigation and dispersal
            operation
Fido   sonobuoy
FIDS   Falkland Islands Dependencies Survey
Fieldguard Conar, fire control radar for
            rocket artillery by Contraves
FIFO   first-in first-out (inventory)
FlFor   flight forecast
fig   figure
FightRon   fighter squadron
FigS   figure shift

FII   Federal Item Identification
FIIG   Federal Item Identification Guide;
            flight instructions indoctrination
            group
FIIGS   Federal Item Identification Guide
            System
FIIGSC   Federal Item Identification Guides
            for Supply Cataloguing
FIILS   full integrity instrument landing
            system
FIIN   Federal Item Identification Number
fil   filter; filament
Fil-Am   Philippine-America
FilCen   filter centre
filg   filing
FILL   fleet issue load list
FILO   first in last out (Commando's motto)
Filopur   combat water purifier (UK)
FIM   field ion microscope
FIM-43   Redeye, portable anti-aircraft
            missile by General Dynamics
FIM-92   Stinger, portable anti-aircraft
            missile by General Dynamics
FImp   field imprisonment
FINA   following items not available
fin   finance; financial
FINABEL   commanders of the land forces of
            France, Italy, Norway, Germany
            (Allemagne), Belgium, England and
            Luxembourg
FINABEL   electronics committee of the land
            forces of France, Italy, Norway,
            Germany (Allemagne), Belgium,
            England and Luxembourg
FINAC   fast interline non-active automatic
            control
final CL   final coordination line
FIND   file interrogation of nineteen-
            hundred data; forecasting institu-
            tional needs for Dartmouth
FinO   finance officer (US Army)
FinSupScol Finance and Supply School (USCG)
FIO   fleet instructor office(r); fleet
            intelligence officer; fleet infor-
            mation officer; fleet in and out;
            force information officer; for
            information only
FIOT   flags and input/output transfer
FIP   force improvement programme; fleet
            improvement programme; flight
            introduction programme; fleet
            introduction programme
FIPS   federal information processing stan-
            dards
FIR   Fiji Infantry Regiment; financial
            inventory reports; flight informa-
            tion region; flight information
            report; functional item replace-
            ment (programme); floating-in
            rate; fuel indicator reading

FIRAA   financial instructions in relation to Army accounts

Firebee AQM-34, BQM-34, supersonic pilotless aircraft family target drone, RPV; chaff dispenser air-to-air rocket carrier by Teledyne Ryan

Firebrand TF-5, torpedo fighter aircraft by Blackburn

Firefinder TPQ-36+TPQ-37 artillery radar sets by Hughes

Firefly aircraft, fighter, recce, ASW by Fairey; M-4 (US) tank WW2; rescue beacon, pocket strobe light

FLIREPLAN fleet improved readiness by expediting procurement, logistics and negotiations (USN)

Firestreak curve-of-pursuit infra-red air-to-air guided missile by de Havilland

Firewire fire protection system by Graviner

FirFlt first fleet (USN)

FIRM fleet indoctrination replacement model

FIRMA firepower and manoeuvre

Firos-6 rocket launcher 48 tubes 51mm by SNIA

Firos-25 rocket launcher 40 tubes 122mm by SNIA

FIRST fleet input reserve support training

FIS family income supplement (UK); flight information service; fleet indoctrination site; fighter interceptor squadron

fis fiscal

FISH fully-instrumented submersible housing

FISO force informational services officer

FISSG fleet issue ship shopping guide

FIST fire integration support team; field intelligence simulation test; fault isolation by semi-automatic techniques

FiST fire support team (vehicle) (M-113 for artillery observation by Emerson)

FIT file information table; fabrication in transit; free of tax; free in truck; Fahrzeug Ingenieurtechnik GmbH (D-6200 Wiesbaden 1)

Fit fighter

Fitr fighter

Fit'Ron fighter squadron

Fittich NBC rpotective suit by Blücher

FITW federal income tax withholding

FIU forward interpretation unit

FiveATAF Fifth Allied Tactical Air Force Southern Europe (Nato)

FIW fighter/interceptor wing (USAF)

fix fixed

Fixer (network) combination of radar and radio aircraft location (Nato)

FJ full jacketed (projectile); fighter jet

FJ-1 Fury, jet fighter aircraft by North American

FJC full jacketed cannelured (projectile)

FJCC Fall Joint Computer Conference

FJP Fünfjahresplan (five year plan)

FJSP full jacketed semi-pointed (projectile)

FK flat keel (boat)

fk fork

FK Feldkanone (field gun); Flugkörper (missile)

F-Kfz Feuerlösch Kraftfahrzeug (fire fighting vehicle)

FKL Fahrzeugkran, leicht (light vehicle-borne crane)

FKM Fahrzeugkran, mittel (medium vehicle-borne crane)

FKS Fahrzeugkran, schwer (heavy vehicle-borne crane)

FL flag lieutenant; front line; fixed line; flight lieutenant; flight level; focal length; flash light

Fl Fliehgewichtsantrieb (centrifugal action fuse)

fl fluid

F&L fuels and lubricants; aviation fuels and lubricants and associated products STANAG

FL-500 low-silhouette cross-country vehicle by Fardier Lohr (FR)

Fla Flugabwehr (anti-aircraft)

FlA flight altitude

Flack jackets bullet-proof jackets (UK)

FlaK Flugabwehrkanone (anti-aircraft gun)

	30	2cm
	18/36	3.7cm
	28	4cm
	41	5cm
	18	8.8cm
	36	8.8cm
	41	8.8cm
	38	10.5cm
	39	10.5cm
	40	12.8cm (GE) WW2

FlakPz-1 Gepard anti-aircraft gun tank

FLAM fault location and monitoring

FLAM-80 Flugabwehr der Marine der 80er Jahre (programme for naval anti-aircraft defence missile of the 1980s)

FlaMG Fliegerabwehr Maschinengewehr (anti-aircraft machine gun)

FLAR forward-looking airborne radar; fault location and repair

FlaRak Fliegerabwehr Rakete (anti-aircraft rocket missile)

FlaRakPz-1 Roland, Fliegerabwehrraketen-
            panzer (tank, anti-aircraft
            missiles)
Flash   anti-ballistic ship defence missile
         by Creusot-Loire/SEP/CSEE
FLAT   foreign language aptitude test
Flatbed project containerized cargo/
         passenger aircraft by Lockheed
FLAW   fleet logistics air wing
FLB   flight line bunker
Fl-BE   filter-band elimination
Fl-BP   filter-band pass
FLC   fleet loading centre; force logis-
         tics command; foreign liquidation
         commission
fld   field
FldArtyGru field artillery group
FldBr   field branch
FldBrBuMed field branch bureau of medicine
         and surgery
FldComDNA field command defence nuclear
         agency
FldCoRE field company Royal Engineers
FldIntO field intelligence office
FldMedSrvScol field medical service school
FldMS   field maintenance shop
FldO   field officer
FldRats field rations
FldTns   field trains
FLE   Eritrean Liberation Front
fle   fleet
FLEA   flux logic element array (radar)
FleAct   fleet activities
FleASWScol fleet antisubmarine warfare
         school
FleASWTacScol fleet antisubmarine warfare
         tactical school
FleASWTracGru fleet antisubmarine warfare
         training group
FleAvnAcctO fleet aviation accounting office
         Lant Atlantic
         Pac   Pacific
FleBalMiSubTraCen fleet ballistic missile
         submarine training
         centre
FLECHT   full length emergency cooling heat
         transfer
Flechettes anti-personnel darts dropped from
         aircraft WW1
FleCompRon fleet composite squadron
FleComputProgCen fleet computer programming
         centre
         Lant Atlantic
         Pac   Pacific
Fledermaus D-VII-B, anti-aircraft fire con-
         trol radar by Contraves
FleMatSuppO fleet material support office
FleNumWeaFac fleet numerical weather
         facility
FleOpInTraCen fleet operational intelligence

         training centre
         Lant Atlantic
         Pac   Pacific
FLE-RC   Eritrean Liberation Front Revolu-
         tionary Council
FLEH-R   Feuerleitrechner (fire control
         calculator by AEG)
FLER-HG fire control calculator by AEG for
         Leopard A-4
FleSOATeam fleet supply operation assis-
         tance team
FleSOAPTeam fleet supply operations assis-
         tance programme team
FleSonarScol fleet sonar school
FleSubTraFac fleet submarine training
         facility
FleTacSuppRon fleet tactical support
         squadron
Fletcher class, destroyers (USN) WW2
FleTraCen fleet training centre
FleWeaCen fleet weather centre
FleWeaCent fleet weather central FWF
FleWeaFac fleet weather facility FWF
FleWorkStudyGru fleet work study group
         Lant Atlantic
         Pac   Pacific
FLEX   fleet exercise
flex   flexible; flexowriter equipment
FLEXAR   flexible adaptive radar by Hughes
         (naval fire control tracks
         multiple targets)
flexo   flexographic
FLF   follow the leader feedback;
         Feuerlöschfahrzeug (fire-fighting
         vehicle)
FlFor   flight forecast
flg   flying; flagging; falling; following
FLG-65   Super Fledermaus, Feuerleitgerät
         (Austrian designation for fire
         control equipment by Contraves)
FLG-75   Skyguard, fire control equipment by
         Contraves
FlgOff   Flag Officer
Fl-HP   filter-high pass
FLIC   fault location indicating console
FliCon   flight control
Fliegerfaust-1 Redeye, man-portable anti-
         aircraft missile by Gene-
         ral Dynamics (GE); WW2 GE
         9-barelled 20mm anti-
         aircraft rocket launcher
FLIP   flight information publication;
         flight information plan; floating
         instrument platform (USN)
FLIR   forward-looking infra-red
FLN   National Liberation Front
Fl-LP   filter-low pass
FLMRad   forward-looking microwave radio-
         meter
FLN   National Liberation Front;
         following landing numbers

fln	flown
FLO	foreign liaison officer; fleet electrical officer
fl/O	flying officer (RAF)
FLOAG	Front for the Liberation of the Occupied Arabian Gulf
FLog	fleet logistics
FLogWing	fleet logistics air wing
FLok	Fehlerlokalisation (fault location)
FLOLS	Fresnel lens optical landing system
FLOOD	fleet observation of oceanographical data
FLOP	Fresnel lens optical practice
floP	floating point
FLOPF	Fresnel lense optical practice, fleet
Florett	anti-aircraft training system by Honeywell
Florida	Swiss early warning and airforce control system
Flower	class, RN corvettes WW2
FLOSY	Front for the Liberation of Occupied South Yemen
FLOT	forward line of own troops
Flot	flotilla
FlOz	fluid ounce
FLP	fault location panel; fighter landplane (USN); field landing practice
FLPC	federal local port controller
FLR	forward-looking radar
flr	filler
FLRG-HG	Feuerleitrechengerät --Leopard (fire control calculator)
FlRng	flash ranging
FlRt	flow rate
flry	flurry
FLS	fault locator system
fls	flashes
FLSA	Fair Labor Standards Act (US)
FLSG	force logistics support group
FLSIP	fleet logistics support improvement plan
FLSIP-COSAL	fleet logistics support improvement plan consolidated stock allowance list
FLSU	force logistics support unit
F/Lt	flight lieutenant (RAF)
flt	fleet; flight
FLT-2	fire control, laser for tanks by Hughes
FltAAWTraCen	fleet anti-air warfare training centre
FltAct	fleet activities
FltBrg	floatbridge
FltCert	fleet certificate
FltComdr	flight commander
FltCon	flight control; fleet control
FLTFM	forward-looking terrain-following mapping (airborne radar)

fltg	floating
FltGt-63	Fledermaus, Feuerleitgerät (anti-aircraft fire control system by Contraves)
FltGt-75	Skyguard, anti-aircraft fire control system by Contraves
FltGunScol	fleet gunnery school
FltLOSCAP	Fleet liaison officer supreme commander allied powers WW2
FltLt	flight lieutenant (RAF)
FltMarFor	fleet marine force
	Lant Atlantic
	Pac Pacific
FltSatCom	fleet satellite communications
FltServScol	fleet service school
FltSerg	flight sergeant
FltSoundScol	fleet sound school
FltSurg	flight surgeon
FltTrackCen	fleet tracking centre
FltTraGru	fleet training group
FltTraSuppRon	fleet training support squadron
FltWeaCen	fleet weather centre
FltWepCen	fleet weapons centre
FLv	foreign leave
flw	follow
Flycatcher	fire control radar by HSA; naval fighter by Fairey
FlyCO	flying control (position) (UK)
Flying Boom	aerial refuelling system
Flying Dustbin	Petard mortar bomb (UK)
Flying Fortress	B-17G, bomber by Boeing
Fylwolf	lightweight naval guidance radar by Marconi
Flzg	Flugzeug (aircraft)
FM	field marshal; flight mechanic; field manual; field music (USMC); foreign military; frequency modulation; frequency multiplexer; fine measure; fan marker; field magnet; field maintenance; titanium tetrachloride (US)
fm	from
FM-200	(1000 15000) mobile directional radio by SEL + AEG
FM-1600B	naval computer by Ferranti
FMA	Foreign Marriages Act; forward maintenance area; foreign military assistance (US); facilities management analysis; flight manual allowance
FmA-Kabine	Fernmeldekabine A (shelter for signals equipment)
FMACC	Foreign Military Assistance Coordination Committee
F-man	foreman
FMAS	Foreign Military Advisory Service
FMAW	fleet marine air wing
FMB	Federal Maritime Board; fast missile boat

FMBT	future main battle tank	FMSCP	foreign military sales credit programme
FMC	Federal Manufacturers' Code; field maintenance centre; field medical card; Federal Maritime Commission; forces motoring club (UK); flutter mode control; Ford Motor Company (Chicago)	FMSgt	field music sergeant (USMC)
		FMSO	foreign military sales order; fleet material support office
		FMSP	foreign military sales programme
FMCBT	full metal case boat tail (projectile)	FMSR	finite mass sum rules
		FMST	foreign military sales trainees
FMCR	fleet marine corps reserve	FMSWR	flexible mild steel wire rope
FMCS	Federal Mediation and Conciliation Service	FMTF	fixed medical treatment facility
		FMTS	field maintenance test station
FMCW	frequency modulated continuous wave (radar)	FMVSS	Federal Motor Vehicle Safety Standards
FMD	ferry movement directive	FmW	Fernmeldewagen (signals vehicle); Flammenwerfer (flamethrower)
FMDM	flexible multiplexer/demultiplexer		
FME	field maintenance equipment	FmWFüllw	Flammenwerferfüllwagen (flamethrower recharging vehicle)
FME-80	Funkmeldeempfänger by Hörmann (communications surveillance receiver)	FMZ	Fernmeldezentrale (signals centre)
		FN	French Navy; Fabrique Nationale d'Armes de Guerre (Herstal Belgium)
FMED	forward medical equipment depot		
FMEO	fleet marine engineering officer	FN-49	rifle by FN
FMetO	fleet meteorological officer	FNA	Fabbrica Nazionale d'Armee (Brescia IT); French North Africa; for necessary action; final approach
FMF	fleet marine force		
	Lant Atlantic		
	Pac Pacific	FNA-4	Fahrzeugnavigationsanlage (land vehicle navigation equipment)
FMIC	flight manual interim changes		
FMICW	frequency modulated intermittent continuous wave (radar)	FNA-615	land vehicle navigation equipment
		FNC	assault rifle 5.56mm by FN
	UK programme 1967-71 for AEW	FNE	following Naval enlisted (personnel)
FMIS	fiscal management information system	FNF	flying needle frame
FMJ	full metal jacketed (projectile)	FNFAL	light automatic rifle by FN
FMLP	field mirror landing practice	FNH	flashless non-hygroscopic (powder)
FMM	French Military Mission	FNI	following named individuals
fmn	formation	FNMA	Federal National Mortgage Association
FMO	flight medical officer; fleet medical officer; forward medical officer; forms management officer; fleet maintenance officer		
		FNMAG	machine gun 7.62mm by FN
		FNO	following named officers; fleet navigation officer
FMP	Federation of Malaysia Police; financial management plan; field marching pack	FNRS	Fondation Nationale de la Recherche Scientifique
		FNS	file nesting store
FMPEC	financial management plan for emergency conditions	fnt	front
		FNWC	fleet numerical weather centre
FMPP	Federal Merit Promotion Program (US)	FO	field officer; flag officer; flying officer; field order; Foreign Office; flight orderly; forward observer; first officer; finance officer; foreign object; fuel oil; field operational (test)
FMR	financial management report; frequency modulated radar		
FMS	Federated Malay States; fleet minesweepers; Foreign Military Sales (US); fleet music school (USN); flight management system by Sperry; fuse maintenance spares; field maintenance shop; field maintenance squadron		
		F/O	flying officer (RAF); flag officer (RN)
		f/o	for orders
		FOA	foreign operations administration; foreign operations agency
fms	fathoms	FOA	Fahrzeugorientierungsanlage (vehicle navigation equipment by AEG)
FMS-90	future medium-altitude SAM (Nato) study a/a missile		
FMSAEG	fleet missile systems analysis and evaluation group	FOAC	flag officer aircraft carriers (RN)
		FOAIB	flag officer Admiralty interview board
FMSC	Federal Manual of Supply Cataloging		

FOAMS	forecasting, order administration and master scheming
FOAP	forward oblique air photograph
FOB	forward observer bombardment; foreign office branch (of the secret service); forward operating base; free on board
FOBLU	forward observation and bombardment liaison unit
FOBS	fractional orbital bombardment system
FOBTSU	forward observer target survey unit
FOBty	forward observation battery
FOC	final operational capability; flight operations centre; flight operations costs; free of charge; full operational capability; faint object camera by Dornier
FOCAS	Flag officer, carriers and amphibious ships (RN)
FOCC	fleet operations control centre
FOCSL	fleet-oriented consolidated stock list
FOCT	flag officer, carrier training (RN)
FOD	Flag Officer, Denmark; field officer of the day; forward ordnance depot; foreign object damage; follow-on development; free of damage
Foden	UK firm trucks
FOE	follow-on evaluation
FofE	field of fire
FOF-1	flag officer first flotilla
FofS	foreman of signals
FOG	Flag Officer, Germany
FOGib	Flag Officer, Gibraltar
Föhn	unguided barrage rockets WW2 (GE)
FOI	fleet operational investigation; field operations intelligence; follow-on interceptor (US programme)
FOIC	flag officer in charge (RN)
Foil	artillery free-flight rocket system (UK)
FOInTraCen	fleet operational intelligence training centre
	Lant Atlantic
	Pac Pacific
FOITC	fleet operational intelligence training centre
FOITCL	fleet operational intelligence training centre Atlantic
FOITCP	fleet operational intelligence training centre Pacific
FOL	forward operating location (Nato air forces)
fol	follow; following
Folgore	anti-tank rocket system by Breda
FOLIS	following information is submitted
FolNoAval	following items not available
FolUp	follow/up

FoMCat	foreign material catalogue
FONAC	Flag Officer Naval Air Command
FONAP	Flag Officer Naval Air Pacific
fone	telephone
FoneCon	telephone conversation
FONF	Flag Officer Newfoundland
FOO	forward observation officer; field ordnance officer; fleet operations officer
FOOBS	fire out of battery system (soft recoil principle)
Foote MG-69	5.56mm machine gun (US)
FOP	forward observation post
FOR	fellowship on reconciliation
for	force; foreigner; fourth round charge
FOR	flying objects research
ForAc	for action
FORACS	fleet operational readiness accuracy check sites (Nato)
FORD	foreign office research department (UK)
Ford	class, patrol boats (RN)
Fordson	.75 ton truck WW2
ForDu	for duty
FoReconCo	Force reconnaissance company (USMC)
Foresters	The Sherwood Foresters Nottinghamshire and Derbyshire Regiment
ForeWAS	force and weapon analysis system
forf	forfeiture
formn	foreman; formation
fornn	forenoon
ForPay	forfeiture of pay
Forrestal	class, attack aircraft carriers CV CVA (USN)
Forrest Sherman	class, destroyers (USN)
ForsCom	Forces Command (US Army)
ForsIC	forces intelligence centre
ForStat	forces status report
fort	fortification
FORTL	force requirement troop list (reporting system)
ForTran	formula translation (computer language)
ForTsk	for task force
FORWARD	feedback of repair workshop reliability data REME data system
Forward Scatter	Nato communication system
FORY	Flag Officer Royal Yachts
FOS	full operational status; faint object spectograph by Dornier
FOSAT	fitting out supply assistance team
	Lant Atlantic
	Pac Pacific
FOSDIC	film optical sensing device for input to computers; field optical sending device
FOSH	Flag Officer, Schleswig Holstein

FOSM   Flag Officer Submarines
FOST   Flag Officer Sea Training
FOT   optimum traffic frequency
Fotac   Formationsflugsystem im TACAN
          Frequenzbereich by SEL
FOTALI   Flag Officer, Taranto and Adriatic
          and for Liaison
FOT&E   follow-on operational test and
          evaluation
Foto Möwe   A-21, reconnaissance aircraft by
          Focke Wulf WW2
Fouga-90 jet trainer aircraft by AS
Fouga Magister   jet trainer aircraft tacti-
          cal support aircraft
          fighter/bomber by Potez
FOUO   for official use only
FourATAF fourth Allied Tactical Air Force
          Central Europe
FOV   field of view
FOW   first open water
FOWABF   Flag Officer, Western Area British
          Pacific Fleet (RN)
Fox   FV-721, CVR, combat vehicle recon-
          naissance wheeled
Foxer   towed acoustic countermeasures
          equipment
Foxhunter airborne interception radar by
          Marconi
FP   fixed price; firing platoon; fool
          proof; field punishment; forfei-
          ture of pay; flag plot; freezing
          point; fire plug; flight plan;
          firing phase; flash point; flame-
          proof; full point; foot pound
          (system); fighter propeller air-
          craft; freight and passenger
          vessel; flat point (projectile)
FPA   Federal Preparedness Agency; Food
          Production Administration; force
          planning analysis; funding pro-
          gramme advice; focal plane arrays
          (detectors)
FPB   fast patrol boat
FPB-37M   class, twin fast patrol boats (IT),
          one is gun-armed, one missile-
          armed by CNL
FPB-46   class, missile patrol boats by
          Vosper
FPB-57   class, 400 ton by Lüerssen
FPBG   final programme and budget guidance
FPC   for private circulation; Federal
          Power Commission; fixed price con-
          tract; fishery protection craft;
          fish protein concentrate
FPCA   Federal Post Card Application (for
          absentee voting)
FPCE   fission product conversion encapsu-
          lation
FPD   predetermined fragmentation
FP&DB   facilities planning and development
          branch

FPDS   fleet probe data system
FPE   forces preliminary examination;
          fixed price with escalation (con-
          tract)
FPF   final protective fire
FPG   force planning guide
FPH   floating point hardware
FPHA   Federal Public Housing Authority
FPI   fixed price incentive (contract);
          Federal Prison Industries Inc.
FPIC   fixed price incentive contract
FPIS   fixed price incentive successive
          (target) contract; forward propa-
          gation by ionospheric scatter
FPJMC   Four Power Joint Military Commission
FPL   final protection line; forest pro-
          ducts laboratory; functional probe
          log; Foxbro programming language;
          flight plan
FPLE   Eritrean People's Liberation Front
FPM   Federal Personnel Manual
fpm   feet per minute
FPMR   Federal Property Management Regula-
          tion
FPN   fixed pattern noise
FPN-62   PAR, ground navigation radar by
          Raytheon
FPO   field post office; fleet post
          office; forces post office; fire
          prevention officer
FPP   firepower potential; floating point
          processor
FPPS   flight programme processing system
FPQA   fixed portion queue area
FPR   fixed price redetermination (con-
          tract), field personnel record
FPRC   flying personnel research committee;
          fixed price redetermination con-
          tract
fprf   fire proof
FPRL   forest products research laboratory
FPS   foot pound second (system); fishery
          protection service; forces postal
          service; feet per second; full
          pressure suit; flight path stabi-
          lization; height-finding radar
FPS-17   long-range tracking radar
FPS-19   long-range radar
FPS-49   tracking radar
FPS-80   tracking radar
FPS-85   sea-surveillance early warning radar
          by Raytheon
FPS-108   Cobra Dane, detection and tracking
          radar against Soviet ICBMs and
          satellites by Raytheon
FPSK   frequency and phase shift keying
FPSPS   feet per second perssecond
FPSTU   full pressure suit training unit
FPT   full power trial; fixed price
          tenders; fixed price type (con-
          tract); fore peak tank

FPt	flat point (projectile)
FPTS	forward propagation by tropospheric scatter (Nato)
FPU	first production unit
FPur	for the purpose of
FPW	firing port weapon SMG for ICV
FQ	fiscal quarter
FQ&P	flight qualities and performance (branch)
FQS	federal quarantine service
FQT	final qualification test
FR	France; fleet reserve; fighter/recce aircraft; frigate; flash ranging; fragmentation (bomb); frequency reader (measuring device); frequency rate; Fairchild Republic Company (New York)
FR-500	high-performance naval target drone by Flight Refuelling (UK)
FRA	food restricted area; federal railroad administration; fleet reserve association
FRAes	Fellow of the Royal Aeronautical Society
frag	fragmentation (bomb)
FRAG-HE	fragmentation + high explosive shell Soviet HEP/HESH
FRAM	fleet rehabilitation and modernization (programme) (US)
FRAMP	fleet replacement aviation maintenance programme
FRAN	fleet readiness analysis system
FRAS-1	free-flight anti-submarine rocket (SU)
FRAT	free radical assay technique
FRATE	formulae for routes and technical equipment (railways)
Frauenlob Klasse	Klasse 394 inshore minesweepers (FGN)
FRB	field research board; federal reserve bank; federal reserve branch; fitness reports branch BUPERS
FRC	Federal Records Centre GSA; facility review committee; flight research centre; federal radiation council; federal radio commission
FrCan	French Canadian
FRCS(E)	Fellow of the Royal College of Surgeons Edinburgh
FRCVS	Fellow of the Royal College Veterinary School
FRD	field remount depot; formerly restricted data
frd	friend
FRD	fibre resin developments
FrdEnl	fraudulent enlistment
FRDist	federal reserve district
FRE	field representative Europe
Freccia	class, small torpedo boat destroyers
	(IT) WW2; guided missile patrol boats
FRED	fatastically reliable electronic device; fast reactor experiment Dounreay; figure reading electronic device
Freedom Fighter	F-5, fighter/bomber/interceptor 1959 by Northrop
Freeloader	light adjustable ramp
Freia	coastal radar (GE) WW2
FRELIMO	Mozambique Liberation Front
FRELOC	relocation of US-CA troops from France to outside France
FREM	fleet readiness enlisted maintenance (trainees) (USN)
Freon-1301	inert vapour, fire extinguishing agent ---SAFE
freq	frequency
FeEqA	French Equatorial Africa
FRESH	foil research hydrofoil (vessel) --HTC
Frev	for further review
FrF	Free French WW2; automatic precision rifle (FR)
FRF-A	fire resistant fuel (with water)
FRF-B	fire resistant fuel (with diesel fuel)
FRFE	field representative Far East
FRFS	fast reaction fighting system
FRG	Federal Republic of Germany
FrG	French Guinea
FRG-RFL-40	fragmentation rifle grenade 40mm by MECAR; BT fragmentation rifle grenade for 5.56mm rifle
FRG-70	Flugregelgerät by BGT (digital flight control equipment)
FRI	Fulmer Research Institute
FR&I	financial regulations and instructions
fric	friction
FRID	four round illumination diamond
FRIS	families rations issue scheme (British troops in Berlin)
FRISCO	fast-reaction integrated submarine control
FRITALUX	France Italy Benelux (customs union project)
Fritz	SD-1400, guided glide bomb by Ruhrstahl; modern US helmet synthetic material
FRL	field radiological laboratory
FRMO	Fleet Royal Marines Officer
FRMP	forward recovery mission profile
FRN	force requirement number
FRNA	foreign rations not available
FRNWC	French naval war college
FRO	field recruiting officer; field recreation officer; fleet recreation officer; fleet record office

fro	front
FrOf	freight office (USN)
FROG	free rocket over ground (SU); battlefield support spin stabilized unguided
fron	frontier
FroPa	frontal passage
Frosch	class, East German landing ships medium
FroSf	frontal surface
FRP	fragmentation (bomb) parachute (US); fibre reinforced plastic
frpf	fireproof
FRRS	foreign research
FRS	fighter and reconnaissance Squadron (RN); federal reserve system; fleet repair service; fuel research station; future rifle system (US programme)
FrS	French Somaliland
FRS	Sea Harrier, fighter/recce aircraft ship-based V/STOL by Hawker Siddeley
FRS-1	Flieger Rettungs Schlauchboot für 1 Person by Autoflug (1-person rescue rubber boat for pilots)
FRSB	frequency referenced scanning beam
frst	frost
FRT	figure reasoning test; forward repair team
frt	freight
FRT	flight rating test
frtns	fortifications
FRTV	forward repair test vehicle
FRU	fleet radio unit; fleet requirements unit; field replacement unit
Frunze	class, cruisers (SU)
FRUPac	fleet radio unit Pacific
FRUS	foreign relations of the US
FRWI	Framingham relative weight index
frwk	framework
frwy	freeway
frz	freeze
frzn	frozen
FS	France Star; field sergeant; flight surgeon; fleet surgeon; foreign service; financial statement; feasibility study; field service; field security; final settlement; fleet support; flight service; factor of safety; fuel ship; firing set; film strip; full scale; freight supply (ship) (USN); field separator; file separator; frequency synthesizer; flight safety STANAG; filler for smoke shells; forecast/surface; feet per second; fire station; far side; facsimile
FS-powder	flashless-smokeless powder
FS-ships	fire support ships; freight supply ships
FS-method	federal standard method
2-FS	double frequency scatterometer radar
FS-2000	electronic teleprinter by TeKaDe
FSA	foreign service allowance; federal security agency; family separation allowance; fire support area; foreign service availability; finance service; Army; fuel storage area; final site acceptance
FSA-1550	teleprinter analysis equipment by AEG
FSAA	flight simulator for advanced aircraft
FSAO	family services and assistance officer
FSAPDS	fin stabilized armour piercing discarding sabot (shot)
FSA-R	family separation allowance - restricted station
FSA-S	family separation allowance - shipboard operations
FSA-T	family separation allowance - temporary duty
FSB	fire support base; final staging base; federal specifications board; Faltschwimmbrücke (inflatable pontoon bridge)
FSC	Friends' Service Council (Quakers); forces study centre; federal supply catalogue; federal supply classification; foreign service credits; federal supreme court; federal supply code, forward scatter (communications)
FSCC	fire support coordination centre
FSCen	flight service centre
FSCL	fire support coordination line
FSCM	federal supply code for manufacturers; federal supply class management
FSCoord	fire support coordinator
FSCP	firing site command post
FSCS	fire support coordination section
FSCT	Floyd satellite communications terminal
FSCV	fire support combat vehicle by FMC + Rheinmetall + Krauss-Maffei
FSD	field supply depot; field survey detachment; fuel supply depot; foreign sea duty; full scale development
FSE	fire support element, field support equipment
FSEC	Federal Specifications Executive Committee --FSB
FSED	full scale engineering development
FSEE	federal service entrance examination

FSF	fleet sweeping flotilla; fully submerged foil (hydrofoil); fin stabilized fragmentation (shell); flight safety foundation
FSG	Flensburger Schiffsbau Gesellschaft since 1980 FFG
Fsg	flash signal; flash spotting
F/Sgt	flight sergeant
FSHC	fin stabilized hollow charge (shell)
FSHOB	fall-out safe height of burst
FSI	federal stock item
FSIF	flight suit with integrated floatation
FSK	frequency shift keying
FSKLF	frequency shift keying low frequency (converter)
FSL	First Sea Lord; full stop landing
FSLP	first Spacelab payload ESA
FSM	flying spot microscope; flight sergeant major; field service manual
FSMAMS	field service manual for Army medical services
FSML	fleet support material list
FSMS	firing set maintenance spares
FSMT	fleet service mine test
FSN	federal stock number; fiscal station number
FSO	fleet signals officer; fleet supply officer; fuel supply office(r); fleet supply office(r); force supply office(r); fire service officer; field security officer; field service operations
FSP	field security personnel; field security police; foreign service pay; fixed station patrol (naval)
fsp	flashspotting
FSPB	field service pocket book
FSR	field service representative; field service regulations (UK); foreign separate rations; force service regiment; fleet spotter reconnaissance (aircraft); frequency scan radar; fin stabilized rocket; forward space record; frequency surveillance receiver
FSR-1000	frequency surveillance receiver by Fairchild
FSRD	fighting services research department
FSRS	frequency selective receiver system by Dalmo Victor
FSS	field security service, fleet supply ship, fixed signal service; forward scatter (communications) system, federal supply schedule; fire support station; fleet service school; flight service station (automated ATC); foreign shore service; flight support system; flight standards service

FSSD	foreign service selection date
FSSE	forward service support element
FST	field surgical team; foreign service tour; field survey team
FS-T-2	fighter aircraft by Mitsubishi
FSTC	foreign science and technology centre
FSU	field surgical unit; Friends' Service Unit (Quakers); field storage unit; ferry service unit; family service unit; field select unit
FSV	fire support vehicle
FSW	field security wing; forward swept wing (aircraft)
FSWF	forward swept wing fighter (aircraft)
FSWO	financial secretary of the war office
FSWR	flexible steel wire rope
FS-X-20	airborne nuclear missile (SU)
FSyO	fleet security officer
FT	fresh target; flight test; foretop (division); fire trench; fitter and turner; field training; formal training; flame thrower; fully tracked; firing tables; flying tanker; full terms
ft	fort; fortified; foot; feet
FT	Funktelegraphie (wireless telegraphy)
F&T	fuel and transportation
FT-17	light tank by Renault WW2
FTA	Commandement des Forces Terrestres Anti-aeriennes (anti-air defence command)
FTACE	Forces Terrestres Allies Centre Europe (Allied Land Forces Central Europe)
FTAS	fast time analyser system ASW by Rockwell
FTB	functional training branch BUPERS; fleet torpedo boat; fleet torpedo bomber; fast torpedo boat
ftbrg	footbridge
FTC	flying training corps; federal trade commission; flight test centre; fleet training centre; flying training command (RAF); first time constant; fast time constant; full technological certificate
Ft-C	foot candle
FTD	foreign technology division (USAF); foreign traffic division; freight terminal department; field training detachment; folded triangular dipole
FTDMA	frequency time division multiple access
FTE	factory test equipment; fracture transition elastic

FTFET   four terminal field effect transistor
FTG   fleet training group; Fuji Texaco Gas
         Corporation
ftg   fitting; footage
FtgDv   footage dives
FtgDives footage dives
ftgs   fittings
fth   fathom
fthm   fathom
FTHMA   frequency time hopping multiple
         access
fthr   further
ft/hr   feet per hour
FTI   fixed target information
ft-lb   foot - pound
ft-lb-f foot pound force
FtLieut flight lieutenant (RAF)
FTLO   fast tuned local oscillator by
         Philips
FTM   flying training manual; folded tri-
         angular monopole (antenna)
ft/min   feet per minute
FTMT   final thermomechanical treatment
ftn   fortification
FTn   field train
FTO   fleet torpedo officer
FtoF   face to face
FTP   field transport pack; fleet training
         publication; federal test proce-
         dure; final technical proposal
FTPC   flight test change proposal
ft/pd   foot pounds
FTR   factory thoroughly reconditioned
ftr   fighter (aircraft)
FTrac   fully tracked (vehicle)
FTS   flying training squadron; fleet
         target service; field training
         services; flying training school;
         flight traffic specialist; federal
         telecommunications system
ft/s   feet per second
FTT   field transfusion team; free Terri-
         tory Trieste WW2
FTT-3500 tractor for semi-trailers by DAF
FTTD   full time training duty
fttr   fitter
FTU   field transfusion unit; field
         torpedo; first training unit
FTVLSIC fault tolerant VLSI circuit (very
         large scale integration)
FTW   free trade wharf; Flugfeldtankwagen
         (airfield tanker)
FTX   field training exercise
FU   fire unit; feed unit; forecast -
         upper air (Nato)
Fu   Funk (wireless)
FUA   fire unit analyser
FUB   facilities utilization board
Fuchs   TPz-1, 6x6 armoured transport
         vehicle by Krauss-Maffei

FUFO   fly under - fly out CLGP mode
FüFu-Netz Führungsfunknetz GAF (guidance
         and control network)
FuG   Funkgerät (wireless set)
FuG-10   Funkgerät air-to-ground radio 1940
FuG-16   Funkgerät air-to-air radio 1940
FuG-203 Funkgerät remote control transmit-
         ter for HS-293 WW2
FüGruSysH-80 Führungsgrundsystem Heer 1980
         (command management and
         information system Army)
FüH   Führungsstab des Heeres (Army
         Command)
FUIF   fire unit integration facility
FüInfoSysLw Führungsinformationssystem
         Luftwaffe GAF (command and
         information system)
FüInfoSysMHQ Führungsinformationssystem
         Marinehauptquartier (command
         and informations system
         Naval Headquarters)
FUKS   Ferngelenktes unbemanntes Kampf-
         panzersystem GST (study remote-
         controlled unmanned battle tank
         system)
FüL   Führungsstab der Luftwaffe (German
         Air Force Command)
Fulmar   8-gun fighter aircraft by Fairey
         (RN) WW2
FULRO   United Front for the Liberation of
         Oppressed Races (Montaignards)
         (Viet Nam)
Fulton   class, submarine tenders (USN)
Fum   fumigating smoke shell
FüM   Führungsstab der Marine (Federal
         German Navy Command)
func   functions
FUP   forming up place
FUPOSAT follow-up on supply action taken
FUR   failure and unsatisfactory report
fur   further; furlong; furlough
FurAs   for further assignment
FUR/EFR failure and unsatisfactory report
         electronics failure report
FuRept   and further report to
furn   furnish
FurOrdMod orders further modified
FU-RU   multi-option proximity fuse by TRT
Fury   FJ-1, FJ-2, fighter/bomber by
         Hawker/North American 1946
fus   fusilier; fuselage
FurTS   furnished this station
FUt   fleet utility
FV   fighting vehicle (UK)
FV-101   Scorpion, CVRT, combat vehicle
         reconnaissance tracked by Alvis
FV-102   Striker, tank destroyer
FV-103   Spartan, armoured personnel carrier
         tracked
FV-104   Samaritan, armoured ambulance

FV-105	Sultan, command post vehicle tracked
FV-106	Samson, armoured recovery vehicle
FV-107	Scimitar, combat vehicle reconnaissance tracked
FV-180	CET, combat engineer tractor
FV-400	mechanical combat vehicle for the 1980s by GKN
FV-432	Trojan, armoured personnel carrier by GKN-Sankey
FV-433	Abbot, 105mm self-propelled gun
FV-434	armoured workshop vehicle by GKN
FV-436	radar vehicle with Green Archer mortar locating radar
FV-438	tank destroyer vehicle with Swingfire
FV-601	Saladin, wheeled gun carrier
FV-602	Saracen, command vehicle wheeled
FV-604	Saracen, command vehicle wheeled
FV-604	Saracen, armoured personnel carrier wheeled
FV-604	Saracen, ambulance vehicle wheeled
FV-610	Saracen, command vehicle wheeled
FV-611	Saracen ambulance vehicle wheeled
FV-622	Stalwart, high-mobility amphibious load carrier wheeled
FV-623	Stalwart, high-mobility amphibious load carrier with hydraulic crane wheeled
FV-624	Stalwart, high-mobility amphibious load carrier mobile workshop wheeled
FV-651	Salamander, fire crash tender on Saracen hull
FV-652	Salamander, fire crash tender on Saracen hull
FV-712	Ferret, scout car
FV-721	Fox, CVRW, combat vehicle reconnaissance wheeled
FV-722	Vixen, communications and command version of Fox
FV-1100	Martian, 6x6 artillery tractor by Leyland
FV-1119	truck-mounted crane by Leyland
FV-1601	truck by Humber
FV-1609	Hornet, 1 ton armoured car, rocket carrier
FV-1611	Pig, 1 ton armoured truck by Humber
FV-3001	semi-trailer 60 tons
FV-3011	semi-trailer 50 tons
FV-4002	AVLB Centurion, scissors type bridgelayer
FV-4003	Centurion AVRE, armoured vehicle Royal Engineers
FV-4016	Centurion Ark, Ark-type bridgelayer
FV-4030	Shir Iran, future main battle tank project cancelled
FV-4030/3	Challenger, future main battle tank by Vickers
FV-4202	Chieftain ARV, armoured recovery vehicle
FV-4203	Chieftain AVRE, armoured vehicle Royal Engineers
FV-4204	Chieftain ARLV, armoured recovery vehicle
FV-4205	Chieftain AVLB, armoured vehicle-launched bridge
FV-4333	armoured personnel carrier prototype
FV-11000	Militant, 6x6 10 ton truck by AEC
FV-11400	Big Ben, 6x6 truck by Thornycroft
FV-12000	Constructor 6x6 tractor by Scammell; Antar 6x6 tractor by Thornycroft
FV-12001	tank transporter Mk 1
FV-12002	tank transporter Mk 2
FV-12004	tank transporter Mk 3
FV-12003	Antar, tank transporter
FV-13100	4x4 truck by Bedford
FV-13581	Albion Clansman 6x6 3 tons
FV-14001	6x6 5 ton truck
FV-16000	4x4 1 ton by Humber
FV-18000	Land Rover
FVD	friction volume damper
FVDE	fighting vehicles design establishment; fighting vehicles development establishment
FVN	failed vector numbers
FVPE	fighting vehicles proving establishment (Chobham)
FVRDE	fighting vehicles research and development establishment (Chobham) since 1970 ---MVEE
FVS	fighting vehicle system by FMC
FVTT	fighting vehicle, troop transport
FW	fixed wing (aircraft); fresh water
F&W	Forehand and Wadsworth (Worcester USA)
FW-aircraft	fixed wing aircraft
Fw-39	recce aircraft WW2 by Focke Wulf
Fw-40	recce aircraft WW2 by Focke Wulf
Fw-44	Stieglitz, trainer aircraft WW2 by Fw
Fw-47	meteorological aircraft WW2 by Fw
Fw-56	Stösser, trainer aircraft WW2 by Fw
Fw-57	combat aircraft WW2 by Fw
Fw-58	Weihe, aircraft by Fw
Fw-62	maritime recce aircraft WW2 by Fw
Fw-159	interceptor WW2 by Fw
Fw-187	interceptor WW2 by Fw
Fw-189	V1 short-range recce aircraft
	V1a combat aircraft
	V1b combat aircraft
	V3 short-range recce
	V4 smoke screening aircraft
	V6 combat aircraft
	A Army recce aircraft
Fw-190	interceptor WW2 by Fw
Fw-191	bomber WW2 by Focke Wulf
Fw-200	Condor, long-range bomber/recce WW2
Fw-300	medium long-range transport aircraft

Fw-491 horizontal bomber WW2 by Fw
FWA federal works agency; forces wives' association (UK); Free Wales Army
FWAD Fort Wingate Army Depot
FWB four wheel brakes
FWC fleet weapons centre; federal warning centre
FWCL field wire command link
fwd forward
FWD four wheel drive; front wheel drive; free water damage
FwdBAA forward brigade administrative area
FwdBL forward bomb line
FwdDelSqn forward delivery squadron
FWDP foreign weapons development programme
FWEO fleet weapons engineering officer
FWF fleet weather facility
FWG Forschungsanstalt für Wasserschall und Geophysik Kiel des BWB (maritime acoustic and geophysical research establishment)
FWHM full width half maximum
FWI French West Indies; Federation of West Indies
FWIC fighter weapons instruction course (USAF)
FWK Feuerwerkskörper (firework)
FWM Feinmechanische Werke Mainz
FWMAF free world military assistance forces
FWNEOFAP funds will not be entrusted to others for any purposes
FWO field work officer, fleet wireless officer
FWOP furlough without pay
FWPC federal women's programme coordinator
FWPCA federal water pollution control administration
FWS fighter weapons squadron; fighter weapons school; fleet work study; flexible weapon system --TAT

FWS fixed wireless station
FWSG fleet work study group
    Lant Atlantic
    Pac Pacific
FWT fair wear and tear
FWTT fixed wing tactical transport (aircraft)
FWV Feldwählvermittlung (field telephone switching centre)
FWVP fallout wind vector plot
FX foreign exchange; forecastle
fx fix(ed)
FX-kit frequency extension (non-communication)
fxd fixed; foxed; fixed fire
fxg fixing
fxle forecastle
FXO food executive officer
FXP fleet exercise publication
FXR Foxer, towed acoustic anti-torpedo device
FY fiscal year; financial year
fy fishery
FYDP five year defence programme; five year defence plan
FYFS&FP five year force structures and fiscal programme
FYI for your information
FYIG for your information and guidance
FYMP five year material programme
FYP five year programme; five year plan; four year programme, four year plan
FYPB five year planning base
FYPP five year procurement programme
FYTP five year test programme
FYU harbor utility unit (USN)
FZ French zone; free zone
fz fuse
Fzg Fahrzeug (vehicle)

G

G   gunnery; group; guilty; German;
           garrison; general staff; Guinea;
           general branch; gun; grid; gravity;
           gauge; generator; tracer (projec-
           tile)
G-bomb   gravitational bomb
G-hour   (day) operation starts
G-man   government man FBI
G-Patrone Gewehrgranatpatrone (rifle
           grenade propelling charge)
G-suit   gravity suit for pilots
5-G   mine sweeping system (FR)
G-1   Grundmine mit Fernzündung (seabed
           loiter mine with remote ignition)
G-1   US Assistant Chief of Staff
              1   personnel
              2   intelligence
              3   operations
              4   logistics and supply
              5   civil affairs
              SHAEF
              5   psychological warfare
              6   civil affairs
G-1   UK general staff officer first grade
              lieutenant colonel
              2 major
              3 captain
G-2   general staff officer operations (UK)
G-3   general staff officer intelligence
           (UK)
G-3   Gewehr, assault rifle by Heckler &
           Kock; A4 assault rifle with re-
           tractable stock
G-5   gun 155mm (South Africa)
G-7a   torpedo
G-11   Gewehr, rifle 4.7mm for caseless
           ammunition by HK
G-12D   parachute for 1 ton loads
G-24   transport aircraft WW2 by Junkers
G-38   transport aircraft WW2 by Junkers
G-41   Gewehr 1941, self-loading rifle
              M by Mauser
              W by Walther
G-91   aircraft, jet, light tactical sup-
           port by FIAT

G-222   transport aircraft by Aeritalia
GA   General of the Army (US); garrison
           artillery; gross average; general
           assembly; general average; general
           alert; ground attack (aircraft);
           graze action (fuse); general
           aviation; Tabun nerve gas (Soviet
           code)
G/A   ground-to-air (radio missile);
           general alert
ga   gauge
G&A   general and administrative
           (services)
GA   Fabrique d'Armes de Guerre
           Haute Precision Armand Gavege
           (Liege BE)
GAA   general agency agreement; general
           account of advance
GaAs   gallium arsenide (laser diodes)
Gabriel   naval missile by IAI
GAC   Gloster Aircraft Company; general
           advisory council
GACS   gun alignment and control system
GAD   Guards Armoured Division; gun 20mm
           turret-mounted by Oerlikon
GADO   general aviation district organiza-
           tion
GAE   general classification test/
           arithmetic test/Electronics tech-
           nician selection test (USN);
           Grumman Aerospace Engineering
GAELIC   GAE language for instructional
           check-out
GAF   (Federal) German Air Force (Nato);
           government aircraft factory
           (Australia)
GAFAWG   general aviation fuel allocation
           working group (UK)
GAFCON   German Air Force Communications Net
           by Siemens
GAFSC   Ghana Armed Forces Staff College
GAF-TO   German Air Force Technical Order
           (Nato)
GAI   general accounting instructions;
           generalized area of intersection;
           anti-aircraft gun 20mm by Oerlikon

gal   gallery; gallon
GALAXY   general automatic luminosity X&Y
             (high speed scanner)
Galaxy   C-5, cargo aircraft by Lockheed
GalCap   gallon capacity
GALCIT   Guggenheim Aeronautical Laboratory
             of California Institute of Tech-
             nology
Galil   M-139, ARM assault rifle/machine gun
             (Israel); SAR short assault rifle
             5.56mm (Israel)
Galileo   Jupiter mission satellite 1983 by
             Martin Marietta
Galliot   muzzle brake, recoil reducing to
             make 32pdr gun airportable
GALT   gut associated lymphoid tissue
galv   galvanic; galvanized; galvanometer
GAM   guided aircraft missile (medium-
             range air-to-ground); ground-to-
             air missile; general aeronautical
             material; graphic access
             method
GAM-204GK naval a/a gun 20mm by
             Oerlikon
GAMA   general aviation manufacturers'
             association (US)
Gama Goat M-561, 1.25 ton articulated 6x6
             vehicle
Gamma Gerät 42cm mortar WW1 (GE)
Gammexane insecticide (malaria)
Gammon bomb No.82MK1 hand grenade (US)
GAMTA   general aviation manufacturers' and
             traders' association (UK)
Gannet   maritime patrol aircraft by Fairey
GAO   (US government) general accounting
             office; general administration
             orders; general alert order
GAONOE   general accounting office notice of
             execution
GAP   general aviation propeller; gun
             aiming point; gun aiming post,
             general assembly programme; govern-
             ment aircraft plant
GaP   gallium phosphide
GAP   Generalausbildungsplan (comprehen-
             sive training scheme)
GAPA   ground-to-air pilotless aircraft
GAPAN   guild of air pilots and air naviga-
             tors (UK)
GA&PB   grade assignment and placement branch
             BUPERS
GAQ-4   laser range finder for a/a guns by
             Hughes
GAR   grand Army of the Republic
gar   garrison
GAR   guided air-to-air rocket
GAR-8   AIM-9, Sidewinder, air interception
             missile, infra-red by Philco
GAR-11   AIM-26, Nuclear Falcon, nuclear air
             interception missile, infra-red by
             Philco

Garand   M-1, self-loading rifle (US)
GARD   gamma atomic radiation detector;
             general address reading device
GAREX   ground aviation radio exchange
             system
Gargoyle   air-to-ground guided missile WW2
             (US)
GARIOA   government aid and relief in
             occupied areas (US) WW2
GARL   group action request lists
garn   garrison
GARP   global atmospheric research pro-
             gramme
GAS   general air staff; general automotive
             support; get-away specials (NASA
             programme); Gorki Automobile
             Factories (SU)
gas   gasoline
GASER   gamma ray laser
Gas Gun   38.1cm grenade launcher by Matheu
gasohol   alcohol as petrol substitute (US)
GASS   guidance accuracy study for Sprint
             (missile)
GAT   Greenwich apparent time; general
             aviation transponder FAA;
             general air traffic
GATCO   guild of air traffic control
             officers (UK)
GATD   graphic analysis of three-dimen-
             sional data
GATE   GARP Atlantic tropical experiment
GATF   graphic arts technical foundation
Gatling gun rotating barrel gun
Gato   class, submarines WW2 (USN)
GATOR   air-dropped mine system (USAF)
             BLU-91 anti-tank mines
             BLU-92 anti-personnel mines
GATR   ground-to-air transmitter receiver
GATT   general agreement on trade and
             tariffs (UN)
GATTC   general aviation technical training
             conference
GATV   Gemini-Agena test vehicle
GAU-8   Avenger, airborne 30mm rotating
             barrel gun by GE
             --CHAG --A-10
GAU-28   7.62mm gun
GAV   gross annual value (tax)
GAW   guaranteed annual wage
GAWR   gross axle weight rating (US)
GAZ   grosskalibriger Annäherungszünder
             (larger calibre proximity fuse)
             (for 105mm, 155mm, 203mm)
GAZ-46   wheeled amphibious vehicle 1.9 tons
             (SU)
GAZ-51   truck 2.7 tons (SU)
GAZ-63   66 truck 3.4 tons (SU)
GAZ-69   jeep 1.5 tons (SU)
Gazelle   SA-341, light helicopter by
             Westland/AS

GB	Great Britain; general board; grand bounce; government bunkers (USN); Sarin (nerve gas) Soviet code; Gemeinschaftsbüro (Büssing, Henschel, KHD, Krupp, MAN); glide bomb; gun boat; grid bias; gun branch
G-B	Geo Brothers; Great Barrington
GB-8	glide bomb, 2000 lbs radio-guided WW2 (US)
GBAD	Great Britain and Allied Dominions
GBC-8	truck by Berliet (FR)
GBD	truck by Berliet (FR); tank-mounted gun 25mm by Oerlikon
GBE	Knight Grand Cross of the Most Excellent Order of the British Empire
GBH	grievous bodily harm (offence); gamma benzene hydrachloride; truck by Berliet (FR)
GBI	anti-aircraft gun 25mm by Oerlikon
GB&I	Great Britain and Ireland
GBL	government bill of lading
GBLading	government bill of lading
GBMS	Great Britain Merchant Ship
GB&NI	Great Britain and Northern Ireland
GBT	tracked amphibious vehicle (SU)
GBU	truck by Berliet (FR); guided bomb unit; guided bomb universal; glide bomb unit; glide bomb universal (USAF)
GBU-8	laser-guided bomb
GBU-10	Paveway, laser-guided bomb 100 kgs by TI
GBU-12	Paveway, laser-guided bomb 225 kgs by TI
GBU-15	HOBOS, homing bomb system by Rockwell (laser+TV+imaging IR)
GBU-16	Paveway, laser-guided bomb 450 kgs by TI
GBW	vehicle turret gun 25mm by Oerlikon
GBX	group branch exchange
GC	government contribution; general counsel; good conduct; George Cross (UK); Grand Commander; grand cross; group captain (RAF); Geneva Convention (protection of civilian persons in times of war 1949), Geiger counter; general contractor; gyro-compass; gun carriage; gas chromatography; Guards Coldstream
GCA	1st Battalion Coldstream Guards
GCB	2nd Battalion Coldstream Guards
GCC	3rd Battalion Coldstream Guards
G&C	guidance and command (unit)
GC-45	howitzer 155mm by SRC
GC-130	Hercules, aircraft gunnery trainer version

GCA	ground controlled approach; guidance and control assembly
GCA-68	gun control act of 1968 (US)
g/cal	gramme calories
GCapt	group captain (RAF)
GCB	good conduct badge; Knight Grand Cross of the Most Ancient and Noble Order of the Bath (UK); generator circuit breaker
GCBS	ground controlled bombing system
GCC	ground control centre; group control centre
GCD	general and complete disarmament; great circle distance
GCE	general college entrance (examination); general certificate of education (UK); gun control equipment
GCE-576	gun control and stabilization equipment by Marconi
GCE-581	gun control and stabilization equipment by Marconi
GCF	gunnery cooperation flight
GCFR	gas-cooled fast reactor
GCG	guidance control group
GCH	Knight Grand Cross of the Hanoverian Order
GCHQ	government communications headquarters (Cheltenham)
GCI	ground-controlled interception; ground-controlled interceptor
GCI/ADC	ground controlled interceptor air defence centre
GCIE	Knight Grand Cross (Commander) of the Order of the Indian Empire
GCL	ground-controlled landing
GCLH	Knight Grand Cross of the French Legion of Honour
GCM	good conduct medal (UK); general court martial (US); naval a/a gun 30mm by Oerlikon
GCMdl	good conduct medal (US)
GCMed	good conduct medal (US)
GCMG	Knight Grand Cross of the Order of St Michael and St George
GCMO	general court martial order
GCMP	general court martial prisoner
GC-MC	gas chromatography-mass spectrometry
GCN	Greenwich civil noon
GCO	Gurkha commissioned officer; ground control officer; gun control officer
GCP	gear control pedal; guidance control package
GCR	The Gold Coast Regiment; ground controlled radar; generator control relay; gas-cooled reactor
GCRVO	Knight Grand Cross of the Royal Victorian Order
GCS	gate controlled switch (Thyristor);

guidance and control section;
gigacycles per second

GCSG Knight Grand Cross of the Order of
St Gregory the Great

GCSI Knight Grand Cross (Commander) of
the Order of the Star of India

GCSIS Georgetown Centre for Strategic
and International Studies

GCSS Knight Grand Cross of the Order of
St Sylvester

GCStJ Bailiff (Dame) Grand Cross of the
Order of St John of Jerusalem

GCT general classification test;
Greenwich civil time; government
competitive testing; ground control
tower, self-propelled gun 155mm
(FR)

155-GCT self-propelled gun 155mm (FR)

GCU guidance computer unit; generator
control unit

GCVO Knight Grand Cross of the Royal
Victorian Order

GCVS general catalogue of variable stars

GD Grand Duke; Grand Duchess; gun drill,
gun digest; general duties;
general discharge; Greenwich date;
ground detector; green dot;
gravimetric density; Soman (nerve
gas); General Dynamics (Fort Worth
Texas)

GDA gun defended area

Gdansk class, patrol craft (Poland)

GDB general duties branch

GDC General Dynamics Corporation

GDES government department electrical
specifications

GDF Gibraltar Defence Force; ground
defence forces; twin a/a gun 35mm
by Oerlikon

GDG general data group

gdhse guardhouse

GDL gas dynamic laser; Gasdrucklader
(gas operated selfloading)

GDM naval a/a gun 35mm by Oerlikon

GDM-A twin naval a/a gun 35mm by Oerlikon

GDMS generalized data management system

GDO gun direction officer

GDOP geometric dilution of precision

GDP gross domestic product; general
defence plan; gun defence position;
gun director pointer
  LL cross leveller
  L leveller
  P pointer
  SS sight setter
  T trainer

GDP-BO3 twin a/a gun 30mm by Oerlikon
--Gepard

GDR German Democratic Republic; general
design requirement; ground delay
response

Gds The Grenadier Guards

gdsm guardsman

GDTA ground for development of aerospace
telediction

GDU gun display unit

GE Germany (Nato); ground engineer;
garrison engineer; general
expenses; general election;
group of experts; General Electric
Company (Cincinnati US)

GE-120 automatic gun 20mm by GE

GE-592 three-dimensional long-range radar
by GE, fixed version of TPS-59

GEADGE German air defence ground environment (radar by Hughes)

GEANS gimballed electro-static aircraft
navigation system by Boeing

Gearing class, destroyers (USN)

GEASEC electronic outdoor alarm system by
AEG

GEB general engine bulletin

geb gebirgs- (mountain ...)

GEBA government excess baggage authorization; government employees'
benefits association

GEBCO general bathymetric chart of the
oceans

GebH Gebirghaubitze (mountain howitzer)

GEC generalized equivalent cylinder;
General Electric of Canada

GECo General Electric Corporation

GECOS general comprehensive operating
supervisory

GED general education development (test)

GEDA Goodyear electronic differential
analyser

GEDP general education development programme

GEDT general educational development test

Gee airborne navigation radar WW2 (RAF)

GEE-H radar navigation and homing system
(RAF)

GEEIA ground electronics engineering
installation agency

GEG generalized Eucliedan geometry

GEGB general electricity generating board
(UK)

GEHS government's emergency hospital
scheme

GEI Gesellschaft für Elektronische
Informationsverarbeitung (Bonn)

G&EIC Gilbert and Ellis Island Colony

GEICo government employees insurance
company

GEIS general electric information service

gel gelatine

gelignite gelatine + igneous (explosive)

GEM ground electronics maintenance;
ground effect machine ACV;
guidance evaluation missile

GEMD   ground electronics maintenance
          division
Gemini   twin fast attack craft (IT) (one
          carries gun, one carries missiles);
          inflatable dinghy (RN); chaff/
          flare decoy cartridge
GEMM   generalized electronics maintenance
          model
GEMSS   ground emplaced mine scattering
          system
Gen   General of the Army (US); general
          (UK)
gen   generator
GENDET   general detail
Genie   AIR-2, airborne (nuclear) intercep-
          tion rocket
Genl   general
GENMISH   US military mission with the
          Imperial Iranian Gendarmerie
GenNo   general number
GeNot   general notices
GENP   general expenses, naval personnel
genr   generate
GenRep   general reports
GenSurg   general surgery
gent   gentleman
Gentex   DH-152, tank crewman's helmet by
          Bauer
geo   geographic
geod   geodetic
geol   geological
geom   geometric
geoloc   geographical location
GEON   gyro-erected optical navigation
geophy   geophysics
georef   geographical reference system
GEORGE   general organizational experiment
Georges Leygues   class, anti-submarine
          frigates (FR)
George Washington   class, nuclear ballistic
          missile submarines SSBN
          (USN)
GEOS   geostationary scientific satellite
          by ESA
GEOVOR   geophysikalische Vorhersagen zur
          Einsatzunterstützung (geophysical
          forecasts for tactical support)
GEPAL   Groupement d'Etudes et de Promotions
          pour les Avions Légères (trainer
          aircraft)
Gepard   FlakPz-1, a/a tank
GEPOD   General Electric gun pod 30mm
          --CHAG
GER   German educational reconstruction
Ger   Germany
GERA   guard's expense in returning absentee
Gerät-040   Karl, Thor, 60cm self-propelled
          mortar WW2
Gerät-56   automatic 5cm a/a gun by Mauser WW2
Gerät-58   automatic a/a gun 5.5cm by
          Rheinmetall

Gerät-104   Münchhausen, larger calibre
          recoilless airborne gun WW2
          project
Gerät-1003 ... 1004, anti-tank gun 4.2cm
          WW2
Gerät-2004 ... 2005, anti-tank gun 4.2cm
          WW2
GerNorSea   German North Sea Subarea (Nato)
GESAMP   group of experts on the scientific
          aspects of marine pollution
GESCo   General Electric Supply Corporation
GET   ground elapsed time
GETA   government employees training act
GETC   Gurkha engineering training centre
GETI   Groupe d'Etudes Tactiques Inter-
          alliée (inter-allied tactical
          study group)
GETIS   ground environmental team of the
          international staff (electronics)
GETOL   ground effect take-off and landing
GETRAG   Getriebe und Fahrradfabrik Hermman
          (Hagemeyer D-7140 Ludwigsburg)
GEV   giga electron volts
Gew   Gewehr rifle
GewGra   Gewehrgranate (rifle-launched
          grenade); HL Gewehrgranate (holow
          charge)
GEX   government employees exchange
GF   gunfire; ground forces; government
          form; gap filler (radar); Group of
          Fourteen Nato nations (France
          excluded); ground fog
GFA   gun fire area; government freight
          agent; government freight agency
          (UK)
GFAC   ground forward air controller
GFAE   government furnished aircraft equip-
          ment
GFCM   general fisheries council for the
          Mediterranean FAO
GFCS   gunfire control system
GFD   general functional description
GFDC   group fire distribution centre
GFE   government furnished equipment
GFF   Gurkha Field Force
GFH   Gesellschaft für Flugtechnik
          (Hamburg)
GFFHQ   Gurkha Field Force Headquarters
          (Hong Kong)
GFI   government free issue
GFK   Glasfaserkunststoff (glass reinfor-
          ced plastic)
GFM   government furnished material
GFN   growth to full NADGE
GFP   government furnished property
GFR   German Federal Republic; gap filler
          radar
GFS   Girls' Friendly Society; gunfire
          support; Gesellschaft für Führungs-
          systeme (Köln)

GFSR   general functional system require-
        ment
GFT   graphical firing table
GFV   guided flight vehicle
GG   gas generator; Girl Guides; Governor
        General;
        The Grenadier Guards
        GGA   1st Battalion the GG
        GGB   2nd Battalion the GG
        GGC   3rd Battalion the GG
GGA   Girl Guides' Association
GGC   gun group commander
GGFG   Governor-General's Foot Guard
        (Canada)
GGHG   Governor-General's Horse Guard
        (Canada)
GGP   Geneva Gas Protocol
GGP-40 Gewehrgranate zur Panzerbekämpfung
        (rifle-launched anti-tank grenade)
GGS   gun gyro (stabilized) sight; air-
        craft gaseous system STANAG
GH   The Gordon Highlanders; The Green
        Howards; general hospital; grid
        heading; gyro (stabilized) horizon
G&H   Griffin & Howe
GH-14   gyro horizon for helicopters by
        Sperry
GHA   Greenwich hour angle
GHAMS   Greenwich hour angle of mean sun
GHATS   Greenwich hour angle of true sun
GHE   ground handling equipment
GHH   Gute Hoffnungs Hütte (GE)
GhN   Ghana Navy
GHOST   global horizontal sounding technique
GHQ   general headquarters
GHQAF   great headquarters Air Force
GHz   gigahertz
GI   gunnery instructor; government issue;
        general issue; general inspection;
        Government of India; galvanized
        iron; Graseby Instruments (UK)
GI-750 active/passive sonar medium/long
        range by Graseby
GI-768 ... 777, improved GI-750
GI   The Irish Guards
        GIA   1st Battalion GI
Giant Talk   world-wide HF communications net-
        work for the USAF SAC
Giant Viper   rocket-assisted mine clearing
        system by ROF
GIAT   Groupement Industriel des Armaments
        Terrestres (Saint-Cloud)
GIB   Gurkha Infantry Brigade
Gib   Gibraltar
GibMed Gibraltar Mediterranean Command
Giboulee   airborne bomblet dispenser by
        Matra
Gibson Girl   miniaturized transceiver WW2
GIC   General Instrument Corporation (New
        York)

GIC   general institute committee (Naafi
        organization) (UK); generalized
        immitance converter
GICo   Gain Implement Company
GID   Gurkha Infantry Division
GIDEP   government industry data exchange
        programme
GIER   general industrial equipment reserve
Giesskanne   WB-81, Waffenbehälter (six-fold)
        airborne machine gun pod) WW2
GIFAS   Groupement des Industries Françaises
        Aeronautiques et Spatiales (Paris)
Gigant Me-321, Me-323, giant aircraft
        transport
GIGN   Groupe d'Intervention de la Gendar-
        merie National (French anti-
        terrorist squad)
GIGO   garbage in/garbage out (badly
        handled computer)
GIISG   graduate,institute of international
        studies (Geneva)
Gillois   bridging equipment by EWK
GIM   gaining inventory manager
GIMRADA   geodesy intelligence and mapping
        research and development agency
GIP   ground instructor pilot
        --ACMRI
GIPC   Guards' independent parachute
        company
Giraffe   PS-70/R, search radar for RBS-70
        by LME; fork lifter by Liner
        (UK); telescopic illumination
        mast (GE)
GIRL   infra-red telescope --Spacelab
GIRLS   general information retrieval and
        listing systems
GIRO   general instructions for routing
        (and reporting) officers
GIS   generalized information system
GISD   general intermediate stores depot
GIU   general intelligence unit
GIUK   Greenland-Iceland-United Kingdom
        (gap) (Nato)
GJAB   groups joint administration board
GJAC   groups joint administration
        committee
GJP   graphic job processor
GKart   Gewehr(granat)Kartusche (rifle-bore
        propelling charge for rifle
        grenade)
GKN-Sankey Ltd   Wellington Guest, Keene &
        Nettlefold
GKrKW   Grossraum Krankenwagen (large
        ambulance)
GKSS   Gesellschaft für Kernenergieverwer-
        wertung in Schiffahrt und Schiffbau
        (D-2054 Geesthacht) (Society for
        Nuclear Application in the Navy)
GL   gunnery lieutenant; general ledger;
        gun limbers; gun layer (radar)

GL   gear lubricant; ground level;
            grenade launcher, government
            laboratories; Garbe-Lahmeyer & Co.
            (Aachen); Gasdrucklader (gas-
            operated machine gun)
gl   geländegängig (cross country capable)
GLAAD   gun low altitude air defense (US
            programme); gun for light anti-
            aircraft defense (US programme)
Gladiator   biplane fighter by Gloster (UK)
GLADS   Great Lakes Auxiliary to Dependents
            Service
Glaive   class, patrol boats 1976 (FR)
GlasH   The Glasgow Highlanders
GLASS   geodetic laser survey system
Glavkos   class, submarines Greece 1970-2 by
            HDW
GLB   Girls' Life Brigade
GLC   gas liquid chromatography
GLCM   Tomahawk, ground-launched cruise
            missile
gldr   glider
GLEEP   graphite low energy experimental
            pile
gli   glider
GliderP   The Glider Pilot Regiment
GLIPAR   guideline identification programme
            for anti-missile research
GLLD   ground laser locator designator by
            Hughes
GLO   ground liaison officer; gunnery
            liaison officer
GlobeCom   global communications system
GloCom   global communications system
Globemaster C-124, cargo aircraft by Douglas
glomb   glider bomb
GLOMEX   Global oceanographic and meteorologi-
            cal experiment 1975-80
GLORIA   geological long-range ASDIC
GlosterH   The Royal Gloucestershire Hussars
Glover   armoured Land Rover by Glover & Webb
GLP   government lent property; general
            layout plan; ground liaison party
GLQ-3   jammer equipment by Fairchild
GLS   ground liaison section; general line
            school; Gesellschaft für Logisti-
            schen Service (München) (Krauss-Maffei
            subsidiary)
GLSect   ground liaison section
Gl'spur   Glimmspur (tracer, dark ignition)
GLV   Groep Lichte Vliegtuigen (Dutch Army
            Air Corps)
GM   Gunner's mate; guided missile; George
            Medal (for Gallantry); general
            message; Grand Master; general
            maintenance (area); guard mail;
            group mark; gyro-magnetic
GM-counter Geiger-Müller counter
GM-15   machine pistol 9mm (Rhodesia)
GMA   guided missile ammunition

GMAS   ground munitions analysis study
GMAT   Greenwich mean astronomical time
GMB   Grand Master of the Most Ancient and
            Noble Order of the Bath
GMBE   Grand Master of the Order of the
            British Empire
GMC   General Motors Corporation; general
            medical council; general manage-
            ment committee; general musketry
            course; ground movement control
GMCM   guided missile counter-measures
GMDEP   guided missile data exchange pro-
            gramme
GMEC   guided missile equipment carrier
GMFCS   guided missile fire control system
GMIE   Grand Master of the Order of the
            Indian Empire
GMKP   Grand Master of the Knights of
            St Patrick
GML   guided missile launcher
GMLS   guided missile launching system
GMM   Guild of Master Mariners; general
            matrix manipulator
GMMG   Grand Master of the Order of
            St Michael and St George
GMMP   guided munition modification pro-
            gramme
GMOBE   Grand Master of the Most Excellent
            Order of the British Empire
GMOCU   guided missile operations and con-
            trol unit
GMod   Grundmodell (basic model)
GMP   Gurkha Military Police; Grand Master
            of the Order of St Patrick; ground
            movement planner
GMR   ground mapping radar
GMRMR   general mobilization material
            requirements
GMRS   general mobilization reserve stock
GMS   guide missile school (Fort Bliss);
            general military science; ground
            meteorological station; geo-
            stationary meteorological satel-
            lite
gms   grammes
GMS-2   second generation geo-stationary
            meteorological satellites by Hughes
GMSA   German Minesweeping Administration
GMSC   general medical services council
GMSER   guided missile service report (eval-
            uation)
GMSI   Grand Master of the Order of the
            Star of India
GMST   general military subjects test
GMT   Greenwich mean time
GMTO   general military training office
GMWM   group mark/word mark
GN   graduated nurse
GNAT   galosh, not attributable tread
            (UK-NI)

Gnat   light jet fighter by HS
GNav   graphic area navigation (computer-
           printed charts)
GNC   General Nursing Council
           EW for England and Wales
GNC   graphic numerical control; global
           navigation chart
gnd   ground
GndCon   ground control
GndFg   ground fog
GNP   gross national product
G-NP   gas, non persistent
GNPC   global navigation and planning chart
gnr   gunner
gnry   gunnery
GNS   general naval staff
gns   guineas
GNS-500   global navigation system by Global
GNTC   Girls' Nautical Training Corps
GNTS   Girls' Naval Training Service
GO   general orders; general officer;
           grand officer; group officer;
           garrison officer; grenade officer;
           grenadier officer; gunnery officer;
           gas operated
GO-242   244, 345, assault and combat glider
           by Gotha (GE)
GOA   general operating agency
Goalkeeper SEM-30, quadruple naval gun by
           SEM
Goat   UK WW2 AVRE demolition tank;
           US wheeltrain for Craig detachable
           containers
GOC   general officer commanding; ground
           observer corps; gunnery officer's
           console; ground observer centre
GOCinC   general officer commanding in chief
GOCNIC   General Officer Commanding Northern
           Ireland's Commendation
GO/CO   government-owned/contractor-operated
           (facility)
GOCRA   General Officer Commanding Royal
           Artillery
Godolphin shelter tin hut on stakes Malaysia
Goer   cross-country truck by Caterpillar
           M-520 8 ton cargo truck
           M-553 10 ton recovery vehicle
           M-559 2500 gal tanker
GOES   geo-stationary operational environ-
           ment satellite (long-term weather
           forecast) (NASA)
GOF   government ordnance factory
           (Maribyrnong Australia)
GOFAR   global geological and geophysical
           ocean floor analysis and research
GOGO   government-owned/government-operated
           (facility)
GOI   government of Indonesia
Golden Lions parachute free-fall team of
           the Scottish Division

Goldhaube Austrian anti-aircraft warning
           and control system by Selenia
Golfswing Swingfire anti-tank missile in
           infantry launch container
Goliath   SdKfz-302, leichter Ladungsträger
           (remote controlled demolition
           tank) WW2 by Borgward
GOMA   general officer money allowance
GOMAC   government micro-circuit application
           conference
GOMS   geo-stationary orbiting meteorologi-
           cal satellite; geo-stationary
           operational meteorological satel-
           lite (SU)
GOO   ground operation order; ground
           observer organization
GOOF   general on-line oriented function
           (computer)
Gooney Bird C-47, Skytrain, transport air-
           craft by Douglas
GOP   ground observation post; general
           outpost; general operational plot
GOPL   general outpost line
GOR   gun operational room; Gurkha other
           rank; general operational require-
           ments
Gorgon   ship-to-shore bombardment missile
           WW2 (US)
Gorijunov M-44, machine gun 7.62mm (SU)
Gorloff guns Gatling guns sold to Russia
GOS   global observation station; global
           observation satellite; graphische
           Operationssystem by Dornier
           (for CL-89)
GOSE   ground operational support equipment
Gosport tube speaking tube
GOSS   ground operational support system
GOT   ground observer team
gov   governor; government
GovAir   travel by government aircraft
GovGen   governor general
govt   government
GovtQtrs   government quarters
GOW   gunnery officer's writer
GOX   gaseous oxygen
GP   gun pointer; general purpose;
           general practitioner; general
           principal; geographical point;
           glide path; geometrical progres-
           sion
G-P   gas, persistent
gp   group
GPA   guidance platform assembly; general
           purchasing agent; general purpose
           amphibian; grade point average
GPAS   general purpose airborne simulator
GPATS   general purpose automatic test
           station
GPB   ground power breaker
GPC   general purpose committee

GPC	gross profit contribution; gel permeation chromatography
GpC	Group Captain (RAF)
GpCapt	Group Captain (RAF)
GpComdr	Group Commander
GPD	gallons per day
GPDC	general purpose digital computer
GPE	guided projectile establishment
GPF	Gibraltar police force
G-PF	gas proof
GpFl	group flashing
GPH	gallons per hour
GPI	ground point of impact; ground position indicator; glide path indicator
gpKw	gepanzerter Kampfwagen (armoured combat vehicle)
GPL	grammes per litre
GPLAN	generalized data base planning system
GPLD	government property lost or damaged (US form)
gpm	gallons per minute
GPM	gepanzerter Pioniermaschine (combat engineer tractor) by MaK EWK
GPMG	general purpose machine gun
Gpmt	groupment
gpMTW	gepanzerter Mannschaftstranportwagen (armoured personnel carrier)
GPN	Groupe des Plans Nucleaires (nuclear planning group) (Nato)
GPN-22	precision approach radar by Raytheon
GPO	gun position officer; general post office (UK); government printing office (US)
GPOA	gun position officer's assistant
GpOcc	group occulting (lights)
GPOS	general purpose operating system
GPR	The Glider Pilot Regiment; general purpose radar
GPS	gradual pensions scheme; global positioning satellite NAVSTAR; ground positioning system; Güteprüfstelle (quality evaluation office)
gps	gallons per second
GPSC	general purpose sub-committee (of the military budget committee)
GPSPAC	global positioning system for spacecraft compatible with NAVSTAR
GPSS	general purpose simulation studies
GPU	ground power unit
GPV	general purpose vehicle
GPW	Geneva Convention, Treatment of Prisoners of War 12 August 1949, 27 July 1929
GPW	general purpose Willys Jeep by Ford; gross plated weight
GPWS	ground proximity warning system
GPzGr	Gewehrpanzergranate (rifle-launched anti-tank grenade)

GQ	general quarters; government quarters
GQA	government quality assurance
GQE	generalized queue entry
GR	The Gibraltar Regiment; The Gurkha Rifles; general reserve; general reconnaissance; Greece (Nato); gross requirement; gunnery range
gr	grade, grenadier; gunner; grenade officer; gravity; grain; gramme; group
2GR	The 2nd King Edward VII's Own Gurkha Rifles
4GR	The 4th Prince of Wales's Own Gurkha Rifles
6GR	The 6th Gurkha Rifles
7GR	The 7th Gurkha Rifles, The Sirmoor Rifles
10GR	The 10th Princess Mary's Own Gurkha Rifles
GRA	government report announcement
GRACE	group routing and charging equipment
grad	gradient graduate
GRAFAC	rifle-launched a/t or a/p grenade for 5.56mm rifles by SERAT
GRAN	global rescue alarm net
gran	granulate(d)
Grand Slam	bomb WW2 (RAF), 22000 lbs DP or HC bomb; tracked rocket launcher 18.3cm 24 tubes (US)
Grant	M-3, medium tank WW2 (US)
Grasshopper	BLU-181, ...81, multi-sensor land mines (USAF), WW2 1080 bombarding rocket to prepare a landing
Grayback	class, conventionally-powered ballistic missile submarine (USN) --Regulus
GRB	government reservation bureau
GrB-39	Granatbüchse, (grenade launching rifle)
GRC	Government of the Republic of China; glass reinforced cement; ground radio communications
GrCapt	Group Captain (RAF)
grd	guard
GRD	Groupe sur la Recherche pour la Défense (FR) (Defence Research Group); Gruppe für Rüstungsdienste (Switzerland) (Swiss Procurement Authority)
grdl	gradual
GRE	The Gurkha Royal Engineers
Gre	Greenland
Grease Gun	M-3A1, .45 cal. submachine gun (US)
Great Panjandrum	rocket driven roller filled with 2 tons of explosives project WW2
GREB	galactic radiation experiment background (satellite)

GreeMain orders contingent upon agreement
          to remain on active duty til ...
Green Archer RFA No. 8, mortar location
          radar by EMI
Green Baron airborne recce pod, forward-
          looking daylight camera by FFV
Green Beret Royal Marines; Commandos;
          WRACs
Greenfinches Women of the UDR
Green Pine UHF early warning system for the
          arctic region SAC (USAF)
green salt depleted uranium
Greif He-177, four-engined bomber WW2 by
          Heinckel; Austrian recovery tank by
          Steyr
GREMEX Goddard Research and Engineering
          Management Exercise
gren grenade
Grenadier 4x4 6 ton armoured personnel
          carrier by MOWAG
grendr grenadier
GrenGds The Grenadier Guards
GrePat Greenland Patrol
Gretacoder cryptographic equipment by
          GRETAG
          -102 speech scrambler
          -201 digital encryption unit
          -505 telex encryption unit
          -521 teleprinter encryption
                unit
          -515 data and fax encryption
                unit
          -805 portable encryption unit
          -601 bulk communications
                encryption unit
          -812 radio teletype encryption
                unit
          -905 hand-held encryption unit
Greyhound M-8, armoured wheeled recce
          vehicle; C-2, carrier on-board
          delivery plane by Grumman
Greys The 2nd Dragoons the Royal Scots
          Greys
GRFO gun rangefinder operator
grGPzGr grosse GewehrPanzergranate (big
          rifle-launched anti-tank grenade)
          Ub rifle-launched anti-tank
              grenade practice
GRI Government of the Ryukyu Islands,
          Glasgow Royal Infantry
GRID graphical inter-active display
Grille anti-tank plastic charge (FR),
          108mm SP field howitzer WW2
GRIP Groupement pour la Réalisation Indus-
          trielle de Programmes MBB +
          Thomson-CSF
Grisha class, anti-submarine corvettes (SU)
Grizzly wheeled armoured personnel carrier
          by MOWAG + General Motors of
          Canada

GrL gunner lieutenant
GRMP Gurkha Royal Military Police
GRN ground radio navigation system Tacan
grn green
GRNC groups not counted; German radio
          navigation committee
GRO general routine order; general
          register office; Greenwich Royal
          Observatory
GROBDM general register office for Births
          deaths and marriages
GROPE ground operational exercise (RAF)
Groundsat portable automatic radio
          repeater station by Plessey
Group-9 ...-12, navigation radar by Decca
groups group movement system
GROWIAN Grosswindanlage (giant wind-driven
          power station) project (GE)
Growler airborne voice digitizer by MSDS
GRP glass reinforced plastic
grp group
GRR ground radio receiver
GrReg graves registration
GRS Gurkha Royal Signals; general recon-
          naissance squadron; graves regis-
          tration service; Gesellschaft für
          Raketensysteme AEG+DNAG+Honeywell
          (Bonn)
GrSL gunner Sub-lieutenant
GRSM graduate of the Royal School of
          Music
GRT gross registered tons
GRTM gross ton miles
GRTS Groupement Turbomeca SNECMA (FR)
GRU graves registration unit; Soviet
          main intelligence directorate
gru group (US)
GRU-7 ejection seat by Martin-Baker
GruCom group commander
GrW Granatwerfer (mortar)
grwt gross weight
GS Germany Star; general staff;
          general schedule (civilian
          employee) (US); general service;
          general support; gunnery school
          ground surveillance (radar);
          ground speed; guard ship; group
          separator
GS-20 Claribel, ground surveillance radar,
          hostile fire indicator by MESL
GSA general services administration;
          games and sports in the Army;
          Girl Scouts of America; gun
          sighting apparatus; Mk-1 gun
          sighting apparatus; artillery by
          BMARCO
GSB government savings bank
GSC general service corps; gunnery staff
          course; general staff corps;
          general staff council; ground
          speed continuing

GSCG	ground systems coordinating group
GSD	geographical survey department; general supply depot; general system description; graphic systems division; general starter drive
GSDA	ground speed drift angle
GSDF	ground self-defence forces (Japan)
GSDFJ	ground self-defence forces Japan
GSE	ground support equipment; ground service equipment
GSF	general support forces; gulf sea frontier; The Grey and Simco Forresters (Commonwealth Regiment); general scientific framework (for the world oceanographic study)
GSFC	Goddard Space Flight Center NASA
GSFG	group of Soviet forces in East Germany
GSG	general support group
GSG-1	general staff, first section (operations)
GSG-10	battlefield data processing system
GSGB	geographical survey of Great Britain
GSGS	geographical section, general staff (UK)
GSh-23	twin airborne gun 23mm (SU)
GSgt	gunnery sergeant
GSI	geographical survey of India
GSK	general storekeeper
GSL	group scout leader
GSM	general stores material; general service medal; garrison sergeant major; general situation map; grammes per square meter
GSMT	general service mechanical transport
GSNol4Mk-l	ZB-298, battlefield surveillance radar by Elliot
GSO	German service organization with BAOR; general staff officer
GSOR	general staff operational requirements; general staff operational research
GSP	good service pension; general syntactic processor; amphibious bridge-layer vehicle (SU)
GSQ	general staff quarters
GSR	general service recruit; general support reinforcing; ground surveillance radar; gun sound ranging; ground speed returning; galvanic skin response
GSRS	general support rocket system; ground support rocket system --MLRS
GSS	general service school; generaly supply schedule; geo-stationary satellite; global surveillance system
GSSS	gyro-stabilized sight system by Tamam

GST	geographical specialist team; general service test; general staff target; Gesellschaft für Systemtechnik (Essen) (Krupp daughter); ground sensor terminal; Greenwich Standard Time; Greenwich Sideral Time
GSTD	general standardization of tactical doctrines (Nato); Gruppe der Sowjetischen Streitkräfte in Deutschland ----GSFG
GSU	general support unit; general service unit; guidance shaping unit
GSV	ground-to-surface vessel (radar)
GSW	general service wagon; gun shot wound
GSWT	general staff with troops
GT	general transport; general technical (aptitude area) (US); gross tonnage; gas tight; Groupe de Travail (working group); Groupement Tactique (regimental combat team)
GTA	graphic training aids; gas tungsten arc (welding)
GTACS	ground target attack and control system
GTC	Girls' Training Corps; government training centre; good till cancelled; good till countermanded; gas turbine compressor; gain time control
CTCoy	general transport company
GTCP	gas turbine compressor and power (unit)
GTD	geometrical theory of diffraction
GTDMU	glossary of terms and definitions for military use (Nato)
GTES	gun training evaluation system
GTE-Sylvania	General Telephone and Electronics (Needham Heights, Mass. USA)
GTGS	Gatling type gun system; gas turbine generator set
GTgt	gun target
GTL	gun target line
GTM	general traffic manager
GTMAH	Groupe de Travail Mixte ad hoc (ad hoc mixed working group) (Nato)
GTMSICC	Groupe de Travail Militaire sur les Systèmes d'Information de Commandement et de Contrôle (Military Command, control and informations systems working group)
GTP	gas turbine power (unit); ground track plotter
GTR	The Gurkha Transport Regiment

GTRE   The Indian Gas Turbine Research Establishment (Bangalore)

GTS   Greenwich time signal; general technology satellite by HSD; global telecommunications system; gas turbine ship; geo-stationary technology satellite

GT-S   snow vehicle (SU)

GT-SM   snow vehicle (SU)

GTSC   German Territorial Southern Command

GT-T   snow vehicle (SU)

GTTAD   Groupe de Travail Inter-armées de Traitement Automatique des Donnes (automatic data handling inter-service working group)

GT-TM-1970   tracked multi-role APC (SU)

GTTT   glossary of training technology terms (Nato)

GTV   group transport vehicle; guidance test vehicle; ground test vehicle; guided test vehicle

GU   guidance unit; Generalunternehmer (general contractor)

Guacolda class, fast torpedo boats (Chile)

Guardian anti-aircraft defence system by HSA + Breda (Flycatcher + twin 40mm)

Guard Rail   signal intelligence and direction finding system by SEMA

Guarini   Argentinian COIN aircraft

Guayaquil class, TNC -45, guided missile patrol boats by Lürssen for Equador

GUB   government Union of Burma

GUCL   general use consumables list

Guepard   ERC TG-120 (FR)

GUF   Gesellschaft für Ungelenkte Flugkörper (Bonn-Beuel) now GRS (society for unguided missiles)

Gufo   reconnaissance drone by Meteor; ESM system for naval helicopters by Elettronica

Gufone   camera carrying RPV by Meteor

GUIDAR   guided intrusion detection and ranging by CDC

guidn   guidance

Gulfstream   executive aircraft by Grumman

gun   gunner; gunnery; gunboat

Gunfighter   mobile fire control radar by Westinghouse

Gunkote   anti-corrosive and self-lubricating metal finish

GUPPY   greater underwater propulsion power

Guppy   class, submarines (USN)

Gur   Gurkha

GUS   hovercraft (SU)

GV   grosse Verzögerung (long-time fuse); grid variation; gravimetric volume; gross valuation

gv   grave

GVA   Gloucestershire Volunteer Artillery

GVC   Girls' Venture Corps

GVN   Government of (South) Viet Nam

GVS-1   low-cost computer-generated image system (simulator) by Gould

GVS-5   laser rangefinder sight, portable hand-held by RCA

GVT   tracked test vehicle by MaK

GVW   gross vehicle weight (rating) (US)

GVWR   gross vehicle weight rating

GW   guerilla warfare, general warning, guided weapons (course), ground waves

GW III   Hummel, Geschützwagen (heavy armoured howitzer 15cm) WW2

GWA   1st Battalion the Welsh Guards

GWC   Greek War Cross

Gwennie   anti-aircraft gun WW1

GWG   guided weapons group (UK)

GWG-58   Gewehrgranate (rifle-launched grenade) (Switzerland)

GwNbGr   Gewehrnebelgranate (rifle-launched smoke grenade)

GWO   general watch officer

GWOA   guerilla warfare operational area

GWOB   guerilla warfare operational base

GWP   government white paper

GWR   general war reserves, guided weapons regiment

GWR RA   Guided Weapons Regiment Royal Artillery

GWS   Geneva Convention 12 August 1949 for the Amelioration of the Condition of the Wounded and Sick in Armed Forces in the Field

GWS 1929 Geneva Convention 17 July 1929 for the Amelioration of the Condition of the Wounded and Sick of Armies in the Field

GWS-1   Sea Slug, guided weapon system, medium-range ship-to-air missile (RN)

GWS-20   ...22, ...24, Seacat, naval point defence anti-aircraft missile by Shorts

GWS-25   Seawolf, naval defence anti-ballistic missile by BAe

GWS-30   Sea Dart, anti-aircraft missile by BAe

GWS Sea   Geneva Convention 12 August 1949 for the Amelioration of the Condition of the Wounded, Sick and Shipwrecked Members of the Armed Forces at Sea

GWT   Gurkha Welfare Trust, gross weight

GXC-7   tactical facsimile transceiver by Magnavox

GY   The Glamorgan Yeomanry

gy   gyro, gyroscope

GYFM   general yielding fracture mechanics

GYK-290	MC-1800, artillery battery computer system by Marconi	GySgt	gunnery sergeant
		GZ	ground zero

H

H	hour; hull; heavy; hard(ness); height; hits; horizontal; howitzer; helicopter; hydrogen; headphones; handset; Hussars; class; coastal submarines (RN) WW1; passive light intensification system (FR)
H-hour	hostilities begin hour (US); hostilities commence hour (Nato)
H-table	area in SACC where TacRon controls air support (USN)
2-H	3-H, hard pencil
4-H	very hard pencil
3-H	The 3rd the King's Own Hussars
4-H	The 4th the Queen's Own Hussars
7-H	The 7th the Queen's Own Hussars
8-H	The 8th Regiment the King's Royal Irish Hussars
10-H	The 10th Regiment the Prince of Wales's Own Royal Hussars
11-H	The 11th Regiment Prince Albert's Own Hussars
13/18-H	The 13th/18th Regiment Queen Mary's Own Royal Hussars
14/20-H	The 14th/20th Regiment the King's Hussars
15/19-H	The 15th/19th Regiment the King's Royal Hussars
H_2X	airborne bombing radar WW2 (US)
H_2S	airborne bombing radar WW2 (UK)
H-5	short-range helicopter by Sikorsky
H-5	Mi-4, Chinese designation transport helicopter
H-6	explosive ---torpedoes
H-13	OH-13. Sioux, light (observation) helicopter by Bell
H-19	S-55, Chicksaw, transport helicopter by Sikorsky
H-21	Shawnee, Work Horse, transport helicopter by Vertol
H-23	trainer helicopter by Hiller
H-24	24 hours a day, continuous operation
H-25	Army Mule, helicopter by Vertol
H-34	transport helicopter by Vertol
H-37	Mojave, heavy transport helicopter by Sikorsky
H-43	Husky, helicopter
H-46	helicopter by Boeing-Vertol
H-3742	tactical tropo-spheric scatter communications system by MSDS
HA	heavy artillery; horse artillery; hostile aircraft; height angle; Hindustan Aircraft Ltd (Banga-lore); hour angle; high angle; high altitude (aircraft)
H&A	Hopkins & Allen Manufacturing Comp. (Norwich Mass.)
HA-200	Super Saeta, jet trainer aircraft (Spain)
HAA	Helicopter Association of America; height above airport; heavy anti-aircraft (gun); heavy anti-air-craft artillery
HAARegt	heavy anti-aircraft artillery regiment
HAAW	heavy anti-tank assault weapon
HAB	high-altitude bombing; high-altitude burst (bomb)
Habicht	A-28, transport aircraft WW2 by Focke-Wulf
HABS	high-altitude bomb sight
HAC	The Honourable Artillery Company (TA); house appropriations committee; Haitian Air Corps; heavy anti-tank convoy; heavy attack aircraft; Helicoptre Anti-Char (anti-tank helicopter); high acceleration cockpit; high alumina cement
HACK	holiday activities club for kids BAOR
HAD	home aircraft depot; hereafter described; head acceleration device
HADAR	artillery digital message handling device by PEAB
HADES	hypersonic air data entry system
Hades	French strategic nuclear missile Pluton replacement
HADR	heavy air defence regiment; Hughes air defence radar (long range)

Hadrian   CG-15, cargo glider WW2 by WACO
HADS   helicopter air data system by GEC-
        Marconi; hypersonic air data
        sensor
HAECo   Hong Kong Aircraft Engineering
        Company Ltd
HAES   high-altitude effects simulation
HAF   home air force; high angle firing;
        headquarters, allied forces;
        helicopter assault forces;
        Hellenic Armed Forces; Hellenic
        Air Force; high altitude fluores-
        cence
HAFAG   Haller & Flüchinger AG (Switzerland)
HAFB   Holloman Air Force Base (New Mexico)
HAFC   high altitude forecast centre
HaFla   Handflammpatrone (dazzling and in-
        cendiary torch by Buck)
Haflinger   truck by Stey-Daimler-Puch
HAFMed   Headquarters, Allied Forces Mediter-
        ranean
HAFO   home accounting and finance office
HAFSE   Headquarters, Allied Forces Southern
        Europe
HAG   heavy artillery group; hardware
        analysis group (computers)
HAH   Hubschrauberabwehrhubschrauber
        (anti-helicopter helicopter)
HAI   handbook of artillery instruments;
        Hellenic Aerospace Industry
Hai   class, anti-submarine corvettes
        (GDR)
Hai Dau   class, Chinese patrol boats, guided
        missiles + mines + torpedo
Hai Nam   Chinese patrol boats
HAIS   Hartley Anglo Iranian Siemens
Hakim   Egyptian self-loading rifle 7.62mm
HAKO   HOT Abschussanlage,kompakt by MBB
        (compact HOT launcher)
HAL   Hindustan Aircraft Ltd (Bangalore)
HA(L)   helicopter attack squadron, light
Halbran   ballistic flight target
Haldane   apparatus   oxygen respirator
HALE   high altitude long endurance RPV
        (USAF programme)
Halifax   bomber/transport aircraft WW2 by
        Handley Page
HALO   high altitude low opening (para-
        chute)
HALP   Hawk equipment logistics programme
HALTATA   high and low temperature accuracy
        testing apparatus
HAM   hardware associative memory (com-
        puter); horizontal action mine
Hamburg   class, destroyers (FGN)
HAMCO   Hawk assembly and missile check-out
HAMD   helicopter ambulance medical detach-
        ment
Hamel cables   Hamick & Ellis, submarine
        pipeline tubes WW2

Hamilcar   cargo glider by General Aircraft
Hamilton   cargo glider WW2 (RAF)
Hammer   recoilless anti-tank gun WW2
Hampden   torpedo bomber by Handley Page WW2
HAMRon   headquarters and maintenance
        squadron
HAMS   headquarters and maintenance
        squadron; hour angle of mean sun
HAMT   heavy artillery mechanical transport
Hansajet   HFB-320, VIP transport aircraft by
        HFB
HAO   hardware action officer
HAP   home owner assistance program (US);
        high altitude platform
HAPDAR   hard point demonstration array radar
HAPDEC   hard point decoy
HAPI   horizontal approach path indicator;
        Harrier approach path indicator
HAPR   high altitude photo reconnaissance
        (aircraft) --U-2
har   harbour
HAR   heavy assault rifle
Harakaze   class, destroyers (JMSDF)
Harava   tactical transport aircraft by IAI
HarCft   harbour craft
HARDEX   harbour defence exercise
HARM   AGM-88, high-speed anti-radiation
        missile (anti-radar) by TI
HARP   home air raid precautions; high
        altitude research project; high
        altitude relay platform
HARPIS   horizontal approach path indicators
        (RN)
Harpon   anti-tank guided weapon by DTAT/
        SNIA
Harpoon   RGM-84, AGM-84, UGM-84, cruise
        missile by McDD
HARPY   hydrofoil advanced research study
        (program) (US); high altitude
        research project
Harrier   AV-8, vertical take-off and landing
        aircraft by Hawker-Siddeley
HARS   (light-weight) heading and attitude
        reference system
HARTRAN   Hartwell Atlas Fortran (computer)
HARU-Präzision   Hans Rustige & Co. KG
        (7022 Leinfelden-
        Echterdingen GE)
Haruna   class, helicopter carrying destroy-
        ers (Japan)
Harvard   fighter aircraft (Israel)
Harvey projector   naval anti-aircraft
        rockets
HAS   helicopter air service; hospital
        advisory service; heading attitude
        system; hardened aircraft shelter;
        helicopter aboard ship; high
        altitude sample; hydrographic
        automated system; Houston auto-
        matic spooling (priority system)

HASAC   Hawaiian armed services athletic
         council
HASC   house armed services committee (US)
HASCO   Hawk assembly and systems check-out
HASP   high altitude sounding projectile;
         high altitude sampling program
         --U-2; high altitude space plat-
         form, hardwares assisted software
         polling (computer); high level
         automatic scheduling programme
HASR   high altitude sounding rocket
HAST   high altitude supersonic target
         drone or RPV by Beech
Hastelloy X alloy for turbines and after-
         burners
HAT   height above touchdown (landing
         minimum)
HATRon   heavy attack squadron
HATS   hour angle of true sun; helicopter
         advanced tactical system
HATWing heavy attack wing
HAV   Her (His) Majesty's Army Vessel
         (RCT); heavy armed vehicle
Have Quick spread spectrum Modem
         jam-resistant by Magnavox
Havoc   A-20, Moonfighter, attack bomber by
         Douglas
HAW   helicopter assault wave; heavy anti-
         armour weapon; heavy anti-tank/
         assault weapon (US); heavy assault
         weapon (Nato)
HAWK   homing all the way killer air-to-
         ground missile (Israel); pistol 9mm
         parabellum (South Africa); PW-8
         VTB, VPB, P-1, fighter/dive bomber
         WW2 by Curtiss; jet aircraft,
         trainer/ground attack by Hawker-
         Siddeley
MIM-23   MIM-23, anti-aircraft missile system
         by Raytheon (Nato)
Hawk-I   infra-red line-scan equipment by
         Hawker
Hawkeye E-2C, naval early warning aircraft
         by Grumman, air-controlled RPV
Hawkins grenade Mine No. 75, anti-tank high-
         explosive hand grenade
Hawklite large surveillance night sight by
         Pilkington
Hawkswing helicopter-borne Swingfire anti-
         tank missile
HAWS   heavy anti-tank weapon system
HawSeaFron Hawaiian Sea Frontier
Hayabusa class, corvettes (JMSDF)
Hayashio class, submarines (JMSDF)
HAZ   heat affected zone
haz   hazard(ous)
HB   howitzer battery; heavy battery;
         heavy bomber; horizontal bomber;
         heavy barrel (machine gun);
         hollow base (projectile)

         hard black (pencil); Brinell
         Hardness (number); homing beacon
H&B   head and breast (set)
HB-81   mortar 81mm by Hotchkiss-Brandt
HBAR   M-16A1 heavy barrel automatic
         rifle by Colt; ...
         airborne rockets by
         Forges
HBC   high breaking capacity
HBDC   home base development committee
HbDv   habitability division (US) WASP
HBG   heavy bomber group
HBH   Herbert Bauer (GmbH&Co) (Hamburg)
HBk   hollow back
HBM   Her (His) Britannic Majesty('s)
HBMS   Her (His) Britannic Majesty's ship
HBn   hazard beacon
HBP   hospital benefits payments
HBS   harbour boat service
HBWC   hollow base wad-cutter (projectile)
HBWR   Halden boiling water reactor;
         heavy boiling water reactor
HC   Household Cavalry; high commissioner;
         high command; home counties;
         helicopter combat (support squad-
         ron); health certificate; higher
         certificate; Hague Convention;
         host country; helicopter carrier
         (ship); hand control; heavy
         cruiser (tank); high carbon
         (steel); high capacity (bomb);
         heating coil; hollow charge
         (shell); hanging ceiling
H/C   helicopter
H&C   hot and cold
HC-130   Hercules, hospital (rescue) version
HC-12000 lbs Tallboy, USAF high capacity
         bomb
HC-22000 lbs Grand Slam, USAF high capacity
         bomb
HCA   heading crossing angle, held by
         civil authorities
HC   discharged under honourable condi-
         tions
     CG convenience of the government
     CM convenience of the man
     DP dependency existing prior to
         enlistment
     EE expiration of enlistment
     MS medical survey
     MU minor age of authorized
         enlistment
     MW minor without consent
     US unsuitable
HCC   hydraulic cement concrete
HCD   high current density
hcd   handcarried
HCDP   high current density projector
HCE   human caused error
HCEX   hyper-charge exchange

HCF	honorary chaplain to the forces; high cycle fatigue
HCG	hardware character generator; horizontal (location of) centre of gravity
HCH	hexa-chloro-cyclo-hexane (insecticide)
HCHE	high capacity high explosive (shell) 40mm
HCIL	Hague Conference on International Law
HCJ	high court of justice
HCL	high cost of living; homing control logic (torpedoes); horizontal centre line
HC Mk1	Chinook, helicopter, cargo (RAF designation)
HCMM	heat capacity mapping mission (satellite) NASA
HCO	hangar control officer; higher clerical officer; headquarters catalogue office
HCo	head commander
HCP	hangar control position
hcp	handicapped
HCP	hollow copper point (projectile); heat of combustion under constant pressure
hcptr	helicopter
HCR	high chief ranger; helicopter cruiser
HCRon	helicopter combat support squadron
HCS	home civil service; hollow charge shell; helicopter computer system; high carbon steel; Haut Commandement Subordinée (major subordinate command)
HCS-500	helicopter computer system by computer avionics Corp.
HCSHT	high carbon steel heat treated
HCT	high commission territories; heater centre tap
HCTC	high commission territories corps
HCU	helicopter clearance unit; hydraulic cycling unit; hard copy unit
HCV	heat of combustion under constant volume
HD	Highland Division; headquarters detachment; honourable discharge; home defence; harbour defence; heavy duty (lubricant); height to distance; horse-drawn; high density (alloy); hourly difference; half duplex; horizontal distance
HDA	hydrographic department, admiralty; high duty alloy
HDAF	home defence air force; High Duty Alloys Forgings Ltd (Hawker-Siddeley, Redditch)
HDATZ	high density air traffic zone
HDC	harbour defence command; helicopter

		direction centre; helicopter direction control; hydrogen de-polarized (CO_2) concentrator
HdCr		hard chromium
HD		honourable discharge
	CG	convenience of the government
	CM	convenience of the man
	DP	dependency existing prior to enlistment
	DS	dependency arising since enlistment
	EE	expiration of enlistment
	MS	medical survey
	MU	under age of authorized consent
	MW	minor enlisted without consent
HDD		head-down display
HdeH		Hawker de Havilland (Australia)
HDF		home defence force; high-frequency direction finder
hdg		heading
HDH		Hawker de Havilland (Australia)
HDH-10		Enmoth, target drone by HDH
HDH-11		Beemoth, chemical spraying drone by HDH
HDI		horizontal display indicator
HDL		Harry Diamond Laboratories (US Army)
hdlg		handling
hdlr		handler
HDM		high density magnum (projectile); high duty metal; hydrodensimeter
HDML		harbour defence motor launch
HDMR		high density moderated reactor
HDMS		His (Her) Danish Majesty's Ship
hdh		harden(ed)
HDP		high destructive power (mine)
Hdqrs		headquarters
HDR		home dockyard regulations
hdr		horse-drawn
HDS		head of defence sales DSO (UK)
HDS-1200		Hochdruckspritze Dampfreiniger (high pressure steam cleaning device) by Kärcher
	EK	Elektrokraft (electric driven)
	BK	Benzinkraft (petrol driven)
HDST		high density shock tube
HDT		Hochdruckturbine (high pressure turbine)
HDUE		high dynamics user equipment NAVSTAR
HDV		horse-drawn vehicle, heavy duty vehicle
HDv		Heeres Dienstvorschrift (Army duty manual)
HDW		hemisphere defence weapon --Superfortress, Howaldswerke Deutsche Werft AG (Kiel)
hdw		hardware (computers)
hdwe		hardware (computers)

HDX	half duplex
HDY	heavy duty
HE	home establishment; His Excellency; high explosive; horizontal equivalent; hydrophone effect; height of eye; hammerless ejector; heat engine; hub end; hall effect
He-59	seaplane by Heinkel
He-72	trainer aircraft by Heinkel
He-111	combat aircraft by Heinkel
He-112	interceptor aircraft by Heinkel
He-115	floatplane torpedo bomber by Heinkel
He-162	jet interceptor 880 kmph by Heinkel
He-177	Greif, four-engined bomber by Heinkel
He-178	jet interceptor 1939 by Heinkel (world's first jet aircraft)
HEA	Henschel Engineering Antwerpen
HEAC	higher education advisory council
HEAFS	high-explosive anti-tank fin-stabilized
HEAO	high energy astronomy observatory NASA
HEAP	high-explosive armour-piercing (shell)
HEAP-T	high-explosive armour-piercing (shell) with tracer (anti-aircraft shell)
HEAP-T-SD	high-explosive armour-piercing (shell) with tracer self-destructing
HEAR	human error analysis record
HEAT	high-explosive anti-tank shell
HEAT-FS	high-explosive anti-tank shell fin stabilized
HEAT-PT	high-explosive anti-tank shell practice tracer (shell)
HEAT-T	high-explosive anti-tank shell with tracer (shell)
HEAT-T-MP	high-explosive anti-tank multi-purpose shell with tracer
HEAT-TP-T	high explosive anti-tank shell target practice with tracer
HEC	higher education centre; high explosive cargo (vehicle)
Hecht	midget submarine WW2
HECP	harbour entrance control post
Hector	double decker aircraft WW2 (UK)
HECTOR	heated experimental carbon thermal oscillator reactor
Hector	infra-red sight for HOT by TRT/Siemens
HECVes	harbour entrance control vessel
Hed	headquarters (US)
HedCom	headquarters command
Hedgehog	RN anti-submarine projector WW2
Hedgerow	explosive land mines sweeping system WW2
HEDP	M-433, high-explosive dual purpose (mortar shell)
HedRon	headquarters squadron

HedRonFAirWing	headquarters squadron fleet air wing
HedRonFMF	headquarters squadron fleet marine force
	Lant Atlantic
	Pac Pacific
HedSuppAct	headquarters support activity
HEF	high energy fuel; high explosive fragmentation (bomb); high expansion foam
HEFS	high explosive fin stabilized (shell)
HEFU	high energy firing unit
HEHC	high explosive hollow charge (shell) UK
HEI	high explosive incendiary (shell)
HEIC	The Honourable East India Company
HEICN	The Honourable East India Company Navy
HEICS	The Honourable East India Company Service
HEIP	high explosive incendiary plugged (shell)
HEIPNP	high explosive incendiary plugged and nose plug (shell)
HEISD	high explosive incendiary self-destructing (shell)
HEI-T	high explosive incendiary with tracer (shell)
HEITDISD	high explosive incendiary with tracer dark ignition self-destructing (shell)
HEITSD	high explosive incendiary with tracer self-destructing (shell)
HEL	human engineering laboratory Aberdeen Proving Ground (US); Hunting Engineering Ltd
hel	helicopter
HelAntiSubRon	helicopter anti-submarine squadron
HELBAT	human engineering laboratory battalion artillery tests (US)
HelCAT	helicopter close air support team (UK)
HelCIS	helicopter command instrument system (for IFR) by Spreey
HelCombSuppRon	helicopter combat support squadron
HELEN	hydrogenous exponential liquid experiment
HELFOTT	human engineering laboratory forward observer transportability tests
HeliBras	Helicopteros do Brasil SA
HeliCol	Helicopteros Nacional del Colombia (Bogota)
Helios	OSO, orbiting solar observatory NASA/ESA
HELIP	Hawk European limited improvement programme (Nato)

HeliPATH   helicopter position and terrain
           height (indicator)
Heliplane UK 1939 VTOL aircraft tilting
           rotor combat aircraft by Baynes
Helistab   helicopter stabilizer autopilot by
           SFEMA
HeliTeam   helicopter team
Helitele   helicopter-borne closed circuit
           television system (UK)
Hell Bowp phosphorous grenade
Hellcat   FGF, naval fighter WW2 by Grumman;
           M-18, tank destroyer (US)
Helldiver SB-2D, naval dive bomber WW2 by
           Curtiss, SBC-4, biplane
Hellebarde unguided anti-tank rocket by
           Rheinmetall
Hellfax   BS-1015Y, Blattschreiber, by Hell,
           weather map teleprinter
Hellfire   helicopter borne anti-tank missile
           laser-guided by Rockwell;
           helicopter rotor mast mounted
           target illuminator and sight by
           Rockwell
Helmer   HF radio, long-range SSB by ELMER
HELMS   helicopter multi-function system
helo   helicopter
Heloise   PGS-600, helicopter-borne stabili-
           zed electronic platform by SFIM
HELOS   highly eccentric lunar observation
           (occultation) satellite
HELP   help establish lasting peace;
           haulage emergency link protection;
           helicopter electronic landing path
HelRec   health record
HelSRon   helicopter anti-submarine squadron
HelSuppRon helicopter combat support
           squadron
HelTraRon helicopter training squadron
HEM   handbook of emergency measures
hem   hemisphere
HEMAC   hybrid electro-magnetic antenna
           couplers
HEMLAW   helicopter-mounted laser weapon
HEMP   horizontal electro-magnetic pulse
           generator AWRE
Hengam   class, landing crafts (Iran)
Henley   target towing aircraft WW2 (RAF) by
           Hawker
HEO   higher executive officer
HEOS   high eccentric orbiting satellite
HEP   high explosive plastic (shell) (US)
HEPA   high efficiency particulate air
HEPAT   high explosive plastic anti-tank
           (shell)
HEPC   hydro-electric power commission (US)
HEPCC   heavy electrical plant consultative
           council
HEPDNP   high explosive point detonating nose
           plug (shell)
HEPFS   high explosive plastic fin stabili-
           zed (shell)

HEPL   high energy physics laboratories
           (Stanford University US)
HEP-T   high explosive plastic with tracer
           (shell)
HERA   high explosive rocket-assisted
           (shell)
Heracles   helicopter avionics programme by
           OMERA/SEGID; ORB-31 airborne
           target designation radar by
           OMERA
Herald   highly enriched reactor (Aldermaston
           AWRE)
HERALDS   harbour echo-ranging and listening
           devices
Herc   Nike-Hercules (missile)
Hercules   C-130, transport aircraft by
           Lockheed
HERF   high energy rate forming
HERFC   high energy Royal Flying Corps
           (bomb) WW1
HERMES   heavy element and radio-active
           material electro-magnetic
           separator
Hermes II 1st supersonic aircraft (US
           Fort Bliss)
HERO   hot experimental reactor of Zero
           power; hazards of electro-magnetic
           radiation to ordnance
Heron   target drone/bomb and flare carrying
           RPV by AEL
Heros   Heeresführungssystem by Siemens
           (Army command and control system)
HERU   higher education research unit
HES   high explosive shell
HE-SD   high-explosive self-destructive
           (shell)
HE-SD-T   high-explosive self-destructive
           (shell) with tracer
HESH   high-explosive squash head anti-tank
           shell (UK)
HESH-T   high-explosive squash head anti-tank
           shell with tracer
HESO   hospital educational services officer
HET   higher education test; heavy equip-
           ment transporter
HE-T   high-explosive with tracer (shell)
HE-T-DI   high-explosive with tracer (shell)
           dark ignition
HETS   hyper-environmental test system
           (USAF)
HE-T-SD   high-explosive tracer self-destruct-
           ing (shell)
Hetzer   killer tank WW2 (GE)
HEU   hydro-electric unit
Heuschrecke 150mm self-propelled field
           howitzer
HEv   health and environment
HEW   health education and welfare
           (department of)
Hex   uranium hexafluoride

Hexofol explosive (mines)

HF high frequency; harassing fire;
    home fleet; home forces; horse
    and foot

H/F height finder (radar)

HFA headquarters field army

HFAC house foreign affairs committee

HFB-320 Hansajet, VIP transport aircraft
    by HFB

HFC The Highland Fusiliers of Canada;
    high frequency current

HFDF high frequency direction finding

HFE human factors engineering

HFG high frequency gas

HFG-FI Hohlstab Fernräumgerät by MaK
    German remote-controlled mine-
    sweeping system

HFI height finding instrument;
    GS-20, Claribel, hostile fire
    indicator by MESL

HFIR high fluy isotope reactor

HFlaAFüSys Heeres Flugabwehr und
    Aufklärungs Führungssystem
    (Army anti-aircraft and recon-
    naissance command system)

HFP hostile fire pay

HFPS high frequency phase shifter

HFS hyper-fine structure

HFSSB high frequency single side band

HG The Horse Guards; Home Guard;
    His (Her) Grace; hand generator

H&G Hensley & Gibbs

HG-43 Handgranate (Switzerland)
    (hand grenade)

HGDH His (Her) Grand Ducal Highness

HGH human growth hormone

HGM Home Guard Medal

HGR hypervelocity guided rocket by Ford

hgr hangar

HGr Handgranate (hand grenade)

HGT hyper-geometric group testing

HGÜ Hochspannungsgleichstromübertragung
    (high-tension direct-current
    energy transportation)

HGV heavy goods vehicle

hgy highway

HH His (Her) Highness; His (Her) Honour;
    heavy hydrogen; double hard
    (pencil); heavy helicopter

H&H Holland & Holland

HH-3F Sea King, amphibious helicopter SAR
    by Sikorsky

HH-19 S-55, SAR helicopter by Sikorsky

HH-43 H-43, Husky, fire-fighting helicopter
    by Kaman

HH-53 S-65, Black Knight, rescue helicopter
    by Sikorsky

HHB headquarters and headquarters battery

HHC headquarters and headquarters company

HHCL H-hour coordination line

HHD headquarters and headquarters
    detachment

HHDWS heavy hand deadweight scrap

HHE household effects

HHG household goods

HHGW heat-homing guided weapon

HHH treble hard (pencil)

HHMU hand-held manoeuvring unit

HHR hand-held radar

HHT headquarters and headquarters troop

HHTV hand-held thermal viewer

HHW higher high water

HI human interest (story); Hawaiian
    Islands; high intensity; humidity
    index; horizontal interval; high
    intercept (aircraft) 20-30 kms

H&I harassing and interdiction (fire)

HIA hold in abeyance

HIAB truck-mounted hydraulic crane (UK)

HiAc high accuracy

HiAlt high altitude

HIBEX high acceleration booster experiment

HIC hydrographic information committee;
    hybrid integrated circuits

HiCapCom high capacity communications
    (system)

HICAT high altitude clear air turbulence

HICOG High Commission for Germany

HiCom High Command; High Commission for
    Germany; high command communica-
    tions system (Nato)

HiComRy high commissioner of the Ryukyu
    Islands

HiComTerPacIs high commissioner trust
    territory Pacific Islands

HIDA helicopter insecticide dispersal
    apparatus
    D dry
    L liquid

HIE hibernation information exchange
    ONR (US)

HIFAM high-fidelity amplitude modulation

HIFAR high flux Australian reactor

HiFi high fidelity

HI-FIX-6 North Sea positioning system (RN)
    by Decca

Hi-Flex high flexibility and pressure
    (hydraulic hoses)

HiFor high-level forecast

HIFR hover in-flight refuelling (heli-
    copters)

Highball anti-ship bomb skip bomb WW2 (RN)

High system ACE High, Allied Command Europe
    exclusive military communica-
    tions system (tropo scatter
    technique)

HIH His (Her) Imperial Highness

HILS high-intensity light-weight search-
    light by Spectrolab

HIM His (Her) Imperial Majesty

HIMAD	high-to-medium altitude air defence
HIMAG	high mobility agility (tank test rig)
Himat	highly manoeuvrable aircraft technology RPV by NASA
Himawari	geo-stationary satellite (Japan)
HIMet	high iron (content) metallized agglomerate
HInt	high intensity (light)
HIP	Hawk improvement programme (Nato); heat iso-static pressing
HIPAR	high power acquisition radar
HIPAS	high-intensity patrol aircraft searchlight system by Spectrolab
HIPEG	high performance experimental gun
HIPERNAS	high performance navigation system
HIPIR	high power illumination radar
HIPOE	high pressure oceanographic equipment
HiPot	high potential
Hippo	land-mine clearing system (washed out by water jet); truck by Leyland; mine-protected truck (South Africa)
Hip Pocket	sonar modernization program (USN)
HIPR	high power (illumination) radar
HiPri	high priority
HIPS	high impact polystyrene
HIR	handbook of inspection regulations; Halden international reports; hydrostatic impact rocket
HI-R	high intensity survey meter
Hiram-1	...2, naval infra-red decoy
HIRAN	high precision short-range navigation
HiRel	high reliability
HIRF	handbook of infantry rangefinders; high intensity reciprocity failure (photogr)
HIRIS	high resolution interferometer spectrometer
HIRL	high intensity runway lights
HIRS	high resolution infra-red radiation sounder
Hirundo	A-109, helicopter by Agusta Bell
HIS	hood inflation system; Honeywell information system; Haushalt-Informationssystem (budget information system)
HISA	headquarters and installation support activity
HISAM	high altitude surface-to-air missile
hist	history; historian; historical
histn	historian
HIT	Holzman inkblot technique; Hughes improved terminals
Hi-T	high torque
HITA	tactical communications system by SAIT
HiTemp	high temperature
HITS	Holloman infra-red target simulator
hittile	direct hitting missile

HIVAC	high value asset control; high value transaction (report)
HIVOS	high vacuum orbital simulator
Hiyo	class, aircraft carriers WW2 (Japan)
HJ	Honest John (missile); utility helicopter
HJ-1	Hornet, baby helicopter (ramjets) by Hiller
HJT-16	Kiran, jet trainer by HAL
HK	Hong Kong; Heckler & Koch (Oberndorf); Hartkern (hard core, tungsten core)
H/K	hunter/killer (submarine)
HK-4	pistol 9mm by HK
HK-11	machine gun 7.62mm by HK
HK-13	self-loading rifle 5.56mm by HK
HK-21	machine gun 7.62mm by HK
HK-23	machine gun 5.56mm by HK
HK-32	assault rifle 7.62mm by HK
HK-33	assault rifle 5.56mm by HK
HK-36	assault rifle 4.6mm by HK
HK-53	machine pistol 5.56mm by HK
HK-69	riot control gun 40mm by HK
HKAAF	Hong Kong Auxiliary Air Force
HKCC	Hong Kong Colonial Cemetery
HKDC	Hong Kong dog company
HKDF	Hong Kong defence force
HKF	hunter killer force
HKG	hunter killer group
HKG-5	Hubschrauberkartengerät by BGT, helicopter mapping equipment
HKGCA	Hong Kong Good Citizen Award
HKGFF	Hong Kong Gurkha field force
HKGSS	Hong Kong Gurkha signal squadron
HKJ	Hashemite Kingdom of Jordan
HKJSPC	Hong Kong Joint Services parachute centre
HKMSC	Hong Kong military service corps
HKNF	Hong Kong naval force
HKO	hunter killer operations
HKPC	Hong Kong provost company RMP
HKR	The Hong Kong Regiment
HKWVF	Hong Kong Women's Volunteer Force
HL	hard labour; House of Lords; honours list; heavy lift (helicopter); hearing level; Hohlladung (hollow centre)
HL-Boot-351	Hohlstablenkboot (remote-controlled minesweeper) (GE)
HL-10	experimental spaceflight aircraft by NASA Northrop
HLAD	high level air defence; hearing look-out assist device
HLAHWG	high-level ad hoc working group (Nato)
HLC	heavy lift cargo (aircraft)
HLCC	high level command and control
Hlds	highlands
HLG	Hawk logistics group
HLH	heavy lift helicopter; high level heating

HLHS	heavy lift helicopter system
HLI	The Highland Light Infantry (the City of Glasgow Regiment)
HLL	high level language (computer)
HLM	Hawk logistics management
HLMR	Hunter-Leggit military reservation (US)
HLO	Helicoptre Légère d'Observation (light observation helicopter)
HLR	high-level run (missile)
HLS	heavy logistics support; heavy lift ship
HLSP	high-level search pattern (interceptors)
HLTC	hard limiting transponder channel
HLU	house logic unit
HLW	higher low water
HLWN	higher low water at neap tides
HLWOC	hard labour without confinement
HM	Her (His) Majesty; Harbour Master
HM-3	submachine gun 9mm by Mendoza
HM-55	AIM-26B, Hughes missile
HM-58	AIM-4D, Hughes missile
HMA	handbook of military artificers
HMAC	His (Her) Majesty's aircraft carrier
HMAF	His (Her) Majesty's Armed Forces
HMAS	His (Her) Majesty's Australian Ship
HMAV	His (Her) Majesty's Army Vessel
HMB	handbook of military bicycles
HMBDV	His (Her) Majesty's boom defence vessel
HMBS	His (Her) Majesty's British Ship
HMC	His (Her) Majesty's Customs; hospital management committee; horizontal motion carriage
HMCIF	His (Her) Majesty's Chief Inspector of Factories
HMCN	His (Her) Majesty's Canadian Navy
HMCS	His (Her) Majesty's Canadian Ship
HMCSC	His (Her) Majesty's Civil Service Commissioner
HMD	His (Her) Majesty's Dockyard; His (Her) Majesty's Destroyer; hydraulic mean depth
hmd	humidity
HMDS	His (Her) Majesty's Diplomatic Service
HMF	His (Her) Majesty's Forces
HMFI	His (Her) Majesty's Factory Inspectorate
HMFSC	His (Her) Majesty's Forces Savings Committee
HMG	His (Her) Majesty's Government; heavy machine gun
HMH	marine heavy helicopter squadron
HMHS	His (Her) Majesty's hospital ship
HMI	His (Her) Majesty's Inspector; handbook of maintenance instructions
HMIS	His (Her) Majesty's Indian Ship;

	His (Her) Majesty's Inspector of Schools
HMIT	His (Her) Majesty's Inspector of Taxes
HMIW	handbook of modern irregular warfare
HML	His (Her) Majesty's Lieutenant
HMLF	His (Her) Majesty's land forces
HMM	Helicoptre Moyen de Manoeuvre (medium manoeuvre helicopter); marine medium helicopter squadron (US)
HMML	His (Her) Majesty's motor launch
HMMMS	His (her) Majesty's motor mine sweeper
HMMS	His (Her) Majesty's mine sweeper
HMNZS	His (Her) Majesty's New Zealand Ship
HMO	Hawk Management Office (Nato)
HMOBC	Hawk Management Office budget committee
HMOCS	His (Her) Majesty's Overseas Civil Service
HMOW	His (Her) Majesty's office of works
HMP	His (Her) Majesty's Prison
HMR	marine helicopter squadron (US)
HMRP	hurricane micro-seismic research platform
HMRT	His (Her) Majesty's rescue tug
HMS	His (Her) Majesty's Service; His (Her) Majesty's Steamer; headquarters and maintenance squadron; helmet mounted symbolic (display) by Marconi-Elliott; hours minutes seconds
HM'sG	His (Her) Majesty's Government
HMSM	His (Her) Majesty's submarine
HMSO	His (Her) Majesty's Stationery Office
HMT	His (Her) Majesty's trawler; His (Her) Majesty's tug; His (Her) Majesty's treasury
HMTM	handbook of mechanical transport maintenance
HMU	Hawk maintenance unit
HMW	height of maxwind
HMWC	XM-966, high mobility weapon carrier
HMX	marine helicopter squadron, octogene (explosive)
HMY	His (Her) Majesty's Yacht
HN	host nation
HNC	higher national certificate
HND	higher national diploma
HNLMS	Her (His) Netherlands Majesty's Ship
HNMS	high Nato military structure
HNS	helicopter, naval by Sikorsky; hyberbolic navigation system
HNS-1	R-4, Hoverfly helicopter, naval by Sikorsky
HNTD	highest non-toxic dose
HO	Home Office; head office; hostilities only (report); holding

HO   operation (command); Hydrographic
            Office of the USN; high order
            (computer language); observation
            helicopter
HO-3S   multi-purpose helicopter by Sikorsky
HO-43   S-55, naval helicopter by Sikorsky
            S   anti-submarine warfare
            G   rescue version
            H-19   USAF designation
HOA   heavy observation aircraft
HOB   height of burst
Hobart project joint tactical communications
                project cancelled (UK)
HoBo   homing bomb
HOBOS   GBU-15, MGB, MGGB, homing bomb
            system by Rockwell
HOBS   high orbital bombardment system
HOC   held on charge, heavy organic chemi-
            cals
HoD   head of department
HOE   homing overlay experiment by Lock-
            heed (for anti-ballistic missile);
            height of eye
HofC   House of Commons
HofK   House of Keys
HofL   House of Lords
HofR   House of Representatives
HOG   height over ground
Hohlstab   HFG-FL, Troika, German remote con-
            trolled mine sweeping system
Hohne box   demoralization machine simulates
            machine gun cracks
HOI   handbook of overhaul instructions
HOJ   home-on jam (missile)
HOK-1   naval helicopter by Kaman
HOL   (common) high order language
            (computers)
HOLWG   high order language working group
            DoD (US)
Home Chain early warning radar WW2 (UK)
HOMP   Halifax ocean meeting point
hon   honorary, honourable
Hond   Honduras
Honest John M-50 surface-to-surface tactical
             missile MGR-1B
Hono   Honolulu Hawaii
HonSec   honorary secretary
HOOP   handbook of operating procedures
HOPE   help organize peace everywhere;
            health opportunity for people
            everywhere
HOR   home of record
hor   horizontal
HORACE H_2O reactor Aldermaston critical
            experiment
horiz   horizontal
Horizon   domestic communications satellite
            (SU)
Hornet   F-18, multi-role combat aircraft by
            McDD; tank destroyer Malkara

            rocket (UK); HJ-1, baby helicopter
            by Hiller
Hornisse   killer tank WW2 (GE)
HORSA   hut operation raising school-leaving
            age
Horsa   WW2 cargo glider by Airspeed
HORSE   hydrofoil operated rocket submarine
HORU   home office research unit
HORV   hydraulic and optical repair vehicle
HOS-1   R-6A, Hoverfly, helicopter, observa-
            tion by Sikorsky
hosp   hospital
HospCo   hospital company
HospRats   hospital rations
HOSS   homing optical systems study
HOT   Haut Subsonique Optiquement Télé-
            guide by Euromissile (high sub-
            sonic speed optically guided anti-
            tank weapon); holographic one-tube
            (night vision goggles) by Hughes;
            Hot Isostatic Pressings Ltd
            (Chesterfield)
HOTAS   hands on throttle and stick (air-
            craft control concept)
HotchKiss   French firm
Hot Dog   infra-red decoy by Buck
Hotspur   cargo glider WW2 (RAF)
Hound Dog   AGM-28A, airborne nuclear stand-
            off missile by Rockwell
hov   hovercraft
Hoverfly   R-4, HNS-1, helicopter, naval by
            Sikorsky
Hoverfly II R-6, HOS-1, helicopter observa-
             tion by Sikorsky
Hovertrain TACV tracked air cushion vehicle
HOVI   handbook of overhaul instructions
HOW   Hercules over water (aircraft)
how   howitzer
HOW-FAR   rockets (Thailand)
How-FI   rockets (Thailand)
HP   half pay; holiday pay; hire purchase;
            high proficiency; Houses of Parlia-
            ment; hollow point (projectile);
            high pressure; high power;
            helicopter (Nato); heating plant;
            hot pressed; horse power;
            horizontal parallax; high preci-
            sion; high performance; high pass
            (filter); heliport; Heerespistole
            (Army pistol); Hirtenberger
            Patronen Zündhütchen & Metallwaren-
            fabrik (Austria); Hewlett Packard
HPA   head of procuring activity;
            He re Probable d'Arrivee (estima-
            ted time of arrival); high power
            amplifier
HPB   harbour patrol boat
HPBT   hollow point boat tail (projectile)
HPBW   half power beam width
HPC   helicopter plane commander,

	Hendon Police College (UK); history of present complaint
HPCbr	high pressure chamber
HPCS	high pressure core spray (system)
HPCyl	high pressure cylinder
HPD	home postal depot; hard point defence; high performance drone; highest posterior density; horizontal polar diagram; anti-tank mine by TRT
HPEW	high power early warning radar
HPF	highest possible frequency
HPHG	high power high gain (amplifier)
HPHGMA	high power high gain microstrip amplifier
HP/Hr	horse power hour
HPI	homing position indicator (radio goniometer); high power illuminator (radar)
HPM	mine countermeasures helicopter (Nato)
HPN	horse power nominal
HPNS	high pressure nervous syndrome
HPOX	high pressure oxygen
HPPP	high priority production programme
HPR	Hungarian People's Republic; high-power radar
HPRP	highpower radar post; high performance reporting post
HPS	highest possible score; helicopter, anti-submarine; hot pressed sheet; high pressure steam; high protein supplement
HPSS	house purchase savings scheme
HPT	high pressure test
HPt	high point
HPTS	high performance third stage (missile) ----Spartan
HPU	hydraulic pumping unit; hydraulic power unit
HPUU	high performance user unit --Navstar
HQ	headquarters
HQASC	headquarters air support command
HQBA	headquarters base area
HQBC	headquarters bomber command (RAF)
HQC	headquarters commandant; headquarters company
HQCC	headquarters coastal command (RAF)
HQCLF	headquarters Cyprus land forces
HQComdt	headquarters commandant
HQComdUSAF	headquarters command (USAF)
HQCS	Heraldic quality control system
HQDP	headquarters department of the Pacific
HQE	high quality environment
HQER	headquarters, engineer resources (Long Marston UK)
HQFC	headquarters fighter command (RAF) now HQSTC
HQGRO	headquarters grave registration office
HQLFHK	headquarters land forces Hong Kong
HQMC	headquarters marine corps
HQNavMatCom	headquarters naval material command
HQ&S	headquarters and service
HQ&Serv	headquarters and service
HQSC	headquarters signals command (UK)
HQServBn	headquarters and service battalion
HQservBnFMF	headquarters and service battalion, fleet marine force Lant Atlantic Pac Pacific
HQServCo	Headquarters and Service Company
HQSqn	headquarters squadron
HQSTC	headquarters strike command (RAF)
HQTC	headquarters transport command (RAF)
HQWesTransAFMATS	headquarters Western transport air force military air transport service
HR	home rule; The Highland Regiment; House of Representatives (US); house record; hospital recruit
HR	heart rates; high reconnaissance (aircraft), 20-30 kms; transportation helicopter (USN)
hr	hussar; hour
H&R	Harrington & Richardson (Worcester USA)
HR-1	Dragonfly, helicopter by Westland
HR-2S	early warning helicopter (USMC) by Sikorsky
HR-14	Sycamore, helicopter by Bristol
HR-6915	The House of Representatives Bill No. 6915 (against firearms in private hands) (US)
HRD	heavy repair detachment
HRDS	handbook on repair to dial sight
HRec	health record
HRFax	high resolution facsimile
HRH	His (Her) Royal Highness
HRF	height ranger finder; high rate of fire
HRMP	home recovery mission profile
HRO	housing referral office(r)
HRP	highway regulating point; holding and reconsignment point; high resolution photometer by Dornier
H&RP	holding and reconsignment point
HRP-1	Rescuer, PV-3, naval helicopter by Piasecki/Vertol
HRPC	high-speed rotating prism camera by Handland
HRPT	high resolution (rate) picture transmission
HRR	higher reduced rate (tax); high repetition rate

HRRAALRF high repetition rate anti-aircraft laser rnagefinder by LM Ericsson
HRS   housing referral service (US)
Hrs   Highlanders
HRS   hydraulics research station; host resident software
hrs   hours
HRS-1   helicopter, rescue by Sikorsky (USMC), S-55 or H-19 USAF designation
HRSCO   housing referral service coordinating office
HRSEM   high resolution scanning electron microscope
HRV   hydraulic repair vehicle
hrzn   horizon
HS   high standard; home service; home secretary; hospital ship; highest score; history sheet; high school (US); high speed; helicopter anti-submarine squadron; Hawker-Siddeley Aviation (Kingston upon Thames UK); Hispano-Suiza; H. Suhner Elektronik GmbH (München)
H&S   headquarters and service
H-S   Hy Score Arms Corporation (US)
HS-30   armoured personnel carrier by Hispano
Hs-117   Schmetterling, anti-aircraft rocket WW2 by Henschel
Hs-122   multi-purpose aircraft WW2 by Henschel
Hs-124   combat aircraft WW2 by Henschel
HS-123   turbofan VIP transport by HS
Hs-125   trainer aircraft WW2 by Henschel
Hs-129   attack bomber with 75mm anti-tank gun
HS-146   transport aircraft by H-S
Hs-293   radio-controlled anti-ship missile WW2 by Henschel
Hs-294   radio-controlled naval anti-surface missile WW2 by Henschel
Hs-298   glide bomb WW2 by Henschel
HS-669   anti-aircraft field mount for Rh-202 gun
HS-748   Coastguarder, Andover, aircraft by H-S
HS-820   automatic gun 20mm by Hispano-Suiza
HSA   health service area; headquarters support activity; Hollandse Signaal Apparaten (Hengelo)
HSAS   headquarters support activity (Saigon)
H-Sat   European regional communications satellite
HSBR   high-speed bombing radar
HSC   health services command (US Army); higher school certificate
HSCP   high-speed card punch
HSCR   high-speed card reader
HSD   Hawker-Siddeley Dynamics (UK);

higher anti-submarine detector (UK); horizontal situation display
HSDE   Hawker Siddeley Dynamics Engineering (Hatfield UK)
HS/DUAV-4 active/passive sonar for helicopters by CIT-Alcatel
HSEP   high-speed explosive Paravane RN towed anti-submarine weapon
HSF   high sea fleet; Hawaiian sea frontier; Hubschrauberflugführung (integrated all-weather helicopter command and control)
HSG   horizontal sweep generator
HSGTC   high speed ground test centre
HSH   His (Her) Serene Highness
HSI   handbook of service instructions; horizontal situation indicator
HS/JC   high school/junior college (graduate training program) (US)
HSL   health service laboratory; high speed launch
HSL-1   anti-submarine helicopter by Bell
HSLA   high strength light alloy
HSM   His (Her) Serene Majesty; hard structure munition (concrete dibber bomb) by McDD + MBB
HSNS   high school news service FHTNC
HSO   headquarters signal officer
HSP   hollow soft point (projectile); heavy stressed platform; high speed printer; high speed photometer by Dornier
HSP-155   howitzer, self-propelled 155mm (Japan)
HSPTP   high speed paper tape punch
HSR   health service region; high speed reader
HSRI   highway safety research institute
HSS   helicopter support ship; high speed
H&SS   headquarters and service squadron
HSS-1   SH-34, Seabat, naval helicopter by Sikorsky
HSS-2   S-61, anti-submarine helicopter by Sikorsky
HSS-28   heavy anti-submarine helicopter by Sikorsky
HSS-831   automatic cannon 30mm by Hispano-Suiza
HSSR   high school seaman recruit
H&SS   headquarters and service squadron
HSST   heavy section steel technology
HST   helicopter support team; highest spring tide; hypersonic transport (aircraft); hypervelocity shock tunnel
HSTCO   high stability temperature compensated crystal oscillator
H&STr   headquarters and service troop
HSTVL   high survivability test vehicle, light by AAI (armoured car for USAF)

HSW	helicopter-borne IR sensor indicating a tank on the ground by Eltro
HT	helicopter training squadron; homing torpedo; homing Terrier (missile); horizontal tab; half track; high tide; horsed transport; heat treated (steel); high tension; high temperature; heavy tank
ht	heat; height
H&T	hardened and tempered
HTA	heavier than air (aircraft)
HTap	heat tap
HTB	high tension battery
HTC	hydrofoil test craft --FRESH
HTD	hand(held) target designator
htd	heated
HTES	high technology ejection seat
HTGCR	high temperature gas-cooled reactor
HTK-1	K-225, helicopter, trainer by Kaman (USN)
HTL	high threshold logic (computers)
HTM	heat transfer medium
HTO	hospital transfer order; highway transportation office
HTOL	horizontal take-off and landing (aircraft)
HTP	hardness test plan
HTPB	hydroxy-terminated-poly-butadiene (rocket propellant)
HTR	highway traffic regulation; high temperature reactor
htr	heater
HTrac	half-track (vehicle)
HTRE	heat transfer reaction experiment
HTS	half time study; high tensile steel
HTSSD	high technology solid state device
HtSup	height supervisor
HTT	heavy tactical transport (aircraft)
HTU	heat transfer unit
HTV	homing test vehicle; hypersonic test vehicle
HTW	high temperature water
HTWS	high tension wireless station
Hubcap	Australian air defence system
HuChwan	class patrol hydrofoils (China)
HuCo	Hughes Corporation
HUCR	highest useful compression ratio
HUD	department of housing and urban development;head-up display
Hudson	patrol bomber WW2 by Lockheed
HUDWAC	head-up display weapon aiming computer by Marconi
Huey Cobra	UH-1, helicopter by Bell
HUF	hamlet upgrading force
Huff-Duff	HF/DF high-frequency direction-finder
Hughes-500D	Defender, TOW-armed helicopter
Hugin	class, fast patrol boats (Sweden)
HUGO	highly unusual geophysical operation
HUK	hunter-killer (submarine)
HUKFor	hunter-killer (submarine) forces Lant Atlantic Pac Pacific
HUKS	hunter-killer submarine
Humber	FV-16000 truck (UK)
HumInt	human intelligence
Hummel	SP howitzer 150mm WW2
HumRRO	human resources research organization
hums	humanitarian reason
Hun	F-100, Super Sabre, fighter aircraft
Hunley	class, USN submarine tenders
Hunt	class, minesweepers (RN)
Hunter	fighter aircraft 1951 by Hawker
Hunter Robot	SA-100, remote control bomb disposal vehicle by SAS
HUP-1	Retriever, naval helicopter by Vertol
hurcn	hurricane
HurrEvac	hurricane evacuation
Hurricane	fighter aircraft WW2 by Hawker
Hurricat	fighter aircraft naval, catapult WW2 by Hawker
HUS-1	UH-34D, helicopter, utility by Sikorsky
Huskey	armoured support and maintenance vehicle by GM of Canada
Husky	H-43, HH-43, helicopter by Kaman
HUSTLE	helium underwater speech translating equipment
Hustler	B-58A, atomic bomber Mach 2 1960 by Convair
HUtRon	helicopter utility squadron
HV	high voltage; hydrographic vessel; high vacuum; high velocity; hyper velocity; hardware virtualizer
H&V	heating and ventilating
hy	heavy
HVAC	heating ventilation and air conditioning; high voltage alternating current
HVACI	high value asset control item
HVAP	hypervelocity armour piercing (shot)
HVAPDS	hypervelocity armour piercing discarding sabot (shot)
HVAPDSFS	hypervelocity armour piercing discarding sabot fin stabilized (shot)
HVAPSS	hypervelocity armour piercing spin stabilized
HVAP-T	hypervelocity armour piercing (shot) with tracer
HVAR	high velocity aircraft rocket
HVAT	high velocity anti-tank (shot)
HvAtkRon	heavy attack squadron
HVC	high velocity clouds

HVD	high velocity detonation; high velocity drop
HVDF	high + very high frequency direction finder
HVDp	heavy drop
HVE	horizontal vertex error
HVG	high velocity gun; high voltage generator
HVI	high value item
HVIS	hypervelocity impact symposium
HVOSM	highway vehicle object simulation model
HvPhotoRon	heavy photographic squadron
HVPS	high voltage power supply
HVRA	heating and ventilating research association
HVSA	high voltage slow activity (fuse)
HVSS	horizontal volute spring suspension
HVTP	high velocity target practice (shot)
HVTP-T	hypervelocity target practice with tracer (shot)
HVTS	hypervelocity technique symposium
hvy	heavy
HW	highway; high water
HWA	helicopter obstacle warning device by Eltro
HWC	hot water circulating
HWCC	Harpoon weapon control console
HWE	home war establishment
HWF&C	high water full and change
HWI	high water interval
HW-K-10	German post-war tank project cancelled, anti-tank/anti-air missile carrier
HW-K-11	APC
HW-K-12	tank hunter 90mm recoilless rifle recce tank
HW-K-14	mortar carrier
HW-K-15	command tank

HW-K-16	ambulance tank
HWL	high water line
HWLB	high water London Bridge
HWM	high water mark
	NT neap tide
	ONT ordinary neap tide
	OST ordinary spring tide
	ST spring tide
HWS	hot water soluble; hurricane warning system
HWT	handbook of weapons training
hwy	highway
HXM	helicopter experimental for the Marines, medium transport and attack helicopter (US)
HY	hydrography STANAG
hy	heavy
HY-30	special submarine steel
Hycatrol	flexible material for fuel tanks by FTF
Hycafloat	floating equipment for tanks by FTF
hyd	hydraulic; hydrographic; hydrostatic
HYDAC	hybrid digital - analog computer
HYDRA	hydrographic digital positioning and depth recording system
Hydrotrack	air-transportable TOW carrier tracked project by IBH
hydt	hydrant
Hyena	mine-protected wheeled counter-insurgency vehicle (South Africa)
HYFIX	signal processing mode
hyg	hygiene
HYLO	hybrid LORAN navigation system
HyRegt	heavy regiment Royal Artillery
HYSTU	hydrofoil special trials unit
HYWEMA	Hydraulische Wekzeuge Maschinenfabrik Solingen
Hz	Hertz

I

I	India; intelligence; inspector; instructor; island; interpreter; independent; inactivated; Irish; Italy; Italian; interceptor; instrument; iodine; incendiary; (airborne) intercept
I-tank	infantry tank
I-16	fighter WW2 (SU) by Polikarpov
IA	instructions for armourers; Indian Army; Italian Army; immediate action (fuse); inspector of armourers; infected area; immediately available; inspection administrative; incorporated account; identical additional (position); indicated altitude; intermediate amplifier
IAA	initial approach area; International Academy of Astronautics
IAAA	integrated advanced avionics for aircraft
IAAC	international agricultural aviation centre
IAACC	inter-allied aeronautical commission of control
IAAE	institution of automotive and aeronautical engineers
IAB	industrial advisory board
IABG	Industrieanlagen Betriebsgesellschaft Ottobrunn
IABSE	international association of bridge and structural engineering
IAC	Irish Air Corps; Inter-Allied Command; initial approach course; integration, assembly and check-out
IACC	inter-agency air cartographic committee
IACCP	inter-American council of commerce and production
IACO	international army control organization
IACOMS	international advisory committee on marine sciences FAO
IACS	International Annealed Copper Standard; ASQ-166, integrated avionics control system (for helicopters) by Grumman
IAD	interception air defence; intermittent arming device; initiation area discriminator; International Astrophysical Decade 1965-75
IADB	Inter-American Defence Board; Inter-American Development Bank
IADC	Inter-American Defence College
IADF	Inter-American Association for Democracy and Freedom
IADPC	inter-agency data processing committee
IADT	initial active duty training; integrated automatic detection and tracking (radar)
IAE	Institute of Army Education (Eltham London); Institute of Automobile Engineers
IAEA	International Atomic Energy Agency (UN Vienna)
IAEC	International Atomic Energy Commission
IAECOSOC	Inter-American Economic and Social Council
IAeE	Institution of Aeronautical Engineers (UK)
IAEE	International Association of Earthquake Engineers
IAEF	intransit aeromedical evacuation facility (US)
IAeS	Institute of Aeronautical Sciences
IAF	Israeli Air Force; Indian Air Force; Italian Air Force; Independent Air Force; Inter-Allied Force; International Astronautics Federation; Informations for the Armed Forces (Office) (US); Indian Auxiliary Force; instrument approach fix; initial approach fix; impact action fuse; interview after flight
IAFB	interim airframe bulletin
IAFF	international airfreight forwarder
IAFV	infantry armoured fighting vehicle

IAG	Industria Armi Galesi (Brescia IT)
IAGC	instantaneous automatic gain control
IAGS	Inter-American Geodetic Survey
IAI	Institute of Atomic Information (for the lay-man); inactive aircraft inventory; Israeli Aircraft Industries (Ben Gurion International Airport)
IAI-201	Arava, light transport aircraft by IAI
IAL	international algebraic language; International Aeradio Ltd (Southall UK)
IALCE	international airlift control element
IAMAP	International Association of Meteorological and Atmospheric Physics
IAMC	Indian Army Medical Corps
IAMSO	Inter-African and Malagesy States Organization
IAMT	Inter-Allied Military Tribunal
IANAP	inter-agency noise-abatement programme
IANC	International Air Navigation Council
IANEC	Inter-American Nuclear Energy Commission
IANF	Inter-Allied Nuclear Force
IAO	Inter-Agency Committee (on Oceanography); information activities office(r)
IAOC	Indian Army Ordnance Corps
IAP	international airport
IAPA	Inter-American Police Academy; Industrial Accident Prevention Association (US)
IAPG	Ibero-Atlantic Planning Guidance (Nato); Inter-agency Advanced Power Group
IAPO	International Association of Physical Oceanography
IAPS	Incorporated Association of Preparatory Schools (UK); International Academy of Political Science
IAR	International Authority of the Ruhr; inventory adjustment report; intersection of air routes; instruction address register
IARA	Inter-Allied Reparation Agency
IARDTS	SYS-CG, integrated automatic radar detection and tracking system by Norden
IARO	Indian Army Reserve of Officers
IAS	Indian Administrative Service; interdepartmental agency support; indirect air support; indicated air speed; Institute of Aeronautical Science; Institute of Aerospace Sciences (US); infantry assault ship; instrument approach system;

	immediate access storage (computer); integrated avionics system; immediate air support
IASA	International Air Safety Association
IASB	International Aircraft Standards Bureau
IASHM	indicated air speed hold mode
IASC	Indian Army Service Corps
IASOR	ice and snow on runway
IAT	indicated air temperature; inside air temperature; international automatic time; Iranian Advanced Technology MBB
IATA	International Air Transport Association, is amended to add
IATCB	Interdepartmental Air Traffic Control Board
IATD	is amended to delete
IATME	International Association of Terrestrial Magnetism and Electricity
IATOD	in addition to other duties
IATR	is amended to read
IAU	Infrastructure Accounting Unit (Nato); International Accounting Unit (currency); interface adaptor unit (radar dataprocessor); International Astronomical Union
IAVC	instantaneous automatic volume control
IAW	in accordance with
IAZ	inner artillery zone
IB	Intelligence Branch; information bureau; instruction book; infantry brigade; inquiry branch; inner belted; ice breaker; incendiary bomb
IBA	International Board of Auditors (Nato)
IBAC	International Bullet and Ammunition Comp
IBB	Ingenieurbüro Bölkow (Stuttgart)
IBCAM	Institute of British Carriage and Automobile Manufacturers
IBCS	integrated battlefield control system
IBD	infantry base depot; International Bureau for Declaration of Death; inhabited building distance
IBDA	indirect bomb damage assessment
IBEN	incendiary bomb with explosive nose
IBERLANT	Iberian Atlantic Area (Nato)
IBH	initial beachhead (US Army)
IbH	Ingenieurbüro Hopp (München)
Ibis	mine-hunting sonar by Thomson-CSF
IBHd	initial beachhead
IBM	intercontinental ballistic missile; International Business Machine Corp.
IBP	international balance of payments; initial boiling point

IBRD   International Bank for Reconstruction and Development (UN Washington)
IBRL   initial bomb release line
IBS   Iceland Base Station (USN)
IBWM   International Bureau of Weights and Measures
IC   in charge (of); in command; individual counsel; Iceland (Nato); information centre; identity card; intermediate course; Imperial College (of Science and Technology London); intelligence corps; independent company; internment camp; intelligence committee; interceptor (aircraft); improved choke (barrel); input circuit; instrument correction; internal connection; internal conversion; internal combustion (engine); interior communications; ice crystals (weather); inspected condemned; index correction; integrated circuit; internal combustion
I/C   in charge of
I-C   Indo-China
I&C   installation and check-out (spares)
2IC   second in command
ICA   International Cooperative Alliance; ignition control additive (tricresyl phosphate); initial cruise altitude; International Cartographic Association; International Communications Association
ICAF   Industrial College of the Armed Forces; International Committee on Aeronautical Fatigue
ICAMRS International Civil Aviation Message Routing System
ICAN   International Commission for Air Navigation
ICAO   International Civil Aviation Organization (UN Montreal)
ICap   increased capability (Prowler aircraft EA-6 by Grumman)
ICAR   integrated command accounting and reporting
ICAS   International Council for Aerospace Sciences (UK); Interdepartmental Committee for Aerospace Sciences (US)
I-CAS independent collision avoidance system
ICB   International Container Bureau; international competitive bid (Nato); interior control board
ICBM   intercontinental ballistic missile 3000 m-8000 nm
ICC   information coordination centre; Interstate Commerce Commission; inventory control centre; intermediate cryptoanalysis course; International Control Commission; International Chamber of Commerce; integrated crystal circuit; internal conversion coefficients; International Computation Centre (Rome); intercept controller coordinator
ICCA   initial cash clothing allowance
ICCAIA International Coordinating Council of Aerospace Industries Association
ICCB   intermediate configuration control board
ICCC   Inter-Council Coordinating Committee
ICCJ   International Committee for the Cooperation of Journalists
ICCP   intelligence civilian career programme; Institute for Certification of Computer Professionals
ICCS   International Commission for Control and Supervision; integrated carrier catapult station; integrated cataput control system
ICCTM Interstate Commerce Commission Transport Mobilization
ICD   information control division; initiative communication deception; industrial cooperation division; inventory control department; Institute of Civil Defence
ICDM   International Consortium of Defence Magazines (Interconair UK, Hamilton Burr Calif., Editora Aero Brazil, Comilit Press Hong Kong)
ICDO   International Civil Defence Organization
ICDP   International Confederation for Disarmament and Peace
icdt   incident
Ice   Iceland
ICE   internal combustion engine; increased combat effectiveness; Institution of Civil Engineers (UK)
IceDeFor Iceland Defence Force
ICEM   Intergovernmental Committee for European Migration; inverted coaxial magnetron
ICES   International Council for Exploration of the Sea; integrated civil engineering system
ICEWG Interim Communications and Electronics Working Group
ICF   installation confinement facility; intelligence contingency funds; International Contract Furnishing Inc.

ICFC	Industrial and Commercial Finance Corp.
ICFPW	International Confederation of Former Prisoners of War
ICG	Interviewer's Classification Guide; interactive computer graphics
icg	icing
IcgIC	icing in clouds
IcgICIP	icing in clouds in precipitation
IcgIP	icing in precipitation
ICHCA	International Cargo Handling Co-ordination Association
ICI	International Commission on Illumination; Imperial Chemical Industries
ICIASF	integrated circuit instrumentation in aerospace simulation facilities
ICIE	International Council of Industrial Editors
ICIP	International Conference on Information Processing
ICIR	in commission, in reserve (vessel) (USN)
ICIREPAT	International Cooperation in Information Retrieval among Patent Offices
ICIS	Interdepartmental Commission on Internal Security
ICJ	International Court of Justice (UN The Hague)
ICL	International Computers Ltd (Westinghouse + Sintra + HSA); index contour line; intermediate contour line
ICM	improved capabilities missile; improved conventional munitions; inverted coaxial magnetron; integral charge-control model
ICMA	initial clothing monetary allowance
ICNS	integrated communications navigation system RPV TV sensor
ICO	in case of; inter-governmental committee on oceanography
ICOC	instructions for commodores of convoys
ICODS	instructions to cryptographic officers custodians and distribution sections (of Allied Command Europe) (Nato)
ICOMP	Iceland ocean meeting point
ICOR	Inter-governmental Conference on oceanic research
ICP	intelligence collecting plan; integrated circuit package; instrument calibration procedures; indicator control panel; interconnected processing; inventory control point; international civilian personnel (with Nato)

ICPE	inventory control point Europe
ICPO	Interpol, International Criminal Police Organization
ICPOA	intelligence centre Pacific ocean area
ICPP	interactive computerized presentation panel
ICPR	industrial cost and performance report
ICR	initial contact report; infantry company radar (portable)
I&CRB	investigation and censure review branch BUPERS
CIRC	International Committee of the Red Cross
ICRL	individual component repair list
ICRP	International Commission on Radiological Protection
IC&RR	inventory control and requirements review (branch) CNO
ICRU	International Commission on Radiological Units and Measurements
ICS	international code of signals; information control system; inter-agency communications system; Indian Civil Service; Imperial College of Science and Technology (London); intercommunications system; input control system; integrated communications system by MCSDS; Integrated Computer Systems (Brussels, Los Angeles)
ICSC	Interim Communications Satellite Committee
ICSE	intermediate current stability experiment
ICSLS	international convention for saving of life at sea
ICSMP	international continuous systems modelling programme
ICSP	Integrated Computer Systems (Pebblecombe/Tadworth Surrey)
ICST	Imperial College of Science and Technology (London)
ICSU	International Council of Scientific Unions
ICT	Imperial College of Technology (London); inter-active control table; international call for tenders; International Computers and Tabulators (ICL)
ICTC	infantry clerks' training centre
ICTOC	independent corps tactical operations centre
ICTP	international centre for theoretical physics; intensified combat training programme
ICTT	intensified confirmatory troop test
ICU	information control unit; international code use

ICV	infantry combat vehicle
ICVA	International Council of Volunteer Agencies
ICW	in connection with; interrupted continuous wave (radar)
ICWA	Indian Council of World Affairs
ICWAR	improved continuous wave acquisition (radar)
ICX	inter-command exercise
ID	infantry division; infantry depot; intelligence department; immigration department; intelligence duties; information department; inner diameter; inner dimension; induced draught; identification; indicator
IDA	Institute for Defense Analysis (Washington); integrated digital avionics; indirect damage assessment; International Development Association (UN Washington)
IDAC	inter-connecting digital analog converter
IDAD	internal defence and development
IDAF	International Defence and Aid Fund (South Africa)
IDB	intelligence data base; Infantry Demonstration Battalion (Warminster)
IDC	Imperial Defence College (London); Indian Defence College (Quetta); Imperial Defence Committee; item detail card; individual defence counsel; information design change; inter-departmental committee
IDCAS	Industrial Development Centre for Arab States
IDCS	integrated data coding system
IDCSP	initial defence communications satellite programme
IDCSS	initial defence communications satellite system
IDD	inter-director designation
IDDD	international direct distance dialing
IDE	interim data element; inter-service data exchange
idef	indefinite
ident	identity; identify; identification
IDEP	inter-service data exchange programme
IDF	Israeli Defence Forces; interceptor day fighter (aircraft); intermediate distribution frame
IDF/AF	Israeli Defence Force/Air Force
IdFor	idle waiting convoy forward
IDG	inspector of degaussing; integrated drive generator; Innerdeutsche Grenze (inter-German border)
IdHom	idle waiting convoy homeward
IDHS	intelligence data handling systems
IDI	Israeli Defence Industries
IDIIOM	information display incorporation input output machine
IDIOI	Industrial Development and Innovation Organization of Iran
IDIOT	instrumentation digital on-line transcriber
IDL	international date line
IDLt	identification light
IDM	integral and differential monitoring
IdNo	identification number
IDOE	International Decade of Ocean Exploration 1970-80
IDP	initial delay position; international driving permit; integrated data processing
IDPC	integrated data processing centre
IDQA	individual document quality assurance
IDR	infantry drill regulations; imagery data recording
IDS	infra-red discrimination system; intelligence data system; interdictor/strike (aircraft); instrument development section; integrated data storage; interim decay storage; integrated dynamic system (helicopters); ionisation detector system (gas analyser) by Honeywell
IDSCS	initial defence satellite communications system
IDSM	Indian Distinguished Service Medal
IDSOT	interim daily system operational test
IDT	inactive duty training; industrial design technology; inter-active display terminal by Litton
IDTC	indefinite delivery type contract
IDW	Institut für Dokumentationswesen (Institute for Documentation)
IE	Indo-European; in excess; industrial engineer; Member of the Order of the Indian Empire; installation equipment; initial equipment; index error
I&E	information and education
IEA	International Energy Agency
IEC	Imperial Economic Committee --CEC; International Electrotechnical Commission; Interstate Electronics Corporation (US)
IECG	interagency emergency coordination group
IED	improvised explosive device (UK) (terrorist bomb)
IEE	Institution of Electrical Engineers; Institute of Electronic Engineering
IEEE	Institute of Electrical and Electronics Engineers (New York), --AIEE --IRE

IEEPA	international emergency economic powers act (for the US President) 1977
IEF	Indian Expeditionary Forces
IEG	information exchange group
IEI	indeterminate engineering items
IEIS	integrated engine instrument system
IEL	information exchange list
IEM	Impulsion Electromagnetique (electromagnetic pulse)
IEME	Inspectorate of Electrical and Mechanical Engineers
IEMS	initial entry into military service
IEN	Imperial Ethiopian Navy
IEP	instrument for evaluation of photos; information exchange project
IEPB	interagency emergency planning board
IEPC	interagency emergency planning commission
IEPG	Independent European Programme Group (Nato)
IER	industrial equipment reserve; individual education record
IERE	Institution of Electronic and Radio Engineers
IES	international explorers society; internal environment simulator
IET	initial engine test
IETC	interagency emergency transportation committee
IF	The Royal Inniskilling Fusiliers; insular force; intermediate fix; intermediate frequencies; ice fog; intermittent frequency; information feedback
IFA	International Federation of Air-worthiness
IFAB	integrated fire-control for Artillery Battery (GE)
IFAC	International Federation for Automatic Control
IFALPA	International Federation of Air Line Pilots' Associations
IFARS	individual flight activity reporting system
IFATCA	International Federation of Air Traffic Control Associations
IFB	invitation for bid
IFBh	intermediate force beach-head
IFC	instructor of fire control; International Financial Cooperation (UN Washington); International Finance Corporation; integrated fire control (radar); independent fire control (area)
IFCS	integrated fire control system by Marconi
IFD	inter-fighter director; initial fill date
IFF	identification friend or foe

IFF-880	anti-aircraft artillery IFF system by Cossor
IFF-3500	air-to-air IFF system by Cossor
IFFPI	identification friend or foe personal identifier
IFF/SIF	identification friend or foe selective identification feature
IFI	in-flight insertion
I-file	interface file
IFIP	International Federation for Information Processing
IFIS	instrument flight instructors school; independent flight inspection system by Eltro
IFL	initial flight level; international frequency list
IFM	instantaneous frequency measurement; International Fluggeräte & -Motoren GmbH (Weinheim)
IF/MF	intermediate frequency/medium frequency
IFMIS	integrated facilities management informations system
IFMS	integrated financial management system
IFPA	Institute for Foreign Policy Analysis (UK)
IFPM	in-flight performance monitor
IFR	instrument flight rules; in-flight refuelling
IFRB	International Frequency Registration Board
IFReq	industrial forecast requirements
IFS	Irish Free State; integrated facilities system; inshore fire support ship (USN); interchange file separator
IFSS	international flight service station
IFT	intermediate frequency transformer
IFTACCA	intermediate frequency time averaged clutter coherent airborne radar
IFTAD	initial and final terminal arrival date
IFTRS	individual flying time report system
IFTU	intensive flying trials unit (Yeovilton RAF)
IFTUs	inhabitants friendly to us or US
IFU	intelligence field unit
IFV	inspectorate of fighting vehicles; infantry fighting vehicle
IFV/CFV	infantry fighting vehicle/cavalry fighting vehicle (M113 replacement)
IG	The Irish Guards; instructor of gunnery (RA); inspector general; inner guard; inertial guidance; Imperial gallon
IG-42	Infanteriegeschütz 1942 (GE) (7.5cm infantry gun)

IGC	inspector general of communications	IHO	International Hydrographic Organization
IGCR	Inter-governmental Committee on Refugees	IHP	indicated horse powers
IGD	inspector general's department (US Army)	IHSBR	improved high-speed bombing radar
IGds	The Irish Guards	IHTU	interservice hovercraft trials unit
IGE	in ground effect	IHU	interservice hovercraft unit
IGESUCO	infrastructure ground environment sub-committee (Nato)	IHX	intermediate heat exchanger
IGF	inspector general of fortifications	II	initial issue; image intensifier; item identification; imagery interpretation
IGFET	insulated gate field effect transistors	I/I	item identification
IGFVP	interservice group for flight vehicle power	I&I	inventory and inspection (report)
IGIA	interagency group for international aviation	IIA	igniter incendiary airdropped WW2 (RAF)
Igloo White	land acoustic sensors by Sperry --QU-22	IIAF	Imperial Iranian Air Force
		IIASA	International Institute of Advanced Systems Analysis (Vienna)
IGM	inter-galactic medium	IID	intermittently integrated doppler (radar)
ign	ignition		
IGO	inspecting general officer; Inter-governmental Organization	II/DAOPS	image intensifier/daylight aiming and observation periscopic system by Philips
IGOR	intercept ground optical recorder (NASA); injection gas oil ratio	IIET	inspection instructions for electron tubes
IGOR-TT	intercept ground optical recorder tracking telescope (NASA)	IIFV	improved infantry fighting vehicle (XM-723 + Chain Gun)
IGOSS	integrated global ocean station system	IIGF	Imperial Iranian Ground Forces
IGS	Imperial General Staff; independent grammar school (UK); information generator system; integrated graphic system; interchange group separator	IIM	India Independence Medal
		IIMC	International Instrumentation Marketing Company Ltd
		IIMS	intensive item management system
		IIN	Imperial Iranian Navy
IGSC	inspector general, supply corps	IIP	instantaneous impact point; International Institute of Peace
IGSM	Indian General Service Medal	IIR	imaging infra-red (sight)
IGT	inspector general of transportation; inspector general to the forces for training	IIRC	interrogation and information reception circuits
		IIRD	international and independent research and development
IGTAVR	inspector general of the territorial army and volunteer reserve	IIRS	imaging infra-red seeker; Institute for Industrial Research Standards (Eire)
Iguane	airborne long-range maritime ASW surveillance radar by Thomson-CSF	IISL	International Institute for Space Law
IGY	International Geophysical Year 1957-8	IISLS	improved interrogator side-lobe suppression
IH	initial heading; interaction handler	IISS	International Institute for Strategic Studies (London)
IHA	interim housing allowance		
IHAS	integrated helicopter avionics system	IIT	Indian Institute of Technology; Israel Institute of Technology
I-Hawk	improved Hawk (missile) (Nato)	IITEC	interservice/industry training equipment conference (USN)
IHB	International Hydrographic Bureau (Monaco)	IITV	image-intensified television
IHC	International Harvester Corp (US)	IJ	Iver Johnson Arms and Cycle Works (Fitchbury US)
IHCA	in hand of civil authorities		
IHD	International Hydrological Decade 1965-74	IJA	Imperial Japanese Army
		IJBS	integrated joint broadband system
IHDS	integrated helmet display system	IJC	International Judiciary Committee
IHI	Ishikawajima-Harima (heavy industries)	IJCS	integrated joint communications system
IHIA	include this headquarters information address		

IJD	international job description
IJLB	infantry junior leaders' battalion (UK)
IJLR	infantry junior leaders' regiment
Ikara	Australian air-to-submarine missile RPV drops ASW homing torpedo
IKL	Ingenieurkontor Lübeck (GE)
IKV-91	Infanterikanonvagn (destroyer tank) by Hägglund & Söner
IL	infantry of the line; Iceland; international logistics; inside lubricated; indication lamp; instrument landing
Il-2	Schtormovik (attack bomber) WW2 by *Ilyushin (SU)*
Il-4	twin-engined bomber WW2 (SU)
Il-12	Coach, transport aircraft
Il-14	Crate, twin-engined tactical transport
Il-18	4-engined long-range transport
Il-28	Beagle, Mascot, jet aircraft
	R recce
	T torpedo bomber
	U trainer
Il-38	May, seaplane maritime recce ASW
Il-62	Classic, long-range transport
Il-68	4-engined transport aircraft by *Ilyushin (SU)*
Il-76	Candid, long-range cargo/tanker aircraft
Il-86	high-capacity aircraft
ILA	instrument landing aid, instrument landing approach
ILAAS	integrated light attack avionics system
ILC	international logistics centre; instruction length counter
ILCEP	interlaboratory committee on editing and publishing (US)
	E East Coast
	W West Coast
ILCOP	international liaison committee of organizations of peace
ILDTF	item logistics data transmission form
ILF	integrated lift fan
ILFO	international logistics field office
ILIMS	integrated logistics information and management system
Ill	illumination (shell); illustration
illum	illumination (shell)
Illustrious	class, aircraft carriers WW2
ILMIS	integrated logistic management and information system
ILMP	integrated logistics management plan
ILO	intelligence liaison officer; in lieu of; International Labour Organization (UN Geneva); International Labour Office; injection locked oscillators
ILOUE	in lieu of until exhausted

ILP	international logistics programme
ILS	instrument landing system; integrated logistic support; international logistic support
ILSCB	improved launcher section control box for Hawk
ILS-LOC	instrument landing system localizer
ILSP	integrated logistics support plan
Iltis	jeep by VW; class, light torpedo boats (EG)
ILTS	international logistic transport service
ILW	international low water
IM	intramural; inventory manager; instrument mechanic; instrument man; intermodulation; inner marker (beacon); image intensifying (apparatus); intensity measuring (device); interceptor missile (long-range); impulse modulation; intermediate modulation; item mark
I&M	improvement and modernization (programme); inspection and maintenance
IMA	intermediate maintenance activity; Indian Military Academy
IMAAWS	infantry man-portable anti-armour/assault weapon system
IMACON	image intensifier camera by Handland
IMAK	Interministerieller Ausschuss für die einheitliche Materialkatalogisierung in der Bundesverwaltung (Interministerial Committee for Uniform Material Cataloguing in the Federal Administration)
IMAS	International Marine and Shipping (Conference)
IMB	independent maintenance battery; independent mortar battery
IMC	International Maritime Committee; International Meteorological Committee; item management coding; item master card; international manpower ceiling (Nato); intensity mine circuit; image movement compensation (aerial photography); instrument meteorological conditions
IMCC	integrated mission control centre; item management control code
IMCCB	International Mine Clearance Control Board (London) (after WW2)
IMCO	Inter-governmental Maritime Consultative Organization (UN London)
IMCOS	international meteorological consultative service
IMD	Indian Medical Department; intermodulation distortion

IMDC	internal message distribution centre
imdt	intermediate
IME	international material evaluation; international magnetosphere explorer; Institution of Mechanical Engineers
IMechE	Institution of Mechanical Engineers
IMET	international military education and training
IMETP	international military education and training programme
IMF	International Monetary Fund (UN Washington)
img	immigration
IMHE	industrial materials handling equipment
IMI	improved manner interceptor (aircraft) (US programme); Israeli Military Industries (Tel Aviv); Imperial Metal Industries Ltd
IMIP	industrial management improvement programme
IMM	integrated material management; integrated maintenance management; international mercantile marine
imm	immune
IMMAC	inventory management and material control applied system (computers)
immed	immediate
IMMP	integrated maintenance management programme
IMMTS	Indian Mercantile Marine Training Ship
IMNS	Imperial Military Nursing Service
IMO	International Meteorological Organization; International (raw) Materials Organization
IMP	initial military programme; integrating motor pneumotachograph; improved manoeuverability package (for drones); integrated maintenance programme; inflatable micrometeroid paraglide; interactive microprogrammable control/display by Litton; interplanetary monitoring platform; industrial mobilization programme; interface message processor; international military personnel; portable mine-detector (SU)
Imp	Imperial
IMPACT	implementation planning and control technique; improved management procurement and contracting technique (US)
Impact	training system for manually controlled missiles by Ferranti
IMPATT	impact avalanche transit time
impreg	impregnate
IMPS	interplanetary measuring probes
impt HL	imprisonment with hard labour
IMR	improved military rifle; individual medical record; immediate mission request; engineer tank T-54 hull (SU)
IMRAN	international marine radio aids to navigation
IMRAP	infra-red mono-chromatic radiation pyrometer
IMRC	International Marine Radio Company (London)
ImRep	immediate report
IMRL	individual material readiness list
IMS	International Military Staff (Nato); Indian Medical Service; industrial manpower section; information management system; industrial methylated spirit; inshore minesweeper (RN); international magnetospheric study; inertial measurement system by Ferranti; International Military Services (UK) (commercial MoD arms trade)
IMSC	International Military Standardization Council (Nato)
IMSCOM	International Military Staff Communication (to commands, staffs, offices and agencies outside IMS) (Nato)
IMSM	Indian Meritorious Service Medal, International Military Staff Memorandum (to commands, staffs, offices and agencies outside IMS) (Nato)
IMSO	initial material support office
IMSUM	International Military Staff Summary (for internal IMS use)
IMSWM	International Military Staff Working Memorandum (to the members of the Military Committee for comment, approval and future discussion) (Nato)
IMT	International Military Tribunal
imt	immediate
IMTD	inspectors of the military training directorate
IMTNE	international meteorological teletype netowrk Europe
IMTP	industrial mobilization training programme
IMU	inertial measurement unit
IMUA	interservice material utilization agency
IMVC	Interstate Motor Vehicle Company (Pretoria South Africa)
IN	Indian Navy; Italian Navy; internal note; infantry aptitude area
In	interpreter; inside (lubricated)
I&N	immigration and naturalization service

INA	inspector of naval aircraft; Indian National Army; initial approach; Integrierte Navigations Anlage für Fregatten by Teldix (integrated navigation system for frigates) (FGN)
INAA	instrumental neutron activation analysis
INA	Industria Nacional de Armes (Brazil)
inact	inactive; inactivation
InactFlt	inactive fleet
	Lant Atlantic
	Pac Pacific
INA/	inactive vessel (USN)
	IC in commission in reserve
	IS in service in reserve
	OC out of commission in reserve
	OS out of service in reserve
INAS	inertial navigation and attack system (airborne) by Ferranti; industrial naval air station
INBBL	International Navy Beam Ball League
InC	instructor captain; instrumental (meteorological) conditions
INC	item name code
inc-bomb	incendiary bomb
IncAir	including air (transportation)
incd	incendiary
incep	interceptor
InCiv	innocent civilian
incl	included
INCO-718	turbine components alloy
INCONEL-625	high-strength alloy
INCOS	integrated control system
InCr	instructor commander
Ind	Indian; independent; industry; index
InD	interceptor director (aircraft)
IND-451	airborne DME equipment by Collins
indc	indicated
INDEC	inter-departmental committee; independent nuclear disarmament election committee
indef	indefinite
IndElSec	industrial electronic security
indep	independent
Independencia	class, patrol boats guided missiles by Vosper-Thornycroft
Indigo	anti-aircraft missile system by SISTEL
IndMan	industrial manager
IndMgr	industrial manager
INDOR	internuclear double resonance
INDRB	inactive non-disability retirement branch BUPERS
IndT	Indian Territory
induc	induction
INEA	International Electronics Association
INEWS	integrated naval electronic warfare system by General Instruments

INF	interceptor night fighter (aircraft); international nuclear forces (Nato); infantry; information; in following
INFANT	Iroquois night fighter and night tracker (helicopter borne LLTV by Hughes)
INFCE	international nuclear fuel circulation evaluation
infl	inflammable; inflatable; inflated
info	information; for the information of
InfoCen	information centre
InfoReq	information is requested on ...
Infoscan	passive infra-red alarm system for perimeter outdoor surveillance
Infra	infrastructure
ING	inactive national guard
INO	international non-governmental organization
Ingram	machine pistol by Ingram (UK)
INH	improved Nike Hercules (missile)
INIS	international nuclear information system
init	initial, initiate
InitCCA	initial cash clothing allowance
InitCCCA	initial civilian cash clothing allowance
InitUnifAlw	initial uniform allowance
inj	injured
InjFacs	injection facilities
InL	instructor lieutenant
INLAW	infantry laser weapon; infantry light anti-tank weapon
In-lb	inch-pounds
InLCr	instructor lieutenant commander
INLR	item no longer required
INM	inspector of naval material; inspector of naval machinery
INWARSAT	international maritime (telecommunications) satellite (US + Europe)
INO	issue necessary orders; inspectorate of naval ordnance
inoc	inoculation
INOC	inter-governmental oceanographic omission
inop	inoperative
INP	if not possible
InRepl	incoming replacement
InReqs	information requests
INS	Institute of Naval Studies; infantry night sight; inertial navigation system
ins	insulated; inches
INS	immediate nuclear support; Irish Naval Service; international news service; Indian Naval Ship
ins	inspect(ion); inspector; insular; insurance
InsAir	inspector of (naval) aircraft

Insat   Indian national satellite (communi-
         cations + meteorological) by Ford
INSAV   interim shipboard availability
INSCAIRS instrument calibration and inci-
         dent repair service
InsCruit inspector of (naval) recruiting
         and induction (US)
INSDOC   Indian National Scientific Documen-
         tation Centre
InSec   internal security
in/sec   inches per second
InsEng   inspector of (naval) engineering
         (US)
insgcy   insurgency
InsGen   inspector general
Inshore Pat inshore patrol
InshorUnSeaWar inshore undersea warfare
              Div   division
              Gru   group
              SurvU surveillance unit
InsSL   instructor sub-lieutenant
InsMach inspector of (naval) machinery
InsMat   inspector of (naval) material
InsMatPet inspector of (naval) material
         and petroleum products
InsNavMat inspector of navigational
         material
insol   insoluble
InsOrd   inspector of (naval) ordnance
insp   inspector; inspection
InsPat   inshore patrol
INSPEC   informations services in physics
         electrotechnology computers and
         control of the institution of
         electrical engineers
InspecGen inspector general
InsPetRes inspector of petroleum reserves
InspGen inspector general
Insp/Inst inspector/instructor
inst   instant; instrument; instructor;
         installation
Inst   Institution of
         CE   Civil Engineers
         D   Directors
         EE   Electrical Engineers
         F   Fuel
         GasE   Gas Engineers
         HE   Highway Engineers
         ME   Machine Engineers
         MM   Mining and Metallurgy
         P   Physics
         Pckg   Packing
         Pet   Petroleum
         PI   Patents and Innovations
         R   Refrigeration
         W   Welding
         WE   Water Engineers
INSTAB   information service on toxicity and
         biodegradability
InstiLux Institute Luxembourg EuroControl
         air traffic control simulator

instl   installation
instn   instruction
instr   instrument(al); instruc(ed);
         instructor
InstRate instrument rating
insuf   insufficient
insur   insurance
InSurv   inspection and survey
int   intelligence; international;
         interest; interned; interceptor;
         intermediate; interpreter;
         interior; internal; interjection;
         interval; interchangeable; inter-
         cept(ion)
INT   Intelligence procedures STANAG
INTAC   intercept tracking and control
         (group)
INTACS   integrated tactical communications
         system (US Army)
INTASGRU inter-allied tactical study group
intcl   inter-coastal
IntCo   international code of signals
IntComb internal combustion (engine)
IntCorps intelligence corps
intcp   intercept
IntDiv   intelligence division
intel   intelligence
IntelCen intelligence centre
IntelO   intelligence officer
IntElPost international electronic postal
         service
InTelSat international telecommunications
         satellite (consortium 80 nations)
Intelsat I...V geo-stationary telecommuni-
         cations satellite by Ford
intens   intensive
inter   intermediate
INTERALIS international advanced life
         information system
InterCom intercommunication
Interkosmos Skean, satellite transport
         missile (SU)
interm   intermediate
IntermSta intermediate station
interp   interpretation
InterPol International Criminal Police
         Organization
InterpRon interpretation squadron
intg   interrogation
INTIPS   integrated information processing
         system
intl   international
intmed   intermediate
IntO   intelligence officer
intrd   interned
IntRep   intelligence report
Intrepida class, fast torpedo boats by
         Lürssen
intrmt   internment
introd   introduction

Intruder   A-6, KA-6, EA-6, carrier-based
            aircraft by Grumman,
            bomber, tanker, AEW
IntSecGS intelligence section, general staff
IntSum   intelligence summary
intxn   intersection
INU   inertial navigation unit
INucE   Institution of Nuclear Engineers
InUS   inside the (continental) USA
inv   inverted, invoice, inventory
Invader   A-26, attack bomber by Douglas
Invar   invariable expansion Ni-Fe alloy
inves   investigation, investigator
Invincible class, anti-submarine cruisers
            (RN)
InvolEx   involuntary extension
IO   intelligence officer; information
          officer; inspecting officer;
          intercept officer; investigating
          officer; issuing office, inventory
          objective; inspection order; Indian
          Office; independent operators;
          inverse osmosis (pure water from
          sea water)
I/O   inspecting order; input - output
IOB   installation operating budget;
          information officer basic (course)
IOBC   Indian Ocean Biological Centre
          (India)
IOBS   input - output buffering system
IOC   initial operational capability (R&D)
          interim operational capability;
          indirect operating costs; input-
          output controller; Intergovernmen-
          tal Oceanographic Commission
IOCA   International Organization for
          Civil Aviation
IOCD   initial operational capability date
IOCE   input - output control element
IOCS   input - output control system; inter-
          office comment sheet
IODE   Imperial Order of the Daughters of
          the Empire (Canada)
IOF   Institute of Fuel; Indian Ordnance
          Factory (Jabalpur) (vehicles)
IofA   inspector of artillery; instructor
          of artillery
IofM   inspector of musketry; Isle of Man
IofPATA   inspector of physical and adventu-
          rous training, Army
IofR   inspector of recruiting
IofW   Isle of Wight
IOH   item on hand
IOIC   integrated operational intelligence
          centre
IOIS   integrated operational intelligence
          system
IOJ   International Organization of
          Journalists
IOL   initial outfitting list

IOLS   input - output label system
IOM   Indian Order of Merit; Isle of Man;
          inert operational missile;
          institute of office management .
IOMMP   International Organization of
          Masters, Mates and Pilots
ION   institute of navigation
IOO   inspecting ordnance officer
IOOP   input - output operation
IOP   input - output processor;
          installation operating programme
IOR   issue on request; issue on requisi-
          tion; immediate operational
          readiness
IORA   intelligence officer, Royal
          Artillery
IORB   input/output record block
IOReq   input/output request
IOS   International Organization for
          Standardization
IOSA   integrated optic spectrum analyser
          (wafer) by Hughes
IOT   institute of transport
IOTA   institute of traffic administration;
          inbound/outbound traffic analysis
IOT&E   initial operational test and
          evaluation
IOU   input/output unit; industrial
          operation unit
IOVST   International Organization for
          Vacuum Science and Technology
IOW   Isle of Wight
IP   instructor pilot; in active pay;
          intelligence police; issuing
          point; implementation of plan;
          initial point; identification
          point; initial phase; input
          primary; instalment plan; impact
          point; imaginary part; identifica-
          tion of position; indicator
          (cathode ray type)
IP-2   directorate of military personnel
IPA   indicated pressure altitude;
          initiation of procurement action;
          iso-propyl alcohol
IPAD   integrated programme for aerospace
          vehicle design
IPARS   international programmed airline
          reservation system by IBM
IPAT   inspector of physical and adventu-
          rous training (UK)
IPB   installation property book;
          illustrated parts breakdown
IPBM   inter-planetary ballistic missile
IPC   independent parachute company;
          industrial planning committee
          (Nato); Icelandic prime contractor;
          intermittent positive control (air-
          craft ground control)
IPCE   independent parametric cost estimate

IPCo   Industrial Products Company
IPCP   improved platoon command post
IPD   individual package delivery;
        issue priority designator
IPDMS   Sea Sparrow, RIM-7H, improved point
        defence missile system
IPD/TAS improved point defence target
        acquisition system (radar + IR
        sensors)
IPE   industrial production equipment
IPER   industrial production equipment
        reserve
IPF   international peace force; initial
        production facilities; indicative
        planning figures
IPG   international planning group (BE-
        GE-NL), international payments
        group
IPH   impressions per hour
IPIR   initial photo interpretation report
IPL   information processing language;
        initial programme load; interim
        parts list; illustrated parts list
IPM   industrial preparedness measures;
        input position map; inches per
        minute
IPMS   international polar motion service
IPN   initial priority number
IPNL   integrated perceived noisiness level
IPP   industrial preparedness programme
IPPC   infrastructure payments and progress
        committee (Nato)
IPQC   in-process quality control
IPR   inter-departmental procurement
        request; individual pay record;
        in-process review; intelligence
        production requirement; institute
        for public relations; institute
        for Pacific relations
IPRB   inter-allied post-war requirements
        bureau
IPS   intercept pilot simulator; inter-
        planetary propulsion system;
        inches per second; interpretative
        programming system; impact polysty-
        rene; independent parachute squad-
        ron (airborne sappers) (RE);
        independent public school (UK);
        Indian police service; initial
        path sweeping
IPSRE   independent parachute squadron
        (Royal Engineers)
IPT   initial production test; inter-
        national planning team; inter-
        national programmes and technology
IPTM   interval pulse time modulation
IPTS   international practical temperature
        scale
IPU   input preparation unit (computer);
        instruction processing unit

ipv   improve
IPW   interrogation, prisoners of war
IPY-43 portable laser illuminator (FR)
IQ   intelligence quotient
IQO   initial quality order; initial
        quantity order
IQSY   international quiet solar year 1965
IR   Ireland; internal review; informa-
        tion report; inspection report;
        infra-red; instrument reading;
        incident rate; interval rate;
        intermediate range (missile);
        ice on runway; index register;
        isoprene rubber; inside radius;
        information retrieval; intermed-
        iate register; illuminator radar;
        interrogator responder
IR-18   Surfire, infra-red fire-control and
        surveillance system, naval by Barr
        & Stroud
IRA   Irish Republican Army; intelligence-
        related activities
IRAA&A increase and replacement of armour
        armament and ammunition
IRAC   interdepartmental radio advisory
        committee
IRAH   infra-red alternate head (Side-
        winder)
IRAM-D improved reliability and maintenance
        development
IRAN   inspect and repair as necessary
Iransat Iranian regional communications
        satellite
IRAS   infra-red astronomical satellite
        (UK-US-NL)
IRASA   international radio air safety
        association
IRASER infra-red amplification by stimula-
        ted emission of radiation
IRASI   internal review and systems improve-
        ment
IRATE   interim remote area terminal equip-
        ment
IRAWS   infra-red attack weapon system
IRB   Irish Republican Brotherhood;
        industrial readjustment board;
        industrial relations board;
        inspection requirements branch;
        infinitely rigid beam
IRBA   intermediate range bomber aircraft
        1000-2500nm (US)
IRBM   intermediate range ballistic missile
        1500-3000nm
IRC   International Red Cross; inter-
        national rescue committee; infantry
        infantry reserve corps; industrial
        relations counsellors; inter-
        national research council;
        inspection record card; item
        responsibility code

IRCCD	infra-red charge coupled devices	IRMPC	industrial raw materials planning committee
IRCCM	infra-red counter counter-measures	IRNV	increase and replacement of naval vessels
IRCGS	infra-red command guidance system	IRO	industrial relations office(r); international refugee organization (UN)
IRCM	infra-red counter-measures		
IRC&M	increase and replacement of construction and machinery	IROAN	inspect and repair only as needed
IRD	industrial relations department; international research and development	Iron bomb	ordinary free-fall HE bomb
		Iroquois	UH-1 light helicopter
IRDA	industrial research and development authority	IROS	increased reliability operational system
IRDC	international rubber development committee	IROSB	inactive reserve officers status branch
IRDF	infra-red direction finder; Infrarotdoppelfernrohr (infra-red binoculars)	IRP	intelligence reporting plan; industrial readiness planning; instrument recording photography
IRDL	information retrieval and display language	IR-P	ice on runway, patchy
IRDS	infra-red disturbance system	IRP	integrierte Raumplanung by Dornier (integrated environmental planning)
IRE	immediate ready element; institute of radio engineers		
IREC	increase and replacement of emergency constructions	IRPP	industrial readiness planning programme
IRER	infra-red extra-rapid	IRPS	Irish Republican Socialist Party
IRET	Industria Radio Electrica Telecomunicazioni	IRR	individual ready reserve; individual ready reservist; infra-red rays; integral rocket ramjet; intelligence radar reporting; infra-red reflectance; Israel Research Reactor
IRETS	infantry remoted target system by Sperry (battlefield simulator)		
IRF	immediate reaction force; interrupted rapid fire		
IRFAA	international rescue and first aid association	IRRS	individual ready reserve system
IRFG	Infrarotfahrgerät (infra-red driver's viewer)	irrt	irritation
IRFNA	inhibited red fuming nitric acid (rocket propellant)	IRS	internal revenue service; induction and recruiting station (USMC); infra-red sensor; infra-red spectroscope; Indian remote sensing satellite; interchange record separator; infinitely rigid system
IRG	interdepartmental regional group		
IR&G	international relations and government		
IRH	inspection requirements handbook		
IRHS	infra-red homing system	IRS-500	(passive) infra-red surveillance sensor (anti-aircraft) by Saab
IRIG	inertial guidance integrated gyro; inter-range instrumentation group	IRSM	infra-red support measures
IRIS	infra-red intruder system; infra-red imaging seeker; infra-red interferometer spectrometer; industrial research and information services; infra-red information symposium	IRST	infra-red search and tracking system by Spar
		IRSTDS	infra-red surveillance and target designation system by Marconi
		IRTAL	infra-red transmission aspheric lense
IRIS-35M	computer for Pluton (FR)	IRTE	institute of road transport engineers
IRISH	infra-red imaging seeker, homing	IRU	international rescue union
IRL	intersection of range legs	IRUS	infantry rifle unit study
IRLS	infra-red line scanning system; interrogation recording location system	Irvin suit	cold weather flying suit (RAF)
		IRWBC	infra-red wide beam capture
IRM	image rejection mixer; isothermal remnant magnetization	IRZF	Infrarotzielfernrohr (infra-red aiming telescope)
IRMC	international radio maritime committee; inter-service radio measurements committee	IS	internal security; Italy Star; intelligence service; interior secretary; information service;

inventory schedule; invalidated from service; international staff; Iceland; input secondary; information system; information separator; isomer shifts; Infanteriespitzgeschoss (infantry pointed projectile)

I&S   inspection and survey; interchangeability and substitutability

ISA   international standards association; inspector of small arms; international federation of the national standardizing associations; international security affairs; inductee special assignment; instrument society of America; international security assistance; international studies association; international standard atmosphere; interrupt storage area; ice-safe air (temperature)

ISAC   international structural analysis committee (Nato) (bridging equipment); industrial safety advisory council; international security affairs committee; Indian Space Applications Centre (Ahmedabad)

ISAM   Indexed Sequential Access Method

ISARC installation shipping and receiving capability

ISAR   inland search and rescue region

ISAT   interrupt storage area table

ISB   information service branch; independent side band; intermediate side band

ISBC   interdepartmental savings bond committee

ISBIC interservice Balkan intelligence committee

ISC   information services centre; information services control; infrastructure special committee (Nato); intelligence subject code; Indian Staff Corps; Imperial Service College; informal staff communications (Nato); intermediate switching centre ETS; initial slope circuit; item status code

ISCB   inter-allied staff communications board

I&SCD indoctrination and special courses department

ISCII international standard code for information interchange

IsCom island commander

IsCoMadeira island commander Madeira

IsComAzores island commander Azores

IsComBermuda island commander Bermuda

IsComFaroes island commander Faroes

IsComGreenland island commander Greenland

IsComIceland island commander Iceland

ISD   information services division; industrial survey division; individual sponsored dependent; initial ship design; initial selection done; internal symbol dictionary; initial search depth; international subscriber dialling; international standard depth

ISDAIC international staff disaster assistance information coordinator

ISDO   international staff duty officer

ISDS   integrated ship design system

ISE   individual ship exercise; independent ship exercise; Indian Service of Engineers; intercept system environment; inter-service education

ISect intelligence section

ISEE-B international sun earth explorer by British Aerospace

ISEES institute of Soviet and East European Studies,(University of Glasgow)

ISEPS international sun earth physics programme

ISI   Indian Standards Institution; initial support increments

ISIB   inter-service ionospheric bureau

ISIC   international standard industrial classification (of all economic activities) (US); immediate superior in command

ISinC immediate superior in command

ISIR   in service in reserve (USN vessel)

ISIS   inter-service information service; independent schools information service; international shipping information service; international satellites for ionospheric studies

Isis-209 airborne laser gunsight by Ferranti

ISIT   initial system integration test

Iskra TS-11, jet trainer aircraft (Poland)

ISL   item survey list; item study listings; informal staff letter (Nato); Institut St Louis (Franco-German Artillery experimental establishment)

Island class, oil rig protection vessels (RN)

Islander BN-2, light aircraft by Britten/Norman

ISLD   inter-service liaison department (UK)

ISLS   interrogator side lobe suppression; improved side lobe suppression

ISLW   Indian spring low water

ISM   Imperial Service Medal; informal staff memorandum (Nato); insulation systems modules

ISMA	international management systems association
IS&MD	instructional standards and materials division
ISMF	inactive ship maintenance facility
ISMRC	inter-service metallurgical research council
ISN	internment serial number
ISO	Companion of the Imperial Service Order; international standardization organization; information systems office; information service office(r)
Isocon	image intensifier valve
isold	isolated
ISP	Imperial Smelting Process (zinc + lead simultaneously)
ISPI	Instituto per gli Studi di Politica Internazionale (IT)
ISPM	international solar polar mission satellite by ESA; international staff planners message (Nato military committee)
ISPMemo	international staff planners memorandum (Nato)
ISPO	instrumentation ships project office
ISPP	inter-service plastic panel
ISPR	infantry systems programme review
ISR	image storage retrieval, intersecting storage rings
ISRB	inter-service research bureau
ISRCSC	inter-service radio components standardization committee
ISRFCTC	inter-service radio frequency cables technical committee
ISRO	Indian space research organization
ISS	institute for strategic studies -IISS; industrial security section; integrated sealift study; inter-service supply; inter-service support; inertial subsystem; image sharpness scale; integrated spacecraft system; ionosphere sounding satellite; international seismologic summary; institute for space science
iss	issue(d)
ISSA	inter-service support agreements
ISS&AHS	incorporated solider's, sailor's, and airman's help society
ISSB	inter-service security board
ISS-B	ionospheric satellite system (Japan)
ISSC	inter-service supply support coordinator (US); inter-service staff college (UK)
ISSG	illustrated shipboard shopping guide (USN)
ISSMIS	integrated support services management information system
ISSP	inter-service supply support programme

ISSRO	inter-service supply support records office
ISSS	installation service supply support; integrated submarine sonar system
ISSSMD	imaging-seeker surface-to-surface missile, demonstration by McDD (all-weather ship-to-ship missile prototype)
ISSST	integrated submarine sonar system technician
ISSTO	instructions for superintending sea transport officers
IST	Indian standard time; initial service test; institute of science and technology; inter-service training
IStaff	intelligence staff
ISTD	inter-service topographical department (UK)
ISTM	international society for testing materials
ISTS	international schok tube symposium
ISTVS	international society for terrain vehicle systems
ISU	inertial sensor unit; integrated sight unit
ISU-122	... 152, SP assault guns (SU)
ISum	intelligence summary
ISU-TB	armoured recovery vehicle (SU)
Isuzu	class, frigates (JMSDF)
ISV	international scientific vocabulary
ISVD	informations system for vocational decision
ISWG	Imperial standard wire gauge
IT	infantry training; inspector of trooping; Indian Territory (US); Italy (Nato); income tax; improved technology; information theory; internal thread; international tolerance; inspection tag
I&T	installation and test
ITA	industrial training act (UK) 1964; independent television authority (UK); instrument time, actual; international telegraph alphabet; inner transport area; Integrationstestanlage für F-122 (integration test facility)
ITACS	integrated tactical air control system
ITAG	Internationale Tiefbohr AG Celle (Bergewinden winches)
Italtel	SIT, Societa Italiana Telecommunicazioni (Milan)
ITASS	SQR-14, interim towed array surveillance system (sonar) by Gould
ITAY-105	airborne laser designator/rangefinder by Cilas
ITC	infantry training centre; initial

training centre; international telecommunications convention (Madrid); instructor training course; industry trade and commerce (ministry CA); international training cell (Erndtebrück Nato); intertropical confluence (weather); ionic thermo-conductivity; ionic thermo-current; interval timer control; incentive type contract

ITCC   Industrial Times and Controls Company

ITCRM   infantry training centre Royal Marines

ITCS   integrated target control system (multiple drone control)

ITCZ   inter-tropical convergence zone

ITD   initial training division; integrated tactical display

ITDA   indirect target damage assessment

ITDE   integrated tactical display equipment; inter-channel time displacement error

ITE   institute of telecommunications engineers; inter-city transportation efficiency

ITEP   integrated test/evaluation programme

ITF   interactive terminal facility

ITI   international technical institute (of flight engineers); industrial turbines Incorporated (Los Angeles) (KHD+Mack Trucks+ Garrett)

itin   itinerary

ITIU   inventory temporarily in use

ITL   industrial test laboratory Philadelphia Navy Yard; intent(ion) to launch; integrate transfer launch

ITM   inspector of torpedoes and mines

ITMIS   integrated transportation management information system

ITMJ   incoming trunk message junction

ITMT   intermediate thermo-mechanical treatment

ITNS   Italian Navy's Ship; integrated tactical navigation system

ITO   international travel order; invitational travel order; inspecting torpedo officer

ITOS·   infra-red television observation satellite (Nasa) (polar orbiting, weather); improved TIROS operational satellite

ITP   initial trial phase; instruction to proceed

ITPA   independent telephone association

ITPP   institute of technical publicity and publications

ITPR   infra-red temperature profile radiometer

ITR   infantry training regiment (USMC); in-core thermionic reactor; inspection test report

ITRM   inverse thermoremnant magnetization

ITS   initial training school; intersectional transportation service; Italian ship; international tracing service; infantry transportable Swingfire, Beeswing by BAe; instrument time simulated; industrial training service; invitation to send

ITSA   institute for telecommunication sciences and aeronomy

ITSO   international telecommunications satellite organization

ITT   inter-theatre transfer; interrogator-translator team; International Telephone & Telegraph Corp.

ITTAC   international telegraph and telephonic advisory committee

ITU   international telecommunications union (UN Geneva); inter-America telecommunications union

ITV   M-901, improved TOW vehicle by Emerson

ITW   infantry training wing; initial training wing (RAF)

IU   immunizing unit

IUCAF   inter-union committee on frequency allocation for radio astronomy and space science

IUCSTP   inter-union commission on solar terrestrial physics

IUE   international ultra-violet explorer satellite

IUGG   international union of geodesy and geophysics

IUPAC   international union of pure and applied chemistry

IUPAP   international union of pure and applied physics

IUrgRqr   item urgently required

IUS   interim upper stage (missile) by Boeing; interchange unit separator

IUW   inshore undersea warfare
     D   division
     G   group
     SU   surveillance unit

IV   initial velocity inverted vertical increased value

Ivan Susanin   class, armed icebreakers (SU)

IVC   intermediate velocity clouds; immediately vital cargo

IVCS   integrated vehicular communications system by Gould

Iveco   industrial vehicles corporation (FIAT+OM+Lancia/UNIC+Magirus-Deutz)

IVG   Industrieverwaltungsgesellschaft (Bund) (Bonn)

IVHM	in-vessel handling machine		IWPC	institute of water pollution control
IVM	initial virtual memory		IWS	Industriewerke Saar, Freisen
IVSN	initial voice switch network			infantry weapon system 5.56mm
IVSP	international voluntary service for peace			(UK)
IVVS	instantaneous vertical velocity sensor		IWST	individual weapon systems trainer
			IWT	international working team, inland waterways transport
IW	Isle of Wight; inspector of works; inside width; indirect waste; isotropic weight; index word			A authority
				D department
				DS department section
IWC	individual weapons captured			WG working group (Nato)
IWCS	integrated wide-band communications system		IWW	inland water way
			IX	unclassified miscellaneous ship (USN)
IWD	inland waterways and docks; intermediate water depth (mine) (US)		IXR	intersection of runways
IWG	international working group; Imperial wire gauge		IXSS	unclassified miscellaneous submarine (USN)
IWGC	Imperial war graves commission		IY	Imperial Yeomanry
IWIStk	issue while in stock		IYQS	international year of the quiet sun
IWKA	Industriewerke Karlsruhe Augsburg (Karlsruhe)		IZ	inspection zone; Innenzünder (internal fuse)
IWM	Imperial War Museum (London)		IZTO	inter-zonal trade office
IWMAVF	Imperial War Museum associate volunteer force		Izumrud	Scan Odd, airborne interception radar (SU)
Iwo Jima	class, amphibious assault ships LPH (US)			

J

J	joint; junior; judge; jet (fuel); junction (device)
J-Code	justifications code (Nato)
J-	1 personnel directorate (US)
	2 intelligence directorate (US)
	3 operations directorate (US)
	4 logistics directorate (US)
	5 plans and policy directorate (US)
	6 communications electronics directorate (US)
J-1	transport aircraft by Junkers
J-2	interceptor aircraft by Junkers
JA	judge advocate; justice of appeal; Jewish Agency
JAAF	Japanese Army Air Force WW2; joint action armed forces (Nato)
JAAOC	joint anti-aircraft operation centre (Nato)
JAAS	Jaroslawl automobile factories (SU)
Jabo	Jagdbomber, fighter/bomber
JAC	joint advisory committee; joint airworthiness committee; joint apprenticeship committee
JACARI	joint action committee against racial interference
JACC	joint airborne communications centre
JACC/CP	joint airborne communications centre/command post; joint airborne communications control and command post
JACCI	joint allocation committee - civil intelligence (US-UK)
JACFA	Japanese-American cultural friendship association
JACO	joint actions control office
JACP	joint airborne command post
JACPAC	joint air communications of the Pacific WW2
JACWA	joint actions control western approaches (Nato)
JADB	joint air defence board
JADE	Japanese air defence environment
JADOC	joint air defence operations centre
JADRep	joint resource assessment data base report

JAdv	judge advocate
JAdvG	judge advocate general
JAE	joint atomic exercise
JAEC	joint atomic energy committee; joint atomic energy commission
JAF	judge advocate of the fleet
JAFC	Japan atomic fuel corporation
JAG	judge advocate general
Jagaren	class, patrol boats, torpedoes + guided missiles (Sweden)
JAGC	judge advocate general's corps
JAGD	judge advocate general's department
Jagdpanther	killer tank 8.8cm gun WW2 (GE)
Jaguar	missile-armed killer tank by TH; Klasse, fast patrol boats (FGN), II, 250 tons, III, 400 tons; XF-10F, variable sweep jet 1953 by Grumman; strike aircraft by SEPECAT
JAGUAR-V	jamming guarded radio VHF by Racal
JAI	Jorgen Andersen Ingeniorfirma (Glostrup Denmark)
JAIEG	joint atomic information exchange group
Jak	Soviet helicopters, see Yak
JAL	jet approach landing (chart)
JAMAC	joint aeronautical materials agency
JAMAG	joint American military assistance group, joint American military advisory group (Nato)
JAMB	joint air movements board
JAMMAT	joint allied military mission to aid Turkey
JAMPO	joint allied military petroleum office (Nato)
JamRep	jamming report
JAMTO	joint airlines military traffic office
JAN	joint Army-Navy
JANAF	joint Army-Navy-Air Force
JANAIR	joint Army-Navy aircraft instrument research
JANAP	joint Army-Navy air procedure (Nato); joint Army-Navy-Air Force publication

JANAST   joint Army-Navy-Air Force sea trans-
          portation message
JANCom   joint Army-Navy communications
JANET   joint Army-Navy experimental and
          testing (board)
JANGO   joint Army-Navy guild organization
JAN/GRC   joint Army-Navy ground radio commu-
          nication HF SSB transceivers
          N-1   10 watts
          N-2   100 watts
JANGrid   joint Army-Navy Grid (map system)
          (Nato)
JANIC   joint Army-Navy information centre
JANIS   joint Army-Navy intelligence studies
JANP   joint Army-Navy publication
JANStd   joint Army-Navy standard (Nato)
JANWSA   joint Army-Navy war shipping admin-
          istration
JAO   joint amphibious operation
JAOC   joint air operations centre
Jap   Japanese
JAPC   joint air photo centre
JAPIB   joint air photographic intelligence
          board
JAPC   joint area petroleum office
Jararaca EE-3, 4x4 armoured car by Engesa
JARC   joint air reconnaissance centre
          (Nato); joint avionics research
          committee
JAS   jet advisory service (US) (ATC radar)
JASASA   joint air-surface anti-submarine
          section (USN)
JASCO   Joint American study commission
          office (of alien property);
          joint assault signal company
JASDA   Julie automatic sonic data analyser
JASDF   Japanese air self-defence forces
Jason   Roland missile, ship-defence version
JASS   joint anti-submarine school
          (Londonderry UK)
JASU   jet aircraft starting unit
JAT   joint airborne training
JATCC   joint air traffic control centre;
          joint aviation telecommunications
          coordination committee
JATCRU   joint air traffic control radar unit
JATE   joint air transport establishment
          (RAF Brize Norton)
JATF   joint amphibious task force
JATO   jet-assisted take-off
JATP   joint air transportation plan
JATS   joint air transportation service
Jav   Java(nese)
Javelin   GA-5, jet fighter/naval interceptor
          1951 by Gloster
Javelin-221 ... 228, ... 238, night viewer
          by Javelin
Javelot   anti-aircraft missile, close point
          defence by Thomson-CSF
JAWPS   joint atomic weapons publications
          system

JAWS   joint attack weapons system
          (attack helicopters)
JB   junction box; jet barrier; jet bomb;
          joint (Army-Navy) board
JBar   jet barrier
JBDAAFES joint board of directors, Army
          Air Force exchange service
JBES   Jodrell Bank experimental station
JBMTO   joint bus military traffic office
JBUSDC   joint Brazil-US defence commission
JBUSMC   joint Brazil-US military commission
JC   justice clerk; junior college;
          joint compound
JC-130   Hercules, special instrumentation
          for satellite recovery aircraft
JCA   joint communications activity
JCAC   joint civil affairs committee
JCADIS   joint continental aerospace
          defense integration staff (US)
JCAE   joint committee on atomic energy
JCAR   joint commission on applied radio-
          activity
JCASR   joint committee on avionics systems
          research
JCB   joint communications board, joint
          consultative board (Nato)
JCC   joint consultative committee;
          joint computer conference;
          joint communication centre;
          joint control centre
JCCRG   joint command and central require-
          ments group (Nato)
JCDSIPS   joint continental defense systems
          integration planning staff (US)
JCEC   joint communications electronics
          committee
JCENS   joint communication electronics
          nomenclature system
JCI   joint communications instruction
JCII   Japan camera inspection institute
JCL   job control language
JCLABS   jet conventional low altitude
          bombing system
JCMPO   joint cruise missile project office
JCNAAF   joint Canadian Navy Army Air Force
JCOC   joint command operations centre;
          joint civilian orientation confer-
          ence
JCP   joint committee on printing
JCPX   joint command post exercise
JCS   joint chiefs of staff
JCSAN   joint chiefs of staff alerting net-
          work
JCSO   joint chiefs of staff office
JCSRE   joint chiefs of staff representative
          Europe
JCSTR   joint commission on solar and
          terrestrial relationships
jct   junction
jct pt   junction point

JCUI	joint common user item
JD	joint determination; job description
jd	joined
JDA	Japanese defence agency
JDC	job description cards
JDCS	joint deputy chiefs of staff
JdEnl	joined by enlistment
JDF	Jamaican defence force
JdFr	joined from ...
JdInd	joined by induction
JDL	job description language
JDPC	joint defence production committee --JWPC
JDReenl	joined by re-enlistment
JDREMC	joint departmental radio and electronics measurements committee
JDS	joint defence staff (Nato); job data sheet
JdSRs	joined by staff returns
JE	junction exchanges
JEA	joint engineering agency
JEC	joint economic committee (of US Congress)
JECMOS	joint electronic counter-measures operation section
JEDEC	joint electron device engineering council
JEDPE	joint emergency defence plan Europe
JEEP	joint emergency evacuation plan
Jeep	general purpose (car) (US)
JEF	Jewish expeditionary force
JEFF	experimental hovercraft (amphibious assault landing craft)
	A by Aerojet
	B by Bell
JEG	joint exploratory group
JEHU	joint experimental helicopter unit
JEIA	joint electronic information agency
JEM	Jerusalem and the East mission
JEMC	joint engineering management conference
JEOCON	joint European operational communications network
JEOS	Japanese earth observation satellite
JEP	Jahreserhaltungsplanung (annual maintenance planning)
JEPS	joint emergency planning staff
JEq	jump equal
JERC	joint electronics research committee
JERI	Japan economic research institute
Jericho	two-stage nuclear tactical missile (Israel)
JERS	Japanese ergonomics research society
JES	job entry subsystem
JESA	Japanese engineering standards association
JEST	jungle environmental survival training
JET	joint European transport (aircraft); joint European torus (reactor)
JETCC	joint export traffic control centre
JETD	joint electronics type designator
Jetfoil	combat hydrofoil by Boeing
Jet Jeep	XH-26, experimental helicopter rotor-tip pulse-jets by AHC
JetP	jet propelled
Jetplan	computerized flight plan service by Lockheed
Jetranger	AB-206, light helicopter by AB
JETRO	Japan external trade organization
JETS	joint en-route and terminal system (radar)
Jet Shot	silent mortar, single hand percussion by PRB
JetStar	C-140, small transport aircraft hy Lockheed
Jetstream	light transport aircraft, maritime patrol (RN) by BAe
JEWT	jungle exercise without trees
Jezebel	SSQ-41, helicopter-borne omnidirectional passive sonar buoy by Ultra (UK)
JFACTSU	joint forward air controllers training and standards unit
JFAI	joint formal acceptance inspection
JFB	jet flying belt
JFET	junction field effect transistors
JFM	joint forces memorandum
JFN	jacketed flat nosed (projectile)
JFRO	joint fire research organization
JFTX	joint field training exercise
JFUB	joint facilities utilization board
JG	junior grade
JgdPzRak	Jagdpanzer Rakete, missile-armed killer tank (GE)
JGS	joint general staff
JGSDF	Japanese ground self-defence forces
JGTC	junior girls' training corps
JHA	job hazard analysis
JHC	jacketed hollow cavity (projectile) (US)
JHD	joint hypo-centre determination
JHGSO	joint household goods shipping office
JHMO	junior hospital medical officer
JHP	jacketed hollow point (projectile)
JHQ	Joint Headquarters (Mönchengladbach Rheindahlen) (NORTHAG+BAOR+2ATAF)
JHS	junior high school
JIB	joint intelligence bureau
JIC	joint intelligence committee (UK); joint intelligence center (US); joint industrial council
JICA	joint intelligence collecting agency
	CBI China, Burma, India
	ME Middle East
	NA North Africa
	RC reception committee
	joint intelligence centre; Africa
JICPOA	joint intelligence centre, Pacific Ocean area

JICS   joint intelligence coordination
          staff (CIA)
JICTAR   joint industry committee for tele-
          vision advertising research
JIEP   joint intelligence estimate for
          planning
JIFDATS   joint in-flight data transmission
          system by Northrop
JILO   joint information liaison office
JIM   jammer intercept missile
JIMA   Japan industrial management associa-
          tion
JIMRT   job instruction method and relations
          training
Jindalee OTH radar (Australia)
Jindivik recce RPV, air cushion landing
          system by GAF/BAe
JINR   joint institute for nuclear research
JINTACCS joint interoperability of tactical
          command and control systems (US
          programme)
JIO   joint information office
JIOA   joint intelligence objectives agency
JIS   joint intelligence staff; Japan
          industrial standard
JISPB   joint intelligence studies publica-
          tion board
JIT   job instruction training
JJ   jungle jeep (US)
JKT   job knowledge test
JLC   joint logistics committee
JLOIC   joint logistics operations intelli-
          gence centre
JLPC   joint logistics planning committee
JLR   junior leaders regiment (UK)
JLRB   joint logistics review board
JLRSS   joint long-range strategic study
JMA   Japan management association,
          Japanese meteorological agency
JMAC   joint munitions allocation committee
JMAHEP   joint military aircraft hurricane
          evacuation plan
JMB   joint movements branch
JMC   joint meteorological committee
JMCC   joint movements coordinating
          committee (UK); joint mobile
          communications centre (Nato)
JMCOL   JUMPS monthly computer listings
          (joint uniform military pay system)
JMED   jungle message encoder/decoder
JMEM   joint munitions effectiveness manual
JMM   J.M. Marlin (New Haven US)
JMne   junior marine
JMP   joint manpower programme
JMPAB   joint material priorities and allo-
          cation board
JMPTC   joint military packaging training
          centre
JMRO   joint medical regulating office
JMRP   joint meteorological radio propaga-
          tion (sub-committee)

JMS   joint movement staff
JMSAC   joint meteorological satellite
          advisory committee
JMSDF   Japanese maritime self-defence
          forces
JMT   job method training
JMTB   joint military transportation board
JMTC   joint military transportation
          committee
JMTG   joint military terminology group
JMUSDC   joint Mexican-US defence commission
JMVB   joint military vessels board
jn   junction
JN   jet navigation; trainer aircraft by
          Curtiss
JNACC   joint nuclear accident coordinating
          centre
JNC   joint negotiating committee
jnc   junction
JND   just noticeable difference
JNE   jump not equal
JNF   joint national facsimile
jng   joining
jnr   junior
JNROTC   junior naval reserve officers train-
          ing course
JnrTech   junior technician (UK)
JNS   just noticeable shift
jnt   joint
JNW   joint committee on new weapons and
          equipment
JNWPU   joint numerical weather prediction
          unit
JO   junction office
JobMan   job management
JOBS   job opportunities in the business
          sector
JOC   joint operations centre
JOD   joint occupancy date
JODC   Japanese oceanographic data centre
JOEG   joint operations evaluation group
JOG   junior offshore group
Johnson   rifle M-1941, semi-automatic
          infantry rifle (US); M-1944,
          machine gun (US)
JOIA   joint operational intelligence
          agency
JON   job order number
J-OO   jet route
JOO   junior officer of the
          D deck
          W watch
JOP   Jupiter orbiter probe by NASA
JOpRep   joint operations reporting system
JOPS   joint operations planning system
JOS   joint operational staff (Nato) (oil)
JOSPro   joint overseas (shipping) procedure
JOSS   joint overseas switching system
Jostle   airborne jammer WW2 (RAF)
JOT   joint observer team

Jour-J	D-day (FR)
Jour-M	M-day (FR)
JOV	armed reconnaissance aircraft (US)
JOVIAL	Jules own version of the international algorithmic language
JP	justice of peace; jet pilot; jet propelled; jet propulsion; jet petrol
JP-fuel	jet propulsion fuel
JP-4	jet propulsion fuel for USAF aircraft
JP-5	jet propulsion fuel for USN aircraft
JP-7	jet propulsion fuel high temperature
JP-233	LAAAS, runway cratering bomb by Hunting Eng.
JPA	Japanese procurement agency
JPA-9	jet petrol ... for Tomahawk
JPB	joint procurement board; joint planning board; joint purchasing board; joint production board; Julius Peters GmbH (Berlin)
JPC	joint planning committee; joint production committee; jet propulsion centre
JPCAC	joint production consultative and advisory committee
JPCC	joint petroleum coordinating committee; joint petroleum coordinating centre
JPG	Jefferson proving ground; job proficiency guide; joint planning group
JPI	joint public information (office)
JPL	jet propulsion laboratory (Pasadena)
JPMR	joint projected manpower requirement
JPNL	judged perceived noise level
JPO	joint program office NAVSTAR; joint petroleum office
JPPL	joint personnel priority list
JPPSOWA	joint personal property shipping office (Washington)
JPRS	joint publications reserach service
JPS	joint planning staff (US-UK); jet propulsion system
JPSC	joint production survey committee
JPTO	jet-propelled take-off
JPWC	joint post-war committee
JPz-4	Jagdpanzer by Rheinstahl (killer tank)
JRB	joint reconnaissance board
JRC	joint reconnaissance centre; junior red cross
JRCC	joint rescue coordination centre
JRDOD	joint research and development objectives document
JrGr	junior grade
JRMTO	joint rail military traffic office
JROTC	junior reserve officers' training corps
JRRC	joint regional reconnaissance centre
JRS	joint reporting structure; jet repair service

JRT	job relations training
JS	joint staff; junior seaman
JS-2	Joseph Stalin, amphibious tank (SU)
JS/A	Joseph Stalin, tracked rocket launcher --FROG (SU)
JSARC	joint search and rescue centre
JSATC	joint services air trooping centre (UK)
JSAWC	joint services amphibious warfare centre
JS/B	tracked launcher --SCUD (SU)
JSBS	joint strategic bomber study
JSC	Johnson space centre; junior soldiers company (UK); junior staff course; joint security control; joint strategic committee; joint support command
JS/C	tracked rocket launcher 300mm (SU)
JSCC	joint services communications centre (UK)
JSCM	Joint Service Commendation Medal (US)
JSCMPO	joint service cruise missile programme office
JSCO	joint staff communications office
JSCP	joint strategic capabilities plan
JS/D	tracked rocket launcher 400mm (SU)
JSDF	Japanese self-defence forces
JSGC	joint services gliding centre (RAF Bicester)
JSIA	joint service induction area
JSKLT	joint services Kuwait liaison team
JSL	job specification language; joint support list
JSLO	joint services lisison organization (UK)
JSLS	joint services liaison staff
JSM	joint staff mission (UK)
JSMB	joint sealift movements board
JSMTC	joint service mountain training centre (Morfa Camp, Tywyn/Fort George, Inverness)
JSO	joint service office
JSOC	joint ship operating committee
JSOP	joint strategic objectives plan
JSOR	joint services operational requirement
JSP	jacketed soft point (projectile); joint staff planners
JSPC	joint services parachute centre (UK)
JSPO	joint system programme office Eglin AFB
JSPR	joint services public relations (UK)
JSRC	joint ship repair committee
JSRU	joint services rehabilitation unit (Chessington UK)
JSS	joint surveillance system (US-Canada); joint services standard
JSSAP	joint services small arms program (US) MC management committee

JSSC	joint services staff college --NDC (UK); joint strategic survey committee (US); joint service sailing centre (UK) (HMS Hornet, Gosport Hants)
JSSDC	joint service subaqua diving centre (Fort Bovis Plymouth)
JSSG	joint service sub-group (Nato)
JSSL	joint services school of linguistics
JSSM	joint services staff manual
JST	Japanese standard time
JStaffOfc	joint chiefs of staff offices
JSTPS	joint strategic target planning staff
JSU-122	SP assault gun 122mm (SU)
JSU-152	SP assault gun 155mm (SU)
jt	joint
JTA	joint table of allowances
JTAMR	MisRep, joint tactical air reconnaissance surveillance mission report
JTB	joint transportation board
JTC	junior training corps; jungle training centre (Canugra)
JTCCG	joint technical configuration control group
JTCO	joint tactical communications office
JTCP	joint tactical communications program (US)
JTD	joint table of distribution
JTDE	joint technology demonstrator engine (USN+USAF programme) -1 for hypersonic aircraft -2 for subsonic aircraft
JTF	joint task force Rep reports
JTG	joint task group
JTIDS	ARC-191, joint tactical information distribution system by Hughes (jam-resistant)
JTDMLS	joint tactical microwave landing system by Bendix
JTO	joint test organization; jump take-off (aircraft)
JTR	joint travel regulations
jt/r	joint rate
JTRC	joint theatre reconnaissance committee
JTS	job training standards; joint tactical school
JTSG	joint trials sub-group
jt/str	jet stream
JTWC	joint typhoon warning centre
JTWU	joint Tornado weapons unit (Nato) (RAF Homington)
JTX	joint training exercise
jty	jointly
Ju-46	mail plane by Junkers (GE)
Ju-52	cargo aircraft WW2 by Junkers
Ju-87	dive bomber WW2 by Junkers
Ju-88	bomber by Junkers WW2

Ju-90	cargo aircraft by Junkers WW2
Ju-188	torpedo bomber by Junkers WW2
Ju-252	cargo aircraft by Junkers WW2
Ju-287	six-jet giant aircraft by Junkers WW2
Ju-322	Mammut, giant glider 82 mtrs span by Junkers WW2
JUD	radar/sonar display by Kelvin
JUEP	Jahresübungs und Erhaltungsplan (annual training and maintenance plan)
JÜEP	Jahresübersicht Einsatz- Ausbildungs-planung (annual schedule for mission and training planning)
JULEM	Justier- und Prüfgerät für Laserent-fernungsmesser (calibration and testing equipment for laser rangers) by Siemens
Julie	JASDA, Julie automatic sonic data analyser
Jumbo	air-to-ground missile by MBB, 6x6 heavy weight transport vehicle by ÖAF
JumpCert	jump certificate
JUMPS	joint uniform military pay system
Jupiter	orbital transport missile/IRBM (US)
JUSCIMPC	joint US-Canada industrial mobili-zation planning committee
JUSMAG	joint US military advisory group, joint US military aid group (Greece)
JUSMAGG	joint US military aid group Greece
JUSMAP	joint US military advisory and planning group
JUSMG	joint US military group (Spain)
JUSMMAT	joint US military mission for aid to Turkey
JUSPAO	joint US public affairs notice
JUSSC	joint US strategic committee
JUTPCS	joint uniform telephone communica-tions system
JUWAT	joint unconventional warfare assessment team
JUWTF	joint unconventional warfare task force A Atlantic P Pacific
JVC	jet vane control (system) missile guidance
JW	junction wide
JWB	joint wages board
JWBC	joint whole blood centre
JWE	joint warfare establishment (Old Sarum UK)
JWF	job work folder
JWGA	joint war games agency
J&WO	jettison and washing overboard
JWPC	joint war plans committee, joint war production committee

JWS	jungle warfare school; joint warfare staff (UK)	JWTC	jungle warfare training centre
		JWVUS	Jewish war veterans of the US
JWT	jungle warfare training	JXCG	joint exercise control group

K

K	king; knight; killer submarine
k	killed; kilo; keel; knot
K-class	RN WW1 fleet submarine
K-day	konvoy day (when regular convoys commence); carrier aircraft assault day
K-powder	smoke powder
K-ration	for 1 day 3726 calories
K-rocket	anti-aircraft barrage rockets (bomb+2 parachutes + cable)
K-system	automatic bomb aiming system
K-Wagen	(Gro)Kampfwagen WW1 heavy tank (GE)
K-II	Kaiserslautern, Gillois type ferry by EWK
K³	Kommando-Kontrolle-Kommunikation (GE) (command control communication)
K-5E	Eisenbahnkanone 28cm (railway gun) (GE)
K-12E	Eisenbahnkanone 21cm
K-13A	Atoll, AA-2, air-to-air missile (SU)
K-61	tracked amphibious vehicle (SU)
K-63	tracked armoured personnel carrier (China)
K-98	Karabiner 1898 carbine (GE) k kurz (short version)
K-225	...600, ...125, helicopters with intermeshing rotors by Kaman
K-273	Kreisel by Litef, gyro
KA	King of Arms; Knight of the Order of St Andrews
KA-3	tanker aircraft by Douglas
KA-6D	Intruder, carrier-based tanker aircraft by Grumman
Ka-8	light helicopter 1947 *by Kamow (SU)*
Ka-10	naval recce helicopter *by Kamow (SU)*
KA-15	Hen, maritime recce ASW *by Kamow (SU)*
Ka-18	Hog, utility helicopter *by Kamow (SU)*
Ka-20	Harp, transport helicopter ASW SAR *by Kamow (SU)*
Ka-22	Hoop, transport helicopter *by Kamow (SU)*
Ka-25	Hormone, transport helicopter *by Kamow (SU)*

Ka-26	helicopter *by Kamow (SU)*
Ka-430	assault and combat glider by Ing. Kalkert WW2 (GE)
KAA	20mm anti-aircraft gun by Oerlikon
KAB	kapok assault bridge (project WW2) (UK); 20mm machine gun by Oerlikon
KAD-B	20mm anti-aircraft gun by Oerlikon
KADU	Kenya African Democratic Union
KAE	Krupp Atlas Elektronik (Bremen); Kaiser Aerospace and Electronics (US)
KAF	Kuwait armed forces
KAFS	killer submarine action and fire control system by Ferranti
KaFüAnl	Kampfführungsanlage (operation control system) (GE)
Kagero	class, destroyers WW2 (Japan)
Kaiten	guided torpedoes WW2 (Japan)
Kalashnikow	assault rifle (SU)
Kalle	fire control system for coastal batteries (TV + laser ranger) (Sweden)
KAM-3D	Kawasaki anti-tank missile ATGW
KAM-9	Kawasaki anti-tank missile
Kaman	class, patrol boats guided missiles by CMN
Kaman-43	fire-fighting helicopter by Kaman (US)
Kangaroo	provisional armoured personnel carrier WW2
Kanin	class, destroyers (SU)
KanJPz	Kanonenjagdpanzer (gun-armed killer tank) (GE)
KANU	Kenya African National Union
KANUPP	Karachi nuclear power plant
KAPB	20mm anti-aircraft gun by Oerlikon
KAR	Kalashnikow assault rifle (SU)
Kara	class, all-purpose cruisers (SU)
Kari	class, corvettes (JMSDF)
Karin	heavy mobile coast artillery battery FH-77 (Sweden)
Karl	Thor, Gerät 040, mortar 60cm WW2 (GE)
Karldap	Karlsruhe automatic data processor Eurocontrol

Karl Gustav anti-tank recoilless rifle by
 FFV
Kartal class, patrol boats guided missiles
 for Turkey by Lürssen
Kartoscan digitalized map by MBB
Kasado class, minesweepers (JMSDF)
Kashin class, destroyers (SU)
Katjusha artillery rocket WW2 (SU)
KATUSA Korean augmentation to US Army
Kauper gun gear fire control equipment
KAZ kleinkalibriger Annäherungszünder
 (GE) small calibre proximity fuse
 (35mm 40mm)
KB Knight of the Most Exalted Order
 of the Bath; kite balloon; key-
 board; kilobits; kilobytes
KB-29 tanker aircraft by Boeing 1949
KB-44 kleine Hohlladungsbombe (small
 hollow-charge (cluster) bomb 44mm
 (GE)
KBA killed by aircraft; 25mm automatic
 cannon by Oerlikon
KBE Knight of the Most Excellent Order
 of the British Empire; Knight of
 the Order of the Black Eagle
KBO kite and balloon officer
KBS kite balloon section; kite balloon
 station; Kernbrennstoffsicherheit
 (GE) (nuclear fuel safety)
KC Knight Cross; Knight Commander;
 King's College; King's Cross
KC-10 Extender, ATCA, advanced tanker/
 cargo aircraft by McDD
KC-97 Stratotanker, tanker aircraft
KC-130 Hercules, tanker aircraft
KC-135 Stratotanker, tanker aircraft by
 Boeing
KCA 30mm airborne gun by Oerlikon
KCB Knight Commander of the Most Exalted
 Order of the Bath; 30mm anti-
 aircraft gun by Oerlikon
KCBE Knight Commander of the Most Excel-
 lent Order of the British Empire
KCC kathodic closure contraction;
 Knight Commander of the Order of
 the Crown and the Congo Free State
KCH Knight Commander of the Hanoverian
 Guelphic Order
KCHS Knight Commander of the Order of the
 Holy Sepulchre
KCIE Knight Commander of the Order of the
 Indian Empire
KCLS Knight Commander of the Lion and Sun
 (Iran)
KCLY The Kent and City of London Yeomanry
KCMG Knight Commander of the Most Disting-
 uished Order of St Michael and
 St George
KCRVO Knight Commander of the Royal
 Victorian Order

KCSG Knight Commander of the Order of
 St George the Great
KCSI Knight Commander of the Order of
 the Star of India
KCSS Knight Commander of the Order of
 St Sylvester
KCVO Knight Commander of the Royal
 Victorian Order
KD Kabeltechnik Dietz Gmbh (München);
 knocked down
kd killed
KDA 35mm twin anti-aircraft gun by
 Oerlikon/Contraves
KDE 35mm cannon by Oerlikon
KDG The First, the King's Dragoon Guards
KDH Korean direct hire
KDLCL knocked down in less than carloads
KdoRe Kommandorechner (fire control
 calculator) (GE)
KDP known datum point
KDS key data station
KE kinetic energy (shot)
KEAS knots equivalent air speed
KEE Komponenten und Experimentalen-
 twicklungen (GE) (components and
 experimental development)
KEH King Edward's Horse (regiment)
KEHA Kurt Eichweber Hamburg
Keiler experimental tank --Leopard (UK)
KEL Komponentenexperimentalprogramm
 Luftfahrt (aerospace component
 experimental programme) (GE)
KEOG King Edward VII's Own Goorkhas
KEOGR King Edward VII's Own Gurkha Rifles
KEP Komponentenerprobungsprogramm (GE)
 (component evaluation programme)
kero kerosene
KESP Courtauld's edible spun protein
 (artificial meat)
Kestrel light-weight night-vision rifle
 sight by Pilkington; VTOL air-
 craft Harrier predecessor
KEV kilo-electron-volts
Kevlar jacket armoured jacket
KF Kaiser Fraeser Aircraft Corp.
Kfir jet fighter aircraft (Israel)
KFK Kohlefaserverbundkunststoff
 (carbon-reinforced plastic)
KFL key facilities list
KFU Kernreaktorfernüberwachungssystem
 by Dornier (nuclear reactor
 remote monitoring system)
Kfz Kraftfahrzeug (motor vehicle) (GE)
Kfz-13 medium armoured passenger car by
 Adler
Kfz-14 medium armoured signals vehicle by
 Adler
Kfz-67 SdKfz-231, heavy reconnaissance
 vehicle
KG Knight of the Most Ancient and Noble
 Order of the Garter

KG-10   Kartengerät by Teldix (helicopter-
        borne mapping equipment)
KGC   Knight Grand Cross; Knight Grand
        Commander
KGCB   Knight of the Grand Cross of the
        Most Exalted Order of the Bath
KGCSG   Knight of the Grand Cross of the
        Order of St Gregory the Great
KGE   Knight of the Order of the Golden
        Eagle
KGF   Knight of the Order of the Golden
        Fleece
KGFS   King George's Fund for Sailors
Kgs   King's
KGStJ   Knight of the Grace of the Order of
        St John of Jerusalem
KH   The King's Hussars; Knight of the
        Royal Guelphic Order of Hanover;
        Kelvin & Hughes Company Ltd
Khalid P-4030/2, Shir I, main battle tank
        (without Chobham armour) for
        Jordan by ROF
KHC   honorary chaplain to the King
KHD   Klöckner Humboldt Deutz (GE)
KHDS   honorary dental surgeon to the King
KhF-1   chemical anti-personnel mine (SU)
KHI   Kawasaki Heavy Industries (Tokyo)
KHM   King's Harbour Master
KHN   Knoop hardness number
KHNS   honorary nursing sister to the King
KHP   honorary physician to the King
KHS   honorary surgeon to the King;
        Knight of the Holy Sepulchre
KIA   killed in action
KIACS   Kenya independent armoured car
        squadron
KIAS   knots indicated air speed
Kiebitz S-24, trainer aircraft by Focke
        Wulf WW2; Do-32 ... 34, tethered
        cold jet helicopter, battlefield
        surveillance platform by Dornier
Kiew   class, aircraft carriers ASW heli-
        copters + VTOL strike aircraft (SU)
Kih   kilometres in the hour
KiH   Kaiser i Hind (Emperor of India)
Kilauea class, ammunition ships AE (USN)
Kildin class, destroyers guided missiles
        (SU)
Kilfrost anti-icing chemical (RAF)
KingAir T-44, twin-engined trainer aircraft
        by Beechcraft
KingCobra Bell-309, combat helicopter by
        Bell
Kiowa   OH-58, OH-4a, observation helicopter
        by Bell
KIP   key intelligence position
Kiran   HJT-16, trainer aircraft by HAL
Kirov   class, cruisers (SU)
KISIM   King Idris Senussi Independence Medal
        1951

KISS   keep it simple, stupid
Kite   towed minesweeping device
Kitten submarine-transported airplane 1922
        by Martin
Kitty Hawk class, aircraft carriers CV
        (USN)
Kittyhawk P-40, interceptor aircraft by
        Curtiss
KJStJ   Knight of Justice of the Order of
        St John of Jerusalem
KK   Kurskreisel (navigational gyro) (GE),
        Kleinkaliber (small calibre) (GE)
KK-62   7.62mm machine gun by Valmet
Kl...   Klasse
KLA   Khmer Liberation Army (Cambodia)
Klasse 101 destroyers (FGN)
        A missile-armed
Klasse 103 guided missile destroyers
Klasse 119 destroyers
Klasse 120 frigates
Klasse 142 Zobel, fast patrol boats
Klasse 143 fast patrol boats
            torpedo + missiles + a/a gun
Klasse 148 patrol boats guided missiles
Klasse 162 patrol hydrofoils
Klasse 205 submarines
Klasse 206 submarines
Klasse 209 submarines for Turkey
Klasse 210 submarine German/Norwegian
Klasse 320 Lindau, coastal minesweepers
Klasse 321 coastal minesweepers
Klasse 331B mine hunters
Klasse 340 fast mine-sweepers (FGN)
Klasse 341 Schütze, fast minesweepers
Klasse 343 fast mine sweeper/layer
Klasse 355 ERMISS minesweeper
Klasse 393 Ariadne, inshore minesweeper
Klasse 394 Frauenlob, inshore minesweepers
Klasse 401 patrol boat tender
Klasse 402 Mosel, mine-sweeper tender
Klasse 403 Lahn, submarine tender
Klasse 420 Thetis, submarine hunter
Klasse 520 Butt, MP landing craft
Klasse 521 landing craft mechanized
Klasse 701 logistic support ships
Klasse 703 ocean tugs
Klasse 704 fleet tanker
Klasse 751 oceanographic vessel
Klasse 753 oceanographic vessel
Klasse 760 ammunition support ship
Klasse 762 mine transporting ship
Klasse 766 fleet tanker
Klasse 780 fleet tanker
KLH   Knight of the Legion of Honour
KLI   The King's Light Infantry
KLJ   Knight of Justice of the Order of
        St Lazarus of Jerusalem
KLu   Koninklijke Luchtmacht (royal Dutch
        Air Force)
KM   Korea Medal, Knight of Malta,

King's Medal, Krauss Maffei
(München)

KMA   Korean military academy
KMAG   Korean military advisory group
KMB   Küstenminensuchboot (coastal mine-
          sweeper)
KMC   Korean marine corps
KMJ   Knight of the Military Order of
          Maximilian Joseph
KMM   truck-mounted treadway bridge 7 mtrs
          long (SU)
KMOM   Knight Magistral of the Order of
          Malta
KMR   Kwajalein missile range
KMT   Klöckner Mannstaedt (Troisdorf)
KMU-388   guidance system for smart bombs
KMU-421   Paveway, laser guided smart bomb by
          TI
KN   Kenya Navy
KN-150   night viewer by Simrad
KNA   killed, not enemy action
Knebsworth chaff dispensing rockets (RN)
KNG   Koppelnavigationsgerät für Uber- und
          Unterwasserschiffe by Litef
Knickebein wireless air navigation system
          WW2 (GE)
KNL   Knight of the Order of the Nether-
          lands Lion; Kombiniertes Naviga-
          tions- und Landesystem by Teldix
Knox   class, frigates (USN)
KNS   Knight of the Order of the Royal
          Northern Star
KO   King's Own
KOB   The King's Own Royal Border Regiment
KOC   Knight of the Order of the Oak Crown
KOD   kick-off drift
Kola   class, corvettes (SU)
KOLLR   The King's Own Loyal Lancaster
          Regiment
Köln   class, frigates (FGN)
KOM   Knight of the Order of Malta
Komar   class, guided missile patrol boats
          (SU)
Komet   Me-163, rocket interceptor by
          Messerschmitt WW2
KOMR   The King's Own Malta Regiment
Kondor   class, East German mine-sweepers
Kongu   class, Japanese battleships WW2
KORBR   The King's Own Royal Border Regiment
Kormoran air-to-ship guided missile by MBB
KORR   The King's Own Royal Regiment
          (Lancaster)
KOSB   The King's Own Scottish Borderers
Kosmos   orbital transport missile (SU)
Kotlin   class, destroyers guided missiles
          (SU)
KOYLI   The King's Own Yorkshire Light
          Infantry
KP   Knight of the Order of St Patrick;
          King's parade, key personnel

KPA   Korea procurement agency
KPC   Koblenz procurement centre
KPFSM   The King's Police and Fire Service
          Medal
KPH   kilometres per hour
KPM   The King's Police Medal
KPR   Kenya Police Reserve
KPU   rocket launcher 16 barrels 140mm
          (SU)
KPVT   14.5mm machine gun Vladimirov (SU)
KPz   Kampfpanzer (main battle tank)
KPz-3   FMBT, future main battle tank Anglo/
          German project
KPz-70   main battle tank of the 1970s pro-
          ject (GE)
KR   The Kenya Regiment; The King's
          Regiment; The King's Regulations;
          Knight of the Order of the
          Redeemer
Krad   Kraftrad (motor cycle) (GE)
Kraftei   Me-163, Komet, rocket interceptor
          WW2
Kraka   Kraftkarren (light air-transportable
          vehicle by Faun)
KR&AL   King's Regulations and Admiralty's
          Instructions
KRAZ   Soviet trucks
          214   12.3 tons
          255   11.9 tons
          219   11.3 tons
KRC   Knight of the Order of the Red Cross
KRE   Knight of the Order of the Red Eagle
Kresta   class, cruisers (SU)
KRH   The King's Royal Hussars
KRIH   The King's Royal Irish Hussars
Krivak   class, combat hydrofoils (SU)
KrKw   Krankenkraftwagen (ambulance) (GE)
KRO   Küstenradarorganisation (coastal
          radar organization (FGN)
Krogulec class, minesweepers (Poland)
Kromantse class, patrol boats by Vosper/
          Vikers
KROMUSKIT Kroger & Muser, recoilless rifle
          (US)
Kronstadt class, corvettes (SU)
KRR   The King's Royal Rifles
KRRC   The King's Royal Rifle Corps
KRT   Kampfraumtrainer by Honeywell (tank
          turret simulator)
Krupny   class, destroyers guided missiles
          (SU)
KS   Kugelsplittergeschoss (spherical)
          fragmentation projectile)
KS-2   anti-aircraft sight for machine guns
          by Jungner Instruments
KS-19   100mm anti-aircraft gun (SU)
KS-30   130mm anti-aircraft gun (SU)
KSA   Knight of St Anne
KSC   Korean service corps; Kennedy space
          center (Florida)

KSF	keel shock factor
KSG	Knight of the Order of St George
KSH	Knight of the Order of St Hubert
KSI	Knight of the Order of the Star of India
KSK	ethyl iodo-acetate (tear gas)
KSL	Knight of the Order of the Sun and Lion
KSLI	The King's Shropshire Light Infantry
KSM	Korean Service Medal
KSP	Knight of the Order of St Stanislaus of Poland
KSS	Knight of the Southern Star
KSSU-group	KLM+SAS+Swissair+UTA
KStJ	Knight Commander of the Order of St John of Jerusalem
KSV	Knight of the Order of St Vladimir
Kt	Knight
KT	Knight of the Most Ancient and Most Noble Order of the Thistle; Knight templar; kilotons
KTAS	knots true air speed
KTK	Kaufmann Thuma Keller, American Missile Industry
KTRHA	The King's Troop Royal Horse Artillery
KTS	Knight of the Order of the Tower and Sword; Kleine Torpedoschnellboote (GDR) (fast small torpedo boats)
KUA	kit upkeep allowance
Kudu	tactical transport aircraft (South Africa)
Kugelblitz	anti-aircraft tank WW2
Kuha	class, minesweepers GRP hull (Finland)
KUKA	Keller und Knappich Ausgburg, IWKA consortium
KUMAR	Kurzstreckenmarineflugkörper (short-range naval a/a missile) by AEG+Dornier+VFW+Matra project
KUR	Kyoto university reactor (Japan)

Kürassier	killer tank by Puch (Austria)	
Kuril	class, aircraft carriers (SU)	
KURRI	Kyoto university research reactor institute	
KV	kilovolts; Karlskrona Varvet Karlskrona; Keine Verzögerung (no delay) (fuse)	
KV-1	Kliment Voroshilov (tank) (SU)	
KV-2	Kliment Voroshilov assault gun (SU)	
KV-107	transport helicopter by Kawasaki	
KVP	Kasernierte Volkspolize (EG) (People's Police in barracks)	
KWAC	key word and context	
KWE	Knight of the Order of the White Eagle	
KWIC	key word in context	
KWIT	key word in title	
KwK	Kampfwagenkanone (tank gun)	
	30 2cm	
	38 2cm	
	39 5cm	L/60
	40 7.5cm	L/43
	42 7.5cm	L/70
	36 8.8cm	L/55
	43 8.8cm	L/71
KWKG	Kriegswaffenkontrollgesetz (war weapons control act) (GE)	
KWOC	key word out of context	
KWS	Kampfwertsteigerung (improved combat effectiveness)	
KY	keying device	
	100 secure voice by Milcom	
	200 secure voice by Milcom	
	500 digital data burst by Milcom	
kybd	keyboard	
Kymothoi	class, patrol boats guided missiles + torpedoes (Greece)	
Kynda	class, cruisers guided missiles (SU)	
KZ	killing zone	
kzV	kurze Verzögerung short delay (fuse)	
KZX-16	impact fuse for DIRA by Oerlikon	

L

L	lieutenant; navigator (USN); learner; lady; electrical; Atlantic; landing; leaf; league; left; light; line; longitude; Lancers; low; lead; lubaloy; length; lightning; lumen; locator beacon; light gun; blank cartridge

L-hour   landing hour (of the first helicopter wave) (USN)

4 L's   lead, log, latitude, lookout (Navy)

9L   The 9th The Queen's Own Royal Lancers

12 L   The 12th The Prince of Wales's Royal Lancers

42L28   howitzer 15cm (Switzerland)

101L1/GTG   20mm gun by Oerlikon

407 L   air defense communications system (US)

412 L   radar command and operations system (US); semi-automatic ground environment (USAF-G)

413 L   distant early warning radar (US)

414 L   OTHB radar project (US)

416 L   BUIC radar interceptor guidance system (US)

474 L   BMEWS, ballistic missile early warning system (US)

496 L   Spacetrack air defence radar (US)

L   class, patrol and minelaying submarines WW1 (RN)

L-1   light aircraft WW2 (RAF); BAT, battalion anti-tank (weapon) (UK)

L1A1   SLR, FN rifle built under licence by RSAF; electrical grenade launcher for riot control by RSAF

L2A1   grenade hand/rifle by ROF

L2A3   Sterling machine pistol

L3A1   9mm Sterling submachine gun

L4   air-droppable torpedo

L4A1   ..., Bren gun, machine gun

L4/5   fire control equipment by HSA

L4A1   tripod for L7A2

L-5   Sentinel, light aircraft WW2 (RAF)

L5A1   gun 76mm (UK)

L5,97   Lauf, Versuchslauf, experimental bore 5.97mm WW2 (GE)

L7A1   ...3, tank gun 105mm by Vickers

L7A2   machine gun 7.62mm by FN or RSAF

L7Tk   tank gun 105mm by Vickers

L8A1   screening smoke grenade system by ROF

L8A1Tk   tank machine gun 7.62mm by RSAF

L11   konischer Lauf, experimental conical bore 15mm-11mm WW2 (GE)

L11A   rifled tank gun 120mm (UK)

L11Tk   tank gun 120mm by ROF for Chieftain

L16   mortar 81mm by ROF

L19   0-1, Bird Dog, light plane COIN, by Cessna

L20A1   machine gun for helicopters

L21A2   RARDEN, 30mm automatic cannon by RSAF

L23Tk   tank gun 76mm

L27   25Pdr, field gun/howitzer 88mm

L-29   Delfin, trainer aircraft by Aero Czechoslov

L32   impact fuse for 105mm light gun (UK)

L33   time and impact fuse for 105mm light gun (UK)

L-33SP   SP gun Sherman hull/155mm Tampella gun (Israel)

L34A1Tk   Patchett Sterling machine pistol (firing port weapon)

L-39   Albatros, trainer aircraft (Czechoslovakia)

L39A1   7.62mm sniper's rifle by RSAF

L42A1   7.62mm sniper's rifle by RSAF

L43A1   ranging machine gun

L48   1.5in signal pistol/riot gun (UK)

L50   90mm gun US on M-47/M-48

L-51   105mm gun (UK)

L54   100mm Soviet gun on T-54/55

L55   120mm tank gun on Cheiftain, Soviet gun 155mm on T-62

L60   40mm anti-aircraft gun on M-42; 57mm towed anti-aircraft gun by Bofors

L64   tank round 105mm APFSDS (UK)

L67   riot gun by RSAF

L70   40mm light anti-aircraft gun by Bofors; 40mm anti-aircraft gun by Breda

L73	57mm anti-aircraft gun on ZSU-57
L80	23mm anti-aircraft gun on ZSU-23-4
L81	time fuse for 105mm shells (UK)
L-83	Adler, airliner by Albatros WW2 (GE)
L92	MK20Rh202, 20mm anti-aircraft gun by Rheinmetall
L-100-50	Stretched Hercules by Lockheed
L419	konischer Lauf, 14mm-9mm, experimental conical bore WW2 (GE)
L-500	low-silhouette cross-country vehicle by Lohr (FR)
L-1011	transport aircraft by Lockheed
L1111	konischer Lauf 14mm-9mm, conical bore
L8202	konischer Lauf 28mm-20mm (GE), conical bore
LA	light artillery; local authority; local agent; leave allowance; letter of activation; letter of advice; letter of authority; leave advance; lieutenant-at-arms; lighter than air (aircraft); light automatic; low altitude; light alloy
La-3	Soviet aircraft *Lavochkin* (single-engined fighter) WW2
La-5	single-engined fighter
La-7	single-engined fighter
La-9	single-engined fighter
La-11	single-engined fighter 1948
La-15	Fantail, jet fighter 1949
LAA	lieutenant-at-arms; light aircraft (artillery) (guns)
LAAAS	JP-233, low-altitude airfield attack system (USAF programme)
LAADS	Los Angeles air defense sector
LAAF	Libyan Arab Air Force
LAAM	light anti-aircraft missile (battalion)
LAAR	liquid air accumulator rocket
LAARegt	light anti-aircraft regiment (RA)
LAAT	laser-augmented airborne TOW by Hughes
LAAV	light airborne attack vehicle
LAACC	light anti-aircraft control centre
LAB	low-altitude bombing
lab	laboratory; labour
Lab	pioneer and labour service
LABIFF	laser IFF interrogation and reply system by Eichweber
Labo	Landungsboot (tank landing craft) (EG)
LABS	low altitude bombing system; low approach bombing system
LAC	lunar aeronautical chart; light aircraft club; local advice centre; London assembly centre; local agency check; liberated areas committee
L/AC	leading aircraftman (RAF)

LaCBW	La Crosse boiling water reactor
LACE	liquid air cycle engine; local automatic circuit exchange
LACES	London airport cargo electronic processing scheme
Lacom	laser communications system by Eichweber
LACONIQ	laboratory computer on-line inquiry
LACV-30	landing air cushion vehicle 30 tons, light air cushion vessel 30 tons
L/ACW	leading aircraftwomen
LAD	light aid detachment; liquid agent detector; landing assistance device; look-out assist device
LADA	light air defence artillery; London air defence area
LADAR	laser detection and ranging
LADR	light air defence regiment
LAdv	lord advocate
LAF	legal aid fund; low angle fire
Lafayette	class, nuclear powered ballistic missile submarines (USN) SSBN
LAFM	Libyan Army Force Medal 1940-3
LAFRA	ladies auxiliary of the fleet reserve association
LAFTA	Latin American free trade association
LAG	light aircraft group
LAGEOS	laser geodynamic satellite 1976 (Nasa)
LaGG-1	... 3, single-engined monoplane fighter by Lavochkin WW2 (SU)
LAGS	laser activated geodetic satellite
Lahn	Klasse, submarine tenders (FGN)
LAHS	low-altitude high-speed
LAI	leaf area index
LAIR	Letterman Army institute of research (San Francisco)
LAIT	logistics assistance and instruction team
LALB	low-angle loft bombing
LALO	low-altitude observation
LAM	land arm mode (automatic landing)
lam	laminated
Lama	SA-315B, utility helicopter by AS
LAmafon	antisubmarine torpedo (FR)
LAMB	light armoured motor battery
Lambda	ESM/ECM system by Elettronica
LAMC	Letterman Army medical center
LAMCS	Latin American military communications system
LAMP	lunar analysis and mapping programme; low-altitude manned penetration (aircraft)
LAMPS	light airborne multi-purpose system (helicopter) (US programme)
LAMS	launch acoustic measuring system; load alleviation and mode stabilization

LAMSAC local authorities management services and computer committee
LAN   local apparent noon
LanarkYeo The Lanarkshire Yeomanry
Lancaster bomber by AVRO WW2
Lance   MGM-52, surface-to-surface tactical missile (US); class, patrol boats (RN)
Lance-bomb hand-thrown depth charge (RN)
Lancelot tank turret quadruple HOT, launcher by MAS
Lancer Boss-3500 side-lift container transporter for US Army by (UK firm Lancer Boss)
Lanciabas depth-charge launcher (IT)
LanCra   landing craft
LANCRAB landing craft and bases
          NAW North West African Waters WW2 (USN)
LANCENT Allied Land Forces Central Europe (Nato)
LANDENMARK Allied Land Forces Denmark (Nato)
LANDJUT Allied Land Forces Schleswig-Holstein and Jutland
Land Mattress artillery rockets WW2
LANDNON Allied Land Forces North Norway (Nato)
LANDNORWAY Allied Land Forces Norway
Land Rover FV-18000, jeep (UK)
Landsat earth resources technology satellite (US)
          -1 23 July 1972
          -2 22 January 1975
LANDSONOR Allied Land Forces South Norway
LANDSOUTH Allied Land Forces Southern Europe
LANDSOUTHEAST Allied Land Forces Southeastern Europe
Land Sparrow anti-aircraft missile system by Raytheon
Landtrain truck by Leyland
LANDUEALAND Allied Land Forces Zealand
LanForASCU landing force air support control unit
LanForTraCom landing force training command
LanForTraU landing force training unit
LanFus The Lancashire Fusiliers
lang   language
Langer Max 38cm quick-firing railway gun WW2 (GE)
LANRAC land army reunion association committee
LanRPWV The Lancashire Regiment The Prince of Wales's Volunteers
LANS   land navigations system by Taman
LANSEC SACLANT security messages
Lansen Saab-32, jet aircraft 1957 by Saab
LanShipRon landing ship squadron
Lant   Atlantic

LantCom Atlantic Command
LantComOpCen Atlantic (fleet) commander operational control center (USN)
LANTCOMPLAN SACLANT communications plan
LANTEX SACLANT Exercise
LANTFAP SACLANT frequency allocation plan
LantFleASWTacScol Atlantic fleet anti-submarine warfare tactical school
LantFlt Atlantic fleet
LantFltWpnRan Atlantic fleet weapons range
LantIntCen Atlantic intelligence centre
LANTIRN low-altitude navigation targeting infra-red for night (attack system) by Marconi/Oldelft
LantNavFacEngCom Atlantic naval facilities engineering command
LANTO SACLANT policy messages
LantResFlt Atlantic reserve fleet
LANSUMINT SACLANT intelligence summary
Lanze PLL, Panzerfaust, leicht, leistungs-gesteigert, light product improved anti-tank weapon by DNAG
LAO   legal assistance officer
LAOAR Latin American office of aerospace research (USAF)
LAP   load, assemble, pack; low altitude performance --Sidewinder, laboratory of aviation psychology (US); Lagearbeitsplatz by SEL (situation display)
LAPADS light airborne processing and display system (sonobuoy data) by Marconi
LAPES low altitude parachute extracting system
Laplander scout car by Volvo
LAR   local acquisition radar; liquid aircraft rocket; long-range aircraft rocket; light automatic rifle
LAR-II leichte Artillerierakete 110mm (light artillery rocket)
LARA   light armed reconnaissance aircraft (US programme) --Bronco
LARA/COIN light armed reconnaissance aircraft counter-insurgency (US)
Larak class, landing crafts (Iran)
LARAT-II anti-tank warhead for LAR-II
LARC   lighter amphibious resupply cargo, low altitude ride control --B-1; large automatic research computer; Liste d'Articles de Rechange à Codifier (spare parts list for codification)
LARC-5 lighter amphibious resupply cargo 5 tons by Consolidated
LARC-15 lighter amphibious resupply cargo 15 tons, wheeled amphibious vehicle by Fruehauf

LARC-60	lighter amphibious resupply cargo 60 tons by Pacific Car
LARC	Libyan American reconstruction commission
LAREC	Los Angeles reactor economics code
Lark	naval anti-aircraft missile, radar directed radio controlled WW2 (US)
LARO	Latin American regional office FAO
LA-RPV	Luftangriffs RPV (air attack remotely piloted vehicle)
LARS	London airways radar station; light artillery rocket system; low altitude radar system
LAS	large automated satellite; low altitude satellite; low airspace; line apparatus shops; legal aid service; leichter Ackerschlepper WW2 (GE) (Krupp tank prototype)
LASA	large aperture seismic array
LASCO	Latin American science co-operation office (UNESCO)
LASER	light amplification by stimulated emission of radiation
Lasercom	space-to-ground laser communications system
LASH	lighter aboard ship
LASL	Los Alamos scientific laboratory
LASP	low altitude space platform
LASR-2	Litton airborne surveillance radar
LASS	land surveillance satellite; lighter-than-air submarine simulator
LAsso	SS/AS-12, AM-10, light anti-surface semi-automatic optical missile, airborne anti-ship missile by AS
LAT	Lockheed air terminal; local apparent time; laser acquisition and tracking
LATAR	laser augmented target acquisition and recognition (system, airborne) by Northrop
LATCC	London air traffic control centre (West Drayton)
LATCRS	London air traffic control radar station
LatHt	latent heat
LATIL	cross-country tractor by CL
latrl	lateral
LATS	light air-transportable Swingfire by BAe
LAU	local administration unit
LAU-10	airborne rockets 5 in
LAU-19	airborne rockets 5 in
LAU-32	airborne rocket pod 7 fold 2.75 inch FFAR
LAU-51	airborne rocket pod for FFAR 2.75
LAU-68	airborne rocket pod for FFAR 2.75
LAU-117	airborne launcher for --Maverick by VARO

Lauster Gerät	jet-operated mine-sweeping equipment
LAV	The Lancashire Artillery Volunteers
Lavie	jet fighter/bomber CAS (Israel)
Lavochkin	Soviet planes --La-...
LAW	local air wing; library, amphibious warfare; M-72, light anti-tank weapon; laminated aluminium wing
LAW-80	light anti-tank weapon of the 1980s by Hunting Engineering
LAWA	Laserwarngerät by Eichweber (laser warning receiver)
LAWDS	LORAN inertial aided weapon delivery system
LAWRS	limited airport weather reporting system; limited airport weather reporting station
LAWS	light anti-tank weapon system
LAWTRAIN	indoor LAW-80 trainer by Miltrain
LAX	limited area auto-extractor by Ferranti (for CAAIS for MCMV)
LAZ-59	Echograph by Elac
Lazaga	class, patrol boats ASW, torpedoes guided missiles by Lürssen
LB	logistic base; litter bearer; liaison branch; landing barge; light bomber; letter box; link belt; local battery; line buffer
LBA	truck by Scania Vabis
LBAD	Lexington Blue Grass Army Depot
LBAT	towing vehicle by Scania Vabis
LBC	Liaison Branch, Capitol BUPERS
LbCHU	pound centigrade heat unit
LBCM	locator at the back course marker
L/Bdr	lance bombardier (RA)
LBE	landing barge, emergency repair
LBG	light bomber group
LBH	length, breadth, height
LBHorse	The Lothians and Border Horse (Regiment)
LBM	lever breech mechanism
LBMS	land-based ballistic missile system
LBn	labour battalion
LBNP	lower body negative pressure
LBP	landing boat, personnel; length between perpendiculars
LBR	line of bomb release
L/Br	lance bombardier
lbr	labor (US)
LBRC	The Leyland & Birmingham Rubber Company Ltd (BTR daughter)
LBS	landing barge, support; life boat station; light bomber, strike (aircraft)
lbs	pounds
LBT	lorry-borne troops
LBTS	land-based test site
LBV	landing boat, vehicles
LC	lieutenant colonel; lieutenant commander; lord chancellor; lines

of communications; Lower Canada;
logistic capacity; legitimate
child(ren); letter contract;
landing craft; lower case;
latent crimp (bi-component acrylic
fibre); links and chargers STANAG;
launching control; light case
(bomb); lead covered; little
change

L/C   lance corporal
LC-bomb light case bomb (USAF)
LC-130 Hercules, arctic version cargo air-
craft
LC-4561 Litton computer, naval digital
computer
LCA   lord commissioner of the admiralty;
launcher control area (missiles);
logistic control activity; landing
craft, artillery; landing craft,
assault; low-cost aircraft; low-
cost automation
LCAC   landing craft, air cushion
LCAO   linear combination of atomic
orbitals
LCAT   landing craft availability table
LCAVAT landing craft and amphibious vehicle
assignment table
LCAX   landing craft, assault, experimental
LCB   landing craft, barge; linear control
block; longitudinal centre of
buoyancy; lord chief baron
LCC   landing craft, control; launch control centre; life cycle cost(ing);
lead coated copper; amphibious
command ship; London county
council; labour class code; London
communications committee; logistic
coordination centre ACE
LCCB   local configuration control board
LCCE   life cycle cost estimate
LCD   light cruiser division; liquid
crystal display
L/Cdr lieutenant commander
LCE   landing craft, emergency repair;
land-covered earth; latest cost
estimate
LCEHV low-cost expandable harassment
vehicle (US programme) drones
LCEOP landing craft, engine overhaul
parties
LCF   landing craft flotilla; laminar flow
control; longitudinal centre of
floatation; low-cycle fatigue;
landing craft, flak
LCFF   landing craft, flotilla flagship
LCFL   landing craft, flotilla leader
LCFlotPac landing craft flotilla, Pacific
fleet
LCG   landing craft, gun; longitudinal
centre of gravity

LCGL   landing craft, gun, large
LCGM   landing craft, gun, medium
LCGP   landing craft group
LCHQ   local command headquarters
lchr   launcher
LCHTF low-cycle high-temperature fatigue
LCI   launcher control indicator;
landing craft, infantry
LCIDiv landing craft, infantry division
LCIFF   landing craft, infantry flotilla
flagship
LCIFlot landing craft, infantry flotilla
LCIG   landing craft, infantry gunboat
LCIGrp landing craft, infantry group
LCIL   landing craft, infantry large
LCILFlot landing craft, infantry large
flotilla
LCIM   landing craft, infantry mortar
LCIR   landing craft, infantry rocket
LCJ   lord chief justice
lcl   local
LCL   landing craft, logistic (UK); less
than car-load (lot); lower control
limit; library control language;
low capacity link
LCLU   land control and logic units
LCM   life cycle management; M-224,
light-weight company mortar;
landing craft, mechanized (USN)
(tracked) Mk I ... VII
LCMM   life cycle management method
LCMSO landing craft material supply
officer
LCN   local civil noon; landing craft,
navigator; load classification
number
LCNN   land commander North Norway (Nato)
LCNT   Link celestial navigation trainer
LCO   launching control officer; landing
craft officer; land control
operations
LCOCU landing craft, obstruction clearing
unit
LCol   lieutenant colonel
LCOP   logistics control office Pacific
L/Corp lance corporal
LCP   landing craft, personnel; light
company patrol; League of Coloured
Peoples; launch control post;
logistic capabilities plan; local
calibration procedures; last
complete programme; low cost
production
LCPFCS low cost precision force control
system
LCP-FY logistics capabilities plan, fiscal
year
LCpl   lance corporal
LCPL   landing craft, personnel, large
LCPM   landing craft, personnel, medium

LCPN	landing craft, personnel, nested
LCPP	landing craft, personnel, plastic
LCPR	landing craft, personnel, ramped
LCPSy	landing craft, personnel, survey
LCR	landing craft, raiding; limited combat ready (pilot)
LCr	lieutenant commander
LCRL	landing craft, rubber, large
LCRR	landing craft, rubber, rocket
LCRS	landing craft, rubber, small
Lcrs	Lancers (UK)
LCRU	lunar communications relay unit; landing craft recovery unit
LCS	landing craft, support; load carrying structure; large capacity store; large core storage; light cruiser squadron
LCSL	landing craft, support, large
LCSM	landing craft, support, medium
LCSR	landing craft, swimmer recovery; landing craft, swimmer reconnaissance; landing craft, support, rocket
LCSS	land combat support system; landing craft, support, small
LCT	latest closing time; local civil time; landing craft, tank; linear combination technique; launching control trailer; Laboratoire Central de Telecommunications (Velizy FR)
LCTA	landing craft, tank, armoured
lctd	located
lctr	locator (beacon)
LCU	large close-up (photography); landing craft, universal; landing craft, utility
LCV	landing craft, vehicles
LCVP	landing craft, vehicles and personnel
LCW	line control word
LCWM	list of changes in war material
lczr	localizer (beacon)
LD	London division; Lowland division; London Docks; list of drawings; line of departure; line of duty; light dragoons; laser detector; lift(over) drag (ratio) plane; lethal dose; light difference; low density
Ld	Lord
ld	land; lead; load; limited
L&D	loss and damage
LD-50	medium lethal dose
LD-55	tractor for semi-trailers by Scammell
LDA	localizer, direction aid; land development aircraft
LDA-01	land development aircraft by Lockspeiser
LDAPS	long duration auxiliary power system
LDB	light distribution box
LDC	less developed countries; long distance call; lower dead centre; link driving computer; local defence centre; logistic data centre
LDD	local defence division; letter of determination dependency; laser decoy device
LDEF	long duration exposure facility (materials testing satellite) (Nasa)
LDF	linear discriminate function; local defence forces
ldg	leading; landing; logging; loading
Ldg	Ladung (charge)
LDG	Lagedarstellungsgerät (situation display) (GE)
ldg&dely	landing and delivery
ldgs	lodgings
LdgSto	leading stoker (RN)
LdgW	Ladungswerfer (mortar)
LDH	London district headquarters
LDisFFD	line of departure is friendly forward disposition
LDisPPos	line of departure is present position
ldk	lower deck
LDL	lower deviation level
LDLF	large distributed load freighter aircraft by Boeing
LDMWR	limited depot maintenance work requirements
LDMX	local digital message exchange
LDNS	Litef doppler navigation system by Litef
LDO	liaison duty officer
LDOT	limited duty officer, temporary
Ldp	Lordship
LDP	local data processor
LDPC	London district provost company
LDPE	low density poly-ethylene
ldr	leader; ledger
LDR	laser designator/rangefinder
ldry	laundry
Lds	Lords
lds	loads
LDSRA	logistic doctrines systems and readiness agency (US Army)
LDTR	long dwell time radar NADGE
LdTTy	land line teletype
LDV	Local Defence Volunteers (UK) --Home Guard; Luftwaffendienstvorschrift (Air Force manual) (GAF)
LDVI	low dollar value item
LDX	long distance xerography
LDY	Leicestershire and Derbyshire Yeomanry
LE	leading edge; lower establishment; labour exchange; large end; left eye; logic element; low explosive (powder); light equipment

LEA local education authority

LEAA law enforcement assistance administration (US)

LEAD Letterkenny Army Depot (US)

Leahy class, cruisers, guided missiles (USN CG)

LEA vesssle leased to ... (US)

  EC Equador
  BZ Brazil
  CH China
  FR France
  GR Greece
  MX Mexico
  NE The Netherlands
  NO Norway
  PA Panama
  PE Peru
  PG Paraguay
  RU Russia
  UK The United Kingdom
  UR Uruguay

Leander class, frigates (RN)

LEAP lift-off elevation and azimuth programmer

Learstar-600 Challenger, twin jet by Canadair

LEASAT world-wide satellite communications system for USN by Hughes

LEC local employment committee; Lachmüller Engineering Company

led ledger

LED light emitting diode

Lee M-3, giant tank WW2

LEED low energy electron diffraction

Lee Enfield rifle WW2 (UK) --SMLE

LEES Loral electronic environment simulator

LeFlaSys Lenkwaffenfliegerabwehrsystem (anti-aircraft guided missile system) (GE)

LEFM linear elastic fracture mechanics

LEG logistical expediting group

LegOff legal officer

LeicesterYeo The Leicestershire Prince Albert's Own Yeomanry

Leigh Light airborne search light against surface vessels WW2 (RAF)

LeinsR The Royal Leinster Regiment

LEKO-70 trainer aircraft by Valmet

LeIs Leeward Islands

LEM lunar excursion module; laser exhaust measurement

LEM-3 Laserentfernungsmesser by SEL (laser rangefinder)

LEMDAT Datenaufbereitungsgerät für Laserentfernungsmesser by SEL (data processing equipment for LEM-3)

LEMSTAR laser fire control system by AEG

Leningrad class, helicopter cruisers (SU)

Lentra class, spy ships (SU)

LEO Lyons Electronics Office

Leon mine drifting mine

Leonidas armoured fighting vehicle by Steyr (Greece)

Leopard (1...2) main battle tank by Krauss-Maffei

Leopard-8 8x8 amphibious vehicle by MCS Giletti

LEP locally enlisted personnel

LEPORE long-term and expanded programme of ocean research and exploration

LEPT long-endurance patrolling torpedo

LertCon alert condition

LERX leading edge root extension --Harrier wing

LES leave and earnings statement; local engineering specifications; Lincoln experimental satellite; launch escape system (Nasa); lunar escape system (Nasa); light emitting switch; light exposure speed; support landing boat

LESC light emitting switch control

LESS least cost estimating and scheduling

LEST low energy speed transmission

LET launch escape tower; leading edge trigger; linear energy transfer

LETE land engineering test establishment (Ottawa)

LEV lunar excursion vehicle (Nasa)

Lewis gun light machine gun

Lewisite cholo-vinyl-di-chlor-arsine (war gas)

LeWS leichter Wehrmachtschlepper (light (Army tractor) WW2 (GE)

LEX land exercise

Lexgard bullet-proof glass by GE-Plastics

LF The Lancashire Fusiliers; Legion of Frontiersmen; land forces; landing force; ledger folio; limiting fragmentation; low frequency; line feed; logic function; light face; laser rangefinder; life float; luminous flash (rocket); live (real) flying; live firing

LF-2 laser rangefinder by Barr & Stroud

LF-11 tank gunner's sight by Barr & Stroud

LF-57 submachine gun 9mm by Franchi

LFA local freight agent; light field ambulance; Land Force, Airmobility STANAG

LF-ADF low frequency airborne (automatic) direction finder

LFB London Fire Brigade

LFC low frequency current

LFCM low frequency cross modulation

LFCS land forces classification system

LFD least fatal dose; low fat diet

LFFET	low frequency field effect transistor
LFH	Lenkflugkörperhubschrauber by MBB (missile-armed helicopter)
LFK	Lenkflugkörper (guided missile)
LFM	landing force manual, limited area fine mesh model
LFMTS	low-frequency field maintenance test set --Roland
LFNGFT	landing force naval gunfire team
LFTC	landing force training command
LFTCU	landing force training command unit
LFTU	landing force training unit
LFU	light fighting unit
LFPS	low frequency phase shifter
LFR	light field reconnaissance; light fighter/reconnaissance (aircraft); low frequency range; inshore fire support ship -IFS -LSMR
LFRD	lot fraction reliability deviation
LFS	landing force support ship; logical file structure
LFSD	landing force support device (weapon)
LFSS	landing force support ship
lft	lift; leaflet; linear foot
LFTD	land force tactical doctrine (Nato)
LG	The Life Guards; landing ground; large grain (powder); line graph; linear gate; linkage groups
lg	long
LG	Lewis Gun; light (automatic) gun; Lasergage Limited (Croydon UK)
LG-240	(290, 310), Leichgeschütz 15cm (light gun)
LGA	lieutenant general in charge of administration
LgA	lodging allowance
LGB	laser guided bomb (USAF); local government board
LGBC	local government boundary commission
LGC	laboratory of the government chemist; lead gas-check (projectile); lunar (module) guidance computer (Nasa)
LGDM	Paveway family, laser guided dispenser munition
lge	large
LGEB	local government examination board
LGen	lieutenant general
LGIO	local government information office (for England and Wales)
LGK-019	Leuchtgefechtskopf --DIRA (illumination warhead)
LGM	land-based guided missile; anti-tank trip-wire mine (SU)
LGM-25C	Titan, land-based guided missile inter-continental ballistic missile by Martin

LGM-30	Minuteman inter-continental ballistic missile by Boeing
LGM-30F	Minuteman II
LGM-30G	Minuteman III
LGO	Lamont geological observatory (US)
LGS	landing guidance system
LGSL	light general service lorry
LGSW	limbered general service wagon
lgt	light
lgtd	lighted
lgth	length
LgthColm	length of column
LgTn	long ton
LGU	laser guidance unit
LH	Legion of Honour; left hand (drive); linear hybrid; light house; locating head
LH^2	liquid hydrogen
LH-66	high-performance anti-submarine radar
LHA	Lord High Admiral; local health authority; landing platform helicopter assault; local hour angle; light helicopter, assault; amphibious assault ship (USN) (general purpose)
LHAMS	local hour angle of mean sun
LHAO	The Lord High Admiral's Office
LHC	Lord High Chancellor; Lord High Commissioner; left hand circular
LHD	left hand drive
LHDC	lateral homing depth charge
LHOX	low and high pressure oxygen; liquid high pressure oxygen
LHP	left hand pusher (engine); leadless hermetic package
LHr	lumen hour
LHS	left hand side
LHSV	liquid hourly space velocity
LHT	Lord High Treasurer
LHWN	lowest high water, neap tides
LI	longitudinal interval; light infantry; Leeward Islands; line item; letter of introduction
Li-2	tactical transport aircraft by Lisunov (SU)
LI-11	wooden pressure mine (Sweden)
lib	liberal
LIB	lorryborne infantry brigade
LbCon	Library of Congress (US)
LibDes	Libyan Desert
Libelle	class, torpedo boats (EG)
Liberator	B-24, bomber by Consolidated
LibMish	US Military mission to Liberia
Librascope	submarine fire control system by Singer
LIC	logistics indoctrination course; Atlantic intelligence centre; linear integrated circuit

lic   licence
Lichtenstein airborne radar WW2 (GE)
LICROSS League of the International Red
       Cross Societies
LID   light infantry depot; laser image
       display
LIDAR light detection and ranging

LIDB   logistics intelligence data base
LIDF   Leeward Islands defence force
LIDO   Lindauer Dornier GmbH (Lindau)
LIDS   lift improvement devices --Harrier
LIE   light identification equipment
Lieut lieutenant
      Cdr Lieutenant Commander
      Com Lieutenant Commander
      Col Lieutenant Colonel
      Gen Lieutenant General
      Gov Lieutenant Governor
LiF   lithium fluoride
LIF   logistics intelligence file;
      layway of industrial facilities
LifeSta lifeboat station
LIF-MoP linerally frequency modulated pulse
LIFO   last in - first out
LIFRAM liquid fuel ramjet (engine)
LIFTU Lynx intensive flying trials unit
       AAC (UK)
Light AAMisBn light anti-aircraft missile
        battalion (USMC)
Light Gun 105mm (UK)
Lightning jet fighter 1957 by BAC; P-38,
       fighter/interceptor by Lockheed
LightPhotoRon light photographic squadron
Light Water Purple K-Powder (US)
LIL   large ionic lithophile
LILO   last in - last out
LILS   lead in light system (for aircraft)
LIM   losing inventory manager; locator
      at inner marker
lim   limit(ed)
Lim-2   Mig-15, Polish version
Lim-5   Mig-5, Polish version
      P fighter
      M close support aircraft
Lim-7   Mig-19, Polish version
LIM-49A Spartan, anti-ballistic missile by
       MDA
Limbo   mortar bomb depth charge (RN)
LimDat limiting date
LimDis limited distribution
LimDu   limited duty
LIN   line item number
lin   linear
LinAc   linear accelerator(AWRE Aldermaston)
LINAS laser inertial navigation and attack
      system by Ferranti
Lince   naval target tracker IR/TV by OTO-
      Melara; laser improved naval
      combat equipment

LINCLOE lightweight individual combat
       clothing and equipment
Lincoln strategic bomber by AVRO (UK)
LincolnR The Royal Lincolnshire Regiment
LinCompEx linked compressor and expander
Lindau class, coastal mine sweepers (FGN)
Lindormen class, mine-layers (Denmark)
Linescan infra-red airborne scanner by BAC
Linesman air defence ground environment
       (UK) (radially linked radar
       stations)
Link   between computerized naval command
      and information system
      1   cable
      11 wireless
      14 teleprinter
Linse   remote controlled explosives boat
      WW2 (GE)
LIO   lesser included offence
LIOD   laser infra-red optical (passive)
      (fire) director by HSA; laser
      inflight obstacle detector;
      lightweight optronic (fire)
      director HSA
Lion   Leopard MBT export version by OTO-
      Melara
LIR   The London Irish Rifles
LIRF   low-intensity reciprocity failure
      (photo
LIROD   lightweight radar/optronic director
      by HSA
LISV   light infantry support vehicle
LIT   light inter-theatre transport;
      logistic implications test
Litas   visual approach system by Metalite
LITEF   Litton Technische Werke (Freiburg)
Little Boy Hiroshima bomb
Little David mortar 91.4cm WW2 (US)
Little Feller nuclear bomb 1962 (Nevada)
Little Henry XH-20, experimental helicopter
       ramjets by McDonnell
Little Joe short-range anti-aircraft
       missile flare-sighted radio
       controlled WW2 (USN)
Little John M-51, tactical nuclear missile
       (US)
Littlejohn adapter taper bore barrel
          attached to normal
          barrel
Littler miniature remotely piloted vehicle
Little Willie tank WW2 (UK)
LIVEX   live exercise (Nato)
LivplScot The Liverpool Scottish
LIY   The Lincolnshire Imperial Yeomanry
LJ   Little John; life jacket; Lord
      Justice
LJD   laser jamming device
Ljungman 6.5mm semi-automatic rifle
       (Sweden)
LKA   amphibious attack cargo ship -APA;
      5 ton light tank by Krupp

LKR	Lieferkoordinierungsrichtlinie (guideline for procurement coordination)	LMF	last meal furnished
Lkw	Lastkraftwagen (lorry, truck)	LMFBR	light metal fast breeder reactor; liquid metal cooled fast breeder reactor
LL	Lord Lieutenant; light line; land line; load line; double L sweep (RN); Luftlande (airborne)	LMG	light machine gun
L-L	mortar 81mm by ECIA	LMG-1	lightweight machine gun 7.62mm by Maremont
LL sweep	double loop magnetic mine sweep (RN)	LMI	logistics management institute (US)
LLAD	low level air defence (system)	LMM	locator at middle marker
LLBS	low level bombing system; low level bomb sight	LMMF	local maintenance and management of facilities
LLC	long lines coordination	lmn	lineman
LLD	low level discriminator	LMO	lens-modulated oscillator; light machine oil
LLDLBR	low level defence land based radar	LMP	lead, metal point (projectile); light marching pack; lunar module pilot
LLDV	Lue Luong Dac Viet (Vietnamese Special Forces)		
LLEIS	low level end item subdivision	LMPT	logistics and material planning team
LLFK	Luft-Luft Flugkörper (air-to-air missile)	LMS	Lockheed Missile & Space Corporation; light pontoon bridge (Czech)
LLFM	low level flux monitor	LMT	local mean time; length mass time; low mobility tanker (vehicle) (UK)
LLH	low level heating		
LLI	low level interdiction; longitude and latitude indicator; Lord Lieutenant of Ireland	lmt	limit
		LMT	Le Matériel Téléphonique (Boulogne) (Thomson-CSF daughter)
LLL	Lawrence Livermore Laboratory (University of California); low level logic; loose leaf ledger	LMVD	Lower Mississippi Valley Division
		LMW	land mine warfare; Luftminenwerfer (compressed air mortar)
LLLGB	low level laser guided bomb	LN	local national; Lorenz Navigation System; Litton Navigation System
LLLO	lend-lease liaison officer		
LLLTV	low light level television	LN-33	Litton navigator twin inertial platforms
LLP	leased long-lines programme (Nato)		
LLR	line of least resistance	LNC	local naval commander
LLS	lunar logistic system; large lot storage	LNDH	local nationals direct hire
		LNFB	linear negative feedback
LLSP	low level search pattern (interceptors)	LNG	liquified natural gas; Luftfahrtnavigationsgerät by LITEF (aeronautical navigation system)
LLSV	lunar logistic system vehicle		
LLT	long lead time NADGE	LNI	land navigation installation
LLTI	long lead time items	LnO	liaison officer
LLV	lunar logistics vehicle; link lift vehicle	LNR	low noise receiver
		LNS-517	land navigation system
LLW	low level waste (nuclear)	LNU	Luftnahunterstützung (close air support)
LLWDS	low level weapon delivery system		
LM	Lord Mayor; Legion of Merit; linesman; list of materials; linear monolithic (computer); lower melting; land mine; lunar module	LO	liaison officer; landing officer; left observer; letter order; legal officer; launch operator; lubrication order; local oscillator; level off; low order; lubricating oil
LM-2	underwater grenade by ALR		
LMA	low moisture avidity; launcher mechanical assembly	LO-20000	electronic teleprinter by SEL
		LOA	local overseas allowance (UK); leave of absentee; length overall; light observation aircraft
LMB	liquidation and manpower board; local message box		
LMC	large megallanic cloud	load&dischg	loading and discharging
LMCo	Elm City Manufacturing Company	LOAL	lock-on after launch (missile target mode)
LMD	light mechanical digger by Thornycroft		
		LoAlt	low altitude
LMEC	liquid metal engineering centre	LOAN	vessel loaned to ... (US)

	A Army
	C Coast Guard
	M miscellaneous activity
	S States
	W War Shipping Administration

LOB   line of balance; left out of battle
LOBAL   long base line buoy
LOBAR   long base line radar
LOBL   lock-on before launch (missile
           target mode)
LOC   launch operations centre; launch
           operations complex; lines of com-
           munications; Liberty of Congress
loc   localizer; location; locality
LOCA   loss of coolant accident
LOCALS   low cost airborne laser seeker
LOCI   list of cancelled items
LOCK   logistical operational control key
loco   locomotive
LOCPORT   lines of communications ports
LOCU   landing craft obstruction clearance
           unit
LOCUS-16   air defence data handling system
           by Marconi
Locust   anti-radiation drones by GD+VFW
LOD   line of departure; line of duty;
           locally one-dimensional; location
           dependent; list of drawings
LODC   local defence district craft
LODI   list of deleted items
LODOR   loaded, waiting orders
LOEP   list of effective parts PURS
LOF   line of fire
LOFAAD   low altitude forward area air defence
LOFAADS   low altitude forward area air
           defence system --Roland
LOFAR   low frequency acquisition and
           ranging
LofC   lines of communication
LOFT   line-oriented flight (simulation)
           training
LOFTI   low frequency trans-ionospheric
           (satellite)
LOG   land force logistics STANAG;
           logistics management oriented file
           NARDIS
Logair   US contract logistic airlift service
LogC   logistics centre
LogDESMAP DoD logistics data element stan-
           dardization and management
           programme
LogDESMO   DoD logistics data element stan-
           dardization management office
LogDiv   logistics division
LogEx   logistics exercise
LOGMAP   US Army logistics system master plan
LogMIS   logistics management information
           system
LogOIS   logistics operating information
           system

LogPlan   DoD logistics systems plan
LogR   logistical ratio
LogRep   logistics representative
LogReqs   logistics requisitions
LogSystLW Logistisches System der Luftwaffe
           (German air force logistics
           system)
LOH   light observation helicopter
LOHAP   light observation helicopter
           avionics pack by GTE Sylvania
LOI   lunar orbit insertion; letter of
           instruction; letter of interest;
           list of items
LOLA   lunar orbit and landing approach;
           library on-line acquisition
Lolite   portable small surveillance device
           night sight by Pilkington
LOM   locator at outer marker;
           Legion of Merit (US)
LOMAD   low-to-medium altitude air defence
LondScot   The London Scottish Regiment
long   longitude
Long Tom   M-59, 155mm field gun (US)
Lonsborough lamp/portable illumination
           light (UK)
Loon   flying bomb V-1 copy (US)
Loopwheel new tank track-laying system by
           Lockheed
LOP   line of position; logistics officer
           programme; local operational plot
LOPAC   load optimization passenger accep-
           tance and control (computer)
BOPAIR   long path infra-red
LOPAR   low power acquisition radar
LOPS   length of patient's stay
LOPU   logistics organization planning unit
LOR   light output ratio; lunar orbital
           rendezvous
lor   lorried; lorryborne
LO-R   low intensity survey meter
LORAAS   VPX, long-range airborne ASW system
LORAC   long-range accuracy (radar);
           long-range accuracy (hyperbolic
           navigation system)
LORAD   long-range air defence; long-range
           active detection (system)
LORAN   long-range radio aid to navigation
           D   mobile ground control station
           DM   double master
           DS   double slave
           S   slave
           long-range air navigation
LORAP   long-range aerial panoramic camera
           by Fairchild
LORAPH   long-range passive homing (system)
LORD   long-range detection (radar)
Lorenz   approach beam --LN
LORIDS   long-range Iranian detection system
           (anti-aircraft defence)
LORO   lobe-on receive-only (passive ECCM
           scan technique)

LOROC   long-range off-board countermeasures
LOROP   long-range optical camera
LORV   low observation re-entry vehicle
Lory   anti-personnel mine (IT)
LOS   logistic operation streamline;
             length of service; line of supply;
             line of sight; loss of signal;
             level of supply
LOSAM   low altitude surface-to-air missile
Los Angeles class, nuclear powered attack
             submarines (USN SSN)
LOSAT   lunar orbiter satellite
LOSS   large object salvage system
Lost   Lommel & Steinkopf, Gelbkreuz war gas
             vessel lost by ... (USN)
             A accident
             E emergency action
             P perils of the sea
LOT   live operational training (course);
             large orbital telescope; load on
             top (oil tanker)
LOTADS   long-term world-wide air defence
             study
LOTCIP   long-term communications improvement
             plan
Lothians   The First and Second Lothians and
             Border Horse Regiment
LOTS   logistics over the shore (vehicle);
             logistics over the shore operation;
             LORAN operational training school
LOUH   light observation utility helicopter
Loutch   Soviet domestic communications
             satellite
LOX   liquid oxygen; liquid oxygen
             explosive
Loyals   The North Lancashire Loyal Regiment
LP   listening post; Lord Provost; last
             paid; litter patient; Last Post;
             low pressure; low power; line
             printer; limited production; low
             pass; liquid petroleum; long
             playing; list of parts; launch
             platform; linear programming
LP-3   ...8 laser distance measuring equip-
             ment by Simrad
LPA   linear pulse amplifier; link pack
             area; log periodic antennas;
             amphibious transport vessel
LPB   light patrol boat
LPB-500   light patrol boat by Zodiac (rubber)
LPC   last pay certificate; linear periodic
             coding; low pressure chamber;
             launch pod container; Lockheed
             Propulsion Company; Laser Products
             Corporation (Fountain Valley Cal.)
LPC-24   Vocoder, narrow-band digital lang-
             uage processor by E-Systems
LPCbr   low pressure chamber
LPCI   low pressure coolant injection system
LPD   landing platform, dock; low perfor-

           mance drone; landing point desig-
             nator; linear phasing device
LPD-20   pulse doppler search radar by
             Contraves
LPE   launch preparation equipment
LPEC   launch preparation equipment com-
             partment
LPES   launch preparation equipment set
LPF   low pass filter
LPG   liquified petroleum gas (tanker)
LPH   landing platform, helicopters
LPI   lines per inch; low power illumina-
             tor; low probability of intercept
             (system)
LPL   list processing language
LPM   lines per minute; lunar portable
             magnetometer
LPMES   logistics performance measurement
             and evaluation system
LPO   local purchasing officer; local
             post officer; land projection
             operation
LPO-50   portable flame-thrower (EG)
LPR   local payment receipt; leadership
             potential rating; amphibious
             transport vehicle, small APD
LPRE   liquid propellant rocket engine
LPS   lines per second; linear pulse
             sector; Lord Privy Seal
LPSS   amphibious transport submarine APSS
LP-T   limited production - test
LPT   low pressure test
LPTI   limited production type item
LPTIS   Laguna Peak tracking and injection
             station
LP-U   limited production - urgent
LPV   landing platform, vehicles;
             launching point vertical
LPW   lumens per watt
lPzMi   leichte Panzermine (light anti-tank
             mine)
LR   long range; long rifle; landing
             radar; light railway; log run;
             The London Regiment; The Loyal
             Regiment; The Lowland Regiment;
             local rank; leave rations
lr   learner
LR   mortar 60mm by Thomson/Brandt
LR-1416   ... 1432, Litef Rechner by Litef
             (mobile digital calculator)
LRA   long-range aviation
LRAC-89   STRIM, anti-tank rocket launcher
             (FR)
LRADP   long-range active duty programme
LRANS   long-range area navigator system
LRAP   long-range acoustic propagation
             programme
LRAssault 9mm submachine gun by MAC
             Marietta
LRB   The London Rifle Brigade (Rangers)

LRBA	long-range bomber aircraft 2500 nm; Laboratoire de Recherches Ballistiques et Aerodynamiques (ballistics and aerodynamics research laboratory)
LRC	Lewis Research Center (Nasa); Langley Research Center (Nasa); longitudinal redundancy check; long-range cruise (speed)
LRCA	long-range combat aircraft
LRCS	long range cruise speed; League of Red Cross Societies
LRD	labour research department
LRDC	long range defence concept
LRDG	long range desert group WW2
LRDMM	long-range dual mission missile
LReg	leading regulator
LREW	long-range early warning
LRF	laser rangefinder
LRFax	low resolution facsimile
LRG	long-range gun
LRI	Luft- & Raumfahrtindustrie (aerospace industry)
LRL	Lawrence Radiation Laboratory; lunar receiving laboratory
LRMG	lockless rifle/machine gun by Hughes (5.56mm plastic cartridges)
LRMP	long-range maritime patrol (aircraft)
LRMR	long-range maritime reconnaissance (aircraft)
LRMTS	laser ranger and marked target seeker (airborne for LMTR) by Ferranti
LRN	lay reference number (mine warfare)
LRNC	long reference number code
LRNOD	long range night observation device
LRP	long range patrol (aircraft); logistic research project
LRPA	long range patrol aircraft
LRR	long range radar; long range requirement; lower reduced rate (tax)
LRR-103	portable laser rangefinder (artillery)
LRRA	Light Regiment Royal Artillery
LRRP	long range reconnaissance patrol
LRRS	long range radar site
LRRT	long range radio telephone
LRS	light recovery section; light repair section; link-route segments
Lrs	Lancers
LRS	laser rangefinder system; log and reporting system
LRS-3	... 4, laser ranger system with integrated computer by OIP
LRSOM	long-range stand-off missile
LRSS	long range survey system
LRSTPP	long range scientific technical planning programme
LRT	long range transport (aircraft); long range typhoon
LRTA	long range transport aircraft 2500 nm
LRTgt	last resort target
LRTNF	long range theatre nuclear forces (Nato)
LRU	line replaceable unit; least recently used; less than release unit
LRV	lunar roving vehicle (Nasa); Lincoln Rifle Volunteers
LRWES	long range weapons experimental station
LS	line scan; long shot; long sight; loud speaker; list of specifications; landing ship; left side, launch station; lead sheet; local sunset; leading seaman; The London Scottish Regiment; land service; letter service; labour service; lump sum (pay); leichtes Spitzgeschoss (light pointed projectile)
L+S Munition	Leucht & Signalmunition (illumination and signals ammunition)
LSA	landing ship assault; labour service agency; labour surplus area; logistics support area; logistics support arrangement (for helicopter parts) (RN RNN FN BAOR); Landsimulationsanlage (der Marinewaffenschule) (land-based simulator of the FGN weapons school)
LSAC	London Small Arms Company
L-SAT	large satellite communications platform by ESA
LSB	landing ship, bombardment; lower side band; least significant bit; library services branch
LSBA	leading sick bay attendant
LSC	London salvage corps; lower school certificate
LSCP	low speed card punch
LSD	landing ship, dock; language for systems development; large screen display; least significant digit; lysergic acid diethylamide (drug); lightermen, stevedores and dockers
LSE	longitudinal section electric; landing signal enlisted; life support equipment; Laurence, Scott & Electromotors (UK)
LSES	large surface effect ship
LSF	landing ship, fighter direction; lumped selection filters
LSFA	logistic system feasibility analysis
LSFF	landing ship, flotilla flagship
LSFO	logistics support field office
LSG	light and sound grenade (stun grenade) (UK); limited sub-group
LS&GC	long service and good conduct (medal)

LS&GCM	long service and good conduct medal
LSGR	logistic support group regiment RCT
L/Sgt	lance sergeant
LSH	Lord Strathcona's Horse Regiment (Canada); landing ship, headquarters; landing ship, helicopters
LSHL	landing ship, headquarters, large
LSH/LSF	landing ship, helicopters/landing ship fighter direction
LSHS	landing ship, headquarters, small
LSI	large scale integration; landing ship, infantry; limited standard item; Lear Siegler Incorporated (Santa Monica)
LSIC	large scale integrated circuits
LSIG	landing ship, infantry, gunboat; linear scan image generator
LSIL	landing ship, infantry, large (USN); landing ship, infantry, little (Nato)
LSIM	landing ship, infantry, mortar
LSI-MOS	large scale integration of metal oxide silicon ----semi-conductors
LSIR	landing ship, infantry, rockets
LSK	leichtes schwebefähiges Kampfflugzeug (light hovering combat aircraft) (GE); Luftstreitkräfte (EG air forces)
LSK/LV	Luftstreitkräfte/Luftverteidigung (EG air defence)
LSL	landing ship logistic; long service list; low speed logic; ladder static logic; lump sum leave (payment)
	BP basic pay
	PMA personal money allowance
	QTRS quarters
	SUBS subsistence
LSL-Spur	leichtes Spitzgeschoss mit Leuchtspur (light pointed projectile with tracer)
LSM	landing ship, medium; long service (and good conduct) medal; longitudinal section magnetic; lunar surface magnetometer; Landminenschnellräummittel (rapid land-mine clearing equipment); Lanceur Strategique Mobile (mobile strategic missile)
LSMR	landing ship, medium, rockets
LSMS	lightweight Sea Sparrow missile system
LSMSO	landing ship material supply officer
LSOC	logistical support operations centre
LSP	logistical support plan; lump sum payment
LSPC	logistic system policy committee
LSPET	lunar sample preliminary examination team

LSPTP	low speed paper tape punch
LSPU	Lear Siegler project update US program land sonobuoys geophones dispensed by RPVs
LSQA	local system queue area
LSR	landing ship, rocket; The London Scottish Regiment; logistic support requirements (system); lump sum (payment) on return; The Lone Scouts Regiment (Canada); loose snow on runway
	-P loose snow on runway patchy
LSR-20000	IFF responder by Siemens
LSRV	The London Scottish Rifle Volunteers
LSS	life saving service; life saving station; limited storage site; logistic support system; landing ship, support; lunar soil simulator
LSSC	light SEAL support craft (sea-air-land team)
LSSF	limited service storage facility; land special security force
LSSG	logistics studies steering group
LSSL	landing support ship, large
LST	laser spotter tracker; landing ship, tanks; low supersonic transport (aircraft); local sideral time; local standard time
LSTH	landing ship, tank, hospital (casualty evacuation)
L/Sto	leading stoker
LST/SCAM	laser spot tracker/strike camera airborne pod by Martin Marietta
LSU	landing ship, utility; labour service unit
LSV	landing ship, vehicles; vehicle cargo ship
LSW	light support weapon
LSZ	Luftschleppziel (towed aerial target)
LSZ-075	towed aerial target by RFB
LT	letter telegram; local time; landing team
lt	left; light
1Lt	first lieutenant
2Lt	second lieutenant
LT	low tension; line telegraphy; line telephony; large tug; long ton; light ton; line telecommunications
LTA	lighter than air; light transport aircraft; Leichtes Transport- & Arbeitsflugzeug (light transport and utility aircraft)
LTB	line term buffer; low tension battery
LTBT	limited test ban treaty
LtC	lieutenant colonel
LtCdr	lieutenant commander
LtCol	lieutenant colonel
LtCom	lieutenant commander

LtComdr	lieutenant commander	Luger SL	9mm pistol by Mauser
LtComm	lieutenant commander	LuH	lumen hours
LTD	long term disability	LUHF	lowest useful high frequency
ltd	limited	LULS	lunar logistic system
LTD	laser target designator	LUMAS	lunar mapping system
LTDP	long-term defence programme (Nato)	Luna	Soviet designation FROG-7
LTDR	laser target designator and ranger	Lunatron	night viewer by Eiselt
LTDS	laser target designating system	LUNR	land use and natural resources (satellite)
LTE	letter to the editor; London Transport Executive; local thermodynamic equilibrium	LUOTC	London university officers' training corps
LTFCS	laser tank fire control system	Lupo	class, frigates (IT)
LTFRD	lot tolerance fraction reliability deviation	LUR	Luftraumüberwachungsradar by AEG (air surveillance radar)
LtG	lieutenant general	LUSI	lunar surface inspection
LTG	local tactical grid	LUT	launch umbilical tower
LtGen	lieutenant general	Lütjens	class, guided missile destroyers (FGN) (former Charles F. Adams class)
LtGov	lieutenant governor		
LTH	light transport helicopter; light training helicopter	LUU-2B	airborne parachute flare by Thiokol
LTI	land training installations	LUZIVER	Luftkampfzielverfolgungsgerät by Dornier (air combat target tracking system)
LtInf	light infantry		
LTJG	lieutenant junior grade		
LTL	less than truckload	LV	luncheon voucher; low voltage; landing vessel; low velocity; landing vehicle; light vessel; Luftverteidigung (air defence)
ltl	little		
LtlCg	little change		
LTM	laser target marker		
LTMR	laser target marker and ranger by Ferranti	lv	leave
		LV-2	... 3, tank laser ranger by Simrad
LTMS	laser target marking system	LVA	liaison officer, department of veterans' affairs (Canada); landing vehicle, assault (USMC programme)
Ltn	lightning		
LtnArr	Lightening arrester		
LTN-72	inertial airborne navigation system by Litton		
LTO	leading torpedo operator	LVD	leave from duty; low velocity drop; low velocity detonation
LTon	long ton		
LTPD	lot tolerance per cent defective	LVDT	linear variable differential transformer; low voltage differential transformer
LtPhotoRon	light photographic squadron		
LTQ-17	ECM equipment by Fairchild		
ltr	letter, lighter	LVHX	landing vehicle, hydrofoil, experimental
LTRP	long term requirement plan		
LtRN	lieutenant, Royal Navy	LVI	low viscosity index; low value item
LTRS	low temperature research station	LVL	low velocity layer
LtTk	light tank	lvl	level
LTS	landfall technique school	LLVMA	light light marine attack aircraft
LTU	line termination units	LVO	low visibility operation; Luftverteidigungsorganisation (air defence organization)
LTV	launcher test vehicle; long tube vertical; Ling-Temco-Vought Inc. later: E-Systems		
		LvRats	leave rations
Lu	lubaloy		SL sick leave
LU	logistical unit		SPEC special leave
LUAZ-969	light vehicle (SU)	LVRJ	low volume ramjet --STM
lub	lubricated, lubaloy	LVT	Buffalo, landing vehicle, tracked 1...3 unarmoured Buffalo, Amtrack, landing vehicle, tracked 4 unarmoured with turret
lubr	lubricant		
LuCom	lunar communications (system)		
LUC	living under canvas		
Luchs	SpähPZ-2, wheeled armoured recce vehicle by Thyssen-Henschel	LVTA	landing vehicle, tracked, armoured + turret
LUF	lowest usable frequency	LVTAA	landing vehicle, tracked, anti-aircraft
LUG	light utility glider		

LVTC-7   landing vehicle, tracked, command
LVTE-1   landing vehicle, tracked, engineers
LVTE-7   landing vehicle, tracked, engineers
     (mine-clearing)
LVTH-7   landing vehicle, tracked, howitzer
LVTP-5   landing vehicle, tracked, personnel
LVTP-7   landing vehicle, tracked, personnel
LVTPX-7   landing vehicle, tracked, person-
     nel, experimental
LVTR-7   landing vehicle, tracked, recovery
     by FMC
LVW   landing vehicle, wheeled
LW   large warship; long wave; low water;
     light warning; light weight
     (radar); lumen per watt;
     limited war
LWA   light wounded in action
LWAR   lightweight attack/reconnaissance
     (aircraft)
LWB   longwheelbase
LWCM   lead wadcutter, match (projectile)
LWCMS   XM-224, lightweight company mortar
     system 60mm
LWCS   limited war capabilities study
LWEST   low water equinoctial spring tide
LWF   lightweight figher (aircraft)
LWG   logistics working group
LWG-F-104 logistics working group for the
     F-104 Starfighter (Nato BE-IT-
     NL-GE)
LWL   length on the waterline; low water
     line; load water line
LWM   low water mark
LWO-2   naval long range air surveillance
     radar by HSA
LWONT   low water ordinary neap tide
LWOP   leave without pay

LWOST   low water ordinary spring tide
LWP   limited war plan
LWR   local wage rate; light water
     reactor; lightweight radar
lwr   lower
LWRecce   lightweight reconnaissance (air-
     craft)
LWRU   lightweight radar unit
LWS   light (radar) warning set; light
     (radar) warning system; Land-
     Wasser-Schlepper (amphibious
     tractor) WW2 (GE)
LWSF   lightweight strike fighter (air-
     craft)
LWSR   lightweight strike reconnaissance
     (aircraft)
LWT   lightweight turret; amphibious
     wharping tug
LX   landing ship, experimental
LX(LSD)   landing ship, experimental,
     landing ship dock
LY   The Queen's Own Lowland Yeomanry;
     Prince Albert's Own Leicestershire
     Yeomanry
LY&LT   lastex yarn and lactron thread
Lynx   W-613, helicopter by Westland
     (anti-submarine/anti-tank);
     command and reconnaissance
     vehicle, tracked (Canada) (M-113)
Lyran   illumination mortar by Bofors
Lysander light commando aircraft hy
     Westland WW2
LZ   landing zone, loading zone
LZC   landing zone control
LZCP   landing zone control party
LZT   lead zirconate titanate
LZZ   Langzeitzünder (long time fuse)

M

M
marshal; model; mark; medium; motor; modified; microphone; mile; morphium; meridian; military; militia; married; manpower; thousand

M-Boot Minensuchboot (minesweeper)

M-day mobilization day

M-Geschoss Minengeschoss (HE projectile)

M-Patrone Messpatrone (sounding projectile)

3M maintenance and material management (system); Minnesota Mining & Manufacturing Company

M-1 Garand carbine (self loading rifle); anti-aircraft gun 40mm (US); howitzer 155mm, 203mm propelling charge; mortar 81mm (US); towed anti-tank gun 57mm (US)

M-2 howitzer 105mm;
IFV infantry fighting vehicle by FMC;
heavy barrel machine gun by Ramo; propelling charge 203mm;
Carl Gustav, 84mm anti-tank recoilless rifle by FFV;
Alligator, amphibious bridging vehicle by EWK

M-2A4 fragmentation mine (US)

M-2HB heavy barrel cal. 50 machine gun by Browning

M2-F2 multi-mode fire and forget (missile) (US Army); experimental space-flight aircraft by Northrop

M-3 halftrack; Grease Gun, submachine gun by Thompson; General Grant, medium tank WW2; anti-tank mine by PRB; anti-tank gun 37mm (US); Lee, giant tank WW2; steel anti-personnel mine (US)
CFV cavalry fighting vehicle; propelling charge 155mm

M-3 VTT, wheeled armoured personnel carrier by Panhard

M-4 Sherman, Firefly, tank WW2; floatbridge equipment (US)

M-4A2 propelling charge 155mm

M-5 halftrack; helicopter-borne grenade launcher

M-6 cool burning propellant

M-7 Priest, SP howitzer 107mm

M-7A1 vehicular flame thrower

M-8 Greyhound, recce tank;
SP howitzer;
tracked tractor (US); smoke hand grenade (US); portable chemical warfare detector (automatic) by Bendix

M-9 armoured tractor/dozer FAMECE

M-10 GMC, gun, motor carriage;
SP anti-tank gun;
gun 152mm (SU)

M-11/16 mortar 035mm WW1 (Austria)

M-12 machine pistol 9mm by Beretta; tank (US); pistol 9mm by Steyr; Be-12, recce/utility amphibian plane (SU)

M-13 vehicular NBC filter unit

M13A new US gun; IT improved technology; ESR electro slag refined steel

M-14 automatic rifle 7.62mm (US); mine, plastic, anti-personnel (US); hand grenade, incendiary (US)

M-15 anti-tank mine metallic (US); hand grenade, smoke WP (US); semi trailer 50 tons

M-16 AR-15, assault rifle 5.56mm by Colt; anti-aircraft halftrack; twin airborne machine gun; submachine gun 9mm by Atchinsson; Max, howitzer 38cm WW1 (Austria)

M-16A1 mine, anti-personnel (US)

M-17 tank vision scope; gas mask; respirator (US); howitzer 42cm WW1 (Austria)

M-18 Hellcat, killer tank (US); howitzer 10mm (SU)

M-18A1 anti-personnel mine, prefragmented

M-19 propelling charge 155mm; mortar 60mm (US); mortar 51mm (UK) ROF; anti-tank mine, rectangular (US); blank firing attachment for Browning HBMG

M-19A1	rifle grenade, smoke WP (US)
M-20	Bazooka, anti-tank rocket launcher 88mm; howitzer 75mm; command car; fire control system, artillery (Nato); mini combat system by HSA
M-21	twin M-134 TAT for helicopters; anti-tank mine, round (US)
M-22	rifle grenade, smoke (US)
M-23	helicopter borne M-60; rifle grenade, smoke (US)
M-24	Chaffee, recce tank by CG; helicopter borne M-60
M-25	mortar fuse 120mm/160mm
M-25C	fragmentation warhead for Chapparral
M-26	armoured tank transporter (US); AVLB on M-47 hull by Astra; gun 105mm (Spain); hand grenade prefragmented by IMI
M-27	helicopter borne M-134 by Hughes; cupola for ITV + M-113
M-29	mortar 81mm by Watervliet Arsenal; rifle grenade, training (US)
M-30	mortar 106mm by Watervliet Arsenal; high energy propellant charge (US); gun/howitzer 122mm (SU)
M-31	heavy rifle grenade HE (US)
M-31A2	illumination shell 105mm
M-32	recovery tank (US)
M-35	6x6 truck 2.5 tons; anti-personnel mine by PRB; pistol 9mm by VKT
M-36	killer tank (US); 6x6 truck 2.5 tons; anti-aircraft gun 40mm by Bofors
M-37	SP howitzer 105mm; 4x4 vehicle .75 ton; machine gun by Maremont; mortar 82mm (SU)
M-38	jeep; field howitzer 122mm (SU); mortar 120mm (SU)
M-38V	anti-aircraft gun 20mm by Rheinmetall
M-39	gun 20mm; truck 6x6 5 tons; armoured personnel carrier, tracked (US)
M-40	SP gun 155mm (US); recoilless rifle 106mm by Watervliet Arsenal; mortar 120mm by Tampella; rifle grenade anti-personnel 50mm (FR)
M-41	Walker Bulldog, air-transportable recce tank (US) B for Brazil; SP howitzer 155mm (US)
M-41E2	Redeye, portable anti-aircraft missile (GD)
M-42	Duster, anti-aircraft tank twin 40mm guns; howitzer 57mm (SU)
M-43	SP howitzer 203mm (US); anti-personnel mine (Sweden); field howitzer 152mm (SU); mortar 120mm (SU); standard round 7.62x39 (SU)
M-44	SP gun 155mm (US); truck 6x6 2.5 tons
M-45	truck 6x6 2.5 tons
M-46	tank (US); truck 6x6 2.5 tons; anti-personnel mine (Sweden); gun 130mm (SU)
M-47	Patton, main battle tank by Chrysler; Dragon, anti-tank guided weapon by McDD; anti-tank mine, metallic (Denmark)
M-48	medium tank by Chrysler; cannon 20mm (Swiss); anti-aircraft gun 40mm (Sweden); fragmentation mine (Sweden); anti-tank gun 76mm (SU)
M-48A3	combat tank 90mm gun (US)
M-49	rifle, self-loading 7.62mm; anti-personnel mine (Sweden); truck 6.4 tons by AM General; mine cylindrical TNT (Swiss)
M-50	round 20mm, electrical fuse; anti-tank rifle grenade 73mm (FR); Honest John, artillery rocket (US); machine pistol 9mm by Madsen; truck .6 tons by AM General
M-51	Little John, artillery rocket (US); jeep, anti-aircraft gun 75mm (US); truck 5 tons; rocket launcher 130mm 32 tubes (Czech); machine gun 7.5mm by SIG
M-52	SP gun 105mm and 155mm (US); rifle grenade anti-personnel (FR); anti-tank mine, bakelite (Denmark); tractor for semi-trailers by AM General; anti-tank gun 85mm (Czech)
M-53	SP gun 155mm (US); anti-tank gun 100mm (Czech); anti-aircraft gun 12.7mm and 30mm (Czech)
M-53/59	twin anti-aircraft gun 30mm (Czech)
M-54	field gun 130mm; anti-aircraft gun 57mm by Bofors; truck by AM General
M-55	Maxton, quadruple a/a mount for 12.7, Browning M-2HB; SP field howitzer 203mm (US); truck by AM General; gun 122mm and 152mm (SU); a/a gun 20mm (SU)
M-56	howitzer 105mm (US); pack howitzer 105mm by OTO; airborne round 20mm; helicopter-delivered mine system; rifle grenade anti-tank/anti-personnel (FR)
M-57	anti-tank missile launcher 45mm; hand grenade, impact fuse, fragmentation (US)
M-58	recoilless gun 95mm (Finland); mortar 106mm by Tampella
M-58EF	--M-58F (400-7000m)
M-58F	mortar round 120mm for Tampella 120mm 400-6200m

M-59	Long Tom, field gun 155mm (US); mortar 60mm; armoured personnel carrier M-113 forerunner; recoilless rifle 82mm (Czech); SP a/a gun
M-60	Patton, MBT, 105mm gun; general purpose machine gun 7.62mm by SACO; smoke shell WP 105mm; gun 122mm by Tampella; self-loading rifle 7.65mm by Valmet; armoured personnel carrier (Yugoslavia); mortar 120mm by Thomson/Brandt
M-60A1	Redeye, anti-aircraft missile; battle tank by Chrysler
M-61	Vulcan, 20mm a/a gun rotating barrels (GE)
M-62	wrecker truck; portable mine detector (Bulgaria)
M-64	mortar 81mm by IMI; mortar 120mm (Swiss)
M-63	recoilless rifle 82mm (Yugoslavia); Shmel, rocket launcher 128mm 32 tubes (SU)
M-65	howitzer 155mm (US); mortar 120mm MO-120; FAZ, automatic rifle 7.62mm; respirator, panoramic glass by Auer; a/a gun 35mm by Oerlikon
M-66	mortar 160mm by IMI
M-67	flame throwing tank (US); recoilless rifle 90mm (US); MAW, medium anti-tank weapon (US); hand grenade, fragmentation (US)
M-68	gun/howitzer 155mm by Soltam/Tampella; hand grenade, impact fuse, fragmentation (US); mortar, long barreled, 82mm (SU)
M-70	MP shell 20mm by Raufoss; class, mine hunters GRP (Sweden)
M-71	field gun 155mm (Israel)
M-72	LAW, light anti-tank weapon; mortar 81mm (Swiss)
M-73	machine gun 7.62mm vehicle-borne
M-74	medium armoured recovery vehicle M-4 hull
M-75	helicopter borne grenade launcher 40mm; APC M-113 forerunner
M-76	rifle by Valmet 7.62mm and 5.56mm
M-78	gun/howitzer 155mm by Tampella
M-79	hand-held grenade launcher 40mm (US)
M-85	TAT with M-2 HBMG by GE
M-86	propelling charge 175mm
M-88	RVM, recovery vehicle medium, tracked M-48 hull by Bowen
M-90	cartridge 20mm
M-92	pistol 9mm by Beretta
M-100	cartridge 20mm
M-101	light field howitzer 105mm (US); shell 155mm HE
M-102	engineer tank (US); air-transportable howitzer 105mm (US)
M-106	M-113 with mortar 107mm; shell 203mm HE
M-107	SP gun 175mm by BMY; shell 155mm HE
M-108	SP gun 105mm (US); recovery truck by Reo (US)
M-109	SP gun 155mm by BMY (G for Germany); truck 6x6 2.5 tons
M-109R	SHORADS, Roland AFV
M-110	SP gun 203mm by BMY; shell WP 155mm; bomb GP 22000 lbs, Grand Slam
M111	tank shot 105mm APDS-FS-T
M-113	APC MICV by Ford, gun 175mm
M-113CR	Dutch version
M-114	T-114, ARSV, by Cadillac
M-114	field howitzer 155mm
M-115	field howitzer 203mm
M-116	FAE fire bomb 750 lbs; anti-tank gun 75mm; snow vehicle by Pacific Car, shell, high capacity 155mm
M-117	anti-aircraft gun 90mm
M-118	anti-aircraft gun 90mm
M-118A2	shell illum 155mm
M-118E1	bomb 3000 lbs 1.360 kgs
M-119	propelling charge 155mm
M-121	shell chemical 155mm
M-122	tripod mount for M-60
M-123	truck 6x6 10 tons; shell HEP 165mm; howitzer M-114 with auxiliary engine; tractor for semi-trailers by Consolidated
M-125	truck 6x6 by Mack; APC M-113 with mortar 81mm
M-130	chaff and flare dispenser for helicopters
M-132	M-113 with flame thrower
M-134	TAT electric 7.62mm gun by GE
M-135	demolition gun 165mm for CEV
M-139	HSS-820, gun 20mm; assault rifle Galil
M-151	jeep
M-158	rocket pods helicopter borne
M-160	mortar 160mm (SU)
M-162	howitzer/missile launcher 152mm
M-163	Vulcan ADS, a/a tank 20mm M-113 hull
M-167	VADS towed version
M-168	automatic cannon 10mm by GE
M-172	semi-trailer 15 tons
M-176	smoke system
M-179	SP howitzer 155mm
M-193	round 5.56mm, ball
M-196	round 5.56mm tracer
M-197	automatic gun 20mm by GE
M-198	towed howitzer 155mm
M-202	multi-shot flame rockets
M-203	rifle-fitted grenade launcher 40mm for M-16 by Colt; propelling charge 155mm
M-204	soft recoil howitzer 105mm, project cancelled
M-211	truck by GM

M-215   truck 6x6 2.5 tons
M-219   machine gun 7.62mm vehicle borne
M-224   LWCM, mortar 60mm
M-234   one-axle trailer Lance transporter
M-239   smoke system
M-240   machine gun 7.62mm vehicle borne;
        M-1953, mortar 240mm (SU)
M-246   wrecker truck; electrical fused
        round
M-251   Lance warhead 860 cluster bombs
        BLU-63
M-261   adaptor kit for M-16 to fire LR
        fire rounds
M-274   Mechanical Mule, 4x4 5 tons
M-314   shell illum 105mm
M-342   truck by AMG
M-344   round 105mm for recoilless rifle
M-371   shell HEAT 90mm for M-67
M-386   wheeled rocket launcher for Honest
        John
M-406   round HE 40mm
M-409   anti-personnel mine by PRB
M-430   round HEDP 40mm
M-433   mortar round HEDP 40mm
M-437   round HE 175mm
M-449   ICM round 155mm
M-454   nuclear round 155mm
M-456   round HEAT 105mm
M-459   RAP fragmentation 155mm
M-483   ICM 155mm contains 88 1.5 in bomblets
        a/a
M-485   shell illum 155mm
M-520   Goer articulated truck 8 tons
M-530   air-to-air missile by Matra
M-533   truck by Caterpillar
M-543   wrecker truck; RAP 155mm
M-548   RCM-748, M-113 hull cargo carrier
M-549   RAP 155mm
M-551   Sheridan, ARAAV, recce tank by GM
M-552   Goer 10 ton articulated recovery
        vehicle
M553   wrecker truck by Caterpillar
M-557   command vehicle M-113 hull
M-559   Goer, 2500 gal articulated tanker
M-561   Gama Goat, 6x6 1.25 ton articulated
        truck
M-577   command post vehicle, M-113 by
        Henschel
M-578   tracked a/a vehicle twin 40mm guns;
        light armoured recovery vehicle by
        Bowen
M-579   field workshop M-113
M-587   time fuse for HE rounds
M-590   anti-personnel round 90mm
M-593   round HEI 20mm by Diehl
M-621   automatic gun 20mm by GIAT
M-650   RAP for M-110
M-656   8x6 truck 5 tons by Ford
M-667   launching vehicle for Lance M-113 hull
M-687   shell 155mm binary gas

M-688   Lance transporter M-113 hull
M-692   ADAM, shell 155mm contains 36
        a/p mines
M-693   automatic gun 20mm by GIAT
M-700   ARGUS, microprocessor by Ferranti
M-705   4x4 light truck
M-712   Copperhead, CLGP
M-715   4x4 light truck; SLR 5.56mm by
        Valmet
M-718   RAAM, shell 155mm
M-724   time fuse for submunitions
M-727   Hawk carrier vehicle
M-728   CEV combat engineer vehicle M-60
        hull
M-730   Vulcan/Chaparral a/a tank M-548
M-731   ADAM, shell 155mm contains 36 a/p
        mines
M-734   multiple option mortar fuse
M-735   Shot 105mm APFSDA DU penetrator
M-740   Lance transporter/launcher towed
M-741   Vulcan/Chaparaal a/a tank M-113;
        RAAM shell 155mm
M-746   8x8 truck 60 tons, tractor for semi-
        trailers by Ward
M-747   tank transporter
M-752   Lance launcher M-113
M-764   truck telephone line construction
M-774   shot 105mm Staballoy penetrator
M-794   trailer
M-802   PVS-5, night vision goggles by
        Litton
M-806   recovery vehicle M-113 by FMC
M-809   truck 6x6 5 tons
M-813   truck 5 tons by AMG
M-814   truck by AMG
M-816   wrecker truck by AMG
M-817   truck 5 tons by AMG; proximity fuse
        for a/a missiles
M-818   tractor for Patriot; tractor for
        semi-trailers by AMG
M-819   wrecker truck by AMG
M-820   truck by AMG
M-825   smoke shell 155mm
M-876   truck telephone line construction by
        IHC
M-880   truck 2.1 tons by Dodge
M-890   truck 2.5 tons by Dodge
M-901   ITV, by Emerson
M-911   tractor for semi-trailers by Oshkosh
M-915   tank transporter by AMG
M-916   tractor for semi-trailers by AMG
M-917   truck 20 tons
M-918   cement mixer truck
M-920   tractor for semi-trailers by AMG
M-980   infantry combat vehicle (SU)
M-1897 howitzer 75mm (FR)
M-1898 mortar 24cm WW1 (Austria)
M-1910 pistol 7.65mm by FN
M-1911 pistol 11.43mm by Remington/Colt
M-1917 gun 15mm

M-1919   machine gun 7.62mm
M-1929   round 7.5mm (FR)
           C   standard round
           P   armour piercing
           TO   tracer
           TP   APT
M-1934   pistol 9mm by Beretta
M-1937   round 7.5mm salvo type (FR)
M-1939   a/a gun 37mm and 85mm (SU)
M-1941   Johnson rifle
M-1942   a/t gun 45mm and 76mm (SU)
M-1943   a/t gun 57mm (SU)
M-1944   a/t gun 100mm (SU)
M-1951   pistol 9mm by Beretta
M-1953   M-240, mortar 240mm (SU)
M-1955   a/t gun 100mm (SU); field howitzer
           180mm (SU)
M-1965   towed rocket launcher 140mm 16
           tubes (SU)
M-1967   amphibious APC (SU)
M-1971   pistol 9mm by Colt
M-1972   rocket launcher 122mm 40 tubes
           (Czech); tracked transporter (SU)
M-1973   SP howitzer 152mm (SU)
M-1974   SP howitzer 122mm (SU)
M-8117   proximity fuse for M-25C
MA   military attache; military assistant;
           medical assistant; mental age;
           military academy; maintenance area;
           mountain artillery; ministry of
           agriculture fisheries and food
           (UK); militia act (Canada);
           marshalling area; monitoring
           agency; mileage allowance; map
           analysis; main amplifier; mass
           analyser; methyl acrylate; multi-
           channel analyser; manufacturing
           and assembly
mA   mili-Ampere
M&A   maintenance and assembly
MA-4   half track APC
MA   automatic morse system by RAcal
           -4230   transmitter
           -4231   reader
           -4233   miniature printer
MAA   master-at-arms; master army aviator;
           medium anti-aircraft (weapon);
           maximum authorized altitude;
           minimum attack altitude; missile
           air/air; air-to-air missile
MAAC   mastic asphalt advisory council
MAACS   multi-address asynchronous communica-
           tions system
MAAD   manual of anti-aircraft defence
MAAF   Mediterranean allied air force
MAAG   military assistance advisory group
MAAHL   maximum aircraft arresting hook load
MAARegt medium anti-aircraft regiment,
           Royal Artillery
MAASL   military assistance articles and
           services list

MAATC   mobile anti-aircraft training centre
MAAW   medium anti-aircraft weapon
MAB   marine amphibious brigade; marine
           air base; mobile (floating)
           assault bridge; missile assembly
           building; minimum altitude
           bombing; medium altitude bombing;
           Manufacture d'Armes Automatiques
           Bayonne (France)
MABD   marine air base defence
           G   group
           W   wing
MaBo   Marinanas Bonin group
MABP   mean arterial blood pressure
Mabra   bomb aiming altimeter audible by IAI
MABRon   marine air base squadron
MABS   marine air base squadron; maritime
           application bridge system
MAC   military airlift command (USAF);
           maritime air command (Canada);
           mission assignment code (Nato);
           manoeuvre area command; military
           assistance command; maintenance
           allocation chart; maintenance
           advisory committee; marine
           amphibious corps; motor ambulance
           convoy; medical administrative
           corps; military affairs committee;
           military aid to the community;
           merchant aircraft carriers;
           maximum allowable concentration;
           mean aerodynamic chord; machine
           aided cognition; multiple access
           computer; maritime air control
           (ship) (RN); Manufacture d'Armes
           Chatterault (FR)
MACA   maritime air control authority
           (Nato); military airlift clear-
           ance authority
MACADS   military airlift command automated
           deployment reporting system
MACAF   Mediterranean allied coastal air
           force
MACAir   munitions assignment committee, air
MACC   military aid to the civilian
           community
MACCS   marine air command and control
           system
MACDAC   machine communication with digital
           automatic computer
           Sys   system
MACCS   marine (corps) air command and
           control system
MACE   military air cargo export (system);
           military airlift centre Europe
Mace   TM-76B, MGM-13, CGM-13, tactical
           missile, cruise missile 1000 kms
MACE   minimum area crutchless ejector by
           MBB
MACES   military air cargo export system

MACF   missile assembly and checkout facility

MACG   marshalling area control group; marine air control group

mach   machine

MachGr   machine group

MACI   anti-tank TNT charge by Alsetex; military adaption of commercial items

MAC-Marietta   Martin Aerospace Corporation Marietta

MACO   marshalling area control office

MACom   major army command

MACOV   mechanized and army combat operations (Viet Nam)

MACRI   mercantile Atlantic coastal routing instructions

MACRIT   (terms of enlistment) manpower authorization standards and criteria

MACRon   marine air control squadron

MACS   marine air control squadron; military airlift command service; management and control system; mobile acoustic communications study (Nato); multiple access communications system AWACS; military aeronautical communications system GEC; multi-mode airborne communications system GEC-Marconi; multi-purpose acquisition control system

MACSS   medium altitude communications satellite system

MACTU   mine and countermeasure technical unit

MACV   military assistance command Viet Nam OI office of information

MAD   marine aviation detachment; mine assembly depot; mutual assured destruction; military assistance division; maintenance, assembly and disassembly; mass analyser detector; magnetic anomaly detector; magnetic airborne detector; mathematical analysis of downtime (computer); mean absolute deviation; Michigan algorithm decoder (computer); machine ANSI data (American national standards institute)

MADAEC   military applications division of the atomic energy commission

Madakara   class, patrol boats by Brooke Marine

MADAM   Manchester automatic digital machine; moderately advanced data management

MADAP   Maastricht automatic data processor (ATC Eurocontrol)

MADepSq   marine air depot squadron

MAD/EuCom   military assistance division USCINCEur

MADGE   microwave aircraft digital guidance equipment (landing aid) by MEL; Malaysian air defence ground environment

MADM   medium atomic demolition munition

MADP   main air display plot

MADRE   magnetic drum receiving equipment

MAD-SADE   magnetic anomaly detection - self adaptive estimation

MAE   mutual assistance executive; mobile ammunition evaluation, mean absolute error

MAE-15   automatic scoring system for aerial targets by SFENA

MAECon   Mid-America electronics converence

MAEE   marine aircraft experimental establishment

MAeroE   master of aeronautical engineering

MAERU   mobile ammunition evaluation and reconditioning unit

Maestrale   class, ASW frigates (IT)

MAF   metropolitan air force; marine amphibious force; maintenance action form; marine air facility; minister of armed forces; mobile air force

MAF-1   Materiel Amphibie de Franchissement by DTCN (bridging equipment)

MAF-2   bridging equipment by EWK

MAFA   military and air force act

MAFac   marine air facility

MAFC   major army field command

MAFF   ministry of agriculture fisheries and food

MAFFST   Middle Atlantic field food service team

Mafius-600   hydrofoil by Navaltecnica

MAFL   manual of air force law

MAFOG   Mediterranean area fighter operations grid

MAF/TDL   maintenance action form/technical direction compliance

MAG   marine aviation group; marine aircraft group; military assistance group; military advisory group; main armaments group

mag   magazine; magnetic; magneto; magnum (projectile); magnesium

MAG-58   Mitrailleur à Gaz (gas-operated machine-gun 7.62mm) by FN

MagBrg   magnetic bearing

MagCoM   magnetic contour matching

Magic   R-550, short-range air-to-air missile by Matra

Magic Dragon   AC-47, attack cargo aircraft, gunship aircraft by Douglas

Maginot line   French fortifications against Germany before WW2

MAGLAD   marksmanship and gunnery laser device
MagLog   magnetic logic (computer)
Magnalium magnesium and aluminium (alloy)
MagSat   magnetic particle mapping satellite
MAGTF   marine air ground task force
MAHC   maximum allowable housing cost
MAI   military assistance institute
MAIDS   multi-purpose automatic inspection
         and diagnostic system
MAIG   Matushita Atomic Industrial Group
         (Japan)
MAIN   military authorization identifica-
         tion number
maint   maintenance
MaintSupOfc maintenance supply office
MAirEastLant maritime air Eastern Atlantic
MAIRU   mobile aircraft instrument repair
         unit
MAISAC   Middle Atlantic inter-service
         athletic conference
MAIT   maintenance assistance and instruc-
         tion team
Maj   major
MAJAC   maintenance anti-jam console
MajGen   major general
MaK   Krupp Maschinenbau GmbH (Kiel)
Makarov pistol 9mm (SU)
Makurdi class, patrol boats by Brooke
         Marine
MAL   monthly army list; material allow-
         ance list
Mal   Malaya; Malaysia
Malafon MQ-1, airborne anti-submarine
         missile by Latecoere (FR)
MalArch Malay Archipelago
MALB   medium altitude loft bombing
MALI   material annex line item
Maliotka Soviet designation Sagger
Malkara anti-tank guided weapon (UK/
         Australia)
Mallard programme for secure trunk communi-
         cations system (US-UK-AUS-CND)
         cancelled later: JTCS
MalPenin Malay peninsula
MALS   medium height approach light system;
         medium intensity approach light
         system; motor airline section
Malyutka class, submarines (SU)
MAM   military air movement (number)
Mamba   anti-tank weapon system by MBB;
         automatic pistol 9mm (South
         Africa)
MAMC   Madigan Army medical center (US)
Mammoth Major heavy truck (UK)
Mammut   Ju-322, giant cargo glider 82m span
         WW2 (GE)
MAMRon   marine aircraft maintenance squadron
MAMS   marine aircraft maintenance squadron
MAMT   mobile air movements team
MAN   military aviation notice; Maschinen-
         fabrik Augsburg (Nürnberg GE)

man   manual; manager; manifest
MANCAN   man-carried automatic navigator
Manch   The Manchester Regiment
Manchester bomber by Avro
ManD   managing director
Mandator heavy truck (UK)
ManDir   managing director
Mandragore semi-active radar homing
         missile project (FR)
Mandrel airborne radar jammer WW2 (RAF)
MangB   manganeze bronze
Mangusta A-129, armed helicopter by Agusta
MANIAC   mechanical and numerical integrator
         and calculator
Manila Pact between Australia, France, New
         Zealand, Philippines,
         Thailand, UK, USA
MANIX   machine aids to Nike-X
ManMedDept manual of the medical department
Mannheim type, river ferries (GE)
ManOp   manually operated
Manpack PRC-104, portable transceiver
         280 000 channels by Hughes
MANPADS man-portable air defense system
         (US)
ManPatr Manöverpatrone (blank cartridge)
MANT   mobile amphibious news team
manuf   manufacturer
MANURHIN Manufacture de Machines du Haut-
         Rhin
MAO   mail address only
MAP   military assistance programme;
         mutual assistance plan; medical
         aid post; ministry of aircraft
         production (UK); modified American
         plan; multiple aim point (US
         missile basing system); manifold
         absolute pressure; missed approach
         point; message acceptance pulse;
         maximum average price; minimum
         association price; minimum audible
         pressure
MAPAG   military assistance programme
         advisory group (Nato)
MAPDV-59 plastic anti-personnel mine by
         SAEA
MAPED-F-1 anti-personnel mine by SAEA
MAPH   manned ambient pressure habitat
         (sub-aqua house)
MAPP   manpower and personnel plan
MAPRC   Mediterranean allied photographic
         reconnaissance command
MAPROS   maintain production schedules
MAPS   multiple address processing system;
         multivariate analysis and predic-
         tion of schedules
MAPSAC   machine-aided planning scheduling
         and control
MAPT   military assistance programme
         training

MAPTOE management practices in TOE units (term of enlistment)
MAPU multiple address processing unit
MAPUC modified area production urgency committee
MAQ money allowance for quarters
MAR major assembly release; marginal age relief (tax); multifunction (phased) array radar; memory address register; minimal angle of resolution
mar marine; maritime
MarAd maritime administration
MarAerialRflTransRon marine aerial refuelling transport squadron
MarAirMed maritime air forces Mediterranean HQ
MarAirWing marine air wing
MarARüst Marineamt, Abteilung Rüstung Wilhelmshaven (FG Naval Office Procurement division/department)
Marathon 6x6 truck for Greece by Steyr
MarAtkRon marine attack squadron
Marauder remote handling device (UK); B-26, bomber by Martin
MarAWAtkRon marine all-weather attack squadron
MarAWFitRon marine all-weather fighter squadron
MarBasScol marine corps basic school
MarBks marine barracks
MarBrig marine brigade
MARC Morris armoured reconnaissance car; material accountability/recoverability codes
MarCAD marine corps aviation cadet
MarCAMP marine corps accured military pay system
MARCE material asset redistribution centre Europe
MarCompReconRon marine composite reconnaissance squadron
MarConFor maritime contingency force Lant Atlantic
MarCor US marine corps
MarCorB marine corps base
MarCorCruit marine corps recruiting
        Dep depot
        Sta station
MarCorCampDet marine corps camp detachment
MarCorDist marine corps district
MarCoResTraCen marine corps reserve training centre
MarCorDS kmarine corps data system
MarCorps US marine corps
MarCorSup marine corps supply
        Act activity
        Cen centre
MarCryp Marconi cryptographic equipment

        Data for data transmission
        Fax for facsimile
        Mux for trunk communications
        Tel for telegraph/teleprinter
        Flex for HF/VHF radio
        Fone for telephone lines
Marder tracked infantry combat vehicle by Rheinstahl; tank hunter WW2 (GE); midget submarine WW2 (GE)
MarDet marine detachment
MARE months after receipt of equipment
MaRec maritime reconnaissance (airborne radar) by MEL
MARECS maritime European communications satellite; maritime reconnaissance and communications
MARegSq marine air regulations squadron
MarEngrLab marine engineering laboratory
MarFAir marine fleet air
MarFitAtkRon marine fighter attack squadron
MarFitRon marine fighter squadron
MarHeavHelRon marine heavy helicopter squadron
MarHelRon marine helicopter squadron
MARI mercantile Atlantic routing instructions
Marindin infantry ranger (UK)
MARINE management analysis reporting information on the naval environment (system)
Mariner PBM, patrol flying boat by Martin; shipborne MARTE system by SISTEL
Marisat maritime Communications satellite for Naval and commercial shipping by Comsat
MariSP maritime strike plan
MaritA maritime airfield
Maritime F-27, maritime patrol aircraft by Fokker
MarLic marriage licence
Marlin P-5M, flying boat
Marl of RAF Marshal of the Royal Air Force
MarMedHelRon marine medium helicopter squadron
MARNET military area radio network (South Africa)
MARO maritime air radio organization
MarObsRon marine observation squadron
MAROTS maritime orbiting communications satellite
MARP manpower allocation requirement plan; months after receipt of problem
MarPhibFor marine amphibious force
MARR marine accident requiring rescue
MARRon marine aircraft repair squadron
MARS Manuel astronomical research station (San Diego); market analysis research system; multiple access retrieval system; mobile ammunition repair section (RAOC);

military affiliate radio system;
mobile Atlantic range station;
marine aircraft repair squadron;
mid air retrieval system; Marconi
automatic relay system; multiple
artillery rocket system; minimally
attended radio system (Seek Igloo
Alaska JSS by Gilfillian); master
agents research system; meteorological automatic reporting system;
RS-80, medium artillery rocket
system

MArs   Marine Arsenal (Kiel, Wilhelmshaven)
Mars   class, combat stores ships AFS
MarSat maritime satellite
MarSettl marriage settlement
MarSO   marine corps shipping order
MarSta marital status
MarSupBn marine support battalion
Marte   helicopter-borne anti-ship missile
        system by SISTEL
Martel USGW, underwater to surface guided
        weapon;
        air-to-ground missile by BAC/Matra
        AJ-168   TV-guided
        AS-37   radar homing
Martello long-range three-dimensional anti-
        aircraft radar by Marconi
Marti   class, patrol boats guided missiles
        for Turkey by Lürssen
Martian FV-1100, artillery tractor by
        Leyland
Martin Baker seat   ejection seat
MarTra&ReplCom marine training and replace-
        ment command
Marut   HF-24, fighter/ground attack air-
        craft by HAL
MARV   manoeuvrable re-entry vehicle;
        manoeuvrable anti-radar vehicle;
        multi-element articulated research
        vehicle
MarWgHQGru marine air wing headquarters
        group
Maryland reconnaissance bomber WW2 (RAF-
        USAF)
MAS   military agency for standardization
        (Nato Brussels); missile assembly
        site; military alert system;
        middle air space; military anti-
        quarian society; manual of artil-
        lery survey; machine accounting
        school; medical administration
        school; military airlift squadron;
        Minsk Automobile Factory (SU);
        Manufacture Nationale d'Armes
        (St Etienne FR); maritime avionics
        system (for naval helicopters) by
        ESG
MAS-1   Marinearbeitsschwimmweste (navy
        working life jacket)

MAS-36 repeater rifle 7.5mm (FR) by MAS
MAS-49/56 repeater rifle 7.5mm (FR) by MAS
MAS-5.56 A-3MAS, assault rifle 5.56mm by
        MAS
MASAF   Mediterranean allied strategic air
        force
MASAMBA mobile advance support and main-
        tenance base by Vosper
MASB   motor anti-submarine boat
Masby   motor anti-submarine boat
MassCons mass concentrations (astronomy)
MASCOT military air-transportable satellite
        communications terminal
Mascot remote-controlled tear gas launcher
        by GIAT; tank turret by GIAT
MASCU   marine air support control unit
MASEC   MAS message (military agency for
        standardization) (Nato)
MASER   microwave amplification by stimula-
        ted emission of radiation
MASF   military assistance service funded
MASG   marine air support group
MASH   mobile army surgical hospital
MASINT measurement and signature intelli-
        gence
MASK   manoeuvring and sea-keeping
        (facility)
MASL   military assistance articles and
        services list
MASRon marine air support squadron
MASS   mobile automatic switching system;
        mobile automatic signal suppressor;
        modular ESM signal processor;
        maritime air support squadron;
        modern army supply system
MassCal mass casualties
MASSTER modern army selected system test
        evaluation and review Fort Hodd;
        mobile army sensor system test
        evaluation and review
MAST   missile automatic supply technique;
        military assistance for safety and
        traffic; microwave antenna system
        technology
MastArAv master army aviator
MastDiv master diver
MasterGunner training system for forward
        artillery controllers by
        Marconi
Mastiff miniature recce RPV by Tadiran
MastPrcht master parachutist
MASTR   modular airborne search and track
        radar by RCA
MASTU   mobile anti-submarine training unit
Masurca naval surface-to-air missile by
        DEFA
MAT   mechanical aptitude test; mobile
        assistance team; microprocessor
        application trainer; micro alloy
        transistor; Mitsubishi anti-tank

MAT   (missile); Manufacture National
           d'Armes de Tulle (FR)
MA&T   missile assembly and test
MAT-49   machine pistol 9mm by MAT
MAT-385   microprocessor applications trainer
           by Feddback Instruments
MATA   multiple answering teaching aid
MatABW   Materialamt der Bundeswehr (German
           Army procurement office)
Matador   anti-aircraft tank twin 30mm by
           Rheinmetall; MGM-1, TM-1, ground-
           launched tactical missile by
           Martin; artillery tractor (UK);
           TV-8A, Spanish designation
           --Harrier
MATAF   Mediterranean allied tactical air
           force
MATC   mobile automatic telegraph centre by
           Philips
MATCALS   marine air traffic control and
           landing system TRS-65 by
           Westinghouse
MATCH   medium-range anti-submarine torpedo-
           carrying helicopter (Nato);
           MTMTS automated transportation
           scheduler (US)
MATCO   military air traffic coordination
           office(r)
MatCom   material command
MATCON   microwave aerospace terminal control;
           mobile air traffic control unit by
           Fieldtech
MATCU   marine air traffic control unit;
           marine air tactical control unit
MATD   mine and torpedo detector
MATE   modular automatic test equipment by
           Westinghouse
MATELO   maritime air telecommunications
           organization (Nato)
Matenin   wheeled trench digger (FR)
MatErh   Materialerhaltung (maintenance)
MatErhSt   Materialerhaltungsstufe
           (maintenance echelons)
Matilda   'infantry' tank WW2 (UK); ESM equip-
           ment by MEL
Matilda Baron minesweeper tank 'flail' WW2
MATMU   mobile aircraft torpedo maintenance
           unit
MATP   military assistance training pro-
           gramme
MA-TPM   maritime administration transporta-
           tion planning mobilization
Matra-181 airborne rocket pod 37mm rockets
           by Matra
Matra-511 air-to-air IR missile by Matra
Matra R-530 air-to-air radar homing missile
Matra-2008 parachute bomb retarding system
MATS   military air transport service
           --MAC;
           Mediterranean air transport service

           WW2; target drone, medium altitude
           target system by AEL; mobile auto-
           matic telegraph system by Philips;
           scatter mine GP by Tecnovar
MATSG   maritime aviation training support
           group
MATT   mobile acoustic torpedo target
Matta   AR-51, jeep by Alfa Romeo
MATTS   multiple airborne target trajectory
           system
MATZ   military aerodrome traffic zone
MAU   maintenance augmenting unit;
           marine amphibious unit; million
           accounting units (EC)
Maule   STOL aircraft
Mauler   XM-546, short-range anti-aircraft
           system; AM-1, naval attack air-
           craft by Martin
Maultier   SdKfz-4, half track by Opel WW2
Maus   super heavy tank 188 tons WW2 (GE);
           plastic anti-personnel mine (IT)
Maverick   AGM-65, air-to-ground guided
           missile anti-tank by Hughes
           A good-weather TV guidance
           B with scene magnification
           C with laser + TV
           D infra-red guidance
MAW   marine air(craft) wing; military
           airlift wing; medium anti-armour
           weapon; medium anti-tank/assault
           weapon; Maverick alternate war-
           head; mission adaptive wing AFTI;
           mountain and arctic warfare
MAWC   marine air West Coast
MAWCS   mobile air weapons control system
MAWEC   maritime aircraft weather code;
           maritime aircraft exercise code
MAWLOGS   models of the US Army world-wide
           logistics system
MAWP   marine air wing Pacific
MAWS   medium anti-tank weapon system;
           mobile aircraft weighing system;
           marine air warning squadron
max   maximum
MaxCap   maximum capacity
Maxi decoy small ECM decoy RPV by Maxwell
Maxton   M-55, quadruple anti-aircraft mount
           for 12.7mm Browning machine gun
Mayak   class, spy ships (SU)
Mayday   m'aidez (FR) (international distress
           sign
MAZ   Marineannäherungszünder (naval proxi-
           proximity fuse 76mm 100mm 127mm)
MAZ-500   truck 6.5t (SU)
MAZ-529   single axle tractor (SU)
MAZ-535   truck (SU)
MAZ-538   wheeled loader (SU)
MAZ-543   8x8 erector launcher transporter
           for SCUD (SU)
Mazur D-350 tracked transporter (Poland)

MB   medical branch; military band; missile base; marine barracks; mortar battery; main battery; motor battery; militia book (Canada); militia bureau; music branch; maritime board; mooring buoys; magnetron branch; magnetic bearing; munitions board; medium bomber; motor boats; methyl bromide (fire extinguisher)

M-B   Mauser Bauer Corporation

MB-326   close support aircraft by Aermacchi

MB-329   jet trainer aircraft by Aermacchi

MB-339   jet trainer aircraft by Aermacchi

MBA   main battle area; magnetic bearing assembly; Mainhardt & Biel Associates; minimum burst altitude

M-BAR   multi-beam acquisition radar by SLMS

MBB   Messerschmitt-Boelkow-Blohm (Munich)

MBBA   military benefits base amount

MBB-Transtechnika Gesellschaft für Technologietransfer

MBC   matchbox camera; manual battery control; maximum breathing capacity; Mediterranean bombardment code; military budget committee (Nato)

MBD   manual burst disable

MBDG   marine base defence group

MBE   Member of the Most Excellent Order of the British Empire

MBF   military banking facility; molecular beam facility

MBFR   mutual balanced force reduction

MBGE   missile borne guidance equipment

MBGTS   missile borne guidance test set

MBI   may be issued

MBK   missing believed killed

MBL   master bidders list; marine biological laboratory

mbl   mobile

MBLE   Manufacture Belge de Lamps et d'Electronique (Brussels)

MBMU   mobile base maintenance unit

MB   marine barracks
- NAD naval ammunitions depot
- NAS naval air station
- NMD naval mine depot
- NOB naval operating base
- NS naval station
- NYd navy yard
- SB submarine base

MBO   management by objective; motor burn out (missile)

MBOH   minimum break-off height

MBOL   motor burn-out locking

MBP   mean blood pressure; mechanical balance package; Mathematischer Beratungs- & Programmierungsdienst GmbH (Dortmund) (mathematical consultative and programming service)

MBPA   military blood programme agency

MBPAS   monthly bulk petroleum accounting summary

MBPO   military blood programme office

mbr   member

MBR   multiple bomb rack; marker beacon receiver

MBRUU   may be retained until unserviceable

MBRV   manoeuvrable ballistic re-entry vehicle

MBS   motor battery subsection; mutual broadcasting system; multiple batch station; magnetron beam switching (tube); medium bomber, strike (aircraft); muzzle bore sight by MSDS

MBST   magnetron beam switching tube

MBT   mobile boarding team; motor burning time; main battle tank; mean body temperature; mechanical bathythermograph

MBT-80   main battle tank of the 1980s (UK-GE project)

MBT-Mk-3   main battle tank by Vickers

MBTTF   main battle tank task force (Fort Knox)

MBU   memory buffer unit

MBU-2500   anti-submarine missile (SU)

MBVR-120   mittleres Ballonverfolgungsradar (medium balloon tracking radar) by ES

MBY&D   maintenance, bureau of yards and docks

MC   message centre; motor convoy; Military Cross; military committee (Nato); military college; military code; member of Congress (US); medical corps; marine corps; movement control; medical certificate; maritime commission; master commandant; military characteristics; mine clearance; major component; maps and charts STANAG; miles on course; magnetic course; metal case; main channel; medium capacity (bomb); Muiden Chemie Koninklijke Nederlandse Springstoffenfabrieken (Royal Dutch Explosives Factories); submarine chaser

MC-1-1   steerable parachute

MC-1800   GYK-29, artillery battery computer system by Marconi

MCA   ministry of civil aviation; military construction, Army; maritime control area; material coordination agency; military civic action; minimum crossing altitude; multi-channel analyser

MC-A   modified conventional alloy

MCAAC	medium calibre automatic cannon 75mm (US)
MCAAF	marine corps auxiliary air field
MCAAS	marine corps auxiliary air station
MCAB	marine corps auxiliary air base
MCABM	manner common among businessmen
MCAC	military common area control
MCACS	modular command and control system by Norden
MCAD	marine corps air depot
MCAF	military construction, air force; marine corps air facility; marine corps air field; Mediterranean coastal air force HQ
MCALF	marine corps auxiliary landing field
MCAR	military construction, army reserve; machine check analysis and recording
MCARNG	military construction, army national guard
MCAS	marine corps air station
MCAT	maritime central analysis team (Nato)
MCAUTO	McDonnell Douglas Automation Company
MCAWS	marine corps amphibious warfare school
MCB	mobile construction battalion; marine corps base; miniature circuit breaker
MCBM	Marine Corps Brevet Medal
MCC	military communications control; military coordination committee; movement control centre; master control centre; master control console; main computer control; manual control centre; missile controller's console; military climb corridor; mid-course correction; meteorological communications centre; multi-channel communications control; mixing cross-bar connectors; mission control centre
MCC-H	mission control center Houston
MCCIS	military command control and informations system (Nato)
MCCISWG	military command control and informations system working group (Nato)
MCCS	military committee chiefs of staff session (Nato); modular command and control system; mine-countermeasures command system by Ferranti
MCCSC	marine corps command and staff college
MCCUSCUSRPG	military coordinating committee US element Canada US regional planning group
MCD	manager constructive department; marine corps district; military coordinating detachment; mine warfare and clearance diving;

	manipulative communications deception; magnetic circular dichronism; mathematics and computer division STC
MCDEC	marine corps development and evaluation command
MCDRF	manual of coast defence range finding
MCDS	management control data system
MCE	military corrective establishment; maximum capability envelope; mobile command element; mapping and charting establishment (UK); multiple cycle engine; modulated carrier envelope (signal); maximum capability element
MCEB	military communications electronics board; marine corps equipment board; microprocessor controlled exterior, ballistic measurement by AVL
MCEC	marine corps education centre
MCEM	machine pistol (Australia)
MCEWG	multi-national communications electronics working group (Nato)
MCF	mine clearing force; mutual coherence function
MC&G	mapping charting and geodesy
MCGD	milimetre wave contrast guidance demonstration by Boeing
MCGH	marine corps good conduct medal
MCGS	microwave command guidance system
MCH	machine check handler; medium cross-hairs (sights)
60-MCHB	mortar 60mm by Thomson/Brandt
MCI	meal combat individual; marine corps institute; Microwave Communications Incorporated; malleable cast iron
MCIAS	marine corps industrial air station
MCL	mid-Canada line; master configuration list; mathematics computation laboratory
MCLFDC	marine corps landing force development centre
MCLG	mobile civilian labour group RPC
MCLOS	manual control to line of sight
MCLP	military committee representative liaison paper (Nato)
60-MCLR	mortar 60mm by Thomson/Brandt
MCLWG	major calibre lightweight gun
MCLWGS	major calibre lightweight gun system naval 203mm (USN)
MCM	manual for courts martial; marine corps manual; military committee memorandum (Nato); mine countermeasures; moving coil motor --ship
MCMG	military committee meteorological group

MCMOT	marine corps mobilization operational test
MCMU	mass core memory unit
MCMV	mine counter-measures vessel (Nato) --Tripartite
MCN	management control number
MCNRF	military construction, naval reserve facilities
MCO	movements control officer; mine clearing officer; motor contact officer; mine clearing office; main civilian occupation; marine corps orders; missile check-out; main communications office
MCOAG	marine corps operations analysis group
MCON	military construction
MCOT	missile control officer trainer
MCOY	military citizen of the year
MCP	medical continuation pay; military construction plan; micro-channel plates; master control programme; message control programme; military construction programme; missile control point
MCPD	marine corps personnel district
MCPHA	multi-channel pulse height analyser
MCPO	military committee representative communication to the private office of the Nato secretary general; master chief petty officer (USN)
MCPON	master chief petty officer of the US Navy
mcps	megacycles per second
MCPS	military committee in permanent session (Nato)
MCPT	maritime central planning team (Nato)
MCR	mass communications research; mobile control room; missile cruiser; master control routing; marine corps reserve; master change record; master control record (system); movement control regiment RCT
MCRB	magnetic compass record book
MCRD	marine corps recruiting depot
MCRDMS	missile certified round data management system
MCREP	military committee representative to the North Atlantic council
MCRL	master component repair list; material cross-reference list
MCROA	marine corps reserve officers' association
MCRR	machine check recording and recovery
MCRT	maximum cruise thrust
MCRS	marine corps recruiting station
MCRTC	marine corps reserve training centre
MCS	mini combat system radar M-20 by HSA; management computing service; medium close shot (photo); master control system; management and control system; mine counter-measures ship; missile control system; military college of science; movement control staff; marine corps station; marine corps school (Quantico Va); maintenance control section; marine casualty statistics; modular (naval) communications system by ES
Mcs	megacycles (per second)
MCS-205	multi-channel (modular) communications system (285000 channels) by Gould
MCSA	marine corps supply activity
MCSC	marine corps supply centre
MCSDS	Marconi Communications and Space and Defence Systems (UK)
MCS-Giletti	Motor Construction Systems Giletti (Monte Carlo)
MCSJC	marine corps schools junior course
MCST	mobile combat systems trainer (electronic warfare) by AAI
MCSTSC	military communications systems technical standards committee
MCSWG	multinational command systems working group (Nato)
MCT	mobile combat teams; mechanical comprehension test; mobile contact teams; mercury cadmium thermal (detectors); magnetic compass table; maximum continuous thrust; mobile communications terminal; Milan compact turret by BDX
MCTC	maritime cargo transportation conference; military corrective training centre (UK)
MCU	memory control unit, multiplexer control unit; microprogrammed control unit
MCV	maritime commission Victory (ship) WW2
MCV-80	mechanized combat vehicle of the 1980s by GKN Sankey
MCVG	marine carrier group (USN)
MCW	modulated continuous wave
MCWM	military committee working memorandum (Nato)
MCWU	military committee of the Western (European) Union
MCX	marine corps exchange
MD	medical doctor; meteorology department; military district; months after date; mentally deficient; mine depot; mine disposal; mechanically drawn; map distance;

MD   military division; medical depart-
            ment; mobilization department;
            material development; movement
            directive; marine detachment;
            mechanized division; mean devia-
            tion; message dropping; methyl di-
            chlorarsine; manual damper;
            modulator; mine detector;
            Mitteldruck (medium pressure)
M&D   medicine and duty
Md-22   plastic anti-personnel mine (Dutch)
Md-25   steel anti-tank mine (Dutch)
Md-26   wooden anti-tank mine (Dutch)
Md-47   anti-tank mine (Sweden)
Md-51/55   anti-personnel mine (French)
Md-52/53   plastic anti-tank mine (Denmark)
MD-106   mine detector (UK)
MD-450   Ouragan, jet fighter 1949 by Marcel
            Dassault
MD-452   Mystere, jet aircraft by Marcel
            Dassault
MD-660   tactical missile (Israel)
Md-1948   anti-tank mine (French)
Md-1953   anti-tank grenade + launcher by
            Luchaire
Md-4021   portable mine detector by Dr
            Förster
Md-4100   portable mine detector by Dr
            Förster
Md-4114   portable mine detector by Dr
            Förster
MDA   malicious damage act; military
            damage assessment; mutual defence
            assistance; minimum descent alti-
            tude; methylene di-aniline;
            multi-dimensional access; multi-
            dimensional array; multiple
            docking adapter (Nasa); McDonnell
            Douglas Astronautics (St Louis)
MDAA   mutual defence assistance act
MDAI   multi-disciplinary accident investi-
            gation
MDAL   McDonnell Douglas Astrophysics
            Laboratory
MDAP   machine and display application pro-
            gramme; mutual defence assistance
            programme
MDB   main distribution board,
MDC   mobile defence corps; message distri-
            bution centre; maintenance data
            collection; mine destruction
            charge (naval) by NWM; miss dis-
            tance calculator; movement desig-
            nator code; mechanical development
            committee; Modern Defence Corpora-
            tion (Spain); McDonnell Douglas
            Corporation
MDC-80   miss distance calculator by Air
            Target
            ATG   air-to-ground
            GTA   ground-to-air

MDCE   monitoring and duplicate control
            equipment
MDCS   maintenance and material data
            collection system
MDD   machine dependent data
MDCS   medical and dental corps special
            (pay)
MDE   mechanism drive electronic;
            missile destroyer
MDF   medium-frequency direction finder;
            main distribution frame; mobile
            defence force; multi-purpose
            rifle grenade by Losfeldt
MDFMR   M-day force material requirement
MDG   medical director general of the RN
MDH   maximum diameter heat; maximum
            descent heigh
MDI   miss distance indicator; M-day
            increment
MDIC   multilateral disarmament informa-
            tion centre
MDK   tracked mechanical digger (SU)
MDL   main deck container/pallett loader
            by FMC; mine defence laboratory;
            main defence line; management
            data list; material deviation
            list; mine detonating line; main
            detonating line
mdl   model
Mdl   mortar 105mm 120mm by ECIA
MDM   multiplexer/demultiplexer
mdm   medium
MDRM   M-day material requirement
MDMS   miss distance measuring system
M-DN-141   electronic base fuse for 120mm
            MP shell by Diehl
mdnt   midnight
MDP   meteorological datum plan; missile
            data processor
MDR   minimum daily requirement; mark-
            sense document reader; mainten-
            ance data report; Moyen de Deminage
            Rapide (AMX-30 minesweeper flail tank)
MDRCT   maritime detachment Royal Corps of
            Transport
MDS   main dressing station; medical dis-
            tributing station; mail distribu-
            tion scheme; maintenance data
            system; material (management)
            data system; mine dispersing sub-
            system; minimum discernible
            signal; Mohawk data system
mdse   merchandize
MDSOR   monthly depot space and operating
            report
MDSR   Malaya district signal regiment
MDST   mountain daylight saving time
MDT   mean down time; minimum down time;
            maximum diameter of the thorax;
            mountain daylight time; Mittel-

druckturbine (medium pressure turbine)

MDTS   modular data transaction system

MDU   main display unit; medical defence union; mine disposal unit; mobile development units

MDUS   medium-scale data utilization station

MDV   military designed vehicle

MDv   Marinedienstvorschrift (Navy manual)

MDW   mine disposal weapon; military district of Washington (US Army); military defence works

ME   military education; military engineering; manual of engineering; married establishment; Middle East; management engineering; mechanical and electrical; marine engineer; mechanical engineer; mining engineer; military engineer; muzzle energy; multi-engine; magneto-electric; mobility equipment; memory error; metabolizable energy; magnetic estimation; Martinie Enfield (rifle) (UK)

M&E   maintenance and equipment; manoeuvres and exercises

Me-109   interceptor aircraft WW2 by *Messerschmitt*

Me-110   night interceptor   "

Me-163   Kraftei, Komet, rocket interceptor "

Me-210   combat aircraft   "

Me-262   jet interceptor 870 kmph   "

Me-263   rocket interceptor   "

Me-264   combat aircraft   "

Me-321   Gigant, giant aircraft   "

Me-328   light high-speed combat aircraft   "

Me-410   recce/bomber   "

MEA   marine engineering artificer; maintenance engineering analysis; minimum en-route altitude; measurements STANAG

MEAD   maintenance engineering analysis division

MEADS   maintenance engineering analysis data system

MEAF   Middle East air force

MEAFSA   Middle East, South Asia and Africa South of the Sahara

MEAR   maintenance engineering analysis record

meas   measure; measurable

MEAT   multiple edge adaptive tracker

MEB   marine expeditionary brigade; military engineers branch (Canada)

MEBD   medical examining board

MEC   Middle East command; marine expeditionary corps; meteorology engineering centre; military

essentiality code; manoeuvre enhancement control; maximum endurable concentration

MECA   missile electronics and computer assembly of M-X by RI

Meca   105mm tank gun minimum spiral rifled (finned projectiles) (FR)

Meca/APX   semi-self propelled anti-tank round (FR)

Mecar   Société Anonyme Belge de Méchanique et d'Armaments (Nivelles)

MECAS   Middle East centre for Arab studies

mech   mechanic; mechanical; mechanized (UK)

Mechanical Mule   M-274, small tractor

MechE   mechanical engineer

MECO   main engine cut-off; manual equipment check-out

MECU   main engine control unit

mecz   mechanized (US)

MED   manager engineering department; minimal effective dose; medical STANAG

Med   Mediterranean

med   medium; medical

MEDAC   medical electronic data acquisition and control; military electronics data advisory committee

MEDAL   micro-mechanized engineering data for automated logistics

MedAlSa   Mediterranean Algeria Sahara (zone) (Nato)

MedBn   medical battalion

MedBr   medical branch

MedCAP   medical civic action programme

MedCaSE   medical care support equipment

MedCen   medical centre

MedCent   Mediterranean central area (Nato)

MedCom   Mediterranean communications

MedComPlan   Mediterranean communications plan

MedCOOP   medical continuity of operations plan

MEDD   Middle East development division

MEDDA   mechanized defence decision anticipation

MedDAc   medical department activity

MedDS   medical data specialist

MedEast   Mediterranean Eastern area

MedEvac   medical evacuation

MediCare   medical care

MEDICO   model experiment in drug indexing by computer; medical international cooperation

MEDICOS   Mediterranean instructions for convoys

Medit   Mediterranean

Medium SAM   improved SAM-D project

MEDLARS   medical literature analysis and retrieval system

MedLOC   Mediterranean lines of communication
(route: France-Mediterranean-
Middle East)
MEDMATS   medical material management system
MEDMIS   medical management information
system
MED/NBC   medical NBC STANAG
MedNorEast   Mediterranean North East area
(Nato)
MEDO   Middle East Defence Organization
MedOC   Mediterranean Western area (occiden-
tal)
MedOfCom   medical officer commanding
MedP   medium port
MedRC   medical reserve corps
MedRgt   medium regiment Royal Artillery
MEDSARS   maintenance engineering data
storage and retrieval system
MedSch   medical school
MEDSEA   ministerial conference for the
economic development of South East
Asia
MedSerWrnt   medical service warrant
MedSouEast   Mediterranean South East area
MedSupDep   medical supply depot
MEDT   military equipment delivery team
MedTech   medical technician; medical tech-
nology
Meduse AT-II, DM-711, Larat-II, mine dispen-
ser warhead by DNAG
MEE   minimum essential equipment
MEECN   minimum essential emergency communi-
cations network
MEES   multi-purpose electronic environment
simulator by Martin
MEETAT   maximum improvement in electronics
effectiveness advanced techniques
MEF   Mediterranean expeditionary force;
Middle East forces (UK); marine
expeditionary force
MEFET   metal semiconductor field effect
transistor
Meflex   Mechanisch Flexible Fernbedienungen
Ehrigghausen (GE)
Meg   mega
C   megacycle
T   megaton
W   megawatt
O   megaohm
MEG   Materialerhaltungsgruppen (mainten-
ance echelons); Marine Elektronik
Planungs GmbH (AEG+HSA+KAE+Siemens
+SEL+VFW Fokker)
Mehari   jeep (FR)
MEI   maintenance and engineering inspec-
tion; manual of engineering
instructions; mathematics in edu-
cation and industry; Mirador-
Eldorado-Indigo anti-aircraft
missile system by SISTEL

MEIS   military entomology information
service
MEIU   middle East interpretation unit
(UK); mobile explosives investi-
gation unit (US); management
education information unit
MEK   methyl ethyl ketone (solvent)
MEKO   Mehrzweck-Kombinations Fregatte by
B&V (multi-purpose combination
frigate)
MEL   manoeuvring element; material
engineering laboratory; marine
engineering laboratory; Mullard
Equipment Ltd (Crawley)
MEL-A   marine engineering laboratory
Annapolis
MELCO   Mitsubishi Electric Corporation
(Japan)
MELF   Middle East land forces
MELG   Middle East liaison group
MEM   maximum entrophy method; Marine
Expeditionary Medal; mission
essential material; marine
engineering mechanic (UK)
mem   member; memorandum
MEMA   micro-electronic modular assembly
MEMIS   maintenance and engineering manage-
ment information system by
Alitalia
MemlActv   memorial activities
memo   memorandum
MEMQ   married enlisted men's quarters
MEN   master equipment number
Mena   safety device for grenades
MENA   mixed manned element in Nato's
armament
MEND   medical education for national
defence (Nato programme)
MENEX   maintenance engineering exchange
(programme)
MEO   major engine overhaul; marine
engineering officer (UK)
MEOOW   marine engineering officer of the
watch
MEP   mean effective pressure
Mephisto   6x6 anti-tank vehicle HOT missile
(FR)
Mepracine   tablets anti-malaria
MER   medical examination room; maximum
effective range
mer   mercantile; meridian
MERADCOM   mobility equipment research and
development command (US Army
Fort Belvoir)
MERB   mechanical engineering research
board
merc   mercantile
MERCAST   (allied) merchant (ships) broadcast
(Nato)
MERCO   (allied) merchant (ships) movement
control and reporting system (Nato)

MERCOS   merchant ships code system
Mercure   transport aircraft by Dassault
Mercury   seaplane 1937 by Short
MERDC   mobile equipment research and devel-
         opment command
MEREP   (allied) merchant ships report,
         (arrival and departure) (Nato)
MERINTREP   (allied) merchant ships intermed-
         iate report (arrival and depar-
         ture) (Nato)
Merkava   main battle tank (Israel)
MERINT   merchant ship intelligence
MERL   mechanical engineering research
         laboratory
MERLIN   medium energy reactor light water
         industrial neutron source
Merlin   VIP transport aircraft by Fairchild;
         AEL-4020, camera-carrying RPV by
         AEL
Mermaid   midget rescue submarine by Bruker
MERMOT   mobile electronic robot manipulator
         on TV
MEROD   message entry and read-out device
         (data burst) by Racal
Meroka   close-in anti-aircraft gun
         12 barrels 20mm by CETME
MERRA   Middle East refugee and relief
         administration (UNRAA)
MERSEX   merchant ships code system (Nato)
MERSIGS   merchant ships signal book
MERT   maintenance engineering review tech-
         nique; maintenance engineering
         review team
MERU   mechanical engineering research unit
         (South Africa)
MERZONE   merchant ships control zone (Nato)
MES   main equipment supplier; manual of
         engineer services; military
         engineer services; Materialerhalt-
         ungsstufen (maintenance echelons);
         Magnetischer Eigenschtz (magnetic
         self-protection)
MESA   modularized equipment storage
         assembly; marine eco-systems
         analysis
MESC   Middle East supply centre
Mescalero   T-41, trainer aircraft by Cessna
MESCO   Middle East science cooperation
         office (UNESCO)
Mesh   electronic alarm system
MESH   Matra-ERNO-Saab-Hawker consortium
         for OTS further consorts: FVW-INTA-
         BAC
MESL   Microwave and Electronic Systems Ltd
         (Lingithgow)
MESEM   multi-echelon supply model
MESO   military embarkation staff officer
MESP   modular ESM signal processor
MEST   missile electrical system test
MET   mission entry time; mean European

         time; meteorology STANAG,
         mechanical enemy tranport
met   meteorology; metallurgy
Met   meteorological committee;
         Metropolitan
meta   dry spirit
metal   metallurgy
Metascope   IR night reading instrument
meteor   meteorological; meteorology
Meteor   jet fighter 1943 by Gloster;
         environmental satellite (SU)
Meteor-2   CT-2, controlled target RPV by
         Northrop Ventura
Meteosat   global meteorological satellite
Metex   metal detector by Dr Förster
methS   methylated spirit
METIMP   meteorological equipment improvement
         program (US)
METO   Middle East Treaty Organization
MetO   meteorological officer
meton   measured tons
METOXI   military effectiveness in a toxin
         environment
MetPierc   metal piercing (projectile)
MetPt   metal point (projectile)
METRI   military essentiality through
         readiness index
METRIC   security designation for the Western
         European union
MetRL   meteorology requirements listings
Metropolitan   CV-440, VIP transport aircraft
         by Convair
METS   mechanized export traffic system;
         modular engine test system
MetSat   meteorological satellite
METSO   sodium metasilicate
METT   mission, enemy terrain and (weather)
         troops (available)
METU   mobile electronics training unit
MetVic   Metropolitan Vickers
MEU   marine expeditionary unit
MEV   million electron volts
MEW   microwave early warning system
         (radar); ministry of economic war-
         fare (UK)
MEWS   modular electronic warfare system
MEXE   military engineering and experimen-
         tal establishment (Christchurch)
         since 1970: MVEE
MEXEFLOTE   bridging equipment by Fairey
MF   Medal of Freedom (US); Mediterranean
         Fleet; militia form; ministry of
         food; mark for; medium frequen-
         cies; magnetic field (generator);
         machine finish; mill finish;
         Manufacture d'Armes et Cycles
         (St Etienne France)
MFA   military functional appropriation
MFA&A   monuments, fine arts and archives
MFAirWest   marine fleet air, West Coast

MFACo	Meriden Firearms Company (US)
MFAR	modernized fleet accounting and reporting system (USN)
MFB	motional feedback system (loudspeaker); Metropolitan fire brigade
MFBS	multi-frequency binary sequence
MFC	mobile fire controller; mortar fire controller; The Military Forces of the Crown
MFCS	missile fire control system
MFD	minimum fatal dose; multi-function display
mfd	manufactured
MF/DF	medium frequency direction finder
MFDP	maintenance float distribution point (centre) NADGE
MFE	manual of field engineering; military field engineering
MFG	Marinefliegergeschwader (naval aviation squadron) (FGN)
mfg	manufacturing
MFGG	Marinefliegergefechtsstand (naval air operations centre) (FGN)
MFGT	manual of flying and ground training (UK) BLAC
MFH	military families' hospital; mobile field hospital
MFI	major force issues; melt flow index (polymers)
MFI-17	Supporter, close air support aircraft by Saab
MFK	multi-function key (set)
MFL	mobile force Atlantic
MFlgFlaStaff	Marinefliegerflugabwehrstaffel (naval air arm anti-aircraft squadron) (FGN)
MFM	missile farm monitor; mine firing mechanism; multistage frequency multiplexer
MFMR	M-day force material requirement
MFMS	Marinefernmeldeschule Flensburg (naval signals school) (FGN)
MFN	most favoured nation
MFNG	motion for a finding of not guilty
MfNV	Ministerium für Nationale Verteidigung (East German national defence ministry)
MFO	master frequency oscillator; military forwarding organization
MFOI	major force-oriented issues
MFP	military foot police (UK); minimal flight path
MFPS	mobile field photographic section; mobile fuel pumping station
MFR	missile frigate; mutual force reduction; memorandum for record
mfr	manufacturer
mfre	manufacture
mfrs	manufacturers
MFS	military flight service; missile firing station; missile firing simulator; magnetic flux sensor; manned flying system; multiple frequency shift; medium future SAM programme (Nato)
MFSS	medical field service school (US)
MFT	mechanized flame thrower; monolayer formation time; multiposition frequency telegraphy; multiprogramming fixed task; motor freight tariff; Metaalwaren Fabriek Tillburg (NL)
MFTU	medical forward treatment unit
MFu	The Royal Munster Fusiliers
MFÜSys	Marineführungssystem (Naval CCIS)
MFV	motor fishing vessel; motor fleet vessel; military flight vehicle
MFWC	marine fleet (air) West Coast
MG	military government; master gunner (RA); marine gunner; major general; master general; machine gun; mid-course guidance; mixed grain; motor generator
M&G	mapping and geodesy
MG-1	... 2, ... 3, machine gun by Rheinmetall
MF-42	machine gun 1942 (GE)
MG-81	machine gun 7.62mm by Mauser
MG-710-3	machine gun by SIG
MG-320	x-ray explosives detector by Philips
MGA	major general in charge of administration
MGas	motor gasoline
MGAWD	make good all works disturbed
MGB	modular glide bomb; motor gun boat; missile gun boat; medium girder bridge by Fairey
MGC	machine gun corps; machine gun company
MGCI	master ground controller interception (radar)
MGCS	missile guidance and control system
MGD	million gallons per day; military geographic documentation
MGDA	multiple degaussing cable
MGE	machine gun emplacement
mge	message
MgF	magnesium fluoride (IR domes)
MGFA	Militärgeschichtliches Forschungsamt Freiburg im Breisgau (military historical research institute)
MGGB-2	modular guided glide bomb TV homing
MGGS	major general, general staff
MGI	military geographic information
MGID	military geographic information and documentation
MGIEC	Magnavox Government & Industrial Electronics Company (Torrance Cal.)

mgm	mailgram
MGM-1	Matador, ground-launched tactical missile by Martin
MGM-13	Mace, CGM-13, ground-launched tactical missile
MGM-29A	Sergeant, ground-launched tactical missile nuclear
MGM-31	Pershing, mobile ground-launched tactical missile by Martin
MGM-32A	Entac, anti-tank guided missile by SNIA
MGM-51C	Shillelagh, gun-launched guided projectile by Ford
MGM-52	Lance, ground-launched tactical missile by Vought
MGO	machine gun officer; master general of ordnance; military government officer; military government ordnance (US)
MGr	Minengranate, high-explosive shell
MgR	Mündungsgeschwindigkeits Radargerät (muzzle velocity radar)
mgr	manager
MGR-1B	Honest John, ground-launched tactical nuclear missile
MGRA	major general, Royal Artillery
MGRS	military grid reference system
MGS	machine gun section; machine gun school
mgs	metre-gram-second
MGSgt	master gunnery sergeant
MGT	machine gun training; machine gun troop
mgt	management
MGU	mid-course guidance unit; military government unit
MGun	marine gunner
MGunSgt	master gunnery sergeant
MGySgt	master gunnery sergeant
MGVP	military government vehicle permit
MH	military hospital; military history; Medal of Honor (US); master of horse; ministry of health; man hole; magnetic heading; man hours; Martini-Henry (rifle) (UK); materials handling STANAG
M&H	Mervin, Hubert & Co.
MHA	Medal for Humane Action (US); mental health administration; minimum holding altitude; minehunter, auxiliary
MHB	master horizontal bomber
MHC	minehunter, coastal; mechanical height computer
MHCO	minehunting control officer
MHCP	mean horizontal candle powers
MHCS	mental hygiene consultation service
MHD	medical holding detachment; military history detachment; magneto-hydro-dynamics (power supply); meter heading differential
MHDF	medium and high frequencies direction finder
MHE	materials handling equipment
MHEI	mine, high-explosive incendiary (anti-aircraft shell)
MHEIT	mine, high-explosive incendiary with tracer
MHF	medium high frequency
MHHW	mean higher high water
MHK	Materialhauptkatalog (material master plan)
MHLW	mean higher low water
MHon	most honourable
MHQ	Marinehauptquarter (FGN) CCIS maritime headquarters (Nato)
MHR	Member of the House of Representatives
MHS	ministry of home security; military historical society; medical history sheet
MHS-1285	message handling system by AEG
MHSS	material handling support system
MHT	mild heat treatment
MHTU	materials handling trials unit RAOC
MHVDF	medium, high and very high frequencies direction finder
MHW	mean high water
MHWI	mean high water interval
MHWLR	mobile hostile weapon locating radar
MHWN	mean high water, neaps
MHWNT	mean high water neap tides
MHWS	mean high water, springs
MHWST	mean high water spring tides
MHz	mega Hertz
MI	military intelligence; mounted infantry; material inspection; medical illustration; middle initial; musketry instructor; ministry of information; missed interception; malleable iron
mi	miles; minutes
M&I	modernization and improvement
Mi-1	helicopter by *Mil (SU)*
Mi-2	Hoplite helicopter by *Mil (SU)*
Mi-4	Hound, ASW helicopter by *Mil (SU)*
MI-5	military intelligence department counter-espionage
MI-6	military intelligence department foreign office secret intelligence
Mi-6	Hook, world's biggest transport helicopter by *Mil (SU)*
Mi-8	Hip, Haze, medium range transport helicopter by *Mil (SU)*
Mi-10	Harke, flying crane 15 tons payload helicopter by *Mil (SU)*
Mi-12	Homer, world's heaviest helicopter 105 tons
Mi-14	Haze, Hip, ASW helicopter naval Mi-8
Mi-24	HindD, combat transport helicopter by *Mil*

Mi-28   Hind, anti-tank helicopter *by Mil*
Mi-103   anti-tank plastic mine (Sweden)
MIA   missing in action; missile intelli-
           gence agency; military inspection
           agency
MIAC   material identification and account-
           ing code
MIACAH   mine by GIAT
MIACF   meander inverted auto-correlated
           function
MIACS   manufacturing information and con-
           trol system
MIAPC   FV-432, mechanized infantry
           armoured personnel carrier
MIARS   maintenance information automatic
           retrieval system
MIAS   major item automated system AMC
MIB   marine index bureau; master instruc-
           tion book; mechanized infantry
           battalion
MIBARS   military intelligence battalion air
           reconnaissance support
MIBK   methyl iso-butyl ketone (solvent)
MIC   management information centre;
           Malayan Indian Congress; mono-
           lithic integrated circuit;
           miniaturized integrated circuit;
           mast interrupt control; meteorolo-
           gical information committee
mic   microphone
MICB   Meck Island control building
Michigan   heavy wheeled tractor with dozer
           blade (UK RE)
MICNS   modular integrated communications
           (command) and navigation system by
           Harris
MiCom   missile command (US Army)
Micon   anti-aircraft guided weapon (Swiss)
MICR   magnetic ink character recognition
MicRad   microwave radiation
             --MTCN
Micradet   PSS-502, microwave radiation
             detector, radar warning
             receiver portable by CGE
micro   microfilm, microscope
Microcam   world's lightest TV camera by
             Thomson
Micropuff passive sonar RAN by Sperry
MicroPUFFS passive sonar RAN passive rang-
             ing sonar for submarines by
             Sperry
MICRS   main instrument console and read-out
           stations
MICS   manufacturing information and con-
           trol system
MICV   XM-723, mechanized infantry combat
           vehicle by FMC
MICV-65   XM-701, mechanized infantry combat
           vehicle 1965 by FMC
MID   military intelligence department;

military intelligence division;
mentioned in despatches; manpower
information division; missile
intelligence directorate; message
input device; minimum infective
dose; median incapacitating dose
Mid   Midshipman
mid   middle; midnight
MIDA   major item data agency
MIDAC   Michigan (university) digital auto-
           matic computer
MIDAS   missile detection and alarm system;
           missile defence alarm system;
           measurement information and data
           system; media investment decisions
           analysis system
MidEastFor Middle East force (USN)
MIDF   major item data file
Midge   USD-501, surveillance drone by
           Canadair
MIDIZ   Mid-Canada identification zone
Midn   Midshipman
midn   midnight
MIDP   major item distribution plan
MidPac   middle Pacific
MIDR   military intelligence division
           reserve; mandatory incident and
           defect reporting
MIDS   movement information distribution
           station; multi-functional informa-
           tion distribution system (Nato)
Midway   class, aircraft carriers CV (USN)
MIEETAT   major improvement in electronic
           effectiveness through advanced
           technologies
MIFASS   USMC marine integrated fire and air
           support system by TRW
MIFF   Mine flach-flach double hollow-
           charge dispersal mine (GE)
MIFLA   mittlere Flugabwehr (project)
           (medium a/a missile (command via
           radar link)
MIG   magnesium inert gas (welding),
           metallic inert gas
MIG   minimum income guarantee
MiG-1   single-engined fighter aircraft WW2
           by Mikoyan-Gurevich (SU)
MiG-3   single-engined fighter aircraft WW2
           by Mikoyan-Gurevich (SU)
MiG-5   single-engined fighter aircraft WW2
           by Mikoyan-Gurevich (SU)
MiG-9   Fargo, jet fighter 1946 *by Mikoyan-
           Gurevich (SU)*
MiG-15   Fagot, Midget, jet fighter 1947 *by
           Mikoyan-Gurevich (SU)*
           U   trainer version
MiG-17   Fresco, jet day fighter 1950 *by
           Mikoyan-Gurevich (SU)*
           P   fighter
           PF   all-weather fighter
           PFU guided missile fighter (4Alkali)

MiG-19   Farmer, supersonic fighter 1953 *by Mikoyan-Gurevich (SU)*
MiG-21   Fishbed, Mongol, supersonic fighter/strike bomber 1955 *by Mikoyan-Gurevich (SU)*
    U   trainer version
    F   Fishbed C
    PF   Fishbed D
    PFM Fishbed F
    PFMA Fishbed J (MRCA)
MiG-23   Flogger, variable sweep strike bomber 1964
    U trainer
MiG-25   Foxbat, fighter/strike bomber/all-weather interceptor
MiG-27   Flogger D, strike fighter/bomber
MIHPED   microwave-induced helium plasma emission detection
Mighty Antar   tank transporter (UK)
Mighty Atom   motor bicycle (UK)
Mighty Mite   jeep short version (US)
Mighty Mo   air-to-air rocket 40mm (USAF)
Mighty Mouse air-to-air rocket 40mm (USAF)
Migrator   airborne navigation system by EAS
mih   miles in 1 hour
mi2h   miles in 2 hours
MiJ-331B   Minenjagdboot by VFW-Fokker (mine sweeper)
MiJB   Minenjagdboot by VFW-Fokker (mine sweeper)
MIJI   meaconing, intrusion, jamming and interference
Mike   first hydrogen bomb (USAF)
MIL   military standard specification
mil   military; mileage; militia; militärische Sonderentwicklung (GE) (special military development)
mila   militia
Milan   Missile d'Infanterie Leger Anti-Char (anti-tank guided missile by Euromissile)
MilAtt   military attache
MilCom   military committee communication (message) (Nato)
MilComSat   military communications satellite
MilCon   military construction
MilConf   military confinement
MilDAT   military damage assessment team
MilDec   military decision
MilDeps   military departments
MilDept   military department
MILES   multiple integrated laser engagement system by Xerox
milglFzg   militärisches geländegängiges Fahrzeug (GE) (military cross-country vehicle)
MilGov   military government
MilGp   military group
MiliMetS   military meteorological system for artillery

MiliPAC   military portable artillery computer by ComDev
Militant   FV-11000, 10 ton truck (UK)
MILLIE   maximum interchange of the latest logistic information is essential (system) (US)
Mills bomb   (spud) No. 36 hand grenade
Milotka   AT-3, Sagger, anti-tank missiles (SU)
MilPAC   military personnel accounting activity
MilPerCen   military personnel center (US Army)
MilPers   military personnel
MilPHAP   military provincial hospital assistance programme
MilPO   military personnel office
MilRep   military representative to the Nato military committee
MILS   missile impact location system
MILSCAP   military standard contract administration procedures (US)
MilSpec   military specifications
MILSTAAD   military standard activity address directory
MILSTAC   military staff communication (message) (Nato)
MILSTAM   Nato international military staff memorandum
MILSTAMP   military standard transportation and movement procedures (US)
MilStd   military standard
MILSTEP   military supply and transportation evaluation procedures (US); military standard evaluation procedures
MILSTICCS   military standard item characteristics coding structure (US)
MILSTRAP   military standard transactions reporting and accounting procedures (US)
MILSTRIP   military standard requisitioning and issue procedures (US)
MILTRA   military Training Aids Company (UK)
MilVan   military owned demountable container (US)
mily   military
MIM   maintenance instruction manual
mim   minimum, mobile intercept missile
MIM-14B   Nike-Hercules, anti-aircraft missile by Western Electric
MIM-23A   Hawk, anti-aircraft missile by Raytheon
MIM-23B   I-Hawk, improved Hawk, anti-aircraft missile
MIM-72A   Chaparral, SHORADS, short-range air defence system by Ford
MIM-104   Patriot, SAM-D, surface-to-air missile by Raytheon/Martin
MIME   ministry of information, Middle East

mi/min   miles per minute
MIMS   major item management system
min   minutes; minimum; mine
Min   minister; ministry
MIN   minecraft
MIN-77   mine identification and neutraliza-
        tion system (wire-guided unmanned
        submersible) by SMIN
MinBatFor   minecraft battle force (USN)
MinDiv   mine division
Mine M-24   Fido, Wandering Annie, sonobuoy
Mine No. 75   Howkins grenade, anti-tank mine
        (UK)
MineStrMeaSta   mine counter-measures station
MineDefLab   mine defence laboratory
Mineguma   class, destroyers (JMSDF)
MINEX   Mine (laying-sweeping-hunting)
        exercise (Nato)
Minfap   minimum facilities project ATC
        computer EUROCONTROL Maastricht
Mini   RPV with laser target illuminator
        RPAODS-1 by Philco-Ford
Mini-14   self-loading rifle 5.56mm by Sturm
        Ruger
MiniAPT   miniature automatic picture trans-
        mission
Miniature Jezebel   passive omnidirectional
        sonobuoy by Ultra
MiniCam   miniature camera
Minicat   infra-red night firing camera by
        SAT
Mini-Drone   miniature recce drone, camera-
        carrying by Allen International
Minigun   machine gun 7.62mm electrically
        driven rotating barrels by GE
Minilaser   artillery laser by Oldelft
Mini-lite   light earphones by Racal
Miniman   anti-tank rocket launcher by FFV
Minimi   light machine gun 5.56mm by FN
Mini-Nukes   miniature nuclear warheads
        (tactical)
Mini-Ranger   tracking and surveillance radar
        by Motorola
MiniRPV   laser target designator RPV by McDD
MiniSadang   sonobuoy system for ASW helicop-
        ters by Thomson-CSF
Ministab   stabilizing gear for helciopters
        by SFENA
MiniTAT   tactical armament turret with mini-
        gun
MiniTrack   minimum-weight tracking system
        (Nasa)
Mini-Ubiquitous   portable frequency analyser
        by Nicolet
MinLant   mine warfare forces, Atlantic
MinPac   mine warfare forces, Pacific
Minotaur   remote-controlled mine removing
        vehicles by Volvo
Minry   class, spy ships (SU)
mins   minutes

MINS   Mare Island Naval Shipyard
MinSuppU   minecraft support unit
MINT   material identification and new
        item control technique (US)
MinTech   ministry of technology
MINU   mobile instrument investigation unit
MINUET   minimum energy trajectory model (US)
Minuteman   LGM-30, land-based intercontinen-
        tal missile by Boeing
MinWarTech   mine warfare technician
MinWt   minimum weight
MINY   Mare Island Naval Shipyard
MIO   mobile issuing office; material
        inventory objective; M-day inven-
        tory objective
MIP   material improvement plan; mean
        indicated pressure; malleable
        iron pipe; management improvement
        programme; maintenance improvement
        programme; manual index pages;
        mobiles integrations- und Prüf-
        system (mobile integration and
        test system)
MIPR   military inter-departmental purchase
        request (US)
MIPROC-16M   military micro computer by
        Plessey
MIR   memory information register; medical
        inspection room; material inspec-
        tion report
MIRA   motor industry research association
        (UK)
Mira   artillery rocket 108mm 12-cell
        launcher by SAI Ambrosini
Mira-2   Milan infra-red adapter (sight) by
        TRT/Siemens
MIRAC   management information research
        assistance centre
Mirach-100/150   RPV by Meteor
Mirach-300   multi-purpose RPV by Meteor
Mirador III   coherent pulse-doppler search
        and target designation radar
        by Thomson
Mirage IIIE   jet fighter/bomber/recce by
        Dassault
Mirage IVA   jet nuclear bomber by Dassault
Mirage-2000   jet interceptor by Dassault
Mirage F-1C   jet all-weather interceptor by
        Dassault
MIRCOM   missile material readiness command
        (US)
MIRD   medical internal radiation dose;
        minor irregularities and
        deficiencies
Mirka   class, frigates (SU)
MIRPL   major item repair parts list
MIRR   material inspection receiving report
MIRROS   modulation inducing reactive retro-
        directive optical system (Nasa)
MIRS   military intelligence reserve

society; military intelligence
research station

MIRV   multiple independently targetable
re-entry vehicles (missile warheads)

MIS   military intelligence service;
management information system;
manpower information system;
material inspection service;
mine issuing ship; midget submarine; master implementation
schedule NADGE; mobile information
system; metal insulation semi-
conductor

MISC   miscellaneous STANAG

mis   missile

MISA   military industrial supply agency

MISAR   micro-processed sensing and automatic regulation 1977 by Olds-
mobile

misc   miscellaneous

MiscDoc   miscellaneous documents

M&ISD   mathematical and informational sciences division ONR

MISER   microwave space electronic relays

MISFET   metal insulation semi-conductor
field effect transistor

misg   missing

MISL   manpower information systems laboratory

MISMA   major item supply management agency

MISO   management information systems
office

MISP   medical information systems programme

MISPC   mechanized infantry squad proficiency course

MISR   major item studies report; minimum
industrial sustaining role

MisRan   missile range

MisRep   joint tactical air reconnaissance/
surveillance mission report

MISS   MS-150, modular instructional servo
system by Feedback Instruments

Missile Minder   TSQ-73, by Litton

Mission Master   utility transport plane by
GAF

Mistel   parasite aircraft WW2 (GE)

MisTraU   missile weapons systems training
unit
Lant   Atlantic
Pac   Pacific

MIT   methods of instruction team;
Massachusetts Institute of Technology, master instruction tape

MiTAC   micro TACAN by SEL

Mitchell   B-52B, medium bomber WW2 (USAF)

MITE   missile integration terminal equipment

MITI   ministry of international trade and
industry

Miticide   insecticide

MITMS   military industry technical manual
specifications

MITO   minimum interval take-off

MITRE   Massachusetts Institute of Technology Research Establishment

MITS   man in the sea; multiple independent
threat simulator by General
Instruments (RWR test set)

Mitscher   class, guided missile destroyers
(DDG USN)

Miura   class, amphibious attack vessels
(JMSSDF)

MIUS   modular integrated utility system

MIUTC   military intelligence unit training
centre

MIUW   mobile inshore underseas warfare

MIUWSU   mobile inshore underseas warfare
surveillance unit

MiVRS   Minenverlege- und Räumsystem (mine
dispersing and clearance system)

MiWS   MSM, Minenwurfsystem (mine dispersing system)

MIX   master index

Mixture VII   incendiary charge

MIZ   missile intercept zone;
Materialinformationszentrum
(Gesellschaft für Logistik mbH
Wilhelmshaven)

Mizutori   class, corvettes (JMSDF)

MJAO   Mediterranean joint air orders

MJC   military junior college

MJD   management job description

MJG   management job guide

MJQ-20   power generator

MJS   Mariner-Jupiter-Saturn (missile)

MJU-7B   infra-red flare by Tracor

MK   miscellaneous kits;
Maschinenkanone (automatic cannon)

Mk   mark

mK   mit Kappe (capped) (projectile)

Mk-1   horizontal anti-tank mine (FR);
illumination hand grenade (US);
anti-aircraft gun 40mm (UK)

Mk-1/3   battle tank 105mm gun by Vickers

Mk-2   Pineapple, hand grenade (US);
arming device for Mk-48 torpedo

Mk-3   hand grenade HE (US); main battle
tank by Vickers (UK)

Mk-4   steel helmet (UK)

Mk-5   SMLE, short magazine Lee Enfield
rifle, jungle version

Mk-5S   class, very fast missile patrol
boats (IT)

Mk-7   anti-tank mine, round by ROF

Mk-8   43/44, homing torpedo (Nato);
114/55, naval gun by Vickers

Mk-9   corvettes for Nigeria by Vosper/
Thornycroft

Mk-10   naval IFF radar

MK-10   Meridiankreisel by BGT (vehicular navigation gyro)
Mk-11   helicopter-borne depth charge (UK)
Mk-12   weapon direction system for Aegis by Raytheon; electronic assembly for torpedo Mk-48; MIRV warhead for Minuteman (3 W-62 warheads 200 KT each)
Mk-15   Phalanx, CIWS, close-in weapon system (USN); Snake-Eye, bomb retarding system (USAF)
Mk-16   unguided ship/submarine torpedo (USN)
Mk-20   passive homing submarine torpedo; Rokeye, airborne laser pod
Mk-20   Rh-202, Maschinenkanone 20mm (automatic cannon) by Rheinmetall
Mk-21   exploder for warhead Mk-107 torpedo Mk-48
Mk-23   torpedo, passive homing and wire guidance
Mk-24   Tigerfish, wire-guided acoustic homing torpedo by Marconi
Mk-26   twin naval multi-purpose ramp --Harpoon, Subroc, Standard
Mk-27   Maschinenkanone 27mm by Mauser (automatic cannon)
Mk-29   eight-cell launcher for Sea Sparrow
Mk-30   training torpedo mobile target (USN); air-launched passive homing torpedo
Mk-31   Tigerfish, airborne version
Mk-32   triple torpedo tubes 324mm --Mk-44, Mk-46
Mk-33   Septar, target boat (5.4m) (USN)
Mk-35   Septar, target boat (15.5m) (USN)
Mk-37   homing torpedo (Nato)
Mk-38   mini mobile target (USN)
Mk-42   naval gun 5in (USN)
Mk-43   torpedo airborne and shipborne
Mk-44   mortar ammunition 120mm for MO-120 (FR); standardized light-weight homing torpedo (Nato)
Mk-45   127/45 anti-aircraft gun (USN)
Mk-46   light-weight active homing anti-submarine torpedo
Mk-48   ADCAP, advanced capability anti-submarine torpedo
Mk-60   CAPTOR, capsuled torpedo, anti-submarine mine
Mk-61   mortar round HE
Mk-61/63 plastic anti-personnel mine by SAEA
Mk-62   mortar smoke shell 120mm (FR) FD flare mortar shell 120mm (FR)
Mk-71   MCLWG, major calibre light-weight gun naval (USN) 203mm 8in
Mk-72   mortar shell 60mm HE
Mk-75   gun mount for 76mm gun
Mk-76   ballistic training bomb
Mk-82   bomb 500 lbs; Snake Eye, airborne

laser pod;bomb 654 lbs, laser-guided
Mk-83   GP bomb 1000 lbs; bomb 1025 lbs laser-guided
Mk-84   bomb, 2000 lbs
Mk-86   naval fire-control system by Lockheed
Mk-99   naval fire control, illuminating and tracking radar by Raytheon and GE
MK-101   Maschinenkanone by Rheinmetall (30mm airborne automatic cannon)
Mk-105   towed magnetic mine sweeping system by EDO
Mk-107   warhead for torpedo Mk-48
Mk-112   eight-cell launcher for extended range ASROC
Mk-115   naval fire control system for Sea Sparrow
Mk-116   anti-submarine fire director system by Singer Librascope
Mk-118   bomb (USAF)
Mk-152   naval computer by Univac
Mk-500   Evader, terminally guided warhead
Mk-545   ORTS, operational readiness and test system for Aegis
mkd   marked
MKG   main killing ground
MKM   Master of the King's Musick (UK); marksman (US)
MKMS   Mehrkammermüllsystem by Dornier (multi-chamber garbage system)
mkr   marker (radio beacon)
MKR   rifle 4.5mm (Sweden)
mks   marks, metre-kilogramme-second (system)
MKS   MaK und Krauss-Maffei Sondertechnik; 5.56mm assault rifle by Inter-dynamics
mksA   metre-kilogramme-second-Ampere (system)
MKTU   marksmanship training unit
MKVA   Jet Provost aircraft
MKW   Military Knight of Windsor
ML   mobile laboratory; military law; military landing; money list; motor launch; small minesweeper (USN)
M/L   mine layer (RN)
ML   meteorological device; mobile land (radio station); muzzle loader; mission load; machine language; mean level
ml   miles; milli-litres
ML-30   gun 152mm (SU)
ML-1611   ... 1665, metal locator, portable by Vallon GmbH
ML-1750   metal locator, vehicle-mounted portable by Vallon GmbH
MLA   mean line of advance; motor launch, auxiliary

MLAF	missile lot acceptance firings	mls	miles
MLAGB	muzzle loaders' association of Great Britain	MLSRE	movement light squadron Royal Engineers
MLB	metal link belt	MLT	mean life time
MLBCoy	mobile laundry and bath company	MLTR	military land transportation resources
MLBM	modern large ballistic missile	MLU	memory loading unit
MLC	master labour contract; military liaison committee; main landing craft; motor landing craft; military landing craft; mechanized landing craft; manoeuvre land control; military load classification	MLV	Medal for Labour Valour; short-range radar
		MLW	mean low water; maximum landing weight
		MLWI	mean low water interval
		MLWN	mean low water, neaps
MLCAEC	military liaison committee to the atomic energy commission	MLWNT	mean low water, neap tides,
		MLWS	mean low water, springs; minimum level water stand (Nato)
MLCP	mobile land command post	MLWST	mean low water spring tides
MLD	main line of defence; minimal lethal dose; median lethal dose; medium lethal dose --LD-50; minimum line of detection; masking level difference; mixed layer depth	MLZ	Marinearsenal Liegezeit (time in FGN naval yard)
		MM	Medal for Merit (US); Military Medal; missile master; master of music; ministry of munitions; manual of movement; motor maintenance (aptitude test) (US); mercantile marine; motor machine gun; mechanic machine gun; middle marker (landing system); magnetic mine; memory module; Mariner Mars (project) (Nasa); maintenance manual; materials measurement; minelayer (USN)
mld	moulded		
mldr	moulder		
MLE	magazine Lee Enfield (rifle); maximum loss expectancy; maximum likelihood estimates		
MLES	multiple line encryption system		
MLF	multi-lateral force (nuclear); mobile land force; motor launch, fast (Nato)		
M/LF	medium/low frequency	MM-38	naval anti-ship missile by AS, Naval Exocet
MLG	main landing gear; Methyl-L-glutamate	MM-39	naval anti-ship missile by AS, Naval Exocet II
MLGW	maximum landing gross weight	MM-40	naval anti-ship missile by AS, Super Exocet
MLHW	mean lower high water		
MLL	manned lunar landing	MM-100	ASEM, marine missile 100km range, anti-ship Euromissile
MLLW	mean lower low water		
MLM	magazine Lee Medford (rifle)	MMA	medical material account; motor mileage allowance (UK); multi-mission aircraft (USCG) --Falcon; manual metal arc (welding); methyl-methacrylate; minelayer, auxiliary (USN)
MLMS	multi-purpose light-weight missile system by GD		
MLNS	ministry of labour and national service (UK)		
MLO	military landing officer; military liaison officer; movement liaison officer	MMACW	manual of medical aspect of chemical warfare
		M-MARP	mobilization - manpower allocation requirements plan (US)
MLP	master logistics plan; multi-level procedure; mirror landing practice	MMAT	mobile mine assembly team
MLQ-24	ground-based counter-measures transmitter	MMBF	mean miles between failures
		MMBP	military medical benefits property
MLR	main line of resistance	MMC	Malaya military college; manual of military cooking and dietry; military mini cooler; maximum metal condition; micro meteroid capsule; material management code; minelayer, coastal (USN)
MLRG	muzzle loading rifled gun		
MLR	muzzle loading rifle		
MLRO	maritime labour relations organization		
MLRP	marine (corps) long-range plans		
MLRS	multiple (medium) launcher rocket system by Boeing/Vought GSRS		
MLS	microwave landing system; mixed language system; multi-language system; medium long shot	MMC-80K	military mini cooler 80K by Philips (for thermal imaging equipment)

MMCMP	mobilization, military and civil manpower program (US)
MMCS	mobile military computer system
MMD	master monitor display (avionics); minelayer, fast (USN)
MMDTSA	memoranda on military diseases in tropical and subtropical areas
MME	manual of military engineering; missile maintenance equipment; motion measuring equipment
MMES	master material erection schedule
MMF	magnetomotive force; moving magnetic features; minelayer, fleet (USN)
MMFF	multi-mode fire and forget (missile) program (US Army)
MMG	medium machine gun
MMGT	medium mobility gun tractor (UK)
MMH	manual on military hygiene; maintenance man hours
MMH/FH	maintenance man hours/per flight hour
MMk	material mark
MML	manual of military law
MMLME	Mediterranean, Mediterranean Litoral and/or Middle East
MMM	medical material manager
MMMC	medical material management centre
MMMF	multinational mixed manned force (Nato)
MM Mk.11	magnetic mine sweeping loop (RN)
MMMS	multi-mission modular spacecraft
MMN	Metallurgie et Mécanique Nucleaires (Belgium)
MMNIC	main Mediterranean naval intelligence centre
MMO	main meteorological office; medium machine oil
MMP	military mounted police; masters, mates and pilots (association); merchant marine personnel; military musical pageant; monitoring metering panel
MMPC	mobilization material procurement capability
MMPDABC	medical material programme for defence against biological and chemical agents
MMPF	master military pay file
MMPNC	medical material programme for nuclear casualties
MMPR	missile manufacturers planning report
MMPVS	modified military pay voucher system (US)
MMR	minimum marginal return; mobilization material requirement; management milestone records; mass miniature radiography; multiple match revolver
MMRA	mobilization material requirements adjustment
MMRBM	mobile medium-range ballistic missile

MMRFS	manual of map reading and field sketching
MMS	motor mine sweeper (USN); multi-mission ship; magnetic median surface; manpower management survey; munitions maintenance squadron (USAFE); multi-mission modular spacecraft
MMSA	mercantile marine service association
MMSC	Mediterranean marine sorting centre
MMSS	magnetic mine sweeping system
MMT	missile maintenance technician; manufacturing methods and technology
MMU	million monetary units; manned manoeuvring unit by Martin
MMV	mittlere maximale Verfügbarkeit (medium maximal availability)
MMW	millimetre wave, main magnetization winding
MMY	military man years
MN	merchant navy; magnetic north; motor number
mn	minute; midnight
MN-1	5.56mm rifle by NWM
MNA	missing, no (enemy) action; mobile naval airfield
MNAO	mobile naval airfield organization
MNAOA	merchant navy and airline officers' association
MNAU	mobile naval airfield unit
MNB	main naval base; mobile naval base
MNBA	minimum normal burst altitude
MNBDO	mobile naval base defence organization (UK)
MNC	multi-national corporations; major Nato command(ers)
MND	minister of national defence
Mne	marine
MNECP	mobile national emergency command post
mng	managing
mngmt	management
mngr	manager
MNI	Madras Native Infantry; ministry of national insurance --MPNI
MNKERR	Marlow nylon kinetic energy recovery rope (UK)
MNLA	Malayan national liberation army
mnm	minimum
MNOMU	mobile nuclear ordnance maintenance unit
MNOPF	merchant naval officers' pension fund
MNOS	metal-nitride oxide semiconductors; metal nitride oxide silicon
MNOSFET	metal nitride oxide semiconductor field effect transistor

MNP	military nuclear power
MNPO	mobile navy post office
MNPS	(North Atlantic) minimum navigation performance specification
MNPT	meta-nitro-para-toluidine (dye)
MNR	mean neap rise (tide); minimum noise routes
MNS	modernized number service
MNT	mean neap tide
MO	medical officer; medical orderly; mining officer; mail order; meteorological office; military operation; money order; monthly order; municipal officer; The Monmouthshire Regiment; management office; mobile object; master oscillator; mixed oxide; mass observation; method of operation; motor operated; manually operated
mo	mobile
MO-9	commando branch of the war office
M&O	maintenance and operation
MO-120-60	mortar 120mm by Thomson/Brandt
MO-120LT	mortar 120mm by Thomson/Brandt
MO-120-RT	rifled mortar 120mm by Thomson/ Brandt
MOA	management operations audit; minute of angle; medium observation aircraft
MoA	ministry of aviation; memorandum of agreement
MOAMA	mobile air material area
Moaning Minnie	WW1 German mine thrower; WW2 German rocket launcher
MOB	main operating base; mobile operating base
mob	mobile; mobilization
M&OA	maintenance and operations branch BUPERS
MOBA	mobility operations in built-up areas
MoBas	model basin
MOBAT	modified BAT battalion anti-tank 120mm recoilless rifle
MobConBat	mobile construction battalion
MobDes	mobilization designee
Möbelwagen	anti-aircraft tank WW2 (GE)
MobiDiC	mobile digital computer
MOBIS	management oriented budget and information system
MOBS	multiple orbital bombardment system
MOBTDA	mobilization table of distribution and allowances
MobTr	mobile trainer
MOBU	mobilization base units
MOC	minimum operational characteristics; Mace operating centre
MOCA	minimum obstruction clearance altitude
MOCAS	mechanization of contract administrative service

MoCom	mobility command
MOCS	Mons officer cadet school
MOD	mobile observation device; miscellaneous obligation document; military obligation designator; month of detachment; ministry of overseas development (UK)
MoD	ministry of defence
mod	model; modified; modulator; modification
ModAp	modified Apollo
MODAS	modular data acquisition system by Plessey
MODB	military occupational data bank
ModCat	modified catamaran
MoDem	modulator-demodulator
ModF	naval gun 30mm by Mauser
MODFB	ministry of defence finance branch
MODFLIR	modularized forward-looking infrared (passive) (US-GE project)
modg	modifying
modn	modification
MODIA	methods of designing instructional alternatives
modif	modification
MODILS	modular instrument landing system
MoDN	ministry of defence, naval department
MODS	mobility planning data system; manned orbital development system
MoE	ministry of education
MOE	measure of effectiveness; mobile telemetry station (radio)
MOEP	meteorological and oceanographic equipment program (US)
MoF	ministry of food
MofA	ministry of agriculture fisheries and food
MOFAB	mobile floating assault bridge
MofP	ministry of pensions and national insurance
MofRAF	marshal of the Royal Air Force
MofW	ministry of works
MOG	material ordering guide
MoGas	motor gasoline
MOH	Medal of Honour; ministry of health; medical officer of health
MoH	ministry of housing and local government
Mohawk	OV-1, EV-1, STOL turboprop aircraft by Grumman
MOHLG	ministry of housing and local government
Moho	Mohorovicic discontinuity
MOI	ministry of information; ministry of the interior; military occupational information; military operations and intelligence; mission-oriented items
MOIC	medical officer in charge; medical officer in command

MOIV	mechanically operated inlet valve
Mojave	H-37, CH-37, heavy transport helicopter by Sikorsky
MOJMRP	meteorological office; joint meteorological radio propagation (sub-committee)
MOL	manned orbiting laboratory; machine oriented language; mirror optical landing
MoL	ministry of labour
mol	molecule; molecular
Molch	midget submarine WW2 (GE)
Molniya	regional telecommunications satellite (SU)
MOLNS	ministry of labour and national service
Molotov	Bred Basket, incendiary bomb; Cocktail, incendiary hand grenade
MOLS	mirror optical landings
molwt	molecular weight
MOM	military official mail; military overseas mail; middle of month
Moma	class, spy ships (SU)
MOMAT	mobile mine assembly team Lant Atlantic Pac Pacific
MOMP	mid-ocean meeting point
Momsen Lung	submarine emergency escape apparatus (USN)
MON	The Monmouthshire Regiment; motor octane number
Mona	airborne radio navigation system by Decca
MONAB	mobile naval air base
Monaghan Respirator	iron lung (US)
Monarch	road tractor (UK)
Mongoose	A-12, Mangusta, armed helicopter by Agusta
Monica	airborne tail-warning radar WW2 (RAF)
Monitor	armoured gun boat; tank; remote-controlled fire hose, water gun, TV screen
MoNoB	mobile noise barge (sound laboratory) (USN)
MONOHUD	helicopter-borne head-up display by Marconi
Montedel	Montecatini-Edison-Elettronica
montrg	monitoring
MOO	money order office
MOON	meeting our operational needs
Moonfighter	Havoc, A-20, attack bomber WW2 by Douglas
MOP	mustering out pay; multiple on-line programming
MoP	ministry of power; ministry of pensions and national insurance
MOPAR	master oscillator power amplifier radar
Moped	motorized pedal bicycle

MOPH	Military Order of the Purple Heart (US)
MoPic	motion pictures
MoPix	motion pictures
MOPMS	modular pack mine system for XM-77...78
MOPP	mission oriented protection posture
MOPR	manner of performance rating
Mops	military operations
MOPTAR	multi-object phase tracking and ranging (system)
MOQ	married officers' quarters
MOR	management operating radios; medical officer's report; ministry of reconstruction; mean observed range; magnetic optical radiation; mandatory occurrence reporting
mor	mortar
MorbRept	morbidity report
MorbTgRept	morbidity telegraphic report
MORC	medical officers' reserve corps
MORCOS	mortar control calculator by Marconi
MORE	minority officer recruitment effort
MoRest	mobile arresting (gear)
Moritzer	mortar howitzer
morn	morning
Morris Tube	sub-calibre barrel inset
MORS	military operational research symposium
MorSeaFron	Moroccan sea frontier
MORSL	mobilization reserve stockage list
mort	mortar
MortRep	mortar bombing report
MORU	military operations research unit
MOS	mounted orderly section; military occupational specification; major operating system; ministry of state (UK); management operating system; marking of overseas shipment; material ordering schedule; ministry of supply; maintenance and operations support; maritime observation satellite (Japan); metal oxide semi-conductor; metal oxide silicon; Marineortungsschule Wilhelmshaven (naval location school)
mos	months
MOSAR	modulation scan array radar
MOSC	military occupational specialty code; military oil sub- committee NAEB
Mosel	Klasse-402, SM-Boot Tender (FGN)
Mosette	AEL-4041, small RPV by AEL
MOS/FET	metal oxide semi-conductor/field effect transistor
MOSID	ministry of supply, inspection department

MOSJJ   Medal of the Order of St John of
         Jerusalem
Moskva   class, helicopter cruisers (SU)
MOS/LSI metal oxide semi-conductor/large-
         scale integration
Mosquito fighter/bomber WW2 by DeHavilland;
         wire-guided anti-tank missile by
         Contraves
MOSS   manned orbital space system (Nasa);
         maintenance and operations support
         set
MOST   mobile optical surveillance tracker;
         metal oxide silicon transistor
MOSU   mobile ordnance service unit
MoSuppU mobile support unit
MOT   month of travel; ministry of trans-
         port; military ocean terminal;
         maximum operating time
mot   motor(ized)
MoTarDiv mobile target division
MOTBA   military ocean terminal Bay area
MOTBy   military ocean terminal Bayonne
MOTG   marine operational training group
MOTKI   military ocean terminal, King's Bay
MOTNE   meteorological operational telecom-
         munications network Europe
mot-op   motor operated
MotPix   motion pictures
MOTSU   military ocean terminal, Sunny Point
MOTU   mobile ordnance technical unit
MoU   memorandum of understanding (Nato)
Moujik   Su-7U, trainer aircraft (SU)
Mountbatten SR-N-4, hovercraft (UK)
Mounty   member of the RCMP
MOUSE   manager owner user systems engineer;
         minimal orbital unmanned satellite
         of earth
Mouse   aerial navigation ground station
         WW2 --Oboe
Mousetrap rocket-propelled depth charge WW2
         (USN)
MOUT   military operations in urban terrain
MOV   military owned vehicle
mov   movement
MovCap   movement capability
MOVEM   movement overseas verification of
         enlisted members
MOVP   military owned vehicle plan
MovRep   movement report
MOVS   military owned vehicle service
MovSum   (daily) movement summary
MOW   ministry of works
Mowag   Motorwagenfabrik AG Kreuzlingen
MOWASP   mechanization of warehousing and
         shipping procedures
MOWB   ministry of works and buildings
Möwe   A-17 ... 29 ... 38, transport air-
         craft by Focke Wulf
MOWT   ministry of war transportation (UK)
MoYr   month year

MP   mineplanter; member of parliament
         (UK); master pilot; military
         police; Mauritian Pioneers;
         municipal police; marching pack;
         melting point; metropolitan
         police; months after payment;
         Mercator's projection (map);
         maintenance period; maritime polar
         (air mass); medium pressure;
         medium pattern; Micro Precision
         Corporation; Maschinenpistole
         (submachine gun); Militärpistole
         (military pistol)
M/P   memorandum of partnership (Nato)
MP-5   machine pistol 9mm by HK
MP-18   machine pistol 9mm 1918 (GE)
MP-28   machine pistol 9mm 1928 (GE)
MP-35   machine pistol 9mm 1935 by Bergmann
MP-38   machine pistol 1938 by ERMA
MP-40   machine pistol 1940 by ERMA
MP-100   hydrofoil by DHC
MPA   main propulsion assistant; maritime
         patrol aircraft; missile procure-
         ment, Army; manpower and personnel
         administration; military personnel,
         Army
MPA/C   maritime patrol aircraft
MPB   material and production branch
         BUPERS; merit promotion bulletin;
         missing persons bureau; mean
         point of burst
MPBB   military personnel budget branch
MPBN   military police battalion (USMC)
MPB&W   ministry of public building and
         works
MPC   member of the parliament of Canada;
         metropolitan police commissioner;
         master pilot's certificate;
         metropolitan police college
         (Hendon); military pay certifi-
         cate; military police corps (US);
         manpower priorities committee;
         maximum permissible concentration;
         multi-purpose communications;
         mathematics, physics, chemistry;
         message processing centre; multi-
         purpose console
MPCA   Merseyside Police Committee Award
MPCo   military police company
MPCRI   mercantile Pacific coastal routing
         instructions
MPCSW   multi-purpose close support weapon
MPD   metropolitan police district;
         Mauritian Pioneer Depot; medical
         pay date; maximum permissible
         dose; map pictorial display;
         meta-phenylene-diamine
MPDA   meta-phenylene-diamine
MPDB   manpower distribution board
MPDR   mobile pulse doppler radar by Siemens

MPDR	12	12km range for Gepard
	16	16km range for Roland
	18	18km range surveillance and target recognition
	30	by SEL, low-level air attack alarm
MPDR-3002S		TUR, Tieffliegerüberwachungs-radar (low-level air attack alarm radar on Marder hull)
MPDS		metropolitan police detective school (Hendon)
MPE		maximum permissible exposure; maximum permissible error; monthly project evaluation; Maschinenpistole Fabrikat ERMA
MPen		ministry of pensions
MPES		mobile photographic enlargement section
MPF		metropolitan police force; Malaya police federation; multi-purpose food
mpg		miles per gallon
MPG		Modulares Prüfgerät (modular test set)
mph		miles per hour
MPI		military police investigator; mean point of impact
MPi-69		machine pistol by Steyr
MPIO		mission payload integration office ESA
MPIP		miniature precision inertial platform
MP-K		machine pistol 9mm by Walther
MPL		maintenance parts list; maximum permissible level; mine planter
MPLA		Mozambique People's Liberation Army
MPLO		Mozambique people's liberation organization
MPM		message processing module; metres per minute; multi-purpose meal; major programme memorandum; maintenance planning manual
MPMIS		military police management information system
MPN		most probable number
MPNI		ministry of pensions and national insurance
MPO		military payment orders; movie projector operator; metropolitan police office; military posting officer; military post office; military permit office; mobile printing office; mobile publishing office; military projection operation; Soviet sea border guard
MPOS		movie projector operators' school
MPP		master programme plan; military pay procedures; member of the provincial parliament; most probable position; mission planning programme

MPPL	multi-purpose programming language
MPPS	military personnel procurement service
mpps	multi purpose
MPPWCOM	military police prisoner of war command
MPQ-3	track via missile guidance radar --Patriot
MPQ-4	mortar locating radar by GE
MPQ-10	artillery locating radar
MPQ-49	forward area alerting radar (anti-aircraft)
MPR	medium power radar
mpr	manpower
MPRJ	military personnel records jacket (US Army)
MPS	multi-purpose ship; mobile radar, search; material planning study; manufacturer's part specification; multi-programming system; modular programming system
mps	metres per second; megacycles per second
MPSA	military petroleum supply agency
MPSB	military production and supply board (Nato)
MPSC	military provost staff corps; material planning schedule and control
MPSD	military personnel security division
MPSM	multi-purpose sub-munition
MPSX	mathematical programming system, extended
MPS	military potential test
MPT	multi-lateral preparatory talks; missile pre-flight tester
mpt	melting point
MPTD	metropolitan police Thames division
MPTS	metropolitan police training school (Hendon)
MPts	metal parts
MPTSWG	military police tripartite standing working group
MPUL	military production urgency list
MPV	military pay voucher; motor powered vehicle
MP/VAP	maritime patrol/reconnaissance/attack aircraft
MPVSCS	military pay voucher summary and certification sheets
MPWS	mobile protected weapon system (USMC programme) (amphibious tank)
MQ	metol-quinol (photo developer)
MQ-1	Malafon, air-launched anti-submarine missile by Latecoere
MQAD	materials quality aussrance directorate (UK)
MQF	mobile quarantine facility (Nasa)
MQM-74C	Chukar, TEDS, target drone by Northrop

MQM-86	Talos missile with Bendix guidance as target drone by PMTC
MQM-107	Streaker, VSTT, target drone by Beech
MQMS	mechanist quartermaster sergeant
MQO	Marksmanship Qualification Order (US)
MQS	military quarantine station; minimum quality surveillance (petrol)
MQT	military qualification test
MR	morning report; medium range; maritime reconnaissance; machine records; marginal return; manufacturer's representative; maintenance review; ministry of reconstruction; military representative; map reference; marine reserve (USN); The Malay Regiment; The Duke of Cambridge's Own Middlesex Regiment; mobilization regulation; memory register; moment of resistance; Modèle de Référence (reference pattern)
M&R	maintenance and repair
M/R	map reading; morning report; memorandum of receipt; muster report
MR-flight	meteorological research flight
MR-2	standards microwave ranging radio (search radar, sonic and tactical systems communications)
MR-8.01	wheeled armoured personnel carrier by Mowag
MR-36	optical fire control system for light anti-aircraft guns by OG
MR-73	.3in pistol by ManRhin
MRA	minimum reception altitude; microwave ranging apparatus; morale re-armament; machine records activity; Maritime Royal Artillery
MRAAM	medium-range air-to-air missile
MRAF	marshal of the Royal Air Force
MRASM	medium-range air-to-surface missile by GD
MRB	microwave distance measuring equipment by Plessey
MRBA	medium-range bomber aircraft (1000 nm)
MRBF	mean rounds between failures (gun)
MRBM	medium-range ballistic missile (600 nm to 1500 nm)
MRC	medical research council; maintenance requirements card; movement reporting centre; material redistribution centre; medical reserve corps; material release confirmation; Mississippi River commission; military representative committee
MRC-108	mobile radio communication 400 Watts HF SSB by Rockwell Collins
MRCA	multi-role combat aircraft --Tornado
MRCC	movement report control centre
MRCP	member of the Royal College of Physicians; mobile radar control post
MRCPA	mobilization reserve components program of the Army (US)
MRCS-403	mobile reporting and control system (modular low-cost air-defence radar 3-dimensional by Selenia)
MRCS	member of the Royal College of Surgeons
MRCVS	member of the Royal College of Veterinary Surgeons
MRD	mandatory retirement date; material release denial; material redistribution division; microbiological research department
MR&D	material redistribution and disposal
MRDC	military requirement and development committee (Nato)
MRDR	material receipt discrepancy report
MRE	Malayan Royal Engineers; mid-range estimate; medical research establishment (Porton); microbiological research establishment; meal, ready to eat (ration) (US)
MRES	material requirements estimation system
MRF	modern rangefinder; maintenance replacement factor
MRFL	master radio frequency list
MRFS	multi-regime frequency scanner (radar) Martello
mrg	mooring; medium range
MRGS	Member of the Royal Geographical Society
mr/hr	milli-roentgen per hour
MRI	machine records installation; meat research institute
MRIC	morning report indicator code
MRK	magnetische Regelkompensation (magnetic control compensation)
mrkr	marker
MRL	master repair list; multiple rocket launcher; material requirement list; missile release line
MRLS	multiple rocket launcher system
MRM	maintenance reporting and management; military representatives memorandum (Nato); miles of relative movement
MRMO	mobilization reserve material objective
MRMR	mobilization reserve material requirement
mrng	morning

MRNLI	medal of the Royal National Life-boat Institution
MRO	message releasing officer; medical regulating officer; management review officer; manning and records office (UK); material release order; motor route order (number); maintenance repair and operating (supplies); mid-range objective; movement report office
MRP	malfunction reporting programme; manual reporting post; military requirements plan; military rated power
MRPB	mobilization and reserve plans branch BUPERS
MRPF	maintenance of real property facilities
MRPL	material requirements planning list
MRPPS	Maryland refutation proof procedure system
MRPS	modular runtime-linkable programming system
MRPV	miniature remotely piloted vehicles recce drones
MRR	military railroad; material readiness report; material rejection report; medical research reactor; mechanical reliability report; mission review report (photo recce)
MRRC	material requirements review committee
MRRW	minimum residual radioactivity weapon
MRS	muzzle reference system (guns); maritime reconnaissance system; manned repeater station; medical reception station; memo routing slip; muzzle reference system; mobilization requirement study; mobilization reserve stocks; military representative; standing group (Nato); material routing sheet; military railway service; movement report system; movement report sheet
Mrs	Mörser (mortar)
MRS-3	naval fire control system by Sperry
MRSA	medium-range surveillance aircraft; mandatory radar service areas
MRSE	microwave remote sensing experiment Spacelab by Dornier
MRSI	mobilization requirements, secondary items
MRSL	Marconi Radar Systems Ltd
MRSM	medium-range stand-off missile (USAF programme)
MRSP	multi-function radar signal processor
MrsTrg	Mörserträger (mortar carrier)

MRT	munitions railway transport; military rated thrust; mid-range trajectory; medium-range Typhoon (missile)
MRTA	medium-range transport aircraft
MRTF	medium rounds to fire (reliability)
mrtm	maritime
MRTT	modular record traffic terminal TRI-TAC
MRTU	multiplex remote terminal unit (fire control system for helicopters by Sperry)
MRU	mobile repair unit; much regret, unable (UK); machine records unit; material recovery unit; manpower research unit
MRUASTAS	Supervisor, Wideye, medium-range unmanned aerial surveillance and target acquisition system by Westland + Marconi-Elliott
MRUSI	member of the Royal United Service Institution
MRV	multiple re-entry vehicle --MIRV
MRVO	Member of the Royal Victorian Order
MS	mess sergeant; military secretary; minister of science; military science; military services; medical science; medical service; medical staff; margin of safety; ministry of supply; ministry of shipping; medical survey; military standards; mast subpart; mine sweeper (Nato); motor ship (USN); multi-spectral; mobile system; medium steel; metric system; medium shot; maximum stress; mild steel
M/S	minesweeping
m/s	metres per second
ms	milliseconds
M&S	maintenance and supply; (bureau of) medicine and surgery (US)
MS-45	echo sounder by Kelvin Hughes
MS-150	MISS, modular instructional servo system by Feedback Instruments
MSA	mutual security association; mutual security agency; merchant shipping act; military service act; medical services account; minesweeper, auxiliary (USN); mission system avionics for AEW by Elliott; maritime safety agency; minimum sector altitude; minimum safe altitude; Manufacture Stepanoise d'Armes J. Gauther, Exporter (St Etienne)
MSA-1	personnel carrier, half-track by White
MSAAB	military service ammunition allocation board

MSAM	multiple sequential access method
MSAO	medical services accountable officer
MSAR	mine safety appliance research
MSARR	maritime search and rescue region
MSB	military security board; manpower services branch BUPERS; minesweeping boat (USN); maritime safety board; most significant bit; missile storage building
MSBS	Mer-Sol-Ballistique-Stratégique (fleet ballistic missile by AS) -1 range 2500km -2 range 3000km
MSC	military service committee; military sealift command (US); medical service corps (US); material status committee; manned spacecraft center (Nasa); manpower services commission (UK); Madras Staff Corps; meteorological service of Canada; metropolitan special constabulary; major subordinate command (Nato); moved, seconded and carried; microwave sounding unit; minesweeper, coastal (Nato); minesweeper, non-magnetic (USN); metric system conversion STANAG; Master Specialities Comp. (Munich)
msc	miscellaneous
MSC-59	mobile satellite communications terminal by RCA
MSCA	military support to civil authorities
MSCB	missile site control building
MSCD	military support of civil defence
MSCI	Mediterranean secret convoy instructions
MSCo	minesweeper, coastal (USN)
MSCP	mean spherical candlepower
MSCS	merchant ship control service
MSCU	missile selection and control unit; microwave sounding and control unit
MSD	material services division; military systems division; missiles and space division; minesweeper, drone (USN); most significant digit; minesweeping division; mechanical supply division; mutual security director; master surgeon dentist; minimum safe distance; metering suction differential
MSDP	missile site data processor
MSDPS	missile site data processing system
MSDPSS	missile site data processing subsystem
MSDS	Marconi Space & Defence Systems Ltd (Stanmore, Middlesex)
MSE	member of the society of engineers; material status evaluation; mobile subscriber equipment TRI-TAC

	missile setting equipment; mean square error; modern ship equipment
msec	milliseconds
MSECU	missile setting equipment control unit
MSEIU	missile setting equipment interface unit
MSER	management system evaluation review
MSF	minesweeping flotilla; mobile striking force; minesweeper, fleet (Nato); minesweeper, steel-hulled (USN); master source file; multi-stage flash; medium standard frequency
MSFC	Marshall Space Flight Center (Nasa)
MSFN	manned space flight network
MSG	master sergeant; mobile support group; models, simulations and games; manpower scaling guide; Marine Schiffstechnik Planungsgesellschaft (Orenstein & Koppel, + Lürssen + HDW + Bremer Vulkan + Blohm & Voss)
msg	message
MSG-1	Minensuchgerät by Eltro (mine detector)
MSG-64	mine detector (EG)
MsgCen	message centre
MSGO	Mediterranean secret general orders
MSGR	mobile support group
msgr	messenger
MSgt	master sergeant
MSHB	minimum safe height of burst
MSHC	military service hardship committee
Mshl	marshal
MSI	military service institution (US); manned satellite inspection; minesweeper, inshore (USN); medium scale integrated (circuits); manned satellite interception
MSIIP	missile installation interruption for parts
MSIR	master stock item record
MSK	minimum shift keying (signals)
MSL	mean sea level; minesweeping launch (USN); military school of languages (Beaconsfield UK)
msl	missile
MSL-2001	language encryption system by Siemens
MSM	meritorious Service Medal (UK/US); minesweeper, river (converted LCM-6) (USN); minesweeper, medium (Nato); Minenstreumittel MiWS (vehicle-borne mine dispenser) (GE)
MSM(EDATS)	mine sweeper, medium, extra-deep armed team sweep (RN)
MSM-Hs	Minenstreumittel für Hubschrauber

MSM-Hs   (helicopter-borne mine dispenser)
          by Dornier
MSMLCS   mass service main line cable system
MS/MS   mutual security military sales (US)
msn   mission
MsNA   mission not accomplished
msngr   messenger
MSO   minesweeper, ocean (Nato); mine-
          sweeper, non-magnetic (USN);
          mixed service organization RCT;
          main signal office (UK)
MSOC   maritime sector operations centre
          (Nato)
MSOP   measurement system operating proce-
          dure
MSP   maintenance support plan; mutual
          support programme; mutual security
          programme; medium stressed plat-
          form; maintenance support package;
          medium speed printer; multi-
          spectral multi-channel polarimeter
MSPLT   master source programme library tape
M&SPB   materials and special projects
          branch
MSPG   material support planning guidance
mSPW   mittlerer Schützenpanzerwagen
          (medium armoured personnel
          carrier)
MSQ-103   Teampack, special purpose receiver
          by Emerson
MSQ-104   engagement control station
          --Patriot
MSR   The Malaya Signal Regiment; mixed
          signals regiment; military service
          register; main supply route; main
          supply road; monthly status report;
          missile site radar; missile surface
          radar; mechanical strain recorder
          by Leigh; mobile sea range (config-
          uration BQM-74); modular surveil-
          lance radar; mean spring rise
          (tide); machine status register;
          minesweeper, reconnaissance
MS&R   merchant shipbuilding and repairs
MSR-400   mobile secondary (vehicular) radar
          by SEL
MSRD   mobile servicing and repair detach-
          ment
MSRE   molten salt reactor experiment
MSRP   massive selective retaliatory power
MSRS   multiple stylus recording system
MSS   mounted service school; military
          supply standard; multi-spectral
          spin scanner (camera for Landsat)
          by Hughes; moored surveillance
          system ASW (USN); maximum sus-
          tained speed; minesweeper, special
          (USN)
MSSA   maintenance supply services agency
MSSC   medium SEAL support craft (USN)
          (sea air land (team))

MSSCS   manned space station communications
          system
MSSR   mobility system support resources
MSSS   maintenance supply services system
MST   mean summer time; mountain standard
          time; missile systems test; mean
          spring tide
mst   measurement
mSt   mit Stössel (fuse) (with pushing rod)
MStd   master steward
mstr   master
MstrMech master mechanic
MSTS   military sea transportation service
          Lant Atlantic
          Pac   Pac
MSTSO   military sea transport office
          M&R   maintenance and repair
          OCPO operations cargo passenger
                office
          SA   supply assistant
MSTU   military sea transport unit
MSU   management study unit (Canada);
          material salvage unit (USN);
          message switching unit; microwave
          sounding unit; modern sharing
          unit; main storage unit
MSV   marine services vessel (UK)
MT   military training; mountain train;
          mandated territory; mechanical
          transport; military transport;
          mechanized transport; motor trans-
          port; Mediterranean Theatre (of
          operations); missile technician
          (US); medical technician (UK);
          mechanical time (fuse); mail
          transfer; multiplex terminal;
          magnetic tape; master time;
          message table; empty; maritime
          tropical (air mass); megaton; mean
          time; motor traction; motor
          tanker; machine translation;
          maximum torque; metric ton;
          missile test
M&T   movements and transport STANAG
MT-1   TGPS, tactical gliding parachute
          system by Para-Flite
MT-34   Czech AVIB T-34 hull
MT-250   hydrofoil by Rolls-Royce/Supramar
MTA   military training act; major train-
          ing area; MAC transportation
          authorization (military airlift
          command) (US); minimum terrain
          altitude (clearance); military
          training airspace
MTACS   marine tactical command system
          (USMC)
MTAF   Mediterranean tactical air force HQ
MTAI   meal tickets authorized and issued
MTB   marine test boat, motor torpedo boat;
          maintenance of true bearing

MTBCF   mean time between confirmed failures
MTBF   mean time between failures
MTBFA   mean time between false alarms
MTBFC   mean time between flight cancellations
MFBMA   mean time between maintenance actions
MTBn   motor transportation battalion
MTBRon   motor torpedo boat squadron
MTBSTC   motor torpedo boat squadron training centre
MTC   mechanical transport corps (women) (UK); mechanical transport company; manoeuvre training command; military terminal control; military transportation committee; modulation transfer curves; Mach trim compensator
MTCA   military terminal control area; ministry of transport and civil aviation; multiple terminal communications adapter
mtcl   motorcycle
MTCN   MICRAD terrain correlation navigation (microwave radiation)
MTCP   ministry of town and country planning (UK)
MTD   material testing directorate; military training directorate; maintenance training department; mobile target division; mean temperature difference; meta-tolyene-diamine; moving target detection (radar)
mtd   mounted
MTDA   modification table of distribution and allowances
MTDE   maintenance technique development establishment; maritime tactical data exchange
MTDP   medium term defence plan
MTDS   marine (corps) tactical data system (US) by Litton
MTE   mechanical training establishment
MTF   medical treatment facility; mechanical time fuse; mean time to failure; modulation transfer function
mtg   meeting; mounting
MTG   multiple target generation (radar); Marinetechnik Planungsgesellschaft (Hamburg) (MEG+MSG+MUG)
MTgas   mechanical transport gasoline
MTH   medium transport helicopter
MTI   mechanical transport instructor; moving target indicator; Mobility Technology International (Chrysler)
MTIL   maximum tolerable insecurity level
MTIRA   machine tool industry research association (UK)

MTIS   material turned into store
MTk   medium tank
MTL   mean tide level; merged transistor logic
mtl   material
MT-LB   10 ton armoured personnel carrier (SU)
MTM   methods of time measurement
MTMA   military terminal major aerodromes
MTMA-UK   methods-time measurements association of the United Kingdom
MTMC   military traffic management command
MTMCTEA   military traffic management command transportation engineering agency
MTMCTTU   military traffic management command transportation terminal unit
MTMTS   military traffic management and terminal services
mtn   mountain
MTO   Mediterranean theatre of operations; mission task objective; military transport office; motor transport officer; mechanical transport officer; medical transport officer
MTOE   modification table of organization and equipment
MTOGW   maximum take-off gross weight
Mton   measurement ton
MTOUSA   Mediterranean theater of operations (US Army)
MTOW   maximum take-off weight
MTP   military training pamphlet; mobilization training programme; minimum time path
MTPT   minimum total processing time
MTR   missile tracking radar; mean time to restore; material testing reactor; migration traffic rate
mtr   motor; meter
mtrcl   motorcycle
MTRE   missile test and readiness equipment
MTRF   mobile tactical reconnaissance facility by Fairchild (dark-room shelters)
mTrP   mittlerer Treffpunkt (mean point of impact)
mtrs   metres
MTS   marine technology society; mechanical transport school (UK); motor transport service; mine training ship; missile test station, missile test set; message transmission system; mercurized turf sand; Millbank Technical Services, now: IMS; machine tractor station; Michigan terminal system

MT/SC   magnetic tape/selectric composer
MTSgt   master technical sergeant
MTSQ   mechanical time super quick (fuse)
MTSS   military test space station

MTT   mobile training team; moving target
           tracker
MTTF   mean time to failure
MTTFF   mean time to first failure
MTTR   mean time to repair; maximum time
           to repair; mean time to restore
MTU   mobile test unit; mobile training
           unit; maintenance training unit;
           missile tracking unit; missile
           training unit; mobile technical
           unit; magnetic tape unit; Motoren
           und Turbinen Union (Munich)
MTU-20   bridgelayer tank (SU)
MTV   motor transport volunteers;
           mechanical transport vehicle;
           motor torpedo vessel; motor tank
           vessel; motor tank vehicle
MTW   mechanical transport wing;
           Mannschaftstransportwagen
           (personnel carrier)
MTWF   militärisch technische wirtschaft-
           liche Foderung (military technol-
           ogical economical requirement)
MTX   military traffic expediting service
MT-X   Mitsubishi trainer experimental
           (sub-sonic jet aircraft)
mtz   motorized
MTZ   militärisch technische Zielsetzung
           (military technological target)
MU   maintenance unit; monetary unit;
           mounted unit; mass unit
MU-2   transport plane (Japan)
MUAC   Maastricht (upper area control)
MUAS   mobile underwater acoustic system
MUAT   mobile underwater acoustic trainer
MUAU   mobile underwater acoustic unit
MUC   Meritorious Unit Commendation (US)
MUCHA   multiple channel analysis
MUDAS   multiple universal data acquisition
           system by Dornier; modular univer-
           sal data acquisition system
MUE   Meritorious Unit Emblem
MUF   maximum usable frequency
MUG   Marine Unterwasser Regelanlagen
           Planungsgesellschaft (KAE+MaK+HSA+
           AEG)
MUI   modular interface unit
MUKdo   Marineunterstützungkommando (naval
           support command) (FGN)
MUL   master urgency list
Mulberries transportable docks WW2 D-day
MULE   modular universal laser equipment by
           Hughes
Mulloka   sonar for Australia by EMI
MULTEWS   electronic warfare system (radar
           jammer) (US) SEMA

MULTOTS   multiple units Link-11 test and
           operational training system by
           Logician
MUMMS   marine (corps) unified material
           management system
mun   munitions
Münchhausen Gerät-104, large calibre
           recoilless airborne gun WW2
           (GE)
Munga   Lkw o,5t gl, jeep by DKW
muni   municipal
Munroe effect hollow-charge effect
Murasme   class, destroyers (JMSDF)
Murene/Mureca anti-aircraft missile (FR)
MURF   material utilization referenced file
MURFAAMCE mutual reduction of forces and
           armaments and associated
           measures in Central Europe
Murola   grenade launcher 4 barrels 60mm by
           Mecar
MUS   manual on the use of smoke,
           manned underwater station
mus   music(ian)
MUSA   Multi-Splittermunition mit aktivem
           Sensor (Submunition, multi-
           fragmentation munition with
           active sensor); multiple unit
           steerable antenna
MUSARC   major US Army reserve command
Mushroom   atomic detonation position
           report (US)
MUSPA   Multi-Splittermine mit aktivem und
           passivem Sensor Submunition (multi-
           fragmentation munition with active
           and passive sensor)
MUST   medical unit, self-contained,
           transportable (field hospitals)
           (Canada)
Mustang   P-51, F-51, fighter/bomber by
           North American
MUT   minimum up time; mission up time
MUTA   multiple unit training assemblies
MUTE   mobile universal test equipment
Mutt   truck by Ford
Mutton   parachute and cable and bomb, air-
           defence project WW2 (UK)
mux   multiplex(er)
muz   muzzle
MuzVel   muzzle velocity
MV   manpower voucher; military vigi-
           lance; muzzle velocity; medium
           vessel; motor vessel; motor
           vehicle; mean value; market value;
           medium voltage; mean variation;
           measured vectors
M/V   merchant vessel, cargo ship (RN)
M&V   meat and vegetable (tinned stew)
mV   millivots; mit Verzögerung (delay
           fuse)
MVA   modern volunteer army (programme),
           mega-Volt-Ampere

MVAP	modern volunteer army programme
MVCG	military vehicles conservation group
MVD	(Army) motor vehicle driver
MVDF	medium and very high frequency direction finder; modular VHF direction finder
MVDSB	motor vehicle driver selection battery
MVEE	military vehicles and engineering establishment (Christchurch) (since 1970)
MVF	Miller vneturied freebored
MVFTS	multi-vehicle filed test system
MVG	Medal of the Victory over Germany
MVI	merchant vessel inspection; medium value item NADGE
MVLUE	minimum variance linear unbiased estimator
MVM	minimum virtual memory, motor vehicle mechanic (UK)
MVO	Member of the Royal Victorian Order; money value only
mvr	manoeuvre
MVS	Mennonite volunteer service; Mannschaftsvollschutz study by IBH, crew's total protection tank
MVSB	motor vehicle storage building
MVSS	motor vehicle storage shed
MVT	manual of vehicle training; motor vehicle technician (UK); multi-programming variable tasks
mvt	movement
MVTO	motor vehicle transportation officer
MVU	minimum variance unbiased
MVUE	manpack/vehicular user equipment for NAVSTAR by TI
MW	medium wave; mine warning; molecular weight; medium warship; manual of works; most worthy
MW-1	Mehrzweckwaffe (air-dispensed multi-purpose weapon) (anti-tank/anti-runway)
MW-72 ... 74	Minenwerfer (mortar)
MWas-A	Marinewaffenschule A Eckernförde (FGN naval weapons school)
MWaS-B	Marinewaffenschule B Kappeln (FGN naval weapons school)
Mwave	microwave
MWB	mechanical warfare board; Metropolitan water board; ministry of works and buildings; motor whaleboat (USN); multi-programme wire broadcasting
MWBAS	mail will be addressed to show
MWD	military works department; multi-weapons dispenser; molecular weight distribution
MWDEA	mutual weapons development data exchange agreement
MWDP	mutual weapons development programme

MWF	mine warfare forces (USN)
MGW	musical wire gauge
MWH	mega Watt hours
MWHGL	multiple wheel heavy gear load
MWI	ministry of war information
MWIC	millimetre wave integrated circuits
MWL	mean water level
MWM	Motorenwerke Mannheim
MWMTR	millimetre wave monopulse track radar
MWNT	mean water neap tide
MWO	modification work order; meteorological watch officer
MWP	mechanical wood pulp
MWPA	married women's property act
MwPz	Minenwerferpanzer (Switzerland) (M113 mortar carrier)
MWr	magnetic tape write (memory)
MWS	major weapon system
MWSG	marine wing service group
MWSS	marine wing service squadron
MWST	mean water spring tide
MWT	ministry of war transport; major water terminal; minimum warning time
MWTR	ministry of war transport representative
MW-X	Mehrzweckwaffe X (multi-purpose bombs, anti-tank/anti-runway)
MWV	mechanical wheeled vehicles,
MX	The Duke of Cambridge's Own Middlesex Regiment; miscellaneous; multiplex
M-X	missile X, mobile intercontinental ballistic missile (US project)
MX-1107	dual-channel satellite navigator ELNA
mxd	mixed
mxm	maximum
MY	motor yacht
MY-Dis	my dispatch
MY-Ltr	my letter
MY-MGM	my mailgram
MY-MSG	my message
MY-RAD	my radio
MY-SER	my serial
MY-SPLTR	my speedletter
MY-TEL	my telegram
Mya-4	Bison, four-jet bomber/recce by Myasischev (SU)
Mya-50	Bounder, jet bomber
MYP	multi-year procurement
MYS	man year space
Mystere MD-452	jet fighter/bomber by Dassault 1955
Mystic Link	TDMA communications link AWACS
mZ	mit Zusatzpanzerung (additional armour)
MZ	Mehrzweck (multi-purpose)
MZL	Mehrzwecklandungsboot (multi-purpose landing craft)

N

N   Navy; naval; north; noon; new;
nuclear; navigational; number;
nitrogen; non-self-propelled; net;
nuclear-powered

N-bomb nuclear bomb; neutron bomb

N-hour nuclear operation starts

1124-N Westwind, fanjet maritime recce aircraft by IAI

N-3 submarine carried cruise missile
(SU)

N-7 submarine carried cruise missile
(SU)

N-22 Nomad, light transport aircraft by
GAF

N-37 airborne gun 37mm Nudelmann (SU)

N-500 Noratlas, cargo aircraft by Nord
Aviation

NA naval attache; naval aviator;
naval auxiliary; nursing auxiliary;
North America; national army;
national assembly; naval academy;
naval aviation; not appropriated;
nautical almanach; not assigned;
not available; numerical aperture;
not applicable; not above (loading
position)

N/A non acceptance; no account; no
advice; not available; not applicable

nA neue Art, new pattern, new model

NA-10 naval search and fire control radar

NAA national aeronautic association;
national automobile association;
not always afloat; naval air
attache; national assistance act
1948; naval air arm (UK); North
Atlantic Assembly (Nato); northern
attack area; national artillery
association; North American
Aviation Inc.

NAABSA not always afloat but safe aground

NAACP national association for the advancement of colored people (US)

NAADS new army authorization documents
system

NAAF naval auxiliary air facility;
Northwest African air force WW2

NAAFI navy, army and air force institutes

NAAG Nato armaments advisory group;
Nato army advisory group

NAAI North American Aviation Inc.

NAAN national association of assistant
nurses

NAAO navy area audit office

NAAS navy area audit service; naval
auxiliary air station

NAATS national association of air traffic
specialists

NAB national assistance board; nuclear
air base; naval air base; naval
amphibious base; naval advanced
base

NABA naval amphibious base annex

NABMO Nato Bullpup management office

NABPARS navy automatic broadcasting and
routing system

NABPO Nato Bullpup production organization

NABS nuclear-armed bombardment satellite

NABTC naval air base training command

NABTraCom naval air base training command

NABU naval advanced base unit

NAC national advisory council; national
air council; national air communications (pool); North Atlantic
Council (Nato); naval air command
(UK); naval air centre; national
agency check

NAc naval academy

NACA national advisory committee for
aeronautics
--Nasa

NACAF Northwest African coastal air force
WW2

NACAL navy art co-operation and liaison
(committee)

NACB national agency check branch BUPERS;
navy and army canteen board now:
NAAFI

NACC naval academy computer centre

NACCAM national coordination committee for
aviation meteorology

NACIO	naval air combat information officer
NACI	national agency check and (written) inquiries
NACIS	naval air combat information school
NACL	Nippon Aviotronics Co. Ltd --Hughes
NaCo	navy cool (propellant)
NACom	northern area command
NACRO	national association for the care and resettlement of offenders
NACSB	naval aviation cadet selection board
NACTU	naval attack combat training unit
NACU	national association of colleges and universities
NAD	naval air division; naval air detachment; naval air depot; naval air detail; not on active duty; national armaments director (Nato); naval ammunition depot; naval aircraft department; nothing abnormal detected; nothing abnormal discovered; no appreciable difference; naval air defence; Nato air doctrine STANAG
NAd	naval advisor
nad	nadir (lowest point)
NADAC	national damage assessment centre
NADC	naval aide-de-camp; naval air development center (Johnsville); national air development center (Johnsville)
	AC aeronautical computer laboratory
	ACEL aerospace crew equipment laboratory
	AML aeronautical materials laboratory
	ASL aeronautical structures laboratory
	ED engineering development laboratory
NADECOL	Nato defence college (Rome)
NADEEC	national air defence electronic environment committee; Nato air defence electronic environment committee
NaDefCol	Nato Defence College (Rome)
NADGE	Nato air defence ground environment
NDGECO	NADGE consortium (AEG+HSA+Hughes+ Marconi+Selenia+Thomson-CSF)
NADGEMO	NADGE management organization
NADIG	Nato air defence integration group
NADIR	helicopter doppler navigation system by Crouzet
NAdm	naval administration
NADO	naval accounts disbursing office
NADOP	North American defense operational plan
NADPB	North Atlantic defence production board

NADReps	national armament directors representatives (Nato)
NADU	naval aircraft delivery unit
NaDWarn	national disaster warning system
NAE	naval aircraft establishment (UK); national aeronautical establishment (Canada); national academy of engineers (US); national administrative expenses.(Nato)
NAEB	naval aviation evaluation board BUPERS; North African economic board
NAEC	national aeronautical establishment (Canada); naval air engineering center (Philadelphia)
	AML aeronautical materials laboratory
	ASL aeronautical structures laboratory
	ACEL aerospace crew equipment laboratory
	AEL aeronautical enginer laboratory
	AEng air engineering laboratory; national aerospace education council
NAEL	naval air engineering laboratory SI ships installation
NAES	naval air experimental station
NAESU	naval aviation engineering service unit
NAEW	Nato airborne early warning (system)
NAF	naval avionics facility (Indianapolis); naval air facility; naval aircraft factory (US); not appropriated funds; northern attack force
NAFAG	Nato air force advisory group; Nato air force armaments group
NAFC	northern attack force commander; naval air ferry command
NAFCB	non-appropriated fund control branch BUPERS
NAFEC	national aviation facilities experimental center (Atlantic City)
NAFF	national association for freedom (right-wing pressure group) (UK)
NAFI	naval avionics facility (Indianapolis); naval air fighting instructions
NAfr	North Africa
NAFS	naval air fighter school
NAFSA	no American flag shipping available
NAFSONW	non-appropriated fund statement of operations and net worth
NAFTA	North Atlantic free trade area
NAG	Northern Army Group (UK+BE+NL) (Nato); new approach group,

NAG   naval advisory group (Nato); navy
           astronautics group; naval augmen-
           mentation group; net annual gain;
           Netherlands Aerospace Group
           (Eindhoven)
NAGARD   Nato advisory group for aeronautical
           research and development
NAGC   naval air-ground centre
NAGCO   naval air-ground centre office
NAGE   Nato air (defence) ground environ-
           ment
Nagrafax   meteorological chart receiver by
           Kudelski
NAGS   naval air gunnery school
NAGTS   national association of girls'
           training corps
NAI   Navigazione Alta Italia (Genoa)
NAIAD   nerve agent immobilized enzyme alarm
           and detector by Thorn
NAIC   nuclear (weapons) accident incident
           control
NAICC   nuclear (weapons) accident incident
           control centre
NAICO   nuclear (weapons) accident incident
           control officer
NAICP   nuclear (weapons) accident incident
           control plan
NAIG   Nippon Atomic Industry Group (Japan)
NAIIU   not authorized if issued under ...
NAIRU   naval air intelligence reserve unit
NAIT   naval air intermediate training
NAITC   naval air intermediate training
           command
Naja   optronic fire control system for
           small boats by CSEE
NAk   negative acknowledgment
NAKWV   national association of Korean war
           veterans (UK)
NAL   national astronomical league;
           national accelerator laboratory
NALCO   naval air logistics control office
           EurRep   European representative
           Lant   Atlantic
           Pac   Pacific
           Rep   representative
NALF   naval auxiliary landing field
NALGO   national association of local
           government officers
NALLA   National long lines agency (Nato)
NALO   naval air liaison officer
NALS   national advisory logistics staff
           (Nato)
NAM   night attack missile by Raytheon
           (air-to-ground); naval aircraft
           modification; nautical air miles;
           national army museum (London UK);
           national association of manufac-
           turers
NAm   North America
NAMA   naval aeronautical material area

NAMAC   Nato advisory group for military
           application of MAS communications
NAMAP   northern air material area Pacific
NAMAPUS   naval assistant to the military aid
           to the President of the US
NAMainTraDet naval air maintenance training
           detachment
NAMainTraGru naval air maintenance training
           group
NAMD   naval academy midshipman branch
           BUPERS
NAmB   naval amphibious base
Nambu-57   pistol 9mm (Japan)
NAMC   naval air material center (Philadel-
           phia); Nippon Aircraft Manufactur-
           ing Company
NAmD   naval ammunition depot
NAMDI   national marine data inventory
NAMedCen   naval aviation medical center
NAMFI   Nato missile firing installation
           (Crete)
NAMI   heavy stuck (SU)
NaMiBa   plastic anti-tank mine (Czech)
NAMilCom   North Atlantic military committee
           (Nato)
NaMilPo   Nato military posture
NAM/lb   nautical air miles per pound
NAMMA   Nato MRCA management agency (Munich)
NAMMO   Nato MRCA (development and produc-
           tion management) organization
NAMO   naval aircraft maintenance order
NAMP   naval aircraft maintenance programme
NAMPA   Nato maritime patrol aircraft agency
NAMRG-3   US navy medical research group
           (Ciaro) (study of tropical ill-
           nesses, bacteriological warfare)
NAMRU   navy medical research unit
NAMS   naval amphibious school
NAMSA   Nato maintenance and supply agency
           (Luxembourg)
NAMSA-SD   Nato maintenance and supply agency
           Southern depot (Taranto)
NAMSO   Nato maintenance and supply
           organization
NAMT   naval air maintenance trainer;
           naval aircraft mobile trainer
NAMTD   naval air maintenance training
           detachment
NAMTG   naval air maintenance training
           group
NAMTraDet naval air maintenance training
           detachment
NAMTraGru naval air maintenance training
           group
NAMU   naval aircraft maintenance unit;
           naval aircraft material, utility
NAn   neutron activation analysis
Nana-Go   class, minesweeping boats (JMSDF)
NANCF   North Atlantic naval coastal
           frontier

NANEP   naval air navigation electronics
         project --NESTEF
NANFAC   naval air navigation facility
         advisory committee
NANS   naval air navigation school
NANTS   national association of naval tech-
         nical supervisors
Nanuchka class, guided missile patrol boats
         (SU)
NAO   naval aviation observer
         B bombardier/navigator
         C controller
         I airborne intercept
         N navigator
         S ASW tactical evaluator
         T tactical
         V recce/attack navigator
NAOC   naval air operations centre; naval
         air operations cell (with Nato
         flag officer, Germany); naval
         aviation officer candidate
NAORPG   North Atlantic Ocean regional plan-
         ning group (Nato)
NAOT   naval air operational training
NAOTC   Naval air operational training centre
NAOTS   naval aviation ordnance test station
NAP   naval airborne project --PRESS
         (Pacific range electromagnetic
         signature studies); naval aviation
         pilot; naval academy preparatory
         (student); non-agency purchase;
         naval air priorities
Napalm   naphthenic and palmitic acids
         fire-bomb charge
NAPATMO Nato Patriot management organization
         (Munich) (US+UK+GE+DK+FR+GR+NL)
NAPC   naval air priorities centre
NAPG   naval aviation pilot, glider
Naph   naphta
NAPMA   Nato AEW programme management agency
         (Brunssum)
NAPMO   Nato AWACS programme management
         organization
NAPO   Nato AEW programme office
NAPOG   naval airborne project PRESS operat-
         ing group (Pacific range electronic
         signature studies)
NAPP   naval aviation preparatory programme
NAPR   Nato armament planning review
NAPRW   North African photographic reconnais-
         sance wing
NAPS   navy ASW patrol squadron
NAPSAC   naval atomic planning support and
         capabilities
NAPT   naval air primary training
NAPTC   naval air propulsion test centre;
         naval air primary training command
NAPTCRO naval air primary training command
         regional officer
NAPUS   nuclear auxiliary power unit system

NAR   notice of ammunition reclassifica-
         tion; net assimilation rate;
         no answer required; no action
         required; naval air representa-
         tive; naval air reserve; Nato
         refugees agency
NARAD   naval air research and development
NARANEXUS name, rate, service number and
         expiration of obligated service
         (USN)
NARANO   name, rate, service number
NARASPO naval regional airspace officer
NARAT   Nato request for air transport
         (supply)
NARC   non-automatic relay centre
NARDIS   navy automated research and develop-
         ment information system
NARDiv   naval air reserve division
NARDivFA naval air reserve division fleet
         air
NARETU   naval air reserve electronics
         training unit
NARF   naval air rework facilities
NARL   naval arctic research laboratory
         (US); national aero research
         laboratory (Canada)
NARMU   naval air reserve maintenance unit
NARS   naval air reserve staff; naval air
         rescue service
NARSTC   naval air rescue service training
         command
NARTC   North America regional test center;
         naval air reserve training
         command
NARTEL   North Atlantic radio telephone
         committee
NARTS   naval air rocket test station
         (Lake Denmark, Dover NJ)
NARTU   naval air reserve training unit
NAS   national aeronautical studies;
         national academy of sciences;
         naval air station; naval air
         service; national airspace system;
         national aircraft standards;
         naval armament supply; nursing
         auxiliary service; national allot-
         ments society
NASA   national aeronautics and space
         administration; naval air station
         association (Johnsville)
NASARR   North American search and ranging
         radar (airborne)
NASC   naval air systems command; naval
         aviation safety centre
NASCO   national academy of sciences
         committee on oceanography
NasCom   NASA communications
NASD   naval air supply depot
NASDA   national aerospace development
         agency (Japan)

NASEAB   naval air systems effectiveness
          advisory board
NASEES   national association for Soviet and
          East European studies (UK)
Nashorn   tank destroyer WW2
NASL   naval applied science laboratory
          (Brooklyn)
NASM   national air and space museum
NASMO   Nato Starfighter management office
NASNI   naval air station North Island
          (Calif.)
NASP   national airport systems plan
NASPO   Nato Starfighter production organi-
          zation
NASR-7511 naval air staff requirement for
          air-launched torpedo (RN+RAF)
          --Stingray
NASS   naval air signal school
NASTAD   national aerospace laboratory,
          STOL aircraft design consortium
          (Kawasaki+Mitsubishi+Fuji+Shin
          Meiwa)
NASTC   naval air station Twin Cities
          (Minn.)
NASTRAN   Nasa structural analysis (programme)
NAT   normal allowed time; navigation aids
          technician
NAt   North Atlantic (regional area)
          (Nato)
NAT   North African theatre WW2; North
          Atlantic Treaty
NATA   northern air training area
          (Alconbury UK)
NATAF   Northwest African tactical air force
NATB   naval air training base
NATC   naval air test center (Patuxent
          River); North Atlantic treaty
          council; naval air training
          command; naval air training centre
NATCG   national association of training
          corps for girls
NATCO   navy air traffic coordinating office
NatCom   national communications (symposium)
          (US); Nato communication (message)
NATCS   national air traffic control service;
          national air traffic control system
NATDEC   naval air training division engineer-
          ing command
NATEC   naval air training and experimental
          command
NATechTra naval air technical training
NATechTraCen naval air technical training
          centre
NATINAD   Nato integrated air defence
NATIS   North Atlantic treaty information
          service; national technical infor-
          mation service (Springfield Va)
natl   national
NATMC   national advanced technology manage-
          ment conference

NatMilComSys national military command
          system
NatNavMedCen national naval medical centre
NatNavResMastConRadSta national naval
          reserve master
          control radio
          station
NATO   North Atlantic treaty organization
NATO-III communications satellite by Ford
NATO-68   naval surface-to-air missile
NATODC   Nato defence college (Rome)
NATODefCol Nato defence college (Rome)
NATOMilOcGrp Nato group on military
          oceanography
NATOPS   naval air training and operating
          procedures standardization
NATOUSA   North African theater of operations
          (US Army)
NATraCom naval air training command
NATraDivEngCom naval air training division
          engineering command
NATRI   naval air training requirements
          information
NAT-RPG   North Atlantic treaty regional
          planning group
NATS   naval air transport service (US);
          national air traffic services (UK)
NATSAA   Nato air traffic service advisory
          agency
NATSF   naval air technical services
          facility
NATSFerry naval air transport service ferry
          command
NATSLant naval air transport service
          Atlantic
NATSPac   naval air transport service Pacific
NATSPG   North Atlantic systems planning
          group ICAO
NAtt   naval attache
NATT   naval air technical training
NATTC   naval air technical training centre
Natter   rocket-propelled interceptor by
          Bachem WW2
NATTS   naval air turbine test station
          (Trenton NJ)
          -ATL aeronautical turbine
          laboratory
NATTS   national association of trade and
          technical schools (UK)
NATTU   naval air technical training unit
NatUS   naturalized US citizen
NATW   naval air transport wing
NatW   national war college
Natya   class, minesweepers (SU)
NAU   naval administrative unit
NAUS   national airspace utilization study
naut   nautical
NEV   net asset value; naval equipment
          STANAG
nav   naval; navigation; navigator

NAV-101 navigation satellite (US)
NAVAC national audio-visual aids centre
NavAcd naval academy
NavAct naval activities
NavAdGru naval administrative group
Nav-Admin navigation-administragion (pro-
gramme)
NavAdminCom naval administrative command
NavAdminO naval administrative office(r)
NavAdminU naval administrative unit
NavAdUSeaWpnScol naval advanced underseas
weapons school
NavAerAudO naval area audit office
NavAerAudServ naval area audit office
service
NavAeroRecovFac navy aerospace recovery
facility
Navaho SM-64, long-range ramjet missile by
NAAI
NavAid navigational aids
NavAide naval aide
NavAir naval air systems command
NavAirBasicTraCom naval air basic training
command
NavAirDevCen naval air development centre
NavAirEngCen naval air engineering centre
NavAirEngLab naval air engineering labora-
tory
NavAirFac naval air facility
NavAirLant naval air forces, Atlantic
NavAirMainTraDet naval air maintenance
training detachment
NavAirMainTraGru naval air maintenance
training group
NavAirMineDefDevU naval air mine defence
development unit
NavAirPac naval air forces, Pacific
NavAirPropTestCen naval air propulsion test
centre
NavAirResTraU naval air reserve training
unit
NavAirReworkFac naval air rework facility
NavAirSysComd naval air systems command
HQ headquarters
Rep representative
RepLant representative
Atlantic
RepPac representative
Pacific
RepPncla representative
Penascola
NavAirTechServFac naval air technical
service facility
NavAirTestCen naval air test centre
NavAirTestFac naval air test facility
NavAirTurbTestSta naval air turbine test
station
NavAirTorpU naval aircraft torpedo unit
NavAirTraCen naval air training centre
NavAirTransWing naval air transport wing

NavAmmoDep naval ammunition depot
NavApScienLab naval applied science labora-
tory
NAVAR navigation and ranging (by ground
control); navigation and radar
NavARA navy appellate review activity
Navarrho location transmitter system (USAF)
NavASO naval aviation supply officer
NavAstroGru naval astronautics group
NavASWDataCen navy anti-submarine warfare
data centre
NavAuth naval authority
NavAviaEngServU naval aviation engineering
services unit
NavAvionicsFac naval avionics facility
NavAvMedCen naval aviation medical centre
NavAvMuseum naval aviation museum
NavAvnSafeCen naval aviation safety centre
NavAvScolCom naval aviation school command
NAVBALTAP allied naval forces Baltic
approaches (Nato Kiel)
NavBase naval base
NavBeachGru naval beach group
NavBioLab naval biological laboratory
NavBoiLab naval boiler laboratory
NavBrOceanOs navy branch oceanographic
offices
NAvC naval aviation cadet
NavCad naval cadet
NavCAMSSoAm naval communications area
master station South America
NavCargoHnBn naval cargo handling battalion
NavCBCen naval construction battalion
centre
NAVCENT allied naval foaces Central Europe
(Nato)
NavCIntSuppAct naval counter-intelligence
support activity
NavCIntSuppCen naval counter-intelligence
support centre
NavCIntSuppGru naval counter-intelligence
support group
NavCIntSuppU naval counter-ingelligence
support unit
NavCivEngLab navy civil engineering
laboratory
NavCloDep naval clothing depot
NavCM navigation counter-measures
Nac/Com (airborne) navigation and communi-
cations (equipment)
NavCom naval communication
NavComSta naval communications station
NavCommSys naval communications systems
HQ headquarters
SuppAct support activity
NavCommTraCen naval communications training
centre
NavCommU naval communications unit
NavCompt comptroller of the US Navy
NavComsyStore navy commissary store

NavConstr naval constructor
NavConsTraCen naval construction training
          centre
NavConsTraU naval construction training
          unit
NavCorCourseCen naval correspondence course
          centre
NavCoSSAct navy command systems support
          activity
NavConvHosp naval convalescent hospital
NavCruitArea navy recruiting area
NavCruiTraCom navy recruit training command
NavCruitSta navy recruiting station
NavDAC navigational data assimilation
          computer
NavDamConTraCen navy damage control centre
NavDanConTraCen navy damage control train-
          ing centre
NavDefEastPac naval defence forces Eastern
          Pacific
NavDegSta navy degaussing station
NavDen naval dental
          Cen   centre
          Clin   clinic
          Scol   School
          TechScol technicians school
NavDep naval deputy (to SACEUR)
NavDepCent naval deputy to CINCENT
NavDept navy department
NavDesScol naval destroyer school
NavDisBar navy disciplinary barracks
NavDisCom navy disciplinary command
NavDiseaVectorConCen navy disease vector
          control centre
NavDisp navy dispensary
NavDist naval district
NavElecSysCom naval electronics systems
          command
NavElex naval electronics systems command
NavEODFac naval explosive ordnance disposal
          facility
NavEu US naval forces in European waters
NavEx navy exchange
NavExam naval examining (board)
NavExamCen naval examining centre
NavExamCenAdvAuthList naval examining centre
          advancement authori-
          zation list
NavExhibCen naval exhibition centre
NavFac naval facility
NavFacEngCom naval facilities engineering
          command
NavFacEngContr naval facilities engineering
          contractor
NavFamAlwAct navy family allowance activity
NavFEC naval facilities engineering command
NavFinCen navy finance centre
NavFinOff navy finance office
NavFldIntO navy field intelligence office
NavFldOpIntO navy field operational intelli-
          gence office

NafFor Naval forces
          Eu   Europe
          Ger   Germany
          Jap   Japan
          Kor   Korea
          V   Viet Nam
NavFrOf navy freight office
NavFuelDep navy fuel depot
NavFuelSupO navy fuel supply office
NavGen navy general (publication)
NavGMScol navy guided missile school
NavGMU navy guided missile unit
NavGun naval gun (factory)
NavHistDisplayCen navy historical display
          centre
NavHome naval home (Philadelphia US)
NavHos naval hospital
NavHosCorpsScol naval hospital corps school
NavHousingAct naval housing activity
NavIC navy information center (US)
NAVICERT naval certificate (for merchant
          ships)
navig navigation, navigator
NavILCO navy international logistics con-
          trol office
NavInsGen navy inspector general
NavIntel naval intelligence
Naviplane N-500, hovercraft by SEDAM
NavJustScol naval justice school
NavLOS navy liaison officer for security
NavMag naval magazine
NavMAirComCon naval and maritime air commu-
          nications electronics con-
          ference (Nato)
NavMar naval forces, Marianas(US)
NavMarCoResTraCen navy and marine corps
          reserve training center
          (US)
NavMarJudAct navy marine corps judiciary
          activity
NavMatCom naval material command
NavMaTransOfc navy material transportation
          office
NavMed naval forces, Mediterranean (US)
NavMedAdminU naval medical administrative
          unit
NavMedCen navy medical centre
NavMedFldRschLab navy medical field
          research laboratory
NavMedNPRschU navy medical neuro-psychiatric
          research unit
NavMedRsch navy medical research
          Inst   institute
          Lab   laboratory
          U   unit
NavMedScol naval school of medicine
NavMedSupU navy medical supply/support unit
NavMgtSysCen navy management systems centre
NavMinDefLab navy mine defence laboratory
NavMinDep naval mine depot

NavMis   naval mission
NavMisCen   naval missile centre
NavMobConstBn   navy mobile construction
            battalion
NavNAW   naval forces, North-West African
            waters
NavNetDep   naval net depot
NavNON   allied naval forces North Norway
            (Nato)
NavNorSols   naval forces Northern Solomons
NavNorth   allied naval forces Northern
            Europe (Nato)
NavNuPwrSco   naval nuclear power school
            TraU   training unit
            U   unit
NavNZ   naval forces New Zealand
NAVO   Dutch name for NATO
NavObsy   naval observatory
NavOceanDistO   navy oceanographic distribu-
            tion office
NavOceanO   navy oceanographic office
NavOceanOfc   navy oceanographic office
NavOCForMed   naval on-call force Mediter-
            ranean (Nato)
NavOCS   naval officer candidate school
NavOpSuppGru   naval operations support group
            Lant   Atlantic
            Pac   Pacific
NavOrd   naval ordnance
NavOrdFac   naval ordnance factory
NavOrdMisTestFac   naval ordnance missile
            test facility
NavOrdSysCom   naval ordnance systems command
NavOrdU   naval ordnance unit
NavPECO   naval production equipment control
            office
NavPers   Bureau of naval personnel
NavPersCen   naval personnel centre
NavPersProgSuppAct   naval personnel pro-
            grammes support
            activity
NavPersRschAct   naval personnel research
            activity
NavPetRes   naval petroleum reserves
NavPetResO   naval petroleum reserve office
NavPhiBase   naval amphibious base
NavPhibScol   naval amphibious school
NavPhil   naval forces Philippines
NavPhotoCen   naval photographic centre
NavPlantRepO   naval plant representative
            officer
NavPorCO   naval port control officer
NavPostGradScol   naval post graduate school
NavPowFac   naval powder factory
NavPris   naval prison
NavProPlt   naval propellant plant
NavPubPrintO   naval publications and print-
            ing office
NavPubPrintServO   naval publications and
            printing service office

NavPubsConBd   naval publications control
            board
NavPubWksCen   navy public works centre
NavPubWksDept   navy public works department
NavPurO   navy purchasing office
NavPvntMedU   navy preventive medicine unit
NavRadCon   naval radiological control
NavRadSta   naval radio station
            R   receiving
            S   sending
NavRdlDefLab   navy radiological defence
            laboratory
NavReconTacSuppCen   navy reconnaissance and
            tactical support
            centre
NavRecSta   naval receiving station
NavRegAirCarConO   naval regional air cargo
            control office
NavRegFinCen   naval regional finance centre
NavRegs   naval regulations
NavRes   naval reserve
            ManPwrCen   manpower centre
            MidScol   midshipmen's school
            ORecAct   officer records
                        activity
            TraCen   training centre
            TraFac   training facility
            TraCom   training command
NavRschLab   naval research laboratory
NavSafeCen   navy safety centre
NavSat   navigational satellite
NavScAp   allied naval forces Scandinavian
            approaches (Nato)
NavScienTechIntelCen   navy scientific and
            technical intelli-
            gence centre
NavScolCEOff   naval civil engineer corps
            officers school
NavScolCom   naval schools command
NavScolConst   naval school of construction
NavScolCryptoRep   naval cryptographic
            repair school
NavScolDeepSeaDiver   navy deep sea divers
            school
NavScolEOD   naval explosive ordnance dis-
            posal school
NavScolHqspAdmin   naval hospital administra-
            tion school
NavScolMinWar   naval mine warfare school
NavScolPreFlt   naval pre-flight school
NavScolTransMgt   naval school of transporta-
            tion management
NavSCon   naval schools, construction
NavSCScol   naval supply corps school
NAVSEA   navy avionics support equipment
            appraisal
NavSEC   naval ship engineering centre
NavSecEngrFac   navy security engineering
            facility
NavSecGruAct   navy security group activity

NavSECNorDiv naval ship engineering centre
            Norfolk division
NavSEEAct naval shore electronics engineer-
            ing activity
NavServScolCom naval service school command
NAVSEX naval standing (orders) exercises
            (Nato)
NavShipEngSuppAct naval ship engineering
            support activity
NavShipLO naval shipbuilding liaison office
NavShhipMisSysEngSta naval ship missile
                    systems engineering
                    station
NavShipRepFac navy ship repair facility
NavShipRschDevCen naval ship research and
            development centre
NavShipStO navy ships store office
NavShipSysCom naval ships systems command
NavShipYd naval ship yard
NavShorElecEngAct navy shore electronics
            engineering activity
NavShorElecEngCen navy shore electronics
            engineering centre
NavSO department of the navy staff offices
NavSouth naval command Southern Europe
            (Nato Malta) since 1971: Naples
NavSpaSur naval space surveillance system
            (Dahlgren Va)
NavSpecWarGp naval special warfare group
NavSta naval station; naval staff
NavStar global positioning satellite system
            (USN)
NavSTRIP navy standard requisitioning and
            issuing procedure
NavSubBase naval submarine base
NavSuBInSurv naval sub-board of inspection
            and survey
NavSubMedCen navy submarine medical centre
NavSubScol navy submarine school
NavSubSOfc navy subsistence office
NavSubSuppFac navy submarine support
                facility
NavSup naval supply
        Cen   centre
        Dep   depot
        Dept   department
NavSupp naval support
        Act   activity
        For   force
NavSupRanDFac navy supply research and
            development facility
NavSupSysCom naval supply systems command
NavTacDocDevProdAct navy tactical doctrine
                development and pro-
                duction activity
NavTechMisJap naval technical mission
                Japan
NavTechMisEu naval technical mission Europe
NavTorpSta naval torpedo station
NavTra naval training

NavTraCen naval training centre
NavTraDevCen naval training device centre
NavTrAidsCen naval training aids centre
NavTrAidsFac naval training aids facility
NavTransCO naval transportation coordina-
            tion office
NavTraPubCen naval training publications
                centre
NavTraSta naval training station
NavU   naval unit
NavUArmCmlScol navy unit, Army chemical
                school
NavUSSEC navy underwater weapons systems
            engineering centre
NavUwtrOrdSta navy underwater ordnance
            station
NavUwtrSoundLab navy underwater sound
                laboratory
NavUwtrSoundRefLab navy underwater sound
                    reference laboratory
NavWAG naval warfare analysis group
NavWarCol naval war college
NAVWASS navigation and weapon aiming sub-
            system for Jaguar by Marconi-
            Elliott
NavWepEvalFac naval weapons evaluation
                facility
NavWesPac naval forces, Western Pacific
NavWpnCen naval weapons centre
NavWpnQualAssurO naval weapons quality
                assurance office
NavWpnsTraCen naval weapons training centre
NavWpnSuppAct naval weapons support activity
                activity
NavWpnSysAnalO naval weapons systems
                analysis office
NavWpServO naval weapons services office
NaWAC national weather analysis centre
NAWAPA North American water and power
            alliance
NaWC   naval war college
NAWCH national association for the welfare
            of the child in hospital (UK)
NavXDivingU naval experimental diving unit
NaWAG naval warfare analysis group
NaWaS national warning system
NAYCYA national association of youth clubs
            and youth aid (UK)
NB   North Britain; naval base; nota
            bene; non-battle (casualties);
            navy band; North Borneo; narrow-
            bore; narrow beam (radar)
Nb   Nebel (smoke)
NBAA   national business aircraft associa-
            tion (US)
NBAD   naval bases air defence
NBC   nuclear biological chemical;
            national broadcasting company;
            navy beach commander
NBCAO   nuclear biological chemical area of
            observation

NBCCC	nuclear biological chemical collection centre; nuclear biological chemical control centre
NBCD	nuclear biological chemical defence; nuclear biological chemical damage (control system)
NBCDX	nuclear biological chemical defence exercise
NBCFD	naval base consolidated fire department
NBCW	nuclear biological chemical warfare
NBCZO	nuclear biological chemical zone of observation
NBER	national bureau of economic research; national bureau of engineering registration
NBF	The North British Fusiliers later: RNBF
NBFM	narrow-band frequency modulation
NbFz	Neubaufahrzeug (tank before WW2) (GE)
NBG	naval beach group
NbHgr	Nebelhandgranate (smoke hand grenade)
NBI	nuclear burst indicator; notice board information
NBK	NbK, Nebelkerze (smoke tube)
NBL	national book league, navy biological laboratory
NBMR	Nato basic military requirement
NBMRs	Nato basic military requirements
NBMT	Nato basic military techniques
NBOO	Naval branch oceanographic office
NBPA	Navy board for production awards
NBPI	national board of prices and incomes (UK)
NBPO	Nato Bullpup production organization
NBPRP	national board for the promotion of rifle practice
NBr	naval brass
NBRI	national building research institute RSA
NBS	national bureau of standards; night bomber, short (range)
NBS-1	night bomber, short (range) 1921 by Martin
NBS-4	Condor, night bomber, short (range) 1920 by Curtiss
NBSS	naval beach signal station
nb st	nimbo stratus
NBT	narrow beam transducer; navigator-bombardier training (programme)
NBTL	naval boiler and turbine laboratory (Philadelphia)
NBU	naval beach unit
NBV	naval book value
NbW	Nebelwerfer (smoke dispenser); artillery rocket launcher WW2 (GE)
NC	Navy Cross (USN); naval cadet; naval chaplain; national certificate; Northern Command; no change; not carried; Nurse Corps; Naval Command; naval communication; newspaper conference; Nato confidential; Nato Centre; non-corrosive; numerical control; no connection; non-crystalline; nitro-cellulose; numbering counter; number of cetane
NC-2	light tank by Renault
NC-130	Hercules, research version (boundary layer control)
NCA	national communications agencies; national command authority; naval communications annex, no copies available
NCACC	national civil aviation consultative committee
NCAP	naval combat air patrol; night combat air patrol (nightCAP)
NCAPC	national center for air pollution control (US)
NCAR	national center for atmospheric research (US)
NCAT	navy college aptitude test
NCAVAE	national council for audiovisual aids in education (UK)
NCB	naval communications board (US); national codification bureau (Nato); navy clerical branch (UK); national cargo bureau (US); navy comptroller budget (US); naval construction bulletin (US)
NC&B	naval courts and boards (US)
NCBC	naval construction battalion centre
NCC	national computing centre (certificate); network computer centre; non-combatant corps; NORAD control center (North American air defense); Northern Counties committee (Ireland)
NCCAT	national committee for clear air turbulence
NCCD	normal construction completion date
NCCDPC	Nato command control (and information systems and automatic) data processing committee
NCCI	national committee for Commonwealth immigrants
NCCIS	Nato command control and information system
NCCL	national council for civil liberties
NCCP	Nato commanders communications publication
NCCPC	Nato civil communications planning committee
NCCR	new construction/conversion requirements (system) (US)
NCCS	national command and control system; net chain cell system (US)
NCCVD	national council for combating venereal diseases

NCD	naval construction department; navy cargo documents; notice of credit due; no can do; not considered disqualifying
NCD C	national civil defence corps; naval contract distribution centre; national centre for disease control
NCDO	navy central distribution office
NCDT&EBase	navy combat demolition training and experimental base
NCDU	naval combat demolition unit
NCE	nuclear capability exercise
NCEL	naval civil engineering laboratory (Port Hueneme Cal.); naval contractor experience list
NCERT	national council for educational research and training
NCET	national council for educational technology
NCF	naval construction force
NCFEP	FX, non-communication frequency extension program (US)
NCGG	national council for geodesy and geophysics (Pakistan)
NCHC	navy cargo handling capacity
NChemL	national chemical laboratory
NCI	naval cost inspector; no common interest
N CIC	national crime information centre
NCIRB	naval communications improvement review board
NCIS	navy cost information system
NCL	navy calibration laboratory; national chemical laboratory (Teddington)
NCLC	non-combatant labour corps
NCLT	night carrier landing trainer
NCM	navy correspondence manual; Navy Commendation Medal (US)
NCMC	NORAD Cheyenne Mountain Complex
NCO	non-commissioned officer;
NCOA	non-commissioned officers' academy (US); non-commissioned officers' association
NCOES	non-commissioned officers' education system (US)
NCOIC	non-commissioned officer in charge
NCOLP	non-commissioned officer logistics programme
NComnd	Northern Command
NCOOM	non-commissioned officers' open mess
NCP	national command post; naval capabilities plan; normal circular pitch
NCPI	naval civilian personnel instructions
NCPL	national centre for programmed learning
NCPS	non-contributory pensions scheme
NCPT	navy central planning team (Nato)
NCQR	national council for Quality and Reliability

NCR	no carbon (paper) required; national capital region (US); naval construction regiment; National Cash Register Company
NCRD	national council for research and development (Israel)
NCRE	naval construction research establishment (UK)
NCRF	naval coastal and riverine forces
NCRL	national chemical research laboratory (RSA)
NCRP	national council for radiation protection
NCS	naval canteen service; Nato codification system; net control station (radio); naval control of shipping (Nato); national communications system; national communications station; naval communications system; naval compass stabilizer by Marconi; navigation and communications system; numerical category scaling; net call sign
NCS-31A	airborne navigation and communication system by Collins
NCSC	naval communications security course
NCSL	naval code and signal laboratory
NCSLO	naval control of shipping liaison officer (Nato)
NCSNE	naval control of shipping Northern European (command area) (Nato)
NCSO	naval control of shipping officer; naval control of shipping organization (Nato); naval control service office (RN)
NCSOrg	naval control of shipping organization
NCSS	national council of social service (UK)
NCSSA	naval command systems support activity
NCSSC	naval command systems support centre
NCSX	naval control of shipping exercise
NCSTR	Nato communications systems technical recommendation
NCT	nitro-cellulose tubular (powder)
NCTAEP	national committee on technology automation and economic progress
NCTC	naval construction training centre
NCTR	naval commercial traffic regulations; non-co-operative target recognition
NCTRU	naval clothing and textile research unit
NCTS	navy civilian technical specialist
NCU	navigation control unit
NCUP	no commission until paid
NCUSA	navy club of the USA
NCV	no commercial value
NCW	ncse cone warhead
NCWA	Nato civil wartime agency

NCWSF	naval commander, western sea frontier
ND	national defence; navy department; naval district; naval dispensary; not dated; nuclear device; nuclear detonation; Niederdruck (low pressure)
ND-7	Northrop dispenser for bomblets
ND-100	Observer, multi-purpose mini RPV by National Dynamics
NDA	naval discipline act (UK); national defence act; nuclear damage assessment; not dated at all
NDAC	national defence advisory committee; nuclear defence affairs committee (Nato)
NDA&LB	naval district affairs and logistics branch BUPERS
NDB	non-directional beacon; navy department bulletin; naval disciplinary barracks
NDB-ADF	non-directional beacon for (airborne) automatic direction finding (medium wave) by SEL
NDBS	naval dispatch boat service
NDBulCumEd	navy department bulletins cumulative editions
NDC	national defence college (Latimer); national defence contribution; national defence company; Nato defence college (Paris) now: Rome; naval dental clinic; negative differential conductivity; national drug code; national data communications
NDCC	national defence cadet corps
NDCO	naval disarmament control officer
NDD	navigation and direction division
NDDC	NORAD division direction centre
NDDP	Nato defence data programme
NDD&RF	naval dry dock and repair facility
NDDRS	nuclear detonation detection and reporting system
NDEA	national defence education act
NDEI	national defence education institute (US)
NDF	non-linear distortion factor
NDGO	navy department general order
NDGS	national defence general staff
NDHQ	national defence headquarters (Canada)
NDID	non-deferrable issue demand
NDIR	non-dispersive infra-red
NDMB	national defense mediation board (US)
NDMC	Nato defence manpower committee
NDMTB	non-deployment mobilization troop basis
NDO	navy department office
NDOS	national defence operation section
NDP	normal diametric pitch; navy department personnel; national disclosure policy
NDPA	Nato defence procurement agency
NDPC	national disclosure policy committee
NDPIC	national defence public interest committee; national defence public information committee; navy department programme information centre
NDPR	Nato defence planning review
NDPS	national data processing service (UK)
NDQA	national director for quality assurance (Nato)
NDRB	new developments research branch BUPERS
NDRC	national defence research committee (UK)
NDRE	Norwegian defence research establishment
NDRF	national defence reserve fleet (US)
NDRG	Nato defence research group
NDRO	non-destructive read-out
NDRSWG	Nato data requirements and standards working group
NDS	non-parametric detection scheme; night driver's sight; naval dental school
NDS-2	tank driver's night viewer by Baird
NDSB	navy dependents school branch BUPERS; narcotic drugs supervisory body (UN)
NDSM	Naval Distinguished Service Medal; National Defence Service Medal
NDT	non-destructive testing; non-distribute trade; nil-ductility transmission; Niederdruckturbine (low pressure turbine)
NDTA	national defence transportation association
NDU	newspaper distribution unit
NDuSta	new duty station
NDUV	non-dispersive ultra-violet
NDW	naval district Washington
NE	nuclear explosive; nuclear explosion; naval engineer; nuclear engineer; national executive; New England; national emergency
NEA	national education association (US)
NEAC	North East Air Command
NEACP	national emergency airborne command post
NEAF	Near East Air Force
NEAFC	North East Atlantic fisheries commission
NEAB	nuclear exo-atmospheric burst
NEAR	national emergency alarm repeater (system)
NEARTIP	near-term torpedo improvement programme (Nato) Mk.46 ASW torpedo conversion

NEASP   navy enlisted advanced school programme

NEAT   navy electronic application trainer;
NCR electronic auto-coding technique

NEATO   North East Asian treaty organization

Neb   Nebelwerfer (rocket launcher) WW2
(GE)

Nebelwerfer artillery   rocket launcher WW2
(GE)

            35   10cm
            40   10cm
            41   15cm
            42   21cm

NEBSS   national examination board for
supervising studies

NEC   national emergency council;
Northern European Command (Nato);
national executive committee;
navy enlisted code; navy enlisted
classification (US); Northern
Europe Committee (oil); not elsewhere classified; national electronics conference (US); naval
examining centre; national exhibit
centre; newspaper editors course;
Nippon Electric Company (Tokyo);
Netherlands Electrotechnical
Committee

nec   necessary

NECC   North East computer center (US);
navy enlisted classification code
(US)

NECOS   Northern European Chiefs of Staff
(Nato)

NECPA   national emergency command post
afloat (US)

NECS   national electrical code standards

necy   necessary; necessity

NED   naval equipment depot

NedAp   Nederlandse Apparatenfabriek
(Groenlo)

NEDC   national economics development
council; North-East development
council

NEDEP   navy enlisted dietetic education
programme

NEDN   naval environment data network

NEDO   national economic development office

NEDU   navy experimental diving unit

NEES   naval engineering experimental
station

NEEWSSOP   Nato Europe early warning system
standard operating procedures

NEF   net energy for fattening; noise
exposure forecast; naval emergency
fund

NEFA   North-East frontier agency

neg   negative

NEGDEF   navy enlisted ground defence emergency force

negRS   negative report submitted

Neher-Harper   circuit, sophisticated Geiger
counter

NEI   new equipment introduction;
Netherlands East Indies; not elsewhere indicated

NEIAC   New England inter-service athletic
conference

NEIT   new equipment introductory team

NEL   naval electronics laboratory
(San Diego); naval explosives
laboratory; national engineering
laboratory

NELIAC   naval electronics laboratory international ALGOR compilers

NELINET   New England library information
network

Nellie   Naval land equipment, trenching
machine Mk-1 WW2

NELM   naval element Atlantic and
Mediterranean

NEM   navy expeditionary medal

NEMA   national electrical manufacturers'
association

NEMCA   Nato electro-magnetic compatibility
agency

NEMEDRI   Northern Europe and Mediterranean
routing instruction

NENEP   navy enlisted nursing education
programme

NEO   navy embarkation officer; non-combat
evacuation order

NEOPAC   North East overseas publicity
advisory committee

NEMP   nuclear electro-magnetic pulse

NEMS   nimbus-E microwave spectrometer

Neosho   class, fleet oilers (USN) AO

NEP   nursing education programme; navy
evaluation, preliminary; penta-
erythritol-tetra-nitrate

Nep   Nepal

NEP-I   ...II, navy evaluation, preliminary
phase 1 ... 2

NEPA   nuclear energy for propulsion of
aircraft; national environmental
policy act (US)

NEPCon   national electronic packaging
conference

NEPO   Nato equipment policy objective

NEPR   Nato electronic parts recommendation

NEPRS   new equipment personnel requirement
summary

Neptune   DP-2E, maritime patrol aircraft;
ASW by Lockheed

NER   North Eastern region

NERA   national emergency relief administration

NERAIC   North European region air information centre (Nato)

NERC   national electronic research

council; natural environment research council

NEREM North-east electronics research and engineering meeting

NERO Natrium experimental reactor of zero power

NERPG North European regional planning group (Nato)

NERRA new equipment resources requirements analysis

NERVA nuclear engine for rocket vehicle applications

NES navy experimenting station; navy engineering station; naval education service; national extension service (India); not elsewhere specified

NESC naval electronics systems command; national environmental satellite centre; nuclear engineering and science conference; national electric safety code (US)

NESCNSC net evaluation sub-committee, national security council (US)

NESEP navy enlisted scientific education programme

NESM non-expendable supplies and material

NESS national environmental satellite service (US department of commerce)

NEST naval experimental satellite terminal; node execution selection table (computer); national emergency survivable troop (system)

NESTEF naval electronic systems testing and evaluation facility --NANEP

Nester VHF cryptographic equipment (US)

NESTOR neutron source thermal reactor

NET new equipment training; nuclear emergency team; not earlier than

NETAC nuclear energy trade association's conference

NETC national emergency transportation centre

Neth Netherlands

NETOPS nuclear emergency teams operations

NETP new equipment training programme

NETR Nato electronic technical recommendation

nets network techniques

NETS navy engineering technical services

NETSO Northern European trans-shipment organization (Nato)

NETT notes on elementary tactical training

Nettuno sea-to-sea missile (IT)

NEWAC Nato electronic warfare advisory committee

NewCon 70-75 New concepts 1970-5 StrikeCom

NewEnGru New England Group

NewFo New Foundland

NEWLC Nato electronic warfare liaison committee

Newport class, tank landing ship (USN) LST

NEWRadS nuclear explosion warning and radiological system

NEWS naval electronic warfare simulator

Newton naval electronic warfare system by Elettronica

NEWTS naval electronic warfare training system by AAI

NEx navy exchange (US)

NEXT Nato experimental tactics

NF New Foundland; national formula; The Northumberland Fusiliers; no fund; nose fuse; noise figure; noise factor; night fighter (aircraft); Niederfrequenz (low frequency)

NF-1 machine gun 7.62mm by GIAT

NF-5 F-5, Freedom fighter, lightweight jet fighter by Northrop for Netherlands

NF-22 airborne remote-control view finder for cameras

NFA new fighter aircraft (Canada); naval fuel annex; national food administration; no further action

NFB naval frontier base

NFC national flag code; national fitness council; naval finance committee; not favourably considered

NFCDA national federation of civil defence associations (of Great Britain and the Commonwealth)

NFCU navy federal credit union

NFD naval fuel depot

NFDC national flight data centre

NFE not fully equipped

NFEC naval facilities engineering command

NFIS naval fighting instruction school

NFL no-fire line

NFLSV national front for the liberation of South Viet Nam

NFM narrow frequency modulation

NFO naval flight officer (USN)
    B bombardier
    C controller
    I radar intercept
    N navigation
    S anti-submarine warfare
    naval finance officer (US); national freight organization (UK)

NFOO naval forward observing officer

NFOV narrow field of vision (camera)

NFP Nato frigate programme

NFPA national fire prevention association

NFPDB Nato force planning data base

NFPE Nato force planning exercise

NFPS	naval flight preparatory school	NHC	national hurricane centre
NFR	no further requirement	NHDC	Nato Hawk documentation centre; navy historical display center (US)
NFS	national fire service (UK); not in flying status (US); not for sale		
NFSA	national fire services association	NHDVS	national home for disabled volunteer soldiers
NFSAIS	national federation of science abstracting and indexing services (US)	NHF	naval historical foundation
		NHI	national health insurance
NFSO	navy fuel supply officer	NHIS	national health insurance scheme
NFT	no filling time	NHMilCom	Nato Hawk military committee
NFTB	naval fleet training base	NHMO	Nato Hawk management office
NFTS	naval flight training school	NHMRCA	national health and medical research council of Australia
NG	National Guard (US); New Guinea; The Army National Guard and the Air National Guard (US); no good; not guilty; nitro-glycerine; narrow gauge		
		NHO	navy hydrographic office
		NHP	nominal horse power
		NHP-47	Navire à Hautes Performances (fast patrol boats 380 tons) (FR)
NGAC	national guard air corps (US)	NHPLO	Nato Hawk production and logistics organization
NGB	national guard bureau		
NGCM	Navy Good Conduct Medal	NHPO	Nato Hawk production organization
NG-EGDN	nitroglycerine-ethylene-glycol-di-nitrate	NHRP	national hurricane research project
		NHS	national health service
NGF	naval gunfire; naval gun factory (US)	NHSA	national health service act
NGH	Northern general hospital	NHSB	national highway safety bureau
Ngl	nitro-glycerine	NHSD	Nato Hawk support department
NGL	Normalair-Garrett Ltd (Yeovil Somerset)	NHSR	national hospital service reserve
		NHTDC	Nato Hawk technical documentation centre
NGLO	naval gunfire liaison officer		
NGLT	naval gunfire liaison team	NHTSA	national highway traffic safety administration
NGO	non-governmental organization		
NGOC	naval gunfire operation centre	NI	native infantry; national insurance; naval intelligence; naval instructor; Northern Ireland; nuclear institute; noise index
NGPS	NAVSTAR global positioning system (24 satellites on 3 orbits)		
NGR	national guard regulations		
NGRI	national geophysical research institute (India)	ni	night
		NIA	national intelligence authority; navy industrial association
NGS	nominal guidance system; naval gunnery school; naval general staff; naval gunfire support		
		NIABC	Northern Ireland association of boys' clubs
NGSDS	national geophysical and solar data center (US)	NIAD	Nato integrated air defence
		NIAG	Nato industrial advisory group
NGSFO	naval gunfire support forward observer	NIATM	new international association for testing materials
NGSM	Naval General Service Medal	NIB	naval intelligence bureau; non-interference basis
NGST	naval gunfire spotting team		
NGSTDS	national geophysical and solar terrestrial data system (US)	NIBMAR	no independence before majority African rule
NGT	next generation trainer (aircraft) (USAF)	NIC	national insurance commission (UK); new installation concept (electric power in aircraft); not in contact; negative immittance converter; network information centre; national inventors council
ngt	night		
NGTE	national gas turbine establishment (UK)		
NH	non-hygroscopic (powder); The Northumberland Hussars; Naval Home (Philadelphia); naval hospital	NICAP	national investigating committee for aerial phenomena
		NICB	national industrial conference board
NH-500M-D	night combat helicopter by Breda Nardi	NICEIC	national inspection council for electrical installation contracting
NHA	next higher assembly; national housing association	NICHD	national institute of child and human development

NICO navy inventory control office

Nico-Pyrotechnik, Rheinmetall subsidiary Nicolaus

NICP national inventory control point; nuclear incident control plan; Nato international civilian post

NICRISP navy integrated comprehensive repairable item scheduling programme

NICS Nato integrated communications system

NICSMO Nato integrated communications system management organization

NICSMA Nato integrated communications system management agency

NICSO Nato integrated communications system organization

NICS/TARE Nato integrated communications system/telex automatic relay equipment by Litton

NID Northern Ireland district; naval intelligence division; naval intelligence department

NIDC Northern Ireland development council

NIDCC national internal defence coordination centre

NIDU navigation instrument development unit

NIE national intelligence estimates; national institute of education (UK); normal impact effect

NIEM national industrial engineering mission

NIER national industrial equipment reserve

NIESR national institute for economic and social research

NIF navy industrial fund

NIFES national industrial fuel efficiency service

NIG navy inspector general

NIGA nuclear induced ground radio activity; neutron induced gamma activity

Mighteye light intensification periscope by Bonaventure (UK)

Nightingale C-9, cargo aircraft by McDD

Night Intruder B-57, bomber by Martin

Nightsun helicopter-borne illumination device (UK)

Night Tracker powerful car battery torch

Night Window night vision instrument with windscreen display by Kollsman

NIGSM Northern Ireland general service medal

NIH North Irish Horse Regiment; national institute for health (US)

NIHOE nitrogen helium and oxygen experiment

NII Nato item identification; Netherlands industrial institute

NIIG Nato item identification guide

NIIN national item identification number (US)

NIIP national institute for industrial psychology

Nike anti-aircraft missile

Nike-Ajax anti-aircraft missile system

Nkolauv class, combat hydrofoils (SU)

Nikolayev class, cruisers (SU)

NILCO navy international logistics control office

Nike-Hercules MIM-14B, anti-aircraft missile by Western Electric

NIM The North Irish Militia; naval inspector of machinery; nuclear instrument module

Nimbus-6 polar orbiting weather satellite

Nimitz class, aircraft carriers (USN) CVN

NIMMS nineteen-hundred integrated modular management system

NIMR national institute of medical research

Nimrod maritime recce/ASW aircraft AEW by Hawker Siddeley; double-decker fighter WW2 by Hawker

NIMS nationwide improved mail service

NIMWACS Nimrod warning and control system

NIN national information network

NINST NInst, nose instantaneous (fuse)

NIO naval intelligence officer; naval inspector of ordnance; navigational information office; national institute of oceanography

NIOSH national institute of occupational safety and health

NIP navy interceptor programme; nucleus initialisation procedure; NADGE improvement programme; notice of intelligence potential

NIPR national industrial plant reserve; national institute of personnel research (South Africa)

NIPS national (military command) information processing system; Nato information processing system; navy intelligence processing system

NIPSSA navy intelligence processing system support activity

NIPTS noise induced permanent threshold shift

NIR normal intelligence reports; nose impact rocket

NIr Northern Ireland

NIRA national industrial recovery act

NIRC national industrial relations court

NIRNS national institute for research in nuclear science

NIRPL navy industrial readiness planning list

NIS	national insurance scheme; not in stock; national intelligence survey (US); national interdepartmental seminar; naval inspection service; non-interference system; Nato identification (IFF) system
NISC	national industrial safety committee; national industrial space committee; Nato intelligence subject code
NISCON	national industrial safety conference ROSPA
NISER	Nigerian institute for social and economic research
Nishan	annual military small arms competition of the CENTO
NISMF	naval inactive ship maintenance facility
NISO	naval intelligence support office
NISOR	naval intelligence support office representative
NISP	navy integrated space programme
NISRA	navy investigative services resident agent
NISRF	Northern Ireland special relief fund ABF
NISSC	national industrial safety study conference ROSPA
Nissen hut	corrugated iron shelter
NISTEX	national industrial safety trade exhibition ROSPA
NITAT	Northern Ireland training advisory team
Nitec	Zeniscope, image intensifying telescope
Niteroi	class, frigates for Brazil by Vosper
Nixe	torpedo by MaK
Nixie	SLQ-25, towed anti-torpedo system
NJ	network junction
NJAC	Nato joint advisory council
NJC	navy job classification (manual); national joint council
NJCC	national joint consultative committee; national joint computer committee
NJCEC	Nato joint communications electronics committee
NJE	New Jersey experiment
NJIC	national joint industrial council
NJNC	national joint negotiating committee
NJP	non-judicial punishment
NJPMB	navy jet-propelled missile board
NJROTC	naval junior reserve officer training corps
NJSC	Nato Jaguar steering committee
NJSD	national joint services delegations
NK	not known
NK-11-2	rifle night sight by Bofors
NK-21-2	portable night viewer by Bofors
NK-22-2	portable night viewer by Bofors
NKA	Navigations Koppeltisch, automatisch by Litef
NKA-40	nordsuchende Kreiselanlage by Teldix
NKERR	nylon kinetic energy recovery rope by Marlow (UK)
NKF	neues Kampfflugzeug (new fighter aircraft)
NKPz	neuer Kampfpanzer by Contraves (new battle tank) Switzerland
NKZ	nuclear killing zone
NL	navy lighter; net layer; new line; Northern latitude; The North Lancashire Regiment; native levies; naval law; Netherlands; Navy League; navy list
nl	national
NL-5-30	inflatable patrol craft (SU)
NLabs	Nattick Laboratories (US)
NLANS	Nattick Laboratories land navigation system by Tamam
NLat	Northern latitude
NLB	national labor board (US)
NLC	NADGE logistics committee; navy law centre
NLCP	naval logistics capability plan
NLD	not in line of duty; navy lighter dock (USN) pontoon
NLDF	naval local defence forces
NLECS	national law enforcement communications system
NLF	national liberation front; nearest landing field; naval landing force
NLFED	naval landing force equipment depot
NLFM	noise level frequency monitor
NLG	noise landing gear
NLGI	national lubricating grease institute
NLH	non-locating head
NLI	national lifeboat institution --RNLI
NLM	nuclear logistic movement
NLMC	national labour management council
NLN	no longer needed
NLO	naval liaison officer
NLon	New London Conn.
NLP	non-linear programming
NLR	national liaison representative to SACLANT
NLRB	national labor relations board department of labor (US)
NLSC	navy Lockheed service centre
NLRSS	naval long-range strategic studies
NLT	not later than; night letter; non-linear transmission (channel)
NM	nautical mile; nuclear magnetron; non-metallic; night and morning; no mark; noise meter; noise margin; naval militia; naval magazine

NMA	non-medical attendant; Nato military authorities; national military authorities
NMAA	navy mutual aid association
NMag	naval magazine
NMAs	Nato military authorities
NMB	national mediation board, department of labor (US); national maritime board
NMC	naval medical center (Bethesda Md); Nato manual on codification; no more credit; naval missile center (Point Mugug Cal.); naval material command; national meteorological centre; network measurement centre; Nordac Manufacturing Corp. (Stafford Va)
NMCA	navy mothers' club of America
NMCC	national military command center (Pentagon)
NMCCIS	Nato military command control and information system
NMCGRF	navy-marine corps-coast guard residence foundation
NMCM	Navy and Marine Corps Medal (US)
NMCJS	naval member, Canadian joint staff
NMCS	national military command system
NMCSSC	national military command system support centre
NMD	navy marine diesel (fuel); naval mine depot
NMDL	naval mine defense laboratory (Panama City Fla)
NMDS	naval mine disposal school
NMDZ	Nato maritime defence zone
NME	national military establishment
NMEA	national marine electronics association
NMES	naval marine engineering station
NMFRL	naval medical field research laboratory (Camp Lejeune NC)
NMG	navy military government
NMGC	national marriage guidance council
NMi	nautical miles
NMI	no middle initial
NMIL	new material introductory letter
NMIS	navy manpower information system
NMIT	new material introductory team
NMM	national maritime museum (Greenwich UK)
NMN	no middle name
NMNRU	naval medical neuropsychiatric research unit (San Diego Cal.)
NMO	navy management office
NMP	national maintenance point; navy management programme
NMPA	Nato maritime patrol aircraft
NMPASC	Nato maritime patrol aircraft steering committee
NMPC	national maintenance publication centre

NMPNC	naval medical programme for nuclear casualties; naval material programme for nuclear casualties
NMPS	navy motion picture service
NMPX	navy motion picture exchange
NMR	national military representative to SHAPE; naval management review; naval management requirements; normal mode rejection; nuclear magnetic resonance
NMR&D	naval material redistribution and disposition
NMRF	navy-marine corps residence foundation
NMRI	naval medical research institute (Bethesda Md)
NMRL	naval medical research laboratory (New London Conn.)
NMRO	navy mid-range objectives
NMRU	naval medical research unit
NMS N	navy mid-range study; navy meteorological service
NMSB	navy manpower survey board
NMSC	national merit scholarship corporation; navy management systems centre
NMSD	next most significant digit
NMSE	navy material support establishment
NMSQT	national merit scholarship qualification test
NMSSA	Nato maintenance supply services agency since 1964: NAMSO
NMSSS	Nato maintenance supply services system
NMSU	naval motion study unit; naval medical supply unit
NMT	national maritime trust; not more than
NMTC	naval mine testing centre
NMTF	non-fixed medical treatment facility
NMU	national maritime union
NMVO	naval manpower validation office
NMVP	naval manpower validation programme
NMVT	naval manpower validation team
NMWS	naval mine warfare school
NMWTS	naval mine warfare test station
NN	Nigerian navy; no name
N/N	not to be noted
NNAG	Nato naval advisory group; Nato naval armaments group
NNC	navy nurse corps
NNCC	navy nurse candidate
NND	naval net depot
NNI	noise and nuisance index
NNMC	national naval medical center (Bethesda Md)
NNPTU	naval nuclear power training unit
NNPU	naval nuclear power unit
NNRC	neutral nations repatriations committee

NNS   national nautical school; Nigerian
           navy ship
NNSA   Norfolk naval sailing association
NNSB&DDCO Newport News Shipbuilding and
           Drydock Company
NNSC   neutral nations supervisory commis-
           sion (Korea)
NNSN   no national stock number
NNSS   Transit, navy navigation satellite
           system (USN)
NNSY   Norfolk Naval Shipyard (Portsmouth
           Va)
NNWO   navy nuclear weapons officer
NNYd   Norfolk Naval Shipyard
NO   naval operations; naval officer;
           neutral officer, Norway (Nato);
           navigation officer; naval observa-
           tory; no orders; not out
No   number
NO-1   fragmentation hand grenade (Dutch)
No-1 ... 4 hand grenades by Alsetex
No.4C   portable mine detector by USI Ltd
           (UK)
No.5   Mills bomb, hand grenade WW2; smoke
           grenade by IMI
No.7   bomb, rocket and cable anti-aircraft
           system WW2
NO-10   smoke hand grenade (Dutch)
NO-12   incendiary hand grenade (Dutch)
NO-13   offensive hand grenade (Dutch)
No-14   hand grenade by IMI
NO-16   smoke hand grenade WP (Dutch)
NO-17   offensive hand grenade (Dutch)
No.36   egg-shaped hand grenade
No.36M   (Mesopotamia) rifle grenade by ROF
No.66   class, missile patrol boats (IT)
No-80   smoke grenade WP (Dutch)
NOA   Nato oil authority; new obligation
           authority; not otherwise authorized
NOAA   national oceanographic and atmos-
           pheric administration (US)
NOAA-A   national oceanographic and atmos-
           pheric administration satellite
NOAA-5   national oceanographic and atmos-
           pheric improved Tiros by RCA
NOACT   navy overseas air cargo terminal
NOAH   national ocean agency headquarters
NOAIA   noise-operated automatic level
           adjustment
NOB   naval operating base; naval ordnance
           bulletin; national oil board
NOBC   navy officer billet codes
NOBS   navy operating base supplies
NObsy   naval observatory
NOC   naval officer classification (code);
           not otherwise classified; notation
           of content
NoConInt   no continued interest
NOCT   naval overseas cargo terminal
Nocticon   night vision instrument by
           Thomson-CSF

NOD   night observation device; naval
           ordnance department; new offshore
           dischargement (Nato)
NODAC   naval ordnance data automation
           centre
Noda-Matic helicopter vibration-damping
           suspension
           ----UH-1
NODC   national oceanographic data center
           (Washington); naval operating
           development centre
Noddy-suit NBC protective suit (UK)
NODECA   Norwegian defence communications
           agency
NoDel   not to delay
NoDeSta   will not depart this station
NODEX   new offshore dischargement exercise
           (Nato); new over the beach dis-
           charge exercise (USN)
NODI   notice of delayed items
NODLR   TAS-6, night observation device,
           long range by TI
NODO   naval oceanographic distribution
           office
NODS   navy overseas dependents' schools
NOE   nap of the earth (flying); notice of
           exceptions; notice of execution;
           not otherwise enumerated
NOEB   Nato oil executive board
           E   East
           W   West
NoEff   no effects
NOESS   national operational environmental
           satellite system
NOF   naval operating facility
NOf   (international) NOTAM office
NOFI   national oil fuel institute
NoForn   not releaseable to foreign nationals
NOFT   notice of foreign travel; naval
           overseas flight terminal
NOGS   OV-10, night observation gunship
           (plane)
NOHP   not otherwise herein provided
NOI   non-operational intelligence
NOIBN   no otherwise indicated by name
NOIC   naval officer in charge (Nato);
           national oceanographic instrumen-
           tation center (US)
NOIL   naval ordnance inspection laboratory
NOIO   naval ordnance inspecting officer
NOK   next of kin
NOL   naval ordnance laboratory (White
           Oak Md)
NOLAC   national organization of liaison for
           allocation of circuits (Nato)
NOLC   naval ordnance laboratory (Corona
           Cal.)
NOLTF   naval ordnance laboratory test
           facility
nom   nominal; nomenclature

NOMA   national office management associa-
        tion
NOMAD   navy oceanographic and meteorologi-
        cal automatic device (buoy) (USN)
Nomad   N-22, light STOL transport aircraft
        by GAF
nomen   nomenclature
NOMSS   national operational meteorological
        satellite system
NOMTF   naval ordnance missile test facility
NoN   North Norway (Nato)
NONA   notice of non-availability
NonCit non-citizen (US)
NonCnst non-consent
NonCom non-commissioned (officer)
NonComECM non-communications electronic
        counter-measures
NonComJam non-communications jamming
NoNeg   no negative replies required
NonFrag non-fragmentation (bomb)
NonRes non-resident
NonStand non-standard
NonTOE non-table of organization and equip-
        ment
NonTSDSL not included in technical service
        demand stockage list
NOO   navy oceanographic office (Washing-
        ton)
NOP   navy objectives plan; notice of pro-
        curements; naval ordnance plant;
        numerical oceanographic platform;
        not otherwise provided; naval
        officer procurement; navy opera-
        tion plan
NOPCL   naval officer personnel circular
        letter
NoPref no preference
NoProCan if not already proceeded, cancel
Nor   Northern
nor   normal
NOR   notice of revision; not operationally
        ready
Nora   man-portable anti-tank rocket
        (Switzerland)
NORAD   North American air defense command
NorASDefLant North American anti-submarine
        defence forces, Atlantic
Noratlas N-2501, transport aircraft by Nord
NORATS navy operational radio and telephone
        switchboard
NorBS   Northern base section
NORC   naval ordnance research calculator
        (UK); naval ordnance research
        center (US)
Nord   AS-30, guided missile by Nord
NoRdA   non-radio aircraft
Norden-gear arrester landing gear, naval
NoreChan North-East Channel subarea (Nato)
NorIP   NORAD intelligence plan
NorIs   North Island (San Diego Cal.)

NorLant North Atlantic
NORM   not operationally ready, maintenance
norm   normal(ised)
NormShor normal tour of shore duty
NorOEC NORAD operational employment concept
NorPac Northern Pacific
NorQR   NORAD qualitative requirement
Norrkoping class, torpedo boats (Sweden)
NORRS   naval operational readiness report-
        ing system
NORS   not operationally ready, supply
NORSAIR not operationally ready, supply
        awaiting item reports
NorSeaCent North Sea Central subarea (Nato)
NorSols Northern Solomons
NORTHAG Northern Army Group (Central
        Europe) (Nato Mönchen-Gladbach)
NORVA   Norfolk Va
NORVAGRP Norvolk Va group
NORVATEVDET Norfolk Va test and evaluation
        detachment
NorWesSeaFron North Western Sea Frontier
NorWesSec North Western Sector
NOS   Nato office of security; not other-
        wise specified;
        OV-10D, Bronco, night observation
        system, aircraft by Rockwell;
        national ocean survey
Nos   numbers
NOSA   naval ophtalmic support activity
NOSC   Nato operations support cell
        (USAFE); naval ocean systems
        center (San Diego); naval ordnance
        systems command
NOSS   Nimbus operational satellite system
NOSTA   naval ophtalmic support and training
        activity
not   notice
NOTAL   notice to all
NOTAM   notice to airmen (aircraft safety)
NOTAP   naval occupational task analysis
        programme
NOTestFac naval ordnance test facility
NotFltCk not flight checked
NOTS   naval overseas transport service;
        naval ordnance test station (Nato)
NOTU   naval operational training unit
NotUn   notice of unreliability
notwg   notwithstanding
NotWT   not to be transmitted by wireless
        (Nato)
NOV   National Order of Viet Nam
Nova   navigational satellite (US)
Novoview CGIVS, night carrier landing
        simulator by Redifon
NOY   not out yet
NP   non-permanent; neuro-psychiatric;
        naval prison; new pattern; new
        paragraph; penta-erythritol-tetra-
        nitrate; nitro-proof (cartridge);

NP	nickel-plated; normal pitch; normal pressure
Np	napalm
NPA	naval prize act; national planning association; national port assoc-iation; national production assoc-iation; non-programme aircraft; numerical production analysis
NPAB	naval price adjustment board
NPacCur	North Pacific Current
NPACI	national production advisory council on industry
NPAM	non-permanent active militia (Canada)
NPB	NADGE policy board; naval patrol boat
NPC	national patents council; Nato pro-gramming centre; Nato pipeline committee; national prime contrac-tor; nucleus port crew; naval photographic centre; national peace council; naval personnel committee
NPCCE	national pollution control confer-ence and exhibition
NPCO	naval port control officer
NPCs	national prime contractors
NPD	navy procurement directives; North polar distance
NPDI	no performance of duty because of imprisonment
NPE	navy preliminary evaluation
NPF	naval procurement fund; naval powder factory; not provided for
NPFA	national playing fields association (UK)
NPFC	North-West Pacific fisheries commis-sion
NPFS	no prior Federal service (US); navy and personal family service (UK)
NPG	nuclear planning group (Nato); naval proving ground; Nile provisional government (Sudan)
NPh	nuclear physics
NPIC	national photographic interpretation center (Washington)
NPIS	national physics information system
NPL	national physical laboratory (Teddington); new programming language
NPLO	Nato production and logistics organization
NPN	non-protein nitrogen; negative-positive-negative (transistor)
NPNA	no protest for non-acceptance
NPO	navy purchasing office; navy pro-gramme objectives; naval port officer
NPOPR	not paid on prior rolls
NPorD	no place or date
NPP	national policy paper; no passed proof; naval propellant plant (Indian Head Md)

NPPE	nuclear power propulsion evaluation
NPPO	navy programme and planning office; navy publications and printing office
NPPS	navy publications and printing service
NPPSO	navy publications and printing service office
NPPS	Nato POL pipeline system
NPR	noise power ratio; naval petroleum reserves; nozzle pressure ratio
NPRA	naval personnel research activity
NPRC	national personnel records centre
NPRO	naval petroleum reserves office
NPS	nominal pipe size; Nato pipeline system; no prior service; navy personnel survey; naval postgrad-uate school
NPSC	navy personnel separating centre
NPSD	neutron power spectral density; naval photographic services depot
NPSH	net positive suction head
NPSP	non-prior service personnel
NPT	neuro-psycho-therapy; nuclear proliferation treaty; non-proliferation treaty; Nato prepa-ration time; normal pressure and temperature
NPTC	national postal and travellers censorship
NPTCO	national postal and travellers organization (US)
NPTF	nuclear power task force
NPTRL	naval personnel and training research laboratory
NPV	net present value
NPWC	navy public works centre
NPWD	navy public works department
NPWS	Nato planning workshop
NQA	net quick assets
NQR	nuclear quadruple resonance
NQT	non-language qualification test
NR	not recommended; not released; non-returnable; naval reserve; navy regulations; national register; not required; non-registered; naval rating; Nato restricted; net register; narrow resonance; no risk; natural rubber; non-reactive; nuclear research (submarine)
Nr	number
nr	near
NR-30	airborne gun (SU) 30mm Nudelmann-Richter
NR-32	airborne gun (SU) 23mm Nudelmann-Richter
NRA	national rifle association (UK); national recovery administration; naval radio activity; naval

	reserve association; Nato refugee agency; non-registered accountable; no repair activities
NRAB	naval reserve aviation base
NRAC	naval research advisory committee
NRACCO	navy regional air cargo control office
NRAD	no risk after discharge
NRAF	naval reserve auxiliary field; navy recruiting aids facility
NRAO	navy regional accounts office
NR-AP-1A	airborne MicroTacan interrogator by LMT
NRAS	nuclear release authentication system; navy readiness analysis system
NRat	non-rationed
NRB	naval repair base; navy reservations bureau
NRC	naval research company; national research council; nuclear research council; national research corporation; nuclear regulatory commission (US); noise rating curves; notch root contraction; national research centre; natural resource carrier by Boeing (liquified gas transport); naval radiological control; Netherlands red cross
NRCC	national research council of Canada; NORAD region combat centre
NRCD	national reprographic centre for documentation
NR-CP-1A	mobile Tacen beacon by LMT
NRCST	national referral centre for science and technology
NRD	national range division AFSC; naval research and development; national register of designers; naval recruiting department; national recruiting department
NRDC	national research and development council; national research and development corporation
NRDFS	naval radio direction finder service
NRDL	naval radiological defense laboratory (San Francisco Cal.)
NRDO	national research and development organization
NRDS	nuclear rocket development station
NRE	non-rotating Earth (hypothesis)
NREC	national resource evaluation centre
NREB	naval reserve evaluation board
NRES	naval receiving station
NRF	naval reserve force; naval repair facility; national relief fund
NRFC	navy regional finance centre
NRFO	navy regional finance officer
NRFI	not ready for issue
NRFS	naval reserve force study (group)

NRI	net radio interface, Tri-Tac
NRL	naval research laboratory; Nelson research laboratory; national reference library of science and inventions
NRLSI	national reference library of science and inventions
NRM	natural remnant magnetization
NRMA	national resources mobilization act (Canada)
NRMC	naval reserve manpower centre
nrml	normal
NRMS	naval reserve midshipmen's school
NRN	negative run number
NR&NDAD	naval reserve and naval district affairs division BUPERS
NRO	non-returnable outer
NROS	naval reserve officers school
NROTC	naval reserve officers training corps; naval reserve officers training course
NRP	non-registered publication
NRPAC	naval reserve public affairs committee
NRPB	national resources planning board; naval reserve policy board; naval research planning board
NRPIO	naval registered publications issuing officer
NRPM	non-registered publications memoranda
NRR	naval research requirement; The Northern Rhodesia Regiment; net retail requirement
NRRC	naval reserve research company
NRRS	no remaining radiation service system
NRS	nose radar system; naval recruiting station; naval recruiting service; navy relief society; naval radio station
	R receiving
	S sending
NRSA	national remote sensing agency (India)
NRT	net register ton(nage); naval reserve training
	B branch
	C centre
NRTS	not repairable this station; national reactor testing station
NRV	non-return valve
Nrw	Norwegian
NRZ	non-return to zero
NRZI	non-return to zero inverted
NS	The Prince of Wales's North Staffordshire Regiment; national service; naval station; naval service; naval stores; not sufficient; new series; new style;

NS	nursing service; nursing sister; nursing staff; Nato secret; neck sizing; not specified; nuclear submarine; nuclear ship; nuclear science; nickel steel; non-standard; graduate of the Royal Naval Staff College Greenwich; navigation system
NS-11C	navigation system for --Minuteman
NS-20	updated guidance system for Minuteman by Rockwell
NS-23	23mm airborne gun by Nudelmann-Suwarov (SU)
NSA	national shipbuilding authority; national security agency; national service act (UK) 1947; national security act (US) 1947; national shipping authority; navy stock account; naval support activity
NSACG	nuclear strike alternate control group
NSACSS	national security agency central security service
NSAFA	national service armed forces act
NSAM	naval school of aviation medicine; national security action memorandum
NSAS	nuclear sealed authentication system
NSB	naval submarine base; Nato security board; nuclear surface burst; national science board
NSBISS	Nato security bureau industrial security section
NSBY	North Somerset and Bristol Yeomanry
NSC	national safety council; national safety council; national steel corporation; Nato supply centre (Chateauroux); naval supply centre; Nato steering committee; national security committee; navy safety centre; naval sea cadet
NSC-68	national security council report for 1968
NSCA	national safety council of Australia; national society for clean air
NSCC	naval sea cadet corps
NSCCLO	naval sea cadet corps liaison officer
NSCF	naval small craft facilities
NSC&MP	national stock control and maintenaance point
NSCO	naval supply center (Oakland Cal.)
NSD	naval supply department; naval supply depot; naval stores department; navigation situation display; non-soapy detergent
NSDA	naval supply depot annex
NSDR	national ships destination room (Nato)
NSE	naval shore establishment
NSEC	national service entertainment council
NSF	not sufficient funds; naval stock fund; national science foundation
NSFO	navy special fuel oil (Nato)
NSG	national security group
NSGOC	naval security group orientation course
NSGT	non-self governing territory
NSHO	naval service headquarters, Ottawa
NSI	non-standard item
NSIA	national security industrial association (US)
NSIC	next senior in command
NSK	nordsuchender Kreisel, gyro
NSKPz	neuer Schweizer Kampfpanzer (new Swiss MBT)
NSL	nuclear safety line; national service league; navy standards laboratory
NSLA	national service life assurance (US)
NSLI	national service life insurance
NSLIN	non-standard line item number (US)
NSM	naval school of music
NSMATCC	Nato small arms test control commission
NSMB	Netherlands' ship model basin (Wageningen)
NSMCM	navy supplement to the manual of courts martial (US)
NSMES	naval ship missiles systems engineering station
NSMG	naval school of military government
NSMG&A	naval school of military government and administration
NSMS	Nato Seasparrow missile system
NSN	national stock number; Nato stock number
NSO	national service officer; naval store officer (RN); navy subsistence office (USN); naval staff officer
NSOC	national service officer cadet
NSOF	navy special operations force
NSomYeo	North Somerset Yeomanry
NSP	nuclear strike plan
NSp	new species
NSP-2	infra-red night sight for rifles (SU)
NSPD	naval shore patrol detachment
NSPE	national society of professional engineers
NSPF	not specially provided for
NSPLO	Nato Sidewinder production and logistics organization
NSPO	Nato Seasparrow project (support) office; Nato Sidewinder production organization; Nato Sidewinder programme office
NSPP	nuclear safety pilot point

NSPSC   Nato Seasparrow project steering committee

NSPV   number of scans per vehicle (photo)

NSPVD   national society for the prevention of venereal diseases

NSR   normal sinus rhythm; natural sinus rhythm; nursing service reserve; national shipping report (Nato); national shipping representative (Nato); Northern Sea Route (Nato); no staff responsibility (US)

NSRA   national smallbore rifle association (UK)

NSRB   national security resources board

NSRDC   national ship research and development center (US) --DMTB

NSRF   Nova Scotia research foundation

NSRS   navy supply radio station

NSS   national stockpile site; nuclear support ship; national sample survey; normal saline solution

NSSC   naval sea systems command (US)

NSSL   national severe storms laboratory (US)

NSSMS   RIM-7H, Nato Seasparrow surface missile system

NSSO   navy ships store officer

NSSP   national security studies programme

NSSS   nuclear steam supply system

NST   Newfoundland standard time; non-slip thread; naval staff target (UK); no sooner than

NS&T   naval science and tactics

NST-7079   naval staff target for command cruisers

NStaffs   The Prince of Wales's North Staffordshire Regiment

NSTIC   Navy scientific and technical information centre (UK), navy scientific and technical intelligence center (US)

NSTL   national strategic target list; national space technology laboratories (Mississippi)

NSTP   Nuffield science teaching project (UK)

NSU   naval scout unit

NSV   net sales value; Niederhol-Sicherungs- und Verbringeeinrichtungen (naval decklanding winches and harnesses for helicopters)

NSW   New South Wales (Australia); nuclear strike warning

NSWC   naval surface weapons center (White Oak Md)

BSWP   Non-Soviet Warsaw Pact Countries

NSWSES   naval ship weapons systems engineering station (Port Hueneme Cal.)

NSY   The North Somerset Yeomanry; naval shipyard; New Scotland Yard

NSYd   naval shipyard

NT   naval training; night time; Northern Territory; not titled; naval torpedo; net tonnage; normal temperature; neap tide

Nt   night

NT-Nebel   smoke by NICO-Technik (GE)

NT-37C   naval torpedo

NTAC   naval training aids centre

NTAF   naval training aids facility

NTC   normal tour of duty completed; naval training centre; national territorial commander; negative temperature coefficient; national test centre

ntc   notice

NtcAval   notice of availability

NTCO   navy transportation coordinating office

NTDC   naval training devices center (Port Washington LI USA)

NT&DC   naval training and distribution centre

NTDDPA   naval tactical doctrine development and production activity

NTDO   naval technical data office

NTDS   naval tactical data system (USN)

NTE   not to exceed; navy technical evaluation; navy teletypewriter exchange

NTEC   naval training equipment centre

NTF   national transsonic facility (US); national tactical force (Nato)

ntfy   notify

nthn   northern

NTI   no travel involved; naval travel instructions

NTIS   national technical information service (of the Department of Commerce) (Springfield Va) UK office: Hamlet House, High St, Alton Hants.)

NTL   no time lost

NTM   net ton mile

NT-MAR   NICO-Technik Nebel für Marine (naval smoke) by NICO

NTO   naval transport officer; not taken out

NTorS   naval torpedo station

NTP   normal temperature and pressure; no title page

NTPI   navy technical efficiency inspection

NTR   nothing to report

NTRE   naval tropical research establishment (Singapore UK)

NTRL   national telecommunications reserach laboratory (South Africa)

NTS   Nevada test site; notch tensile strength; not to scale; naval training station; naval torpedo

NTS	station; non-tariff size; naval target subdivision; naval training school; naval transportation service;
NTSA	national traffic safety agency
NTSB	national transportation safety board
NTTR	non-tactical telecommunications requirement
NTU	naval training unit
NTV	network television
NtWt	net weight
NTX	navy teletypewriter exchange
NU	name unknown (UK); number (US); Nato unclassified; naval unit
NUB	nuclear underground burst
Nubian	6x6 fire fighting vehicle (UK)
nuc	nuclear (Nato)
NUC	navy unit commendation (US)
NUCAS	nuclear authentication system (US)
NucDef	nuclear defence
NucDet	nuclear detonation
NUCDETS	nuclear detonation detection and reporting system
NuChem	Nuclearchemie und Metallurgie (GE)
NuCo	numerical code
NucRep	nuclear damage report
NucStatRep	nuclear operational status report
NucWpn	nuclear weapon
NUDETS	nuclear detonation detection and reporting system
NuFCor	nuclear fuels corporation (South Africa)
NUMEC	Nuclear Materials & Equipment Corp. (US)
NUMIS	navy uniform management information system (US)
NUOS	naval underwater ordnance station (Newport RI USA)
NUP	Nato unified product
NUPOC	nuclear propulsion officer candidate (programme) (USN)
NuPwr	nuclear power
NuPwrU	nuclear power unit
nur	nurse
NUSC	naval undersea systems centre
NUSL	navy underwater sound laboratory
Nutcracker	twin-engine multi-purpose VTOL aircraft by Grumman
nutr	nutrition
NUTC	Nottingham University Training Corps
NUTS	new universal terminology subjects
NUWB	nuclear underwater burst
NUWC	navy underwater warfare centre
NuWepSA	nuclear weapons supply annex
NuWpnsTraCen	nuclear weapons training centre Lant Atlantic Pac Pacific
NUWRES	naval underwater weapons research and engineering station
NV	needle valve; new version; North Viet Nam
NVA	nuclear vulnerability assessment (Nato); North Vietnamese Army; Nationale Volksarmee (national people's army) (EG)
NVAC	North Vietnamese Army Soldier captured
NVA-211	night vision goggles by Baird
NVAL	not available
NVB	national volunteer brigade
NVCT	non-verbal classification test
NVD	no value declared
NVE	night vision equipment
NVEOL	night vision and electro-optics laboratory (US Army)
NVG	night vision goggles; Nichtverbrauchsgüter (non-consumable goods)
NVK	Nachrichtenmittelversuchskommando (Kiel) (naval communications experimental command)
NVL	night vision laboratory (Fort Belvoir)
NVM	non-volatile matter
NVM-2	Northrop Ventura Meteor RPV
NVN	North Viet Nam
NVPO	nuclear vehicle projects office (Nasa)
NVR	no voltage release
NVS	night visual system, airborne by Link; night vision sight by Bofors
NVSB	Nederlandse Verenigde Scheepsbouw Bureaus, s'Gravenhage
NW	nuclear weapon; nuclear warfare; nominal width; no wind; North West; net weight
NWA	North West Africa
NWAC	Netherlands Women's Army Corps
NWAIB	nuclear weapons accident investigation board
NWB	naval weapons bulletins
NWC	naval weapons center (China Lake); national war college; naval war college
NWCA	navy wives clubs of America
NWCAA	national war college alumni association
NWC/CS	naval war college/command and staff (course);
NWCR	nuclear weapons correction report
NWCS	Nato-wide communications system
NWD	nuclear weapon degradation
NWEF	naval weapons evaluation facility (Albuquerque NM USA)
NWEO	nuclear weapons employment officer
NWEP	nuclear weapons effects panel

NWES	nuclear weapons electronics specialist		nwt	non-water tight
NWET	nuclear weapons employment time		nwtd	non-water tight door
NWF	navy working fund (US); North West Frontier (Pakistan)		NWTC	nuclear weapons training centre

NWES nuclear weapons electronics specialist
NWET nuclear weapons employment time
NWF navy working fund (US); North West Frontier (Pakistan)
Nwfld New Foundland
NWFP North West Frontier Province (Pakistan)
NWG national wire gauge
NWI Netherlands West Indies
NWIP naval warfare information publication
NWISO naval weapons industrial support office
NWL naval weapons laboratory (Dahlgren Va); natural wave length; National Water Lift Company (Kalamazoo Mich.)
NWLB national war labor board (US)
NWM nuclear warning message; nuclear weapons manoeuvre
NWM de Kriuthoorn BV Nederlandsche Wapen- en Munitiefabriek, s'Hertogenbosch
NWMF nuclear weapons maintenance foreman
NWMP North West Mounted Police now: RCMP
NWMS nuclear weapons maintenance specialist
NWOO Nato wartime oil organization
NWP numerical weather prediction; naval weapons plant; naval warfare publication; North Western Pro- vinces; Nato and Warsaw Pact (projects)
NWPA Nato weapons procurement agency
NWPAG Nato wartime preliminary analysis group
NWR nuclear weapons report
NWRF navigational weather research facility
NWS normal water surface; national weather service; nuclear weapons surety (US)
NWSA nuclear weapons supply annex
NWSC national weather satellite centre
NWSD naval weather service department
NWSF nuclear weapons storage facility; North West Sea Frontier
NWSO naval weapons service office
NWSS nuclear weapons support section
NWT North West Territories (Canada); Nato warning time
NWt net weight

nwt non-water tight
nwtd non-water tight door
NWTC nuclear weapons training centre
  L Atlantic
  P Pacific
NWX nuclear weapon exercise
NX Nike X
  DO development office
  PM project manager
  PO project office
  PRG programme review group
  SM system manager
NY navy yard; New York
NYA national youth administration (US)
NYATCC New York air traffic control center
NYC neighborhood youth corps (US)
Nyclad nylon-jacketed bullet by Smith & Wesson
NYAL National Yugoslav Army of Liberation WW2
NYAO New York area officer ONR
NYBos navy yard Boston
NYCharl navy yard Charleston
NYd naval yard
NYD not yet diagnosed
NYP not yet published
NYNor navy yard Norfolk
NYNYd New York navy yard
NYPE New York port of embarkation
NYPH navy yard Pearl Harbour
NYPhil navy yard Philadelphia
NYPort navy yard Portsmouth
NYPS navy yard Puget Sound
NYR not yet returned; nuclear yield requirement
NYWash naval yard Washington
NZ New Zealand; neutrality zone
NZAI New Zealand Aerospace Industries
NZD New Zealand division
NZDSIR New Zealand Department of Scientific and Industrial Research
NZEF New Zealand expeditionary force
NZEI New Zealand electronics institute
NZJCB New Zealand joint communications board
NZLO New Zealand liaison officer
NZMF New Zealand military forces
NZMS New Zealand meteorological service
NZNB New Zealand naval board
NZR New Zealand rifles
NZSeaFron New Zealand sea frontier
NZSI New Zealand standards institute

O

O   office; officer; order; ocean; operations; ordnance; observation; occupation; orange; ordinary; observer; airborne intercept (US); immediate (message) (US); oscillator; oxygen; Ohms; overcast; observation aircraft (US); class, submarines 1923 (RN)

O-level   ordinary level GCE (UK)

O-license   operator's license

O-1E   Bird Dog, observation plane by Cessna

O-2TT   Armed Porter, observation aircraft for FAC by Cessna

OA   operating assemblies (electronics); oil absorption; operation analysis; over all; outside air; officers' association; ordnance artificer (RN); operating agency (US); officer administering; on or about; official address; operationally available (aircraft) MBFR; office of application (Nasa)

O/A   on account of ...

O&A date   oath and acceptance date (US)

OA-1   double-decker amphibious plane by Loening

OAA   old age assistance

OAASN   office of the administrative assistant to the secretary of the navy

OAB   officers' accounts branch

OAC   optimally adaptive control; oceanic area control; operation of aircraft costs

OACC   oceanic area control centre

OAD   operational availability date; over all depth; ordered to active duty; operations analysis division; officers' accounts division

OADiv   operations/weather service division (USN)

OAF   overseas air force

ÖAF-   Gräfe & Stift AG Österreichische Automobilfabrik (Wien)

OAFU   observers' advanced flying unit

OAH   over-all height

OAI   outside air intake

OAL   over-all length; obstruction and apron lighting; obstacle and apron lighting

OALS   observer air lock system

OAMS   orbital attitude manoeuvring system

OAN   ocean aids to navigation

OandOS   ordnance and ordnance stores

OandT   organization and training division (SHAPE)

OANFE   operational aircraft not fully equipped

OAO   orbiting astronomical observatory; orthoganalized astronomic orbital; off and on

OAP   observation amphibious plane; old age pension(er) (UK); office of alien property (Washington); office of allied property

OAPC   office of the alien property custodian (US)

OAR   office of aerospace research; Ocean Applied Research (San Diego)

OARS   ocean area reconnaissance submarine; ocean area reconnaissance satellite

OART   office of advanced research and technology (Nasa)

OAS   organization of American states (Washington); occupied areas section; offensive air support; offensive avionics system (bombers) by Boeing; on active service; old age security

OASC   officer and aircrew selection centre (RAF Biggin Hill)

OAS/CMI   offensive avionics system/cruise missile integration (USAF)

OASI   old age and survivors insurance

OASIS   operational advantages of special intelligence system (USAF) by Martin Marietta; Oberon (class submarines) acoustic system improvement (Canada)

OASN   office of the assistant secretary of
               the Navy (US)
               FM   financial management
               I&L   installations and logistics
               P&RF   personnel and reserve forces
               R&D   research and development
OASP   organic acid soluble phosphorous
OASPL   overall sound pressure level
OASU   oceanographic air survey unit
OAT   operational acceptance test;
               operational air traffic; outside
               air temperature
OATC   oceanic air traffic control;
               oceanic air traffic centre;
               overseas air traffic control
OATS   optimum aerial targeting sensor
OAU   organization for African unity
OAVCSA   office of the assistant vice chief
               of the Army (US)
OB   oil bomb; optical bench; observed
               bearing; ordnance board; outside
               broadcasts; order of battle
               (ground forces) (Nato); official
               business; operating bases;
               operational bases; passive light
               intensification system (FR)
O/B   on berth (USN)
ob   obsolete; obligation
OBA   oxygen breathing apparatus; optical
               bleaching agent; old boys'
               association (UK)
OBAWS   on-board aircraft weighting system
OBB   old battleship (USN)
OBC   on-board computer
obc   old boys' club (UK)
OBD   open blade damper
OBDH   on-board data handling (unit)
OBDk   observation deck
OBE   Officer of the Most Excellent Order
               of the British Empire
Oberon   class, submarines (RN)
               RAN ---Oxley class
OBF   one-bar functions
OBI   Order of British India; obligated
               involuntary officer (US)
obj   object; objective
objn   objection
obl   oblique; obligation
OblAuth   obligation authority (US)
oblg   obligate
OBLI   The Oxfordshire and Buckinghamshire
               Light Infantry
ObliServ   obligated service
Obluze   class, fast patrol boats (Poland)
OBO   oil, bulk and ore (carrier) ship;
               official business only
Oboe   airborne radar navigation system WW2
               (RAF) (ground stations Cat and
               Mouse)
OBOGS   on-board oxygen generating system by
               Dräger

OBP   ortsfeste Bewegungsplattform
               (stationary motion platform)
               (simulator)
ObPh   oblique photography
OBR   on-board recorder; office of budgets
               and reports (US)
OBS   orbital bombardment system
obs   observation; observatory; obscuring;
               obsolete; observed (position)
obsc   obscure
Observer   ND-100, multi-purpose mini RPV by
               National Dynamics
ObsHt   obstacle height
obsn   observation
obsol   obsolescent
OBSPL   octave band sound pressure level
obsr   observer
ObsRon   observation squadron (USN)
OBSS   ocean bottom scanning sonar
obst   obstruction
obsy   observatory
OBTM&M   on-board test maintenance and
               monitor (capabilities) AWACS
Obus-G   OCC-61, spin-stabilized hollow-
               charge anti-tank shell (FR)
OBV   ocean boarding vessel
ObV   obligated volunteer officer (US)
obv   obverse
OC   ordnance committee; open circuit;
               on centre; official classification;
               open cover; over-charge; office of
               censorship; operations control;
               operational command; observer
               corps; office copy; Oslo Conven-
               tion; Ottawa Convention; officer
               cadet (UK); officer candidate
               (US); officer commanding
O/C   officer in charge (US Army)
OCA   officer in charge of the apes
               (Gibraltar); oceanic control area;
               operational control authority
               (Nato); office, comptroller of the
               Army (US)
OCAC   office of chief of Air Corps
OCALC   Oklahoma City air logistics center
OCAMA   Oklahoma City air material area
OCan   officer candidate airman programme
OCAR   office of the chief, Army reserve
OCAS   officer in charge of armament
               supplies (US); office, coordinator
               of Army studies (US); organization
               of central American states
OCB   operations conducting board
OCB/L   ocean bill of lading
OCBM   CS, tear gas
OCC   officer, commanding camp; officers'
               country club; officer candidate
               course (US); officer correspon-
               dence course; operational control
               centre; oceanic control centre;
               operational control console

occ   occupation; occidental; occasion(al)
OCC-61   Obus-G, spin-stabilized hollow-
            charge anti-tank shell (FR)
OCCC   oil control coordination committee
OCCh   office, chief of chaplains
OCCIS   operational command and control
            intelligence system (US);
            operations control and command
            information system
OccMed   occupational medicine
OCCS   operational command and control
            system; office of the combined
            chiefs of staff
OCC/TBS   officer candidate course/the basic
            school (USMC)
OCD   office of civil defence; office of
            civil defence; ordnance classi-
            fication of defects; on-line com-
            munications driver (computer)
OCDA   officer commanding divisional
            artillery
OCDE   officer commanding divisional
            engineers
OCDiv   operations control division
OCDM   office of civil defense mobiliza-
            tion (US)
OCDS   officer commanding divisional
            signals; Otomat coastal defence
            system
O/Cdt   officer cadet
OCE   ocean covered earth; officer conduct-
            ing exercise (Nato); office, chief
            of engineers (US)
OceanLant   ocean (sub-area) Atlantic (Nato)
OceanoAirSurvU   oceanographic air survey unit
OCE&TB   officer candidate training and
            education branch BUPERS
OCF   officiating chaplain to the forces
OcFnt   occluded front
OCHAMPUS   office of the civilian health and
            medical program of the uniformed
            services (US)
OCI   office, coordinator of information;
            operator control interface;
            optically coupled isolator
OCIAA   office of the coordinator of inter-
            American affairs
OCInfo   office of the chief of information
OCL   obstacle clearance limits;
            obstruction clearance limits
            (landing minimum); old cruiser,
            light (USN); ordnance circular
            letters
OCLL   office of the chief of legislative
            liaison
OCM   optical counter-measures
OCM/ECM   optical counter-measures/electronic
            counter-measures
OCMH   office of the chief of military
            history

OCMM   office of civilian manpower manage-
            ment
OCNPR   operation and conversion of naval
            petroleum reserves
OCO   operational capability objective
OConUS   outside the continental US
OCP   obstacle clearance panel;
            operations computer programme;
            office of civilian personnel;
            operational capability plan
OCPO   operations cargo passenger office
OCR   optical character reader;
            optical character recognition;
            organic cooled reactor; over-
            consolidated ratio; office of
            civilian requirements (US);
            Officer of the Order of the Crown
            or Romania
OCRA   officer commanding Royal Artillery
OCRD   office of the chief of research and
            development
OCRE   optical character recognition
            equipment
OCS   office of contract settlements WPB;
            optical contact sensor; output
            control sub-system; operations
            characteristics (Nato); officer
            cadet school; officer candidate
            school (Newport US)
OCSA   office, chief of staff, Army (US)
OCSigO   office of the chief signal officer
            (US)
ocst   overcast
OCT   operational cycle time; off-course
            target; officer candidate test;
            office of the chief of transporta-
            tion (US); overseas countries and
            territories (EC)
oct   octane
Octopus   sonar system by Thomson-CSF
OCT/RR   off-course target remote reference
            (display)
OCTU   officer cadet training unit (UK)
OCU   operational control unit;
            operational conversion unit (RAF);
            operational command unit (RAF)
OCV   open circuit voltage; old aircraft
            carrier (USN)
OD   ordnance department; outer diameter;
            optical density; observed drift;
            ordnance data; on demand; olive
            drab; ordnance depot; operations
            division; on deck; overdraft;
            ordinary seaman; officer of the
            day
ODA   overseas development administration
            (UK); Operations de Défense
            Aerienne;(air defence operations)
ODC   overseas defence committee; officer
            data card

ODandMC	operational direction and management control (Nato)	OEA	officers' employment association; organizational expense accounts
ODCR	officer distribution and control report (US)	OEB	officers' employment bureau
ODCSLog	office, deputy chief of staff for logistics (US)	OEC	operational employment concept; Ocean Engineering Corporation (US); output exception code
ODCSOps	office, deputy chief of staff for operations	OECD	Organization for Economic Co-operation and Development
ODCSPer	office, deputy chief of staff for personnel	OECO	out-board engine cut-off
		OECon	offshore exploration conference
ODCSRDA	office, deputy chief of staff for research, development and acquisition	OECQ	Organisation Européenne de Contrôle de Qualité (European Organization on Quality Control)
ODD	old destroyer (USN); officer distribution division BUPERS	OEDiv	operations electronics division
		OEDO	ordnance engineering duty officer
ODDRE	office of the director of defence research and engineering	OEEC	organization for European economic cooperation now: OECD
ODECo	Ocean Drilling & Exploration Company	OEG	operations evaluation group; organization and equipment guide (US)
ODESSA	Ocean Data environmental sciences Services acquisition		
ODIn	optical design integration	OEGCMJ	officer exercising general courts martial jurisdiction (US)
Odin	field artillery computer (Norway)		
ODM	office of defense mobilization (US); overseas development ministry (UK)	OEH	Oxford Eye Hospital
		Oeil Noir	fire control radar by Thomson-CSF
ODO	operations duty officer	Oeil Vert	fire control radar by Thomson-CSF
ODP	officer distribution plan; original departure point; organized reservists in drill pay status (US); open door policy; office development permit; official development planning; over-all development planning; orbit determination programme; optical data processor; over-all documentation plan NADGE	OEL	organizational equipment list; ordnance equipment list
		OEM	office for emergency management; on equipment material; original equipment manufacturer
		OEMI	office equipment manufacturers' institute
		OEO	office of economic opportunity; ordnance engineer overseer
ODPCS	oceanographic data processing and control system	OE/OTO	twin automatic gun 35mm by OTO
ODR	omni-directional range; oxygen diffusion rate; official duty rate; office of defense resources (US)	OEP	office of emergency planning; operational employment plan
		OER	organization for European research; officer evaluation report; officer emergency reserve
ODRI	office of the US defense representative, India		
ODRP	office of the US defense representative, Pakistan	OERC	optimum earth re-entry corridor
		OERS	officer evaluation reporting system; Organisation Européenne de Recherches Spatiales ESRO
ODS	ordnance delivery schedule; ocean data station		
ODT	office of defense transportation (US)	OES	operations and engineering squadron; Order of the Eastern Star; organization of European states; office of emergency service; order entry system
ODTS	optical discrimination and tracking system		
ODUSIPT	office of the deputy under-secretary for international programmes and technology		
		OESBR	oil-extended styrene-butadiene rubber
ODWSA	office of the directorate of weapon systems analysis	OESPCMJ	officer exercising special court martial jurisdiction
ODX	ultra-light rapid intervention, mine-sweeping system (FR)	OET	office of emergency transportation; office of education and training
OE	ordnance engineer (UK); office of education; omissions excepted; original error; original equipment	OE&TB	officer education and training branch
O&E	operations and engineering	OEW	office of economic warfare (US); operating empty weight
O2E	officer in charge of the 2nd echelon GHQ	OEWG	operation evaluation war-time group; open-ended working group

OEX   office of educational exchange
OF   optional form; operating forces; operational forces; oil fired (boiler); oil fuel (UK) FFO; oceanographic facility; outside face; oxidating flame
OF-37   hand grenade by Luchaire
OFA   oil fired appliances
ofc   office
OfcofAsstSecNav   office of the assistant secretary of the Navy
  FinMgt
    financial management
  Inst&Log
    installations and logistics
  Pers&ResFor
    personnel and reserve force
  Rsch&Dev
    research and development
OfcofInfo   office of information
OFEA   office of foreign economic administration (US) (lend-lease)
OFEC   office of federal employees' compensation; office of foreign economic coordination
OFEMA   Office Française d'Exportations de Matériels Aeronautique (Paris)
Ofenrohr   Panzerschreck, RPzB-54 (infantry anti-tank rocket launcher) WW2
OFERRA   office of foreign economic relief and economic rehabilitation administration
OFF   office of facts and figures
off   officer; official; office
OffBusOnly   official business only
OFFHE   ordinary free-fall high-explosive (bomb)
OffNavHist   office of naval history
OffNavWeaServ   office of naval weather service
OFPP   office of federal procurement policy
OFGR   objective force gross requirement
OfIndMan   office of industrial management
OFL   own front line; 105mm APFSDS with slipping driving band (FR)
OFLA-M   Optronische Feuerleitanlage – Marine (naval optronic fire control equipment) by AEG
OFLC   office of foreign liquidation committee
OFP   ordnance field park RAOC; operating force plan (US)
OFRR   office of foreign relief and rehabilitation
OFRRO   office of foreign relief and rehabilitation operation
OFS   office of field service; Orange Free State

OfShr   off-shore
OFT   orbital flight test; operational flight trainer
OF/WST   operational flight/weapons system trainer
OFZ   obstacle free zone
OG   officer of the guard; outside guard; Officine Galileo (Florence IT)
OG-14   tank prediction computing system by OG
OGA   Office Général de l'Air (Paris)
OGC   office of general counsel --PLD
OGE   out of ground effect; operational ground equipment
OGLA   officer grade limitations act
OGM   ordinary general meeting
Ognevoi   class, missile destroyers (SU)
OGO   orbiting geophysical observatory (Nasa)
OGR   ordnance, Gunnery and Readiness division (USCG)
OGT   outlet gas temperature
OGU   outgoing unit
OGW   overload gross weight
OH   on hand; office hours; overhaul; observation helicopter; opposite hand; overhead; open hearth
OH-4A   Kiowa, observation helicopter by Bell
OH-6   Cayuse, observation helicopter by Hughes
OH-13   Sioux, observation helicopter by Bell (Bell 47G)
OH-58   Kiowa, observation helicopter by Bell
OHA   oxygen haemoglobin affinity
OHB   optimum height of burst
OHBMS   On Her (His) Britannic Majesty's Service
OHC   overhead camshaft (engine)
OHDetS   over the horizon detection system
OHI   ordnance handling instruction
Ohio   class, nuclear-powered ballistic missile submarines SSBN (USN)
OHMS   On Her (His) Majesty's Service
oHoB   optimum height of burst
O/HRS   oceanographic/hydrographic research ship
OHS   open hearth steel
OHT   oxygen at high temperature
OHTA   observation helicopter, target acquisition (US programme)
OHV   overhead valve (engine)
OI   operating instruction; office of information; office instruction
OIAA   office of Inter-American affairs
OIAF   office of information for the armed forces --DAFIE

OIC	officer in charge
OIC2ndEch	officer in charge of the 2nd echelon
OICC	officer in charge of construction
OIDiv	operations information centre, division
OIDP	overseas internal defence policy
OIL	operating information lines; ordnance investigation laboratory; orbiting international laboratory
OinC	officer in charge
OinCABCCTC	officer in charge advanced base combat communications training centre
Oionoskop	anti-aircraft gunnery training equipment 1937 by Contraves
OIP	Société Belge d'Optique et d'Instruments de Précision (Gent)
OIP	operations improvement programme; operational improvement plan
OIPAAR	office of industrial personnel access authorization review
OIR	office of industrial relations
OIRA	Oakland industrial recreation association
OIRT	Organisation Internationale de Radio-diffusion et de Télévision
OIS	organiser industrial safety
OISP	overseas internal security plan; open improved storage space
OJ	open joint
OJCS	office, joint chiefs of staff; organization of joint chiefs of staff
OJT	on the job training
OK	all correct
O&K	Orenstein & Koppel AG (Dortmund)
OKA	otherwise known as
Okba	class, attack torpedo boats by SFCN
Okean	class, spy ships 680 tons (SU)
ÖKG	Österreichische Klimatechnik Gesellschaft
Oksywie	class, patrol craft (Poland)
OL	operating level; operating location; Officer of the Order of Leopold (Belgium); ordnance lieutenant; outside lubricated; oil lighter; overhead line; overflow level; overhead links
OL77/ASQ	fighter control and navigation computer by Litton
OLA	officer of legislative affairs
OLAS	organization of Latin American solidarity (Cuba)
OLBM	orbital launched ballistic missile
OLC	on-line computer
OLCr	ordnance lieutenant commander
Oldelft	NV Optische Industrie de Oude Delft
OLDiv	operation, lookout and recognition division

OLF	outlaying field
OLGA	open loop gust alleviation
OLH	officer of the Legion of Honour
OLI	The Oxfordshire and Buckinghamshire Light Infantry
Olifant	observation limitée du fantassin (portable battlefield radar) by Thomson-CSF
OLIVER	on-line instrumentation via energetic radio-isotopes
Oliver Hazard Perry	class, RAN FFG bought from US
OLLA	office of lend-lease administration
OLMC	ordnance light maintenance company (US)
OLMR	organic liquid moderated reactor
OLOS	out of line of sight
OLP	observation landplane; office of labor production (US)
OLPARS	on-line pattern analysis and recognition system
OLQ	officerlike qualities
OLRT	on-line real-time (computer)
OLS	optical landing system
OL&S	ocean and lake surveys
OLSS	overseas limited storage site
OLTEP	on-line test executive programme
OLTI	office of liaison and technical information
OLTS	on-line test system
OM	Member of the Order of Merit; observer's mate; office messenger; operational memorandum; ordnance manual; ordnance map; observations means; outer marker; old measurement; overturning moment; operator maintenance
O&M	operation and maintenance; organization and methods
OM	officers' model; Oto Melara SpA (La Spezia IT)
OMA	operation and maintenance, Army; organizational maintenance activities
OMAC	obus mine anti-char (anti-tank mine (shell))
OMAR	operation and maintenance, Army Reserve
OMArNG	operation and maintenance, Army National Guard
OMAS	one-man atmospheric submersible by Vickers
OMB	office of management and budget; ordnance maintenance battalion (US)
OMCI	French IMCO
OMD	operations maintenance division
OMDA	office of mutual defence affairs (Nato)
OME	office of management engineer; ordnance mechanical engineer

Omega	airborne VLF navigation system by Bendix; southern hemisphere positioning system	OND	own number dialling; ordinary national diploma
Omera-Segid	Argenteuil (FR)	ONERA	Office Nacional d'Etudes et de Recherches Aerospatiales
OMF	operation and maintenance of facilities; officer master file; originating medical facility	Ongar	project, Mk.23 homing torpedo successor
OMFBAA	operation and maintenance of facilities budget activity account	ONH	office of naval history
		ONI	office of naval intelligence
OMFCA	operation and maintenance of facilities cost account	Onion	AVRE demolition tank version WW2
		ONM	office of naval material
O&MFH	operation and maintenance, family housing	ONO	office of naval operations; or near offer
OMFSCA	operation and maintenance of facilities summary cost account	ONOO	outline Nato operational objectives
		ONOP	office of naval officer procurement
OMGUS	office military government (for Germany) US	ONP	office of naval procurement
OMI	office management information; ordnance modification instructions; Ottico Meccanica Italiana SpA	ONR	operational non-radar (directed flight); official naval reporter; office of naval research Washington
			BRO branch research office
			L London
OMIS	office management information system	ONS	overseas nursing service
OMJ	outgoing message junction	ONS-25	Omega navigation system VLF by Bendix
OML	Order of Merit List		
OMM	officer message mail	OnShr	on shore
OMMC	officer message mail centre	ONT	ordinary neap tide
OMM	officers' model match (pistol); Organisation Métérologique Mondiale (world meteorological organization)	Ontos	light tracked vehicle (US)
		Ontrac-2	long wave navigation system by CCCC
O&MN	operation and maintenance, Navy	ONU	French UNO
OmniDME	omni-range distance measuring equipment; omni-directional distance measuring equipment	ONWARD	organization of the North West authorities for rationalized design (US)
OMO	one man operated	OO	operational order; own occupation; operations officer; ordnance officer; orderly officer; observation officer; on order; order of
OMPA	octa-methyl pyrophosphor-amide; one man pensions arrangement		
OMPF	official military personnel file		
OMPR	optical mark page reader		
OMQ	officers' married quarters	OOB	order of battle Naval (Nato)
OMR	optical mark reader; optical mark recognition	OOC	office of censorship
		OOD	officer of the day; officer of the deck
OMS	officers' model Springfield; orbital manoeuvring system (Nasa); organizational maintenance system ; output per manshift; Organisation Mondiale de Sante --WHO; organizational maintenance shop; organizational maintenance squadron	OOE	out of ecliptic (mission) satellite
		OofB	order of battle
		OOG	officer of the guard
		OOM	officers open mess
		ooo	out of order
OMSF	office of manned spaceflight (Nasa)	OOQ	officer of the quarters
OMT	organizational maintenance technician	OOR	office of ordnance research
OMTS	organizational maintenance test station	O&OS	ordnance and ordnance stores
		Ooshio	class, submarines (JSDF)
OMUX	optical multiplexing	OOSS	overseas operations storage site
OMVTO	office(r), motor vehicle transportation	OOW	officer of the watch
ON	octane number (clear) (no additive)	OP	observation post; old price; ordnance publication; operational procedures STANAG; old pattern; out of print; open pattern; over proof; open point (projectile); original pack; observed position; ordnance pamphlet;
ONA	optical navigation attachment		
OnApp	on approval		
ONC	operational navigation chart; ordinary national certificate; overall Nato command		

	operational project; ownership purpose (code); operational priority; ordnance personnel; order policy; original policy
op	operator
OPA	other procurement, Army; office of price administration; office of programme appraisal; officer personnel act (US) 1947; optical plotting attachment
OPAL	optical platform alignment linkage
OpAnal	operations analysis
OpAttyGen	opinion of the attorney general
OPB	officer programme branch
OPC	ownership, purpose and condition (code); operational performance category; ordinary Portland cement
OpC	operational control centre
OpCode	operations code
OpCom	operations communications
OpCon	operational control
OpCtr	operations centre
OPCW	office of petroleum coordinator for war
OPD	officer personnel directorate; officer performance division
OpD	operations division
OPDAR	optical detection and ranging
OpDatS	operational performance data system
OpDevFor	operational development force
OpDiv	operations/air intelligence division (phot)
OPE	open point expanding (projectile)
OPEC	organization of petrol exporting countries
OPED	other pay entry date
OPEG	OEEC petroleum emergency group
OPEP	orbital plane experiment package (Nasa)
OPers	officer personnel
OPET	organization, personnel, equipment and training
OpEval	operational evaluation
OpEx	operational extension; operational, executive and administrative (personnel)
OPF	official personnel folder
OpFor	opposing forces (exercises)
OPGE	OEEC petroleum industry emergency group
OPGENS	optical pollution surveillance schedule generating system
OPH	offshore patrol helicopter; ocean patrol hydrofoil by Boeing
OPI	office of public information
OP&I	office of patents and inventions
OPIS	operational priority indicating system
OPL	outpost line (US Army)
OPlan	operational plan (Nato)

OPLE	Omega position locating equipment
OPLO	Organisation de Production et de Logistique de l'OTAN (Nato production and logistics organization)
OPLOH	French NHPLO
OPLR	outpost line of resistance (US Army)
OPM	office of production management; office of procurement and material; operating plane months; operations per minute; output position map
OPMAC	operations for military aid to the community
OPMACC	operations for military aid to the civilian community
OPMG	office of the provost marshal general (US)
OPMS	officer personnel management system
opn	operation; opinion; option
OPN	other procurement, Navy
OpNav	office of the chief of naval operations
	CommO communications office
opns	operations
O&POMB	officers' and petty' officers management branch BUPERS
OpOrd	operation order
OPP	out of print at present
OpPlan	operation plan
OPQ	occupying public quarters
OPR	ordnance property regulations; operational project requirements; office of public relations
OpRdy	operationally ready
OpRep	operational report
OprEx	operational exercise (Nato)
oprg	operating
Ops	operations (general staff) operations (division SHAPE)
OpsArmyJAG	opinions of the Army judge advocate general
OpSec	operations security
OPSKS	optimum phase shift keyed signals
OpsRep	operations report (Nato)
OpStr	operating strength
OpStatusRep	operation status report
OPT	optical equipment STANAG
OpTar	operations target
OpTEVFor	operational test and evaluation force (Norfolk)
OPTIM	order point technique for inventory management
OpTra	operational training
OpTraU	operational training unit
OpU	operational unit
OPUR	objective programme utility routines (computer)
OPV	offshore patrol vessel; offshore protection vessel

OPW	office of public works
Opy	operating authority
OPZ	Operationszentrale (operations room)
OQMG	office of the quartermaster general
OQR	officer's qualification record
OR	operational requirement; operational readiness; operations research; out of range
O&R	overhaul and repair
OR	other ranks; orderly room; organized reserve; operations room; operational reliability; official receiver; owner's risk
O/R	on request
OR-130	EOD operator's three-way communications equipment (UK)
ORA	office of research analysis; operational radar (directed flight); operations research analyst
Orange	defoilant agent (US)
ORB	oceanographic research buoy; officer record brief; officers' records branch BUPERS; owner's risk of breakage
ORB-31D	Heracles, airborne target designation radar by Onera
OrBat	order of battle (report)
ORBIS	orbiting radio beacon ionospheric satellite
ORBIT	on-line retrieval of bibliographic information; (Feuerwehrsystem zur) optimalen Rettung & Brandbekämpfung und integrierten technischen Hilfeleistung (fire brigade system for optimal rescue and firefighting operation with integrated technical aid)
Orbiter-101	STS, Enterprise, shuttle transportation system (Nasa)
ORC	overseas research council; operational requirements committee (UK); Member of the Order of the Red Cross; officers' reserve corps; Orange River Colony OFS
ORCA	ocean resources conservation association
ORCen	overseas record centre
OrCon	organic control
ORD	once-run destillate; operations research division; office of rubber director WPB; owner's risk of damage; overseas replacement depot; ordnance (Nato)
Ord	ordnance; orderly; ordinary (seaman)
OrdAlt	ordnance alteration
ORDAP	organization for development assistance programme
OrdBd	ordnance board (UK)
OrdC	ordnance corps

ORDC	ordnance research and development centre
OrdCan	orders cancelled
OrdConTech	ordnance control technician
OrdCor	orders corrected
OrdEng	ordnance engineering
OrdDept	ordnance department (US)
OrdFac	ordnance facility
ORDIR	omni-range digital radar (Nato)
OrDis	ordnance discharge
ORDiv	operations/radio communications division
OrdM	ordnance manual
OrdMod	orders modified
OrdSgt	ordnance sergeant
OrdSta	ordnance station
OrdU	ordnance unit
ORE	operation readiness evaluation; office for research and experimentation; operational readiness evaluation
OResCo	overseas research council
OREST	Ortungsradar mit elektronischer Strahlschwenkung by Siemens (phased array location radar)
ORF	operational readiness float; owner's risk of fire
OrFS	Orange Free State
ORG	operations research group; ordnance research group
org	organic; organized; organization
ORGDP	Oak Ridge gaseous diffusion plant
ORI	office of research and inventions (US); ocean research institute (Japan); operational readiness inspection
Orion-10X	naval fire control radar (IT)
Orion P-3C	patrol aircraft anti-submarine by Lockheed 1959
Orion-80	N-80, night aiming device for infantry weapons by Eltro
ORIT	operational readiness inspection test
ORL	owner's riks of leakage
ORLL	operational reports lessons learned
OR/MC	operational requirements military characteristics
OrMod	orders modified
ORNL	Oak Ridge National Laboratory
ORO	operational research organization (US Army)
Oropesa	wire cutting mine-sweeping float (RN)
Orphel	Observatoire Radar sur Platforme à hélice (propeller-driven radar observation platform)
ORR	Oak Ridge Reactor; owner's risk rates
ORS	orderly room sergeant; operational research study; operational

research section; operational
research society Ltd (London)

ORSA   operations research society of
America

OR/SA   operations research/systems analysis

ORT   operating room technician;
operational readiness training;
operational readiness test;
optical relay tube

ORTAC-M Ortungsverfahren im TACAN Band,
Monopulsverfahren by SEL
(mono-pulse location system
TACAN band)

ORTS   Mk-545, operational readiness and
test system

ORTU   organized reserve training unit
(USCG)
AG   augmentation
EL   electronics
PS   port security
RCC rescue coordination center

ORTU   other ranks training unit

ORV   optical repair vehicle; Oxfordshire
Rifle Volunteers;

ORVC   Oxfordshire Rifle Volunteers Corps

OS   optical sight; outsize; old style;
outside; oil switch; ordnance
specification; old series;
ordnance survey; out of stock;
output secondary; on spot; ocean
station; on sale; oblique sounding;
operating system; ordnance stores;
observer school; out of service;
ordnance services; ordinary seaman

OS-shell proximity-fused fragmentation
shell 76/62 by OTO

OSA   official secrets act; office of the
secretary of the Army; order for
simple alert

Osa   class, fast patrol missile boats (SU)

OSAF   office of the secretary of the Air
Force

OSAP   ocean surveillance air patrol (aircraft)

OSAS   overseas service aid scheme

OSB   officer selection battery; officer
services branch BUPERS; office
services branch

Osborn acoustic mine-sweeping system by
Sperry

OSBT   officer selection battery test

OSC   ordnance service corps;
organizational supply code; own
ship's course

osc   oscillator; oscillating

OScAd   office of the scientific advisor

OSCAR   oxygen steelmaking computer and
recorder; orbital satellite
carrying amateur radio; optical
submarine communication by aerospace relay by GTE

OSD   office of the secretary of defence;
ordnance survey department; on-
line systems driver (computer);
over, short and damaged (report);
overseas duty

OS&D   over, short and damaged (report)

OSE   officer scheduling exercise (Nato)

OSect   operations section

OSEcy   office of the secretary to the staff
SHAPE

OSFCo   office of the solid fuels coordinator

OSFCW   office of the solid fuels coordinator for war

OSHA   occupational safety and health act;
occupational safety and health
administration

OSHC   occupational safety and health
commission

OSI   office of strategic information;
office of special investigation
(USAF); operations security
indicators

OSIA   office, services information agency

OSigO   office of the (Chief) signal officer

OSIL   operating systems implementation
league

OSIP   operation and safety improvement
plan

OSJJE   Order of St John of Jerusalem in
England

Oskol   class, repair ships (SU)

OSL   ordnance sub-lieutenant

OSM   option select mode; ordnance supply
manual

OSN   office of the secretary of the navy

OSO   officer selection office; ordnance
supply officer; other supply
officers; orbiting solar observatory

OSOD   over, short or damaged (report)

OSP   office of surplus property; off-
shore procurement (programme);
US pay arms for their allies

OSPA   overseas service pensioners'
association

OSPE   organizational spare parts and
equipment

OSPRD   officers' selection, promotion,
reclassification and disposal
branch (CA)

Osprey class, off-shore protection vessels
(UK)

OSPro   ocean shipping procedures

OSR   office of scientific research;
optical solar reflector; over-the-
shoulder rating; operational
status release; optimum ship
routing; office of security
review; ordnance status report

OSRB	overseas service resettlement bureau
OSRD	office of scientific research and development
OS&RD	officer services and records division BUPERS
OSRepl	overseas replacement
OSRet	overseas returnee
OSS	office of strategic services WW2 (US military espionage and sabotage); operational storage site; office of space sciences (Nasa); orbiting space station
OSSR	office of selective service records
OST	ordinary spring tide; operational suitability test; order ship time
OSTAN	Organisations Stärke & Aus-rüstungsnachweise (organizational personnel and equipment tables)
OSTCOOP	office of the secretary of trans-portation continuity of operations plan
OStd	ordnance standards
OS&TD	ocean science and technology division ONR
OSTI	office of scientific and technical information
OStJ	Officer of the Order of St John of Jerusalem
Ostwind	anti-aircraft tank WW2 (GE)
OSU	ordnance supply unit
OSV	ocean station vessel (SUCG); ordnance spares vehicle (for missiles); on station vehicle; ordnance spares vessel
OSW	office of saline waters; office of the secretary of war
OT	off time; over time; operational test; occupational therapy; observer target; overseas trade; one-time; other times
O&T	organization and training
OT-1	... 2, ... 3 operational test phase 1
OT-1/DT-1	operational test phase 1/ development test phase 1
OT-62	Topas, tracked personnel carrier (Czech)
OT-64	Skot, wheeled personnel carrier (Czech)
OTA	other than air (USNR programme); outer transport area
OTAC	ordnance, tank and automotive command (US)
OTAD	overseas terminal arrival date
OTAN	Organisation du Traité de l'Atlantique Nord French: NATO
OTASE	Organisation du Traité de l'Asie du Sud-Est French: SEATO
otbd	outboard

OTC	overseas telecommunications commission; one-stop tour charter; Ocean Technology Centre (Schneverdingen (GE); officers' training corps; officers' training camp; officers' training college; office of the theatre chaplain; officer in technical command; officers' transit camp; operational training command (USN)
OTCLANT	operational training command Atlantic
OTCPac	operational training command Pacific
OTCS	office of the theatre chief surgeon
OTCSigO	office of the theatre chief signal officer
OTCT	office of the theatre chief of transportation
OTD	operational tactics development; overseas travel development; original transmission density; observer-target distance
OTDS	optronic target designation system
OTE	operational test and evaluation
OTE	Telecommunications (Florence IT) (subsidiary of Montedel)
OTEA	operational test and evaluation agency
OTEC	ocean thermal energy conversion
OTEF	overseas troops entertainment fund
OTF	observation-target factor; optical transfer function; optimum traffic frequency
OTH	over the horizon (radar)
OTH-B	over the horizon back scatter
OTH-F	over the horizon forward scatter
OTHR	over the horizon radar
OTI	ordnance technical instructions
OTIG	office of the inspector general
OTIS	ordnance telemetry instrumentation station
OTIU	overseas technical information unit (UK)
OTJAG	office of the judge advocate general
OTL	order trunk lines; observer-target line
otlk	outlook
OTMJ	outgoing trunk message junctions
OTng	observer training
OTO	operations training and organization (Nato)
OTO-Melara SpA	La Spezia (IT) Odero-Terni-Orlando
OTO-76/62	naval compact gun 3in by OTO-Melara
OTO-127/54	naval compact gun 5 in by OTO-Melara
Otomat	sea-skimming anti-ship missiles by OTO
OTOSel	OTO-Melara + Selenia

OTP	one-time pad; one-time process; outline test plan
OTPI	on top position indicator
OTPM	office of the theatre provost marshal
OTPMG	office of the provost marshal general
OTQ	office of the theatre (chief) quartermaster
OTR	Oxford territorial regiment; observer-target range
otr	other
OTRA	other than regular Army
OTRAG	Orbital Transport & Raketen AG (Neu Isenburg GE)
Otrag-200	500 1000 2500 5000 10000 orbital transport missile (project) by OTRAG 200kgs payload ...
OTS	office of technical services; orbital test satellite (1st European); orbital telecommunications satellite; officers' training school
OTSG	office of the surgeon general
OTSR	optimum track ship routing
OTS-SCTS	orbital test satellite control and station (Fucino/Rome)
OTT	one-time tape
Otter	towed mine-sweeping device
OTU	office of technology utilization (Nasa); operational taxonomic unit; operational training unit;
OU	observation unknown, out of use; official use only (UK)
O&U	over and under (shotgun)
O/U	over and under
OUAS	Oxford University Air Squadron
OUDP	officer undergraduate degree programme
OUO	official use only (US)
OURA	Oxford University Rifle Association
OURC	Oxford University Rifle Club
Ouragan	MD.450, light bomber by Marcel Dassault
OUSArmA	office of the US Army attache
OUSN	office of the under-secretary of the Navy
OUSW	office of the under-secretary of war
outbd	outbound
OutConUs	outside the continental USA
OutUS	outside the continental USA
OV	operational value
oV	ohne Verzögerung (instantaneous) (fuse)
OV-1	Mohawk, observation STOL turboprop
OV-10	Bronco, observation plane night observation system NOS; LARA/COIN light armed recce aircraft, counter-insurgency by North American
OV-10B	Bronco, target towing version
OVAC	overseas visual aids centre
ovbd	overboard
ovc	overcast
ovckd	overchecked
OvckdFldRats	overchecked field rations
ovded	overdeduction
ovpd	overpaid
OveRep	overseas unit replacement system
ovfl	overflow
OVH	overhead (projector)
ovhd	overhead
ovhl	overhaul
ovld	overload
ovrd	override
ovsp	overspeed
ovr	over
ovrn	overrun
OvS	overhaul specifications
OW	ordnance workshop; one-way; order wire; office of works (UK); open wire (land over land) (Nato)
O/W	oil in water
OWAEC	organization for West African economic co-operation
OWC	ordnance weapons command (US Army)
OWE	operating weight, empty
Owen gun	machine pistol (Australia)
OWF	optimum working frequency
OWI	office of war information
OWL	over water and land (aircraft); observation and surveillance vehicle (truck + hydraulic platform) by MDC
OWM	office of war mobilization
OWMR	office of war mobilization and reconversion
OWR	obligated war reserve
OWRMR	other war reserve material requirements
OWRR	office of water resources research
OWRS	other war reserve stocks
OWS	operation weather support (circuits) (circuits); ocean weather ship; ocean weather station; ocean weather service; orbital workshop station
OWU	office of war utilities
ox	oxygen
oxy	oxygen
OXFAM	Oxford Committee for Famine Relief
OxfBucks	The Oxfordshire and Buckinghamshire Light Infantry
Oxley	class, submarines (RAN) (Oberon class RN)
OxRB	oxygen replacement bottles
Oxyport-2000	portable oxygen apparatus by Dräger
OZM	anti-personnel mine (SU)

P

P	paymaster; pilot; pupil; prince; photo/navigator (USN); park; pole; post; page; planning; priority (message); phosphorous; photography; pistol; patchy (runway); percussion; period; pipe; pitch; positive; pressure; particle; peak; print; power; patrol (aircraft); prosecutor (aircraft); pursuit (aircraft); prototype (aircraft); parabellum (projectile); pointed (projectile); practice (projectile, shell); phosphorous (shell)
P-boat	patrol boat
P-day	production day
P-Gerät	Platzpatronengerät (practice bore)
P-hour	parachute operation starts
P-lines	pole line; power lines; pole-power lines
P-plane	unmanned explosive carrying aircraft
P-01	MRCA, multi-role combat aircraft by Panavia
P-1	Lightning, jet fighter aircraft by BAC '57; Hawk, interceptor by Curtiss 1920; Pershing missile
P-1a	Pershing 1a
P-1	pistol 9mm by Walther
P-2A1	signal pistol by HK
P-3C	Orion, ASW patrol aircraft by Lockheed
P-3	Versuchsträager, amphibisch by EWK (wheeled amphibious vehicle, experimental)
P-03	Alpha Jet, tactical support/trainer aircraft by Dornier/Dassault/Breguet
P-3T	Sea Eagle, air-launched anti-ship missile project by BAC
P-4	class, coastal torpedo boats (SU)
P-5M	Marlin, flying boat
P-5Y	Tradewind, flying boat
P-6	class, torpedo boats (SU)
P-6/2	mine detector by Plessey
P-6M	Seamaster, four jet flying boat
P-9	pistol 9mm by HK

P-12	Tornado, MRCA by Panavia
P-14	Tall King, early warning radar (SU)
P-15	pistol 9mm by MAB
P-25	anti-personnel mine, HE by MISAR
P-26	single-seat all-metal fighter/bomber by Boeing
P-27	bazooka (Czech)
P-35	interceptor by Seversky WW2
P-36	interceptor WW2 by Curtiss
P-38	Lightning, interceptor WW2 by Lockheed
P-39	Airacobra, interceptor by Bell
P-39	assault and combat glider WW2 (GE)
P-40	Kittyhawk, Warhawk, interceptor by Curtiss; floating HE anti-personnel mine by MISAR
P-47	Thunderbolt, interceptor WW2 by Republic
P-50	Bar Lock, ground-controlled fighter direction radar (SU)
P-51C	Mustang, interceptor WW2 by North American
P-59	Airacomet, jet fighter by Bell; TNT mine (Switzerland)
P-61	B-15, Black Widow, night fighter WW2 by Northrop
P-64	pistol 9mm (Poland)
P-68R	Victor, light twin-engined aircraft by Partenavia
P-80	Shooting Star, jet fighter by Lockheed
P-82	Twin Mustang, fighter by North American
P-96	ECA, project future European combat aircraft by BAe
P-103	ECA, project future European combat aircraft by MBB
P-166	twin turboprop aircraft by Piaggio
P220	pistol by SIG
P-230	pistol by SIG
P-391	SLAR, side-looking airborne radar by EMI
P-420	Sparviero, Italian hydrofoil (USN designation)
P-1040	Sea Hawk, carrier-borne fighter by Hawker

P-1051   class, patrol boats by Halter Marine
P-1067   interceptor/ground attack fighter
          1951 by Hawker
P-1127   VTOL jet 1960 Harrier prototype by
          Hawker
P-4030/1 Chieftain, main battle tank proto-
          type by ROF Leeds
P-4030/2 Shir I, redesigned Khalid
          MBT projected for Iran then sold
          to Jordan without Chobham armour
          by ROF Leeds
P-4030/3 Shir II, MBT project cancelled
          (with Chobham armour) by ROF
          Leeds
P-4030/4 Challenger project future main
          battle tank by ROF Leeds
P-5000   4x4 ambulance vehicle for RAF by
          Stonefield
PA   personal assistnat; presidential
          assistant; press attache; post
          adjutant; public affairs (officer);
          Pakistan Army; pattern analysis
          (test); pending availability;
          per annum; performance analysis;
          procurement appropriation;
          permanent appointment; port agency;
          programme account; public appoint-
          ment; position approximate;
          position of assembly; probation
          act; provisional allowance; pre-
          computed altitude; patrol aircraft;
          particular average; pola-amide
          nylon; power amplifier
P/A   precision alignment; private account;
          put away
P&A   personnel and administration;
          procedures and analysis; procure-
          ment and assignment
PA-system public address system
PA-3DM   machine pistol 9mm by FMDAP
PA-005   Peilanlage, radio direction finder
          by R&S
PA-37   Pre luftatmer by Auer
          (compressed air breathing
          apparatus)
PAA   procurement of ammunition, Army;
          pay adjustment authorization;
          primary aircraft authorization;
          poly-acrylic acid; phased antenna
          arrays; Pont Automoteur
          d'Accompagnement (bridging equip-
          ment by DCAN)
PAAC   programme analysis adaptable control
PAACS   prior active army commissioned
          service
PAADC   principal air aide-de-camp
PAAES   prior active army enlisted service
PAAFCS   prior active air force commissioned
          service
PAAFES   prior active air force enlisted
          service

PAB   price assignment board; pulse
          adsorption bed; policies allotment
          board; primary adhesively bonded
PABST   structure technology (USAF pro-
          gramme)
PABX   private automatic branch exchange
PAC   preventive ablution centre;
          parachute and cable (apparatus);
          public aid committee; public
          assistance committee; political
          action committee; personnel and
          administration centre; Pacific
          air command (USAF); programme
          adjustment committee; Pan African
          Congress; Pan American Congress;
          passed advancec class (at MCS);
          package assembly circuit; primary
          address code; panoramic air
          camera; parachute and cable
          apparatus (apparatus, air defence,
          type L RN WW2)
Pac   Pacific
PacAdv   Pacific advanced headquarters
PacAF   Pacific air forces
PACas   patient care system
PacCom   Pacific command
PacComOpConCen Pacific fleet commander
                operational control centre
PACCS   post attack command and control
          system SAC
PACDA   personnel and administration combat
          development activity
PACE   precision analog computing equipment;
          performance and cost evaluation
          (programme);
          package CRAM executive (card random
          access memory);
          phased array control electronics;
          programme for afloat college
          education
PaCens   patient census
Pacer   artillery muzzle velocity measuring
          system by Ferranti
PacEx   Pacific exchange (system)
PACF   periodic auto-correction
          function
PacFlt   Pacific Fleet
PacFltCom Pacific Fleet command
PACGCS   prior active Coast Guard
          commissioned service
PACGES   prior active Coast Guard enlisted
          service
PacHedPearl Pacific headquarters Pearl
             Harbour
PacIntCen Pacific intelligence centre
Packet   C-82, cargo aircraft by Fairchild
PACM   pulse amplitude code modulation
PacMisRan Pacific missile range
PacMisRanFac Pacific missile range
              facility

PacNavFacEngCom Pacific naval facilities
     engineering command
PaCom Pacific command (USAr-USN-USAF)
PaComDet Pacific command detachment
PACORNALOG Pacific Coast coordinator for
     naval logistics
PacDiv Pacific division
PAcRep port activities report
PacResFlt Pacific reserve fleet
PACS Pacific area communications system
PACT production analysis control tech-
     nique; project for the advancement
     of coding techniques
PACUSA Pacific air command US Army
PAD preferred arrival date; public
     affairs division (US); personnel
     affairs division BUPERS; pilotless
     aircraft; pontoon assembly detach-
     ment; primary aeronautical desig-
     nation; payable after death;
     passive air defence; propellant
     actuated device; pressure acutated
     device; positioning arm disc;
     provisional acceptance date
PADAR passive detection and ranging;
     programme approval disposal and
     redistribution
PADC Philippines Aircraft Development
     Corp.
PADD planned active duty date
PADLOC passive detection and location of
     counter-measures (USAF)
PADMIS patient administration management
     information system
PADO proposed advanced development
     objective
PADOC pay adjustment document
PADS position + azimuth determining
     system (helicopter navigation by
     Ferranti); personnel automated
     data system; performance analysis
     and design synthesis
PAEC Pakistan atomic energy commission;
     Philippines atomic energy commis-
     sion
PAECT pollution abatement and environment
     control technology
Paek Ko class, guided missile patrol boats
     (Korea)
PAF peripheral address field
PAFB Patrick air force base (Fla)
PAFC phase-locked automatic frequency
     control
PAFCS prior active foreign commissioned
     service
PAFES prior active foreign enlisted service
PAFMECA Pan American Freedom Movement for
     East and Central Africa
PAG project advisory group; protection
     against gas; preliminary analysis
     group

PAGE piston arrestment gas entrapment
     (system) Sprint launch cell
PAGTU Pan-American ground training unit
PAH-1 BO-105M, Panzerabwehrhubschrauber by
     MBB (anti-tank helicopter)
PaHel pay and health (records)
PAHO Pan-American health organization
PAI primary aircraft inventory
Pai-force Palestine and Iraq force
PAID press agent of information depart-
     ment
PAIL post attack intercontinental line
PAInt post attack intelligence
PAIR precision approach interferometer
     radar by MEL; performance and
     integration retrofit (hull-mounted
     sonar) SQS-23 by Sperry
PAIT programme for the advancement of
     industrial technology
Pak Pakistan
Pak Panzerabwehrkanone (anti-tank gun)
     WW2 (GE)
     41   4.2cm
     38   5cm
     40   7.5cm
     41   7.5cm
     97/38 7.5cm
     43/2 8.8cm
PAL phase alternation line (colour TV);
     permissive action link;
     peripheral availability list;
     parcel air lift (mail);
     prisoner at large (US)
Pal Palestine
Palapa-1 ... 2, regional communications
     satellite (Indonesia) by Hughes
PALCru pay and allowance accrue (form) (US)
PALM precision altitude and landing
     monitor
PALO port amenities liaison officer
PALR permissive action link report
PALS permissive action link system;
     precision approach lighting system
PALSG personnel and logistics systems
     group
PAM payload assist module rocket system
     by McDD; pulse amplitude modula-
     tion; peripheral adapter module;
     process automatic monitor;
     parametric amplifier; permanent
     active militia; priorities alloca-
     tion manual; partial mobilization
     (expansion plan) (US); Programme
     d'aide our la Défense Mutuelle
     (mutual defence assistance pro-
     gramme)
pam pamphlet
PAMC Pakistan Army Medical Corps
PAMCE (naval) propulsion and auxiliary
     machinery control equipment
     -- Spruance class by Litton

PAMCS   prior active marine corps commis-
            sioned service
PAMES   prior active marine corps enlisted
            service
PAMETRADA Parsons and Marine Engineering
            Turbine Research and Develop-
            ment Association
PAMI   personnel accounting machine
            installation
            Lant Atlantic
            Pac   Pacific
PAMISE   (naval) propulsion and auxiliary
            machinery information system
            equipment by Litton
PAMN   procurement of aircraft and
            missiles, Navy
pamph   pamphlet
PAMUSA   post attack mobilization of the US
            Army
Pan   Panama
PAN   pilot assumed navigation
Panavia Aircraft GMBH (Munich) (Aeritalia +
            BAC + MBB)
PanCan   Panama Canal
PanCanCo Panama Canal Company
Pancerovka RPG anti-tank rocket launcher
            (Czech)
PANDA   personnel and administration SHAPE
Panda   optronic fire-control system by CSEE
PandL   pioneer and labour (UK);
            pay and allowances
PandLChar pay and allowances chargeable
Pandora AT-I, DM-701, rocket warhead con-
            taining 8 anti-tank bar mines by
            DNAG
PANDP   Plans and Policy Division SHAPE
PandS   pay and supply (USCG)
PANES   prior active navy enlisted service
PANGCS   prior active national guard commis-
            sioned service
PANGES   prior active national guard enlisted
            service
Panhard M-4 VAB-4 wheeled APC
            M-6 6
            M-8 8
PANS   procedures for the air navigation
            services
PANSDOC Pakistan national scientific and
            technical documentation centre
PanSeaFron Panama Sea Frontier
Pantera truck 8.2 tons (Poland)
Panther PzKpfW-V, SdKfz-173, killer tank
            WW2 by MAN (GE)
Panther F-9F, naval jet fighter 1949 by
            Grumman
Panzerblitz air-launched anti-tank missile
            WW2 (GE)
Panzerfaust rocket-propelled anti-tank
            hollow charge WW2 (GE)
            30 30m range
            60 60m range

Panzerschreck RPzB-54, Ofenrohr,
            Raketenpanzerbüchse WW2
            (GE) (anti-tank rocket
            launcher)
PAO   principal administrative officer
            (UK); primary action office (US);
            public affairs officer (US)
PAOC   principal administrative officers'
            committee (UK)
PAP   patrol amphibious plane (USN);
            pilotless aircraft programme;
            personnel assistance points;
            product assurance plan; people's
            action party (Singapore)
Pap   Papua
PAP-104 Poisson Auto Propulse (wire-guided
            mine-sweeping system)
PAPC   poster advertising planning
            committee
PAPE   programme analysis, planning and
            evaluation
PAPI   precision approach path indicator by
            ADB
PAPS   periodic armaments planning system
            (Nato)
PAQ-1   laser target designator by Hughes
PAR   precision approach radar (TPN-19);
            perimeter acquisition radar;
            pulse acquisition radar; progres-
            sive aircraft rework; processor
            address register; programme
            appraisal and review; public
            affairs regulations
par   paragraph, parallel
Para   The Parachute Regiment (UK);
            Paraguay(an)
para   paragraph; parachute; parallel
PARACS   perimeter acquisition radar attack
            characteristics system
            ---Safeguard (US)
Para-Flite Inc. Pennsauken NJ (USA)
parafrag parachute fragmentation (bomb) WW2
Para-Point remote-controlled aerial
            delivery parachute system by
            Para-Flite
Paras   parachute troops
Paravane towed mine-sweeping system
PARB   perimeter acquisition radar building
Parca   surface-to-air missile prototype by
            DEFA
ParCor   parameter-correlation (synthetic
            language)
PARCS   perimeter acquisition radar (attack)
            characterization system
PARD   personal actions and records
            directorate
            MilPerCen
PARDP   perimeter acquisition radar data
            processor

PaRec   pay record
P&AReg   pay and allowance regulations
Parkhill voice cryptographic equipment HF
          (US)
Parl   parliamentary
ParlSec parliamentary secretary
Parlt   parliament
ParM   participating manager
PARM   programme analysis of resources
          management
Parrot   IFF transponder (US)
PARS   portable anti-tank rocket system;
          perimeter acquisition radar system;
          passenger automatic reservation
          system IBM; Programmsystem (EDV)
          zur Steuerung der Kapazitäten der
          Marinearsenalbetriebe (programme
          for capacity management for the
          FGN Naval arsenal facilities);
          Panzer-Abwehr Raketen System
          (anti-tank rocket system)
pars   paragraphs
parsq   para-rescue (US)
ParSyn   parametric synthesis
part   participate; participating;
          particular
partn   partnership
PAS   primary alerting system SAC (USAF);
          public address system; power-
          assisted steering; perigee and
          apogee system; prisoners' aid
          society; personnel accounting
          system
pas   passage; passenger
PAS-3   infra-red telescope (US)
PAS-7   HHTV, hand-held thermal viewer
PASB   Pan-American sanitary bureau PAHO
PASC   Palestine armed struggle command
          (al Fatah)
PASEP   (being) passed separately)
PASGT   personnel armour system for ground
          troops (plastic helmet and fragmen-
          tation vest) Kevlar material
PASI   precision approach slope indicator
PASO   principal armament supply officer
          (UK); port anti-submarine officer
          (US); Pan-American sanitary
          organization
PASRAN   passive ranger (submarine sonar for
          tracking surface ships by Sperry)
pass   passage; passenger; passive
PASSIM   presidential advisory staff on
          scientific management (US)
PasTraM passenger traffic management system
PASU   patrol aircraft service unit
PASWEPS passive anti-submarine warfare
          environmental protection system
          (Nato)
PAT   passive acoustic torpedo; prelim-
          inary acception trials; production

acceptance test; programmable
automatic tester; pattern analysis
test; priority air travel; politi-
cal action team
pat   patent; pattern
PATA   pensions appeal tribunals act
PatBomRon patrol bombing squadron (USN)
PATCA   phase-lock automatic tuned circuit
          adjustment
PatCent patching central (US)
Patchett machine pistol (UK)
Patchett-Sterling machine pistol (UK)
patd   patented
PATCUA   professional air traffic control-
          lers' union of America
PatFor   patrol force
Pathfinder BGM-34B, carrying LLLTV by
          Philco Ford; naval automatic
          tracking radar by Raytheon
PatOff   patent office
PatPend patent pending
Patr   Patrone (cartridge)
Patras   class, patrol boats (FR)
PatrH S Patronenhülse Stahl (steel
          cartridge case) WW2 (GE)
Patriot MIM-104, SAM-D, anti-aircraft
          guided missile by Raytheon
Patrol   programmierbares Abfeuer- und
          Konturenbegrenzungsgerät by
          Rheinmetall (programmable anti-
          aircraft fire and contour limita-
          tion equipment)
PatRon   patrol squadron
PATS   precision automated tracking system
          by GTE Sylvania
PATSU   patrol aircraft service unit
PATSY   programmer's automatic testing
          system
Patton   M-60, main battle tank
PatWing patrol wing
PatWingLant patrol wing Atlantic
PatWingPac patrol wing Pacific
PatWingScoFor patrol wings scouting force
PAU   Pan-American Union; pilotless air-
          craft unit; programmes analysis
          unit
PAV   pressure altitude variable;
          personnel allotment voucher;
          pay adjustment voucher
PAVE   principles and applications of valve
          engineering
Pave Eagle Igloo White + CU-22
Pave Knife airborne pod for point target
          designation LLLTV by Philco
          Ford
Pave Low night/adverse weather SAR helicop-
          ter HH-53, Black Knight
Pave Mover TAWDS, airborne target acquisi-
          tion and weapons delivery
          radar by Hughes

Pave Nickel   RPV programme for monitoring
                Soviet Electronic activities
                and missile tests
                YQM-94A by Boeing
                YQM-98A by Teledyne Ryan
Pave Paws   ground early warning radar by
                Raytheon
Pave Penny   AAS-35, airborne laser target
                identification set
Pave Pronto   USAF project COIN gunship
                aircraft
Pave Spike   AVQ-23A, pod day-only TV/laser
                target designator by
                Westinghouse
Pave Strike   guided glide bomb
Pave Tack   ARN-101, pod FLIR/laser target
                designator
Pave Way   GBU-10, KMU-421, laser guided
                bomb by Texas Instruments
                GBU-10   300 kgs
                GBU-12   225 kgs
                GBU-16   450 kgs
                Mk-82   500 lbs
                Mk-117   750 lbs
                Mk-83   1000 lbs
                Mk-84   2000 lbs
                Mk-118   3000 lbs
PAVN   People's Army of Viet Nam
PAW   powered all the way; petroleum
            administration for war
PAX   private automatic exchange
pax   passenger
PAYE   pay as you earn; pay as you enter
Paymr   paymaster
PB   permanent base; postage book;
            provisional battalion; ports and
            beaches (Nato); property book;
            publications board; premium bond;
            porous base (shell); parabellum
            (bullet); peripheral buffer;
            power buzzer; push button;
            picket boat; patrol (flying) boat;
            patrol bomber; Pietro Beretta
            (Gardone IT)
PB-2Y   Coronado, flying boat by Consolidated
PB-4Y2   Privateer, naval aircraft
PB-35H   helicopter-borne LLLTV observation
            system by AEG
PBA   Pine Bluff Arsenal (US); public
            buildings administration (US)
PBAA   poly-butadiene acrylic acid
            (rocket propellant)
PBAC   programme budget advisory committee
PB-AESRS property book - Army equipment
            status reporting system (US)
PBC   practice bomb contained; practice
            bomb container; packed by carrier
            (household goods)
PBCS   post boost control system
PBD   programme/budget decision; parallel
            blade damper

PBd   power building
PBDI   position bearing and distance
            indicator
PBE   pulsed bridge element
PBEIST   planning board for European inland
            surface transport (Nato) CEP
PBF   patrol boat, fast (over 30 knots)
            (Nato); potential benefit factor
PBFG   patrol boat, fast, guided missiles
            (Nato)
PBH   patrol boat, hydrofoil (Nato)
            (missiles)
PBI   partial background investigation;
            protein-bound iodine; poly-benz-
            imidazoles
PBL   public broadcast laboratory
PBM   principal beachmaster; Mariner,
            flying boat by Martin
PB MAT   machine pistol by MAT
PBMR   provisional base military require-
            ments
PBO   property book officer; packed by
            owner (household goods)
PBOS   planning board for ocean shipping
            (Nato) CEP
PBR   payment by result; power barge with
            ramp (RN); patrol boat, river
            (USN); precision bombing range
PBRA   practical bomb rack adapter
PBERP   permanent board for review of
            enlisted retention programme
            BUPERS
PBRERS   permanent board for review of the
            enlisted rating structure BUPERS
PBRF   Plum Brook reactor facility
PBS   production base support; peninsular
            base section
PBT   President of the board of trade
Pbv-301   armoured personnel carrier by
            Hägglund
PBX   private branch exchange (telephone)
PBXN-103 explosive composition (torpedo
            Mk/48)
PC   plane commander; plane captain;
            pay clerk; postal clerk; peace
            commissioner; police constable;
            paymaster captain; postmaster
            captain; post commander; port
            committee; preparatory commission;
            prophylactic centre; pension code;
            post card; Philippine Constabu-
            lary; post captain; privy council;
            port call; Pharmacy Corps (US);
            Pioneer Corps; Press Council;
            Prison Commission; per cent;
            prices current; petty cash;
            patrol craft; printed circuit;
            printing cylinder; predictor con-
            trol; purchasing and contracting;
            pressure chamber; power control

PC | (hydraulics); pre-stressed concrete; poly-carbonate; punch card; programme computer; processor controller; coastal escort (Nato); submarine chaser (USN); patrol craft (RN); Poste de Commandement (command post)

PC-7 | Turbo Trainer, trainer aircraft by Pilatus

PC | principal chaplain
(P)   Protestant
(RC)   Roman Catholic

PCA | principal control authority; positive controlled airspace; polar cap absorption; prevention of crimes act; permanent change of assignment; personal cash allowance; Parachute Club of America; parliamentary commissioner for administration; permanent court of arbitration

PCAM | punched card accounting machine

PCB | printed circuit board; plenum chamber burning; poly-chlorinated-biphenyl; parts control board; policy control branch BUPERS; petty cash book

PCC | postal and courier communications; planning coordination conference; postal concentration centre; production compression capability; political consultative committee (Warsaw Pact); power control centre; precipitated calcium carbonate; peripheral control computer; Portland Cement concrete; submarine chaser, control (USN)

PCCB | project configuration control board

PCCEMRSP | permanent commission for the conservation and exploitation of the maritime resources of the South Pacific

PCCN | port call control number

PCCNL | Pacific Coast coordinator of Naval logistics

PCCS | programme change control system; ported coaxial cable sensor ComSec by CDC

PCCU | punched card control unit; postal and courier communications unit

PCD | programme change decision; production common digitizer; programme control display (system) Nadge

P&CD | planning and computer department NSC

PCDA | Poste de Commandement de la Défense Aerienne (air defence command post)

PCDesig | plane captain, designated

PCDG | prestressed concrete development group

PCE | patrol craft escort (USN); punch card equipment; programme cost estimates

PCEC | patrol craft, escort, control (USN)

PCEM | parliamentary council for the European movement

PCEP | preliminary call for an experimental proposal Spacelab

PCER | patrol craft, escort, rescue (USN)

PCF | patrol craft, coastal, fast; patrol craft, inshore; pistol, centre-fire; pounds per cubic foot; personnel control facility

PCG | patrol craft, guided missiles SAM (Nato); phonocardiogram; patrol craft (chaser) guided missiles (USN); corvette

PCGN | permanent committee on geographical names

PCH | patrol craft, hydrofoil (USN); submarine chaser, hydrofoil (Nato); post and cross-hairs (sights)

Pchela | class, patrol hydrofoils (SU)

PCHT | packaging, crating, handling and transportation

PCI | peripheral command indicator; plant control interface; programmed control interrupt

PCIFC | permanent commission of the international fisheries convention

PCIZC | permanent committee of international zoological congresses

PCL | pointed core lokt (projectile); project control ledgers; process control language

pcl | parcel

PClk | pay clerk

PCLU | pioneer civil labour unit

PCM | planning and control memorandum; pulse code modulation; pulse cycle modulation; punch card machine; patrol craft, medium (Nato); penalty cost model

PCMC | provided chief of mission concours (US)

PCMCM | permanent chairman military committee memorandum (Nato)

PCMI | photo-chromic micro image

PCMO | principal colonial medical officer

PCMS | punched card machine systems

PCN | part control number; procurement control number; Poste de Commandement et de Navigation (control and navigation panel); Premier Contractant National (national prime contractor)

PCO | passport control office; principal control officer (UK); procuring

	contracting officer (US); publications control officer (US); prospective commanding officer
PCOB	permanent central opium board
PCOLA	pulse coded optical landing aid
PCOp	port changes operator
PCOS	process control operating system
PCP	programme change proposal; product change proposal; primary control programme; programmable communications processor; platoon command post (vehicle); passenger control point; progressive constitutional party (Malta); ploy-chloro-prene (rubber); phencylidin (drug) (Serylan)
pcpn	precipitation
PCPV	pre-stressed concrete pressure vessel
PCR	programme change request; publications contract requirements; positive control routes; programme control register
PCr	paymaster commander
P&CR	planning and compensation reports
PCS	permanent change of station; post, camp or station; postal and courier service (UK); principal clerk of session; patrol craft, submarine chaser (USN); power conditioning system; print contrast system; project control system; passive communications satellite
PCSC	patrol craft, submarine chaser, control (USN)
PCSIR	Pakistan council for scientific and industrial research
PCSP	programme communications support programme
PCSP	permanent commission for the South Pacific
PCT	patent co-operation treaty
pct	per cent
PCTFE	poly-chloro-trifluoro-ethylene
PCU	printed control unit; programme control unit; power control unit; petrol control unit; pressure control unit; Plans Civils d'Urgence (civil emergency planning)
PCV	primary control vessel (USN); passenger controlled vehicle; positive crank-case ventilation; peace corps volunteer
PCW	previously complied with
PCZ	Panama Canal Zone
PCZST	Panama Canal Zone standard time
PD	police department; plans division; position doubtful; position

	description; port director; preventive detention; programme, directive; procurement, directive; priority directive; plain drunk; postal district; preference of duty; presidential directive; pulse doppler; pulse duration; power doubler; potential difference; polar distance; principal distance; passive detection; pitch diameter; preliminary design; port dues
pd	passed; paid; period; per diem (by day)
p/d	post dated
P&D	pioneer and demolition (US)
PD-aid	programme determination aid
PD-2	... 3, explosivess detector by Pye
PD-59	presidential directive for retargeting (USN) SLBMs
PDA	property disposal agent; principal development activity; proposed development approach; predicted drift angle; photon detector assembly
PDAD	probate, divorce and admiralty division
PDAPS	pollution detection and prevention system
PDB	primary demolition belt
P&DD	procurement and distribution branch BUPERS
PDC	practice depth charge; power distribution cabin; power distribution cubicles; physical development centre; personal data card; personnel dispatch centre; personnel dispersal centre; public dividend capital
PDCO	property disposal contracting officer
PDCS	(airborne) performance data computer system by Lear Siegler
PDD	priority delivery date; projected data display; pulse delay device; physical damage division
P&DD	procurement and distribution branch BUPERS
PDDA	power-driven decontamination apparatus
PDDLS	post D-day logistics support
PDE	projectile development establishment; post-strike damage estimation; prospective data element
PDES	pulse doppler elevation scan (radar mode)
PDF	point detonation fuse; principal direction of fire; point of demonstrated feasibility; probability density function

PDFD	pulse doppler frequency diversity
PDFLP	Popular Democratic Front for the Liberation of Palestine
PDG	paymaster director general; point designation grid
PDGW	principal director of guided weapons
PDH	parachute deployment height
PDI	powered descent initiation; pre-delivery inspection
PDIR	priority disassembly and inspection report
PDL	procedure definition language
PDM	pulse duration modulation; pay duties manual; programme decision memorandum
PDM-6	anti-personnel mine (SU)
PDME	precision distance measuring equipment by SEL
PDMM-47	stores dropping parachute system (SU)
PDMS	point defence missile system (Nato)
PDn	petition denied
pdn	production
PDNES	pulse doppler non-elevation scan (radar mode)
PDO	property disposal officer
PDP	procurement data package; programme definition phase; programme development plan (Nasa); programmed data processor
PDP-11/45	airborne computer by Link
PDP-11/M	military micro computer by SEL
PDR	pilot's display recorder; pre-determined route CEAC; Philippine Defence Ribbon
pdr	pounder
6Pdr	anti-tank gun 57mm (UK)
17Pdr	anti-tank gun 76.2mm (UK)
25Pdr	anti-tank gun 87.6mm (UK)
PDRC	professional recruitment and career development
PDRY	People's Democratic Republic of (South) Yemen
PDS	personnel data summary; programme data sheets; portable dynamic simulator for EW by Antekna; passive detection system (airborne); programming documentation standards
P&DSec	pioneer and demolition section (US)
PDSJ-1	oil drum dropping parachute system (SU)
PDSMS	point defence surface missile system Sea Sparrow
PDSQ	point detonating super quick (fuse)
PDSR	principal director of scientific research
PDST	Pacific daylight saving time
PDT	Picatinny (Arsenal) detonation trap;

	Pacific daylight time; power distribution trailer; practice delivery torpedo by Marconi
PDT-1	Picatinny Arsenal detonation trap No. 1
PDU	pilot's display unit; printing and distributing unit
PDUS	primary data users station (Marex Wefax) by Dornier
PDy	principal duty
PDZC	pathfinder drop zone control
PE	post engineer; production engineer; programme element; point of explosion; pilot error; probable error; permissible error; poly-ethylene; plastic explosive; port of embarkation; practical exercise; personal estate; personal effects; professional examination; post exchange; physical education; physical examination; patrol vessel, Eagle (USN); point expanding (projectile); power equipment; processing elements; Pilkington Electronics (UK)
P&E	planner and estimator; procurement and expedition (US); propellants and explosives (US)
P/E	port of embarkation; price-earnings (index)
Pe-2	light bomber by Petlyakov WW2 (SU)
Pe-8	four-engined transport by Petlyakov
PE-48T	... 47eT, ... 452T fire control radar by LM Erisson
PEA	primary expense account; poly-ethyl acrylate; Portuguese East Africa
PEAB	professional engineers' appointment bureau; Philips Elektroindistrier AB
Peace Crown	Iranian national air defence system
Peacekeeper	wheeled armoured vehicle for USAF by CG
Peacemaker	AU-23A, COIN plane by Cessna
Peace Peck	Atlantic EW modernization by E-Systems
Peace Scepter	Iranian air defence communications system
PEAD	presidential emergency action document
PEAL	Power Engineering Associates Ltd (London)
PEARL	process and equipment automation real-time language
PEAS	production engineering advisory service
PEB	physical evaluation board; performance evaluation board BUPERS
PEBD	pay entry basic date
PEC	principals of equipment collabora-

tion (Nato); production equipment code; production executive committee; photo-electric cell; platform electron cards

PECM passive electronic counter-measures
PECO production equipment control office
PED personnel - equipment data; promotion eligibility date; pulse edge discrimination; probable error deflection
ped pedal; pedestrian
PEDC personal effects distribution centre
Peder Skram class, Danish frigates
PEE proof and experimental establishment (Shoeburyness, Eskmeals UK)
PEEK periodically elevated electronic Kibbitzer
PEEP pilot's electronic eye-level presentation
PEF Palestine exploration fund
PEG poly-ethylene glycol
Pegasus satellites 96ft span micro-meteorites research (US); class, hydrofoils PHM
PEGE programme for evaluation of ground environment
PEHOB probable error height of burst
PEI Prince Edward Islands (Canada)
PELSS precision emitter location strike system
PEM production engineering measure; photographic equipment and materials STANAG
PEMA procurement of equipment and missiles Army; procurement of equipment and munitions appropriations
PEMARS procurement of equipment and missiles Army management and accounting reporting system
Pembroke twin-engined photo aircraft by Hunting Percival
PemYeo Pembroke Yeomanry
PenAids penetration aids
Penelope encryptic procedure (Nato)
PEng registered professional engineer (Canada)
Penguin naval surface-to-surface guided missile (Norway)
PEnO prospective engineer officer
PenRad penetration radar
Pent Pentagon
pent penetration
Pentane project, 460mm active/passive homing torpedo (RN) Mk.30 replacement
PEO programme evaluation office; programme evaluation organization (India); poly-ethylene oxide; prospective engineering officer
People Sniffer E-63, helicopter-borne amonia analyser by GE

PEP producibility engineering and planning; performance effectiveness programme; political and economic planning; programme evaluation procedure (USAF); peak envelope power; (power) point expanding (projectile); propulsion and energetics panel
PEPA mortar round 120mm HE rocket-assisted 6,500m range (FR)
PEPA/LP mortar round 120mm HE rocket-assisted 9,000m range (FR)
PEPG port emergency planning group
PEPP professional engineers in private practice
PEPSU Patiala and East Punjab States Union
PEquA production equipment agency
PER performance evaluation report; probable error range; Professional Executive and Recruitment (agency) (London)
per permission; person
PERA Production Engineering Research Association of GB; planning and engineering for repair and alterations (US)
per an per annum (yearly)
perc percussion
Perdana class, fast patrol boats (Malaysia)
PERDDIMS personnel development and distribution management systems
PerEf personal effects
Peregrine night driving sight by PEL
perf perforated; performance
Perfectos airborne IFF locator and jammer WW2 (RAF)
PERFIS Personal-Führungs und Informations-system Soldaten (personal management and information system - service personnel)
PERG production equipment redistribution group
PerGra permission granted
PERI production equipment redistribution inventory
peri perimeter
Peri-12 Periskop (periscopic sight) --Leopard
perigee closest point of orbit to the earth --apogee
PerIntRep periodic intelligence report
PerIntSum periodic intelligence summary
Peri R-12 Periskop Rundblick (gyro-stabilized panoramic periscope + IR night sight)
Peri-Z-11 Periskop Zielfernrohr (aiming and observation periscope)
Perkasa class, patrol boats missiles + torpedoes by Vosper
Perla class, submarine WW2 (IT)

perm   permanent; permission
PERMACAP   personnel management and accounting card processors
Permasep   inverse osmosis permeators for pure water generation from sea water by DuPont
PERME   propellants, explosives and rocket motor establishment (Westcott UK)
Permit   class, nuclear attack submarines SSN (USN)
PermR   permanent residence
PermRep   permanent representation to the North Atlantic Council
perms   permission
PerNoGra   permission not granted
PERO   president's emergency relief organization
perp   perpendicular
Perry   class, guided missile frigates (USN)
PERS   professional executives recruitment section of the Manpower Services Commission
pers   personnel; persons
PersCen   personnel centre
PersD   personnel department
PerSepComd   personnel and separation command
PersExp   personal expense
Pershing   T-25, tank WW2; MGM-31, tactical ground-to-ground missile by Martin
Persid-4A   battlefield surveillance seismic equipment by Defence Electronics
PersInSD   personnel information systems directorate MilPerCen
PersIR   personnel inventory report
PersO   personnel officer
Perspex   splinter-proof glass
PersProc   personnel processing
PerStatRep   personnel status report
PersTran   personnel transportation
PERT   programme evaluation and review technique; performance evaluation and review technique; programme evaluation research task
pert   pertain(ing)
PERT-CS   programme evaluation and review technique cost system (expanded PERT)
Perth   bomber aircraft by Blackburn
perto   pertaining to
PerUn   permanent and universal (space station)
PES   production engineering specifications; programmer electronic switch; PULHEEMS employment standard (physical capacity, upper limbs, locomotion, hearing, eye-eye, mental capacity, stability)
PESC   public expenditure survey committee

PESD   programme execution sub-directive; programme element summary data
PESR   planning element system report
PET   periodic evaluation test; paper equilibrium tester; penta-ery-thritol; ploy-ethylene-terephthalate
pet   petroleum; petition
Petard mortar   mortar, recoiling, spigot (UK); bomb   demolition bomb
Peter fuse   proximity fuse radar principle (US)
PETN   penta-erythritol-tetra-nitrate Peri-thrite (explosive)
petn   petition
PETP   poly-ethylene-tereph-thalate
Petrel   supersonic anti-submarine missile (USN)
PetRes   petroleum reserves
PetResO   petroleum reserves office(r)
petrl   petroleum
PETS   Pacific electronics trade show (US); posting and enquiring terminal system (computer); prior to expiration of term of service
PETS-1   ... 2, electro-magnetic pulse simulators at AWRE (UK)
PetSec   petroleum section
PetSta   petroleum station
Petya   class, frigates (SU)
Pevicon   thermal imaging tube by EEV
PEWS   platoon level early warning system
PEX   projectable excitation
PF   Pacific Fleet; permanent forces; Police Federation; popular forces (RVNAF); performance factor; practicable factors; procurator fiscal; pilot flying; patrol frigate (RN); patrol escort (USN); position finder; power factor; proximity fuse; protection factor; pneumatic float; phenol-formaldehyde (resin); panchromatic film
pf   pre-flight; proof
PFA   pure food act; pulverized fuel ash
Pathfinder   battlefield surveillance and control vehicle (study) by IBH
PFB   pre-formed beams (sonar)
PFC   private first class; passed flying college; preliminary flight certification; pack feed and converter; phase frequency characteristics; patrol frigate, Canadian
PFCCG   Pacific fleet combat camera group
pfce   performance
PFCO   position field classification officer
PFCS   primary flight control system
PFD   pulse frequency diversity; position

finding device; position fixing
device; power flux density

pfd   preferred

pfdr   pathfinder

PFE   purchaser furnished equipment

PFF   pre-formed fragmentation (warhead);
       pathfinder force (bombers)

PFGM   patrol frigate, guided missiles
       SSM+SAM (Nato)

PFI   post-flight inspection

PFLO   People's Front for the Liberation of
       Oman

PFLOAG People's Front for the Liberation of
       the Occupied Arab Gulf (Oman)

PFLP   People's Front for the Liberation of
       Palestine

PFL-RFL-40 parachute illumination grenade
       rifle-fired by Mecar
       BT for 5.56mm rifles

PFM   pulse frequency modulation; proto-
       flight model; power factor meter;
       Pont Flottant Motorisé by CNIM
       (floating bridge vehicle)

PFMA   peacetime force material assets (US)

PFMPG Pacific fleet mobile photographic
       group

PFMR   peacetime force material requirements
       (US)

PFN   pulse forming network; permanent
       file name

PFNS   position finding navigation system

PFO   postal finance officer

PFP   post-flight processor

PFPC   precision flight path control

PFPC/MEC precision flight path control
       manoeuvre enhanced control

PFR   prototype fast reactor; personal
       financial record

PFRT   preliminary flight rating test
       (Sprint)

PFSS   particles and field sub-satellite

PFSV   pilot to forecaster service

PFT   portable flame thrower; physical
       fitness test

PFTE   poly-fluoro-tetra-ethylene

PFW   pre-determined fragmentation warhead

PF   pay grade; pay group; paying guest;
       prison graduate; permanent grade;
       post graduate; prospective gain;
       preacher, general; procurator,
       general; proving ground; photogram-
       metry; patrol gunboat (USN); power
       gate; pulse generator; project
       group

PG   Portugal

pg   pistol grip; proof gallons

PGA   pressure garment assembly; public
       general acts

PGA-1 hovercraft by Angeveniere

PGB   patrol gunboat (Nato)

PGC   Persian Gulf command; panoramic
       ground camera; per gyro compass

PGCE   post-graduate certificate of educa-
       tion

PGE   primary group equipment

PGG   patrol gunboat, guided missiles

PGH   patrol gunboat, hydrofoil (Nato)

PGHSM precision guided hard structure
       munition (USAF programme)

PgLin page and line

PGM   precision guided munitions (bombs);
       patrol gunboat, motor (USN)

PGM-Systems (precision guided munitions)
       Copperhead production consor-
       tium (Nürnberg) (Martin-
       Marietaa + Diehl + BAe + SNIA
       + HSA + GSG + MSDS)

pgnd   propaganda

PGNoDsr pay grade number designator

PGO-7 optical aiming system for RPG-7 (SU)

PGR   popular growth rate; psycho-galvanic
       reflex

P Gr   petition granted

PGRC   programme guidance and review
       committee

PGS   predicted ground speed

PGA-600 Heloise, helicopter-borne stabili-
       zed optronic platform by SFIM

PGS-5000 air-drop pallet + parachute +
       retro rockets (SU)

PGT   pilot ground trainer; per gross ton

PGU-17 20mm round for airborne guns (US)

PH   Purple Heart (US); plane handler;
       public health; precipitation
       hardening; phosphorous

ph   phase; photographic

PHA   pulse height analyser; public health
       act; public housing administration

Phalanx CIWS, close-in weapon system
       anti-aircraft gun 20mm sub-
       calibre shots

Phantom FH-1, twin-engined naval jet
       fighter by McDD

Phantom II F-4, jet recce, interceptor by
       McDD; target aircraft by
       Flight Refuelling

PHAROS phased array radar operational
       simulation

PhBrz phosphorous bronze

PHD   public health department

PHDC   parachute heavy drop company RAOC

PHE   POL handling equipment (petrol oil
       lubricants)

Phebus communications satellite by AS +
       MBB + ETCA

PHEI   plastic high explosive incendiary
       (shell); penetrating high explo-
       sive incendiary (shell)

PHG   passive homing guidance

phib   amphibious
PhibCB   amphibious construction battalion
PhibCorPac amphibious Corps Pacific fleet
PhibCorps amphibious Corps
PhibDet   amphibious detachment
PhibDetInd amphibious detachment India
PhibEu   amphibious forces Europe
PhibEx   amphibious exercise
PhibFor   amphibious forces
PhibGru   amphibious group
PhibLant amphibious forces Atlantic
PhibMaintSuppU amphibious maintenance
                  support unit
                Lant Atlantic
                Pac   Pacific
PhibNAW   amphibious forces North West
            African Waters
PhibOps   amphibious operations
PhibOpTraU amphibious operations training
              unit
PhibPac   amphibious forces Pacific
PhiBrigLEx amphibious brigade landing
              exercise
PhibRon   amphibious squadron
PhiBsUK   amphibious bases UK
PhibTra   amphibious training
PhibTraBase amphibious training base
PhibTraLant amphibious training command
               Atlantic
PhibTraPac amphibious training command
              Pacific
PhibTrans amphibious transport
PhibWarTraCen amphibious warfare training
                 centre
Phil   Philippine Islands
Philax chaff grenade launching system by
          Philips
PhilCAG Philippine civic action group
PhilCAGV Philippine civic action group
            Viet Nam
PhilI   Philippine Islands
PhilIns Philippine Islands
PhilPUC Philippine Presidential Unit
           Citation Badge
PhilSeaFron Philippine sea frontier
Ph/Jo   photo journalist
PHLS   public health laboratory service
PHM   patrol craft, hydrofoil, missiles
          (Nato)
PHN   public health nursing
PHNY   Pearl Harbour Navy Yard
PHO   port health officer
PHOENIX plasma heating obtained by energetic
           neutral injection experiment
Phoenix AIM-54, air intercept missile long-
           range by Hughes
PhonCon telephone conversation
Phosgene war gas
PhotInt photographic intelligence
Photogrid vertical air photograph grid

photom photometry
PhotR   photographic reconnaissance
PHP   pump horse power; pouds per horse
          power
PHPC   post hostilities planning committee
PhR   photographic reconnaissance
PHS   public health service
PHS-32 advanced medium-range sonar system
          by KAE
PHT   physical therapy technician
PHTC   pulse height-to-time converter
PHTH   Pearl Harbour Territory of Hawaii
PhysEd physical education
PhysExam physical examination
PhysQual physical defects disqualifying
            from military service (US)
PhysTer physical therapy
PI   parachute infantry; Philippine
          Islands; preliminary inquiry;
          public information; programmed
          instruction --CAI; photographic
          interpretation; precision instru-
          ment; position indicator; petrol
          injected; programmer's interface;
          proportional plus integral; point
          initiating (fuse)
Pi   Pistole (pistol) (GE)
PI-3   hollow-charge warhead for DIRA
PIA   primary insurance amount; public
          information adviser MC (Nato);
          Plan d'Intervention Atomique
          atomic strike plan
PIAC   petroleum industry advisory
          committee
PIANC   permanent international association
          of navigation congresses
PIAPDS product improved armour piercing
          discarding sabot (anti-tank shot)
PIAT   projector, infantry, anti-tank WW2
          (UK)
PIB   petroleum information bureau;
          poly-iso-butylene; prices and
          incomes board
PiBal   pilot balloon (observation)
PiBals pilot balloon reports
PIBD   point initiating base detonating
          (shell)
PIBL   PEMA item baseline list (procurement
          of equipment and missiles, Army)
PIC   procurement informations for con-
          tracts; particle in cell; polymer
          impregnated concrete; process
          interface control; pursuant to
          instruction contained in ...;
          Pacific intelligence centre;
          photographic interpretation
          centre; programmed information
          centre; programmed instruction
          centre; purpose identification
          code; public information committee
          MC (Nato)

pic   picture
PICA   procedures for inventory control
        afloat
PICAO   provisional international civil
        aviation organization
        --ICAO
PICCOE programmed initiations, commitments
        obligations and expenditures
PICIC   Pakistan Industrial Credit and
        Investment Corporation
Picket light infantry anti-tank missile by
        IAI
PICLS   Purdue instructional and computa-
        tional learning system
PICME   political intelligence centre
        Middle East (UK)
PICMME provisional inter-governmental
        committee for movement of migrants
        in Europe
PIC-MOD purpose identification code - month
        of detachment
PICS   production information and control
        system
pict   picture
PID   political intelligence department WO
        (UK); political intelligence
        division (US); public information
        division SHAPE; proportional
        integral derivative; pseudo
        interrupt device
PIE   pulmonary infiltration (associated
        with blood) Eosinophilia
PIES   packaged interchangeable electronic
        system
PIF   pilot information file; place in
        inactive file; provision of indus-
        trial facilities; Punjab Irregular
        Force
Piffers Punjab Irregular Frontier Force
Pig   midget submarine (human torpedo)
        WW2 (IT); FV-1611, armoured
        vehicle 4x4 by Humber
Pigeon class, submarine rescue ships (ASR
        USN)
Pig Trough naval anti-air rocket launcher
PIHESH product improved high explosive
        squash head (shell)
PIIN   procurement instrument identification
        number (file)
Pijao   class, Columbian submarines 1975 by
        HDW
PIL   pest infestation laboratory
Pilica class, coastal patrol vessels
        (Poland)
Pillar Box naval anti-aircraft rocket
        launcher
PILO   public information liaison officer
PILOT   piloted low speed test
pilt   pallet (Nato)
PIM   pulse interval modulation; position

and intended movements (Nato);
        position in miles
PIMISS Pennsylvania interagency management
        information support system
PIN-diodes positive-intrinsic-negative
PINAC   permanent international association
        of navigation congresses
Pineapple Mk-2, hand grenade (US)
Pinguin ship-to-ship missile (Norway);
        mine sweeping system by VFW;
        armoured vehicle for arctic
        regions (SU)
PINS   personnel information system
Pinwheel RH-1, one-blade tip-ramjet heli-
        copter by Rotorcraft
PINZ   plastic institute of New Zealand
Pinzgauer cross-country vehicle by Steyr-
        Puch
        710 4x4
        712 6x6
PIO   public information office(r);
        preliminary inquiry officer;
        photographic interpretation
        officer
pion   pioneer
Pioneer light observation plane (Canada)
PIOSA   Pan-Indian ocean science association
PIOU   parallel input/output unit
PIP   pilot integrating pendulum;
        peripheral interchange programme;
        progressive inspection programme;
        product improvement programme
        (for Nato Hawk by Raytheon)
PIPACE peacetime intelligence plan, allied
        central Europe
PIPER   pulsed intense plasma for explora-
        tory research
Piper   L-18 L-21, light aircraft by Piper
Piperack airborne radar jammer WW2 (RAF)
PIPS   pulsed integrating pendulums
PiPz-1 Pionierpanzer 1 by MaK (engineer
        combat vehicle)
PIQSY   probes for the international quiet
        solar year
PIR   pressure ignition rocket; personnel
        information roster; periodic
        intelligence review SACLANT;
        periodic intelligence report;
        Philippine Independence Ribbon
Piranha midget submarine by Vickers;
        amphibious combat vehicle 8x8 or
        6x6 by MOWAG; small sonar by
        Thomson-CSF; naval infra-red
        tracker by SAT
Pirat   armoured personnel carrier by MOWAG
PIRAZ   positive identification and radar
        advisory zone
PiRep   pilot report(s)
PIRMW   patents for inventions relating to
        munitions of war

PIS product improved smoke (shell);
  petroleum intersectional service

Pistol No. 710 photo-electric proximity
  fuse

PITAC Pakistan industrial technical assistance centre

PIU photographic intelligence unit

PIV production inspection verification

PIW pensions increase warrant

pix pictures

Pixels picture elements

PJ procurement justification; photo
  journalist; probate judge; police
  justice; presiding judge

PJBD permanent joint board on defense
  (US-Canada)

PJI parachute jumping instructor

PJOP Pioneer-Jupiter orbiter probe (Nasa
  programme)

pk pack

pkg package

PK Pakistan; Pelemet Kalashnikov
  (machine gun 7.62mm) (SU)

PK-300 portable night viewer by PK

PK-1250 portable night viewer by PK with
  monitor

PK-1255 underwater viewer by PK

PKB vehicle-mounted machine gun 7.62mm
  (SU)

PkHow pack howitzer

PKM dual-purpose machine gun 7.62mm
  Kalashnikov (SU)

PKMS machine gun 7.62mm (SU)

PKP Light Water, purple K powder (smoke)

PKS general purpose machine gun 7.62mm
  (SU)

pkt packet; pocket

PKT general purpose machine gun 7.62mm
  (SU)

PKw Personenkraftwagen (car, jeep)

PL plain language; packing list; post
  laundry; paymaster lieutenant;
  prospective loss; public law;
  pipe line; Plimsoll line; position
  line; phase line; positioning land
  (station, radio); power lokt
  (projectile); patrol land (aircraft); programming language

pl platoon; place; plane; plate; plain

P&L profit and loss

P/L pipe line

PL/1 programme language No. 1 (nearly
  English)

PL-41 naval navigation system by Litef

PLA Port of London Authority; People's
  Liberation Army (China); Palestine
  Liberation Army; practice landing
  approach; production loss appraisal

PLAA positive low angle of attack

PLACE programming language for automatic
  check-out equipment

PLADS parachute low altitude delivery
  system

PLAKO-Verfahren Plexiglas Anlagen Konstruk-
  tionsverfahren (Modell-
  bau) (plexi-glass design
  modelling)

PLAN programme language nineteen hundred

PLANAT North Atlantic treaty regional
  planning group (London) and the
  North Atlantic regional planning
  sub-group (Paris)

PlanNet planning network

PLAT pilot landing aid television
  (system)

plat platoon

PLATO programmed logic for automatic
  teaching operation (for pilot
  instruction by Control Data)

PLAT/VLA pilot landing aid television/
  visual landing aid

PLB personal locator beacon

PLC platoon leaders class (US)

plcy policy

PLD procurement legal division;
  probable line of deployment

pld payload

PLE prudent limit of endurance

Plejad class, fast patrol boats (Sweden)

PLF precise local fix

PLHP power lokt hollow point (projectile)

PLI pre-load indicator

plk plank

PLK Princess Louise's South Kensington
  Regt

PLL prescribed load list; peripheral
  light loss; phase locked loop
  (synthesizer)

PLL Lanze, Panzerfaust, leicht,
  leistungsgesteigert by DNAG
  (anti-tank charge, light, product
  improved)

PlLdr platoon leader

PLM power line modulation; pulse length
  modulation; production line maintenance

Pl-N place name

plng planning

PLO Palestine Liberation Organization;
  passenger liaison officer;
  personal liaison officer; Pacific
  launch operations (Nasa)

PLOBS pilot's log observation

PLOCSA personal liaison officer chief of
  staff Army (US)

PLOM prescribed loan optimization model
  (US)

PLOP pressure line of position;
  planetary landing observation
  package

Plotaid data terminal for smaller ships
  compatible with SENIT + NTDS by ECA

PLP	prudent limit of patrol
PlPatr	Platzpatrone (blank cartridge)
PLPN	training round 105mm (FR)
PLR	parachute logistic regiment; programme life requirement; Philippine Liberation Ribbon
PLS	potential leaders' school
PLRACTA	position location reporting and control tactical aircraft
PLRS	position location reporting system by Hughes
PLS	pre-launch survivability
pls	please; plates
PlSgt	platoon sergeant
PLSS	precision location strike system (USAF) by Lockheed; personal life support system (Nasa); portable life support system
plst	plastic
PLT	procurement lead time; production lead time
plt	pallet; platoon; pilot
PLT	pipe line time; post loading test
PlT	pilot training
PLU	platoon leaders unit; Pierburg Luftfahrtgeräte Union, Neuss (GE)
PLUCON	plutonium decontamination (team); plutonium contamination (emergency team)
PLUM	payload launch module
Plume	pipe line under mother earth WW2
PLUS	programmed learning under supervision; potential long-term supply utilization screening (Nato); plus reinforced (equipment)
Pluto	pipe line under the ocean WW2
PLUTO	parts listing and used on techniques
Pluto	low-altitude surveillance radar by Selenia
Pluton	land-based tactical nuclear missile by AS
PLW	production lost by waiting
PlyInst	application for instructions
PlymChan	Plymouth Channel sub-area (Nato)
PlyPassport	application for passport
PLZC	pathfinder landing zone control
PM	prime minister; pipe major; police medal; polar medal; pay master; post master; provost marshal; project manager; post meridiem (after noon); post mortem (after death); practice message; police magistrate; Pacific mail; phase modulation; pulse modulation; positioning mobile (radio station); preventive maintenance; procurement and material (US); parachute mine; permanent magnet; photo-multiplier; mechanical mine-layer (SU); automatic pistol 9mm Makarov (SU)

PM-12	pistol 9mm parabellum by Beretta
PM-60	plastic anti-tank mine (GDR)
PMA	Pacific Maritime Association; permanent mailing address; personal money allowance; project military adviser; poly-methyl-acrylate
PMap	photo map
P-MARP	peacetime manpower allocation requirements plan (US)
PMC	programme management control; physical medicine centre; president of the mess committee (UK); Plainfield Machine Company
PMCL	peacetime material consumption and losses
PMCR	Poste Mobile de Contrôle Radar (target director post)
PMCT	permissive (action link) management control team
PMD	projected map display; programme module dictionary
PMDA	pyro-mellitic di-anhydride
PMDD	personnel management development directorate
PMDL	post M-day deployment list
PMD	phosphorescence microwave double resonance
PME	planmässige (programmierte) Material-erhaltung (planned (programmed) material maintenance)
PMEL	precision measurement equipment laboratory (USAFE)
PMF	professional medical film; personnel master file
PMG	provost marshal general; pay master general; postmaster general
PMGS	predictable model guidance scheme
PMH	(production) per man hour; past medical history
PMI	preventive maintenance inspection
PMIP	post-maintenance inspection pilot
PMIS	patient medical information system
PmK	Phosphorpatrone mit Stahlkern (armour-piercing, incendiary (projectile)
PML	prime minister's list; production music library
PMLO	principal military landing officer (UK); Philippine military liaison officer
PMM	planar motion mechanism (submarine); pulse mode multiplex; Princess Mary Medal (Royal Signals)
PMMA	poly-methyl-methacrylate(acrylic)
PMMS	planar motion mechanism system (submarine simulator) --DTMB --DTNSRDL
PMN	anti-personnel mine (SU)

PMO   Princess Mary's Own The 10th Gurkha
          Rifles Regiment; principal medical
          officer; project management office;
          provost marshal's office; Polaris
          material office; Polaris missile
          office
PMOFF   Presidential Medal of Freedom
PMOGAR   Princess Mary's Own Glasgow and
          Ayrshire Regiment (Royal Highland
          Fusiliers)
PMOGR   Princess Mary's Own Gurkha Rifles
PMOLant   Polaris material office Atlantic
PMOPac   Polaris material office Pacific
PMOS   primary military occupational
          speciality
PMOSC   primary military occupational
          speciality code
PMP   project master plan; programme
          management plan; pressure measure-
          ment package; bridging equipment
          pontoons (SU)
PMR   Pacific missile range; proton
          magnetic resonance; mechanical mine
          layer (SU); permanent military rep-
          resentative
PM&R   physical medicine and rehabilitation
pmr   paymaster
pmrinC   paymaster in chief
PMRAFNS   Princess Mary's RAF Nursing Service
PMRM   periodic maintenance requirements
          manual
PMRMO   protectable mobilization reserve
          material objective
PMS   professor of military science;
          preventive maintenance school;
          provost marshal school; planned
          maintenance system; programme
          management support; projection map
          system; project management system;
          public message service; portable
          monitoring set; pontoon equipment
          (SU)
PMS-26   ... 27, hull-mounted active/passive
          sonar by Plessey
PMS-32   hull-mounted active/passive sonar
          for escort vessels by Plessey
PMS-35   hull-mounted active/passive sonar
          for larger ships by Plessey
PMSE   programme management simulation
          exercise
PMSgt   paymaster sergeant
PMS&T   professor of military science and
          tactics
PMT   parachute medical team
pmt   payment
PMTC   Pacific missile test centre (Point
          Mugu)
PMTraDe   project manager for training devices
PMTS   pre-determined motion time system
PMVI   periodic motor vehicle inspection

PMvr   prime mover
PMW   photo mapping wing (USAF)
PMX   private manual exchange (telephone)
PN   Pakistan Navy; please note; part
          number; positive negative
PNA   para-nitro -aniline; passed but not
          advanced; purchase notice agree-
          ments
PND   pictorial navigation display
PNdB   perceived noise decibels
pndg   pending
PNEC   primary navy enlisted classification
pneu   pneumatic
PNF   pilot, not flying
PNG   persona non grata
PNI   pictorial navigation indicator
PNIO   priority national intelligence
          objectives
PNL   perceived noise level; prescribed
          nuclear load
pnl   panel
PNMO   provided no military objection
          (exists)
PNNCF   Pacific northern naval coastal
          frontier
PNOK   primary next of kin
PNP   precision navigation processor;
          positive-negative-positive (tran-
          sistor); People's National Party
          (Jamaica)
PNR   preliminary negotiation reports;
          prior notice required
pnr   pioneer
PNS   Portsmouth naval shipyard (US);
          prescribed nuclear stockage
PNSO   principal naval store officer
PNS&T   professor of naval science and
          tactics
pnt   patient
PntCens   patient census (report)
PNTO   principal naval transport officer
PNUAR   pull nose up at ramp
PNUB   permanent naval uniform board
PNVAL   previously not available
PNVD   passive night vision device
PNVS   pilot night vision system
PO   pilot officer (RAF); petty officers
          (RN-USN); port officer; plotting
          officer; press officer; planning
          officer; Province of Ontario
          (Canada); post office; patent
          office; Portugal (Nato); postal
          order; previous orders; planning
          objective; programme objective;
          project order; purchase order;
          production offset; power operated
P&O   Peninsular & Oriental Steam Naviga-
          tion Company Ltd; plans and
          operations
PO-1   petty officer class 1 (USN)
          ...2; ...3

PO-1 ...11, ...111 hand grenade by
       Plasticas Oramile (Spain)
PO-2   light bi-plane Polikarpov (SU)
PO-300 automatic optical landing system TV
       by Saab Scania
POA   public order act; probation of
       offenders act; plotting officer's
       assistant; Pacific Ocean area;
       psychological operation approach;
       position of advantage; police
       officers' association; prison
       officers' association; purchasing
       officers' association
POACS prior other active commissioned
       service
POAES prior other active enlisted service
POAHedPearl Pacific Ocean area headquarters
       Pearl Harbour
POAN   procurement of ordnance and ammuni-
       tion Navy
POAR   project order action report
POATSC Pacific Ocean air terminal service
       command
POB   permanent order book; place of birth;
       persons on board; post office book;
       post office box
POC   post office corps; point of contact;
       privately owned conveyance; port of
       call; process operator's console
Pocketscope hand-held image intensifier by
       Pilkington
POCU   Puma operational conversion unit
       (RAF)
POD   port of debarkation; post office
       department; plan of the day; pay on
       delivery
PODREP Soviet Bloc submarine reporting
       system
POE   port of embarkation
POED   post office engineering department;
       provincial officer of establish-
       ment division
POERS post office engineering research
       station (Dollis Hill London)
POG   port operating group; petty officer's
       guide
POGO   polar orbiting geophysical observa-
       tory (Nasa); programmer oriented
       graphics operation
POI   programme of instruction; principal
       operational interest
POINTER partial orientation interferometer
PoinTerm appointment terminated
PointMail letter appointed in mail
POL   port of loading; petrol oils lubri-
       cants; patent office library;
       programme oriented language;
       Pacific oceanographic laboratory
pol   police; polar(ized); polished
PolAd political advisor

PolAng polarization angle
Polaris UGM-27, submarine-launched ballis-
       tic missile (nuclear) by Lockheed
POLDam POL installations damage report
       (Nato)
POLIC POL intersectional command
POLIS POL intersectional service
polit political
Pollux navigation and fire control radar
       by Thomson-CSF
Polnocny class, landing ships, tanks
       (Poland)
POLO   Pacific (command) operations liaison
       office
POLP   popular organization for the libera-
       tion of Palestine
PolWar political warfare
POM   priority of movements; preparation
       for overseas movement (units);
       programme objective memorandum;
       poly-oxy-methylene; offensive
       hand-grenade by Plasticas Oramile
POMA   petty officers' military academy
       (US)
POMAR positive operational meteorological
       aircraft report
POMCUS prepositioning of material config-
       ured to unit sets
POME   principal ordnance mechanical
       engineer
POMF   Polaris missile facility
       Lant Atlantic
       Pac   Pacific
POMM   preliminary operating and mainten-
       ance manual
POMO   production oriented maintenance
       organization (USAF)
pom pom quick-firing gun
POMR   problem oriented medical record
POMS   panel on operational meteorological
       satellites
POMSEE performance, operating and mainten-
       ance standards for electronic
       equipment
POMZ-2 anti-personnel mine (SU)
pon   pontoon
PonBn pontoon battalion
PONSE personnel of the naval shore estab-
       lishment (report) (USN)
POO   post office order; priority opera-
       tional objective
POOD   permanent officer of the day;
       permanent officer of the deck (US)
POOF   peripheral on-line oriented function
       (computer)
POP   printing-out paper, point of pur-
       chase; perpendicular ocean
       platform; plaster of Paris;
       practical ordered programme
pop   population; popular

POPGUN   policy and procedure governing the
          use of nicknames (US)
POQ   provided otherwise qualified (US)
por   porous; porosity
POR   preparation for overseas replacement;
          personnel occurrence report; pay on
          receipt; pay on return
PORCO   port control office
PORIS   post office radio interference
          station
port   portable
Port   Portugal; Portuguese
              Chi   Portuguese China (Macao)
              Ind   Portuguese India (Goa)
              Tim   Portuguese Timor
Porta Phone   UHF radio set by Harris
Portee   gun mounted on lorry (UK)
Porter   STOL aircraft by Pilatus/Fairchild
Porthus   helicopter-borne IR viewing and
          aiming system by SFIM
Port Said   machine pistol 9mm licensed
              Carl Gustav for Egypt
POS   petty officer stoker; preferred over-
          seas shore (duty); period of
          service; Port of Spain (Trinidad);
          period of sale; partially ordered
          set
pos   positive; position
POSA   payment outstanding suspense accounts
POSARE   offensive hand grenades by Plasticas
          Oramile
POSB   post office savings bank
POSD   personnel on station date; post
          office savings department
Poseidon UGM-73, submarine-based inter-
              continental missile by Lockheed
POSH   port-side out/starboard home
          Britain-India cooler cabin reser-
          vation
posit   position
posn   position
POSS   passive optical surveillance system;
          passive optical satellite surveil-
          lance
POST   passive optical seeker technique for
          Stinger
POSTER   post-strike emergency reporting
POT   propeller order transmitter
pot   potential
Potato Digger   automatic machine gun 1895 by
              Colt
POTel   petty officer telegraphist
POTF   polychromatic optical thickness
          fringes
Poti   class, corvettes (SU)
POut   power output
POV   privately owned vehicle
POW   prisoner of war; please oblige with;
          petty officer of the watch;
          The Prince of Wales

pow   powder
POWBC   prisoner of war branch camp
POWC   prisoner of war camp; prisoner of
          war censorship (US); prisoner of
          war compound
POWCP   prisoner of war collecting post
POWPR   prisoner of war personnel record
POWPS   prisoner of war processing station
POWS   pyrotechnic outside warning system
POWU   post office work unit
Pozit fuze   proximity fuse (radar principle)
              (US)
PP   permanent party; physical profile;
          petroleum point; public prosecu-
          tor; promotion pamphlet; post
          paid; pedic perspiration; parcel
          post; preparation phase; permanent
          pass; pressure pattern; pilotless
          plane; proportional part; present
          position; push pull; power point
          (projectile); power plant; peak-
          to-peak; parallel processor;
          peripheral processor; plane
          parallel; poly-propylene;
          Polizeipistole (pistol) 7.65mm by
          Walther
P&P   packaging and preservation; plans
          and policies; procurement and
          production; plans and programmes;
          postage and packing; payments and
          progress (committee)
P/P   point-to-point
PP-64   folding pontoon bridge (Poland)
PPA   Provincial Police Award (certifi-
          cate) (UK); parallel processing
          automaton; photo peak analysis;
          poly-phosporic acid
PPAA   Personal Protection Armor Associa-
          tion (US)
PPAS   pre-planned air support
PPB   programmes, planning and budgeting;
          parts per billion; provisioning
          parts breakdown; private posting
          box
PPBAS   planning programming budgeting
          accounting system
PPBS   planning programming and budgeting
          system
PPC   petroleum planning committee (Nato);
          pistol practice course; partial
          pay card; peace promotion code;
          patrol plane commander
PP&C   production planning and control
PPCLI   Princess Patricia's Canadian Light
          Infantry
P&PCtte   payments and progress committee
PPD   project planning directive; pulse
          phase detector; proficiency pay
          designator
ppd   postage paid

PPDA	poor prisoners' defence act	PPRM	population protection and resources management
PPDC	programming panels and decoding circuits	PPS	pre-positioned stocks; principal private secretary; parliamentary private secretary; projected planning system; plant protection system; pulses per second; submachine gun (SU)
PPE	protected point expanding (projectile); pre-production evaluation; philosophy, politics and economics; Pilkington PE Ltd (St Asaph, Clwyd UK)		
PPF	provision of production facilities	PPS-4	portable radar, search, battlefield surveillance radar
PPFRT	prototype preliminary flight rating test	PPS-5	medium battlefield surveillance radar AIL
PPG	personnel processing group; planning and programming guidance; PEMA policy and guidance	PPS-6	medium battlefield surveillance radar for USMC by RCA
		PPS-9	medium battlefield surveillance Infantry radar by RCA
PPGM	planning and programming guidance memorandum	PPS-10	Infantry radar by GD
PPH	petroleum pipehead	PPS-11	Infantry radar by RCA
pph	pamphlet	PPS-12	Infantry radar by RCA
pphm	parts per hundred parts of mix	PPS-15	Infantry radar by GD
PPI	plan position indicator (radar); policy proof of interest	PPS-17	battlefield surveillance radar + IFF by GIC
PPK	Polizeipistole, Kurz 7.65mm (pistol by Walther)	PPS-18	battlefield surveillance radar by RCA
PPL	preferential planning list; private pilot licence	PPS/AutoNet	automatic network
ppl	pipeline	PPSC	physical profile serial code
PPL-64	anti-tank shot 105mm tungsten penetrator APFSDS (UK)	ppsd	proposed
		PPSh	submachine gun (SU)
PPLA	practice precautionary landing approach	PPSIA	pamphlet 'personnel property shipping information' is applicable (US)
PPM	pulse position modulation; phase pulse modulation; parts per million; position and pay management	PPSMEC	procurement, precedence of supplies material and equipment committee
		PPSR	periodic personnel strength report
PPMR	pre-planned mission request	PPT	pre-production test
PPN	procurement programme number	ppt	precipitation
PP&NA	private plants and naval activities	pptd	precipitated
Ppndg	petition pending	pptg	precipitating
PPNS	pre-planned nuclear support	pptn	precipitation
ppnt	proponent	PPU	peace pledge union
PPO	projected programme objective; precedence partition and out-degree; power projection overseas; publications and printing office	P&PW	publicity and psychological warfare
		PPWR	pre-positioned war reserves
		PPWRR	pre-positioned war reserves requirement
PPP	pesos for progress plan (Philippines); packaged petroleum product	PPWRS	pre-positioned war reserves stocks
		PQ	previous question; physically qualified; Province of Quebec (Canada)
PPPC	petroleum pool Pacific coast		
PPPI	precision plan position indicator; projection plan position indicator	PQEP	product quality evaluation plan
		PQM	post quartermaster (USMC))
PPPP-RC	promptly prepared professional and polite - reference and check (journalism)	PQM-102	target drone by Sperry
		PQMDO	proposed quality material development objective
PPQA	pageable partition queue area	PQQPRI	provisional qualitative and quantitative personnel requirements information
PPR	proprietary procurement request; precedence partition and random (assignment); permanent pay record; prior permission required; printed paper rate		
		PQR	personnel qualification roster (US)
		PQS	progressive qualification scheme; promotion qualification score
ppr	proper		
PPRept	periodic personnel report	PR	parachute rigger; The Parachute

PR   Regiment; proportional representa-
          tion; photographic reconnaissance;
          public relation; purchase request;
          procurement regulations; procure-
          ment request; plotting and radar;
          prepare reply; payroll; press
          release; priority regulations;
          Puerto Rico; ply rating (tyres);
          patrol (boat) river; river gunboat;
          postal regulations; press representa-
          tive
P/R   payroll
pr   present; price; print; proper;
          proved; preferred (stock)
Pr   Prince; protestant; province
PR I ... II processing and reporting course
          phase 1
Pr-Patrone Phosphorpatrone, incendiary pro-
          jectile
PR-14   mortar shell 120mm (FR)
PR-72S   fast attack craft, guided missiles
          SFCN
PR-500BC combined airborne tank + bomb rack
          by IMI
PRA   President of the Royal Academy;
          paymaster rear admiral; The Para-
          chute Regiment Association;
          projected requisition authority;
          pay readjustment act; pay record
          access; personnel research
          activity; permanently restricted
          area (USSR); precision radar
          altimeter; paint research associa-
          tion (UK)
PrA   programmierte Ausbildung
          (programmed instruction)
pract   practice
Praerie   miniature RPV for target illumina-
          tion by Philco Ford
Prairie   propulsor air emission (naval
          propeller)
PRAP   provisions of following reference
          apply
PRARS   pitch, roll, azimuth reference
          system
PRASD   personnel research activity (San
          Diego Cal.)
Pravda   class, patrol submarines (SU)
PRB   psychological research branch;
          personnel records branch;
          planned requirements bureau;
          pay review body (UK); ammunition
          manufacturer (Brussels)
PRB-8/7   defensive/offensive hand grenade by
          PRB
PRB-403   illumination trip flare by PRB
PRB-404   rifle-fired fragmentation grenade
          by PRB
PRB-406   illumination rifle grenade by PRB
PRB-408   protected anti-tank mine by PRB

PRB-410   trip-wire anti-personnel mine by
          PRB
PRB-412   rifle-fire smoke grenade by PRB
PRB-413   fragmentation mine by PRB
PRB-416   demolition charge by PRB
PRB-422   high-explosive hand grenade by PRB
PRB-423   hand grenade by PRB
          PHD   practice version
PRB-424   disposable grenade launcher (7
          rounds) by PRB
PRB-426   grenade launcher by PRB
PRB-434   rifle-fired anti-personnel
          grenade by PRB
PRB-446   offensive hand grenade by PRB
PRB-Smoke smoke hand grenade by PRB
PRBS   pseudo-random binary sequence
PRC   People's Republic of China; price
          regulation committee (US);
          Planning Research Corporation
          (US); passenger reservation
          centre; Polish Resettlement Corps
          (RAF); personnel reporting code;
          planned requirements conversion;
          production readjustment committee
          WPB; portable radio, communication
PRC-74   portable radio, communication by
          Hughes
PRC-77   portable radio, communication VHF
          manpack
PRC-99   portable radio, communication VHF
          transceiver by Liberty Inter-
          national
PRC-104   portable radio, communication
          HF 280,000 channels by Hughes
PRC-105   portable radio, communication
          two man portable 100 Watts
PRC-349, 350, 351, 352, by Racal
PRC-353   vehicle-borne by Racal
PRC-390   HF SSB manpack by Plessey
PRC-515   HF manpack by Rockwell
PRC-2077 HF manpack by Tadiran
prchst   parachutist
prcht   parachute
PRCM   passive radiation counter-measures
PR/COM   partially completed (vessel status)
PRD   personnel readiness date; personnel
          records division; personnel
          research division; postal regula-
          tory detachment; public relations
          division
prd   period
P&RD   promotion and retirement division
prec   precision; precedence
precip   precipitation
Preclair mortar flare 120mm (FR)
PRECOM   preliminary communications search
          precommissioning
          Det   detail
          Scol school
pred   predict

pref   preference
prefab   prefabricated
PreFlt   preflight
PreFltScol   preflight school
prelim   preliminary
PreMarFrench   maritime prefect
             I   1st region Cherbourg
             II   2nd region Brest
             III   3rd region Toulon
PreMedU   preventive medicine unit
prep   preparation; preparatory
PrePoStor   pre-positioned storage
PrepScol   preparatory school
pres   president; present; pressure
PresAir   air compressors
PresProc   presidential proclamation
PRESS   Pacific Range electro-magnetic
      signature studies
PRESTO   programme reporting and evaluation
      system for total operation
PreTechRep   preliminary technical report
prev   preventive; previous
PrevMedDiv   preventive medicine division
PrevMedU   preventive medicine unit
PRF   personnel readiness file; pulse
      repetition frequency; pulse
      recurrence frequency; position,
      radar, fixed
PRFD   pulse recurrence frequency discrimi-
      nation
PRFS   pulse recurrence frequency stagger
prgs   prognosis
PRH   petrol railhead
PRI   preliminary rifle instruction;
      public recreation institute
      (Naafi); public relations institute
      of Ireland; president of the regi-
      mental institutes (UK); pulse
      repetition interval; pulse recur-
      rence interval; photographic
      reconnaissance and interpretation
      STANAG; production rate index;
      projection read-out indicator;
      projected reticle image (sights)
pri   priority; prison
PriBag   priority baggage
PriBil   priority billet
PRIDE   personal responsibility in daily
      effort
Priest   M-7, SP howitzer 105mm
prim   primary; primitive
PRIMAR   program to improve management of
      army resources (US)
PRIME   precision recovery including
      manoeuvring re-entry
Prime   priority management effort
Primorye   class, spy ships 4000 tons (SU)
Primus-40   airborne weather radar by RCA
prin   principal(ity)
PRINCE   parts reliability information center
      (Nasa)

Princess   flying boat by Saunders Roe
print   printing and stationery
PriNOB/NEC   primary navy officer billet and
      navy enlisted classification
      (code) (USN)
PRIOR   programme for in-orbit rendezvous
PRIS   personnel record information system
pris   prisoner
PRISE   program for integrated shipboard
      electronics (USN)
PRISIC   photographic reconnaissance inter-
      pretation section, intelligence
      center (US)
PRISM   programmed integrated systems
      management; programme reliability
      information system for managementt
prism   prismatic
PriTra   primary training
Privateer   PB-4Y2, naval aircraft
PrivAuth   travel with private vehicle
      authorized
PrivProp   private property
prkg   parking
PRL   publications requirements list;
      print lister
prly   partly
PRM   pressure remnant magnetization;
      position, radar, mobile
prm   premium
PRM-4041   Plessey radio manpack
      light-weight HF transceivers by
      Plessey
PRM-5041   light-weight HF transceivers by
      Racal
PRNC   Potomac River naval command
PRO   pilot radio operator; public rela-
      tions officer; personnel relations
      officer; pay and records office
      (UK); public records office (UK);
      planned requirements outfitting
PrO   press officer
pro   provost; profession; procedure;
      prophylactic; proficiency
prob   problem; probable; probability
ProB   Projektbeauftragter (project manager)
PR&OBB   procurement, research and operations
      budget branch BUPERS
ProbCost   probable costs; probabilistic
      budgeting and forward costing
      (US)
Probeye   hand-held infra-red viewer by
      Hughes
ProbOff   probation officer
probout   proceed on or about (US)
PROC   proposed required operational
      capability
proc   process; procure(ment); proceedings
PROCAER SrL   Progetti Construzioni Aero-
      nautiche (Milan IT)
prod   product(ion); producer

ProdAC   production advisers consortium
PROD-EL   Prodotti Elettronici SpA (IT)
ProDutAs   proceed on duty assigned
prof   professor; profession; proficiency
ProFAGTrans   proceed by first available
    government transportation
PROF-E   programmed review of operator
    functions - elementary
Profilair-70   inflatable tent by Angeviniere
PROFIT   programme for financed insurance
    techniques
ProfP   proficiency pay (US)
PROG   programmes division SHAPE
prog   progress; programme; prognosis;
    progressive
ProgaV-35   armoured anti-aircraft truck
    (Czech)
prop   propeller
ProImRep   proceed immediately and report
proj   projectile; project; projector
Project-7511   Stingray, airborne light-
    weight torpedo by MSDS
ProjMgr   project manager
    ASWS   anti-submarine warfare
        systems
    SMS   surface missile systems
ProjTrns   project transition
PROM   programmable read-only memory
prom   promotion
PROMAP   program for the refinement of the
    material acquisition process (US)
PROMIS   project management information
    system
PROMPT   project reporting, organization and
    management planning technique;
    production reviewing organizing
    and monitoring of performance
    technique
PromStat   promotion status
PRON   procurement request order number (US)
PROP   planetary rocket ocean platform;
    profit rating of projects
prop   propeller; property
ProPay   proficiency pay
propl   proportional
propn   proportion
propul   propulsion
ProRep   proceed and report
PRORM   pay and records office Royal Marines
pros   prospective
ProsAtty   prosecuting attorney
ProSig   procedure signal
ProSign   procedure signal
PROSPER   profit simulation planning and
    evaluation of risk
ProSPro   process systems programme
prot   protection
Protean   ECM equipment by MEL
Proteus   UYS-1, acoustic processor by IBM
ProTimeRep   proceed in time to report

PROUS   proceed to continental US port
prov   provide; provision; provisional
Prov   provost; province
ProvGr   proving ground
Provider   C-123, twin-engine transport by
    Fairchild
ProvMain   other provisions to basic orders
    remain in effect (US)
Provo   members of the provisional IRA
PROVOST   priority research and development
    objectives for Viet Nam opera-
    tions support
Provost   jet aircraft (UK)
ProWDelRep   proceed without delay and report
Prowler   EA-6, ElInt aircraft by Grumman;
    ICR, infantry company radar by
    Marconi
ProWord   procedure word (US)
prox   proximity (fuse)
PRP   petrol refilling point; program
    review panel (US); people's revo-
    lutionary party; personnel
    requirements plan; progressive
    rework plan; public relations
    personnel; personnel requirements
    programme; pulse repetition period
PRPA   rocket-assisted mortar shell 120mm
    HE (FR)
PRPC   public relations policy committee
PRR   pulse repetition rate; The Puerto
    Rico Regiment
PRS   photographic reconnaissance
    squadron (RAF)
PRS-3   passive ranging sonar by KAE
PRS-7   portable mine detector by Fourdee
PRSA   public relations society of America
PRSB   progress, reports and statistics
    branch
prsd   pressed
prsd met   pressed metal
PRSec   payroll section
PrST   Prairie standard time (US)
prsvn   preservation
PRT   personnel research test; personnel
    reaction time; power recovery
    turbine; pulse repetition time;
    personnel rapid transit; platinum
    resistance thermometer; primary
    ranging test; programme reference
    table
P&RT   physical and recreational training
PRT-402   missile transponder by Marconi
prtg   printing
PRTI   physical and recreational training
    instructor
PRTR   plutonium recycling test reactor
PRTS   pseudo-random ternary sequence
PRU   photographic reconnaissance unit;
    pay research unit (UK Civil
    Service)

PRUDR   province reserve Ulster defence
         regiment
PRV   pressure reducing valve; Peugeot-
         Renault-Volvo (engine manufactu-
         rers' consortium)
PRVT   production reliability verification
         testing
PS   Pacific Star; police sergeant;
         provost sergeant; pistol sharp-
         shooter (US); parliamentary secre-
         tary; press secretary; passed
         school (of instruction); privy
         seal; permanent staff; pioneer
         school; personal service; parade
         state; penal servitude; personnel
         sub-system; prior service; project
         stock; Philippine Scouts (US Army);
         programme summary; Puget Sound
         (Washington); patrol sea (air-
         craft); programme stores; passenger
         steamer; pull switch; phasing
         system; problem specification;
         programming system; pumping
         station; Pferdestärke (horse power)
P/S   power section
ps   per second
3-PS   perimeter protection system by
         Plessey
3Ps   Plessey perimeter protection
         (system)
PS-1   patrol flying boat by Shin Meiwa
PS-11   Tornado, MRCA by Panavia
PS-7p/R Giraffe, surveillance radar by
         LM Ericsson
PSA   property services agency (UK); post-
         shakedown availability; passed
         staff college (RAF); phase-steered
         array (radar); parametric semi-
         conductors amplifiers; prefix
         storage area; provisional site
         acceptance
PSAC   the president's scientific advisory
         committee
PSALI   permanent supplementary artificial
         lighting installation
PSandT   pay, subsistence and transportation
PSAR   phase-steered array radar; prelimi-
         nary safety analysis report
PSB   public safety branch; performance
         separations branch; personal
         services branch; procurement
         security branch; publications
         support branch; Pacific science
         board; pistol, small bore
psbl   possible
PSC   per standard compass; Pacific science
         committee; Pacific science council;
         power supply circuits; programme
         sequence control; plastic surgery
         centre (Queen Victoria Hospital

East Grinstead); principal subordinate command (Nato); personnel
service company (US); public
services commission (UK); passed
graduation staff course; passed
staff college
PSC-2001 language encryption set by Siemens
PSCD   patrol service central depot
PSCLA   petroleum supply committee for Latin
         America
PSCO   personnel survey control officer

PSD   physical sciences division ONR;
         power spectral density; pulse
         shape discrimination; personnel
         service division; professional
         service dates; preferred sea duty;
         pay supply depot
PSDE   post-strike damage estimation
PSDetn   particle size determination
PSDistn particle size distribution
PSDP   programmable signal data processor
         (airborne) by Sperry
PSDS   permanently separated from duty
         station
PSE   personnel subsystem elements;
         priority standardization efforts;
         prevention of stripping equipment
         (Nato)
PSect   phototype section
PS&ER   production support and equipment
         replacement
PSET   permanent service on earth tides
PSF   Panama sea frontier; Philippine sea
         frontier; pounds per square foot
PSG   phopho-silicate glass; pre-set
         guidance; platoon sergeant
psg   passage
PSG-2   digital message device for FOO by
         Magnavox
PSGI   permanent service for geo-magnetic
         indices
psgr   passenger
PSgt   platoon sergeant
PSH   pre-select heading
PSHFA   public servants' housing and finance
         association
PSI   pounds per square inch; plan speed
         indicator; present serviceability
         index; permanent staff instructor;
         programmed student input; presi-
         dent of the service institute;
         public services international;
         personnel security investigations
P&SI   pay and supply instructions
psia   pounds per square inch absolute
psig   pounds per square inch gauge
PSK   phase shift keying
PSK/PCM phase shift keying/pulse code
         modulation

PSK   Philipp Scherer GmbH Koblenz (GE)
PSL   programme specification language;
      paymaster sub-lieutenant
PSL-003 inflatable hovercraft by Michel
      Peissel
PSM   platoon sergeant major; provost
      sergeant major; personnel sub-
      systems manager; partial storage
      monitoring; passed Royal Military
      School of Music; parallel slit map
PS&M   personnel supervision and management
      SELP
PSMLG   public services microfilm liaison
      group (UK)
PSMR   part specification for maintenance
      and reliability
PSMSL   permanent service for mean sea level
PSN   public switched network; package
      sequence number
psn   position
PSN-6   portable position locating system
      by Litton
PSNCF   Pacific southern naval coastal
      frontier
PSNCO   personnel staff non-commissioned
      officer
PSNS   programmable sampling network
      switching; Puget Sound naval Ship-
      yard (Bremerton Washington)
PSO   public safety officer; principal
      scientific officer (RNSS);
      political survey officer;
      personnel selection officer;
      primary standardization office;
      performance and structure oriented
      (language); provisions supply
      office
PSO-1   telescopic sight for SVD (SU)
PSOL   performance structure oriented
      language
PSOTC   public schools officers training
      corps
PSP   product support programme;
      personnel subsystem process;
      pointed soft point (projectile);
      pierced steel planking (runway);
      patrol sea-plane (aircraft);
      programmable signal processor
      (radar) by Hughes; planned
      schedule performance; plastic
      spray packaging (cocooning);
      phenol-sulphone-pthalein
PSPBT   pointed soft point, boat tail
      (projectile)
PSPP   proposed system package plan
PSPR   personnel subsystem products
pspt   passport
PS&QS   planning and quotes
PSR   packed snow on runway
PSR-P   packed snow on runway - patchy

PSR   picket, support, reserve;
      parachute status report; perfor-
      mance summary report; post-strike
      reconnaissance
PSRD   personnel shipment ready date;
      personnel support research
      division
PSRO   passenger standing route order
PSS   personnel support system; power
      supply system; printing and
      stationery service (UK)
PSS-10 portable radar warning receiver by
      GI
PSS-11 portable mine detector by Fourdee
PSS-502 Micradet, microwave radiation
      detector radar warning receiver
      by Canadian GI
PSSI   primary speciality skill identifier
PST   Pacific standard time; pre-service
      training; personnel subsystem team
PS&T   pay, subsistence and transportation
PS/t   Pferdestärken pro Tonne (horse
      powers per ton)
pst   past; passed time
PSTCO   per steering compass
PSTE   personnel subsystem test and evalua-
      tion
pstl   postal
PSTN   pay, subsistence and transportation,
      Navy
PSTO   principal sea transport officer
PSU   power supply unit
PSU-1   ... 2, passive sonar by KAE
PSurg   plastic surgery
PSV   public service vehicle; pre-set
      vector; psychologische
      Verteidigung (psychological
      warfare -- defence)
PSVP   pilot secure voice project (US
      programme)
PSW   programme status word
PSWB   patented steel wire bureau
psy   psychological
psy-div psychological sciences division ONR
PsyOp   psychological operation
PsyWar psychological warfare
PT   project transition; physical train-
      ing; primary target; purchase tax;
      plan table; proceed time;
      preferential treatment; production
      test; penetration test; primary
      trainer (aircraft); point of turn;
      patrol torpedo (boat) (Nato);
      paper tape
pt   pint; point; part; platinum; post;
      payment
PT-boat patrol torpedo boat
PT-11   class, patrol torpedo boats by
      Mitsubishi
PT-20   Panzerturm (tank turret) 105mm gun
      (GE)

PT-21   Panzerturm (tank turret) 120mm gun
        (GE)
PT-76   amphibious recce tank 76mm gun (SU)
PT-85   amphibious tank (SU)
PT-428 all-weather anti-aircraft missile
        (UK) project cancelled
        --Mauler bought instead
PTA   proposed technical approach;
        programmed time of arrival;
        proficiency training aircraft;
        primary target area; public
        transport authorities
PT/A   tracked transporter/launcher
        -FROG-2 (SU)
PTAB   photographic technical advisory
        board
PTACV   prototype tracked air cushion
        vehicle
Ptarmigan tactical communications system
        by Plessey
PTAS   productivity and technical assis-
        tance secretariat
PTB   patrol torpedo boat
PT/B   tracked transporter/launcher
        -FROG-3 (SU)
ptbl   portable
PTBT   partial test ban treaty (nuclear
        bombs)
PTC   photographic type composition;
        personnel transfer capsule;
        positive temperature coefficient;
        passive thermal control; patrol
        torpedo (boat) submarine chaser
        (USN); primary training centre;
        personnel transit centre
PT/C   tracked transporter/launcher
        -FROG-4 (SU)
PTCAD   provisional troop carrier airborne
        division
PTCR   positive temperature coefficient of
        resistivity
PTD   pilot to dispatcher; personnel
        transportation division
ptd   printed; pointed (projectile)
PTDP   preliminary technical development
        plan
PTE   passenger transport executive
pte   private
PteLtd private limited (company)
PtEx   part exchange
PtExch part exchange
PTF   port task force; patrol torpedo
        (boat) fast; phase transfer
        function
PTFCE   poly-tri-fluoro-chloro-ethylene
PTFE   poly-tetra-fluoro-ethylene
PTFMPO peacetime force material procurement
        objective
PTFMR   peacetime force material requirement
        A   acquisition
        R   retention

PTFS   pilot to forecast service
ptg   printing
PTgt   primary target
PTH   patrol (boat) torpedo, hydrofoil
        (Nato)
PTI   physical training instructor; pre-
        trial investigation; Philips Tele-
        communicatie Industrie BV
        (Hilversum)
PTIDG   presentation of technical informa-
        tion discussion group
PTL   petroleum testing laboratory; power
        transmission line; primary target
        line; process and test language
ptl   patrol
PTM   pulse time modulation; pulse time
        multiplex; performance test model
PTMA   phospho-tungsto-molybdic-acid
PTMiBa anti-tank mine (Czech)
        -2   rectangular
        -3   circular
PTMiD   anti-tank bar-shaped mine (Czech)
PTMiK   mechanical anti-tank mine (Czech)
ptn   pattern; portion
PTO   project technical officer; power
        take-off; physical training
        officer; port transportation
        officer; please turn over
PTOS   peacetime operating stock
P-TOTS portable-transportable optical test
        system (USAF) (rainbowing of wind-
        screens)
PTP   pre-fire testing phase; production
        test procedure; paper tape
        printer; point-to-point
pt/pt   point-to-point
PTPU   portable test and programme unit
PTR   paper tape reader; part throttle
        reheat; public transport rate
ptr   printer; painter
PTR-1410 VHF radio system by Plessey
PTR-2411 high performance VHF manpack radio
        by Plessey
PTRD   heavy anti-aircraft machine gun
        Degtyarev (SU)
PTRF   peacetime rate factor
PTRM   partial thermo-remnant magnetization
PTRO   personnel transaction register by
        originator
PTRS   heavy anti-aircraft machine gun
        Simonov (SU)
PTS   parachute training school; physical
        training staff; tracked amphibious
        vehicle (SU)
pts/hr parts per hour
PTS-M   tracked amphibious tractor for field
        howitzer (SU)
PTSO   personnel transaction summary by
        originator
PTST   personnel transaction summary by
        type transaction

PTT	post telegraph telephone; push to talk (switch); part task trainers
PTTI	post telegraph telephone international
PTTS	post telegraph telephone systems
PTU	personnel transport/utility (truck); power transformation unit
PTV	propulsion test vehicle
pty	party
PU	processor unit; pick up (truck); power unit; propellant utilization; public utility; paid up
Pu	plutonium
PUAZO-6/19	anti-aircraft aiming system (SU)
pub	publication; public
pubd	published
PubDoc	public documents
PubInfo	public information
publ	publication; published
pubn	publication
PubRel	public relations
PubWkCen	public works centre
PubWkDept	public works department
PubWks	public works
PUC	production urgency committee; pick-up car; provided you concur; port utilization committee; papers under consideration; public utilities commission
Pucara	twin-engined COIN aircraft (Argentina)
PUC(Army)	presidential unit citation (Navy)
PUE(Army)	presidential unit emblem (Navy)
PUE-1	Pegelüberwachungsempfänger für Lautsprecherbeschallung by W&G (volume monitoring receiver for acoustic PsyWar)
PUFFS	passive underwater fire-control feasibility system by Sperry (sonar traces propeller noise)
PUI	pilot under instruction
PUL	palletized unit load
Pulau	class, minesweepers by Abeking & Rasmussen
PULHEEMS	physical capacity, upper limbs, locomotion, hearing, eye, eye, mental capacity, stability (employment standard) (UK)
PULHES	physical capacity or stamina, upper extremities, lower extremities, hearing and ears, vision and eyes, psychiatric (physical profile serial code (numerical)) (US)
PULO	Pottani united liberation organization (Thailand)
Pulse-8	North Sea positioning system by Decca/Kongsberg
PUMS	permanently unfit for military service

PUMA	Panzer unter minimalem Aufwand Studie von GST (minimal effort tank study)
Puma	SA-330, tactical transport helicopter by AS; SdKfz-234/2 8x8 heavy armoured car WW2; 6x6 armoured personnel carrier by Mowag
PUP	plutonium utilization programme; people's united party (British Honduras)
pup	pupil pilot
Puppchen	RW-43, Raketenwerfer 8.8cm (anti-tank rocket launcher) WW2
PUr	poly-urethane
pur	purchase; pursuit
PURA	Pacific command utilization and re-distribution agency
purch	purchase
purif	purification
Purple Heart	US decoration for the wounded
purs	pursuit
PURS	programme usage replenishment system
PURV	powered underwater research vehicle
PUS	parliamentary under-secretary; permanent under-secretary; permanently unfit for service
PUTGBIL	recoilless gun (Sweden)
PUVA	plutonium value analysis (system)
PV	Paravane (UK); patrol vessel; private venture; physical vulnerability; production validation; public voucher
PV-Zünder	Pulver-Verögerungszünder (powder delay fuse)
PV-1	... 2, Private E- 1 (US)
PV-2	Piasecki Vertical single-seat single-rotor helicopter by Piasecki
PV-3	HRP-1, Flying Banana, tandem helicopter by Piasecki-Vertol
PV-11	...10, recoilless anti-tank gun 90mm by Bofors
PV-1641	digital message terminal by Plessey
PV-1712	radio altimeter by Plessey
PVA	poly-vinyl-alcohol; poly-vinyl-acetate; prevention of violence act; amphibious tank (SU)
PVAC	poly-vinyl-acetate
PVAL	poly-vinyl-alcohol
PVB	poly-vinyl-butyrol
PVBr	poly-vinyl-butyrol
PVC	poly-vinyl-chloride; pulse voltage converter; pigment volume concentration
PVCH	poly-vinyl-cyclo-hexane
PVD	plan video display
PVDA	prevention of venereal diseases act
PVDC	poly-vinyl-idene-chloride
PVDF	poly-vinyl-idene-fluoride

PVF	poly-vinyl-fluoride
PVG	poly-vinylene-glycol
pvl	prevail
PVMS	projectile velocity measurement system
pvnt	prevent
PvntMed	preventive medicine
PVO	principal veterinary officer; Soviet air defence troops
PVOR	precision VOR
PVO-Strany	Soviet air defence of the Home Land
PVO-Voisk	Soviet air defence theatre forces
PVP	poly-vinyl-pyrolidone
PVRC	pressure vessel research committee
PVS	panoramic vision system; portable (night) vision system; principal veterinary surgeon
PVS-2	Starlight Scope, portable light intensification scope for rifles
PVS-5	M-802, night vision goggles by Litton
PVS-5A	night vision goggles by Varo
PVS-1310	HF radio system (UK)
Pvt-1	...2, private E-1 (US)
PVT	production validation test; poly-vinyl-toluene
PVTCA	poly-vinyl-tri-chlor-acetate
PVT/POE	production validation test/follow-on evaluation
PW	prisoner of war (UK); pay warrant (royal warrant for pay and promotion); public works; pulse width; private wire; per week
PW-8	Hawk, single-engined fighter/dive bomber by Curtiss
PW-42	SdKfz-4/1, Panzerwerfer 15cm (half-track artillery rocket launcher) WW2
PWA	public works administration
PWB	pulling whaleboat; psychological warfare branch
PWC	prisoners of war camp; Pacific war council; provincial warning centre; psychological warfare consolidation
PWCen	public works centre
PWD	procurement work directive; psychological warfare department; psychological warfare division; public works department
pwd	powered
PWDG	The Prince of Wales's Dragoon Guards
PWDT	pre-withdrawal demolition target
PWE	political warfare executive (UK) ME Middle East
PWG	permanent working group (Nato)
PWHQ	peace war headquarters
PWI	pilot warning indicator
PWL	power level
PWLB	public works loan board

PWM	public works maintenance; Panzerwurfmine (anti-tank hand grenade)
PWO	public works office; principal warfare officer
PWOf	principal warfare officer
PWOGR	The Prince of Wales's Own Gurkha Rifles
PWOP	pregnancy without permission
PWORY	The Prince of Wales's Own Regiment of Yorkshire
PWOWYR	The Prince of Wales's Own West Yorkshire Regiment
PWP	plasticized white phosphorous
PWR	pressurized water reactor
pwr	power
PWR	police war reserve
PWR-FLECHT	pressurized water reactor full length energy cooling heat transfer
PWRR	pre-positioned war reserves requirements MF for medical facilities
PWRS	pre-positioned war reserve stocks
PwrSup	power supply
PWS	permanent working staff
PWT	Pacific war time; propulsion wind tunnel; public works transportation
PWTC	public works transportation centre
PwTn	power train
PWTVA	procurement of weapons and tracked vehicles, Army
PWU	public works utilities
PWV	The Prince of Wales's Volunteers The South Lancashire Regiment
PWVols	The Prince of Wales's Volunteers The South Lancashire Regiment
PWW	planar wing weapon (glide bomb) HOBOS
PWX	permanent working staff
PX	post exchange (telephone) (Nato); post exchange (US Naafi); physical examination
PXO	prospective executive officer
PY	patrol (vessel), yacht (USN); prior year
py	party
PYC	patrol (vessel) yacht, coastal (USN)
PYR	prior year report
Pyricon	pyro-electric vidicon valve by Thomson-CSF
pyro	pyrotechnics
Pyroxyline	gun cotton (explosive)
Pyroxylol	nitro-cellulose (explosive)
PZ	pick-up zone (fleet/squadron manoeuvres) (RN)
Pz	Panzer (tank/armoured car)
Pz-51	AMX-13, Swiss designation, recce tank

Pz-55	Centurion Mk.III Swiss designation
Pz-57	Centurion Mk.VII Swiss designation
Pz-61	Swiss home-made tank
Pz-65	Swiss recovery tank by Arsenal Thun
Pz-68	main battle tank by Arsenal Thun
PzAbw	Panzerabwehr (anti-tank)
PzB-41	Panzerbüchse (anti-tank rifle taper-bore) 28mm to 20mm WW2
PZB-200	passives Fernseh Ziel- und Beobachtungsanlage by AEG,(passive TV aiming and surveillance equipment)
PzBefWg	Panzerbefehlswagen (command tank)
PzF	Panzerfaust (anti-tank launcher)
PzFGr	Panzerfaustgranate (grenade for anti-tank launcher)
PzF-44	Panzerfaustgranate 1944
PzGr	Panzergranate (anti-tank grenade)
PzGrPatr	Panzergranatpatrone (armour-piercing round for 2cm a/a gun)
PzH	Panzerhaubitze (self-propelled howitzer)
PzH-70	Panzerhaubitze 155mm
PzHb-66	M-109, Swiss designation
PzKpfW	Panzerkampfwagen (tank) WW2
PzKW	Panzerkampfwagen
PzJg	Panzerjäger (killer tank)
PzMi	Panzermine (anti-tank mine)
PzMrs	Panzermörser (SP mortar)
PzSpWg	Panzerspähwagen (armoured recce vehicle)
PZT	photographic Zenith tube
PzTrspWg	Panzertransportwagen (tank transporter)

Q

Q	queen; question; quarter(master); quartermaster general's branch; quartering and logistics (UK); quarterly (report)
Q-boat	quiet boat, disguised submarine destroyer
Q-card	qualification card
Q-cartridge	quiet cartridge, proof cartridge
Q-factor	quality factor
Q-fighter	quiet fighter, remotely controlled
Q-helicopter	quiet helicopter, remotely controlled
Q-message	navigational security and safety message
Q-ships	quiet, disguised submarine destroyers
Q-staff	quartermaster staff
Q-star	quiet aircraft, remotely controlled
992-Q	naval surveillance and target designating radar by Marconi
QA	quality assurance; qualification approval
Q&A	questions and answers
QAD	quality assurance directorate MoD; quality assurance division
QADS	quality assurance data system
QAET	quality assurance evaluation test
QAIMNS	Queen Alexandra's Imperial Military Nursing Service --QARANC
QAM	queued access method
QAMDO	quadripartite agreed material development objective
QAMH	Queen Alexandra's Military Hospital (London Millbank)
QAMR	quadripartite agreed material requirement
QAP	quality assurance procedures; quality assurance provisions
QAPED	quadripartite agreed plans of engineering design
QAPET	quadripartite agreed plans of engineering test

QAPST	quadripartite agreed plans of service test
QAR	quick access recorder
QARANC	Queen Alexandra's Royal Army Nursing Corps
QARNNS	Queen Alexandra's Royal Naval Nursing Service
QAS	quiet armed Scout (helicopter); quality assurance standard; quaternary ammonium compound; The Queen's Army Schoolmistresses
QAST	quality assurance service test (nuclear)
QAT	qualification approval test
QB	The Queen's Bays, The 2nd Dragoon Guards; Queen's Bench
QBD	Queen's Bench Division
QBYG	The Queen's Bodyguard of the Yeoman of the Guard
QC	Queen's commission; Queen's Counsel; quality control; quarter credit; quick change (magazine); quantum count
QCB	queued control block; quality control board (US Army); qualifications control board; The Queen's Commendation for Bravery
QCBC	The Queen's Commendation for Brave Conduct (Oak Leaves) for civilians
QCE	quality control engineering; quality control evaluation
QCG	Quartier Générale de Guerre (war headquarters)
QCI	quality control information
QCIs	Queen Charlotte Islands
QCM	quartz crystal microbalance
QCMG	quartz crystal microbalance gravimetry
QCPSK	quadrature coherent phase shift keying
QCR	qualitative construction requirement; quality control representative; quality control reliability
QCSEE	quiet clean STOL experimental eengine

QCT	quality control technology		QMAC	quadripartite material and agreements committee
QCVS	The Queen's Commendation for Valuable Service		QMAO	qualified for mobilization ashore only
QD	quickly detachable; quarterdeck		QMC	quartermaster corps (US)
QDD	qualified for deep diving (RN)		QMDO	qualitative material development objective
QDG	The 1st the Queen's Dragoon Guards		QMess	The Queen's Messenger
QDO	quadripartite development objective		QMG	quartermaster general (USMC)
QDRI	qualitative development requirement information		QMGF	quartermaster general to the forces
			QMM	quartermaster's manual
QE	quadrant elevation; quality evaluation; quantum electronics		QMO	qualitative material objective
			QMov	quartermaster general's branch, movements
QEAF	Qatar Emiri Air Force		QMOW	quartermaster of the watch (USN)
QEAM	quick-erecting antenna mast by GTE-Sylvania		QMR	qualitative military requirement; qualitative material requirement
QEC	quick engine change		Qmr	quartermaster
QECA	quick engine change assembly		QMS	quartermaster sergeant
QECK	quick engine change kit		QMSI	quartermaster sergeant instructor; quartermaster service instructor
QECS	quick engine change stand		
QEL	quality evaluation laboratory		QMSO	quartermaster supply officer (US Army)
QEMH	Queen Elizabeth Military Hospital (Woolwich)		QM-T	quartermaster trainee (US)
QEOGR	Queen Elizabeth's Own Gurkha Rifles		Qn	queen
QER	qualitative equipment requirements		qn	question; quotation
QEST	quality evaluation systems test		QNS	quantity not sufficient
QF	quality factor; quick-firing (gun); quiet fighter (remotely controlled aircraft)		qnty	quantity
			QO	qualified in ordnance (RN)
			QOCH	The Queen's Own Cameron Highlanders
QF-4B	Phanton, remote control by NADC		QOH	The Queen's Own Hussars; The Queen's Own Highlanders; quantity on hand
QF-8	Crusader, remote control by NADC		
QF-86	Sabre, remote control by PMTC		QOMAC	quarter orbit magnetic altitude control
QFE	quiet, fuel efficient (engine)		
QFSM	The Queen's Fire Service Medal		QOMY	The Queen's Own Mercian Yeomanry
QG-035	class, small multi-role corvettes (Israel)		QOOH	The Queen's Own Oxfordshire Hussars
QGE	The Queen's Gurkha Engineers		QOps	quartermaster general's branch operations
QGM	The Queen's Gallantry Medal for civilians		QOR	qualitative operational requirement
QGO	Queen's Gurkha Officer		QORC	The Queen's Own Rifles of Canada
QGS	The Queen's Gurkha Signals		QORGY	The Queen's Own Royal Glasgow Yeomanry
QH	quiet helicopter, remotely controlled		
QH-50	DASH, drone anti-submarine helicopter RPV carrying homing torpedoes by Gyrodyne		QORWKR	The Queen's Own Royal West Kent Regiment
			QP	qualification pay; quasi-peak
QHC	Queen's Honorary Chaplain		QPL	qualified products list
QHM	Queen's Harbour Master		QPM	The Queen's Police Medal
QHNS	Queen's Honorary Nursing Sister		
QHP	Queen's Honorary Physician		QQPRI	qualitative and quantitative personnel requirements information
QHS	Queen's Honorary Surgeon		
QI	quality index		QR	The Queen's Regulations (for the Army and the Royal Army Reserve); The Queen's Royal Regiment quantity requested; quick reaction; quality requested; quality requirement
QISAM	queued indexed sequential access method		
qk	quick		
QL	query language; The Queen's Lancers		
Qld	Queensland		
QLR	The Queen's Lancashire Regiment		qr	quarter
qlty	quality		QRA	quick reaction alert
QM	The Queen's Medal; quartermaster; The Queen's Messenger		Q&RA	quality and reliability assurance
			QR&AI	Queen's Regulations and Admiralty Instructions
QMA	qualitative material approach		
QMAAC	Queen Mary's Army Auxiliary Corps WW1 --WRAC		

QRC quadripartite research committee; quick reaction contract; quick reaction capability

QRC-35 electronic warfare pod program by Westinghouse

QRC-255 electronic warfare pod program by Westinghouse

QRC-559 electronic warfare pod program by Westinghouse (USAF)

QRCan The Queen's Regulations and Orders for the Canadian Militia

QRI Qualitative requirements information

QRIH The Queen's Royal Irish Hussars

QRL The Queen's Royal Lancers; quadripartite research list

QRMF quick-reacting mobile force (Nato)

QrMr quartermaster

QRPS quick-reaction procurement system

QRR The Queen's Royal Regiment (West Surrey); The Queen's Royal Rifles; qualitative research requirements (for nuclear weapons effects information) (US)

qrs quarters

QS quadruple splitting; Question Standard (standard requirement); quota source; quarantine station; qualified for staff employment

QSAL quadripartite standardization agreements list

QSAM queued sequential access method

QSATS quiet short-haul air transportation system

QSEE quiet STOL experimental engine

QSG quasi-stellar galaxy

QSO quasi-stellar object (quasar)

QSOP quadripartite standing operating procedures

QSP quick search procedure

QSR quick strike reconnaissance (aircraft)

QSRA quiet short-haul research aircraft (Nasa)

QSRS quasi-stellar radio sources

QSS quasi-stellar source; quick supply store

QSSR quarterly stock status report

QSTAG quadripartite standardization agreement

QSTS quadruple screw turbine ship

qt quantity

QT-33A remotely piloted aircraft by PMTC

QTAM queued telecommunications access method

QTD quadruple terminal digits

qtr quarter; quarterly

qty quantity

QtyDesReq quantity desired as requested

Qu Queen

qu quarter; quasi; question

QU-22 Bonanza, remotely piloted aircraft as data relay station by Beech

quad quadrant

qual qualify

quar quarantine

Quadrad US defence policy based on strategic bombers + land-based missiles + submarine-based missiles + cruise missiles

Quail ADM-20, air-launched decoy missile ECM

QUANGO quasi-autonomous non-governmental organization

QUARANC Queen Alexandra's Royal Army Nursing Corps

QUARNNS Queen Alexandra's Royal Naval Nursing Service

QUAS The Queen's Army Schoolmistresses

Que Quebec

Queen Bee remotely piloted targer aircraft (RAF)

Queen Gull remotely piloted target ship

Queen Mary wheeled aircraft transporter

Queens The Queen's West Surrey Royal Regiment

Queensl. Queensland

Queen Wasp target drone (RAF)

ques question (mark)

questn questionnaire

QUEST quality evaluation technical system

QUESTOL quiet experimental STOL

Quiang-5 Chinese MiG-19 ground attack version

Quick Fix SEMA, helicopter-borne electronic warfare system

Quick Look side-looking airborne radar SEMA, RPV wide-band signal location

Quick Strike air-dispensable shallow-water mines (USN)

Quicktrans long-term airlift service contract (US)

Quiet Advanced Scout helicopter by Hughes + mast-mounted aiming equipment anti-tank

QUIP query inter-active processor; questionnaire interpreter programme

Quito class, guided missile patrol boats by Lüerssen

Quonset hut corrugated iron hut (US)

quot quotation

QVCF Queen Victoria Clergy Fund

QVR Queen Victoria's Rifles

QVS Queen Victoria's School

QW The Queen's Westminsters The King's Royal Rifle Corps

QWG quadripartite working group

qy query

qz quartz

R

R	Rex; Regina; reserve (officer); retired (officer); runner; Royal; Rupee; river; replenishment; resistance; rimmed (cartridge); round nose (projectile); receiver; reconnaissance (aircraft); rain; radiological; radius;
R-Boot	Räumboot (minesweeper)
R-day	replenishment day; redeployment day
R-hour	release hour; retaliation hour (Nato)
R-Patrone	Rauchpatrone (smoke cartridge)
R-ship	refrigerating ship
3R's	reading, writing, arithmetic; readiness, reinforcement, rationalization (Nato)
R-1	Rheintochter (radar-guided anti-aircraft rocket) WW2 (GE)
R-1L	Spin Scan, airborne intercept radar (SU)
R-4	HNS-1, Hoverfly, helicopter by Sikorsky
R-6A	HOS-1, Hoverfly II, helicopter by Sikorsky
R-6B2	rocket launcher 108mm 32 tubes (Spain)
R-20	surveillance drone by AS
R-22	two-seat helicopter by Robinson
R-35	light tank by Renault
R-76	light-weight low-cost precision fire control system by RCA
R-80	ELINT system by GTE-Sylvania
R-405J	ground-based mobile radar jammer by Plessey
R-440	... 460, Crotale, anti-aircraft missile by Thomson/Matra
R-530	air-to-air missile by Matra
R-550	Magic, dog-fight missile by Matra
R-2000	... 2010, infantry radar by GIC
RA	rear admiral; Royal Academy; Royal Artillery; resettlement administration; The Royal Regiment of Artillery; regular army; rental agreement; reviewing authority; reinforced alert; refugees agency; reconnaissance aircraft; right

	ascension; return air; readiness of action; Raufoss Ammunisjonsfabrikker (Norway)
R&A	review and analysis
RA-3B	Skywarrior, reconnaissance aircraft
RA-5	Vigilante, long-range recce by Rockwell
RA-20	anti-aircraft radar by EMD
RA-73	gamma radiation detector by Autophon
RA-1781	receivers by Racal
RAA	rear admiral, aircraft carriers EF eastern fleet (RN); Royal Australian Army; Royal Australian Artillery; Royal Artillery Association; random access array; radar altimetry area; radar approach aids
RAAAC	the Royal Artillery and anti-aircraft command WRAC
RAAC	Royal Australian Armoured Corps
RAADB	Royal Artillery air defence battery
RAAEF	rear admiral, administration Eastern fleet
RAAF	Royal Australian Air Force; Royal Afghanistan Air Force; Royal Auxiliary Air Force
RAAFNS	Royal Australian air force nursing service
RAAM	Royal Alderney artillery militia; remote anti-armor mine (US)
RAAMC	Royal Australian army medical corps
RAAMS	remote anti-armour mine system
RAANC	Royal Australian army nursing corps
RAANS	Royal Australian army nursing service
RAAO	Royal Australian army order
RAAOC	Royal Australian ordnance corps
RAAP	residue arithmetic associative processor; resource allocation and planning; Radford army ammunition plant (US)
RAAR	random access address register
RAAS	racial adjustment action society
RAB	Royal Artillery band; recruiting administration branch; radar beacon

RABAR   Raytheon advanced battery acquisi-
        tion radar
RABFAC radar beacon, forward air controller
RAC   Royal Air Force College; Royal
        Armoured Corps; Rhine Army College
        (Göttingen); requisition advice
        care; regional advisory council;
        restricted air cargo; rear admiral
        commanding (RN); request for
        authority to contact; rubber
        allocation committee; Research
        Analysis Corporation (US)
Racal Acoustics Ltd   (Wembley UK)
RACC   Royal Army catering corps;
        reporting activity control card
        (US)
RACD   Royal Army clothing depot; Royal
        Army chaplains' department
RACDC   Royal Army chaplains' department
        centre (Bagshot)
RACE   restoration of aircraft to combat
        effectivity; radiation adaptive
        compression equipment; random
        access computer equipment; rapid
        automatic check-out equipment
RACEP   random access coreelation for exten-
        ded performance (communications)
RACES   radio amateur civil emergency
        service
RACF   Royal Army clothing factory; Royal
        Artillery charitable fund
RACFOE research analysis corporation field
        office Europe
RACGS   Royal Armoured Corps gunnery school
        (Lulworth)
RAChD   Royal Army chaplains' department
RAChDC Royal Army chaplains' department
        centre (Bagshot)
RACI   Royal Australian chemical institute
RACM   radar altitude control mode
RACOB   rear admiral commanding combined
        operational bases (RN)
        WA Western approaches
RACOMS rapid combat mapping system
RACON   radar beacon
RACR   Rhodesian armoured car regiment
RACS   Royal Australian corps of signals
RACSS   Robertshaw air capsule safety system
        (5 minutes supply of air)
RACT   Royal Australian corps of transport
RAD   rear admiral, destroyers (RN);
        Royal Albert docks; regional
        accountable depot; return to active
        duty; released from active duty;
        recruiting aids division; radio
        analysis diagram; rapid access
        device; rapid access disc; rela-
        tive air density; radiac equipment
        STANAG; radiation abosrbed dose;
        rapid automatic drill;

                Rechnergestütztes Ablaufsteue-
                rungs- und Datenerfassungssystem
                by MaK (computerized process
                control and data acquisition
                system)
rad   radical; radio; radar; radiology
radA   radio active
RADA   random access discrete address
RADAG   radar area (correlation) guidance
        by Goodyear
RADAR   radio detection and ranging
RADAS   random access discrete address
        system
RadBn   radio battalion (USMC)
RADBPF rear admiral commanding destroyers
        British Pacific Fleet
RADC   Royal Army dental corps; Rome air
        development center (USAF); Rome
        air defence centre; regimental
        air defence centre
RADCD   radar counter-measures + deception
RADCM   radar counter-measures
RADCOM radar counter-measures
RadCon radiological control
RADEM   random access delta modulation
RADEX   radioactive (contaminated) airspace;
        radar data extractor by Hughes
RadFal radioactive fallout; radiological
        prediction fallout plot
RadHaz radiation hazards; hazards from
        electro-magnetic radiation
rad/hr rads per hour
RADIAC radio-activity meter instrument;
        radio-active detection, indication
        and computation (equipment);
        radio-activity detection, indica-
        tion and computation;
        radiation detective indicating and
        computating (equipment)
Radiator naval anti-aircraft rocket
          launcher
Radiaura air raid warning set
Radieschen Bv-246, anti-radiation missile
            WW2 (GE)
RadInt radio intelligence (US)
RaDist radar distance indicator
RADks   Royal Albert Docks
radl   radiological; radiology
RadlDefLab radiological defence laboratory
TadlFO radiological fall-out
RadlMon radiological monitor(ing)
RadlOps radiological operations
RadlSafe radiological safety
RadlSO radiological survey officer
RadlSv radiological survey
RAdm   rear admiral
RadMon radiological monitor
radn   radiation
RADOBS Radar Objecktschutz-Sensor by
        Dornier

RADOBS   radar object protection sensor
        R   rundum. all around
        L   linear
        intruder alarm radar

RADOC   regional air defence operations
        centre

Radom   arsenal (Poland) (pistols)

radome   radar dome

radon   radio-active argon

RADOP-10   ... 20, ... 30, ... 40   naval
        radar and optical gun director by
        CSEE

RadOp   radio operator

RADOT   real-time automatic digital optical
        tracker (Nasa); recording auto-
        matic digital optical tracker

RadPlanBd   radio planning board

RADR   Royal Association for Disability and
        Rehabilitation (UK)

RadRel   radio relay

RadRon   radar squadron (USAF)

rad/s   radians per second

RadSafe   radiological safety

RADU   ram-air-driven unit

RADVA   rechnergestützte automatische
        Datenverarbeitungsanlage
        (computerized automatic data
        processing installation (equip-
        ment))

RAE   Royal Aircraft Establishment
        (Bedford) (Farnborough);
        radio astronomy explorer;
        Royal Australian Engineers

RAEC   Royal Army Educational Corps

RAeC   Royal Aero Club

RaEm   radium emanation

RAEME   Royal Australian electrical and
        mechanical engineers

RAeS   Royal Aeronautical Society;
        research aerospace

RAETU   reserve airborne electronic
        training unit

RAF   Royal Air Force; Royal Aircraft
        Factory

RAFA   Royal Air Force Association;
        reserve and auxiliary forces act;
        Royal Australian field artillery;
        Rhine Army fishing association

Rafale   artillery rocket launcher 145mm
        18 tubes by SEP

RAFBF   Royal Air Force benevolent fund

RAFBU   Royal Air Force balloon unit

RAFCC   Royal Air Force coastal command;
        Royal Air Force cinema corporation

RAFEOER   Royal Air Force ex-officers'
        emergency reserve

RAFES   Royal Air Force educational service

RAFFC   Royal Air Force ferry command
        --RAFTC

RAFG   Royal Air Force Germany

RAFGSA   Royal Air Force gliding and
        soaring association

RAFLO   Royal Air Force landing officer

RAFLTC   Royal Air Force language training
        centre (Rheindahlen)

RAFMS   Royal Air Force medical service

RAFO   Royal Air Force order; Reserve of
        Air Force Officers

RAFOAC   Royal Air Force outdoor activities
        centre (Grantown-on-Spey,
        Llanwrst Wales)

RAFR   Royal Air Force reserve; Royal Air
        Force requirement

RAFRO   Royal Air Force reserve of officers

RAFS   regulations for the army fire
        services

RAFSA   Royal Air Force sailing association

RAFSAA   Royal Air Force small arms associa-
        tion

RAFSAC   Royal Air Force school of army co-
        operation (Old Sarum)

RAFSC   Royal Air Force strike command
        1   strike group
        11   air defence group
        18   maritime group
        38   air transport group and
            offensive air support group
        Royal Air Force staff college

RAFSGC   Royal Air Force soaring and gliding
        centre (Bicester)

RAFT   rear admiral fleet train(ing)

RAFTC   Royal Air Force transport command

RAFVR   Royal Air Force volunteer reserve

RAFWSP   The RAF's Wilkinson Sword of Peace

RAG   replacement air group; river
        assault group; returned ammunition
        group

RAGA   Royal Australian garrison artillery

RAGRO   Rhine army's general routine orders

RAGs   river assault groups

RAI   Royal Artillery Institution

RAID   river assault interdiction division

RaidEx   (anti-surface) raider exercise
        (Nato)

RAIF   Royal Australian Imperial Forces

Raikka-41   ... recoilless anti-tank gun
        counter-mass principle by
        Raikka (Finland)
        41   41mm
        55   55mm
        81 ... 120 ... 150 mm

RAIL   revised individual allowance list
        (US), runway alignment indicator
        lights

RAIL   remote area instrument landing
        system

Rak   Rakete (rocket)

RakJPz   Raketenjagdpanzer (missile-armed
        killer tank)

RAL   radio annoyance level

RALLA   regional allied long lines agency (Nato)

Rallye-235   single-engined COIN aircraft by AS

RAM   Royal Artillery Museum (Woolwich); reliability, availability and maintainability (Nato); right ascension of the meridian; random access memory; radio attenuation measurement; radar absorbing material; XRIM-116, re-entry anti-missile; rocket assisted motor; rolling airframe missile by GD; anti-aircraft missile (US)

Ram   tank WW2 (UK)

RAMAC   random access memory accounting; random access method of accounting and control

RAM-ASMD   rolling airframe missile - anti-ship missile defence by GD

RAMB   Royal Artillery mounted band

RAMC   Royal Army medical corps; Royal Army medical college (Millbank London)

RAMCD   Royal Army medical corps depot (Aldershot)

Ramco   International Inc. (Mohawk NJ)

RAMD   receiving agency material division

RAM-D   reliability, availability, maintainability and durability

RAMF   Royal Australian military forces; Royal Australian militia forces

RAMIS   receive, accept maintain issue and store (for Regulus missiles) (US)

RAMIT   rate-aided manually implemented tracking

RAM-J   ground attack aircraft project (SU) (Ramskorye experimentation centre)

RAM-K   MRCA project (SU) (Ramskorye experimentation centre)

Ram Kangaroo   provisional armoured personnel carrier WW2; gutted Sherman tank

RAM-L   air superiority fighter project (SU)

RAMMS   responsive automated material management system

RAMNAC   radio aids to marine navigation application committee

RAMP   Raytheon airborne microwave platform

RAMPART   radar advanced measurement programme for analysis of re-entry techniques

RAMPS   resources allocation and multi-project scheduling

RAMR   Royal Australian military regulations; Royal Artillery maritime regiment

RAMRO   Royal Artillery manning and records office (York)

RAMS   right ascension of the mean sun; random access measuring system (buoys for tracking oil slicks)

Ramses   active/passive naval ECM system by HSA

Ramta   jeep (Israel)

RAMVAN   reconnaissance aircraft maintenance van (US)

RamWing   X-114, WIGE, wing in ground effect giant naval transport aircraft project Nasa/Lockheed

RAN   Royal Australian Navy; reporting accounting number; request for authority to negotiate; radar navigation; Ryan automatic navigator; reconnaissance and attack navigator; regional air navigation

RAN-11LX   radar air-to-surface naval

Rana   hyperbolic navigation system (FR)

RANC   Royal Australian naval college

RanCom   random communications (satellite)

RAND   research and no development (US institutes)

RandD   research and development

RandR   rest and recreation

Ranger   DHC-7, maritime patrol aircraft by DHC; SSQ-47, helicopter-borne active sonar buoy; mine-launching system 72 tubes 18 mines in each for anti-personnel mines by EMI

Range Train   rifle fire simulator by Miltrain

Ranken   air-dispensed anti-personnel darts WW1

RANN   research applied to national needs (US)

RANR   Royal Australian naval reserve

RANVR   Royal Australian naval volunteer reserve

RANXPE   resident army Nike-X project engineer

RAO   resettlement advice officer (UK)

RAOB   radiosonde observation; radar observation

RAOC   Royal Army ordnance corps; regional air operations centre

RAOCAC   Royal Army ordnance corps apprentices college (Blackdown)

RAOCETS   Royal Army ordnance corps employment training school (Deepcut)

RAOCMRO   Royal Army ordnance corps manning and records office (Wigston)

RAOCPC   Royal Army ordnance corps petroleum centre (West Moors, Fendown)

RAOCTB   Royal Army ordnance corps training battalion

RAOCVD   Royal Army ordnance corps vehicles depot (Ludgershall)

RAOO   Royal Artillery operation orders

RAOP   regional air operations plan

RAOS	regulations for army ordnance services
RAP	regimental aid post; rear area protection; rocket-assisted projectile; reliable acoustic path (sonar)
RAP-14	rocket launcher 138mm 21 tubes by CNIM
RAPA	Rhine Army parachute association
Rapace	Radar pour l'Acquisition des Chars-Ennemis (battlefield surveillance radar) by EMD
RAPC	Royal Army pay corps
RAPCCC	Royal Army pay corps computer centre (Worthy Down)
RAPCO	regional air priorities control office
RApCon	radar approach control (centre)
RAPEC	rocket-assisted personnel ejection catapult
RAPIDS	random access personnel information discrimination system
Rapids	naval ESM system by HSA
Rapier	F-108, mach 2 interceptor anti-aircraft missile by BAC
Rapiere	RASIT-72, medium-range battlefield surveillance radar by LCT/LMT
RAPP	registered air parcel post
RAPPI	random access plan position indicator
Rapport	airborne EW self-protection system by Loral
Rapport II	rapid alert programmed power management system of radar targets (anti-aircraft battery ECM system) MBLE
RAPR	Rhine Army public relations
RAPRA	rubber and plastics research association (UK)
RAP-TAP	releaseable assets programme-transferable assets programme
RAPWI	rehabilitation of allied prisoners of war and internees
RAR	Royal Army reserve; The Rhodesian African Rifles; The Royal Australian Regiment; The Royal Anglian Regiment; radio acoustic range-finding (equipment)
RARC	revoked appointment and returned to civilian (status) (US)
RARDE	Royal armament research and development establishment (Sevenoaks)
RARDEN	Royal armament research and development establishment Enfield; cannon 30mm by RARDEN
RaRep	radar reports
RARI	regular army recruiting instructions; reporting and routing instructions
RARO	regular army reserve of officers
RAS	resettlement advice service; replenishment at sea; rear area

	security; requirements audit system; radar analysis system; rocket alarm system (airborne) by Tadiran; rectified air speed; radar assembly spaces; Royal Astronomical Society; Royal Aeronautical Society; radar analysis system (anti-missile); Radar Abstandssystem by SEL; vehicular proximity warning radar
RASAU	reserve anti-submarine warfare systems analysis (mobilization) unit (USN)
RASB	Rhine army sports board
RASC	Royal Army service corps since 1965: RCT; Royal Australian staff corps; rear area security controller
RASCAL	random access secure communications anti-jam link
RASCC	rear area security control centre
RASC/EFI	Royal Army service corps expeditionary force institute
RASER	radio frequency amplification by stimulated emission of radiation
Rashid	self-loading rifle 7.62mm (Egypt)
RASIF	Radarsimulator Flugsicherung Kaufbeuren (ATC radar simulator) by Datasaab
Rasit-72	Rapiera, DDMT-1A, medium-range battlefield surveillance radar LCT/LMT
RASO	rear airfield supply organization
RASP	refined aeronautical support programme
RASPE	resident army SENSCOM project engineer
RASS	rotating acoustic stereo scanner
RAST	recovery assist secure and traverse (helicopter shipboard landing system) by DAF Inc.; recovery and secure traversing system for helicopters (USN)
Rasura	DRPT-2A, battlefield surveillance radar EMD
RAT	rocket-assisted torpedo (Nato); ram air turbine
rat	rations; rating
RAT-31S	medium-range land-based 3D surveillance radar by Selenia
Ratac	DRPC-1A, Radar de Tir de l'Artillerie de Campagne (battlefield and artillery radar); TPS-75 by SEL
RATAN	radio and television aid to navigation
RATCC	regional air traffic control centre
RATE	radar automatic telemetry equipment
RaTel	radio telephone
Ratel	wheeled armoured car (South Africa)
RaTelO	radio telephone operator

RaTg   radio telegram; radio telegraphy
RATO   rocket-assisted take-off
RATOG   rocket-assisted take-off gear
          (naval aircraft)
RatP   ration point
rats   rations
RATSEC   Robert A. Taft sanitary engineering
          center (US)
RATT   radio tele-type (writer)
RAT/T   radio telephone and telegraph
Rattle Box light infantry rocket launcher
          50mm 16 tubes by SARMAC
RAU   remote acquisition unit
RAuxAF   Royal Auxiliary Air Force
RAV   restricted availability
RAVC   Royal Army veterinary corps
RAVCC   Royal Army veterinary corps centre
          (Melton Mowbray)
Raven   repeater jammer for tactical air-
          craft
RAVS   Royal Army veterinary school;
          regulations for army veterinary
          services
RAW   rifleman's assault weapon
RAWA   rear admiral West Africa (RN); radar
          warning antenna by Eichweger;
          rail-water (transport)
RAWARA   rail-water-rail (transport)
RAWARC   radar warning circuit
RAWI   radio and wire integration
RAWIN   radar wind sounding
RAWINSONDE radiosonde and radar wind
          sounding
RAWS   remote area weather system
RAX   rural automatic exchange (telephone)
RayChem   Radiation Chemistry (Dorcan/
          Swindon UK)
RayCom   Raytheon communications (equipment)
Raydist   hyperbolic navigation system (US)
Raynger-2 portable IR temperature measuring
          system by Raytek
RaySistor Raytheon (electro-optical)
          resistor
RaySpAn   Raytheon spectrum analyser
RayTAS   Raytheon technical and administration
          services Ltd (Bagneux FR)
RayTel   Raytheon telephone (CB radio)
RAZ   Radarannäherungszünder (radar proxim-
          ity fuse); DM-54 Raketen Radar-
          annäherungszünder (missile radar
          proximity fuse)
Razon-bomb range and azimuth only bomb WW2
RB   The Prince Consort's Own Rifle
          Brigade; rescue boat (USN);
          reconnaissance bomber (RAF);
          relative bearing; radio beacon;
          rubber band
Rb-04   ... 05, ... 08, air-to-sea missile
          by Saab
Rb-27   AIM-26B license-built by Saab

Rb-28   AIM-4D license-built by Saab
RB-36   reconnaissance bomber by Convair
RB-57   Canberra, ultra-high reconnaissance
          bomber by Martin
RB-66   Destroyer, ultra-high reconnaissance
          bomber
Rb-69   FIM-43 licence-built by Saab
Rb-72   air-to-air missile by Saab
RBA   rescue breathing apparatus
RBAC   Royal British Attendants Company
          (ex-servicemen's security organi-
          zation)
RBAF   Royal Belgian Air Force
RBD   rapid beam deflector
RBDE   radar bright display equipment
RBDNRQ   received but did not return ques-
          tionnaire
RBE   relative biological effectiveness
RBerks   Princess Charlotte of Wales's
          Royal Berkshire Regiment
RBF   read bit feedback (computer)
RBFC   retract before firing contractor
RBGM   real beam ground map (radar mode)
RBH   regimental beachhead
RBI   require better information
RBKOM   The Royal Buckinghamshire King's
          Own Militia
RBL   Royal British Legion (veterans)
RBLG   rifled breech-loading gun
RBM   real-time batch monitor
RBMR   Royal Brunei Malay Regiment
RBMRAW   Royal Brunei Malay Regiment air wing
RBn   radio beacon (omnidirectional)
RBNA   Royal British nurses association
RBOC   rapid blooming off-board chaff
RBP   registered business programmer;
          ration breakdown point
RBR   rotor blade radar by Ferranti
RBS   radar bomb scoring (group);
          random barrage system; radar
          bombardment system
RBS-15   anti-ship missile by SBMC
RBS-70   portable anti-aircraft missile by
          Bofors
RBV   return beam vidicon (satellite TV)
RBW   Röchling-Burbach Weiterverarbeitungs
          GmbH (Völklingen GE)
RBY Mk.1 patrol car by RAMTA
RC   Red Cross; reception centre;
          reserve corps; reserve components;
          radio code (aptitude area);
          request for checkage; Royal
          College; Royal Commission;
          release clause; rifle calibre;
          remote control; reinforced
          concrete; resistance capacitance
          (time); rotary combustion
          (engine); rubber cushioned;
          research centre; reconnaissance
          cargo aircraft (USAF)

RC-10	Superaviogon, airborne camera
RC-47	Dakota, reconnaissance version
RC-121	airborne early warning aircraft by Lockheed
RC-130	Hercules, recce version
RC-135	recce aircraft
RCA	reach cruising altitude; repair cycle asset; riot control agent (gas); Royal Canadian Army; Royal Canadian Artillery; Royal Company of Archers; Royal commission on awards; Radio Corporation of America Ltd
RCACS	readiness command and control system (US)
RCAF	Royal Canadian Air Force
RCAG	remote-controlled air/ground
RCAGCSD	Radio Corporation of America government communications systems division (Camden USA)
RCAMC	Royal Canadian Army medical corps
RCAPC	Royal Canadian Army pay corps
RCASC	Royal Canadian Army service corps
RCAT	radio-controlled aerial target
RCAVC	Royal Canadian Army veterinary corps
RCB	railway construction battalion; ready crew building
RCC	Radio-chemical centre (Amersham); rescue coordination centre (Nato); resistance-capacitance coupling; road/railway construction company; recovery control center (Nasa); region control center (Norad); resources control centre
R&CC	riots and civil commotions
RCCC	reserve component career counselor (US)
RCCF	reserve components contingency force
RCCS	Royal Canadian Corps of Signals
RCD	Royal Canadian Dragoons; regional co-operation for development (Iran + Iraq + Turkey); rocket cushioning device
RCDC	radar course directing central; Royal Civil Defence Corps; Royal Canadian dental corps
RCDCB	regional civil defense coordination board (US)
RCDS	Royal College of defence studies (London)
RCE	Royal Canadian Engineers
RCERIP	reserve component equipment readiness improvement program (US)
RCF	repair cycle float; relative centrifugal force
RCFD	Red Cross field director;
RCG	regular coast guard; radio-activity concentration guide
RCGRI	rules for the conduct of garrison and regimental institutes
RCH	Royal Canadian Hussars
rch	reach
RCHA	Royal Canadian Horse Artillery
RCI	rating cone index; radar coverage indicator; Royal Colonial Institute --RCS
RCID	recruiter code identification
RCIU	receiver control and indicator unit (module)
RCIWCS	radar combat information and weapon control system by HSA
RCJ	reaction control jet; Royal Courts of Justice
RCL	ramped cargo lighter (USN); runway centre line
rcl	recoilless
rclm	reclaim
RCLO	reports control liaison officer
rclR	recoilless rifle
RCLS	runway centre-line light system
RCM	regimental corporal major; regimental court martial; Royal College of music; radar countermeasures (Nato); radio countermeasures; Rapier carrier, mechanized
RCM-748	M-548, Rapier carrier, anti-aircraft missile carrier
RCMA	reservist clothing maintenance allowance
RCMAT	radio-controlled miniature aerial target by GE
RCMI	Royal Canadian military institute
RCMP	Royal Canadian mounted police
RCMS	Royal college of military science
RCN	Royal Canadian Navy; Royal college of nursing; record control number
rcn	reconnaissance
RCNC	Royal corps of naval constructors
RCNR	Royal Canadian naval reserve
RCNVR	Royal Canadian Navy volunteer reserve
RCO	railway control officer; railway construction officer; reports control officer; remote control officer; riot control operations
r	
RCo	rifle company (US)
RCOC	Royal Canadian ordnance corps
RCP	Royal college of physicians; regimental command post; rotation ccombat personnel (US); reserved circuits programme
RCPA	reserve components programme of the army
RCPAC	reserve components personnel and administration center (US Army)
rcpt	reception
RCR	The Royal Canadian Regiment; M-40, recoilless rifle; runway conditions reading

RCRC   revoked commission, returned to civilian (status) (US)

RCRDC   radio components research and development committee

RCS   reaction control system (Nasa); reactor control system; radar control ship; radar cross section; remote control system; report control symbol SHAPE; Royal Corps of Signals; Red Cross Society; Royal College of Surgeons; Royal College of Science; regimental conduct sheet; regional crime squads (UK); Radio Control Specialists Ltd (UK)

RCSC   radio components standardization committee; Royal Canadian signal corps

RCSigsS   Royal Corps of Signals School (Catterick)

RCSS   random communications satellite system; remote control special service (pistol WW2 (RAF))

RCST   Royal College of Science and Technology

RCT   Royal Corps of Transport before: RASC; regimental control team; regimental combat team (Nato); received copy of temporary (pay record) (US); radar control trailer; region control task; road clearance time

rct   recruit

RCTB   reserve components troop basis

rctg   recruiting

RCTL   resistor capacitor transistor logic

RCTP   reserve components troop programme; reserve components test programme

RCTSR   radio code test, speed of response

RCTV   Royal Corps of Transport Volunteers

RCU   remote control unit; rocket countermeasures unit; requisition control unit; road construction unit

RCV   radar control van

rcv   receive

rcvr   receiver

RCVW   readiness attack carrier air wing (USN)

RCyN   Royal Ceylon Navy

RCZ   rear combat zone

RD   The Royal Dragoons; rifle depot; regimental depot; research department; records department; Royal dockyard; Royal (Naval Reserve) Decoration; readiness date; required date; recruiting division; restricted data (atomic energy act 1954); replenishable demand; revolutionary development (team) (US); red dot (illum shot); radiation damage; read direct (data); recording demand; reference drawing

rd   round; radar; road; received

R&D   research and development

RDA   regional duty activity; recommended daily allowance; Royal Danish Army

RD&A   research, development and acquisition

RDAF   Royal Danish Air Force

RDB   research and development board; ramped dump barge (USN)

RDC   recording doppler comparator; Royal Defence Corps

RDD   required delivery date; range development department; rapid demolition device

RDE   research and development establishment

RD&E   research, development and evaluation

R&DElSec   research and development electronic security

RDem   released, demobilized

RDep   recruit depot

RDF   Royal Dublin Fusiliers; rapid depoloyment force (US); radio direction finding; radial distribution function; repeater distribution frame

RDFDB   radio direction finding data base (US)

RDFSta   radio direction finding station

RDG   reference drawing group

rdg   ridge

RDG-1   ...2, hand grenade, smoke (SU)

rdH   roadhead

RdHd   roundhead

RDI   relief driver increment; Royal Designer for Industry; Radar, Doppler à Impulsions (pulse doppler radar) by Thomson-CSF

RDL   naval radar warning receiver by Decca

RDM   radar, doppler, multi-function by Thomson

RDN   Royal Danish Navy

rdo   radio

RDOS   real-time disc operating system

RDP   radar detector processor; radar data processing

RD&P   research, development and production (Nato)

RDP   ration distribution point

RDPC   radar data processing centre

RDPE   radar data processing equipment

RDPJ   rail discharge point, jet (fuel)

RDPM   rail discharge point, MOGAS

RDR   raider (USMC); radiation dose rate; Rhodesian Defence Regiment;

rdr   radar

RDR-160   Weathervision, airborne radar by
          Bendix
RDS   relational data system; robust
          detection scheme; remote display
          sub-system
rds   rounds
RDS-390   passive night vision equipment by
          Siemens
RDS-400   passive night vision equipment by
          Siemens
RDSS   rapidly deployable sonobuoy system
          (USN); rapidly deployable surveil-
          lance system
RDT   reactor development and technology;
          reserved demolition target
RDTE   radar differential tracking element
          GWS-22
RDT&E   research, development, test and
          evaluation
RDT&EN   research, development, test and
          evaluation Navy
RDTR   radiographic di-electric track
RDU   receipt and dispatch unit
RDUFP   radar display unit, front panel
rdvu   rendezvous
RDX   research department formula X
          (explosive)
          Hexogene, cylonite
RDX/TNT   composition explosive
RDY   Royal Dockyard
rdy   ready
RDZ   radiation danger zone
RE   Corps of Royal Engineers; Régiment
          Étranger; radium emanation; ram
          effect; relative efficiency
re   regard(ing)
R&E   research and engineering
REA   re-entry angle; radar echoing area
ReAcDu   recalled to active duty
REACT   register enforced automated control
          technique (computer)
readj   readjust(ed)
ReadjP   readjustment pay
REAF   Royal Egyptian Air Force
REAMS   resource evaluation and management
          system
reapt   reappoint(ed)
RearAdm   rear admiral
REB   radar evaluation branch; relativistic
          electron beam; Royal Engineer Board
          (inspectorate); regional examining
          board
REBA   relativistic electron beam accelera-
          tor
REBC   Royal Engineers bridging camp
          (Wyke Regis)
Rebecca   airborne navigation receiver BABS
rec   receiver; recover; recorder; recipe;
          recording; recovery; record;
          recreation

recap   recapitulation
RECAT   remote controlled agile target
          (tank shooting target) by Marconi
RECAU   receipt, acknowledged and understood
RecBaks   receiving barracks
RECC   Rhine evacuation control command
          (Nato)
recce   reconnaissance
RecCFO   received in connection with fitting
          out
recd   received
RecDuIns received fur duty under instruc-
          tion
RecDut   received for duty
recl   reclamation
recm   recommendation; recommended
recmpt   recomputation
recncln   reconciliation
RecNo   no record in this office
recog   recognize; recognition
recom   recommendation
ReComp   recommended completion (date)
recon   reconnaissance
ReconAtkRon   reconnaissance attack squadron
          (USN)
ReconAtkWing reconnaissance attack wing
          (USN)
ReconCo   reconnaissance company (USMC)
recond   recondition
ReconDO   reconnaissance by direct observa-
          tion
reconst   reconstruct(ion)
recov   recover(y)
recr   receiver; recreation
RecSec   recording secretary
RecShip   receiving ship
RecSta   receiving station
RecTAD   received for temporary additional
          duty
RecTADIns received for temporary additional
          duty under instruction
RecTD   received for temporary duty
RecTemDuIns received for temporary duty
          under instruction
RecTreat received for treatment
RED   rapid excess disposal; reflection
          electron diffraction
red   reduced
Red Baron reconnaissance pod, passive
          infra-red by FFV
          --Green Baron, Blue Baron
Red Berets paratroopers
Red Capes QARNNS
Red Caps Royal Military Police
Red Cross ---George Cross (UK)
Red Devils Parachute Regiment
Red Schield Club Salvation Army Club
RedAS   reduced to apprentice seaman (USN)
RedCom   readiness command
RedCon   readiness condition

Redeye   FIM-43A, M-41E2, portable anti-air-
         craft missile by General Dynamics;
         M-60A1, laser target designator
RED HORSE   rapid engineer deployable and
         heavy operations repair squad-
         ron engineer (organization)
         (USAFE)
         --RRR
RedOps   readiness operations (report)
Redoutable   class, strategic nuclear sub-
         marines (FR)
redsg   redesignate
Redstone   missile (US)
Red Top   air-to-air missile by BAC
Red, White & Blues   QARANCS
REE   rare earth elements
reefer   refrigerator (vehicle)
reenl   re-enlist(ment)
ReenlA   Re-enlistment Allowance
ReenAllow   Re-enlistment Allowance
ReenlB   Re-enlistment Bonus
REES   reactive electronic equipment simu-
         lator by Gould
ref   reference; refresher
refd   refund
refg   refrigeration
refl   reflex; reflection
ReForGer   redeployment of forces to Germany;
         reinforcement of forces in
         Germany (annual exercise) (Nato)
RefP   reference papers
ReFrAD   released from active duty
ReFrADT   released from active duty for
         training
ReFrAT   released from annual training
refrig   refrigeration; refrigerator
RefSyst   reference system
RefUrDis   reference your dispatch
RefUrLtr   reference your letter
REFT   released from experimental flight
         test
reg   regulated; regulation; regular;
         register; region; regiment
REGAL   range and elevation guidance for
         approach and landing
REGLOS   reserve and guard logistics opera-
         tion streamline (US)
regs   regulations; registers
regt   regiment(al)
RegTM   registered trade mark
Regulus   naval guided nuclear missile by
         Chance Vought
REIC   Reeves electronic integrator and
         computer
REIG   rare-earth iron garnets
REIL   runway end identifier lights
ReimbJTR   reimbursed in accordance with joint
         travel regulations
reinf   reinforced; reinforcements
reinfmt   reinforcement

REINS   radar-equipped inertial navigation
         system
rejn   rejoin
REKR   The Royal East Kent Regiment
rel   relief; release; relieved (UK);
         related; reliable; religion (US)
RE1   radio electrician (UK)
RELE   radio electrician (US)
RelAcDu   released from active duty (US)
RelBy   relieved by
RelDet   when relieved, detach
RelDirDet   when relieved and directed,
         detach
RELLA   regional European long lines agency
         (Nato)
RELR   railway end loading ramp
REM   Roentgen equivalen man (mammal);
         rapid eye movement; replacement
         micrographs
rem   remit(ted); remove
REM-500   railway and road bridge (SU)
REMAD   remote magnetic anomaly detection
REMBASS   remotely monitored battlefield
         sensor system by RCA (airdropped
         combined sensors, IR seismic,
         acoustic, magnetic)
REMC   radio and electronics measurements
         committee
REME   Royal Electrical and Mechanical
         Engineers
ReMo   reorganization and modernization
Remora   omnidirectional active sonar by
         Thomson
REMS   registered equipment management
         system (USAF)
RemS   remote sensors (intelligence)
REMSCO   Raytheon European Management and
         Systems Comp.
RemStgs   remaining stages
REMT   radiological emergency medical teams
REMUS   Rechnergestütztes einheitliches
         Mess-und automatisches Prüfsystem
         by AEG (computerized uniform auto-
         matic measuring and test system)
Ren-leave   re-enlistment leave; re-engage-
         ment leave
RENM   request for next message
RENMR   reconnaissance medium range
         (aircraft)
RENOT   request notices
RENT   re-entry nose tip
REO   regional education officer;
         registration for employment order;
         reinforcement officer; regional
         officer
reorg   reorganize
REP   range error probability; Roentgen
         equivalent physical; recovery and
         evacuation program (USMC)
rep   repair; report; reporting point;
         representative; republican

REP-63   reserve enlistment program 1963 (US)
REPAG   Raketen Einstell- Prüf- und Abfeuer
          gerät by Honeywell (missile pro-
          gramming testing and firing
          equipment)
repat   repatriate
REPB   Royal Engineers pocket book
REPC   regional economic planning council
REPCAT report corrective action taken
RepComDesPac   representative of commander,
                destroyers, Pacific fleet
RepDu   report(ing) for duty
RePerMsg   report in person or by message
RepForMaint   representative for maintenance
               force
RepIN   reply if negative
RepISIC   report to the immediate superior in
           command
repl   replace(ment)
repln   replenish(ment)
RepLtr report by letter
Repm   repairman
RepNAResTraProg   report to naval air
                   reserve training program
                   (as aviator) (USN)
RepNavResTraCen   report to nearest naval
                   reserve training centre
RepO   reporting officer
Reporter   radar equipment providing omni-
            directional reporting of targets
            at extended ranges by HSA (naval
            air surveillance)
RepPt   reporting point
REPR   real estate planning report
repr   reprint; represent(ed)
repro   reproduce; reproduction
REPS   Royal Engineers postal service; rail
         express parcel service
reps   repairs
RepShips   reports of shipments
RepSNO report through senior naval officer
rept   report
ReptInerary   report address and itinerary
ReptOf reporting officer
RepTrans   report for transportation
req   request; requirement
ReqAFA request advice as to further action
ReqAns request answer
ReqAuRqn   request authority to requisition
ReqDI   request disposition instructions
ReqFolInFO   request following information be
              forwarded this office
ReqIBO request item be placed on back order
ReqInt request interim reply
reqn   requisition
ReqNom request nomination
ReqRec request recommendation
ReqSI   request shipping instructions
ReqSSD request supply status and expected
         delivery date

ReqSupStaFol   request supply status of
                following
ReqTat it is requested that
ReqTrac   request tracer be initiated
requal requalify; requalified
ReqUChRd   request unit of issue be changed
            to read
ReqWQ   requisition work queue
RER   rubberized equipment repair
RERO   Royal Engineers reserve of officers
RES   regulations for engineer services;
         remote entry service; radar
         environment simulation; radiation
         exposure state; reticulo-
         endothelial system
res   research; restore; reserve;
         resident; resign(ed)
ResAntiSubCarAirGru   reserve anti-submarine
                       warfare carrier air
                       group
ResASWCarAirGru   reserve anti-submarine war-
                   fare carrier air group
RESAR   reference safety analysis report
ResCAP rescue combat air patrol
Rescuer   HRP-1, Flying Banana, helicopter by
           Piasecki/Vertol
ResDat restricted data (atomic energy act
         1954) (US)
ResDesDiv   reserve destroyer division
ResDesRon   reserve destroyer squadron
ResDist reserve district
resgd   resigned
Reshef class, patrol boats, guided missiles
         (Israel)
resig   resignation
Res/IC reserve - in commission (vessel
         status)
Res/IS reserve - in service (vessel status)
Resnatron   radar jammer tube
ResofOff   reserve of officers
Resojet resonating (air intake) jet engine
Resolution   class, ballistic missile sub-
              marines) (RN)
resp   responder (beacon); responsible
RespBn responder beacon
ResPO   responsible property officer
resr   resources
ResRep resident representative
ResSec resident secretary
REST   range, endurance, speed and time
rest   restricted
REST   routine execution selection table
         (computer)
RESTA   reconnaissance, surveillance and
         target acquisition
RESTAT reserve components status reporting
restd   restricted
RETORC research torpedo configuration
restr   restrict
ResTraCen   reserve training centre

ResTraFac   reserve training facility
resup   resupply
ret   retired; retained
RetAbstee   returned absentee

ReTat   it is requested that
RETC   regional emergency transportation
  centre; Royal Engineers training
  camp (Wyke Regis)
RETCO   regional emergency transportation
  coordinator
retd   retired (UK); returned (US)
RetnDu   returned to duty
RetI   Rex et Imperator
RetP   retired pay; retirement pay
ReTrans   return transportation
RETRep   regional emergency transportation
  representative
Retriever   HUP-1, ... 2, naval helicopter by
  Vertol
retro   retro-active
retro-bomb   rocket-retarded bomb
RetroFA   retro-active family allowance
RetSer   retained in service
RetUlSign   retain on board until assignment
ReURad   refer your radio message
Rev   Reverend (UK Army Chaplain)
REV   re-entry vehicle
rev   revolution; revolve;
  reverse; review; revise; revision
REVA   recommended vehicle adjustment
REVAR   revisit above mentioned place and
  vary itinerary
revd   reversed
revg   reversing
rev/min   revolutions per minute
rev/s   revolutions per second
revo   revoke
rew   reward
REWS   Royal Engineers works services
rexmit   retransmitted
RF   The Royal Fusiliers; regional forces;
  (City of London Regiment);
  regular forces; replacement factor;
  range finder; radio frequency;
  reconnaissance fighter (aircraft);
  rimfire (cartridge); roof fan;
  rapid fire; reactive factor;
  radio (direction) finder;
  release fraction; red fumes
R&F   Riehl & Fuller (rifle manufacturers)
RF-Energie   Radar/Funk Energie (radio and
  radar energy)
RF-4   Phanton, recce/fighter jet by McDD
RF-5   Tiger, Freedom Fighter, recce/fighter
  jet by Northrop
RF-8   Crusader, recce/fighter by Vought
RF-84   Thunderflash, recce/fighter jet by
  Republic
RF-101   Voodoo, recce/fighter jet by McDD

RFA   Royal field artillery; reserve
  forces act; Royal fleet auxiliary
  (vessel); relieved from assigned;
  radar, field artillery
RFA No. 8   Green Archer, radar, field
  artillery, mortar location radar
RFA No. 15   Cymbeline, radar, field artil-
  lery, mortar location by EMI
RFAA   relieved from attached and assigned
RFAD   released from active duty
RFALROU   request follow-up action on listed
  requisitions indicated still outstanding in unit
RFASix   reserve forces act (US 1955)
  six months trainee
RFAT   relieved from attached
RFAThree   reserve forces act (US 1955)
  three months trainee
RFB   regimental fund board;
  Rhein Flugzeugbau (VFW daughter)
  Mönchengladbach (GE)
RFC   Royal Flying Corps WW1 later: RAF;
  reconstruction financial co-
  operation; relative force capa-
  bility; radio frequency choke
RFD   ready for delivery; rural free
  delivery; reporting for duty;
  radio frequency device
RFDS   Royal flying doctor service
  (Australia)
RFDU   reconfiguration and fault detection
  unit
RFE   Radio Free Europe
RFEA   regular forces employment associa-
  tion
RFG   rapid fire gun; rifle fine grain
  (powder)
RFI   radio frequency interference;
  radio frequency interface, ready
  for issue; request for information
RFI/ECM   radio frequency interference/
  electronic countermeasure
  (immunity)
RF/IR   radio frequency/infra-red (homing)
RFL   requested flight level
rfl   refuel
RFM   rimfire magnum (projectile)
rfn   rifleman
rflmn   rifleman
RFNA   red fuming nitric acid
RFO   radio frequency oscillator
RFP   radio finger printing; restricted
  fire plan; request for proposal;
  retired on full pay
RF/PF   regional forces popular forces
  (Viet Nam)
RFPP   radio frequency propagation pro-
  gramme; reserve forces policy
  board
RFQ   request for quote (price); request
  for quotation

RFR	reduced frequency responses; Royal fleet reserve
rfrd	referred
RFS	ready for sea (RN + US); ready for service
RFSB	regional forward scatter branch
RFSM-3	(mobile multi-purpose) radio frequency surveillance and monitoring system by AEL; radio frequency spectrum motorvan by AEL
RFT	refresher training
rftHU	reinforcement holding unit
RFTS	reserve flying training school; radio frequency test set
rftSU	reinforcement sub-unit
rfty	reformatory
RFU	reference frequency unit
RG	readiness group; reserve grade; reserve guard
rg	range
RG	rifle grenade; right gun; reduction gearbox
RG-34	hand grenade (Czech)
RG-42	hand grenade (SU)
RGA	residual gas analyser; Royal garrison artillery; Royal Guernsey artillery
RGCFT	radar guidance captive flight test
rgd	registered
RGD-5	hand grenade (SU)
rge	range
RGF-4	Regenerationsfilter 40 kgs by Auer (breathing oxygen regeneration cartridge)
RGF	Royal gun factory
RGG	The Royal Grenadier Guards
RGH	The Royal Gloucestershire Hussars
RGJ	The Royal Green Jackets
RGLET	rise-time gated leading edge trigger
RGM	Royal Guernsey Militia; rotor governing mode (helicopter)
RGM-66	Standard ARM, AGM-78, ship-to-ship anti-radiation missile by GD
RGM-84	Harpoon, ship-launched guided missile by McDD
rgn	region
RGO	Royal Greenwich Observatory
RgPh	registered pharmacist
RGR	receipt for goods received
rgr	ranger
RGS	Royal Geographical Society
RGS-2	airborne optical sight system computed HUD by Saab
rgt	regiment; right
rgtl	regimental
RGWS	radar guided weapon system air-to-air missile by Grumman
RGZ	recommended ground zero
RH	The Royal Highland Regiment (Black Watch); Royal Highness; roadhead;

	railhead; right hand (drive); relative humidity
RH-1	Pinwheel, one-blade tip ramjet helicopter by Rotorcraft
RH-3A	Sea King, naval helicopter by Sikorsky
RH-53	Sea Stallion, naval helicopter by Sikorsky
Rh-202	cannon 20mm by Rheinmetall
Rh-205	cannon 25mm by Rheinmetall
RHA	Royal Horse Artillery; records holding area; Royal Hellenic Army
RHACo	Robin Hood Ammunition Company
RHAF	Royal Hellenic Air Force
RHamps	The Royal Hampshire Regiment
RHAW	radar homing and warning system
RHC	re-heat coil; right hand circular; rubber hydro-carbon (content)
RHD	right hand drive
rhd	railhead
Rheinbote	4-stage ground-to-ground rocket by Rheinmetall 1944
Rheintochter	R-1, radar-guided anti-aircraft rocket WW2 (GE)
RHEL	Rutherford high energy laboratory
RHF	The Royal Highland Fusiliers; River Hall Foundation for Maritime Research (Kent UK)
RHG	The Royal Horse Guards
RHH	The Royal Herbert Hospital (Woolwich)
RHI	range-height indicator
Rhino	assault landing craft, out-board motor; mine protected car (Rhodesia)
RHIO	rank has its obligation
RHIP	rank has its privileges
RHIR	rank has its responsibilities
RHKAAF	Royal Hong Kong auxiliary air force
RHKDF	Royal Hong Kong defence force
RHKPF	Royal Hong Kong police force
RHlGr-4592	Raketen-Hohlladungs-Granate 38cm WW2 (rocket-assisted projectile, hollow-charge)
RHLI	Robert Hamilton light infantry
RHMA	railhead maintenance area; roadhead maintenance area
RHMS	Royal Hibernian (Irish) Military School
RHMSTS	regulations on Her (His) Majesty's sea transport service
RHN	Royal Hellenic Navy
RHO	railhead officer; regimental hospital officer
Rhod	Rhodesian
Rhodoid	cellulose acetate (windscreens)
RHP	rated horsepower
RHQ	regimental headquarters
R/Hr	Roentgens per hour
RHR	The Royal Hampshire Regiment;

The Royal Highland Regiment
(Black Watch)

RHS   right hand side; round headed screw

RHT   right hand tractor (engine)

RHU   regimental holding unit; reinforcement holding unit

RhUzi   machine pistol 9mm Uzi manufactured
in Rhodesia

Rhyolite   early warning satellites

RI   Royal Institution; Regimental institute; recruit induction; Rex et
Imperator; report of investigation;
radiation intensity; reflective
insulation; refractive index;
radio influence; read in

RIA   Rock Island Arsenal (US); sighting
and aiming equipment by PEAB

RIASC   Royal Indian Army service corps

RIB   reservists' instruction book

Ribbon Bridge   floating assault bridge

RIBS   restructured infantry battalion
system

RIC   relocation instruction counter;
routing identification code;
Royal Irish Constabulary;
replaceable item code; representative in charge

RICC   reportable item control code

RICE   relative index of combat effectiveness; rationalized internal communications equipment (naval) by
Plessey

RICMO   radar input counter-measures officer

RID   released to inactive duty

RIDG   The 5th the Royal Inniskilling
Dragoons

RIETCom   regional inter-agency emergency
transportation committee

RIF   reduction in force; resistance
inducing factor; Royal Inniskilling
Fusiliers; Royal Irish Fusiliers

RifBrig   rifle brigade

RIFT   reacto in-flight test

RIG   receiving and transmitting gear
(transceiver)

Riga   class, frigates (SU)

RIGS   runway identifier and glide slope

RIIA   Royal Institute of International
Affairs

RIK   replacement in kind

RILOP   reclamation in lieu of procurement

RILS   rapid integrated logistic support
system

RIM   receipt, inspection and maintenance;
regulations for the issue of maps;
Royal Indian Marines

RIM-2   Terrier, surface-to-air missile

RIM-7   Sea Sparrow, surface-to-air
point defence by Raytheon

RIM-8   Talos, surface-to-air long-range

naval air defence by Bendix
F   high-altitude version
H   anti-radiation version
anti-ship

RIM-24   Tartar, surface-to-air missile

RIM-66   ... 67, Standard, surface-to-air
anti-radar missile by GD

RIMOB   reserve indication of mobilization

RIMS   radiation intensity measuring
system

RIN   report identification number;
Royal Indian Navy

RINA   Royal Institute of Naval Architects;
resident inspector of naval aircraft

RINM   resident inspector of naval material

RInniks   The Royal Inniskilling Fusiliers

RINO   resident inspector of naval ordnance

RIns   resident inspector

RInsMat   resident inspector of (naval)
material

RInsOrd   resident inspectof of (naval)
ordnance

RIO   regimental intelligence officer;
radar intercept operator; retail
issue outlets; reporting in and
out

RIP   recoverable item program (USMC);
re-enlistment incentive programme;
roll-in point (aircraft attack);
ring index pointer; radiological
information plot

RIPA   Royal Institute of Public Administration

RIPH&H   Royal Institute of Public Health
and Hygiene

RIPOM   report if present otherwise by
message

RIPPLE   radioactive isotope powered pulsed
light equipment

RIPS   range instrumentation planning
study; radio-isotope power study

RIR   Royal Irish Rangers

RIRF   Princess Victoria's Royal Irish
Fusiliers

RIS   research information service; radar
instructional system; receipt
inspection segment

RIS-10   radar instructional system by
Litton

RISE   reliability improvement selected
equipment; research in supersonic
environment

RISOP   red integrated strategic offensive
plan

RISS   range instrumentation and support
systems; receipt into the supply
system PLT

RIT   radio (network) for Inter-American
telecommunications; Rochester
Institute of Technology

RITA	reuseable interplanetary transport approach (vehicle); Reseau Integre de Transmissions Automatiques (FR)
RITE	rapid information technique for evaluation
RITTER	French tropospheric infrastructure network by Thomson-CSF
RIV	repayment issue voucher
riv	river
River	class, frigates WW2 (RN RAN); submarines (RN) 1929
RivFlot	river flotilla
RivPatFlot	river patrol flotilla
RivPatFor	river patrol force
RivRon	river (assault) squadron
RivSec	river section
RivSuppRon	river support squadron
RJ	ramjet; repeater jammer; road junction
RJA	Royal Jersey artillery; Royal Jordanian artillery
RJAF	Royal Jordanian Air Force
RJE	remote job entry
RJLI	Royal Jersey Light Infantry
RJM	Royal Jersey Militia
RJPz-2	Raketenjadgpanzer by Rheinmetall (anti-tank missile carrier)
RKG-3	rifle-fire anti-tank grenade (SU)
RKO	range keeper operator
rkt	rocket
rktr	rocketeer
RL	Royal laboratory; report leaving; rocket launcher; radio link; resistor logic; radio location; radiation laboratory; research laboratory; radio relay (mobile)
RLB	radar locating battery
RLC	rotating litter chair
rlcd	relocated
RLD	hand-held laser range-finder by Iskra
RLE	relative luminous efficiency
RLG	rifle large grain (powder)
RLI	Rhodesian Light Infantry
RLIEVDP	request line items be expedited for vehicles (or equipment) deadlined for parts
RLincolns	The Royal Lincolnshire Regiment
RLK-1	portable laser transceiver by Molenda
RLN	radio LORAN station
RLO	repair liaison officer; railway liaison officer; returned letter office
RLOS	retention level of supply
RLP	rail loading point
RLPA	rotating log periodic antenna
RLPJ	rail loading point jet (fuel)
RLR	The Royal Leicestershire Regiment

RLSS	Royal Life Saving Society
RLT	record lead time; regimental landing team
rlt	relating to
RLW	rules of land warfare
rly	railway; relay
RM	Royal Marines; Royal Mail; remount manual; riding master; regulations for mobilization; resident magistrate; radioman; radio monitoring; range mark; raw material; research memorandum; ring micrometer; record mark; remote multiplexer (module) SDMS
r/m	revolutions per minute
R&M	reports and memoranda; reliability and marketing; reliability and maintainability
4RM/62F	armoured car by FN
RM-70	rocket launcher 40 tubes 12mm (SU)
RM-916	naval search/navigation radar by Decca
RM-1226	naval navigation radar by Decca
RMA	The Royal Military Academy; The Royal Military Asylum; Royal Malta Artillery; reserve of military aviators; rear maintenance area; Royal Marine Artillery; Rocky Mountains Arsenal; request for manufacturers of articles; reserve maintenance allowance; Royal Marines Association; reactive modulation (type) amplifier; Rückgewinnung von Metallen aus Abwässern by Dornier (recycling of metals from sewage (method))
RMAB	Royal military academy band
RMABC	Royal military academy band corps
RMAF	Royal Malaysian Air Force
RMalaN	Royal Malaysian Navy
RMAM	Royal military academy museum (Sandhurst)
RMAS	Royal military academy Sandhurst
RMASBC	Royal military academy Sandhurst band corps
RMASG	Royal Marine armoured support group
RMB	Royal Marine brigade
RMC	Royal Marine Corps; Royal Marine commandos; Royal military college (Sandhurst) --RMA radio modifications committee; rod memory computer
RMCB	reserve mobile construction battalion (US)
RMCC	Royal military college of Canada (Kingston Ontario)
RMCCC	Royal military college club of Canada

RMCS	Royal military college of science (Shrivenham UK)
RMD	ready money down
RME	rocket motor establishment (Westcott UK); Royal Marine Engineers (UK); resident maintenance engineer
RMetS	Royal Meteorological Society
RMF	The Royal Munster Fusiliers; required military force
RMFVR	Royal Marine forces volunteer reserve
RMG	recommended for medal and gratuity; ranging machine gun (tank); Regel- & Messtechnik GmbH (Kassel) (IWKA group)
RMI	reliability maturity index; radio magnetic indicator
r/min	revolutions per minute
RMIS	readiness management information system
rmks	remarks
RML	Royal Mail lines; rescue motor launch
2.5 RML	2.5 in rifled muzzle loader (mountain gun) (UK)
RMLI	Royal Marine light infantry
RMMP	Royal mounted military police
RMMU	removable media memory units
RMN	Royal Malayan Navy; Royal Malaysian Navy; reserve material (account) Navy
rmn	remain
RMNS	Royal Merchant Navy School
RMO	regimental medical officer (UK); regional medical officer; resident medical officer; records management officer (US); Royal Marine office; recruiting and manning organization (US) WSA; radar material officer; radio material officer
RMOC	recommended maintenance operation chart
RMonRE	Royal Monmouthshire Royal Engineers
RMonREM	Royal Monmouthshire Royal Engineers Militia
RMP	Corps of Royal military police; Royal Marine police; re-entry measurement program (US); round maximum pressure
RMR	Royal Marines reserve; Royal Montreal Regiment
RMRA	Royal Marines rifle association
RMRE	Royal Monmouthshire Royal Engineers
RMRESR	Royal Monmouthshire Royal Engineers supplementary reserve
RMS	Royal Mail steamer; railway mail service; Royal Meteorological Society; Royal Medical Society; resources management system; radar maintenance spares; recovery management support

RMSA	regulations for the medical services of the army (UK)
RMSchMus	Royal Marines school of music
RMSM	Royal Marines school of music
RMSO	render mines safe officer (RN)
RMSP	refractory metal sheet programme
RMSPC	Royal Mail steampacket company
RMTR	redesigned missile tracking radar
RMU-10	aerial towed target
RMV	re-entry measurement vehicle
RN	Royal Navy; registered nurse; residual number; round nose (bullet); reception nil; research note
rn	radon; region
RNA	radio navigational aid (Nato); Royal Naval Association; rations not available
RNAAC	reference number action activity code
RNav	route navigation (airborne area
RNAB	Royal Navy air branch
RNAD	Royal naval armament depot
RNAF	Royal naval air force later: FAA
RNAMY	Royal naval aircraft maintenance yard
RNAR	Royal naval air reserve (60 pilots)
RNAS	Royal naval air service WW1; Royal Navy air station; Royal Navy air school
RNATE	Royal naval air training establishment
RNAV	Royal naval artillery volunteers
RNAW	Royal naval aircraft workshop
RNAY	Royal naval aircraft yard
RNB	Royal naval barracks
RNBC	Royal naval beach commander
RNBF	The Royal North British Fusiliers
RNBT	Royal naval benevolent trust
RNCC	reference number category code
RNC	Royal naval college
RNColl	Royal naval college
RND	Royal naval division
rnd	round
rnds	rounds
RNEC	Royal naval engineering college
RNEColl	Royal naval engineering college (Plymouth)
RNEE	Royal naval equipment exhibition (Greenwich)
RNethAF	Royal Netherlands' Air Force
RNF	receiver noise figure; The Royal Northumberland Fusiliers
RNFC	Royal Navy film corporation
RNFP	radar not functioning properly
rng	range; radio-range
RNGHQ	Royal Navy general headquarters
rngt	re-negotiate
RNH	Royal naval hospital
RNHS	Royal naval helicopter squadron (Malaysia)

RN1A	Royal Netherlands' Army
RN1AF	Royal Netherlands' Air Force
RNLI	Royal National Lifeboat Institution
RN1N	Royal Netherlands' Navy
RNLO	Royal naval liaison officer
RNMS	Royal Navy medical school; Royal Navy medical service
RNMWS	Royal naval mine watching service
RNN	Royal Netherlands Navy (Nato)
RNO	resident naval officer
RNoA	Royal Norwegian Army
RNoAF	Royal Norwegian Air Force
RNOCA	Royal Navy old comrades' association
RNoN	Royal Norwegian Navy (Nato)
RNorAF	Royal Norwegian Air Force
RNorfolk	The Royal Norfolk Regiment
RNPL	Royal naval physiological laboratory
RNPS	Royal Navy patrol service
RNR	Royal naval reserve
RNRA	Royal naval rifle association
RNS	radar netting station
rns	runs
RNSA	Royal naval sailing association
RNSC	Royal naval staff college
RNSD	Royal naval stores depot
RNSG	reserve naval security group (US)
RNSGC	reserve naval security group course
RNSP	round nose soft point (projectile)
RNSQ	Royal naval sick quarters
RNSR	Royal naval special reserve
RNSS	Royal naval scientific service
RNSTS	Royal naval supply and transport service
RNSWR	The Royal New South Wales Regiment
RNTE	Royal naval training establishment
RNTU	Royal naval training unit
RNU	radar netting unit
RNVR	Royal naval volunteer reserve
RNVC	reference number verification code
RNVSR	Royal naval volunteer supplementary reserve
RNWAR	Royal naval wireless auxiliary reserve
RNWMP	Royal North West Mounted Police (Canada)
RNWSP	The Royal Navy's Wilkinson Sword of Peace
rnwy	runway
RNZA	Royal New Zealand artillery
RNZAC	Royal New Zealand armoured corps
RNZAF	Royal New Zealand Air Force
RNZAMC	Royal New Zealand Army medical corps
RNZAOC	Royal New Zealand Army ordnance corps
RNZASC	Royal New Zealand Army service corps
RNZCS	Royal New Zealand corps of signals
RNZEME	Royal New Zealand electrical and mechanical engineers
RNZIR	Royal New Zealand infantry regiment
RNZN	Royal New Zealand Navy
RNZNC	Royal New Zealand nursing corps
RNZNVR	Royal New Zealand naval volunteer reserve
RO	regimental orders; reference object; routine order; route order; requisitioning objective; retro-fit order; routing office; right observer; radio operator; room orderly; recruiting officer; retired officer; reporting officer; routing officer; receive only; reference oscillator; reverse osmosis; radio navigation (mobile station) (Nato)
ROA	radio altimeter (station); reserve officers' association
ROAD	rotocraft audio detector by Tadiran (helicopter identification); reorganized objective army division
Roadtrain	truck by Leyland
ROAMA	Rome air material area
ROAR	return of army repairables; right of admission reserved
ROB	regimental order book; report on board (USN); remaining on board
Robbe	class, tank landing ships (EG)
RObCo	readiness objective code
Robert	long-range surveillance radar on FV-610 by Decca
RoBIn	rocket balloon instrument
Robomb	robot bomb
ROC	Republic of China; Royal observer corps; reserve officer candidate (US); required operational capability; reduced operating costs; research on oral communications (US); reconnaissance and operations centre (Nato); required obstruction clearance; receiver operating characteristics; remote operation console; required operational capacity
Roc	fighter aircraft, four-gun turret by Blackburn WW2; TV-guided bomb (USAF)
ROCALDIS	routine call may be dispensed with (US)
ROCAP	fragmentation rocket by SARPAC
ROCAR	anti-tank rocket HE by SARPAC
ROCCM	remotely operated and controlled counter-measures (and deception)
ROCE	return on capital employed
ROCID	reorganization of combat infantry division
Rockan	influence seabed mine by Bofors
Rockeye	Paveway, smart bomb (USAF)
Rocket Spear	airborne anti-submarine rocket WW2 (RN)
ROCLAIR	illumination rocket by SARPAC

ROCM   Royal Observer Corps Medal
ROCMM   regional office of civilian manpower
          management (US)
ROCP   radar out of commission for parts
ROD   rate of descent; Royal ordnance
          department; railway operating
          division; range operation depart-
          ment (US) PMR
RODAC   reorganization objectives Army
          division and Army corps (US)
Rodar   rotor blade radar by Ferranti
Rodeo   anti-aircraft gunfire control radar
          by EMD
RODRE   railway operating division Royal
          engineers (Longmoor)
ROE   Royal Observatory Edinburgh; reflec-
          tor orbital equipment; rules of
          engagement; roster of exceptions
          (US)
ROF   rate of fire;
          Royal Ordnance Factory
          Leeds   armoured vehicles
          Nottingham artillery
          Radway Green ammunition
          Chorley ammunition
          Glascoed ammunition
          Birtley ammunition
          Patricraft ammunition
          Blackburn fuses
          Bridgewater explosives
          Bishopton propellants
          Fazackerley small arms
          Enfield small arms
RofO   reserve of officers
RoFor   route forecast
ROG   rise of ground
ROH   required obstruction height; regular
          overhaul
Rohini   RS-1, satellite (India)
ROI   return on investment; report of
          investigation
ROIC   resident officer in charge
ROICC   resident officer in charge of con-
          structions
ROID   report of item discrepancy
ROinC   resident officer in charge
ROJ   range-on jamming
ROK   Republic of Korea
ROKA   Republic of Korea Army
Rokeye   Mk.20, airborne laser pod
ROKN   Republic of Korea Navy
ROKPUC   Republic of Korea presidential unit
          citation
ROLAC   regional organization of liaison for
          allocation of circuits
Roland   anti-aircraft missile tank by
          MBB/EM
          1   optical guidance
          2   all-weather version;
          4x4 armoured personnel carrier by
          Mowag

Rolligon low-pressure tyres
ROM   research office memorandum; radar
          operator mechanic; read-only
          memory; rough order magnitude;
          red oxide of mercury
ROMACC   range operational mounting (monitor-
          ing) and control centre
Romney hut large corrugated iron shelter
RON   research octane number; remain over
          night; receiving only
Ron   squadron (US)
Ronly   range only (radar); receiver only
RONS   reserve officers of the naval
          service
ROO   railhead ordnance officer; roadhead
          ordnance officer
ROOST   reusable on-stage orbital space
          truck
ROP   run of paper; recorder point
ROPA   reserve officer personnel act (US)
ROPB   reserve officers promotion branch
rope   low frequency chaff
Ropucha   class, landing craft tanks (SU)
ROR   range-only radar
RORC   Royal ocean racing club
Ro/Ro   roll-on/roll-off (ship)
ROS   read only storage; reduced opera-
          tional status; return from over-
          seas
ROSIE   reconnaissance by orbital ship
          identification equipment
ROSLA   raising of school-leaving age (UK)
RoSPA   Royal Society for Prevention of
          Accidents
ROSR   regulations for officers of the
          supplementary reserve of officers
          and for the supplementary reserve
Ross   rifle WW1 (Canada)
ROT   re-usable orbital transport
rot   rotor; rotation; rotary
Rota   autogyro WW2 (RAF) by Avro-Cierva
Rotaplane autogyro WW2 (1 paratrooper/
          1 Bren gun)
ROTC   reserve officers' training corps
          (US); reserve officers' training
          camp; reserve officers' training
          course; regulations for the
          officers' training corps
ROTCM   reserve officers' training corps
          manual (US)
Rothesay class, frigates (RN)
RotLt/Bcn rotating light or beacon
Rotor   air defence radar station (UK)
RotProj   rotation projection
ROTR   receive only typing re-perforator
Rotterdam H_2S, airborne radar WW2
Roubaix   booster rocket by Bayern Chemie
RO/UF   reverse osmosis ultra filtration
rout   routine
ROVD   remotely operated volume damper

ROvnite   remain overnight
ROW   rise of water; right of way
ROWIS   remotely operated window scanner
           (listening device) by Gesellschaft
           für Mini-Elektronik
RP   rules of procedure; regimental
           police; refilling point; reference
           point; replenishment park; release
           point; retained personnel; raid
           plotter; replacement pilot; report
           passing; reserve personnel;
           Republic of the Philippines;
           revision proposal; reply paid;
           radar plot; rocket projectile;
           reaction product; reception poor;
           reinforced plastic; research
           paper; real part; record proces-
           sor; rated pressure; reporting
           post; reference pattern; Remington-
           Peters
RP-46   Rouchnoi Pelemet, machine gun 7.62mm
           (SU)
RPA   radium plaque adaptometer; reserve
           personnel army; regional port
           authorities; record of personal
           achievement
RPAE   regulations for the preservation of
           artillery equipment (UK)
RPAO   radium plaque adaptometer operator
RPAODS-1   remotely piloted aerial observa-
           tion designation system (battle-
           field laser)
RPB   regional preparedness board
RPBG   revised programme and budget
           guidance
RPC   Royal pioneer corps; request pleas-
           ure of company; reporting to
           commander; regional preparedness
           committee; registered publications
           clerk; registered publications
           custodian; reports of patents
           decision and trade mark cases;
           reporting post, coastal; reversed
           phased chromatography
RPCAP   radar picket combat air patrol
RPCTC   Royal pioneer corps training centre
           (Northampton)
RPD   rocket propulsion department; radar
           planning device; regional port
           director; Ruchnoi Pelemet
           Degtyarev (light machine gun
           7.62mm) (SU)
rpd   rapid
RPE   rocket propulsion establishment
           (Westcott UK); relative price
           effect; range probable error;
           radio production executive
RPEP   register of planned emergency pro-
           cedures
RPF   real property facilities

R&PFB   recreation and physical fitness
           branch
RPG   regional planning group (Nato);
           random pulse generator; report
           programme generator; rounds per
           gun; radiation protection guide;
           rocket propelled grenade
RPG-2   rocket propelled grenade anti-tank
           (SU)
RPG-6   anti-tank hand grenade WW2 (SU)
RPG-7   anti-tank grenade launcher (SU)
RPG-43   anti-tank hand grenade (SU)
rpgpm   rounds per gun per minute
RPH   remotely piloted helicopter;
           relative pulse height; revolutions
           per hour
RPI   radar precipitation integrator;
           retail price index; real property
           inventory; Rank Precision Indus-
           tries
RPIO   registered publications issuing
           office
RPK   Ruchnoi Pelemet Kalashnikov (light
           machine gun 7.62mm) (SU)
RPKS   light machine gun with folding
           stock (SU)
RPL   repair parts list; ramp powered
           lighter (UK)
rplca   replica
RPM   reliability performance measure;
           resale price maintenance; random
           phase model; revolutions per
           minute; rounds per minute;
           registered publications manual
RPMA   real property maintenance activities
RPMF   reserve personnel master file
RPMIO   registered publications mobile
           issuing office
rpmn   repairman
rpmorpm   round per mortar per minute
RPN   reserve personnel Navy
RPO   railway post office; regimental pay
           office; regulating petty officer;
           registered publications officer;
           regional personnel officer;
           Radiophare Omnidirectional (omni-
           directional radio beacon)
RPOA   recognized private operating
           agencies
RPOD   resident to place of duty rate (UK)
RPP   regional priority plan; requisition
           processing point
RPPI   remote plan position indicator
RPQ   request for price quotation
RProP   receiving proficiency pay
RPRV   remotely piloted retrievable
           vehicle; remotely piloted
           research vehicle
RPS   radiological protection service;
           rapid processing system; radar

	plotting sheet; revolutions per second; rounds per second; rotations per second; registered publications system; registered publications section
	-PL personnel library
RPSTL	repair parts and special tools list
rpt	repeat; repeater; reprint
RPT	recruit performance test
R&PT	rifle and pistol team
RPTC	Royal physical training corps
RPtPt	reporting point
RPU	radio priority unit; registered publications unit
RPV	remotely piloted vehicles
RPzB-54	Raketenpanzerbüchse, Panzerschreck WW2 (infantry anti-tank rocket launcher)
RPzGr	Raketenpanzerbüchsengranate (hollow charge grenade for anti-tank launcher)
RQ	respiratory quotient
RQE	relative quantum effectiveness
RQL	reference quality level
RQMCM	regimental quartermaster corporal major
RQMS	regimental quartermaster sergeant
rqmt	requirement
rqn	requisition
RQN-1	radar interceptor
RQS	ready qualified for standby
RQT-9X	Sentinel, battlefield surveillance radar by Selenia
RR	The Rhodesia Regiment; relegated to reserve; remount regulations; recruiting regulations; register of recruits; regimental register; railroad; ready reserve (US); retired reserve (US); recommended for re-engagement (UK); rifle range; recruit roll; radio relay; radio ranging; radiation resistance; research reactor; retro rocket; rendezvous radar; respiratory rate; Rolls Royce
R&R	rest and recreation; rest and recuperation (US); rest and rehabilitation; rest and relaxation; recovery and reconstruction
RR-170	chaff cartridge by Tracor
RRA	The Royal Regiment of Artillery; retraining and re-employment administration
RRAC	regional resources advisory committee
RRAD	Red River army depot
RRAF	Royal Rhodesian Air Force
RRB	railroad retirement board; radio research board; rapid response bibliography

RRC	radio relay centre; The Royal Regiment of Canada; (Lady of the) Royal Red Cross; requirements review committee; rubber reserve committee
RRCM	Royal Red Cross Medal
RRCT	regional railway control team
RRE	Royal radar establishment (Malvern UK); radar research establishment
RR/EO	race relations/equal opportunity (US)
RRF	The Royal Regiment of Fusiliers; rapid reaction force; ready reserve force; radio range finding
RRI	Rowett Research Institute (Bucksburn); rubber research institute; radio recognition and identification
	--IFF
RRIC	rubber research institute of Ceylon
RRIM	rubber research institute of Malaysia
RRIS	remote radar interrogation station
RRL	road research laboratory; radio research laboratory (Japan); radio relay link; radio relay (station); regiment reserve line (US)
RRMRP	ready reserve mobilization reinforcement pool
RRP	radar reporting post
RRPC	reserve reinforcement processing centre
RRR	rapid runway repair; range and range rate
RRRA	regulations for recruiting of the regular army
RRRT	runway rapid repair team
RRS	radio research station
	--RSRS
	remaining radiation service; Royal research ship; Royal research station; radio range system; range rate system; radio relay station; ready reserve status (US)
RRSRS	rapid runway (road) surface repair system by Laird
RRSTRAF	ready reserve, strategic army forces (US)
RRT	railroad transport; ready round transporter
RRTC	retractable replaceable thermocouple
RRTS	range-rate tracking system
RRU	radio research unit
RRV	rate of rise of voltage
RRW	The Royal Regiment of Wales

RS	receiving station; regulating station; report of survey; road space; recruiting station; recruiting service; revised status; recording secretary; revised statutes; Royal Standard; The Royal Scots Regiment; radio supervisor; reconnaissance squadron; rifle, survival; reader stop; receiver sight; roll stabilization; resolver; repair ship; research station; recorder separator; right side; rejection slip; Reizstoff (tear gas); Rohde & Schwarz (Hamburg)	RSDU	radar storm detection unit
		RSEE	Royal school of electronic engineering (Arborfield)
		RSF	The Royal Scots Fusiliers; radiological survey flight
		RSFA	radiological survey flight altitude
		RSFPP	retired servicemen's family protection plan (scheme)
		RSFSR	Russian Soviet Federated Socialist Republic
		RSG	The Royal Scots Greys
RS-1	Rohini, research satellite (India)	rsgn	re-assign; rising
RS-80	MARS, Mittleres Artillerie Raketensystem (medium artillery rocket system)	rsg	resign; re-assign
		RSI	Royal signals institution; record status indicator; replacement stream input; regional staff inspector; rationalization, standardization and interoperability (US programme) (Nato); research studies institute
RS-80	Foil, free-flight rocket system (UK)		
RS-700	... 710, ... 730, airborne infra-red line scanner		
RSA	Royal Signals Association; Royal Scottish Academy; Redstone Arsenal; Rechnergestützte Schussdatenanalyseanlage by MaK (computerized firing data analysis system)	R-SI	restricted - security information (US)
		RS&I	receipt, storage and issue (US)
		RSigs	Royal corps of signals
		RSIUFL	release suspension for issue and issue following lots
		RSJ	rolled steel joist
RSA-20	Rettungssystem Aussenlast by Autoflug (external load rescue system)	RSK-100	Raketensperre, Kurzzeit by Rheinmetall WW2 (barrage rockets)
RSAAC	Royal signals Army apprentices college (Harrogate)	RSL	returned service league (Australia); remote Sprint launch; Ruckstosslader (recoil feeding gun)
RSAAF	Royal South African Air Force; Royal Saudi Arabian Air Force		
		RSLA	raising of school-leaving age (UK)
RSAC	reactor safety advisory committee (Canada)	RSM	Royal school of mines; regimental sergeant major; reconnaissance strategic missile
RSAF	Royal small arms factory (Enfield); Royal Saudi (Arabian) Air Force		
		RSME	Royal school of military engineering
RSB	reduced size blueprint; range safety beacon; regimental stretcher bearer; regional shipping board	rsn	reason
		RSNP	registered student nurse program (US)
RSC	runway surface condition; revised statutes of Canada; research status code; rescue sub-centre; reserve service control; recruit selection centre (Sutton Coldfield UK)	RSO	railway sorting office; recruiting staff officer; regimental special order; regimental surveillance officer; regimental supply officer; railhead supply officer; roadhead supply officer; range safety officer; reconnaissance and survey officer
rsch	research		
Rsch&Dev	research and development		
RschOpsDet	research operations detachment	RSOD	Royal school for officers' daughters (Bath)
RSD	recovery salvage and disposal; rolling steel door; rescue shoring and demolition squads (RN); returned stores depot; reserve supply depot; regimental salvage depot	RSOP	reconnaissance, selection and occupation of position
		RSP	reconnaissance and security positions; render- safe procedures; reserve stock point
		RSPCA	Royal Society for the Prevention of Cruelty to Animals
RSDG	Royal Scots Dragoon Guards		
RSDP	remote site data processing	RSPI	resident shared page index
RSDS	Royal soldiers' daughters' school (Hampstead)	RSPL	recommended spare parts list
		R-Sprenggr	Raketensprenggranate 38cm

	(rocket assisted HE shell) WW2 (GE)	RTAFB	Royal Thailand Air Force base
rsq	rescue	RTAG	range technical advisory group
RSR	route surveillance radar; required supply rate; ready service ring; The Royal Sussex Regiment	RTAM	remote terminal access method
		RTB	return to base
RSRA	rotor systems research aircraft by Sikorsky	RTC	reference transfer calibrator; radio transmission control; Royal Tank corps; replacement training centre; railway training centre; recruit training centre; recruit training command
RSRE	Royal signals and radar establishment (Malvern)		
RSRI	regional science research institute	RTCA	radio technical commission for aeronautics
RSRS	radio and space research station (Slough UK)	RTCC	real time computer complex (Nasa)
RSS	rifle, shotgun, survival; relaxed static stability	RTCM	radio technical commission for marine services
RSSAILA	returned soliders' sailors' and airmen's imperial league of Australia	RTCP	radio transmission control panel
RSSP	reporting secondary stock point	RTCW	recruit training command, women
R&SSQ	repair and salvage squadron	RTD	return to duty; research and technology division; resistor temperature detector
RSSR	The Royal South Sascatchewan Regiment (Canada)		
rst	resistance	rtd	returned
RSTBS	regulations for supply transport and barrack services	RTDA	returned absentees
		RTDS	real time data system
rstd	restricted	RTE	radio transmission equipment; radio trunk extension; railway transport establishment; real time executive
RSTM&H	Royal Society of Tropical Medicine and Hygiene		
RSTO	regimental supply transport office	rte	route
RSU	road safety unit; recovery storage unit	RTEB	radio trades examination board
		RTEL	runway and taxiway edge lighting
RSTR	Royal signals training regiment	RTG	radio-isotope thermal generator; radio-isotope thermo-electric generator
rstr	restricted		
RSTW	Royal signals training wing		
RSupO	railhead supply officer; roadhead supply officer; regimental supply officer	rtg	rating; routing
		RTG	Raketentechnik GmbH (Schobenhausen) (Diel + MBB)
RSussex	The Royal Sussex Regiment	RTg	Raketen Tauchgranate 38cm WW2 (GE) (hand-launched anti-submarine rocket)
RSV	Rhine-Schelde-Verolme (Rotterdam)		
RSVP	re-startable solid variable pulse (rocket); random signal vibration protector; répondez s'il vous plait		
		RTI	radar target identification; referred to input; reporting time interval
rsvr	reservoir		
RSwN	Royal Swedish Navy	RTIP	radar target identification point
RT	receiver transmitter; radio telephony; radio telegraphy; range table; road transport; register tonnage; right turn; reaction time; rocket target; room temperature; raise top; re-perforator transmitter; record of trial; rough terrain; reading test; regular time	RTITB	road transport industry training board
		RTk	The Royal Tank Regiment
		RTL	resistor transistor logic; regimental training line (US)
		RTLA	road transport lighting act
		RTN	Royal Thai Navy
R&T	research and technology	RTM	rapid turning magnetron; reconnaissance tactical missile; receiver transmitter modulator; real time monitor; response time module; registered trade mark
rt	route; right		
RT-61	mortar, 120mm by Thomson-Brandt		
RTA	receiver transmitter antenna; reciprocal trade agreements; relative target altitude; regulations for the Territorial Army; road traffic act; Royal Thai Army	RTN	registered trade name; Royal Thai Navy
		rtn	return; retain
		RTN-10X	naval tracking system by Selenia
RTAF	Royal Thai Armed Forces; Royal Thailand Air Force	RTNE	radio technical new entrant

RTO	referred to output; rail traffic officer; railway transportation office(r); regimental transportation officer
R/TOL	reduced take-off and landing aircraft
RTOS	real-time operating system
RTP	reinforced theatre plan; requirement and test procedures
RTR	Royal Tank Regiment
rtrd	retarded
rtrn	returned
RTS	reserve tug service; real-time subroutines; remote testing system; rural telephone system; radar target simulator; radar tracking station
RTSCS	ruggedized transportable synthesized communication system by Granger
RTST	radio technician selection test
RTT	radio teletype (Nato); reservoir and tube tunnel
RTTY	radio teletype(writer)
RTU	remote terminal unit; returned to unit; reinforcement training unit
RTV	rocket test vehicle; re-entry test vehicle; remote television
R&TV	radio and television
RTW	road tank wagon; ready to wear
RTX	real-time executive
RU	ready-use; reusable (mine); registered user; release unit; radio unit
R&U	repairs and utilities
RÜAK	Rüstungswirtschaftlicher Arbeitskreis (GE) (armaments industrial working group)
RUAT	report upon arrival threat
rub	rubber
RUC	riverine utility craft; Royal Ulster Constabulary; reporting unit code
RUCR	Royal Ulster Constabulary Reserve
rud	rudder
RUD	report unsatisfactory or defective
	AOE aviation ordnance equipment
	M material
	MIN mine
	MINDE mines, depth charges or associated equipment
	TorpE torpedo equipment
	Rieger & Dietz (Unterkochen GE)
RUDI	restricted use digital instrument
RUFAS	remote underwater fishery assessment system
Rufbus	demand-controlled public passenger bus by Dornier
RUKBA	Royal United Kingdom beneficient association
RUM	remote underwater manipulator
Rumbling Rhino	amphibious tank

RUN	rewind and unload
RüPl	Rüstungsplanung (GE) (armaments planning)
RUPP	road used as public path
RUPPERT	reserve unit personnel performance report
RUQ	rifle unqualified
RUR	The Royal Ulster Rifles
RUR-5A	ASROC, anti-submarine rocket by Honeywell
RURLAM	replacement unit repair level analysis model
Rushton	aerial towed target
Rushton LL	aerial towed target height-keeping by Flight Refuelling
RUSI	Royal United Services Institute for Defence Studies (London)
RUSIJ	Royal United Services Institute for Defence Studies Journal
RUSI/RMAS	Royal United Services Institute for Defence Studies/Royal Military Academy Sandhurst
RUSM	Royal united service museum
RUSNO	resident US naval officer
Rutgar	electronic warfare radar simulator by LME
Rutu	wheeled combat vehicle Embraer
RV	rescue vessel; research vessel re-entry vehicle; remaining velocity; rendez-vous; rifle volunteers; electronic reconnaissance aircraft; Richtverbindung (directional radio link)
RVA	Ruhr Valley Authority; regular veterans' association of the US
RVAH	carrier-borne long-range reconnaissance squadron (USN); recce attack squadron (USN)
RVC	rifle volunteer corps; Royal veterinary college
RVD	residual vapour detector
RVH	Royal Victoria Hospital (Netley) (closed)
RVHR	road vehicles headlamps regulations
RVLExR	road vehicles lighting (standing vehicles) exemption regulation
RVLR	road vehicles lighting regulations
RVM	M-88, recovery vehicle, medium; Royal Victorian Medal;
RVN	Republic of (South) Viet Nam
RVNAF	Republic of (South) Viet Nam Air Force
RVNAFHM	Republic of (South) Viet Nam armed force honour medal
	-FC first class
	-SC second class
RVNCAM	Republic of (South) Viet Nam civil actions medal
RVNGCUCWP	Republic of (South) Viet Nam gallantry cross unit citation with palm

RVO	Member of the Royal Victorian Order
RVO-TNO	Rijksverdedigings Organisatie Toegepast Natuurkundig Onderzoek Den Haag (Netherlands' National Defence Research Council)
RVP	Reid vapour pressure
RVR	runway visual range; runway visibility range
rvr	river
RVS	reserve vehicle stores
rvse	reverse
RVT	Räderversuchsträger (wheeled experimental vehicle)
RVU	research vessel unit
RVV	runway visibility value
R W	rotary wing (aircraft); radiological warfare; right of way; runway; read write; Royal warrant (for pay and promotion); repair workshop
R&W	recreation and welfare
RW-43	Puppchen, 8.8cm rocket launcher anti-tank WW2 (GE)
RWAFF	The Royal West African Frontier Force
RWarR	The Royal Warwickshire Regiment
RWBH	records will be hand-carried
RWC	relative water content; regional welfare committee
RWE	Radarwarnempfänger (radar warning receiver)
RWF	The Royal Welsh Fusiliers
RWI	radio wire integration; radar warning installation
RWiltsYeo	The Royal Wiltshire The Prince of Wales's Own Yeomanry

RWK	The Queen's Own Royal West Kent Regiment
RWK-007	rocket launcher by Oerlikon
RWL-004	twin rocket launcher by Oerlikon
RWNBH	records will not be hand-carried
RWO	reimbursable work order
RWPAP	Royal warrant for the pay, promotion and non-effective pay of the Army
RWR	radar warning receiver; remain well right of ...; Royal Winnipeg Rifles (Canada)
RWRW	radar warning and reconnaissance wing (USAF)
RWS	receiver waveform simulation
RWSR	The Royal West Surrey Regiment
RWTC	recruits' weapon training course
rwy	runway
RX	radio receiver
RY	residual yield
ry	railway
RYE	retirement year ending
RYM	reference your message
RZ	return to zero; recruiting zone; reconnaissance zone
RZ-	Rauchzylinder WW2 (GE) (airborne rockets)
65	65cm
73	73cm
15/8	150mm
100	420mm
RZF	Rundblickzielfernrohr (panoramic aiming telescope)

S

S   situation (report); section; staff
         South; (air raid) shelter; signals;
         stores; supply company; supply and
         secretariat; snow; short; sub-
         marine; super; silenced; super-
         sonic; sulphur; Sheridan Products
         Inc. (Racine US); schwer (heavy);
         sicher (safe); Spitzgeschoss
         (pointed projectile); Stahlhülse
         (steel cartridge case)
S-class coastal submarines (RN)
S-Boot   Schnellboot (fast patrol boat)
S-day   submarine deployment day (Nato)
S-gun   40mm automatic airborne gun by
         Vickers
S-Mine   Schützen (spring) Mine (anti-person-
         nel mine)
S-Rolle Stacheldrahtrolle (barbed wire coil)
4S   Sperry Secor Simulations Systems
         (Fairfax Va)
6S   small surface-to-air ship self-
         defence system (Nato programme for
         the 1980s)
S-1   adjutant (US Army) personnel planning
S-2   intelligence officer (US Army)
         intelligence and security
S-2E   Tracker, anti-submarine patrol air-
         craft by Grumman
S-3   operations and training officer (US
         Army) operations department
S-3A   Viking, carrier-based anti-submarine
         aircraft by Lockheed
S-4   supply officer (US Army) quarter-
         master's department
S-5   civil affairs officer (US Army);
         silent reconnaissance aircraft by
         VFW
S-6   service respirator (UK)
S-23   180mm gun (SU)
S-24   Kiebitz, trainer aircraft WW2 by
         Focke-Wulf
S-53   smoke hand grenade (EG)
S-55   Whirlwind, helicopter by Westland
         helicopter by Sikorsky, US designa-
         tion: HRS-1, HO-4S, H-19 (USAF)

S-58   SH-34, medium transport helicopter
         by Sikorsky
S-60   57mm anti-aircraft gun (SU)
S-61   RH-3, Sea King, transport helicopter
         by Sikorsky
S-62   amphibious helicopter by Sikorsky
S-64   Skycrane, CH-54, Tarhe, heavy-lift
         helicopter by Sikorsky
S-65   CH-53, Sea Stallion, heavy helicop-
         ter by Sikorsky
S-67   Black Hawk, assault helicopter by
         Sikorsky
S-70   Black Hawk, UTTAS, YH-60, SH-60,
         assault helicopter by Sikorsky
S-76   Spirit, helicopter by Sikorsky
S-80   engineer tractor (SU)
S-1000   engineer tractor (SU)
S-103   MiG-15, Czech version
S-104   MiG-17, Czech version
S-105   MiG-19, Czech version
S-107   MiG-21, Czech version
S-142   Zobel class, torpedo boats (FGN) by
         Lürssen
S-143   Schnellboot, fast patrol boats (FGN)
S-148   fast patrol boat guided missiles
         (FGN) by Lürssen CMN
S-150   anti-personnel mine WW2
S-162   fast patrol boat project (FGN)
S-211   jet trainer aircraft by SIAI
S-373   battlefield electronic warfare
         system by Marconi
S-800   naval light-weight surveillance
         radar by Marconi
S-1019   forward air controller aircraft by
         SIAI
S-1148   UHF naval multi-coupler by E-Systems
S-1722   US Senate Bill against firearms in
         private hands
S-8600   military computer system by IAI
SA   Secretary of the Army (US); seaman
         apprentice; service adviser;
         supply assistant; supply accoun-
         tant; special agent; salvation
         army; subject to approval; see
         also; South Afirca; South America;

South Australia; servant's allowance; semi-annual (report); supervisory authority; supplemental
agreement; simple alert; self
acting (fuse); semi automatic;
surface-to-air (missile); small
arms; shop accessory; submerged
arc (welding); safe arrival;
Savage Arms Company; Springfield
Armory; Société d'Armes (Paris)

S&A safety and arming (device); bureau
of supplies and accounts (US)

SA-1 Guild, surface-to-air missile (SU)

SA-2 Guideline, surface-to-air missile
(SU)

SA-3 Goa, surface-to-air missile (SU)

SA-4 Ganef, surface-to-air missile (SU)

SA-5 Gammon, Griffon, long-range, high-
altitude surface-to-air missile
(SU)

SA-6 Gainful, surface-to-air missile (SU)

SA-7 Grail, Strela, portable IR guidance
high-altitude surface-to-air
missile (SU)

SA-8 Gecko, surface-to-air missile (SU)

SA-9 Gaskin, short-range surface-to-air
missile (SU)

SA-11 surface-to-air missile

SA-13 laser communications system by SAS
Industries

SA-16 Albatros, amphibious plane (US)

SA-100 Hunter Robot, remote-controlled bomb
disposal vehicle by SAS

SA-200 Saeta, jet trainer aircraft by
Hispano

SA-315 Lama, utility helicopter by AS

SA-319 Alouette III, utility helicopter by
AS

SA-321 Super Frelon, heavy transport helicopter by AS

SA-330 Puma, medium transport helicopter by
AS

SA-332 Super Puma, anti-submarine helicopter by AS

SA-341 ... 342, Gazelle, light helicopter
by AS

SA-355 Twin Star, anti-submarine helicopter
by AS

SA-360 Dauphin, transport helicopter by AS

SA-365 Dauphin II, military version by AS

SA-3130 Alouette II, helicopter by AS

SAA South African Army; summary activity
account; staff administrative
assistant; single action Army
(revolver); small arms ammunition;
Standards Association of Australia;
surface active agents

SAAB Svenska Aeroplan Aktie Bolag
(Linköping)

Saab-17 tactical bomber by Saab

Saab-21R jet fighter 1949

Saab-29 J-29, jet fighter aircraft 1951 by
Saab

Saab-32 Lansen, jet aircraft 1951 by Saab

Saab-35 Draken, Mach 2 jet aircraft by
Saab

Saab-37 Viggen, combat aircraft by Saab

Saab-105 trainer/tactical support aircraft
by Saab

Saab-372 air-to-air missile by Saab

Saab Sub remote-controlled submersible by
Saab

SAAC special assistant for arms control;
small arms ammunition column

SAAD school of anti-aircraft defence;
small arms ammunition depot

SAAEB South African atomic energy board

SAAF South African Air Force

SAAM special assignment airlift mission

SAAMA San Antonio air material area

SAAMI Small Arms and Ammunition Manufacturers Institute; Sporting Arms
and Ammunition Institute (Hamden
CT USA)

SAAR special assignment airlift requirements

Saar class, Israel patrol boats guided
missiles by CMN

SAARF special allied airborne reconnaissance force

SAAS standard army ammunition system (US)

SA-AT sub-ammunition anti-tank by SNIA
(Firos-25 rocket warhead)

SAATC South African air transport control

SAB scientific advisory board; solar
alignment bay; subject as above

sab saboteur

SABA Sol Air Basse Altitude (FR-GE)
(anti-aircraft missile programme)

Sabalo class, submarines (Venezuela) by
HDW 1977

SABCA Société Anonyme Belge de Constructions Aeronautiques (Brussels)

SABMIS sea-based anti-ballistic missile
intercept system

sabo sabotage

Saboteur 8x8 light amphibious vehicle by
Bedford

Sabra tank (Israel)

SABRA South African bureau of racial
affairs

SABRE secure airborne radar equipment

Sabre F-86, YF-85, jet fighter by North
American; air-launched anti-tank
missile by BAe

Sabrebat forward swept wing jet project by
Rockwell

SABS stabilizing automatic bombsight;
South African bureau of standards

SAC standard aircraft characteristics;

SAC	small arms committee; scientific advisory council; senior aircraftman; supreme allied commander; special agent in charge (CIA); supporting arms coordinator; signal analysis course; state appeal court (US); strategic air command (USAF); South Atlantic Coast; security and administration council (Burma); Sullivan Arms Corporation
SACA	supreme allied commander Atlantic
SACAD	stress analysis and computer aided design
SACANGO	Southern African committee on air navigation and ground operation
SACC	supporting arms coordinating centre
SACCS	strategic air command automated control and communications system
SACE	semi-automatic check-out equipment
SACEUR	supreme allied commander Europe (Casteu Belgium)
SACEUREP	supreme allied commander Europe representative
SACI	South Atlantic co-operative investigation
Saci-54/7	Italian pressure anti-tank mine
SACLANT	supreme allied commander Atlantic (Norfolk Virginia)
SACLANTCEN	SACLANT anti-submarine warfare research centre (La Spezia IT)
SACLANTREPEUR	SACLANT representative in Europe
SACLEX	SACLANT standing exercise orders
SACLAU	SACLANT authentification system
SACLOS	semi-automatic command to line-of-sight
SACM	Société Alsacienne de Constructions Mécaniques de Mulhouse
SACMDR	site activation commander
SACMED	supreme allied commander Mediterranean
SACO	Sino-American co-operative organization
SACo	Service Armament Corporation
SACOM	southern area command (US); secretary (of the navy) advisory committee on manpower (US)
SACP	Crotale, Surface-Air Courte Portee (naval anti-aircraft missile)
SACREP	messages from SACLANTREPEUR to SACLANT
SACS	structure and composition system
SACSEA	supreme allied commander South East Asia
SACSIR	South African council for scientific and industrial research
SAD	search and destroy; safety and arming device; special artificer's device; systems automation division;

	Sacramento army depot; support air division; support arms department
SADANG	sonobuoy and data processor for Atlantic Nouvelle Generation by Thomson-CSF
SADARM	sense and destroy armor (smart artillery anti-tank munition) (US programme)
SADAS	Sperry airborne data acquisition system
SADC	sector air defence commander
SADF	South African defence forces
SADIE	scanning analog-to-digital input equipment
SADM	special atomic demolition munition
SADMG	special artificer device, machine gun
SAdO	senior administrative officer; station administrative officer
SADS	Soviet air defence system
SADTC	SHAPE air defence technical centre The Hague now: STC
SAE	society of automotive engineers (US); self-addressed envelope; stamped addressed envelope; site acceptance evaluation
SAEB	special army evaluation board (US)
SAED	small aircraft engine department
SAEDA	subversion and espionage directed against US Army and deliberate security violations
SAES	special assistant for environmental sciences (USN)
Saeta	SA-200, jet trainer aircraft by Hispano
SAF	Swiss Air Force; strategic air force; secretary of the air force; special action force; Southern attack force; The Sultan (of Oman's) armed forces; stability augmentation feature
SAFA	South African freedom association
SAFAB	Sailors' and families' advice bureau (UK)
SAFB	Stead air force base
SafCmd	US Army Safeguard command
SafCPM	Safeguard communications programme manager
SafCPMO	Safeguard communications programme management office
SAFE	Spectronix automatic fire extinguishing; San Andreas fault experiment; save a friend in Europe (organization); South African Friends of England; self-addressed foolscap envelope
SafeCen	safety centre
Safeguard	anti-ballistic missile system (US)

SAFEPlan submarine air frequency plan
SAFER sequential action flow routine (UK)
SAFF South Arabian Federal forces
SafPACC Safeguard public affairs coordinating committee (US)
SAfr South Africa
SAfrD South African Dutch
SAFS safety, arming and fusing system
SafTCP Safeguard tactical communications plan
SafTCS Safeguard tactical communications system
SafTrans Safeguard transportation system
SAFU store and forwards unit (to FACE) by MSDS
SAFUS under-secretary of the USAF
SAG Southern army group; study advisory group; scientific advisory group; service advisory group; Swiss aerospace group
SAGA short arc geodetic adjustment; scout and guide activity
Sagaie ERC-90, anti-aircraft gun 90mm (FR)
SAGE stratospheric aerosol and gas experiment (satellite) (Nasa); semi-automatic ground environment by Western Electric (CONUS IFF system)
SAGE/BUIC SAGE back up interceptor control
SAGEM Société d'Applications Générales d'Électricité et de Mécanique (Paris)
SAGGA scout and guide graduate association
SAGW surface-to-air guided weapon
SAH semi-active homing; supreme allied headquarters;
SAHG
SAHG semi-active homing guidance
SAHQ supreme allied headquarters
SAHR society of army historical research
SAHRIU standby attitude heading reference interface unit
SAHRS secondary attitude and heading reference system
SAI senior army instructor (US); special artificer, instruments (USN); South African infantry; Seemine, anti-invasion (anti-invasion seabed mine)
SAIC small arms inter-post competition
SAIL ship armament inventory list
SAILS standard army intermediate level system (US)
Sailwing propeller-driven RPV by Fairchild
SAIMR South African institute of medical research
SAINT satellite interceptor; system analysis of integrated networks of tasks
SAINS satellite inspection system
SAINTS single attack integrated system

Saiqa commandoes (Egypt)
SAIR semi-automatic inventory report
SAIRR South African institute of race relations
SAK-40 naval anti-aircraft gun by Bofors
SAKI self-organizing automatic keyboard instructor
SAL special ammunition load; station allowance list; salvation army; salvage; salary
Saladin FV-601, wheeled armoured car
Salamander FV-651 ... 652, fire crash tender
SALH South Alberta Light Horse Regiment (Canada)
Salisbury class, frigates (RN)
SALORS structural analysis of layered orthotropic ring-stiffened shells
SALP semi-active laser-guided projectile
SALS standard army logistics system (US); super (height) approach light system; short (height) approach light system
SALT strategic arms limitation talks
SALTI summary accounting for low-dollar turn-over items (US)
salv salvage
SalvDiv salvage diver
SalvDv salvage dives
Salvo project, infantry training system (US Army)
Salvus apparatus, oxygen respirator
SALWIS shipboard air-launched weapons installation system
SAM surface-to-air missile; screen for aeronautical material (US); school of aviation medicine; special air mission (detachment) (US); space available mail (US)
SAm South America; sequential access method; strong absorption model
SAMAA special assistant for military assistance affairs (US)
SAMAP southern air material area, Pacific
SAMAR ship activation, maintenance and repair; surface-to-air missile availability report
Samara class, spy ships (SU)
Samaritan FV-104, armoured ambulance by Alvis
Sam Browne UK officer's belt and shoulder strap
SAMBUD system for automation of material plan for army material budget (US)
SAMC South African medical corps
SAM-D Patriot, surface-to-air missile (in) development (US programme)
SAME society of American military engineers
SAMGS small arms and machine gun school

SAMI   socially acceptable monitoring
          instrument; single action main-
          tenance instructions
SAML   standard army management language
SAMM   Société d'Applications des Machines
          Motrice (Issy-les-Moulineaux)
SAMMS   standard automated material manage-
          ment system (US)
SAM-NIS   screen for aeronautical material
          not in stock (US)
SAMOS   satellite and missile observation
          system
SAMP   Surface-Air Moyenne Portee (FR)
          (anti-aircraft missile); Société
          des Ateliers Mécaniques de Pont-
          sur-Sambre (FR)
SAMPAM   system for automation of material
          plans for army material (US)
SAMPAN   system for automation of material
          plan
SAMPE   society of aerospace material and
          process engineers (US)
SAMS   standard army maintenance system
          (US); sample method survey (for
          family housing requirements) (US);
          satellite and missile surveillance
SAM/SAT   South American South Atlantic area
SAMSO   space and missile systems organiza-
          tion AFSC
SAMSON   strategic automatic message switch-
          ing operational network (Canada)
Samson   FV-106, recovery tank (UK);
          magnetic mine
SAMTEC   space and missile test center (US)
Samuel Gompers class, destroyer tenders
          (USN)
Samurai   76mm missile by CSTM air-to-ground
          and ground-to-ground
SAN   styrene-acrylo-nitrile (copolymer);
          school of air navigation
san   sanitary; sanitation
SA-N   surface-to-air, naval missile (SU)
SA-N-1   Goa, surface-to-air, naval missile
          (SU)
SA-N-2   Guideline, surface-to-air, naval
          missile (SU)
SA-N-3   Goblet, surface-to-air, naval
          missile (SU)
SA-N-4   Gecko, surface-to-air, naval
          missile (SU)
SAN-4   surface-to-air naval missile (RN)
SANA   State, army, navy, air (US)
SANCIP   SACLANT approved Nato common infra-
          structure programme
SANCOR   South African national committee for
          oceanographic research
SandA   (bureau) of supplies and accounts
          (US)
SandFSD   sea and foreign service division
Sandringham four-engined flying boat by
          Shorts; 6x6 Land Rover

SANDT   school of applied non-destructive
          testing
SANF   South African naval forces
SanInsp   sanitation inspector (US)
Sanna-17 machine pistol 9mm (South Africa)
SANR   subject to approval, no risk
SANS   South African naval service
SANU   South African national union
SANZ   standards association of New Zealand
SAO   Smithsonian astrophysical observa-
          tory; survivors' assistance
          officer; support air observer;
          special artificer, optical (US);
          senior accountant officer;
          squadron accountant officer
SAOC   space and astronautics orientation
          course
SAODAP   special action officer for drug
          abuse prevention
SAP   scouting and amphibious plane
          (USCG); semi-armour piercing
          (bomb); special airfield pavement;
          system assurance programme;
          system alignment procedure; soon
          as possible; spot authorization
          plan; South African Police;
          search and attack priority;
          search and attack pattern
SAPF   South African permanent force
SAPFR   South African permanent force
          reserve
SA-PFF   sub ammunition pre-formed fragmen-
          tation (warhead for Firos-25)
SAPHEI   semi-armour piercing high-explosive
          incendiary (anti-aircraft shell)
SAPHEI-T semi-armour piercing high-explo-
          sive incendiary with tracer
Saphir   class, minelaying submarine (FR)
SAPI   semi-armour piercing, incendiary
          (anti-aircraft shell)
SapNo   saponification number
SAPO   sub-area petroleum office
SAPP   special airfields pavements pro-
          gramme; security, accuracy,
          propriety and policy (in informa-
          tion release)
Sapphire naval fire-control system by
          Marconi
SAR   search and rescue; short assault
          rifle; sea-air rescue; semi-
          active radar; semi-automatic
          rifle; synthetic aperture radar;
          site acceptance review; special
          aeronautical requirement; stan-
          dardized abnormality ratio;
          selected acquisition report;
          selected air reserve; South
          African Republic
Sar   class, advanced construction patrol
          boats for Turkey by Lürssen

SAR-8	IRTS, infra-red tracking system by Spar
SAR-33	patrol boats guided missiles for Turkey by Abeking & Rasmussen
SARA	search and rescue aid; Southern Arizona rescue association
Saracen	FV-603, wheeled armoured personnel carrier by Alvis
SARAH	search and rescue and homing (equipment); semi-active radar alternate head
SARBE	search and rescue beacon equipment by Burndept (UK)
SARC	search and rescue coordinator artillery rocket system by Breda
SARCC	search and rescue coordination centre
SARCen	search and rescue coordination centre
SARCom	search and rescue communicator; search and rescue command
SARD	special airlift requirement document
SARDA	state and regional defense airlift (US); state and regional disaster airlift
SARDIP	stricken aircraft reclamation and disposal programme
SAREx	search and rescue exercise
SAR&H	South African railway and harbours
SARIC	search and rescue incident classification
SARIE	radar warning receiver with analyser by EMI
SARLant	search and rescue Atlantic
SARMA	Société Anonyme de Recherches de Mécanique Appliquée (St Vallier)
SARMC	search and rescue mission coordinator
SAROO	search and rescue operation officer
SAROS	Satellite de Radiodiffusion en Orbite Stationaire (broadcasting satellite in stationary orbit)
SARPac	search and rescue Pacific
Sarpac	anti-tank rocket launcher by Thomson/Brandt
SARPS	standard and recommended practices ICAO
SARSAT	search and rescue satellite (FR+CA)
SARR	search and rescue region
SARTEL	search and rescue telephone
SAS	special air service (regiment) (UK); sealed authentication system (US); special ammunition stockage; school of air support (Old Sarun UK); staff administrative specialist; stability augmentation system; survival avionics system (USAF) by Motorola; segment arrival storage; small angle

	scattering; small astronomical satellite; support amplifier station; Schnellbrücke auf Stützen (assault bridge on supports)
SASB	special air service battalion (UK)
SASC	small arms school corps (UK) senate armed services committee (US)
SASCOM	special ammunition support command
SASF	SIDPERS authorized strength file (standard installation division personnel system) (US)
SASLO	South African scientific liaison office
SASM	special assistant for strategic mobility (US)
SASMS	special assistant for surface missile system (US)
SASO	senior air staff officer; superintending armament supply officer (UK)
SASP	special ammunition supply point
SASR	special air service regiment (UK)
SASS	standard ammunition supply point; special aircraft service shop
SASSMP	Senate armed services subcommittee on manpower and personnel (US)
SASTE	semi-automatic shop test equipment
SASWREC	SACLANT anti-submarine warfare research centre --SACLANTCEN
SAT	space available travel; summer accelerated training; scholastic aptitude test; site acceptance test; small arms training; spatial apperception test; society for acoustic technology; system approach to training; ship's apparent time; security alert team; sabotage alert team; Société Anonyme de Télécommunications (Paris)
SAt	South Atlantic
sat	satisfactory; satellite
SATAF	site activation task force; second allied tactical air force
SATCC	southern air traffic control centre
SATCO	signal automatic air traffic control; senior air traffic control officer
SatCom	satellite communications by RCA
SatComA	satellite communications agency
SatCon	satellite condition
SATCP	Sol Air Très Courte Portée (infantry anti-aircraft missile) by Matra
SATD	Seattle army terminal detachment
SATE	study of army test and evaluation
SATEX	semi-automatic telegraph exchange
SATF	shortest access time first

SATFor	special air task force (US)
satfy	satisfactory
SATGCI	satellite ground controlled interception
SATIF	scientific and technical information facility (Nasa)
SATIN	semi-automatic air traffic integration (ground environment)
SATIR-Z-103	system zur Auswertung taktischer Informationen für Raketen-Zerstörer der Klasse 103 (FGN) (naval tactical information processing system)
SAtk	strike attack (US)
satl	satellite
satn	saturation
SatNav	satellite navigation
SATO	South Atlantic Treaty Organization (planned); strategic air transport operation
SATP	small arms target practice
SATS	short airfield for tactical support; solar alignment test site
SATU	small arms training unit
Saturn	orbital transport missile (US)
SAU	surface attack unit; search and attack unit
Saurer	infantry combat vehicle by Steyr
Sauro	class, submarines (IT)
SAus	South Australia
SAV	stock at valuation; salvage vessel
SAVA	South African veterans' association
SavDep	savings deposit
SAVE	shortages and valuable excesses; society of American valve engineers
SAVER	study to assess and validate essential reports (US)
SAVES	sizing of aerospace vehicle structures
SAVIEM	Société Anonyme de Véhicules Industriels et d'Équipements Mécaniques (Renault)
SAW	surface acoustic wave; XM-248, squad automatic weapon (US programme) 5.56mm
SAWAS	South African Women's auxiliary services
SAWBET	supply action will be taken (US)
SAWG	special advisory working group
SAWRS	supplementary aviation weather reporting station
SAWS	squad automatic weapon system 5.56mm (US); small arms weapons system; small arms weapons study
SAWVA	South African war veterans' association
SA-X-10	surface-to-air nuclear missile (SU)
SAXS	small angle X-ray scattering
SAYE	save as you earn

SB	South Britain; special branch (of the intelligence service) (UK); simultaneous broadcasting; siege battery; signal book; supply branch; searchlight battery; shipbuilding; submarine base; sick bay; sick berth; selection board; supply bulletin; services branch; service bulletin; stretcher bearer; signal boatswain; single breasted; single box; secondary battery; short barrel; switchboard; smooth bore; steamboat; single barrelled
SB-2	medium bomber WW2 by Tupolev (SU)
SB-2D	Helldiver, dive bomber by Curtiss WW2
SB-2U	Vindicator, dive bomber by Vought
SB-33	air-droppable plastic anti-personnel mine by MISAR
SB-81	helicopter-dispensable anti-tank mine by MISAR
SB-301	Shorland, armoured land rover by Short Brothers
SB-3614	automatic tactical switchboard by GTE Sylvania
SBA	sovereign base area (Cyprus); small business administration; sick bay attendant; standard beam approach
SBA-111	Tgb-30, 4x4 5 ton truck by Saab/ Scania
SBAC	society of British aerospace companies Ltd (London); society of British aerospace constructors
SBAE	stabilized bomb approach equipment
SBAMA	San Bernadino air material area
SBAO	Schiffsbesatzungs- & Ausbildingsordnung der Handelsmarine (merchant navy manning and training regulations)
SBAT-1113	Tgb-40, 6x6 8 ton truck by Scania
SBC	signal books correct
SBC-4	Helldiver, combat biplane by Curtiss
SBCA	sensor based control adapter
SBCo	shipbuilding company
SBCorp	shipbuilding corporation
SBCPO	sick bay chief petty officer
SBD	Schottky barrier diode; Dauntless, dive bomber by Douglas
SBE	smoke, base ejection (shell); strategic bomber enhancement (USAF programme)
sBeGr	schwere Betongranate (heavy concrete piercing grenade) WW2 (GE)
SBEUA	small business and economic utilization advisor
SBG	small box girder (bridge)
SBGB	small box girder bridge
SBH	safe burst height
SBL	shore bombardment line

SBLG	small blast load generator
SBM	single buoy mooring; short barrel model
sbm	submission; submit
SBMC	Saab Bofors Missile Corporation
SBML	smooth-bore muzzle loader
SBMS	submarine-launched ballistic missile system
SB-MVT	anti-tank mine by MISAR
SBN	standard book number
SBNO	senior British naval officer
	-WA western Atlantic
SBO	senior British officer; summary (plot) board
SBP	shore based prototype (reactor); systolic blood pressure
S³BP	systems source selection board procedure (US)
SBP-04	... -07, non-magnetic anti-tank mine by MISAR
SBP	service benefit plan (US)
SBPH	single burst probability of hit (US)
SBR	serial bullet rifle (4.32mm) (US programme FRS future rifle system); standard busy rate (air traffic)
SBS	special boat service (RN); strategic Balkan services (US); Satellite Business Systems (US) (consortium: IBM, Comsat General, Aetna Life & Casualty)
SBSB	selection board services branch BUPERS
SBT	surface barrier transistor
sBt	small boat
sbtg	sabotage
SBU	station buffer unit
SBV	sea-bed vehicle
SBWS	Systembeauftragter, Waffensystem (GE) (system manager)
SBX	sub-sea beacon transponder
sby	standby
SC	Silver Cross (RAF); special constable; section commander; station commander; staff captain; second in command; senior council; staff college; signal corps; security council (UN); survey company; supply column; school certificate; supreme court (US); statement of charges; sanitary corps (US); science committee (Nato); supply catalog (US); standing committee (Nato); Star of Courage (Canada); Suffolk & Cambridgeshire Regiment; shipping contract; stepchildren; salvage corps; service certificate; senior staff course; Sandia Corporation; submarine chaser (USN); space craft; shaped charge; set clock; sub-contractor; shaping circuit; specific conductivity; special conventional (alloy); steering committee (Nato); strato-cumulus (clouds); small craft; self contained; steel casing
sc	score
S/C	statement of charges
S-C	secret and confidential (files)
S&C	strategic and critical (raw material); search and clear (operation)
SC-70.233	short carbine 5.56mm by Beretta
SCA	section chief assembly, part of GDU; special conventional alloy single channel analyser; summary cost account; service cryptologic agencies (US); stock control activity (US)
SCAAP	Special Commonwealth Africa Assistance Plan
SCAD	AGM-86, subsonic cruise armed decoy (USAF); Schenectady Army Depot (US)
SCADAR	scatter detection and ranging
SCADS	Sioux City air defense sector
SCAEC	submarine classification and analysis evaluation centre
SCAEF	supreme commander allied expeditionary forces
SCAF	supreme commander of allied forces
SCAJAP	shipping control administrator, Japan
SCAM	spectrum characteristics analysis and measurement
SCAMA	station conferencing and monitoring agreement (Nasa)
SCAMP	small calibre ammunition modernization program (US); automatic modular programmed control system; standard configuration and modification program (US); space controlled array measurements programme
Scamp	low-silhouette vehicle 4x4 or 6x6 by Tyrac (UK)
SCAMPI	small manpack battlefield radar by RSRE
SCAN	switched circuit automatic network (US); stock market computer answering network; stock control and analysis; schedule analysis; system for collection and analysis of near collision (reports)
Scan	Scandinavia(n)
Scand	Scandinavia(n)
Scanray	portable X-ray equipment (UK)
SCANS	scheduling and control by automatic network system

SCAO   senior civil affairs officer

SCAP   silent compact auxiliary power (unit); supreme command(er) for the allied powers

SCAR   sub-calibre aircraft rocket; supersonic cruise aircraft research; scientific committee on antarctic research; Scandinavian council for applied research

Scarff ring   airborne machine gun mount

SCARS   software configuration accounting and reporting system; status control alert reporting system; status control alerting and reporting system (Nato)

SCAT   security control of air traffic; systems consolidation of accessions and trainees (US); service command air transport; South (Pacific) combat air transport; speed control approach - take-off; submarine classification and tracking; supersonic commercial air transport

SCATANA   security control of air traffic and air navigational aids

SCATER   security control of air traffic and electro-magnetic radiations

SCATHA   spacecraft charging at high altitudes (experiment) by Martin Marietta

SCATS   sequentially controlled automatic transmitter start

SCB   ships characteristics board (US); segment control bits; site control block; system control block

SCBD   Service Central Book Depot (W.H. Smith & Son London)

SCC   SAM control centre; ship control centre (RN); sequence control charts (US); single cotton covered (wire); stress corrosion cracking; satellite communications control (office) SHAPE; surveillance co-ordination centre; specific clauses and conditions; submersible compression chamber; sea cadet corps (UK); standard commodity classification; security coordination committee; supply control centre; Somaliland Camel Corps (UK); submarine chaser, control (USN); training round 105mm (FR)

ScC   Scottish command (UK)

SCCEp   steering committee for civil emergency planning

SCCF   security clearance case files

SCCO   security classification control officer

SCCo   Strong Cartridge Company

SCCPG   satellite communications contingency planning group

SCCS   STRICOM command and control system (US) (strike command); standard commodity classification system

SCD   security coding device

scd   schedule(d)

SCD,OCSA   staff communications division, office chief of staff Army (US)

SCD   staff communications division; supply commissary and disbursing; surface craft division

SCE   schedule compliance evaluation; single charge exchange; separated career employee (US); staff civil engineer (US); superintendent civil engineer (UK); school certificate examination; Scottish certificate of education

SCEA   service children's education authority

SCEB   SHAPE communications electronics board

SCEO   station construction engineering officer; system civil engineering office(r)

SCEPC   senior civil emergency planning committee

SCEPTRON   special comparative pattern recognizer

SCER   scientific committee on the effects of radiation

SCE&PWD   staff civil engineer and public works department

SCF   satellite control facility; senior chaplain to the forces (UK); support carrier force (USN)

SCFMO   self consistent field molecular orbital

SCGRL   signal corps general research laboratory

SCGSA   signal corps ground signals agency

SCGSS   signal corps ground signals service

SCH   safe course home

sch   school

Schalmei   chaff dispenser missile system by AEG DNAG

sched   schedule

Schildkröte   prototype amphibious car WW2 (GE)

Schmetterling   Hs-117, anti-aircraft rocket WW2 by Henschel (GE)

Schneeorgel   array of 10 torpedo tubes WW2 (GE)

SchüMi   Schützenmine (anti-personnel mine)

Schütze   class, Kl-134, minesweeper by Abeking & Rasmussen

SCI   supervisor cost inspector; special counter-intelligence (branch); ship-controlled interception (radar); switched collector impendance; sensitive compartmented information; Servo Components Incorporated (München)

sci   short circuit; science; scientific

SciCon   scientific control

SCIM   speech communications index meter

Scimitar   carrier-borne transsonic strike fighter 1956 by Supermarine; naval ECM system by Elettronica; naval EW jammer by HSA; FV-107, CVRT, combat vehicle recce, tracked by Alvis

SCIP   ship's capability impeded by lack of parts (USN)

SCL   standard classification list

SCLAR   multiple artillery rocket launcher, naval by Breda/Elsag

SCLI   The Somerset & Cornwall Light Infantry

SClk   ship's clerk (USN)

SCLO   statistical clearance liaison officer

SCL&SB   staff corps liaison and services branch

SCM   summary court martial; sender's composition message; state certified midwife; security countermeasures; software configuration management; STARAN control module

SCMN   Service de Contrôle du Matériel Naval (FR)

SCMO   summary court martial order

SCMPL   Société de Constructions Mécaniques Panhard et Levassor (Paris)

SCMS   signal command management system (US)

SCN   shortest connected network; shipbuilding and conversion, navy; ship control number

SCNO   senior Canadian naval officer

SCNR   standing committee on naval research (Nato); scientific committee of national representatives

SCNVYO   standing conference of national voluntary youth organizations

SCO   statistical control officer (US); staff communications office SHAPE; sea control operation; shipping control office

SCo   signal company

Sco   scouting

SCOCE   special committee on compromising emanations

SCODA   scan coherent doppler attachment

SCOFA   shipping control office forward area

SCofCS   sub-committee of chiefs of staff

ScoFor   scouting force (USN)

SCO-IN   staff communications office SHAPE in-coming messages

scol   school

SColl   staff college

SColm   supply column

SCom   scientific committee

SCOMA   shipping control office, Marianas

SCon   self contained

SCOOP   scientific computation of optimum programmes; support plan to continuity of operations plan (US)

SCO-OUT   staff communications office SHAPE out-going message

SCOP   student controlled on-line programming

SCOPT   special committee on programming technology (US)

SCOR   scientific committee on oceanographic research

SCORE   satellite computer-operated readiness equipment; signal communications by orbiting relay equipment; serial control of Racal equipment; selective conversion and retention (USN)

ScoRon   scouting squadron (USN)

SCORPIO   subcritical carbon moderated reactor assembly for plutonium investigations

Scorpion   F-89, jet fighter by Northrop; FV-101, CVRT, combat vehicle recce, tracked by Alvis; target illumination radar for Bloodhound

SCOT   ship-borne satellite communications terminal for Skynet
-1 lightweight 1m antenna
2 for command ships 2m antenna ship control and operation terminal (RN)

Scot   Scotland; Scottish

ScoTraCen   scouting training center (USN)

SCOTUS   Supreme Court of the United States

Scout   light helicopter by Westland; articulated high-mobility truck by Lockheed; light reconnaissance car 4x4 by CG; mini RPV by IAI

Scout-D   orbital transport missile by LTV

SCP   security classification procedure; survey control point; special career programme; self-contained package; section command post (vehicle); serial character printer; surveillance communication processor

SCPC   small channel pulse coding; single channel per carrier (communication)

SCPD   staff civilian personnel division OCSA

SCPO   senior chief petty officer (USN)

SCPt   security control point

SCR   signal corps radio (code) then AN/... now: JETDS; silicon control rectifier

SCR-584 anti-aircraft radar
SCRA   single-channel radio access
        staff captain, Royal Artillery
SCRAM   space capsule regulator and
        monitor;
        special criteria for retrograde
        Army material (US)
SCRAMJET supersonic combustion ramjet
SCRAP   selective curtailment of reports and
        paperwork (US)
SCR-DC silicon controlled rectifier -
        direct current
SCRDE   stores and clothing research and
        development establishment
        (Colchester)
Screw Gun 2.5 in rifled muzzle loader
        mountain gun
ScRif   The Scottish Rifles The Cameronians
SCRL   signal corps research laboratory
SCS   sea control ship (USN);
        security container system;
        satellite communications system;
        space communications system;
        screening and costing staff;
        stationing capability system;
        Somaliland Camel Scouts (UK);
        society of civil servants;
        Scientific Control Systems GmbH
        (Hamburg)
SCSC   semiconductor standardization sub-
        committee; satellite communications
        system control
SCSS   self-contained starting system;
        staff colleges sailing society
        (UK)
SCT   sustained concept testing; special
        crew time; satellite control
        terminal; Schottky clamped transis-
        tor; surface charge transistor
sct   scout
Sc&T   science and technology
SCTC   submarine chaser training centre;
        security council truce commission
        (UN)
sctd   scattered (weather)
SCTF   SHAPE centralized training facility
SCTR   standing conference on telecommuni-
        cations research
sctr   sector
SCTraCen submarine chaser training centre
SCTS   satellite control and test station
SCTTL   Schottky clamped transistor-
        transistor logic
scty   security
SCU   station control unit
SCUA   Suez Canal users' association
SCUBA   self-contained underwater breathing
        apparatus
SCV   sub-clutter visibility
SCW   super critical wing

SCZ   Suez Canal Zone
SD   submarine detector (aircraft);
        self destructing (fuse); safety
        destructor (fuse); sea drome;
        sectional density; semi-diameter;
        sailing direction; system demon-
        stration; standard displacement;
        standard deviation; synchronous
        detector; semi-detached; secretary
        of defense (US); signal department;
        staff duties; state department;
        service dress; secret document;
        supply depot; special duty;
        special delivery; supply depart-
        ment; supporting document to ...;
        same date; several dates; sine die
        (without dates); site defence;
        Schalldämpfer (silencer)
S&D   search and destroy; single and
        double (reduction gear)
SD-3M   maritime patrol aircraft by Shorts
SD-44   anti-tank gun 85mm (SU)
SD-1400 Fritz, guided glide bomb WW2 (GE)
SDA   source data automation; symbolic
        device address; ship destination
        authority
SDAA   servicemen's dependents' allowance
        act
SdAh   Sonderanhänger (special trailer)
SDandT staff duties and training (section)
        GS
SdAnh-121 Sonderanhänger 60t (special
        trailer)
SDAS   source data automation system
SDAT   symbolic device allocation table
SDB   seaward defence boat (RN); skill
        development base
SDBP   small data base package
SDC   shipment detail card; space defense
        center (US); southern defense
        command (US); seaward defence
        craft (Nato); signal data conver-
        ter; submersible decompression
        chamber
SDCD   sea duty commencement date
SDCP   supply demand control point
SDCR   source data communication retrieval
SDD   system definition directive;
        special devices division NTDC;
        system development department;
        selectable digital display;
        synthetic dynamic display
SDDTTG stored data definition and transla-
        tion task group
SDE   standard data element
SDECE   Service de Documentation d'Etudes
        Contre-Espionage (FR) (counter-
        intelligence)
s det   semi detached
SDF   ship design file; self-destroying

fuse; simplified directional facility; standard data format; strategic defence forces; Sudan Defence Force (UK)

SDHE spacecraft data handling equipment

SDHS ship's data highway system (RN)

SDI selective discrimination of information; selective dissemination of information; situation display indicator

SDIT Service de Documentation et d'Information Technique (Paris)

SdKfz Sonderkraftfahrzeug (special vehicle) WW2 (GE)

  2 light tracked motorbike

  3 Maultier, 4x4 APC

  4 halftrack APC

  6 halftrack artillery tractor

  8 12 ton artillery tractor

  9 18 ton artillery tractor

  10 light halftrack tractor

  101 PzKpfW I tank

  121 PzKpfW II tank

  123 Luchs tracked recce tank

  124 Wespe 105mm SP howitzer

  132 Marder 76.2mm SP anti-tank gun

  138 Marder III 75mm SP anti-tank gun

  139 Marder 76.2mm SP anti-tank gun

  141 PzKpfW III tank 3.7cm gun

  161 PzKpfW IV

  162 Jagdpanzer 75mm SP a/t gun

  173 Panther, 8.8cm SP a/t gun

  181 Tiger a/t SP gun

  186 Tiger B, 128mm a/t SP gun

  221 light recce car

  222 light recce car

  223 light recce car with wireless

  231 8x8 recce car heavy

  232 6x6 recce car with wireless

  234 Puma, 8x8, heavy armoured car

  247 6x6 armoured car

  250 half track

    2 telephone line vehicle

    3 light wireless vehicle

    5 light artillery surveillance

    7 mortar carrier 80mm

    10 platoon command post

    12 artillery survey vehicle

  251 medium armoured half track

    3 wireless

    4 gun tractor

    5 engineer assault version

    6 command post vehicle

    8 ambulance

    10 anti-tank gun carrier

    16 flame thrower carrier

    11 telephone line layer

    12..15 artillery survey vehicle

    17 anti-aircraft carrier

  253 light surveillance half track

  254 medium armoured observation vehicle

  260 command post vehicle

  261 command post vehicle

  263 6x6 heavy wireless vehicle

  301 heavy remote controlled demolition charge carrier

  302 heavy remote controlled demolition charge carrier 320 kgs

  303 heavy remote controlled demolition charge carrier 365 kgs

  3026 heavy remote controlled demolition charge carrier 430 kgs

  304 Springer, heavy remote controlled demolition charge carrier 2400 kgs

SDL special duties list

SdLdg Sonderladung (special charge)

SDLO strategic defense liaison office (US)

SDM site defence of Minuteman

SDMA space division multiple access

SDMS shipboard data multiplex system by Rockwell

SDNCO staff duty non-commissioned officer

SDO staff duty officer; special duty officer; station duty officer; squadron duty officer; signal despatch office; special duty only; senior dental officer; squadron dental officer

SDoc Senate Document (US)

SdOpr sound operator

SDOS standard day of supply

SDP splash detection radar; single department purchasing (agency); system development plan; supply dropping point

SDPL Safeguard data processing laboratory

SDPO site defence project office; space defence project office

SDpo stores depot

SDR small development requirements; special drawing rights; signal data recorder; system design report; ship destination room; ship diversion room; special despatch rider (UK)

SDr special driver

SDRT slot dipole ranging test

SDS science data store; shared data set; scientific data system; satellite data system; signal despatch service; secret defence service;

SDS	supplemental data sheet; space documentation service; Surveillance du Sol (FR) (heavy battle-field radar)
SDSS	self-deploying space station
SDSW	sense device status word
SD&T	staff duties and training
SDUS	small-scale data utilization station; secondary data users station
SDV	swimmer delivery vehicle
SDX	satellite data exchange
SE	single ended; system effectiveness; single engined (aircraft); shared electronics (double lines); spherical equivalent; special equipment; standard error; slip end; small end; spherical eyeball; single entry; Southern Europe; South East; staff engineer
SE-2000	Sender/Empfänger (portable transceiver) (Switzerland)
SE-3130	Alouette, light helicopter by AS
SE-6861	Sender-Empfänger (portable transceiver) by AEG
SEA	subterranean exploratory agency; statistical energy analysis; spherical electrostatic analyser; South East Asia; service educational activities; ship's editorial association
SEAAC	South East Asia air command
SEAACE	South East Asia air combat experience
Sea Archer	optical fire control system by Sperry
Seabat	SH-34, HSS-1N, naval helicopter by Sikorsky
Seabees	construction battalion Royal Engineers; construction battalion civil engineer corps (USN)
SEAC	South East Asia Command (Admiral Viscount Mountbatten); standard electronic automated computer
Seacat	GWS20 ... 22 ... 24, naval anti-aircraft missile by Shorts
SEACDT	South East Asia Collective defence treaty
Sea Cobra	AH-1, ASW helicopter by Bell
SEACOM	underwater telephone cable (Australia-New Guinea-Guam-Hong Kong-Malaysia-Singapore 1967)
SEACOP	strategic sealift contingency planning system
SE/ACT	Southern Europe - Actisud
SEAD	Seneca Army Depot (US)
Sea Dart	XF-2Y, hydroski jet fighter 1953 by Convair; GWS-30, anti-aircraft missile by BAe
Sea Devon	maritime patrol aircraft (UK)
SEADEX	seaward defence exercise (Nato)

Sea Dragon	class, patrol boats guided missiles for Singapore 1974 by Hong Kong Lürssen
SeaDu	sea duty
Sea Eagle	P-3T, naval surface-to-surface missile by BAe
Sea Fan	chaff rocket launcher by Plessey
Seafarer	submarine communications system ELF (US)
Seafire	naval version Spitfire WW2 (RN); naval laser target designator + EO gunfire control system (USN)
Sea Flash	naval anti-air missile by BAC; high-speed remote controlled target boat (RN)
Seaforth	The Seaforth Highlanders, the Duke of Albany's Ross-Shire Buffs
Sea Fox	naval multi-rocket anti-aircraft system (RN); special warfare craft by Uniflote
SeaFron	sea frontier
Sea Fury	naval fighter aircraft by Hawker
Sea Gnat	naval chaff rocket by Plessey
Seaguard	naval anti-aircraft fire control system for guns by Contraves
Sea Guard	naval a/a system by Plessey+ Oerlikon+Siemens Albis
Seagull	catapult floatplane by Curtiss
SeaH	The Seaforth Highlanders Regiment
Sea Harrier	FRS, fighter/recce aircraft ship-based V/STOL aircraft by Hawker Siddeley
Sea Hawk	P-1040, carrier borne day jet fighter by Hawker; LAMPS-III, helicopter project; light airborne multi-purpose system
Sea Hornet	carrier-borne two-seat all-weather fighter
Sea Hunter	search and fire control radar + TV camera by Contraves
Sea Indigo	naval anti-aircraft missile (IT)
Sea Killer	sea-to-sea missile by SISTEL
Sea King	SH-3D, medium anti-submarine helicopter by Sikorsky
Sea Knight	UH-46, medium helicopter by Boeing/Vertol
SEAL	sea-air-land (craft); sea-air-land (team); signal evaluation airborne laboratory
Seal	wire-guided homing torpedo
SeaLab	underwater laboratory
SEALF	South East Asian land forces
SEAM	Sidewinder expanded acquisition mode (guidance system)
Seamaster	P-6M, long-range bomber; four-jet flying boat 1950 by Martin
Sea Mattress	1080 bombarding rockets to prepare a landing WW2
Seamew	all-weather anti-submarine aircraft (RN)

SEAMIC   South East Asia management informa-
          tion centre
SEAMOD   sea systems modification and moderni-
          zation by modularity (USN pro-
          gramme)
Sea Mosquito   carrier-borne torpedo bomber
          by deHavilland
SEAN   senior enlisted advisor, Navy (US);
          state enrolled assistant nurse
SEAOPSS   South East Asia operational sensor
          system
SEAPAC   sea activated parachute automatic
          crew release by Vought
Sea Pig   miniature submarine, human torpedo
          WW2 (IT)
Sea Prince   WP-308, patrol aircraft (RN)
SEAR   systematic effort to analyse results
SEARCH   system for electronic analysis and
          retrieval of criminal histories
SEARCHEX   sea-air search exercise (Nato)
Search Master   maritime patrol aircraft by
          GAF (modified Nomad)
Searchwater   naval air-to-surface radar by
          EMI
SeaS   sea school
Seasat   polar orbiting sea surveillance
          satellite
Sea Scan   maritime patrol aircraft by IAI
          (modified Westwind)
Sea Searcher   naval helicopter-borne search
          radar by MEL
Sea Sentry   passive electronic surveillance
          system by Kollmorgen
          I   for FPB
          II   for surface ships
          III   for submarines
Sea Serpent   naval optronic ire control
          system by Kollmorgen
Sea Skimmer   AQM-37A, target drone by Beech
Sea Skua   helicopter-borne anti-ship missile
          BAC
Sea Slug   GWS-1, medium-range naval anti-
          aircraft missile
Sea Sparrow   RIM-7H, point defence ship
          missile system by Raytheon
Sea Spray   naval search radar
Seasprite   UH-2, light naval rescue helicop-
          ter by Kaman
SEASTAGS   SEATO standardization agreements
Sea Stallion   S-65, RH-53, heavy helicopter
          by Sikorsky
Sea Strike   Mosquito fitted with 32 pdr gun
          WW2
SEATAF   Southern European atomic task force
SEATELCOM   South East Asia telecommunications
          system
Sea Tiger   naval surveillance radar by
          Thomson-CSF
SEATO   South East Asia treaty organization
Sea Truck   landing craft (FR)

Sea Vampire   carrier-borne all-weather
          fighter
Seavan   shipping container
Sea Venom   naval all-weather fighter by
          de Havilland
Sea Vixen   DH-110, twin-engined naval all-
          weather fighter by de Havilland
Sea Warrior   SF-260, maritime patrol air-
          craft SIAI
SeaWea   sea weather (report)
Sea Wolf   class, patrol boats guided
          missiles by Lürssen
Seawolf   GWS-25, naval anti-missile missile
          by BAC
Seawolf/Dardo   naval point defence system
Sea Zenith   naval radar Sea Guard + special
          gun by Oerlikon/Contraves
SEBQ   senior enlisted bachelor quarters
          (US)
SEBS   submarine emergency buoyancy system
SEC   scientific estimates committee;
          simple electronic computer; studio
          equipment complex; South European
          command; securities and exchange
          commission; ship engineering
          centre; South Eastern command;
          sssupply executive committee
sec   section; security; sector; second;
          secretary; secretariat
SECAL   selective calling
SECAM   Sequentielle a Memoire (FR) (colour
          TV system)
SECAN   military committee communications;
          security and evaluation agency
          (Washington); standing group
          security and evaluation agency
SECAPEM-30   target and fire training system
          SFENA
SecBase   section base
SECBAT   Société Européenne de Construction
          du Breguet Atlantique
secd   second(ary)
SecDef   secretary of defense (US)
SecFlt   second fleet (USN)
SecGen   secretary general
SecGenNATO   secretary general of Nato
SecGruHQ   security group headquarters
SecLantFAP   secretary of the allied command
          Atlantic frequency allocation
          panel
SecLeg   secretary of the legation
SecNav   secretary of the Navy
SECOR   sequential collation of ranges
          (satellite)
SECP   shore establishments and civilian
          personnel
secr   secret
SECS-80   severe environment computer system
          by EMM/SESCO
SecState   secretary of state (US)

sect   secretary; section; sector
Sectascan high definition sector scanning
             sonar by Plessey
SecTaskFlt second task fleet (USN)
Sec-Treas secretary treasurer
SecWar secretary of war
secy   secretary
SED   special electronic devices;
           South Eastern department;
           shore establishment
           division
SEDAM   N-500, hovercraft by SEDAM
SEDAR   submerged electrode detection and
           ranging
SEDEMS Société et Études et de Développe-
           ment de Matérials Spéciaux
SEE   signals experimental establishment;
           school of electric engineering;
           senior electrical engineer (UK)
SE&E   survival, evasion and escape
Seeing Eye submarine TV camera
Seehund midget submarine WW2 (GE)
Seek Igloo minimally attended radar system
             Alaska by Gilfillian
Seek Talk spread spectrum modem, jam resis-
             tant (US programme) by GE
Seekuh remote controlled mine-sweeping
           system; Troika predecessor by
           Blohm&Vo
SEER   systems engineering evaluation and
           research; submarine explosive echo
           ranging
Seeschlange anti-submarine guide torpedo
             (FGN)
SEF   small end forward
SEFAN   Sektor Fahrzeug Navigationssystem by
           SEL (vehicle navigation system)
SEFIC   seventh fleet intelligence centre
SEFOR   southwest experimental fast oxide
           reactor
SEFT   Section d'Études et Fabrication de
           Télécommunication (FR) DTAT
SEG   systems evaluation group
SEI   stockpile entry inspection
SEIE   submarine escape immersion equipment
SEIS   submarine emergency identification
           signal; submarine escape immersion
           suit
SE/IWT Southern Europe inland waterways
           transport
SEL   sound effects laboratory; Standard
           Elektronik Lorenz AG (Stuttgart)
sel   selectee (selective service trainee
           US national service man)
SelCal selective calling system
SelCom select committee
SELD   selectadata equipment
SELIN   Societa per l'Elettrotecnica Indus-
           triale & Navale SpA (Genova IT)
SElokaH System Elektronische Kampfführung

           (Heer) (Army electronic warfare
           system)
SELS   severe local storm
SEM   scanning electron microscope; space
           environment monitor; Signaal,
           Emerson & Mauser (Corporation)
SEM-25 ... 35, Sender-Empfänger, mobil by
           SEL (mobile transceiver)
SEM-30 Goalkeeper, Shortstop, 30mm quad-
           ruple naval anti-aircraft system
           by SEM
SEM-52 Sender-Empfanger mobil by SEL (VHF
           portable transceiver)
SEM-70 Sender-Empfänger mobil by SEL (VHF)
           portable transceiver)
SEM-80 ... 90, Sender-Empfanger mobil by
           SEL (vehicular VHF portable trans-
           ceiver) by SEL
SEM-170 ... 180, ... 190, vehicular VHF
           portable transceiver with inte-
           grated encryption system
SEMA   special electronic mission aircraft
SEME   school of electrical and mechanical
           engineering (Bordon UK)
SEMET   self-evident meteorological code
           (Nato)
SEMO   system engineering and management
           organization
SEMRE   Sprint electromagnetic radiation
           evaluation
SEMS   severe environment memory system
           EMM/SESCO
SEMTR   Sprint early missile test radar
SEN   single edge notch; state enrolled
           nurse
sen   senator; senior
SeNavAv senior naval aviator (USN)
SenCd   senior commissioned
SenClk senior clerk
SenDentalO senior dental officer
SenDoc Senate Document
SEng   single engine
SEngO   senior engineering officer
SENIT   Système d'Exploitation Navale des
           Informations Tactiques by Thomson-
           CSF (naval tactical data handling
           system)
SENL   standard equipment nomenclature list
           (US)
SenMedO senior medical officer
SenMem senior member
sent   sentence
SentConf sentenced to be confined
SentLP sentenced to lose pay
Sentinel L-5, light aircraft WW2 (RAF);
           RQT-9, medium battlefield sur-
           veillance radar by Selenia
Sentry E-3, AWACS, airborne warning and
           control system by Boeing
SenWtO senior warrant officer

SEO state of emergency order; senior executive officer; senior equipment officer; senior experimental officer; satellite for Earth observation (India); Software Entwicklungsordner (GE) (software development register)

SEOCS sun earth observatory and climatology satellite by Dornier

SEODSE special explosive ordnance disposal supplies and equipment

SEOP SHAPE emergency operating procedures

SEP separation parameter; system engineering process; scientific and engineering personnel; selective employment payment; Société Européenne de Propulsion Puteaux

sep separate

SEP-6 ... 10, automatic flight control system by Smith

SEPA Societa di Elettronica per l'Automazione SpA

SEPAC space experiments with particle accelerators by University of Tokyo Spacelab

SEPacFor South East Pacific force

separ separately

SE/PB Southern Europe ports and beaches (Nato)

SEPCO services electronic parts coordinating committee

SEPE single escape peak efficiency

SEPI Smith's electrical pilot instrument

SEPORT supply and equipment report

SEPOS selected enlisted personnel for overseas service

SEPROS separation processing; separate processing

SEPS solar electric propulsion system

SEPTAR sea-borne powered target (boat) (USN)

seq sequence

SER The Singapore Engineer Regiment; state of emergency regulations; single electron response

ser service; servicing; serial

SERANDA service and health records, pay accounts and personel effects

SERE survival, evasion, resistance and escape

SerForSoPacSubCom service force South Pacific subordinate command

Serg sergeant

Sergeant MGM-29, ground-to-ground nuclear tactical missile

SeRGrad selected rotated graduate

SERI Société d'Études et de Réalisation Industrielle

SERL services electronics research laboratory (Baldock UK)

SerLant service force Atlantic (USN)

SerNo service number; serial number

SeRon service squadron

SerPac service force Pacific (USN)

Serrate night interceptor location equipment WW2 (RAF)

SE/RRT Southern Europe railroad transport

SERT spinning satellite for electric rocket test

SE/RT Southern Europe road transport

SERTH satisfactory evidence received this headquarters

serv service

SERV surface effect rescue vessel

ServBn service battalion (USMC)

ServComFMFPac service command, fleet marine force, Pacific

ServDiv service division

ServFor service force

ServGrp service group

ServHel service and health (records)

ServLant service force Atlantic

ServPa service and pay (records)

ServPac service force Pacific

ServPaHel service, pay and health (records)

ServRec service record

ServRegt service regiment (USMC)

ServRon service squadron

ServScoCom service schools command

ServSoWesPac service force South West Pacific Fleet

servt servant

SES Society of Engineers and Scientists; strategic engineering survey; scientific exploration society; surface effect ship; super-excited electronic states

SES-100 surface effect ship (USN)
    A by Aerojet
    B by Bell

Sesam-69 computer programme for construction (finite element method)

SESAME Station d'Écoute de Satellite Météorologique (meteorological satellite monitoring station); mobile electronic equipment test system by SFENA

SESCO secure submarine communications; Severe Environment Systems Company (EMM daughter) (US)

SESE secure echo-sounding equipment (sonar)

SESG Southern European shipping group

SESL space environment simulation laboratory

SESO senior equipment staff officer

SeSta Senkrecht startende See-Lenkflugkörper by VFW (vertical take-off naval guided missile)

SET	single escape tower; solar energy thermionic (Nasa program); satellite experimental terminal; submarine engineering technician; selective employment tax
SETAC	Sektor TACAN by SEL (microwave landing system)
SETAF	Southern European task force (Nato)
SETEL	Société Européenne de Téléguidage (Paris)
SETF	Staran evaluation and training facility
SETS	severe environment tape system by EMM; solar energy thermionic conversion system (Nasa)
SETS-1	severe environment tape system by EMM
SETT	submarine escape training tank
sev	serve
SEV	special equipment vehicle
SEVAC	secure voice access console
SEVAS	secure voice access console systems
SevFlt	seventh fleet (USN)
SevP	severance pay
SevrPay	severance pay
SEW	safety equipment worker
SEWACO	sensor weapons and control system, naval by HSA
SEWLROM	special end of war leave for regular officers and men
SEWMRPG	Southern European Western Mediterranean regional planning group
SEWT	simulation for electronic warfare training by AAI
Sextan	inertial laser gyro for helicopter navigation by SFENA
Sexton	SP field gun WW2 (UK)
SEZ	sector engagement zone; selector engagement zone, a/a missiles
SF	fleet submarine (USN); square foot; semi-fixed (ammunition); statement of functions; subject field; separate function; stepping factor; signal frequency; surface foot (feet); ship fitter; standard form; special forces; scouting force (USN); The Sherwood Forresters Regiment; Selbstfahr(lafette) (self-propelled gun)
S&F	sound and flash
110-SF	multiple rocket launcher 110mm by Wegmann
280-SF	multiple rocket launcher 280mm MARS, medium artillery rocket system
SF-260	single-engined aircraft by SIAI
M	trainer
W	Warrior, light attack plane
SW	Sea Warrior, maritime patrol
SFA	single frequency approach; special foreign activities

S&FA	shipping and forwarding agents
SFADS	San Francisco air defense sector
SFAO	San Francisco area office ONR
SFAW	solid fuels administrator for war
SFBNSY	San Francisco Bay naval shipyard
SFC	sergeant first class (US); specific fuel consumption
sfc	surface
SFCN	Société Française de Construction Navales
SFCP	shore fire control party (Nato)
SFCS	submarine fire control system by Singer; simplified fire control system
SFCS-6000	simplified fire control system by Marconi
SFD	sudden frequency deviation
SFDS	standby fighter director ship
SFEL	standard facility equipment list
SFENA	Société Française d'Équipements pour la Navigation Aerienne (Velizy)
sferics	athmospherics
SFF	site field force
SFG	sweep function generator; signal frequency generator; special forces group (US)
SFG-606	sweep function generator by Feedback
sfgd	safeguard
SFH	Selbstfahrhaubitze (self-propelled howitzer)
SFIC	San Francisco information center
SFIM	Société de Fabrication d'Instruments de Mésure (Massy)
SFL	sequenced flashing lights (landing system); Selbstfahrlafette (SP carriage)
SFM	Sinai field mission (tactical ground early warning system by E-Systems); switching-mode frequency multiplexer; ship fitter metal smith (USN)
SFMS	Shipwrecked Fishermen and Mariners Royal Benevolent Society
SFN	ships and facilities Navy (US)
SFNS	San Francisco naval shipyard
SFO	senior flying officer; senior flag officer
SFOB	special forces operational base
SFOD	special forces operational detachment
SFOF	space flight operations facility (Nasa)
SFP	slack frame programme; ship fitter pipefitter; supplementary fire party
SFP-ANGS	standardization field panel for artillery and naval gunfire support (US)

SFPOE   San Francisco port of embarkation
SFR   XM-19, ... 70, serial flechette rifle
          AAI; signal frequency receiver
SFS   senior flight surgeon (US); student
          flight surgeon (USN); Sperry Flight
          Systems (Phoenix Ariz.)
SFSCL   shunt feedback Schottky clamped logic
SFSD   Star field scanning device
S&FSD   sea and foreign service duty (pay)
          A aviation
          S submarine
SFSS   satellite field service stations
SFT-800   Selbstwählfeldtelefon by Siemens
          (self-switching field telephone)
SFTS   synthetic flight training system;
          services forebody test set
          --Sky Flash
SFU   signals flying unit
SG   The Scots Guards; surgeon general
          (US); seaman gunner; security
          guard; steam generator; signal
          generator; super group (telephone)
          (Nato); stabilized gyro; steel
          girder; screen grid; super granule;
          specific gravity; snow grains
Sg   surgeon
S+G   Strassen- & Geländereifen (road and
          cross-country tyres)
1-SG   first sergeant (US)
SG-43   medium machine gun Goryunov (SU)
SG-510-4 Sturmgewehr 7.62mm by SIG
          (assault rifle)
SG-530   Sturmgewehr 5.56mm
SG-540   Sturmgewehr 5.56mm
SG-542   Sturmgewehr 7.62mm
SG-543   Sturmgewehr 5.56mm short by SIG
SGA   standards of grade authorization
SGAC   special group for arms control (Nato)
SGAD   Safeguard army depot
SGAW   sub-group on assessment of weapons
SGB   steam gunboat
SGBC   S.G. Brown Communication Ltd
          (Watford)
SGC   Spartan guidance computer
SgC   surgeon captain
SGCEC   standing group communications elec-
          tronics committee
SgCr   surgeon commander
sgd   signed
SGE   secondary group equipment
SGE-30   Shortstop, Signaal- General Electric
          30mm naval anti-missile gun radar
          directed by HSA + GE
SGED   supervisory grade evaluation guide
          (US)
SGET   Sous-groupe d'Experts Techniques
          (technical experts sub-group)
SGF   southern group of Soviet forces
SGFS   Scottish Girls' Friendly Society
SGH   Southern Gernal Hospital; Spezial-
          gerätebau Hamburg

SGHW   steam generating heavy water
          (moderated reactor)
SGHWR   steam generating heavy water reactor
SGIC   standing group, intelligence
          committee
SGJP   satellite graphic job processor
sgl   single
SgLCr   surgeon lieutenant commander
SGLI   Servicemen's Group Life Insurance
          (US)
SGLP   standing group representative
          liaison paper to the international
          staff (Nato)
SGLS   space-to-ground link sub-system
          (Nasa); satellite to ground link
          system
SGM   spark gap modulation; Stanhope Gold
          Medal; sergeant major of the Army
          (US); sergeant major (USMC);
          standing group memorandum (Nato);
          Sea Gallantry Medal; medium
          machine gun 7.62mm (SU);
          Stankovy Goryunov Modernizovaniji
          SGMT coaxial machine gun
          SGMB infantry version
SGM-80   Seegrundmine 1980, sea-bed mine
SGMC   standing group meteorological
          committee
sgmn   signalman
SGN   standing group Nato
sgnr   signature
SGO   squadron gunnery officer
SGP   secondary gun pointer
SGPO   standing group representative commu-
          nication to the private office of
          the SecGen (Nato)
SgRA   surgeon rear admiral
SGRep   standing group representative to
          NAC
SGRS   steering group on rationalization
          and standardization (US)
SGS   secretary of the general staff (US)
SGSC   standing group security committee
          (Nato)
SGSO   senior general staff officer
SGT   satellite ground terminal
sgt   sergeant
1-Sgt   first sergeant (US)
SGTIA   standing group technical intelli-
          gence agency (Nato)
SgtMaj   sergeant major (US)
SGTR   standardized government travel
          regulations (US)
SGU   Sidewinder generator unit; single-
          gun unit (UK)
SgVA   surgeon vice admiral
SGWM   standing group working memorandum
SGZ   surface ground zero
SH   squash head (shell); scratch hard-
          ness; sea helicopter; supreme

SH   headquarters; Scottish Horse
         Regiment; Schleswig-Holstein;
         second hand; ship's serviceman
         (USN)
Sh   shipwright
SH-2   Sea Sprite, LAMPS, naval helicopter
         by Kaman
SH-3   Sea King, naval helicopter by
         Sikorsky
SH-4   hypersonic anti-ballistic missile
         (SU)
SH-19   S-55, anti-submarine helicopter by
         Sikorsky
SH-34   S-58, Sea Bat, anti-submarine heli-
         copter by Sikorsky
SH-55   plastic anti-tank mine (IT)
SH-60   LAMPS III, by Sikorsky naval helicop-
         ter
SHA   sideral hour angle; side hour angle
SHAC   shelter housing aid centre
Shackleton AEW-2, airborne early warning
         aircraft (UK)
SHAD   Sharpe army depot
ShAdCom shipping advisory committee
SHAEF   supreme headquarters allied expedi-
         tionary forces WW2
Shafrir air-to-air infra-red missile
         (Israel)
Shahine anti-aircraft missile system by
         Thomson/Matra
Shanghai class, fast patrol boats (China)
SHANICLE short-range navigation vehicle
         (Nato)
SHAPE   supreme headquarters allied powers
         Europe (Nato)
SHAPEX   SHAPE annual command exercise (Nato)
Shapirit class, coastal and river patrol
         boats IAI
SHAPTO   SHAPE to standing group (message)
SHARP   ships analysis and retrieval project
Sharpshooter digital fire control system
         for 20mm to 40mm guns by
         Lockheed
Sharpshooters The 3rd/4th County of London
         Yeomanry the Sharpshooters
SHAS   shared hospital accounting system
SHASEC   SHAPE secretariat (messages);
         SHAPE to military committee
         (messages)
SHATC   SHAPE technical centre
SHAWL   special hard target assault weapon,
         light-weight by GD
Shawnee H-21, transport helicopter by
         Vertol
SHC   super heat control; synthesized
         hydro-carbons (lubricator); sur-
         veillance helicopter company (US)
SHD   slant hole distance; Scottish Home
         Department; ship's diver (RN)
Sheffield class, guided missile destroyers
         (RN)

Shelduck propeller-driven RPV target drone
ShelRep shelling report
Sheridan M-551, reconnaissance tank (US)
Sherman M-4, main battle tank (US)
Shershen class, torpedo boats (SU)
Shet   Shetland Islands
SHF   super high frequencies
shft   shift
SHG   semi-active homing guidance;
         second harmonic generation
SHHD   Scottish home and health department
Shil   Shillelagh
Shillelagh MGM-51, gun-launched guided
         missile infra-red guidance by
         Ford
SHINPADS UYK-502, ship integrated proces-
         sor and display system by CDC/
         Sperry
SHIP   standard hardware interface pro-
         gramme; self-help improvement
         programme
ShipAlt ship alteration
ShipCon shipping control (Nato)
ShipDa   shipping data
ShipDaFol shipping data follows
ShipDat shipping date
ShipDTO ship on depot transfer order (US)
ShipGo   shipping order; ship goods
ShipIm   ship immediately
shipmt   shipment
ShipRepTech ship repair technician (USN)
ShipReq ship to apply on requisition (US)
ShipSto ship store office
shipt   shipment
Shipyard MIS shipyard management informa-
         tion system
Shir Iran FV-4030, main battle tank for
         Iran project cancelled
SHIU   steering/hover indicator unit
shkdn   shakedown
ShL   shipwright lieutenant
shlw   shallow
SHM   simple harmonic motion
SHMO   senior hospital medical officer
SHO   Scottish Home Office; senior house
         officer
sho   shore
SHOC   SHAPE operations centre
Shokaku class, aircraft carriers WW2
         (Japan)
Shooting Star P-80, jet fighter aircraft
         1944 by Lockheed
SHOP   pre-launch missile control system
SHORAD   short-range air defence (Nato)
Shorad EZ short-range air defence engage-
         ment zone
SHORADS short-range air defence system
SHORADS/LOFAADS short-range air defence
         system/low-level forward
         area air defence system
         --Roland

SHORAN short-range radio aid to navigation (air)
ShorDu shore duty
Shore Buffer naval air defense system (USN)
Shorland armoured Land Rover by Short & Harland
ShorOutPubInt shore duty beyond the sea is required by public interest
ShorPubInt shore duty is required by public interest
SHORSTAS short-range surveillance and target acquisition system (UK)
Shortstop SGE-30 or SEM-30, naval anti-missile gun, radar directed by SGE or SEM
Shot Bravo hydrogen bomb test Nevada 1954
Shot Smokey nuclear bomb test Nevada 1957
SH/P squash head practice (shell)
SHP shaft horse power
shpmt shipment
shpsd shipside
SHPTARBY ship to arrive by ...
SHQ supreme headquarters; station head-quarters
shrap shrapnel
SHRF ship regular freight
Shrike AGM-45, ARM, air-to-ground missile, anti-radar missile
Shrimp transportable battlefield surveil-lance radar by RRE
ShropsYeo The Shropshire Yeomanry
shrtg shortage
SHS squash head shell
SHVD sex hygiene and venereal diseases
SHW safety health and welfare
shwr shower
SHyRegt super-heavy regiment Royal Artil-lery
Shyri class, submarines for Equador by HDW
SI spark ignition; sample interval; shift-in; specific inventory; surveillance and inspection; standardization and interopera-bility; signal-to-interference (ratio); sergeant instructor; seriously ill; staff inspector; special intelligence; spot inven-tory; Sandwich Islands; Shetland Islands; member of the Order of the Star of India
Si silicon
SIA standard instrument approach; service information analysis; stereo image alternator; station of initial assignment
SIAD Sierra army depot
SIAL-MD-60 electronic distance measuring equipment by Siemens Albis
SIAM self-initiating anti-aircraft missile by Ford; signal information and monitoring

SIAP standard instrument approach procedure
SIAR Service de la Surveillance Indus-trielle de l'Armament (FR)
SIB special investigations branch (police)
Sibmas 6x6 armoured personnel carrier by BN
SIC scientific information centre; survey information centre; sonar information centre; specific inductive capacity; standard industrial classification; semi-conductor integrated circuit; second in command
Sic Sicily
SICA sampling and identification of chemical agents
Sica tracked Crotale anti-aircraft missile launcher
SICAT tank fire control system by MSDS
SICC Safeguard inventory control centre
SICMA special initial clothing monetary allowance
Civ civilian
NAOC naval aviation officer candidate
NAvCad naval aviation cadet
Siclamen IFF interrogator by LMT
SICR specific intelligence collection requirement
SID special intelligence department; Scottish Infantry Depot (Glen-corse); strategic intelligence digest; security and intelligence division (US Army); standard instrument departure; syntax improving device; systems integra-tion demonstration; sudden iono-spheric disturbances
Sida automatic anti-aircraft surveillance and fire control system (IT)
SIDC supply item design change
SidCot-suit Sidney Cotton RAF uniform
SIDE superthermal ion detector experiment
Sidewinder AIM-9, GAR-8, air-to-air missile by Raytheon; MIM-72, Chapparal, ground-to-air version
SIDL system identification data list
SIDPERS standard installation/division personnel system (US)
SIE science information exchange
Siegfried railway cannon 38cm WW2 (GE)
Siegfried line Westwall, German system of fortifications WW2
SIF selective identification feature IFF
SIFLIR Siemens forward-looking infra-red
SIFS special instructors flying school
SIG senior interdepartmental group (US);

SIG   ship improvement guide (USN);
         Schweizerische Industriegesellschaft
         Neuhausen/Rheinfall
sig   signal; signalman
sIG   schweres Infanteriegeschütz 15cm
         (heavy infantry gun)
SIG-510 assault rifle 7.62mm by SIG
SIG-542 assault rifle 7.62mm by SIG
SIG-710 dual purpose machine gun 7.62mm by
         SIG
SigC   signal corps
SigCen   signal centre
SigCo   signal company
         A airline
         C cable
         D with division
         W wireless
SIG-D   simplified inertial guidance (system)
         - demonstration by LTV
SigDiv   signals division SHAPE
SIGESO   sub-committee, intelligence German
         electronic signals organization
SIGEX   signal exercise (Nato)
Sightline anti-aircraft missile by BAC
         (Rapier prototype)
SIGI   system for interactive guidance and
         information
SigInt   signals intelligence
SigL   signals Lieutenant
SIGMA   shielded inert gas metal arc
         (welding); site information
         generation and material accounta-
         bility (plan) (US); science in
         general management (US)
SIGMA-9 air training computers ACMR
SIGMALOG simulation and gaming methods for
         analysis of logistics
SigMets significant meteorological informa-
         tions
sigmn   signalman
sign   signature
SIGNE-1 ... 2, ... 3, scientific satellite
         (FR/SU)
SigO   signal officer
SigOp   signal operation
SIGr   schwere Infanteriegranate, Stiel-
         granate (super-calibre grenade)
SIGS   simplified inertial guidance system
sigs   signals
SigSec   signals security
SIH   The South Irish Horse Regiment
SII   statements of intelligence interest
SIL   speech interference level; seriously
         ill list
SILKA   Simulation Luftkampf Mehrfachduell-
         modell by Dornier (multiple aerial
         combat simulation)
SILLACS Siemens low-level air defence
         control system
SILO   security intelligence liaison office

SILOS   Shiffs-Identifikations- und
         Ortungssystem by SEL (naval iden-
         tification and location system)
SILSP   Safeguard integrated logistics
         support plan
Silver Dog naval chaff launcher by Buck
Silverfish naval static balloon
Silver Stars free-fall team RCT
SIM   selected item management; sergeant
         instructor of musketry; staff
         instruction manual SACLANT;
         scientific inventory management;
         scientific instrument module
sim   simulation; similar
SIM-74   laser tank combat simulator
SIM-80   gamma ray simulator by Autophon
Simcat   simulator, combat, anti-tank
         Solartron
SIME   security intelligence Middle East
Simfics improved Simfire by Solartron
Simfire tank firing training system by
         Solartron
Simflak laser simulator for anti-aircraft
         guns by Solartron;
         helicopter-mounted a/a fire
         evasion simulator
Simgun   gun fire simulator by Solartron
Simlan   Milan laser fire simulator by
         Solartron
SIMNS   simulated navigation system
Simon Lake class, submarine tenders (USN)
SIMP   shipboard integrated maintenance
         programme
SIMPL   scientific industrial and medical
         photographic laboratories
Simray   laser fire simulation equipment
SIMS   selected item management system
Simstrike anti-tank helicopter crew
         simulation system by Solartron
SIN   study item number
SINBADS submarine integrated battle and
         data system by Signaal
SINCGARS single channel ground and air-
         borne radio subsystem VHF,
         cryptographic and ESM system by
         ITT
SINEWS   ship integrated electronic warfare
         system
Sing   Singapore
Single Hand grenade launcher for Jet Shot
         PRB
SINK   simulated inter-active naval
         Kriegsspiel
SINS   ship's inertial navigation system
         (USN)
SINT   single informal negotiating text
SINTAC   French air force navigation commu-
         nication and IFF system by
         Thomson
SIO   Scripps Institute of Oceanography;

service information officer;
senior intelligence officer

SIOP   single integrated operation plan;
strategic integrated operation
plan (US)

Sioux OH-13, AB-47, light helicopter by
Bell

SIP   systems implementation plan;
standard information package;
stay in place; standard inspection
procedure; standardization
instructor pilot

SIPD   supply item provisioning document

Siplex bullet-proof glass by Haller

SIPRI Stockholm International Peace
Research Institute

SIPS   Spartan improved performance study

SIR   serious incident report; selected
item report; specialist intelligence report; search and interrogation radar; selective information retrieval

SIRA   scientific instruments research
association

SIRAD semi-automatic data handling equipment for the early warning system

Sir Bedivere class, logistics landing craft
(RN)

SIRCS shipboard intermediate-range combat
system (US programme a/a missile)

SIRE   satellite infra-red experiment
(USAF)

Sirena airborne radar warning receiver (SU)

SIRETRAC Siemens infra-red tracker

Sirio fire control radar by Selenia;
telecommunications satellite by
AS+ESA

Sir Lancelot logistic landing craft (RAN)

Sirocco Station Integrée Radar d'Observation Continué de Courants Aero-
logiques (meteorological radar)
by EMD

SIRS   ship installed radiac system by
Plessey; satellite infra-red
spectrometer

SIS   satellite intercept system; secret
intelligence service; special
investigation section; strategic
intelligence summary

SISMS standard integrated support management system

SISR   selected items status report

SISS   submarine integrated sonar system

SISSI Schiff-Schiess-Simulator by ES (on-
board fire control simulator)

SIST   self-inflating surface target

SISTEL Sistemi Elettronici SpA (Rome)

SISTER special institution for scientific
and technological education and
research

SISTMS standard integrated supply/trans-
portation manifest system (US)

SISU-1 active/passive sonar for submarine
by Selenia

SIT   self ignition temperature; spontan-
eous ignition temperature; silicon
intensifier tubes; silicon intensifier targets; storage inspection
test; statement of inventory
transactions

sit   situation

SIT-Italtel Societa Italian Telecommuni-
cazioni (Milan)

SIT-301 airborne UHF system by Italtel

SITA   Société Internationale de Télécommu-
nications Aeronautiques

SITC   standard international trade classification

SitCen situation centre MC (Nato)

SITE   satellite instructional television
experiment (India)

Sit-map situation map

SITRAC Siemens infra-red tracker

SitRep situation report

SITS   systems integration test station

SitSum (intelligence) situation summary

SIUFL suspend issue and use of following
lots

SIUSM suspend issue and use as suspect
material

SIW   self-inflicted wound

SixATAF Sixth allied tactical air force

SixFlt sixth fleet

SIZ   security identification zone;
Sprachsythese im Zeitbereich
(synthetic language) (Holtz
Institute Berlin)

SIZE   Sicherheitszentrale by Dornier
(security centre)

SJ   selective jamming; spot jamming

SJA   staff judge advocate

SJAA   St John Ambulance Association

SJAB   St John Ambulance Brigade

SJAC   Society of Japanese Aerospace
Companies

SJC   supreme judicial court (US);
standing joint committee

SJCM   special job cover map

SJP   special job procedure

SJS   secretary, joint staff

sk   sketch; storekeeper

SK   Schnelladekanone (rapid firing gun)

SK-105 Kürassier (killer tank) by Steyr

SKAMP station keeping and mobile platform
(unmanned sailing boat)

Skatan miniature recce RPV (Sweden)

Skate class, nuclear attack submarine
(USN)

SKC   The Services Kinema Corporation
(UK)

sked   schedule
Skeet   target drone by Short
Skeeter   AOP-10, light helicopter by
           Saunders Roe
SKF   superkritischer Flügel (supercritical
           wing)
SHFNbK   Schwimmkörper für Nebelkerze (float
           for smoke tube)
SKG   Schweizerische Kriegstechnische
           Gesellschaft (Swiss Society for
           War Technology)
SkiDoo   motor sledge (Canada)
SKILA   Southern Korean interim legislative
           assembly
SKill   satellite kill
Skipjack   class, nuclear attack submarines
           (USN)
SKL   skip lister
SKMC   sickness due to misconduct
skmr   hydroskimmer (boat) (USN)
Skory   class, destroyers (SU)
Skot   wheeled armoured personnel carrier
           (Czech)
SKP   skip (line) printer
SKP-5   armoured recovery vehicle (SU)
SKR   WG-34, Sea King Replacement,
           helicopter by Westland project;
           South Korean Republic
skr   skipper
SKS   assault rifle (SU)
SKT   skill knowledge test
Skua   fighter/dive bomber by Blackburn
Skybolt   airborne ballistic missile (UK-US)
Skycrane   CH-54, Tarhe, heavy lift helicop-
           ter by Sikorsky
Sky Eye   reconnaissance drone by DSI
Sky Flash XJ-521, medium-range air-to-air
           guided missile by BAe
Skyguard   FLG-75, anti-aircraft fire-control
           system by Contraves
Skyhawk   A-4, supersonic fighter/bomber by
           McDD
Skylark   sounding rocket by BAe
Skyliner   19-passenger commuter aircraft by
           Shorts
Skymaster C-54, four-engined cargo aircraft
           by Douglas
Skymonster CL-44, cargo aircraft
Skynet   naval communications satellite system
           by Marconi
Skynight   F-3, all-weather fighter by Douglas
Skyraider A-1, fighter/bomber
Skyray   F-4, transsonic fighter by Douglas
Skyservant Do-28, STOL aircraft by Dornier
SkyShadow ECM pod by Marconi
Skyshark   A-2, attacker aircraft by Douglas
Skyschield Italian territorial air defence
           system
Skyspy   unmanned helicopter platform for
           surveillance and SIGINT by Short

Skysweeper M-51, 75mm radar controlled
           anti-aircraft gun
Skytrack   recce drone by Dornier
Skytrain   C-47, Gooney Birds, tactical
           transport by Douglas
Skyvan   A-40, transport aircraft by Shorts
Skywagon   tactical transport aircraft by
           Cessna
Skywarrior A-3, bomber by Douglas
SL   salvage loss; search light; sound
           locator; sea level; safety level;
           subscriber line; stock list;
           super long (range); sub-lieuten-
           ant; secretary of labour; squad
           leader; squadron leader; section
           leader; start line; storage loca-
           tion; south latitude; supplemen-
           tary list; support line
SLA   supply loading airfield; sequential
           launch adapter (one LCC fires 3
           Pershings); single line approach;
           Sandia Laboratories Albuquerque
SLAC   Stanford linear accelerator center
Sladen-suit shallow water diving suit
SLAE   standard light-weight avionics
           equipment
SLAET   society of licensed aircraft
           engineers and technologists
           (Kingston UK)
SL/ALQ   ECM pod by Selenia
SLAM   submarine launched airflight missile
           (a/a 6 Blowpipes + TV camera by
           Vickers); supersonic low altitude
           missile (US)
Slammer VI experimental artillery rocket
           launcher (US)
SLAMMR   side-looking airborne multi-mission
           modular radar by Motorola
SLang   systems language
SLanR   The South Lancashire Regiment The
           Prince of Wales's Volunteers
SLAR   side-looking airborne radar
SlaR   slant range
SLAT   special logistic action Thailand
SLat   south latitude
SLATE   small light-weight altitude trans-
           mission equipment FAA
SLAW   school of land/air warfare (Old
           Sarun UK)
SLB   side lobe blanking
SLBM   ship-launched ballistic missile;
           sub-surface-launched ballistic
           missile; sea-launched ballistic
           missile
SLC   surgeon lieutenant commander;
           side lobe cancellation; support
           landing craft; super-light car;
           simulated linguistic computer
SLCM   Tomahawk, sea-launched cruise
           missile (GD)

SLCP   Saturn launch computer program
SLCU   standard landing craft unit
SLD   sea-landing division (Nato);
          ships logistic division
sld   sealed; solid; sailed
SLDAA   SACLANT distributing and accounting
          agency
sLdgW   schwerer Ladungswerfer (heavy mortar)
SLdr   squadron leader
sldr   soldier
SLE   superheat limit explosion
SLEP   service life extension program for
          USN ships
SLEW   static load error washout
SLF   special landing force; straight line
          frequency; system library file;
          Schaumlöschfahrzeug (foam fire-
          fighting vehicle)
SLFCS   survivable low frequency communica-
          tions system (US)
slght   slight
SLI   shelf life item
SLIC   simulation linear integrated
          circuits
SLIM   standards laboratory information
          material
SLIN   standard line item number
SLIS   shared laboratory information system
SLL   Sandia Laboratories Livermore (US)
SLM   ship-launched missile
SLMF   Sierra Leone Military Forces
slmr   sailmaker (RN)
SLMR   speed limit on motorways regulation
          1966
SLMS   Sea Sparrow light-weight missile
          system
SLN   Sri Lanka Navy
SLO   staff legal officer; senior liaison
          officer
slo   slow
SLOC   sea lines of communication
SLOCOP   specific linear optimal control pro-
          gramme
SLOE   special list of equipment
SLOMAR   space logistics maintenance and
          rescue
SLP   supply landing point; scouting land-
          plane
slp   slope; slip
SLPP   Sierra Leone People's Party
SLQ-17   shipboard ECM system by Hughes
SLQ-25   Nixie, torpedo counter-measures
          system
SLQ-31   anti-missile ECM system by Hughes
SLQ-32   naval ECM system by Raytheon
          V1 for small craft identifies
              hostile missiles
          V2 for bigger craft V1 + early
              warning + hostile radar iden-
              ifier
          V3 V1 + V2 + jamming + deception

SLR   self-loading rifle; super long-
          range; side-looking radar;
          special light rifle; The Sierra
          Leone Regiment; slush on runway
SLR-600   naval ESM system by GIC
SLR-P   slush on runway, patchy
SLRV   Surveyor lunar roving vehicle
SLS   side lobe suppression; small lot
          storage
SLt   sub-lieutenant
SLT   solid logic technology
slt   searchlight; sleet
SLT   Schwerlasttransporter (heavy weight
          transporter) (road vehicle)
          Elefant
SLTF   shortest latency time first
SLT&SDL   search light and sound locator
SLUFAE   surface launched unit, fuel air
          explosives
SLUMINE   surface launched unit mine system
          (scatter mines)
SLUR   shared library user report
SLURP   self-levelling unit to remove
          pollution
SLUTT   ship-launched underwater transponder
          target by GI
SLV   space launch vehicle
SLV-3   space launch vehicle 4-stage Indian
          missile
slw   slow
SM   submarine (RN); submarine, mine-
          laying (USN); set mode; service
          module; storage mark; strategic
          missile; Soldier's Medal (US);
          state militia; surgeon major;
          signalman mechanic (RN); station
          master; sergeant major; salvage
          mechanic (USN); signalman (USN);
          staff major; sappers and miners;
          service member; system manager;
          semi-monthly (report); supply
          manual; shipment memorandum
S&M   supply and maintenance
SM-Boot   schnelles Minensuchboot (fast mine-
          sweeper)
SM-1   sea-to-sea guided missile (GE)
SM-1A   Standard missile, anti-aircraft
          missile
SM-4-1   gun 130mm (SU)
SM-8   4x4 truck 5.5 tons by Saviem
SM-38   submarine-launched Exocet missile
          by AS
SM-62   Snark, strategic missile, long-
          range ground-to-ground by Northrop
SM-64   Navaho, strategic missile,
          long-range, ramjet by
          North American
SM-65   Atlas, ICBM, inter-continental
          ballistic missile
SM-75   Thor, IRBM, intermediate range
          ballistic missile

SM-1019   single-engined STOL by SIAI-
          Marchetti
SMA   SUBROC missile assembly; surface
          modeling and analysis; small arms
          STANAG; Soviet military adminis-
          tration (in Germany); ship's
          material account; sergeant major
          of the US Army; standard mainten-
          ance allowance (clothing); surplus
          marketing administration;
          Segnalemento Maritimo et Aero SpA
          (Firenze IT)
SMAA   submarine movement advisory
          authority
SMAB   solid motor assembly building
SMAC   standing medical advisory committee;
          scene matching area correlator
          --ALCM
SmaCTraCen   small craft training centre
SMAF   shipboard maintenance action form;
          special mission aircraft flights
SMAlp   school of military Alpinism (Aosta)
SMAMA   Sacramento air material area
SMAr   Schallmessanlage, Artillerie by SEL
          (artillery acoustic location
          equipment)
SMARADAR Canada Inc.   Consortium SMA + Leigh
                       Instruments
SMART   satellite maintenance and repair
          techniques
smart bomb   HOBOS homing bomb
SMASH   South-East-Asia multi-sensor armament
          system for Huey Cobra day/night
          sight
SMATS   source module alignment test site
SMAW   second marine air wing; shoulder-
          fired multi-purpose assault weapon
          by McDD
SMAWT   short-range man-portable anti-tank
          weapon technology
smaze   smog and haze
smbl   semi-mobile
SMC   staff message control; servicemen's
          centre; supply and maintenance
          command (US); Sandhurst military
          college (UK); submachine carbine;
          STEN machine carbine; semi-
          automatic maintenance control;
          sheet moulding compound
smcln   semicolon
SMCO   semi-automatic (ground environment)
          maintenance control office
SMCSG   special military construction study
          group
SMD   submarine detector; Sony magnetic
          diode; superintendent of mine
          design; submarine mine depot
SMD,OCSA staff management division, office,
          chief of staff, Army (US)
SME   school of military engineering

SmE   Spitzgeschoss mit Eisenkern
          (pointed projectile with iron
          core)
SMEAT   Skylab medical experiments altitude
          tests
SMEC   special mission for economic co-
          operation
SMERE   Sprint missile electromagnetic
          radiation evaluation
SME/SC   Sprint missile engineering service
          course
SMETO   staff meteorological officer
SMetO   senior meteorological officer
SMF   system management facilities
SMG   submachine gun (UK); Sterling
          machine gun; submarine gun (USN)
SMI   sergeant major instructor (UK);
          Saturday morning inspection;
          Südsteirische Metallindustrie
          (Austria)
SMIC   study of man's impact on climate
SMIG   sergeant major instructor of
          gunnery (UK)
SMIN   MIN-consortium (ELSAG+Riva Calzoni)
          mine identification and neutrali-
          zation system
SMIS   supply management information
          system; Safeguard management
          information system
SMISOP   Safeguard management information
          system operating programme
Smith gun   3 in. smooth-bore gun (UK Home
            Guard)
smk   smoke
SmK   Spitzgeschoss mit Stahlkern (pointed
          projectile with steel core)
SmKBr   Spitzgeschoss mit Brandsatz (pointed
          projectile with incendiary)
SmKGl'spur   Spitzgeschoss mit Glimmspur
             (pointed projectile with
             dark ignition tracer)
SmKH   Spitzgeschoss mit Stahlkern gehärtet
          (pointed projectile with hardened
          steel core)
SMK-RFL-40   rifle-fired smoke grenade by
             MECAR
             BT for 5.56mm rifles
SML   support material list; symbolic
          machine language
sml   small; simulation
SMLE   short magazine Lee Enfield rifle
SMM   start of manual message
SMMC   systems maintenance monitor console
SMMR   scanning multi-channel microwave
          radiometer (pollution monitoring
          satellite by RCA)
SMNO   Singapore Malays National Organiza-
          tion
SMO   senior medical officer; ship's
          medical officer; squadron medical

officer; stabilized master oscil-
lator; so much of; ship's material
office; supplementary meteorologi-
cal office
SMOA single manager operating agency
SMOAF Sultan of Muscat and Oman's Armed
Forces
smog smoke and fog
SMOLant ship's material office, Atlantic
SMOPac ship's material office, Pacific
SMOM Sovereign and Military Order of
Malta
SMOP so much of paragraph
SMOPS school of maritime operations (RN)
SMOS secondary military occupational
speciality (US)
SMOSC secondary military occupational
speciality code
SMP scanning microscope photometer
SMPO sound movie projector operator
SMPR supply and maintenance plan and
report (US); semi-monthly progress
reports
SMR special money requisition; stock
management report; standardized
mortality ratio; super metal rich
(star); standard military requirement
SM&R source maintenance and recoverability
(code)
SMRAS Safeguard maintenance and reporting
analysis system
SMRE safety in mines research establishment
SMR/MIS supply maintenance and readiness
management information system
--LOGMIS (US)
SMS sequence milestone system; surface
missile system; synchronous
meteorological satellite; standard
modular system; systems maintenance service; satellite and
missile surveillance; marine
service squadron (USMC); signal
messenger service; sensor monitoring set; heavy pontoon bridge
(Czech); Société des Matériels
Spéciaux (Saviiem - Creussot-
Loire) (Saint-Cloud FR)
SMSD submarine detector ship's magnet
SMSgt senior master sergeant
SMSO senior maintenance staff officer
SMSPO surface missile systems project
office
SMSTD surface missile systems training
division
SMT SUBROC missile technician (USN)
shop mechanics test; ship's mean
time; Système Modulaire Thermique
(SAT + TRT)

SMT-1 truck-mounted treadway bridge
(Poland)
SMTAG standard micro-teaching appraisal
guide
smth smooth
SMTO senior mechanical transport officer
SMU secondary multiplexing unit
SMV standardized modular display system
SINTRA
SMW standard metal window
smwht somewhat
SN seaman; staff nurse; sergeant navi-
gator; secretary of the navy;
serial number; service number;
shipping note; stock number;
submarine, nuclear
S/N signal-to-noise (ratio)
SNA submarine, nuclear-powered, attack;
student naval aviator
SNAB stock number action bulletin
Snake rocket-driven mine-clearing pipe
Snakeeye bomb retarding system (USAF) Mk-15
Snakeye Mk-82, airborne laser equipment
SNAME society of naval architects and
marine engineers
SNAP student naval aviation pilot;
senior naval aviator present;
short notice annual practice;
shelter neighbourhood action pro-
ject; satellite, nuclear-powered;
systems for nuclear auxiliary
power; structural network analysis
programme; steerable null antenna
processor (interference protec-
tion) by Hazeltine
Snap-report joint tactical air/recce/sur-
veillance mission report
SNAR fire control radar (SU)
Snark SM-62, strategic missile, long-
range by Northrop
SNB secondary naval base
SNCASE Société National de Constructions
Aeronautiques du Sued-Est
SNCASO Societe National de Constructions
Aeronautiques du Sud-Ouest (Paris)
SNCO senior non-commissioned officer
SNDL standard navy distribution list
SNDS stock number data section
SNDV strategic nuclear delivery vehicles
SNEB unguided airborne rockets (FR)
SNEB-4 47 37mm airborne rockets by Matra
SNEC secondary navy enlisted classifica-
tion
SNECMA Société Nationale d'Étude et de Con-
struction de Moteurs d'Aviation
(Paris)
SNEP Saudi-Arabian naval expansion pro-
gramme
SNF system noise figure
SNFA standing naval force, Atlantic

SNFO	student naval flight officer
SNFS	student naval flight surgeon
S ng	Singapore
SNH	South Nottinghamshire Hussars RHA
SNIAS	Société Nationale Industrielle Aero-spatiale short: Aerospatiale AS
SNIES	special national intelligence estimates
Sniffer	No. 2 explosives detector (UK-NI)
Snipe	small RPV for anti-aircraft training AEL; passive nightsight by Pilkington
SNIT	stock number identification tables
SNIWB	Scottish National Institute for War-blinded
SNJ	switching network junction
SNL	standard name line; standard nomenclature list
SNLE	Sous-marine Nucleaire Lançeur d'Engines (nuclear-powered ballistic missile launching submarine (French Navy)
SNLR	services no longer required (RN)
SNM	senior naval member
SNMMMS	standard navy maintenance and material management system (US)
SNO	senior naval officer (UK); senior navigation officer
SNOAD	senior naval officer Adriatic (RN)
Snogg	class, patrol boats guided missiles (Norway)
SNOK	secondary next of kin (US)
SNOL	senior naval landing officer (RN)
SNOP	senior naval officer present (RN)
SNOPG	senior naval officer Persian Gulf (RN)
Snora	81mm air-to-ground rocket by SNIA + Oerlikon
SNORSCA	senior naval officer, Red Sea and Suez Canal area (RN)
SNORT	supersonic naval ordnance research track (China Lake, Cal. US)
SNOT	senior naval officer, transportation (RN)
SNOWCAT	support of nuclear operations with conventional air tactics
SNOWI	senior naval officer, West Indies (RN)
Snowtrac	snow tractor (Swedish-make)
SNPE	Société Nationale des Poudres et Explosives (FR)
SNPO	space nuclear propulsion office
SNPRI	selected non-priority list items
SNPS	satellite nuclear power station
SNR	signal-to-noise ratio; society for nautical research
SNS	Spanish navy ship; space navigation system
SNSN	standard navy stock number

SNSO	superintending naval stores officer (RN)
SNTI	integrated ship's communications system TRT
SO	senior officer; staff officer; signals officer; supply officer; section officer; sonarman; sorting office; statistical office; special order; sub-office; standing orders; shipment order; (Her/His Majesty's) Stationery Office; stockage objectives; secretary's office; signal orders; systems orientation; shift out; slow operate; signal oscillator
SO-1	class, corvettes (SU)
SOA	special open allotment; special operating agency; speed of advance (over ground); staff officer, administration; submarine operating authority; speed of approach
SOAC	scene of action commander
SOAD	staff officer, air defence
SOAF	Sultan of Oman Air Force
SOAG	senior officer, assault group (UK)
SOAP	supply operation assistance programme; spectrographic oil analysis programme; side oblique air photograph
SOAS	School of Oriental and African Studies
SOASC	senior officer, assault ships and crafts (RN)
SOASCI	senior officer, assault ships and crafts, India
SOBLIN	self-organizing binary logical network
SOBM	stand-off ballistic missile
SOC	sector operation centre NADGE; special operations command (US); mine planting equipment by GIAT
soc	society
SOC-2	Seagull, catapult floatplane by Curtiss
SOC-3	Seagull, catapult floatplane by Curtiss interchangeable float or undercarriage
SoCalSec	Southern California Sector
Socata	TB-30, trainer aircraft by AS
SOCE	staff officer, construction engineering
SoChinaFor	South China Force
SOCMC	Special Order of the Commandant of the US Marine Corps
SOD	special operations detachment; special operations department; small object detector
SODATSS	sonar data tape storage system by Plessey
SOE	special operations executive (UK);

secret operations equipment; status of equipment

SoEastPac South East Pacific

SOEDETE Société d'Études Techniques et d'Enterprises Générales (French arms trade)

SOEF senior officer, Eastern fleet (RN)

SOEP solar-oriented experiment package (Nasa)

SOES station operating and engineering squadron

SOF strategic offensive forces; schedule of fire

SOFA status of forces agreement; antenna pointing mechanism for TDF-1

SOFAR sound fixing and ranging ASW

SOFCS self-organizing flight control system

SofM school of musketry

SOFMA Société Française de Matériel d'Armament

SOFPAC special operating forces, Pacific

SOFREGIAT Société Française d'Exportation du GIAT

SOFREMAS Société Française d'Exportation de Matériels et Systèmes d'Armament

SOFREXAN Société Française d'Exportation de Matériels Navals Militaires

SofS the school of signals (Catterick Blandford); secretary of state

SofSA secretary of state for air

SofTT school of technical training

SOG seat of government; special operations group; speed over ground

SOGEPA Société de Gestion de Participations Aeronautiques (French government)

SoGru southern group

SOH start of heading

SOHKS senior officer Hong Kong squadron (RN)

SOI signal operation instruction; staff officer, intelligence

SOIC supply officer in charge

SOinC supply officer in charge (US); signal officer in chief (UK)

SOIS senior officer, inshore squadron (RN); shipping operations information system

SOJ stand-off jamming

Sokol class, submarines (Poland) (ex-Whisky)

sol solar; solution; soluble

SoLant South Atlantic

SoLantFor South Atlantic force (USN)

Solar high-power flashlight by Eiselt

Solar Riser solar energy-powered aircraft by Ultralight Flying Machines (Cal.)

Soldati class, destroyers WW2 (IT)

SOLF The Sultan of Oman's Land Forces

SolG solicitor general

SolGen solicitor general

soln solution

SOLO status of logistics, offensive (US)

SOLOG standardization of certain aspects of operations and logistics (US)

SOLOMON simultaneous operation linked orbital modular network

SolRad solar radiation

Sols Solomon Islands

solv solvent

soly solubility

SOM start of message; scheme of manoeuvres; SACLANT staff organization manual; stand-off missile by MBB; self-orientation mechanism

SOM-9A anti-aircraft radar

SOME secretary's office management engineer; senior ordnance mechanical engineer

SOMELER Société de Mécanique et d'Electronique de Ruelle

SOMF SIDPERS organization master file (standard installation/division personnel system) (US)

SOMISS study of management information systems support (US)

SOMLI Prince Albert's Somerset Light Infantry

SOMP Sydney ocean meeting point

SOMRB senior officers material review board

SOMS selection on military studies

SOMUA Société d'Outillage Mécanique et Usinage d'Artillerie

SON The Sultan of Oman's Navy

SONAR sound navigation and ranging

SONCM sonar counter-measures (and deception)

SOND secretary's office, navy department

Sonda-III Avibras-X-40, atmospheric research rocket (Brazil)

SONNTLAN solar energy project, Mexico by Dornier

SoNoAn sonic noise analyser

Sonobuoy sonar buoy

SONRD secretary's office, naval research and development (department)

SONS statistics of naval shipyards (US)

Sonya class, minesweepers (SU)

SOO senior operations officer; senior ordnance officer; staff officer, operations

SOO-2 second staff officer in charge of operations

SOOBE self-operating outside broadcasting equipment

SOP standard operating procedure;

SOP   standing operating procedure;
        senior officer present; staff
        officer, pensioners; sum of
        products
SOPA   senior officer present, afloat
SOP(A) senior officer present, ashore
SoPac   Southern Pacific
SoPacBaCom Southern Pacific base command
SoPaComs Southern Pacific communications
SoPat   South (China) patrol (USN)
SOPMET standing operating procedure meteo-
        rological plan
SOPUS   senior officer present (US Navy)
Sopwith Baby submarine carried airplane
        1916 (RN)
SOQ   senior officers' quarters; sick
        officers' quarters
SOR   services off-shore race (UK);
        specific operational requirement
SORA   secretary's office, records
        administration
SORB   subsistence operations review board
        (US)
SORC   sound ranging control
SORD   submerged objects recovery device
SORG   submarine operations research group
SORNEI senior officer, Royal Naval estab-
        lishment India
SoRng   sound ranging
SORR   signal (intelligence) operations
        readiness review (US); submarine
        operations research report (USN)
SORT   simulated optical range tester by
        Hughes (for testing tank range-
        finders)
SORTI   satellite orbital track and inter-
        cept
SOS   senior officers' school; service
        observers' school; struck off
        strength; sniping, observation and
        scouting; statement of service;
        save our ship; save our souls
        (distress call); senior officer
        seminar (course); services of
        supply (US Army); special opera-
        tions squadron (US); sonar techni-
        cian, submarine (USN); Sprint
        operating shelter; silicon-on-
        sapphire; Sentinel on station;
        start of significant (information)
SOSC   Smithsonian Oceanographic Sorting
        Center (US)
SOSED   secretary's office, shore establish-
        ment division
SOSS   shipboard oceanographic survey
        system
SOSSPA service of supply, South Pacific
        area
SOSTEL solid state electric logic
SOSU   scout observation service unit

SOSUS   sound surveillance system (USN);
        passive long-range sea-bed micro-
        phones
SOT   superintendent of training; simula-
        ted operational training;
        secretary of transportation (US);
        schedule of targets (US); systems
        operability test
SOT-I ... II ... III simulated operational
        training course phase 1 2 3
SOTA   state of the art
SOTAS   stand-off target acquisition system
        (helicopter borne)
SOTB   secretary's office, transportation
        branch
SOTFE   support operations task force Europe
        (US)
SOTIM   sonic observation of the trajectory
        and impact of missiles
SouthAG Southern army group (Nato)
SouWesPac South West Pacific Headquarters
SOV   shut-off valve; seabed operations
        vehicle (RN)
SOVMedRon Soviet Mediterranean squadron
        (Nato)
SOW   stand-off weapon (missile, helicop-
        ter-borne, anti-tank)
SoWes   South West
SoWesPac South West Pacific
SoWesPacCom South West Pacific command
SoWesSeaFron South West sea frontier
Soyuz   orbital transport missile (SU)
SOZ   Soviet occupied zone
SP   service policeman; staff paymaster;
        steam propulsionman (USN); shore
        patrol (USN); signal publication;
        shore party; shore police; ship
        police; secret police; starting
        point; Spain; section patrol;
        security publication; special
        programmes; sub-professional;
        summary plotter; standing proce-
        dure; soft point (projectile);
        self-propelled (gun); signalling
        projector (RN); single purpose;
        special purpose; seaplane (USN);
        shore patrol (boat) motor;
        service pistol; single phase;
        smokeless powder; supply point;
        stirrup pump; snow pellets
        (weather); service package;
        summary punch; supervisory package;
        supervisory printer; short page;
        starting price; starting pay;
        stop payment; single point
        (sights)
sp   special; specific; speed; specimen;
        support; spearhead
SP   Simmonds Precision NV (Brummen NL)
SP-group support group

SP-4	... 7, Specialist 4th class (US Army)
SP-70	self-propelled gun 1970; howitzer 155mm by UK-IT-GE
SP-73	self-propelled gun 152mm (SU)
SP-74	SP amphibious howitzer 12mm (SU)
SPA	strategic posture analysis (US); shore patrol advance (pay); South Pacific area; submarine patrol areas; small parts analysis
SPAB	supply priorities and allocation board
SPACE	symbolic programming anyone can enjoy
Spacelab	space laboratory by ERNO ESA
Space Shuttle	orbital transport recoverable aircraft (NASA)
Space Track	NORAD National space surveillance control center (US)
Spacetrack	SLBM radar warning system
SpACon	space assignment committee
SpaCon	space control
SPAD	satellite protection for area defence; simplified procedure for analysis of data (systems)
Spada	low-level anti-aircraft system by Selenia; missile Aspide
SPADATS	NORAD space detection and tracking system
SPADS	STRATCOM program automated data system (US) (satellite position and display system); Sprint air directed defence system; simplified procedure for analysis of data systems
SpaePz-2	Luchs, Spähpanzer, recce vehicle 8x8
SPAM	special air mission; spiced ham; special aeronautical material; servo-pneumatic altitude meter; satellite processor access method
SPANDAR	space and range radar (Nasa)
SPANDRA	space and range radar (Nasa)
SPAR	sea-going platform for acoustic research; surveillance and (super) precision approach radar; staff payroll allocations and records; semper paratus (USCG motto)
SPARC	shore (establishment) planning analysis and review co-operation
SPARM	solid-propellant augmented rocket motor
Sparrow	AIM-7, RIM-7, anti-aircraft point defence missile system by GD; recce mini-RPV (US)
Spartan	FV-103, armoured personnel carrier by Alvis; LIM-49A, anti-ballistic missile by MDA
Spartan viewer	night observation device by Pilkington
SPARTIATE	Système Polyvalent d'Atterisage, Recueil, Télécommunications et Identification de l'Armée de Terre (French Army CCC-IFF-ILS system)
Spartron-set	low-cost Navstar GPS receiver
Sparviero	P-420, hydrofoil (IT designation); anti-tank missile by Breda
SPASM	system performance and activity software monitor
SpAsst	special assistant
SpAst	special assistant
SPASUR	space surveillance system NAVSPASUR Navy part of NORAD
SPAT	self-propelled anti-tank (gun); self-propelled acoustic target (ASW practice torpedo)
SPATC	South Pacific air transport council
SPATG	self-propelled anti-tank gun
SPATGM	self-propelled anti-tank, guided missile (vehicle)
SPATS	South Pacific air transport service
SPBn	shore party battalion (USMC)
SPBT	soft point boat tail (projectile)
SPC	South Pacific commission; senior (level) political committee; special purpose code; standard products committee; stored programme control; standard plate count; Systems Planning Corporation (Rosslyn Va)
SPCC	ships parts control centre; standardization policy and coordination committee
SPCE	stored programme control exchange
SPCM	special court-martial (US)
SPCMO	special court-martial order
SPD	separation programme designator; self-protection depth; synchronous phased detector; South polar distance; ship project directive
spd	speed
SPDC	spare parts distribution centre (UK); soft point dual core (projectile)
spdltr	speedletter
SPDT	single pole double throw
SPE	school of preliminary education (Corscham, Wiltshire UK); semi-pointed expanding (projectile); special purpose equipment
Spear	class, patrol boats by Fairey; class, submarine tenders (USN)
SPEARD	satellite photo-electronic analog rectification device
SPEARS	satellite photo-electronic analog rectification system
spec	specification; specific; spectrum
SPEC	speech predictive encoding communication
Spec-1	...-4, specialist 1st class (US Army)
SpecAppt	special appointment

SpecAstSecNav special assistant to the
              secretary of the navy
SpeCat special catalogue MMIS
SpecEmp specially employed
SpecForCom special forces command
specif specifical(ly); specification
specl specialize(d)
SpeComME specified command, Middle East (US)
SpecProjLOUK special projects liaison
              office United Kingdom
Spectre AC-130, armed cargo aircraft
         Gunship Hercules by Lockheed
SPEDE system for processing educational
       data electronically
SPEED system-wide project for electronic
       equipment and depots (US);
       special project for emergency
       employment development; signal
       processing in evacuated electronic
       devices; subsistence prepared by
       electronic energy diffusion
SPEEDEX system-wide project for electronic
         equipment and depots - extended
         (US)
speedo speedometer
Speer/Pfeil anti-tank missile project by
             Diehl
SPEF single program element funding (US)
SpeNavO special naval observer (USN)
Sperber A-33, passenger aircraft by Focke-
         Wulf
Sperrin SR-4, jet bomber by Short
Sperry-Cat mine-sweeping catamaran by Sperry
SPERT scheduled programme evaluation review
       technique
SPF SIDPERS personnel file
SPFP soft point flat point (projectile)
SPG special patrol group; self-propelled
     gun
SPG-9 self-propelled gun anti-tank 73mm
       (SU)
SPG-51 naval illuminator radar
SPG-55 naval missile guidance system
SPG-60 3-dimensional air surveillance and
        tracking radar, naval by Lockheed
SPG-63 naval anti-aircraft search and
        tracking radar
SPG-51 naval missile guidance radar
SPG-62 naval tracking and illuminating radar
sp gr specific gravity
SPH statement of personal history
SPH-4 helmet for attack helicopter crews
       Bauer
SPHERIC security classification (Nato)
Sphinx naval ECM system (UK+NL); DC-4 four-
        engined airliner by Douglas
SPHQ shore patrol headquarters
sp ht specific heat
SPI single programme initiator; symbolic
     pictorial indicator

Spica class, small torpedo boat destroyers
       WW2 (IT)
SPICE SPACELAB payload integration and
       coordination in Europe by ESA
SPIDAC specimen input to digital automatic
        computer
SPIDACSYS specimen input to digital auto-
           matic computer system
SPIE society of photo-optical instrumen-
      tation engineers
SPIL ships parts integration list
SPIN space inspection; selected physics
      information notice
Spinne monoplane aircraft 1913 by Fokker
SPIRE space infra-red experiment
Spirit S-76, helicopter by Sikorsky
SPIS services packaging instruction
       sheet
SPIT selective printing of items from
      tape
Spitfire fighter aircraft WW2 (RAF) by
          Supermarine
SPIV suspected persons and itinerant
      vagrants
SPIW special purpose individual weapon
      (US) 5.56mm programme
SPL sound pressure level; space pro-
     gramming language; spare parts
     list
spl special
SPLC spare parts list for codification
SPLL self-propelled launcher-loader
SPLSM single position letter sorting
       machine
SplW special warrant
SPM self-propelled mount; small pertur-
     bation method; solar proton
     monitor
SpM-75 Splittermine (fragmentation mine)
        by Arges
SPMS special purpose manipulation system
SPN-10 naval navigation radar
SPN sponsor programme number
SPN-42 ... 43, ... 44, naval navigation
        radar; carrier-borne air traffic
        control
SPN/GEANS standard precision navigator/
           gimballed electrostatic air-
           craft navigation system by
           Honeywell
SpNWC Spanish naval war college
SPO senior planning officer; spare parts
     officer; shore patrol officer;
     special projects officer; senior
     press officer; signal property
     office; systems programme office;
     sea projection operations
SPOC single point orbit calculator;
      spacecraft oceanography
SPOMCUS selective prepositioning of mate-
         rial configured to unit sets (US)

SPOOL simultaneous peripheral operation on-line

SPOT spot inventory (US); spotter; Satellite pour Observation de la Terre CNES

SPP system package programme; standard psycho-physiological preparation

SPPBT soft point pointed boat tail (projectile)

SPPO scheduled programme print out

SpPz Spähpanzer (reconnaissance tank)

SPQ-9 naval surface surveillance radar

SPR system programming review; semi-permanent repellent; supervisory printer read

spr sapper

SPRAUS synthetic language by AEG

SP&RB special projects and review branch

SprBr Sprengpatrone mit Brandsatz (high-explosive incendiary)

sprd spread

SprGr Sprenggranate (HE shell)

SPRI Scott Polar Research Institute

Springer remote-controlled demolition tank 240 kgs WW2 by NSU (GE)

SPRINT solid propellant rocket intercept

Sprint anti-ballistic missile by Martin-Orlando

SPRN soft point round nose (projectile)

SPRS single passenger reservation system

SPRT school of physical and recreational training BAOR Sennelager; standard platinum resistance thermometer

SPRU science policy research unit

Spruance class, guided missile destroyers (USN DDG)

SPS special services; ship planning system; sharpshooter; symbolic programme system; soft point semi-pointed (projectile); seismic point processor; secondary power system; solar probe spacecraft (Pioneer)

SPS-10 naval surface search radar

SPS-30 3-dimensional naval air surveillance radar

SPS-40 naval long-range search radar

SPS-48 naval 3-dimensional long-range search radar

SPS-49 naval long-range surveillance radar by Raytheon

SPS-52 naval long-range 3-dimensional surveillance radar

SPS-55 naval surface search and navigation radar by Cardion Electronics

SPS-58 low-altitude search radar, naval

SPS-503 naval surveillance radar by Litton

SPSA signal phase statistical analyser

SPSO senior personnel staff officer; senior principal scientific officer

SPSP soft-point semi-pointed (projectile)

SP&SPB special programmes and special projects branch

SPST single pole single throw

SPT shared page table; star point transfer; school of physical training

spt support; seaport

SPTF sodium pump test facility

sptL support line

SpTrps special troops

SPTU staff pilots training unit

SpSurf specific surface

SPUR space power unit reactor (Nasa-AEC); source programme utility routines

SPURV self-propelled underwater research vehicle

SPV special purpose vehicle

SPVD society for the prevention of venereal diseases

SPW self-protection weapon (for aircraft); short-range missile (USAF programme)

SpWar special warfare

SPWM single-sided pulse-width modulation

SPY-1 naval multi-function phased-array radar (tracks multiple targets) by RCA

SPZ submarine patrol zones

SPz Schützenpanzer (armoured personnel carrier)

sPzB-41 schwere Panzerbüchse 2.8cm WW2 (GE) (heavy anti-tank rifle conical bore)

sPzFuWg schwerer Panzerfunkwagen (6x6 armoured wireless vehicle)

sPzSpWg schwerer Panzerspähwagen (heavy armoured reconnaissance car)

SQ sick quarters; survival quotient; second quality; safety quotient; super quick (fuse)

sq square; squadron

SQA system queue area

SQA-502 mechanical sonar by Fleet

SQAP supplementary quality assurance provisions

SQAT ships qualification assistance team

sqd squad

sqdn squadron

SqdnLdr squadron leader (RAF)

SQF subjective quality factor

SQI special qualification identifiers

SQUID superconductivity quantum interference device

SqIn square inch

SQL school quota letter (US)

SqLn squall line

SQMS squadron quartermaster sergeant; staff quartermaster sergeant

SQN	school quota number (US)
sqn	squadron
SqnQMS	squadron quartermaster sergeant
SqnSM	squadron sergeant major
SquO	squadron officer
SqO	squadron officer
SQPN	staggered quadraphase pseudo-noise (signal)
SQQ-14	variable-depth mine-hunting sonar CGE/FIART
SQQ-23	PAIR, performance and integration retrofit single array ASW sonar by Sperry
SQ$-14	ITASS, interim towed array surveillance system (sonar receiver) by Gould
SQR-15	TASS, towed array sonar system by Gould
SQR-18	... 19, TACTAS, tactical towed array sonar
SQS-23	keel sonar by Sperry
SQS-26	active search and attack keel sonar
SQS-35	passive variable depth sonar
SQS-53	active search and attack sonar
SQS-56	active/passive hull-mounted lightweight modular ASW sonar by Raytheon
SQS-508	digital active-passive sonar by WCL
SQS-509	Dutch version SSQ-505, active/passive sonar by WCL
SQT	ship qualification trial; system qualification test
SQU-505	mechanical sonar by Fleet
Squid	anti-submarine projectile
SR	seaman recruit; sound ratings (US Army); special regulations; service record; study requirements; shipment request; storage and repair; South Rhodesia; special reserve; supplementary reserve; The Sherwood Rangers; The Sarawak Rangers; standby reserve; separate rations; supporting research; standard requirement; surface raider (aircraft); short range (aircraft); seaplane reconnaissance (aircraft); spotter reconnaissance (aircraft); surveying recorder (UK); scanning radiometer; semi-regular; slow release; sorter reader; station radio; sound ranging; service rifle; self raising; short rate, anti-tank gun (Sweden); Sturm, Ruger & Co. (Southport USA)
SR-53	Saunders Roe, jet fighter prototype 1957
SR-71	Blackbird, YF-12A, special strategic recce aircraft Mach 3.2 by Lockheed
SRA	surgeon rear admiral; ship radio authorization; special rules airspace; spring research association (UK); surveillance radar approaches; standards of readiness and availability
SRA-1	jet fighter flying boat by Saunders Roe
SRAA	senior army advisor (US)
SRAACE	short-range air-to-air combat environment
SRAAG	senior army advisor, army national guard
SRAAM	short-range air-to-air missile by Hawker-Siddeley
SRAAR	senior army advisor US army reserve
SRAM	AGM-69, short-range attack missile by Boeing
SRAP	service record and allied papers
SrArAv	senior army aviator
SRAS	southern region additional sites (Nasa)
SRATS	University of Tokyo astronomical satellite
SRB	selective re-enlistment bonus (US); seaplane repair base; service record book (USMC); sorter reader, buffered; solid rocket booster
SRBM	short-range ballistic missile
SRBOC	super rapid bloom outboard chaff
SRBP	synthetic resin-bonded paper
SRC	Space Research Corporation Inc. (Quebec); science research council (UK); scheduled removal components; sample return container; standard requirements code; sanitary reserve corps; Swiss Red Cross
SRCC	strikes, riots and civil commotions
SRC-International	Space Research Corporation (Belgium)
SRCP	special reserve components programme
SRCT	standard recovery completion time
SRD	supply reserve depot; service revealed difficulty; service rum diluted
SRDE	signals research and development establishment (Christchurch)
SRDL	Saunders Roe Development Ltd (Hayes UK)
SRDS	shop repair data sheets; systems research and development service
SRE	surveillance radar element; surveillance radar equipment; scientific research and experiments (department); sound reproduction equipment; single round effectiveness

SRF   selected reserve force; submarine repair facility; ships repair facility; sorter reader flow
SRg   sound ranging; short-range
SRG-103   naval medium-range surveillance radar by HSA
SRH   supply railhead; structural repair handbook
SRI   standby request information; Stanford Research Institute (US)
SRIB   SAC strike route information book (US)
Sri Kudat class, fast patrol boats for Malaysia 1977 by Hong Kong Lürssen
SRILTA   Stanford Research Institute lead time analysis
SRIP   ship readiness improvement plan; specification review and improvement plan
SRL   system reference library
srl   serial
SRM   speed of relative motion; short-range missile; shock remnant magnetization
SRMU   space research management unit
SRN   state registered nurse (UK)
SR-N-4   Mountbatten, hovercraft by BHS/Saunders/Roe
SR-N-6   Winchester, hovercraft by BHS/Saunders/Roe
SRN-17   naval radio navigation set
SRNC   Severn River naval command
SRO   supplementary reserve of officers; station recruiting officer; standing room only; standing route order; squadron recreations officer; shop repair order; short-range order; special regional operations
SR&O   statutory rules and orders
SROTC   senior reserve officers' training corps (US)
SRP   supply refilling post; Safeguard readiness posture
SRPB   selected reserves programme branch
SRR   supplementary reserve regulations; short-range rescue (helicopter)
SRRA   searchlight regiment, Royal Artillery WW2
SRRL   sound-ranging radio link by Plessey
SRS   special raiding squadron SAS; sound ranging section; substitute route structure; supply response station; strategic reconnaissance squadron; satellite radar station
S/Rs   staff returns (USMC)
SRSA   scientific research society of America
SRSC   short-range secure communication

SRSM   short-range stand-off missile (USAF programme)
SRSM/WAAM short-range stand-off missile wide area anti-armor munition (USAF programme)
SRT   sheltered tactical radio; slow run-through (trials); secondary ranging test; supply response time; short-range transport (aircraft); space requirement travel; strategic rocket troops; Standard Radio & Telefon
SRTA   short-range transport aircraft
SRTU   ship repair training unit
SRU   signal recording unit; seaplane reconnaissance unit; ship repair unit; submarine repair unit
SRW   strategic reconnaissance wing (USAF)
SRWBR   short-range wide-band radio by ITT
SRY   The Sherwood Rangers Yeomanry
SS   Silver Star (US); staff surgeon; supply sergeant; steel shrinker; secretary of state; sharpshooter; secret service; service school; store section; signal station; short service; selective service; Somaliland Scouts; special staff; summary sheet; sworn statement; surveillance station; submarine studies; simplified spelling; special strike (aircraft); surface-to-surface (missile) (SU); sight setter; standard size; spectrum signature; silk screen; side by side; smoke shell; single seated (aircraft); single shot; submersible ship; submarine seeker; solid solution; stream-lined supersonic (bomb) Talloby WW2; stainless steel; spherical symmetry; steamship; submarine; support ship; screw steamer; ship-to-ship (missile)
S&S   The Stars and Stripes; supply and service
SS   sehr schwer (super heavy)
sS   schweres Spitzgeschoss (heavy pointed) (projectile)
SS-forms special strike forms (nuclear employment)
SS-1   Scunner, surface-to-surface missile (SU)
SS-1C   Scud B, surface-to-surface missile battlefield support (SU)
SS-2   Sibling, surface-to-surface missile (SU)
SS-2B   Samlet, surface-to-surface missile (SU)
SS-3   Shyster, surface-to-surface missile MRBM (SU)

SS-4	Sandal, surface-to-surface missile IRBM (SU)
SS-5	Skean, surface-to-surface missile IRBM (SU)
SS-6	Sapwood, surface-to-surface missile ICBM (SU)
SS-7	Saddler, surface-to-surface missile ICBM (SU)
SS-8	Sasin, surface-to-surface missile ICBM (SU)
SS-9	Scarp, surface-to-surface missile ICBM FOBS (SU)
SS-10	Scrag, surface-to-surface missile ICBM (SU); anti-tank missile by AS (FR)
SS-11	Sego, surface-to-surface missile ICBM 3 warheads (SU); anti-tank guided missile by AS
SS-12	Scaleboard, surface-to-surface missile tactical (SU); ATGW by AS
SS-13	Savage, surface-to-surface missile ICBM (SU)
SS-14	Scapegoat, Scamp, surface-to-surface missile IRBM (SU)
SS-15	Scrooge, surface-to-surface missile land-mobile strategic (SU)
SS-16	mobile ICBM
SS-17	ICBM 4 warheads
SS-18	ICBM 8 warheads
SS-19	ICBM 6 warheads
SS-20	IRBM
SS-20	individual infra-red weapon sight by Rank
SS-21	short-range battlefield support missile (SU) FROG replacement
SS-22	tactical missile SS-12 replacement (SU)
SS-23	SCUD-3, replacement
SS-30	CSWS, crew served weapons sight by Rank
SS-32	Twiggy night sight, image intensifying night sight by Rank
SS-70	night vision goggles by Rank
SS-92	5.56mm round, ball by FN
SS-109	5.56mm round, ball extended range by FN
SS-125	tank day/night sight by Rank
SS-126	tank day/night sight by Rank
SS-130	driver's night periscope by Rank
SS-901	day/night binocular by Rank
SS-9117	Pocketscope, day/night viewer by Rank
SSA	cargo submarine (USN); selective service act; social security administration (US); source selection authority; staff supply assistant; supply support arrangements; ship's stores activities; signal security agency; secretary of state for air; senior service accountant; security supporting assistance (US)
SSAC	section of small ammunition carts; source selection advisory council
SSAFA	soldiers' sailors' and airmen's family association (UK)
SSAG	strategic studies advisory group
SSALS	simplified short approach light system
SSAN	social security account number
SSASSDS	small surface-to-air ship self-defence system for the post-1985s
SSB	ballistic missile submarine (USN); ballistic missile submarine diesel-powered (Nato); special studies branch SHAPE; single side band (radio)
S&SB	strength and statistics branch
SSBAM	single side band amplitude modulation
SSBC	stock status balance card
SSBN	ballistic missile submarine, nuclear powered (Nato)
SSBN-X	next generation ballistic missile submarine, nuclear powered (USN)
SSBS	Sol-Sol Ballistique Stratégique (nuclear missile by AS)
SSC	ship systems command BuShips (USN); secondary strike capacity; services standardization sub-committee; coastal submarine (Nato); stellar simulator complex; senior service college; supply status code; service schools command; submarine supply centre; supply support centre
SSC-1	Shaddock, surface-to-surface, coastal missile (SU)
SSC-1B	Sepal, surface-to-surface, coastal missile (SU)
SSC-2A	Salish, surface-to-surface, coastal missile (SU)
SSC-2B	Samlet, surface-to-surface, coastal missile (SU)
SSC-3	Shaddock, surface-to-surface, coastal missile (SU)
SSCA	strobed single-channel analyser
SSCC	spin scan cloud camera
SSCCB	Safeguard system configuration control board
SSCDS	small-ship combat direction system
SSCF	space subsystems control facility
SSCMA	special supplementary clothing monetary allowance
SSComm	short service commission
SS-CPA	single-site coherent potential approximation
SS&CS	ship's stores and commissary stores
SSD	secret service division; specialized support depot; scrap salvage

	division; space system division; special services division; special sales division; solid state device; stabilized ship detector
S/SD	ship/shore department
S SD	Spitzgeschoss für Schalldämpferwaffen (pointed projectile for silenced weapons)
SSDB	shore station development board
SSDR	steady state determining routing
SSDRS	Safeguard system design release schedule
SSE	signal security element; system status evaluation; special support equipment
SSEB	source selection evaluation board
SSEC	secondary schools examination council (UK)
SSE/EWE	SIGINT support element/electronic warfare element
SSF	service storage facility; ship's service force; special service force (Canada); single seater fighter (aircraft); super-sonic frequency; system support facility
SSG	staff sergeant; guided missile submarine (diesel-powered) (USN)
SSG-69	Scharfschützengewehr 7.62mm by Steyr (sniper's rifle)
SSGN	guided missile submarine, nuclear powered
SSgt	staff sergeant
SSGW	surface-to-surface guided weapon
SSI	staff sergeant instructor; standing signal instructions; shoulder sleeve insignia (US); sustaining support increment; speciality skill identifier; sites of scientific importance; Startbahnschellinstand- setzung (rapid runway repair)
SSIM	statistical sampling inventory method
SSINS	secure survivable integrated network system (air defence ground environ- ment)
SSJ	self-screening jamming
SSK	killer submarine (Nato); single shot kill; Schallsignalkörper by Diehl (acoustic signalling device for submarines)
SSK-018	Splittergefechtskopf für DIRA by Oerlikon (fragmentation warhead for artillery rocket)
SSK-1500	killer submarines for India by HDW
SSKP	single shot kill probability
SSL	system stock list; submarine safety lines; Software Sciences Ltd
SSLS	Standard space launch system
SSLT	stock status lag time
SSM	staff sergeant major; squadron sergeant major; system support
	manager; Silver Star Medal (US); surface-to-surface (guided) missile; standard service module; single side (band) modulation; single-side-band signal multi- plexer; spread spectrum modulation
SSMA	spread spectrum multiple access
SSMCNP	Safeguard system management communi- cations network programme
SSME	Space Shuttle main engines
SSMR	single senior military representa- tive
SSMsn	surface-to-surface mission
SSN	social security number (US); specification serial number; severely sub-normal; nuclear- powered (attack) submarine (USN)
SS-N-1	Scrubber, surface-to-surface, naval missile (SU)
SS-N-2	Styx, surface-to-surface, naval missile (SU)
SS-N-3	Shaddock, SS-C-3, surface-to-sur- face, naval missile (SU)
SS-N-4	Sark, SLBM, surface-to-surface, naval missile (SU) 700 km
SS-N-5	Serb, SLBM, surface-to-surface, naval missile 1500 km (SU)
SS-N-6	Sawfly, SLBM 3 warheads
SS-N-7	surface-to-surface, naval missile submarine-launched (SU)
SS-N-8	surface-to-surface, naval missile SLBM, MIRV, 7000 km (SU)
SS-N-9	Siren, surface-to-surface, naval missile (SU)
SS-N-10	surface-to-surface, naval missile supersonic cruise missile (SU)
SS-N-11	surface-to-surface, naval missile (SU)
SS-N-12	surface-to-surface, naval missile cruise missile (SU)
SS-N-13	surface-to-surface, naval missile 370 nm (SU)
SS-N-14	surface-to-surface, naval missile RPV carrying homing torpedoes (SU)
SS-N-15	surface-to-surface, naval missile anti-submarine nuclear missile (SU)
SS-N-16	surface-to-surface, naval missile submarine-launched anti-submarine (SU)
SS-N-15	surface-to-surface, naval missile anti-submarine missile submarine- launched nuclear
SS-N-17	surface-to-surface, naval missile SLBM (SU)
SS-N-18	surface-to-surface, naval missile long-range SLBM (SU)
SSNS	standard study numbering system

SS-NX-12 surface-to-surface naval nuclear missile (SU)
SS-NX-13 submarine-launched ballistic nuclear missile (SU)
SS-NX-17 submarine-launched ICBM, solid-fuelled nuclear (SU)
SS-NX-18 SLBM 2 warheads 8000 km nuclear
SSO oiler submarine (USN); special service office; station staff officer; senior scientific officer; senior supply officer; squadron signals officer
SSP SACEUR scheduled programme; ship's stores and profit; semi-self propelled (shell); stores stressed platform (UK); single-shot probability; sustained superior performance; scouting seaplane (USN); transport submarine (USN); signalling and switching processor
sSP schwerer Spähwagen (heavy recce car)
SSPF signal structure parametric filters
SSPN ship's stores and profit, Navy
SSQ station sick quarters
SSQ-36 Bathy, helicopter-borne sonar buoy
SSQ-41 Jezebel, helicopter-borne passive omnidirectional sonar buoy
SSQ-47 Ranger, helicopter-borne active sonar buoy
SSQ-50 CASS, helicopter-borne sonobuoy command-active sonobuoy system
SSQ-53 DIFAR, helicopter borne sonobuoy directional low-frequency analyser and ranging system
SSQ-62 DICASS, helicopter-borne sonobuoy directional command-active sonobuoy system
SSQ-75 ERAPS, expandable reliable acoustic path sonobuoy
SSQ-77 VLAD, vertical line array DIFAR sonobuoy
SSQ-418 passive ASW sonobuoy
SSQ-505 active/passive sonar by WCL
SSQ-517 passive sonobuoy by Spartron
SSQ-522 Canadian designation for SSQ-47 by Spartron
SSQ-523 CANCASS, Canadian command-active sonobuoy system by Spartron
SSQ-801 BARRA-CAMBS, Australian helicopter-borne sonobuoy; command-active multibeam sonobuoy by Marconi
SSR social security report; Soviet socialist republic; supply support request; SACEUR strategic reserve; secondary surveillance radar; spin-stabilized rocket; radar picket submarine (USN); short-range sea rescue (aircraft)
SSR-90 Sauerstoffselbstretter (90 Minuten) (oxygen self-rescue breathing apparatus 90 minutes) by Auer

SSRA Soldiers' and Sailors' Relief Act; spread spectrum random access
SSRC Social Science Research Council; Soviet studies research centre (RMA Sandhurst)
SSRN submarine, radar picket, nuclear-powered
SSR-UW Sauerstoffselbstretter - Unterwasser (oxygen self-rescue breathing apparatus - underwater) by Auer
SSS submarine support ship; single screw ship; shipboard surveillance system; sea surveillance system; shipboard survey sub-system; selective service system (US); strategic satellite system (USAF); standard supply system (US); storage serviceability standard; synchro self shifting (gears); Solid State Sources (Pittsburgh US)
S/SS steering and suspension system
SSSBP system source selection board procedure
SSSC self-service supply center (US)
SSSI sites of special scientific interest
SSSO specialized surplus sales office (US)
SSSR semi-automatic (ground environment) systems status report
SSSS 4S, Sperry Secor Simulation Systems (Fairfax, Va USA)
SSSSSS 6S, small surface-to-air ship self-defence system (Nato programme for the 1980s)
SST super-sonic transport (aircraft); super-sonic telegraphy; sea surface temperature; submarine, target and training (USN); set strobe time; special strike tele-type; standard sonar transmitter; shore survey team MMVO
SST-4 torpedo by AEG-Telefunken
SSTA selective service and training act
SSTD solid state track detectors
SSTM semi-automatic (ground environment) system training missile
SSTO senior sea transport officer; superintending sea transport officer
SSTU semi-automatic (ground environment) system training unit
SSTV sea skimming test vehicle (missile); submarine shock test vehicle; supersonic shock test vehicle
SSU special service unit; squadron service unit; strategic services unit; stratospheric sounding unit
SSupO senior supply officer
SSUS spin stabilized upper stage (Nasa)

SSV   supersonic (test) vehicle; ship-to-
         surface vessel
SSvc   selective service
SSVF   Straits Settlements volunteer force
SSW   Secretary of State for War (US)
SSWS   strike support weapon system RPV
SSWS   ski and snow warfare school
SS-X-16 surface-to-surface nuclear missile
         (SU) ICBM MIRV
SS-X-20 surface-to-surface nuclear missile
         (SU)
SSZ   specified strike zone (US); pocket
         submarine (Nato)
ST   signal training; supply and trans-
         port; service test; special test;
         shock troops; seaman tropedoman
         (RN); sonar technician (USN);
         strategic transport (aircraft);
         space telescope; spoon type (pro-
         jectile); sticky type (anti-tank
         grenade); silver tip; sabre tip;
         segment table; skin temperature;
         sound trap; surveillance test;
         summer time; spring tide; short
         ton; sonic telegraphy
S&T   supply and transport; scientific and
         technical (intelligence)
st   street; stone; staff; strait;
         stratus (cloud)
St   mit Stahlkern (with steel core)
ST-901   ... 802, anti-ship gun and missile
         control radar by Marconi
STA   straight-in approach; science and
         technology agency (Japan); staff
         training assistant (US);
         Schiesstaktische Auswertanlage
         (for Roland) by Dornier (Roland
         tactical shooting system evalua-
         tion)
sta   station
StAAA   St Andrew's ambulance association
STAAG   standard tachymetric anti-aircraft
         gun (UK)
STAAS   surveillance and target acquisition
         aircraft system (US)
STAB   strike assault boat (USN)
stab   stabilizer
Staballoy high-density depleted uranium for
         armor-piercing penetrators (US)
Stabileye surveillance mini-RPV by BAe
StaBo   Startbahnbombe (runway dibber bomb)
         (retarded + hollow-charge + follow-
         on charge)
STAD   special temporary aviation duty
         (USMC)
STADAC   station data acquisition and control
STADAN   space tracking and data acquisition
         network (Nasa)
STADIN   standing administrative instruction
         (for US Army attaches)

STAF   strategic and tactical air force
STAFEX   staff exercise (Nato)
STAFF   smart target-activated fire and
         forget anti-tank weapon program
         (US); stand-off target acquisition
         fire and forget (sensor) (US Army
         programme)
Staffs Yeo The Staffordshire Yeomanry
STAG   special task air group; strategy and
         tactics analysis group
STAGG   small turbine advanced gas generator
         (US)
Staghound armoured recce car
STAGS   S-tank agility/survivability tests
         (Fort Knox 1976); structural
         analysis of general shells (USAF)
STALO   stabilized local oscillator
Stalwart high-mobility 6x6 amphibious truck
         by Alvis
         FV-622
         FV-623
STAM   statistical (section) (standing
         group) memorandum (Nato)
STAMP   standard amphibious plan; small
         tactical air-manoeuvrable platform
         by Garret
STAMO   stabilized automatic modulated
         oscillator
STAN   Stärke- und Ausrüstungsnachweisung
         (personnel and equipment tables)
stan   standard
STANAG   standardization agreement (Nato)
StaNavForChan standing naval force Channel
         (Nato)
StaNavForLant standing naval force Channel
         Atlantic
STAND   policy message originated by
         Standing group (Nato)
stand   standard
Standard multi-role missile by General
         Dynamics
         AGM-78   anti-radar missile ARM
         RGM-66 D
         RIM-66A MR medium-range
                  ER extended range
         RIM-67A   anti-aircraft and
                  anti-ship
StanFlt standardization flight
StanLanCrU standard landing craft unit
STANO   surveillance target acquisition and
         night observation (equipment)
STAP   shipbuilding temporary assistance
         programme (Canada)
STAPSC   Senate tactical air power sub-
         committee (US)
STAR   scientific and technical aerospace
         reports (Nasa); selective training
         and reassignment program (US Army);
         selective training and retention
         programme; special treatment and

STAR   review; standard terminal arrival
          route (US); ship-tended acoustic
          relay (US); storage array radar;
          stacked array radar; Satellites de
          Télécommunication d'Application et
          de Recherches (consortium 12 firms)
STARCOM   strategic Army communications
          system (US)
Starfighter F-104, multi-role jet by
          Lockheed
STARFIRE system to accumulate and retrieve
          financial information with
          random extraction
Starfire F-94, all-weather fighter by
          Lockheed
Starfish RAF WW2 mock airfields in England
Starlifter C-141, 4-turbofan cargo by
          Lockheed
Starlight Scope PVS-2, light intensifying
          rifle night sight (US)
Starnet   static relay network for British
          forces in Germany
STARS   study of tactical airborne radar
          systems

START   spacecraft technology and advanced
          re-entry tests
STARTLE   surveillance and target acquisition
          for tank location and engagement
          by Martin
Star-tron Mk.700 passive night vision system
          for assault rifles by S&W
Starwheels special rough-terrain wheels
Star Z-62 machine pistol 9mm by Echeverria
STAT   Seebee technical assistance team
          (construction battalion); Section
          Technique de l'Armée de Terre
          (French procurement office)
stat   statuary; statistics
STATE   simplified tactical approach and
          terminal equipment; simulator for
          tank/anti-tank evaluation STC
STATEM   shipment status system (US)
Stationar domestic communication satellite
          (US)
StaTrafO standard transfer order
StatsCentre statistical centre
STATSEC   administrative messages from the
          standing group (Nato)
StatServOff statistical service office SHAPE
STB   sun's true bearing
stbd   starboard
stblz   stabilized
stbt   steamboat
stby   standby
STC   signal training centre; sea transit
          centre RCT; SHAPE technical centre
          (The Hague); senior (officers')
          training corps (UK); sensitivity
          time control; satellite test centre
          (US); standard telephone cables

STD   sea transport division; services
          telephone directory (UK); subscri-
          ber dialling; salinity-temperature-
          depth (sensor)
Std   steward (RN)
std   standard; standing
STDN   spacecraft tracking and data network
stdy   steady
stdzn   standardization
STE   simplified test equipment
Steadyscope portable gyro-stabilized sight
          by BAe
Stealth   USAF program invisible aircraft
STECC   Scottish technical educational con-
          sultative council
STE/ICE   simplified test equipment for
          internal combustion engines by RCA
Steinbock wheeled forklifter by Steinbock
          (GE)
STELLA   satellite transmission experiments
          linking laboratories (for CERN,
          SACLAY, DESY, Rutherford by OTS-
          ECS)
Stellite barrel lining material (US)
STEM   Seebee technical equipment manage-
          ment; stay time extension module;
          storable tubular extendable
          member
Sten   Shepherd & Turpin (Enfield UK)
          (submachine gun)
Stenka   class, torpedo boats (SU)
Stentor   long-range ground surveillance
          radar LCT
STEP   satellite telecommunications experi-
          ments project (India); supervisory
          tape executive programme; Safe-
          guard test and evaluation program
          (US); standard test equipment
          procedures; special training
          enlistment program (US); supple-
          mentary training and enlistment
          program (US)
Stereomat anti-aircraft gunnery trainer
          1937 by Contraves
STE/T   simplified test equipment/transi-
          tional
STE/X   simplified test equipment/expendable
stf   staff
STFF   Safeguard tactical field force (US)
STFG   staffing guides (department of the
          Army US)
STG   sonar technician, surface (USN);
          special task group
stg   sterling; strong; staging (US)
STG   Schiffbautechnische Gesellschaft
          e.V. (GE)
STG-58   Sturmgewehr 1958, assault rifle by
          Steyr
StgAr   staging area (US)
StgB   staging base (US)

stge   storage
STgt   secondary target
StGw-57   SG-510, Sturmgewehr (assault rifle)
          by SIG
S&TI   scientific and technical intelligence
          (US); scientific and technical
          information (UK)
STIB   scientific and technical intelligence
          branch
STIC   scientific and technical intelligence
          centre
Stick bomb hand-launched depth charge (RN)
Stickleback Grasshopper, Sea Mattress, Land
          Mattress; 1080 naval bombard-
          ing rockets array
Sticky bomb anti-tank adhesive hand grenade
          (UK)
STID   scientific and technical information
          division (Nasa)
Stieglitz Fw-44, trainer aircraft WW2 by
          Focke Wulf
Stiletto propeller-driven target drone by
          Short
Stina   coastal and offshore surveillance
          system (Sweden) by Philips
STInfo   scientific and technical information
          (US)
Stinger   FIM-92, shoulder-fired anti-air-
          craft missile by GD
Stinger Alternate XFIM-92A, shoulder-fired
          anti-aircraft missile by Ford
Stingray Project 7511, airborne light-weight
          torpedo by Sperry + MSDS
STINGS   stellar inertial guidance system
StInv   static inverter
STIR   surplus to immediate requirements;
          ship target illumination radar by
          HSA
Stirling bomber/transport WW2 (RAF) by
          Short; submachine gun
STIT   scientific and technical information
          team
          Conus   continental US
          Eur   Europe
          FE   Far East
StJABde   St John of Jerusalem's Ambulance
          Brigade
stk   stock
StkF   stock fund
StkFA   stock fund accounting
StkFS   stock fund statement
StkR   stockroom
StL   stockage list
STL   studio-to-transmitter link; standard
          telecommunications laboratories;
          static test load
StLI   stockage list items
STLO   scientific and technical liaison
          office
stlr   semi-trailer

STM   supersonic tactical missile (long-
          range air-to-ground by Vought);
          short-term memory; structural
          thermal model; standard thermal
          model
stm   storm
StMrs   Sturm Mörser (self-propelled assault
          mortar)
STNI   stabiloy/tungsten nickel Iron (pro-
          jectile)
stn   station
STNIFS   stabiloy/tungsten nickel iron fin-
          stabilized (projectile)
STO   sea transport officer; standard
          transfer order; senior technical
          officer; standing orders, short
          take-off
sto   stores
Stockade decoy launcher by Wallop
STOL   short take-off and landing (air-
          craft)
STOL/VCD short take-off and landing (air-
          craft)/vertical climb and
          descent
STon   short ton
Stonefield P-5000, medium-mobility truck
          1.5 tons (UK)
Stoner-63 machine pistol 5.56mm by CG
Stooge   radio-controlled anti-aircraft
          missile naval WW2 by Fairey
stor   storage
STORADS   site tactical optimized range air
          defence system by Siemens/
          Thomson
Storch   Fi-156, STOL communications aircraft
          WW2 by Fieseler (GE)
Storm   class, guided missile patrol boats
          (Norway)
StoS   ship to shore; station to station
Stösser   Fw-56, trainer aircraft WW2 by
          Focke-Wulf (GE)
STOVL   short take-off and vertical landing
          (aircraft)
STP   systems technology program (US Army)
          (anti-ballistic missile)
STP-man   SCUBA-trained para-rescue man (USN)
          (self-contained underwater breath-
          ing apparatus)
STP   standard temperature and pressure;
          scientific and technical potential
STPTC   standardization of tar products test
          committee
STPX   systems training programme exercise
STR   sea transport regulations; surplus
          to requirements; standard taxiway
          routing; synchronous transmitter
          receiver
str   strike; street; strait; strength;
          seater; steamer; string; stringer
STR-700   airborne transponder by SEL

StraBAD   strategic base air defense (US)
StrAC   strategic air command (US);
          strategic army corps
STRAD   signal transmission and reception
          automatic device
STRAAD   special techniques for repair and
          analysis of aircraft damage
STRAD   signal transmitting, receiving and
          distribution
STRADAP   storm radar data processor
STRAF   strategic army forces (US)
STRAFIP   strategic army forces (readiness)
          improvement program (US)
STRAFPOA strategic air force Pacific ocean
          area
strag   straggler
stragL   straggler line
strat   strategic
StratAD   strategic aerospace division (USAF)
StratAnalSuppGru strategic analysis support
                  group
strato   stratosphere
Stratofortress B-52, SAC bomber by Boeing
Stratofreighter C-97, cargo aircraft by
                 Boeing
Stratojet B-47, jet bomber by Boeing
Stratolifter C-135, cargo aircraft by
              Boeing
Stratotanker KC-135, tanker aircraft by
              Boeing
stratR   strategic reconnaissance
STRE   specialized team, Royal Engineers
Streaker MQM-107, VSTT, variable speed
          training target by Beech
Streamlite halogen flashlight (US)
StreBo   Streubombe (cluster bomb, dispersal
          bomb)
StricFltLant striking fleet Atlantic (Nato)
StriCom   strike command (US)
STRIDA   Systeme de Traitement et de Visuali-
          sation des Donnes de la Défense
          Aerienne (French national air
          defence system)
Strike Eagle F-15, long-range bomber by
              McDD
Strikemaster BAC-167, low-cost jet bomber,
              recce, trainer by BAC
Striker FV-102, CVRT + Swingfire, anti-tank
         combat vehicle tracked by Alvis
STRIKEX   Nato naval strike exercise
StrikFltLant striking fleet Atlantic (Nato)
StrikForSouth naval striking and support
               forces southern Europe
               (Nato)
STRIL   air defence radar by ITT (Sweden)
STRIM-89 LRAC-89, anti-tank rocket 89mm by
          Brandt
STRINGS   stellar inertial guidance system

STRIP   specification technical review and
          improvement programme; stock turn-
          in and replenishment invoicing
          procedures; standard taped rout-
          ings for image processing
STROBE   satellite tracking of balloons and
          emergencies
struc   structure
STRUDL   structural design language
STRV-103 Tank -S, Swedish tank by Bofors
STS   sonar technician, submarine (USN);
          Orbiter-101, shuttle transportation
          system by Nasa; space transporta-
          tion system; standard test signal;
          stockpile to target sequence (nuc.
          weap.); Sicherheitstechnische
          Anlagen & Systeme Friedrichshafen
          (GE) (Dornier daughter)
STSO   senior technical staff officer
STT   standard tube test
STTA   Service Technique des Télécommunica-
          tions de l'Air
STTEA   Service Technique des Télécommunica-
          tions et des Equipements de
          l'Aeronautique
stu   student
STU   service trials unit; submersible
          (material) test unit
Stuart   Honey, tank WW2 (UK)
Stubby   homing bomb system
STube   steel tubing
STUFF   system to uncover facts fast
StuG   Sturmgeschütz (SP assault gun)
StuK   Sturmkanone (SP assault cannon)
StuKa   Sturzkampfflugzeug (dive bomber)
STUP   spinning tubular projectile (target
          practice shell 105mm); stabiloy/
          tungsten projectile (UK)
STUP-C-62 Stabiloy-tungsten projectile
           105 mm by ROF
StuPz   Sturmpanzer (assault tank)
Sturgeon class, attack submarines nuclear-
          powered (USN)
StuTng   student training
STV   single transferable vote; steam tank
          vessel (USN); sensitivity time
          vectoring; standard test vehicle;
          subscriber television; standard
          tar viscometer; separation test
          vehicle; substitute transport-type
          vehicle (US)
stvdr   stevedore
STVW   symmetrical triangle voltage wave-
          form
STW   speed through water; Strassentankwagen
          (street tanker)
STWS-1   ship's torpedo weapon system by
          Plessey
STX   start of text
Styx   SS-N-2, naval missile (SU)

SU	strontium unit; station unit; service unit; set up; Soviet Union
su	substitute
Su-2	tactical recce bomber WW2 by Sukhoi (SU)
Su-7	Fitter A, ground attack aircraft WW2 by Sukhoi (SU)
Su-9	Fishpot, all-weather fighter jet WW2 by Sukhoi (SU)
Su-11	Fishpot C, Mach 2 fighter/interceptor
Su-11U	Maiden, trainer version by Sukhoi (SU)
Su-15	Flagon A, all-weather fighter by Sukhoi (SU)
Su-17	Fitter C, multi-role combat aircraft (SU)
Su-19	Fencer, fighter bomber by Sukhoi (SU)
Su-20	Fitter C, variable geomatry attack aircraft (SU)
SU-57-2	twin gun anti-aircraft tank (SU)
SU-76	SP assault gun (SU)
SU-85	assault gun 85mm (SU)
SU-85T	armoured recovery vehicle (SU)
SU-100	SP assault gun 10mm (SU)
SU-122	SP assault gun 122mm (SU)
sub	substitute; submarine; subaltern; sub-lieutenant; submachine gun; subordinate; subscription
SubACLant	submarines allied command Atlantic (Nato)
SubAD	submarine air defence (missile system)
SubBase	submarine base
SubCAP	submarine combat air patrol
SubCom	sub-committee; subordinate command
SubComitSE	regional permanent sub-committee (of PBEIST -petrol-) Southern Europe
SubConsent	(assignment to active service is) subject to consent
subD	sub-division
SubDiv	submarine division (USN)
SubEastLant	submarine forces Eastern Atlantic
SubEx	submarine exercise (Nato)
SubFlot	submarine flotilla
SubGru	submarine group
Sub-Harpoon	sub-surface-to-surface missile
SubIC	submarine integrated control (FCS)
SubInSurv	sub-board of inspection and survey
subj	subject
subL	sub-lieutenant
SubLant	submarine forces Atlantic
SubLt	sub-lieutenant
subm	submitted; submerged
SUBMACOM	major Army subcommand (US)
Sub-Martel	sub-surface-launched Martel
SubMed	submarine forces Mediterranean (Nato)
SubMedNorEast	submarine forces North-Eastern Mediterranean (Nato)

SubNo	substitutes not desired
SubOK	substitutes acceptable
subor	subordinate
SuborCom	subordinate command
SuborComServ	subordinate command service force
	Lant Atlantic
	Pac Pacific
SubPac	submarine forces, Pacific
subQ	subsequent
Subroc	UUM-44A, submarine-launched rocket nuclear by Goodyear
SubRon	submarine squadron
SubRU	submarine repair unit
subs	subsistence; subsidiary; substitute; subscription
SubSafeCen	submarine safety centre
SubScoFor	submarine scouting force
SubScol	submarine school
subsec	subsection
SubsEls	subsisting elsewhere (US)
subsGM	subsisted in general mess
SubsLant	submarines Atlantic
SubsPac	submarines Pacific
SubsSoWesPac	submarines South West Pacific
subst	substantive rank; substitute
substan	substandard
SubTacGru	submarine tactical group
SubU	substitution unit
subv	subversion
SubWestLant	submarine forces Western Atlantic (Nato)
SUC	senior unit commander
suc	suction
SuchTrans	such transportation as designated
SuchTransAvail	such transportation as available
SUD	sudden unexpected death
SuDam	sunk or damaged (vessel report)
Sucuri	EE-17, 6x6 tank hunter vehicle by Engesa
SUD	symbol unit designator (computer)
SUDS	submarine detection system
SUE	signal underwater exploding
suf	sufficient
sug	suggested
SUIT	rifle sight (UK)
SUL	simplified user logistics
SULF	Speedball up-range launch facility
Sultan	FV-105, command post vehicle by Alvis
sum	summary; summer
SUM	surface-to-underwater missile (Nato)
SUMT	sequential unconstrained minimization technique
SUN	symbolic unit number (computer)
Sunderland	flying boat by Short
SUNEC	sea-borne supply of the North East Command
SUNFED	special United Nations fund for economic development

SUNI   Southern Universities Nuclear
          Institute (Canada)
SUNS   sonic underwater navigation system
sup   supply
SupAnx   supply annex
SupCom   support command; supreme command
SupCon   superintending contractor
SupD   supplementary division
SupDpo   supply depot
Supdt   superintendent
super   superintendent
Super-50 air-intercept missile by Matra
Super-530 air-intercept missile by Matra
Superaviogon RC-10, airborne camera
Super-Bazooka anti-tank rocket launcher (US)
Super Buffalo transport aircraft by DHC
Super Constellation C-121, transport air-
          craft
Super Constructor truck-mounted crane by
          Scammell
Super Dart infantry training simulator by
          ATA
Super Etendard naval fighter aircraft by
          Dassault/Breguet
Super Flagstaff hydrofoil by Grumman
Super Fledermaus FLG-65 anti-aircraft FCS
          by Contraves
Super Fortress B-29, bomber WW2 by Boeing
          (USAF)
Super Frelon SA-321, heavy transport heli-
          copter by AS
Super Haulmaster articulated truck by Foden
superhet super-hetrodyne receiver
Super Jaguar jet by BAe
Super King Air C-12A, light transport air-
          craft by Beech
Super Lepus parachute illuminating bomb by
          Bofors
Super Loki sounding rocket (US)
Super Magister CM-170, trainer aircraft by
          Fouga
Super Mystere B-2, fighter/interceptor Mach
          2 by Dassault
Super Puma AS-332, heavy transport helicop-
          ter by AS
Super Sabre F-100, supersonic fighter
          bomber by North American
Super Saeta HA-200, jet trainer aircraft
          (Spain)
Super Sherman SP gun 105mm WW2
Super Star pistol 9mm by Echeveria
Super Tampella 120mm rocket-assisted mortar
          bomb
Supervisor battlefield surveillance and
          target acquisition system by
          Westland/Marconi (MRUASTAS +
          Wideye)
Super Wal DoR-4, transport floatplane WW2 by
          Dornier
SuPier   supply pier

SupInsMat supervising inspector of naval
          material
SupIntRep supplementary intelligence report
SupO   supply officer
SupOHDU   supply from stock on hand or due in
          (US)
supp   support
SupP   supply point
SuppAct   support activity
SuppBaS   supplementary basic allowance for
          subsistence
suppl   supplement(ary)
Supporter MFI-17, close air support air-
          craft by Saab
SupPt   supply point
supr   supreme; supervisor
SupResofOff supplementary reserve of
          officers
SupSgt   supply sergeant (USMC)
SupShip   superintendent of shipbuilding;
          supervisor of shipbuilding
supt   superintendent
supv   supervisor
sur   surplus; surgical; surrender;
          surrounding; survivor; surface
SURA-FL   80mm airborne rocket by Oerlikon
SURANO   surface radar and navigation
          operator; surface radar and
          navigation operation
SURCAL   surveillance calibration satellite
Surefire naval optical fire control system
          IR-18 by Barr& Stroud
surfA   surface area
surg   surgeon; surgical
SurgCdr   surgeon commander
SurgComdr surgeon commander
SurgGen   surgeon general
SurgLtComdr surgeon lieutenant commander
SurgMaj   surgeon major
SURIC   surface-ship integrated control
          system (US)
SurObs   surface observation
SurOrdTech surface ordnance technician
Surprise Package USAF project COIN gunships
SURS   surface export cargo system (US);
          sonar by Simrad
SURTASS   surveillance towed array sensor
          system (ASW towed hydrophones) by
          Hughes
SURV   standard underwater research vehicle
surv   surveillance; survey; surveyor
Surveymaster Nomad photographic plane by
          GAF
SurvFor   surveillance force
SurvGen   surveyor general
survl   surveillance; survival
SurvM   surveillance and maintenance
SurWONCO surplus warrant officers and NCOs
          WW1 (UK)
SUS   sound underwater signals (Nato);
          soldier under sentence

SUSAC	Soviet Union strategic air command
Susie I	... II, ... III, ESM equipment by MEL (RWR + display)
SUSM	Scottish United Services Museum (Edinburgh)
SUSMOP	senior US military observer, Palestine
SUSNO	senior US naval officer
susp	suspension; suspect
SUSREP	senior US representative (to the defense production board)
SUSREP-NADPB	senior US representative North Atlantic Defence production board
SUT	society for underwater technology Seeziel/U-Jegd Torpedo by AEG
SUU-13	airborne bomblets dispenser (80 Canisters)
SUU-25	airborne flares
SUU-54	CADM, clustered airfield demolition munition
SUW-N-1	naval multi-purpose missile launcher (SU)
SUW-N-3	naval anti-submarine missile launcher (SU)
SV	super velocity (cartridge); small vessel; surface vessel; sailing vessel; synchronous voltage; surveyor (USN); selective volunteer (US); South Vietnam; Super Vel Cartridge Corp. (US)
SV-500	Strahlenspur- & Verstrahlungsmesserät (radiation detector)
SVA	Seebee veterans of America
SVAD	Savanna army depot
SVC	Singapore volunteer corps
svc	service(d); serving
SvC	supervisory call
SVCS	star vector calibration sensor
SvcStrs	service stars (US)
SVD	self-loading precision rifle 7.62mm (SU) by Dragunov
SVE	secure voice equipment
SVER	spatial visual evoked response
Sverdlov	class, cruisers (SU)
SVH	solar vacuum head
SVI	stroke volume index
SVK	Sperrwaffenversuchskommando Kiel (mine warfare experimental command) (FGN)
SVM	silicon video memory
SVNRF	State of Vietnam Ribbon of Friendship (US)
SVOC	Standard Vacuum Oil Company
SVP	small vessels pool; small vessels patrol
SVR	slant visual range
svr	severe
SVRC	Singapore volunteer rifle corps
SVSO	superintending victualling stores officer (UK)

SVSS	small voice switching system by Litton
SVTL	services valve testing laboratory (UK)
SVTOL	short/vertical take-off and landing (aircraft)
SVTP	sound velocity temperature and pressure
svy	survey
svyr	surveyor
SW	security watch; ship's warrant (USMC); secretary of war; steel worker; small warship; special weapon; short wave; static water; standard weight; salt water; sea water; specific weight; sea-worthy
sw	switch
Sw	Sweden; Switzerland
S&W	Smith & Wesson (Springfield USA)
SW-1	Sonderwagen (wheeled personnel carrier) by MOWAG
SWA	seriously wounded in action (US); South-western Approaches
SWACS	space warning and control system
SWADS	scheduler work area data set
SWAFAC	Southwest Atlantic fisheries advisory commission
SWAG	standard written agreement
SWANU	Southwest African National Union
SWANUF	Southwest African National United Front
SWAPO	Southwest African People's Organization
SWAS	social workers advisory service
SWASU	South West African Special Units (against SWAPO)
SWAT	Sidewinder angle tracking; special warfare armoured transporter; stress wave analysis technique
SWATH	small waterplane twin hull (surface-effect ship)
SWB	The South Wales Borderers; special weapons branch; short wheelbase; switchboard
swbd	switchboard
SWBOD	Sidewinder Board of Directors (Nato)
SWBS	ship work breakdown structure
SWC	service women's club; semi wad-cutter (projectile)
SwCent	switching central
SWD	surface wave device
Swed	Sweden; Swedish
Sweep P-6	metal detector (UK-NI)
SWETTU	special weapons experimental tactical test unit
S&W/F	Smith & Wesson/Fiocchi
SWG	special working group; standard wire gauge; single weight gloss (photo paper)
SWIA	seriously wounded in action

SWIEEECO Southwestern institute of electricians and electronics engineers conference
SWIFT strength of wings including flutter
Swift swept-wing jet fighter by Supermarine; RPV (recce or target) by RCS
Swiftscope daylight zoom telescope (UK)
Swiftshure class, submarines by Vickers (RN)
Swingfire anti-tank guided missile by BAC
SWIO SACLANT war intelligence organization
SWIP super-weight improvement programme
SWIR special weapons inspection reports; short-wave infra-red
Swit Switzerland
Switz Switzerland
SWL safe working load; surface wave lines
SWLT strategic warning lead time
SWM special warfare mission; ship-board wave meter; short-wave meter
SWNCC State War Navy coordinating committee
SWO senior works officer; senior woman officer NFS (UK); staff weather officer (US); squadron wireless officer; station warrant officer
SWOC special weapons operations centre (US)
SWOD special weapons ordnance division
Swod radar-guided air-to-surface missile (US)
SWOP special weapons ordnance publication; stop without pay
SWORD shallow water oceanographic research data system (US)
Sword class, patrol boats by Fairey (RN)
Swordfish torpedo bomber WW2 by Fairey
SWP special working party (US); safe working pressure
SWPA Southwest Pacific area; surplus war property administration
SWPC Smaller War Plants Corporation
SWPF Southwest Pacific force
SWPT strategic warning post-decision time (US)
SWR steel wire rope; standing wave ratio
SWRA selected water resources abstracts
SWRI Southwest research institute
SWS static water supply
SWSI single width single inlet
SWSM special weapons supply memorandum (US)
SWT secondary water terminal
SWTI special weapons technical instructions

SWTTEU special weapons test and tactical evaluation unit
Swtz Switzerland
SX class, midget submarines; ballistic strategic missile (FR)
SX-765 midget submarine by Cosmos (IT)
sxt sextant
Sy Seychelles
sy security; survey; supply
Syd Sydney
SYd Scotland Yard
SY-AT helicopter-borne mine-laying system by MISAR
Sycamore B-171, helicopter by Bristol
SYCOMORE Système de Commandement Operationnel et de Renseignement (French CCCI system)
Sydade land navigation system by Crouzet
SyG secretary general
SYLA-20 anti-aircraft gun by Thomson
Syledis naval navigational data system
Sylosat satellite navigation system by CSEE
SYLT System für Lufttransport (aerial transport system)
sym symbol
Symphonie European communications satellite by CIFAS-Dornier
SYMWAR system for estimating wartime attrition and replacement requirements (US)
sync synchronize; synchro-mechanism
SynCom Synchronous communications satellite by Hughes 1963
SyPO supply petty officer
SYR-1 down-link missile communications system (standard missile) by E-Systems
Syra demolition charge artillery rocket 142mm by SEP
sys system
SYSCAP system of circuit analysis programmes
SYSB Scotland Yard Special Branch
SYS-CG integrated automatic radar detection and tracking system by Norden
SysCon systems control
SysGen system generation
SysIn system input
SysOut system output
SysRC system reference count
SysTEP system test and evaluation plan
SZG Soviet Zone in Germany
SZOG Soviet Zone of Occupation in Germany

T

T	Turkey; territorial; tactical; transportation; temporary; treasury; trainer (aircraft) (US); target aircraft; transport; tanker; time (fuse); black powder (charge); transmitter; tracer (projectile); torpedo; telegraphy; test; temperature; prototype tank (US)
T-air	transportation (by) air (Nato)
T-group	training group
T-light	paradrop landing aid
T-man	treasury agent
T-mine	anti-tank mine
3T-s	Tanks, Troops, Time (Warsaw Pact) Nato response: 3R-s: readiness, reinforcement, rationalization
52-T-2	anti-aircraft gun 20mm (FR)
800-T	class, multi-role corvette by CMN
T-1	standard parachute
Tl Cl 4	titanium tetrachloride (smoke charge)
T-2	Buckeye, trainer aircraft by Rockwell
T2G	technician 2nd grade
T-4	Hexogen (explosive)
T-5E	Soviet designation FROG-4
T-6	piston-engined trainer aircraft by North American
T-10	steerable parachute; Soviet main battle tank 122mm gun
T-12	100mm anti-tank gun (SU); GP bomb 44000 lbs (USAF)
T-14	GP bomb 22000 lbs, Grand Slam (USAF); heavy tank WW2 (UK)
T-16	experimental Patriot missile by Martin
T-22	experimental Patriot missile by Martin; CSWS, corps support weapons system; missile by Vought
T-24	tank 1939 (SU)
T-25	Pershing tank (US)
T-28	super-heavy tank WW2 (US)
T-28	Trojan, trainer aircraft by North American
T-33	jet trainer by Lockheed
T-34	Turbo Mentor trainer aircraft by Beech; Josef Stalin, tank (SU)

T-37	Tweety Bird, jet trainer by Cessna; light amphibious tank (SU)
T-38	Talon, jet trainer by Northrop
T-40	metallic anti-tank mine (Dutch); light tank (SU)
T-41	Mescalero, piston-engined trainer by Cessna
T-43	class, ocean-going mine-sweepers (Poland)
T-44	experimental machine gun 7.92mm (US); King Air twin-engined trainer by Beech
T-52	experimental machine gun 7.62mm
T-54	battle tank 100mm gun (SU)
T-55	Vampire, jet trainer aircraft; battle tank 100mm gun (SU)
T-59	battle tank 100mm gun (SU)
T-60	amphibious tank 85mm gun (SU)
T-62	light tank 115mm gun
T-64	combat tank 115mm gun (SU)
T-65	7.62mm cartridge 47.5mm long (US) E2 49mm long E3 51mm long (Nato) round
T-70	combat tank (SU)
T-72	combat tank 122mm gun (SU)
T-80	combat tank 125mm gun (SU)
T-88	recovery tank M-88 (US)
T-95	heavy assault tank (gun motor carriage) (US)
T-97	US tank M-53
T-98	US tank M-52
T-99	US tank M-44
T-100	tractor (Yugoslavia)
T-113	US tank M-113
T-117	US prototype M-113
T-119	recovery tank (US)
T-120	recovery tank M-578
T-161	experimental machine gun 7.62mmx51
T-195	helicopter-borne dunking sonar by Plessey; tank howitzer M-108
T-196	tank M-109
T-235	tank M-107
T-236	tank M-110
T-245	experimental 155mm gun SP (US)
T-250	anti-aircraft gun 35mm by Sperry

T-252   tank howitzer 105mm
T-378   trainer aircraft
T-1148   teleprinter by E-Systems
T-17161 sonar beacon by Plessey
         --T-195
TA   Territorial Army; treason act;
         target area; technical assistance;
         theatre army; transport animal;
         table of allowances; time and
         attendance (card); training
         advisor; traffic agent; Turkish
         army; temporary assistant; tax
         authorization (plan); technical
         analysis; travel allowance;
         transition altitude; true altitude;
         track adjustment; time analyser;
         target aircraft; turbulence
         amplifier; tape address
TA-1   PFM, Pont Flottant Motorisé by CNIM
         (motorized floating bridge)
TA-4   Skyhawk, trainer aircraft by Douglas
TA-20   gunfire control radar by EMD
TA-23   long-range air surveillance radar by
         Thomson
TA-43   target (acquisition) aircraft for FAC
TA-838   field telephone (US)
TAA   territorial army associations; test
         of academic aptitude; tactical air
         army
TAABS   the automated army budget system (US)
TAACom   theater army area command (US)
TAADCom theater army air defense command
         (US)
TAADS   the army authorization documents
         system (US)
TAAFA   territorial army and air force
         association
TAAG   textbook of anti-aircraft gunnery
TAAM   transportation army aviation main-
         tenance; Tomahawk airfield attack
         missile
TAARS   the army ammunition reporting system
TAAS   traffic accident analysis system
TAB   target acquisition battalion (US);
         training aids branch; technical
         assistance board; technical assis-
         tance bureau; typhoid, paratyphoid
         A and paratyphoid B (vaccine)
tab   tabular; tabulated
TABL   tropical Atlantic biological labora-
         tory (US)
TabSim   tabulating simulator
TAB-V   theater air base vulnerability
         shelters (USAFE)
TAC   technical assistance committee (UN);
         (landforce) tactical doctrine
         (Nato); tactical coordinator
         (Nato); tactical air command
         (USAF); tactical air control;
         tactical atomic command; transpor-

         tation account code; tactical
         (headquarters); type of activity
         code; training aids centre;
         telemetry and command;
         terminal area control (ATC);
         time amplitude converter
TACA   tactical air coordinator, airborne
         (US)
TACAC   theater army civil affairs command
         (US)
TACAMO   take action charge and move out;
         EC-130, tactical communications
         aircraft by Lockheed (airborne
         communication with submerged
         ballistic missile submarines)
TACAN   tactical air navigation (system)
         SEL
TACC   tactical air control; tactical air
         command; TYQ-1, tactical air
         control centre
TACCAR   time averaged clutter coherent air-
         borne radar
         ---APS-125
TACCO   tactical control officer; tactical
         coordinator
TACCS   telecommunications and command and
         control system (US)
TACCTA   tactical commander's terrain analy-
         sis (US)
TACDEW   tactical advanced combat direction
         and electronic warfare (training
         system) by Hughes
TacElecWaRon tactical electronics warning
         squadron
TacEval tactical evaluation
TACFDC   tactical fire direction center (US)
Tacfire tactical fire direction system by
         Litton
TacFtrWing tactical fighter wing (US)
TACG   tactical air control group (US)
TACGru   tactical air control group (US)
TacJam   tactical (mobile communications)
         jammer by GTE
TACL   theater authorized consumption list
         (US); training for action centered
         leadership (US); technical
         advisory committee on electronics
TACLOG   tactical-logistical group (ship-to-
         shore)
TACMAR   tactical multi-function array radar
         (US)
Tac-Nav tactical navigation (system)
TACO   tactical coordinator
TACOM   tank automotive command (Warren,
         Michigan US)
TACOS   tactical air combat simulation
TACOT   tactical air control operations team
TACP   tactical air control party
Tacprox tactical fighter ground proximity
         warning system by Litton

TACPST   tactical air control party support
         team
tacR   tactical reconnaissance
TacRecce tactical reconnaissance
TacRecon tactical reconnaissance
TACRon   tactical air control squadron
TACRV   tracked air cushion research vehicle
TACS   tactical air control system; theatre
         army communication system
TACSAT   tactical communications satellite by
         Hughes
TacSatCom tactical satellite communication
TACT   tank and armoured car training;
         transsonic aircraft technology
tacT   tactical transport (aircraft)
TACTAS   (variable depth passive) tactical
         towed array sonar (USN)
tacTMR   tactical transport medium-range
         (aircraft)
tacTSR   tactical transport short-range
         (aircraft)
TACV   transport air cushion vehicle;
         tracked air cushion vehicle
TAD   temporary additional duty; tactical
         air direction; tactical air
         doctrine; training aids division;
         thrust-augmented delta (Nasa);
         transistor amplifier demonstrator;
         Traitement Automatique des Donnes
         (automatic data processing)
TAD-510 transistor amplifier demonstrator
         by Feedback
TADAR   target acquisition designation and
         aerial reconnaissance TV + laser
         (US programme)
TADC   tactical air direction centre;
         training aids distribution centre
TADCOM   consortium for JTIDS (Hughes + ITT)
TADF   tactical air defence fighter
TADIL   tactical airborne defence identifica-
         tion link
         ---IFF ---AWACS
TADM   tactical atomic demolition munitions
TADOC   tactical air defence operations
         centre
TADP   tactical air direction post
TADS   tactical automatic digital switch
         (US); target acquisition and desig-
         nation system by Martin-Marietta
TADS/PNVS target acquisition and designation
         system/pilot night vision system
         (helicopter-borne)
TAF   tactical air force; training aids
         facility; terminal aerodrome fore-
         cast; time and frequency; toxoid-
         antitoxin flocules
TaF   Taktische Forderungen (tactical
         requirements)
T&AFA   territorial and auxiliary forces
         association

TAFC   target acquisition and fire control
TAFCSD   total active federal commissioned
         service to date (US)
TAFDS   tactical airfield fuel dispension
TAFFS   the army functional file system (US)
TAFMSD   total active federal military
         service to date (US)
TAFNORNOR allied tactical air force North
         Norway
TAFOR   terminal aerodrome forecast
TAFOT   terminal aerodrome forecast in
         units of English system
TAFSONOR allied tactical air force South
         Norway
TAG   telegraphist airman gunner; training
         aids guide; transport air group;
         tactical air group (Canada); the
         adjutant general (US)
TAGCen   US Army adjutant general center
TAGL   territorial army general list
TAGO   the adjutant general's office (US);
         auxiliary general ocean surveil-
         lance with civilian crew (US)
TAHQ   theatre army headquarters
TAIDHS   tactical air intelligence data
         handling system
Taifun   barrage rocket WW2 (GE); infantry
         combat vehicle by Mowag
Taildog air-to-air missile (UK)
TAIU   technical aircraft instrument unit
Taiyo   class, aircraft carriers WW2 (Japan)
TAJAG   the assistant judge advocate general
         (US)
TAK   attack cargo ship of the MSTS
Takami   class, minesweepers (JMSDF)
Takao   class, cruisers WW2 (USN)
Takatsui class, destroyers (JMSDF)
TAKD   landing ship dock of the MSTS
TAKV   anti-submarine warfare support
         carrier of the MSTS
TAKX   RoRo cargo ships for prepositioning
         of stocks for the RDF of the MSTS
TAL   training aids library
TALAFIT tank level aiming and firing
         trainer by SABCA
TALAR   Talos activity report
talas³M tactical laser system military
         modular multi-functional by
         Eichweber
TALC   tactical air lift center (USAF)
TALCM   Tomahawk air launched cruise missile
Talisman-46 coastal patrol boat; police
         boat
TALISSI taktischer Licht (laser)
         Schusssimulator by Eichweber
Tallboy 12000 lbs bomb WW2 (RAF USAF)
Tallin   class, destroyers (SU)
TALOG   theater army logistical command (US)
Talon   T-38, trainer aircraft by Northrop;
         35mm lightweight cannon by Stoner

Talos   RIM-8, naval intercept missile by
            Bendix
TALS   transfer air lock section
TALUS   transportation and land use study
TALZ   tactical air landing zone
TAM   tactical air missile; terminal
            access method; light tank Marder
            hull (Argentina)
TAMA   territorial army and militia act;
            training aids management agency
TAMC   Tripler army medical center (US);
            time and material contract (US)
TAMET   terminal aerodrome (forecast) in
            units of the metric system
TAMIRAD   tactical mid-range air defense
            program (US)
TAMMS   the army maintenance management
            system (US)
TAMO   training aids management office
Tampella-120 mortar 120mm by Tampella
TAMS   tactical aircraft maintenance system
            (USAF)
TandAVR   territorial army and army volunteer
            reserve
Tang   Tanganjika
Tang   class, submarines (USN)
Tank Breaker shoulder-fired anti-tank
            weapon by Rockwell ATGW
            3rd generation
Tannoy system naval loudspeakers
TANS   terminal area navigation system by
            Decca; tactical airborne naviga-
            tion system; territorial army
            nursing service QARANC
Tansam   anti-aircraft missile by Toshiba
TANU   Tanganjika African National Union
TAO   tactical air observer; technical
            assistance operation (UN); tactical
            air observation procedures STANAG;
            auxiliary oiler of the MSTS
TAOA   tactical air officer, afloat
TAOC   TYQ-2, tactical air operations
            centre; the army operations centre
TAOCC   tactical air operations control
            centre
TAOR   tactical area of responsibility (US)
TAP   Trans Arabian pipeline; technical
            area plans; technical assistance
            programme; table of authorized
            personnel; target approach point;
            MSTS attack transport
TAPAC   transportation, allocations, priori-
            ties and controls (committee) (US)
TAPE   tape automatic preparation equip-
            ment
TAPER   temporary appointment pending estab-
            lishment of register (US)
TAPFOR   the army portion of force status and
            identify report (US FORSTAT)
Tapiron   Th.D.3201, radar detector and warn-
            ing receiver by Thomson-CSF

TAPS   time analysis of programme status
TAPIT   tactical photographic image trans-
            mission sub-system
TAPS   tactical area positioning system
TAQ   transient airmen quarters (USAF)
TAR   territorial army reserve; territor-
            ial army regulations; technical
            action request; tactical air
            reconnaissance; total assets
            reporting; training and adminis-
            tration of reserves; tri-annual
            review; terrain avoidance radar;
            thrust augmented rocket
tar   target
TARA   technical assistant, Royal Artillery;
            territorial army rifle association
TARABS   tactical air reconnaissance and
            aerial battlefield surveillance
TARADCOM   tank automotive research and
            development command (US)
Tarakan   class, combat hydrofoil (SU)
TARAN   test and replace as necessary
Tarasnice   recoilless gun (Czech)
Tarasque   towed anti-aircraft gun by EFAB
Tarawa   class, amphibious support ship (USN);
            amphibious assault helicopter
            carrier LHA (USN)
TARC   the army research council (US);
            theater army replacement command
            (US); cable repair ship (US)
TARE   telegraphic automatic relay equip-
            ment
TarEx   target exploitation
TARGET   team to advance research for gas
            energy transformation
Tarhe   Skycrane, CH-54, heavy transport
            helicopter by Sikorsky
TARIF   telegraph automatic routing in the
            field by Marconi
Tarmac   tar macadam
TARMOCS   the army operations center system
            (US)
TARO   territorial army reserve of officers
Tarpon   DUBA-25, hull-mounted sonar by
            Thomson
TARS   theater army replacement system (US);
            technical assistance recruitment
            service (UN); tender and repair
            ship (USN)
TARSLL   technical assistance recruitment
            service load list (USN)
TARSP   tactical air radar signal processor
Tartar   RIM-24, naval anti-aircraft missile
            by Raytheon
Tartaruga   armoured personnel carrier by
            Saurer
TARTC   theater army replacement and train-
            ing command (US)
TARVH   aircraft repair ship, helicopters
            (USN)

Tarzon   12000 lbs radio-guided targetable
           bomb (US)
TAS   torpedo and anti-submarine (RN);
           the army staff (US); training aids
           section; tactical airlift squadron
           (USAF); true air speed; time air
           speed; tactical automatic switch;
           target acquisition system by
           Hughes; (airborne) tracking adjunct
           system by Northrop
TAS-4   passive infra-red night sight for
           TOW by TI
TAS-6   NODLR, night observation device,
           long-range by TI
TAS-23   naval target acquisition system by
           Hughes
TASA   task and skill analysis
TASAMS   the army supply and maintenance
           system (US)
TASB   target area survey base
TASC   training and support component (USN);
           tactical articulated swimmable
           carrier
TASCOM   theater army support command (US)
TASE   tactical air support element (US)
Taser   Tom Swift and his electric rifle
           (stun gun) (fires two thin electric
           wires and needles) (US)
TASES   tactical airborne signal exploitation
           system ELINT (USN)
TASI   torpedo and anti-submarine instructor
           (RN); time assignment speech inter-
           polation
TaskFlot   task flotilla
TaskForNON allied task force Northern Norway
           (Nato)
TASL   theater authorized stockage list (US)
TASM   tactical air to surface missile
TASMO   tactical air support of maritime
           operations (concept) (Nato)
TASO   training aids service office (US)
TASP   the army studies program (US)
TASR   terminal area surveillance radar;
           terminal air surveillance radar;
           submarine rescue ship (USN)
TASRA   thermal activation strain rate analy-
           sis
TASS   tactical air support squadron;
           tactical air support section (US);
           the army study system (US); trans-
           port aircraft servicing specialist
           (RAF); tactical air support system
           (Nato); SQR-15, towed array sonar
           system by Gould
TASSO   tactical special security office (US)
TASTA   the administrative support theater
           army (US)
TASYLL   Trefferanzeigesystem für Luftschlepp-
           ziele by Dornier (scoring system
           for aerial towed targets)

TAT   to accompany troops (US); temporary
           ambulance train; torpedo attack
           teacher; trans-Atlantic telephone
           (cable); true air temperature;
           tactical armament turret (air-
           borne); thrust-augmented Thor
           (Nasa)
T&AT   tank and anti-tank (ammunition)
TAT-101   tactical armament turret 2x M-60
           by Emerson
TAT-102   tactical armament turret 1x M-134
TAT-141   tactical armament turret 1x M-134 +
           1x XM-129 by Emerson
TAT-161   tactical armament turret 1x Vulcan
           by Emerson
TATAC   temporary air transport advisory
           committee
TATAWS   tank-anti-tank/assault weapons
           (requirements) study (US)
TATC   terminal area traffic control
TATO   tactical air transport operation
TATS   tactical aircraft training system
           by Cubic
TATSA   transportation aircraft test and
           support activity (USAF)
TATF   fleet tug (USN)
TATTES   Talos tactical test equipment
TAUN   technical assistance of the UN
Taurus   recovery tank for Canada by MaK
TAV-8   Harrier, VTOl aircraft by BAe
TAVE   Thor-Agena vibration experiment
Tavitac   plotter desk by Thomson
TAVR   territorial army and volunteer
           reserve (UK); territorial and
           auxiliary volunteer reserve (UK)
TAW   twice a week
TAWC   tactical air warfare center (US)
TAWDS   Pave Mover, target acquisition and
           weapon delivery system (airborne)
           by Hughes
TAZ   tactical alert zone
TB   torpedo boat (USN); torpedo bomber
           (Nato); technical bulletin (US);
           tactical bulletin; training
           battalion; troop basic (US);
           training branch; traffic branch;
           tuberculosis; true bearing;
           temporary buoy; target bombing;
           torpedo bombing; trial balance
t&b   top and bottom
TB-30   Epsilon, primary trainer aircraft by
           AS
TB-76   proximity fuse by Borletti
TBA   table of basic allowance; to be
           activated; to be announced; test-
           bed aircraft; torsional braid
           analysis
TBAn   to be announced
TBAT   TOW/Bushmaster armoured turret for
           MICV

TBCEP	tri-beta-chloro-ethyl-phosphate (flame retardant additive)
TBCF	to be called for (poste restante)
TBD	to be determined (US); terminal bomber defence; target bearing designator; torpedo boat destroyer; torpedo bomber by Douglas
TBD-1	torpedo bomber by Douglas Devastator WW2 (USN)
TBE	time base error
TBF	time between failures; torpedo bomber/fighter (aircraft)
TBF-1	torpedo bomber/fighter (aircraft) Avenger, by Grumman
TBFFU	naval Twin-Ball fire-fighting unit (USN)
TBGTA	travel by government transportation authorized (US)
TBH	test bed harness
TBI	to be inactivated (US); test bed installation
TBL	through bill of lading; target base line
TBM	tactical ballistic missile; tera-bit memory (computer)
TBMD	terminal ballistic missile defence
TBN	to be nominated
TBO	transaction by others; territorial command East Netherlands (Nato); time between overhauls
TBOI	tentative basis of issue
TBOIP	tentative basis of issue plan (US)
TBP	true boiling point
TBPO	tertiary butyl per-octoacte
TBR	torpedo bomber, reconnaissance (aircraft)
TBS	the basic school; talk between ships (radio); training battle simulation; tolerance for bureaucratic structure
TB&S	top bottom and sides
TBTA	turbine blade temperature amplifier by BGT
TBX	tactical ballistical experimental (missile)
TBZ	territorial command South Netherlands (Nato)
TC	training cadre; training centre; training camp; training corps; training circular; traffic control; tank corps; transport command; till cancelled; transport column; transport capacity; technical centre; tactical command; transport cargo; torpedo control, technical characteristics; transaction code; total cost; transportation corps (US); turret captain; torpedo coxswain; troop commander; temporary constable; town council-

	lor; tape command; telescoping collar; temperature coefficient; threshold circuit; transmitting circuits; true complement; twin carburettor; tungsten carbide (core); truncated cone (projectile); true cylinder (map); time charter; true course; transceiver code; time check, temperature control
TC-3	... 6, electronic anti-tank mine by Tecnovar
TCA	terminal control area; theatre commander's approach; tender-controlled approach; tactical combat aircraft; turbulent contact absorber; track crossing angle; transcontinental aviation; Télécommande Automatique
TCAB	travel cost analysis branch
TCAC	technical control and analysis centre SIGINT
TCAD	technical control and analysis division
TCAM	TCAM telecommunications access method
TCAP	target combat air patrol
TCATA	tactical combined arms testing agency
TCB	title certificate book; terminal control block; task control block
TCBM	trans-continental ballistic missile
TCC	Technical Communications Corp. (Concord USA); traffic control company; temporary council committee (Nato); troop carrier command (US); transportation control card; transport control center (US); tracking and control center (US); transportation control committee; travel classification code; Transport and Communications Commission (UN); time compression coding; thermo-catalytic cracking; technical coordination committee; thermal control coatings; transportation commodity classification; tactical control console; test control commission
TCC-39	ACCO, automatic communications central office
TCCF	tactical communications control facility TRI-TAC by Martine Marietta
TCCPSWG	tactical command and control procedures standardization working group (US)
TCCS	technical committee on communications satellites; tide communication control ship

TCCSR	telephone channel combination and separation racks	TCRA	telegraphy channel reliability analyser
TCD	tentative classification of defects; time code division; tour completion date	TCS	traffic control station; temporary change of station (US); target cost system; tactical control squadron (USAF); target control system; traffic control system; tactical computer system by Singer; type classified standard; terminal communications subsystem
TCDD	tetra-chloro-di-benzo-para-dioxine (defoilant)		
TCDU	transport command development unit (RAF)		
TCE	thermal control electronic; thermal control element; tetra-chloro-ethane		
TCEA	training centre for experimental aerodynamics	TCSP	tactical communications satellite programme
TCF	troop carrier force; tactical control flight (USAF); temporary chaplain to the forces; time correction factor	TCSS	tactical control surveillance system
		TCT	tactical computer terminal by Singer of TCS; total controlled tabulation; trunk coin telephone
TCFB	trans-continental freight bureau	TCTC	transportation corps technical committee (US)
TCG	tactical control group (USAF)		
tchg	teaching		
tchr	teacher	tctl	tactical
TCJCC	trade council's joint consultative committee	TCTM	(aircraft) time compliance technical manuals (US)
TCL	tri-chloro-ethylene	TCTMT	two-colour thermal measuring technique
TClas	type classification		
TCLE	thermal coefficient of linear expansion	TCTO	time compliance technical order (USAF)
TCLSC	theater COMSEC logistics support center (US)	TCTS	Trans-Canada telephone system
		TCU	transmission control unit
TCM	theatre combat model (simulator); troop corporal major; tactical cruise missile; temperature control model; temperature control module; terminal capacity matrix	TCV	troop carrying vehicle
		TCVS	anti-submarine warfare support aircraft carrier of the MSTS
		TCW	tactical control wing (USAF); tactical communications wing (RAF)
TCM-20	towed twin anti-aircraft gun 20mm by IAI	TCWO	train conducting warrant officer
TCMD	transportation control and movement document (US)	TD	Territorial Decoration (UK); training devices man (USN); transport driver; topographic draftman; telegraph department; telegraph depot; temporary duty; tactical division; tables of distribution (US); torpedo depot; traffic director; treasury department; treasury decisions; tank destroyers WW2 (US); tractor-drawn (gun); transmitter distributor; target discrimination; target drone; time devices; through-deck (cruiser); torpedo dive (bomber) (USN); touch-down (of aircraft); temperature datum; technical development; technical data; test data; top down; tunnel diode
TCN	transportation control number (US); tactical communications network		
TCNA	tank corps US national army		
TCNE	tetra-cyano-ethylene		
TCNQ	tetra-cyano-quinodi-methane		
TCO	train conducting officer; tactical control officer; traffic control officer; torpedo control officer; termination contracting officer; test control officer; transport company (US Army); tactical combat operations (USMC computer)		
TCP	traffic control post; technical co-operation programme (AUS/CAN/UK/US); tri-cresyl-phosphate; tri-chloro-phenyl-iodo-methyl-salicyl (antiseptic)	TDA	tables of distribution and allowances (US); transcript deserter's account; target designating assembly
		TDAMTB	tables of distribution and allowances mobilization troop basis (US)
TCR	transportation corps release; total controlled return; temperature coefficient of resistance	TDB	total disability benefit
tcr	transceiver	T&DC	training and distribution centre;

TDC	through-deck cruiser (RN); top dead centre; torpedo-firing data computer; track detection circuit --ED-135
TDCA	tactical development and control aircraft
TDCC	through-deck command cruiser
TDCO	torpedo data computer
TDD	target detection device
TDDL	time division data link
TDF	territorial defence force; tactical data facsimile by Litton TRI-TAC
TDF-1	French regional broadcasting satellite by Eurosatellite
TDFO	temporary duty pending further orders
TDFS	terminal digit fitting system
TDG	twist drill gauge
TDHGA	travel of dependents and household goods authorized (US)
TDH	toxic dose high
TDI	target data inventory; tolyene-di-iso-cyanate
TDIP	total disability income provisions (US)
TDis	time distance
TDL	toxic dose low
TDM	torpedo detection modification (sonar); time division multiplex-ing; telemetric data monitor
TDMA	time division multiple access (jam-resistant communications) by Hughes
TDM/PCM	time division multiplex/pulse code modulation
TDMPDRT	tactical digital message prepara-tion dispatching and receiving terminal
TDMS	time-sharing data management system
TDMTB	tables of distribution mobilization troop basis (US)
TDN	travel as directed is necessary (US)
tdn	torpedoman
TDO	technical directives, ordnance
TDOA/DME	time difference of arrival dis-tance measuring equipment
TDP	technical development plan; technical data package; target director post; temporary detention of pay
TDPAC	time differential perturbed angular correlation
TDPJ	trunk discharge point, jet (fuel)
TDPL	technical data package list
TDPM	trunk discharge point, MOGAS
TDR	training device requirement; Talos discrepancy report; teacher demon-stration rating; torque differen-tial receiver
TDRL	temporary disability retired list
TDRSS	tracking and data relay satellite

	system by Western Union Space Com-munications
TDS	training duty status; tactical data system; tactical display system by Litton; target designation system; tertiary data set; total dissolved solids
TDSCC	Tidbinbilla deep space communica-tion complex
TDSS	time dividing spectrum stabilization
TDT	target designation transmitter; task dispatch table
TDTG	true date-time group
TDTL	tunnel diode transistor logic
TDTS	tactical data transfer system; tandem digital tactical switch-board GTE
TDU-10	target demonstration unit (aerial towed target)
TDX	time division exchange; torque differential transmitter
TDy	temporary duty
TDZ	touch-down zone
TDZL	touch-down zone lights
TE	topographical engineer; tank element; task element; tables of equipment; time expired; terminal exchange; trunk equalizer; trailing edge; tangent elevation; test equipment; turbo-electric; twin engined; tape equipment; telecommunications engineering
T&E	test and evaluation
TEA	transferred electron amplifier; transversely excited atmospheric; tri-ethyl-amine
TEAC	turbine engine analysis check
TEAL	top European Atlantic leaders
Teal Ruby	satellite-borne infra-red multi-spectral sensing system
TEAM	the European-Atlantic movement
Teampack	MSQ-103, special-purpose receivers by Emerson
TEAMUP	test evaluation analysis and management uniformity plan (US)
TEC	training extension course; techni-cian education council; Tiros evaluation centre; ternary eutectic eutectic chloride (fire exting-uisher); total electron content; transient electron current; track evaluation computer
tec	technical college
tech	technician; technical; technology
TechAd	technical advisor
TechDok	Gesellschaft für technische Dokumentation (Mainz)
TechEval	technical evaluation
techn	technical; technician; technology
technol	technology; technological

Tech-Set-I ... III, technology demonstrator
          AFTI
TechSgt   technical sergeant
TechTra   technical training
TECom   US Army test and evaluation command
TECR   test equipment change requirement
TecR   technical requirement
TecRep   technical representatives (Nato)
          (manufacturer)
TECSTAR   technical missions structures and
          career development
TED   Territorial Efficiency Decoration
          (UK); trading with the enemy
          department; training equipment
          development; (airborne) tactical
          environment display; targets for
          economic development; Traitement
          Electronique des Données (elec-
          tronic data processing)
TE/DC   traffic enforcement driver control
TEDS   tactical expandable drone system
TEE   torpedo experimental establishment;
          telecommunications engineering
          establishment
Tee-Bird T-33, jet trainer aircraft by
          Lockheed
TEEL   temporary expedient equipment list
TEEM   transportable engineered environment
          modules (containers) (RN)
TEI   target extraction and indication
          (radar); trans-earth insertion
TEIU   target extraction and indication
          unit (radar)
Tek   Tel el Kebir (Egypt) (stores)
Teknikit communications system by Feedback
          TK-295 basic model
          TK-296 advanced model
TEL   transporter, erector, launcher
          (vehicle); tetra-ethyl-lead
tel   telephone; telegraph; telegram
TelBn   telegraph battalion
TelCom   telephone communications; telecommu-
          nication
TelCon   telephone conversation
TELD   teledate equipment
tele   telephone; telegraph; television
Telecin   distance measuring equipment by TRT
Telecom   telecommunications
Telecom-1 French domestic communications
          satellite by Thomson
TeleCon   Teletypewriter conference (US)
Teledac   VHF system with language encryption
          AEG
TeleDis   teletypewriter distribution
Teledrone TV-carrying drone by RCS
teleg   telegram; telegraphy
Telegon-7 ... 8, directional radio system
          by AEG
Telekrypt radio encryption system by AEG
Telemux   trunk communications encryption
          system by AEG

teleph   telephone; telephony
Teleran   television radar air navigation
          (US)
Telesat   ANIK, US designation for Canadian
          ANIK
Telespace Thomson-CSF daughter space tele-
          communication
Teleterminal mobile data acquisition system
          by AEG
TELETTRA Laboratori di Telefonia Elettron-
          ica e Radio SpA
Televoice language encryption system by AEG
Telex   teletypewriter exchange
telg   telegram
Tellurometer microwave distance measuring
          instrument
TelNo   telephone number
TELOPS   telemetry on-line processing system
TELS   transporter erector launcher shelter
tels   telecommunications
Telstar   telecommunications satellite (US)
TEM   Territorial Efficiency Medal (UK);
          transmission electron microscopy;
          Tiefflieger Erfassungs- und
          Meldenetz (low-level aircraft
          acquisition and reporting network)
tem   temperature
TEM-2   Turmentfernungsmesser by Zeiss
          --Leopard
          turret distance measuring instru-
          ment
TemAc   temporary active duty
TemAcDIFOT temporary active duty in flying
          status involving operational
          or training flights
TemAcDIFOTIns temporary active duty in
          flying status involving
          operational or training
          flights under instruction
TemAcIns temporary active duty under
          instruction
TemAdd   temporary additional duty
          Con in connection with
          Ins under instruction
Tem-Cas   temporary casualty (pay record)
TemCon   temporary duty in connection with
TemDIFOT temporary duty in flying status
          involving operational or train-
          ing flights
          Ins under instruction
TemDu   temporary duty
          Con in connection with
          Ins under instruction
TemFly   temporary duty involving flying
          Ins under instruction
Tem-Gen   temporary general (pay record)
TemIns   temporary duty under instruction
temp   temporary (rank) (UK); temperature
TempAtt   temporarily attached
TempDetD temporary detached duty

Tempest   fighter aircraft by Hawker
Tempistor   temperature compensating resistor
TemProx   temporary duty for approximately
tempy   temporary
Tem-Ret   temporary (pay record) for retired
    member called to active duty
TemWait   temporary duty awaiting
TENEC   total estimated net energy consumed
TEng   technician engineer
Tenley   encryption equipment for TRI-TAC (US)
TENOC   ten-year oceanography plan (US)
TEO   torpedo engineer officer; transferred
    electron oscillator
TEP   transmitter experimental package;
    transportation energy panel;
    tetra-ethyl-pyro-phosphate;
    Truppenentgiftungsplatz (personnel
    decontamination site)
TEPA   tetra-ethyl-enepentamine
TEPIGEN   television picture generation
    computer-generated image system
    by Marconi
TEPIS   tidewater enlisted public informa-
    tion specialists (US)
ter   territory
TerCom   terrain comparison (guidance)
TERCOM   terrain contour matching
TERCON   terrain contour matching (aircraft
    navigation system)
TEREC   ALQ-125, tactical electronic recon-
    naissance system (USAF)
TerEnvSvc   terrestrial environmental
    services (US)
Terex   medium wheeled tractor forklift or
    shovel (UK)
Terex-4021   Italian detector avalanche rescue
    (people have to wear magnets)
TERI   torpedo effective range indicator
term   terminate; terminology; terminal;
    termination
TERMS   terminal management system
TerminAcTraOrd   termination of active duty
    training orders
Tern-100   airborne area navigation system by
    Sperry
Terne   Norwegian anti-submarine rocket
TerPacIs   trust territory of the Pacific
    Islands
TERPS   terminal instrument procedures SIAP
    (USMC)
terr   territory
TerrA   territorial army
Terranger   8x8 amphibious vehicle by
    Terranger (UK)
TERRE   trans-Europe road rail express
TerRes   territorial residents
Terrier   member of the TAVR (UK); RIM-2, sea-
    to-air missile project (Nato);
    6x6 armoured vehicle for para-
    troopers project by Faun

Tertyl   explosive
TES   technical enquiries section; total
    ELINT system by Singer
Tesed   naval Otomat missile
TESS   thermocouple emergency shipment
    service
TestComDNA   test command defense nuclear
    agency (US)
TET   turbine entry temperature
TETA   tri-ethylene-tetramine
TETAM   tactical effectiveness testing
    anti-tank missiles (US)
TETOC   technical education and training
    for overseas countries
Tetrach   light glider-transportable tank
    WW2 (UK)
Tetrin   explosive (mines)
Tetryl   explosive
TetTox   tetanus toxin
TEV   terminal equipment vehicle
TEW   tactical electronic warfare (air-
    craft)
TEWA   threat evaluation and weapon assign-
    ment
TEWS   tactical effectiveness of weapon
    systems; tactical electronic
    warfare squadron (US); ALQ-135,
    tactical electronic warfare
    system by Northrop
TEWT   tactical exercise without troops (UK)
TEx   target excitation
tex   textile
Texas Tower   maritime radar platform (USAF)
Text   textural file for NARDIS
TEXUS   Technologische Experimenta unter
    Schwerelosigkeit (Spacelab techno-
    logical experiments under zero
    gravity)
TF   technical forecasting; territorial
    force; tax free; task force; till
    forbidden; total forfeiture (US);
    terminal frame; tank farm POL;
    training film; thin film; torpedo
    fighter (aircraft); tactical
    fighter (aircraft); trainer
    fighter (aircraft); threshold
    factor
tf   telephone
TF-5   Firebrand, torpedo fighter by
    Blackburn
TF-15   Eagle, trainer by McDD
TF-104   Starfighter, trainer version by
    Lockheed
TFA   territorial forces association;
    timing filter amplifier; transfer
    function analyser; tri-fluoro-
    acetic
TFC   time first call; tactical fusion
    centre AAFCE intelligence;
    terminal flight control

tfc	traffic
TFCS	tank fire control system by SABCA
TFCNN	task force commander, North Norway (Nato)
TFCSD	total federal commissioned service to date
TFD	tactical fusion division (Nato) intelligence; thin film detector
TFF	tactical fighter force (RAAF)
TFFET	tactical fighter force evaluation team (RAAF)
tfg	typefounding
TFNS	territorial forces nursing service
TFNZ	territorial force New Zealand
TFO	transactions for others
TFP	temporary forfeiture of pay
TFR	territorial force reserve; terrain-following radar
tfr	transfer
TFS	tactical fighter squadron; terrain-following system
TFT	thin film transistor; thin film technology; tubular firing tables (US); time-to-frequency transformation
TFTAS	tactical fighter training aggressor squadron (USAF)
TFTR	Tokamak fusion test reactor (Princeton University)
TFU	telecommunications flying unit
TFWC	tactical fighter weapons centre
TFW	tactical fighter wing (USAF)
TFWM	territorial force war medal WW1 (UK)
TFX	tactical fighter, experimental (USN) F-111 MRCA
TFZ	transfer zone; traffic zone
TG	textbook of gunnery; training group; task group; tail gear; turbo generator; total graph; thermo gravimetry; top grille
T&G	tongued and grooved
tg	telegraphy; telegraph; telegraphist
TGB	tongued grooved beaded
TGB-30	4x4 truck by Scania Vabis
TGB-40	6x6 truck by Scania Vabis
TGBL	through government bill of lading (US)
TGCGM	textbook of gun carriages and gun mountings
TGG	third generation gyroscopes; temporary geographic grid
TGH	Tripler General Hospital (US)
TGL	touch-and-go landing
TGM	torpedo gunner's mate
TGPS	MT-1, tactical gliding parachute system by Para-Flite
TGS	Turkish general staff; telemetry ground station
TGSM	terminally guided sub-missiles by Vought (for Lance IR homing anti-tank missiles)
TGSO	tertiary groups shunt operation
TGT	turbine gas temperature; tactical graphics terminal by Magnavox
tgt	target
TGW	terminally guided warhead
TH	true heading; trans-hdyro (US); transport helicopter; tapered heel (projectile); territory of Hawaii; Trinity House; Thailand SEATO
th	thermal
T&H	testing and handling
T-HA	terminal high-altitude FLIP
THAFE	thousand hours accident free each
ThC	thermal converter
thd	thunderhead
thdr	thunder
ThE	thunderstorm event
Theodor	240mm railway gun WW2 (GE)
therm	thermometer
Thermite	steel melting composition incendiary
Thes	Thesaurus file for NARDIS
Thetis	class, anti-submarine patrol boats (FGN)
THHM	Trinity House high water mark
THI	time handed in; temperature humidity index; total height index
THIS	total hospital information system
thk	thick
thn	thin
thou	thousand
Thomaston	class, assault transports LSD (USN)
Thompson	Tommy gun, machine pistol (US)
THOR	tape handling option routines
Thor	SM-75, intermediate-range ballistic missile; Karl, Gerät-40, SP 600mm mortar WW2 (GE)
THQ	theatre headquarters
thq	troop headquarters
Thracian	armoured special support vehicle by Glover & Webb
thrftr	thereafter
ThroBL	through bill of lading
ThS	thermal stress
Exper	experiment
Thud	F-15, Thunderchief
Thunderbird	anti-aircraft missile by BAC
Thunderbolt	P-47, interceptor by Republic
Thunderbolt II	A-10A, close air support aircraft by Fairchild
Thunderchief	F-105, tactical bomber Mach 2 by Republic
Thunderflash	RF-84, recce fighter by Republic
Thunderjet	F-84, jet fighter by Republic
Thunderstick	all-weather blind attack system (for Thunderchief)
Thunderstreak	F-84, jet fighter/bomber by Republic

THWM	Trinity House high water mark
TI	torpedo instructor; technical institute; technical inspection; technical intelligence; terminal island; Treasure Island; technical instructor; training instructor; target indicator (grenade); tracer incendiary (projectile); temperature indicator; Texas Instruments (Dallas, Tx US)
TIAS	target identification and acquisition system (missiles)
TIB	time interval bell; travel information bureau; technical information branch; trimmed in bunkers
TIBT	Turnvill infinity balance test (spectacles)
TIC	technical intelligence centre; target intercept computer; task interrupt control
TICACE	technical intelligence centre Allied Command Europe
TICAS	taxonimic inter-cellular analytic system
TICC	technical intelligence coordination centre
TICCI	technical information centre for the chemical industry (India)
TICCIT	time shared interactive computer controlled information television Hazeltine
TICF	transient installation confinement facility
TICM	thermal imaging common modules (UK programme)
TICO	tri-services identities organization (Canada); technical information contact officer
TICP	theatre inventory control point
TICTAC	time compression tactical communications
TID	total ion detector
TIDE	tactical international data exchange
TIDOC	technical information documentation centre AGARD
TIDU	technical information documents unit
TIE	totally integrated environment
TIF	telephone interference; telephone influence factor
TIFR	Tata institute of fundamental research (Bombay)
TIFS	total in-flight simulator
TIG	the inspector general (US); tungsten inert gas (welding)
Tiger	YF-9F, F-11F, jet fighter by Grumman; mobile tactical radar by Thomson --Aladin SdKfz-181, tank WW2 88mm gun (GE)
Tiger-II	F-5, Freedom Fighter, lightweight jet fighter by Northrop
Tigercat	low-level anti-aircraft missile by Short; F-7F, carrier-borne fighter WW2 by Grumman
Tigerfish	Mk-24, wire-guided acoustic homing torpedo by MSDS
TIH	Their Imperial Highnesses
TIIC	technical industrial intelligence committee
TIIF	tactical imagery interpretation facility
TIL	Technology Investment Ltd (Dublin) (Timoney vehicles)
TILS	technical information and library service; tactical instrument landing system
TIM	target incendiary marker (bomb)
TIMAR	near-term improvement in material asset reporting (US)
TIMI	technical informations maintenance instructions
TimIG	time in grade (US)
TimInt	time interval
TIMM	thermionic integrated micro-module
TIMMS	total integrated manpower management system
TIMMs	thermionic integrated micro-modules
TIN	temporary identification number; temperature independent
Tinsel	airborne jammer WW2 (RAF)
TINSY	Treasure Island naval shipyard
TinT	track in track
TINTS	turret integrated night thermal sight
Tiny Tim	12in air-to-ground rocket WW2 (USAF)
TIO	target indication officer; technical information officer
TIOHUSA	the institute of heraldry (US Army)
TIOM	telegraph input/output multiplexer
TIOS	tactical information organization system for submarines by Vickers
TIP	technology integration programme (Nato); technical information programme; target identification point; technology integrator prototype (aircraft); Transit im improvement programme (satellite)
TIPI	tactical information processing and interpretation (system) (US)
TIPS	time index of performance and sales; telemetry impact prediction system
TIPTOP	tape input/tape output
TIR	time in rate; target indicating room; target illumination radar; tracking and interrogation radar
Tirailleur	wingless air-to-air missile project by BGT
TIREC	TIROS ice reconnaissance
TIRH	terminal infra-red/radar homing

TIROS   television infra-red (radiation of the earth) observation satellite NOAA

TIS   target identification system; target information system; tracking and injection station; technical information service; thermal imaging system by Hughes; transponder interrogation system; technical interface specification; theatre intelligence service

TISEO   TVSU, target identification system electro-optical by Northrop (airborne) (television sight unit)

TISL   target identification set, laser ---Pave Penny

TISU   Trilux infantry sight unit

TIT   turbine inlet temperature

TITAL   Titan Aluminium Feinguss GMBH (Bestwig GE)

Titan   LGM-25, land-based intercontinental ballistic missile by Martin

Titan-III   land-based intercontinental ballistic missile orbital transport version

Titan-Coder   bridging equipment for tanks by GIAT

TIU   tactical information unit (naval FCS)

TJ   junction temperature

tj   trajectory

TJADC   theater joint air defense command (US)

TJAG   the judge advocate general (US)

TJAGSA   the judge advocate general's school (US Army)

TJC   trajectory chart

TJD   trajectory diagram

Tjeld   class, patrol torpedo boats (Norway)

TJId   terminal job identification

TJOC   theater joint operations center (US)

TK   tool kits

tk   tank

TK-gescho   Treibkäfiggeschoss (discarding sabot shot)

TKB-481   12.7mm gun pod (SU)

TkBn   tank battalion (USMC)

TKF-90   taktisches Kampfflugzeug der 90 er Jahre (tactical fighter of the 1990s)

TK-KE-Gescho   Treibkäfig-Kinetische Energie Geschoss (discarding sabot, kinetic energy shot)

TKP   tonne kilometre performed

tkr   telephone talker; tanker

tks   tahnks

TL   troop leader; torpedo lieutenant; telegraphist lieutenant; time loss; total loss; truck load; target loss; transport/loader; time lengths

thermoluminescence; Technische Lieferbedingungen (technical procurement requirements)

tl   trial; tool

TLA   temporary lodging allowance (US); transition layer

T-LA   terminal low-altitude FLIP

T-LANS   Tamam's land navigation system by IAI

TLAS   tactical logical air simulation

TLB   temporary lighted buoy

TLC   tank landing craft; thin layer chromatography

TLD   technical logistic data; transmission line demonstrator; thermoluminescence dosimeters

TLD-511   transmission line demonstrator by Feedback

TLDI   technical logistics data and information

TLF   Tanklöschfahrzeug (fire engine with water-tanks)

TLI   trans-lunar injector (Nasa)

Tlm   telemeter

T-LMD-2   tank laser rangefinder by ISKRA

TLO   tracking local oscillators; technical liaison officer; total loss only

TLP   total loss of pay; tactical leadership programme (Nato air forces); torpedo landplane; truck loading point; transient lunar phenomena

TLPJ   truck loading point/jet (petrol)

TLPM   truck loading point/MOGAS

TLQ-17   transportable communications counter-measures set by Fairchild

tlr   trailer

TLR-31   transportable ECM receiver by Watkins

TLRV   tracked levitated research vehicle

TLS   tank laser sight by Barr & Stroud; Territorial Long Service (Medal) (UK); typed letter, signed

TLT   transportable link terminal

tltr   translator

TLU   table look up; terminal logic unit (module)

TLV   threshold limit values

TLWM   Trinity low water mark

tlymn   tallyman

TM   torpedoman's mate (USN); trained man; traffic manager; town manager; tropical medicine; technical manual; training memorandum; technical memorandum; training manual; tape mark; tele-metry; tone modulation; transverse magnetic; torque meter; trade mark; target marker (shell); tactical missile (ground-to-

TM   ground) (US); trench mortar;
            Thyssen Maschinenbau (Witten GE)
tm   team
TM-Zentrale Tieffliegermeldezentrale (low-
            level aircraft reporting post)
TM-4-4   truck by Bedford
TM-12   light artillery rangefinder by DTAT/
            SEFT
TM-46   anti-tank mine (pressure) (SU)
TM-47   anti-tank mine metallic (SU)
TM-61   Matador, tactical missile by Martin
TM-69   6x6 artillery tractor by FIAT
TM-76   Mace, tactical missile,cruise missile
TM-90   4x4 armoured internal security
            vehicle by TM
TM-120   4x4 armoured internal security
            vehicle by TM
TM-170   4x4 amphibious armoured internal
            security vehicle by TM
TM-1226   naval navigation radar by Decca
TMA   Taiwan maintenance agency (US); total
            material assets; terminal manoeuv-
            ring area ATC airspace

TMAO   troop movement assignment order
TMB   torpedo motor boat   .
tmbr   timber
TMC   Thompson machine carbine; test and
            monitor console; transportation
            material command (US)
TMCC   theater movement control center (US)
TMCRL   tailored master cross reference list
TMCV   Eridan, tripartite mine-counter-
            measures vessel (BE-NL-FR)
TMD   training management division;
            tactical munitions dispenser
            (USAF); Tieffliegermeldedienst
            (low-level aircraft reporting
            service)
TMD-B   bar-shaped anti-tank mine (SU)
TMDE   test, measurement and diagnostic
            equipment
TME   telemetric equipment; strapdown
            Trägheitsmesseinheit by Litef
            (inertial navigator for RPVs)
TMEDA   tetrammethyl-ethylene-di-amine
TMG   track made good; tactical missile
            group
TMi   Topfmine (anti-tank mine)
TMICP   topographic map inventory control
            point
tmil   teilmilitarisierte Sonderentwicklung
            (partially militarized version)
TMIS   technician's maintenance information
            system by Hughes; television
            measurement information system
tmkpr   timekeeper
tml   terminal
TML   three mile limit; tetra-methyl-lead
TMLD   Tieffliegermelde und Leitdiest (low-

            level aircraft reporting and
            directing service)
TMM   truck-mounted treadway bridge 10.5mm
            (SU)
TMMC   theatre material management centre
TMN-46   automatic-layable anti-tank mine
            (SU)
TMO   total material objective; transpor-
            tation movements office(r); tele-
            graph money order
TMort   trench mortar
TMP   training material part RAOC;
            technical manual parts; transpor-
            tation motor pool; thermal
            mechanical processing; terminal
            monitor programme; twin MAG pod
            by FN
tmp   temperature
TMPO   total material procurement objective
tmpry   temporary
TMR   training and manoeuvre regulations;
            transportation movements release;
            total material requirement
TMRRCT   transport and movement regiment
            Royal Corps of Transport
TMS   transportation management school;
            transportation management squad-
            ron (RCT); trooping medical staff
            (UK); time and motion study;
            Technische Marineschule (Kiel)
            naval technical school
T/M/S   type model series
TMS-65   decontamination vehicle (SU)
TMS-401   LLLTV camera by Thomson
TMSD   total military service to date
TMSVCS   TOW missile sight video camera
            system by Fairchild (for airborne
            practice)
TMT   transportation motor transport;
            turbine motor train
TMTC   telemetry and telecommand (sub-
            system)
TMV   true mean value
TMV-596   French computer, tanks
tmw   tomorrow
TMXO   tactical miniature crystal oscilla-
            tor
TMY-83..113 laser rangefinder by CILAS
TN   transportation notice; telephone
            number; technical note; thermo-
            nuclear; true north; air transport
            STANAG
tn   transportation; telephone
TN   Telephonbau und Normalzeit (Frank-
            furt GE)
TNA   transient network analyser
TNC   total numerical control; tide net
            controller
TNC-45   guided weapons patrol boat by
            Lürssen

tndcy	tendency
TNF	theatre nuclear forces
tnf	trainfire
tng	training
TNG	tactical and negotiations game
TngLit	training literature
tngt	tonight
TNI	traffic noise index
TNIWT	transport Navy, inland waterway transport
TNM	tactical nuclear missile; tetra-nitro-methane (explosive)
TNO	thermo-nuclear
TNPG	the nuclear power group
tnr	trainer
TNS	tow night sight
TNSW	Thyssen Nordsee Werke (GE)
TNT	Tolite, tri-nitro-toluol tri-nitro-toluene (explosive) Tragflügel neuer Technologie (advanced technology wing)
tntv	tentative
TNW	tactical nuclear weapon; theatre nuclear weapon
TNWE	tactical nuclear weapons employment (US)
TNX	tri-nitro-xylene
TO	take-off; turn over; technical order; tactical observer; transport officer; torpedo officer; telegraph office; telegraphic order; telephone order; trained operator; trans-ocean; traditional orthography; table of organization (US); theatre of operations; travel order; trainer operation
TOA	term of agreement; total obligational authority; time of arrival; table of allowances; tanker operations assistant MSTS
TOAD	Tolyhanna army depot (US)
TOB	target observation battery; tanker operations board MSTS; temporary office building; take-off boat
tobeDi	(vessel) to be disposed of
tobeLe	(vessel) to be leased
tobeLn	(vessel) to be loaned
Tobias	seismic battlefield surveillance equipment by Elliott (UK)
TOC	tactical operations centre; technical order compliance; theatre of operations command; tanker operation circular; troop operations centre; total operating costs
TOD	time of delivery (Nato); time of despatch (signal) (UK); trade-off determinations; torpedo operations department NTS; trade and operations division; time of day (clock); top of dust; technical objectives documents

TODC	theatre oriented depot complex
TOE	term of enlistment; table of organization and equipment
TO&E	table of organization and equipment
TOEMTB	table of organization and equipment mobilization troop basis
TOES	tables of organization and equipment; trade-off evaluation system
TOET	test of elementary training
TOF	time of filing; time of flight
TofA	terms of agreements STANAG
T/Off	take-off
TOFL	take-off field length
TOG	target-observer-gun (method)
TOGW	take-off gross weight
TOI	term of induction
TOICA	transport officer-in-chief, Army (UK)
TOJ	track on jamming
Tokarev	automatic pistol 7.62mm (SU)
Tolite	--TNT
ToLt	towing light
TOM	topological optimization module
Tomahawk	BGM-109, submarine-launched cruise missile by GD; fighter aircraft WW2 by Curtiss
TOMCAT	theatre of operations (missile); continuous wave anti-tank (weapon)
Tomcat	F-14, naval jet fighter by Grumman
TOMi	anti-tank mine, chemical fuse (Czech)
Tommy gun	Thompson submachine gun
Ton	class, coastal minesweepers (RN)
tonn	tonnage
Tonsil	anti-aircraft barrage rocket WW2
TOO	time of origin (signal)
TOP	total obscuring power; temporarily out of print
TOP-7	panoramic vision tank cupola (FR)
Topas	tracked armoured personnel carrier (Czech) WPT repair and recovery version
Topaze	ballistic missile (Israel)
Top Gun	naval anti-aircraft computer
TOPICS	transport operations for increasing capacity and safety
topo	topographic; topography
TopoCo	topographic company (USMC)
TopoEngr	topographic engineer
topog	topographic; topography
TOPS	the operational PERT system (programme evaluation review technique); telephone order processing system
Top S	
Top Sargent	XA-5, ultra-light helicopter pulse-jets by American Helicopters
TopSec	top secret
TOPSTAR	the officer personnel system the US Army reserve

TOR   time of reception; time of receipt;
          terms of reference (US)
Toran   hyperbolic navigation system (FR)
TORCI-204 torpedo control instrument by
          PEAB
TorDep   torpedo depot
Tornado   MRCA, multirole combat aircraft by
          Panavia
          ADV air defence version
          B-45, jet bomber by North Ameri-
          can; anti-aircraft rocket WW2
          (GE); wheeled APC by Mowag
torp   torpedo
TorpCM   torpedo counter-measures and decep-
          tion
TorpRon   torpedo squadron
Tortoise A-39, heavy assault tank WW2 (UK)
TOS   tactical operations system (US pro-
          gramme); term of service; type of
          shipment; Tiros operational satel-
          lite; tape operating system; test
          operating system; top of steel
Tosca   command, control and information
          system (Denmark)
TOSD   training and operations support
          department
TOSS   Tiros operational satellite system;
          turbine oxidation stability test
ToSto   torpedo stopping
TOT   time on target (artillery support);
          time over target (air support);
          time of transmission; time on
          tape; turbine outlet temperature
tot   total
Totem   tethered TV reconnaissance platform
          by Westinghouse (Canada); naval
          optronic fire control system by
          CSEE
TotForf   total forfeiture (of all pay and
          allowances due) (US)
Toti   class, submarines (IT)
TOTO   Tongue of the Ocean AUTEC site;
          Atlantic underwater test and
          evaluation centre
Toucan-II two-seater anti-aircraft turret
          (FR)
Tours-200 submarine for off-shore work by
          IKL
Tourville class, guided missile frigates
          (FR)
TOVALOP   tanker owners' voluntary agreement
          concerning liability for oil
          pollution
TOvc   top of overcast
TOVS   TIROS operational vertical sounder
TOW   BGM-71, tube-launched optically-
          tracked wire-guided anti-tank
          missile by Hughes; take-off weight
tox   toxicology; toxicological
TP   traffic post; teaching practice;

          technical publication; troop
          program (US); teleprinter;
          transport pack; timing pulse;
          true position; translucent paper;
          toilet paper; target practice
          (ammunition); time and percussion
          (fuse); test procedure
tp   troop; township
TP-3   1.2 ton 4x4 truck by Saviem
TP-4   3.5 ton 4x4 truck by Saviem
TP-42   light wire-guided anti-submarine
          torpedo by FFV
TP-61   high-performance wire-guided torpedo
          by FFV
TP-1050   tank laser range-finder by Bofors
TPA   travel by privately owned vehicle
          authorized; test project agree-
          ment; transfer to pay account;
          track producing area (radar)
TPB   training publications branch
TPB-1   radar for ASRT (air surveillance
          radar team)
TBEIST   transport planning board European
          inland surface transport (Nato)
TPBOS   transport planning board ocean
          shipping (Nato)
TPC   Trenchards police college now:
          MPDS; the US Peace Corps;
          training plans conference;
          transport plane commander; time
          pick-off control
TPCA   test procedure change authorization
TPCU   thermal pre-conditioning unit
TPD   tables of personnel distribution;
          tons per day
TPDS   target practice discarding sabot
          (projectile)
TPE   teleprocessing executive
TPEP   TEREC portable exploitation proces-
          sor
TPF   two photon fluorescence
TPFDD   time phased force deployment data (US)
TPFSDS-T target practice, fin-stabilized
          discarding sabot with tracer
          (projectile)
tpg   topping
TPG   terminal phase guidance
TPH   tons per hour
TPHC   time-to-pulse-height converter
TpHsg   troop housing
TPI   technical proficiency inspection;
          target practice incendiary (pro-
          jectile); target position indica-
          tor; terminal phase initiation;
          tons per inch immersion; trans-
          poly-isoprene (synthetic gutta
          percha); teeth per inch; tons per
          inch; threads per inch; turns per
          inch
tpk   turnpike

TPL   technical publications library

TPM   tons per minute; tri-phenyl-methane
           (dyes)

TPMG   the provost marshal general (US)

TPN-18   GCA radio equipment by ITT

TPN-19   precision approach radar

TPN-22   automatic landing radar

TPN-24   airport surveillance radar by
           Raytheon

TPN-28   radio beacon for FAC

TPO   tree preservation order; travelling
           post office; track production
           officer NADGE; telecommunications
           program objective (US)

TPO-50   flame-thrower on one-axle trailer
           (EG)

TPP   time past a point; total package
           procurement; transit patient and
           prisoner; bridging equipment (SU)

TPQ-10   fire-control radar by GECo

TPQ-31   artillery radar by Raytheon

TPQ-32   FAAR, forward area alerting radar
           anti-aircraft by Gould/Saunders

TPQ-36   mortar locating radar by Hughes

TPQ-37   artillery locating radar by Hughes

TPQ-38   Firefinder, artillery radar by Hughes

TPR   temperature pulse respiration;
           thermo-plastic recording; test
           procedure record

tpr   trooper

TPR-2   Turmperiskop, Rundsicht (panoramic
           turret periscope) by Steinheil-Lear

TPRI   tropical pesticides research insti-
           tute

TPS   transmitter power supply; toughened
           poly-styrene; thermal protection
           system; telecommunications pro-
           gramming system; test pilot school

tps   troops

TPS-1   air surveillance and reporting radar

TPS-21   battlefield surveillance radar by
           Admiral

TPS-25   battlefield surveillance radar by
           Hazeltine

TPS-32   air surveillance radar by ITT

TPS-33   heavy battlefield surveillance radar
           by Admiral

TPS-43   air defence radar by Westinghouse

TPS-44   radar for FACP

TPS-58   battlefield radar integrated into
           TACFIRE

TPS-59   long-range radar by GE

TPS-64   air surveillance radar NADGE by ITT

PTS-63   USMC radar surveillance + ATC by
           Westinghouse

TPS-65   USMC radar surveillance + ATC by
           Westinghouse

TPS-75   RATAC, artillery fire control radar

TPSN   troop programme sequence number

TPSU   transmitter power supply unit
           (module)

TPT   tail pipe temperature

TP-T   target practice with tracer (projec-
           tile)

tpt   transport(er)

TPtn   transportation WW2 (US)

tptr   trumpeter

TPTRL   time phased transportation require-
           ments list (US)

TPU   troop program unit (US); time pick-
           off units

TPWB   three programme wire broadcasting

TPz-1   Transportpanzer Fuchs, by Krauss-
           Maffei (6x6 armoured transport
           vehicle)

TQA   total quality assurance

TQCA   textile quality control association
           (US)

TQE   technical quality evaluation

TQM   transport quartermaster (US) EMBO;
           naval electronic warfare antenna
           by Selenia

TQMS   technical quartermaster sergeant
           (UK); troop quartermaster sergeant

TR   transportation request; technical
           regulations; training reserve;
           temporary rank; army transport
           service regulations; territorial
           reserve; tariff reform; tracking
           radar; test run; target rifle;
           tons registered; transmitter
           receiver; tactical reconnaissance
           (aircraft); transport reconnais-
           sance (aircraft); trainer recon-
           naissance (aircraft); torpedo
           reconnaissance (aircraft);
           Teledyne Ryan Corporation (US)

tr   translation; trace; track; truck;
           transfer; troop; trooper; trainer;
           translator; trumpeter

TR-1   updated U-2, tactical reconnaissance
           aircraft 1979 by Lockheed

TR-84   Falke, artillery calculator

TR-1400   submarines by Thyssen

TR-1700   submarines by Thyssen

TRA   temporary restricted area; temporary
           reserved airspace; technical
           requirements analysis; Teledyne
           Ryan Aeronautical (San Diego US)

TRAAC   Transit research and altitude con-
           trol (satellite)

TRABFS   tables of regulations Army books and
           forms and stationery

trac   tracer; tractor

tracdr   tractor-drawn

TRACAB   terminal radar control by CAB

TRACALS   traffic control and landing system

TRACE   taxiing and routing of aircraft
           coordinating equipment; task
           reporting and current evaluation

Tracer   E-1, naval radar platform twin
           rotors (USN)

Tracker   class, fast patrol boats GRP by
           Fairey; S-2E, ASW seaplane by
           Grumman
TraComd   training command
           Lant   Atlantic
           Pac   Pacific
           SubPac   submarines Pacific
TRACON   terminal radar control
trad   tradition(al)
TRADAD   trace to destination and advise (US)
Trader   C-1, carrier cargo aircraft (USN)
TraDet   training detachment
TraDevMan training devices man
Tradewind P-5Y, four turboprop flying boat
           by Convair
TRADEX   target resolution and discrimination
           experiment
TRADOC   training and doctrine command (US
           Army)
TraFac   training facility
Trafalgar class, submarines 1918 (RN) by
           Vickers
TRAFACs   training facilities
TraFolPers transfer following persons
TRAIF   torso restrained assembly with inte-
           grated floatation
Trainfire infantry training system (US)
TRAKX   millimetre wave tracking radar (USN
           Research)
TraLant   training forces Atlantic
TRAM   target recognition and attack multi-
           sensor (night aiming device) by
           Hughes; test reliability and
           maintenance
TRAMPS   temperature regulator and missile
           power supply
tran   transit; transient
TranC   transient center (USMC)
TraNet   training network
trans   transport; transistor; transverse
Trans   Transvaal
Transall   C-160, cargo aircraft Nord/HFB/VFW
transceiver transmitter + receiver
TransDEC   sonar transducer test and evalua-
           tion center (NEL San Diego)
Trans/Dep transportation of dependents
TransDiv   transportation division
TRANSFER   transportation simulation for
           estimating requirements
TransGrPhibFor transportation group amphib-
           ious force
TransGrpSoPac   transportation group South
           Pacific force
TRANSIT   NNSS, US Navy navigation satellite
           system
transl   translation; translator
TransLant transportation, Atlantic
TransMan   (enlisted) transport manual
TransMgtScol transportation management
           school

TransPhib transports, amphibious force
           Lant   Atlantic
           Pac   Pacific
transp   transportation
Transponder receiver, transmitter + respon-
           der for IFF
           I   international civil avia-
                tion
           S   selective identification
                feature
           T   mark X basic
TransRon   transport squadron
TransTEC   sonar transducer test and evalua-
           tion centre (NEL)
TraPac   training force, Pacific
TRAPATT   trapped avalanche triggered transit
TRAPP   training and retention as permanent
           party (US)
TraRon   training squadron
TraSta   training station
TraU   training unit
trav   traverse; travel
TravChar   cost of travel is chargeable
TravNec   travel is necessary
Trax   jeep (South Africa) by IMVC
TRC   type requisition code; troposcatter
           radio communication; tactical
           radio communication; tilt-rotor
           concept (V/STOL); technology
           reports centre (UK); tape relay
           centre
TRC-97A   tropospheric scatter communications
           system
TRC-170   TROPO, tactical digital tropo-
           scatter terminal by Raytheon
           TRI-TAC
TRC-372   540 552, tactical radio communica-
           tion by Thomson-CSF
TRC-645   field radio system UHF/FM by
           Tadiran
TRCCC   tracking radar central control
           console
TrColl   training college
Trd   Trinidad
TRDTO   tracking radar data take-off
TRE   telecommunications research estab-
           lishment (Malvern UK)
Treas   treasury; treasurer
TreasDept treasury department
TReCom   transportation research command
TREE   transient radiation effect on elec-
           tronics
TrEm-card transport emergency card (tank
           vehicles)
TREND   tropical environment data
TRF   tuned radio frequency
trf   transfer; tariff
TRFA   territorial and reserve forces act
Tr/FlRes   transferred to fleet reserve
trg   training (general staff)

TRH   Their Royal Highnesses
TRI   total response index
Triad   US defense policy (strategic bombers
          + land-based missiles + submarine-
          based missiles)
Triad of initiatives Nato concept
                      1 memoranda of under-
                         standing
                      2 dual production
                      3 family of weapons
Trialene high explosive composition
          (mines)
Tribal   class, frigates (RN)
TriCap   triple capability
TriCon   tri-service container (US programme)
          (special vehicle, self-loading)
Trident   class, submarines (USN) SSBN
Trident-I UGM-96, submarine-launched ICBM
          8 or 14 warheads by Lockheed
Triffid   transportable UHF radio relay
          equipment by Marconi
Trident   class, patrol boats guided missiles
          by CMN
trig   trigonometry; triangulation; trigger
TRIGA   trigger reactor
trigon   trigonometry; trigonometric
Trik.   tri-chloro-ethylene (degreasing
          harmful vapour)
Trilite   night sight for small arms by
          Pilkington
Trilumin microlights, prosphorescent
Trilux   small arms sighting unit
TRIM   training records and information
          management system
Trinity   class, patrol boats by Vosper
Trion   underwater winch + buoy + sensors by
          Dornier
trip   triplicate
TRIP   Tartar reliability improvement
          programme
Tripartite Eridan class, mine hunter FRP
          (BE+FR+NL)
Trislander aircraft by Britten Norman
Tristar   L-1011-1, transport aircraft by
          Lockheed
TRI-TAC   tri-service tactical communications
          network by Sylvania (US)
Tritol   explosive (mines)
triphibious working on land/at sea/in the
          air
Triptane trimethyl + butane (fuel)
Triton   jet aircraft by SNCASO; search and
          navigation radar by Thomson
trk   truck
trkdr   truck-drawn
trkhd   truckhead
trmt   treatment
TRLB   temporarily replaced by lighted buoy
TRLFSW   tactical range landing force support
          weapon

TRLP   transport landplane (USN)
TRM   time release mechanism (ejection
          seat)
TRM-500   jeep by Renault
TRM-920P UHF-VHF manpack transceiver by
          EAS
TRM-1200 4x4 truck by Saviem
TRM-2000 4x4 truck by Saviem
TRM-4000 4x4 truck by Saviem
TRM-6000 4x4 truck by Berliet
TRM-9000 6x6 truck by Berliet
TRM-12000 6x6 truck by Berliet
TRMF   transportable rocket maintenance
          facility
trml   terminal
TRMS   Tiefflieger Radarmeldesystem by AEG
          (low-level aircraft radar report-
          ing system); Telefunken Radar,
          mobil, such (mobile surveillance
          radar by Telefunken)
TRN   transportable radio navigation
          system; television relay network;
          technical research note
TRN-26   portable TACAN system by Decca
trne   trainee
trng   training
T&RNP   transportation and recruiting, naval
          personnel
trns   transition
TRO   truck route order; temporary
          restraining order; Turkey red oil
TRODI   touch-down rate of descent
          altitude
Troika   HFG, remote-controlled minesweepers
          (GE)
Trojan   T-28, trainer aircraft by North
          American; FV-432, tracked armoured
          personnel carrier
TROL   tape-less rotor-less on-line (crypto
          equipment)
TROMEX   tropical oceanographic and meteoro-
          logical experiment 1971/2
trop   tropical
TropMed   tropical medicine
Tropo   TRC-170, tactical digital tropo-
          scatter terminal by Raytheon
          TRI-TAC
TROSCOM   troop support command (US Army)
TroTLF   Trockentanklöschfahrzeug (dry fire-
          fighting vehicle)
Trotyl   tri-nitro-toluol
TRP   traffic regulation point; track
          reporting post (air defence)
trp   troop
TRP-2   Turm Rundblickperiskop by Steinheil
          (turret panoramic periscope)
TRR   tactical range recorder; target
          ranging radar
TRRA   tilt-rotor research aircraft
trrn   terrain

TRRS	tactical radio relay system
TRS	tactical reconnaissance squadron; tactical reconnaissance system; test requirement specification; tetrahedal research satellite; transversing rake system; Torry research station (UK)
trs	transfer
TRS-65	MATCALS, marine air traffic control and landing system by Westinghouse (USMC)
TRS-906	naval optronic fire control system by Thomson
TRS-3405	coastal surveillance and command radar (FR)
TRS-3410	coastal surveillance and command radar (FR)
TRSA	terminal radar service area
TRSB	time-referenced scanning beam (landing system) by Hazeltine
TRSBMLS	time-referenced scanning beam microwave landing system
trsd	transferred
TRSP	transport seaplane (USN)
trsp	transport
TRSR	taxi and runway surveillance radar
TRSSGM	tactical range surface-to-surface guided missile
TRSSM	tactical range surface-to-surface missile
trsy	treasury
TRT	TEREC remote terminal; Télécommunications Radioelectroniques et Téléphoniques (Paris)
trt	turret
TRTG	tactical radar threat generator
TRTT	tactical record teletypewriter terminal by Tracor
TRU	thrust reversion unit
TRUB	temporarily replaced by unlighted buoy
TRUMP	target radiation measurement programme
TRUST	Trieste US Troops Headquarters WW2
TRV	torpedo recovery vessel (RN); tank recovery vehicle
TR-VP	FM radio set (FR)
TRW	troop carrier wing (USAF)
TS	technical secretariat; transport and supply; tensile strength; type script; terminal service; top secret; transit storage; type specification; torpedo shell; testing set; tape status; target strength; transformer substation; transition set; transmitting station; twin screw; time shack; training ship; tool steel; test summary; turbine steamship; temperature switch
T&S	transport and supply
T-S	terminal seaplane ELIP
TS-Gramate	Treibspiegelgranatae (discarding sabot shot)
TS-8	initial trainer aircraft (Poland)
TS-11	Iskra, trainer aircraft (Poland)
TS-14	scraper vehicle by Terex
TS-50	anti-personnel scatter mine by Tecnovar
TSA	textbook of small arms; troop support agency (US Army); total scan area; time series analysis
TSAM	trainer, surface-to-air missile
TSARC	test schedule and review committee (US)
TSARCOM	troop support and aviation material readiness command (US Army)
TSB	twin side band; technical support building
TSC	tactical support centre; technical sub-committee; territorial army staff course (UK); terminal switching centre ETS; thermally stimulated currents; time sharing control; transmitter start code; transportation systems centre; tactical support centre AEW
TSC-89	FLTSATCOM operating centre by E-Systems
TSCA	timing single channel analyser
TSCC	top secret control channel; twin swirl combustion chamber (in piston engines)
TSCDP	technical service career development program (US)
TSCO	top secret control officer (US)
TSCP	top secret control procedures
TSCS	top secret control section
TSD	theatre shipping document; toured sea duty; thermally stimulated depolarization; touch sensitive digitizer
TSDS	two-speed destroyer-sweeper
TSE	tactical support equipment; time slice end
TSEC	telecommunications security; tactical support equipment cryptographic
TSEE	thermally stimulated emission of exo-electronics
TSF	two-seater fighter (aircraft); télégraphie sans fil (wireless telegraphy)
TSFO	transportation support field office (US)
tsfr	transfer
TSG	technical sub-group; technical speciality group; transport support group (UK); the surgeon general (US)

TSGAD	tri-service group on air defence (Nato)	TSX	telecommunications satellite experiment; time sharing executive
TSGCEE	tri-service group on communications and electronic equipment (Nato)	TSW-7A	mobile air traffic control system by RCA
TSgt	technical sergeant	TSW-10	remote control system for RPVs by Motorola
TSH	Their Serene Highnesses	TT	torpedo tube; time trial; technical test; technical training; tank top; transit time; tank technology; total time; tetanus toxid; tuberculin tested; tele-type-writer; troop training; telegraphic transfer; Tanganjika Territory; target towing (aircraft); turret trainer
tshwr	thundershower		
TSI	technical standardization inspection; task status index; tons per square inch		
TSIT	technical service intelligence team		
TSL	troop safety line		
TSLS	tri-service laser seeker by Rockwell		
TSM	troop sergeant major; technical service manual		
TSMC	technical supply management code	T&T	Trinidad and Tobago
TSMG	Thompson submachine gun	TTA	tactical transport aircraft
TSMV	twin screw motor vessel	TTAB	trade mark trial and appeal board
TSO	technical staff officer; transportation supply officer; TACAN systems operator; textbook of service ordnance; time since overhaul; technical standard order; time sharing option	TTAC	telemetry tracking and command
		TTAT	torpedo tube acceptance trials
		TTC	technical training command (RAF); technical training centre
		TTC-39	transportable telephone communication automatic circuit switch by GTE TRI-TAC
TSO-73	command and control system	TTCC	the technical cooperation committee (US)
TsOET	tests of elementary training		
TSOP	tactical standing operating procedures (US)	TTCP	the technical cooperation programme (AUS+US+CAN+UK)
TSOR	tentative specific operational requirement	TTCU	teletypewriter control unit
TSOT	telephone switchboard operating troop	TTD	temporary travel document
		TTE	tropical testing establishment
TSP	torpedo seaplane (USN); titanium sublimation pump	TTF	training task force; test to failure; time to failure
TSPP	total ship procurement package (USN)	TTF&T	technology transfer fabrication and test (contract phase)
TSQ	time-super-quick (fuse)	TTG	test target generator
TSQ-73	Missile Minder, surveillance radar by Litton	TTI	time to intercept
TSQ-111	CNCE, communications nodal control element by Martin TRI-TAC	TTJE	training tactical jamming equipment
		TTL	transistor transistor logic; to take leave
TSR	tactical strike reconnaissance (aircraft); torpedo spotter reconnaissance (aircraft) (Barracuda) (RN)	TTM	two-tone modulation
		TTMA	truck trailer manufacturer's association
TSRI	technical skill re-enlistment incentive	TTMCFO	theater type mobilization corps force objective (US)
TSS	technical support services; twin screw steamer; turbine steamship; time sharing system	TTP	total taxable pay
		TTPE	total taxable pay earned (US)
		TTP	tri-tolyl-phosphate (plastic)
TSs	typescripts	TTP&S	trainees, transients, patients and students (programme) (US)
TSSC	target system service charge; temporary short service commission (UK)	TTR	target tracking radar; time temperature recorder
TST	Tele Security Tinman (Pöcking GE)	TTRC	thrust travel reduction curve
TST-1221	hand-held text encryption system by C+S	TTRM	transition thermo-remnant magnetization
tstm	thunderstorm	TTS	tank transporter squadron RCT; transitional training school; tank thermal sight; turret thermal sight; tactical telephone
tstr	tester		
TSTS	twin screw turbine steamer		
TSTV	tracked and semi-tracked vehicles		
TSU	tariff selection unit; TOW telescopic unit; this side up		

TTS	switchboard; teletypesetting; teletypesetter; temperature threshold shift; transportable transformer sub-station
TTS-4	TINTS, turret thermal sight by TI
TTSA	transitional training squadron Atlantic
TTSP	transitional training squadron Pacific
TTSPF	transitional training squadron Pacific fleet
TTT	time to turn; team time trial; time temperature transformation
TTTC	technical teachers training college
TTTE	tri-national Tornado training establishment (RAF Cottesmore)
TTTT	Tartar-Talos-Terrier-Typhoon
TTTU	tri-national Tornado training unit (RAF Cottesmore)
TTU	tank transporter unit RCT
TTWG	training technology working group (Nato)
TTY	teletypewriter
TTZL	threshold and touchdown zone lighting
TU	transmitter unit; transmission unit; transfer unit; tape unit; top up; thermal unit; toxic unit; Turkey (Nato); turbopump unit; task unit; thank you (US)
tu	tug
Tu-2	bomber WW2 by Tupolev (SU)
Tu-4	Bull (licence-built B-29), bomber WW2 by Tupolev (SU)
Tu-14	Bosun, jet bomber by Tupolev (SU)
Tu-16	Badger, jet long-range bomber by Tupolev (SU)
	A radar bomber
	B 2 Kennel missiles
	C 1 Kipper missile
	D maritime recce and ECM
	E multi-sensor recce
	F ECM + ESM
	G updated B version
Tu-20	Bear, nuclear bomber WW2 by Tupolev (SU)
Tu-22	Blinder, nuclear bomber WW2 by Tupolev (SU)
	U trainer version
Tu-26	Backfire, bomber/maritime recce WW2 by Tupolev (SU)
Tu-28P	Fiddler, super-sonic interceptor WW2 by Tupolev (SU)
Tu-95	Bear, bomber/missile/director/maritime recce WW2 by Tupolev (SU)
Tu-104	passenger aircraft Aeroflot
Tu-105	passenger aircraft Aeroflot
Tu-114	passenger aircraft by Tupolev
Tu-124	Cookpot, cargo aircraft by Tupolev
Tu-126	Moss, AEW aircraft by Tupolev
Tu-134	Crusty, cargo aircraft by Tupolev
Tu-144	supersonic transport aircraft Aeroflot
Tu-154	long-range passenger aircraft
TUAASL	theory and use of anti-aircraft sound location
tub	tubular
Tucan	re-usable RPV by VFW-Fokker
TUCC	Tri-lateral universities computation centre
TÜR	Tieffliegerüberwachungsradar by Siemens (low-level aircraft surveillance radar)
Turana	surveillance RPV by GAF
Turbo Mentor	T-34C, trainer aircraft by Beech
Turbo Porter	single-engined plane by Pilatus
turboprop	turbine and propeller (aircraft)
Turbo Sky	So-28, Sky Servant turboprop version by Dornier
Turbo Trainer	PC-7, trainer aircraft by Pilatus
TURCO	turn round control organization
TURPS	terrestrial unattended reactor power system
Turtle	first submarine USA 1778 by David Bushnel
Turunma	class, corvettes (Finland)
Turya	class, patrol hydrofoils (SU)
TUSA	the 3rd US Army
TUSAB	the US Army band
TUSAC	the US Army chorus
TUSLog	Turkey US logistics group (USAF Ankara)
TV	travel voucher; terminal velocity; television; test vector; test vehicle; tube tester; transport vehicle; transport vessel
TV-8A	Matador, Spanish designation Harrier
TVA	Torpedoversuchsanstalt Eckernförde (torpedo experimental establishment) (FGN)
T-VASIS	T-visual approach slope indicator system
TVAT	television air trainer
TVC	thrust vector control; technical valve committee; total variable counts; temporary visual display; tactical visual display
TVDR	tag vector display register
TVDS	television distribution system
TVF	tape velocity fluctuations
TVG	time variation of gain
TVI	television interference
TVIS	turbine vibration indicator system
Tvl	Transvaal
tvl	travel
TvlAlwS	travel allowance on separation (US)
TVM	track via missile (control system)

TVO	translation verification office
TVOR	terminal VHF omni-directional range
TVP	transit vehicle park
TVR	temperature variation of resistance; tag, vector response
TVRB	tactical vehicle review board (US)
TVS-2	CSWS, crew-served weapons sight
TVS-4	medium-range night observation device
TV-SAT	Germany-covering regional communications satellite project by Euro-satellite
TVSU	TISEO, airborne television sight unit by Northrop
TVT	television translator; television tracker
TVT-300	television target tracker by Saab
TVTD	television tabular display
TVW	tag, vector word
TW	tapes and recording wires; type writer; tape word; tail warning (radar); tail wind
TWA	time weighted average
TWA-80	Torpedowaffenanlage der 80 er Jahre torpedo weapons system of the 1980s (FGN project)
TWB	typewriter buffer
TWEB	transsscribed weather broadcasts
Tweety Bird	T-37B, jet trainer by Cessna
TWERLE	tropical wind energy (conversion) and research level experiments
TWG	technical working group (Nato)
TWI	training within industry
TWIC	theatre watch intelligence condition
Twiggy-	night sight SS-32, image intensifying night sight by Rank Pullins
Twin Mustang	P-82, interceptor WW2 by North American
Twin Star	SA-355, US designation for Ecureuil helicopter by AS
Twister	XM-808, 6x6 cross-country vehicle by Lockheed
twix	teletypewriter message
TWK	Trängaswurfkörper by Buck (tear gas grenade)
TWL	teeny weeny laser; total weight loss
TWL-50	teeny weeny laser, miniature laser for RPVs
twlt	twilight
TWM	tactical weapons meet (Nato) 76 ---1976
TWOATAF	2nd allied tactical air force (Central Europe Nato)
twp	township
TWPD	tactical and weapons policy division
TWPL	teletypewriter private lines
TWR	torpedo weapons receiver
twr	tower; transceiver
TWS	teletypewriter service; timed wire

	service; tactical weather station; track while scan (radar mode); tail warning system EW; torpedo weapons system by Plessey
TwSc	twin screw (vessel)
TWSS	TOW weapons sub-system
TWT	travelling wave tube; telephone-teletypewriter exchange; trans-sonic wind tunnel; two week training
TWTA	travelling wave tube amplifier
TWX	teletypewriter exchange; teletype-writer message
twy	taxiway
TX	torque transmitter; transmitter
Tx/Rx	windows for laser sensors (material)
TY	total yield
ty	territory
TyCom	type commander
Tyglass	glass roving mat for GRP
Type-21	frigate RN by Yarrow-Vosper
Type-22	frigate (RN)
Type-42	missile launching destroyer; patrol frigate (RN)
Type-58	howitzer 15mm (Japan)
Type-60	recoilless gun carrier 106mm (Japan)
Type-62	machine gun 7.62mm (Japan)
Type-64	mortar 81mm (Japan); automatic rifle 7.62mm (Japan)
Type-73	armoured personnel carrier (Japan)
Type-74	tank (Japan)
Type-75	SP howitzer 155mm (Japan)
Type-140	helicopter navigation system by Crouzet
Type-162	side scan sonar for detection and classification of seabed targets by Kelvin-Hughes
Type-184M	sonar developed by AUWE manufactured by Graseby
Type-193M	mine search and classification sonar by Plessey
Type-195	helicopter-borne dipping sonar by Plessey
Type-199	variable depth sonar by EMI
Type-500B	airborne cartridge dispenser 20 x 74mm 80 x 40mm by Alkan
Type-909	naval fire control radar (RN)
Type-910	missile guidance radar for Sea-wolf by Marconi
Type-965	naval long-range air surveillance radar by Marconi
Type-967	naval surveillance radar D-band
Type-968	naval surveillance radar E-band
Type-978	naval surface and tactical radar by Decca
Type-992Q	naval surveillance and target indicator radar by Marconi
Type-1006	naval navigation radar (RN)
Type-1092	sea control ship by Italcantieri

Type-1107	ocean submarine by Italcantieri	typw	typewriter
Type-1113	landing ship/helicopter carrier by Italcantieri	TYQ-1	tactical air command central (US)
Type-2016	advanced long-range sonar for fleet escort ships by Plessey	TYQ-2	TAOC, tactical air operation centre
		TZ	tactical zone
Type-2020	chin-mounted sonar for submarines by Plessey	TZD	true zenith distance
		TZE	Telezielerfassungsgerät (airborne target acquisition set)
Typhoon	fighter-bomber by Hawker WW2 (US missile)	TZF-1	Turmzielfernrohr by Zeiss (turret telescopic sight)
TYPOE	ten year plan of ocean exploration		

U

U   unit; universal; university; unclas-
        sified (Nato); upper (airspace);
        utility; ultra-high (flying)

U-Boot Unterseeboot (submarine)

U-cartridge inspector's dummy cartridge

U-factor utilization factor; insulation
        factor

U-film unfit for public show film

U-rocket anti-aircraft barrage rocket (UK)

U-1   anti-personnel mine (Belgium)

U-2   Aquatone, ultra-high flying recce
        aircraft by Lockheed

U-5TS 55mm smooth-bore gun (SU)

U-10   Speaker Bird, light PSYWAR aircraft

UA   un-identified aircraft; under age
        (UK) (20); unauthorized absentee
        (US); uniform allowance (US);
        underwriting account

UAAF   unified action armed forces (US)

UAB   until advised by

UAC   upper area control ATC; United Air-
        craft Corporation
        --Sikorsky

UACC   upper area control centre ATC

UACM   unilateral arms control measure

UACS   underwater acoustic communications
        system

UACTE universal automatic check-out
        and test equipment

UAD   unit air defence

UADF   UHF automatic direction finder

UADPS uniform automatic data processing
        system

UADPS/INAS uniform automatic data proces-
        sing system/industrial naval
        air station

UADS   user attribute data set

UAE   United Arab Emirates

UAF   Union Air Force (South Africa)

UAI   United Aircraft International
        (Cologne/Paris) helicopters

UAIMS uniform aircraft information manage-
        ment system

UAL-11201 laser rangefinder by Ericsson

UAM   underwater-to-air missile

UAN   uniform automatic network;
        Unterauftragnehmer (sub-contrac-
        tor)

UANC   united African national council

UAP   utility amphibious plane; upper air
        project

UAP-40301 battlefield surveillance radar
        by Ericsson

UAR   upper air route; United Arab
        Republic (of Egypt)

UARRSI universal aerial refuelling recep-
        tacle slipway installation

UARS   unmanned arctic research submarine

UAS   upper air space ATC; university air
        squadron (UK)

UAS-4   airborne infra-red surveillance
        equipment

UATP   universal air travel plan

UAZ-469 jeep (SU)

UB   uniforms bill

UB-16   rocket pod for 57mm unguided rockets

UB-32   rocket pod for 57mm unguided rockets

UBA   Umweltbundesamt (Federal GE environ-
        ment agency)

UBAF   Union of Burma air force

UBFC   underwater battery fire control

UBITRON undulation beam interaction elec-
        tron (tube)

UBM-52 mortar 120mm (SU)

UbmZerl Ubungsgranate mit Zerleger (prac-
        tice round self-destructing)

UboZerl Ubungsgranate ohne Zerleger (prac-
        tice round not self-destructing)

UbR   Ubungsgranate, rote Sprengwolke
        (practice grenade red smoke)

UbS   Ubungssprengladung (practice demoli-
        tion charge)

UbW   Ubungsgranate, weisse Sprengwolke
        (practice grenade white smoke)

UC   undercarriage; upper case; unit
        cost; undercart; uranium carbide;
        under conversion; under construc-
        tion; upper Canada; unclassified

UC-12   utility/cargo aircraft by Beech

UCA   upper control area ATC

UCAR	Union of Central African Republic
UCB	unit control block
UCC	upper (airspace) control centre; umpire coordination centre
UCDWR	University of California division of war research
UCI	unit construction index
UCK	unit check
UCL	upper control limit; upper cylinder lubricant
UCMJ	uniform code of military justice (US)
UCMR	upon completion thereof will return to ... (US)
UCNI	unified communication navigation and identification
UCO	universal (weather) code
UCODES	united identification system report (US)
UCP	unified command plan
UCR	unsatisfactory condition report
UCS	universal character set
UCSTR	universal code synchronous transmitter receiver
UCWRE	underwater countermeasures and weapons research establishment
UD	unit diary; undesirable discharge
	CA trial by civil authorities
	DE desertion
	FE fraudulent enlistment
	UF unfitness
UDA	Ulster defence association
UDAS	unified direct access system
UDC	universal decimal classification; upper dead centre
UDE	underwater development establishment
UDEC	universal digital electronic computer (US)
UDF	UHF direction finder; Union defence force (South Africa); Ulster defence force
UDI	unilateral declaration of independence
UDICON	universal digital communications network by Ford
	STS synchronous time sharing
	ADB asynchronous data bus
	BSB bit synchronous bus
	VCB voice communications bus
UDMH	unsymmetrical di-methyl hydracine
UDR	Ulster Defence Regiment; universal document reader
UDT	underwater demolition team; underwater destruction team; universal document transport; uncharged demolition target
UDU	underwater demolition unit
UE	unit equipment; until exhausted
UE-31	Chenillette, tank WW2 (FR)
UEE	unit essential equipment
UEEO	unexploded explosive ordnance

UEF	universal extra fine (thread)
UEIC	United East India Company
UEO	unexploded explosive ordnance; unit education officer; unit emplaning officer
UEP	underwater electric potential
UEPR	unsatisfactory equipment performance report
UER	unsatisfactory equipment report; university entrance requirements
UERT	universal engineer tractor rubber-tyred (USN)
UET	universal engineer tractor (US programme)
UETA	universal engineer tractor armoured
UETRT	universal engineer tractor rubber-tyred (US)
UEUAF	United Emirates Union Air Force
UF	unit of fire (US); utilization factor; ultrafiltration; urea-formaldehyde (resin)
UFA	until further advised (US)
UFC	up-front control (avionics)
UFD	universal firing device
UFN	until further notice
UFO	unidentified flying object; unit families officer
UFOP	ultra-fast opening parachute
UFORA	unidentified flying objects research association
UFP	unemployed with full pay
UFU	utility flight unit
ug	undergoing; underground
UG-3rd	upgraded third generation ATC system
Ugan	Uganda
UGC	University Grants Committee
UGC-129	tactical record teletypewriter terminal by tracer
UGK-020	Ubungsgefechtskopf for Dira (practice warhead)
UGM	underwater-launched guided missile
UGM-27	Polaris, underwater-launched guided missile fleet ballistic missile by Lockheed
UGM-73	Poseidon, underwater-launched guided missile by Lockheed
UGM-84	Harpoon, underwater-launched guided cruise missile (USN)
UGM-93	... 96A, Trident, SLBM by Lockheed
ugnd	underground
Ugra	class, submarine depot ship (SU)
UGS	unattended ground sensors
UH	upper half; utility helicopter
UH-1	utility helicopter by Bell, Huey, Iroquois
UH-2	Seasprite, utility helicopter
UH-19	S-55, utility helicopter by Sikorsky
UH-34	S-55, utility helicopter by Sikorsky
UH-46	Sea Knight, utility helicopter by Boeing Vertol

UH-60	Black Hawk, LAMPS, UTTAS, by Sikorsky
UH-61	Black Hawk, LAMPS, UTTAS, by Boeing
UHA	ultra-high altitude
UHC	under honorable conditions (US)
UHE	ultra-high efficiency (filter)
UHF	ultra-high frequencies
UHT	ultra-high temperature; ultra heat treated
Uhu	tank-borne infra-red search light WW2 (GE)
IHV	ultra-high vacuum; ultra-high voltage
UI	unidentified installation; unit of issue; under instruction
UIC	upper (flight) information centre CEAC; unit identification code
UICA	united Irish counties association
UICIO	unit identification code information officer
UICP	unit inventory control point (system)
UIL	united Irish league
UIR	upper (flight) information region ATC
UIW	universelle Infanteriewaffe spater AUG, 5.56mm by Steyr (universal infantry weapon)
UJ	Union Jack
UJC	Union Jack club
UJm	uncorrelated jet model
UK	United Kingdom
UKA	United Kingdom Alliance
UKAC	United Kingdom Automation Council
UKADGE	United Kingdom air defence ground environment
UKADR	United Kingdom air defence region
UKAEA	United Kingdom atomic energy agency
UKAIR	United Kingdom air defence region; United Kingdom air forces
UKB	universal keyboard
UKBC	United Kingdom bomber command
UKCATR	United Kingdom civil aviation tele-communications representative
UKF	unbemanntes Kampfflugzeug (unmanned combat aircraft)
UKFC	United Kingdom fortifications club
UKIP	United Kingdom import plan
UKJATFOR	United Kingdom joint airborne task force (Nato)
UKLF	United Kingdom land force
UKMF	United Kingdom mobile force
UKNF	United Kingdom nuclear force
UKOOA	United Kingdom offshore operators' association (North Sea oil)
UKPA	United Kingdom pilots' association
UKSL	UKADGE Systems Ltd (Marconi, Plessey, Hughes)
UKSLS	United Kingdom service liaison staff (Australia)
UKSM	United Kingdom scientific mission
UKSTC	United Kingdom strike command (RAF)

UKV	underground keybox vault
UL	upper limit; underleaver
ULAS	University of London air squadron
ULC	unit-load container (for Chieftain)
ULCC	ultra-large crude (oil) carrier
ULCS	unit level circuit switching system TRI-TAC
ULD	unit load device (air cargo)
UlDest	ultimate destination
ULF	upper limiting frequency; ultra-low frequency
ULISS	universal light inertial system by SAGEM (airborne laser gyro)
ULISS-53	universal light inertial system by SAGEM (airborne laser gyro)
ULLA	ultra-low-level airdrop (system) (UK)
ULLV	unmanned lunar logistics vehicle
ULM	ultrasonic light modulator; universal logic module
ULMS	underwater long-range missile system system; unit level message switching system TRI-TAC
ULO	unit landing officer
ULP	utility landplane
ULRGW	ultra-long-range guided weapon
ULS	unit level switchboard TRI-TAC
Ultrafax	tape transmission in shorter time by higher speed (system)
UltSign	ultimate assignment
ULV	ultra-low volume
Ultratek	explosive vapour sniffer by SAS
um	infra-red light wave length
2.2.5um	sunrays reflected from clouds
5 um	exhaust gas
UM	urgent memorandum; unorganized militia; underwater mechanic (US); under mentioned; unmanned
UMA	unmanned aircraft; united maritime authority
UMAD	Umatilla army depot (US)
UMBR	universal multiple bomb rack
UMC	unit mail clerk (US); unit manning code (report) (US); Union Metallic Cartridge Comp
UMD	unit movement data (US); unit management document
UMF	marine fighter squadron
UMFAW	marine fighter squadron all-weather
UMG	universal machine gun 7.62mm by Maremont
UMI	unit movement identifier
UMIDS	universal mine dispensing system
Umitaku	class, corvettes (JMSDF)
UMIV-1	mine detector (SU)
UML	universal mission load
UMMIPS	uniform material movement and issue priority system (US)
UMNO	United Malays national organization

UMR	unsatisfactory material report; unipolar magnetic regions
UMS	Unfederated Malay states
UMT	universal military training
UMTA	urban mass transportation administration (US DoT)
UMTS	universal military training system; universal military training and service
UN	United Nations; underneath; urban network
UNA	United Nations assembly; United Nations association
UNAAF	unified action armed forces
UNACOM	universal army communications system
UNADA	UN atomic development authority
UNAEC	UN atomic energy commission
unalot	unallotted
unasgd	unassigned
unauthd	unauthorized
UNB	universal navigational beacon
UNC	UN charter; UN command
UNCAST	UN conference on the applications of science and technology
UNCC	UN cartographic commission
UNCCP	UN conciliation commission for Palestine
UNCIO	UN conference on international organizations
UNCIP	UN commission for India and Pakistan
UNCivPol	UN civilian police (Cyprus)
UNCKorea	UN command Korea
unclass	unclassified
UNCLE	united network command for law enforcement (TV)
UNCMAC	UN command military armistice commission
UNCO	UN civilian operations (mission Congo Rep.)
UNCOK	UN commission on Korea
uncond	unconditioned
uncor	uncorrected
UNCP	UN conference of Plenipotentiaries
UNCR	UN command, rear
UNCTAD	UN conference on trade and development
UNCURK	UN commission for the unification and rehabilitation of Korea
UND	urgency of need designator
unded	underdeduction
UndelOrdCan	undelivered orders cancelled
undetm	undetermined
undg	undergoing
UNDOF	UN forcesGolan Heights
UNDP	UN development programme
UNDRO	UN disaster relief organization
undsgd	undersigned
UNEC	UN education conference
UNECA	UN economic commission for Asia
UNECAFE	UN economic commission for Asia and the Far East
UNECE	UN economic commission for Europe
UNEDA	UN economic development administration
UNEF	UN emergency force
UNEP	UN environmental programme
UNESCO	UN educational scientific and cultural organization (Paris)
UNETAS	UN emergency technical aid service
unex	unexecuted
unexpl	unexploded; unexplored; unexplained
UNF	UN forces
UNFAO	UN food and agricultural organization
unfav	unfavourable
UNFC	UN food conference
UNFICyp	UN (peacekeeping) force in Cyprus
UnFurNote	until further notice
UNGA	UN general assembly
UNHCR	UN high commissioner for refugees
UNHQ	UN headquarters (New York)
UNI	UN intelligence
UNI-52	inertial navigation unit (FR)
Uni-Air	united defence force air force (Brussels Treaty)
UNIC	UN information centre
Unic	logistic truck (FR)
UNICEF	UN children's fund
UNICOM	universal integrated communications (system)
unident	unidentified
UNIDO	UN industrial development organization
unif	uniform(ity)
Uniflote	light floating bridge equipment by Mabey Acrow
Uni-Force	the combined staff of the united defence force (Brussels Treaty)
Uni-Gun	single 12.7mm gun pod by FFV
UNIHEDD	LLLTV for helicopters by Ferranti
Unillion	chairman of the united defence force (Brussels Treaty)
Uni-Mer	united defence force Navy (Brussels Treaty)
Unimog	4x4 truck by Daimler Benz
UNIO	UN information organization
UNIS	UN information service; UN international school
UNISCAN	consultative economic association of UK Sweden Norway Denmark
UNISIST	universal system for information in science and technology
UNITAR	UN institute for training and research
UNITAS	united international anti-submarine (warfare exercise)
Unitel	united telephone system
Unit-Terre	united defence force land force (Brussels Treaty)
UNITOPOS	unit to operate overseas (for at least 1 year)

univ	universal; university
Univac	universal automatic computer
Universal	Bailey, bridging equipment by Mabey
Universal	carrier Bren gun tracked carrier WW2
UNJSPB	UN joint staff pensions board
unkn	unknown
UNKRA	UN Korean reconstruction agency UN Korean relief administration
unl	unlimited
UNLC	UN liaison committee
unlgtd	unlighted
unliq	unliquidated
unlod	unloaded
unltd	unlimited; unlighted
UNM	United Nations Medal
unm	unmarried
UNMC	UN Mediterranean commission
UNMIPS	uniform material maintenance and issue priority system
UNMOGIP	UN military observer group in India and Pakistan
UNMSC	UN military staff committee
UNNSAD	unit neutral normalized spectral analytical density
UNO	United Nations Organization
UnODir	unless otherwise directed
UNOGIL	UN observation group in Lebanon
UnOIndc	unless otherwise indicated
unop	unopposed
UnOrdCan	unexecuted orders cancelled
UNPA	UN postal administration
UNPC	UN Palestine commission
UNPCC	UN Palestine conciliation commission
unpd	unpaid
UNPIK	UN peacekeeping force in Korea
UNPOC	UN peace observation commission
unpub	unpublished
unqual	unqualified
UNREF	UN refugees' fund; UN refugees' emergency fund
unrel	unreliable
UnRep	underway replenishment
UNRISD	UN research institute for social development
UNRPR	UN relief for Palestine refugees
UNRRA	UN relief and rehabilitation administration
unrstd	unrestricted
UNRWA	UN relief and work agency (for Palestine refugees in the Near East)
UNRWAPRNE	UN relief and work agency for Palestine refugees in the Near East
Unryu	class, aircraft carriers WW2 (Japan)
unsat	unsatisfactory
UNSC	UN security council; UN social commission
UNSCC	UN standards coordinating committee
UNSCCUR	UN science conference on the conservation and utilization of resources
UNSCEAR	UN scientific committee on the effects of atomic radiation
UNSCOB	UN special committee on the Balkans
UNSCOP	UN special committee on Palestine
UNSF	UN special fund
UNSFH	UN security forces Hollandia
UNSG	UN secretary general
UNSM	UN service medal
unstdy	unsteady
UNSR	UN space registry
unstbl	unstable
unstdy	unsteady
Unsvc	unserviceable
UNTA	UN technical assistance
UNTAA	UN technical assistance administration
UNTAB	UN technical assistance board
UNTAM	UN technical assistance mission
UNTC	UN trusteeship council
UNTCoK	UN temporary commission on Korea
UNTEA	UN temporary executive authority (West New Guinea)
UNTSO	UN truce supervision organization
UNTT	UN trust territory
UNUK	UN unified command Korea
UNWCC	UN war crimes commission
UNYOM	UN Yemen observation mission
UO	unobserved; unidentified object(ive); undelivered orders
u/o	used on ...
U&O	use and occupancy
UOC	ultimate operation capability
UOD	ultime oxygen demand; units of optical density
UofSAf	Union of South Africa
UOHC	under other than honorable conditions (US)
UON	unless otherwise noted
UOS	undelivered orders schedule
UOTC	university officer training corps
UOU	underwater operations unit (Philippines)
UP	unidentified position; under proof; under provision (of US); Ulster Parliament; United Province (India); unrotated projectiles (rockets) WW2 (UK); unsaturated polyester
up	upper
UP-3	unrotated projectile (anti-aircraft rocket) WW2 (UK)
UPA-59	IFF decoder by Italtel
UPC	unit production costs; unit processing code
upd	unpaid
UPD-2	airborne surveillance system by

UPD-2	Motorola; APS-94 SLAR, AKT-18 data transmitter (TKQ-2 data receiver)
UPD-4	airborne reconnaissance radar by Goodyear
Update-3	US program to update P-3/S-3 Viking
UPE	unnatural parity exchange
UPO	unit personnel officer
UPOA	Ulster public officers' association
UPP	ultra precision parachute
upr	upper
UpRec	upon receipt
UPS	under provision of section; unit personnel section; uninterrupted power supply; universal polar stereographic (grid)
upslo	upslope
UPSTART	universal parachute support tactical and research target
UPT	undergraduate pilot training (programme)
UPTT	unit personnel and tonnage table
UPU	Universal Postal Union (Berne)
ÜPz	Überwachungspanzer (surveillance tank)
UR	unregistered; uniform regulations (US Army); unfinanced requirements; unsatisfactory report; unattended repeaters
UR-416	armoured car by Rheinstahl
UR-425	Condor, 4x4 armoured car by Thyssen/Henschel
UrActy	your activity
URAD	your radio
Ural-375	truck 8.4 tons (SU)
Ural-377	truck 7.2 tons (SU)
URBM	ultimate range ballistic missile
URC-93	anti-jam frequency-hopping radio by Rockwell/Collins
URC-94	radio by Harris
URC-96	HF SSB transceiver by Southcom
UrDis	your dispatch
URG	underway replenishment group
urg	urgent
URGR	underway replenishment group
URIS	Unite Rapide d'Intervention Sous-marine (submarine rescue ship) by COMEX
URLtr	your letter
URMgm	your mailgram
UrMsg	your message
URN	UHF radio navigation station TACAN
URR	unit readiness report
URP	underwing rocket projectiles
URQ-28	ATDMA terminals by Singer
URS	unmanned repeater station; unit reference sheet
URS-1	Unfallrettungsschere, Hydraulisch by Petig (hydraulic rescue scissors)
URT	upper respiratory tract; unit recruit training
UrTel	your telegram
URu	submachine gun 9mm by INA
Urutu	EE-11, wheeled amphibious personnel carrier by Engesa
URV	undersea research vehicle; undersea rescue vehicle
URZ	universal small arm (Czech) 7.62mm
	AP assault rifle
	LK light machine gun
	TK medium machine gun
	T vehicle mounted machine gun
US	United States (of America); united services; under secretary; underside of slab; unit separator
U/S	unserviceable; useless
US-1	flying boat by Shin Meiwa
US-3A	Viking, utility version by Lockheed
USA	United States of America; Union of South Africa; the United States Army
USAA	US arctic army; United services automobile association (UK)
USAAA	US Army audit agency
USAAvS	US Army agency for aviation safety
USAABMU	US Army aircraft base maintenance unit
USAAC	US Army ambulance corps; US Army air corps --USAAF
USAACDA	US Army aviation combat development agency
USAADCenFB	US Army air defense center and Fort Bliss
USAADEA	US Army air defense engineering agency
USAADS	US Army air defense school (Fort Bliss)
USAADTC	US Army armor and desert training center
USAAF	US Army Air Force
USAAFIME	US Army Air Force in the Middle East
USAAFO	US Army avionics field office
USAAGPC	US Army adjutant general's publication center
USAAPDT	US Army aviation precision demonstration team
USAARL	US Army aeromedical research laboratory (Ft Rucker AL)
USAArmA	US assistant army attache
USAArmHRU	US Army human research unit (Ft Knox KY)
USAArmS	US Army armor school
USAARSB	US Army aviation research safety board (Ft Rucker)
USAAS	US Army air service
USAASC	US Army air service command
USAASD	US Army aeronautical service detachment
	E Europe
	LA Latin America
	Pac Pacific

USAASO   US Army aeronautical service office
USAATC   US Army arctic test center
USAATCO   US Army air transport coordination
  organization
USAAVA   US Army audio-visual agency
USAAvLabs   US Army aviation material
  laboratories
USAAvnC   US Army aviation center
USAAvnHRU   US Army aviation human research
  unit (Ft Rucker)
USAAvnS   US Army aviation school
USAAvnTBd   US Army aviation test board
USAABMDA   US Army advanced ballistic missile
  defense agency
USAAGAR   US Army advisory group army reserve
USAAGNG   US Army advisory group national
  guard
USAAENBD   US Army armor and engineer board
USAArmC   US Army armor center
USAB   US Army Berlin
USABAAR   US Army board for aviation accident
  research
USABioLabs   US Army biological laboratories
USABRL   US Army ballistic research labora-
  tories
USABVAPac   US Army broadcasting and visual
  aids activities Pacific
USAC   US Army commission; US Army corps;
  US air corps
USA/CA   USA/Canada
USACAA   US Army concept analysis agency
USACAC   US Army combined arms center;
  US Army continental army command
USACAK   US Army construction agency Korea
USACAT   US Army culinary arts team
USACATB   US Army combat arms training board
USACC   US Army communications command

A	Alaska
AMC	Army material command
CommAgcy	communications agency
HSC	health services command
MTMC	military traffic management command
USACIDIC	US Army criminal investigations command
USAIntC	US Army intelligence corps

USACC-ConUS   US Army communications command
  contintental USA
USACC-EUR   US Army communications command
  Europe
USACC-Forces   US Army communications command
  Forces
USACCL   US Army coating and chemical
  laboratory
USACC-Pac   US Army communications command
  Pacific
USACC-SAFCA   US Army communications command
  Safeguard communications
  agency

USACCSD   US Army command control
  support detachment
USACC-SigGpAD   US Army communications
  command signal group air
  defense
USACC-SO   US Army communications command
  south
USACC-T   US Army communications command
  Thailand
USACC-TraDoc   US Army communications command
  training and doctrine
  command
USACDA   US Army catalog data agency
USACDC   US Army combat development command
USACDEC   US Army combat developments
  experimentation command
USACEBD   US airborne communications and
  electronics board
USACEEIA   US Army communications electronics
  engineering installation agency
  WH   Western Hemisphere
USACENCDCSA   US Army corps of engineers
  national civil defense
  computer support agency
USACERCOM   US Army communication and elec-
  tronics research command
USACGSC   US Army command and general staff
  college
USAChB   US Army chaplain board
USAChS   US Army chaplain school
USACIDC   US Army criminal investigation
  command
USACIU   US Army command information unit
USACMA   US Army club management agency
USACMR   US Army court of military review
USAComZEur   US Army communications zone
  Europe
USACPEB   US Army central physical evaluation
  board
USACRREL   US Army cold regions research and
  engineering laboratory
USACS   US Army courier service; US Army
  chief of staff
USACSA   US Army communications systems
  agency
USACSC   US Army computer systems command
USACSLA   US Army communications security
  logistics agency
USACSSEA   US Army computer systems support
  and evaluation agency
USADCJ   US Army depot command Japan
USADEG   US Army dependents' education group
USADIP   US Army deserter information point
USADJ   US Army depot Japan
USADP   uniform shipboard automatic data
  processing
USADRB   US Army discharge review board
USAE   US Army engineer
USAEAGSC   US Army Europe adjutant general
  support center

USAEC   US atomic energy commission
USAECBde US Army engineer center brigade
USAEC   US Army electronics command
USAECA   US Army electronic command computa-
          tion agency
USAECFB   US Army engineer center and Fort
          Belvoir
USAEDH   US Army engineer division Huntsville
USAEDLMV US Army engineer division lower
          Mississippi valley
USAEDM   US Army engineer division Mediter-
          ranean
USAEDMR   US Army engineer division Missouri
          River
USAEDNA   US Army engineer division North
          Atlantic
USAEDNC   US Army engineer division North
          Central
USAEDNE   US Army engineer division New
          England
USAEDNP   US Army engineer division North
          Pacific
USAEDOR   US Army engineer division Ohio
          River
USAEDPO   US Army engineer division Pacific
          Ocean
USAEDSA   US Army engineer division South
          Atlantic
USAEDSP   US Army engineer division South
          Pacific
USAEDSW   US Army engineer division South-
          western
USAEEA   US Army enlistment eligibility
          activity
USAEEC   US Army enlisted evaluation center
USAEFMA   US Army electronics command finan-
          cial management agency
USAEHA   US Army environmental hygienic agency
USAEIS   US Army electronic intelligence and
          security
USAEMA   US Army electronics material agency
USAEMCA   US Army engineer mathematical
          computation agency
USAEMSA   US Army electronics material
          support agency
USAEngComEur US Army engineer command Europe
USAEPA   US Army electronics command patent
          agency
USAEPG   US Army electronics proving ground
USAEPMARA US Army Europe personnel manage-
          ment and replacement activity
USAERA   US Army electronics command logistics
          research agency
USAERC   US Army enlisted records center
USAERDAA US Army electronics research and
          development activity Fort
          Huachuca Arizona
USAERDAW US Army electronics research and
          development activity White Sands
          NM

USAERDC   US Army electronics research and
          development command (Adelphi)
USAERDL   US Army electronics research and
          development laboratory
USAERG   US Army engineer reactor group
USAET&DL US Army electronics technology
          and devices laboratory
          ECOM electronics command
USAETL   US Army engineer topographic
          laboratory
USAEU   US Army exhibit unit
USAF   United States armed forces; United
          States Air Force
USAFA   United States Air Force academy
USAFABd   US Army field artillery board
USAFAC   US Army finance and accounting
          center
USAFACFS US Army field artillery center and
          Fort Sill
USAFAL   US Air Force armament laboratory
          (Eglin AFB)
USAFALADTC US Air Force armament laboratory
          armament development and test
          center (Eglin AFB)
USAFAS   US Army field artillery school
USAFB   US Army field band
USAFE   US air forces Europe
USAFESA   US Army facilities engineering
          support agency
USAFI   US armed forces institute (corres-
          pondence courses)
USAFICPA US Army forces in Central Pacific
          Area
USAFIK   US Army forces in Korea
USAFIME   US Army forces in Middle East
USAFINZ   US Army forces in New Zealand
USAFISPA US Army forces in South Pacific
          Area
USAFLant US air forces Atlantic
USAFMS   US Air Force medical service
USAFOCA   US Army field operating cost agency
USAFOF   US Army flight operations facility
USAFR   US Air Force reserve
USAFRed   US Air Force readiness command
USAFSA   US Army forces in South Africa
USAFSBL   US Air Force space biological
          laboratory
USAFSG   US Army field support group
USAFSMS   US Air Force special mission
          service
USAFSo   US Air Force southern command
USAFSS   US Air Force security service
USAG   US Army garrison
USAGMPC   US Army general material and ports
          center
USAH   US Army hospital
USAHC   US Army health clinic
USAHEL   US Army human engineering labora-
          tories
USAHSDSA US Army health services data
          systems agency

USAHTN	US Army hometown news center
USAI	US Army intelligence
USAIA	US Army institute of administration
USAIB	US Army infantry board
USAIC	US Army infantry center
USAICA	US Army inter-agency communications agency
USAICS	US Army intelligence center and school
USAID	US Agency for international development
USAIDR	US Army institute of dental research
USAIG	US aircraft insurance group
USAIIA	US Army image interpretation agency
USAILG	US Army international logistics group
USAIMA	US Army institute for military assistance
USAIMC	US Army inventory management center
USAInfHRU	US Army infantry human research unit (Ft Benning GA)
USAIntA	US Army intelligence agency
USAIntC	US Army intelligence corps
USAirA	US air attache
USAIRE	US aerospace industries representative in Europe
USAirMilComUNO	US Army air corps representative military staff committee UNO
USAIRR	US Army investigation records repository
USAIS	US Army infantry school
USAISR	US Army institute for surgical research (Ft Sam, Houston TX)
USAITFG	US Army intelligence threats and forecasts groups
USAJFKCenMA	US Army John F. Kennedy center for military assistance
USAJSC	US Army joint support command
USAKorSCom	US Army Korea support command
USALAPA	US Army Los Angeles procurement agency
USALdrHRU	US Army leadership human research unit (Presidion of Monterey CA)
USALEA	US Army logistics evaluation agency
USALMC	US Army logistics management center
USALSA	US Army legal services agency
USALWL	US Army limited war laboratory
USAMAA	US Army memorial affairs agency
USAMCFG	US Army medical center Fort Gordon
USAManRRDC	US Army manpower resrouces research and development center
USAMBRDL	US Army medical bio-engineering research and development laboratory (Ft Detrick MD)
USAMC	US Army material command; US Army missile command; US Army mobility command; US Army munitions command; US Army missile corporation -- Honest John
USAMCC	US Army metrology and calibration center
USAMD	US Army missile detachment
USAMDAR	US Army medical depot activity Ryukyu Islands
USAMedComEur	US Army medical command Europe
USAMedS	US Army medical service
USAMedTC	US Army medical training center (Ft Sam, Houston TX)
USAMedSVS	US Army medical service veterinary school
USAMEOS	US Army medical equipment and optical school
USAMERC	US Army mobility equipment research center (Ft Belvoir)
USAMERDC	US Army mobility equipment research and development center (Ft Belvoir)
USAMFSS	US Army medical field service school
USAMHRC	US Army military history research collection
USAMIDA	US Army major item data agency
USAMIIA	US Army medical intelligence and information agency
USAML	US Army medical laboratory
USAMMA	US Army medical material agency Pac Pacific
USAMMCS	US Army missile and munitions center school
USAMMT	US Army military mail terminal
USAMP	US Army mine planter
USAmphibFor	US amphibious forces
USAMPS	US Army military police school; US Army motion pictures service
USAMRDC	US Army medical research and development command (Washington DC)
USAMRIID	US Army medical research institute of infectious diseases (Ft Detrick MD)
USAMRL	US Army medical research laboratory (Ft Knox KY)
USAMRNL	US Army medical research and nutrition laboratory (Denver Co)
USAMRU	US Army medical research unit (Panama, Malaysia)
USAMS	US Army management school
USAMSSA	US Army management systems support agency
USANCG	US Army nuclear cratering group
USANCSG	US Army nuclear and chemical surety group
USANDL	US Army nuclear defense laboratory
USANWTC	US Army northern warfare training center
USAOC&S	US Army ordnance center and school
USAOD	US Army ordnance department
USAORRF	US Army ordnance rocket research facility

USAOTEA   US Army operational test and evaluation agency
USAPACDA   US Army personnel and administration combat developments agency
USAPAE   US Army procurement agency Europe
USAPDA   US Army physical disability agency
USAPDCE   US Army petroleum distribution command Europe
USAPDSC   US Army personnel data support center
USAPDSK   US Army petroleum distribution system Korea
USAPEB   US Army physical evaluation board
USAPersCen   US Army personnel center
USAPG   US Army participation group
USAPHC   US Army primary helicopter center
USAPHS   US Army primary helicopter school
USAPIA   US Army personnel information activity
USAPOP   US Army port operations Pusan
USAPRC   US Army physical review council
USAPSG   US Army personnel security group
USAQMCenFL   US Army quartermaster center and Ft Lee
USAQMS   US Army quartermaster school
USAR   US Army reserve
USArADBd   US Army air defense board
USArADCom   US Army air defense command
USArRAE   US Army reserve affairs Europe
USArAl   US Army Alaska
USARB   US Army retraining brigade
USArBCO   US Army base command Okinawa
USARC   US Army reserve center
USARCPC   US Army reserve components personnel center
USArCS   US Army claims service
USARDA   US Army regional dental activity
USARDL   US Army research and development laboratories
USARDORAG   US Army research and development operational research advisory group
USARec   US Army recruiting command
USARecSta   US Army reception station
USARet-RsgSta   US Army returnee- reassignment station
USArEur   US Army Europe
USArEurAGLO   US Army Europe adjutant general liaison office
USArEurCSTC   US Army Europe combat support training center
USArFT   US Army forces Taiwan
USARIBSS   US Army research institute for the behavioral and social sciences
USARIEM   US Army research institute of environmental medicine (Natick MA)
USArJ   US Army Japan
USArLant   US Army forces Atlantic
USArmA   US Army attache
USArMis   US Army mission

USArmLO   US Army liaison officer
USAROTCR   US Army reserve officers' training corps region
USARP   US arctic research program; US Atlantic research program
USArPA   US Army publications agency
USArPacIntS   US Army Pacific intelligence school
USARR   US Army readiness regions
USArRed   US Army forces readiness command
USArSo   US Army forces southern command
PR   Puerto Rico
USArSupThai   US Army support Thailand
USArV   US Army Viet Nam
USAS   Univac standard airlines system (computer)
USASA   US Army security agency (Ft Devens Mass.)
USASACDA   US Army security agency combat development activity
USASACDSA   US Army security agency command data systems activity
USASADEA   US Army signal air defense engineering agency
USASAE   US Army security agency Europe
USASAFO   US Army signal avionics field office
USASAPac   US Army security agency Pacific
USASARC   US Army system acquisition review council
USASASA   US Army small arms systems agency; US Army security agency systems activity
USASASSA   US Army security agency signal security activity
USASatComA   US Army satellite communications agency
USASATC&S   US Army security agency training center and school
USASATEC   US Army security agency test and evaluation center
USASCA   US Army satellite communications agency
USASCAF   US Army service center for the armed forces
USASCC   US Army strategic communications command
USASC&FG   US Army signal center and Ft Gordon
USASCH   US Army support command Hawaii
USASCS   US Army signal center and school
USASD   US Army student detachment
USASESS   US Army Southeastern signal school
USASETAF   US Army Southern European task
USASEXC   US armed services exploitation center (Australia)
USASF   US Army special forces
USASFV   US Army special forces Viet Nam
USASG   US Army standardization group
CA   Canada
UK   United Kingdom

USASI   USA standards institute
            --ANSI
USASigC   US Army signal corps
USASigS   US Army signal school
USASMA   US Army sergeants major academy
USASMC   US Army supply and maintenance
            command
USASMSA   US Army signal material support
            agency
USASOPac US Army support office Pacific
USASOS   US Army service of supplies
USASPSAE US Army special services agency
            Europe
USASPTCM US Army support center Memphis
USASptAP US Army support activity Philadel-
            phia
USASRDL   US Army signal research and devel-
            opment laboratory
USASSA   US Army signal supply agency
USASSG   US Army special security group
USASupCom US Army support command
            CRB   Cam Ranh Bay
            QN   Qui Nhon
            Sgn   Saigon
USAT   US Army transport
USATACom US Army tank automotive command
USATAWH   US Army transportation agency
            White House
USATC   US Army training center; US armor
            training center (Ft Knox KY)
USATCEFLW US Army training center engineer
            and Ft Leonard Wood
USATCEur US Army terminal command Europe
USATCFA   US Army training center field
            artillery Ft Sill Okla
USATCFE   US Army transportation center and
            Ft Eustis
USATCInf US Army training center infantry
            Ft Dix NJ, Ft Jackson SC,
            Ft Ord CA, Ft Polk LA
USATDGL   US Army terminal detachment Great
            Lakes
USATEC   US Army test and evaluation command
USATMACE US Army traffic management agency
            Central Europe
USATMC   US Army troop medical clinic
USATopoCom US Army topographic command
USATP   US Army tank plant (Detroit)
USATrEOG US Army transportation environmen-
            tal operations group
USATrfSta US Army transfer station
USATSA   US Army technical support activity
USATSC   US Army terrestrial sciences center
USATSch   US Army transportation school
USATTAY   US Army transportation test activity
            Yuma
USATTC   US Army tropical test center
USATUC   US Army terminal unit Canaveral
USAWC   US Army weapons command; US Army
            war college

USAWES   US Army waterways experiment station
USB   United States of Brazil; United
            States band; upper surface blowing
            (STOL aircraft)
USBATU   US-Brazil aviation training unit
USBC   US bureau of the census
USBer   US mission Berlin
USBRO   US base requirements overseas
USBSS   US bureau of service standards
USC-... digital communications system by
            Collins
USC   Ulster special constabulary;
            US code; US citizen; under
            separate cover; united service
            corps; united service club;
            United States of Columbia
USCA   US civil authorities; US code
            annotated; united services
            catholic association
USCAEC   US congressional atomic energy
            commission
USCAO   US civil administration Okinawa
USCC   US circuit court
USCCA   US circuit court of appeals
USCCPA   US court of customs and patent
            appeals
USCG   US coast guard
USCGA   US coast guard academy
USCGAD   US coast guard air detachment
USCGAS   US coast guard air station
USCGC   US coast guard cutter
USCGR   US coast guard reserve
USCGS   US coast and geodetic survey
USC&GSS US coast and geodetic survey ship
USCIIC   US civilian internees information
            center
USCinCAFRed commander in chief, US air
            forces readiness command
USCinCEur US commander in chief Europe
USCinCMEAFSA   US commander in chief Middle
            East, Southern Asia and
            Africa South of the Sahara
USCinCRed commander in chief US readiness
            command
USCinCSo commander in chief Southern
            Command
USCMA   US court of military appeals
USCOA   uniformed services contingency
            option act
USCoB   US commander Berlin
USCom-   US commander
USComEastLant US naval commander Eastern
            Atlantic
USComSubGruEastLant US naval commander
            submarines group
            Eastern Atlantic
USConArC US continental army command
USCorps united service corps
USCSB   US communications security board
USCSC   US civil service commission

USCSupp   US code supplement
USD-501   Midge, CL-89, universal surveillance
          drone by Canadair
USD-502   CL-289, improved Midge by Canadair
USDA   US department of agriculture
USDAO   US defense attache office
USDB   US disciplinary barracks
USDC   US department of commerce
USDCFO   US defense communication field
          office
USDelIADB   US delegation inter-American
            defense board
USDHEW   US department of health education and
          welfare
USDI   US department of the interior
USDL   US department of labor
USDocOLandSouthEast   US document office
                      allied land forces
                      Southeastern Europe
USDLGI   US defense liaison group Indonesia
USDRE   under-secretary of defense for
          research and engineering (US)
USDSEA   US dependents' schools European area
USE   United States of Europe
usea   undersea
USec   under-secretary
USED   US engineer department
USEES   US (naval) engineering experimental
          station
USElmCENTO   US element central treaty
             organization
USEP   US escapee program
USER   user interest file (for NARDIS)
USES   US employment service
USESSA   US environmental sciences services
          administration
USEuCom   US European Command
USF   US forces; US fleet
USFAirWingMed   US fleet air wing Mediter-
                ranean
USFBI   US forces in the British Isles;
          US federal bureau of investigation
USFC   united service flying club
USFET   US forces European Theater
USFG   US forces in Germany
USFK   US forces in Korea
USForAz   US forces in the Azores
USFR   US fleet reserve
US/FRG   US/Federal Republic of Germany
USG   US government; US standard gauge
USGB   US geographic board
USGLI   US government life insurance
USGPO   US government printing office
USGS   US geological survey
          universal space guidance system
          --Titan
USGW   underwater-to-surface guided weapon
USH-24   analog sonar tape recorder by Bell
          & Howell
USH-32   ASW acoustic data recorder by Bell
          & Howell

USHBP   uniformed services health benefits
          program (US)
USHL   US hygienic laboratory
USHP   US helium plant
USI   united services institution
          --RUSI
          user system interface
USIA   US information agency
USIB   US intelligence board
USICA   US international communications
          agency
USIS   US intelligence service; US infor-
          mation service
USJCA   US joint communications agency
USJCS   US joint chiefs of staff
USJTF   US joint task force
USJUWTF   US joint unconventional warfare
          task force
USL   underwater sound laboratory
          (Ft Trumbell); US lines;
          US legation
USLADR   Ulster Scottish light air defence
          regiment TAVR
USLant   US Atlantic subarea (Nato)
USLO   US (Navy) liaison officer
USM   US mail; US Marines; underwater-to-
          surface missile; ultra-sonic
          machining
USM-407   EQUATE, electronic quality assur-
          ance test equipment by RCA
USMA   US military academy
USMAC   US military assistance command
          Thai   Thailand
          V   Viet Nam
USMAPS   US military academy preparatory
          school
USMAPU   US military academy preparatory unit
USMB   US marine barracks
USMC   US marine corps; US maritime
          commission
USMCEB   US military communication elec-
          tronics board
USMCR   US marine corps reserve
USMCRF   US fleet marine corps reserve
USMCRO   US organized marine corps reserve
USMCRV   US volunteer marine corps reserve
USMCW   US marine corps women
USMCWR   US marine corps women's reserve
USMD   US medical department
USMemMilComUNO   US members military staff
                 committee UNO
USMG   US military government
USMH   US marine hospital
USMI   US military intelligence
USMilComUNO   US delegation military staff
              committee UNO
USMLMCinCGSFG   US military liaison mission
                to commander in chief group
                of Soviet forces in Germany
USMPC   US military pay certificate

USMS   US maritime service
USMSCIAP US manual of criteria of standard
            instrument approach procedures
            --TERPS
USMSFFT US military service funded foreign
            training
USMSI   US military service institution
USMSOS US maritime service officers school
USMSTS US maritime service training school
USMTMSA US military training mission to
            Saudi Arabia
USN   United States Navy
USNA   US naval academy (Annapolis Md.);
            US national army
USNAA   US naval air arm
USNAS   US naval air services
USNato US mission to the Nato
USNavForConAD US naval forces continental
            air defense command
USNavM US naval mission
USNavMilComUN US navy representative mili-
            tary staff committee UN
USNavSo US naval forces Southern command
USNavWeaServ US naval weather service
USNavyMilComUNO US navy representative
            military staff committee
            UNO
USNC   US national committee
USND   US naval department
USNDD   US Navy dry docks
USNEES US naval engineering experimental
            station
USNESC US naval electronic systems command
USNF   US naval forces
USNFR   US naval fleet reserve
USNG   US national guard
USNH   US naval hospital
USNHO   US Navy hydrographic office
USNI   US naval institute (Annapolis Md.)
USN-I   US Navy inductee
USN-I-CB US Navy inductee construction
            battalion
USN-ISA US Navy inductee special assignment
USNLO   US naval liaison officer
USNM   US naval mission; US naval militia
USNMI   US Navy medical institute
USNMPS US Navy motion picture service
USNMR   US national military representative
USNMRC US naval manpower (research) center
USNOSC US naval ordnance systems command
USNOO   US naval oceanographic office
USNObsySubSta US naval observatory (time
            service) sub-station
USNPGS US Navy post graduate school
USNR   US naval reserve; US Navy retired
USN-Ret US Navy retired
USNR-R US naval reserve retired
USNR-S1...2 US naval reserve standby 1
            (mobilization)
USNR-SV US naval reserve selective volunteer

USNS   US Navy ship (civilian crew);
            US naval station
USNSSC US naval sea systems command
USN-SV US Navy selective volunteer
USNTEC US naval training equipment center
            (Orlando Fla)
USNTI   US Navy travel instructions
USNTS   US naval torpedo station (Keyport)
USNUSL US Navy underwater sound laboratory
USN&USMCRTC US Navy and US Marine Corps
            reserve training center
USO   united services organization (US);
            unit security officer; under
            secretary's office; US (presiden-
            tial) order
USofA   under secretary of the Army (US)
USofS   under secretary of State (US-UK)
USOID   US overseas international defense
USOM   US operations mission
USOWI   US office of war information
USP   US patent; utility seaplane;
            US property
USPat   US patent
USPFO   US property and fiscal officer
USPHS   US public health service
USPO   US post office
USPS   US postal service
USPSR   US public service reserve
USPWIC US prisoner of war information
            center
USQ-20 digital computer by Univac
USR   US reserves; Usher of the Scarlet
            Rod,Officer of the Most Honour-
            able Order of the Bath (UK)
USRA   universities space research associa-
            tions (US)
USRC   US reserve corps
USRD   underwater sound reference division
            ONR
USRedCom US readiness command
USRepMilComUNO US representative, military
            staff committee UNO
USRepO US (naval) reporting officer
USRL   underwater sound reference
            laboratory
USRNMC US representative to Nato military
            committee
USRO   US routing office; US mission to
            the Nato and European regional
            associations
USS   US ship; US senate; US standard
            (thread)
USSA   US security authority (for Nato
            affairs)
USSAC   US security authority for CENTO
            affairs
USSAF   US strategic air force; US strate-
            gic army force
USSAFE US strategic air force Europe
USSAH   US soldiers' and airmen's home

US-SALEP US-South Africa leader exchange
          program
USSAS   US security authority for SEATO
          affairs
USSB   US shipping board
USSBS   US strategic bombing survey
USSC   US supreme court
USSCt   US supreme court
USSD   US state department
USSDP   uniformed services savings deposits
          program (US)
USSecMilComUNO the secretary US delegation
                military staff committee
                UNO
USSG   US standard gauge
USSID   US signal intelligence directive
USSM   united systems simulation model
USSouthCom US Southern command
USSP   universal sensor signal processor
          (USAF)
USSR   Union of the Soviet Socialist
          Republics
USSS   US secret service; US steam ship
USSSO   US sending state office
USStAFE   US strategic air force Europe
USTC   US training camp; US tariff
          commission
USTDC   US Taiwan defense command
USTOL   ultra-short take-off and landing
          (aircraft)
USTS   US travel service
USV   US volunteers
USVB   US veterans' bureau
USVH   US veterans' hospital
USW   ultra-short waves; undersea warfare;
          under secretary of war
USWACC   US women's army corps center
USWACS   US women's army corps school
USWB   US weather bureau
USWBC   US war ballot commission
USWD   US war department; under-surface war-
          fare division
USWDiv   undersea warfare division
USWI   US West Indies
USWP   ultra-short wave propagation panel
USWV   united Spanish war veterans
UT   underway trial; universal time;
          user test; under training;
          universal trainer
ut   utilities
UTA   upper terminal (control) area; unit
          training assembly
UTAD   Utah army depot (US)
UTAP   unified transportation assistance
          programme
UTC   universal time coordinated; unit
          training camp; unit training
          center; university training corps;
          United Telephone Company; United
          Technologies Corporation

UTCS   urban traffic control system
utd   united
UTE   universal test equipment
UTIAS   university of Toronto institute for
          aerospace studies
util   utility
UTM   universal transversal Mercator
          (grid)
UTN   urban telephone network
UTP   upper turning point
UTrnsRon utility transport squadron
UTROAA   units to round out the active
          (US Army)
UtRon   utility squadron
UTS   universal time standards; universal
          time sharing (system); United
          Telephone System; underwater
          telephone system; ultimate
          tensile strength
UTTAS   utility tactical transport aircraft
          system (US helicopter programme)
UTU   underwater training unit
UtWing   utility wing
UtWingServ utility wing service force
            Lant Atlantic
            Pac   Pacific
UU   Ulster Unionist
UUI   United Utilities Incorporated
UUM   underwater-to-underwater missile
UUM-44A   underwater-to-underwater missile
          nuclear anti-submarine rocket by
          Goodyear
UUT   unit under test
UUUC   United Ulster Unionist Council
          (Armagh)
UV   ultra-violet (light); unidentified
          vessel
UV-18   Twin Otter, utility aircraft
UVAS   ultra-violet astronomical satellite
UVASER   ultra-violet amplification by
          stimulated emission of radiation
UVC   unidirectional voltage converter
UVCo   united veterans' council (US)
UVDC   urban vehicle development competi-
          tion
UVE-ROM   ultra-violet erasable read only
          memory by Litton
UVF   Ulster volunteer force
UVFDS   ultra-violet flame detection system
UVL   ultra-violet light
UVP   Union pour les Ventes des Produits
          late: Euromissile MBB+Nord
          Aviation
UW   unconventional warfare; under-
          water; underwater weapon (UK);
          unladen weight
UWayTU   underway training unit
UWayTUNorVa underway training unit Norfolk
             Va
UWCE   underwater weapons counter-measures
          establishment

UWF	unconventional warfare forces	UXO	unexploded ordnance
UWFCS	underwater fire control system	UXOI	unexploded ordnance incident
UWOA	unconventional warfare operations area (US)	UYA-4	data display by NTDS by Hughes
UWordTech	underwater ordnance technician	UYK-7	digital naval computer
UWSEC	underwater weapons systems engineering centre	UYK-20	standard shipboard computer by Univac
		UYK-502	SHINPADS by Sperry
uwtr	underwater	UYQ-19	digital tactical computer by Singer
UWWP	underwater working party (RN)	UYQ-21	standard display console by Hughes
UXB	unexploded bomb	UYS-1	Proteus, acoustic processor by IBM
UXC-4	tactical laser facsimile transceiver by Litton	UZI	machine pistol 9mm by IMI
		UZRG	fuse for hand grenades (SU)
		Uzushio	class, submarines (JMSDF)

V

V	volunteer; vice; victory; Viscount; venerable; versus; Volt; vector; vanadium; valve; velocity; ventral; vertical; voice; volume; Bremer Vulkan Schiffbau & Maschinenfabrik
V-day	victory day
V-1	Fi-103, Vergeltungswaffe WW2 (GE) (flying bomb)
V-2	A-4, Vergeltungswaffe WW2 (GE) (ballistic missile)
V-40	small fragmentation grenade by NWM
V-100	wheeled armoured vehicle by Cadillac Gage
V-150	infantry combat vehicle by Cadillac Gage
V-538	Fantrainer, aircraft by VFW/Vought
VA	vice admiral; voucher attached; Member of the Order of Victoria and Albert; vital area; vulnerable area; volunteer army; veterans' administration (US); veterans' association; carrier-borne light attack squadron (USN); value analysis; visual aids; volt amperes; Vickers Armstrong Ltd
VAAC	vanadyl-acetyl-acetonate
VAAFA	vintage aircraft and flying association (Brooklands UK)
VAB	vertical assembly building (Nasa); vehicle assembly building
VAB	Vehicule de l'Avant Blindee by Creussot Loire (wheeled armoured vehicle)

	VCAC	anti-tank
	VMP	riot control
	ECH	recovery workshop
	AMB	ambulance
	VTM	mortar carrier
	VPM	mortar carrier
	VTT	troop carrier

VABPF	vice admiral British Pacific fleet
VABM	vertical angle bench mark
VAC	Volts alternating current; vector analogue computer; veterans' administration center (US)

vac	vacuum; vacant; vacancy; vacation
VACNAS	vice-admiral commanding North Atlantic station
VACR	variable amplitude correction rack
VAD	voluntary army department; voluntary ambulance detachment; voluntary aid detachment WW1 (UK); veterans' administration domiciliary; vice-admiral, destroyers (RN)
VADAR	Vehicule Autonome de Defense Anti-aerienne by Saviem (anti-aircraft vehicle twin guns + radar)
VAdm	vice admiral
VADS	Vulcan air defence system
VAF	department of veterans' affairs (Canada)
VAG	vice adjutant general
VAH	heavy attack squadron (USN); veterans' administration hospital (US); fixed-wing attack aircraft, heavy naval
VAJ	fixed-wing attack aircraft, jet; fixed-wing attack aircraft squadron (USN)
VAK-191	experimental VTOL aircraft by VFW/Fokker
VAK-702	IR line-scanner pod
VAL	vehicle authorization list; vertical assault lift; fixed-wing attack aircraft, light; fixed-wing attack aircraft, light squadron (USN)
val	value; valley
Valentine Tank	WW2 (UK)
Valentine Scorpion	mine-sweeper tank flail WW2 (UK)
Valiant	class, submarines RN 1962-71 by Vickers; bomber/tanker/recce aircraft by Vickers; FV-4030/3 interim main battle tank by Vickers
Valkyrie	XB-70, Mach 3 bomber by North American
Valmara-69	anti-personnel jumping mine by Valsella

Valmet-76   assault rifle 7.62mm or 5.56mm
            by Valmet
VAM   virtual access method; vice-admiral,
          Malta (RN)
VAMCo   Valley Automatic Machine Company
VAMOS   verified additional military occupa-
          tional speciality
VAMP   visual approach for management plan-
          ning; variable anamorphic motion
          picture; visual acoustic magnetic
          pressure
Vamp   modular automatic portable test set
          for field maintenance by SFENA
VAMPIR   Veille au mer Panorama Infra-Rouge
          by SAT (airborne infra-red sur-
          veillance equipment)
Vampire   jet fighter aircraft by DeHavilland
VAN   value added networks
van   advanced
VAND   vacuum air nitrogen distribution
          system
VANDPF   Viet Nam alliance of national demo-
          cratic and popular forces
Vanessa   naval anti-aircraft missile by OTO
Vanguard aircraft by Vickers
Vanneau   AQM-37, target drone by Beech (FR
          design)
Van Speijk   class, frigates (NL)
VANWACE   vulnerability analysis of nuclear
          weapons in allied command Europe
          (US)
Vanya   class, coastal minesweepers (SU)
VAO   veterans' administrative office;
          voting assistance officer
VAP   video audio participative;
          fixed-wing attack/patrol aircraft;
          attack squadron (propeller) (USN);
          4x4 amphibious logistic support
          vehicle by ENASA
VAP-3550 amphibious truck by ENASA
VAPI   visual approach path indicator
VAPO   vaporizing oil
VapPrf   vapour proof
VAPS   VSTOL approach system
VAQ   carrier-borne electronic warfare
          squadron (USN)
VAQ-3   tank laser rangefinder by Selenia
VAQBPF   vice-admiral, administration British
          Pacific fleet
VAR   volunteer air reserve; visual aural
          range; vertical air rocket
var   variation; variant; variety
VAR-10   anti-personnel mine by Tecnovar
VAR-100   anti-personnel mine by Tecnovar
          SP extended action
varactor variable capacitor
Varan   airborne surveillance radar by
          Thomson
VarCond   variable condenser
VARES   Vega aircraft enhancing system

VARIG   illumination mine by Tecnovar
varistor variable resistor
varN   variation of direction (magnetic
          north - true north)
VARO   veterans' administration regional
          office
VARP   Viet Nam asset reconciliation
          procedure
VARS   vertical and azimuth reference
          system
VAS   visible infra-red spin-scan radio-
          meter atmospheric sounder
          (satellite weather forecast
          system) by Hughes
VASI   visual approach slope indicator
VASRD   veterans' administration schedule
          for rating disabilities (US)
VAST   versatile avionics shop test (equip-
          ment) by Rockwell; versatile auto-
          matic shop test
VAT   value-added tax
VATE   versatile automatic test equipment
VATLS   visual airborne target location
          system
VATS   versatile avionics test shop
Vautour   light bomber by SNCASO
VAW   carrier-borne early warning and
          fighter guidance squadron (USN);
          Vereinigte Aluminiumwerke
          (Hannover)
VAX   fixed-wing attack aircraft experi-
          mental
VB   volunteer battalion; dive bomber
          squadron (USN); vertical bomber;
          vehicle-borne
VBC   Vehicule Blinde de Combat by
          Renault (6x6 combat vehicle)
VBC-90   Vehicule Blinde Cenon 90mm (6x6
          armoured combat vehicle) by Saviem
VBF   fighter bomber squadron (USN)
VBH   Verbindungs- und Beobachtungs-
          Hubschrauber (liaison and recon-
          naissance helicopter)
VBS   Vehicule Blinde Sanite (ambulance
          tank) AMX-13
VBTP   Vehicule Blinde de Transport de
          Personnel (armoured personnel
          carrier)
VC   (winner of the) Victoria Cross (UK);
          veterinary corps (US); Viet Cong;
          Vietnamese communist; voyage
          charter; fleet composite squadron
          (USN); vice-chairman; vice-consul;
          vice-chancellor; variable contrast
          (photo paper); vector control;
          voice control; vinyl chloride;
          valuation clause
VC-9   carrier-borne cargo aircraft by McDD
VC-10   strategic transport aircraft by BAC
VC-400   VTOL project (cancelled) by VFW/
          Fokker

VCA   virtual crystal approximation; volunteer civic association (US)

VCAC   Mephisto, Lancelot, Vehicule de Combat Anti-Chars by Saviem (6x6 anti-tank vehicle with HOT)

VCAS   vice chief of the air staff; visual close air support

VCC   vice-chancellor's committee; Viet Cong captured; valve control coordinator

VCC-80   armoured personnel carrier by OTO

VCCS   vehicle command and control system by Hazeltine; voltage controlled current source

VCD   variable centre distance

VCDS   vice chief of the defence staff (UK-CAN)

VCE   voltage, collector-emitter; variable cycle engine (for aircraft)

VCG   vice consul general; vertical centre of gravity; Vehicule de Combat du Génie (engineer combat vehicle)

VCH   vinyl-cyclo-hexane

VCI   volatile corrosion inhibitor; Vehicule de Combat d'Infanterie by Saviem (6x6 infantry combat vehicle)

VCIGS   vice chief of the Imperial general staff

VCIM   Vehicule de Combat d'Infanterie Mécanisée (mechanized infantry combat vehicle)

VCL   Vehicule de Commandement et de Liaison (4x4 amphibious jeep Eurojeep by Saviem + MAN + FIAT

VCM   vacuum condensable material

vcm   vacuum

VCNM   vice chief of naval management

VCNO   vice chief of naval operations

VCNS   vice chief of the naval staff

vcnty   vicinity

VCO   viceroy's commissioned officer (Indian Army); voltage controlled oscillator

VCOAD   voluntary committee on overseas aid and development

VCofGwBS   Vietnamese Cross of Gallantry with bronze star

VCofGwGS   Vietnamese Cross of Gallantry with gold star

VCofGwP   Vietnamese Cross of Gallantry with palm

VCofGwSS   Vietnamese Cross of Gallantry with silver star

VCP   visual control post; vehicle collection post; vehicle check post

VCR   variable compression ratio (piston); video cassette recorder; visual control room

VCR   wheeled armoured personnel carrier by Panhard
    TT 6x6 troop transport by Panhard
    TH 6x6 anti-tank HOT by Panhard

VCS   vice chief of staff; Viet Cong suspect; cruiser scouting squadron; versatile console system by Vosper; Vehicule Canon by Saviem

VCSA   vice chief of staff (US Army)

VCS/LNS   vehicle command system land navigation system by Bendix

VCT   Vehicule à Combat à Tourelle by Saviem (6x6 combat vehicle with turret)

VCVS   voltage controlled voltage source

VCXO   voltage controlled crystal oscillator

VD   venereal disease; various dates; Volunteer (officers') decoration (RN); Veteran (officers') decoration (RN); photographic squadron (USN); volume damper; vapour density

VDA   variable depth ASDIC; anti-aircraft defence vehicle by Panhard

VDAA   Vehicule d'Auto-Defense Anti-Aerienne

VDC   volunteer defence corps (Thailand); venereal disease clinic; volts direct current

VDDS   very deep draught ship

VDev   Victory device (US)

VDF   VHF direction finder

VDFS   VHF direction finder system

VDG   vertical display generator

VDP   very displaced persons; volunteer (reservist) in drill pay status

VDR   variable diameter rotor

VDRL-test   venereal disease research laboratory

VDS   variable depth sonar

VDT   variable density (wind) tunnel; video tape terminal

VDU   visual display unit

VE   vocational education; air evacuation squadron (USN); value engineering; valve engineering; vibration eliminator; nerve gas

VE-day   victory in Europe day 8 May 1945

VEA   vehicles excise act 1962

VEB   variable elevation beam

vec   vector

VECP   value engineering change proposal (US)

Vector-V   airborne radar warning receiver by Itek

VEES   vehicle engine exhaust smoke system

veg   vegetation

Vega   fire control system by Thomson

Vegesack   class, coastal mine sweepers (FGN)

VEH   vehicles and vehicle equipment
           STANAG
VEI   value engineered indicator
vel   velocity
Vela   nuclear detection satellite (US)
Veltro-II MB-339K, close air support air-
           craft by Aer Macchi
Vengeance dive bomber WW2 (India)
           by Vultee
VENISS   visual education national information
           service for schools
Venom   DH-112, jet fighter 1949 by
           deHavilland
vent   ventilated; ventilation
Ventura   day bomber WW2 by Lockheed
Venus   night-vision system for helicopters
           TRT
VEOS   versatile electro-optic system IR+
           TV+laser naval surveillance by
           Hughes
VEP   value engineering proposal
VEPM   value engineering program manager
           (US)
VEQ   visiting enlisted quarters (US)
VER   visual evoked response
ver   verify
VERA   versatile experimental reactor
           assembly; vision electronic
           recording apparatus; Verfahren zur
           Ermittlung der Rangfolge von
           Alternativen
Verey   light illumination cartridge
Vericrypt cryptographic system by BBC
           (Switz)
Verograph anti-aircraft trainer by Contraves
           1937
vert   vertical
Vert-2-exp vertical double expansion
           (engine)
Vert-3-exp vertical triple expansion
           (engine)
Vert-4-exp vertical quadruple expansion
           (engine)
Vertical-4 satellite transport missile (SU)
VertRep   vertical replenishment (Nato)
Very light illumination cartridge
ves   vessel
VesCa   vessels and cargo
VESPER   voluntary enterprises and services
           and part time employment for the
           retired
VET   verbal test
vet   veteran (US); veterinarian; veterin-
           ary
VetAdmin   veterans' administration (US)
Vetronix   Veterans Electronics Communications
           Inc. (Manila)
VetSci   veterinary science

VetSurg   veterinary surgeon
VF   day fighter squadron (USN); carrier-
           borne interceptor day fighter;
           voice frequency; variable frequen-
           cy; video frequency; frequency
           voltage; very fine; visual field;
           rail movements and transport
           STANAG
VF-band   voice frequency band
VFA   visiting forces act
VFAW   carrier-borne fixed-wing fighter
           all-weather capable
VFB   fixed-wing carrier-borne fighter
           bomber; fixed-wing carrier-borne
           fighter squadron (USN)
VFC   video film converter; voltage-to-
           frequency converter
VFGH   Valley Forge general hospital (US)
VFN   carrier-borne fixed-wing night
           fighter; carrier-borne fixed-wing
           squadron (USN)
VFO   voice frequency operated; variable
           frequency oscillator
VFOAR   Vandenberg field office for aero-
           space research (USAF)
VFP   variable factor planning; light
           photographic squadron (USN)
VFR   visual flight rules
VFT   voice frequency telegraphy
VFTG   voice frequency telegraphy (terminal)
VFU   vertical format unit (computer)
VFW   veterans of foreign wars (US);
           Vereinigte Flugtechnische Werke
           (Bremen)
VFW-614   maritime patrol aircraft by VFW
VG   vicar general; very good; Vickers
           gun; voice grade; velocity gravity;
           vinylene-glycol; vertical gyro-
           scope; variable geometry (air-
           craft)
VGA   vocational guidance association
VGC   very good condition; viscocity
           gravity constant
VGF   escort fighter squadron (USN)
VGPI   visual glide path indicator; visual
           ground position indicator
VGS   escort/scouting squadron (USN)
VH   helicopter rescue squadron (USN);
           helicopter (USN); very heavy;
           very high; heater voltage
VHA   very high altitude
VHB   very heavy bombardment
VHC   very highly commended
VHF   very high frequencies
VHFDF   VHF direction finder
VHF/UHF   VHF and ultra high frequencies
VHMCP   voluntary home mortgage credit programme
VHO   very high output
VHRR   very high resolution radiometer
           (satellite camera) by RCA

VHSI   very high speed integrated(circuits)
VHSIC   very high speed integrated circuits
VI   volume indicator; viscosity index;
            vertical interval (map);
            Virginian Islands; Vancouver
            Island
VIAS   voice interference analysis system
VIB   vertical integration building
vib   vibration
vic   vicinity; victualling; Victoria
ViceAdm   vice admiral
VICI   velocity indicating coherent
            integrator
Vickers-303 medium machine gun by Vickers
VICOM   visual communications management
VICON   visual confirmation (of voice take-
            off clearance) green light box
Victor   bomber, tanker, recce by Handley
            Page 1958; P-68, light twin engined
            aircraft by Partenavia
VID   very important document; volunteers
            for international development
VIDAR   velocity indication detection and
            ranging; visual detection and
            ranging
VideoTrack electro-optic naval fire control
            system by SAAB
VIDIAC   vidicon input to automatic computer
VIFF   (thrust) vectoring in forward flight
Viggen   jet combat aircraft by Saab
            AJ-37 ground attack version
            JA-37 all-weather interceptor
Vigilant light anti-tank guided weapon by
            BAC
Vigilante 35mm anti-aircraft gun project by
            Sperry (cancelled); A-5, Mach 2
            bomber, recce, EW aircraft;
            class, coastal patrol boat by
            CMN
VII   viscocity index improver
Vikasol   vitamin K solution (tablet)
Viking   Mars probe by Martin Marietta;
            S-3, anti-submarine aircraft by
            Lockheed
vil   village
VIM   very important mail; vertical
            improved mail (service)
VIMS   vertical improved mail service
VIM-625   metallic mine detector (SU)
Vimy   double-decker aircraft 1919 by
            Vickers
VIN   vehicle identification number
Vindicator SB-2U, dive bomber WW2 by Vought/
            Sikorsky
VINS   very intensive neutron source
VIO   visual intercept officer;
            veterinary investigation officer
viol   violation
VIP   very important person; versatile
            information processing; visual

            image processor; value improvement
            project; visual identification
            point
Viper   light un-guided anti-tank rocket by
            GD; mine-clearing system
            (rockets); infra-red air-to-air
            missile (project cancelled) by BGT
ViPre   visual precision
Virginia class, nuclear-powered guided
            missile strike cruiser (USN CGN)
VIS   veterinary investigation service
vis   viscount; visibility; visual;
            viscocity
visby   visibility
VISF-46   mine detector Bulgaria
Visionar passive laser/infra-red fire
            control system by HSA
VISSR   visible infra-red spin-scan radio-
            meter (satellite weather and
            cloud surveillance) by Hughes
VISSRAS   visible infra-red spin-scan
            radiometer atmospheric sounder
            by Hughes VAS
VISTA   volunteers in service to America;
            visual-talking (recce platform
            WISP + TV camera + ground
            station) by Westland; viewing
            instantly/security transactions
            automatically
Visulink helicopter flight simulator by
            Link
VIT   vertical interval test
vit   vitreous
VITA   volunteers for international techni-
            cal assistance
Vital-IV flight simulator by McDD
VITAL   variably initialized translator for
            algorithmic languages; VAST inter-
            face test application language
            (versatile automatic shop test)
Vitamer   vitamin + isomer
VitStat   vital statistics
Vixen   wheeled combat reconnaissance
            vehicle
Vizir   data display for SENIT by SINTRA
VJ   utility squadron (USN)
VJ-day   Victory in Japan day 14 August 1945;
            2 September 1945
VJ-101   experimental VTOL aircraft
VK   vertical keel; volume kill
VK-155   self-propelled gun by Bofors
VKI   Van Karman Institute (for fluid
            dynamics)
VL   vice lieutenant
VLA   very low altitude; very large array
VLAD   vertical line array DIFAR (sonobuoy)
            (direction finding and ranging)
Vl/Az   velocity azimuth (aircraft display)
VLB   vertical lift bridge; very long
            baseline

VLBI   very long baseline interferometry
VLC   Vehicule de Combat Léger (light combat vehicle)
VLCC   volunteer leader's certification course (Boy Scouts); very large crude (oil) carrier
VLD   visual laydown delivery
VLF   very low frequency; vectored lift flight (aircraft)
VLN   very low nitrogen
VLPE   very long period experiment
VLR   very long range (aircraft)
VLS   vapour liquid solids
VLSI   very large scale integration
vltg   voltage
VLTT   Vehicule Légère Tous Terrains (jeep by Peugeot)
vlv   valve
vly   valley
VM   victory medal; veterinary manual; velocity modulation; volatile matter; virtual machine
v/m   volt per metre; volt per mile
VM-40   Seawolf, lightweight GWS-25 with two starters by BAC
VMA   virtual memory allocation; marine attack squadron (USN)
VMAAW   marine attack squadron all-weather
Vmap   video map equipment
VMB   marine patrol bombing squadron (USN)
VMBS   marine fighter bomber squadron (USN)
VMC   visual meteorological conditions; vertical motion carriage
VMCB   virtual machine control block
VMCJ   marine composite recce squadron (USN)
VMD   marine photographic squadron (USN); vertical magnetic dipole; vector meson dominance
VMF   marine fighter squadron
VMFAW   marine fighter squadron all-weather
VMFA   carrier-borne marine fighter/attacker squadron (USN)
VMFN   marine night fighter squadron (USN)
VMGR   marine aerial refueller/transport squadron (USN)
VMI   Virginia military institute
VMID   virtual machine identifier
VMJ   marine utility squadron (USN); vertical multi-junction
VML   marine glider squadron (USN)
VMM   vertical machine monitor
V&MM   vandalism and malicious mischief
VMO   marine observation squadron (USN)
VMOAS   marine observation squadron artillery spotting
VMO   Vehicule Maintien de l'Ordre by Saviem (4x4 anti-riot vehicle)
VMR   Victorian mounted rifles (Australia); volunteer militia regiment

marine transport squadron (US); visual meteorological (flight) rules
VMRMDS   vehicle-mounted road mine detector system by Cubic
VMSB   marine scouting bombing squadron (USN)
VMT   very many thanks (UK); video matrix terminal
VMTAB   virtual machine table
VN   ventral nozzle; volatile nitrogen; vulnerability number; Viet Nam; passive light intensification system (FR)
VNAF   Viet Nam Air Force
VNMC   Viet Nam marine corps
VO   verbal orders; veterinary officer; Member of the Royal Victorian Order; observation squadron (USN)
VOA   voice of America
VOC   observation spotter squadron (USN); volunteer officer candidate; vehicle observer corps
VOCall   voluntary recall to service (US)
VOCG   verbal orders of commanding general
VOCO   verbal orders of commanding officer
Vocoder   LPC-24, narrow-band digital language processor by E-Systems
VOCOSS   voluntary organizations co-operating in overseas social service
VOCS   verbal order of chief of staff
VOD   vertical on-board delivery (aircraft); velocity of detonation
VODAT   voice-operated device for automatic transmission
VODP   verbal order by the direction of the president
VOEST-Alpine   Vereinigte Öesterreichische Stahlwerke Linz
VOF   observation fighter squadron (USN); variable operating frequency
VOG   observation plane squadron (USN)
VOGov   verbal orders of the governor
VoiceCon   telephone conference
vol   volunteer; volume; volatile
VolAr   volunteer army (US)
VolAsh   volcanic ash
VOLFD   volume (adjustable) fire damper
volm   volume; volumetric
VolMain   voluntary remain in service
VolMet   meteorological information for aircraft in flight
voly   voluntary
VOM   Volt Ohm meter
VONA   vehicle of the new age (computer-controlled short-distance)
Voodoo   F-101, super-sonic all-weather fighter by McDD
VOQ   visiting officers' quarters
VOR   vehicle off the road; VHF omnidirec-

VOR	tional range; visual omnidirectional range
VOR/Loc	VHF omnidirectional range localizer
VORTAC	VHF omnidirectional range tactical air navigation
VOS	vocabulary of ordnance stores
VOSA	verbal orders of the secretary of the army
VOSC	VAST operating system code
VOSL	variable operating and safety level
VOTAG	verbal orders of the adjutant general
VOTEC	vocational training in existing civilian centers (US)
VOTEM	video-operated typewriter employing morse
Votrax	synthetic language system (US)
vou	voucher
vouded	voucher deduction
VOX	voice operated exchange switch
Voyager	Jupiter+Uranus Saturn probe (Nasa)
VP	vulnerable point; vital point; vice president; vice principal; fixed-wing patrol squadron (USN); variable pitch (airscrew); vertical planning; virtual processor; vapour pressure; vanishing point
VP-70	9mm pistol by HK
VP-90	Voltigeur Patrouilleur (light tracked vehicle) by Lohr
VPA	Verey pistol ammunition; veterans' preference act
VPAM	virtual partitioned access method
VPB	medium/heavy patrol bomber squadron (USN); Hawk-III medium/patrol bomber WW2; vertical plot board
VPC	armoured personnel carrier (FR)
VPD	vehicles per day; variations per day; vertical polar diagram
VPG	Vorflugprüfgerät (pre-flight test set)
VPG-608	variable phase generator by Feedback
VPH	vehicles per hour; variations per hour; vertical photography
VPM	vendor part modification; vehicles per mile; mortar carrier (FR)
VPMOS	verified primary military occupational speciality
VPN	vendor part number
VPP	validation phase procurement
VPR	virtual PPI reflectoscope (US) (plan position indicator radar) NMP with navigational microfilm projector
VPres	vice president
VPS	vibrations per second; volume pressure setting
VPS-2	anti-aircraft radar for VADS by Lockheed
VPSB	veterans' placement service board
VPSW	virtual programme status word
VPX	LORAAS, long-range anti-submarine aircraft project
VPX-110	light tracked vehicle by Lohr
VQ	fleet air recce squadron (USN)
VQMG	vice quartermaster general
VQX	TACAMO aircraft project
VR	ventilated rib; voyage regulations; veterinary and remount (service) (UK); volunteer reserve; fleet tactical transport squadron (USN); very respectfully; transport aircraft (USN); variety reduction; vertical retort (zinc); voltage regulator; vulcanized rubber
VRB	voice rotating beacon; variable re-enlistment bonus
VRBM	variable re-enlistment bonus multiple
VRC	volunteer rifle corps; air transport squadron (USN); vehicular radio communication; vertical ride control; visual record computer; vertical redundancy check; vehicular radio communication
VRC-600	vehicular radio communication by MBLE
VRCS	veterinary and remount conducting section
VRD	vehicle reserve depot; (Royal Naval) Volunteer Reserve Decoration
VRE	Viet Nam regional exchange; volume review exercises
VRF	aircraft ferry squadron (USN)
VRFWS	vehicle rapid fire weapon system
vrg	veering
VRI	visual rule instrument (aircraft)
4(V)RIrish	the 4th volunteer battalion the Royal Irish Rangers
VRL	Vehicule de Reconnaissance Léger (light recce vehicle)
VRM	viscous remnant magnetization
VROC	vertical rate of climb
VRP	vehicle reserve park
VRT	vehicle, reconnaissance, tracked
VRTS	volunteer reserve training school
VRU	utility transport squadron (USN); vertical reference unit
VRV	vorderer Rand der Verteidigung (forward edge of defence)
VRW	vehicle reconnaissance, wheeled
Vry	viceroy
VS	visual signal (man); veterinary surgeon; veterinary school; shore-based scouting squadron (USN); fixed-wing ASW squadron (USN); variable stores; vertical sounding; anti-submarine search and attack aircraft; variable speed; Vickers & Sons (UK); Vought Sikorsky (US)
VS-2.2	anti-tank mine by Valsella

VS-3.6   plastic anti-tank mine by Valsella
VS-50   anti-personnel mine by Valsella
VS-300   helicopter by Vought Sikorsky
VS-316   XR-4, helicopter by Vought Sikorsky
VSA   voice stress analyser; Vought
          Sikorsky Aircraft Corp.
VSAM   virtual storage access method;
          virtual sequential access method
vsb   visible
vsby   visibility
VSC   volunteer staff corps
VSCF   variable speed constant frequency
          (electrical generator)
VSD   vendor's shipping document; vertical
          situation display
VSE   Verkehrssimulationseinrichtung by
          SEL (switchboard operation simula-
          tor)
VSF   antisubmarine fighter squadron (USN)
VSG   vocational school graduate (pro-
          gramme) (US); vertical sweep
          generator
VSG-2   tank thermal sight
VSI   very seriously ill (US); vertical
          speed indicator
VSL   variable safety level
VSM   Viet Nam Service Medal; vestigial
          sideband modulation; Vickers Sons
          & Maxim
VS/MD   Valsella mines distributor
VSMF   visual search microfilm file
VSMOS   verified secondary military occupa-
          tional speciality (US)
vsn   vision
VSO   very senior officer; victualling
          stores officer; voluntary service
          overseas
VSPT   vehicle summary and priority table
          (US)
VSPX   vertical scheduling programme
          extended
VSR   very short range; validation summary
          report; visual security range
VSS   V/STOL support ship (USN) (aircraft
          carrier)
VSSSN   verification status social security
          number (US)
VSTOL   vertical and short take-off and
          landing aircraft
VSTOL/A   VSTOL aircraft to replace assault
          helicopters (US programme USN)
VSTOL/B   VSTOL aircraft to replace ASW heli-
          copters (USN programme)
VSTT   variable speed training target
VSU   voice security unit
VSWR   voltage standing-wave ratio
VT   varmint/target (projectile); variable
          time (fuse); variable transmission;
          vertical tabulation; visual tele-
          graphy; visual telephony; torpedo

          bomber squadron (USN); training
          squadron (USN); Vosper & Thorny-
          croft (Portsmouth)
V&T   volume and tension
VT-1-2   Versuchsträger by MaK (two-gun
          experimental tank 120mm on M-113
          hull
VT-1   hovercraft by Vosper
VTB   Hawk-IV, vertical torpedo bomber WW2
VTC   volunteer training corps
VTF   variable time fuse; Versuchsträger
          mit Fronttriebwerk by MaK (experi-
          mental tank with frontal engine)
VTIP   visual target identification point
VTL   variable threshold logic (computer)
VTM   vehicle test meter; voltage turnable
          magnetron; vehicles to the mile
VTM-120   Vehicule Tracteur de Mortier 120mm
          (mortar tractor) by Saviem
VTN   night torpedo bomber squadron (USN)
VTO   vocational training officer;
          vertical take-off (rockets)
VTOC   volume table of content
VTOGW   vertical take-off gross weight
VTOHL   vertical take-off and horizontal
          landing (aircraft)
VTOL   vertical take-off and landing (air-
          craft)
VTOVL   vertical take-off and vertical
          landing (aircraft)
VTPR   vertical temperature profile radio-
          meter
VTR   vehicle, tracked, recovery (USN);
          video tape recorder
VTS   vocational training scheme; Vulcan
          training system by GE
VT-S-1   Versuchsträger mit Scheitellafet-
          tierter Kanone by MaK
VTT   troop transport vehicle 4x4 by
          Saviem
VTTM   troop transport vehicle 4x4 + mortar
          by Saviem
VTU   volunteer (reserve) training unit
          (USCG)
VTVM   vacuum tube voltmeter
VTX   trainer aircraft project (USN)
VTS-TS   trainer aircraft project + training
          system (simulator)
VU   voice unit; volume unit; fleet com-
          posite squadron (USN); utility and
          general aircraft (USN)
VUA   Valorous Unit Award (US)
VUDFS   VHF/UHF direction finder system
Vulcan   bomber by Hawker Siddeley 1956;
          M-61, 20mm Gatling gun by GE
Vulcan-ADS M163, anti-aircraft tank with
          Vulcan gun (air defense system)
Vulcano   sea-to-sea missile (IT)
Vulcan/Phalanx naval anti-aircraft point
          defence system

Vultee	B-38, bomber	VWG	vibrating wire gauge
VUNC	voice of the United Nations command	VWO	voluntary welfare organization
VUV	vacuum ultra-violet	vx	vertex top
VV	visibility variable	VX	air experimental squadron (USN); nerve gas
V-VAC	Vickers versatile aircraft carrier		
VVE	vertical vertex errors	VXB	Vehicule Experimental Berliet (wheeled armoured car)
VVS	vehicular viewing system		
VVS-2	vehicular viewing system drivers viewer by Varo	VXO	variable crystal oscillator
		VY	victualling yard
VW	airborne early warning squadron (USN); airborne early warning squadron aircraft (USN); Volkswagen AG (Wolfsburg GE)	Vydra	class, landing craft (SU)
		VZ	Zener voltage

W

W	Watts; wheeled; warhead; weight; Wales; Western; weekly (report);
W-62	warhead nuclear 200 KT
W-80	warhead, nuclear for SRAM AGM-69
W-613	Lynx, helicopter by Westland
WA	West Africa; West Australia; Western Approaches (UK); will adjust
WAA	war assets administration; West African artillery
WAAAF	Women's Australian auxiliary air force --WRAAF
WAAC	Women's auxiliary army corps --WRAC
WAACP	Western Atlantic airlift command post (US)
WAADS	Washington air defense sector
WAAF	Women's auxiliary air force --WRAF
WAAM	wide area anti-armour munition
WAAS	wide aperture array sonar
WAAS	Women's auxiliary army service
WAB	wage adjustment board (US); when authorized by (US)
WABCo	Westinghouse Air Brake Company
WABTOC	when authorized by the overseas commander
WAC	weapons assignment console; world aeronautical chart; Women's army corps (US); Women's auxiliary corps; women's advisory committee; Western Arms Corporation (Los Angeles); Wright Aeronautical Corporation
WACB	women's army classification battery (US)
WACCC	world air cargo commodity classification
Wachtel	outdoor perimeter surveillance electronic fence by Zettler
WACI	Western approaches convoy instructions (UK); Women's army corps of India
WACO	written advice of contracting officer
WACRES	Women's army corps reserve (US)
WACSM	Women's army corps service medal (US)
WADC	Wright air development center (US); Wright Patterson AFB (Dayton)
WADD	Wright air development division
WADF	Western air defense force (US)
WADS	wide area data service
WAE	when actually employed
WAEC	war agricultural executive committee WW2 (UK)
WAF	West African forces; with all fault; women in the air force (US)
WAFF	West African frontier force
WAFFLE	wide angle fixed field locating equipment (US)
WAfr	West African
WAfrR	West African regiment
WAFS	women's auxiliary ferrying service (USAF); women's auxiliary fire service (UK)
WÄGA	Wärme-Gastechnik GmbH (Kassel) (IWKA group)
WAGGGS	world association of girl guides and girl scouts
Wagoneer	station wagon (US)
WAGR	Windscale advanced gas-cooled reactor
WAIS	Wechsler's adult intelligence scale
Walid	wheeled armoured vehicle (Egypt)
Walleye	AGM-62, TV guided air-to-ground missile
Walker Bulldog	M-41, light tank (US)
Walross	remote-controlled mine-sweeping system (GE)
Walrus	double-decker seaplane WW2 (RAF) by Supermarine
WAM	work analysis and measurement
WAMO	weapon allocation and mode of operation system
WAMS	weapon aiming mode selector
WAMTMTS	Western area military traffic management and terminal service (US)
WANAP	Washington national airport
Wandering Annie	sonobuoy FIDO

WANEF   Westinghouse astronuclear experimental facility
WANL   Westinghouse astronuclear laboratory
WANS   Women's Australian national service
WAOCA   Washington area officers club association
WAP   work assignment procedure; work assignment plan
WAPC   Women's auxiliary police corps
WAR   the West African regiment
War   the Warwickshire regiment
WARC   Western air rescue center (US); world administrative radio conference
WARC-ST world administrative radio conference for space telecommunications
WARES   workload and resources evaluation system (US)
WARF   wartime active replacement factors
Warhawk P-40, interceptor by Curtiss
WARLOCE wartime lines of communications Europe
WARM   walking and road marching (UK)
Warrior SF-260, single-engined plane by SIAI
WARS   worldwide ammunition reporting system (US)
WAS   Women's auxiliary services
WASAC   working group of army study advisory committee (US)
WASAG-Chemie Westfälisch-Anhaltische Sprengstoff Aktiengesellschaft (Essen)
WashADSect Washington air defense sector
WashDC Washington, District of Columbia
WASP   Women's auxiliary service pilot; war air service program (US); white Anglo-Saxon protestant (US); wide area special projectile (US programme) (short-range anti-tank homing missile)
Wasp   flamethrower tank WW2; 100 lbs fire and forget mini-missile by Hughes; anti-submarine helicopter by Westland
Waspaloy special alloy for turbine compressors
WASPs   Women's air force service pilots
Wasserfall radio-guided super-sonic anti-aircraft rocket WW2 (GE)
WAST   Western Australia standard time
WAT   weight, altitude and temperature; Women's auxiliary territorial service
WATCO   water transportation coordination office
Water Buffalo heavy assault landing craft
WATS   wide area telephone service; wide area telecommunications service
WATU   Western approaches tactical unit (UK)

WAus   Western Australia
WAVES   Women accepted for volunteer emergency service (USN)
Wavell field automatic data processing system (UK)
Wavy Navy RNVR Royal Naval Volunteer Service
WB   wave band; water ballast; wheel base; wet bulb; wide beam; wage board (civilian employees) (US); weather bureau; weekly bulletin
WB-Sensor Wärmebildsensor (thermal imaging sensor)
WB-81   Waffenbehälter Giesskanne WW2 (GE) (aerial gun pod)
WBAFC   weather bureau area forecast center (US)
WBAMC   William Beaumont army medical center (US)
WBAN   weather bureau Air Force and Navy (US)
WBAS   weather bureau airport station
WBAWS   weather, briefing, advisory and warning service (US)
WBC   white blood cell
WBG   Wärmebildgerät (thermal imager)
WBGT   wet bulb globe thermometer
WBI   will be issued
WBLC   Wiblics, water-borne logistic craft (US)
WBP   water and boil proof
WBS   walking beam suspension; work breakdown structure; Western base section
WBSCB   work breakdown structure control board (US)
WBT   wet bulb temperature
Wby   Weatherby
WC   war college; war cabinet; wing commander; wage change; war council; war communications; Western command; without charge; wad-cutter (projectile); water column (pressure)
WC-130 Hercules, weather reporting aircraft
WCA   West coast of Africa
WCAB   working committee of the aeronautical board
WCBSU   West Coast base service unit
WCC   war crimes commission; war crimes court; work centre code
WCD   West Coast division; weapons classifications defects
WCdr   wing commander
WCDS   West Coast (naval publications) distribution center (US)
WCE   war crimes executive
WCEE   world conference on earthquake engineering
WCF   Winchester centrefire (cartridge); wind chill factor

WCFM   Winchester centrefire magnum (projectile)
WCIU   war crimes investigation unit
WCL   Westinghouse Canada Ltd
WComm   wing commander
WCP   world council of peace
WCPAB   war control price adjustment board
WCRA   weather control research association (US)
WCS   weapons control system
WCYMSC   world council of young men's service clubs
WD   wind direction; write direct; war department; works department; when directed
wd   withdrawn; warranted
WDA   war damage act; weapons defended area (US)
WDC   war department constabulary; war damage contribution; war damage commission; Washington document center; Western defence command; world data centre
WDClr   war department circular
WDCSA   war department chiefs of staff army
WDE   weapons direction equipment
WDF   Western desert force; wood door and frame
WDGF   war department ground forces
WDgns   the Westminster Dragoons, 2nd County of London Yeomanry
WDGS   war department general staff
WDI   weapons data index; war department intelligence
WDJ   war division of justice
WDL   weapons density list (US)
wdly   widely
WDM   weapon delivery model
WDP   war department pamphlet
WDPC   Western data processing center (US)
WDPMG   war department provost marshal general
    ID intelligence division
wdr   withdrawal; welder; wardmaster
WdrL   wardmaster lieutenant
WDS   weapon direction system
wds   words
WDSS   war department special staff
wdt   width
WDTS   war dogs training school
WE   weapons engineering; watch error; war establishment; with equipment; withholding exemptions; week end(ing); Western Electric Corp.
W&E   windage and elevation
wea   weather; weapon
Weapon Able   forward projecting depth charge (RN)
WEARCON   weather reporting and forecasting control

Weasel   amphibious tractor
weat   weathertight
Webley   service revolver (UK)
WEBASTO   W. Baier, Stockdorf (GE)
WEC   weapon exports control; waterway exports control
WECo   Western Electric Company Inc.
WECOM   weapons command (US Army)
WEDN   war emergency day nursery
Weeping Willie   tear gas
WEF   with effect from; war emergency formula
WEFAX   weather facsimile
WEFT   wings, engines, fuselage, tail (aircraft recognition) (US)
WEG   war emergency grant
Weibull   anti-aircraft artillery trainer by Oerlikon
WEIS   world event interaction survey
WelAdm   welfare administration
WelDept   welfare department
Wellesley   bomber WW2 (RAF)
Wellies   Wellington boots
Wellington   Wimpey, bomber WW2 by Vickers (RAF)
Welman   midget submarine (RN)
WEM   wireless and electrical mechanic
WEMA   Western electronics manufacturers' association (US)
WEMSB   Western European military supply board
WEP   water extended polyester; wide-band exciter and processor
wep   weapon
WEPCOSE   weapon control systems engineering program by UCLA
WEqT   war equipment tables
WERPG   Western European regional planning group
WES   war equipment scale; world economic survey; waterways experiment station (US)
wes   western
WesAusFor   Western Australia force
WesCar   Western Caroline
WESCON   Western electronics show and convention (US)
WesCoSoundScol   West Coast sound school
WESO   weapons engineering standardization office (US)
WesPac   Western Pacific
WESPAR   weapon systems phase analog records
Wespe   SP infantry gun 105mm WW 2(GE)
Wessex   transport helicopter by Westland
WEST   Women's enlistment screening test (US)
WESTAF   Western transport air force
WESTAR   Western Union telecommunications satellite by Hughes

Westbury bomber WW2 by Westland (RAF)
WestLant Western Atlantic area (Nato)
WESTOMP Western ocean meeting point
WestPac Western Pacific
WestSeaFron Western sea frontier
Westwind fanjet aircraft maritime patrol by
           IAI
WET   Washington exploratory talks
WETS   week-end training site (US)
WEU   Western European Union
WF   the Welsh Fusiliers; wing forward
WFA   war food administration
WFCMV   wheeled fuel consuming motor vehicle
WFD   war finance division
WFN   weapons facility, Navy
WFOV   wide field of view (camera)
WFPC   wide field planetary camera by
          Dornier
WF&RDM   Dok en Werf Maatschapij Wilton
          Fijenoord BV & de Rotterdamsche
          Droogdok Maatschapij BV
WFTU   world federation of trade unions
WG   the Welsh Guards; working group;
          wire gauge; water gauge; weight
          guaranteed
wg   wing
W&G   Wandel & Goltermann (Emmingen GE)
WG-13   Lynx, helicopter by Westland
WG-30   transport helicopter by Westland
WG-34   SKR, Sea King Replacement
          helicopter project by Westland
WGC   war graves commission
WgCdr   wing commander (RAF)
WgComdr   wing commander (RAF)
WGD-2   windshield guidance display by SFEMA
WGH   Western general hospital
w gl   wired glass
WGPMS   warehousing goods performance meas-
          urements system
WGPW   Women's group for public welfare
WGSC   wide gap spark chamber
wgt   weight
WGTA   Wisconsin general testing apparatus
WGWC   working group on weather communica-
          tions
WGWP   working group on weather plans
WH   Western hemisphere; watt hour; war-
          heading building
wh   wheeled; wheel; where; withholding
WHAM   work handling and maintenance
WHAMO   winning the hearts and minds of (the
          Vietnamese)
WHAP   where applicable
WHCA   White House communications agency
          (US)
WHD   Western hemisphere defense (US)
whd   warhead
WhdS   warhead section
WHE   Waffe Hydraulik Energieversorgung
          (weapon hydraulics power supply)

Wheelbarrow remote-controlled manipulator
             EOD
Whiplash air-to-air missile (South Africa)
Whippet   tank WW1 (UK)
Whirlaway XHJD-1, twin-engined helicopter
           by McDonnell
Whirlwind helicopter by Westland; fighter
           aircraft WW2 by Westland
Whiskey-3 WSC-3 FltSatCom terminals by
           E-Systems
WHIST   worldwide household goods informa-
          tion system for traffic management
          (US)
White Fox HF radio communications system
           (Nato)
White Helmets Royal Marines band; Royal
               Signals motorcycle display
               team
Whiteout neutral smoke by Wallop Industries
Whitley   transport aircraft by Armstrong/
          Whitworth
Whittle   jet aircraft 1941 by Gloster
Whizz Bang tracked rocket launcher WW2 (US)
whl   wheeled
WHL   Western Helicopters Ltd (UK)
WHNS   wartime host nation support (pro-
          gramme)
WHO   World Health Organization (Geneva)
WHOI   Woods Hole oceanographic institute
          (Mass.)
WHP   water horse power
WHQ   war headquarters
WHR   Western hemisphere reserve
WHRA   Welwyn Hall research association
          (UK)
whs   warehouse
whsmn   warehouseman
WI   West Indies; women's institute; when
          issued; welded iron; welding
          institute (UK); wrought iron
WIA   wounded in action
WIB   war industries board (US)
Wiblics   WBLC, waterborne logistics craft
          (US)
WIC   West India Committee
Wichita   class, replenishment oilers (USN)
          AOA
WID   West India Docks; war information
          department
Widder   gun-armed killer tank Jagdpanzer,
          Kanone (GE)
Wideye   MRUASTAS, Supervisor, recce platform
          by Westland/Marconi Elliott
Widgeon   helicopter by Westland
WIE   with immediate effect
Wiesel   air transportable light tank project
          by Porsche
WIF   West Indies Federation
WIGE   Ramwing, wing in ground effect
          giant maritime transport aircraft
          project by USN/NASA

WilCo   I understand and will comply
Wildcat F-4F, naval fighter WW2 by Grumman
Wild Weasel airborne ECM system against a/a
            radars
Wilga   light communications air craft
            (Poland)
Willemoes class, patrol boats guided
            missiles (Denmark)
WiltsR   the Wiltshire Regiment
WIMERA   Windmessradar by ES (wind sounding
            radar)
Wimex   WWMCCS, world-wide military command
            and control system (US)
Wimpey   Wellington bomber WW2 (RAF)
WIMR   Woolmer instructional military
            railway (UK)
WIMS   wartime instructions for merchant
            ships
WIN   work intensive
win   winter
Win   Winchester
Winchester US carbine
            SR-N-6 hovercraft (UK)
Windfinder high-altitude wind measuring
            radar (EEC)
WindI   Windward Islands
Window   chaff radar jamming technique WW2
            (RAF)
WINE   Webb institute of naval engineering
            (US)
WingCdr wing commander
WINS   Women's industrial and national
            service
WInst   women's institute
WintEx   winter exercise (Nato)
WIP   work in progress; work in process;
            work in place; wartime intelligence
            plan
WIPACE   wartime intelligence plan allied
            command Europe
WIPO   world intellectual property organiza-
            tion
WIR   weekly intelligence report;
            West India Regiment
Wirbelwind anti-aircraft tank WW2 (GE)
WIRDS   weather information reporting and
            display system
WIRE   weapons interference reduction effort
WIRES   women in radio and electrical
            services (US)
WISC   West Indian standing conference
WISP   wide range imaging spectrometer
Wisp   unmanned miniature helicopter by
            Westland
wit   witness
WITS   Westinghouse interactive time sharing
            system
Wits   Witwatersrand
WJC   world Jewish congress
WJCC   Western joint computer conference
            (US)

WJI   Watkins-Johnson International
WK   well known
wk   weak; week; work
wkd   weekday
WKIY   West Kent Imperial Yeomanry
wkly   weekly
WkQDr   work queue directory
wkr   worker; wrecker
wks   works; weeks
wksp   workshop
WL   wave length; waterline; white light;
            workload; waiting list
WLcoeff waterline coefficient
WLA   women's land army
WLB   war labor board (US); weapons log-
            book (US)
WLCS   workload and cost schedule (US)
WLD   west longitude date; war load dis-
            placement
wlf   welfare
WLI   wavelength interval
WLO   wagonline officer
WLong   West longitude
WLR-8   sonar warning receiver by GTE
WM   War Medal; Waterloo Medal; woman
            marine; work measurement;
            Weatherby Magnum (projectile);
            work mark; white metal; Watt
            meter; wave meter; weight or
            measurement; wing main (airfield)
WM-17M   naval integrated search and fire
            control radar by HSA
WM-20   naval integrated search and fire
            control radar by HSA
WM-24   naval fire control system by HSA
WM-25   search and fire control radar by
            HSA
WM-28   search and fire control radar by
            HSA
WMA   women marines association (US)
WMATC   Washington Metropolitan area
            transit commission
WMC   weapons monitoring console; war man-
            power commission; ways and means
            committee
WMEC   USCG medium endurance cutter
WMF   Württembergische Metallwarenfabrik
            (Geislingen) (Rheinmetall daughter)
WMHS   Wessex military historical society
wmk   watermark
WMLWR   wing-mounted lightweight weather
            radar RCA
WMO   world meteorological organization
            (Geneva UN)
WMP   with much pleasure
WMPC   war material procurement capability
WMR   war material requirement; Winchester
            magnum rimfire (cartridge)
WMS   watchmen's service; world magnetic
            survey; wire mesh screen

WMSC	weather message switching centre
WMTC	Women's mechanized transport corps
WMTV	wheeled motor traction vehicle
WN	will not
WNA	winter North Atlantic
WNB	will not be
WNC	WASAG Nitro-Chemie GmbH (Aschau GE)
wnd	wind
wng	warning
WNL	within normal limits
WNLC	Women's national land corps
WNP	will not proceed
WNRC	Washington national records center
WNRE	Whiteshell nuclear research establishment (Canada)
WNTF	Western naval task force
WO	warrant officer; wireless operator; weapons officer; welfare officer; war orientation; war office; written order; warning order; without
WO-1	warrant officer W-1 (US)
WOA	weapons orientation, advanced
WOAG	wireless operator airman gunner
WOB	washed overboard
WOC	without compensation; weight of car
WOCC	war office car company
WOCCI	war office central card index
WOCG	weather outline contour generator
WOCL	war office casualty list
WOCS	women officer candidate school (US)
WOCT	WAC officer candidate test (US)
WOD	war office directorate; wind-over-deck
WODD	war office design department; without equipment
WOG	wrath of God (Israeli conspirative anti-terrorist force); with other goods; water oil or gas
WOHL	war office honours list
WOJG	warrant officer junior grade (US)
WOL	war office library; war office letter; wedge opening load(ed); wedge opening loading
WOM	war office memorandum; wireless operator mechanic
Wom	Woomera (Australia) (tracking station)
Wombat	120mm recoilless gun (UK)
WOO	war office order; western operation office (Nasa); war orientation officer; warrant ordnance officer
Woofers	the Worcestershire and Sherwood Foresters Regiment
Woofus	landing craft rocket launcher WW2 (US)
Woolworth Carriers	MAC, tankers with flight deck WW2
Woomera	bomber WW2 (Australia)
WOP	without pay; wireless operator; without personnel
WOPAG	wireless operator;airman gunner
WOPE	without personnel or equipment
WOQ	warrant officers' quarters
WOQT	warrant officers' qualification test
WORAM	word-oriented random access memory
WORBAT	wartime order of battle
WorcH	the Queen's Own Worcestershire Hussars
WorcR	the Worcestershire Regiment
Work Horse	H-21, transport helicopter by Vertol
WORSAMS	world-wide organization structure for army medical support (US)
WorSe	word selection
WOS	war office staff; woman officer school
WOSAC	worldwide synchronization of atomic clocks
WOSB	war office selection board; weather observation site building
WOSD	weapons operational systems development
WOSG	warrant officer senior grade
WOT	weather over target; wide open throttle
Wotan	4x4 armoured personnel carrier by Mowag
WOTS	women officers' training school
WOW	war on wastefulness; women ordnance workers; waiting on weather
WOWAR	work order and work accomplishment record
WOWN	without winch
WOWS	women ordnance workers service (US)
WP	water point; white paper; weather permitting; West Point; will proceed; waste paper; without prejudice; Warsaw Pact; work programme; working paper; weather patrol (aircraft); white phosphorous (shell); working pressure; working point; working programme
WP-3	Orion, weather patrol aircraft by Lockheed
WP-8	rocket launcher 140mm 8 tubes (Poland)
WP-308	Sea Prince, maritime patrol aircraft (RN)
WPA	works progress administration; works progress agency
WPB	war propaganda bureau; war production board
WPBC	Western Pacific base command
WPC	war pensions committee; woman police constable; world power conference
WPD	Western procurement division (USMC)
WPE	white porcelain enamel
WPESS	within-pulse electronic sector scanning
WPF	Warsaw Pact Forces

wpf	waterproof
wpg	waterproofing
WPHC	Western Pacific high commission
wpig	waterproofing
WPL	war plans; warning point level
WPM	war planning memorandum; words per minute
wpn	weapon
WPNST	war plan, naval transportation service
WpnSta	weapon station
WPP	weapons production programme
WPR	wartime personnel requirements
WPRB	weapons personnel research branch EISO
WPRI	wartime Pacific routing instructions
WPRL	water pollution research laboratory
WPS	with prior service
WPSC	war plan, shipping control
wpt	waypoint
WPT-34	armoured recovery vehicle (SU)
WPU	with power unit
WPWOD	will proceed without delay
WQ	water quenched; Wilhelm Quante Fernmeledetechnik Wuppertal
WQS-2	sonar communications system
WR	the Wessex Regiment; Western region; ward room; weapon requirement; war reserve (US); women's reserve; war risk; water-rail; wet runway; water repellent; weapon range
W&R	welfare and recreation
WRA	ward room attendant; war relocation authority
WRAAC	Women's Royal Australian army corps
WRAAF	Women's Royal Australian air force
WRAC	Women's Royal army corps; Winchester Repeating Arms Company
WRAF	Women's Royal air force
WRAIN	Walter Reed army institute of nursing (US)
WRAIR	Walter Reed army institute of research
WRAMA	Warner Robins air material area
WRAMC	Walter Reed army medical center
WRANS	Women's Royal Australian naval service
WRAP	weapons readiness achievement programme IMM; weapons readiness analysis programme
WRAT	wide range achievement test
WRC	water retention coefficient
WRE	weapons research establishment (Australia)
Wren	Women's Royal naval service
WRF	Winchester rimfire
WR&FSA	welfare recreation and food services association (US)
WRGH	Walter Reed general hospital (Washington)

WRI	war resisters international; war risk insurance; women's rural institute
wrls	wireless
wrm	warm
WRMess	ward room mess
wrmn	wireman
WRMR	war reserves material requirement
WRMS	war reserves material stocks
WRNR	Women's Royal naval reserve
WRNS	Women's Royal naval service
wrnt	warrant
WRO	war records office
WR-P	wet runway patchy
WRR	the West Riding Regiment
WRS	war reserve stocks
WRSIC	water resources scientific information center (US)
WRSK	war readiness spares kits
WRVS	Women's Royal voluntary service
WS	warlike stores; war scale; war substantive; wireless set; wireless station; workshops; Wallops station (Nasa); water supply; weather ship (Nato); weapon system
W&S	Webley & Scott
WS-80	electro-optic naval fire control system by Plessey
WSA	war shipping administration; weapon system analysis; weapon system automation; war supplies agency
WSA-4	weapon system automation (naval fire control system by Ferranti)
WSA-21	weapon system automation laser/TV fire control system for 30mm naval guns by Ferranti
WSA-420	CAAES, fire control system for fast patrol boats by Ferranti
WSA-421	CAAES, fire control system for small and medium naval guns
WSA-422	CAAES, fire control system for guns and missiles
WSA-423	CAAES, fire control system integrated fire control for guns and missiles
WSBA	Western sovereign based area (Akrotiri Cyprus)
WSC	Western sea (frontier) command; working security committee
WSC-3	Whiskey-3, FltSatCom terminals by E-Systems
WSCS	wide-sense cyclo-stationary
WSD	weapon system development (phase); working stress design
WSDA	weapons system data acquisition (unit); anti-aircraft gun trainer by Dornier
WSE	weapons and support equipment; weapon systems efficiency
WSEC	Washington state electronics council

WSED   weapon system evaluation division
WSEG   weapon system evaluation group
WSET   weapon system evaluation test
WSF   Western sea frontier
WSFR   the Worcestershire and Sherwood
        Foresters Regiment
WSG   war service grant
WSH   wind screen heating
WSIM   water separation index, modified
WSL   Warren Spring laboratory MoT
WSMR   White Sands missile range
WSO   weapon systems operator;
        Washington standardization office
WSP   work simplification programme;
        water supply point; water sterili-
        zation pill; water sterilization
        powder
wsp   workshop
WSPACS weapon system programming and control
        control system
WSPC   weapon systems partnership committee
WSPD   weapon systems planning data
WSPG   weapon systems phasing group
WSPO   weapon systems planning office
WSR   weather surveillance radar; weapons
        status report
WSRP   weapons system requisitioning
        procedure
WST   weapon system trainer; weapon system
        test
WSTF   White Sands test facilities
WSTH   weapons systems tactical handbook
WSTM   White Sands transverse Mercator
        (map)
WSZ   wrong signature zero
WT   wireless; telephony; wireless, tele-
        graphy; water tender; weapons
        training; water tight; watch tower;
        war transport
wt   without; weight; warrant
WTA   Women's territorial army
WTB/MTDE wading trials branch of mainten-
        ance technique development
        establishment
WTC   water transport company; women's
        timber corps
WTCA   water terminal clearance authority;
        water terminal clearance activity
WTCB   water tender construction battalion
WTCSS   West Coast tactical (off-shore)
        control surveillance system (US)
WTD   war trade department; weapons train-
        ing detachment (RAF); water-tight
        door
WT/DF   wireless telegraphy direction finder
WTF   Western task force
wthr   weather
WTI   water tight integrity
WTIS   world trade information service
WTL   weapon-target line

WTM   write tape mark
WTMH   water tight man hole
WTO   Warsaw treaty organization;
        weapon training officer;
        wireless telegraph officer
WTP   weapons testing programme
wtr   writer; winter
WTR   Western test range
WTS   Women's transport service
WTT   weapon tactics trainer for F-18 by
        Hughes
WTV   water tank vessel
WU   Western (European) Union; weather
        research aircraft (US)
WUC   work unit code
WUCOS   Western (European) union chiefs of
        staff
WUDC   Western union defence committee
WUDO   Western union defence organization
WUE   water use efficiency
WUFEC   Western union finance economic
        committee
WUIS   work unit information system
WUP   Western union powers
Wurzburg anti-aircraft radar WW2 (GE)
WUSL   women's united service league
WV   wind vector; wind velocity; weight-
        volume; water valve
WVA   Western Valley Arms
WVAS   Wake vortex avoidance system
wvd   waived
WVE   water vapour electrolysis
WVeh   wheeled vehicle
WVF   world veterans' federation
WVR   within visual range (US missile
        programme)
WVRAAM within visual range air-to-air
        missile (US programme)
WVS   women's voluntary service
        --WRVS
WVT   water vapour transfer; water vapour
        transmission
WVTR   water vapour rate
W-W   Winchester-Western
WW   world war; worldwide; waterworks;
        wire wound
WW-Tyres white wall tyres
WW-1   ... 2, World War 1, ... 2
WWAP   worldwide asset position
WWCP   walking wounded collecting post
WWDC   world war debt commission
WWdr   warrant wardmaster
WWDS   walking wounded dressing station
WWG   war widows guild
wwn   with winch
WWO   wing warrant officer
WWIVM   World War 1 victory medal (US)
WWIIVM World War 2 victory medal (US)
WWMCCS worldwide military command and com-
        munications system (US Wimex)

WWIO	worldwide inventory objective (US)
WWO	wing warrant officer
WWSM	World War (1) service medal (Army and Navy)
WWSP	worldwide surveillance programme
WWSSN	worldwide standard seismograph network
WWW	world weather watch WMO
WWY	the Queen's Own Warwickshire and Worcestershire Yeomanry
WX	weather
WXD	meteorological radar station
WXR	weather radar, radiosonde station
WXR-700	colour weather radar system by Collins
WXTRN	weak external reference
WYorks	the Prince of Wales's Own West Yorkshire Regiment
WYR	West Yorkshire Regiment
Wyvern	carrier-borne torpedo bomber by Westland
WZO	world Zionist organization

X

X   experimental, special; zero hour;
exchange; explosive; extension;
xylonite; submersible craft (USN)

X-axis   horizontal axis

X-craft   midget submarine

X-hour   evacuation hour (shipping) (Nato)

X-1   experimental rocket aircraft by Bell

X-2   experimental rocket aircraft by Bell

X-1A2   Carcara, light tank 90mm gun by
Bernardini

X-2   Spartan, preliminary designation

X-3   Advanced Spartan, preliminary
designation

X-4   wire-guided ship-to-ship missile WW2

X-7   wire-guided anti-tank missile WW2

X-15   rocket aircraft by North American

X-23   spaceflight aircraft by Martin-
Marietta

X-24   spaceflight aircraft by Martin-
Marietta

X-40   Avibras, solid propellant rocket
(Brazil)

X-114   Airofoil, floatplane by VFW

XA-5   Top Sargent, ultra-light helicopter
pulse-jets by AHC

XA-6   Buck Private, ultra-light helicopter
pulse-jets by AHC

XACT   experimental automatic code translation

XAR-30   high-hardness steel

XASM-1   experimental air-to-surface missile

XAR-3   jet trainer aircraft prototype
(Taiwan)

X avante   AR-26, close support aircraft
(Brazil)

XB-10   B-10, bomber by Martin

XB-15   XBLR-1, experimental bomber long-
range by Boeing

XB-19   XBLR-2, experimental bomber long-
range by Douglas

XB-29   experimental bomber 1942 by Boeing

XB-42   Mixmaster, by Douglas

XB-43   first jet bomber by Douglas

XB-45   jet bomber by North American

XB-46   jet bomber by Convair

XB-48   jet bomber by Martin

XB-51   jet bomber by Martin

XB-52   bomber by Boeing

XB-53   jet bomber by Convair

XB-70   Valkyrie, Mach 3 bomber by North
American

XB-901   B-9, bomber by Boeing

XB-907   B-10, bomber by Martin

XBLR-1   XB-15

XBLR-2   XB-19

XBQM-106   mini RPV by AFSL

XBT   expandable bathythermograph

XCH-62   experimental cargo helicopter by
Boeing Vertol

XCO-5   experimental single-seat double
decker aircraft (US) 1926

xd   examined

XDC   Nike X control centre

X&DFlot   experiment and development flotilla
(landing craft) (USN)

XDO   extended defence officer (UK)

XDS   Xerox Data Systems

XE   experimental engine; midget submarine

Xecon-SPC   silver and copper coated elasto-
mer by Metex

XF   experimental fighter aircraft;
extra fine

XF-2   Sea Dart, experimental fighter by
Convair

XF-3   Demon, experimental fighter by
McDonnell 1951

XF-10   Jaguar, experimental fighter by
McDonnell 1951

XF-85   Jaguar, parasite fighter by
McDonnell

XF-91   Jaguar, mixed propellant interceptor
by Republic

XF-92   Jaguar, delta wing jet by Convair

XFA   cross fired acceleration

XFBU-1   F-8, jet fighter by Vought

XFD-1   experimental fighter, defensive,
FH-1, Phantom by McDonnell

xfer   transfer

XFIM-92A   Stinger Alternate, portable anti-
aircraft missile

XFM	expeditionary force message	XM-129	helicopter-borne grenade launcher by Ford
xfmr	transformer	XM-130	light-weight airborne gun 30mm by Ford; helicopter-borne chaff dispenser by Tracor
XFV-1	Salmon, experimental fighter, vertical, piston-engined by Lockheed	XM-134	anti-aircraft telescope
XFV-12	Salmon, experimental jet VSTOL multi-role attack fighter by Rockwell	XM-138	155mm self-propelled howitzer, unarmoured
XFY-1	Pogo, naval experimental fighter VTOL piston-engined by Convair	XM-144	grenade launcher 40mm
		XM-156	helicopter-borne rocket launcher
xg	crossing	XM-157	rocket launcher pod for XM-158
XGAM	experimental guided air missile	XM-158	airborne rocket 70mm
XH-16	experimental tandem heavy-lift helicopter by Piasecki	XM-159	pod for 19x 70mm rockets
XH-17	heavy-lift helicopter by Hughes	XM-174	automatic grenade launcher 40mm by Aerojet
XH-20	Little Henry, experimental helicopter, ramjets by McDonnell	XM-179	CLGP, cannon-launched guided projectile 155mm SP howitzer armoured
XH-26	Jet Jeep, single-seat air-droppable helicopter, rotor tip ramjets by AHC	XM-188	airborne automatic gun by GE
		XM-195	six-barrel 20mm gun by GE
		XM-197	three-barrel 20mm gun by GE
XH-59	ABC, advanced blade concept helicopter by Sikorsky	XM-198	towed 155mm gun
		XM-204	air transportable howitzer 105mm
XHJD-1	Whirlaway, naval twin-engined helicopter by McDonnell	XM-224	LWCMS, light-weight company mortar system 60mm
xhst	exhaust	XM-230	Chain Gun, 20mm gun by Hughes
xhvy	extra heavy	XM-233	SAW, squad automatic weapon 6mm by Maremont
XIO	executive input/output	XM-234	SAW by Ford
XJ-521	Skyflash, medium-range air-to-air missile (UK)	XM-235	SAW
XL	extra large	XM-242	Chain Gun, 25mm electric motor gun by Hughes
XL-21-E-1	smoke grenade by ROF	XM-248	SAW, Dover Devil, light machine gun 5.56mm by Dover Arsenal
XLF-40	tracked rocket launcher (Brazil) 3x X-40	XM-251	cluster bomb warhead for Lance contains 836x BLU-63 by Honeywell
XLP-10	AVLB 10m span by Bernardini	XM-252	81mm mortar (UK made)
XLP-30	AVLB 30m span by Bernardini	XM-262	HK-21, SAW 5.56mm by HK
XLWB	extra long wheelbase	XM-287	cartridge 5.56mm ball
XM	experimental model (US designation); experimental missile; research missile	XM-288	cartridge 5.56mm ball tracer
		XM-321	pistol grip machine gun for MICV
		XM-445	electronic remotely set for MLRS
XM-1	experimental MBT by Chrysler by GM	XM-474	M-113 Pershing system launcher/warhead carrier/electronics vehicle/communications vehicle
XM-2	IFV, infantry fighting vehicle by FMC		
XM-3	CFV, cavalry fighting vehicle by FMC	XM-504	towed launcher for Sergeant
XM-8	helicopter-borne grenade launcher	XM-522	30mm round
XM-18	TAT, helicopter-borne tactical armament turret	XM-546	Mauler, anti-aircraft vehicle M-113
		XM-552	30mm round HEDP
XM-19	SFR, serial flechette rifle by AAI	XM-571	Dynatrac, snow vehicle by Flextrac
XM-28	TAT, tactical armament turret for Huey Cobrai guidance system (laser range + passive IR)	XM-577	M-113 radio tank
		XM-639	30mm round
		XM-645	flechette ammunition for XM-19/XM-70
XM-31	helicopter gun pod 20mm	XM-667	M-113 Honest John missile carrier
XM-34	helicopter gun pod 20mm	XM-668	M-113 rocket transport
XM-47	Dragon, ATGW, anti-tank guided weapon	XM-694	155mm artillery shell REMBASS
XM-70	SFR, serial flechette rifle by AAI	XM-696	tracked recovery vehicle
XM-74	anti-personnel mine by Aerojet	XM-701	MICV, mechanized infantry combat vehicle
XM-75	anti-tank mine by Honeywell		
XM-93	TAT with GAU-28 for UTTAS	XM-712	Copperhead, CLGP 155mm by Martin-Marietta
XM-94	helicopter-borne grenade launcher		
XM-106	M-16HB, machine gun 5.56mm		
XM-128	mine dispenser by FMC		

XM-720	improved mortar ammunition for XM-224
XM-723	MICV by Ford
XM-732	6mm cartridge for SAW
XM-734	M-113
XM-735	APFSDS with uranium tip
XM-736	203mm shell combat gas
XM-744	APFSDS 105mm Stabiloy penetrator
XM-752	M-113 rocket launcher
XM-753	nuclear round for M-110
XM-765	AIFV by FMC
XM-774	APFSDS, uranium tip
XM-777	5.56mm round for SAW, ball
XM-778	5.56mm round for Saw, ball tracer
XM-785	rocket-assisted nuclear projectile 155mm
XM-788	30mm round TP
XM-789	30mm round HEDP
XM-790	25mm round
XM-795	155mm HE shell
XM-797	105mm fin stabilized training round ablative nose cone APFSDS
XM-799	30mm round
XM-803	new MBT project cancelled 1971; 105mm red phosphorous smoke shell
XM-804	155mm practice round
XM-806	M-113, recovery tank
XM-808	Twister, articulated high-mobility truck by Lockheed
XM-815	105mm MP shell
XM-825	155mm white phosphorous smoke shell
XM-827	120mm APFSDS by Rheinmetall
XM-829	APFSDS
XM-830	120mm HEAT by Rheinmetall
XM-832	120mm TPFSDS-T
XM-833	105mm KE shot Stabiloy penetrator
XM-861	4x4 truck by Chrysler
XM-869	radar trailer for Patriot
XM-901	launcher unit for Patriot
XM-966	HMWC, high mobility weapon carrier by Cadillac
XM-975	Roland a/a tank by BMY
xmfr	transformer
XMGM-31	Pershing
XMIM-104	Patriot
XMQM-105	Aquila, TV carrying RPV by Lockheed
XMS	experimental development specification
xmit	transmit
xmsn	transmission
xmtr	transmitter
XNBL-1	experimental night bomber, long-range
XO	examination officer; executive officer; expenditure order; extremely old
XOP-2	Pitcairn, autogyro aircraft (USN)
XP-59	Airacomet, jet fighter by Bell
XPC	inshore patrol cutter (USN)
xpd	expedite
XPG	converted merchant ship (USN)
xpl	explosive
XPM	expended metal
XPN	external priority number
xpn	expansion
XPT	external page table
XQM-93	propeller-driven RPV by E-Systems
XR	extended range (missile)
XR-4	VS-316, helicopter by Sikorsky
XR-311	Dune Buggy jeep by FMC
xrds	crossroads
XRep	auxiliary report
XRF	x-ray fluorescence
XRIM-116	RAM, rolling airframe missile; naval anti-aircraft missile by GD
XRL	extended range Lance
XSPT	external shared page table
xstr	transistor
xtal	crystal
xtnd	extend
xtran	experimental translator
xtrm	extreme
XTSI	extended task status index
XV-15	TRC, tilt rotor concept VTOL by Bell
XV-626	radar trials aircraft for Nimrod AEW
XW	experimental warhead
XX-	image intensifier by Philips
	1500 rifle sight
	1380 precision rifle sight
	1410 goggles

Y

Y	yeomanry, prototype (Nato)
Y-gun	depth-charge launcher (RN)
YA-126	Wapendrager (truck) by DAF
YA-314	4x4 3 ton truck by DAF
YA-328	6x6 artillery tractor by DAF
YA-616	6x6 10 ton truck by DAF
YA-4000	4x4 4 ton truck by DAF
YA-4440	4x4 by DAF
YA-5441	4x4 by DAF
YAG	Yttrium Aluminium garnet (laser); miscellaneous auxiliary ship (USN)
YAGR	ocean radar station ship (USN)
YAH-1	helicopter by Bell
YAH-63	Cobra, AAH, advanced attack helicopter by Bell
YAH-64	LAMPS-III, by Hughes
Yak-3	single-engined fighter by Yakovlev (SU)
YAK-9	single-engined fighter WW2 by Yakovlev (SU)
Yak-11	Moose, trainer aircraft by Yakovlev (SU)
Yak-12	Creek, liaison aircraft by Yakovlev (SU)
Yak-15	jet fighter 1946 by Yakovlev (SU)
Yak-17	Feather, Magnet, fighter by Yakovlev (SU)
Yak-18	Max, primary trainer by Yakovlev (SU)
Yak-23	Flora, fighter by Yakovlev (SU)
Yak-24	Horse, large transport helicopter by Yakovlev (SU)
Yak-25	Flashlight, all-weather fighter 1950 by Yakovlev (SU)
Yak-26	Mandrake, high-altitude recce by Yakovlev (SU)
Yak-27	Flashlight, Mangrove, all-weather interceptor by Yakovlev (SU)
Yak-28	Brewer, Firebar, Maestro, bomber, fighter, recce aircraft by Yakovlev (SU)
Yak-36	Forger, Freehand, V/STOL naval attacker by Yakovlev (SU)
Yak-40	passenger plane by Yakovlev (SU)
Yak-42	high-capacity short-haul plane (SU)

Yak-50	aerobatic aircraft by Yakovlev (SU)
Yamagumo	class, destroyers (JMSDF)
YangPat	Yangtse patrol (USN)
YAQM-34	RPV, land sonobuoy dispenser
YAR	Yemen Arab Republic (North)
Y-ARD	Yarrow admiralty research department (UK)
YASM-1	experimental air-to-surface missile by Mitsubishi
YAV-8	AV-8, Harrier VTOL built by McDD
YB-17	B-17, Flying Fortress, bomber by Boeing
YB-35	jet bomber, flying wing by Northrop
YB-49	jet recce bomber, flying wing by Northrop
YB-60	jet bomber by Convair
YBGM-109	Tomahawk, naval cruise missile by GD
YBGM-110	submarine launched cruise missile by Vought
YBR	sludge removal barge (USN)
YC	open lighter (towed) (USN)
YC-14	AMST, advanced medium STOL by Boeing
YC-15	AMST by McDD
YC-141	Stretched Starlifter by Lockheed
YCD	fuelling barge (USN)
YCF	car float (towed) (USN)
YCG-13	experimental cargo glider by Waco
YCH-43	helicopter by Boeing
YCH-53	heavy lift helicopter by Sikorsky
YCK	open cargo lighter (USN)
YCND	youth campaign for nuclear disarmament
YCV	aircraft transportation lighter (towed) (USN)
yd	yard
YD	floating crane (Derrick) (towed) (USN)
Y&D	bureau of yards and docks (USN)
ydi	yard drain inlet
YDT	diving tender (towed) (USN)
YE	aircraft homing system (US); ammunition lighter (USN)
Yellow Fever	FCE AA No7, anti-aircraft fire control equipment (UK)

YEO	youth employment officer; yeomanry
YES	youth employment service
YF	covered lighter (USN)
YF-9F	F-11F, Tiger
YF-12	SR-71, jet interceptor by Lockheed
YF-16	ACF, air combat fighter by GD
YF-17	F-18, low cost air combat fighter Cobra land-based by Mcdd Hornet carrier-based by Northrop
YF-95	F-86, Sabre
YF-96	F-84, Thunderstreak
YF-408	fast armoured caryby DAF
YFB	ferryboat and launch (USN)
YFD	yard floating dock (USN)
YFN	covered lighter (towed) (USN)
YFNB	big YFN
YFND	drydock companion craft dumb (USN)
YFNG	covered lighter general purpose (USN)
YFNX	covered lighter special purpose (USN)
YFP	power barge (towed) (USN)
YFR	refrigerated covered lighter (USN)
YFRN	refrigerated covered lighter (towed) (USN)
YFRT	covered lighter range tender (USN)
YFT	torpedo transportation lighter (USN)
YFU	harbor utility craft (USN)
YG	garbage lighter (USN)
YG-1054	proximity warning radar by Honeywell
YG-1081	proximity warning radar by Honeywell
YGN	garbage lighter (towed) (USN)
YH	ambulance boat (USN)
YHB	houseboat (USN)
YHLC	heavy salvage lift craft (USN)
YIG	Yttrium iron garnet
YIR	yearly infrastructure report
YL	yield limit
Y&L	the York and Lancaster Regiment
YLI	the Yorkshire Light Infantry
YLLC	light salvage lift craft (USN)
YLR	the York and Lancashire Regiment
YLTC	youth leadership training centre
YM	dredge (USN); prototype missile (Nato)
YMCA	young men's christian association
YMLC	medium salvage lift craft (USN)
YMP	motor mine planter (USN)
YMS	auxiliary motor mine sweeper (USN)
YN	net tender; boom (USN); yeoman
YNG	gate craft (towed) (USN)
YNT	district net tender (USN)
YO	fuel oil barge (USN)
YOB	year of birth
YOC	youth opportunity corps (US); young officers' course (UK)
YOD	year of death
YofS	yeoman of signals
YOG	gasoline barge (USN)
YOGN	gasoline barge non-self-propelled (USN)
YOM	yellow oxide of mercury; year of marriage
YON	oil storage barge (towed) (USN)
YOP	youth opportunity program (US)
YorksDgns	the Queen's Own Yorkshire Dragoons
YorksH	the Yorkshire Alexandra Princess of Wales's Hussars
YOS	oil storage barge (USN)
YP	yield point; patrol craft (USN)
YP-104	armoured recce car by DAF
YP-408	wheeled APC by DAF
YPD	floating pile driver towed (USN)
Yperide	di-cholor-di-ethyl-sulphide,war gas
YPG	Yuma proving ground (Ariz.)
YPK	pontoon storage barge (USN)
YPR-765	Dutch AIFV
YQM-94	Compass Cope RPV by Boeing
YQM-98	Compass Cope RPV by Teledyne Ryan
YR	floating workshop (towed) (USN)
yr	year; your
YR-4	experimental helicopter by Sikorsky
YRB	repair and berthing barge (towed) (USN)
YRBM	repair berthing and messing barge
YRDH	floating drydock workshop hull (USN)
YRDM	floating drydock workshop machine
YrFln	year flown
YRL	covered lighter repair
YRR	covered lighter radio repair
YRST	salvage craft tender (USN)
YS	yard stick; yield strength
YS-11	twin turboprop aircraft by NAMC
YS	stevedoring barge (USN); young soldier; yard superintendent
YSD	seaplane wrecking derrick ISN
YSL	youth service league
YSP	years service for severance pay purposes; stowage pontoon
YSR	sludge removal barge (towed) (USN)
YT	harbour tug; Yukon Territory
YT-1500	semi-trailer with 10 ton trailer by DAF
YTB	big harbour tug
YTL	little harbour tug
YTM	medium harbour tug
YTRES	Yankee Tractor rocket escape system
YTS-10050	tank transporter by DAF
YTT	torpedo testing barge (USN)
YUH-60	UTTAS by Sikorsky
YUH-61	UTTAS/LAMPS by Boeing
Yurka	class, ocean minesweepers (SU)
YV	drone catapult and control craft (USN)
YVF	young volunteer force
YVFF	young volunteer force foundation
YW	yeoman warder (of the Tower); water barge (USN)
YWCA	young women's christian association
YWDN	water distilling barge (towed) (USN)
YWN	water barge (Towed) (USN)
YWT	the yeoman warder of the Tower

Z

Z   nitro-cellulose loading; zenith (distance); zone; zero; flash (message)

Z-axis   vertical axis

Z-battery barrage rockets by Harley

Z-barrier barbed wire coil by Graepel

Z-gun   anti-aircraft gun (UK)

Z-man   US army reservist

Z-time   GMT (Nato)

ZA   zone of action

ZAC   zinc ammonium chloride

ZADCC   zone air defence control centre

ZANU   Zimbabwe African National Union

ZAP   zero anti-aircraft potential

ZAPU   Zimbabwe African People's Union

Zastawa recce car (Yugoslavia)

Zaunkönig acoustic homing torpedo WW2 (GE)

ZB-298 GS-14, battlefield surveillance radar by Marconi

ZBQM-11 target drone by Teledyne Ryan

ZC   zone constabulary

ZCS   zone communications station

ZD   zone description; zenith distance; zero defects; Zener diode

ZD-3   dry zeroing device

ZD-300 Zettelmeyer wheeled dozer by Zettelmeyer

ZEBRA   zero energy breeder reactor assembly

Ze'ef   tactical missile (Israel)

ZEEP   zero energy experimental pile

ZEL   zero launch

ZELL   zero length launch

ZEMTR   Zeus early missile test radar

zen   zenith

ZENDA   artillery and rocket locating radar (Nato)

Zeniscope image intensifier by Nitec

ZENITH zero energy nitrogen heated thermal reactor

Zephyr balloon tracking radar by ITT

ZERO   contaminated area no transit area

ZETA   zero energy thermo-nuclear assembly

Zentaur half track Land Rover by Laird

ZETR   zero energy thermal reactor

ZF   zone of fire; zero frequency; zone finder; Zahnradfabrik Friedrichs-hafen

ZFGBI   Zionist federation of GB and Ireland

ZFS   zero field splitting

ZGF   zero gravity facility (Nasa)

ZGS   zero gradient synchrotron

Zhenya class, coastal minesweepers (SU)

ZHr   zero hour

ZI   zone of the interior (US)

ZIP   zone improvement plan; ZIP code (US)

ZIPA   Zimbabwe People's Army

Zipper target dawn and dusk combat air patrol

ZIS-3   76mm anti-tank gun (SU)

ZL   zero line

ZMAR   Zeus multifunction array radar

ZMkr   zone marker

Zn   zone

ZnO   zinc oxide

ZofI   zone of the interior

Zonda   orbital transport missile (SU)

ZOPFAN zone of peace freedom and neutrality (South East Asia)

ZOR   zone of reconnaissance

ZOTS   zoom optical target seeker

ZP   zero point; lighter-than-air air-craft (US)

ZPA   Zeus programme analysis

ZPEN   Zeus project engineer network

ZPG   zero population growth

ZPG-3   cargo airship (USN)

ZPI   zone position indicator

ZPO   Zeus project office

ZPT   zero power test

ZPU   14.5mm anti-aircraft machine gun (SU)
        -2 twin
        -4 quadruple

ZR   zone of responsibility

ZRA   zero range approximation

ZSF   zero skip frequency

ZST   zone standard time

ZSU   Shilka, radar-guided anti-aircraft tank (SU)
        23/4 quadruple gun 23mm
        57/2 twin gun 57mm

ZT	zone time	Zuni	5 in artillery rockets
ZTO	zone transportation office	ZW-06	naval navigation radar by HSA
ZTS	zoom transfer scope	Zwaardvis	class, submarines (Dutch)
ZU-23	23mm automatic gun (SU)	Zytel	hard nylon type material by DuPont
Zubov	class, spy ships (SU)		

BIBLIOGRAPHY

Bluwstein, W.O., 'Dictionary of Abbreviations', Moscow, Soviet Encyclopedia, 1964.

Bonds, R., 'The Soviet War Machine', London, Salamander, 1976.

Brandt, J. and Brücker, E., 'Der Reibert', Frankfurt/Main, Mittler & Sohn, no date.

Bretzke, W., 'Taschenbuch für den Pionierdienst', Darmstadt, Wehr & Wissen, 1968.

Bührle, E.G., 'Oerlikon Taschenbuch', Zürich, Oerlikon, 1956.

Carstensen, 'Wörterbuch der gebräuchlichen Abkürzungen', Lübeck, Oldenbourg, 1966.

Cartier, F.A., 'The Language of The Air Force in English', New York, Regents Publishers, 1976.

Collins, F.H., 'Authors and Printers Dictionary', London, Oxford University Press, 1973.

Dornan, Dr J.E., 'The US War Machine', London, Salamander, 1978.

Eitzen, H., 'The Military Eitzen', Bonn, Offene Worte, 1957.

Flood, W.E. and West, M., 'An Elementary Scientific and Technical Dictionary', London, Longman, 1952.

Forty, G., 'U.S. Army Handbook', London, Ian Allan, 1979.

Freeman, H.G., 'Technisches Taschenwörterbuch Englisch - Deutsch', München, Hueber, 1979.

Glück, C. and Görtz, J., 'Wörterbuch der Waffentechnik', Schwäbisch Hall, Schwendt, 1972.

Goedecke, W., 'Technische Abkürzungen', Wiesbaden, Brandstetter, 1961.

Graver, D.D. and Hoile, K.J.T., 'Military Texts', London, Oxford University Press, 1967.

Grun, P.A., 'Schlüssel zu alten und neuen Abkürzungen', Luneburg, Starke, 1966.

Gunston, B., 'Jane's Aerospace Dictionary', London, Macdonald & Jane's, 1980.

Gurnett, W.J. and Kyte, C.H.J., 'Cassell's Dictionary of Abbreviations', London, Cassell & Co., 1966.

Hayward, P.H.C., 'Jane's Dictionary of Military Terms', London, Macdonald & Jane's, 1975.

Höhne, G. and Rose, H., 'Handbuch der Internationalen Organisationen', Berlin, Dietz, 1969.

Horak, O., 'Elektronische Aufklärungsmittel', München, Lehmanns, 1971.

Hornby, A.S., 'Oxford Advanced Learner's Dictionary of Current English', London, Oxford University Press, 1974.

Kerkhof, H. and Gras, M., 'Lexikon englisch - amerikanischer Abkürzungen', Hamm, Grote, 1956.

Koblischke, H., 'Grosses Abkürzungsbuch', Leipzig, VEB Bibliographisches Institut, 1978.

International Institute for Strategic Studies Report, 'The Military Balance', London, 1977-81.

Lanze, W., 'DABI, Das Abkürzungsbuch für den Ingenieur', München, Vulkan, 1969.

Lichtenstern, H., 'Lexikon der Abkürzungen', München, Heyne, 1973.

Marshall, N., 'Collins Gem Dictionary of Abbreviations', London, Collins, 1980.

Meisinger, H., 'Langenscheidts Grosses Schulwörterbuch Englisch - Deutsch', Berlin, Langenscheidt, 1978.

Mügge, K.A., 'Fernmeldetechnik', Frankfurt/Main, Mittler & Sohn, 1959.

NATO Information Service, 'NATO Facts and Figures', Brussels, 1976.

Nicholson, R.W. and Williams, R., 'The Language of National Defense in English', New York, Regents, 1978.

North Atlantic Council, 'Glossary of Abbreviations Used in NATO Documents', Brussels, 1974.

Ocran, E.B., 'Ocran's Acronyms', London, Routledge & Kegan Paul, 1978.

Palmer, J., 'Jane's Dictionary of Naval Terms', London, Macdonald & Jane's, 1975.

Paxton, J., 'Everyman's Dictionary of Abbreviations', London, Dent, 1974.

Phythian, B., 'A Concise Dictionary of English Slang', London, Hodder & Stoughton, 1965.

Rheinmetall G.m.b.H., 'Waffentechnisches Taschenbuch', Düsseldorf, Rheinmetall, 1972.

Rogers, H.C.B., 'The British Army - Today and Tomorrow', London, Ian Allan, 1979.

495

Rothe, H., AKÜLEX, Frankfurt/Main, Labendiges Wissen, 1956.

Ruppert, F., 'Initials', München, Vulkan, 1966.

Sanson, R.G., 'The Language of the Navy in English', New York, Regents, 1978.

Saur, K.G., 'Internationales Verzeichnis von Abkürzungen', München, Vulkan, 1968.

Schubert, K., 'Internationales Abkürzungslexikon', München, Fink, 1978.

Seek, G., 'Taschenbuch für den Fernmeldedienst', Darmstadt, Wher & Wissen, 1961.

Senger and Etterlin, Dr F.M., 'Das kleine Panzerbuch', München, Lehmanns, 1964.

Sokoll, A., 'Abkürzungen in der Luft- und Raumfahrt', München, Alkos, 1965.

Spillner, P., 'Abkürzungslexikon', Frankfurt/Main, Ullstein, 1967.

Sybertz, G., 'Technisches Wörterbuch für Waffenfreunde, Schützen und Jäger', Melsungen, Neumann & Neudamm, 1969.

United States Department of the Army, Army Regulation 310 - 50, 'Authorized Abbreviations & Brevity Codes', Washington, 1975.

United States Department of Defense, The Joint Chiefs of Staff, 'Dictionary of Military and Associated Terms', Washington, 1979.

Wederz, B., 'Dictionary of Naval Abbreviations', Annapolis, The US Naval Institute, 1970.

Wendt, V.K., 'Abkürzungen und Symbole', Heidelberg, Sauer, 1967.

Wentworth, H. and Flexner, S., 'The Pocket Dictionary of American Slang', New York, Pocket Books, 1968.

Werlin, J., 'Wörterbuch der Abkürzungen', Mannheim, Bibliographisches Institut, 1971.

Williams, R.R., 'The Language of The Army in English', New York, Regents, 1979.

Zuerl, W., '50 moderne mehrsitzige Hubschrauber', München, Luftfahrtverlag, 1962.